Global Problems, Smart Solutions

Every four years since 2004, the Copenhagen Consensus Center has organized and hosted a high-profile thought experiment about how a hypothetical extra $75 billion might best be spent to solve twelve of the major crises facing the world today. Collated in this specially commissioned book, a group of more than fifty experts make their cases for investment, discussing how to combat problems ranging from armed conflicts, corruption, and trade barriers, to natural disasters, hunger, education, and climate change. For each case, "Alternative Perspectives" are also included to provide a critique and make other suggestions for investment. In addition, a panel of senior economists, including four Nobel Laureates, rank the attractiveness of each policy proposal in terms of its anticipated cost–benefit ratio. This thought-provoking book opens up debate, encouraging readers to come up with their own rankings and decide which solutions are smarter than others.

BJØRN LOMBORG is Director of the Copenhagen Consensus Center and Adjunct Professor in the Department of Management, Politics and Philosophy at Copenhagen Business School. He is the author of the controversial bestseller, *The Skeptical Environmentalist* (Cambridge University Press, 2001) and was named one of the "Top 100 Global Thinkers" by *Foreign Policy* magazine in 2010, 2011, and 2012, one of the world's "100 Most Influential People" by *Time*, and one of the "50 people who could save the planet" by the *Guardian*.

Global Problems, Smart Solutions

Costs and Benefits

Edited by
BJØRN LOMBORG

CAMBRIDGE
UNIVERSITY PRESS

CAMBRIDGE
UNIVERSITY PRESS

University Printing House, Cambridge CB2 8BS, United Kingdom

Published in the United States of America by Cambridge University Press, New York

Cambridge University Press is part of the University of Cambridge.

It furthers the University's mission by disseminating knowledge in the pursuit of education, learning and research at the highest international levels of excellence.

www.cambridge.org
Information on this title: www.cambridge.org/9781107612211

First published 2013

Printing in the United Kingdom by TJ International Ltd. Padstow Cornwall

A catalogue record for this publication is available from the British Library

Library of Congress Cataloguing in Publication data
Global problems, smart solutions : costs and benefits / edited by Bjørn Lomborg.
pages cm
Includes index.
ISBN 978-1-107-03959-9 (hardback)
1. Social problems – Economic aspects. 2. Problem solving – Economic aspects. 3. Cost effectiveness. 4. Economics – Sociological aspects. I. Lomborg, Bjørn, 1965–
HN18.3.G544 2013
303.3′72 – dc23 2013013122

ISBN 978-1-107-03959-9 Hardback
ISBN 978-1-107-61221-1 Paperback

Additional resources for this publication at www.ranksmartsolutions.com

Contents

Figures

Tables

Contributors

Experts

Finn E. Kydland, Nobel Laureate in Economic Sciences, is the Jeffery Henley Professor of Economics at the University of California, Santa Barbara. He has had previous appointments at Carnegie Mellon University, the University of Texas at Austin, and the Norwegian School of Economics and Business Administration. He was Research Associate for the Federal Reserve Banks of Dallas, Cleveland, and St. Louis, and a Senior Research Fellow at the IC2 Institute at the University of Texas at Austin. He was also Adjunct Professor at the Norwegian School of Economics and Business Administration, and he has held visiting scholar and professor positions at, among other places, the Hoover Institution and the Universidad Torcuato di Tella in Buenos Aires, Argentina. He was elected a Fellow of the Econometric Society in 1992, selected as a member of the Consulta de San José in 2006, and served on the Expert Panels at the Copenhagen Consensus in 2008 and Copenhagen Consensus on Climate in 2009 because of his high-level knowledge of economics in general and political economy in particular.

Robert Mundell, Nobel Laureate in Economic Sciences, is University Professor at Columbia University in the City of New York. He is adviser to a number of international agencies and organizations including the Government of Canada, the United Nations (UN), the International Monetary Fund (IMF), the World Bank, the European Commission, the Federal Reserve Board, the US Treasury, and numerous governments, institutions, and companies. He prepared the first plan for a European currency and is known as the father of the theory of optimum currency areas and the euro. He developed the international macroeconomic model (the Mundell–Fleming model), the theory of growth, and was an originator of supply-side economics. He has written extensively on economic theory, international economics, transition economies, and the history of the international monetary system. Awards given to him include appointment as Companion of the Order of Canada, the Global Economics Award of the Kiel World Economics Institute, Germany, and appointment as Knight Grand Cross of the Royal Order of Merit. He has served on the Expert Panel at the Copenhagen Consensus in 2004 because of his expertise on international economics and transition economies.

Thomas Schelling, Nobel Laureate in Economic Sciences, is a Distinguished Professor of Economics at the University of Maryland. He has been elected to the National Academy of Sciences, the Institute of Medicine, and the American Academy of Arts and Sciences. He is Former President of the American Economic Association, of which he is now a Distinguished Fellow, and he was the recipient of the Frank E. Seidman Distinguished Award in Political Economy and the National Academy of Sciences award for Behavioral Research Relevant to the Prevention of Nuclear War. In 1990, he left the John F. Kennedy School of Government, where he was the Lucius N. Littauer Professor of Political Economy. He has also served in the Economic Cooperation Administration in Europe, and has held positions in the White House and Executive Office of the President, Yale University, the RAND Corporation, and the Department of Economics and Center for International Affairs at Harvard University. He served on the Expert Panel of the Copenhagen Consensus in 2004, the Copenhagen Consensus in 2008 and the RethinkHIV 2011 because of his expertise in competing development priorities, and he served as a member of the Copenhagen Consensus on Climate in 2009 because of his expertise in global warming policy choices.

Vernon Smith, Nobel Laureate in Economic Sciences, is Professor of Law and Economics and George L. Argyros Endowed Chair in Finance and Economics at Chapman University School of Law. He has authored or co-authored more than 250 articles and books on capital theory, finance, natural resource economics, and experimental economics. He serves or has served on the board of editors of the *American Economic Review*, *The Cato Journal*, *Journal of Economic Behavior and Organization*, *the Journal of Risk and Uncertainty*, *Science*, *Economic Theory*, *Economic Design*, *Games and Economic Behavior*, and the *Journal of Economic Methodology*. He was past president of the Public Choice Society, the Economic Science Association, the Western Economic Association, and the Association for Private Enterprise Education. He served on the Expert Panel at the Copenhagen Consensus in 2004, the Copenhagen Consensus in 2008, the Copenhagen Consensus on Climate in 2009 and the RethinkHIV 2011 because of his expertise in policy trade-offs and development priorities.

Nancy Stokey is Frederick Henry Prince Distinguished Service Professor of Economics at the University of Chicago. She has published significant research in the areas of economic growth and development, as well as papers on economic history and econometrics. She was co-developer, with Paul Milgrom, of the no-trade theorem, a counter-intuitive development of the premises of financial economics. She is a member of the National Academy of Sciences and former vice-president of the American Economic Association, and she has held editorial positions with top journals such as *Econometrica*, *The Journal of Economic Growth*, *Games and Economic Behavior* and *The Journal of Economic Theory*. She served on the Expert Panel at the Copenhagen Consensus in 2004, the Copenhagen Consensus in 2008, and the Copenhagen Consensus on Climate in 2009 because of her expertise in policy trade-offs and development priorities, and her ability to succinctly explain policy choices.

Chapter Authors

Kym Anderson is George Gollin Professor of Economics, foundation Executive Director of the Wine Economics Research Centre, and formerly foundation Executive Director of the Centre for International Economic Studies at the University of Adelaide

J. Eric Bickel is Assistant Professor, Graduate Program in Operations Research, Center for International Energy and Environmental Policy, The University of Texas at Austin

David Bloom is Clarence James Gamble Professor of Economics and Demography and chair, Department of Global Health and Population, School of Public Health, Harvard University, USA

Francesco Bosello is Associate researcher, Fondazione Eni Enrico Mattei (FEEM), Milan; Assistant Professor of Economics, University Statale of Milan; Affiliate Scientist, Euromediterranean Center for Climate Change (CMCC),

Luke Brander is a researcher at the Institute for Environmental Studies, Vrije Universiteit

Carlo Carraro is President, Professor of Environmental Economics and Econometrics, Università Ca' Foscari Venezia; President, Ca' Foscari University Foundation; Chairman, Scientific Advisory Board, Fondazione Eni Enrico Mattei (FEEM)

Enrica De Cian is Senior researcher, Fondazione Eni Enrico Mattei (FEEM)

Rudolf de Groot is Associate Professor in the Environmental Systems Analysis group, Wageningen University

J. Paul Dunne is Professor at the School of Economics at the University of Cape Town, Emeritus Professor of Economics at Bristol Business School, University of the West of England, Bristol, and visiting Professor at the Faculty of Economics, Chulalongkorn University

Isabel Galiana is Lecturer, Department of Economics, McGill School of Environment, McGill University

Christopher Green is Professor of Economics, Department of Economics, McGill School of Environment, McGill University

John Hoddinott is Senior Research fellow, Deputy Director in the Poverty Health and Nutrition Division, International Food Policy Research Institute

Ryan Hum is Special Lecturer, Faculty of Applied Science and Engineering, University of Toronto

Salman Hussain is an Ecological Economics Researcher at the Scottish Agricultural College

Dean T. Jamison is Professor of Global Health, University of Washington, Seattle

Prabhat Jha is Professor of Economics, Canada Research Chair of Health and Development at the University of Toronto, founding director of the Centre for Global Health Research, St. Michael's Hospital; Associate Professor in the Department of Public Health Sciences, University of Toronto; research scholar at the McLaughlin Centre for Molecular Medicine, professeur extraordinaire at the Université de Lausanne, Switzerland

Erwann Michel-Kerjan is Managing Director, Risk Management and Decision Processes Center; Adjunct Associate Professor, Operations and Information Management Department, Wharton School, University of Pennsylvania; Chairman, OECD Secretary General Board on Financial Management of Catastrophes, OECD

Hans-Peter Kohler is Frederick J. Warren Professor of Demography, University of Pennsylvania

Howard Kunreuther is James G. Dinan Professor; Professor of Decision Sciences and Business and Public Policy, Co-Director, Risk Management and Decision Processes Center, Wharton School, University of Pennsylvania

Lee Lane is Visiting Fellow, Hudson Institute; Senior Consultant, NERA Economic Consulting

Ramanan Laxminarayan is Senior Fellow, Development and Environment, Resources for the Future,

Anil Markandya is a Professor at the University of Bath, and Scientific Director at the Basque Centre for Climate Change

Alistair McVittie is a researcher at the Scottish Agricultural College

Rachel Nugent PhD is a research scientist, Department of Global Health, University of Washington, Seattle; former deputy director of Global Health at the Center for Global Development

Peter F. Orazem is Professor of Economics, Department of Economics, Iowa State University

Toby Ord is British Academy Postdoctoral Fellow, Department of Philosophy, University of Oxford

Frank Rijsberman is CEO, CGIAR Consortium

Mark Rosegrant is Division Director in the Environment and Production Technology Division, International Food Policy Research Institute

Susan Rose-Ackerman is Henry R.Luce Professor of Jurisprudence (Law and Political Science), Yale University

Richard S. J. Tol is Professor of Economics, Department of Economics, University of Sussex; Professor of the Economics of Climate Change, Institute for Environmental Studies and Department of Spatial Economics, Vrije Universiteit, Amsterdam

Maximo Torero is Director of the Markets, Trade, and Institutions Division, leader of the Global Research Program on Institutions and Infrastructure for Market Development and Director for

Latin America, International Food Policy Research Institute

Rory Truex is PhD in Political Sciences, Yale University

Olivier Vardakoulias is an analyst, and works in development and environmental economics, and nef-consulting

Peter H. Verburg is Professor of Environmental Spatial Analysis and head of the Department of Spatial Analysis and Decision Support at the Institute for Environmental Studies, VU University, Amsterdam

Stéphane Verguet Researcher, Department of Global Health, University of Washington, Seattle

Alfred Wagtendonk is a researcher at the institute for Environmental Studies at Vrije Universiteit, Amsterdam

Alix Peterson Zwane is Senior Program Officer on the Water, Sanitation, and Hygiene Program, Bill and Melinda Gates Foundation

Perspective Paper Authors

Till Bärnighausen is Assistant Professor of Global Health, Department of Global Health and Population, School of Public Health, Harvard University

David E. Bloom is Clarence James Gamble Professor of Economics and Demography and Chair, Department of Global Health and Population, School of Public Health, Harvard University

David Canning is Professor of Population Sciences and Professor of Economics and International Health, School of Public Health, Harvard University

Paul E. Chambers is Professor, Department of Economics and Finance, University of Central Missouri

Anil B. Deolalikar is Associate Dean of the University of California Riverside's College of Humanities, Arts and Social Sciences; Co-Director of Global Health Institute, University of California

Samuel Fankhauser is Professor, Co-Director of the Grantham Research Institute on Climate Change and the Environment, London School of Economics

Julia Fox-Rushby is Professor, Health Economics Research Group, Brunel University, London

Oded Galor is Herbert H. Goldberger Professor of Economics, Core Faculty, Population and Training Center, Brown University and Fellow, Department of Economics, Hebrew University, Jerusalem

Stéphane Hallegatte is Lead Climate Change Specialist, in special assignment with the World Bank – Sustainable Development Network

W. Michael Hanemann is Chancellor's Professor, Department of Agricultural and Resource Economics, University of California

Anke Hoeffler is Research Officer at the Centre for the Study of African Economies, University of Oxford

Salal Humair is Research Scientist, Department of Global Health and Population, Harvard School of Public Health; Associate Professor, School of Science and Engineering, Lahore University of Management Sciences, Pakistan

David Lam is Professor, Department of Economics, Research Professor, Population Studies Center, Institute for Social Research, University of Michigan

Beatrice Lorge Rogers is Professor of Economics and Food Policy Director, Food Policy and Applied Nutrition Program, Friedman School of Nutrition Science and Policy, Tufts University

Guy Hutton is an International Development Economist

Andrew Mack is Director, Human Security Report Project, School for International Studies, Simon Fraser University

Ilan Noy is Associate Professor, Department of Economics, University of Hawaii, Manoa

Lant Pritchett is Professor of the Practice of International Development, Harvard Kennedy School

George Psacharopoulos is Education Economics Expert, formerly of the London School of Economics and the World Bank

Juha V. Siikamäki is Research Fellow, Resources for the Future

Marc Suhrcke is Professor in Public Health Economics, University of East Anglia

John C. Whitehead is Professor and Department Chair, Department of Economics, Appalachian State University

Acknowledgments

This book and the Copenhagen Consensus 2012 project are only possible because of the efforts of many people. I would like to thank the Copenhagen Business School and Denmark's Foreign Ministry for their support. I am grateful to those who have worked on Copenhagen Consensus projects and related work, including Sandra Andresen, Sara Csepregi, Zsuzsa Horvath, David Lessmann and Roland Mathiasson, Kristine Pedersen, and Tommy Petersen, and especially to the core project team of Sibylle Aebi, Sasha Beckmann, Ulrik Larsen, Henrik Meyer, Kasper Thede Anderskov, and David Young, who saw the Copenhagen Consensus 2012 to fruition. I am particularly grateful to the authors and experts whose work forms these pages. Their enthusiasm and dedication to creating excellent research is to be commended.

Selected abbreviations and acronyms

AAF	average annual number of fatalities
AAL	average annual loss
AARPD	average annual reduction in property damage
AC	air capture
ACA	anti-corruption authority
ACT	artemisinin combination therapy
AEIC	American Energy Innovation Council
AFTA	ASEAN FTA
AGR	area growth rate
AKST	agricultural knowledge, science and technology
ALP	acquisition of life potential
AMFm	Affordable Medicines Facility-malaria
AMMA	African Monsoon Multi-Disciplinary Analysis
APEC	Asia Pacific Economic Cooperation
ARPA-E	Advanced Research Projects Agency – Energy
ART	alternative risk transfer
ASEAN	Association of South East Asian Nations
BAU	business as usual
BAUWMM	business as usual with more money
BCR	benefit-cost ratio
BIT	bilateral investment treaty
BRIC	Brazil, Russia, India, and China
CATS	Community Approaches to Total Sanitation
CBA	cost-benefit analysis
CBD	Convention on Biological Diversity
CCM	chronic care model
CCP	Cyclone Preparedness Program
CCS	carbon capture and storage
CCT	conditional cash-transfer
CDC	Centre for Disease Control and Prevention
CE	climate engineering
CEA	cost-effectiveness assessment
CEE	Central and Eastern Europe
CER	cost-effectiveness ratio
CFS	Committee on World Food Security
CLD	chronic lung disease
CLTS	community-led total sanitation
CMH	Commission on Macroeconomics and Health
CNCD	chronic non-communicable disease
COI	cost of illness
COP	Conference of the Parties
COPD	chronic obstructive pulmonary disease
CoST	Construction Sector Transparency Initiative
CPI	Corruption Perceptions Index
CPIA	Country Policy and Institutional Assessment
CR4	top-4 concentration ratio
CRD	chronic respiratory disease
CRS/PC	constant returns to scale and perfect competition
CT	cash transfer
CV	coefficient of variation
CVD	cardiovascular disease
DAH	donor assistance for health
DALY	Disability Adjusted Life Year
DCPP	Disease Control Priorities Project

DDA	Doha Development Agenda
DEC	dietary energy consumption
DER	dietary energy requirements
DEWS	Distant Early Warning System
DHS	Demographic and Health Surveys
DRR	disaster risk-reduction
DSSAT	Decision Support System for Agrotechnology Transfer
EEA	European Environment Agency
EIA	Energy Information Agency (US)
EITI	Extractive Industries Transparency Initiative
EP	exceedance probability
EPI	Expanded Program on Immunization
ESI	Economics of Sanitation Initiative
ESS	ecosystem services
EU ETS	EU Emissions Trading Scheme
EV	equivalent variation in income
EWS	early-warning systems
FAO	Food and Agriculture Organization
FCPA	Foreign Corrupt Practices Act
FDI	foreign direct investment
FEMA	Federal Emergency Management Agency
FEWS NET	Famine Early Warning Systems Network
FIT	feed-in tariff
FPU	food production unit
FSE	former socialist economies
FSU	former Soviet Union
FTA	free-trade agreement
FTAAP	APEC FTA
GAC	Governance and Anti-Corruption
GATT	General Agreement on Tariffs and Trade
GAVI	Global Alliance for Vaccines and Immunization
GBD	global burden of disease
GCB	*Global Corruption Barometer*
GDI	gross domestic income
GDP	gross domestic product
GHG	greenhouse gas
GTAP	Global Trade Analysis Project
GWP	gross world product
HANPP	human appropriation of net primary product
HDI	Human Development Index
IA	Impact Assessment
IADB	Inter-American Development Bank
IAM	Integrated Assessment Model
IAVI	International AIDS Vaccine Initiative
ICCC	Innovative Care for Chronic Conditions
ICER	incremental cost-effectiveness ratio
ICPD	International Conference on Population and Development
ICRG	International Company Risk Guide
ICSID	International Center for the Settlement of Investment Disputes
ICT	information and communication technology
IEA	International Energy Agency
IFDC	International Fertilizer Development Center
IFI	international financial institution
IFPRI	International Food Policy Research Institute
ILO	International Labor Office
IMF	International Monetary Fund
IMPACT	International Model for Policy Analysis of Agricultural Commodity and Trade
IMR	infant mortality rate
I-NGO	international non-governmental organization
IOM	Institute of Medicine
IPC	Integrated Food Security Phase Classification
IPCC	International Panel on Climate Change
IPR	yield growth rate

IRR	internal rate of return
IRS/MC	increasing returns to scale and monopolistic competition
ITA	International Trade Agreement
ITO	International Trade Organization
IUCN	International Union for Conservation of Nature
IUGR	intrauterine growth restriction
JMP	Joint Monitoring Program (WHO/UNICEF)
LDC	less-/least-developed country
LMIC	lower and middle-income country/countries
MAC	marginal cost of abatement
MD	marginal damage
MDER	minimum dietary energy requirement
MDG	Millennium Development Goal
MDR	multi-drug-resistant
MEA	Millennium Ecosystem Assessment
MMC	Multihazard Mitigation Council
MNC	multinational corporation
MSA	Mean Species Abundance
MYI	multi-year insurance
NCD	non-communicable disease
NGO	non-governmental organization
NIH	National Institute of Health
NOAA	National Oceanic and Atmospheric Administration
NPP	net primary product
NPV	net present value
NRR	net reproduction rates
NTB	non-tariff barrier
NTFP	non-timber forest products
NWP	numerical weather prediction
ODA	Official Development Assistance
ODF	Open Defecation Free
OECD	Organisation for Economic Cooperation and Development
PAL	Physical Activity Level
PAPI	Public Administration Performance Index
PDV	present discounted value
PETS	Public Expenditure Tracking Surveys
PIDI	*Proyecto Integral de Desarrollo Infantil*
PPC	production possibility curve
PPP	polluter-pays principle
PPP	purchasing power parity
PRTP	pure rate of time preference
PTWC	Pacific Tsunami Warning Centre
PV	present value
QALY	quality-adjusted life year
R&D	research and development
RD&D	research, development, and demonstration
REDD	deforestation and forest degradation
REF	Renewable Energy Foundation
RF	risk factor
RIMES	Regional Integrated Multi-Hazard Early Warning System
RML	Reuters Market Light
ROR	rate of return
RPS	renewable portfolio standard
RTA	regional trade agreement
SAI	stratospheric aerosol injection
SEC	Securities and Exchange Commission
SES	socio-economic status
SGR	strong-growth recovery
SMS	self-care and self-management
SRAS	Seismic Risk Assessment of Schools
SRES	Special Reports on Emissions Scenarios
SRM	solar radiation management
SSA	Sub-Saharan Africa
StAR	Stolen Asset Recovery Initiative
SVHL	statistical value of a human life
TB	tuberculosis
TFP	total factor productivity

TFR	total fertility rate
TI	Transparency International
TPP	Trans-Pacific Partnership
TRIPS	Trade-Related Aspects of Intellectual Property Rights
TSSM	Total Sanitation and Sanitation Marketing
UN	United Nations
UNDP	United Nations Development Programme
UNEP	United Nations Environment Programme
UNFCCC	United Nations Framework Convention on Climate Change
UNFPA	United Nations Population Fund
VIP	ventilated improved pit
VOI	value of information
VoL	value of life
VOL	value of lost output
VSL	value of statistical life
VSLY	value of a statistical life year
VTT	Technical Research Centre of Finland
WDPA	World Database on Protected Areas
WEF	World Economic Forum
WHO	World Health Organization
WMO	World Meteorological Organization
WRF	Weather Research Forecasting
WSP	Water and Sanitation Program
WSSD	World Summit on Sustainable Development
WTO	World Trade Organization
WTP	willingness to pay
WVS	*World Values Survey*
YLD	years of life lost due to disability
YLL	years of life lost
YPLL	years of productive life lost

Introduction

BJØRN LOMBORG

The Copenhagen Consensus approach is to look at global issues and to ask: how could economic science help us to improve decision-making?

Each day decisions are made about global political priorities. Governments, philanthropists, and international bodies choose to support some worthy causes while others are disregarded. Unfortunately, these decisions frequently do not take fully into account a comprehensive view of the effects, benefits, and costs of solving one problem instead of another. The conflicting demands of the media, stakeholders, and politicians mean that priorities are set in an obfuscated environment. The idea behind the Copenhagen Consensus is to render this process less arbitrary, and to provide more evidence upon which informed decisions can be made by politicians and others.

Much of the time, society is presented with a menu of choices, but with very little information on their costs and benefits. The Copenhagen Consensus process aims to put prices and sizes on the menu, making choice easier and more informed. To inform this process in practice, we ask: if you were to spend an additional $75 billion over the next four years to do good for humanity and the environment, where would you spend it first?

This book constitutes a concrete contribution designed to improve the debate regarding global priorities: the questions of how we tackle the world's problems, where we start, and what should sensibly be done.

This Introduction sets out the methodological approach to the Copenhagen Consensus 2012 project and adumbrates the research that follows.

In 2004 and 2008, the Copenhagen Consensus Center gathered research on ten key global challenges – from malnutrition to terrorism – and commissioned a panel of expert economists to rank the investments. The research from the Copenhagen Consensus 2004 and the Copenhagen Consensus 2008 is available in Cambridge University Press books, *Global Crises, Global Solutions* and *Global Crises, Global Solutions* (2nd edn.) (Lomborg, 2005, 2009a).

These projects attracted attention from all around the world. Denmark's government spent millions more on HIV/AIDS projects, which topped the economists' "to do" list in 2004. Micronutrient delivery programs in Africa and elsewhere received significant attention and greater resources after they topped the list in 2008. The World Bank quoted Copenhagen Consensus research and findings in 2006 when it created its new strategy on combatting malnutrition: "As documented by the Copenhagen Consensus, we know what to do to improve nutrition and the expected rates of returns from investing in nutrition are high."[1]

In 2006, the Copenhagen Consensus United Nations brought together twenty-four UN ambassadors, including the Chinese, Indian, and American ambassadors, and set them the task of prioritizing limited resources along Copenhagen Consensus lines to improve efforts to mitigate the negative consequences of global challenges.

Consulta de San José in 2007 (the Copenhagen Consensus for Latin America and the Caribbean) was a collaboration with the Inter-American Development Bank (IADB). This project gathered highly esteemed economists to identify the projects that would best improve welfare in Latin America and the Caribbean. The research is available as *Latin American Development Priorities* (Lomborg, 2009b).

In 2009, the approach was applied to climate change. The Copenhagen Consensus on Climate assembled an Expert Panel of five world-class

[1] World Bank (2006).

economists, including three recipients of the Nobel Prize, to evaluate twenty-one research papers on different responses to climate change and to deliberate on which solutions would be most effective; this project was published in *Smart Solutions to Climate Change* (Cambridge University Press, 2009).

In 2011, RethinkHIV – funded by the Rush Foundation – saw the Copenhagen Consensus Center gather teams of economists and medical scientists to perform the first comprehensive, cost-benefit analysis (CBA) of HIV/AIDS investment opportunities in sub-Saharan Africa (SSA). This research was published in 2012 as *RethinkHIV* (Lomborg, 2012).

These projects generated considerable attention and discussion. They showed that an informed ranking of solutions to the world's big problems is possible, and that CBAs – much maligned by some – lead to a compassionate, clear focus on the most effective ways to respond to the real problems of the world's most afflicted people.

This book builds on several of these past projects – particularly the Copenhagen Consensus 2004 and the Copenhagen Consensus 2008 – which each gathered Expert Panels of outstanding economists to deliver ranked lists of the most promising solutions to ten of the most pressing challenges facing the world. Each project involved around sixty leading economists and specialists in ten global challenges.

This effort also draws on the research for the Copenhagen Consensus on Climate and RethinkHIV, to ensure that the most up-to-date and informed analysis is provided for the topics of global warming and HIV/AIDS.

The objective for the Copenhagen Consensus 2012 was to commission new research and data to deliver an informed, current perspective on the smartest investments to respond to global challenges.

Tremendous progress has been made in the fight against humanity's biggest ailments within our lifetimes. People in most countries live longer, healthier lives; air and water quality in the developed world is generally getting better; and a much larger proportion of the global population is being adequately fed.

But there are still many problems to tackle. The minority of us lucky enough to have been born in the developed world can sometimes take for granted universal education, an assured food supply, and clean, piped water. But billions of people are not so lucky. And although the world's problems fall disproportionately heavily on the developing world, rich countries also face problems.

When it comes to global welfare projects, it is easy for decision-makers to pay lip service to prioritization, but to act as though the pool of money is infinite, that all that is lacking is willpower, and that everything should be tackled all at once.

Many of the big decisions are made individually by the governments of donor countries, or by relatively specialist international agencies that receive money from rich nations and use it for the benefit of the world, especially developing countries. Each such organization has its own remit, scope of work, and funding base.

Of course, in principle we ought to deal with all of the world's woes. We should win the war against hunger, end conflicts, stop communicable diseases, provide clean drinking water, step up education, and halt climate change. But we don't do all of this at once. We live in a world with limited resources and even more limited attention for our biggest problems. This means we have to ask the crucial question: if we don't do it all, what should we do first?

This book focuses on the funding that the developed world spends on improving the world in general. Of course, most nations spend the vast bulk of their resources on themselves – perhaps 99 percent of developed nations' GDP. In a well-functioning political system, this internal system is prioritized according to a solid framework of economic principles, as well as by social and ethical concerns.

However, the last 1 percent of spending – the portion that goes outside a nation's borders – is less well developed. This spending ranges from the money that goes from donor nations as Official Development Assistance (ODA) to spending on peacekeeping forces, research into vaccines, and efforts to reduce environmental pollution.

Often, explicit prioritization is ignored altogether by policy-makers. The UN Millennium Development Goals (MDGs), which shaped much of this funding for the first decade of this century, consist of a laundry list of noble causes with no consideration given to relative costs or benefits.

Relying on costs and benefits, as this project does, is a transparent and practical way to establish whether spending is worthwhile or not. It lets us avoid the fear and media hype that often dictate the way that we see the world. Carefully examining where an investment would have the biggest rewards provides a principled basis upon which important decisions can be made. Assigning a monetary value is the best way we have of introducing a common frame for comparison.

Some will argue that it is impossible to put a value on a human life. Yet, refusing to put a value on human life does not help to save lives. In practice, prioritization occurs every day in areas as disparate as health policy and infrastructure. When we decide on a national speed limit we are implicitly putting a price on human life, weighing the benefits of fewer lives lost with a lower speed limit against the dispersed costs of higher transport times. Making such trade-offs explicit allows us all to better evaluate our choices. In this book, we use tools such as the 'Disability Adjusted Life Year' (DALY) which allows economists – and thus, policymakers – to add up the years of life that are lost and establish the impact of disability, and then weigh these with other benefits and costs of different policies. Specifically, we have set low and high values of a DALY at $1,000 and $5,000, respectively, to ensure comparability across areas.

Another economic tool that informs this project is discounting, which allows us to balance our own needs against those of future generations, and ensure that we have a consistent approach across all of the challenges presented in the book. So, what discount rate have we used, and why?

Commercial projects typically discount at the rate of current or expected market interest rates. Economists often recommend a rate of 6 percent for discounting development projects, and we have suggested this as a baseline for the economists who wrote research for this project.

However, some argue that humanity should take a longer view and set a lower discount rate. Hence, we have also asked authors to use a rate of 3 percent for comparison. Such an approach makes virtually all projects look more attractive but especially those (like education or global warming) which take longer to produce significant benefits. Which rate is more appropriate is something we leave up to the individual experts – and you, as a reader – but, crucially, it is important to have a consistent discount rate across all areas.

Using these economic tools, we can then gauge how the relative benefits and costs change as we alter discount rates, the value of DALYs, or change our assumptions about the relative likelihood of outcomes. Such results make the prioritization of different policies much more transparent.

The challenges chosen for the first Copenhagen Consensus exercise in 2004 were drawn from a larger list of areas that receive the attention of UN organizations and winnowed down by the suggestions from the Expert Panel. Likewise, for the Copenhagen Consensus 2012, we asked the panel of Nobel Laureates and economists to provide us with input on the challenges with the most promising solutions on the list, so that the 2012 list is fully updated.

Ideally the project would make a full examination of all possible challenges, but in a world of limited resources we identified the ten top challenges, ensuring a wide coverage of the most important issues of the time. Compartmentalizing all issues within these ten challenges is of course an approximation. This means we can ask a team of expert economists to address the individual area, examine the available literature, and make a proper CBA. However, in reality, of course, boundaries are not clearly defined. Action in one area will often have indirect positive effects in others.

As you will see in both Part I and Part II of this book, authors and the Expert Panel have taken such effects into account as much as possible.

Throughout all the analysis, we have asked authors to use a comparable economic framework. If each chapter is in the same "language," then decision-makers – and you, the reader – will be able to establish what can be achieved with spending in different areas.

We turn now to the research, which forms Part I of this book.

In Chapter 1, J. Paul Dunne looks at armed conflict. Armed conflict is a major global problem that disproportionately affects the world's poorest. Not a single low-income country afflicted by violence has achieved even one of the eight MDGs. Without peace there cannot be development, and solving other challenges becomes impossible. Seen in that light, the benefits of curtailing the costs of conflict are definitely worth considering.

There are now more states than ever and also more disputes, but still relatively few of these lead to war. The types of conflicts range from the ideological struggles that we see in Mozambique, Eritrea, or Nicaragua, to the more fragmented decentralized conflicts such as those of Somalia and Rwanda. Many are a mixture of both.

The nature of war has changed with a decreasing role for formal armies, lack of battlefield engagement, and increased involvement of civilians as victims.

The costs from conflicts can be immense and devastating – yet they are almost always understated because we ignore the legacies that violence leaves behind. The immediately apparent, direct costs are obviously loss of life and injury on the battlefield. But in many countries, conflict leads to far greater casualties because of economic collapse, so that fewer can afford health care, proper food, and education. Because of the long lag in economic recovery after a conflict, people will die for years after a conflict ends. In addition to the direct and legacy costs, there are spinoff costs such as the expense of looking after refugees displaced by one country's internal strife.

Clearly, the complex nature of conflict makes finding solutions immensely challenging. To be able to approach the problem more easily, Dunne focuses on the three obvious points at which we can try to reduce the devastating impact of conflict: preventing it in the first place, intervening to end it when it occurs, and helping to reconstruct a nation after it has ended.

According to Dunne's analysis, conflict prevention is the most cost-effective solution. The causes of conflict are hugely varied and the roots of war are multi-faceted, with important historical contexts. There are a number of factors that can be identified, including colonial legacy, military governments and militaristic cultures, ethnicity and religion, unequal development, inequality and poverty, bad leadership, polity frailties and inadequacies, external influences, greed, and natural resources.

How can we stop conflicts before they occur? Dunne pinpoints early warning mechanisms, peacekeeping operations, economic sanctions, and aid as the tools that have proved most effective.

Dunne calculates that spending about $56 billion over four years on a combination of these measures would lead to benefits on the magnitude of at least $606 billion. Among these benefits, the avoided deaths, injuries, and other conflict-related violence are perhaps the most compelling arguments for the use of available funds for prevention.

Given the high possible benefits of avoided carnage and relatively low costs, conflict prevention has a benefit-cost ratio (BCR) of at least 11. This means that, when we frame it in economic terms so that it can be compared to other interventions, each dollar spent achieves benefits worth at least $11.

If conflicts do break out, the next stage is intervention. At this stage it will be impossible to avoid a significant part of the cost of conflict, and the intervention itself will also be more costly. The projected $100 billion cost of intervention includes better intelligence, economic sanctions, and aid, as well as most likely military intervention. This is nearly double the cost of preventing a conflict in the first place. Yet, with benefits of at least $606 billion, there are still large pay-offs. For each dollar spent, we can avoid conflict damage worth about $5, making intervention a cost-effective use of resources.

When conflicts end, what is needed for reconstruction is contingent on the nature of the conflict and the way that it ended. Most of the costs of conflict have already been incurred, but experience shows that it is possible to speed recovery and reduce the risk of relapse into further violence. Particularly important are the legacy costs of the conflict, such as more general violence within the society. Post-conflict policies can be costly but are also cost-effective in preventing suffering and building up economies that provide new markets and raw materials. According to research by former Copenhagen Consensus Expert Panel member and researcher Paul Collier and others,[2]

[2] Collier *et al.* (2009).

economic reconstruction reduces the risk of a renewed outbreak of conflict by 42 percent in ten years.

The cost of post-conflict policies is higher than intervention at around $140 billion, and the benefits are also smaller, at $404 billion. In total, it is estimated that each dollar will avoid at least $3 of conflict damage. While post-conflict policies may not have the highest BCR, Dunne argues that they are crucial in ensuring that successful development can occur. For that reason, these policies are already attracting considerable resources from the international donor community.

As in past Copenhagen Consensus projects, there is more than one chapter for each topic. The aim of a Copenhagen Consensus Challenge Paper, such as Dunne's Chapter 1, is to present empirically based CBA studies of the highest academic standards within each challenge. These are the central source for the Copenhagen Consensus Expert Panel whose considerations form Part II of this book. Two more subchapters are provided for each main chapter, which are called "Alternative Perspectives." The purpose of these is to balance the Challenge Papers and to indicate any important issues that were not sufficiently dealt with within them. The Alternative Perspective chapters are short, reviewing published research that might have been left out in the original Challenge Paper, and providing alternate interpretations on the estimates or other strengths, weaknesses, and omissions in the economic models. Their role is primarily to spur discussion and reveal substantial professional differences regarding the subject.

In the case of armed conflict, for those wishing to understand the economics of this issue in more depth, an Alternative Perspective by Anke Hoeffler (Chapter 1.1) provides another view on the arguments used by Dunne, as does one by Andrew Mack (Chapter 1.2).

In Chapter 3, Prabhat Jha, Rachel Nugent, Stéphane Verguet, David Bloom, and Ryan Hum look at chronic diseases such as heart disease, stroke, and cancer. These are problems that we associate with rich countries, while infectious diseases such as malaria and HIV/AIDS are more commonly seen as the problems afflicting the poor. But 80 percent of global deaths from chronic diseases occur in low-income and middle-income countries. Cardiovascular disease in low- and middle-income countries killed more than twice as many people in 2001 as did AIDS, malaria, and tuberculosis (TB) combined.

Yet, according to a recent review of donor health funding, chronic disease receives the smallest amount of donor assistance of all health conditions, having lost ground since 1990 relative to infectious diseases. Donor assistance for health was estimated at almost $26 billion in 2009. The amount allocated to chronic disease was $270 million, or a minuscule 1 percent of the total.

Although high-income countries currently bear the biggest economic burden of chronic diseases, developing countries (especially those that are middle-income) will assume an increasing share as their populations grow and the effects of the tobacco epidemic take greater hold. And the costs for governments of achieving maximal adult survival are rising, in contrast to declines in the costs of achieving child survival. This divergence is chiefly a consequence of the lack of tobacco control in most low- and middle-income countries (while smoking rates are declining in many developed countries, they are on the rise in the developing world), the lack of sustained investments in new drugs, and gaps in the strategies and program implementation for chronic diseases.

Jha and his colleagues identify five key priority interventions where the costs are relatively low compared to the benefits.

The most important action is tobacco taxation. Estimating conservatively that tobacco causes about one-third of the vascular disease, half of all cancers and 60 percent of chronic respiratory diseases, the researchers estimate a total economic loss from tobacco of about $12.7 trillion over the next twenty years – or about 1.3 of global GDP annually. Already, tobacco kills up to 6 million people a year, including about 1 million each in China and India. Without increased cessation efforts, tobacco use could account for about 10 million deaths per year by 2030, with most of these occurring in low- and middle-income countries. With no change to current patterns, 1 billion tobacco deaths might occur this century, in contrast to 100 million in the twentieth century.

Reducing tobacco deaths in the next few decades requires current smokers to quit, and tobacco taxation is particularly effective at raising cessation rates: a 10 percent increase in price leads to a 4–8 percent drop in consumption. France, for example, tripled the price of cigarettes quickly (over a decade or so), and this cut consumption per adult in half, while more than doubling tax revenue in real terms. Lung cancer rates for young men in France have fallen sharply since. Tax hikes need not cost anything except the political will to overcome vested interests. Generously estimating a comprehensive tobacco control program including a tobacco tax rise to cost $500 million annually, such a program would avert more than 1 million deaths each year. Put into economic terms, the benefits would be forty times higher than the costs.

The second initiative is using low-cost drugs to avert heart attacks. Jha and his colleagues argue that system-wide efforts to achieve high rates of appropriate drug use administered within hours of an acute heart attack should be a high priority. Up to 300,000 heart-attack deaths could be prevented each year at the cost of $200 million. Jha and his colleagues calculate that, in economic terms, each dollar spent would generate $25 of benefits.

Another approach to the same problem is to create a "generic risk pill." In the absence of any drug therapy, adults with previous stroke, heart attack, diabetes, or any other evidence of some serious vascular disease have about a 7 percent annual risk of either dying or being re-hospitalized with a recurrence. This "generic risk pill" would prevent 1.6 million deaths annually. If the cost per adult patient per year were $100, the total cost would then be $32 billion per year. The higher cost is reflected in a lower "BCR": Each dollar spent on this initiative would see about $4 worth of benefits. Still, this remains an attractive investment.

Next, Jha and his colleagues propose efforts to reduce salt consumption, which is a significant cause of heart disease and strokes. This can be done in food processing or at the cooking or eating stages. The former approach is being tried in Latin America where Brazil, Argentina, and Chile are among the countries with industry agreements to reduce salt in processing. The researchers propose a population-level intervention to reduce salt intake through voluntary manufacturing changes, behavior change using mass media, and other awareness-raising campaigns. An annual expenditure of $1 billion would save more than 1.3 million lives a year from heart disease and strokes, meaning that the benefits are twenty times higher than the costs.

Finally, Hepatitis B is a viral infection that attacks the liver and is the major cause of liver cancer worldwide. The Hepatitis B vaccine can prevent 90 percent of liver cancer deaths, and the Hepatitis B vaccine is safe and very effective when given at birth or in early childhood. The vaccine could cost as little as $3.60 per child vaccinated. Spending $122 million to increase vaccine coverage by 25 percent would avert about 150,000 annual deaths from the disease, forty years into the future. Each dollar spent generates $10 of benefits.

Julia Fox-Rushby (Chapter 3.1) and Marc Suhrcke (Chapter 3.2) present Alternative Perspectives on the topic of tackling chronic disease.

We take a slightly different approach to climate change, tackled in the four-part Chapter 4. This is because we have the results of the 2009 research project, the Copenhagen Consensus on Climate Change, to draw from, in which specialist economists detailed specific ways to respond to climate change, from targeting black carbon emissions to taxing carbon to planting more forests. So we asked some authors from *Smart Solutions to Climate Change* (Lomborg, 2009c) to update their research.

In three cases – geo-engineering, research and development (R&D), adaptation – these authors were chosen for the new volume because their proposed investments were given a relatively high ranking by the Expert Panel in 2009, and in one case (carbon mitigation) because this is the path that the world is currently on.

The latter is discussed first. In Chapter 4.1, Richard S. J. Tol makes the case that there is wide agreement in the economic literature that greenhouse gas (GHG) emission reduction is best done through a carbon tax. Climate policy, he notes, is not about spending money. It is about raising money (and, of course, about finding the best way to spend the revenues raised through a carbon tax).

Tol finds that a low tax of about $1.80 on each ton of carbon would generate benefits (of avoided climate damage) worth between $1.50 and $9. However, a high tax set at $250 would cost much more than it would gain, with benefits of just 2 cents to 12 cents, putting it in the category of "does more damage than it prevents."

In Chapter 4.2, Isabel Galiana and Christopher Green propose a technology-led climate policy. This means dramatically increased R&D, testing, and demonstration of scalable, reliable, and cost-effective low carbon-emitting energy technologies. This will be funded by a low but gradually rising carbon tax, but unlike Tol's proposal the main focus is on innovating cheap, green energy sources.

Galiana and Green argue that the size of the energy technology challenge is huge, and there is a current lack of technological readiness and scalability in low-carbon energy sources. They show that adopting a "brute force" approach to reducing emissions with a carbon tax before green technology is actually ready to take over from fossil fuels could generate economic costs ten times or more than widely published estimates of CO_2 mitigation cost estimates. The authors conclude that increased funding for low-carbon R&D would have benefits ranging from three to eleven times higher than the cost, depending on the rate of success and time horizon.

In Chapter 4.4, Carlo Carraro, Francesco Bosello, and Enrica De Cian look at what can be achieved with adaptation policies. They find that the most important impacts of global warming will be on agriculture and tourism, where nations will lose, on average, about half of 1 percent of GDP from each by the mid-century. However, they point out that much of this damage will actually be avoided by people choosing for themselves to adapt to the change in their environment. Farmers will choose plants that thrive in the heat. New houses will be designed to deal with warmer temperatures.

Taking this into account, rich countries will adapt to the negative impacts of global warming and exploit the positive changes, actually creating a total positive effect of global warming worth about half a percentage point of GDP. However, poor countries will be hit harder. Adaptation will reduce the climate-change-related losses from 5 percent of GDP to slightly less than 3 percent, but this is still a significant negative impact.

The researchers find that, broadly, every dollar spent on adaptation would achieve at least about $1.65 worth of positive changes for the planet.

Finally, in Chapter 4.3, J. Eric Bickel and Lee Lane look at geo-engineering. This essentially means cooling the planet by reflecting more of the sun's rays back to space. There are several different ways to achieve this. One promising approach is stratospheric aerosol injection – where a precursor of sulfur dioxide would be continuously injected into the stratosphere, forming a thin layer of aerosols to reflect sunlight. Another suggested approach is marine cloud whitening, where seawater would be mixed into the atmosphere at sea to make the clouds slightly whiter and more reflective.

Bickel and Lane do not suggest actually implementing such programs at this point, but they look at the costs and benefits of preparing the knowledge of how they might be deployed in the future. They estimate that the cost of a climate-engineering R&D program is on the order of $1 billion: a small fraction of what the United States alone is spending on climate change research each year. They estimate that each dollar spent could create roughly $1,000 of benefits in economic terms.

Such high benefits reflect the fact that solar radiation management holds the potential of reducing the economic damages caused by both warming and costly CO_2 reduction measures (such as carbon taxes). These early-reduction costs tend to be higher than those of climate change; so by lessening the stringency of controls, climate engineering may also provide near-term benefits, compared to strategies relying solely on emissions reductions.

The two Alternative Perspectives tackle all four of the climate change chapters. These are by Samuel Fankhauser (Chapter 4.5) and Anil Markandya (Chapter 4.6).

Next we turn to another major environmental challenge, ecosystems and biodiversity (Chapter 2). The issue of disappearing biodiversity has increasingly received mainstream media attention in the past few years, and is starting to compete with climate change as the most-discussed environmental threat. Biodiversity campaigners have often attempted to capture our attention with pictures of cuddly endangered animals or alarming figures about the rate of disappearing species.

In practice it is difficult to actually quantify the loss of biodiversity, let alone put a value on it. What scientists can do instead is measure "ecosystem services." These are the natural processes by which the environment produces resources used by humans, such as clean water, timber, habitat for fisheries, and pollination of native and agricultural plants. Also included are genetic materials that can help make new life-saving drugs, the recreational and cultural uses of natural environments, the control of agricultural pests, and the value of biomass storing CO_2 (as a counter to global warming).

The links between biodiversity and ecosystem services are still undergoing research. But the most important known fact is that these services have faced major (and measurable) losses. According to the Millennium Ecosystem Assessment (MEA), during the twentieth century the planet lost 50 percent of its wetlands, 40 percent of its forests, and 35 percent of its mangroves. About 60 percent of global ecosystem services have been degraded in just fifty years.

Salman Hussain and his colleagues find that there will be a significant loss of biodiversity over the next forty years. They estimate that this loss could be about 12 percent globally, with South Asia facing a loss of 30 percent and SSA 18 percent. They look at three interventions, and compare these to doing nothing – a "business as usual" (BAU) approach.

The first solution focuses on increasing agricultural productivity through R&D. This may seem like a roundabout way to address biodiversity, but as the global population has increased to 7 billion, we have cut down more and more forest to grow our food. Between now and 2050, we will likely expand agricultural area another 10 percent, and that land will come from forests and grasslands. Thus, if we could increase agricultural productivity, we would need to take less and be able to leave more to nature. The authors estimate that with a $14.5 billion annual infusion into research, we can achieve 20 percent higher annual growth rates for crops and 40 percent higher growth rates for livestock, which over the next forty years will significantly reduce the pressure on nature.

Looking just at tropical forests, this would save an area the same size as Spain, along with a similar amount of temperate forests and more than twice that area of grasslands. In total, the benefits will be on the order of $53 billion. When we take into account that these forests will store more carbon, for every dollar spent, we will do about seven times the amount of good both for biodiversity and climate. And, of course, we will have made more food available and at cheaper prices for future generations, substantially increasing the total benefits. This option is very similar to the one suggested in Chapter 6 on hunger and malnutrition.

Hussain *et al.* note that currently about 10 percent of all land globally is deemed to be "protected" from destruction. They explore increasing protected land to about 20 percent globally (across a large number of ecological regions), over three decades. There are obvious benefits but also significant costs, principally the loss of output from the land that is taken out of use.

Land scarcity arising from such a policy would likely force an increase in agricultural productivity. The cost estimates for the newly protected lands have a big impact on the overall results. With higher assumptions, the program costs more than it achieves, even when the benefits of avoided climate change are included. With lower assumptions it only barely passes, with expenditure of $1 achieving slightly more than $1 worth of good.

However, Hussain *et al.* note that the main reason for this program would be to enhance biodiversity conservation; our current methods of estimation do not fully capture those benefits, so these estimates could be an underestimation.

Forests are one of the main homes to biodiversity. The final program Hussain *et al.* propose seeks to prevent all dense forests from being converted to agriculture over a thirty-year period. They do not attempt to assess the political viability of such an approach. To use the same measure as above, it would save more than seven times the area of Spain in tropical forests.

The benefits are very high, but it must be noted that there is considerable uncertainty about the costs. With estimates they find reasonable, the benefits exceed the costs even without including the CO_2 storage value, and the solution is attractive because it will yield a minimum of $7 for each dollar spent.

Alternative Perspectives are provided by John C. Whitehead and Paul E. Chambers (Chapter 2.2) and Juha V. Siikamäki (Chapter 2.1).

Over the past fifty years, remarkable progress has been made ensuring that children receive a basic education. In Chapter 5, Peter F. Orazem notes that more than 60 percent of adults in low-income countries can read and write, whereas in 1962 just one-third were literate. Today, nearly nine out of ten children globally complete primary school. Most children in developing countries are now already enrolled in school for at least some period, so Peter Orazem points out that we could focus on strategies that improve school quality, either by enhancing the learning that is occurring in school or increasing the number of years of schooling.

Unfortunately, there is very weak knowledge about which inputs actually generate quality schooling outcomes, and many investments are unlikely to generate the desired effects. There is widespread acknowledgment that resources are used inefficiently but, for instance, efforts to improve resource management by devolving authority to local jurisdictions are as likely to fail as succeed.

Peter Orazem thus considers three strategies that appear to offer the best evidence of success to date: nutrition supplements, offering information on returns to schooling, and conditional cash transfers (CCTs) for school attendance. All have been shown to succeed with benefits that exceed the costs.

It may seem surprising to focus on nutrition to achieve better schooling, but malnourished children learn poorly. Ensuring proper nutrition when brain development is occurring makes a significant difference. The benefits are not just educational but also increase health and the child's physical abilities. Provision of nutrient supplements and anti-parasitic medicines is very inexpensive: in Kenya the cost of deworming a child can be as low as $3.50, with benefits twenty–fifty times higher.

Increasing the years a child spends in school simply by providing accurate information to children and parents on the returns of education is another promising and relatively inexpensive intervention. Many children and parents, especially in rural areas, are simply unaware of the long-term benefits that may come from a better education. In Madagascar, for instance, providing children and their parents with accurate information on the value of schooling has been achieved at a cost of $2.30 per child, resulting in total benefits of possibly 600 times the cost.

Although the costs vary across countries, such an intervention could conceivably be built into the standard curriculum at relatively low cost and has the potential of increasing academic effort while in school, as well as increasing years of schooling. However, because of the very few studies available, the benefits from a large-scale information campaign are less certain.

Finally, Orazem argues that the most consistent evidence of success in recent years comes from making payments to underprivileged parents conditional on their children attending school. CCTs have consistently increased child attendance, even when the transfer is modest. Administrative costs have been lower than those of other social interventions. In addition to positive schooling outcomes, these transfers have lowered the poverty rate, improved the nutritional status of poor households, and increased the proportion of children receiving vaccinations and other health services. While there is great variance in performance, a dollar spent on such programs on average produces benefits of about $9.

Because the programs increase the intensity of child investment in school, as well as child time in school, they help to break the cycle of poverty whereby poor parents underinvest in their children's schooling and doom their children to poverty. By increasing child attendance, Orazem argues, we should see an increase in teacher attendance, which will increase the quality of schooling offered to the poorest children.

Yet, cash transfer programs are much more expensive than nutrition or health interventions. That might explain why cash transfer programs are concentrated in wealthier countries while nutrition programs typically focus on the poorest countries.

In general, the climate for all of these interventions is worse where the positive returns are depressed by poor government institutions. Therefore, Orazem argues, the best places to try these interventions are countries that protect individual economic and political freedoms. Of course, those countries would also have better capacity to implement an intervention, whether by distributing medication, transfer payments, or information on the benefits of investing in schooling.

Alternative Perspectives are provided by Lant Pritchett (Chapter 5.1) and George Psacharopoulos (Chapter 5.2).

In Chapter 6, John Hoddinott, Mark Rosegrant, and Maximo Torero tackle the challenges of hunger and malnutrition. The planet creates more than enough food to meet everyone's needs. But there are still around 925 million hungry people in the world, and nearly 180 million pre-school children do not get vital nutrients.

In 2008, the global Copenhagen Consensus project focused attention on the problem of hidden hunger. The Expert Panel found that micronutrient interventions – fortification and supplements designed to increase nutrient intake – were the most effective investment that could be made, with massive benefits for a tiny price-tag.

In Chapter 6, the authors once more propose that decision-makers prioritize micronutrient interventions, and they update the analysis of the costs and benefits of doing so. They find that for a relatively small amount of money – less than $700 million annually – it would be possible to eliminate vitamin A deficiencies in pre-school children, eliminate iodine deficiency globally, and dramatically reduce maternal anemia during pregnancy. But they also offer new solutions, including bundling nutrition interventions, increasing global food production, and improving market functioning through better communications and increased competition in fertilizer markets.

Chronic undernutrition has significant neurological consequences that can damage spatial navigation and memory formation, leading to loss of cognitive abilities and, in time, lower incomes. Hoddinott, Rosegrant, and Torero find that for about $100 per child, by means of a bundle of interventions (including micronutrients and improvements in diet quality and behavior), chronic undernutrition could be reduced by 36 percent in developing countries. Even in very poor countries such as Ethiopia and using very conservative assumptions, each dollar spent reducing chronic undernutrition has a $30 pay-off when seen in economic terms.

Increasing global food production might seem a strange proposal given that, globally, food production actually exceeds food needs. But the researchers argue that lower prices are necessary to make food more affordable and to provide a buffer against some of the negative consequences of climate change. Hoddinott's team looks at how to speed up improvements in agricultural production. This means first and foremost increasing R&D to insure higher yields through extensive breeding. But the researchers also look at ways to increase tolerance to drought, heat, and salt; identifying and disseminating the best varieties of crops; addressing problems like wheat rust; developing resistance to cattle diseases like East Coast Fever; and focusing on soil diagnostics to ensure that optimal combinations of organic and inorganic fertilizers are used.

They propose an $8 billion increase in annual global public investment in agricultural R&D (to $13 billion total annual spending). They use economic modeling to calculate the results on yields, incomes, GDP growth, and prices. This investment would mean that in 2050, canola oil would be 68 percent cheaper, and rice would be nearly 25 percent cheaper than it would otherwise be. There would be 200 million fewer hungry people around the world. Taking global population growth into account, hunger would be 63 percent less prevalent in 2050 than it was in 2010, with the reduction most pronounced in South Asia and SSA. Spending an additional $8 billion per year would, by 2050, reduce the number of hungry people in the world by 210 million and the number of underweight children by 10 million. Put into economic terms, the BCR of this spending is at least 16:1, indicating high returns to expanded investment in agricultural R&D. Moreover, they estimate that reduced price variability could more than double the benefits.

Roughly 80 percent of the global hungry live in rural areas and half are smallholders. The researchers propose a dual approach to improving the economic conditions of the rural poor, by providing market information through cellphones and reducing barriers to fertilizer access.

In India, the Reuters Market Light program sends text messages to smallholders with crop advice. The monthly cost is $1.50, and recipients get configurable, location-specific weather forecasts, local price information, and local and international commodity information. Hoddinott looks at African and South Asian studies into the impact of improved market information, and concludes that with the most pessimistic assumptions this investment can be justified only in a few countries. But under any other set of assumptions, benefits will exceed costs and in some cases do so by a considerable factor, up to 8.35 in return for every dollar spent.

There have been mixed results from policies designed to stimulate sustainable fertilizer use, but Hoddinott and his colleagues note that not much has been said about developing regions and their increasing dependence on imported fertilizer. A small number of countries control most of the production capacity for the main nitrogen, phosphate, and potash fertilizers. In most cases, the top four firms control more than half of each country's production capacity. Policy-makers could consider forcing the breakup of this concentrated industry. But apart from the disruption this would cause, it could lead to a loss of economies of scale. Regulation is another possibility, but imposing price restrictions could lead to unproductive rent-seeking. Instead, the researchers propose investment in the construction of new production capacity. Private companies are deterred from entering the market by high fixed costs and strategic pricing behavior by incumbents, so the researchers outline a case for public investment in production capacity with the understanding that the operation of the facility would be turned over to the private sector. Hoddinott estimates that building fertilizer plants with annual production capacity high enough to be a top-four firm would cost $1.2 billion in South Asia and $700 million in Africa. Put into economic terms, the NPV of doing so is $12.5 billion.

Alternative perspectives on these economic arguments are posited by Beatrice Lorge Rogers (Chapter 6.2) and Anil B. Deolalikar (Chapter 6.1).

Chapter 7 deals with infectious diseases. It is difficult to overstate how much the fight against infectious disease improved the human condition in the twentieth century. Dean T. Jamison, Prabhat Jha, Ramanan Laxminarayan, and Toby Ord point out that improved immunization saves more lives per year than would be saved by global peace. The same is true for smallpox eradication, diarrhea treatment, and malaria treatment. Nonetheless major problems remain, and Jamison and his colleagues explore the ways to step up our battle against the biggest killer diseases, and identify five top priorities.

The most important of these is malaria treatment. The malaria parasite has developed a resistance to the effective, inexpensive, and widely available drugs that have previously provided an important partial check on the high levels of child deaths caused by malaria in Africa.

The resistance to these older drugs is leading to a rise in deaths and illness that could number in the hundreds of thousands. A high priority for additional spending is to reduce the relative prices that poor countries face for new artemisinin combination therapies (through the so-called "affordable medicines facility – malaria"). Every $1 million spent on this financing mechanism of the Global Fund means about 300,000 more children treated, 20,000 with severe malaria. This would prevent 1,000 deaths. Thus, spending $300 million a year would prevent 300,000 child deaths, with benefits, put in economic terms, which are thirty-five times higher than the costs. Various donors have reviewed extending this facility, and this analysis suggests it is one of the best returns on health that could be made globally.

The second intervention is the control of TB, which kills more adults than any other infectious disease besides HIV/AIDS. Nearly 9 million new cases of TB appeared in 2003, causing perhaps 1.6 million deaths, with nine out of ten being in low- and middle-income countries.

Growing drug resistance suggests that the current approach might not be able to bring TB under control, especially in Africa and the former Soviet republics. Addressing resistance increases costs and the short-term benefits in saved lives are limited. This means that compared with 2008, when the costs and benefits were calculated for the Copenhagen Consensus 2008, the benefits for each dollar spent are actually lower. But, with each dollar achieving more $15 worth of benefits in economic terms, TB control remains a very worthwhile investment. Spending $1.5 billion would save 1 million adult deaths annually.

The third approach Jamison and his colleagues outline is expanding case management of acutely ill children and adding several new antigens to routine vaccinations. These include Haemophilus influenza type b (Hib) and Streptococcus pneumonia which are common causes of childhood pneumonia; Hepatitis B which protects against liver cancer; and newer rotavirus and shigella vaccines to prevent diarrhea. The Global Alliance for Vaccines and Immunization estimates that the addition of Hib and pneumococcal vaccines to vaccination programs could save 800,000 lives a year, and rotavirus and shigella vaccines might save 600,000. In total, Jamison's team estimates that spending about $1 billion annually on expanded immunization coverage would save 1 million child deaths annually. Put into economic terms, the benefits would be twenty times higher than the costs.

Another priority is deworming. The costs of worm treatment are low and the prevalence is high, but this remains a neglected infection. From complications with digestion to difficulty absorbing nutrients, worms can be detrimental to a person's overall well-being, hampering productivity, appetite, fitness, and growth. Children are at greater risk of infection than adults and will suffer more severe, lifelong complications if worms are left untreated. Children who experience worm infection often live in poor communities and need a sustainable treatment plan to remedy any loss in education, nutrition, and intellectual development they may experience. Spending $300 million would mean about 300 million children could be dewormed, with benefits in economic terms ten times higher than the costs.

No disease comes close to the HIV/AIDS epidemic in threatening every aspect of development for dozens of countries. Unfortunately, it is also in many ways the hardest to tackle. Jamison and his colleagues draw on research created for the Copenhagen Consensus and Rush Foundation project *RethinkHIV* to identify priorities against this disease. The most effective preventive interventions against HIV/AIDS are those targeting sex workers and those most likely to contribute to increased transmission, as has been done successfully in India and other Asian countries. Voluntary counseling and testing has reduced unsafe behavior in some studies, although the duration of this change is not clear. Prevention of mother-to-child infection is cheap and effective, and needle exchange and blood safety programs can reduce other modes of transmission.

An HIV/AIDS vaccine is the ultimate preventative tool. The researchers use *RethinkHIV* research by Robert Hecht and Dean Jamison on the costs and benefits of increasing research funding to speed up the arrival of a useful vaccine. Jamison concludes that there is a strong case for increasing HIV/AIDS vaccine R&D by $100 million annually. Even with conservative assumptions, each dollar spent would generate benefits worth twenty times the costs. The Alternative Perspectives are by Till Bärnighausen (Chapter 7.1) and David Canning (Chapter 7.2).

In Chapter 8, Howard Kunreuther and Erwann Michel-Kerjan look at natural disasters and argue that hurricanes, earthquakes, and floods impose an economic toll that can disrupt and undermine a fragile country for a long time. This cost is growing. According to the reinsurer Munich Re, direct economic losses from natural catastrophes amounted to $1.6 trillion from 2001 to 2011. Small island economies like St. Lucia and Samoa have suffered high losses to productivity because of disasters. Nature can impose a roadblock to the growth that lifts people out of poverty.

Costs from natural disasters are increasing largely because more people choose to live in harm's way. This trend, combined with the expectation of some events becoming more extreme because of changes in climate patterns, challenges the human capacity to adapt. The researchers propose a series of concrete actions that would reduce the vulnerability of poor nations to such large-scale catastrophes.

They propose investments in four risk-reduction measures. The first three proposals are designed to better protect against damage and loss of life from earthquakes, floods, and hurricanes, and the fourth one is intended to more generally increase the resilience of communities.

First, the authors propose designing schools that can withstand earthquakes to reduce damage and also the number of fatalities to children, teachers, and other staff. Retrofitting the schools in all thirty-five most-exposed countries around the world would save the lives of 250,000 individuals over the next fifty years. Costs vary dramatically from country to country: in the Solomon Islands it would cost just $36 million to retrofit schools with cumulative total benefits worth $187 million, but for all other countries the benefits are dramatically lower, meaning that any program of global reach would probably pay back less than the initial investment.

Kunreuther and Michel-Kerjan's second proposal is to invest in community flood walls and elevated homes to protect areas subject to floods. It would cost $5.2 trillion to elevate by 1 m all houses subject to flooding in the thirty-four countries most susceptible to this hazard and another $940 billion to build walls around the relevant communities in all thirty-four countries. The most cost-effective approach would be to invest $75 billion into building flood walls around some of these communities. Kunreuther and Michel-Kerjan calculate the benefits over the next fifty years as $4.5 trillion, making the benefits a remarkable sixty times higher than the costs. Those benefits would mostly come from reduction in damages, though the walls would also save 20,000 lives.

Thirdly, Kunreuther and Michel-Kerjan propose strengthening the roofs of houses in countries with high exposure to hurricanes and cyclones to reduce losses from wind damage. This would cost $951 billion in the thirty-four countries most prone to high-wind events, with benefits ranging between two and three times this amount. This measure would save 65,700 lives over the next fifty years.

Finally, Kunreuther and Michel-Kerjan explore setting up disaster early-warning systems (EWS). Based on existing studies and research from Stéphane Hallegatte, they find that EWS in developing countries would require less than $1 billion a year and would have direct benefits (reductions in the losses from disasters) of between $1 billion and $5.5 billion per year. There are additional benefits, such as the reduction in evacuation costs, the reduced costs to the health care system, improved continuity of education (from preserving schools), reduced social stress, and avoided business interruption, which are worth at least another $3 billion and possibly $30 billion. In total, the benefits could range from four to thirty-five times their cost.

But who should pay for disaster protection measures? As Kunreuther and Michel-Kerjan point out, there is a need to persuade international donors to start investing more systematically in disaster risk reduction before a disaster strikes, rather than focusing almost exclusively on post-disaster assistance, as they do today. Similarly, non-governmental organizations (NGOs) must put their time and energy into promoting measures that reduce future losses and fatalities rather than focusing on emergency relief. And more governments in developed countries and multinational corporations (MNCs) need to provide funding and technical expertise to assist low-income countries in undertaking these measures.

Kunreuther and Michel-Kerjan point out that the way that we often approach decisions, with short-term costs rather than long-term benefits in mind, can get in the way of policy-makers making their necessary change in approach. To address these issues, they propose new programs such as multi-year insurance coupled with disaster risk-reduction loan programs, as well as alternative risk transfer instruments for covering catastrophic losses.

Ilan Noy (Chapter 8.2) and Stéphane Hallegatte (Chapter 8.1) provide Alternative Perspectives on Kunreuther's and Michel-Kerjan's work.

Population is the challenge tackled in Chapter 9 by Hans-Peter Kohler. In 2011, the world's population reached 7 billion. It added the seventh billion in merely twelve years, similar to the time it took to add the fifth and sixth billion. Despite this rapid growth, the doomsday predictions of previous decades about the potentially disastrous consequences of rapid population growth have not materialized. Indeed, during the recent decades of rapid global population growth, various summary measures of individual well-being have in fact increased.

Kohler looks at SSA nations that, among high-fertility countries, make the dominant contribution to world population growth. These nations are among the poorest and most vulnerable in the world, often having weak institutions and capacities to manage population growth. "High-fertility" countries today account for about 38 percent of the 78 million people that are added annually to the world's population, despite the fact that they are home to only 18 percent of it. After 2060, the world's population is projected to grow exclusively as a result of population growth in today's high-fertility countries.

Kohler argues that many high-fertility SSA countries have a considerable – and possibly growing – "unmet need" for family planning: this means women who are not using any contraception but do not want more children, or want to delay the next child. About 25 percent of sexually active women would like to limit their fertility but do not use family-planning methods.

Family-planning programs that facilitate a decline in fertility and a reduction in population growth rate would seem to be potentially highly beneficial interventions that should be expanded. And yet, as Kohler outlines, this conclusion has been subject to a long-standing and sometimes heated debate, often questioning the very basic pillars of this deduction.

This debate has sometimes raised more questions than answers: how detrimental, if at all, is population growth for economic development, individual well-being, and the attainment of development indicators such as the MDGs? Do family-planning programs have causal effects toward reducing fertility, or would the declines that have been observed in fertility areas have also been observed in the absence of these programs? Is there a window of opportunity in coming decades in which declines in population growth could provide a "demographic dividend" that would facilitate social and economic development in some of the world's most developed countries?

In the last two decades, a growing body of research has substantially strengthened the case for family-planning programs – documenting, for example, the significant effects of such programs toward reducing fertility, increasing education for mothers, improving women's general health and longer-term survival, increasing female labor force participation and earnings, and improving child health.

However, the attempt to obtain reasonably reliable estimates of both the benefits and costs of these programs remains very challenging. Kohler draws on recent estimates to find that expanding family-planning services to all women with unmet needs – 215 million women – would require an additional annual expenditure of $3.6 billion, bringing the total cost to $6.7 billion annually. Three-quarters of these additional expenses would be required for program and other systems costs related to expanding family planning services, while only 16 percent would be required for the supplies and contraceptive commodities.

The benefits are large. Reduced fertility, increased child spacing, and possible reductions in unwanted fertility are likely to reduce infant and maternal mortality, each year leading to 150,000 fewer maternal deaths and 600,000 fewer motherless children. These effects alone, Kohler estimates, are worth more than $110 billion, meaning that each dollar spent will achieve $30–$50 of benefits.

But, moreover, it is also estimated that reduced fertility will lead to higher levels of female education, and increases in female labor force participation and earnings. At the same time, fewer children and more men and women in the work force will increase economic growth over the coming decades. Essentially, reductions in fertility and population growth rates would result in sustained increases in GDP per capita over several decades. This could lead to an extra benefit of perhaps $60 for every dollar spent.

With the caveat that knowledge about the interactions between population and development remains limited and heated discussion surrounds many assumptions, Kohler's research suggests substantial BCRs for family-planning programs. Altogether, he finds that every dollar spent in this area could result in benefits worth about $90–$150.

David Lam (Chapter 9.2) and Oded Galor (Chapter 9.1) present Alternative Perspectives on the topic of population.

Water and sanitation (Chapter 10) is the last of the ten chapters that examine the costs and benefits of competing solutions. Frank Rijsberman and Alix Peterson Zwane argue that development agencies overemphasize safe-water projects and underinvest in sanitation. Rijsberman and Zwane look at what it would cost to improve sanitation services for both the unserved population in developing countries (those 1 billion or so who must defecate in the open), and what it would cost to improve the quality of service for those people in urban areas who are nominally "served" but are confronted with the challenges of emptying and safely disposing of latrine or septic-tank contents. An estimated 200 million latrines and septic tanks are emptied manually, by a worker descending into the pit with a bucket and spade, and subsequently dumped or buried in the immediate environment, often reintroducing pathogens previously contained in the pit or tank.

They propose three solutions which they argue are potentially worthy of large-scale investment.

The first of these is community-led total sanitation (CLTS), the name given to various forms of an approach that emphasizes behavior change, particularly making it the community's responsibility to share in the creation of communities that are free from open defecation, especially in rural areas. Rijsberman and Zwane base their calculations on a large-scale behavior-change program, reaching 23 million with a one-off delivery cost of $3 to $5 per person affected.

Given the rapid adoption of community-led total-sanitation programs aiding tens of millions of people over the last ten years and the relatively high rate of success in achieving "open-defecation free" (ODF) communities, they consider this to be a comparatively low-risk intervention.

Their analysis implies that about 50 percent of people in rural areas – about 600 million people – who lack access to basic sanitation could be reached with a total investment of $3 billion, providing welfare benefits that are four–seven times higher.

The second intervention Rijsberman and Zwane explore is sanitation as a business. For the existing 2 billion latrines and septic tanks in developing countries, a critical bottleneck – one that affects the urban poor particularly – is that there are no affordable and sustainable services to effectively and efficiently empty them and process the fecal sludge safely and economically.

Typically, the sludge is just deposited on the ground, negating almost all of the health benefits of sanitation. The solution is to generate innovation in sanitation services, reducing the cost of this service from between $35 and $91 per household to just $10 per household per year. That cost pays for emptying the latrine or septic tank, transporting the fecal sludge to a treatment plant, and treating it to acceptable levels before reuse or dispersal into the environment. While speculative, the authors provide illustrative calculations that suggest that an investment in innovation to develop these technologies, including an initial subsidized rollout, would provide benefits to about 40 million people at a cost of $320 million and overall benefits worth between twenty-seven and forty-six times higher than the costs.

Third, Rijsberman and Zwane propose the "reinvented toilet" – one of the signature ideas of the Bill and Melinda Gates Foundation: efforts to stimulate technical innovation, particularly harnessing advances in physics, chemistry, and engineering, to create a radically reinvented toilet that recycles human waste into reusable products at the household scale.

Early in 2011, the Bill and Melinda Gates Foundation challenged more than twenty top universities to use modern science and engineering to come up with a significantly different form of processing and recycling human waste that does not depend on sewer networks and large volumes of water for transportation. The challenge was to develop a system that is off the grid, affordable for the poorest members in society (meaning that it costs less than a nickel a day), and an aspirational product – something that everyone will want to use and that over time will replace the flush toilet as the new gold standard.

The foundation awarded eight "reinvent the toilet" challenge grants and funded another fifty-seven small grants in 2011 that aimed to innovate all or part of the non-sewered value chain. All complete reinvented toilets are currently at the laboratory/proof-of-concept to prototype stage and therefore investments in the development of this solution are high risk. The Foundation expected to review the first series of prototypes and proof-of-concept results for parts and processes in August 2012.

Assuming that this investment would lead to 100 percent coverage for all latrines currently emptied manually, this $125 million investment would pay back $40 for each invested dollar, serving 1 billion people. In addition, if successful, the "reinvented toilet" would serve many more of the other 3.5 billion people who currently do not have access to a flush toilet. Presuming a reinvented toilet can be successfully developed, and can become an aspirational product – the smartphone of sanitation – the issues of high cost, slow adoption, and limited benefits that variously plague the current generation of sanitation technologies will be overcome.

W. Michael Hanemann (Chapter 10.1) and Guy Hutton (Chapter 10.2) provide Alternative Perspectives on Chapter 10.

Hutton's chapter ends the section of research that establishes concrete costs and benefits for each investment. But there are two more chapters, that are devoted to major global challenges whose solutions are largely political rather than a matter of spending more money. The chapters on Corruption (Chapter 11) and on Trade barriers (Chapter 12) were considered by members of the Expert Panel, who comment on them in Part II, and they still include cost and benefit estimates. Their inclusion here is to highlight the benefits of responding to these challenges, as well as outline the barriers and implementation issues.

In Chapter 11, Susan Rose-Ackerman and Rory Truex examine different solutions to tackle corruption.

The authors caution that, at present, there is a lack of good data on the relative effectiveness of most reform programs. Yet, even without definitive studies, some options look promising because benefits seem clear and costs are minimal. Even if the benefits cannot be precisely measured, the rates of return appear large.

Perhaps the most often prescribed remedy for corruption is to increase top-down monitoring and punishment. Improved monitoring, whether in the form of an external auditor, an anti-corruption agency, or an international oversight body, increases the probability of being caught. There is some evidence that increased monitoring does have positive effects on government performance.

The natural complements to external monitoring and punishment by formal organization are increased transparency and bottom-up accountability. Citizens have an interest in fighting corruption and, if given a voice, they can be a potent force for its reduction. In 2004, the Ugandan government began publishing the details of education-funding processes in local newspapers, allowing citizens and schoolmasters to better monitor the release of funds from higher levels of government. The analysis shows that communities with better access to newspapers, as well as more informed schoolmasters, experienced lower leakage rates, and that the introduction of the newspaper campaign as a whole substantially reduced leakage rates and associated embezzlement. The release of such vital information to citizens may require little more than a website or a well-placed newspaper story, and the potential returns may be quite large.

Internal bureaucratic reorganization and the improved administration of public programs are equally, if not more, important to the anti-corruption calculus. If bureaucrats have easy access to rents, an abundance of corrupt partners, and a low public service ethos, self-dealing is nearly inevitable. Internal reforms, such as meritocratic recruitment and competitive public salaries, can help ensure that those situations do not occur.

When the state carries out large-scale projects, signs contracts, and sells assets, such deals produce substantial financial gains that are difficult to monitor. Grand corruption may thus be a serious problem. Reforms in this category could include both more competitive and transparent bidding processes and careful evaluation of what is being bought and sold in order to be sure that these choices are not distorted by self-dealing officials.

However, if government bodies are riddled with corruption and inefficiency, a final drastic remedy is to remove certain tasks from the public sector completely, moving their provision to the private sector. Firms have taken over basic service provision in parts of India, tax collection in Uganda, transportation in Mexico City, and parts of customs inspection in over fifty developing countries. The existing record suggests that privatization is a high-risk, high-reward strategy – some reforms seem to have substantially reduced corruption; others appear to have made the situation worse.

Rose-Ackerman and Truex stress the need to focus not only on controls inside states where corrupt deals occur but also on international forums. At the international level, reforms should go beyond the weak enforcement mechanisms in existing treaties and contracts.

Kym Anderson (Chapter 12) looks at the barriers to international trade in goods, services, and capital flows. Such policies hurt the economies imposing them, but are particularly harmful to the world's poorest people. Anderson argues that addressing this challenge would therefore also reduce poverty and thereby assist in meeting several of the other challenges identified in this project, including malnutrition, disease, poor education, and air pollution.

The challenge involves finding politically attractive ways to phase out remaining distortions to world markets for goods and services. Kym Anderson focuses on how costly those anti-poor trade policies are, and examines possible strategies to reduce remaining distortions. He addresses four opportunities in particular.

Among the most feasible opportunities available today for encouraging trade negotiations to stimulate significant market opening, the most obvious is a non-preferential legally binding partial liberalization of goods and services trade following the WTO's current round of multilateral trade negotiations, the Doha Development Agenda (DDA).

The NPV of the future benefits of a Doha Agreement ranges from $12 trillion to $64 trillion. The costs are less than $400 billion in present value (PV) terms, but they are mostly private rather than government costs and are dwarfed by the gross benefits. Today's developing countries would reap just over half of those net gains, as their share of the global economy is assumed to grow throughout this century (although at a progressively slower rate after 2025). Their BCRs from the trade reform opportunity offered by the Doha Round are between 140 and 250, which means it is an extremely high pay-off activity, if only the political will to bring about a successful conclusion to the Doha Round can be found. The global BCRs from Doha are not much lower, at between 90 and 180.

If for political reasons the Doha Round cannot be brought to a successful conclusion with all the flexibilities demanded by developing countries, governments still have the opportunity to form preferential trade agreements.

One involves the proposed Trans-Pacific Partnership (TPP) among a subset of member countries of the Asia-Pacific Economic Cooperation (APEC) grouping. Another subregional agreement involves extending the free-trade area (FTA) among the ten-member Association of South East Asian Nations (ASEAN) to include China, Japan, and Korea (ASEAN+3).

The third opportunity is an FTA among all APEC countries. APEC leaders have endorsed both the TPP and ASEAN+3 integration tracks and see them as potential pathways to an FTA involving all APEC members.

Of the three possibilities among countries in the Asia-Pacific region, the greatest estimated gain would come if all APEC member countries agreed to form a region-wide FTA (FTAAP).

That is assumed to involve completely freeing all trade, albeit preferentially within the Asia-Pacific region (including Russia). This contrasts to a Doha Agreement, which would only partially open up trade, albeit non-preferentially so that all trading partners are involved (as the WTO membership now includes nearly 160 members and thus almost all of world trade).

Since the APEC members are projected to comprise nearly three-fifths of global GDP by 2025, it is not surprising that an FTA among them could yield a benefit to the world that is three-quarters of what Doha is projected to deliver. Furthermore, the FTAAP is projected to deliver a slightly greater benefit to developing countries as a group than is Doha. This is partly because under Doha developing countries are assumed to reform less than high-income countries, and partly because by 2025 the APEC grouping will account for around two-thirds of the GDP of all developing countries.

The two other opportunities analyzed by Anderson involve subregional FTAs in the Asia-Pacific region, and so necessarily yield smaller benefits than an FTA for the entire APEC region: fewer countries are liberalizing, and only for their trade with a subset of APEC members. Of those two, the ASEAN+3 proposal would yield more than twice the global and developing country benefits as the TPP between the United States and a number of small APEC economies.

In Part II, Ranking the Opportunities, an Expert Panel of five economists – including four Nobel Laureates – provides their views of the solutions looked at in Part I. Economists were chosen – as in the past – because they are experts in prioritization and comparing costs and benefits across the many different challenges.

As in the previous Copenhagen Consensus 2008 projects, this group – comprising Finn E. Kydland, Robert Mundell, Thomas Schelling, Vernon Smith, and Nancy Stokey – examined all of the research presented here. They traveled to Copenhagen and engaged with all of the core authors over three days. Each session started with a short presentation by the Challenge Paper author, and then these authors were interviewed by the Panel. The specialists then left, and the experts discussed their considerations and reasons for ranking the solutions, which they would do before they ended the session.

The experts each, individually, came to their own conclusions about the merits of each suggested solution to each Challenge. As in past Copenhagen Consensus exercises, their consensus findings were achieved by taking the median of the expert rankings as the ranking in the common list (found in Figure 1.1). This procedure provided a common ranking while ensuring that one expert changing his or her ranking at the extreme would not make the general ranking change, but would rather require a majority of experts to change their ranking.

In Part II, you can find not only the economists' consensus, shared opinion, but also their individual rankings. Their work highlights some of the most cost-effective responses to global challenges.

It is vital, however, that these important issues are not just left to economists. This book serves to give everybody the opportunity to consider (and reconsider) their own priorities. The framework presented here provides a way for you to compare investments side by side. Which do you find we should focus on first? Which would help the world the most? Which deserve more attention from policy-makers in your region? And, crucially, what are you going to do about it?

Bibliography

Collier, P., L. Chauvet, and H. Hegre, 2009: The security challenge in conflict-prone countries, in B. Lomborg (ed.), *Global Crises, Global Solutions*, 2nd edn., Cambridge

Lomborg, B., 2005: *Global Crises, Global Solutions*, Cambridge

2009a: *Global Crises, Global Solutions*, 2nd edn., Cambridge

2009b: *Latin American Development Priorities*, Cambridge

2009c: *Smart Solutions to Climate Change*, Cambridge

2012: *RethinkHIV*, Cambridge

World Bank, 2006: *Repositioning Nutrition as Central to Development: A Strategy for Large-Scale Action*, World Bank, Washington, DC, www.wphna.org/downloadsnov2011/2006%20Bank%20Repositioning%20Nutrition.pdf

PART I

The Solutions

CHAPTER 1

Armed Conflicts

J. PAUL DUNNE

I am grateful to Kasper Thede Anderskov, Jurgen Brauer, Anke Hoeffler, Guy Lamb, Bjørn Lomborg, Andrew Mack, Ron Smith, and an anonymous referee for comments and suggestions. The usual disclaimer applies.

Introduction: the problem

In each year of the 1980s and 1990s there were between thirty and forty major armed conflicts in progress, though over the 2000s active major armed conflicts have declined. In 2007, there were fourteen major armed conflicts active in thirteen locations around the world, nearly all of which were internal or interstate disputes over government or territory – civil wars. There was a wide variation in the intensity of these conflicts, from "low intensity" guerrilla–government conflicts to conflicts between relatively large and well-equipped armies.[1] While there are less of them they tend to last longer and range from ideological struggles (Mozambique, Eritrea, Nicaragua) to more fragmented decentralized conflicts (Somalia and Rwanda), with many a mixture of both at any particular time. The nature of war has changed, with an increasing role for less formal armies, lack of battlefield engagement, and increased involvement of civilians as victims. There are now more states and more disputes, but still relatively few lead to war.

The causes of conflict are as varied as the nature of conflict and the roots of war are multi-faceted, with important historical contexts. There are a number of potential factors that can be identified, including colonial legacy; military governments and militaristic cultures; ethnicity and religion; unequal development; inequality and poverty; bad leadership and/or polity frailties and inadequacies; external influences; greed/opportunity/feasibility; and natural resources. Very few conflicts are simple, they are often a combination of factors, and this fact can have important implications for the achievement of peace and the success of post-conflict reconstruction policies.

There are differences in opinion on the effects of war. Some suggest a positive role of modernization – conflict and war can be positive or at least have positive effects – but most emphasize that the destructive effects of conflict and war have real costs and impact negatively upon economies. They also have legacy costs that can last for a long time. As we shall see, the actual costs of conflict are huge, both direct and indirect, and tend to fall on some of the world's poorest countries. The true costs are almost invariably understated as the legacy costs can continue for many years in countries the international community would see as peaceful.

The benefits of armed conflict and armed violence

While there is little discussion of the possible benefits of conflict and armed violence, they do exist and can be important. Many modern states owe their form to some conflict or other and conflict and war can have positive economic effects in removing bad leaders or leading to the introduction of structures and governance needed for modernization. In an attempt to rebalance the analysis of civil wars Cramer (2006) points out that conflicts could be important in the process of economic development, allowing the "primitive accumulation" that allows resources to be placed

[1] Low-intensity conflicts are those between 25 and 1,000 battle deaths a year and the "major armed conflict" figure covers conflicts with 1,000 or more battle deaths a year.

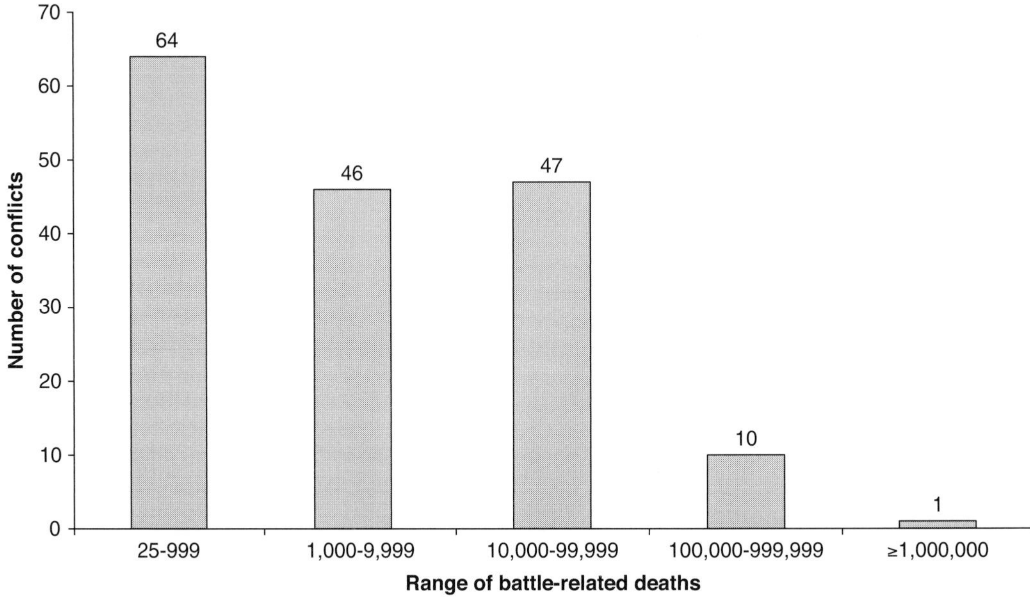

Figure 1.1 *Battle-related deaths, 1946–2005*

Source: Anderton and Carter (2009) based on PRIO data.

in the hands of a ruling class that can use them to support industrialization. In addition, the basic neoclassical models would forecast that countries would just bounce back quickly from conflict to long-term trend, with some sort of phoenix effect – (Organski and Kugler, 1977). But such predictions would be for the long run and it is unclear how long that could take. Certainly the destruction of old capital can have benefits and there may even be human capital gains, while there may be positive effects of spillovers, as immigrants/refugees can boost the labor force in the host country. While there may be such benefits, it is extremely difficult to measure them, or to disentangle them from the negative impacts we consider next. It is, however, important to recognize that conflicts can be complex and have complex effects and that care needs to be taken in any form of intervention.

Measuring the costs of armed conflict and armed violence

The costs of armed conflicts are massive and wide-ranging. We can distinguish a range, starting with the short- and medium-term ones that are generally recognized – the lives lost, permanent injuries, refugees, military expenditure, asset losses (destroyed capital including human), GDP/production losses (income losses), and trade losses (specialization losses). In addition there are the long-term costs which are often not considered, including intergenerational effects, transboundary effects, and environmental effects. Another way of looking at the costs is to distinguish destruction and deferred accumulation and legacy costs.

The immediately apparent costs are loss of life. As Figure 1.1 shows, most wars are relatively small, with most in the 25–999 battle related deaths range. In some datasets these would not be considered as the definition of an active war is >1,000 battle-related deaths. The vast majority of conflicts have fewer than 100,000 battle-related deaths. But this is not the whole story by any means, as in many countries conflict leads to many hidden casualties and the devastation can mean that people die for years after a conflict ends – a legacy cost of the conflict that is often ignored. As Figure 1.2 shows estimated fatalities for genocides and politicides are disturbing. Up to 1992 Afghanistan had seen

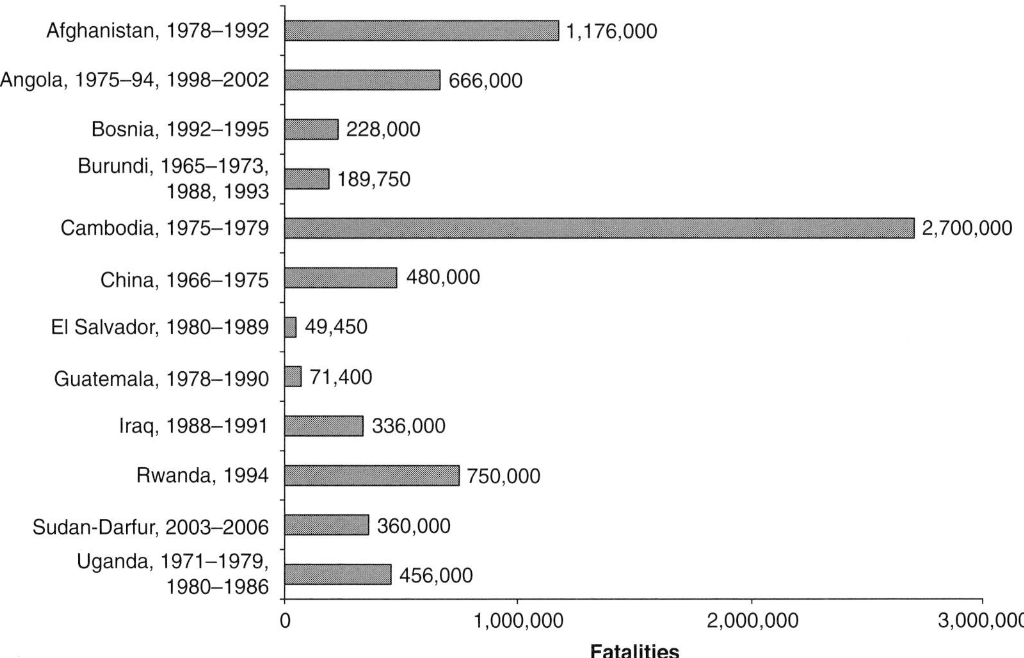

Figure 1.2 *Fatalities, selected conflicts*

Source: Anderton and Carter (2009).

over 1 million fatalities, with estimates suggesting almost 1 million military-related casualties since the US and coalition invasion, a figure that is dwarfed by the genocide in Cambodia which took an estimated 2.7 million lives.

While the accuracy of these data can be questioned, as more recent estimates tend to reduce the figures given here (for example, in Bosnia) and as they contain relatively imprecise estimates of wider/indirect deaths from war, they still give support to the argument that the costs of conflict can be very large. Deaths are, however, only part of the violence engendered by conflict. The World Health Organization (WHO) (2002) differentiates among forms of violence by grouping them into three categories: self-harm (including suicide), interpersonal violence (e.g. violence between intimate partners and other forms of family violence; rape and sexual assault by strangers; violence committed in institutional settings, such as schools, prisons, and workplaces), and collective violence (e.g., armed conflict between, among, and within states; violent political repression and genocide; violent acts of terror; organized crime). Together, these form a system of violence progressing from individual and relationship-related violence to communal and large-scale violence. The existence of conflict in a country creates the environment in which all forms of violence are possible and the less "headline" forms often remain as a legacy when the conflict is supposedly over.

There are two main frameworks used to measure the economic costs. First, the economic growth framework, which considers that if conflict affects performance of the economy it should be through the factors of production or technology, plus the institutions and culture that augments them. Different frameworks can give different conclusions. In a basic neoclassical growth model a one-time shock to capital stock may not affect the equilibrium, but poverty trap, endogenous growth and vintage-type models will create persistent effects that can be damaging. Asymmetric destruction could influence the recovery of an economy and certainly in a Barro-type endogenous growth model a disproportionate loss of human capital could lead to slower recovery. There is also an identification problem, in that countries in conflict could be different to peaceful countries, so that bad performance after the conflict could reflect what a country was like before the conflict rather than the fact that it was damaged by the conflict.[2] As regards physical capital, the evidence suggests that the post-war evolution of capital shows a rapid recovery to equilibrium, consistent with the neoclassical prediction.[3] Such predictions may be overoptimistic, however, as economic devastation may also prevent a durable peace, leading to further costs. In addition, there are also factors that the models do not consider, the destruction of household assets – peasant households, the flight of capital, the effect of uncertainty on the cost of capital – which can play important roles in economic recovery. As mentioned already, many people are killed in conflict and this has an impact on the labor force and human capital, but while there may be mixed evidence on how long the economic effects last, there are clearly negative human capital effects on both combatants and non-combatants. While fatalities may be relatively low, as a proportion of the population, related deaths and injuries can increase the impact significantly. At the same time institutions and economic networks also suffer damage and these can be important in growth, though there is little work on how they evolve, adapt, and decline in civil war. However, war does not have to be destructive to institutions, as it may create a better state or ruler and improve governance, but in general this is not the case and certainly not during the conflict (from a civilian perspective). What effects conflicts have can also vary, depending on how the war started and why and how it ended, such as in stalemate or victory for one side (Blattman and Miguel, 2010). There are also other non-neoclassical frameworks that identify further paths and impacts. Again there is a tendency to see war as destructive and bad for economies in Keynesian approaches, though the preparation may not necessarily be so. There may also be disequilibrium effects on economies and impacts on the path of technology that can reduce potential growth.

To measure the actual impact, the cost of conflict, there are two approaches – the accounting and counterfactual methods. In the accounting approach the researcher would try to work out the total value of goods destroyed. A fairly comprehensive schema would set the direct and indirect costs as in Table 1.1. The task is then to find values for as many of the headers as possible. This is a very difficult task and can really only be attempted for case studies of individual countries; in most cases there will also be many missing values and guesstimates. Some recent effort has been made in this, but it is difficult to compare and aggregate to get a figure for total costs. Different countries are likely to have different headers completed and different levels of detail available (de Groot *et al.*, 2009). The problem with this sort of method is the fact that the more carefully you look, the more cost you can find, and so high costs might simply reflect high effort by the researchers rather than any real difference in cost of conflict.

The second and more commonly used approach is counterfactual analysis, where an attempt is made to compare the path of the economy in and after the conflict with the likely path it would have taken in the absence of conflict. This comparator could be a simple trend, the average for the income bracket of the country, another similar country, or an artificial country (a combination of countries that reflects the characteristics of the one under study). The graph in Figure 1.3 illustrates this using a simple trend line. The curved, solid black line represents the average fall and rise of *per capita* GDP in the sample during and after the war and the dotted line represents the potential GDP growth path had war not interfered. The area in between the lines then indicates cumulative GDP losses (Brauer and Dunne, 2012).

The costs of armed conflict and armed violence

In 2008 the United Nations Development Program (UNDP) Bureau for Crisis Prevention and Recovery provided a useful illustration, graphing the GDP

[2] For example Gates *et al.* (2010) seem to find that fragile states without conflict appear to have worse educational outcomes than countries emerging from conflict.

[3] There are studies of the effect of bombing in the Second World War which suggest that it was not as damaging as hoped or expected.

Table 1.1 Accounting for the costs of conflict

Economic level	Direct costs	Indirect costs
External relations	Foreign debt	Capital flight of domestic capital Capital flight of foreign capital Discouragement of new foreign investments Emigration of skilled workforce Reduction of incoming tourists Less exports Less imports Less development aid Less humanitarian aid Military aid +/−
National economy level	Physical destruction of production capacity, infrastructure, factories, machinery Physical destruction of transport vehicles and routes, agricultural production capacity Physical destruction of land Death and injuries of workforce Higher military expenditure Refugee care Landmines	Non-production because of threat situation Taxation by rebel and government troops Less investment Less developed human resources as less health expenditure Less education expenditure Missed education opportunities for combatants Less production of transport and physically limited intensive production More production for short-term profits, less long-term
Household level	Death, injuries, and illness Extra legal income +	Food scarcity Inflation Emigration, forced migration

Source: Lindgren (2005); De Groot *et al.* (2009).

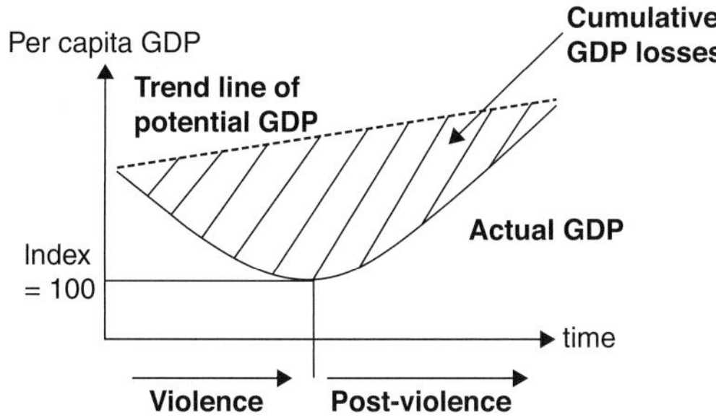

Figure 1.3 *Cost of conflict, illustration*

Note: This is clearly a stylized perspective and there is some debate over what happens during the crisis and how to measure the counterfactual, but it is a useful heuristic device.

per capita for seven countries that had experienced conflict, collecting data on the pre- and post-war real *per capita* gross domestic product (GDP), adjusting for purchasing power differences with the start of the conflict at the same point on the graph, an index of 100, shown by the vertical dashed line in Figure 1.4.[4] An arrow for each state indicates its war's start date. The result is striking. In most cases, before the war began, *per capita* GDP was growing. With the start of the war, GDP collapsed and, with peace, GDP started to grow once more. Three of the countries – El Salvador, Guatemala, and Nicaragua – experienced weak post-war growth and hence are designated as weak-growth-recovery (WGR) states; four others – Cambodia, Mozambique, Rwanda, and Uganda – are considered strong-growth-recovery (SGR) states. But the macroeconomic policies of each country differ from the others, as do the trajectories of their recoveries. Rwanda bounced back strongly after 1994, but since then its growth has been modest, while Mozambique did badly initially before

[4] The war periods are Guatemala, 1965–1995; Cambodia, 1970–1991; Mozambique, 1976–1992; Nicaragua, 1978–1990; El Salvador, 1979–91; Uganda, 1979–1991; and Rwanda, 1990–1994.

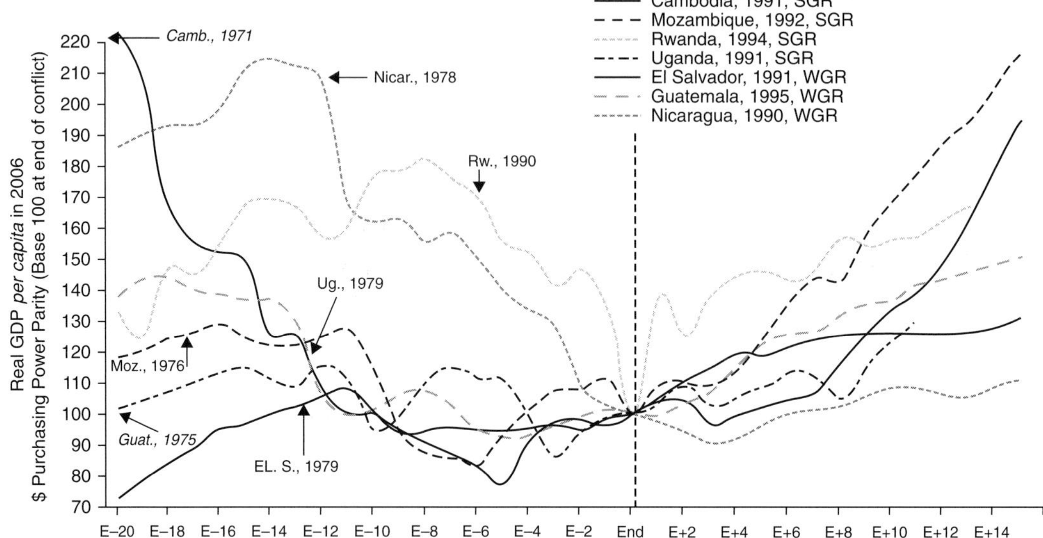

Figure 1.4 *GDP* per capita *in selected SGR and WGR countries (year conflict ended, group)*

Note: SGR = Strong growth recovery, WGR = Weak growth recovery. Arrows point to starting year of conflict, unless where conflict is ongoing over the entire period covered (Cambodia, Guatemala), in which case the arrow points to the first year of the series.

starting to grow more strongly. Cambodia's *per capita* income index had still not recovered to its pre-war *per capita* income levels after thirty-five years. Nicaragua's high-point in *per capita* GDP was fourteen years before the end of the war and by fourteen years after its end, its income level still was only one-half of what it had been. In El Salvador, average income levels improved slightly, but the peace after the war ended was worse than the war itself: it is said that more people were killed there in the ten years after the war than during the twelve-year conflict (Stohl *et al.*, 2007).

The UNDP study suggests that the economic cost of civil war lies somewhere between 1.7 and 3.3 percent of GDP per country per conflict year before 1990 and the average reduction was about 12.3 percent of GDP after 1990, the post-Cold War era (UNDP, 2008). The apparent loss of output is staggering, and while countries do recover it is not for a good number of years.

So measuring the costs of conflict is not straightforward. There are different methods which measure different things, and can give rather different answers. Economists do not agree on how to fully enumerate, let alone compute, the global cost of war, let alone the cost of all violence, war-related or not. What is required are comprehensive and consistent computations of current cost, legacy cost, and spillover cost. The current cost is the direct and indirect cost of violence, the legacy cost includes the cost of past violence that carries into the present (e.g. reduced productivity on account of permanent injury; continuous health care for the injured), and the spillover costs relate to the impact on others (e.g. refugees) (Bozzoli *et al.*, 2008, 2010).

Although the linkage between armed conflict, violence, and development is not explicit in the MDGs, objectives such as reducing poverty, ensuring maternal health, and promoting education are all associated with effective armed violence prevention and reduction initiatives. The World Bank's *World Development Report 2011* (World Bank, 2011) points out that not a single low-income country afflicted by violence has achieved even one of the eight MDGs.[5] An example is Ethiopia, which showed a steady rise in GDP from 1950 to 1974,

[5] Though there could be other reasons than the conflict that the MDGs were not achieved. It is still an interesting observation, however.

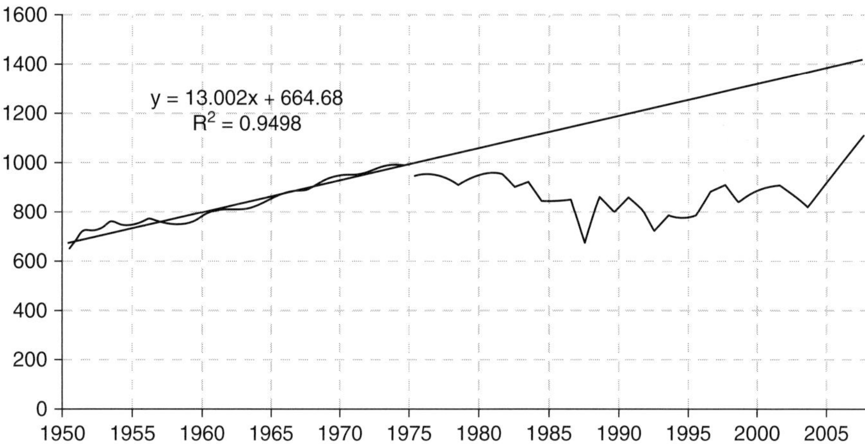

Figure 1.5 *Ethiopia: real GDP, 1950–2007*

Note: Population-, inflation-, and PPP-adjusted GDP, Ethiopia, 1950–2007 (base year = 2005)
Source: Penn World Tables, V.6.3.

with *per capita* GDP $279 in purchasing power parity (PPP) dollars in 1950 and $473 in 1974, an increase of about 70 percent over 25 years, or 2.8 percent per person per year. Then things changed: 1974 saw a violent revolution and 1977 a war with Somalia. The early 1980s saw several massive famines and a brutally repressive political regime, while the early to mid 1990s saw violently contested elections, and long-running secessionist movements in Tigray and Eritrea resulted in more violence. Eritrea gained independence in 1993, but a border war with Ethiopia broke out in 1998 that was only nominally settled in 2000. Over the thirty-year period from 1975 to 2004, economic output per person was flat. Had Ethiopia continued to grow at its 1950–1974 rate average production should have reached about $800 in 2009 instead of the $684 actually achieved, and it reached this level only due to a growth spurt in the last five years of the data series. The size of the cumulative loss of production was $7,721, over eleven years' worth of 2009 income (Brauer and Dunne, 2012) (Figure 1.5).

An even more extreme example is Nicaragua. Its *per capita* production, in PPP dollars, grew from $1,948 in 1950 to $4,554 in 1977, or about 4.8 percent per person per year, a significant achievement despite a repressive political regime. A long-running revolutionary campaign finally gained some success in 1978 and came to power in 1979, provoking an undeclared proxy war with the United States that involved harbour-mining, arms smuggling, and the clandestine support of counter-revolutionaries by the US administration against the express wishes of Congress. An internal war continued until multi-party elections were held in Nicaragua in 1990, resulting in the revolutionaries' electoral defeat. By then the economy had completely collapsed, resulting in production per person of only $2,192 in 2009 – almost equal to the level of $2,148 in 1951. The trend-line projection suggests that average production without conflict would have reached nearly $7,000 by 2009. In other words, in the sixty years from 1950 to 2009, Nicaragua's economy has not grown at all, with stagnation even after the 1990 elections due to political turmoil (Figure 1.6) (Brauer and Dunne, 2012).[6]

Non-war-related homicide can also severely damage an economy as Brauer and Dunne (2012) illustrate with the example of the Dominican Republic. There has been steady production growth from $1,820 in 1951 to $9,911 in 2009, or production growth of 7.5 percent per person per year,

[6] Former President Arnoldo Alemán (1996–2001) was convicted of embezzlement, money laundering, and corruption and sentenced to a twenty-year prison term by his presidential successor, Enrique Bolaños (2001–2006), of the same political party. The former rebel leader, Daniel Ortega, was re-elected to the country's presidency in 2006.

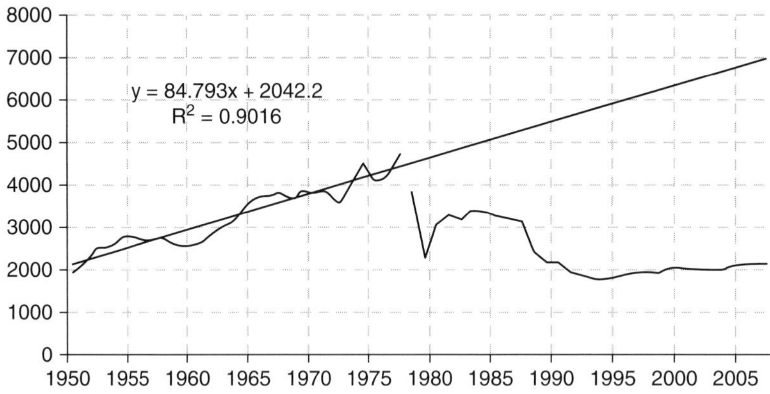

Figure 1.6 *Nicaragua: real GDP, 1950–2007*

Note: Population-, inflation-, and PPP-adjusted GDP, Nicaragua, 1950–2007 (base year = 2005)
Source: Penn World Tables, V.6.3.

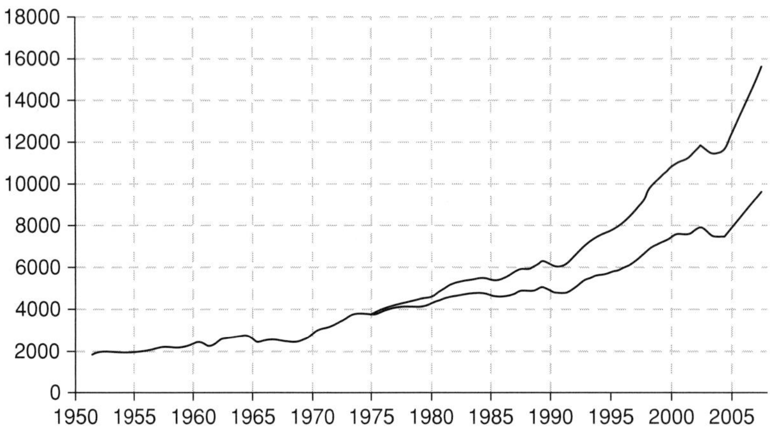

Figure 1.7 *Dominican Republic: real GDP, 1951–2007*

Note: Population-, inflation-, and PPP-adjusted GDP, Dominican Republic, 1951–2007 (base year = 2005)
Source: Penn World Tables, V.6.3.

an impressive achievement. A study by the United Nations Office on Drugs and Crime (UNODC) estimated that since 1975 growth could have been increased by an additional 1.7 percent per person each year if homicide rates in the Dominican Republic could have been halved from over 16 per 100,000 people to Costa Rica's rate of about 8 per 100,000 people (UNODC, 2007). This implies that, by 2009, average production should have been around \$16,456 rather than the around \$10,000 actually achieved, more than a 60 percent difference. This illustrates the validity of the World Bank (2011) conclusion that "violence is a major impediment to development." Clearly, violence prevention, or at least mitigation, and the post-conflict and post-violence reconstruction of a stable social order are necessary conditions for development, while lack of development or even the hope of advancement is a primary cause of violence (Figure 1.7) (Collier and Hoeffler, 2004).

That said, violence rarely permeates the whole of a society. Often it is highly localized, consistently affecting some city neighborhoods, or some districts or provinces, more than others. However, it can also move from one place to another, sometimes in response to policy action.[7]

On the basis of a case study analysis of fifteen countries Harris (1999) argues that war is associated with slow growth, declining food production, and declining exports and while war is generally not the only or essential cause of such economic problems, once it has started it does impact negatively on human development. Nordhaus (2002) considered the costs of the US/Iraq war, considering different scenarios, while Bilmes and Stiglitz (2006: 8) provide a more recent and much higher estimate study. In interesting recent work, Abadie and Gerdeazabal (2003) look at the effect of ETA conflict on the Basque region. They use a counterfactual based on construction of an artificial region, a combination of other unaffected areas to replicate characteristics as closely as possible. They find a difference of around 10 percent.

Rather than using deviations from trends to measure the cost of conflict, one can use some form of counterfactual based on an estimated model. An early example is FitzGerald (1987), who used a regression counterfactual for Nicaragua to estimate the cost of the conflict. More recently and more generally, Collier (1999) used regression analysis, with cross-country data. He estimated the costs of civil war in terms of the reduction in the rate of economic growth, adapting the standard approach of empirical growth econometrics by taking as the dependent variable the growth rate during a decade and introducing the number of months during which the country was at civil war as an explanatory variable. Each year of civil war was found to reduce the growth rate by around 2.2 percent. On average a civil war lasts for around seven years (Collier and Hoeffler, 2002, 2004a). Thus, by the end of a civil war the economy is approximately 15 percent below its counterfactual level.[8] One interpretation of Collier's finding is that countries in violent conflict are essentially stagnant; that all their "natural" growth is negated by violence, or that their "above normal," "catch-up" growth is dampened. Dunne (2007), in the context of arms proliferation, summarizes their estimates of the costs of civil wars (Table 1.2).

Table 1.2 Estimates of the costs of civil wars

Economic growth NPV costs:	105% initial GDP
Increase milex during and after conflicts NPV:	18% initial GDP
Deterioration in health (0.5 DALYs p.a. @ $1th)	£5m
Spillover effects on neighbors	115% initial GDP
Increase milex neighbors	12% initial GDP
Total	255% initial GDP
Benefit of averting war to a low-income country	= £54 bn
Conflict trap cost	= £10.2 bn
Total	= £64.2 bn

Source: Dunne (2007).

Other estimates have been made from aggregations of case studies, and these tend to propose rather higher growth costs of war, but the case studies were not selected randomly and there may have been a tendency to select particularly costly wars. A comparative analysis of the cost of conflict was undertaken by Sköns (2006), who considers the costs of armed conflict to the external actors, with the goal of comparing these costs with the costs to the external actors of the alternative – i.e. policies to reduce the incidence or to prevent violent conflict, the aim being to cost the option of funding international public goods in peace and security. Recognizing the difficulties with making any such estimates and their variation, she suggests external costs of $4.5–$54 billion. Even without considering the country costs, the upper bound of this estimate is around half the value of all development aid. She also reports the estimates of Collier and Hoeffler (2004a) for the internal costs of war and

[7] Colombia's drug-related violence abated in the 2000s, at least partly because concerted efforts by its government, with overseas assistance, made it preferable for drug gangs to move to Mexico. Mexican government counter-measures appear to have led to an explosion of violence since 2006, which has led to bases for narcotics trafficking being set up in El Salvador, Guatemala, and Honduras – that is, in countries with weaker systems of law and order (Brauer and Dunne, 2012).

[8] One difficulty is deciding whether the counterfactual is a linear trend or some other forecast path, or using the experience of a group of similar countries.

Table 1.3 Case studies including conflict costs

Study	1	2	3	4	5
War years	1983–1988	1983–1988	1983–1992	1983–1987+1990–1994	1994–1996
Total costs (billion US$)	6.15	1.99	6.31	16.74	22.34
Average p.a. (billion US$)	1.02	0.33	0.63	1.72	1.93
% of GDP p.a.	2.2	0.7	1.3	3.3	3.5

Sources:
1. Richardson and Samarasinghe (1991).
2. Grobar and Gnanaselvam (1993).
3. Harris (1999).
4. Kelegama (1999).
5. Arunatilake *et al.* (2001).

emphasizes that international (interstate) conflicts would likely have considerably higher costs, especially if a developed country was involved. Hess (2003) estimates a lower bound of the cost of war at an average cost of $72 per person. This gives a total world cost of conflict in 1985 US$ and 1985 population of $399.12 billion, a permanent payment growing with population.[9] To get figures for 1985–2006, one can increase this amount by the growth in world population of around 2 percent p.a. (the 2000 figure).

To get an idea of the range of estimates available, de Groote *et al.* (2009) compare the results of different types of studies for one country (Sri Lanka) (Table 1.3). Costs are in billion US$ (constant 2000 prices).

To give this some perspective, the respected and non-partisan Congressional Research Service estimates that the United States had spent almost $802 on funding the Iraq war by the end of fiscal year 2011, with Stiglitz and Bilmes (2008) putting the true cost at $3 trillion once additional impacts on the US budget and economy were taken into account. In the United Kingdom, the conflict has been funded from the Treasury Reserve Fund (extra money on top of the normal Ministry of Defence budget) and figures released in June 2010 put the cost at £9.24 ($14.32 trillion), the vast majority of which was for the military but which also included £557m ($861 million) in aid. For comparison, UK GDP was around £1.3 trillion and US GDP £8.3 trillion or just over $13 trillion.

In measuring indirect costs, some studies aim to analyze how conflict affects a particular attribute of economic well-being. In doing this it is important to be careful about double counting various costs under different headings when aggregating. The costs include military expenditure effects (opportunity cost; economic effect; international spillovers); intertemporal effects (generational, growth, and welfare effects); human capital effects (health, civil, and military casualties; aftermath; education); effects on inequality; environmental consequences; and international spillovers. Conflict in a particular country or region can have a wider impact. This is obvious for large wars, but a surprising example is Costa Rica – a peaceful country that seems to have suffered from conflict in the region (Figure 1.8).[10]

More generally, Murdoch and Sandler (2002) look at the effect of civil war on *per capita* income growth in a home country and neighboring countries; using a model based on Solow's augmented growth model, they consider human capital, migration, investment, shift factors (such as interrupted supply lines), and measures of neighbors' contiguity and distance. Their results suggest that there are more spillovers in the long run than the short run and that there is smaller reach (less dispersion) in Africa. Africa is also more resilient and recovers faster, with estimated negative neighborhood effects actually stronger than the home-country effect. The spatial reach is both region- and

[9] This is based on estimating the amount of consumption individuals would lose through conflict and hence would be willing to pay to prevent conflict. A Lucas-type new classical model was used.

[10] There are, of course, other possible explanations and other regional effects that could be important, but there does seem to be some justification in suggesting that the security situation in the region has had a negative impact.

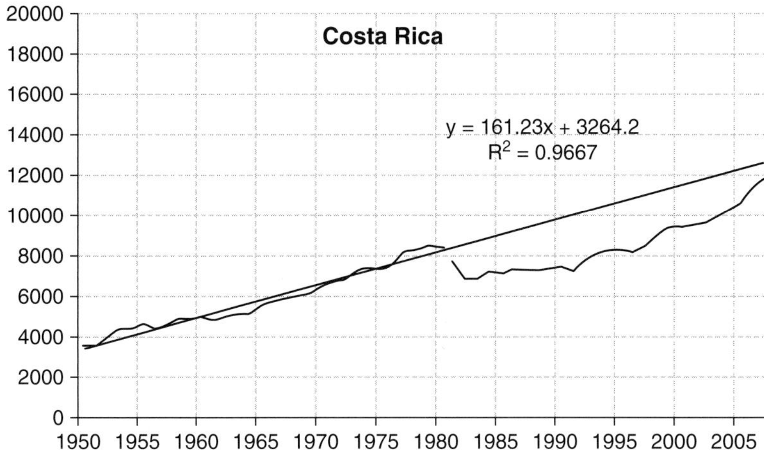

Figure 1.8 *Costa Rica: real GDP, 1951–2007*

Notes: Population-, inflation-, and PPP-adjusted GDP 1951–2007, with base year 2005
Source: Penn World Tables, V.6.3.

time-period-specific. De Groote (2010) provides some updates to these results and there has been further recent empirical work focusing on refugees. Using the number of refugees and internally displaced persons (IDPs) for selected countries of origin, Salehyan and Gleditsch (2006) examine (one of) the mechanisms involved and propose that refugees help spread civil war to neighbors, with some refugee camps acting as bases for military operations. Civil wars are clustered in time and space, suggesting non-independence or knock-on effects, and while states are bound by political borders, their citizens are not. They form "dense networks of social relations that transcend national boundaries." Refugees are also usually highly clustered or concentrated, which can exacerbate their impact in particular regions. But there can also be positive effects as immigrants boost the labor force in the host country (Figure 1.9).

A complete survey of the various estimates for general violence found in the literature does not exist, though Brauer and Tepper-Marlin (2009) partially survey the economic cost of self-harm, interpersonal, and collective violence, including civil wars and terrorism. They conclude conservatively that, if all violence had ceased, the 2007 value of world economic production, called gross world product (GWP) – the sum of GDP across all states – could have been 8.7 percent larger than it actually was. They distinguish between static and dynamic effects. The former recognizes that cessation of violence makes some security services superfluous, freeing expenditure to be shifted to other goods and services. But this substitution effect does not increase GDP; it merely reallocates spending from one sector of the economy to another without increasing GDP. Being more secure does, however, tend to increase the effectiveness of effort and productivity of investment, and so does increase GDP. It is this effect of non-violence that they suggest would have amounted to an 8.7 percent gain in GWP in 2007. To put this in context, it is interesting to note that the International Monetary Fund (IMF) estimates that the world economic crisis of 2009 amounted to a one-time world output loss of 0.5 percent. The world economic crisis would have been worse had it not been for extraordinary policy intervention world-wide, and is still ongoing. Whatever the final cost, it is clear that the cost of violence presents an even more severe economic problem and by comparison receives very little attention.

Overall, there are a wide range of estimates for the costs of armed conflicts. Using an accounting method, the more you look into it the higher the costs can become, though there are informational

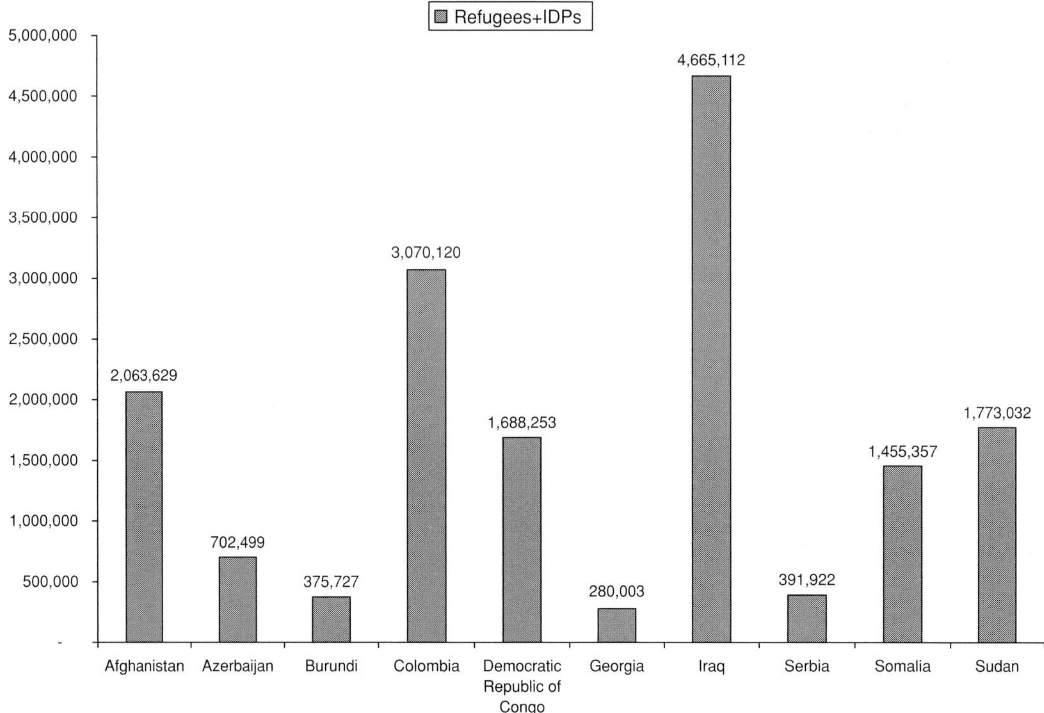

Figure 1.9 *Refugees and internally displaced persons, selected countries*

Source: Anderton and Carter (2009).

constraints. Counterfactual methods have a number of conceptual issues, but tend to be more transparent and readily understood, but again can produce a number of estimates. So in evaluating the costs of conflict it is always important to either offer a range of estimates or to be careful to emphasize the uncertainties involved.

For this study, we return to the estimates in Collier *et al.* (2008a), which derive from those used in Collier and Hoeffler (2004a) and which they find, despite developments in the analysis of the effects of conflict, still seem to be reasonable. They estimate that a country's growth rate is reduced by about 2.2 percent for the duration of the conflict, which is within the UNDP (2008) range of 1.7 percent to 3.3 percent per conflict year. More recent estimates seem to agree that 2.2 percent remains around the center of the estimates. Since the typical civil war lasts about seven years, this implies that the economy is likely to be around 15 percent poorer than if there had been peace. When the conflict is over Collier and Hoeffler (2004a) and Elbadawi *et al.* (2008) estimate that recovery takes about twice as long as the war itself, which fits in with our earlier discussion of the UNDP graph. So they consider a reasonable counterfactual to be growth reduced by 2.2 percent for seven years, during the conflict, and 1.1 percent afterwards for fourteen years, giving an NPV of conflict of 105 percent of one year's GDP measured at the point of conflict onset.

Collier *et al.* (2008a) also consider spillover effects, with Chauvet *et al.* (2006), making efforts to account for neighborhood effects that have nothing to do with the war, such as drought. They estimate that a conflict will create around a 0.9 percent reduction in growth rate if a neighbor is at war, might have three or more neighbors typically, and with gradual recovery post-conflict 1.1 percent p.a., the cost of the conflict to each neighbor 42 percent of onset year GDP. A valuation for the cost of conflict, using figures for civil wars by Collier and Hoeffler (2004a), suggests that the NPV costs of conflict is around 250 percent of initial

Table 1.4 Costs of conflict (relative to GDP)

Discount rate	3%	5%
NPV cost of conflict	1.5	1.2
NPV cost to neighbor	0.58	0.5
NPV cost of military spending	0.01	0.01

Table 1.5 Costs of conflict (US$ billion)

		Discount rate (%)	Cost (US$ billion)
DALY	$1,000	5	13
		3	35
DALY	$5,000	5	33
		3	54

GDP.[11] In calculating a contemporary cost of conflict, Collier *et al.* (2008a) simply update the GDP figures, giving the cost to the country directly affected as $20 billion PPP prices and the cost to neighbors $23 billion (there are more of them and they tend to be larger and richer). This gives them a combined cost of $43 billion, slightly lower than Collier and Hoeffler (2004a). They also consider the cost of the increase in military spending, which tends to increase by 1.8 percent during conflicts (though there are data issues) and remains high, declining by about one-fifth from the conflict level, suggesting 1.5 percent of GDP. Their total is then $56.6 billion and as since 1960 there have been about two wars starting every year they suggest $123 billion per year which, as they remark, is the same order of magnitude as the total for global development aid.

To take account of the severe effect civil war can have on human health, we can express the cost in terms of DALYs. This measures the total number of people affected and the period for which their disability lasts. Collier and Hoeffler (2004a) suggest that an average war causes an estimated 0.5 million DALYs each year and, assuming a recovery period of twenty-one years, gives the NPV of health costs when hostilities start as 5 million DALYs. If each DALY is valued at $1,000 (roughly the *per capita* income in many at-risk countries), the economic cost of harm to human health in a typical war is around $5 billion.[12] Collier *et al.* (2008a) update this, and adopt two values for DALYs, namely $1,000 and $5,000. With a discount rate of 3 percent, these give an additional cost of a civil war of $13 billion and $33 billion, respectively; a 6 percent discount rate gives total war costs of $46 billion and $66 billion, respectively.

For this chapter, we use GDP data for the group of low-income countries and estimate the actual annual growth rates for 1990–2010; rather than extrapolation, we simulate a conflict by introducing a reduction in the growth rate by 2.2 percent for 1991–1997 and then an increase in the growth rate of 1.1 percent until 2010. This takes the GDP figure close to the counterfactual at the end of the twenty-one years. Calculating the NPV using a 5 percent discount rate gives a value of conflict of 120 percent of GDP, which is higher than Collier *et al.* (2008a). Using a reduction of 0.9 percentage points for seven years and a recovery of 0.5 to the counterfactual level by 2010 suggests a cost of conflict to a neighbor of 58 percent of initial GDP. We also add in 1 percent of initial GDP to allow for the increase in military spending. These results are summarized in Table 1.4.

While HSRG (2011) show how the cost of conflict in terms of fatalities continues to decline, there are still considerable effects on the health of the countries, indirectly through disease, etc. as well as directly. To allow for these health costs of conflict we use Collier *et al.* (2008a) figures for the typical war (Table 1.5).

Collier *et al.* (2008a) also add in the cost of coups, arguing that these have become important costs to developing countries. The first cost is the direct loss of income due to the political disruption; they

[11] Murdoch and Sandler (2002) show that conflicts can permeate the whole subregions, meaning the cost to neighbors could well be greater than to the country at war.

[12] Ghobarah *et al.* (2003) use data on twenty-three major diseases, and find significant adverse effects of civil war. Using WHO data, they estimate that during 1999 then-current wars were causing the loss of 8.44 million DALYs, and that a further 8.01 million DALYs were lost as a legacy effect of the civil wars that had ended during the period 1991–1997. Collier *et al.* (2008) use the first of these figures, giving the typical civil war as incurring around 0.5 million DALYs a year of loss during the conflict. This yields a health cost of the typical civil war of around $5 billion. (There are typically around seventeen civil wars at any one time; hence, the loss per war is 8.44/17).

Table 1.6 Costs of conflict, assumptions for different regions (US$ billion)

Assumptions	Low-income	Low- and middle-income	Our estimate	Full
$1,000 DALY, 3%	56	228	142	284.0
$1,000 DALY, 5%	31	173	101	202.0
$5,000 DALY, 3%	75	247	161	322.0
$5,000 DALY, 5%	51	193	121	242.0

quote Collier *et al.* (2006b), who found reduced growth of around 3 percent in the year following a coup, although the effects were not found to be highly persistent. In addition, Collier and Hoeffler (2006b) show that coups lead to an increase in military spending, and this effect is persistent. If the shift was across the political spectrum from full democracy to severe autocracy (using Polity definitions), military spending would be consistently higher by 2 percent. In addition, where coup risk is high governments tend to increase military spending. Like civil wars, coups can be politically beneficial and in some cases may have improved governance. Collier *et al.* (2008a) estimate the cost of coups at 10 percent of one year's GDP, around $2 billion per successful coup.

These studies only deal with civil wars, so they may represent underestimates of the cost of conflict, but the approach taken seems reasonable. The more recent literature does not lead one to consider these estimates unreasonable and they seem consistent with the case studies. However, the focus on the costs of coups does raise further issues of importance and tends to move away from the specific concerns of armed conflict, so in this chapter the focus will simply be on conflict.

For this chapter, we take the 2010 mean GDP for low-income countries in $2000 prices ($8 billion), and for both low- and middle-income combined countries ($72 billion); assuming that a country has two neighbors and that they are the same size we get a cost of one conflict for the average low-income country of $18 billion and for low- and middle-income countries of $160 billion, using a 5 percent discount rate. While conflicts are more common among low-income countries, they do increasingly occur in higher-income groups, which makes the lower-income group too low an estimate and the combined low- and middle-income group too high (Fearon, 2010). It seems reasonable to take an estimate of $40 billion, mid-way between the two means for a representative country with conflict. This gives a cost of war of $107 billion. Adding in the DALYs to our estimates provides figures for the benefits of preventing conflict based on the mean for low-income and the mean for low- and middle-income countries (Table 1.6).

Collier *et al.* (2008a) rightly emphasize that their figure of around $60 billion per year omits a number of factors: that the people affected by the violence are among the poorest and most disadvantaged; that the absence of peace means that other development initiatives and interventions will not work; that the costs are borne by societies least able to cope; that the costs are highly persistent; that there are global spillovers than can be indirect and large – drugs, crime, disease, and terrorism. These costs cannot be readily enumerated and so are generally not considered, but they suggest that each of these factors could increase the cost of conflict by 20 percent; then allowing for four factors increases the cost more than fourfold to around $250 billion for the cost of a typical conflict. They suggest treating $60 billion as a lower bound and consider $250 to be closer to full costs and use both figures. Our estimates for low-income countries are similar to the Collier *et al.* (2008a) lower bound, but our low- and middle-income and our representative estimate are somewhat higher (the comparison is with the $1,000 DALY and 3 percent discount rate). We are comfortable with using a higher GDP estimate, as more recent conflicts reflect this, but we are still missing the wider costs mentioned in the last paragraph, plus the increased probability of conflict that countries that have had a previous conflict experience, and feel the need to increase these figures to take account of this. It seems reasonable to increase by a lower factor than that of Collier *et al.* (2008a) and double the representative value, to take it from $142 billion to $284 billion.

The focus of this chapter is to suggest how some share of additional spending – up to $75 billion per year over the next four years targeted at the challenges identified by the 2012 Copenhagen Consensus – could best be spent to deal with the problem of armed conflict. So the solutions have costs computed over four years, with some allowance for the fact that the benefits may have much longer-run effects. This is particularly important in the solutions proposed here, which are likely to be additions to already existing streams of expenditure, and successful initiatives are likely to attract further funding. So we now move on to consider the proposed solutions in terms of prevention, intervention, and post-conflict reconstruction.

The solutions

In the literature the argument of economic growth reducing the risk of conflict is now more generally accepted than in the past, with evidence that higher income reduces the probability of conflict, both directly and indirectly.[13] Collier (2007) suggested some solutions that aimed to increase growth, to reduce conflict risk, as well as to improve security. These solutions included increased aid; increased aid with limits on military spending; increased peacekeeping forces; and external guarantees of security.

Collier *et al.* (2008a) follow this, but argue that their results are new, as they focus on the two types of what they consider preventable, the recurrence of civil war in post-conflict situations and the prevention of coups in countries that are democratic. They consider two strategies, first an attempt to change the size of the domestic military establishment in post-conflict situations, not only to remove expenditure from the unproductive sector, but also because of the increased risk of recurrence of conflict that can result from high military spending, in contrast to the usual argument that it could increase security and reduce the likelihood of recurrence (Collier and Hoeffler, 2006). They do not bother with the neighborhood arms' race effects[14] that might occur since, with countries being post-conflict, they are unlikely to have a big effect. Second, they suggest providing military services internationally – generally, but not exclusively, under the auspices of the United Nations. They argue that the supply of effective peacekeeping troops is limited and suggest that keeping them in their home countries, but providing over-the-horizon guarantees of rapid intervention when necessary, would be more cost effective. The role of the United Kingdom in Sierra Leone and French support for Francophone Africa until the late 1990s are used to illustrate the feasibility and effectiveness of such a strategy. The troops may be more expensive *per se*, but keeping them at home reduces costs and one group could be used for a number of countries, with a decent transport pool. This might also include over-the-horizon guarantees of external military support to intervene in the case of an attack on a democratic government.

The Alternative Perspective authors had some valid concerns over the suggested solutions. Mack (2008) pointed out that there has been a growing number of negotiated settlements, a significant change in the way conflicts come to an end. At the same time, while grievances may not show up in aggregate as determining conflict this can be because they are specific to groups or areas. If so, it is important to deal with them to prevent wars restarting. This means any "solutions" should reflect the likely need for negotiation, reconciliation, and power sharing. Mack was also concerned about the fact that the small intervention forces, such as the British in Sierra Leone, may have worked there, but might not in other situations. There are political problems – the United States has tended to oppose a permanent UN volunteer force, while in practice any centralized UN force would be mainly OECD country soldiers, and this might not be acceptable to the regional states involved in the conflicts. In addition, Elbadawi *et al.* (2008) were concerned with the focus on economic "feasibility" in determining conflict risk and the downplaying of political legitimacy. This leads to proposals being externally driven and ignoring domestic institutions and regional dimensions, and the importance of the UN mandate for any intervention.

[13] The evidence may now be less strong than in the past (Fearon, 2010).

[14] Where a country increases its military spending, which leads neighbors/rivals to increase theirs, the country then responds with a further increase and so do the rivals, leading to an arms' race.

Table 1.7 Share of conflicts averted for different interventions (costs averted, US$ billion)

Assumptions	Prevention	Intervention	Post-conflict and reconstruction
Conflict cost averted (share)	100%	75%	50%
$1,000 DALY, 3%	284	213	142
$1,000 DALY, 5%	202	151.5	101
$5,000 DALY, 3%	322	241.5	161
$5,000 DALY, 5%	242	181.5	121

Note: We assume prevention will avert 100% of conflict costs while intervention and post-conflict initiatives will avert 75% and 50%, respectively.

These are all valid criticisms that are hopefully more readily dealt with in the solutions proposed in this chapter. We argue that it is hard to take the Collier *et al.* (2008a) approach of compartmentalizing the problems and offering related solutions. First, there is the heterogeneity of conflicts, meaning that it is difficult to generalize and to create generic solutions. Second, there is the issue of seeing "peace" as a process rather than trying to suggest that it is a state that some group – often foreign powers/institutions – defines.

There are three facets to consider, and each of these represents a solution, but really each of these solutions are interlinked and should be running at the same time. The first is prevention, putting networks, organizations, and resources in place to stop a conflict happening; the second is intervention, where a conflict has already broken out; and the third is post-conflict reconstruction, when a conflict has ended. Many of the instruments are already in place, so that in many cases the contributions being considered would be adding to existing initiatives.

These solutions, will also have different benefit profiles, as prevention will stop the conflict from occurring and so will prevent the full cost, while intervention will mean that the conflict is already underway to some extent and post-conflict reconstruction will mean the conflict has come to an end – by some definition – and so the solution can only claim a fraction of the full cost. We argue that the legacy cost of conflict is high and so the post-conflict solution remains relatively high (Table 1.7).

For the period 1990–2008 (eighteen years) there were 132 conflicts, which is around seven a year. The number of conflicts has been declining, as we saw earlier, so we would not expect as many to start. It is also unlikely that war onsets would be spread uniformly, and wars that might have started after the first year would not have continued over the whole period, and not all attempts would be successful. Given this, it seems reasonable to allow for four wars over the four-year period in what follows.

Conflict prevention

The first solution is to set up procedures to try and prevent a conflict from occurring. We now have a wide literature that gives some idea of the countries that are most at risk, and if there were tools that could be used to prevent them moving into conflict then the world would be saved the loss of life and economic costs outlined above. The best means of stopping a conflict is surely to stop it happening in the first place.

Early warning

A major part of this solution would be to establish an effective "early-warning system," (EWS) to provide a warning of the onset of conflict. There is already an established set of tools for this, though as Wulf and Dibeil (2009) and OECD (2009) show, the effectiveness of the response is open to question. There would be some costs in improving data collection and effectiveness of existing systems within the context of regional organizations, such as the African Union (AU). The research has certainly been done to try to identify problem countries, although improvements could be made. A major problem is likely to be the translation of "early warning" into "early action," given past experience, where countries and their allies have resisted conflict prevention methods as a threat to their national sovereignty, and richer countries have been loath to

Table 1.8 Assessment criteria

	Fifteen-year conflict probability estimates		
Income level (2002)	Major conflict in last five years	No major conflict in last five years	Total
Low	80	37	50
Lower middle	61	28	33
Upper middle	11	5	6
Total developing	61	28	34

Source: Chalmers (2004).

intervene unless there is a perceived threat to their national interest

With this in mind Chalmers (2004) considers the cost-effectiveness to the international community of conflict prevention activities. He starts by providing a useful summary of research on the probability of conflict for countries when they have been involved in a major conflict in the last five years and when they have not, disaggregated by income group. The differences are striking. Countries that have been in conflict seem twice as likely to be involved again, while low-income countries are the most likely to be involved in conflict. This information is combined with a series of risk assessment factors, so that case studies can take the relevant probability and then adjust it for the specific characteristics of the individual country (Table 1.8).

In undertaking conflict risk assessment, Chalmers and his collaborators take income and recent conflict history to give a base probability. A judgment is then made of whether the country is greater, equal to, or less than the norm, with the weights based on fourteen characteristics shown to be important in the empirical literature. Whether there is a dominant ethnic group; high dependency on commodity exports; decline in *per capita* GDP over last decade; large population; interregional inequality; if in first year of independence; if an immature democracy; political instability; low Country Policy and Institutional Assessment (CPIA) score; migrant communities in neighborhood; conflicts in neighborhood; violent leaders; international peacekeeping forces; other factors. These are summed to give a judgment of conflict probability.

What is needed is continuous support for research, collection of information, and an increase in coverage, plus resources to develop capabilities at country level and within regional bodies. In addition, some attempt could be made to develop international resources to improve diplomatic engagement at UN level, improve mediation services, and provide resources for fact-finding missions (Cranna, 1994). This would allow the international community to engage with government and groups within countries and between countries when the early warning systems had flagged up problems. The cost of providing this sort of support would be relatively minor, as much of the framework already exists.

Peacekeeping operations

The international community is of course already involved in dealing with conflicts, but to give some context to the effort made the budget for UN peacekeeping operations for the fiscal year 1 July 2011–30 June 2012 was about $7.84 billion. By way of comparison, this was less than 0.5 of 1 percent of world military expenditures in 2010. The estimated cost of all UN peacekeeping operations from 1948 to June 2010 amounted to about $69 billion. The top ten providers of assessed contributions to UN peacekeeping operations in 2011–2012 were: (1) United States (27.14 percent); (2) Japan (12.53 percent); (3) United Kingdom (8.15 percent); (4) Germany (8.02 percent); (5) France (7.55 percent); (6) Italy (5.00 percent); (7) China (3.93 percent); (8) Canada (3.21 percent); (9) Spain (3.18 percent); (10) Republic of Korea (2.26 percent). Many countries have also voluntarily made additional resources available to support UN peacekeeping efforts on a non-reimbursable basis in the form of transportation, supplies, personnel, and financial contributions above and beyond their assessed

Table 1.9 UN interventions, 1948–2011: key statistics

Mission	Country	Date	Troops	Total persons	% troops	Fatalities	Budget ($US million)
UNTSO		1948	0	383	0	50	70.3
UNMOGIP	India/Pak	1949	0	114	0	11	21.1
UNFICYP	Cyprus	1964	857	1,076	79.6	181	58.2
UNDOF		1974	1,046	1,190	87.9	43	50.5
UNIFIL	Lebanon	1978	12,138	13,156	92.3	293	545.5
MINURSO	W. Sahara	1991	24	510	4.7	15	63.2
UNMIK	Kosovo	1999	0	403	0	54	44.9
UNMIL	Liberia	2003	7,812	10,943	71.4	164	525.6
UNOCI	Côte d'Ivoire	2004	9,418	12,363	76.2	89	646.0
MINUSTAH	Haiti	2004	7,699	13,377	57.6	170	793.5
UNMIT	E. Timor	2006	0	2,752	0	12	196.1
UNAMID	Darfur	2007	17,777	27,795	64.0	110	1689.3
MONUSCO	DRC	2010	16,975	23,205	73.2	35	1489.4
UNISFA	Abyei	2011	3,715	3,823	97.2	6	175.5
UNMISS	S. Sudan	2011	4,726	7,369	64.1	1	722.1
Total			82,187	118,756	69.2	1,234	7091.2

Source: UN DPI/1634/Rev. 129, February 2012.

share of peacekeeping costs. However, not all countries pay their contributions in a timely manner.

To undertake such roles properly would require a larger and better-resourced UN force than exists at present, as the ineffectiveness of the UN troops in Lebanon illustrated (Table 1.9).

GAO-06–331 consider the cost of the United States conducting a peacekeeping operation similar to the UN Stabilization Mission in Haiti (MINUSTAH), and estimate that it would cost the United States about twice as much to do the same job. They argue that while the UN budgeted $428 million for the first fourteen months, a US operation in Haiti of the same size and duration would have cost an estimated $876 million, far exceeding the US contribution of $116 million. Virtually all of the cost difference is attributable to civilian police, military pay and support and facilities, and reflects higher costs and standards for police training, troop welfare, and security.[15] In addition to military considerations, including nation-building and development assistance activities in the scope of the operation would increase the cost significantly. Official donors, including the United States, distributed $382 million for these activities during the first year of MINUSTAH.

Political considerations are likely to influence decisions about the role of Western powers and the United Nations in peacekeeping. US-led operations in Haiti between 1994 and 2004 benefitted from a vast military infrastructure, giving strong communications, command and control, readiness to deploy, tactical intelligence, and public information. The United Nations provided multinational participation, extensive peacekeeping experience, and an existing structure for coordinating nation-building activities.

[15] They show how various military and non-military factors can substantially affect the estimated costs of a US operation. They analyzed three military factors: the mix of reserve and active duty troops, the rate of deployment, and the operational tempo. Deploying all reserve troops would increase the cost estimate by $477 million, since it would require paying more reservists a full salary. Deploying troops at a faster rate than the United Nations – within the first 60 days instead of 180 – would cost an additional $60 million. Conducting the operation at a higher tempo – with more intensive use of vehicles and equipment – would increase estimated costs by $23 million.

Chalmers (2004) looks at a number of conflict prevention packages for several conflicts in an attempt to evaluate the cost-effectiveness of such activities. He estimates the likely probability that particular conflict prevention policies, both military and non-military actions, would have stopped the conflict. He then considers the actual cost of the conflict to the international community and works out the breakeven probability. It turns out to be very low: the study estimates that £1 on conflict prevention generates savings of £4.1 to the international community, with a range of £1.2–7.1 based on the case studies. He estimates NPV costs at 2004 prices of between $0.2 billion and $139.4 billion, the latter being for Afghanistan.

Again there is the issue of how intervention operations should be structured and arranged. It is vital that the UN play a major role. Cranna (1994) suggested a range of conflict prevention policy initiatives which would first establish clear principles for international action following precedents in the UN Security Council and then provide guidelines for how and when action would be taken. Some organizational structure would be required to respond to the "sparks of conflict," implying effective early warning, fact-finding missions, diplomacy, and mediation. Sanctions could be applied, targeted for effectiveness and fairness. UN troops could be deployed to prevent conflict (and if that failed, for peacekeeping), to provide support for humanitarian aid, and to shift military balances. The United Nations could also provide safe havens and even UN trust territories, a much longer-term commitment. They also suggest policies to curtail the arms' trade, some of which have already been pursued, but with limited effectiveness. Brown and Rosecrance (1999) undertook a similar exercise and argued for the need to distinguish the long-term efforts of reducing security concerns, promoting political justice and human rights, promoting economic development and justice, and overturning patterns of discrimination, from focussed efforts. The latter are such things as fact-finding missions, mediation missions, confidence-building missions, traditional peacekeeping operations, multi-functional peacekeeping operations, military and economic technical assistance, arms embargoes and economic sanctions, and finally the use of military force.

There has also been some analysis of the costs and benefits of setting up a free-standing UN rapid reaction force. Klein (2006) discusses the cost of setting up a UN rapid reaction force and its benefits, which in Klein and Marwah (1996) was costed at $50 billion for 1 million persons ($50,000 per person per year), with a "standing" UN rapid reaction force of 15,000 plus back-up reaching 45,000 persons. More recently Kaysen and Rathjens (2003) used a measure of £30,000 per person, but to give perspective recent pseudo-official estimates suggest that the cost of a US soldier in Afghanistan or Iraq is $390,000–900,000.

It is unlikely a UN force would be as expensive as this, and for conflict prevention it may be that heavily armed troops are not required, though there may need to be some stronger units in reserve. So a reasonable estimate for a force of this type would be, say, $200,000 p.a. for each of the 15,000 including back-up, giving a cost of 3 billion p.a. These are in fact similar to the p.a. costing of Collier (2008a) for peacekeeping troops, when over-the-horizon guarantees are ignored. In addition, as we have argued that peacekeeping operations need strong non-military support. So we add in another $1 billion for non-military personnel, such as police, administrators, professionals, and mediators, to assist in peacemaking activities.

Aid and economic sanctions

Both of these have long been tools of foreign policy, and sanctions have noticeably increased in use in recent years. There are a range of available types that can be categorized as comprehensive, targeted general; targeted financial; targeted commodity. Comprehensive sanctions, such as those against Iraq, can be an effective foreign policy tool and achieve concessions, but targeted sanctions can also be effective and less damaging. Targeted commodity sanctions – for, example on oil and diamonds – have been common, though UN monitoring and enforcement capabilities need to be improved. In the United Kingdom, the costs to business of sanctions policy has been seen as relatively minor (House of Lords, 2007). Research by Escriba-Folch (2010) found strong evidence for the effectiveness of economic sanctions in reducing the duration of conflicts, finding that total economic embargoes were the most effective. While embargoes by all actors had negative effects, those imposed by international organizations were more likely to lead to conflict resolution, while those imposed by others tended to increase the probability of military victory. This is supported by Petrescu (2010), who found that countries involved in a dispute were less likely to participate in another in the future if they were sanctioned by a large country or group of countries.

Targeted sanctions could play an important part in policies intended to prevent conflict, aimed at one or both sides in the dispute. The obvious instruments include arms sanctions (to prevent further militarization), financial sanctions (to limit income) and commodity sanctions (to prevent exports/reduce income flows to protagonists) (as Collier and Hoeffler, 2004a, have shown most civil wars need defined income sources for both rebels and government). Such sanctions are best organized through the United Nations and are unlikely to be particularly costly to the world economy; they would need to be designed to minimize suffering for individuals within the targeted countries, to maximize the impact on the elite, and minimize the impact on ordinary citizens. When sanctions are being used to prevent conflict, the threat may be the most important and so there may be no cost.

To get some idea of potential costs, consider Hufbauer *et al.* (1997), who estimate that the United States in 1997 had sanctions on twenty-six target countries and that this led to between $15 and $19 billion in forgone earnings. This suggests costs of about $0.6–0.7 billion per country. Given the type of sanctions we are looking at and the small size of most countries in conflict, these are overestimates, but there may also be costs of enforcement and there are other countries involved.

In a situation where attempts are being made to prevent conflict there may also be carrots as well as the stick of sanctions. Indeed, one might even see the sanctions as threats and aid as the main instrument. In these situations the aid could be targeted in such a way as to deal with any stated grievances, provide needed humanitarian assistance, or even contribute to more infrastructural investments – even actions that might be tantamount to bribes. Dumas (2006) argues that minimizing economic stress points also helps minimize the potential for conflict, These actions would obviously be in addition to any other aid programs within the target countries.

Aid can also play an important role in preventing the onset of conflict, by targeting any of the problems that seem to be increasing its probability. Official development assistance (ODA) reached about $100 billion in 2006. If we assume that an extra 1.5 percent would provide the necessary leverage, a reasonable figure seems to be $1.5 billion. It is also possible that targeted economic sanctions may be necessary, which we put at a cost of $0.5 billion.

This gives a cost of $2 billion p.a. for economic sanctions and aid combined, to reflect the contributions and sacrifices of a number of countries, some of whom may need to be compensated. This allows for different mixes of the two approaches.

Action on arms' trade

Certainly sanctions can be imposed on countries at risk of starting a conflict, but these may not be particularly successful given the nature of the arms' trade. It may be that the major suppliers withhold arms, making it difficult to get high-tech equipment in particular, but there are also other ways of getting arms, particularly the low-tech equipment of most wars, through countries not committed to sanctions and through the private and second-hand arms' market, especially the illicit one. While the flow of small and light weapons (SALW) is difficult to control, there are actions that can be taken to try to deal with it, through agreements and treaties, assistance with border controls and anti-smuggling measures, and the international investigations of illegal arms' flows and those involved in the trade. If nothing else, these actions would increase cost and lower affordability, so it is worthwhile adding in some funds to support such activities. It is not clear how one would cost this, but $0.5 billion a year should provide some effective activities (Table 1.10).

Summarizing these, the costs per year per conflict for this solution are as shown in Table 1.11.

This means a total cost of around 7.5 billion per year, which over four years will cost 30 billion; discounting this by 3 percent over four years gives $28.7 billion and by 5 percent give $27.9 billion in 2000 prices.

Table 1.10 Conflicts, by region and intensity

	1946–2008					1990–2008				
	Major	Medium	Small	Minor	All	Major	Medium	Small	Minor	All
SSA	24	22	8	40	94	8	11	3	28	50
Asia	31	21	8	25	85	4	6	7	16	33
MENA	20	6	3	16	45	5	1	0	9	15
Latin America	11	4	3	17	35	0	0	0	5	5
E. Eur/FSU	12	7	2	11	32	10	5	2	10	27
West	1	0	0	5	6	0	0	0	2	2
Total	99	60	24	114	297	27	23	12	70	132

Note: Average kia p.a.: major 1,000, medium 500–999, small 250–499, minor 25–249.
Source: Fearon (2010).

Table 1.11 Conflict prevention, cost p.a. per conflict (US$ billion)

	$bn p.a. per conflict
Early warning, etc.	1
Economic sanctions/Aid	2
UN Troops and backup	3
Non-military forces	1
Action on arms' trade	0.5
Total	7.5

Table 1.12 Conflict prevention, benefits, and costs (US$ billion) and BCRs

Solution	Assumptions	Benefits	Costs	BCR
Prevention	$1,000 DALY, 3%	852	56	15.2
	$1,000 DALY, 5%	606	54	11.2
	$5,000 DALY, 3%	966	56	17.3
	$5,000 DALY, 5%	726	54	13.4

Note: This assumes that prevention averts three out of four conflicts and so 75% of the full four-year costs.

We allow for four wars over the four years and assume that three of them are successfully prevented, with a cost per war for a 3 percent discount rate and $1,000 DALYs $284 billion. So the total benefits are three-quarters of $1,156. It is unlikely that four conflicts would be dealt with each year and given the cross-subsidization and joint costs spread over conflicts, it seems reasonable to allow for two conflicts per year for the total costs, giving a cost per year per conflict of $15 billion, which discounted over four years at 5 percent gives $54 billion (Table 1.12).

This gives a set of minimum 11:1 and maximum 17:1 BCRs, showing conflict prevention to be an impressively beneficial use of any available funds.

Intervention

Once conflict has started, or is starting, it may be necessary to undertake policies of intervention. Brauer (2006) considers the difficulties real-world peacemakers might be expected to encounter. He identifies eight determinants of intervention that explain why it is relatively rare. First, there must be information that something is amiss; second, externalities such as refugees spill over to non-conflict neighbors; third, the closer the neighbors, the more informed and caring they are; fourth, distance is mediated when relations (e.g. colonial) exist; fifth, problems with a number of neighbors distracts; sixth, problems at home reduce the likelihood of involvement; seventh, the existence of economic and strategic self-interest; eighth, the opportunity to train forces in real-time conditions. Brauer does not include "humanitarian good will," as peacekeeping tends to be done for rather more hard-edged reasons, nor the cost of peacekeeping, as he argues this is usually trivial – at least in relation to the cost of maintaining standing, national armies (Fetterly, 2006, takes issue with this). It is also the case that peacekeeping can provide tangible benefits for the military – e.g. it provides funds, keeps them in the political arena, and provides opportunity for real-life training and equipment testing. This suggests that the problems may be getting countries to engage in the activity at all, and that cost may not be an issue.

Peacekeeping costs cannot be directly generalized to consider peacemaking roles. But as already mentioned, Chalmers (2004) considers the argument that intervention saves the international community money in the long run to be important. He considers a number of hypothetical packages for conflict intervention, estimates their costs, and then considers what the breakeven point is – i.e. at what probability of conflict occurring do the costs of doing something and doing nothing equate. Chalmers (2004) also provides some estimates for the successful British intervention in Sierra Leone. In addition to peacekeeping troops, sanctions and aid can play an important intervention role in conflict, providing the carrot to the stick of military intervention. Collier *et al.* (2008a) suggest that the threat of international involvement has a role to play and the fact that Francophone countries had the support of the French army when needed made them less likely to end up in conflict. As discussed before, we feel a UN rapid deployment force would be a better means to achieve this.

This solution really is intended to deal with an ongoing conflict, to stop it from continuing, and to deal with the immediate aftermath. Any further action would come under the next solution – post-conflict reconstruction support.

Given the likely need for military action, this solution will require some better armed forces than those suggested for prevention, but these "peacemaking" troops would have specific rules of engagement and would need to be supported by both peacekeepers and non-military forces. Of course, no action may be needed, and if the threat is seen as credible that may be enough. To reflect the costs of better armed troops the proposed costs are around $4 billion p.a., a little higher than the force costs proposed by Collier *et al.* (2008a).

In addition, as before, costs of non-military forces – such as police, technicians, doctors, administrators, etc. – are added in to help deal with grievances and the immediate impact of any conflict and/or external action: quick action might reduce the likelihood of reprisals. $1 billion a year is added for this.

Table 1.13 Conflict intervention, cost p.a. per conflict (US$ billion)

	$bn p.a. per conflict
Intelligence, etc.	1
Economic sanctions and aid	1
UN rapid reaction	4
UN peacekeepers	2
Non-military forces	1
Total	9

Intelligence

Improved intelligence could be extremely beneficial for any intervention, providing up-to-date and detailed information on political, military, and social, conditions on the ground, so we allow for $1 billion a year for this.

Economic sanctions and aid

Economic sanctions could be important in putting increased pressure on the protagonists both before and during the military intervention. It may even be enough, when combined with the credible threat of action, to stop the conflict. As before, it is important to have a carrot as well as a stick, and aid can play an important role, as can promises to help deal with grievances. Aid will be important in assisting the intervention and dealing with humanitarian problems, but it is likely that its major role will come once the intervention has ended. The requirement will be considerably less than for intervention, so we allow for $1 billion to cover both.

Summarizing the expected p.a. costs per conflict, it is clear that this solution takes a much more force-heavy form and that this is where the majority of the resources will be required. This is not surprising given the possibility of military action, but we do not lose sight of the concerns about external intervention and the need to plan this carefully through the United Nations and gain political acceptability (Table 1.13).

This gives an NPV cost at a 3 percent discount of around $34 billion and at 5 percent of $33 billion. If conflicts finish early they will be less costly and may reduce the cost of the post-conflict reconstruction that is likely to follow. Given the joint costs,

Table 1.14 Conflict intervention, benefits, and costs (US$ billion) and BCRs

Solution	Assumptions	Benefits	Costs	BCR
Intervention	\$1,000 DALY, 3%	852	100	6.4
	\$1,000 DALY, 5%	606	96	4.8
	\$5,000 DALY, 3%	966	100	7.2
	\$5,000 DALY, 5%	726	96	5.7

Note: This assumes that intervention averts 75% of the costs of conflict, as conflicts have already started.

economies of scale, and cross-subsidization, using four times these costs probably overestimates the costs of dealing with four interventions within the period, so we use three times in the estimates in Table 1.14. It is difficult to judge the true benefits of intervention, but given that the conflict has started the benefits of ending it will be lower than if it had been prevented from happening, but the probability of success will be higher than for prevention. It seems reasonable to allow for benefits of around three-quarters of the full costs for four wars. But this is not true of the DALYs, as the earlier the intervention the fewer health costs will arise; but they are still likely to do so, and in fact the intervention may inadvertently create some extra costs. For this reason, we retain the full estimated cost of the DALYs. This gives the costs and benefits in Table 1.14.

This shows that intervention would still be a highly rewarding use of resources, with a minimum BCR of 5:1 and a maximum of 7:1, not as high as prevention.

Post-conflict reconstruction support

Once peace has been achieved through victory by one side, stalemate, or the effects of intervention in some form, there is the need for reconstruction and repair of the economy and society, in a manner that prevents the country falling back into conflict. Considerable effort is put into post-conflict reconstruction at present, but it has certain weaknesses – most strikingly, it may end before real peace has been achieved and this may leave huge legacy costs.

As discussed earlier, many countries or regions in countries can suffer through more general violence that can remain after the conflict. As we have seen, the criticism of Mack (2008) that the acceptance by Collier *et al.* (2008a) of the dominance of the "feasibility" understanding of conflict tends to reduce concerns over potential grievances that may have existed before the conflict or have developed during the conflict. Putting more resources into this process can be hugely beneficial if used to deal with some of the criticism of present policy, to focus on the legacy costs of conflict, rather than just the attainment of "peace" and economic stabilization.

It is useful to consider post-conflict as a process that goes through a number of stages. Harris (1999) suggests four phases of recovery and reconstruction. The first is ending the fighting, which may continue even as a peace agreement is being drawn up so it can take time to end it and to start to put the agreement into practice. The second is rehabilitation and restoration, which will include the removal of limitations on civil activity, re-establishing civil law and civil institutions, disarming ex-combatants, demining roads, and returning displaced persons. Then comes reconstruction and/or replacement, which will involve gaining financial resources for reconstruction, replacing and repairing capital and infrastructure, demobilization and resettlement, rehabilitating victims of war, introducing or reintroducing democracy, developing and restructuring civil institutions consistent with the post-conflict environment, and beginning reconciliation. Finally development and transformation, which will involve adopting and implementing a new vision for society, undertaking structural changes, establishing new institutions, and continuing reconciliation.

Seeing post-conflict reconstruction in this way is valuable, as it makes the achievement of peace a process and allows more effort to go into creating a "peaceful" country rather than a country no longer in conflict. It is certainly difficult to achieve any form of peace, as the variety of forms and causes of conflict all make recovery from conflict and the reconstruction of the country difficult and fraught with the danger of a return to fighting. The peace will first depend on how the war ended – by victory of one side, by international imposition, or by exhaustion – and whether it does, in fact, end completely. As war moves to peace the country and economy will require reconstruction and this will certainly need to be designed in such a way as to prevent any of the parties reverting to war. This of course raises the question of how "peace" is defined, and different groups are likely to disagree on this. Clearly, the process of transition to a commonly accepted "peace" is as important as the end of hostilities. Rehabilitation and reconstruction is likely to aim for more than a return to the pre-conflict economic, political, and social life. An important concern is the possibility of moving back to conflict simply because it makes economic sense. It has to be clear to the protagonists that they will benefit from the peace more than going back to war (Dunne, 2006).

Economic reconstruction is clearly vital and may start before the complete end of the conflict/crisis. An improving economy would clearly make it easier for all stages to be moved through. Whenever it does start, the first actors involved are likely to be the aid agencies, the World Bank, and the IMF. An important issue to be dealt with by all those involved is the perceived balancing of the demands for greater economic growth with those for greater social justice and human welfare. The fact that conflict has occurred is likely to mean that a series of changes and promises will be needed to deal with grievances and to underpin any peace deal. To ignore these and to impose generic policies for economic growth that may have high short-run costs may well simply lead to a reigniting of hostilities. The protagonists may simply see themselves as being better off fighting.

The end of the war is likely to provide opportunities for government to reallocate spending, but this is likely to be limited in the short run. Conflicts seldom end tidily and continued military action may be required, even if only to defend the peace. Weapons often do not make up the majority of military expenditure in developing economies and demobilizing soldiers is problematic and can take time. If it is done too quickly, the country could end up with disaffected and armed ex-soldiers, and this can be dangerous. Dismissing soldiers can also mean that they are no longer spending their income and this reduction in demand may affect regions damaged by the war particularly badly. More generally, the reduced spending power of the armed forces as a whole can reduce the demand they provide for goods and services in the economy and lead to economic problems. A "war" economy faced with a sudden change in the form and level of demand will find it difficult to adjust. After a civil war the first stage may be to "regularize" all combatants, and this costs money. Unfortunately, given the state of the economy, the fiscal possibilities are also likely to be limited as well. Generally, revenue-raising improvements will be the result of foreign aid and loans and these can cause their own problems (displacement, dependency, interest payments, etc. . . .) (Dunne, 2006). This means that the "solution" of reducing military spending in post-conflict countries proposed by Collier *et al.* (2008) is not so clear-cut, to the extent that we do not consider it as part of the solution here.

The end of war does not necessarily imply economic security. There may be problems of micro-security (with armed inhabitants desensitized to violence and high rates of robbery), and macro-insecurity (the considerable risk that war will be resumed) (Bevan *et al.*, 1994). Political instability can discourage private investment, especially foreign direct investment (FDI) (the growth of small-scale national investment is particularly important as it drives the informal sector, probably the largest potential source of employment). Governments may find it difficult to raise taxes or borrow from the public and will be tempted to print money, possibly resulting in inflation.[16]

Aid can play a vital role in developing infrastructure, and is itself a valuable way of encouraging other investment. There is a need to consider how to develop local investment and encourage entrepreneurs at the same time as encouraging

[16] A post-Keynesian would argue that the assumed causal link from money supply to inflation is not clear, and if anything is likely to be the other way around.

foreign investment. There can be some tension between these two. For example, the policy of keeping government expenditure down to keep inflation down may encourage investment in an economy but damage economic development, which itself may discourage foreign investment (through lack of potential profits).

Agriculture will be affected through the destruction of infrastructure, but it also has its own problems and given the importance of "food security" is vital to reconstruction. In a post-crisis situation, it is necessary to get investment into the sector, support clear-up, and support agricultural development, through the development of public services, credit services, and infrastructure. It is important to consider both subsistence and commercial farming, the former being crucial as it can allow much of the population to become self-sustaining fairly rapidly and the latter important as it may be the only earner of foreign exchange. Land reform policies may also be important, but need to be designed and implemented with care. There is a need to prevent an exodus to urban areas and to take pressure off them, and targeting the development of rural areas is the obvious way to do this. Failing to prevent the break-up of social groups and communities, which is likely to result from moves to urban areas, could cause conflict with return of ex-combatants, who will not be reintegrated into society (ILO, 1995).

In conflict situations, the informal economy can often come to the fore. This can be a complex circuit of exchange with international links (as in Sarajevo). But with the end of conflict the strength of this sector can act as a restraint on the reassertion of the formal economy and can even introduce criminal elements. Indeed, as Duffield (1992) points out, conflict can lead to a transfer of assets to middlemen, which can be extremely destructive and embed inequality. At the same time this is usually a circulation of goods, with little new production of assets. The informal sector is, however, the only viable possibility of a livelihood for many and the impact of destroying it through reconstruction policies may not be compensated for by the growth of the formal sector. International intervention can in fact make things worse and care needs to be taken by both aid agencies and policy-makers. Aid can destroy the existing market structures and lead to anomalies, such as farmers being ruined by inflows of cheap aid.

Given such heterogeneity and complexity, it is likely to be important to carefully research individual countries when attempting to design policies for post-conflict reconstruction, but some generic requirements can be identified. There is also some level of overlap, and it will be important to try to envisage a way in which this can be dealt with.

So there are a number of issues to take into account in looking at how best to contribute to post-conflict reconstruction with the available instruments. Considering the costs of conflict that are relevant to this solution, the first is the increase in military spending resulting from conflict. This is something considered in detail by Collier *et al.* (2008a), but it is a more complex issue than simply reducing spending to create growth and limit the probability of conflicts recurring. It is in fact difficult and dangerous to simply disband the armed forces and, as mentioned already, security sector reform has recently been an important policy issue. In post-conflict situations the security sector is often characterized by politicization, ethnicization, corruption, lack of professionalism, poor oversight, inefficiencies, and excessive military spending. The sector needs to be restructured to free up resources and stop it being a fetter on development, but the need for security while the rebuilding is taking place is still clear. Domestic public security institutions are needed and the re-establishment of the legitimate monopoly of violence. Linked to this provision of physical security, which primarily involves the police and the military, is a proper functioning of the courts and the prison system, as well as small arms' control and security institutions within the realm of rule of law. The international community may need to be directly involved if the relevant state structures have broken down (Brzoska and Heinemann-Grüder, 2005). These will seem to justify some maintenance of security spending, but with some clear guidelines.

Intelligence

Given the complexity and heterogeneity outlined above, it seems important to have good knowledge of the economic, political, and social background of the country, the causes of conflict, the reason for it ending, and the context of the post-conflict period. Many problems have come about from policies designed with a lack of understanding (Dunne, 1996). So it seems useful to allocate about 0.5 billion p.a. to support such efforts.

Peacekeeping forces

These can be important, but will have a different role to the intervention forces discussed above and will more likely be truly peacekeeping forces. Depending upon the situation in the country, the troops may be required to keep the sides apart, but are more likely to be involved in "policing" the peace agreement.

Non-military support

Non-military forces will be useful, such as police to support and train locals and overcome entrenched mistrust. Police and justice "development" projects could ensure reduced corruption, with external auditing and maybe "accreditation" of police and justice forces. Certainly, support is likely to be required for creating credible and non-corrupt institutions of state. This could include support from administrators and civil servants. Mediation and reconciliation services are also likely to be important, as it is also important to recognize that the end of conflict is not necessarily the end of violence and many countries are saddled with the legacy of conflict even when they are considered at peace. We include $2 billion p.a. to cover these services and personnel.

Aid

International aid – economic and humanitarian – will also play an important role, but there is considerable debate over its value and the type of aid that is most useful in a post-conflict environment (Duffield, 2001; Dunne, 2006). The usual post-conflict policies of demobilization, infrastructure development (maybe labor-intensive methods), human capital development, development of banking and finance, and macroeconomic and trade policy support will also be important. Aid will be important initially for humanitarian needs and demobilization and reintegration, but then to assist with economic restructuring and develop institutions and capabilities (including education). Infrastructure development will also be necessary. As discussed above, aid has important roles to play, but it is important to recognize the need for security and the specifics of the individual country's problems when it is in such a fragile condition (Brauer and Dunne, 2012). It is also clear that foreign aid will need to be much larger in post-conflict situations than in the other solutions, as so much damage will already have been created. For this reason we suggest $8 billion p.a. over the four years.

Table 1.15 Post-conflict reconstruction, cost p.a. per conflict (US$ billion)

	$bn p.a. per conflict
Intelligence	0.5
Aid	8
UN troops and back-up	3
Non-military forces	1
Action on arms' trade	0.5
Total	13

A considerable amount has been spent on post-conflict measures already, so really all we can do is look at the marginal effect. It would also be valuable if the resources allowed the programs to be more flexible and deal with the legacy costs of conflict which are often ignored as the more usual indicators start to look better. As mentioned already, the peace accord is often not the end of the fighting and the end of the fighting is often not the end of violence. The violent legacy left behind can be devastating and cause great economic loss. It is difficult to gauge this within the framework here. Certainly the cost of this "solution" is greater than the others, but it is also the final step, the solution needed when the first two fail.

Summarizing the estimated costs is carried out in Table 1.15.

Over four years and discounting at 3 percent would suggest costs of $54 billion and at 5 percent, $52 billion per conflict. The benefits of post-conflict policies will be the increased economic

Table 1.16 Post-conflict reconstruction, benefits, and costs (US$ billion) and BCRs

Solution	Assumptions	Benefits	Costs	BCR
Post-conflict	$1,000 DALY, 3%	568	145	3.9
	$1,000 DALY, 5%	404	138	2.9
	$5,000 DALY, 3%	644	145	4.9
	$5,000 DALY, 5%	484	138	3.5

Note: This assumes that post-conflict reconstruction averts 50% of the costs of conflict, as the conflicts have already ended or are close to it.

growth in the same manner as before. While there will be some cost sharing across the four conflicts we consider, the specific needs of the countries mean that it would be reasonable to expect three times these costs to cover four conflicts. Growth in this case will be slightly slower as the economy takes off, but aid will play a major role. Engaging in the reconstruction of economies would prevent conflict from restarting and this is unlikely to be non-linear, with the largest probability of recurrence occurring in the early years.[17] So we allocate 50 percent of our base estimates to benefits and for speeding up the recovery phase. In this situation the benefits could be more widespread than under the previous solutions, as a focus on the legacy costs could increase the benefits. Brauer and Tepper-Marlin (2010) estimate that the costs of the wider effects of violence internationally are 9 percent of world GDP. When looking at low-income countries there may not always be such a large externality effect, though the development of terrorism in conflict-ridden countries is always a concern. As we are contributing to a post-conflict scenario and can focus on the legacy costs, the benefits of reduced DALY can well be higher than before. After a conflict the health costs are bound to be large, because of what has happened during the conflict, the breakdown in infrastructure, communications, and services. To reflect this and the impact on the chance of recurrence, we maintain the DALY cost per conflict, despite the initial conflict having ended (Table 1.16).

These results show that there are certainly good returns to investing more funds in post-conflict restructuring, but the BCRs are not as high as the other solutions. This is not surprising, given that international organizations, governments, and NGOs already commit a lot of effort and resources to assisting countries coming out of conflict and so additional resources would only have a marginal effect (the easy benefits have already been taken). It is also a long-run process. In fact, post-conflict reconstruction is so important it is a necessity, with our main concern being that the legacy costs may not be identified correctly and that international effort may be ending before an end to violence.

Conclusions

Conflict is a major problem for the world and one that impacts most upon the very poorest individuals. It has potentially huge costs which are generally never fully measured. The direct costs are always very evident in the headlines, but the indirect and legacy costs are much less apparent. It is possible to measure both direct and indirect costs, using accounting and counterfactual methods. Such studies find that conflicts can be devastating in a number of ways, can have high economic costs, can have high spillover effects, and are a major concern for development. Arguments remain that we may be interpreting the role of conflicts wrongly (Cramer, 2006) and that they can play a positive role, representing primitive accumulation, allowing the removal of fetters on production, or making important institutional changes. But given the damage they can do, the main focus is on their costs.

What is being measured by studies of the cost of conflict is unlikely to be the full legacy costs and there always remain the questions of what peace is

[17] Collier *et al.* (2003) suggest that post-conflict countries face a 42 percent risk of returning to conflict in ten years.

Table 1.17 Conflict prevention, benefits, and costs (US$ billion) and BCRs

Solution	Assumptions	Benefits	Costs	BCR
Prevention	$1,000 DALY, 3%	852	56	15.2
	$1,000 DALY, 5%	606	54	11.2
	$5,000 DALY, 3%	966	56	17.3
	$5,000 DALY, 5%	726	54	13.4

Note: This assumes that prevention averts three out of four conflicts and so 75% of the full four-year costs.

Table 1.18 Conflict intervention, benefits, and costs (US$ billion) and BCRs

Solution	Assumptions	Benefits	Costs	BCR
Intervention	$1,000 DALY, 3%	852	100	6.4
	$1,000 DALY, 5%	606	96	4.8
	$5,000 DALY, 3%	966	100	7.2
	$5,000 DALY, 5%	726	96	5.7

Note: This assumes that intervention averts 75% of the costs of conflict, as conflicts have already started.

Table 1.19 Post-conflict reconstruction, benefits, and costs (US$ billion) and BCRs

Solution	Assumptions	Benefits	Costs	BCR
Post-conflict	$1,000 DALY, 3%	568	145	3.9
	$1,000 DALY, 5%	404	138	2.9
	$5,000 DALY, 3%	644	145	4.9
	$5,000 DALY, 5%	484	138	3.5

Note: This assumes that post-conflict reconstruction averts 50% of the costs of conflict, as conflicts have already ended or are close to it.

and when a conflict ends. The high costs and complexity make the creation of solutions very difficult, but in some ways it is better to see the solutions as part of a process to deal with problems at particular stages, rather than simple remedies. For this reason we put together a combination of instruments that are relevant for conflict prevention, intervention, and then post-conflict reconstruction.

In this chapter an attempt has been made to estimate the likely costs and benefits of using new funds to contribute to each of the solutions, which as they are essential phases show a degree of overlap. The analysis starts by considering the solutions presented in Collier *et al.* (2008a), using estimates that still seem reasonable for the valuations involved and adjusting where necessary. The approach taken here is quite different and the instruments focused upon dealt with differently. Each of the solutions contains a number of instruments and trying to determine what the cost of these is illustrates the issues involved. The results of the reasoning and calculations provide the estimates in Tables 1.17–1.19.

Clearly the results suggest that the most cost-effective way of dealing with the cost of conflict is to prevent the conflict taking place, although care needs to be taken that this is not being undertaken against the interests of the citizens of the countries – in some cases conflict may have positive outcomes. If conflicts do break out then the next stage is possible intervention. This is shown to be extremely cost-effective, but again there are a number of political issues and some clear guidelines and procedures need to be agreed and there must be transparency. If intervention succeeds it will lead to the post-conflict reconstruction phase earlier than would have happened otherwise and the costs to the country and the international community are likely to be smaller. When conflicts do end, what is needed for reconstruction is contingent on the nature of the conflict and the way it ended. Already considerable effort has been made on post-conflict reconstruction, but it can be more effective. Particularly important are the legacy costs of the conflict, such as more general violence within the society, and these are usually not picked up. Post-conflict policies can be costly but are also cost-effective in preventing suffering, important externalities, and building up economies to provide new markets and raw materials. While post-conflict policies may not have the highest BCR, they do represent necessities and already command the attention and resources of the international community.

It is important to emphasize that even with the efforts we have made the true costs of armed conflicts are still likely to be hugely underestimated. The unmeasureables are significant and the full legacy costs are not always registered as a cost of the conflict. The existence of drugs, criminal gangs, and violence in South American countries such as Colombia in the present day can be traced back to the ending of an armed conflict without true peace being achieved.

The solutions here have fitted the costs into the four-year window specified for the project, but clearly it would make sense to continue these expenditures. The benefits reflect the long-run impact of the expenditures, but might be greater if a longer time frame were used. It may be possible to have some immediate impacts in prevention and intervention, but the post-conflict reconstruction initiatives are for the long run and in the past have failed because of short-run attitudes. Prevention and intervention have received not nearly enough attention and more research is certainly required to provide consistent and comprehensive CBAs of these potential solutions to conflict.

The bottom line is that without peace there cannot be development and the MDGs and other development targets become unattainable. So one might see the contributions to the solutions discussed here as necessities, to create an environment where the other challenges can have a hope of being attained. If this is accepted, the benefits we have calculated here can only be seen as a mere fraction of what could be achieved.

Bibliography

Abadie, A. and J. Gardeazabal, 2003: The economic costs of conflict: a case study of the Basque Country, *American Economic Review* **93**, 113–32

Adam, C., P. Collier, and V. Davies, 2008: Post-conflict monetary reconstruction, *World Bank Economic Review*

African Development Bank, 2008–2009: African Development Report "Conflict resolution, peace and reconstruction in Africa"

Anderton, C. H. and J. R. Carter, 2009: *Principles of Conflict Economics*, Cambridge University Press

Arunatilake, N., S. Jayasuriya, and S. Kelegama, 2001: The economic costs of the war in Sri Lanka, *World Development* **29**, 1483–500

Azam, J.-P., 1994: Democracy and development: a theoretical framework, *Public Choice* **80**, 293–305

Bevan, D., P. Collier, and J. W. Gunning, 1994: *Controlled Open Economies*, Oxford University Press

Bigombe, B., P. Collier, and N. Sambanis, 2000: Policies for building post-conflict peace, *Journal of African Economies*

Bilmes, L. and J. E. Stiglitz, 2006: The economic costs of the Iraq War: an appraisal three years after the beginning of the conflict, NBER Working Paper **12054**

Blattman, C. and E. Niguel, 2010: Civil war, *Journal of Economic Literature* **48**, 3–57

Bozzoli, C., T. Brück, and S. Sottsas, 2010: A survey of the global economic costs of conflict, *Defense and Peace Economics*, **21**, 165–76

Bozzoli, C., T. Brück, T. Drautzburg, and S. Sottsas, 2008: Economic costs of mass violent conflict: final report for the Small Arms Survey, Geneva, Switzerland, *Politikberatung Kompakt* **42**, Deutsches Institut für Wirtschaftsforschung, Berlin

Brauer, J., 2006a: Environmental consequences of war, in N. Young (ed.), *The International Encyclopedia of Peace*, Oxford University Press, New York

2006b: Theory and practice of intervention, *The Economics of Peace and Security Journal* **1**, 17–23

Brauer, J. and P. Dunne, 2011: Macroeconomics and violence, chapter 14 in D. Braddon and K. Hartley (eds.), *Handbook on the Economics of Conflict*, Edward Elgar, Cheltenham

2012: *Peace Economics: A Macroeconomic Primer for Violence-Afflicted States*, US Institute for Peace, Washington

Brauer, J. and J. Tepper-Marlin, 2009: Defining peace industries and calculating the potential size of a peace gross world product by country and by economic sector, Report for the Institute of Economics and Peace, Sydney

2010: A method to compute a peace gross world product by country and by economic sector, in B. E. Goldsmith and J. Brauer (eds.), *Economics of War and Peace: Economic, Legal, and Political Perspectives*, Emerald Group, Bingley, 13–30

Brown, M. E. and R. Rosecrance (eds.), 1999: *The Costs of Conflict*, Rowman & Littlefield, Boulder, CO

Brück, T., O. de Groot, and F. Schneider, 2011: The economic costs of the German participation in the Afghanistan War, *Journal of Peace Research* **48**, 793–805

Brzoska, M. and A. Heinemann-Grüder, 2005: Security sector reform and post-conflict, chapter 6 in A. Bryden and R. Kossler, *Reform and Reconstruction of the Security Sector*, Lit Verlag, Berlin

Chalmers, M., 2004: Spending to save, *CICS Working Papers* **1–3**, Department of Peace Studies, University of Bradford, www.brad.ac.uk/acad/cics/publications/spending/

Chauvet, L., P. Collier, and A. Hoeffler, 2007: The cost of failing states and the limits to sovereignty, *UNU-WIDER Research Paper* **2007.30**

Collier, P., 1999: On the economic consequences of civil war, *Oxford Economic Papers* **51**, 168–83

2007a: *The Bottom Billion: Why the Poorest Countries are Failing and What can be Done About It*, Oxford University Press, New York

2007b: Conflicts, chapter 12 in B. Lomborg (ed.), *Solutions for the World's Biggest Problems*, Cambridge University Press, 220–8

Collier, P. and D. Dollar, 1998: On economic causes of civil war, *Oxford Economic Papers* **50**, 563–73

2002a: Aid allocation and poverty reduction, *European Economic Review* **46**, 1475–1500

2002b: Aid, policy and peace: reducing the risks of civil conflict, *Journal of Defence and Peace Economics* **13**, 435–50

Collier, P. and A. Hoeffler, 2004a: Greed and grievance in civil war, *Oxford Economic Papers* **56**, 563–95

2004b: Conflicts, in B. Lomborg (ed.), *Global Crises: Global Solutions*, Cambridge University Press

2004c: Aid, policy and growth in post-conflict societies, *European Economic Review* **48**, 1125–45

2006a: Military spending in post-conflict societies, *Economics of Governance* **7**, 89–107

2006b: Grand Extortion: Coup Risk and Military Spending, Department of Economics, Oxford University, mimeo

2007a: Unintended consequences: does aid increase military spending?, *Oxford Bulletin of Economics and Statistics* **69**, 1–28

2007b: Coup risk and military spending, Department of Economics, Oxford University, mimeo

2007c: Civil war, in K. Hartley and T. Sandler (eds.), *Handbook of Defence Economics*, Vol. 2, Elsevier, New York, 711–37

Collier, P. and D. Rohner, 2008: Democracy, development, and conflict, *Journal of the European Economic Association* **6**, 531–40

Collier, P., L. Chauvet, and H. Hegre, 2008: The challenge of conflicts, Copenhagen Consensus 2008 Challenge Paper, Copenhagen

Collier, P., B. Goderis, and A. Hoeffler, 2006: Shocks and growth in low-income countries, Department of Economics, Oxford University, mimeo

Collier, P., A. Hoeffler, and D. Roemer, 2009: Beyond greed and grievance: feasibility and civil war, *Oxford Economic Papers* **61**, 1–27

Collier, P., A. Hoeffler, and M. Soderbom, 2008: Post-conflict risks, *Journal of Peace Research* **45**, 461–78

Collier, P., V. L. Elliot, H. Hegre, A. Hoeffler, M. Reynal-Querol, and N. Sambanis, 2003: Breaking the conflict trap: civil war and development policy, OUP for the World Bank; New York

Coyne, C., 2006: Deconstructing reconstruction: the overlooked challenges of military occupation,

Economics of Peace and Security Journal **1**, 94–100
Cramer, C., 2006: *Civil War is not a Stupid Thing*, Hurst & Company, London
Cranna, M., 1994: *The True Cost of Conflict*, London, Earthscan
De Groot, O. J., 2010: The spillover effects of conflict on economic growth in neighbouring countries in Africa, *Defence and Peace Economics* **21**, 149–64
De Groot, O. J., T. Brück, and C. Bozzoli, 2009: How many bucks in a bang: on the estimation of the economic costs of conflict, DIW *Discussion Papers* **948**
Doyle, M. and N. Sambanis, 2006: *Making War and Building Peace*, Princeton University Press
Duffield, M., 2001: *Global Governance and the New Wars: The Merging of Development and Security*, Zed Books, London
Dumas, Loyd, J., 2006: An economic approach to peacemaking and peacekeeping, *Economics of Peace and Security Journal* **1**, 7–12
Dunne, P., 1996: Economic effects of military spending in LDCs: a survey, in N. Petter Gleditsch, A. Cappelen, Ol. Bjerkholt, R. Smith, and P. Dunne (eds.), *The Peace Dividend*, North-Holland, Amsterdam, 439–64
2006: After the slaughter: reconstructing Mozambique and Rwanda, *Economics of Peace and Security Journal* **1**, 38–46
2007: Arms proliferation, Chapter 11 in B. Lomborg (ed.), *Solutions for the World's Biggest Problems*, Cambridge University Press, 220–28
Dunne, P. and S. Perlo-Freeman, 2003: The demand for military spending in developing countries, *International Review of Applied Economics* **17**, 23–48
Elbadawi, I., I. A. Kaltani, and K. Schmidt-Habbel, 2008: Foreign aid, the real exchange rate, and growth in the aftermath of civil wars, *World Bank Economic Review*, World Bank Group, **22**, 113–40
Escriba-Folch, A., 2010: Economic sanctions and the duration of civil conflicts, *Journal of Peace Research* **47**, 129–41
Fearon, J. D., 2010: Governance and civil war onset, *WDR Background Paper*, World Bank, Washington, DC
Fearon, J. D. and D. D. Laitin, 2003: Ethnicity, insurgency, and civil war, *American Political Science Review* **97**, 75–90
Fetterly, R., 2006: The cost of peacekeeping: Canada, *Economics of Peace and Security Journal* **1**, 46–53
FitzGerald, V., 1987: An evaluation of the economic costs to Nicaragua of US aggression: 1980–1984, in R. J. Spalding (ed.), *The Political Economy of Revolutionary Nicaragua*, Allen & Unwin, Boston, MA, 195–213
GAO, 2006: Cost comparison of actual UN and hypothetical US operations in Haiti, US Government Accountability Office, Washington, DC, www.gao.gov/products/GAO-06-331
Gates, S., H. Hegre, H. M. Nygard, and H. Strand, 2010: Consequences of civil conflicts, *WDR Background Paper*, World Bank, Washington, DC
Ghobarah, H., P. Huth, and B. Russett, 2003: Civil wars kill and maim people – long after the shooting stops, *American Political Science Review* **97**, 189–202
Grobar, L. M. and S. Gnanaselvam, 1993: The economic effects of the Sri Lankan civil war, *Economic Development and Cultural Change* **41**, 395–405
Harris, G., 1999: *Recovery from Armed Conflict in Developing Countries*, Routledge, London
Hartley, K. and T. Sandler (eds.), 2007: *Handbook of Defence Economics*, North-Holland, Amsterdam
Hegre, H., T. Ellingsen, S. Gates, and N. Petter Gleditsch, 2001: Toward a democratic civil peace? Democracy, political change, and civil war, 1816–1992, *American Political Science Review* **95**, 33–48
Hess, G. D., 2003: The economic welfare cost of conflict: an empirical assessment, *CESifo Working Paper* **852**, CESifo, Munich
Heston, A., R. Summers and B. Aten, 2009: *Penn World Table Version 6.3*, Center for International Comparisons of Production, Income and Prices, University of Pennsylvania, https://pwt.sas.upenn.edu/php_site/pwt_index.php
House of Lords, 2007: The impact of economic sanctions, Select Committee on Economic Affairs, The Stationery Office, London
Hufbauer, G. C., K. A. Elliott, T. Cyrus, and E. Winston, 1997: US economic sanctions: their impact on trade, jobs, and wages, Peterson Institute for International Economics, April
Human Security Report Group, 2010: *Human Security Report 2009/2010: The Causes of*

Peace and the Shrinking Costs of War, Oxford University Press

ILO, 1995: Reintegration of demobilised combatants through self-employment and training, *Issues Paper*, International Labour Office, Geneva

International Monetary Fund, 2001: *World Economic Outlook*, IMF, Washington, DC

Kaysen, C. and G. Rathjens, 1995: *Peace Operations by the United Nations: The Case for a Volunteer UN Military Force*, American Academy of Arts and Sciences, Cambridge, MA

2003: The case for a volunteer UN military force, *Daedalus* **132**(1), 91–102

Kelegama, S., 1999: Economic costs of conflict in Sri Lanka, in R. I. Rothberg (ed.), *Creating Peace in Sri Lanka: Civil War and Reconciliation*, World Peace Foundation and Belfer Center for Science and International Affairs, Brookings Institution Press, Cambridge, MA and Washington, DC

Klein, L. R., 2006: Peacekeeping operations: from the birth of the United Nations onward, *Economics of Peace and Security Journal* **1**, 3–6

Klein, L. and K. Marwah, 1996: Economic aspects of peacekeeping operations, in N. P. Gleditsch, A. Cappelen, O. Bjerkholt, R. Smith, and P. Dunne (eds.), *The Peace Dividend*, North-Holland, Amsterdam, 533–53

Lindgren, G., 2005: The economic costs of civil war, Paper presented to the 9th Annual Conference on Economics and Security, Bristol, http://carecon.org.uk/Conferences/Conf2005/Papers/Lindgren.pdf

Mack, A., 2008: Perspective Paper – The security challenge in conflict-prone countries, Copenhagen Consensus, www.humansecuritygateway.info/documents/CP_Mack_securitychallen gesinconflictpronecountries.pdf

Martin, P. and T. Mayer, 2008: Civil wars and international trade, *Journal of the European Economic Association* **6**(2–3), 541–50

Miguel, E., S. Satyanath, and E. Sergenti, 2004: Economic shocks and civil conflict: an instrumental variables approach, *Journal of Political Economy* **112**(4) 725–53

Murdoch, J. and T. Sandler, 2002: Civil wars and economic growth: a regional comparison, *Defence and Peace Economics* **13**, 451–64

Nordhaus, W. D., 2002: The economic consequences of a war in Iraq, *NBER Working Papers* **9361**, National Bureau of Economic Research, Cambridge, MA

OECD, 2009: *Preventing Violence, War and State Collapse*, OECD Publishing, Paris

Organski, A. F. K. and J. Kugler, 1977: The costs of major wars: the phoenix factor, *American Political Science Review* **71**, 1347–66

Petrescu, I. M., 2010: Rethinking economic sanction success: sanctions as deterrents, University of Maryland, mimeo, December

Polity IV, 2010: *Polity IV: Regime Authority Characteristics and Transitions Datasets*, Center for Systemic Peace, Virginia, www.systemicpeace.org/inscr/inscr.htm

Rajan, R. G. and A. Subramanian, 2004: Reconstruction under International auspices, chapter 6, in A. Bryden and H. Hänggi (eds.), *Reform and Reconstruction of the Security Sector*, Geneva Centre for the Democratic Control of Armed Forces (DCAF), Geneva

2005: What undermines aid's impact on growth?, *IMF Working Paper*, 05/126

Richardson, J. M., Jr. and S. W. R. de A. Samarasinghe, 1991: Measuring the economic dimensions of Sri Lanka's ethnic conflict, in S. W. R. de A. Samarasinghe and R. Coughlan (eds.), *Economic Dimensions of Ethnic Conflict*, Printer, London

Rigterink, A. S., 2010: Natural resources and civil conflict: an overview of controversies, consensus and channels, *Economics of Peace and Security Journal* **5**(2), July

Salehyan, I. and K. Gleditsch, 2006: Refugees and the spread of civil war, *International Organization* **60**, 335–66

Sambani, N., 2002: A review of recent advances and future directions in the quantitative literature on civil war, *Defence and Peace Economics* **13**, 215–43

Sköns, E., 2006: The costs of armed conflict, in *Expert Paper Series Five: Peace and Security*, The Secretariat of the International Task Force on Global Public Goods, Stockholm, 169–90, www.regeringen.se/sb/d/6501/a/155614>

Stewart, F. *et al.*, 2001: *War and Underdevelopment*, Oxford University Press

Stiglitz, J. E. and L. J. Bilmes, 2008: *The Three Trillion Dollar War: The True Cost of the Iraq Conflict*, W. W. Norton, New York

Stohl, R. J., M. Schroeder, and D. Smith, 2007: *The Small Arms Trade: A Beginner's Guide*, Oneworld, Oxford, 56

Themnér, L. and P. Wallensteen, 2011: Armed conflict, 1946–2010, *Journal of Peace Research* **48**, 525

UN, 2012: UN Peacekeeping Operations Fact Sheet, DPI/1634/Rev.129, United Nations. http://www.un.org/en/peacekeeping/archive/2012/bnote0112.pdf

United Nations Development Programme, 2008: *Post-Conflict Economic Recovery: Enabling Local Ingenuity*, UNDP Bureau for Crisis Prevention and Recovery, New York, 35

World Bank, 2011: Making societies more resilient to violence: a conceptual framework for the conflict, crime and violence agenda, Conflict, Crime, and Violence Team, World Bank, Washington, DC

World Health Organization, 2002: *World Report on Violence and Health*, ed. E. G. Krug, L. L. Dahlberg, J. A. Mercy, A. B. Zwi, and R. Lozano, WHO, Geneva

Wulf, H. and T. Debeil, 2009: Conflict early warning mechanisms: tools for enhancing the effectiveness of regional organisation?, *Crisis States Working Papers* **2**, WP **49**

Yousif, B., 2006: Economic aspects of peacekeeping in Iraq: what went wrong?, *Economics of Peace and Security Journal* **1**, 23–30

1.1 Armed Conflicts

Alternative Perspective

ANKE HOEFFLER*

Introduction

In his Challenge Paper (Chapter 1) Paul Dunne demonstrates that the costs of armed conflict are not restricted to the fatalities of such conflict, but include deaths and disabilities due to the consequences of war, the economic losses to the country experiencing civil war, and to their neighbors. He builds on previous Copenhagen Consensus attempts to quantify the costs of armed conflict (Collier and Hoeffler, 2004a; Collier *et al.*, 2008) and the costs are estimated by assessing the economic and social impact the armed conflict has had on the society.[1]

My Alternative Perspective Paper has two main sections. I first discuss alternative calculations of the health burden. My calculations suggest that the costs of war – in terms of loss of life, injury, disability, and disease – are possibly much higher than calculated by Dunne; they could be as high as $79 billion.

I then provide a discussion of Dunne's proposed solutions. How effective are they? What works and what does not? Dunne proposes a number of solutions, such as early warning systems, development aid, and peacekeeping operations. Based on the costs of such interventions he calculates the BCRs and concludes that all of the proposed solutions would be highly cost-effective. While I agree with his main conclusion I highlight the uncertainties when evaluating the proposed solutions. I argue that although some interventions are frequently advocated, we know very little about their success, partly because we base our assessment on the implicit assumption that interventions are motivated by the desire to prevent or lessen conflict. This implicit assumption may not be correct.

Cost of armed conflict

Like the 2004 and 2008 Copenhagen Consensus Challenge Papers Dunne uses a counterfactual approach to estimate the economic costs of armed conflict: it is based on a comparison between the path the economy takes during and after the conflict and the likely path the economy would have taken in the absence of conflict. The economic costs are the sum of the cost to the war economy, the spillover cost affecting neighboring economies and the legacy effect of war.

In addition to these economic costs, the social cost in terms of the health costs of civil wars are considered. The concept of DALYs is used to measure such health costs. One DALY can be thought of as one lost year of "healthy" life. The average civil war is estimated to cost half a million DALYs p.a. These DALYs are then priced and discounted to derive an estimate in US$. Two possible prices for a lost year of healthy life are considered, $1,000 and $5,000, and two discount rates of 3 and 6 percent.

Wars kill, but numbers are hard to come by. In the literature there is a wide discrepancy between the number of deaths reported for various wars. One distinction among the number of war deaths is whether people were killed through direct violence or through the indirect consequences of war

* I would like to thank Doug Bond and Nicholas Marsh for information and helpful discussion on early warning systems and the international arms trade. All remaining errors are of course my own.

[1] Armed conflict is understood to be large-scale, and internal to a country where an organized opposition movement is able to inflict fatalities on the government. Only conflicts with more than 1,000 battle-related deaths p.a. are considered. For the purpose of this Alternative Perspective chapter I will use "conflict" and "civil war" interchangeably.

such as malnutrition, increased risk of communicable diseases, and increased crime. Typically the literature distinguishes between "battle deaths" and "total war deaths," which includes deaths due to both direct and indirect causes.

The calculation of DALYs for the Copenhagen Consensus is based on an estimate by Ghobarah *et al.* (2003). They suggest that armed conflicts cause the loss of 8.44 million DALYs p.a. Their estimate includes deaths and disability resulting from twenty-three major diseases, not only from injuries inflicted by fighting. Collier and Hoeffler (2004a) assume that there were on average seventeen ongoing civil wars (based on Collier *et al.*, 2003), and thus suggest that on average civil wars cost 500,000 DALYs p.a. Assuming that the average war lasts for seven years, that the effects of war decrease over time (following the pattern of the economic costs of war), that the effects of the war are zero in the twenty-first year after the start of the war, and a discount rate of 5 percent, they calculate an NPV of 5 million DALYs per war. Using a price of $1,000 per DALY the costs are thus $5 billion. Dunne uses a discount rate of 3 or 6 percent and a price of $1,000 or $5,000. Thus, his costs are estimated to lie between $4.7 billion and $27.8 billion.

My alternative calculation would put these costs substantially higher. The WHO puts the number of DALYs lost due to war and civil conflict at 12.1 million in 2004 (most recent figures). Using the UCDP/PRIO Armed Conflict Dataset (Gleditsch *et al.* 2002) yields an average number of wars per year of 8.4, thus there are 1.4 million DALYs lost per war per year. Following the Collier *et al.* (2008) and Dunne calculation, the NPV is between $13.2 billion and $77.9 billion. The upper bound of the calculation would thus be higher than the total costs of war as suggested by Dunne ($58.6 billion).

However, although this appears plausible it appears that the calculations do not use the same data definitions. Let us assume that the aim is to assess the health costs of civil wars. First, we require a definition of civil war. While the definition of Gleditsch *et al.*, 2002 has become the standard in quantitative social sciences the estimates of the corresponding DALYs by the WHO do not appear to match this classification. The WHO categorization appears to be wider, including all wars and civil conflict. Lancina and Gleditsch (2005) provide estimates of battle deaths that do correspond to the Gleditsch *et al.*, 2002 definition, but they do not provide an estimate of DALYs. The estimates of Murray *et al.* (2002) suggest that the battle deaths are almost equally split between military and civilian fatalities. Second, the health costs of wars are not only due to injuries inflicted in battle but are also consequences of the war, such as malnutrition and a higher incidence of communicable diseases. Lacina and Gleditsch (2005) also provide some estimates for total war deaths, including battle deaths and deaths due to increased one-sided violence, diseases, and crime. Their estimates of total war deaths have very large confidence intervals. On the whole their estimates appear to be conservative. For example, Coghlan *et al.* (2006) use the International Rescue Committee (IRC) household survey to estimate the number of deaths due to the war in the Democratic Republic of the Congo (DRC): they put the total death toll at about 3.9 million and suggest that the Congolese war has been the deadliest since the end of the Second World War. Their total death toll differs markedly from Lacina and Gleditsch (2005), who put the total at 2.5 million.[2]

A relatively small percentage of total war deaths are due to direct violence. For African wars, Lacina and Gleditsch (2005) suggest that battle deaths make up between 3 and 29 percent. In other words more people are killed by the consequences of war rather than in the fighting. This ratio varies considerably across the different civil wars.

Estimating the number of war deaths is very difficult. The use of household surveys enables researchers to estimate excess mortality rates. The study by Degomme and Guha-Sapir (2010) calculates the number of excess deaths for the conflict in Darfur. Using sixty-three mortality surveys gathered from 2004 to 2008 they estimate the overall number of excess deaths at 300,000[3] and find that about 20 percent of excess deaths were the direct result of violence.

[2] Lacina and Gleditsch (2005) provide data for only four years of the war but the corresponding Coghlan *et al.* (2006) estimate for this period is 3.3 million.

[3] This number does not include deaths among the refugees living in Chad.

Why is it important to derive plausible estimates of the number of (civilian) deaths or DALYs? If we want to provide meaningful policy advice for interventions it must be based on hard evidence. Without information it is impossible to design adequate programs to address the health burden that civil wars impose on the population (Checchi, 2010).

A dynamic health cost that has not been considered by any of the Copenhagen Consensus papers is the impact of war on the global eradication of communicable diseases. Global vaccination programs successfully eradicated smallpox (1979) and rinderpest (2010). Civil war countries are pivotal in the global effort of eradicating disease as the following three examples of polio, Guinea-worm disease, and measles show.[4]

Polio

Since the inception of the global eradication plan in 1988 polio cases have decreased by over 99 percent. At the start of the program polio was endemic in 125 countries; today only three countries remain polio-endemic – Afghanistan, Nigeria, and Pakistan. Afghanistan is at war and the others have considerable levels of violence. As long as polio remains endemic in these three countries, neighboring countries are at risk – for example, the continuation of cases in northern Nigeria poses the risk of renewed spread of the virus to other West African states. In the past, polio virus has spread from northern Nigeria to Niger, then on into Burkina Faso and Mali. Given the current security situation in Mali, this is of particular concern.

Guinea-worm disease

Dracunculiasis (guinea-worm disease) is a crippling parasitic disease. It is transmitted exclusively when people who have little or no access to a safe drinking water supply swallow water contaminated with parasite-infected fleas. Dracunculiasis is rarely fatal, but infected people become nonfunctional for months. A global eradication strategy was developed in 1981 and now only four African countries are endemic – Chad, Ethiopia, Mali, and South Sudan. Most cases (97 percent) occur in newly independent South Sudan. The WHO regards insecurity as the major constraint in the eradication of the disease. In the past "periods of tranquillity" have been negotiated to distribute filters, treat infected patients, and apply larvicide.[5] Although Guinea-worm disease is almost eradicated, the security situation in South Sudan raises concern over the final push in the global eradication campaign.

Measles

Measles is a highly infectious disease and one of the leading causes of death among young children. The fourth MDG (MDG 4) aims to reduce the under-5 mortality rate by two-thirds between 1990 and 2015. The global Measles and Rubella Initiative contributed 23 percent of the overall decline in under-5 deaths between 1990 and 2008 and is driving progress towards meeting MDG 4. Routine measles vaccination coverage has been selected as an indicator of progress towards achieving the MDG. Although measles' outbreaks occur worldwide, more than 95 percent of measles deaths occur in low-income countries. The reduction of measles is thus of particular importance to such countries; however, none of the low-income countries afflicted by violence has achieved a single one of the eight MDGs.[6] Security concerns are thus pivotal in the global effort to reduce measles.

To summarize, we still do not have a clear understanding of the health burden of civil wars. Partly, this is a problem of definitions. Social scientists and public health experts use different concepts of large-scale violence. Social scientists also concentrate on the estimate of deaths while public health researchers use the concept of DALYs. The loss of a "healthy" year of life is a more dynamic measure of the health burden of war, which indicates the impact of war long after the shooting stops. Health surveys give more precise estimates of excess mortality rates during and after war, but due to the

[4] The discussion is based on information from the WHO: polio – www.who.int/mediacenter/factsheets/fs114/en/index.html; Guinea worm disease – www.who.int/mediacenter/factsheets/fs359/en/; measles – www.who.int/mediacenter/factsheets/fs286/en/.

[5] The Carter Center leads the global effort of eradicating Guinea-worm disease – www.cartercenter.org/health/guinea_worm/mini_site/index.html.

[6] World Bank (2011).

security situation household surveys are difficult to carry out. Good information on the health burden is essential in the design of appropriate health interventions.

Proposed solutions

Dunne proposes a number of solutions to prevent and shorten conflicts but he does not discuss their effectiveness. Some of the proposed solutions have been assessed in large *n*-studies and I provide a brief overview of the effectiveness of aid, peacekeeping, arms' control, and early warning systems.

Development aid

Dunne regards aid as an effective instrument to prevent and shorten wars, although the mechanisms through which aid can achieve this are not discussed in detail. Aid could potentially reduce the risk of conflict directly. Development aid increases the government budget and since aid is fungible these additional funds can be used to increase military expenditure (Collier and Hoeffler, 2007) and thus deter rebellion or suppress it. Another possible channel is that potential rebel groups can be "bought off." However, there is no empirical evidence that aid decreases the risk of conflict (Collier and Hoeffler, 2002; De Ree and Nillesen, 2009).

What about indirect channels? Aid could potentially decrease the risk of conflict by increasing growth and income. However, although there is a large literature on the economic impact of aid on growth (e.g. Burnside and Dollar, 2000; Dalgaard *et al.*, 2004), I concur with Rajan and Subramanian (2008) that there is no robust positive relationship between aid and growth in cross-country regressions. They also find no evidence that aid works better in better policy or geographical environments, nor that certain types of aid work better than others. Thus, aid is unlikely to affect the risk of conflict through growth.

Does aid affect the duration of a conflict? Most of the aid goes to the government although there is some discussion that food aid can be appropriated by rebel forces. De Ree and Nillesen (2009) provide some evidence that aid shortens the duration of civil wars; they suggest that aid strengthens the government by "leaking" into the military budget. While this appears plausible, they do not examine whether aid results in a military victory for the government.

Another line of inquiry is whether aid can help to stabilize post-conflict countries and reduce the high rate of recurrence. Collier and Hoeffler (2004c) and Hoeffler *et al.* (2011) focus their analysis on whether aid can enhance the peace dividend. In contrast to the general literature on aid and growth (which finds essentially no links), Hoeffler *et al.* (2011) find that aid has a positive effect on growth in post-war economies. However, the effect is moderate: an extra 1 percent of aid increases growth by 0.05–0.1 percent. Importantly, they show that these results do not hold in violent post-war situations: aid in such situations has no growth-enhancing effect. Toft (2010) shows that post-conflict growth is independent of the type of settlement that brought the conflict to an end. Hoeffler *et al.* (2011) examine whether certain types of aid are particularly beneficial to growth in post-war countries. After an armed conflict, countries face particular needs – for example, physical infrastructure reconstruction and rehabilitation, and there will be a health burden. However, they find no statistical evidence that one particular type of aid is more beneficial than another.

UN peacekeeping

There is now considerable evidence that UN peacekeeping operations (UNPKOs) are effective in maintaining peace. Collier *et al.* (2008) use a duration model and conclude that UNPKOs do extend the peace. Fortna and Howard (2008) provide an overview of the peacekeeping literature and conclude that there is robust evidence on peacekeeping's positive effects. One concern in this literature is the possible endogeneity of UNPKOs. If peacekeepers are only sent to less difficult situations, the statistical results would suffer from endogeneity bias. However, Fortna (2008) argues that the United Nations sends peacekeepers to the more difficult situations. There is no evidence that UNPKOs lead to democratization (Fortna and Howard, 2008), nor that they affect growth directly (Hoeffler *et al.*, 2011). Interestingly, Fortna (2008) suggests that the success of UNPKOs is mainly due to non-military mechanisms. The decision of the belligerents to keep the peace is the result of altered incentives, alleviation of fear and mistrust, the prevention of accidental escalation into war, and the reshaping of the political procedures.

Arms trade and arms embargoes

Restrictions of arms transfers to conflict zones could potentially be a useful instrument in the international prevention and intervention strategy. Currently there is no internationally binding international Arms Trade Treaty, but the UN negotiations for such a treaty are on-going. If a Treaty can be concluded the challenge is to ensure that states have the capacity to control arms' transfers. There are a number of regional and national regulations that restrict the arms' trade to countries in conflict or to states with a poor human rights record. Examples are the EU Code of Conduct on Arms Exports and the US Arms Export Control Act (AECA). Some of these arms' trade restrictions appear to be motivated by the self-interest of the manufacturing country rather than concerns for the conflict situation in destination countries. Many arms' manufacturers want to prevent the spread of technology. For the discussion of civil war, the transfer of Small Arms and Light Weapons (SALW) is of most interest. Bourne (2012) discusses how SALW are traded and how they reach conflict zones. He argues that about 90 percent of all conflict countries have managed to obtain SALW from the global market. The SALW are typically obtained within the region: imported by one country but diverted to a different end-user through unauthorized re-export.

How much does it cost to monitor the export controls on SALW? US post-export checks are regarded as the most effective and are known as the "Blue Lantern" program. This includes the checks on foreign consignees and end-users. The operational budget for 2011 was \$2.17 million (this excludes salaries) US Department of State (2011). Considering that the total US arms' trade with developing countries is about \$21.3 billion (Grimmett, 2011), there is scope to improve and finance the monitoring program. The value of the global arms' exports to developing countries is estimated at \$40.4 billion (Grimmett, 2011), and scaling up the controls may be a very effective way of reducing the flow of arms to conflict countries.

Are arms embargoes effective? UN Security Council arms' embargoes are the only global, legally binding prohibition on arms' transfers. Since 1990 the United Nations has imposed twenty-eight arms' embargoes (Holtom and Bromley, 2010). However, there have also been various national and regional embargoes and there is a small emerging literature on the effectiveness of such embargoes. One of the key issues is what is meant by "effectiveness." The objectives of embargoes can be wide-ranging – for example, regime change, end of a civil war, or end of the support for terrorism. Objectives cannot be directly observed and there may be a difference between the aim and the result of the embargo. Brzoska (2008) examines the effectiveness of embargoes and concludes that although they changed import patterns it is less clear that targeted countries changed policies. Multilateral embargoes (for example, EU) appear to be more effective than unilateral (US) ones. Embargoes take time to work and import restrictions only "bite" once stockpiles of arms and ammunition are depleted. Based on seventy-four embargo cases Brzoska (2008) suggests that embargoes of five years' duration are more likely to be effective. The study by Fruchart *et al.* (2007) suggests that embargoes have a higher effectiveness in the presence of UNPKO.

Interventions in ongoing civil wars

There is an implicit assumption that interventions will shorten conflicts, or make them less violent. In comparison to the intellectual attention that civil war onset has received, the duration of war has been relatively understudied. Regan (1996) defines interventions as military, diplomatic, or economic and has generated a dataset which has been used by a number of researchers (e.g. Collier *et al.*, 2008). Military interventions include UNPKOs as well as interventions by neighbors and major powers. Economic interventions include economic assistance as well as sanctions. Regan (2010) provides an overview of the intervention literature and concludes that external interventions increase the expected duration of a civil war.[7] Thus, based on the implicit assumption that interventions should limit conflicts, we conclude that they are not effective in conflict management. However, there are other reasons why external interventions take place, such as strategic considerations. The goals of interventions are often multi-faceted and it is thus difficult to assess their effectiveness. One area that is poorly understood is whether interventions result in a particular form of conflict termination. This is an important question because there is evidence that military victories result in longer-lasting peace. Negotiated settlements are more likely to break down and civil war to reoccur (Toft, 2010).

Interventions before a civil war

The question whether interventions can prevent wars has received very little attention and the relatively recent effort in developing early warning systems has not yet been systematically analyzed. The central questions are whether "early warning" results in "early action," and whether this prevents civil wars. Nyheim (2009) and Wulf and Debiel (2009) provide overviews on early warning and response mechanisms. An example of a regional warning and response system is the Continental Early Warning System (CEWS) in Africa, which was initiated in 2002. It is intended to contain crisis situations and prevent them from further escalation into large-scale violent conflict. The system was generated by the AU and is part of an integrated conflict preventions' mechanism: intelligence is gathered and analyzed in a specialist center, the AU can send additional fact-finding missions, the Peace and Security Council can then decide to intervene.[8] The African Peace Facility Fund and the African Standby Force are used to implement the interventions. Recent missions include: Burundi (2003), Darfur (2004–2006), Somalia (2007–2008) and Comoros (2008). Some of the interventions seem to have been underresourced and a lot of outside funding (for example from the United States) appears to be ad hoc.

While it is too early to assess the effectiveness of AU interventions statistically, Regan's (2010) large *n*-study assesses the success of interventions before civil wars. To my knowledge this is the only study of this kind. Regan (2010) builds on Goldstone *et al.* (2010) and determines countries and periods with a high risk of civil war. Regan (2012) then analyzes whether interventions were successful in preventing conflict. He concludes that military interventions increase the likelihood of civil war, economic interventions have no effect on the likelihood of war, and diplomatic interventions decrease the likelihood of a war.

Conclusions

World-wide, more people die in traffic accidents than in armed conflict. Considering the death statistics, the challenge of "armed conflict" appears to be a comparably minor one. However, as Dunne and previous Copenhagen Consensus authors have suggested, the cost of war is much larger than the loss of life: it is the sum of economic and health losses to the country and their neighbors, and legacy effects due to an increased risk of war. In this Alternative Perspective Paper I have suggested that the number of healthy years lost may have been underestimated and the health burden of war may be considerably higher than previously assumed. However, the discussion highlights the fact that the estimation of the health burden of war is particularly difficult. Part of the problem is that definitions vary across public health and social science research. Household surveys can provide more accurate figures of excess mortality but they are of course dangerous and difficult to carry out in conflict zones. One issue that has not received attention within the Copenhagen Consensus is that civil wars provide a major obstacle in the global fight against communicable disease. Global eradication programs often hinge on a very small number of countries at war. Thus, wars impose considerable dynamic global health costs which could potentially be estimated.

[7] This is in contrast to the findings by De Ree and Nillesen (2009), but this may be due to the fact that they concentrate on the effect of aid, unlike Regan (2010), who considers "economic" interventions which he defines as convention-breaking – i.e. the usual assistance through aid is not considered.

[8] Peace-enforcement missions require a UN Security Council mandate.

In general, the Copenhagen Consensus debates in 2004 and 2008 did not put sufficient emphasis on the links between the challenges. The global challenges have been reviewed in isolation, but civil wars impact on hunger, disease, education, population growth, water and sanitation, and biodiversity. It would be great to see a debate on the links between these challenges.

In the last section I discussed the effectiveness of some of the proposed solutions. Based on large *n*-studies we are fairly confident that UNPKOs keep the peace and that aid increases the peace dividend. There is a much smaller literature on arms' embargoes. They can be effective and seem to be more so in the presence of UNPKOs. Comparatively little work has been done on interventions during conflict. Interventions seem to prolong war: it appears to be very difficult to stop a war once it has started. Interventions to prevent wars starting in the first place may be more promising. However, there is hardly any work on the effectiveness of interventions before a conflict and it is too early to provide a quantitative assessment of early warning and response efforts. The discussion of the proposed solution also shows that some interventions are more effective if they are combined with others. However, we know very little about optimal policy design. Fragile countries require a combination of economic and security assistance. Studies have either concentrated on development or security aspects, paying insufficient attention to the relationship between development and security. This is an important area of future research.

Bibliography

Bourne, M., 2012: Small arms and light weapons spread and conflict, in O. Green and N. Marsh (eds.), *Small Arms, Crime and Conflict: Global Governance and the Threat of Armed Violence*, Routledge, London and New York

Brzoska, M., 2008: Measuring the effectiveness of arms embargoes, *Peace Economics, Peace Science and Public Policy* **14**, 1–32

Burnside, C. and D. Dollar, 2000: Aid, policies, and growth, *American Economic Review* **90**, 847–68

Checchi F., 2010: Estimating the number of civilian deaths from armed conflicts, *The Lancet* **375**, 255–7

Coghlan, B., R. J. Brennan, P. Ngoy, D. Dofara, B. Otto, M. Clements and T. Stewart, 2006: Mortality in the Democratic Republic of the Congo: a nationwide survey, *The Lancet* **367**, 44–51

Collier, P. and A. Hoeffler, 2002: Aid, policy and peace: reducing the risks of civil conflict, *Defence and Peace Economics* **13**, 435–50

2004a: Conflicts, in B. Lomborg (ed.), *Global Crises: Global Solutions*, Cambridge University Press, 129–56

2004b: Greed and grievance in civil war, *Oxford Economic Papers* **56**(4), 563–95

2004c: Aid, policy and growth in post-conflict countries, *The European Economic Review* **48**, 1125–45

2007: Unintended consequences: does aid promote arms races?, *Oxford Bulletin of Economics and Statistics* **69**, 1–28

Collier, P., L. Chauvet, and H. Hegre, 2008: The challenge of conflicts, Copenhagen Consensus 2008 Challenge Paper

Collier, P., A. Hoeffler, and M. Söderbom, 2008: Post-conflict risks, *Journal of Peace Research* **45**(4), 461–78

Collier, P., L. Elliot, H. Hegre, A. Hoeffler, M. Reynal-Querol, and N. Sambanis, 2003: *Breaking the Conflict Trap: Civil War and Development Policy*, Oxford University Press

Dalgaard, C.-J., H. Hansen, and F. Tarp, 2004: On the empirics of foreign aid and growth, *The Economic Journal* **114**(496), 191–216

Degomme, O. and D. Guha-Sapir, 2010: Patterns of mortality rates in the Darfur conflict, *The Lancet* **375**(9711), 294–300

De Ree, J. and E. Nillesen, 2009: Aiding violence or peace? The impact of foreign aid on the risk of civil conflict in sub-Saharan Africa, *Journal of Development Economics* **88**, 301–13

Fortna, V. P., 2008: *Does Peacekeeping Work? Shaping Belligerents' Choices After Civil War*, Princeton University Press

Fortna, V. P. and Howard, L. M., 2008: Pitfalls and prospects in the peacekeeping literature, *Annual Review of Political Science* **11**, 283–301

Fruchart, D., P. Holtom, S. T. Wezeman, D. Strandow, and P. Wallensteen, 2007: *United Nations Arms Embargoes: Their Impact on Arms Flows and Target Behaviour*, SiPri Report, Stockholm

Gleditsch, N. P., P. Wallensteen, M. Eriksson, M. Sollenberg, and H. Strand, 2002: Armed conflict

1946–2001: a new dataset, *Journal of Peace Research* **39**(5), 615–37

Gobarah, H. A., P. Huth, and B. Russett, 2003: Civil wars kill and maim people – long after the shooting stops, *American Political Science Review* **97**, 189–202

Goldstone, J. A., R. H. Bates, D. L. Epstein, T. R. Gurr, M. B. Lustik, M. G. Marshall, J. Ulfelder, and M. Woodward, 2010: A global model for forecasting political instability, *American Journal of Political Science* **54**, 190–208

Grimmett, R. F., 2011: *Conventional Arms Transfers to Developing Nations, 2003–2010*, CRS Report for Congress, Chapter 3, 21–41, www.fas.org/sgp/crs/weapons/R42017.pdf, accessed April 28, 2012

Hoeffler, A., S. S. Ijaz, and S. von Billerbeck, 2011: Post-conflict recovery and peace building, Background Paper for the *World Development Report* 2011, 3, https://openknowledge.worldbank.org/bitstream/handle/10986/9184/WDR2011_0010.pdf?sequence=1

Holtom, P. and M. Bromley, 2010: The international arms trade: difficult to define, measure and control, Arms Control Association, www.armscontrol.org/print/4306, accessed 28 April 2012

Lacina, B. and N. P. Gleditsch, 2005: Monitoring trends in global combat: a new dataset of battle deaths, *European Journal of Population* **21** (2–3), 145–66, the data are available at www.prio.no/CSCW/Datasets/Armed-Conflict/Battle-Deaths

Murdoch, J. and T. Sandler, 2002: Civil wars and economic growth: a regional comparison, *Defence and Peace Economics* **13**(6), 451–64

Murray, C. J. L, G. King, A. D. Lopez, N. Tomijima, and E. G. Krug, 2002: Armed conflict as a public health problem, *British Medical Journal* **324**, 346–9

Nyheim, D., 2009: Preventing violence, war and state collapse: the future of conflict early warning and response, OECD, Paris

Rajan, R. G. and A. Subramanian, 2008: Aid and growth: what does the cross-country evidence really show?, *Review of Economics and Statistics* **90**, 643–65

Regan, P. M., 1996: Conditions of successful third-party intervention in intrastate conflicts, *The Journal of Conflict Resolution* **40**(2), 336–59

2010: Interventions into civil wars: a retrospective survey with prospective ideas, *Civil Wars* **12**(4), 456–76

2012: Interventions before civil wars, Department of Political Science. University of Binghamton, mimeo

Toft, M. D., 2010: Ending civil wars: a case for rebel victory, *International Security* **34**(4), 7–36

US Department of State, 2011: *End-Use Monitoring of Defense Articles and Defense Services Commercial Exports FY 2011*, www.pmddtc.state.gov/reports/documents/End_Use_FY2011.pdf

World Bank, 2011: *The World Development Report 2011: Conflict, Security, and Development*, World Bank, Washington, DC

Wulf, H. and T. Debiel, 2009: Conflict early warning and response mechanism: tools for enhancing the effectiveness of regional organisations? A comparative study of the AU, ECOWAS, IGAD, ASEAN/ARF AND PIF, *Crisis States Working Papers* **2**, Working Paper **49**, London School of Economics and Political Science, London

1.2 Armed Conflicts

Alternative Perspective

ANDREW MACK

Introduction

Paul Dunne's Challenge Paper (Chapter 1), like earlier work produced by Paul Collier and his colleagues, and a more recent background study undertaken for the World Bank, establishes that there is a very clear association between periods of wars and subsequent sustained economic decline from which, on average, recovery is slow. The daunting task the chapter sets itself is to determine the extent of the economic costs of war and suggest the most cost-effective policies for reducing them.

But establishing that there is an *association* between war and post-conflict patterns of economic development is not the same as demonstrating that there is a clear *causal relationship* between the two.

But while the chapter undertakes a thorough review of recent research on these issues, it assumes, with some minor caveats, what really needs to be demonstrated – namely that the "costs" that are identified are in fact primarily a function of political violence – and not other factors.

Armed conflicts are both a consequence and cause of what, for want of a better term, we might refer to as "mal-governance" – the syndrome of governance-related factors that increases the risks of conflict and in turn are increased by it. Mal-governance is central to the perverse feedback system that leads to Paul Collier's famous "conflict trap" – where conflicts exacerbate the very structural conditions, grievances, and political tensions that caused them in the first place – leading to more conflict.

The chapter focuses in considerable and compelling narrative detail on the destruction and disruption wrought by war and its impact on post-conflict economic performance. Little attention, however, is devoted to examining the possibility that in many cases the assumed economic costs of war are in fact determined not by political violence, but by mal-governance factors that pre-date the conflict and persist both throughout it, and long into the post-conflict period.

This is one of the issues that this Alternative Perspective Paper addresses.

This question matters for policy because the prescription that follows logically from the assumption that war is responsible for massive amounts of forgone post-conflict income is to prevent wars – and seek to stop those that cannot be prevented. This is the theme of the second half of Chapter 1.

But where poor economic performance is determined not by war, but mal-governance or other factors, preventing conflicts and stopping those that cannot be prevented may not have the beneficial effects assumed in the chapter, and the other literature on the costs of war.

Case studies

The chapter illustrates the thesis that war has a sharp negative impact on GDP with several case studies. We note two here. In the case of Ethiopia we see a sharp absolute decline in GDP for nearly twenty years, followed by a slow increase. Nearly thirty years after the war started Ethiopia's GDP is still well below the counterfactual projection (Figure 1.2.1).

The same pattern is evident in the case of Nicaragua, though here the decline in GDP after the war begins is even more extreme. In the late 1970s before the war, Nicaragua's GDP was over \$4,000; in 2005 it was barely over \$2,000. What is not clear, however, is how much of this decline should be attributed to the destructive and disruptive impact of the war, and how much to failures of policy.

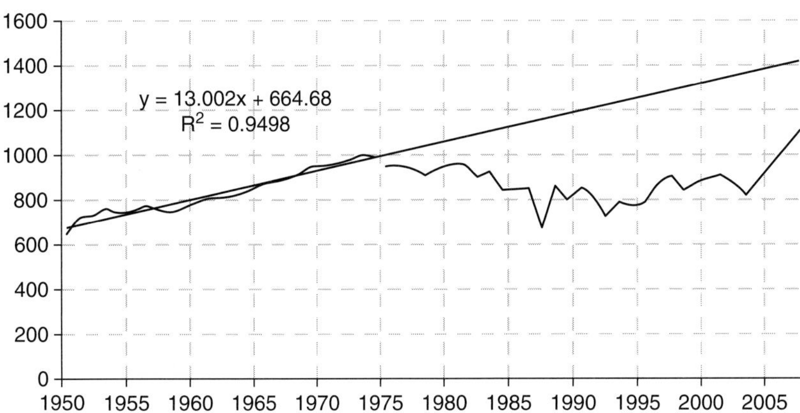

Figure 1.2.1 *Ethiopia: real GDP, 1950–2007*

Note: Population-, inflation-, and PPP-adjusted GDP, Ethiopia, 1950–2007 (base year = 2005)
Source: Penn World Tables, V.6.3.

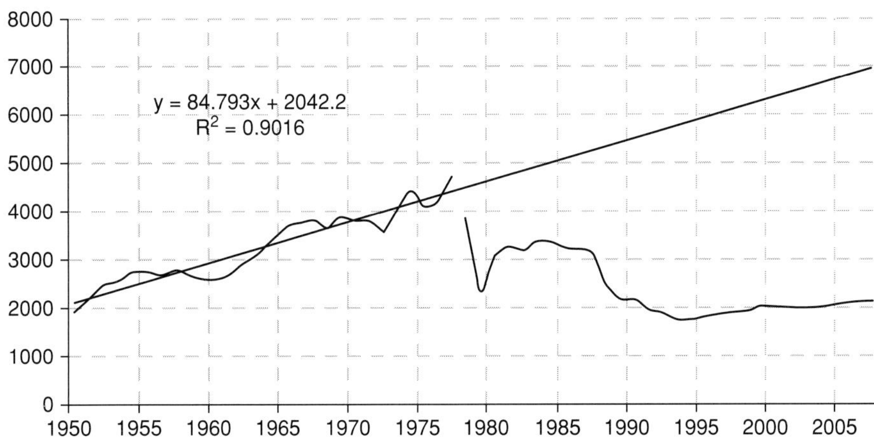

Figure 1.2.2 *Nicaragua: real GDP; 1950–2007*

Note: Population-, inflation-, and PPP-adjusted GDP, Nicaragua, 1950–2007 (base year = 2005)
Source: Penn World Tables, V.6.3.

It is instructive here to compare the Nicaraguan case with that of Rwanda. The severity of the impact of Rwanda's genocidal civil war was far greater than that in Nicaragua. In terms of lives lost as a percentage of the population over a period of less than a year it was the most devastating conflict since the Second World War. Yet Rwanda's economy recovered extraordinarily fast despite the hugely destructive war, while Nicaragua's GDP continued to fall for four years after the war ended in 1990. It is difficult to avoid the conclusion that the difference between the two countries was due in large part not to the impact of the war, but to differences in the effectiveness of governance.

Both cases provide illustrations of the mainstream thesis about the relationship between conflict and economic growth. But it is important to note that the trend that they depict is far from universal.

We illustrate this with reference to the case of the DRC, where the war that started in 1998 has been described as the deadliest since the Second World War. An estimated 5.4 million people are claimed to have died between 1998 and 2007 who would

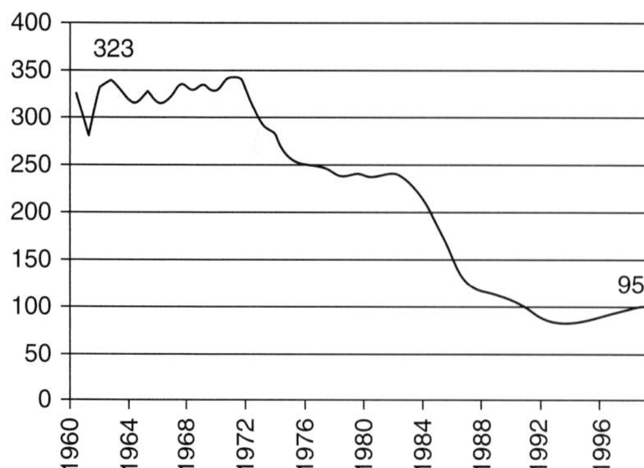

Figure 1.2.3 *Trends in* per capita *GDP (constant 2000 US$)*

Source: WDI (2009).

not have died had there been no war.[1] Here, then, we might expect to see an even greater impact of war on economic growth than in most other war-affected states.

In fact the pattern of pre-war, wartime, and post-war economic growth in the DRC are very different from those in Ethiopia and Nicaragua. Whereas in both these countries GDP was increasing steadily prior to the war, in the DRC it had been declining for more than two decades (Figure 1.2.3):

> By the mid-1990s, the country faced a risk of virtual disintegration due to hyperinflation, financial, economic and growth collapse... From 1990 to 1995, the contribution of the industry, manufacturing and services sectors to the GDP plummeted, pushing the economy into subsistence agriculture. By the end of 1995, income *per capita* was only one third its pre-independence levels.[2]

And this was *before* the war that started in 1998.

What we see in the case of the DRC is the reverse of what happened in Ethiopia and Nicaragua – two decades of steep peacetime economic decline in the DRC was associated in part with exogenous shocks (the decline in the price of copper and cobalt) and in part by the increasing mismanagement of the economy by the corrupt, repressive, and incompetent Mobutu regime.[3]

What is remarkable about the DRC case is that, after more than two decades of freefall the economy begins to recover *shortly after the war starts*. In fact GDI, which had declined until 1997, actually started to increase in the year that the war began, as Figure 1.2.4 makes clear.[4] Between the beginning and the (official) end to the war in 2003, domestic investment increased fourfold.

The point here is not, of course, that war is good for the economy, rather that more powerful forces than warfare were driving the DRC's development path throughout this period.

It may well be true that had there been no war, economic recovery would have been stronger than in fact it was. But this is very difficult to demonstrate.[5] In fact the war was not as devastating as it has so often been portrayed. The numbers killed in the fighting were likely of the order of several hundred thousand, mostly between 1998 and 2003. This is very high, but the DRC is an enormous country with a population greater than 60 million, meaning that deaths as a percentage of the population, which is the most appropriate measure of the human costs of war, would not be nearly as high as countries like Rwanda, which experienced a much higher war death toll (between 500,000 and 800,000) and had a much smaller population (some 7 million). And most of the fighting in the DRC was concentrated in the east of the country, a very small part of the national territory.

It might of course be argued that the DRC case – of GDP increasing during the course of a war – is exceptional, but this is not the case. Figure 1.2.5 shows the number of conflicts (excluding those that lasted for less than a year) in SSA between

1 In fact, the war in the DRC is not the deadliest since the Second World War. That dubious distinction almost certainly goes to the Korean War. Moreover the survey-derived estimate of 5.4 million "excess" deaths is far too high. The exaggerated figure arose because (a) the IRC, which conducted the surveys that produced the headline-catching finding of 5.4 million excess deaths caused by the war, chose a baseline mortality that was too high and (b) because its survey-derived wartime mortality rate was approximately double that of two our major surveys – by UNICEF and the Demographic and Health Survey that covered approximately the same period as the IRC's surveys.

2 www.hks.harvard.edu/fs/drodrik/Growth%20diagnostics%20papers/DRC_Growth_Diagnostic.pdf, p. 15.

3 There was a short period of warfare in 1996–1997.

4 www.hks.harvard.edu/fs/drodrik/Growth%20diagnostics%20papers/DRC_Growth_Diagnostic.pdf.

5 See Chapter 7 of the *Human Security Report, 2009–2010*, http://hsrgroup.org/docs/Publications/HSR20092010/20092010HumanSecurity Report-Part2-ShrinkingCosts OfWar.pdf.

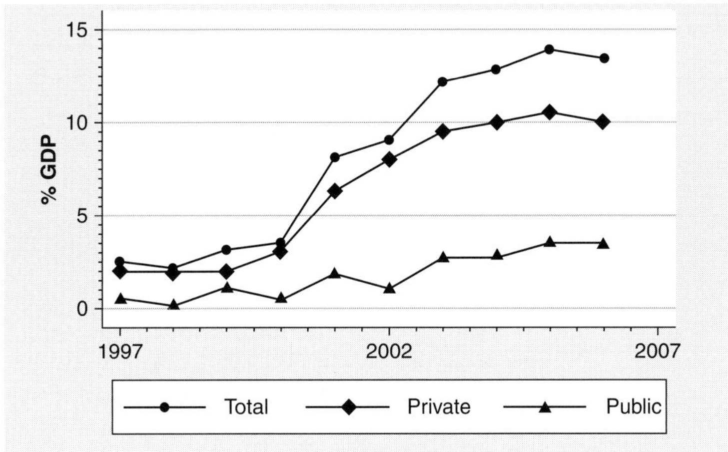

Figure 1.2.4 *GDI*

Source: IMF.

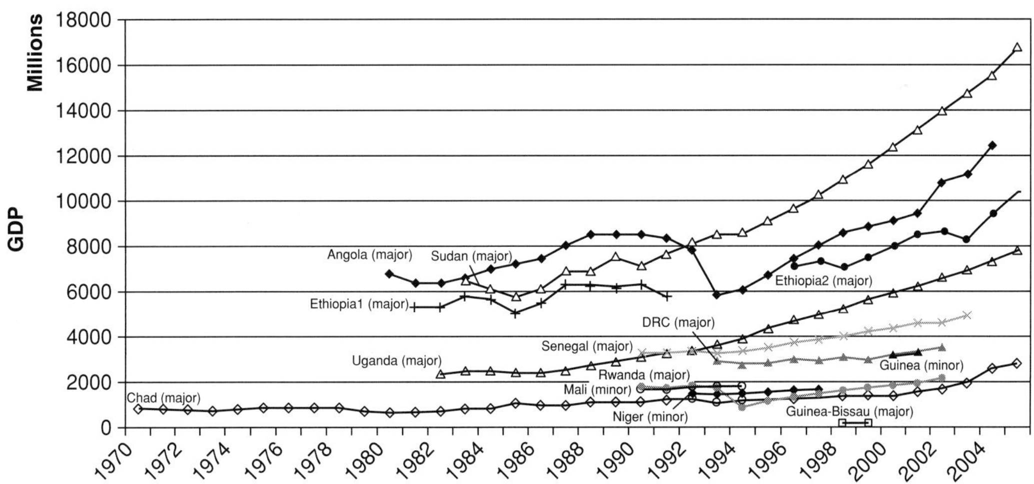

Figure 1.2.5 *GDP increases during conflicts, 1970–2005 (constant 2000 US$, excluding conflicts of one year)*

Source: WDI (2009).

1970 and 2005 in which GDP (*not* GDP *per capita*) increased – i.e. was higher at the end of the war than at the beginning.

This clearly shows that from 1970 to 2005 in the majority of conflicts lasting for more than a year in the world's most conflict-prone region economic growth continued throughout the war.

Figure 1.2.6 shows the pattern that reflects the popular understanding of the impact of war on economic development, namely that it is associated with a decline in economic output. Note that fewer countries (nine out of twenty-one) experience declining GDP during wartime than experience rising GDP (12 out of 21).

The data in Figures 1.2.5 and 1.2.6 came from a presentation by NYU's Sakiko Fukuda Parr, former Director of the UN's *Human Development Report*, at a conference in Wilton Park in 2008. Note that these data are for GDP, not GDP *per capita*.

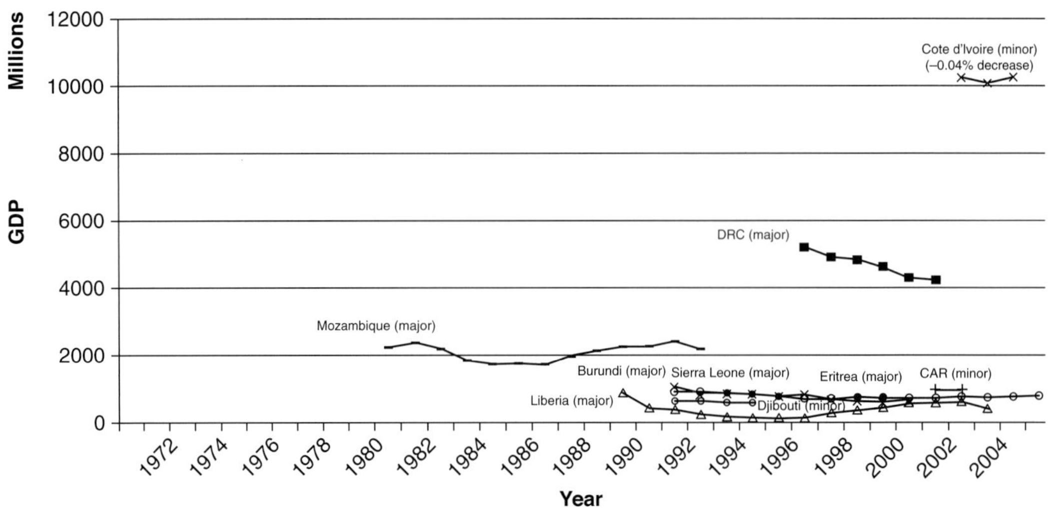

Figure 1.2.6 *GDP decreases during conflicts, 1970–2005 (constant 2000 US$, excluding conflicts of one year)*

There is a major difficulty with attempting to determine counterfactuals in particular cases. It is often assumed that the counterfactual will follow a relatively linear (upward) trend line, as the Ethiopian and Nicaraguan case studies in the chapter suggest. But as Figure 1.4 in the chapter (p. 26) makes clear, pre-war GDP *per capita* trends are very rarely linear, making the task of determining counterfactuals in particular cases often difficult, and sometimes impossible.

Cross-national regression analyses

It is of course also possible to seek to determine the *average* impact of conflicts on a range of development outcomes using regression analysis with large-*N* country-year datasets that include most countries in the world over a number of decades. Recent research in this area is reviewed in depth in the Challenge Paper and in the background paper on the impact of conflict on progress towards achieving the MDGs prepared for the World Bank's much-cited *World Development Report 2011* by researchers from PRIO in Oslo.[6]

The latter report makes it clear that while conflict and "fragility" and poor MDG outcomes are clearly associated, the authors also acknowledge, "the difficulty of analyzing the effect of conflict on a set of indicators that we know are also causally related to the onset of conflict."[7] There is, in other words an endogeneity problem.

What is interesting about the PRIO analysis of the impact of war on the attainment of the MDGs is that the regressions do indeed show a clear association between the impact of conflict and development outcomes. But the analysis does not show that, in Paul Collier's memorable term, "war is development in reverse," but rather that war-affected countries demonstrate a rate of improvement towards achieving the various MDG goals *that is essentially the same as for the countries not affected by war.*

Thus we see in the case of undernourishment – a poverty-related measure – that while conflict-affected countries (solid black line in Figure 1.2.7) clearly suffer from higher levels of malnourishment, the rates of malnourishment actually improve at a slightly faster rate over time than the non-conflict countries. We also note that non-conflict "fragile" states (those that rank low on the Bank's CPIA index and/or host a

6 http://wdr2011.worldbank.org/PRIO.
7 http://wdr2011.worldbank.org/PRIO, p. 1.

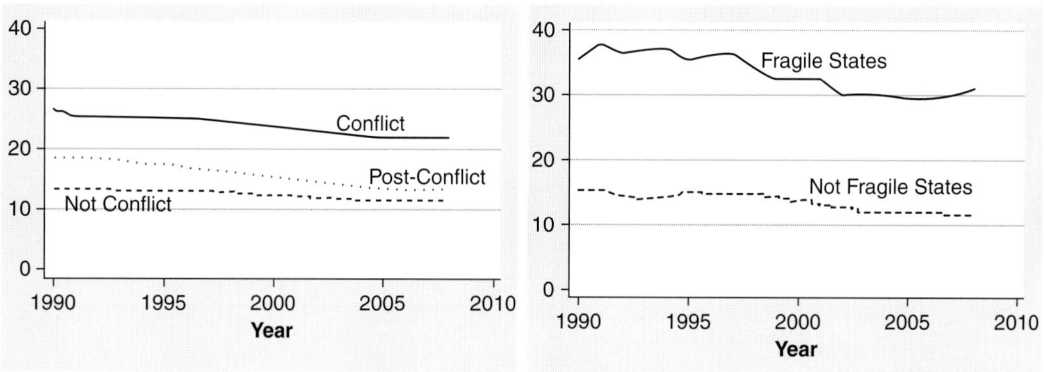

Figure 1.2.7 *Trends in percentage of population that is undernourished, by conflict type and fragility status*

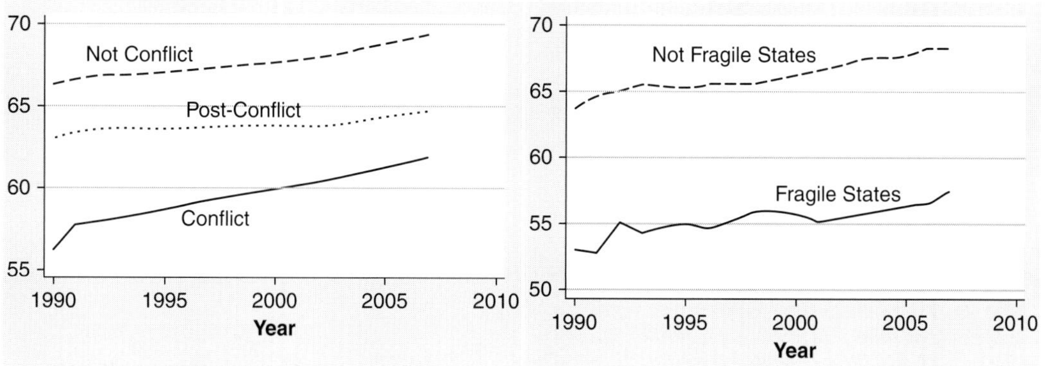

Figure 1.2.8 *Mean life expectancy over time, by conflict and state fragility status*

peacekeeping operation) are considerably more prone to undernourishment.[8]

When we turn from undernourishment to life expectancy we see a very similar pattern. Conflict-affected countries improve their life expectancy at a slightly faster rate than non-conflict countries – albeit from a lower base, as Figure 1.2.8 demonstrates.[9]

When we turn to the impact of conflict on GDP – the most measured of the impacts on development outcomes, we see in Figure 1.2.9 that countries in conflict have *on average* increased their GDP *per capita* slightly over time, but here the non-conflict countries improve at a slightly faster rate.[10]

With respect to secondary education we again find the same pattern (Figure 1.2.10). From 1990 to 2008 secondary education attainment rates for conflict-affected countries improved at approximately the same rate as non-conflict countries – meaning that while they too start from a lower base they are not falling further behind – on average – during periods of warfare.

Finally, we look at infant mortality rates. Again the same pattern is observable between 1990 and 2008: there is a substantial, but again somewhat counterintuitive improvement in infant mortality rates in countries in conflict over time (Figure 1.2.11).[11]

[8] http://wdr2011.worldbank.org/PRIO, p. 29.

[9] http://wdr2011.worldbank.org/PRIO, p. 38.

[10] http://wdr2011.worldbank.org/PRIO, p. 41.

[11] http://wdr2011.worldbank.org/PRIO, p. 48. The "stepped" nature of the trend-lines is because infant and under-5 mortality data derive from surveys undertaken at five-year intervals.

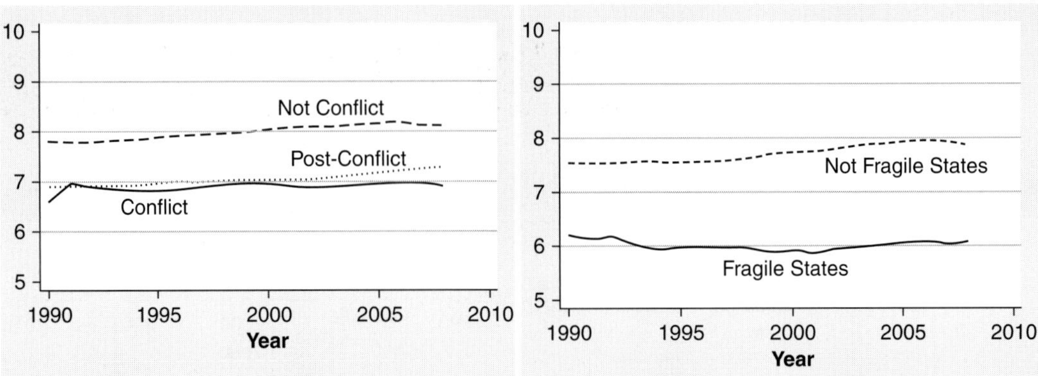

Figure 1.2.9 *Mean GDP* per capita *over time, by conflict and fragility status*

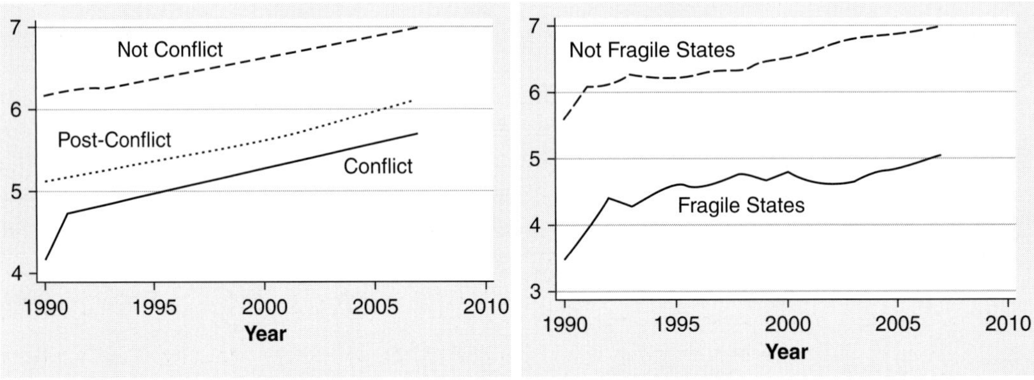

Figure 1.2.10 *Trends in secondary education attainment rates, 1990–2008, by conflict and fragility status*

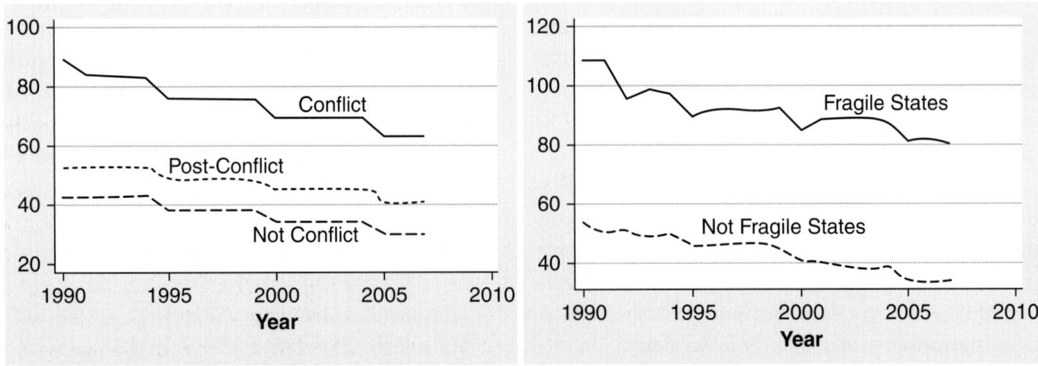

Figure 1.2.11 *Trends in average infant mortality rates, 1990–2008, by conflict and fragility status*

So the image of war being "development in reverse," while striking, is untrue. *On average*, most development outcomes improve during periods of warfare – and they do so at about the same rate as in peacetime – but from a lower base.

This sounds counterintuitive because we know that some wars have devastating effects on development outcomes. But these are the wars that get most attention from the media and the international community. Most conflicts today have relatively low battle deaths and tend to be fought over a very small part of the national territory. In these countries conflict tends to have only a modest impact on development outcomes and gets very little international attention.

In fact, there is so much heterogeneity in this area that it is not so clear how valuable focusing on the "average" conflict is for policy-makers. The one-size-fits all prescription that prescribes policies to prevent the "average" conflict – i.e. one that reduces GDP *per capita* by some 2 percent a year over seven years – may be of little utility in preventing really major wars. We simply don't know.

The World Bank study data raises another interesting question.

Non-conflict "fragile" states perform consistently worse that "conflict states" in making progress towards achieving the MDGs. But almost all the states in conflict are also "fragile." This suggests – no more – that the "fragility" element – essentially the mal-governance factor – in the conflict states may be more important that the conflict element in determining development outcomes. In other words what we may be seeing in the findings on the "impact of war" is *in addition* to an "impact of mal-governance" effect.[12]

As noted above, the policy implications of this puzzle are important. If it is mal-governance, and not conflict *per se*, that is driving negative development outcomes, then preventing and stopping wars will not be enough.

There is one more reason to be skeptical about the effect of the "average" conflict – especially as a guide to the present. There is a broad consensus – including Chapter 1, the work of Paul Collier and his various collaborators, and the PRIO researchers – about the major development impact of the "average conflict" – i.e. it lasts for some seven years and reduces national GDP *per capita* by some 2 percent a year. But this average is derived from country-year data that go back three–five decades.

The problem here is that the average conflict in the Cold War era, and indeed up until the new millennium, was far deadlier and thus far more likely to have a negative impact on development outcomes, than those in the new millennium. In the 1980s, the average conflict involving a state killed more than 5,000 people a year; in the new millennium the average conflict kills fewer than 1,000.

In the 2009/2010 *Human Security Report* we argued that this change was no accident and that low fatality conflicts are likely – not certain, of course – to become the norm. If this is the case then we can expect that the impact of these less deadly recent conflicts on development outcomes could well be substantially less than the "average" impact suggested by Chapter 1 and by other researchers.

Conflict prevention

Chapter 1 offers a comprehensive menu of policy options for preventing conflicts and stopping those that can not be prevented. And it costs them all – a heroic exercise on which I do not feel competent to comment.

Here I simply want to draw attention to some remarkable, and as yet unpublished, research being undertaken by Håvard Hegre and his colleagues at PRIO, that predicts that by 2050 the percentage of countries around the world experiencing armed conflict will have halved from about 15 percent to 7 percent.[13]

The authors' prediction model uses two key "structural" variables – infant mortality and educational attainment. Both variables are predicted, with some confidence, to improve world-wide over the coming decades. Improvements in each are associated with reduced risks of conflict onsets.

[12] The PRIO researchers found that the CPIA index they used as one of the indicators for "fragility" could not explain much of the variance in development outcomes. But a new study by two of the authors of the World Bank study, using a much broader conception of governance, found that it helped explain the variance in conflict recurrence.

[13] Hegre *et al.* (forthcoming).

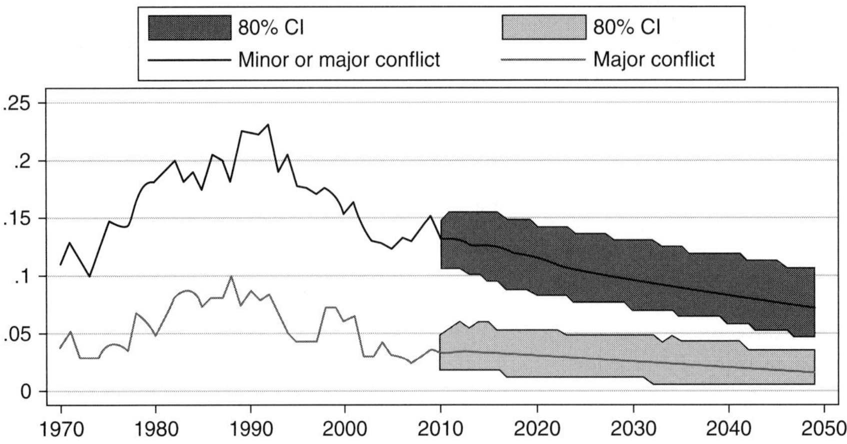

Figure 1.2.12 *Observed and simulated proportion of countries in conflict, 1960–2050*

Note: Averaged over nine model specifications, different conflict levels, all countries, 1960–2050. The upper line in the graph is for all conflicts, the lower line for major conflicts (1,000 or more battle deaths a month). The shaded areas represent the 80 percent confidence interval.

Both infant mortality and educational attainment are also proxy variables for good governance. In addition to these variables, the model also includes variables that relate to conflict history – a past history of conflict increases the risk of conflict recurrence considerably, "neighborhood effects," population size, "youth bulges," and "ethnic dominance."

Having developed a large number of candidate models for the period 1970–2000, they then ran a series of simulations to obtain predictions for the period 2001–2009. They compared the model predictions with the actual observed conflicts in the latter period, and chose the model whose predictions most closely reflected what actually happened in 2001–2009. The best-fit model predicted conflicts in sixteen of the twenty-six countries that had conflicts in 2009. They then used the refined model to predict the share of countries in conflict out to 2050. Figure 1.2.12 was the result.

The model, of course, assumes that variables that impacted the risk of conflict in the past will continue to do so in future, but that seems reasonable in this case.

What is most interesting about these findings is that they indicate that a considerable degree of civil war conflict prevention is already built into the way that poor countries are developing. Yet this prevention mechanism is independent of any consciously articulated prevention policy. No international agencies are arguing for improved child health, nor for better education opportunities, on the grounds that they are long-term security policies.

But one consequence of the trend revealed by the Norwegian researchers is that – other things remaining equal – we can predict that the percentage of countries experiencing conflict in the international system will halve over the next forty years simply as a consequence of a continuation of the status quo.

But this is not the only conflict-reducing trend at work today.

The growth of international security activism

In the two decades since the Cold War ended, there has been an explosion of international security activism, focused mostly on civil wars. This has led to the creation of a new, still-evolving, but little-analyzed, global security architecture, one that is radically different from the bipolar security system of the Cold War years.

The new architecture comprises a loose but ever-expanding network of international organizations, donor and other governments, interagency committees, informal clusters of like-minded states that help countries emerge from conflict, think-tanks, and large numbers of national and international NGOs.

The central rationale of the system is the reduction of political violence – in particular, civil wars – around the world.

The pursuit of this objective is grounded in a growing normative consensus that the international community has a responsibility to prevent war, to help stop wars that cannot be prevented, and to try and prevent those that have stopped from starting again.

This still-emerging system of security governance has been, and remains, rife with coordination problems, disagreements over strategy, and unresolved tensions between international agencies, states, and NGOs. It is a system that is inherently inefficient and disputatious and – as Rwanda and Darfur remind us – prone to tragic failure. But the best evidence that we have suggests that its collective efforts have been a primary driver of the major decline in the deadliest forms of armed conflict since the end of the Cold War.

So we have two powerful long-term trends tending to reduce the incidence of conflict and its associated costs around the world. The one analyzed by the PRIO scholars is "structural" and not conceived as a prevention strategy at all. The other is very consciously focused on the challenges of conflict and its associated costs. They complement one another perfectly.

Bibliography

Hegre, H., J. Karlsen, H. M. Nygård, H. Strand, and H. Urdal, 2012: Predicting armed conflict, 2010–2050, *International Studies Quarterly*, DOI: 10.1111/isqu. 12007

WDI, 2009: *World Development Indicators*, World Bank, Washington, DC

Ecosystems and Biodiversity

SALMAN HUSSAIN, ANIL MARKANDYA, LUKE BRANDER, ALISTAIR MCVITTIE, RUDOLF DE GROOT, OLIVIER VARDAKOULIAS, ALFRED WAGTENDONK, AND PETER H. VERBURG*

Introduction

In this chapter we look at the costs and benefits of three possible interventions that would enhance the planet's biodiversity and improve its ecosystems over the next forty years. The results are based on a study carried out across four research institutes and coordinated by the Scottish Agricultural College (Hussain *et al.*, 2011)[1] that combined a global biophysical model (IMAGE-GLOBIO), which analyzed the biophysical impacts of different development scenarios compared to the counterfactual, with a set of valuation studies that placed monetary values on the outcomes resulting from the different policy options in terms of biodiversity and ecosystem services (ESSs).

While reference is frequently made in the popular press to biodiversity losses, in practice it is difficult to quantify and value them. There are several studies that attempt to do this in specific cases but no one has successfully estimated the value of the loss of biodiversity at a global level.[2] This is because the links between biodiversity and biological systems and the economic and social values that they support are extremely complex. Even the measurement of biodiversity is problematic, with a multi-dimensional metric regarded as appropriate (Purvis and Hector, 2000; Mace *et al.*, 2003), but with further work considered necessary to define the appropriate combination.

For this reason the focus, initiated by the Millennium Ecosystem Assessment (MEA, 2005), has been on measuring ESSs, which are derived from these complex biophysical systems. The Millennium Ecosystem Assessment (MEA) defines ESSs under four headings – provisioning, regulating, cultural, and supporting – and under each there are a number of sub-categories.

The most important fact about these services is that they have been facing major losses. During the twentieth century the planet lost 50 percent of its wetlands, 40 percent of its forests, and 35 percent of its mangroves. Around 60 percent of global ESSs have been degraded in just fifty years (MEA, 2005).

While working at the ecosystem level makes things somewhat easier it is still important to understand the causes of the loss of these services and the links between losses of biodiversity and the loss of ESSs. Indeed, this is a major field of research for ecologists and one thesis that has been articulated over a long period is that more diverse ecosystems are more stable and less subject to malfunction (Tilman and Downing, 1994; McCann, 2000; Haines-Young and Potschin, 2010). The current state of knowledge on the links between biodiversity and ESSs is still a topic of research and while some clear lines are emerging, they are not strong enough to allow a formal modeling to be carried out at a level that would produce credible estimates of

* The authors would like to thank PBL staff (Ben ten Brink, Stefan van der Esch, and Michel Jeuken). We would also like to thank the two Alternative Perspective contributors (John C. Whitehead, Paul E. Chambers, and Juha V. Siikamaki) as well as Kasper Thede Anderskov and his team at the Copenhagen Consensus Center.

[1] Anil Markandya was an advisor to the Project and a reviewer of the report and Salman Hussain was the coordinating lead author. We are interpreting some of the results of the original study in a way that involves additional assumptions and analysis.

[2] For a review see ten Brink (2011: Chapter 5.4).

the global value of biodiversity. The latter therefore remains a topic for research.[3]

If the aim is to obtain estimates of changes in the economic values of services from natural systems at the global level, as it is in this chapter, one has, of necessity, to estimate these services through the ecosystem valuation framework, recognizing that there is a complex link between changes in such values and changes in the measures of biodiversity (appropriately defined). However, the ecosystem methodology used in the chapter does take into account the quality of an ecosystem and the services it produces, based on the species abundance within it. This is derived from the Mean Species Abundance (MSA) approach, which is explained more fully in the next section. To some extent, therefore, the study does build on the linkages between the biodiversity of a biome and its ecosystem functions.

What we attempt to do in this chapter is to link bio-physical modeling (PBL, 2010) with non-market valuation (Hussain *et al.*, 2010). The bio-physical modeling sets out projections for global BAU scenarios for terrestrial ecosystems as well as scenarios with three policy options (increases in agricultural productivity; extending protected areas; reduced reforestation). There is thus a bio-physical comparison between BAU and each policy option in turn, with outputs presented in terms of changes in the extent of terrestrial land cover and also a measure of biodiversity (MSA).

The core economic benefit appraisal is based on changes in land cover. This analysis is carried out at patch level using a geographical information system (GIS). We analyze changes in the extent of c. 2.3 million patches of grassland, temperate forest, and tropical forest. If the size of a particular patch changes (BAU versus policy option) then the value of that patch also changes, owing to a modified provisioning of the suite of ESSs provided by that patch. The novelty in the economic benefit analysis is that, unlike previous analyses, the value change estimates are patch-specific and then aggregated across all c. 2.3 million patches, with the values of some patches increasing under policy-on and the value of others decreasing.

We apply benefits transfer using meta-regression analysis. We have constructed a comprehensive spatially referenced database of primary valuation estimates for the three biomes, using GIS databases on various variables that might influence the estimated per ha value at the patch level. Typically in benefits transfer the only variable which is routinely used in meta-regression-based transfer is the income variable. We extend this by considering a range of variables that are proxies for the ecological characteristics of the patch (e.g. human appropriation of net primary product, a proxy for habitat intactness) as well as context characteristics (e.g. proximity to roads). We use extant databases (where available) to infer the projected values of these variables at the end of the study period (which is 2030 or 2050, depending on the policy). The value of a projected increase in extent for a particular patch in 2030 or 2050 depends on these variables as described by the biome-level meta-regression analyses.

The analysis presented here aims at meeting the setup of the Copenhagen Consensus where a hypothetical, additional budget of $75 billion over the next four years is assumed. The four years and the budget is not viewed as a one-time increase, but rather as a perpetual increase.

We argue in the conclusions that spending a smaller amount than proposed will not lower the BCRs we derive because none of our programs have significant setup costs. In fact the BCRs could be higher for a policy option limited to $75 billion or less, as that would allow one to pick out the options with higher net benefit. We could not undertake such an exercise for this study because it would have involved a lot more disaggregated work.

We also note that our costs and benefits start in 2000 and go forward to 2030 or 2050, depending on the policy option being considered. The starting date is defined by the bio-physical modeling: the model runs use the Global Land Cover 2000 (GLC2000)[4] as a baseline, as described on p. 74. All

[3] Theoretical models of the economic values attached to biodiversity have been developed. See for example, Brock and Xepapadeas (2003). Such models draw simple links between harvesting rates, system biodiversity, and overall system value. As yet, however, they are not supported by empirical estimates that can be used to apply the methods to derive these system values.

[4] http://bioval.jrc.ec.europa.eu/products/glc2000/glc2000.php.

benefits and costs are standardized to 2007 USD. This year for standardization was chosen as, at the time the analysis was being carried out (2010), 2007 was the last year for which World Bank PPP data were available across all primary valuation studies in our valuation databases (see the Appendix, p. 106). To update all benefit and cost figures to 2012 would have involved a lot of detailed re-estimation; we do not expect such an updating to make much difference to the estimates and there was not enough time and resources to undertake that task.

The structure of this chapter is as follows:

The next section sets out the bio-physical modeling and the baseline data and assumptions, the latter providing the rationale for some form of policy intervention, viz. projected losses in biodiversity under BAU. The policy options are a response to this agenda but our assessment is not based on biodiversity loss *per se*, as set out above; we consider benefits to arise from land cover change and the associated changes in ESS provision. The next section sets out the three policy measures in turn, and the following section the cost estimates for each of these policy options. We do not carry out any primary analysis for cost estimation.

The next two sections then turn to the benefit estimation. The first sets out the value functions and underpinning GIS analysis (the discussion of the primary valuation databases underpinning these value functions is found in the Appendix). We then present overall results for the benefit estimates.

The final section provides the overall summary of cost-benefit estimates including sensitivity analysis, and a discussion *vis-à-vis* the wider implications of the study, limitations, and outcomes with regard to the Copenhagen Consensus framework.

Bio-physical modeling and baseline data

The Global Biodiversity Model used here (IMAGE-GLOBIO3) analyzes biodiversity as "the remaining mean species abundance (MSA) of original species, relative to the abundance in pristine or primary vegetation, which are assumed to be not disturbed by human activities for a prolonged period" (Alkemade *et al.*, 2009: 375). Species abundance is a measure of the population size of a species, not a measure of species richness. MSA as estimated by IMAGE-GLOBIO is a composite indicator that indexes the average abundance of original species remaining in disturbed ecosystem patches relative to their abundance in a pristine, undisturbed state.

MSA is calculated based on five drivers of biodiversity change: land use; nitrogen deposition; infrastructure; habitat fragmentation; and climate change. The model consists of a relationship between each of these pressures and the effect on MSA. Based on these "meta-analysis" functions, an MSA value is calculated for a chosen area, given information on the different pressure indicators. The total MSA effect in a particular area is a multiplication of the individual pressure effects.

As IMAGE-GLOBIO is a geographically explicit model, the MSA value of a geographical region is calculated as the area-weighted mean of MSA values for the constituent parts, actually grid cells of about 1 × 1 km. The GLOBIO3 model is used to assess the probable impacts of the selected drivers on MSA for a number of world regions and a future no-new-policies scenario, as well as the impacts of specific pre-defined policy options.

Input data and assumptions in IMAGE-GLOBIO

Data for land cover and land use in IMAGE-GLOBIO came from the IMAGE model at a resolution of 0.5 by 0.5° grid cells (c. 50 km × 50 km). The spatial detail was increased by calculating the proportion of each land cover type within each grid cell from the Global Land Cover 2000 (GLC2000) map (Alkemade *et al.*, 2009); GLC2000 data was at a resolution of 1 km × 1 km. The ten GLC2000 forest classes were converted into four land use categories using national data on forest use[5] with fractions assigned on a regional basis. The five scrubland and grassland classes were converted into three IMAGE-GLOBIO categories. The livestock grazing area was based on estimates from IMAGE, and herbaceous areas were assigned to

[5] FAO (2001), ftp://ftp.fao.org/docrep/fao/003/Y1997E/FRA%202000%20Main%20report.pdf.

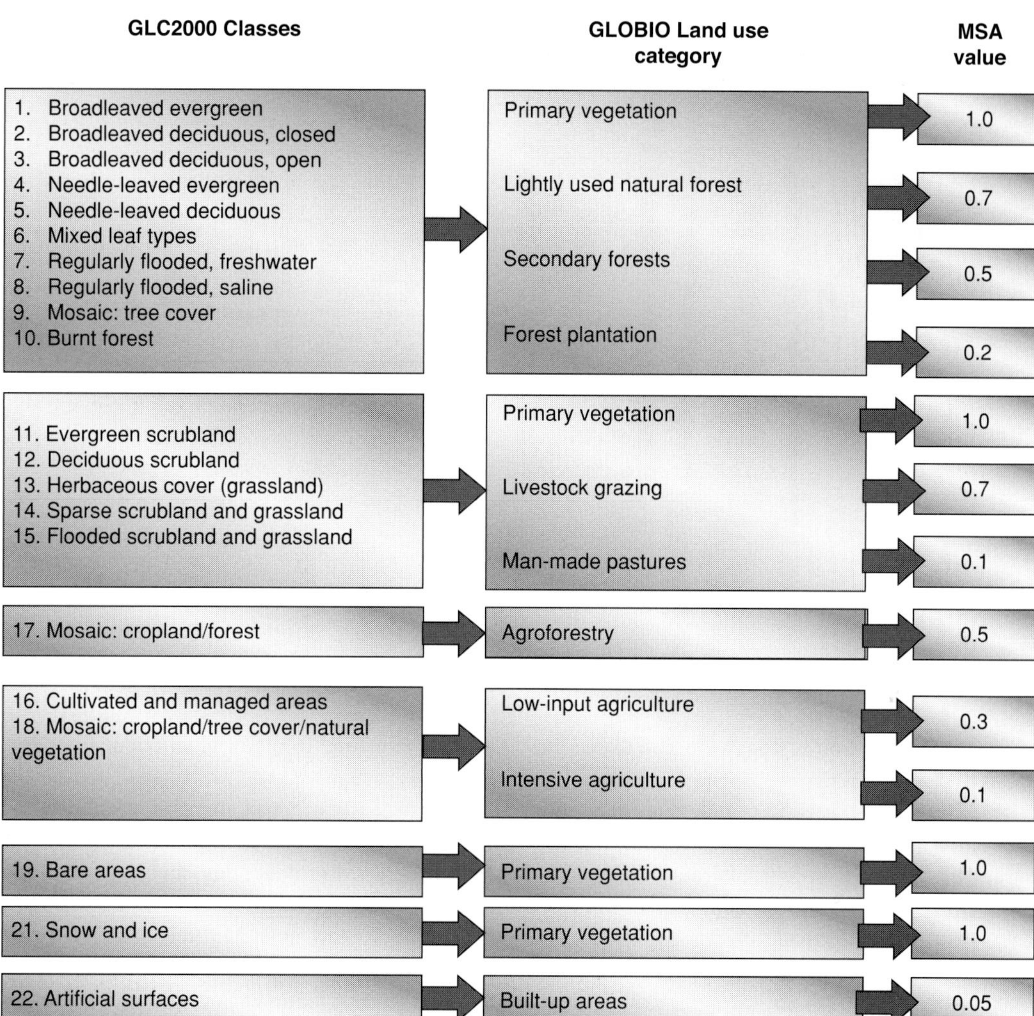

Figure 2.1 *Conversion of GLC2000 classes to IMAGE-GLOBIO land use categories and respective MSA values*

Source: Adapted from Alkemade *et al.*, 2009.

"pasture" if those areas were originally forest. The cultivated and managed areas class was categorized as either low-input or intensive agriculture based on regional distributions of intensity[6]; where no estimates of distribution were available intensive agriculture was assumed. The GLC2000 class of mosaic of cropland and tree cover was treated as a 50/50 mix of low-input agriculture and lightly used forest. This is summarized in Figure 2.1.

Land use change within the IMAGE model was derived from an extended version of the GTAP agriculture and trade model (PBL, 2010). The outputs from GTAP include sectoral production growth rates, land use, and the degree of intensification. Exogenous trends in crop yields (due to technology, science, and knowledge transfer) were adjusted through a process of iteration between IMAGE and GTAP, in which the effects of climate

[6] Dixon *et al.* (2001), ftp://ftp.fao.org/docrep/fao/003/y1860e/y1860e00.pdf.

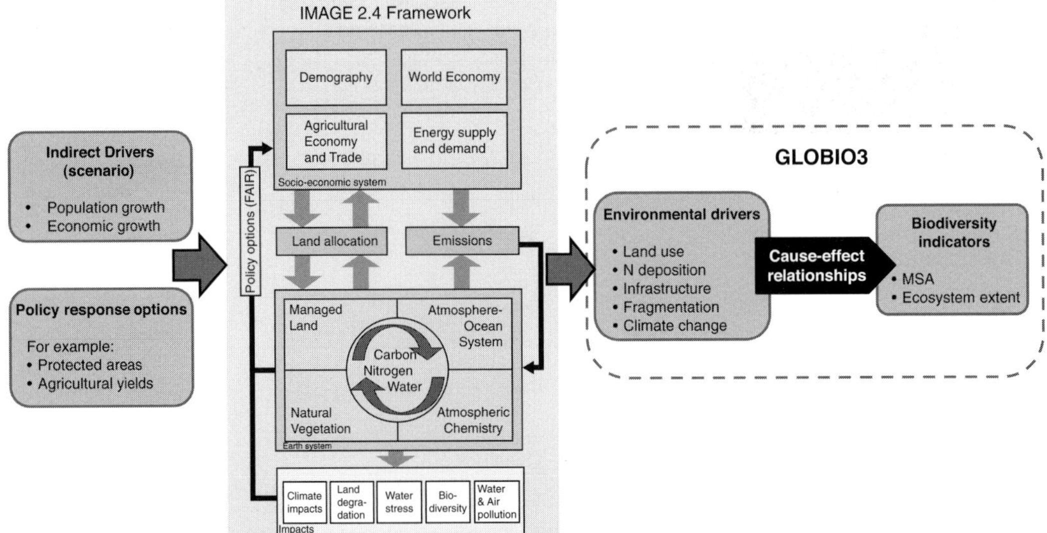

Figure 2.2 *IMAGE-GLOBIO modeling framework*

Source: Adapted from http://themasites.pbl.nl/en/themasites/image/model_details/index.html and http://www.globio.info/what-is-globio/how-it-works.

change and land conversion were calculated in IMAGE (PBL, 2010).

IMAGE was also used to calculate nitrogen (N) deposition, as this also affects the MSA measure. This is based on agricultural and livestock production, energy consumption and the mix of energy sources (Alkemade *et al.*, 2009). Infrastructure data were derived from a GIS map of linear infrastructure (roads, railways, power lines, and pipelines) derived from the Digital Chart of the World database.[7] Buffers representing low-, medium-, and high-impact zones were calculated for each biome (Alkemade *et al.*, 2009).

The IMAGE-GLOBIO modeling framework is illustrated in Figure 2.2.

Losses in mean species abundance, 1900–2000

We start by examining the losses we have suffered in MSA and in terms of "MSA area" across the main biomes and in the different regions of the world. Loss in MSA is, as stated above, the average decrease in all original populations in a particular area as compared to the original population sizes (as a percentage). Lost "MSA area" means the hypothetical size of intact area (100 percent MSA) entirely lost due to human interventions (0 percent MSA). Table 2.1 provides this summary from 1900 to 2000.

Globally we lost about 21 percent of biodiversity expressed in MSA terms in the twentieth century, with the greatest losses in South Asia, followed by Central and South America, China, East and South East Asia, and the OECD regions. In simple terms, this means that on average all biomes in the world have been decreased by about 21 percent due to direct and indirect human interventions (for more information, see www.globio.info).

Baseline scenario and results from biophysical analysis

The baseline for the IMAGE-GLOBIO projections, a no-new-policies scenario, was based on the OECD *Environmental Outlook to 2030* report

[7] www.maproom.psu.edu/dcw/.

Table 2.1 Changes in MSA area, by biome and world region, 1900–2000 (1,000 ha)

Biome	OECD	Central and South America	Middle East and North Africa	SSA	Russia and Central Asia	South Asia	China, East and South East Asia	Total	% on 1900 levels
Ice and tundra	–18,158	–3,200	0	0	–11,629	–1,627	–19,701	–54,316	–6
Grassland and steppe	–174,658	–34,955	-33,475	–46,282	–58,187	–26,498	–76,689	–450,744	-27
Scrubland and savannah	–71,234	-135,528	-13,465	-234,860	0	–119,254	–118	-574,459	-26
Boreal forests	–118,677	–4,062	0	0	–171,040	–3,478	–35,195	–332,452	–16
Temperate forests	–278,755	–82,342	0	–11,238	–41,840	–33,326	–79,433	–526,934	–45
Tropical forests	–13,590	–191,819	0	–76,072	0	–133,360	–1,579	–416,421	-25
Desert	–42,642	–3,905	–49,790	–44,567	–2,793	–22,872	–9,321	–175,890	–8
Total	–717,715	–455,812	–96,729	–413,019	–285,489	–340,414	–222,036	–2,531,216	
% on 1900 levels	–23	–26	–9	–19	–14	–40	–24		–21

Source: Derived from PBL (2010).

(Bakkes *et al.*, 2008; OECD, 2009)[8], which runs from a base year of 2000 upto 2050. The IMAGE-GLOBIO modeling exercise uses a number of specific baselines for different policy options. The ten main characteristics of the OECD baseline are:

(a) Population growth from 6 to 9 billion following the UN medium scenario.
(b) *Per capita* incomes increase in all regions, particularly in dynamic emerging economies such as the Brazil, Russia, India, and China (BRIC) countries.
(c) Global economic output increases fourfold (approximately 2.8 percent per annum), with attendant shifts in consumption patterns including increased luxury foodstuffs and livestock products.
(d) Technical progress and the productivity of labor converge across countries to the long-term industrialized nation trend.
(e) Yields of major staple crops increase by a factor of 1.6, i.e. an average 0.94 percent per annum. This is insufficient to keep pace with either increasing population or changing consumption patterns, necessitating an increase in land under production.
(f) Global energy use increases from 400 EJ to 900 EJ primarily from fossil fuel sources; global average temperature increases by 1.6°C above pre-industrial levels over the period.
(g) No new policies are introduced on environmental and global trade fronts.
(h) No new measures will be taken to promote biofuel use or to reduce CO_2 emissions from deforestation and forest degradation.
(i) There are no incentives to promote sustainable forestry; demand for timber, pulp, and firewood increase with economic and population growth.
(j) The size of protected areas will remain constant (approx. 10 percent of terrestrial area).

The results of the baseline scenario, on biodiversity indicators modeled in IMAGE-GLOBIO, suggest that, for the period 2000–2050, globally:

(a) Biodiversity, as measured by MSA, will decline from 71 percent in 2000 to 62 percent in 2050. PBL (2010). Note that it is unlikely that MSA globally could drop below 30–35 percent as 20 percent of the terrestrial land area is inaccessible; land converted to agriculture has a lower MSA limit of 5–10 percent.

[8] www.pbl.nl/en/publications/2008/BackgroundreporttotheOECDEnvironmentalOutlookto2030; www.oecd.org/document/20/0,3343,en_2649_34283_39676628_1_1_1_37465,00.html.

Table 2.2 Changes in wilderness area, by biome and world region, 2000–2050 (1,000 ha)

Biome	OECD	Central and South America	Middle East and North Africa	SSA	Russia and Central Asia	South Asia	China	Total	% on 1900 levels
Ice and tundra	–23,962	–1,942	0	0	–20,945	–1,483	–12,339	–60,672	–7
Grassland and steppe	–63,278	–14,656	–6,869	–31,315	–37,606	–17,395	–24,171	–195,289	–16
Scrubland and savannah	–46,646	–42,645	–2,273	–197,689	0	–64,980	–39	–354,272	–22
Boreal forests	–56,870	–2,302	0	0	–78,001	–2,079	–11,780	–151,033	–9
Temperate forests	–52,321	–9,476	0	–9,627	–17,456	–12,091	–19,775	–120,744	–18
Tropical forests	–1,897	–48,078	0	–58,835	0	–35,314	–436	–144,560	–12
Desert	–38,357	–1,660	–30,055	–31,671	–9,790	–22,385	–5,205	–139,122	–7
Total	–283,332	–120,759	–39,197	–329,137	–163,798	–155,726	–73,745	–1,165,693	
% on 2000 levels	–12	–9	–4	–18	–10	–30	–11		–12

Source: Derived from PBL (2010).

(b) The extent of natural areas will decline by 8 percent (10 million km^2). "Natural areas" are those not used for urban construction, agriculture, or infrastructure. Natural areas can be intact (MSA 100 percent) but also be affected (low MSA). This indicator is another produced by the IMAGE/GLOBIO model and derived from the 2010 indicators of the Convention of Biological Diversity (CBD).
(c) Wilderness areas (areas which are highly intact MSA > 80 percent) will decline by over 11 percent (15 million km^2).

Within these global projections, some regional variations occur, with MSA forecast to drop below 60 percent in South Asia, China, and the OECD countries due to higher economic and/or population growth and higher proportion of usable land taken into production or development (PBL, 2010). The highest rates in the decline of MSA are expected in South Asia and SSA, where wilderness areas will decline from 30 to 12 percent and 55 to 33 percent, respectively (PBL, 2010). A summary is provided in Table 2.2.

The bio-physical modeling of a suite of policy options set out in the next section is a direct response to the 2010 targets set by the CBD and the World Summit on Sustainable Development (WSSD), primarily the "significant reduction in the current rate of biodiversity loss at the global, regional, and national level; as a contribution to poverty alleviation; and to the benefit of all life on Earth" (Alkemade *et al.*, 2009).

Description of policies and measures

In order to reduce this loss in MSA the chapter considers three policy options. For each of these an estimate is made of both the bio-physical impacts with regards to MSA and also the range of costs and possible benefits under various assumptions. The methodology used for benefit-cost estimation is set out in the next section; here we first outline the three policy options.

Underpinning this choice of policy options is the premise that halting both biodiversity loss and the loss in provision in ESSs is not merely a "conservation" issue; economic development and biodiversity are inextricably linked and should be analyzed as an entity (MEA, 2005). Promoting conservation policies without providing credible alternatives aimed at tackling the causes of habitat destruction through land conversion would likely be doomed to failure (Goklany, 1998).

Investment in agricultural knowledge, science, and technology

The first policy option addresses the potential impacts of a transformation in agricultural production practices. Since the industrial revolution, agricultural productivity has increased more than tenfold world-wide, primarily as a consequence of the intensification of Western agricultural production, although intensification has also occurred in parts of the developing world, particularly following the green revolution (Evenson and Gollin, 2003). Yet disparities exist globally between regions, and there is evidence of the growth rate of agricultural productivity levelling off (van Vuuren and Faber, 2009). Many propositions have been advanced for explaining this trend: reduced investment in agricultural R&D (Pardey *et al.*, 2006); a general decrease of policy focus on, and support of, agriculture (Bello, 2009; McIntyre *et al.*, 2009); and land degradation and desertification (Bai *et al.*, 2008) as a consequence of poor land management or overintensification of agricultural practices (Vitousek *et al.*, 1997; Steinfeld *et al.*, 2006).

The baseline scenario for this policy option is based on Rosegrant *et al.* (2009) and van Vuuren and Faber (2009). Average yields, aggregated at a global level, are projected to increase by about 1 percent for cereals, 0.35 percent for soybeans, roots, and tubers, and 0.8 percent for fruits and vegetables, yet gradually levelling off in most regions. Average livestock and dairy yields (i.e. production per animal) increase by 0.74 percent and 0.29 percent per year, respectively.

Yield differentials can be due to a variety of factors, such as soil and climatic conditions. With regard to bio-physical constraints, van Ittersum *et al.* (2003) synthesize the factors determining attainable crop yields by separating: (1) growth-defining factors, (2) growth-limiting factors, and finally (3) growth-reducing factors. A "yield gap" refers to the difference between potentially attainable yields (given a variety of bio-physical conditions) compared to actual agricultural yields. As stated by Fischer *et al.* (2009): "Yield gaps exist because known technologies that can be applied at the local experiment station are not applied in farmers' fields having the same natural resource endowment."

In the baseline, while the year-on-year increase in yield remains constant, the rate of growth in food demand is projected to outstrip yield growth as a consequence of: (1) population and economic growth, and (2) increased demand for meat (livestock) – itself an outcome of dietary transformations brought about through economic growth in developing countries (FAO, 2006). These parallel developments are expected to put pressure on land conversion of natural areas; expansion is projected to be of the order of a 10 percent increase in current agricultural area, occurring mostly in the tropical and subtropical zones (OECD, 2009).

The following policy option is modeled in our study: globally, productivity growth is spurred by investment in agricultural knowledge, science, and technology (AKST), increasing productivity growth by 40 percent and 20 percent for crop and livestock, respectively, relative to the baseline.

The scope of our analysis is restricted to the benefits arising from changes in land cover relative to the baseline, namely reduced conversion of forest or other natural areas. However, there are a number of other benefits and costs that might arise from investment in AKST but which are not included in our assessment. Previous research focusing on market impacts has indicated that the rate of return on investment in AKST can vary between 36 and 67 percent (IAASTD, 2009: 539), arising from the benefits of investments in an accelerated technological growth in the existing agricultural areas, therein enhancing farmer livelihoods and potentially food security.

The distribution of these returns, however, will clearly impact on the incentives driving investments. Unless private companies are able to capture benefits through technology licensing, increased input prices (seeds, agrochemical, etc.), or expanded markets, the incentives for investment may not be sufficient. This suggests that a role remains for public sector investment in both R&D and extension services, and consequently the implementation of the option becomes contingent on its relative position in governments' spending priorities. Beyond the need for political and commercial will to make the necessary investments in AKST, there remain barriers to technology adoption that will also need to be overcome. PBL (2010) note that new technologies and techniques need to be extensively trialed, tested, and adapted to local conditions and that existing social, institutional, and political conditions may need to change before farmers are prepared to make the necessary management changes.

Extension of protected areas

This policy option explores the effects of increasing protected area coverage to 20 percent of 65 terrestrial ecological regions (Olson *et al.*, 2001). The 20 percent target was developed from earlier work for the second Global Biodiversity Outlook (sCBD, PBL, 2007). Despite the (pre-Nagoya) 10 percent objective set by the CBD,[9] figures vary across biomes and even more across eco-regions.[10] According to Coad *et al.* (2009a), while the 10 percent objective has been achieved for eleven out of fourteen global biomes, only half of global eco-regions reach this protection level. In the baseline, no further policy is applied and thus the baseline (current) level of protection of around 10 percent is maintained.

This policy option results in an even representation of protected areas not only per biome but also per eco-region within each biome. While the expansion of protected areas can severely limit potential agricultural expansion in the context of the baseline projection of rising food demand, land scarcity is also thought to provide incentives for spurring agricultural productivity (Lambin *et al.*, 2001). The IMAGE-GLOBIO model allows for changes in land use intensity when protected area expansion limits the area available for agriculture. Finally, this option assumes that further anthropogenic pressures on ecosystems such as nitrogen deposition and climate change impacts continue to exert their effects within protected areas, thus impacting on biodiversity.

Reduced deforestation (REDD variant)

Approximately 20 percent of greenhouse gas emissions (GHGs) come from deforestation and forest degradation, whether directly or indirectly through land use change; thus, reducing emissions from deforestation and forest degradation (REDD) appeals as a prominent way to reduce GHG emissions of anthropogenic origin, and/or increase natural carbon sinks of global forest areas (IPCC, 2007; Houghton, 2009). Beyond emissions abatement, REDD is also believed to present benefits for biodiversity preservation, since 40–50 percent of the global genetic pool is located in global forests, particularly in tropical forests (Kitayama, 2008; Karousakis, 2009).

The original REDD objectives have been replaced by a so-called 'REDD-plus' objective, which: (1) takes further account of the co-benefits of reduced deforestation, (2) aims to develop schemes spurring participation of local communities, and (3) extends international transfer mechanisms to participating developing countries (Angelsen *et al.*, 2009).

We do not model REDD or REDD-plus *per se*, as PBL (2010) does not model degradation; this is consistent with current and proposed programs. However our analysis focuses on value changes derived from land cover changes. As such our methodology only partially address equality changes *vis-à-vis* degradation; however, if degradation were to have been modeled in the bio-physical analysis in PBL (2010) then our valuation results would not change markedly from those presented. As such, we term this option a variant of REDD.

The baseline assumes no additional actions compared to current standards: in short, deforestation and forest degradation continue due to additional pressures of population and economic growth, with subsequent land use change for agriculture and logging practices (PBL, 2010).

[9] The post-Nagoya target for protected areas is for 2020, and includes "at least 17 percent of terrestrial and inland water areas, and 10 percent of coastal and marine areas" (see www.cbd.int/decision/cop/?id=12268, Target 11). The policy option obviously talks to the outcomes established at the Nagoya CBD COP *vis-à-vis* protected areas but equally the analysis in our report is based on current protection *achieved* as opposed to protection level aspired to.

[10] Defined by Brunckhorst (2000) as a "recurring pattern of ecosystems associated with characteristic combinations of soil and landform that characterize that region."

The policy option assumes that *all* forests with closed tree cover (areas of closed tree cover excluding savannah, scrub, and wooded tundra) are protected from conversion to agricultural land from 2000 onwards (PBL, 2010).[11] Woodlands are not included because of lower tree cover. In PBL (2010) some tropical woodlands are lost while tropical dense forests are preserved, resulting in an overall loss of the tropical forest biome extent (the tropical forest biome includes both woodlands and dense forest).

The analysis of reduced deforestation through IMAGE-GLOBIO allows the assessment of potential trade-offs between climate change mitigation objectives and biodiversity preservation (or the extent of "co-benefits"). On the one hand, protecting forest areas can reduce GHG emissions, thus addressing a critical pressure on global biodiversity. On the other hand, protecting solely forest ecosystems leads to the possibility of agricultural expansion to other natural areas; thus an attempt is made under IMAGE-GLOBIO to capture leakage effects.

The assumption that all dense forests are protected from deforestation will have knock-on effects in that land available for agriculture (to meet rising global demand) will be reduced; consequently there will be pressure to convert other biomes such as grassland to cropping, and more land will also be required for plantation forestry to meet timber demand. The opportunity costs arising from this restriction on land conversion to agriculture form the bulk of the costs of this option as discussed further below.

Estimation of costs for the policy options

No primary research was carried out for the estimation of the costs. However, there are extant cost estimates that can be modified to reflect the three policy options. We have reviewed the existing literature to provide such cost estimates for each policy option in so far as this is possible. Each of the policy options is treated in turn below.

The analysis in Hussain *et al.* (2011) is based on a fifty-year time horizon from 2000 to 2050 for the first option (agricultural productivity) and a thirty-year time horizon for the second and third options (extending protected areas and reduced deforestation–REDD variant). We report the results for these time horizons. Costs and benefits in Hussain *et al.* (2011) are also standardized to 2007 USD, and the figures herein are also reported in 2007 USD, as discussed on p. 74.

Agricultural productivity

This policy option is concerned with closing the agricultural yield gap between the developed and developing world through investment in AKST, leading to an assumed 40 percent increase in crop productivity and a 20 percent increase in livestock productivity relative to the baseline.

Agricultural yields depend, *inter alia*, on access to production inputs, management of the natural environment, and the adoption of techniques and technologies; all of these factors depend on market and institutional constraints (Dreyfus *et al.*, 2009; Neumann *et al.*, 2010) such as agricultural subsidies, institutional incentives, property rights, and land distribution (Morton *et al.*, 2006; Bello, 2009). The extent to which different factors affect overall productivity has been analyzed empirically (e.g. Morris *et al.*, 2001; Alvarez and Grigera, 2005) but there is no consensus in this regard. This in turn implies that the efficacy of AKST policy interventions in terms of increasing agricultural productivity will vary depending on what is assumed about these factors.

The policy option for agricultural productivity is explicitly based upon an influential study assessing the future of agriculture, entitled *Agriculture at a Crossroads* (IAASTD, 2009). This study combines partial equilibrium (IMPACT) and computable general equilibrium (CGE) models (GTEM) to analyze alternative scenarios and their impact on agricultural yield to 2050. The study considers five factors as catalysts of a growth in agricultural yield: (1) investment in education in rural areas,

[11] The PBL (2010) bio-physical model applies this assumption, which we accept is politically unfeasible. Future runs of the iMAGE-GLOBIO model are set to modify this assumption.

particularly focusing on women; (2) investment in rural roads; (3) irrigation management; (4) policies propagating access to clean water; and (5) agricultural R&D.

The "AKST high 2" scenario in IAASTD (2009) is estimated by the authors to cost c. US$30 billion p.a. for total cumulative costs.[12] This "AKST high 2" scenario is used in PBL (2010). The question that is pertinent to our study is whether this cost estimate is realistic and defensible.

There is limited evidence in this regard. Schmidhuber *et al.* (2009) provide an estimate of capital requirements needed for agriculture up to 2050 if developing countries are to meet FAO baseline projections (FAO, 2006). It is not possible to draw a like-for-like comparison between IAASTD (2009) and Schmidhuber *et al.* (2009) as the outcomes for which costs are estimated differ. Notwithstanding this important caveat, the overall total estimate in the latter study is around US$5.2 trillion, a figure considerably higher than the IAASTD estimate of US$30 billion.

The IAASTD (2009) figures might underestimate costs owing to assumptions *vis-à-vis* policy implementation; there is evidence (e.g. Easterly, 2001; Rist, 2001) that "big pushes" in terms of development aid have often not fulfilled the investment requirements of developing countries, and therein not achieved outcomes as predicted *ex ante*. This point links with the discussion concerning market and institutional constraints.

A further issue from a cost perspective with the intensification that often goes hand-in-hand with AKST is losses in agro-biodiversity as a consequence of pollution spillovers (Harris, 1996; Matson and Vitousek, 2006; UNEP, 2009). In this respect, the environmental impacts following the "green revolution" in Asia are particularly illustrative (Matson *et al.*, 1997). Such losses are difficult to fully capture in bio-physical modeling. Some research findings indicate that considerable yield improvements can be made in some agricultural systems at a little or even a positive environmental impact (IAASTD, 2009; Brussaard *et al.*, 2010; Keating *et al.*, 2010). The precise nature of productivity improvements (e.g. education; access to credit; increased inputs and intensification) and their interactions with agricultural systems and local social and environmental conditions will drive both the direction and the extent of these impacts.

Notwithstanding the caveats discussed above, we use the cost estimates provided in IAASTD (2009). The figure of US$30 billion p.a. is not used directly as we consider net costs (i.e. additional investment requirements over and above BAU), rather than total cumulative investments. We assume that the profile of these investments is flat. As such, the figure used for costs is US$14.5 billion p.a. from 2000 to 2050. It is not possible to generate a primary cost estimate range without further primary research.

Protected areas

Despite their numerous benefits, most notably in terms of positive externalities (Naidoo *et al.*, 2008), the establishment of protected areas entails considerable costs; these costs are considered to be the source of both ecological underrepresentation and poor management (Balmford *et al.*, 2003; Bruner *et al.*, 2004; Galindo *et al.*, 2005; Ruiz, 2005). Of these, opportunity costs in terms of forgone alternative use of land are the most critical (Faith and Walker, 1996; Ferraro, 2002). Global level estimations of costs are widely divergent and even contradictory (Pearce, 2007); they require considerable assumptions to be made and extensive modeling analysis (TEEB, 2008).

This policy option refers to a precise percentage increase of 20 percent for the earth's 834 eco-regions rather than biomes; this is an important distinction, as the extant cost literature does not in general estimate costs on an eco-region basis.

We found seven studies on the global costs of conserving protected areas with some variability as regards the types of costs estimated (James *et al.*, 1999; Lewandrowski *et al.*, 1999; James *et al.*, 2001; World Bank, 2002; Balmford *et al.*, 2003; Bruner *et al.*, 2004; Iwamura and Naidoo, 2007). Values from these studies are converted (where possible) to 2007 US$ per ha per year for the

[12] The total cost includes investments in agricultural research, irrigation, rural roads, education, and clean water. The figure of US$30 billion includes spending to achieve the baseline growth in agricultural productivity.

Table 2.3 Global assessments of the costs of protected areas

Authors/study	Scope of study	Type of costs	Type of assessment	Mean cost estimation (2007 US Dollars)
Balmford *et al.* (2003)	Global	Management costs	Costs for adequately financing current PA system	8.2 billion/p.a.
Bruner *et al.* (2004)	Global	Management costs	Costs for adequately financing current PA system, and expansion to high-priority sites	13.8 billion/p.a.
James *et al.* (1999)	Global	Management and opportunity costs	Requirements for protecting and expanding PA system to represent 20% of global biomes	19.1/ha/p.a.
James *et al.* (2001)	Global	Opportunity, management and acquisition costs	Requirements for protecting and expanding PA system to represent 20% of global biomes	20.2–21.4/ha/p.a. (management costs 3.8–5/ha/p.a.)
Lewandrowski *et al.* (1999)	Global	Opportunity costs	Setting aside 5%, 10%, and 15% of global terrestrial area	98/ha/p.a.
Naidoo and Iwamura (2007)	Global	Opportunity costs	Estimation of cost-effectiveness of protection juxtaposing species richness and agricultural returns	58/ha/p.a.
World Bank (2002)	Developing countries	Management and opportunity costs	Additional protection of 800 million ha of land in developing countries	93/ha/p.a. (2000) (management costs 10/ha/p.a.)

Source: Pearce (2007) and authors' synthesis.
PA = Protected areas.

results to be comparable. Bruner *et al.* (2004) estimate total management financial requirements at US$13.8 billion per year (2007 US$ equivalent) for adequately managing and expanding the current protected areas network to cover key unprotected species.

James *et al.* (1999, 2001) estimate values on a per ha basis. As such, adequately managing and expanding the protected area network to represent 20 percent of ecological biomes would cost approximately US$18–27.5 billion per year (or US$23–34 billion). Their estimation includes management costs obtained through surveys of currently protected areas, acquisition costs for new land areas, and finally compensation for forgone land use. The latter is nonetheless based on an estimation of the value of land (in terms of rent) rather than as a flow of forgone benefits from alternative land use.

More methodologically consistent for estimating opportunity costs are the analyses of Lewandrowski *et al.* (1999) and Naidoo and Iwamura (2007). Lewandrowski *et al.* (1999) combine GIS modeling with CGE modeling, the former for identifying potential protected area status, the latter in order to estimate global returns from agricultural production in an input–output fashion. In this way the authors estimate potential forgone revenues for protected areas covering 5 percent, 10 percent, and 15 percent of world biomes. Their approach is, however, more focused on human geography territorial (rather than ecological) criteria. Naidoo and Iwamura (2007) consider global agricultural returns using a GIS model with a view to identifying cost-effective conservation strategies. Their model notably allows the identification of any overlap between relatively low agricultural returns and high biodiversity levels. While not dealing with protected areas *per se*, their figures are relevant to our analysis, since the levels of agricultural returns per bio-geographic realm can be considered as opportunity costs of conservation (Table 2.3).

Comparing opportunity cost results across the studies, it appears that there are significant differences in mean estimates, ranging from more than US$98 per ha per year for management costs alone to around US$21 for opportunity and management costs *combined*. However, there are reasons for this variation in estimates:

(1) James *et al.* (1999, 2001) deal mostly with opportunity costs in developing countries, considering that only these are relevant for

compensation of forgone land uses. This explains the low mean estimate, since the higher land returns in the Lewandrowski *et al.* (1999) and Naidoo and Iwamura (2007) estimations are located in developed countries – with the exception of parts of the developing world in Asia.

(2) Moreover, the divergence in the estimates in Lewandrowski *et al.* (1999) and Naidoo and Iwamura (2007) can partly be explained by the fact that the former does not include parts of the world that have low agricultural returns (such as Greenland or Siberia), whereas the latter does.

Previous studies calculating protected areas' expansion costs, have done so by assuming an area protected per biome or geographic assemblies, not per ecological region; this policy option analysis requires a cost estimate per eco-region, as defined by the CBD (Coad *et al.*, 2009b), which in turn entails inevitable complexities. Data on the total coverage (km^2) of eco-regions were obtained from Coad *et al.* (2009b) and Naidoo and Iwamura (2007). While the World Database on Protected Areas (WDPA[13]) provides specific regional data, and maps of protected areas, we did not find a specific percentage for eco-regions. The policy option developed in PBL (2010) assumes current protection to be 10 percent of all eco-regions, and this figure is used as the counterfactual.

We therefore estimate the total costs of achieving 20 percent coverage assuming that cost increments are linear – i.e. the costs of protecting 20 percent are double the costs of protecting 10 percent. This assumption of linearity is applied in the absence of clear evidence to support an alternative formulation: (1) management and opportunity costs are ongoing irrespective of any incremental protection; (2) opportunity costs can rise when additional area is added to the protected network whereas there is some evidence of countervailing scale economies for management costs (James *et al.*, 2001; Balmford *et al.*, 2003).

In our estimation, the total hectares of eco-regions are scaled up per bio-geographic realm. For both estimations we provide three different cost estimation scenarios based on the availability of data, different cost estimations on a per ha basis (or per km^2), and on different assumptions applied. Table 2.4 summarizes the outcomes across the three scenarios for an expansion across all global eco-regions. A summary of the constituent elements of Scenarios 1–3 are given below:

Table 2.4 Estimated costs of expanding protection (2007 US$ billions) from 10% to 20%.

	Scenario	Costs/p.a.	Marginal annual costs (assuming 10% current protection)
All eco-regions	1	30.9	15.4
	2	132.9	66.4
	3	71.3	35.6

Source: Authors' calculations.

Scenario 1: Data from James *et al.* (1999, 2001) is used which estimates combined management and opportunity costs but excludes land acquisition costs.

Scenario 2: Data from Lewandrowski *et al.* (1999) and Naidoo and Inamura (2007) are used to estimate opportunity costs in forgone land returns; management costs estimates inputted are based on James *et al.* (2001) and Balmford *et al.* (2003) for this scenario.

Scenario 3: As per Scenario 2 but opportunity costs for developed world countries are excluded from the calculations.

As is the case for most global cost estimations, for an expansion to 20 percent results show a wide range from 2007 US$30.9 billion p.a. for Scenario 1 to 2007 US$132.9 billion for Scenario 2 for total costs, and 2007 US$15.4 to 66.4 billion for marginal costs.

We consider Scenario 1 to be our "best-guess estimate" for the reasons set out in this section. The comparison between Scenarios 2 and 3 requires the determination of whether or not to include opportunity costs in developed world nations. From a conceptual point of view, the estimates for global returns from agricultural land use in Lewandrowski *et al.* (1999) and Naidoo and Inamura (2007) do

[13] See www.wdpa.org/Statistics.aspx.

not consider shadow values, in this case agricultural subsidies. As such, the net opportunity cost of conservation should be annual returns from alternative agricultural land use minus potential subsidies. This is particularly (but not exclusively) an issue in the developed world. Payments for protected area establishment *vis-à-vis* opportunity costs are also likely to be restricted in many cases to land-owners in developing world countries. For these reasons we would support estimates from Scenario 3 over those derived from Scenario 2. However we retain Scenario 2 as an "upper-bound" estimate.

Our mid-level (Scenario 3) and upper-bound (Scenario 2) estimates are largely based on the FARM (combined CGE and GIS) model results used by Lewandrowski *et al.* (1999) to compute opportunity costs of conservation, and a similar application in Naidoo and Iwamura (2007). In these studies, opportunity costs are considered to be highest potential feasible p.a. returns from agricultural land for a given geographic area. As Lewandrowski *et al.* (1999) note, one critical assumption made using the FARM model is that all global land can potentially be of economic use. The authors observe that this assumption is a necessary modeling simplification: clearly, protected areas are often located in areas where there is low (or even non-existent) human productive exploitation. As such, opportunity costs are systematically overestimated in their model, and thus in our mid- and upper-bound estimates. The approach combining CGE and GIS is clearly defensible (and arguably potentially the most robust), but of course has its own methodological limitations.

Our rationale for choosing the lower-bound (Scenario 1) estimate as our "best guess" is partially based on these methodological concerns, but is also determined by a stream of potential benefits that is missing, viz. eco-tourism returns (Naidoo *et al.*, 2006; Carret and Loyer, 2003) that are not accounted for in our analysis. Further, other influential global cost estimates such as Bruner *et al.* (2004) and Balmford *et al.* (2003), often cited in the conservation literature (Bruner *et al.*, 2008) as the costs of maintaining and expanding the protected area system, focus on *acquisition* and management costs. James *et al.* (1999, 2001) is used as the basis for the Scenario 1 estimate; the authors consider compensation mechanisms in the developing world derived from land prices, a proxy for acquisition costs. Thus Scenario 1 is consistent with some influential extant estimates (e.g. TEEB, 2010).

The most defensible estimate for costs for an expansion to 20 percent from the 10 percent baseline is US$15.4 billion p.a. The upper-bound estimate for costs for expansion to 20 percent from the 10 percent baseline is US$66.4 billion per annum. The latter assumes compensation payments to landowners in the developed world, and compensation that includes market distortions in the form of agricultural subsidies (Scenario 2).

These values represent (1) one-off acquisition or on-going opportunity costs and (2) on-going management costs implied by the expansion of the protected area network. In summary, we assume one-off acquisition costs at a conservative level of US$2.2 billion occurring during the first implementation year; and ongoing management and opportunity costs of US$15.4 and 66.4 billion p.a. respectively, for scenarios 1 and 2 (our "best-guess" and "upper-bound" estimates) from 2000 to 2030 for a 20 percent coverage of global eco-regions.

Reduced deforestation (REDD-variant)

There are three principal costs of implementing the "reduced deforestation" policy option, a variant of REDD (Pagiola and Bosquet, 2009): (1) opportunity costs; (2) management and monitoring costs; and (3) transaction costs. The most critical cost category is likely to be opportunity costs in terms of forgone revenues either from forest conversion to agricultural land or possible returns from forest exploitation through logging (Chomitz, 2006). Accurately estimating forgone revenues on a global scale is complex, since it implies a generalization of possible alternative land returns to vast geographical areas (Barreto *et al.*, 1998), and the need to predict changes over time. Policy implementation of REDD are highly dependent on the institutional factors prevailing in developing world countries, as well as on equity in the management of payment transfers (Gomez, 2009). These elements might well be determinants of the additionality and efficiency of the scheme (Karousakis, 2009).

Table 2.5 Studies that have estimated global costs for reduced deforestation (REDD)

Study	Study type	Costs assessed	Cost/p.a. (billion US$)	Time horizon	% reduction in GHGs
Eliash (2008)	Global model	OC + MC + TC	17–33	2030	46
Kinderman *et al.* (2008)	Global model	OC + MC + TC	17–28	2030	46
Grieg-Gran (2006)/Stern (2007)	Hybrid approach	OC + MC	5 + 0.5	2030	50
Grieg-Gran (2008)	Hybrid approach	OC + MC	6.8–8 + 0.5	2030	50
Strassburg *et al.* (2008)	Empirically derived	OC	29.6	n/a	100
Boucher (2008)	Global (partial equilibrium)	OC + MC + TC	14–48.5	2030	20–80
Blaser and Robledo (2007)	Global	OC	12.2 (min.)	2030	100

Notes: OC = Opportunity costs; MC = Management costs; TC = Transaction costs.

Adapting from Boucher (2008), methodologies to address costs might be categorized as follows:

(1) Empirical studies that have a local, regional or national scope, which are based on specific bottom-up calculations of REDD implementation or simulation of REDD implementation.

(2) "Hybrid studies" which partly use bottom-up calculations is order to model global costs, notably by using, explicitly or implicitly, benefit transfer methodology, and applying specific assumptions to variables.[14] The estimations used by the Stern Review, for example, are in this category (Grieg-Gran, 2006; Stern, 2007).

(3) Global modeling through partial equilibrium dynamic models. While they may have global coverage, their scope is almost uniquely the assessment of opportunity costs with additional costs generally added to estimated opportunity costs by using the results of empirical studies. The Eliash Review (Eliash, 2008) can notably be classified in this category. A synopsis of studies that have attempted to estimate costs for REDD is provided in Table 2.5.

Results range by an order of magnitude, but there are various factors that might explain this variability. First, the studies do not estimate the same percentage reduction in GHG emissions from deforestation and forest degradation. Second, different categories of cost are assessed. Third, different assumptions are made *vis-à-vis* returns to the land use alternatives and therefore to opportunity costs. Grieg-Gran (2006), for instance, only considers returns from conversion of forests to agriculture: other forms of forestry activity are not considered, and she states that using higher (and plausible) returns for agriculture could increase opportunity costs to US$26 billion p.a. using her data (Grieg-Gran, 2006, 2008). Kinderman *et al.* (2008), a background paper for the Eliash Review (Eliash, 2008), consider not only land returns from agriculture but also from timber activities, and include forgone flows of revenues and also forgone rents to land. In short, the assumptions applied and methodologies used are divergent across the studies in Table 2.5.

One reason to present the study type (empirically derived/hybrid/global) is that analysis by Boucher (2008) suggests that this is influential in determining cost estimates (see Table 2.6).

Table 2.6 Opportunity costs differentials, depending on methodological approach

Approach	Mean opportunity cost (US$/t$CO_2$eq)	
Empirical/Regional	2.51	(Range: 0.84–4.18)
Hybrid	5.52	(Range: 2.76–8.28)
Global partial equilibrium models	11.26	(Range: 6.77–17.86)

Source: Adapted from Boucher (2008).

[14] Assumptions are related to the extrapolation of carbon density levels (per ha) to other sites (from local to regional extrapolation): see Boucher (2008: 15–17).

Although the sample size of studies is small, it is noteworthy that the high-point in the estimate range for empirical studies (4.18) is less than the lower-bound estimate for global partial equilibrium models (6.77).

All the estimates presented in the five studies have been peer reviewed. There is no definitive "correct" approach *vis-à-vis* methodology, assumptions, or data sources. In this sense, choosing an estimate from any single, any combination, or all the studies cited in Table 2.6 would be defensible. Perhaps the most significant estimate as regards the policy perspective is Grieg-Gran (2006). However, since Grieg-Gran (2008) is an update we would recommend using this estimate; it would be a lower-bound estimate (taking the mid-point in the range US$6.8–8 billion + US$0.5 billion). The choice of higher-bound estimate is somewhat arbitrary, but Kinderman *et al.* (2008) might be picked for the following reasons: (1) it is linked with the Eliash Review (Eliash, 2008) and produces very similar estimates; (2) the percentage reduction is similar to the lower-bound estimate from Grieg-Gran (2008) (i.e. 46 percent versus 50 percent); and (3) it covers all three cost categories.

The lower-bound estimate is US$7.9 billion p.a. and an upper-bound estimate is US$22.5 billion p.a. (Both values are mid-points in their respective ranges.) Both estimates take into account the evolution of opportunity costs up to 2030, following possible increases in returns from alternative land use. Hence, non-linearity can be considered as endogenous to these estimations. Two additional non-linear elements were taken into account when calculating aggregate costs:

(1) Grieg-Gran (2008) provides incremental management costs as an additional area is included in the network. Thus management costs represent US$50 million in the first year of implementation, and increase up to US$500 million when full implementation takes place. This cost trajectory has been taken into account when using the Grieg-Gran (2008) figure.
(2) Eliash (2008) proposes additional one-off implementation costs which occur during the first four implementation years (representing globally an additional US$4 billion over five years). This element is also taken into account.

In summary, to assess non-linearities in costs, we analytically separated (1) our lower-bound estimate based on Grieg-Gran (2008) from (2) our higher-bound estimate based on Eliash (2008) for the sake of remaining faithful to the cost quantification of the respective analyses:

(1) Following Grieg-Gran (2008) for our lower-bound estimate, initial management and transaction costs represent US$50 million in year 1 (2001), US$100 million in year 2, and reach US$500 million in year 10 (2010), after which the 500 million figure is constant from 2010 to 2030. Opportunity costs are assessed as constant by Grieg-Gran (2008), and we thus assume costs of US$7.9 billion per annum from 2000 to 2030.
(2) Following Eliash (2008), initial implementation costs were assumed to represent US$4 billion for the period 2000–2005 (evenly distributed in the first five years, i.e, US$800 million p.a.). Ongoing costs are assumed to be US$22.5 billion p.a. for the period 2000–2030.

Summary of policy option cost estimates

Table 2.7 provides an overall synopsis of the cost analysis; the estimates are used in the BCRs presented (where applicable) on p. 88.

Benefit assessment: value functions and the GIS framework

The IMAGE-GLOBIO bio-physical model estimates: (i) ecosystem extent, (ii) MSA, and (iii) carbon storage and carbon sequestration for 0.5 degree × 0.5 degree (c. 50 km × 50 km) grid cells under the assumptions inputted. The benefit estimate depends on the change in these parameters. IMAGE-GLOBIO models the protected area and reduced deforestation (REDD-variant) option to 2030 and the AKST option to 2050. Thus there is a 2000 base year, a BAU (no-new policies)

Table 2.7 Overall summary of cost estimates for policy options (all figures 2007 US$ billion)

Policy option	Annual cost estimate	Program cost estimate[a,b] 3%	5%
Agricultural productivity	14.5	372.1	264.7
Protected areas			
"Best-guess"	15.4	304.6	239.4
Upper bound	66.4	1304.6	1023.7
Reduced deforestation			
Lower bound	7.9	162.6	127.2
Upper bound	22.5	441.0	345.9

Notes:
[a] Agricultural productivity 2000–2050; both protected areas and reduced deforestation 2000–2030.
[b] Plus up to US$500 million p.a. management and transaction costs by year 10 of program (cost rising in US$50 million increments each year from year 1)

2030 or 2050 baseline projection, and a 2030 or 2050 scenario on which the above policy options have been superimposed (e.g. with protected areas expansion). The premise for benefit valuation is as follows:

(a) Patches of land (e.g. a contiguous area of tropical rainforest) deliver a range of ESSs, including a proxy value for biodiversity located in that patch (the ESS termed "gene pool")
(b) One of the ESSs relates to carbon, and this is treated independently
(c) The patches are valued *vis-à-vis* ESSs provisioning in 2000, in 2030–2050 in the baseline scenario), and in 2030–2050 with the policy option
(d) The marginal change in provisioning in 2030–2050 defines the net benefit of the policy option.

Patch-level analysis is applied across 2.3 million patches. A key requirement of the analysis is to determine value appropriately at patch level. There are two elements to the estimation of benefits: (1) valuing overall changes in land use, and (2) valuing changes in carbon.

Biome-level value functions

The valuation of changes in the extent of ecosystem patches follows the methodology set out by Brander *et al.* (2011), which combines meta-analytic value functions with GIS to transfer and scale up ESS values. A biome-level value function explains the variation in value estimates. The explanatory variables that capture site characteristics might include: general characteristics (e.g. site size, ESSs provided); context characteristics (e.g. abundance of the ecosystem in the region, accessibility); and socio-economic characteristics of beneficiaries (e.g. size of relevant population, income). The value functions do not include MSA directly as an explanatory variable of ESS value, but some include variables that represent the underlying determinants of MSA in the IMAGE-GLOBIO model (land use intensity, fragmentation, and site size). Whether these (and other) variables are included in the biome-level value functions varies on a biome-by-biome basis, depending on the relevance of each explanatory variable to each biome and on statistical significance in the meta-regression model.

The aim of benefit function estimation is to produce a model that explains variation in site values (in this case, US$/ha) in both a theoretically and statistically robust manner. That is, the explanatory variables should have some reasonable theoretical justification for both having an effect and the direction of that effect (the sign of the estimated coefficient); that effect should also have reasonable level of statistical significance.

An important decision in function estimation is the choice of functional form; common throughout the meta-analysis and benefit transfer literature is the use of either log or log-log functions. In log forms a natural logarithm transformation of the dependent variable (unit value) is used; in log-log forms the transformation is applied to both dependent and independent variables. There are a number of reasons why a log or log-log functional form is attractive (see Brander *et al.*, 2006). Often values follow skewed (non-normal) distributions with a small number of outlying values; a log transformation counteracts this by reducing the effect of extreme values and the resulting data more closely reflect a normal distribution and have a smaller variance. The use of a log-log specification allows the normalization of both dependent and independent variables and has the further advantage that the estimated coefficients can be interpreted as elasticities, i.e. the coefficients represent the percentage change in the dependent variable (value per ha) of a small percentage change in the explanatory variable (Brander *et al.*, 2006).

In addition to functional form a major consideration in the development of benefit functions is the choice of explanatory variables. As noted on p. 88, these should be theoretically valid and have a significant effect on per ha values. A further consideration with benefit transfer exercises is that they should also be observable for the sites to which benefits are to be transferred. It is common in meta-analyses of valuation studies to include study-specific variables that relate particularly to the methodology that has been applied. The effect of different valuation methods or the different value elicitation approaches have been found to be significant explanatory variables; see Bateman and Jones (2003), Lindhjem and Navrud (2008), and Barrio and Loureiro (2010) for examples of meta-analyses of forest valuation studies where methodological variables were found to be significant. However, although such analyses are of theoretical interest and can be useful in guiding methodological development, they are of little value in benefit transfer as such variables are essentially unobservable. Similarly site-specific variables that cannot be observed across transfer sites are of little use.

We discuss possible reasons for the occurrence of positive or negative signs on various variables, on a biome-by-biome basis; the degree to which we have confidence in this interpretation of the results varies. For instance, we would certainly expect patch value to be positively linked with income. However, the accessibility variable for instance is more complicated to interpret; it shows the potential for the study site to generate positive on-site use values (e.g. for recreation) but also the ease by which the site might be exploited and degraded (which reduces ESS values).

We use a range of spatially referenced variables that are derived from publicly available data sources and are applied to the study sites by GIS analysis of each site's location. Table 2.8 summarizes the spatial variables estimated for the study sites that can also be applied to all transfer sites. GIS is used to transform and integrate a series of global spatial datasets into separate datasets that spatially cover the seven biomes under investigation. Note that spatial variables are applied at three different radii from the patch: 10 km, 20 km, and 50 km.

The GIS is used to transform the different spatial input data, such as global population, infrastructure, urbanization, and human appropriation of net primary product (HANPP) into a dataset of specific spatial variables (e.g. area, abundance). The spatial data selection is based on the following criteria: (1) possible explanatory value for ecosystem value estimates; (2) completeness *vis-à-vis* global extent; (3) spatial and temporal consistency; and (4) credibility, i.e. well-documented and preferably scientifically referenced data.

There are four chronologically executed stages to the GIS integration and analysis work. The first three pertain to the benefit function estimation:

(1) spatial data selection, acquisition, transformation, and integration of input data for spatial variables and biome maps
(2) import of study sites into the GIS database as point locations, based on their estimated geographic coordinates
(3) extraction of spatial variable values to point-based study site locations as input for meta-regression analysis.

The fourth chronological step (upscaling of spatial relationships resulting from the meta-regression analysis between ecosystem values and explanatory spatial variables to a global scale) takes place after the generation of the biome-level value functions. We thus return to GIS Step (4) on p. 92 after discussing the biome-level meta-regressions.

Table 2.8 Spatial variables used in benefit function development

Variable	Description	Comments	Source
Forests	Area (ha) of forest within specified radius of site	Measure of substitute and/or complementary sites	Global Land Cover 2000 database. European Commission, Joint Research Center, 2003, http://bioval.jrc.ec.europa.eu/products/glc2000/glc2000.php
Grassland	Area (ha) of grassland within specified radius of site	Measure of substitute and/or complementary sites	Global Land Cover 2000 database. European Commission, Joint Research Center, 2003, http://bioval.jrc.ec.europa.eu/products/glc2000/glc2000.php
Gross cell product	Measure of gross value added (PPP US$2005) within specified radius of site	Measure of economic output that acts as proxy for ability (willingness) to pay for ESSs	Global Economic Activity G-Econ 3.3 http://gecon.sites.yale.edu/data-and-documentation-g-econ-project
Population	Population density (2000 persons/km^2) within specified radius of site	Measure of population likely to benefit from ESSs and/or proxy measure of pressure	Socio-Economic Data Center (SEDAC), Columbia University, http://sedac.ciesin.columbia.edu/data/collection/gpw-v3
Urban area	Area (ha) of urban land use within specified radius of site	Measure of presence of population likely to benefit from ESSs and/or proxy measure of pressure	Institute for Environmental Studies, University of Wisconsin–Madison www.sage.wisc.edu/people/schneider/research/data.html.
Roads	Length (km) of roads within specified radius of site	Measure of accessibility and/or fragmentation of site	FAO – UN SDRN (1997) Roads of the World, www.fao.org/geonetwork/srv/en/main.home?uuid=c208a1e0–88fd-11da-a88f-000d939bc5d8
Net primary product (NPP)	NPP actual vegetation (gC/m^2/yr) within specified radius of site	Proxy measure for production of ESSs of site and substitutes	Institute of Social Ecology (SEC), IFF – Faculty of Interdisciplinary Studies, Alpen Adria University, Vienna, Austria, http://www.uni-klu.ac.at/socec/inhalt/1191.htm
HANPP	HANPP (gC/m^2/yr) within specified radius of site	Proxy measure of human exploitation of ESSs and/or land management – primarily agricultural land	Institute of Social Ecology (SEC), IFF – Faculty of Interdisciplinary Studies, Alpen Adria University, Vienna, Austria, http://www.uni-klu.ac.at/socec/inhalt/1191.htm
Accessibility index	Index of accessibility based on distance in travel time to urban centers	Measure of accessibility and use of ESSs of site	Aurelien Letourneau, Wageningen University

We now present the benefit functions used in this study for each biome in turn. The dependent variable in each case is US$/ha/p.a. in 2007 price levels (note that the dependent variable is not total value per site). In all cases the value functions are estimated by ordinary least squares regression (OLS) using SPSS 16.0.[15]

What we do not consider is the change in habitat type described in the primary valuation studies; the US$/ha/p.a. value estimate for a particular (say) woodland site depends on what the proposed alternative land use is. We do not apply a filter *vis-à-vis* the alternative land use as to do so would imply having smaller subsets of data points for each biome (e.g. only those studies proposing woodland conversion to pasture land), and in terms of our patch-level analysis there is insufficient spatial resolution to identify the nature of land use changes for each patch.

The transfer pertains to the aggregate value of ESSs at the study site. Although considerable

[15] We use OLS notwithstanding the fact that willingness-to-pay (WTP) is truncated at $0; the truncation is due to the log transformation rather than being otherwise imposed on the data.

Table 2.9 Temperate forest and woodland value function

Variable	Beta	Std error	Sig.
Constant	28.627	6.124	0.000
Natural log of the study site area	–0.420	0.076	0.000
Natural log of gross cell product within 50 km radius	0.247	0.150	0.104
Natural log of urban area within 50 km radius of study site	0.245	0.143	0.092
Natural log of HANPP within 50 km radius of study site	–1.610	0.417	0.000
N	69		
Adjusted R^2	0.348		

Table 2.10 Tropical forest value function

Variable	Beta	Std error	Sig.
Constant	12.960	4.071	0.002
Natural log of the study site area	–0.230	0.070	0.001
Natural log of gross cell product within 50 km radius	0.402	0.173	0.022
Natural log of urban area within 50 km radius of study site	0.424	0.121	0.001
Natural log of HANPP within 50 km radius of study site	–0.394	0.292	0.181
Natural log of area of forest within 50 km radius of study site	–0.336	0.202	0.100
Natural log of length of roads within 50 km radius of study site	–0.204	0.131	0.124
N	102		
Adjusted R^2	0.392		

effort was expended in developing the biome-level valuation database (see the Appendix), the number of studies did not allow benefit transfer for individual ESSs or indeed for a broader split between use and non-use values.

Table 2.8 sets out the spatial variables used in the benefit function development and corresponding data sources.

Temperate forests and woodlands

The average temperate forest and woodland value is US$892/ha/p.a. and the median is US$127/ha/p.a. The benefit function outlined in Table 2.9 was found to have the best performance in terms of variable significance and goodness-of-fit. The estimated coefficients have the expected signs. The negative sign on the log of site area indicates that values per ha decline as the size of the site increases, i.e. diminishing margin values. The log of gross cell product within 50 km is positive indicated that site values increase with income. The positive sign on the log of urban area within 50 km of the sites suggests that values for natural areas increase with the local urban population; this would be expected given the predominance of recreational values in the temperate forest studies. The final independent variable included is the log of HA NPP within 50 km of the study sites, a proxy for land use intensity. The negative sign on the estimated coefficient could be interpreted to mean that more intensive land use surrounding forest sites reduces their value, but we accept that interpreting the sign on this variable is less straightforward.

The coefficients are significant at the widely accepted 5 and 10 percent levels, although the significance of LN_GCP50 (Gross Cell Product) is marginally insignificant under these criteria. However, removal of such variables can serve to reduce the significance of those remaining or the overall model performance. The adjusted R^2 indicates that this model accounts for 34.8 percent of the observed variation in log per ha values.

Tropical forests

The average tropical forest value is US$444.98/ha/p.a. and the median is US$14.86/ha/annum. Table 2.10 outlines the benefit function. There are four independent variables in common with the temperate forest function; these have the same signs and interpretation. The additional variables include

Table 2.11 Grasslands value function

Variable	Beta	Std error	Sig.
Constant	–2.366	5.094	0.444
Natural log of country level GDP *per capita* (PPP US$2007)	0.856	0.514	0.120
Natural log of area of grassland within 50 km radius of study site	–0.029	0.142	0.839
Natural log of length of roads within 50 km radius of study site	–0.225	0.213	0.309
Accessibility index	2.590	1.322	0.072
N	17		
Adjusted R^2	0.27		

the area of forest within 50 km of the site and the length of roads within 50 km; both of these have negative signs. For the former variable, we suggest that this can be interpreted as the effect of having substitute sites in the same area that can provide a similar range of ESSs. This might reflect the greater continuity of forest cover in the tropical forest sites as compared to many of the temperate forest study sites where forest cover was more fragmented. The negative sign on the log of roads within the 50 km variable suggests that this might be a proxy for the degree of forest exploitation. The adjusted R^2 figure indicates that 39.2 percent of observed variation in values is explained by the model. With the exception of the LN_HAN50 and LN_RDS50 variables each variable is significant at either the 5 percent or 10 percent level.

Grasslands

The value function for grasslands is presented in Table 2.11. The estimated coefficients on the explanatory variables all have the expected signs but are mostly not statistically significant.[16] Only the estimated effect of accessibility is statistically significant at the 10 percent level, although the GDP *per capita* variable is significant at the 12 percent level. The positive coefficient on the income variable (GDP *per capita*) indicates that grassland ESSs have higher values in countries with higher incomes, i.e. grassland ESSs are a normal good for which demand increases with income. The negative effect of grassland abundance (area of grassland within a 50 km radius) on value indicates that the availability of substitute grassland areas affects the value of ESSs from a specific patch of grassland. The negative effect of roads on grassland values captures the effect of fragmentation on the provision of ESSs from grassland. Grasslands that are more fragmented by roads tend to have lower values. The positive coefficient on the accessibility index indicates that grassland areas that are more accessible tend to have higher values. In this case, direct use values derived from grasslands (e.g. recreation and food provisioning) appear to dominate values that do not require access (e.g. wildlife conservation).

Confidence in the estimated value function for grassland ESSs is not high. Although the adjusted R^2 of 0.27 for grasslands (which indicates that the estimated model explains 27 percent of variation in the value of grassland) is not much worse than the R^2 of 0.35 that applies for the temperate forests and woodlands biome, all but one of the explanatory variables included in the grasslands model are not statistically significant. The signs and magnitudes of effect of the explanatory variable do, however, make theoretical sense. We therefore cautiously use this value function to estimate site-specific values for grasslands; an alternative would be to transfer mean values. Transferred values are checked for estimates that lie outside the range of values observed in the literature.

GIS analysis: upscaling values

As mentioned on p. 89, there is a fourth substantive GIS step: upscaling of spatial relationships resulting from the meta-regression analysis

16 The presence of insignificant independent variables is of concern; however the estimated model is otherwise theoretically consistent. The lack of significance indicates low precision in the degree to which the coefficients predict the effect of the independent variables on per ha values. We would argue that rejecting the value function for this biome entirely would result in the omission of potentially significant values in our subsequent analysis.

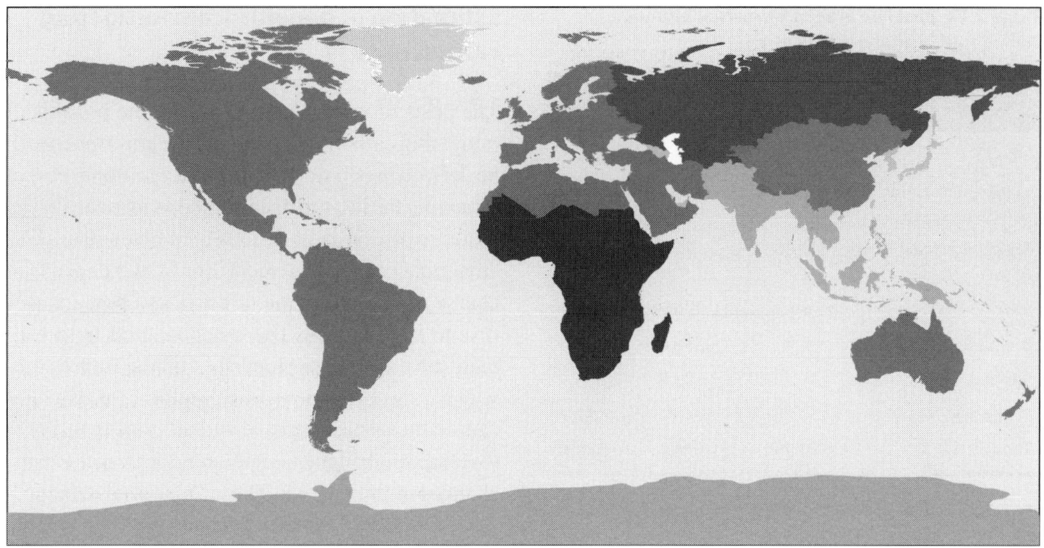

Figure 2.3 *Map of regions*

between ecosystem values and explanatory spatial variables to a global (or regional) scale. The outputs of IMAGE-GLOBIO are changes in the distribution of land cover within grid cells. The pertinent methodological question is as follows: if a patch changes in extent, what is the value of that change given the local spatial characteristics? There are five substeps:

(1) Preparation and mapping of seven different non-overlapping biomes represented at patch level.
(2) Construction of global datasets with selected variables, covering the spatial extent of all considered biomes.
(3) Integration and analysis of IMAGE-GLOBIO modeling data resulting in change factors for all grid cells concerning land use change, infrastructure change, economic change, and water quality change. Spatial transfer to full spatial extent of selected biomes.
(4) Combination for each biome of all relevant spatial variables into one raster map.
(5) Export to tables of all relevant variables and change factors per biome for statistical processing of value functions (outside the GIS environment, using SPSS 16.0).

Estimation of benefits arising from land use change

The value changes for each of the policy options are based on the three terrestrial biomes (temperate forests, tropical forests, and grasslands) which were modeled in IMAGE-GLOBIO.[17] Our results are presented at the level of the regions used by PBL (2010) when presenting land use change within the IMAGE-GLOBIO analysis, as illustrated in Figure 2.3.

[17] GLOBIO presents results for seven distinct biomes; of these we combine "boreal forest" and "temperate forest," and "grassland and steppe" and "scrubland and savannah" into two single biomes: "temperate forest" and "grassland," respectively.

Table 2.12 Baseline area of terrestrial biomes considered in analysis (000 km^2)

	Grassland	Temperate forest	Tropical forest
OECD	14,197.4	9,663.4	872.7
Central and South America	4,255.2	789.3	6,963.9
Middle East and North Africa	1,464.3	71.6	10.0
SSA	7,692.1	296.9	6,401.4
Russia and Central Asia	5,952.6	8,356.8	0.0
South Asia	1,723.9	509.8	2,525.9
China Region	3,983.7	1,940.7	84.7
Total	39,269.1	21,628.4	16,858.6

Table 2.12 presents the area of the terrestrial biomes in each region; discussions of land use change under the policy options below should be considered in the context of these baseline values. The biome sites used for the value transfer were derived from GLC2000 data; forest biomes were classified in our study as either temperate or tropical on the basis of latitude. Our classification of grassland differs from that used by PBL (2010), in that we include patches classified as grassland in cultivated areas; we use this classification because our grassland value function includes values for such pasture sites. The consequence of our grassland classification is that we have a larger area of grassland, but the relative change factors for that biome are lower than those used in the PBL (2010) analysis.

For each landscape patch (i.e. site) the value per ha under the baselines and policy options are calculated. This is done by substituting the site-specific variable values into the value function. The value of a change in a specific site is calculated by multiplying the average value (average across two scenarios) for that site by the change in area at the site. The values for changes in each ecosystem site are then aggregated to a regional and global level to give the annual benefit value at these respective scales to determine the benefits of the policy option *vis-à-vis* land use change. Note that in some cases land use change can have net costs if there is a switch from higher-value to lower-value land-use types.

Estimation of benefits from mitigating carbon release

The costs of carbon (and therefore the benefits of mitigating carbon) released into the atmosphere can be derived in two ways. One is the additional cost of removing the last ton of carbon so as to meet a given target reduction in emissions by a given date. This "marginal cost of abatement" (or MAC) depends of course on how strict the target is and how quickly it is to be achieved. The other method is to estimate the damages per ton based on the future pathway for the economy and the amount of damages caused by a small increase in emissions in terms of losses through higher temperatures, extreme events, changes in rainfall, etc. These "marginal damage"- or (MD)-based estimates depend very much on the expected physical changes from increased carbon emissions and on the monetary values associated with them. Both are highly uncertain.

The IMAGE-GLOBIO models consider changes in three main sources: (1) deforestation, (2) re-growth of vegetation, and (3) increased carbon sequestration by existing forests (CO_2 and Nitrogen fertilization). The policy options generally impact upon all three. For instance, a reduction in agricultural land reduces deforestation, increases the re-growth of vegetation, and affects sequestration by increasing the area of natural forest, but also by reducing atmospheric CO_2 concentrations. Table 2.13 provides the bio-physical data on changes in carbon storage for the three policy options. The economic benefit appraisal is set out in each respective subsection on pp. 95–104.

In the benefits reported in this study, the MAC estimates are taken from the POLES model, where the goal is to reduce global emissions by 80 percent relative to 1990 levels by 2050 (Criqui *et al.*, 1999). The MD damages are taken from the RICE model, which provides a range based on different assumptions about temperature and precipitation changes and their physical impacts (Nordhaus and Yang, 1996). The difference between the two is significant, especially over time. In 2010 the MAC estimate is US$8/ton CO_2, while the MD damages are between US$7 and US$13/ton CO_2. By 2050, however, the MAC estimate is US$406/ton CO_2, while the MD range is US$21–61/ton CO_2. In the

Table 2.13 Modeled projections of changes in net carbon storage relative to the baseline 2000–2050 (billion tonnes CO_2-equivalent)

	Agricultural productivity (high AKST)	Protected areas (20%)	REDD
2000	0.00	–0.29	0.71
2005	–0.57	–0.04	6.34
2010	0.04	–0.02	6.71
2015	1.39	0.66	9.16
2020	0.96	0.49	8.65
2025	2.49	0.31	8.05
2030	2.41	0.76	6.97
2035	3.05		
2040	2.85		
2045	3.70		
2050	3.74		
Total (all years)	90.88	8.18	216.53

analysis of the different options we consider both the MAC estimate based on POLES and the MD estimate based on the mean of the figures from the RICE model.

Assessment of benefits: systemic underestimation

An important point with regard to the estimation of any value changes arising from each policy option is that our analysis is partial for several reasons:

(1) This study focuses on valuing changes in land cover, i.e. the quantity of land cover under a particular categorization (i.e. GLC2000), as opposed to the quality of the ecosystem. We do attempt to capture some aspects of changes in quality by testing various spatial variables which affect habitat quality in the derivation of the value functions, e.g. HANPP, as a proxy for intensity of land use and "roads" as a proxy for habitat fragmentation; such variables are likely to only partially capture changes in habitat quality. The only alternative is to infer changes in quality from MSA changes, but this requires mapping changes in MSA to changes in ESS provision; the evidence base from the scientific literature to support these inferences is limited and thus no attempt is made to do so in this study. The outcome of this methodological choice is that the approach in our study is likely to systematically undervalue changes in habitat quality.

(2) Aside from the results for carbon, values are not transferred across ESS categories. Valuation estimates from primary studies are used once screened for methodological integrity, specificity of study area, etc., but most data points in the valuation database are for study sites where only some subset of ESSs has been valued. Since these site-level values are thus only partial (but are the ones used in the valuation database) this implies a systematic undervaluing of benefits. This second issue of omitted values for ESSs is generic to environmental valuation studies and to site-level benefits transfer (as opposed to ESS-level transfer).

(3) Our value estimations for the policy options are based on changes to only three terrestrial biomes (temperate forest and woodland; tropical forest; grasslands). It is very likely that there are significant value changes to other biomes, but these are not considered in this chapter.

Overall results

Results are presented in turn for agricultural productivity (high investment in AKST), extension of protected areas to 20 percent of eco-regions, and reduced deforestation (REDD-variant).

Agricultural productivity

As noted on p. 82, based on FAO (2006), Rosegrant *et al.* (2009), and Van Vuuren and Faber (2009), the baseline assumes that the current levelling-off of agricultural productivity growth persists: a cumulated growth in productivity of 60 percent to 2050 relative to productivity in 2000. Under the policy option, productivity growth is spurred by investment in AKST, increasing productivity growth by 40 percent and 20 percent for crop and livestock, respectively, relative to the baseline.

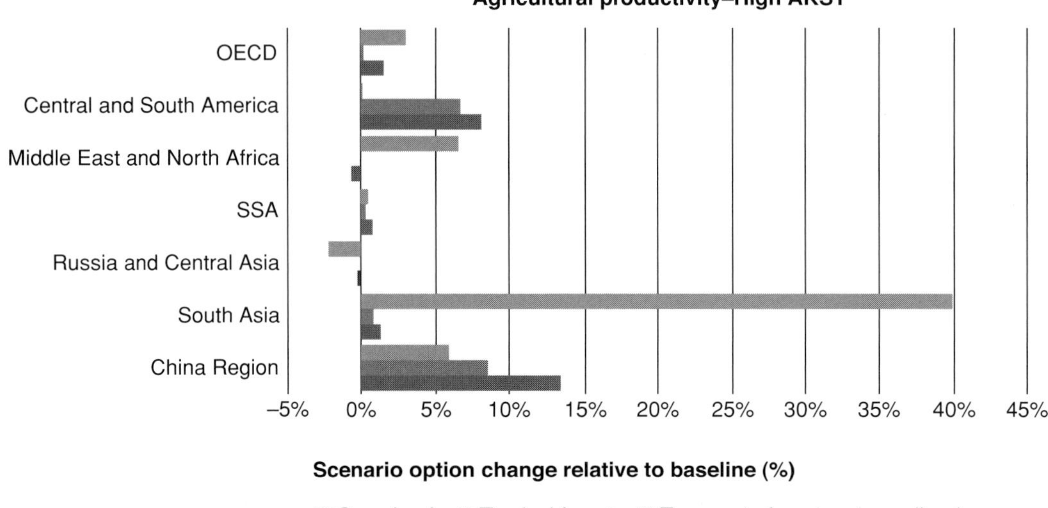

Figure 2.4 *Agricultural productivity: change in area of biomes for policy option relative to the baseline*

Figure 2.4 presents the percentage changes in land use for each biome under the high-AKST policy option relative to the baseline. There are increases in the area of each biome in each region with the exception of small reductions in temperate forest in the "Middle East and North Africa" and in grasslands in "Russia and Central Asia," the latter being due to an expansion of arable cropping in Central Asia into previously unsuitable areas (PBL, 2010). Most of these changes are below 10 percent and so might be described as marginal. The approximately 40 percent increase in grassland area in "South Asia" counteracts a 25 percent decline in that biome under the baseline relative to the 2000 base year; the increase is thus a more modest 5 percent when compared to the 2000 situation. The results are presented by region and by biome (Table 2.14), with the overall aggregated results from 2000 to 2050 at two discount rates (3 percent and 5 percent) for the high-AKST scenario (Table 2.15).

Table 2.14 shows the breakdown on a biome-by-biome basis. The sum of the value changes across the three biomes is US$27.8 billion for grasslands; US$81.7 billion for temperate forest; and US$52.6 billion for tropical forests. These are summed in the second column of the summary table (Table 2.15), i.e. US$162.1. All values are in 2007 prices. This presentational style is repeated for all the policy options below.

A further point to note is that the annual values for each region cannot be calculated directly from the changes in area and the mean per ha values. This is because the value functions include patch size as an explanatory variable, hence the value per ha varies across patches.[18] The patch-size coefficient for each biome is negative, indicating that larger patches have lower per ha values.

Globally, the land use value change is significantly positive, i.e. around US$1,631 billion at the 3 percent discount rate (see Table 2.15). Note that these gains are against the "moderate" counterfactual of (on average) 0.94 percent growth in productivity p.a. The results show that there are significant welfare gains associated with the high-AKST policy option across the three biomes; however there are some variations across regions. Specifically the "Russia and Central Asia" region sees a loss in

[18] As an example, assume we have a region with three patches of biome *X* that are initially 100, 200, and 500 ha in size and per ha values are $400, $300, and $200, respectively. Then if each patch increases by 10 percent the sum of the individual patch values is $(10 \times 400) + (20 \times 300) + (50 \times 200) = \$20{,}000$. If we use the total change in patch-area and mean per ha values the estimated value would be $(10 + 20 + 50) \times 300 = \$24{,}000$.

Table 2.14 Agricultural productivity: value results, by region and by biome relative to 2050 baseline

	Change in area (000 km^2)	Mean per ha value[a] (US$2007)	Annual value (bn US$2007)
Grassland			
OECD	423.7	645.3	20.6
Central and South America	4.7	252.9	0.1
Middle East and North Africa	91.2	326.4	2.4
SSA	35.3	63.6	0.3
Russia and Central Asia	–128.2	351.2	–3.6
South Asia	511.8	146.2	4.8
China Region	229.4	232.3	3.2
Total[b]	1167.8		27.8
Temperate forest			
OECD	155.7	21054.7	26.1
Central and South America	57.0	17673.2	19.1
Middle East and North Africa	–0.4	16464.7	–0.1
SSA	2.4	8135.5	0.2
Russia and Central Asia	–18.0	18170.2	–1.9
South Asia	6.6	9787.0	1.4
China Region	253.6	15765.8	37.0
Total	456.8		81.7
Tropical forest			
OECD	1.7	9958.5	0.6
Central and South America	420.9	8308.7	45.9
Middle East and North Africa			
SSA	21.1	4015.4	0.8
Russia and Central Asia			
South Asia	20.8	7593.5	3.4
China Region	7.1	8502.5	1.7
Total	471.7		52.6

Notes:
[a] Mean per ha values are the average of 2050 baseline and 2050 scenario per ha values.
[b] Total value changes are the sum of individual patch values and are not calculated from regional mean per ha values.

welfare of US$5.5 billion p.a. in 2050; this arises due to an expansion of agricultural production and improved growing conditions in that region (PBL, 2010). This welfare loss reflects a decrease in extent of uncultivated area relative to the baseline, whereas welfare gains in other regions reflect a greater extent of uncultivated areas when compared to the baseline.

The undiscounted annual benefit in 2050 (162.1 billion US$) is the figure for the *year* 2050, i.e. the end of the study period 2000–2050. We assume a linear trajectory of benefits from 2000 to 2050. This is represented in Figure 2.5.

Given the development-focused nature of the policy option, the IMAGE regions that show the largest benefits from land use change include "Central and South America," "OECD," and "China region." These benefits arise largely from increased forest area relative to the baseline across these regions, although there are also substantial

Table 2.15 Annual and discounted aggregated regional benefits (2007 US$ billion) of agricultural productivity increase versus 2050 baseline

	2050 undiscounted annual benefit	2000–2050 discounted total benefit	
		3%	5%
OECD	47.3	476.4	280.4
Central and South America	65.1	655.4	385.7
Middle East and North Africa	2.3	23.0	13.5
SSA	1.3	13.1	7.7
Russia and Central Asia	–5.5	–55.4	–32.6
South Asia	9.6	96.6	56.9
China Region	41.9	422.1	248.4
Total	162.1	1631.3	960.1

Table 2.16 Overall BCRs for agricultural productivity, 2000–2050

		Discount rate	
		3%	5%
Benefits of change in biome areas (bn US$2007)		1,631	960
Carbon values (bn US$2007)			
	POLES	6,019	3,166
	RICE-Mean	1,182	720
Costs (bn US$2007)		373	265
BCRs			
No carbon value		4.4	3.6
Carbon value based on MAC (POLES)		20.5	15.6
Carbon value based on MD (Rice-Mean)		7.5	6.3

benefits from increased grassland area in the "OECD" region.

Alongside the benefits from land use change, the estimated net benefit (relative to the baseline) from additional carbon sequestration is valued at between US$720 million and US$6,019 billion (see Table 2.16). Costs were estimated to be US$373 billion at a 3 percent discount rate. The BCRs across a range of discount rates and carbon values are set out in Table 2.16.

Even without adding the additional carbon storage estimated to occur with the policy option, the BCR is significantly positive, i.e. 3.6 with the higher 5 percent discount rate. The majority of the benefits from land use change come from the forest biomes: of the US$162.1 billion undiscounted annual benefit US$27.8 billion is attributed to the grasslands biome (see Table 2.14), i.e. 17 percent.

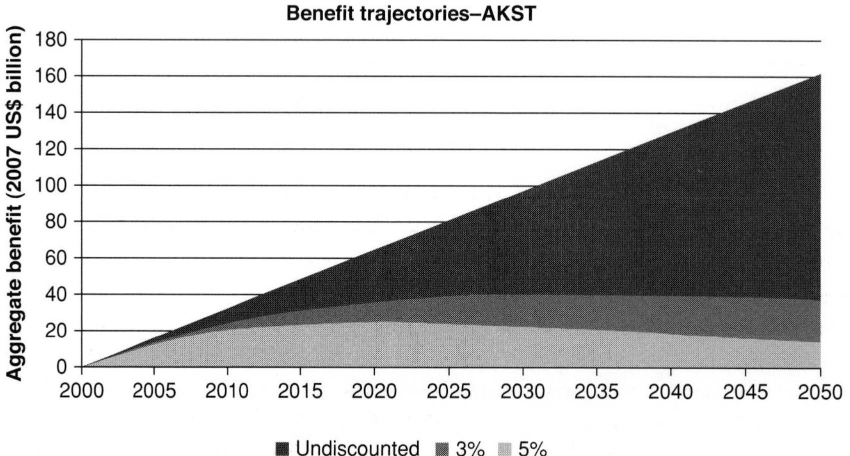

Figure 2.5 *Linear benefit trajectory for increased productivity: undiscounted and discounted benefit estimates over the study period, 2000–2050*

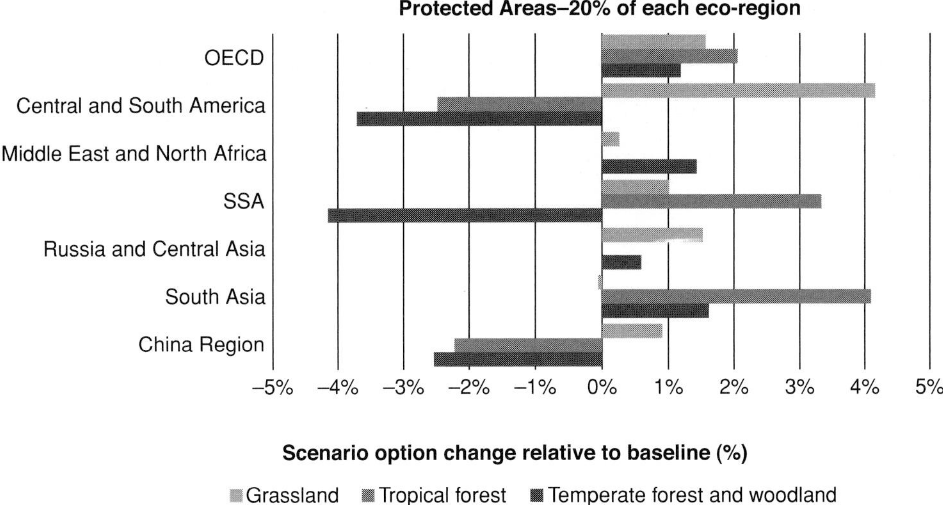

Figure 2.6 *Protected areas: change in area of biomes for scenario option relative to baseline*

This is significant. We also note that although one of the changes in the grasslands biome was arguably non-marginal (e.g. 40 percent for "South Asia"), the average change in the forest biomes is 3 percent, i.e. clearly marginal. Even removing the grasslands benefits (US$510.3 bn) and the carbon benefits leaves a significant positive BCR (~3 at a 3 percent discount rate). Adding the carbon benefits raises the BCR to between 8 and 21 at the 3 percent discount rate and between 6 and 16 at the 5 percent discount rate.

We can say, therefore, with very high confidence, that this policy option is economically efficient on the basis of land use change alone.

Protected areas

The baseline scenario assumes that the current system of protected areas in maintained. No further policy interventions are assumed. The policy option assumes an increase in protected area coverage to 20 percent in sixty-five identified ecological regions.

Figure 2.6 presents the bio-physical changes in land use relative to the baseline. Note that both the BAU and policy option pertain to 2030 (not 2050); the bio-physical modeling is to 2030 (PBL, 2010). The area of grassland increases in each region under this policy option; however, these increases are offset by decreases in forest area in three regions, although land use change does not exceed 4.2 percent of biome area in any region compared to the baseline. These reductions in forest are not direct conversions to grassland, but rather result from deforestation to provide land for agriculture following protection of grassland areas. Grasslands are underrepresented in the existing network of protected areas, and under the baseline these are more likely to be converted to agricultural use than forests. The policy option specifically aims to achieve a more representative network of protected areas across biomes, and consequently there will be displacement of land conversion into forest areas. Value results by region and by biome are presented in Table 2.17, and Table 2.18 presents the overall results with two discount rates.

The overall results for value changes from land use change are positive with the exception of "Central and South America," SSA and "China region," and there are wide variations regionally. As indicated in Table 2.17 the benefits from this policy arise mainly from increases in the area of the grassland biome (609,000 km^2). This compares to a more modest, although valuable, increase in

Table 2.17 Protected areas: value results, by region and by biome relative to 2030 baseline

	Change in area (000 km²)	Mean per ha value[a] (US$2007)	Annual value (bn US$2007)
Grassland			
OECD	210.3	536.5	8.7
Central and South America	182.2	217.1	2.8
Middle East and North Africa	3.9	275.2	0.1
SSA	93.1	53.1	0.6
Russia and Central Asia	89.3	295.7	2.2
South Asia	–0.9	120.6	0.0
China Region	31.8	188.4	0.4
Total[b]	609.7		14.7
Temperate forest			
OECD	110.8	20,132.1	17.8
Central and South America	–27.0	16,988.0	–8.7
Middle East and North Africa	1.0	15,582.6	0.4
SSA	–5.9	10,468.4	–0.6
Russia and Central Asia	49.2	17,217.6	4.9
South Asia	8.1	9,118.5	1.6
China Region	–47.2	15,281.9	–6.7
Total	89.2		8.7
Tropical forest			
OECD	17.8	9,785.8	6.2
Central and South America	–161.3	8,063.5	–16.6
Middle East and North Africa			
SSA	154.3	4,219.7	6.5
Russia and Central Asia			
South Asia	102.9	7,071.8	15.3
China Region	–1.8	8,104.3	–0.4
Total	111.9		11.0

Notes:
[a] Mean per ha values are the average of 2030 baseline and 2030 scenario per ha values.
[b] Total value changes are the sum of individual patch values and are not calculated from regional mean per ha values.

temperate forest (89,200 km^2) and tropical forest (111,900 km^2). The large contribution of grassland values to the total value (43 percent) arises from the predominance of increases in grassland areas across the majority of regions. In contrast, there is a greater degree of balancing of gains and losses for the forest biomes, particularly with respect to values.

Table 2.19 presents overall benefit/cost results for the protected areas option. Taking the "best-guess" estimate for costs (Scenario 1 for protected areas reported on p. 84), the BCR at a 3 percent discount rate is 1 with no carbon values, 1.4 with carbon values based on MAC, and 1.2 with carbon values based on MD. With a discount rate of 5 percent the BCR is <1 with no carbon value and between 1.0 and 1–2 with carbon values, depending on whether we take the MAC or MD figures. If, however, we take the higher estimate of costs the BCR is below 1 in all cases, including those where carbon is added to the benefits.

Table 2.18 Annual and discounted aggregated regional benefits of protected areas versus 2030 baseline

	2030 undiscounted annual benefit	2000–2030 discounted total benefit	
		3%	5%
OECD	32.7	284.2	200.4
Central and South America	−22.4	−195.3	−137.7
Middle East and North Africa	0.4	3.8	2.7
SSA	6.5	56.5	39.8
Russia and Central Asia	7.1	61.4	43.3
South Asia	16.9	146.8	103.5
China Region	−6.7	−58.5	−41.3
Total	34.4	299.0	210.8

The undiscounted annual benefit in 2030 (34.4 billion US$) is the figure for the *year* 2030, i.e. the end of the study period 2000–2050. We assume a linear trajectory of benefits from 2000 to 2030. This is represented in Figure 2.7.

The issue of the distribution of winners and losers regionally should also be considered, particularly with respect to the large losses estimated for

Table 2.19 Overall BCRs for protected areas

		Discount rate	
		3%	5%
Benefits of change in biome areas (bn US$2007)		299	211
Carbon values (bn US$2007)			
	POLES	132	70
	Rice-Mean	63	39
Costs (bn US$2007)			
	"Best guess"	305	239
	Upper	1,305	1,024
BCRs			
No carbon value	"Best guess"	1.0	0.9
	Upper	0.2	0.2
Carbon value based on MAC (POLES)	"Best guess"	1.4	1.2
	Upper	0.3	0.3
Carbon value based on MD (Rice-Mean)	"Best guess"	1.2	1.0
	Upper	0.3	0.2

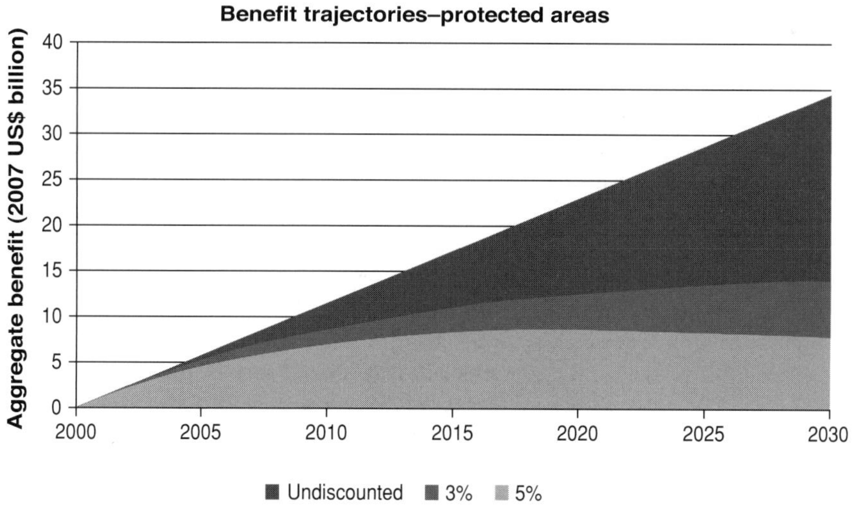

Figure 2.7 *Linear benefit trajectory for protected areas: undiscounted and discounted benefit estimates over the study period, 2000–2030*

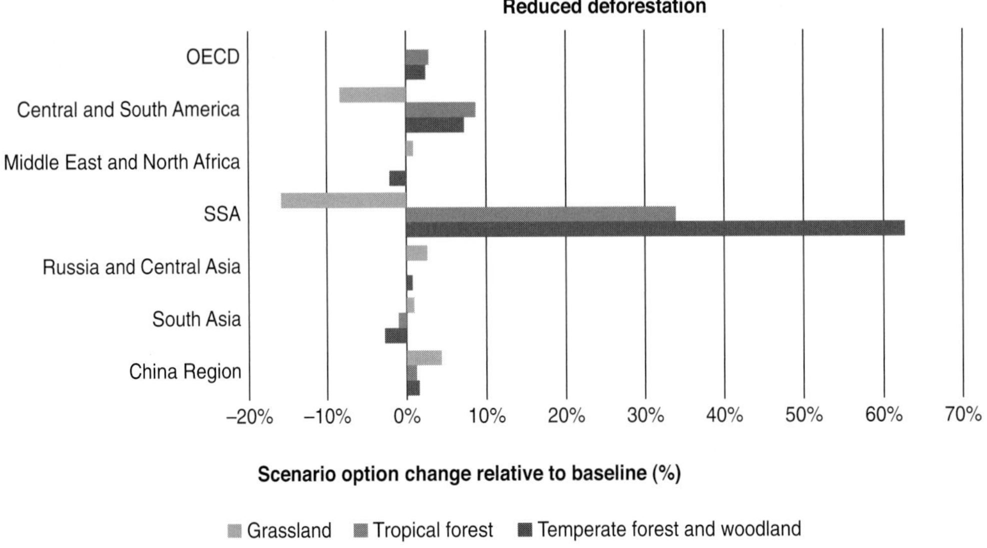

Figure 2.8 *Reduced deforestation: change in area of biomes for scenario option relative to baseline*

"Central and South America." A case can be made for promoting the protected areas option on global welfare grounds with compensation to such affected regions. This is particularly the case for this option, as a main driver of protected area establishment is biodiversity conservation, whereas the value estimates derived in this study are focused on a wider range of ESSs. The protected status of a site will alter the mix of ESSs it provides, i.e. fewer provisioning services but more supporting services, with perhaps more or less regulating and cultural services depending on context. We are unable to "unpick" the relative values of ESSs for different sites, as our value functions implicitly assume an "average" level of ESS provision.

We conclude for the chosen discount rates that the protected areas option is only economically efficient for our lower-bound cost estimate and then only when the associated carbon benefits are included.

Reduced deforestation (REDD-variant)

The baseline scenario assumes no additional actions compared to current standards: in short, deforestation and forest degradation continue due to additional pressures of population and economic growth, with subsequent changes as land use is converted for agriculture. The policy option assumes the protection of all dense forests from agricultural expansion. Note that the study period based on the IMAGE-GLOBIO modeling is 2000–2030, and all calculations are made to 2030.

Figure 2.8 presents changes in the extent of grassland and forest biomes for the reduced deforestation policy option relative to the baseline. The changes in land use for this option are largely marginal across the seven regions: they average 2.7 percent and do not exceed 8.7 percent. The exception to this is "SSA," where changes range from a loss of 15.8 percent of grassland to increases of 34 percent and 62.5 percent of tropical forests, respectively. In absolute terms these changes are large for grassland and tropical forests and reflect an increased conversion of grassland to cultivation and comparable preservation of forest relative to the baseline. The large percentage change for temperate forest and woodland relates to a relatively small change in physical area.

Value results by region and by biome are presented in Table 2.20, and Table 2.21 presents overall results for the two discount rates.

Table 2.20 Reduced deforestation: value results, by region and by biome relative to 2030 baseline

	Change in area (000 km^2)	Mean per ha value[a] (US$2007)	Annual value (bn US$2007)
Grassland			
OECD	–25.9	536.6	–1.1
Central and South America	–360.6	217.4	–5.6
Middle East and North Africa	13.8	275.2	0.3
SSA	–1,481.2	53.2	–9.1
Russia and Central Asia	154.7	295.6	3.8
South Asia	14.6	120.5	0.1
China Region	155.2	188.3	1.8
Total[b]	–1,529.4		–9.8
Temperate forest			
OECD	226.2	20,081.6	36.3
Central and South America	53.0	16,612.6	16.7
Middle East and North Africa	–1.4	15,695.4	–0.5
SSA	87.8	9,426.7	7.9
Russia and Central Asia	66.8	17,210.1	6.6
South Asia	–13.8	9,202.2	–2.7
China Region	28.0	15,152.3	3.9
Total	446.6		68.3
Tropical forest			
OECD	24.8	9,781.3	8.6
Central and South America	567.5	7,955.8	57.1
Middle East and North Africa			
SSA	1,571.9	3,991.8	62.1
Russia and Central Asia			
South Asia	–23.8	7,131.7	–3.6
China Region	1.1	8,057.2	0.2
Total	2,141.5		124.3

Notes:
[a] Mean per ha values are the average of 2030 baseline and 2030 policy option scenario per ha values.
[b] Total value changes are the sum of individual patch values and are not calculated from regional mean per ha values.

The undiscounted annual benefit in 2030 (US$182.8 billion) is the figure for the *year* 2030, i.e. the end of the study period 2000–2050. We assume a linear trajectory of benefits from 2000 to 2030. This is represented in Figure 2.9.

The overall results show strongly positive net benefits for the reduced deforestation/REDD option. "Central and South America" benefits significantly, as does "SSA." Considerable benefits are also observed for the "OECD" region. The loss in forest area observed in the "South Asia" region (and, to a lesser extent, "Middle East and North Africa") arises due to losses of woodlands of lower density that are not protected by the policy option.

We set out the benefit/cost results for reduced deforestation in Table 2.22. A worst-case scenario (applying the upper estimate for costs and excluding additional carbon storage benefits) realizes a BCR of 3.2 at a 5 percent discount rate. With the value of carbon added and the lower cost estimate,

Table 2.21 Annual and discounted aggregated regional benefits of REDD option

	2030 undiscounted annual benefit	2000–2030 discounted total benefit	
		3%	5%
OECD	43.8	381.1	268.7
Central and South America	68.1	592.7	417.9
Middle East and North Africa	–0.2	–1.6	–1.1
SSA	60.9	529.4	373.3
Russia and Central Asia	10.4	90.4	63.7
South Asia	–6.1	–53.4	–37.7
China Region	5.9	51.7	36.5
Total	182.8	1,590.4	1,121.3

the BCR is a very high value (as much as 31.3 at a 3 percent discount rate and 27.8 at a 5 percent discount rate). These values do not account for changes in the opportunity cost of agricultural land.

Given the overall confidence in the results, including the assessment of marginality, there is an unequivocally strong case for supporting the reduced deforestation option as economically efficient on a global basis.

Table 2.22 Overall BCRs for REDD

		Discount rate	
		3%	5%
Benefits of change in biome areas (bn US$2007)		1,590	1,121
Carbon values (bn US$2007)			
	POLES	3,522	2,408
	Rice – Mean	1,866	1,369
Costs (bn US$2007)			
	Lower	163	127
	Upper	441	346
BCRs			
No carbon value	Lower	9.8	8.8
	Upper	3.6	3.2
Carbon value based on MAC (POLES)	Lower	31.3	27.8
	Upper	11.6	10.2
Carbon Value based on MD (Rice-Mean)	Lower	21.2	19.6
	Upper	7.8	7.2

Conclusion

This chapter has analyzed the challenge of ecosystems and biodiversity. Under BAU, there will be a significant loss of biodiversity over the next forty years: our estimates indicate that globally it could

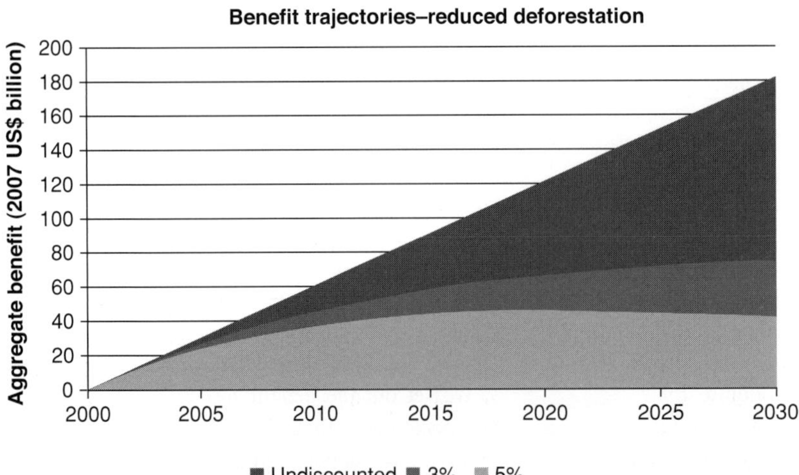

Figure 2.9 *Linear benefit trajectory for reduced deforestation: undiscounted and discounted benefit estimates over the study period, 2000–2030*

be around 12 percent, with South Asia facing a loss of around 30 percent and SSA 18 percent. These losses have a significant value, based on the services that the different biomes provide. These include timber and other forest products, genetic materials, recreational and cultural uses of the biomes, non-use values, and carbon values. They have been estimated in monetary terms in a number of studies for the three main biomes (temperate and tropical forests, and grasslands), using a meta-analysis linking the unit values of the services in each biome to the characteristics of the particular patch of biome over which the estimates were made. From this meta-analysis we derive figures for the losses that will occur when any patch of the same biome is lost. This approach is applied to all biomes and ESSs except for carbon values, which are based on a review of the literature. For the carbon values a range is taken, with the lower bound based on marginal damage studies and an upper bound based on the marginal costs of abatement arising from a target of a 50 percent global reduction in emissions by 2050.

The chapter looked at three interventions relative to BAU. The first was an increase in agricultural productivity (20 percent for crops and 40 percent for livestock), which reduces pressure on land. The BCRs for this program were very favorable: with a total cost over the period 2000–2050 of US$373 billion at a 3 percent discount rate the non-carbon benefits alone were well in excess of that. If we take the carbon benefits valued using the MD (the lower of the two unit values) the BCR goes to 7.5 at a 3 percent discount rate and around 6 at a discount rate of 5 percent. Hence we would argue that there is a strong case for such a program.

The second program was to increase the amount of protected areas globally to around 20 percent of all land across a large number of ecological regions. Currently such areas account for around 10 percent of all land. There are obvious benefits from this but there are also significant costs, principally the loss of output from the land taken out of use. The net benefits are very much dependent on what cost estimates are taken as valid. With these figures set at the best guess, the program was just beneficial with the lower of the carbon values. If, however, the costs were at the upper end, the program did not have a BCR of more than 1, even with higher carbon values. This suggests that only a selective increase in protected areas is warranted – in situations where the opportunity costs are low and the ESSs gained are high.

A further comment about protected areas is warranted. The main reason for these programs is really to enhance biodiversity conservation and our methods of estimation do not fully capture those benefits. Hence the assessment made here underestimates the benefits of such policies.

The final program was one that sought to prevent all dense forests from conversion. In this case the benefits are very high, and while there is considerable uncertainty about the costs (the upper bound is more than four times the lower bound) the BCR exceeds 1 even with the higher-cost figures and without the carbon values. When the carbon values were included the BCR went well above 1, indicating that such a program would be very attractive.

The Challenge specifies that the amount available is around US$75 billion p.a. for four years. The amounts involved in these programs are in excess of that figure but these are spread out over a longer period as well: over fifty years in the case of the first intervention and over thirty years in the case of protected areas and reduced deforestation. The detailed analysis did not indicate that there was any notable non-linearity in the programs; in other words the BCRs should not be significantly different if the programs were conducted at a fraction of the scale considered here. In fact, one could argue that a smaller program could have a higher BCR if one could pick out the areas where it was applied so as to keep the costs lower and the benefits higher. This should certainly be possible in the case of the reduced deforestation option, although perhaps less so for the increasing agricultural productivity option. In any event these two options could easily share the budget of US$75 billion over four years (possibly spending it over a longer period) and generate benefits that would result in BCRs similar to the ones reported here. One caveat we have added is that these programs cannot be readily aggregated. Consequently there is likely to be significant double counting if the programs are combined, i.e. changes in land cover for any one patch may apply over more than one program – e.g. any given patch of forest might not be converted to pasture under high AKST and would not be converted to another use under reduced deforestation.

One final remark about the methodology that merits consideration is the fact that it is based on a partial equilibrium analysis. That is to say, changes in biomes are valued on the assumption that the amounts involved are small compared to the total size of the biome and the services it provides. If that assumption is not valid then the estimates of changes will be flawed to the extent that other prices, as well as the unit values of the services themselves, may change. We have been at pains to note that the size of the change in biomes and services is relatively small but that is a matter of judgment and in one or two cases the proposed measures may be considered as possibly non-marginal. In that case there may have been an overestimate of the benefits.

Appendix: databases of biome-level primary valuation studies

In this section we outline the data collection and development of biome-level primary valuation studies. We summarize the data sources used to develop the benefit databases for each biome and provide a commentary on the respective valuation databases subsequently used in the value functions.

Benefit database development

The valuation studies used for the benefit transfer were identified from the TEEB valuation database (van der Ploeg *et al.*, 2010) developed at Wageningen (forest and grassland biomes). The TEEB database contains 1,298 individual entries across fourteen biomes with temperate and tropical forests accounting for 105 (8 percent) and 260 (20 percent) of values, respectively. Woodlands studies account for 3 percent of the studies in the database, and grasslands are just under 5 percent of the studies. Several entries may arise from a single study, as each entry represents the values for a specific ESS.

The major task in our database development was to undertake a thorough review of the biome values obtained from the TEEB database so as to determine the suitability of the values for their inclusion. The site coordinates listed in the TEEB database were also checked prior to the calculation of site-specific spatial data for use in the value function estimation.

Following completion of the review a number of studies in each biome were considered unsuitable for inclusion in our database. The primary reason for rejection was that the values contained in a study were themselves derived through benefit transfer; only primary valuation estimates are included. Benefit transfer commonly occurred where an existing study was used to provide values for specific ESSs, e.g. bio-prospecting, or where global or regional values were downscaled to a specific country or site. Other reasons for rejection include the value being for an entire country rather than an identifiable site, or there being insufficient information to identify the site size or the benefitting population. In some cases additional values were found – for example, where the published paper aggregated a number of individual site values or where additional values were stated in the paper.

Some additional analysis was undertaken on the selected values – conversion of all values to the common unit of value, viz. 2007 US$/ha/p.a. The data used for the currency conversions and deflations were obtained from the World Bank's World Development Indicators dataset (World Bank, 2010). These calculations involved first estimating the year of study value per ha p.a. in local currency units (if reported in another currency such as US$ these were converted to local units using the appropriate PPP exchange rate). Values given in perpetuity or over a specific time period were converted into PV terms using the discount rates quoted in the study (if none was quoted an appropriate local discount rate was identified through an online search). If values were given in per household terms then these would be aggregated using relevant local, regional, or national household estimates[19] (studies were rejected if the relevant population over which to aggregate could not be

[19] Estimates were obtained for household numbers in Denmark, Finland, and Australia (Queensland) from national statistical agency online databases.

Table A2.1 ESS categories covered by temperate and tropical forest studies

	Temperate forest		Woodlands		Tropical forest	
ESS category		(%)		(%)		(%)
Provisioning services	8	14	10	63	43	42
Regulating services	11	19	1	6	32	31
Cultural services	28	48	2	13	22	21
Supporting services	10	17	2	13	4	4
Total economic value	1	2	1	6	2	2
Total	58		16		103	

identified). The aggregate values were then divided by site area. Finally, per ha values in local currency units were adjusted to 2007 values using appropriate national GDP deflators and then converted to US$ using the relevant PPP exchange rate.[20]

In addition to the variables contained in the studies themselves, we added a number of site-specific spatial variables from a range of bio-physical and socio-economic datasets to the dataset used in this study. These site-specific variables are used in value function estimation and also for the subsequent value transfer.

Forest biome database description

Following the review of the TEEB database, 58 temperate forest and 103 tropical forest values were selected for inclusion in our database. A further sixteen values were obtained for the woodlands biome; given this small number these sixteen studies were included with the temperate forest biome for value function development and transfer.[21] Table A2.1 summarizes the ESS categories represented by the values for temperate and tropical forest biomes. There is a clear difference between the biomes with a higher representation of provisioning and regulating services in the tropical forest biome. The main provisioning services considered are non-timber forest products (NTFP), particularly food resources, and the provision of raw materials. The regulating services cover a range of ESSs, including climate regulation, moderation of extreme events, regulating water flow, waste treatment, erosion prevention, and pollination. The wide range of services included in the tropical biome studies is due primarily to the nature of those studies which deliberately set out to estimate values for all ESSs provided. By contrast, nearly half of the temperate forest biome values relate to cultural services, specifically recreation.

We can speculate that the reason for these differences between studies for the forest biomes is that in temperate regions "natural" forests have been more fully exploited. The motivation for a primary valuation study is often the potential conversion from forest to other land uses (e.g. agriculture). Tropical forests are relatively underexploited (at least in respect of our study sites) and thus more complete information on service provision is needed to balance trade-offs in land use decisions. The other major difference between service coverage between the biomes is that there is a higher proportion of studies (17 percent versus 4 percent) relating to supporting services in the temperate forest studies; these all relate to gene pool protection, i.e. an approximate proxy for biodiversity conservation. Regulating service values make up a fifth of the

[20] The reason for converting a reported US$ estimate to local currency using the appropriate PPP exchange rate and then back to 2007 US$ was so as to track changes in the local currency, which is arguably more methodologically defensible for values elicited from local residents. Those studies that elicited values from foreign visitors were not subject to this two-stage conversion.

[21] We refer in this section and throughout this report to two forest biomes: (1) temperate forests and woodland and (2) tropical forests. However Table A2.1 and Table A2.2 provide the disaggregated analysis for completeness, i.e. temperate forests and presented separately to woodlands.

Table A2.2 Valuation methods used by forest biome

Valuation method	Temperate forest	(%)	Woodland	(%)	Tropical forest	(%)
Contingent valuation	32	55	2	13	10	10
Contingent ranking	3	5	0	0	0	0
Choice experiment	0	0	1	6	2	2
Group valuation	0	0	0	0	1	1
Hedonic pricing	0	0	0	0	0	0
Travel cost	1	2	0	0	8	8
Replacement cost	1	2	2	13	1	1
Factor income/Production function	2	3	0	0	24	23
Market price	11	19	11	69	41	40
Opportunity cost	0	0	0	0	0	0
Avoided cost	7	12	0	0	15	15
Other/unknown	1	2	0	0	1	1
Total	58		16		103	

Figure A2.1 *Forest biome site locations and services*

temperate forest values; however the coverage is less even across ESSs when compared to tropical forest values.

Table A2.2 summarizes the valuation methods used in the studies and distribution of valuation methods used between the two forest biomes reflects the categories of ESSs that the studies cover (an introductory explanation of valuation methods is provided in Pascual *et al.*, 2010). Contingent valuation was used in over half of the temperate forest studies, reflecting the dominance of recreational values collected. By contrast, 40 percent of the tropical forest values were collected using market values – for example, for NTFP these would reflect either the market values of selling those products or the market cost of substitutes; 23 percent of tropical forest values reflect production function or factor income values for regulating services. The locations of the study sites for each of the forest and woodland biomes are illustrated in Figure A2.1 (note that multiple values may have been obtained for individual sites).

Table A2.3 ESS categories valued in grassland studies

ESS	No. of observations	%
Food provisioning	6	32
Recreation and amenity	7	37
Erosion prevention	3	16
Conservation	3	16

Grassland biome database description

We collected and reviewed twenty-seven studies that estimate values for ESSs from grasslands. Of these studies, there are eleven that provide both original value estimates (not benefit transfers) and complete information on all the explanatory variables that we include in the estimated value function. From the eleven selected studies we are able to code nineteen separate value observations. We therefore obtain multiple value observations from single studies, with an average of 1.7 observations per study. Separate value observations from a study were included if they represented different study sites or ESSs.

The studies included in our analysis were published between the years 1995 and 2010. The locations of study sites included in the database are largely in Northern Europe, with studies in the Netherlands, United Kingdom, Sweden, and Germany. We include one study from North America (Colorado, United States), two from Africa (South Africa and Botswana), and two from Asia (Israel and the Philippines). We have no information on the value of ESSs from grasslands in South America. A summary of ESS provision across these selected studies is provided in Table A2.3.

Table A2.4 provides a synopsis of the valuation methods used to estimate ESS values for grasslands. We find that the most commonly employed method is to estimate replacement costs for lost ESSs – food provisioning and erosion prevention. The contingent valuation and choice of experiment methods have been used to value recreational uses of grasslands and wildlife conservation, the hedonic pricing method to estimate the amenity value of grasslands, and the net factor income method and market prices have been used to value food provisioning.

Table A2.4 Valuation methods used in grasslands studies

Valuation method	No. of observations	%
Contingent valuation	5	26
Choice experiment	2	11
Hedonic pricing	1	5
Net factor income	1	5
Replacement cost	6	32
Market prices	4	22

Bibliography

Alkemade, R., M. van Oorschot, L. Miles, C. Nellemann, M. Bakkenes, and B. ten Brink, 2009: GLOBIO3: a framework to investigate options for reducing global terrestrial biodiversity loss, *Ecosystems* **12**, 374

Alvarez, R. and S. Grigera, 2005: Analysis of soil fertility and management effects on yields of wheat and corn in the rolling Pampa of Argentina, *Journal of Agronomy and Crop Science* **191**, 321–9

Angelsen, A., S. Brown, C. Loisel, L. Peskett, C. Streck, and D. Zarin, 2009: Reducing emissions from deforestation and forest degradation (REDD): an options assessment report, Meridian Institute, Washington, DC

Bai, Z. G., D. L. Dent, L. Olsson, and M. E. Schaepman, 2008: *Global Assessment of Land Degradation and Improvement 1: Identification by Remote Sensing*, Report **2008/01**, FAO/ISRIC, Rome and Wageningen

Bakkes, J. A., P. R. Bosch, A. F. E. Bouwman, M. G. J. den Elzen, P. H. M. Janssen, M. Isaac, K. Klein Goldewijk, T. Kram, F. A. A. M. de Leeuw, J. G. J. Olivier, M. M. P. van Oorschot, E. E. Stehfest, D. P. van Vuuren, P Bagnoli, J. Chateau, J. Corfee-Morlot, and Y. G. Kim, 2008: *Background Report to the OECD Environmental Outlook to 2030: Overviews, Details, and Methodology of Model-based Analysis*, PBL Report **500113001/2008**, Bilthoven

Balmford, A., K. J. Gaston, S. Blyth, A. James, and V. Kapos, 2003: Global variation in terrestrial conservation costs, conservation benefits, and unmet conservation needs, *Proceedings of the National Academy of Sciences of the United States of America* **100**, 1046–50

Barreto, P., P. Amaral, E. Vidal, and C. Uhl, 1998: Costs and benefits of forest management for timber production in eastern Amazonia, *Forest Ecology and Management* **108**, 9–26

Barrio, M. and M. L. Loureiro, 2010: A meta-analysis of contingent valuation forest studies, *Ecological Economics* **69**, 1023–30

Bateman, I. J. and A. P. Jones, 2003: Contrasting conventional with multi-level modelling approaches to meta-analysis: expectation consistency in UK woodland recreation values, *Land Economics*, **79**, 235–58

Bello, W., 2009: *The Food Wars*, Verso, London

Blaser, J. and C. Robledo, 2007: *Initial Analysis on the Mitigation Potential in the Forestry Sector*, Report Prepared for the UNFCCC Secretariat, New York

Boucher, D., 2008: *What REDD Can Do: The Economics and Development of Reducing Emissions from Deforestation and Forest Degradation*, World Bank, Washington, DC

Brander, L. M., J. G. M. Florax, and J. E. Vermaat, 2006: The empirics of wetland valuation: a comprehensive summary and meta-analysis of the literature, *Environmental and Resource Economics*, **33**, 223–50

Brander, L. M., I. Brauer, H. Gerdes, A. Ghermandi, O. Kuik, A. Markandya, S. Navrud, P. A. L. D. Nunes, M. Schaafsma, H. Vos, and A. Wagtendonk, 2011: Using meta-analysis and GIS for value transfer and scaling up: valuing climate change induced losses of European wetlands, *Environmental and Resource Economics* **52**, 395–413, **DOI: 10.1007/s10640–011-9535–1**

Brock, W. A. and A. Xepapadeas, 2003: Valuing biodiversity from an economic perspective: a unified economic, ecological, and genetic approach, *The American Economic Review* **93**, 1597–1614

Brunckhorst, D., 2000: *Bioregional Planning: Resource Management Beyond the New Millennium*, Harwood Academic, Sydney

Bruner, A. and R. Naidoo, 2007: Review on the economics of biodiversity loss: scoping the science: review of the costs of conservation, European Commission, **ENV/070307/2007/ 486089/ETU/B2**, Brussels

Bruner, A., R. Gullison, and A. Balmford, 2004: Financial costs and shortfalls of managing and expanding protected-area systems in developing countries, *BioScience* **54**, 119–26

Bruner, A., R. Naidoo, and A. Balmford, 2008: Review on the economics of biodiversity loss: scoping the science. Review of the costs of conservation and priorities for action, European Commission, **ENV/070307/2007/486089/ ETU/B2**

Brussaard, L., P. Caron, B. Campbell, L. Lipper, S. Mainka, R. Rabbinge, D. Babin, and M. Pulleman, 2010: Reconciling biodiversity conservation and food security: scientific challenges for a new agriculture, *Current Opinion in Environmental Sustainability* **2** 34–42

Carret, J. C. and D. Loyer, 2003: *Comment financer durablement les aires protégées à Madagascar?* Agence Française de Dévelopement (AFD) *Notes et Etudes* **3**, Paris

Chomitz, K., 2006: *At Loggerheads?: Agricultural Expansion, Poverty Reduction, and Environment in the Tropical Forests*, World Bank, Washington, DC

Coad, L., N. Burgess, L. Fish, C. Ravilious, C. Corrigan, H. Pavese, A. Granziera, and C. Besançon, 2009a: *Progress on the Convention on Biological Diversity Terrestrial 2010 and Marine 2012 Targets for Protected Area Coverage, WWF Reports*, Washington, DC

Coad, L., N. D. Burgess, C. Loucks, L. Fish, J. P. W. Scharlemann, L. B. Duarte, and C. Besançon, 2009b: *The Ecological Representativeness of the Global Protected Areas Estate in 2009: Progress towards the CBD 2010 Target*, UNEP–WCMC, WWFUS and ECI, University of Oxford

Criqui, P., S. Mima, and L. Viguier, 1999: Marginal abatement costs of CO_2 emission reductions, geographical flexibility and concrete ceilings: an assessment using the POLES model, *Energy Policy* **27**, 585–601

Dixon J., A. Gulliver, D. Gibbon, 2001: Farming systems and poverty: improving farmers' livelihoods in a changing world, FAO and World Bank, Rome and Washington, DC

Dreyfus, F., C. Plencovich, and M. Petit (eds.), 2009: Historical analysis of the effectiveness of AKST systems in promoting innovation, in B. D. McIntyre, H. R. Herren, J. Wakhungu, and R. T. Watson (eds), *Agriculture at Crossroads: International Assessment for Agricultural*

Knowledge, Science and Technology, Island Press, Washington, DC
Easterly, W., 2001: *The Elusive Quest for Growth: Economists' Adventures and Misadventures in the Tropics*, MIT Press, Cambridge, MA
Eliash, J., 2008: *Climate Change: Financing Global Forests*, UK Treasury, London, Crown Copyright 2008
Evenson, R. E. and D. Gollin, 2003: Assessing the impact of the green revolution, 1960 to 2000, *Science* **300**, 758–62
Faith, D. P. and P. A. Walker, 1996: Integrating conservation and development: effective trade-offs between biodiversity and cost in the selection of protected areas, *Biodiversity and Conservation* **5**, 431–46
FAO, 2001: Global forest resources assessment 2000: main report, FAO Forestry Paper **140**, FAO, Rome
2006: *Livestock's Long Shadow: Environmental Issues and Options*, FAO, Rome
Ferraro, P. J., 2002: The local costs of establishing protected areas in low-income nations: Ranomafana National Park, Madagascar, *Ecological Economics* **43**, 261–75
Fischer, R., D. Byerlee, and G. O. Edmeades, 2009: *Can Technology Deliver on the Yield Challenge to 2050*?, FAO, Expert Meeting on How to Feed the World in 2050, FAO, Rome
Galindo, J. *et al.*, 2005: Análisis de Necesidades de Financiamiento del Sistema Nacional de Áreas Protegidas (SNAP) del Ecuador, *Mentefactura*, Quito
Gallagher, E., 2008: *The Gallagher Review: The Indirect Effects of Biofuels Production*, Renewable Fuels Agency, Report to the UK Secretary of State for Transport, London
Goklany, I. M., 1998: Saving habitat and conserving biodiversity on a crowded planet, *Bioscience* **48**, 941–53
Gomez, K., 2009: *Co-benefits of Collateral Damage? The Potential Impacts on the Wellbeing of Forest-dependent People under Different Shades of REDD*, Center for Environmental, Policy and Development, School of Oriental and African Studies (SOAS), Research Reports, SOAS, London
Grieg-Gran, M., 2006: *The Cost of Avoiding Deforestation: Report Prepared for the Stern Review of the Economics of Climate Change*, International Institute for Environment and Development, London
2008: *The Cost of Avoiding Deforestation: Update of the Report Prepared for the Stern Review of the Economics of Climate Change*, International Institute for Environment and Development, London
Haines-Young, R. and M. Potschin, 2010: The links between biodiversity, ecosystem services and human well-being, in D. Raffaelli and C. Frid (eds.), *Ecosystem Ecology: A New Synthesis*, Cambridge University Press
Harris, J. M., 1996: World agricultural futures: regional sustainability and ecological limits, *Ecological Economics* **17**, 95–115
Houghton, J., 2009: *Global Warming*, Cambridge University Press
Hussain, S. S., A. Winrow-Giffin, D. Moran, L. A. Robinson, A. Fofana, O. A. L. Paramor, and C. L. J. Frid, 2010: An ex ante ecological economic assessment of the benefits arising from marine protected areas designation in the UK, *Ecological Economics* **69**, 828–38
Hussain, S. S., A. McVittie, L. Brander, O. Vardakoulias, A. Wagtendonk, P. Verburg, R. Tinch, A. Fofana, C. Baulcomb, and L. Mathieu 2011: *The Economics of Ecosystems and Biodiversity: The Quantitative Assessment*, Draft Final Report to UNDEP, New York
IAASTD, 2009: Agriculture at a crossroads: global report, B. D. McIntyre, H. R. Herren, J. Wakhungu, and R. T. Watson (eds.), *International Assessment of Agricultural Knowledge, Science and Technology for Development*, Island Press, Washington, DC
IPCC, 2007: *Mitigation*, IPCC, Geneva
van Ittersum, M., P. A. Leffelaar, H. van Keulen, M. J. Kropff, L. Bastiaans, and J. Goudriaan, 2003: On approaches and applications of the Wageningen crop models, *European Journal of Agronomy* **18**, 201–34
James, A., K. Gaston, and A. Balmford, 1999: Balancing the Earth's accounts, *Nature* **401**, 323–4
2001: Can we afford to conserve biodiversity?, *BioScienceBioscience*, **51**, 43–52
Karousakis, K., 2009: Promoting biodiversity co-benefits in REDD, *OECD Environment Working Papers* **11**, OECD, Paris
Keating, B., P. Carberry, P. Bindraban, S. Asseng, H. Meinke, and J. Dixon, 2010: Eco-efficient agriculture: concepts, challenges, and opportunities, *Crop Science* **50**, S-1–S-11

Kindermann *et al.*, 2008: Global cost estimates of reducing carbon emissions through avoided deforestation, *Proceedings of the National Academy of Sciences* **105**, 10302–7

Kitayama, K., 2008: Risks and co-benefits of biodiversity conservation in REDD, Meeting of the ad-hoc technical expert group on biodiversity and climate change, Convention on Biological Diversity (CBD), London

Lambin, E., B. L. Turner, H. J. Geist, S. B. Agbola, A. Angelsen, J. W. Bruce, O. Coomes, R. Dirzo, G. Fischer, C, Folke, P. George, K. Homewood, J. Imbernon, R. Leemans, X. Li, E. F. Moran, M. Mortimore, P. S. Ramakrishnan, J. F. Richards, H. Skanes, W. Steffen, G. D. Stone, U. Svedin, T. A. Veldkamp, C. Vogel, and J. Xu, 2001: The causes of land-use and land-cover change: moving beyond the myths, *Journal of Global Environmental Change* **11**, 261–9

Letourneau, A., 2010: MSc student at Wageningen University, personal communication

Lewandrowski, J., R. F. Darwin, M. Tsigas, and A. Raneses, 1999: Estimating costs of protecting global ecosystem diversity, *Ecological Economics* **29**, 111–25

Lindhjem, H. and S. Navrud, 2008: How reliable are meta-analyses for international benefit transfers?, *Ecological Economics* **66**, 425–35

Mace, G. M., J. L. Gittleman, and A. Purvis, 2003: Preserving the tree of life, *Science* **300**, 1707–9

Matson, P. A. and P. M. Vitousek, 2006: Agricultural intensification: will land spared from farming be land spared for nature?, *Journal of Conservation Biology* **20**, 709–10

Matson, P. A., W. J. Parton, A. G. Power, and M. J. Swift, 1997: Agricultural intensification and ecosystem properties, *Science* **277**, 504–9

McCann, K. S., 2000: The diversity–stability debate, *Nature* **405**, 228–33

McIntyre, B. D., H. R. Herren, J. Wakhungu, and R. T. Watson (eds.), 2009: *Agriculture at a crossroads: International assessment for agricultural knowledge, science and technology*, Island Press, Washington, DC

Millennium Ecosystem Assessment (MEA), 2005: *Ecosystems and Human Well-being: Current State and Trends*, Island Press, Washington, DC

Morris, M., V. A., Kelly, R. J. Kopicki, and D. Byerlee, 2007: *Fertilizer Use in African Agriculture: Lessons Learned and Good Practice Guide*, World Bank, Washington, DC

Morton, D. C., R. DeFries, and Y. E. Shimabukuro, 2006: Cropland expansion changes deforestation dynamics in the southern Brazilian Amazon, *Proceedings of the National Academy of Sciences USA* **103**, 14637–41

Naidoo, R. and T. Iwamura, 2007: Global-scale mapping of economic benefits from agricultural lands: implications for conservation priorities, *Biological Conservation* **140**, 40–9

Naidoo, R., A. Balmford, P.-G. Ferraro, S. Polasky, T. Ricketts, and M. Rouget, 2006: Integrating economic costs into conservation planning, *Trends in Ecology & Evolution* **21**, 681–7

Naidoo, R., A. Balmford, R. Costanza, B. Fisher, R. E. Green, B. Lehner, T. R. Malcolm, and T. H. Ricketts, 2008: Global mapping of ecosystem services and conservation priorities, *Proceedings of the National Academy of Science, USA* **105**, 9495–9500

Neumann, K., P. H. Verburg, H. Sethfest, E. and C. Muller, 2010: The yield gap of global grain production: a spatial analysis, *Agricultural Systems* **103**, 316–26

Nordhaus, W. D. and Z. Yang, 1996: A regional dynamic general-equilibrium model of alternative climate change strategies, *American Economic Review* **886**, 741–65

OECD, 2009: *OECD Environmental Outlook to 2030*, OECD, Paris

Olson, D. M., E. Dinerstein, E. D. Wikramanayake, N. D. Burgess, G. V. N. Powell, E. C. Underwood, J. A. D'Amico, I. Itoua, H. E. Strand, J. C. Morrison, C. J. Loucks, T. F. Allnutt, T. H. Ricketts, Y. Kura, J. F. Lamoreux, W. W. Wettengel, P. Hedao, and K. R. Kassem, 2001: Terrestrial ecoregions of the world: a new map of life on earth, *Bioscience* **51**, 933–8

Pagiola, S. and B. Bosquet, 2009: Estimating the costs of REDD at the country level, World Bank, *Working Papers*

Pardey, G., J. M. Alston, and R. Pigott (eds.), 2006: *Agricultural R&D in the Developing World: Too Little, too Late?*, International Food Policy Research Institute, Washington, DC

Pascual, U., R. Muradian, L. Brander, E. Gómez-Baggethun, B. Martín-López, and M. Verma, 2010: The economics of valuing ecosystem services and biodiversity, in *The Economics of Ecosystems and Biodiversity: The Ecological and Economic Foundations* (Chapter

5, TEEB Ecological and Economic Foundations Report), FSD and Wageningen University

PBL, 2010: *Rethinking Global Biodiversity Strategies: Exploring Structural Changes in Production and Consumption to Reduce Biodiversity Loss*, Netherlands Environmental ASSESSMENT Agency, www.pbl.nl/en/publications/2010/Rethinking_Global_Biodiversity_Strategies.html

Pearce, D., 2007: Do we really care about biodiversity?, *Environmental and Resource Economics* **37**(1), 313–33

van der Ploeg, S., Wang, Y., and de Groot, D., 2010: *The TEEB Valuation Database: An Introduction and Overview of Data and Results*, Final Report for TEEB D0 Report, FSD and Wageningen University

Purvis, A. and Hector, A., 2000: Getting the measure of biodiversity, *Nature* **405**, 212–19

Rist, G., 2001: *The History of Development: From Western Origins to Global Faith*, Zed Books London, 1st English edn., 1997

Rosegrant, M. W., M. Fernandez, and A. Sinha, 2009: Looking into the future for agriculture and AKST, in B. McIntyre, H. R. Herren, J. Wakhungu, and R. T. Watson (eds.), *Agriculture at a Crossroads: International Assessment for Agricultural Knowledge, Science and Technology* Island Press, Washington, DC

Ruiz, J. V., 2005: *Análisis de las Necesidades de Financiamiento del SINANPE 2005–2014*, PROFONANPE, Lima

sCBD, PBL, 2007: *Cross-roads of Life on Earth: Exploring Means to Meet the 2010 Biodiversity Target. Solution-oriented Scenarios for Global Biodiversity Outlook 2*, Secretariat of the Convention on Biological Diversity (sCBD), Montreal and the Netherlands Environmental Assessment Agency (PBL), Bilthoven

Schmidhuber, J., J. Bruinsma, and G. Boedeker, 2009: *Capital Requirements for Agriculture in Developing Countries to 2050*, FAO, Expert Meeting on How to Feed the World in 2050, FAO, Rome

Schneider, A., M. Friedl, and D. Potere, 2009: A new map of global urban extent from MODIS data, *Environmental Research Letters* **4**, article 044003

2010: Monitoring urban areas globally using MODIS 500m data: new methods and datasets based on "urban ecoregions," *Remote Sensing of Environment* **114**, 1733–46

Steinfeld, H., P. Gerber, T. Wassenaar, V. Castel, M. Rosales, and C. Haan, 2006: *Livestock's Long Shadow: Environmental Issues and Options*, FAO, Rome

Stern, N., 2007: *The Stern Review: The Economics of Climate Change*, Cambridge University Press

Strassburg, B., K. Turner, B. Fisher, R. Schaeffer, and A. Lovett, 2008: An empirically-derived mechanism of combined incentives to reduce emissions from deforestation, *CSERGE Working Paper*, ECM **08–01**, University of East Anglia, Norwich

TEEB, 2008: *An Interim Report*, Commission of the European Communities, Brussels

2010: *The Economics of Ecosystems and Biodiversity: Ecological and Economic Foundations*, P. Kumar (ed.), Earthscan, London and Washington, DC

Ten Brink, P. (ed.), 2011: *The Economics of Ecosystems and Biodiversity in National and International Policy Making*, Earthscan, London and Washington, DC

Tilman, D. and J. A. Downing, 1994: Biodiversity and stability in grasslands, *Nature* **367**, 363–5

UNEP, 2009: *The Environmental Food Crisis: The Environment's Role in Averting Future Food Crises*, UNEP, GRID-Arendal

Vitousek, P. M., H. A. Mooney, J. Lubchenco, and J. M. Melillo, 1997: Human domination of earth's ecosystems, *Science* **277**, 494–99

van der Ploeg, S., Y. Wang, and D. de Groot, 2010: *The TEEB Valuation Database: An Introduction and Overview of Data and Results*, TEEB Ecological and Economic Foundations Report, FSD and Wageningen University, Wageningen

van Vuuren, D. P. and A. Faber, 2009: *Growing within Limits. A Report to the Global Assembly 2009 of the Club of Rome*, Netherlands Environmental Agency, Bilthoven

World Bank, 2002: Costing the 7th Millennium Development Goal: ensure environmental sustainability, Environment Department and Development Economics Research Group. World Bank, Washington, DC (restricted)

2010: *World Development Indicators*, World Bank, Washington, DC, http://data.worldbank.org/data-catalog/world-development-indicators, accessed August 27, 2010

Ecosystems and Biodiversity

Alternative Perspective

JUHA V. SIIKAMÄKI

Introduction

Does investment in global ecosystem protection warrant its costs? This is the vital question Salman Hussain and his colleagues address in their Challenge Paper (Chapter 2) (Hussain *et al.*, 2012). The chapter focuses on examining the costs and benefits of three global policies: investing in increasing agricultural productivity, extending protected areas, and reducing deforestation. The assessment meticulously evaluates the three policy options, focusing especially on estimating their anticipated benefits. They are first measured in bio-physical units as improvements from the baseline (BAU) land cover and habitat condition (MSA). BAU is projected until 2050 under a set of future economic, demographic, and environmental conditions developed at the OECD. Ecological benefit estimates are then monetized using meta-analyzed ecosystem valuation results from a large number of primary studies from around the globe. Cost estimates are adopted from unrelated assessments, which examine roughly similar policy options to the ones evaluated in the Challenge Paper.

Benefits from ecosystem protection are typically highly heterogeneous spatially. The Challenge Paper addresses this by separately examining three different biomes – temperate forests and woodlands, tropical forests, and grasslands. Added spatial resolution is obtained from grid cell-level benefit estimations. Regional level summaries highlight global heterogeneity and also help understand the incidence of ecosystem degradation in the absence of added protections.

Summing up the estimated benefits and costs of the three global policy options examined, the authors find that investing in increasing agricultural productivity and reducing deforestation have substantial net benefit potential. The estimated BCRs depend heavily on the assumptions and fall between roughly 3 and 30 for reduced deforestation and between about 3 and 20 for agricultural productivity investments. So, according to the Challenge Paper, every dollar invested in reduced deforestation has the potential to return \$3–30 worth of benefits, while agricultural productivity investments could return roughly \$3–20 per each dollar put in.[1] Extending protected areas appears considerably less attractive. It barely reaches and often remains below the breakeven point, with estimated BCRs ranging between 0.2 and 1.4.

Brief assessment

Projecting environmental change far into the future in response to a large-scale policy intervention, let alone economically valuing it, is rife with difficulties and uncertainties. For example, despite considerable methodological progress over the last few decades, the economic valuation of environmental quality remains imperfect even when studying values in one particular location and under a set of known environmental conditions. Here, we need to draw results from primary valuation studies from many different countries, ecological systems, policy settings, and economic conditions to forecast future economic benefits outside the contexts of the original studies. Reflecting these and other uncertainties, the authors usefully consider a

[1] Agriculture is one of the main threats to biodiversity, so the net benefits from improved agricultural productivity probably should be scaled down because of the adverse ecological effects from agricultural intensification.

broad range of assumptions to determine reasonable upper and lower bounds for the benefit estimates. The Challenge Paper also makes a noteworthy contribution by conducting meta-analytic regressions to improve the transfer of the primary valuation results to a new setting. Regardless, huge methodological and empirical difficulties remain at the outset. This is not to criticize the Challenge Paper – it would be tremendously difficult to formulate alternative approaches to provide equally or more robust results – but to help evaluate its findings. Given these difficulties and uncertainties, the benefit-cost estimates in the chapter are probably best viewed as qualitative indicators comprising some quantitatively helpful information.

Regardless, the results are instructive. Developing roughly consistent assessments across different policy options, the Challenge Paper discovers that two of the policy options – agricultural productivity investments and reduced deforestation – are promising from an economic standpoint, whereas the third option – increased protected areas – has difficulty satisfying minimum economic criteria. This is extremely helpful information for ranking and more thoroughly evaluating the policy options examined.

More generally, the results from the Challenge Paper highlight several important aspects of ecosystem protection. First, investing in such protection can have substantial economic potential. Even though the economic importance of the ecosystems and their protection is now widely acknowledged and increasingly well understood, this basic finding derived from a meticulous and geographically broad assessment is powerful and informative. Second, not all potential investments in ecosystem protection pass the benefit-cost test. Therefore, thorough vetting of different policy alternatives is critically important to identify the best options for implementation. Third, estimating the benefits and costs of ecosystem protection is exceedingly feasible, though it involves substantial challenges and uncertainties. Because of the very nature of ecosystem protection, its benefits often are not transacted through markets, so they are difficult to pinpoint accurately. Moreover, complicated and poorly understood ecological processes and human-nature interactions underlie the production of ESSs, further complicating their valuation. Investing in research and data to better understand ESSs and their economic value may therefore be highly beneficial.

Before I go deeper into discussing a few complementary perspectives, it is important to commend the assessment by Hussain and his colleagues. Albeit facing an especially difficult task, the authors have been able to compile rigorous and systematic assessments of the benefits and costs of three important and often-debated policy options. The assessment also acknowledges and discusses some of the chief caveats and presents the main estimates as a range to reflect uncertainties. Moreover, the assessment arrives at meaningful and conceivable results. The research puzzle in the assessment involves so many challenging pieces that constructing a logical assessment at a global scale, as Hussain *et al.* (2012) present, is exceedingly difficult.

I next set aside the inescapable restrictions of the Challenge Paper. Environmental valuation is now so broadly conducted and methodologically assessed that it suffices to note that substantial difficulties and uncertainties remain in any assessment, especially in the context of long time horizons and a global geographic scale. Certainly, one might tweak some of the estimates, assumptions, and methodological approaches in the Challenge Paper, but doing so would be unlikely to dramatically alter the key results, such as the ranking of policy alternatives or overall benefit-cost judgments. Given the task at hand, the Challenge Paper provides an adequately rigorous, thorough, and critical assessment to help experts form informed opinions on whether investments in ecosystem protection are sensible in the context of many other demands for spending.

Overview

The rest of this Alternative Perspective discusses two complementary areas. The first area of discussion – coastal and marine ecosystems – highlights these vast and globally essential ecosystems which are outside the scope of Chapter 2 but include some of the most productive and threatened ecosystems world-wide. The second area of discussion, designing international forest conservation policies, recommends systematically targetting these policies to produce multiple benefits (avoided emissions, biodiversity). This likely will generate greater overall net gains than are feasible by focusing solely on avoided emissions.

Coastal and marine ecosystems

Coastal and marine ecosystems serve a wide range of ecological functions and provide people with many economically valuable products and services (Barbier *et al.*, 2008, 2011; Schipper *et al.*, 2008; Spalding *et al.*, 2010). The importance of coastal and marine ecosystems is heightened by the concentration of human populations near coasts. It is estimated that over half of the world's population lives within 120 miles (about 200 km) of the coast, and in some regions, such as Latin America and the Caribbean, the percentage of coastal populations is substantially higher (Hinrichsen, 1998; Lemay, 1998).

Status

Despite their ecological and economic importance, many coastal and marine ecosystems are degraded and their area has been substantially reduced (e.g. FAO, 2007; Spalding *et al.*, 2010). Coastal ecosystems are particularly vulnerable, and they are considered among the most threatened and rapidly disappearing natural environments world-wide (Valiela *et al.*, 2001). Even the recent increase in protected areas has not stemmed the gradual degradation and disappearance of coastal ecosystems world-wide (Lotze *et al.*, 2006; Halpern *et al.*, 2008; Spalding *et al.*, 2010; Siikamäki *et al.*, 2012).

Some of the ecologically most essential and economically valuable coastal ecosystems, such as mangroves, continue to experience exceedingly high loss rates, which in many areas are multiple times the global rate of tropical deforestation. For example, in the last three decades mangroves in the Americas have already lost about 40 percent of their range (Valiela *et al.*, 2001).

Coral reefs constitute yet another example of important but threatened ecosystems. Coral reefs are biodiversity hotspots, which feed economic benefits to fisheries, tourism, and other sectors. For example, the coral reef system alongside the Caribbean coasts of Belize, Guatemala, Honduras, and Mexico – the second-largest reef system world-wide – provides habitat for an estimated 10,000-plus species and plays a critical role in the broader regional environment. But coral reefs are also exceedingly vulnerable to damage by coastal development, sedimentation and other pollution, water acidification, fishing activities, and several other threats related to human activities. In the Caribbean, coral reefs have already lost almost one-third of their historical range, and it is estimated that another 20 percent or so will be lost in the absence of additional conservation measures over the next few decades (Sherman and Hempel, 2009). Moreover, the remaining corals are frequently degraded, with one study finding that the hard coral on reefs has been reduced from around 50 percent to 10 percent cover in the last three decades (Gardner *et al.*, 2003).

Fisheries

Coastal and marine ecosystems provide a broad range of economically important ESSs. I do not try to cover their full range here but instead highlight their economic importance by focusing on fisheries. Fisheries depend on coastal and marine habitats and provide an important source of food, employment, and income world-wide. Fish accounts for about 15 percent of the global population's intake of animal protein, and over half of this fish protein originates from capture fisheries (FAO, 2010). Fisheries also generate considerable commercial activity, ranging from large commercial operations that export internationally to small-scale and artisanal fisheries along the coasts throughout the world. Coastal populations, especially small-scale fishers, often depend heavily on fisheries for income and food, which also makes them susceptible to any adverse developments regarding available fish catch, such as fisheries stock collapses or otherwise reduced catches.

Coastal and marine fisheries throughout much of the world have developed according to roughly similar trends. Despite increases in fishing capacity, capture fisheries' production has plateaued or is already declining (FAO and World Fish Center, 2008). Global production peaked in 1996 and since then has declined slightly and fluctuated considerably.

Whereas about three decades ago, roughly 10 percent of the world's fish stocks were overexploited or depleted, today about one-third of them fall under this category (FAO, 2010). The proportion of underexploited or moderately exploited stocks has decreased from around 40 percent in the mid 1970s to 15 percent in 2008. When overexploited, harvests reduce the future productive potential of the fisheries and subject them to a potential collapse. Harvests in fully exploited fisheries, which currently comprise about half of the world's fish stocks, match the maximum sustainable production of the stock, without room to increase production or a buffer to allow for unexpected environmental conditions, such as relatively frequent but poorly understood weather patterns (for example, El Niño/La Niña).

Problems in the governance and management of the world's fisheries have substantially reduced the economic contribution of the fish harvest sector. The magnitude of these losses is hard to estimate, but a recent assessment puts them at roughly \$50 billion annually (World Bank, 2009). According to the same assessment, the cumulative losses due to unsustainable fisheries management in 1974–2008 amounted to over \$2 trillion. By improving the governance of fisheries, a portion of the lost economic benefits due to unsustainable management could be recovered.

Several factors have contributed to this natural resource management failure, including: (i) inappropriate economic incentives and subsidies that encourage overcapacity; (ii) high and growing demand for limited resources; (iii) poverty and lack of alternatives in coastal communities; (iv) fisheries' complexities, lack of knowledge, and the associated uncertainties; (v) lack of governance; (vi) interactions of the fisheries' sector with other sectors and their environmental impacts; and (vii) stock fluctuations due to natural causes (Swan and Gréboval, 2004; Salas *et al.*, 2011).

What is the cost of improved fisheries' management? While this is perhaps yet harder to estimate than the value of lost opportunities, it is safe to suggest that for many fisheries and in many parts of the world, even relatively moderate investments in improved governance and management could potentially generate considerable benefits, even assuming fairly high costs of designing and implementing fisheries' reforms. Simple solutions may not be available, however, and it is likely that the most cost-effective approaches would involve a combination of interventions, such as improving fisheries' property and management rights, adapting economically more efficient and sustainable governance systems (for example, catch-share systems), removing perverse subsidies encouraging overfishing and overcapacity, and improving systems for fisheries' science, planning, and monitoring. Focusing on just the few policy interventions with the greatest potential, such as fisheries' governance reform and improved information systems, could probably help recover significant amounts of the estimated \$50 billion annual losses due to unsustainable management.

Designing international forest conservation policies

One of the policy options examined in the Challenge Paper involves a program to reduce emissions from deforestation and degradation (REDD). My purpose next is to illustrate that benefits from REDD programs will crucially depend on whether they address the objective of carbon or biodiversity. I argue that while carbon-focused REDD programs will benefit biodiversity, it is possible to configure these programs to achieve considerably greater biodiversity benefits without a loss of emission reductions. The cost of a more biodiversity-focused REDD program will be greater, but jointly targeting biodiversity and GHG mitigation should be more cost-effective than addressing only one goal.

Considering both climate change and the loss of biodiversity in the context of REDD is also motivated by international agreements and political commitments declared at high-level international gatherings, including Kyoto, Rio de Janeiro, Copenhagen, Cancún, Nagoya, and others. These efforts have resulted in two separate international conventions, the UNFCCC and the CBD, both signed at the Earth Summit in Rio de Janeiro in 1992. The limited achievements as well as the many challenges faced by the UNFCCC are perhaps more widely known, although the CBD is equally or even more ambitious in its goals, seeking to halt biodiversity loss in the near term. However, it is widely acknowledged that the CBD has been unable to substantially slow the rate of biodiversity loss, so improvements are needed (Convention on Biological Diversity, 2010).

REDD programs

REDD programs have received considerable attention for their potential to provide low-cost options to mitigate global GHG emissions by engaging developing countries in some form of international climate policy architecture (Angelsen, 2008; Kindermann *et al.*, 2008b; Sohngen, 2009). Rather than adopt high-cost mitigation actions domestically, developed countries could finance developing countries to achieve similar but less costly emission reductions through reduced deforestation. REDD programs also have the potential to provide emission reductions in the near future, which is particularly important to achieving near-term emission reduction targets with politically acceptable economic costs.

More fundamentally to climate policy, reducing deforestation is central because it is among the chief contributors to global GHG emissions and a particularly pressing problem in the developing world (Gibbs *et al.*, 2007; IPCC, 2007; Angelsen, 2008). According to the most recent estimates, average annual emissions of carbon dioxide from deforestation and forest degradation are roughly 1.2 gigatons (Gt) of carbon, or about 4.4 Gt of carbon dioxide, which represents about 12 percent of total anthropogenic carbon emissions (van der Werf and Morton, 2009). Using another reference point, the estimated current annual emissions from deforestation are roughly equal to the emissions from all sources in the entire European Union in 2009 (UNFCCC, 2011). Moreover, deforestation has the potential to be yet more detrimental if efforts to stem forest losses are not successful. The world's forests store more carbon in biomass and soils than currently resides in the atmosphere (IPCC, 2007; Pan *et al.*, 2011). Much of this carbon pool is not covered by existing reduction targets or management frameworks.

From the perspective of biodiversity conservation, stemming deforestation is critical, because habitat loss is one of the main drivers of biodiversity loss, and the conversion of forests to agricultural uses is among the most detrimental kinds of land use change in its effects on biodiversity (Pereira *et al.*, 2010). The conversion of natural areas to agricultural, residential, and commercial uses reduces the habitat available to support species and populations. As natural habitats continue to disappear, the ranges of many species shrink and become fragmented. Both phenomena reduce species richness and abundance and eventually drive species to extinction when the remaining habitats are unable to support minimum viable populations.

Spatial variation of biodiversity losses and carbon dioxide emissions from deforestation

While any habitat protection will produce some benefits to biodiversity, biodiversity is highly spatially heterogeneous. When REDD focuses on avoiding carbon emissions, biodiversity will benefit in locations where REDD has the greatest economic potential to reduce emissions. As demonstrated below, these areas are generally not where the greatest biodiversity benefit potential exists. The geographic differences between the most attractive target areas of carbon and biodiversity-focused programs are relatively stark.

To help highlight the trade-offs between biodiversity and avoided emissions, Figure 2.1.1a–f shows global maps of aboveground forest carbon, mammal species richness, endemic species richness, potential agricultural revenue, deforestation rates, and opportunity cost of avoided emissions due to deforestation. These maps are drawn from a high-resolution (five-minute resolution, about

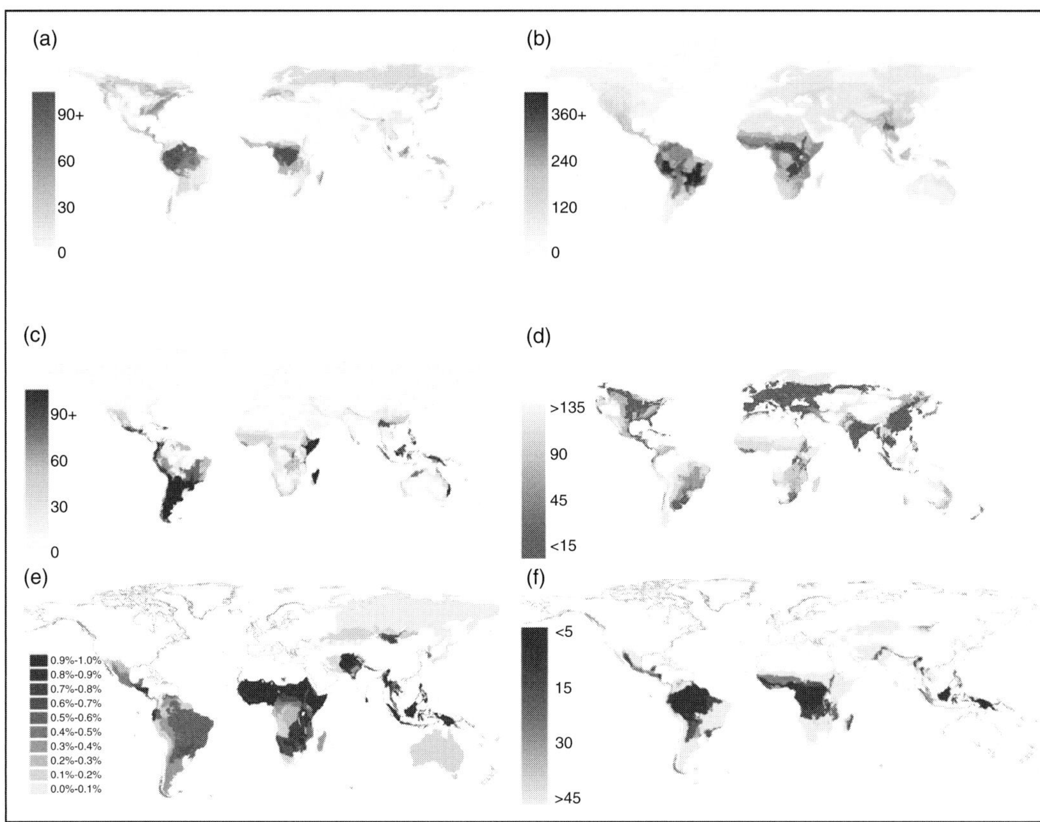

Figure 2.1.1 *Global maps of aboveground carbon, mammal species richness, endemic species richness, potential agricultural revenue, deforestation rates, and opportunity cost of avoided emissions. a. Tons of carbon ha^{-1}, on average per ecoregion. b. Total number of mammal species per ecoregion. c. Total number of endemic mammal, bird, amphibian, and reptile species per ecoregion. d. Potential agricultural revenue, US\$ ha^{-1}, on average per ecoregion. e. Deforestation rate, on average per ecoregion, annually. f. Estimated cost per ton of avoided emissions from deforestation, on average by ecoregion*

Source: Compiled using data from Siikamäki and Newbold (2012).

9 km × 9 km grid cells) global dataset compiled by Siikamäki and Newbold (2012). Forest carbon (Figure 2.1.1a) denotes the mass of aboveground carbon in the forest biomass (metric tons per ha), as estimated by Kindermann *et al.* (2008a). Biodiversity measures (Figure 2.1.1b–c) are compiled using global digitized maps of species ranges from the International Union for Conservation of Nature (IUCN, 2010) and information on endemic species from Olson *et al.* (2001). Annual potential agricultural revenue (Figure 2.1.1d) indicates the opportunity cost of conservation, as estimated using data from Naidoo and Iwamura (2007). Deforestation rates (Figure 2.1.1e) are estimated by ecoregion (Olson *et al.*, 2001) using data from the FAO's Global Forest Resource Assessment (FAO, 2005). The cost of avoided emissions (Figure 2.1.1f) is estimated by ecoregion using data on the opportunity cost of land and total annual emissions.

The geographic distribution of mammal species richness (Figure 2.1.1b) is markedly different from the amount of forest carbon (Figure 2.1.1a). Forest carbon is relatively high in the Amazon region, Central Africa, Indonesia, Malaysia, and Papua New Guinea, while mammal species richness is highest in northeast Colombia, Ecuador, Eastern

Africa, coastal regions in South East Asia, and mountain ranges around Mongolia and Tibet. Endemic species (Figure 2.1.1c) show similar patterns but are even more divergent from forest carbon, with several endemic species hotspots, such as the southern portion of the South American continent, situated in areas relatively low in forest carbon.

Figure 2.1.1e shows that the highest rates of deforestation occur in parts of Indonesia, Papua New Guinea, and several other parts of South East Asia. Several regions in South America, especially the Amazonas, parts of Bolivia, and Nicaragua, also have relatively high rates of deforestation. Central Africa, which is particularly rich in forest carbon, has a relatively low rate of deforestation.

The economically most attractive areas for REDD are shown in the darkest color in Figure 2.1.1f, which illustrates where the cost per ton of avoided emissions is lowest. Here, I focus only on non-Annex I countries (countries not committed to specific GHG reduction targets under the Nyote Protocol, including all developing countries), which are the prime targets of REDD. Overall, Figure 2.1.1f indicates that the Amazonas, much of the broader Central African region, and parts of South East Asia will be the most attractive to REDD programs that would focus on generating net revenue from carbon credits most cost-effectively.

Effectiveness of carbon-focused REDD in promoting biodiversity

Spatial correlations among the key variables that will influence the attractiveness of a region for REDD programs and biodiversity conservation are relatively weak. Although species richness in general tends to be high in areas both rich in carbon and subject to high deforestation, Siikamäki and Newbold (2012) find practically zero correlation between the opportunity cost per ton of emissions avoided (a key measure influencing the attractiveness of REDD investments) and species richness. This suggests that if REDD programs are targeted to deliver carbon emission reductions at the least possible cost, then these programs may not deliver particularly high biodiversity benefits. In fact, REDD programs that focus exclusively on carbon may not be more effective at protecting biodiversity than programs that randomly select forest parcels for protection.

The ecoregions targeted by two alternative forest conservation programs, carbon and species programs (Figure 2.1.2), confirm the above observation. The first program mimics a REDD-type policy focused on maximizing forest carbon emission reductions under a budget constraint. The second program is focused on biodiversity conservation and aims to maximize the number of endemic species protected under a budget constraint. For the available budget, these programs both consider spending about one-fifth of the estimated forgone agricultural net revenue from the total elimination of all deforestation in all non-Annex I countries. This budget is intended to illustrate the potential scope of the large-scale international policy proposals in the context of REDD, such as the proposals presented and rejected in the US Congress in 2008–2009.

Whereas the carbon-focused program (Figure 2.1.2a) concentrates in the Amazonas, Central Africa, Indonesia, and Papua New Guinea, the species-focused program (Fig. 2.1.2b) distributes conservation investments much more broadly, including a large number of ecoregions distributed across the world. The species program targets areas differently from the carbon program and thereby delivers more biodiversity benefits. But as a consequence, the species program also would generate less avoided carbon emissions. In the above example, the reduction in the carbon emissions from the species program is about 44 percent of that from the carbon program. On the other hand, the species program protects nearly six times the number of endemic species as does the carbon program.

Discussion

What are the implications of the above complementary perspectives in the context of the Challenge Paper and global biodiversity conservation more generally? First, expanding the scope beyond terrestrial systems is warranted. Coastal and marine ecosystems are rich in species, ecologically and economically essential, and face threats that are

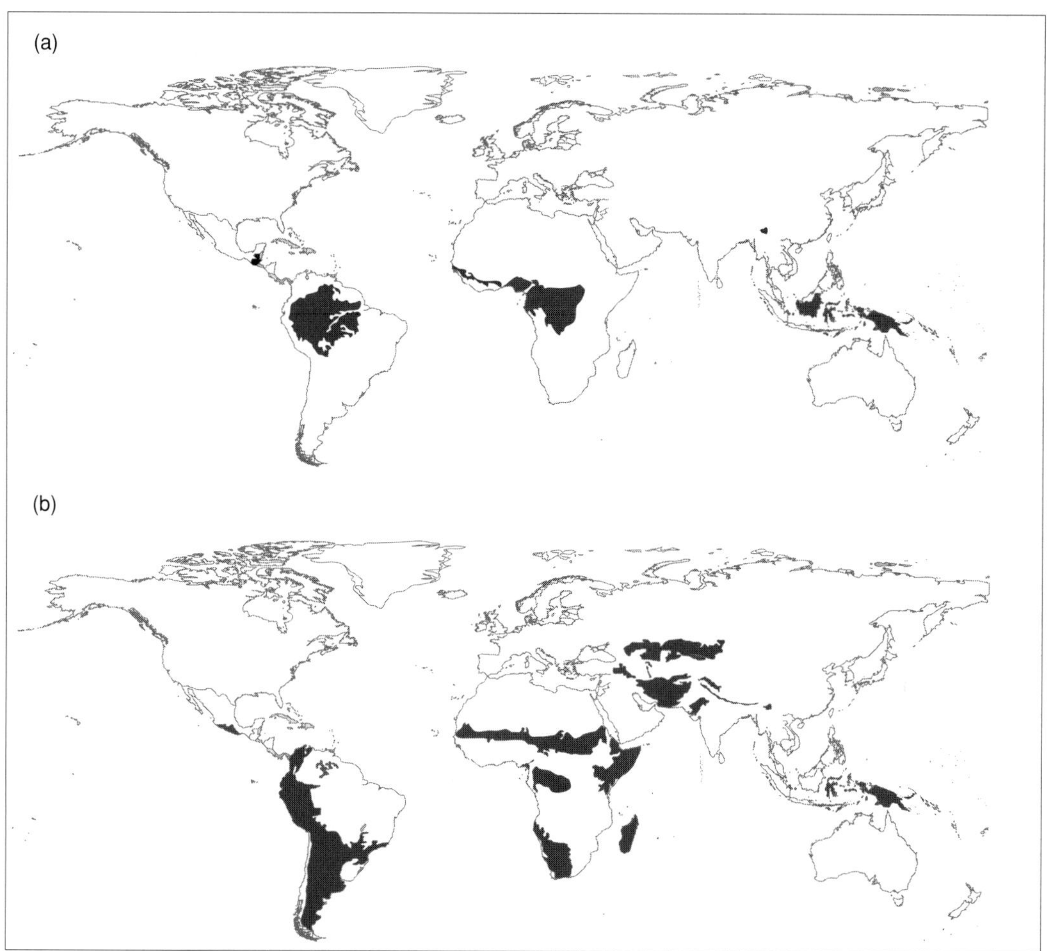

Figure 2.1.2 *Geographic targeting alternative forest conservation programs (ecoregions selected for conservation). (a) Program to generate REDD credits at the least cost per ton carbon. (b) Program to support species richness at the least cost per species*

Source: Compiled using data from Siikamäki and Newbold (2012).

similar in magnitude as threats facing the terrestrial systems, if not greater. Moreover, significant and potentially highly cost-effective policy options may be available in coastal and marine systems. However, pinpointing the most cost-effective options and their BCRs requires further assessments. Improved fisheries' management seems particularly attractive, because it could help protect biodiversity while also improving the economic productivity of the world's fisheries. Second, forest conservation policies have multiple benefits, such as avoided CO_2 emissions and biodiversity, so these policies should be designed and evaluated from the perspective of multiple objectives. This helps generate greater overall benefits per dollar invested in conservation. While the magnitude of potential gains from improved design is an empirical matter, the analysis discussed above suggests that REDD programs could produce substantially greater overall benefits if biodiversity and avoided emissions are considered joint objectives. A related point is that improved spatial targeting of conservation interventions in general can substantially increase their cost-effectiveness. Often, a small subset of all location candidates produces a vast majority of total potential benefits. A key challenge is to identify the most advantageous locations to target for conservation.

Bibliography

Angelsen, A., 2008: Moving ahead with REDD: issues, options and implications, CIFOR, Bogor

Barbier, E. B. *et al.*, 2008: Coastal ecosystem-based management with nonlinear ecological functions and values, *Science* **319**, 321–3

Barbier, E. B., S. D. Hacker, C. Kennedy, E. W. Koch, A. C. Stier, and B. R. Silliman, 2011: The value of estuarine and coastal ecosystem services, *Ecological Monographs* **81**, 169–93

Convention on Biological Diversity, 2010: COP 10 Decision X/2, Strategic Plan for Biodiversity 2011–2020

FAO, 2005: Global Forest Resources Assessment 2005: progress towards sustainable forest management, *FAO Forestry Paper* **147**, FAO, Rome

2007: *The World's Mangroves 1980–2005*, FAO Report, FAO, Rome

2010: *The State of World Fisheries and Aquaculture*, FAO, Rome

FAO and World Fish Center, 2008: Small-scale capture fisheries: a global overview with emphasis on developing countries, www.worldfishcenter.org/resource_centre/Big_Numbers_Project_Preliminary_Report.pdf

Gardner, T. A., I. M. Cote, J. A. Gill, A. Grant, and A. R. Watkinson, 2003: Long-term region-wide declines in Caribbean corals, *Science* **301**, 958–60

Gibbs, H. K., S. Brown, J. O. Niles, and J. A. Foley, 2007: Monitoring and estimating tropical forest carbon stocks: making REDD a reality, *Environmental Research Letters* **2**, 045023,

Halpern, B. S. *et al.*, 2008: A global map of human impacts on marine ecosystems, *Science* **319**, 948–52

Hinrichsen, D., 1998: *Coastal Waters of the World: Trends, Threats, and Strategies*, Island Press Washington, DC

Hussain, S., A. Markandya, L. Brander, A. McVittie, R. de Groot, O. Vardakoulias, A. Wagtendonk, and P. H. Verburg, 2012: *Ecosystems and Biodiversity*, 2012 Copenhagen Consensus Paper Chapter 2 in this volume

IPCC, 2007: *Climate Change 2007: The Physical Science Basis* (eds.) S. Solomon, D. Qin, M. Manning, Z. Chen, M. Marquis, K. B. Averyt, M. Tignor, and H. L. Miller, Intergovernmental Panel on Climate Change, Cambridge University Press

IUCN, 2010: *IUCN Red List of Threatened Species*, International Union for Conservation of Nature, www.iucnredlist.org/technical-documents/spatial-data, accessed October 12, 2009

Kindermann, G. E., I. McCallum, S. Fritz, and M. Obersteiner, 2008a: A global forest growing stock, biomass and carbon map based on FAO statistics, *Silva Fennica* **42**, 387–96

Kindermann, G. E., M. Obersteiner, B. Sohngen, J. Sathaye, K. Andrasko, E. Rametsteiner, B. Schlamadinger, S. Wunder, and R. Beach, 2008b: Global cost estimates of reducing carbon emissions through avoided deforestation, *Proceedings of the National Academy of Sciences* **105**, 10302–7

Lemay, M., 1998: *Coastal and Marine Resources Management in Latin America and the Caribbean*, Technical Study, I ADB, Washington, DC

Lotze, H. K. *et al.*, 2006: Depletion, degradation, and recovery potential of estuaries and coastal seas, *Science* **312**, 1806–9

Naidoo, R. and T. Iwamura, 2007: Global-scale mapping of economic benefits from agricultural lands: implications for conservation priorities, *Biological Conservation* **140**, 40–9

Olson, D. M., E. Dinerstein, E. D. Wikramanayake, N. D. Burgess, G. V. N. Powell, E. C. Underwood, J. A. D'Amico, I. Itoua *et al.*, 2001: Terrestrial ecoregions of the world: a new map of life on Earth, *BioScience* **51**, 933–8

Pan, Y., R. A. Birdsey, J. Fang, R. Houghton, P. E. Kauppi, W. E. Kurz, O. L. Phillips, A. Shvidenko *et al.*, 2011: A large and persistent carbon sink in the world's forests, *Science* **333**, 988–93

Pereira, H. M., P. W. Leadley, V. Proenca, R. Alkemade, J. P. W. Scharlemann, J. F. Fernandez-Manjarres, M. B. Araujo, P. Balvanera *et al.*, 2010: Scenarios for global biodiversity in the 21st century, *Science* **330**, 1496–1501

Salas, S., R. Chuenpagdee, A. Charles, and J. C. Seijo (eds.), 2011: Coastal fisheries of Latin America and the Caribbean region: issues and trends, in S. Salas, R. Chuenpagdee, A. Charles, and J. C. Seijo (eds.), *Coastal Fisheries of Latin America and the Caribbean*, FAO Fisheries and Aquaculture Technical Paper **544**, FAO, Rome, 1–12

Schipper, J., J. S. Chanson, F. Chiozza, N. A. Cox, M. Hoffman, V. Katariya, J. Lampourex, A. S. L. Rodrigues *et al.*, 2008: The status of the world's land and marine mammals: diversity, threat, and knowledge, *Science* **322**, 225–30

Sherman, K. and G. Hempel (eds.), 2009: The UNEP large marine ecosystem report: a perspective on changing conditions in LMES of the world's regional seas, *UNEP Regional Seas Report and Studies* **182**, UNEP, Nairobi

Siikamäki, J. and S. Newbold, 2012: Potential biodiversity benefits from international programs to reduce carbon emissions from deforestation, *Ambio* (Supplement 1), 78–89

Siikamäki, J., J. Sanchirico, S. Jardine, D. McLaughlin, and D. Morris, 2012: *Blue Carbon: Global Options for Reducing Emissions from the Degradation and Development of Coastal Ecosystems*, RFF Report, November

Sohngen, B., 2009: Assessing the economic potential for reducing deforestation in developing countries, in C. Palmer and S. Engel (eds.), *Avoided Deforestation: Prospects for Mitigating Climate Change*, Routledge, Taylor & Francis, Abingdon

Spalding, M., M. Kainuma, and L. Collins, 2010: *World Atlas of Mangroves*, Earthscan and James & James, London

Swan, J. and Gréboval, D., 2004: *Report and Documentation of the International Workshop on the Implementation of International Fisheries Instruments and Factors of Unsustainability and Overexploitation in Fisheries*, Mauritius, 3–7 February, 2003, *FAO Fisheries Report* **700**, FAO, Rome

UNFCCC, 2011: *Summary of GHG Emissions for European Union (27)*, United Nations Framework Convention on Climate Change, http://unfccc.int/files/ghg_data/ghg_data_unfccc/ghg_profiles/application/pdf/eu-27_ghg_profile.pdf, accessed September 8, 2011

Valiela, I., J. L. Bowen, and J. K. York, 2001: Mangrove forests: one of the world's threatened major tropical environments, *BioScience* **51**, 807–15

van der Werf, G. R., D. C. Morton *et al.*, 2009: CO_2 emissions from forest loss, *Nature Geoscience* **2**(11), 737–8

World Bank, 2009: *The Sunken Billions: The Economic Justification for Fisheries Reform*, I BRD World Bank, Washington, DC

Ecosystems and Biodiversity

Alternative Perspective

JOHN C. WHITEHEAD AND PAUL E. CHAMBERS

Introduction

This Alternative Perspective Paper reviews the Copenhagen Consensus 2012 Challenge Paper on Ecosystems and Biodiversity (Chapter 2) (Hussain *et al.*, 2012). The chapter addresses the benefits and costs of three programs: increasing agricultural productivity, increasing protected areas, and reducing deforestation. The major economic problem addressed by these policies is that biodiversity is a public good. Since its consumption is non-rival and non-excludable, households attempt to free-ride on the payments of others and market allocations result in too little protection of ecosystems and biodiversity. CBA can be used to identify government policies that would generate positive net benefits for ecosystems and biodiversity reallocation.

While net beneficial policies can be identified, there is a clear mismatch in the incidence of benefits and costs. Households in rich countries tend to benefit while the less rich countries that host the ecosystems and biodiversity tend to bear the costs. In this context, CBA should not be conducted in a vacuum and policies with appropriate management incentives should be considered when conducting the analysis. In the next section of this paper we describe some of these policies – e.g. an increased funding of taxonomic surveys, efficient environmental agreements, asymmetric information, and ecotourism with a focus on volunteer tourism and ecosystem protection designed to avoid fragmentation. Given the numerous policy missteps in this area, we will focus on well-meaning policies that have resulted in unintended consequences. In addition to traditional empirical studies of policies, our analysis will be enriched with insights from common pool resource and public goods experiments from the field and the laboratory. Finally, we will consider the game theoretical aspects of various policies.

The economic benefit of biodiversity and ecosystems comprises three components (Nijkamp *et al.*, 2008), Market values include medicinal and ecotourism functions of ecosystems. Assuming that prices do not change as a result of policy, these values can be measured as the changes in expenditures that result from changes in habitat protection with relatively small error. Use values include the non-market value of ecotourism and other recreation activities involving ecosystems. Use values can be measured with revealed preference methods (e.g. travel cost method) and stated preference methods (e.g. contingent valuation method). Non-use values (or passive use values) arise from simply knowing that biodiversity and ecosystems are protected for current and future generations. Non-use values can be estimated with stated preference methods. Use and non-use values are estimated with greater error than market values since non-market valuation methods are used. Hussain *et al.* (2012) sums market values, use values and non-use values as if they are equivalently determined dollar values. In the third section of this chapter we survey the meta-analysis and benefit transfer literature to determine the reliability of the benefit estimation approach presented in the Challenge Paper.

The fourth section of the paper will present an analysis of data from the *World Values Survey* in order to gain insights about the value of biodiversity and ecosystems in a large number of countries. The 2005–2008 *World Values Survey* wave contains questions concerning WTP for local and global environmental problems. Analysis of these data offers important insights about benefit transfer of biodiversity values. For example, respondents are willing to give up part of their income for environmental problems as their income rises. Holding income and other socio-economic variables constant, there is considerable heterogeneity in attitudes about WTP across countries.

The next three sections of the paper point to one conclusion: the benefits of ecosystems and biodiversity are difficult to measure and, when measured successfully, subject to a high degree of statistical and other uncertainties. In contrast, the benefit estimates used by Hussain *et al.* (2012) do not address these uncertainties, relying on point estimates of the present value of benefits for the CBA. In the fifth section of this paper we conduct sensitivity analysis over the estimates of benefits and costs presented by Hussain *et al.* (2012) using Monte Carlo simulation over ranges of uncertainty. We conduct a series of simulations in order to determine the level of uncertainty at which the BCRs are statistically unreliable.

Insights from the economics of biodiversity

Uncertainty is considered to be an intrinsic part of biodiversity. The uncertainty of the net benefits of biodiversity takes on numerous forms. Biodiversity is difficult to define, measure, and quantify. With respect to the definition of obscenity in the case of *Jacobellis* v. *Ohio*, 378 US 184 (1964), US Supreme Court Justice Potter Stewart famously wrote, "I shall not today attempt further to define the kinds of material . . . [b]ut I know it when I see it." Similarly, the measurement of biodiversity is not easily defined and it may not even pass Justice Stewart's criterion given that it may not be easily recognizable. While there is no consensus regarding how biodiversity should be measured (DeLong, 1996), there are several theoretical measurements of biodiversity including the widely used Simpson and Shannon Weaver indices (Magurran, 2004) and distance functions (Weitzman, 1992, 1993, 1998; Solow *et al.*, 1993; Weikard, 2002). Weitzman (1995) argues that the value of theoretical measures is not in their practical application but as "a paradigm for guiding and informing conservation decisions, even if the model must be at a high level of abstraction." In terms of practical measures, taxonomic inventories or species censuses are valuable, and Wheeler (1995) described taxonomic inventories as "our only insurance against bio-ignorance."

Commonly, conservation biologists use species richness, the number of species present in a community or a sample, when considering species diversity. Magurran (2004) describes species richness as the simplest way to describe community diversity. However, the global biodiversity model, IMAGE-GLOBIO3, used by Hussain *et al.* (2012) does not focus on species richness but on species abundance. Although species abundance is important, it may occur with limited species richness. Contrasting with the Biodiversity Intactness Index, which gives greater weight to areas with higher species richness, in the MSA metric every hectare is given equal weight (Alkemade *et al.*, 2009). Spatial heterogeneity and the existence of biodiversity hotspots imply that there are significant benefits to parcel selection based on sampling. Biodiversity hotspots may take three forms: overall species richness, threat, and endemism, with the overall species richness hotspots not necessarily being congruent with the threatened and endemic hotspots (Orme *et al.*, 2005). Naidoo *et al.* (2006) found significant cost reductions when the spatial heterogeneity of diversity was considered, suggesting that the use of equal weights results in inefficiencies.

In addition to a greater consideration of species richness, parcel selection should consider the uncertain effects of fragmentation. If fragmentation is present, biodiversity may be compromised (Fahrig, 2003). As Fahrig notes, it is important to distinguish between habitat loss and habitat fragmentation. Habitat loss has negative effects on biodiversity; however, fragmentation may have uncertain effects and disproportionally affect adversely certain species (Ewers and Didham, 2006).

Hussain *et al.*'s (2012) policy prescription of extending protected areas to prevent the loss of biodiversity raises the question: is environmental diversity a substitute for biodiversity?

Environmental diversity is the establishment of reserves for the protection of biodiversity. However, Araújo *et al.* (2001) find that environmental diversity areas are poor surrogates for terrestrial vertebrates. Oliver *et al.* (2004) find support for environmental surrogates but with a caveat of additional sampling of geographic space or range occupied by each land system. If environmental diversity is an imperfect substitute for the maintenance of biodiversity, we recommend expenditures on taxonomic surveys. Since certain taxa (especially invertebrates) are poorly documented (Magurran, 2004), there exists a need for greater sampling. Wilson (1991) has argued that "systematics or the study of biological diversity and its origins has one of the highest benefits to costs ratios of all scientific disciplines." Unfortunately, the collection of biodiversity data is both time-consuming and expensive (Magurran *et al.*, 2010). Although ecotourism has not been the panacea it was once considered (Bookbinder *et al.*, 1998), Brightsmith *et al.* (2008) find that ecotourism, in the form of volunteer tourism, may be a source of funding and labor for conservation research projects.

There are many factors that make the cost of reserve expansion difficult to project accurately (James *et al.*, 2001). We will focus on two factors, the enforcement of property rights and the existence of potential strategic behavior that may lead to greater uncertainty and a systematic underestimation of the costs of conservation. International environmental agreements, such as debt-for-nature swaps, are difficult to enforce given that the resources may be owned by a sovereign nation (see Chambers *et al.*, 1996; Deacon and Murphy, 1997). Chambers and Jensen (2002) show that environmental aid may actually increase environmental degradation if a recipient nation acts in a strategic manner given the presence of asymmetric information. Domestic environmental purchases may be plagued by costly strategic behavior in that the landowner may engage in anticipatory investment (development) to affect his or her bargaining position which in turn would adversely affect the conservation organization's costs (see Richer and Stranlund, 1997; Stranlund, 1999).

Even if the recipient sovereign nation is compliant, the conservation efforts may be ineffective at the local level. Governments may create a national park or reserve, but fail to provide any real protection due to lack of funding or lack of community support. These areas are referred to as "paper parks." Bruner *et al.* (2001) found that 57 percent of the tropical parks in their sample had net clearing since their establishment. They found that even modest increases in funding would directly increase the ability of parks to protect tropical biodiversity. In 1990, The Nature Conservancy began an initiative known as Parks in Peril in order to identify the most-threatened natural areas and work to convert them from paper parks to fully protected areas. Partnering with USAID and local conservation organizations across Latin America and the Caribbean, Parks in Peril protected forty-five parks and reserves covering 44.8 million acres between 1990 and 2007. Their approach involved empowering local residents, developing long-term funding strategies, and developing systems of municipal parks for biodiversity conservation. It is not clear if similar provisions are included in the policies described by Hussain *et al.* (2012).

What is the best practice to avoid paper parks? As Ostrom (1990) and Poteete *et al.* (2010) have shown, there is no single, universal solution to the institutional fragilities that arise with the commons and collective action problems such as the protection of biodiversity. Successful environmental agreements are still evolving with approaches based on field and laboratory experiments. Cárdenas (2004) and Cárdenas and Ostrom (2004) provide insights regarding the effects of social norms and internal versus external regulation which may be useful in the development of more efficient management of common pool resources. However, Ostrom (1990) states "that 'getting the institutional right' is a difficult, time-consuming, conflict-invoking process."

Insights from the benefits transfer literature

Meta-analysis is a general term for any methodology that empirically summarizes a literature from several studies. It requires the collection of a large number of studies related to the policy situation. In the case of environmental benefit transfer, a dataset is constructed with benefit estimates gathered from several studies, with WTP as the dependent variable and characteristics of the individual studies as the independent variables. Regression models are developed which are used to relate benefit estimates to the characteristics of the study and policy context. These regression models are used as benefit function transfer models where the characteristics from the case study are inserted and environmental benefits related to the case study are developed.

Benefit transfer using meta-analysis has three advantages (Shrestha and Loomis, 2001). First, by employing a large number of studies, the WTP estimates will be more rigorous. Second, methodological differences can be controlled. For example, meta-analysis may be used to control for differences in functional form across studies (Smith and Kaoru, 1990). Third, differences between the study site and the policy site can be better controlled. However, meta-analysis suffers from (1) reporting errors and omissions in the original studies, (2) inconsistent definitions of environmental commodities and values, and (3) large random errors. These drawbacks limit the ability to use meta-analysis as a benefit transfer method.

Several early meta-analyses showed the importance of study characteristics (i.e. functional form, publication year) when explaining variations in benefit estimates. Smith and Kaoru (1990) conduct a meta-analysis of WTP estimates derived from travel cost recreation demand models. Smith and Huang (1993) conduct a meta-analysis of air-quality benefits derived from hedonic property value models. Loomis and White (1996) conduct a meta-analysis of WTP estimates from studies of rare and endangered species. Each of these studies finds that study characteristics influence benefit estimates.

Other studies have pooled benefit estimates from different non-market valuation methodologies. Walsh *et al.* (1992) conduct a meta-analysis of outdoor recreation value estimates from travel cost, recreation demand and contingent valuation studies. Woodward and Wui (2001) conduct a meta-analysis of WTP estimates from studies of wetland values using travel cost, contingent valuation, and other methods. Carson *et al.* (1996) conduct a meta-analysis of studies that employ the contingent valuation and hedonic property value, travel cost, and averting behavior methods. In each of these, estimates of WTP from the contingent valuation method are lower than those from the revealed preference methods. These early studies suggest that non-market valuation methodology is an important independent variable for meta-analyses.

More recently, a number of meta-analyses have appeared in the literature for biodiversity. Following previous research, each study includes a large number of independent variables, including study characteristics. Jacobsen and Hanley (2009) consider contingent valuation studies of biodiversity in order to focus on non-use values and find that the income elasticity of WTP across countries is 0.38. Their meta-analytic model includes variables that control for study origin, focus of the study (habitat versus species), payment unit, income unit, payment interval, payment vehicle, valuation question format, and time of the survey. They find that a few of these methodological variables are statistically significant.

Barrio and Loureiro (2010) estimate a meta-analysis model with contingent valuation studies of forest values. They find that a number of study characteristics, forest characteristics, site characteristics and socio-economic characteristics help explain the variation in forest values. Studies that include forests that generate biodiversity values (i.e. "management of flora and fauna") have no statistical effect on the overall values. Recreation opportunities increase forest economic values. In other words, biodiversity is a relatively low component of forest values. The amount of variation in the dependent variable explained by variation in the independent variables ranges (i.e. model R^2) from 83 percent to 91 percent.

Ojea and Loureiro (2011) estimate a meta-analysis model with contingent valuation studies of biodiversity with a focus on the issue of scope (i.e. "more is better"). They find that scope effects exist when it is measured absolutely (instead of relatively), that economic values tend to be lower if the benefits are mostly non-use values, that more recent studies generate lower values, and that methodology is important in explaining economic values.

A few studies have assessed the accuracy of benefit transfers with meta-analyses. Using an update to the meta-analytic data from Walsh *et al.* (1992), Rosenberger and Loomis (2000) find that benefit transfer errors range from 54 percent to 71 percent. Shrestha and Loomis (2001) conduct out-of-sample benefit transfer tests using results from the data from Rosenberger and Loomis (2000). In contrast to other studies reviewed here but similar to Hussain *et al.* (2012) their R^2 statistic is relatively low, 0.26. They use US studies to forecast benefits for international policy sites that are not included in the data. They find that the average prediction error ranges from 24 percent to 30 percent.

Lindhjem and Navrud (2008) consider the accuracy of meta-analysis benefit transfer with particular attention to the role of model specification for relatively homogenous Scandinavian forests. Using regression models of various functional forms, the model R^2 statistic ranges from 86 percent to 89 percent. Even with reliable econometric models the authors find that out-of-sample benefit transfer errors range from 21 percent to 51 percent when using median WTP and 62 percent to 266 percent when using mean WTP. They conclude that meta-analysis benefit transfer may not improve accuracy compared to simpler benefit transfer techniques.

This review raises several concerns about the Hussain *et al.* (2012) meta-analysis. First, Hussain *et al.* (2012) do not include variables that identify the type of benefits (market, use, non-use). This could lead to an "apples versus oranges" problem where one type of benefit is estimated and transferred to a policy situation that would generate another type of benefit. Second, benefit transfer errors from meta-analyses have ranged from 24 percent to 71 percent for recreation studies with relatively low R^2 statistics and 62 percent to 266 percent for forest studies (that use mean WTP) with relatively high R^2 statistics. This is little reason to believe that the benefit transfers in Hussain *et al.* (2012) will be 100 percent accurate. Third, Hussain *et al.* (2012) do not include variables that identify ability to pay, study characteristics, and study methodology. If omitted variable bias is present in these models it could cause the coefficient estimates to be biased. Bias in the coefficient estimates can lead to additional inaccuracies in benefit transfers.

Insights from the *World Values Survey*

We use the most recent wave of data from the *World Values Survey* from 2005 to 2007 (WVS, 2009). This wave also includes responses from 2008, but results from 2008 seem counter to the results from 2005–2007, perhaps due to the effects of the global recession. The countries included in each year of the WVS vary (see the Appendix, p. 134), but include both developed and developing countries. After dropping cases with missing values on key variables, our sample includes 45,435 observations from forty-one countries.

Our dependent variables are attitudinal measures of the economic benefits of global environmental quality. Respondents are presented the following questions: "I am now going to read out some statements about the environment. For each one I read out, can you tell me whether you strongly agree, agree, disagree, or strongly disagree." The two statements assessed in this chatper are: (1) "I would be willing to give part of my income if I were sure that the money would be used to prevent environmental pollution," and (2) "I would agree to an increase in taxes if the extra money is used to prevent environmental pollution," 69 percent of the sample strongly agrees or agrees that they would be willing to give up income and 62 percent of the sample strongly agrees or agrees that they would be willing to pay higher taxes. The frequency of responses across the two questions differ significantly ($p < 0.001$) which indicates that the method of payment matters and that separate analysis of both questions could lead to additional insights (Table 2.2.1).

In order to relate the attitudinal statements of WTP to ecosystem and biodiversity benefits we consider attitudinal statements about global environmental problems: "Now let's consider environmental problems in the world as a whole. Please tell me how serious you consider each of the following to be for the world as a whole. Is it very serious, somewhat serious, not very serious, or not serious at all?" The three global problems are "global warming or the greenhouse effect," "Loss of plant or animal species or biodiversity," and "Pollution of rivers, lakes, and oceans," 56 percent believes that the loss of biodiversity is a very serious problem,

Table 2.2.1 WTP for environmental improvements

	Would give part of my income for the environment		Increase in taxes if used to prevent environmental pollution	
	Frequency	%	Frequency	%
Strongly agree	7,838	18.05	6,283	14.47
Agree	22,015	50.68	20,479	47.15
Disagree	10,111	23.28	12,254	28.21
Strongly disagree	3,471	7.99	4,419	10.17

Table 2.2.2 Perceptions of global environmental problems

	Global warming or the greenhouse effect		Loss of plant or animal species or biodiversity		Pollution of rivers, lakes, and oceans	
	Frequency	%	Frequency	%	Frequency	%
Very serious	25,383	58.44	24,400	56.18	28,870	66.47
Somewhat serious	13,448	30.96	14,220	32.74	11,074	25.50
Not very serious	3,795	8.74	4,055	9.34	2,829	6.51
Not serious at all	809	1.86	760	1.75	662	1.52

33 percent feel that it is somewhat serious, and only 11 percent feel that it is not very serious or not serious at all, 89 percent of the sample believes that global warming is very or somewhat serious, 92 percent believes that pollution of rivers, lakes, and oceans is a very or somewhat serious problem (Table 2.2.2).

While these three variables are highly correlated, the frequency of responses across the three questions differs significantly ($p < 0.001$), which indicates that the three issues could be treated separately in the empirical model. We recode these variables so that each is equal to one if the respondent felt that the problem is very serious.

Respondents were also asked about their attitudes towards local environmental problems: "I am going to read out a list of environmental problems facing many communities. Please tell me how serious you consider each one to be here in your own community. Is it serious, somewhat serious, not very serious, or not serious at all?" The three issues are "Poor water quality," "Poor air quality," and "Poor sewage and sanitation." Attitudes towards local environmental problems are highly correlated, causing multicollinearity in the empirical models, so we code each "very serious" attitude equal to 1 and sum these across respondents. We include this as an independent variable to control for the contribution of concern about local, relative to global, environmental problems. The average level of local environmental concern is 1.24.

In addition to local environmental concerns, we include several socio-economic control variables in the empirical models, 50 percent of the sample is female, the average age is 41 (range is from 15 to 97 years), 54 percent of the sample is married and the average number of years' schooling is 11 (the range is from 6 to 16 years). The income variable is the income decile that the respondent perceives themselves to inhabit. The average income decile is 4.92. Socio-economic summaries for each country in the sample are presented in the Appendix.

In order to conduct the empirical analysis we recode the WTP attitudinal variables to equal 1 if the respondent strongly agrees and 0 otherwise. We estimate the determinants of strongly agree WTP with logistic regression. Similar results are found with ordered logistic regression; however, we estimate simpler models given the limited scope of this chapter. In addition to the above-mentioned independent variables we include dummy variables for countries. We constrain similarly sized coefficient estimates and conduct a series of likelihood ratio tests to determine groups of countries that have like parameters. For the income decile variable, we create dummy variables for each decile and constrain coefficients to be equal using the results from likelihood ratio statistics. We also conduct similar tests for each year of survey dummy variables.

In both models, respondents are more likely to strongly agree with the WTP statements as their perceptions of the seriousness of local environmental problems increase. Respondents also strongly agree about WTP for each of the global environmental problems. In the income model, none of the global environmental problem coefficients are statistically different from each other according to likelihood ratio statistics. According to the odds ratio statistic, respondents are 1.32, 1.26, and 1.21 times more likely to be willing to give up some of their income if they feel that global warming, biodiversity, and water pollution are very serious global problems. In the taxes model, respondents are 1.16, 1.27, and 1.21 times more likely to be willing to pay higher taxes if they feel that global warming, biodiversity, and water pollution are serious global problems. The coefficient on biodiversity is not statistically different from water pollution but is statistically greater than global warming according to likelihood ratio statistics. However, none of the differences in the odds ratios are statistically significant.

In terms of the socio-economic factors, the probability that respondents strongly agree about giving up income increases with age, for those who are married with increasing years of schooling, and with income. Respondents who are in the fourth and fifth, sixth and seventh, and above income deciles are more (and more) likely to strongly agree about willingness to give up some income. The probability that respondents strongly agree about paying taxes increases for those who are married with increasing years of schooling and with income. Respondents who are in the fourth and fifth, sixth, seventh and eighth, and above income deciles are more and more likely to strongly agree about willingness to pay taxes.

In the income model, we find ten separate sets of countries with differing attitudes about willingness to give up income. In the second model (willingness to pay higher taxes), we find nine separate sets of countries with differing attitudes. There are some similarities in groups of countries but the only commonality is Vietnam (no. 39) whose respondents are six and seven times more likely to give up income and pay higher taxes than the baseline group of countries. The next highest odds ratio in the willingness to give up income model is 1.90 and 1.66 in the taxes model. The odds ratios for Vietnam would be even greater if the omitted country group is that which is least willing to pay.

Finally, in terms of survey year fixed effects, respondents in the 2006 and 2007 surveys are more likely to be willing to give up income, relative to 2005. Respondents in 2006 are less likely to be willing to pay more taxes, while respondents in the 2007 surveys are more likely to be willing to pay (Table 2.2.3).

Our analysis of the *World Values Survey* data suggests two salient points for the assessment of Hussain *et al.* (2012). First, if the correlation between concern about environmental problems and WTP is causal, there is world-wide support for protection of biodiversity. However, these attitudinal statements do not provide evidence of the magnitude of WTP. Given that considerable effort has been made by a number of researchers to create meta-analytic databases of biodiversity valuation studies, future effort might usefully be redirected toward the conduct of multi-country contingent valuation surveys of biodiversity (Carson, 1998). Second, meta-analytic models, even if adjusted for income, socio-economic variables, and attitudes about biodiversity, are likely to be less than 100 percent accurate when used for benefit transfers. This is due to country-level fixed effects and the temporal nature of attitudes towards biodiversity. The meta-analyses in Hussain *et al.* (2012) do not incorporate variables of this nature.

Sensitivity analysis

Hussain *et al.* (2012) find that the BCRs for policies that enhance agricultural productivity, protect land, and reduce deforestation are 4.4, 0.2–1.0 and 3.6–9.8, respectively (using a discount rate of 3 percent). Including climate change co-benefits

Table 2.2.3 Logistic regression models (dependent variable = 1 if agree or strongly agree); $n = 43{,}435$

	Would give part of my income for the environment			Increase in taxes if used to prevent environmental pollution		
	Coeff.	S. E	*p*-value	Coeff.	S. E	*p*-value
Constant	0.032	0.070	0.6451	–0.362	0.071	<.0001
Local	0.039	0.010	<.0001	0.029	0.0091	0.0018
Global warming (= 1 if very serious)	0.28	0.028	<.0001	0.15	0.026	<.0001
Biodiversity (= 1 if very serious)	0.23	0.030	<.0001	0.24	0.028	<.0001
Water pollution (= 1 if very serious)	0.19	0.031	<.0001	0.19	0.029	<.0001
Income Decile (= 1)						
4, 5	0.15	0.028	<.0001	0.11	0.027	<.0001
6	0.23	0.037	<.0001	0.22	0.035	<.0001
7				0.40	0.038	<.0001
7, 8, 9, 10	0.32	0.033	<.0001			
8, 9, 10				0.34	0.037	<.0001
Female	0.038	0.022	0.0845	0.019	0.021	0.3468
Age	0.0020	0.00075	0.0071	–0.0007	0.00070	0.3569
Married	0.050	0.024	0.0355	0.065	0.022	0.0034
Schooling	0.066	0.0041	<.0001	0.038	0.0039	<.0001
Countries (= 1)						
12, 28, 36, 38	–1.91	0.043	<.0001			
2, 4, 5, 8, 10, 22, 27, 37	–1.32	0.035	<.0001			
1, 4, 7, 14, 19, 40, 41	–0.98	0.039	<.0001			
20, 23, 26, 30	–0.94	0.045	<.0001			
6, 31	–0.67	0.055	<.0001			
16, 21, 29, 34	–0.43	0.043	<.0001			
13, 17	–0.12	0.058	0.0463			
9, 32	0.64	0.069	<.0001			
39	1.79	0.16	<.0001	1.91	0.11	<.0001
22, 28, 38				–1.05	0.048	<.0001
5, 10, 21, 27, 36, 37, 40				–0.54	0.039	<.0001
2, 4, 8, 19, 20, 23, 26, 31, 41				–0.43	0.037	<.0001
1, 7, 14, 16, 34				–0.20	0.040	<.0001
6, 35				0.15	0.051	0.0037
25, 29, 30				0.12	0.045	0.0066
9, 24				0.50	0.067	<.0001
Year (= 1)						
2006, 2007	0.070	0.027	0.009			
2006				–0.14	0.028	<.0001
2007				0.41	0.037	<.0001
Model χ^2	5638 ($p < 0.0001$)			3583 ($p < 0.0001$)		

increases these ratios to 7.5–20.5, 0.3–1.4 and 7.8–31.3. Best-case and worst-case sensitivity analysis is conducted, but this leads to ranges of BCRs where each ratio might seem to be equally likely. For example, there is little guidance concerning where in the range of 3.6 to 9.8 the BCR for reduced deforestation is most likely to fall.

Our review of biological and institutional issues, the biodiversity valuation, and benefit transfer literature, and analysis of the *World Values Survey* data leads us to question the confidence placed in the BCRs. Each of these issues suggests that the actualization of the economic benefit of ecosystem and biodiversity is highly uncertain or measured with considerable statistical error. A limitation of the Hussain *et al.* (2012) analysis is that only point estimates of the benefits of each of the three policies is considered when calculating BCRs.

Further, considering the data used for the benefits analysis also raises the issue of uncertainty. For two of the three sets of data, the median benefit estimate is much lower than the mean, indicating that the sample is strongly influenced by outliers (the median and mean for the third dataset are not reported). Removal of these outliers could result in much lower PVs of benefits for each policy and lower BCRs. On the other hand, Hussain *et al.* (2012) assume a linear trajectory of annual benefits that begins at 0 in the initial year. Alternative trajectory assumptions, with larger benefits received in the early years, would lead to larger PV of benefit estimates and larger BCRs.

Considering these uncertainties, we conduct a limited Monte Carlo sensitivity analysis in order to (1) provide a mean BCR for each policy and (2) assess the sensitivity of the mean BCRs to assumptions made in the analysis. For each policy we take 1,000 random draws from a normal distribution of the PV of benefits with the coefficient of variation (CV) equal to 0.1, 0.2, 0.3, 0.4, and 0.5.

In addition, the agricultural productivity policy assumes certain costs. 1,000 random draws from a normal distribution with CV equal to 0.05, 0.1, 0.15, 0.2, and 0.25 are used for the agricultural productivity policy, assuming that cost estimates are less uncertain than benefit estimates. Ranges of costs are presented for the other policies. 1,000 random draws are taken from a uniform distribution of the low- and high-cost estimates for the protected areas and deforestation scenarios.

Table 2.2.4 Sensitivity analysis of BCRs

Agricultural productivity				
CV	B/C	Std dev.	95% CV	
0.1	4.39	0.52	3.40	5.41
0.2	4.40	1.03	2.55	6.44
0.3	4.51	1.57	1.80	7.79
0.4	4.70	2.21	0.91	9.86
0.5	4.67	2.72	0.40	10.64
Protected areas with carbon values				
CV	B/C	Std dev.	95% CV	
0.1	0.51	0.24	0.29	1.18
0.2	0.58	0.29	0.27	1.24
0.3	0.57	0.27	0.23	1.29
0.4	0.57	0.28	0.17	1.29
0.5	0.59	0.33	0.13	1.44
Deforestation				
CV	B/C	Std dev.	95% CV	
0.1	5.60	1.78	3.39	9.48
0.2	5.82	2.13	2.77	10.80
0.3	6.00	2.57	1.88	11.77
0.4	5.97	2.93	1.17	12.95
0.5	5.94	3.17	0.25	12.79

These random draws are used to construct 1,000 BCRs for which we report mean and standard deviations. The 1,000 BCRs are ordered from lowest to highest and the twenty-five lowest and highest values are trimmed to create a 95 percent confidence interval. We consider the CBA with carbon values included for the protected areas policy since (1) BCRs are clearly below 1 without carbon values for that policy and (2) BCRs with carbon values included are quite large for the other policies.

In Table 2.2.4 we present the sensitivity analysis of BCRs at a 3 percent discount rate. Considering the agricultural policy, as the CV rises from 0.1 to 0.5 for the PV of benefits and the CV of the PV of cost rises from 0.05 to 2.5, the standard deviation of the BCR rises from 0.52 to 2.72. The 95 percent confidence interval rises from 46 percent to 219 percent of the BCR. At CVs greater than 0.4 the

Table A2.2.1 ***World Values Survey*** **data, 2005–2007**

Country	Code	Year	Cases	Local	Income	Female	Age	Married	Schooling
1	AD	2005	866	0.79	5.60	0.50	40.13	0.41	12.22
2	AU	2005	1242	1.00	5.26	0.53	49.38	0.59	13.30
3	BF	2007	922	2.52	3.84	0.44	33.95	0.52	8.62
4	BG	2006	613	1.90	4.02	0.53	46.17	0.64	12.52
5	BR	2006	1349	1.20	4.32	0.58	39.58	0.41	9.91
6	CA	2006	1562	0.67	5.70	0.56	47.74	0.48	12.43
7	CH	2007	978	0.72	5.45	0.52	51.85	0.54	12.95
8	CL	2005	800	1.27	4.27	0.54	42.25	0.47	11.33
9	CN	2007	783	0.68	4.33	0.47	42.09	0.81	11.00
10	CSS	2006	934	1.91	4.76	0.49	41.56	0.59	12.20
11	CY	2006	1017	1.95	5.69	0.51	41.59	0.65	12.05
12	DE	2006	1517	0.37	4.49	0.53	50.48	0.57	10.74
13	ET	2007	1301	2.11	5.22	0.48	29.62	0.38	10.43
14	FI	2005	874	0.42	4.33	0.51	47.02	0.47	11.75
15	GH	2007	1003	1.39	4.70	0.46	33.12	0.42	9.39
16	ID	2006	1259	1.47	5.37	0.46	34.85	0.18	12.78
17	IN	2006	964	1.62	4.00	0.36	39.76	0.78	11.04
18	IR	2007	2511	2.11	4.88	0.49	32.50	0.60	11.29
19	IT	2005	553	0.61	4.31	0.49	45.59	0.59	12.40
20	JP	2005	524	0.48	4.69	0.48	49.95	0.73	12.81
21	KR	2005	1193	0.21	4.88	0.50	41.35	0.64	13.43
22	MA	2007	677	2.14	5.02	0.46	34.89	0.52	8.92
23	MD	2006	926	1.82	4.99	0.52	41.86	0.64	11.69
24	ML	2007	805	2.30	4.99	0.49	36.59	0.67	8.77
25	MX	2005	1252	1.22	5.10	0.48	38.12	0.54	11.22
26	MY	2006	1192	0.88	5.88	0.50	31.85	0.50	11.73
27	PL	2005	760	1.43	4.08	0.47	45.16	0.58	11.05
28	RO	2005	1113	1.12	6.12	0.50	47.18	0.71	11.37
29	RW	2007	1212	1.35	3.40	0.50	34.26	0.52	8.39
30	SE	2006	880	0.17	6.13	0.47	47.94	0.48	12.97
31	SI	2005	785	0.54	5.08	0.49	44.41	0.51	12.07
32	TH	2007	1446	0.76	5.59	0.51	45.37	0.69	9.85
33	TR	2007	1115	2.22	3.61	0.47	35.82	0.65	10.53
34	TT	2006	833	0.78	4.74	0.54	42.22	0.39	10.80
35	TW	2006	1174	0.34	4.49	0.49	43.21	0.64	12.47
36	UA	2006	650	1.89	4.49	0.64	41.44	0.58	13.25
37	US	2006	1118	1.06	5.03	0.49	47.99	0.58	11.79
38	UY	2006	751	0.95	4.52	0.56	46.41	0.42	10.35
39	VN	2006	1147	1.18	5.62	0.46	40.20	0.73	10.79
40	ZA	2007	1980	1.59	5.14	0.49	38.83	0.42	11.05
41	ZM	2007	854	1.19	5.64	0.47	29.03	0.32	11.37

Note: Country codes can be found at the *World Values Survey*, www.wvesevsdb.com/wvs/wvsdata.jsp.

95 percent confidence interval of the BCR falls below 1, indicating that the ratio is not statistically different from 1. The sensitivity analysis for protected areas including carbon values is trivial, with the 95 percent confidence interval never being statistically different from 1. Considering the deforestation policy, as the CV of the point estimate of PV of benefits rises from 0.1 to 0.5 the mean of the BCR varies between 5.60 and 6.00 and the standard deviation rises from 1.78 to 3.17. The 95 percent confidence interval rises from 109 percent to 211 percent of the BCR. At CVs somewhere between 0.4 and 0.5 the 95 percent confidence interval of the BCR falls below 1, indicating that the ratio is not statistically different from 1.

Conclusions

Hussain *et al.* (2012) have presented a wealth of information and are to be commended for the magnitude of their effort. However, in this chapter we have raised a number of concerns about the analysis.

Uncertainty is an unavoidable component of the study of biodiversity. This inherent uncertainty is reflected in the estimate that the earth is inhabited by 8.7 million species with a standard error of 1.3 million species. Only 1.3 million of these species are currently named (Mora *et al.*, 2011). Not only is the number of species elusive, but a large portion of the biodiversity benefits these species represent is unknown and benefits may occur with unexpected species. For example, the bark of the Pacific yew (*Taxus brevifolia*), a tree previously considered to be a marginal species that was discarded during logging of old growth forests, is the source of the anti-cancer drug, Taxol (see Polasky and Solow 1995; Chivian, 2001). With preserved species, such as the Pacific yew which was once considered to be a trash tree by loggers, there is a positive expected value of the future information that extinction would preclude. This option value, as defined by Conrad (1980), Hanemann (1989), and others, is difficult to measure. However, the discovery of previously unknown species and associated benefits through taxonomic inventories and bioprospecting is a costly undertaking. Finally, accurate acquisition and management costs are clouded by asymmetric information and strategic behavior.

Even without these uncertainties, numerous and restrictive conditions are necessary for a benefit function from a meta-analysis to transfer accurately to a policy site. It is not surprising that few studies generate satisfyingly accurate benefit transfers. These and our other concerns raise questions about overconfidence in the point estimates of the PV of benefits presented in Hussain *et al.*, 2012. Our attempt to conduct *ex post* sensitivity analysis suggests that none of the policies is likely to have benefits greater than costs at the 95 percent level of confidence when the standard deviation is about 40 percent of the point estimate of the PV of benefits. However, more extensive sensitivity analyses are needed for each policy, with Monte Carlo simulation conducted, *ex ante*, over the large number of explicit and implicit assumptions that led to the point estimate of the PV of benefits.

Appendix

The *World Values Survey* data used in this study are shown in Table A2.2.1.

Bibliography

Alkemade, R., M. van Oorschot, L. Miles, C. Nellemann, M. Bakkenes, and B. ten Brink, 2009: GLOBIO3: a framework to investigate options for reducing global terrestrial biodiversity, *Ecosystems* **12**, 374–90

Araújo, M. B., C. J. Humphries, P. J. Densham, R. Lampinen, W. J. M. Hagemeijer, A. J. Mitchell-Jones, and J. P. Gasc, 2001: Would environmental diversity be a good surrogate for species diversity?, *Ecography* **24**, 103–10

Barrio, M. and M. L. Loureiro, 2010: A meta-analysis of contingent valuation forest studies, *Ecological Economics* **69**,1023–30

Bookbinder, M. P., E. Dinerstein, A. Rijal, H. Cauley, and A. Rajouria, 1998: Ecotourism's support of biodiversity conservation, *Conservation Biology* **12**, 1399–1404

Brightsmith, D. J., A. Stronzab, and K. Hollec, 2008: Ecotourism, conservation biology, and volunteer tourism: a mutually beneficial triumvirate, *Biological Conservation* **141**, 2832–42

Bruner, A. G., R. E. Gullison, R. E. Rice, and G. A. B. da Fonseca, 2001: Effectiveness of parks in protecting tropical biodiversity, *Science* **291**, 125–8

Cárdenas, J.-C., 2004: Norms from outside and from inside: an experimental analysis on the governance of local ecosystems, *Forest Policy and Economics* **6**, 229–41

Cárdenas, J.-C. and Elinor Ostrom, 2004: What do people bring into the game? Experiments in the field about cooperation in the commons, *Agricultural Systems* **82**, 307–26

Carson, R. T., 1998: Valuation of tropical rainforests: philosophical and practical issues in the use of contingent valuation, *Ecological Economics* **24**, 15–29

Carson, R. T., N. E. Flores, K. M. Martin, and J. L. Wright, 1996: Contingent valuation and revealed preference methodologies: comparing the estimates for quasi-public goods, *Land Economics* **72**, 80–99

Chambers, P. and R. Jensen, 2002: Transboundary air pollution, environmental aid, and political uncertainty, *Journal of Environmental Economics and Management* **43**, 93–112

Chambers, P. E., R. Jensen, and J. C. Whitehead, 1996: Debt-for-nature swaps as noncooperative outcomes, *Ecological Economics* **19**, 135–46

Chivian, E., 2001: Environment and health: 7. Species loss and ecosystem disruption – the implications for human health, *Canadian Medical Association Journal* **164**, 66–9

Conrad, J. M., 1980: Quasi-option value and the expected value of information, *Quarterly Journal of Economics*, **94**, 813–20

Deacon, R. T. and P. Murphy, 1997: The structure of an environmental transaction: the debt-for-nature swaps, *Land Economics* **73**, 1–24

DeLong, D. C., Jr., 1996: Defining biodiversity, *Wildlife Society Bulletin* **24**, 738–49

Ewers, R., and R. Didham, 2006: Confounding factors in the detection of species responses to habitat fragmentation, *Biological Reviews* **81**, 117–42

Fahrig, L., 2003: Effects of habitat fragmentation on biodiversity, *Annual Review of Ecology, Evolution, and Systematics* **34**, 487–515

Hanemann, W. M., 1989: Information and the concept of option value, *Journal of Environmental Economics and Management* **16**, 23–37

Hussain S., A. Markandya, L. Brander, A. McVittie, R. de Groot, O. Vardakoulias, A. Wagtendonk, and P. Verburg, 2012: *Ecosystems and Biodiversity*, Copenhagen Consensus Paper 2012, Chapter 2 in this volume

Jacobellis v. *Ohio*, 378 US 184 (1964)

Jacobsen, J. B. and N. Hanley, 2009: Are there income effects on global willingness to pay for biodiversity conservation?, *Environmental and Resource Economics* **43**, 137–60

James, A., K. J. Gaston, and A. Balmford, 2001: Can we afford to conserve biodiversity?, *BioScience* **51**, 43–52

Lindhjem, H. and S. Navrud, 2008: How reliable are meta-analyses for international benefit transfers?, *Ecological Economics* **66**, 425–35

Loomis, J. B. and D. S. White, 1996: Economic benefits of rare and endangered species: summary and meta-analysis, *Ecological Economics* **18**, 197–206

Magurran, A., 2004: *Measuring Biological Diversity*, Blackwell, Oxford

Magurran, A., S. R. Baillie, S. T. Buckland, J. Dick, D. A. Elston, E. M. Scott, R. I. Smith, P. J. Somerfield, and A. D. Watt, 2010: Long-term datasets in biodiversity research and monitoring: assessing change in ecological communities through time, *Trends in Ecology and Evolution* **25**, 574–82

Mora C., D. P. Tittensor, S. Adl, A. G. B. Simpson, and B. Worm 2011: How many species are there on Earth and in the ocean?, *PLoS Biology* **9**, e1001127 9

Naidoo, R., A. Balmford, P. J. Ferraro, S. Polasky, T. H. Ricketts, and M. Rouget, 2006: Integrating economic costs into conservation planning, *Trends in Ecology and Evolution* **21**, 681–7

Nijkamp, P., G. Vindigni, and P. A. L. D. Nuñes, 2008: Economic valuation of biodiversity: a comparative study, *Ecological Economics* **67**, 217–31

Ojea, E. and M. L. Loureiro, 2011: Identifying the scope effect on a meta-analysis of biodiversity valuation studies, *Resource and Energy Economics* **33**, 706–24

Oliver, I., A. J. Holmes, M. J. Dangerfield, M. Gillings, A. J. Pik, D. R. Britton, M. Holley, M. E. Montgomery, M. Raison, V. Logan, R. L. Pressey, and A. J. Beattie, 2004: Land systems as surrogates for biodiversity in conservation planning, *Ecological Applications* **14**, 485–503

Orme, C. D. L., R. G. Davies, M. Burgess, F. Eigenbrod, N. Pickup, V. A. Olson, A. J. Webster, T. Ding, P. C. Rasmussen, R. S. Ridgely, A. J. Stattersfield, P. M. Bennett, T. M. Blackburn, K. J. Gaston, and I. P. F. Owen, 2005: Global hotspots of species richness are not congruent with endemism or threat, *Nature*, **436**, 1016–19

Ostrom, E., 1990: *Governing the Commons: The Evolution of Institutions for Collective Action*, Cambridge University Press

Polasky, S. and A. Solow, 1995: On the value of a collection of species, *Journal of Environmental Economics and Management* **29**, 298–303

Poteete, A., M. Janssen, and E. Ostrom, 2010: *Working Together: Collective Action, the Commons, and Multiple Methods in Practice*, Princeton University Press

Richer, J. and J. K. Stranlund, 1997: Threat positions and the resolution of environmental conflicts, *Land Economics* **73**, 58–71

Rosenberger, R. S., and J. B. Loomis, 2000: Using meta-analysis for benefit transfer: in-sample convergent validity tests of an outdoor recreation database, *Water Resources Research* **36**, 1097–1107

Schwartzman, S., A. Moreira, and D. Nepstad, 2000: Rethinking tropical forest conservation: Perils in Parks, *Conservation Biology*, **14**, 1351–7

Shrestha, R. K. and J. B. Loomis, 2001: Testing a meta-analysis model for benefit transfer in international outdoor recreation, *Ecological Economics*, **39**, 67–83

Smith, V. K. and J.-C. Huang, 1993: Hedonic models and air quality: twenty-five years and counting, *Environmental and Resource Economics* **36**, 23–36

Smith, V. K. and Y. Kaoru, 1990: Signals or noise? Explaining the variation in recreation benefit estimates, *American Journal of Agricultural Economics* **72**, 419–33

Solow, A., S. Polasky, and J. Broadus, 1993: On the measurement of biological diversity, *Journal of Environmental Economics and Management* **24**, 60–8

Stranlund, J. K., 1999: Bargaining to preserve a unique eco-system: the role of anticipatory investments to establish stronger bargaining positions, *Ecological Economics* **31**, 425–37

Walsh, R. G., D. M. Johnson, and J. R. McKean, 1992: Benefit transfer of outdoor recreation demand studies, 1968–1988, *Water Resources Research* **28**, 707–13

Weikard, H., 2002: Diversity functions and the value of biodiversity, *Land Economics* **78**, 20–7

Weitzman, M. L., 1992: On diversity, *Quarterly Journal of Economics* **107**, 363–405

1993: What to preserve? An application of diversity theory to Crane conservation, *Quarterly Journal of Economics* **108**, 157–83

1995: Diversity functions, in C. Perrings, K. G. Mäler, C. Folke, C. S. Holling, and B.-O. Jansson (eds.), Biodiversity Loss: Economic and Ecological Issues, Oxford University Press

1998: The Noah's Ark problem, *Econometrica* **66**, 1279–98

Wheeler, Q. D., 1995: Systematics, the scientific basis for inventories of biodiversity, *Biodiversity and Conservation* **4**, 476–89

Wilson, E. O., 1991: *The Current State of Biological Diversity in Learning to Listen to the Land*, N. B. Willers (ed.), Island Press, Washington, DC

Woodward, R. T. and Y.-S. Wui, 2001: The economic value of wetland services: a meta-analysis, *Ecological Economics* **37**, 257–70

World Values Survey (WVS) Association, 2009: *World Values Survey, 2005–2008*, www.worldvaluessurvey.org

Chronic Disease

PRABHAT JHA, RACHEL NUGENT, STÉPHANE VERGUET, DAVID BLOOM, AND RYAN HUM*

Eighty percent of global deaths from heart disease, stroke, cancer, and other chronic diseases occur in low- and middle-income countries. This chapter discusses priorities for control of these chronic diseases as an input into the 2012 Copenhagen Consensus. This chapter and the accompanying Chapter 7 on infectious disease control build on the results of the 2008 Copenhagen Consensus chapter on disease control (Jamison *et al.*, 2008), and is best read as an extension of the latter chapter.

This chapter also draws on the framework and findings of the Disease Control Priorities Project (DCP2).[1] The DCP2 engaged over 350 authors and among its outputs were estimates of the cost-effectiveness of 315 interventions, including about 100 interventions for chronic diseases. These estimates vary a good deal in their thoroughness and in the extent to which they provide regionally-specific estimates of both cost and effectiveness. Taken as a whole, however, they represent a comprehensive canvas of chronic disease control opportunities. This chapter identifies five key priority interventions for chronic disease in developing countries which chiefly address heart attacks, strokes, cancer, and tobacco-related respiratory disease. These interventions are chosen from among many because of their cost-effectiveness, the size of the disease burden they address, their implementation ease, and other criteria. Separate but related 2008 Copenhagen Consensus chapters dealt with other major determinants of chronic diseases such as nutrition, (Behrman *et al.*, 2007), air pollution (Larsen *et al.*, 2008) and education (Orazem *et al.*, 2008). The health-related chapters for the 2012 Copenhagen Consensus focus on infectious diseases (Jamison *et al.*, 2012), sanitation and water (Rijsberman and Zwane, 2012), education (Orazem, 2012), hunger and undernutrition (Hoddinott *et al.*, 2012) and population growth (Kohler, 2012).

There are five main conclusions of this chapter. First, chronic diseases already pose a substantial economic burden, and this burden will evolve into a staggering one over the next two decades. Second, although high-income countries currently bear the biggest economic burden of chronic diseases, countries in the developing world, especially middle-income ones, are expected to assume an increasing share as their economies and populations grow. Third, the marginal costs for governments of achieving maximal adult survival are rising, in contrast to declines in the marginal costs of achieving child survival. This divergence is a consequence chiefly of the lack of tobacco control in most low- and middle-income countries, the lack of sustained investments in new drugs, and gaps in the strategies and in the program implementation

* This chapter was prepared with support from the Copenhagen Consensus Center and from the Bill and Melinda Gates Foundation through the Disease Control Priorities Network grant to the University of Washington. We are indebted to Dean T. Jamison for his advice and guidance. We also thank David Watkins for helpful input.

[1] The DCP2 was a joint effort, extending over four years, of the Fogarty International Center of the US National Institutes of Health, the World Bank, and the World Health Organization (WHO) with financial support from the Bill and Melinda Gates Foundation. While the views and conclusions expressed in this chapter draw principally on the DCP2, others might draw different broad conclusions. In particular, the views expressed in this chapter are not necessarily those of any of the sponsoring organizations.

The DCP2 resulted in two main volumes, both of which Oxford University Press published in 2006. One book deals with the *Global Burden of Disease and Risk Factors* (Lopez *et al.*, 2006a). The second book, *Disease Control Priorities in Developing Countries*, 2nd edn (Jamison *et al.*, 2006) discusses interventions to address diseases and risk factors, and the health systems to deliver those interventions. A first edition was published by Oxford University Press for the World Bank in 1993. This chapter will refer to these two volumes as DCP1 and DCP2.

for chronic diseases. This leads to the fourth conclusion, which is that addressing chronic disease in poor countries requires a concomitant rethinking of developmental assistance, and possibly new delivery approaches. Finally, selected options available to prevent and control chronic diseases appear to justify themselves in economic terms in the sense that the welfare gains and the economic losses that could be averted by investments that would reduce chronic diseases are considerably larger than the financial costs to implement them.

After some brief definitions, the first section of the chapter describes and contrasts the declines in childhood and adult mortality and presents the current burden. The section also summarizes work for the World Economic Forum (WEF) on the cost of illness from selected chronic diseases and the resulting economic costs. The section describes the DCP2 framework for choosing interventions, including issues of poverty, implementation costs, and the intervention demands on health systems. The third section summarizes the cost-benefit methodology. The fourth section presents specific interventions for tobacco control, prevention and treatment of vascular disease, and immunization against liver cancer as opportunities in chronic disease control, and includes very approximate CBAs for these interventions. The chapter concludes with the implications for developmental assistance of increases in chronic disease. As in CC08, the chapter emphasizes, although not exclusively, opportunities relevant to low-income countries in South Asia and SSA.

Progress and challenges

Definitions

Epidemiological transition

The next few decades will see a continuation of rising trends resulting from dramatic fertility declines (and consequent population aging) that has been occurring variously in countries over the last few decades. The combination of an aging population with increases in smoking and other lifestyle changes mean that the major chronic diseases (sometimes called non-communicable diseases (NCDs) or chronic non-communicable diseases (CNCDs)) – circulatory system diseases, cancers, respiratory diseases, and major psychiatric disorders – are fast replacing (or adding to) the traditional scourges – particularly infectious diseases and undernutrition in children. Additionally, injuries resulting from road traffic are adding to or replacing some of the more traditional forms of injury (although these will not be dealt with in this chapter). Responding to this epidemiological transition within sharply constrained resources is a key challenge.

Table 3.1 Causes of chronic (NCD) death in LMICs, age 5 and older

Disease	Deaths (in million)	% of all over 5 deaths
Cancers	5.6	15.0
COPD	2.5	6.7
Diabetes	1.1	2.8
Ischemic and hypertensive heart disease	6.2	16.5
Stroke	5.0	13.4
Other	5.9	15.8
Subtotal	26.3	70.2

Source: Institute for Health Metrics and Evaluation (IHME). Global Burden of Disease Study 2010. Results by cause 1990–2010 Seattle, United States: IHME, 2012.

Table 3.1 provides cause-specific estimates of the number of deaths over age 5 due to major causes in low- and middle-income countries. This summary indicates that chronic disease already accounts for two-thirds of all deaths over age 5 in these countries.

At the same time that most low- and middle-income countries need to address the traditional health problems that are now effectively controlled in high-income countries, they are increasingly sharing the high-income countries' heavy burdens of cardiovascular system disease, diabetes, cancers, respiratory diseases, psychiatric disorders, and automobile-related injuries. DCP2 has chapters addressing each of these chronic diseases and others. Until recently, the public health research and policy communities have been surprisingly silent about these epidemics even though, for example, cardiovascular disease (CVD) in low- and middle-income countries killed over twice as many people in 2001 as did HIV/AIDS, malaria, and TB combined.

Avoidable mortality

A central conclusion from nearly 200 years of epidemiology and demography is that while death in old age (after age 70) is inevitable, death at young ages (below age 30) could become a rare occurrence, and death in middle age (age 30–69) need not be common (Doll and Peto, 1981). Currently, about 60 million deaths occur world-wide per year, of which 50 million are in low- and middle-income countries (as defined by the World Bank). Taking into account some expected increase in HIV/AIDS deaths, then about 20 million deaths occur before age 30 (mostly in the first 5 years of life), about 20 million deaths occur during age 30–69 years, and another 20 million occur at older ages (Peto, 2006). The years of life lost (YLL) are greatest for those at young ages: even in middle age, a premature death incurs 20–25 years of productive life lost (YPLL), often as the head of a household. Rapid reductions in child mortality over the last few decades have meant that the vast majority of the 130 million children born world-wide in 2010 can expect to reach middle age.

Today, there are an estimated 2.9 billion (UN, 2009) adults aged 30–69 in low- and middle-income countries, and currently there are about 40 million deaths over age 30 in these countries. As of 2001, nearly 70 percent of deaths during these ages were from the "non-communicable diseases," shown in Table 3.1. Thus as much as possible, we emphasize the avoidable premature deaths before age 70. This is not to argue that many deaths and much disability can be avoided at older ages. Indeed, Paccaud (Rousson and Paccaud, 2010) points out that the ideal pattern of mortality involves low death rates in young age and middle age, paired with a sharply compressed time before death lived in any disability state.

Finally, although we focus chiefly here on changes in mortality, it is worth noting that chronic diseases also carry considerable disability. Our calculations for cost-benefit take this into account, but for the purposes of tracking changes over time, use of mortality is preferred – simply because it is far less likely to be misclassified than are the more subjective measures of disability.

Trends and burdens

Global life expectancy has increased by about three months per calendar year for the last four decades, with much of this gain from sharp declines in childhood mortality (see Chapter 7 in this volume control by Jamison *et al.*, and Jamison *et al.*, 2012). Notably, adult mortality has also declined overall. Table 3.2 shows the progress in the probability of death between age 15 and 60 for selected countries from 1970 to 2010 (Rajaratnam *et al.*, 2010a). The large increases in adult male and female (not shown) mortality in South Africa and Russia reflect the specific effects of the increases since 1980 in HIV/AIDS and in binge drinking of alcohol in these countries, respectively. Aside from these countries mortality declines have been impressive and have been greater in the high- than in the low- or middle-income countries. Even within the high-income countries, sharp differences in declines have been noted among the G-7 countries, with the United States doing much worse in its decline of adult male mortality than Canada.

Much of the variation in country outcomes appears to result from the very substantial cross-country variation in the rate of diffusion of appropriate health technologies (or "technical progress"). In the case of child mortality, countries range from having essentially no decline in infant mortality rate (IMR) caused by technical progress to reductions of up to 5 percent per year (Jamison *et al.*, 2004). Measham *et al.* (2003) reached a similar conclusion concerning the variation in IMR decline across the states of India. Cutler *et al.* (2006) provide a complementary and extended discussion of the importance of technological diffusion for improvements in health. Differing rates of technical progress are the principal source of the cross-country variation in rate of under-5 mortality decline (Jamison *et al.*, 2012). Controlling for socio-economic and geographic factors, under-5 mortality in low- and middle-income countries has been declining at about 3 percent per year, driven by technical progress.

Table 3.2 Trends in the risk of death between ages 15–59 for males, 1970–2010, selected countries

	% of 15-year-old males dead by age 60				
Country	1970	1990	2010	Change %	Rank 2010
Russia	31	32	41	34	155
South Africa	42	38	53	28	172
Brazil	27	24	19	−29	82
India	33	27	23	−31	103
China	24	20	15	−35	58
France	20	16	12	−42	33
US	23	17	13	−43	44
Germany	19	16	10	−47	24
UK	18	13	9	−48	17
Japan	17	11	8	−51	13
Canada	19	13	8	−55	11
Italy	18	13	8	−55	8
Low-income	34	37	32	−5	
Middle-income	26	23	22	−15	
High-income	23	16	20	−13	
Global average	28	25	25	−10	

Source: Authors from IHME data (IHME, 2010b).

With justification, investment in cost-effective interventions has been disproportionately devoted to child and maternal health (Daar *et al.*, 2007) and more recently to control of HIV/AIDS, malaria, and TB. In a novel analysis, Hum *et al.* (2013) explain that increasing coverage of inexpensive health interventions has not only reduced child mortality, but has also reduced the national income *per capita* required to achieve one-half of the maximal survival seen in a year across countries. They define this as "critical income," which represents the efficiency of mortality gains in relation to available resources, given the maximum that other countries have achieved (Figure 3.1). Critical income has fallen for child survival gains, with the majority of declines occurring since 1990 – coinciding with global efforts to improve child health. For adult survival, however, there is a reversal of fortune. While global adult survival has improved, Hum *et al.* (2008) find that higher income is needed to achieve these improvements. This may explain the lower rate of decline in adult mortality in countries with low income seen in Table 3.2, compared to the more widespread decline in child mortality (Rajaratnam *et al.*, 2010b). High-income countries, where overall income well exceeds the critical income needed, have benefitted from the rise in maximum survival among adults. The key explanation for this greater disparity appears to be the lack of widespread use of treatments for chronic diseases, and sharp reductions in tobacco-attributable deaths that are occurring mostly in high-income countries. This has implications for developmental assistance for health, to which we return at the end of this chapter. More disturbingly, the trend in adult critical-income level continues to rise each year. This suggests that delaying a concerted effort now would escalate costs in the future.

Of course, the importance of technical progress and diffusion should be viewed in a larger context. Factors from outside the health sector also affect the pace of health improvement: education levels of populations appear quite important, although the level and growth rate of income appear much less so. Expanded education improves the coverage and efficiency of disease control, as in the case of

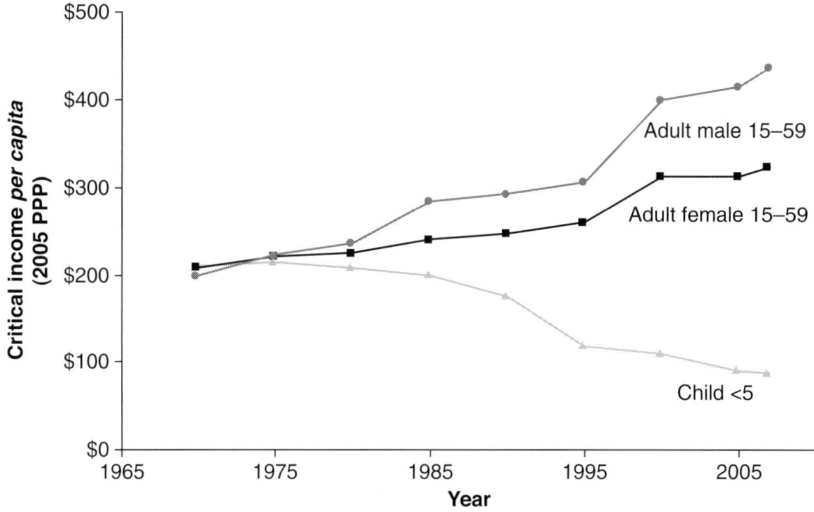

Figure 3.1 *Divergence of "critical income" for child and adult mortality*

maternal education improving child health. Indeed, rapid economic growth in many parts of the world, especially in China and India, might well mean that some can buy their way into better health, but this chapter argues that far more benefit will occur from using public coffers on a relatively limited set of highly effective public health and clinical interventions. This point bears reiterating in a slightly different way: income growth is neither necessary nor sufficient for sustained improvements in health (Preston, 1975). The experiences of Costa Rica, Cuba, Sri Lanka, and Kerala state in India, among others, conclusively show that dramatic improvements in health can occur without high or rapidly growing incomes. Publicly financed health care or insurance can dramatically reduce the social costs of chronic conditions, just as they have with communicable diseases (Jeemon and Reddy, 2010). Today's tools for improving health are so powerful and inexpensive that health conditions can be reasonably good even in low-income countries.

Rising costs of chronic diseases

Recent analysis underscores the very large economic costs imposed on society, broadly defined, by chronic diseases and gives rise to a compelling need for a public response. Bloom *et al.* (2011b) estimate the economic burden of five major categories of NCDs (CVD, cancer, chronic respiratory diseases, and diabetes) and mental health conditions) for 2010 and 2030. They do this by applying three distinct approaches to conceptualizing and measuring that burden.[2]

The *cost-of-illness (COI) approach* views the cost of NCDs as the sum of several categories of direct costs (meaning actual expenditures) and indirect costs (meaning lost output and the implicit cost of pain and suffering). The direct costs typically considered in this approach are personal medical care costs for diagnosis, procedures, drugs, and inpatient and outpatient care; personal non-medical costs, such as the costs of transportation for treatment and care; and non-personal costs such as those associated with information, education, communication, and research. The indirect costs are the income losses that arise because of NCDs (with no attempt made in this chapter to monetize the burden of pain and suffering).[3] Due to the nature of data available on the prevalence and cost of the various conditions covered, the COI method was

[2] The data sources for this study include information on demographics, income *per capita*, mortality rates by disease, DALYs by disease, treatment costs per case by disease, and measures of the value of statistical life.

[3] A key assumption made in this calculation is that if someone stops working because of an NCD, there will not be another worker to take that person's place.

implemented in different ways for each condition. For example, the time frame to which the medical care cost and forgone productivity data apply differ by diseases; in addition, personal non-medical care costs are available for some diseases and not others. Therefore, COI results presented for any one of the conditions are not directly comparable to the results presented for another. In the case of diabetes, prevalence estimates for 2030 are taken from the International Diabetes Federation (2010). For all other conditions, prevalence is assumed to be constant over time. The number of cases in 2010 and 2030 is derived by multiplying incidence by the population in the respective year.

The *value of lost output approach* estimates the projected impact of NCDs on aggregate economic output (GDP) by using the WHO's EPIC model to simulate the macroeconomic consequences of NCDs for the factors of production (labor and capital) that determine economic output and growth. The basic premise is that if there were no NCDs, there would be more labor and capital and hence more output.[4] EPIC calculates the output that is lost because of NCDs on a disease- and country-specific basis in 1997 international (PPP-adjusted) dollars. The EPIC results are then adjusted so they are (a) expressed in 2010 US$ (not PPP-adjusted); (b) scaled up so they refer to all countries;[5] (c) scaled up using WHO data on DALYs to reflect five NCDs;[6] and (d) scaled up further, using WHO data on mental illness DALYs, to include estimates of economic losses from mental health conditions. Estimates for both 2010 and 2030 are based on WHO projections of the mortality trajectory associated with these five conditions.

The *value of statistical life (VSL) approach* reflects a population's WTP to reduce the risk of disability or death associated with NCDs. By placing an economic value on morbidity and mortality, this approach goes beyond the impact of NCDs on GDP alone. Separate analyses are conducted for the five sets of health conditions, as well as for all NCDs taken as a whole. The VSL approach can be carried out in three different ways. The first method requires regression-based projections – for all countries in 2010 and 2030 – of (a) GDP *per capita*, (b) VSL, and (c) DALYs. GDP *per capita* is projected by extrapolation using the annual average growth rate of GDP *per capita* during 2004 through 2009 (drawn from the World Bank's *World Development Indicators*). VSL estimates are constructed by regressing VSL (in US$2000) for the twelve countries reported in Viscusi and Aldy (2003) on GDP *per capita* (in US$2000) and life expectancy at birth (from the UN Population Division).[7] The parameter estimates are then applied to estimates of GDP *per capita* in 2010 (2030) and life expectancy data/projections in 2010 (2030) for all countries to impute VSL estimates for countries where no studies existed in Viscusi and Aldy (2003). DALYs are projected by regressing the most recent estimates of DALYs (in 2004) on GDP *per capita*, total population, and the share of population over age 65, and using projected GDP *per capita* and population projections published by the UN Population Division.[8] The second method builds on a rule-of-thumb proposed by the WHO Commission on Macroeconomics and Health. It values DALYs at 1 times GDP *per capita* (CMH1). The third method is the same as the second, except that it values DALYs at 3 times GDP *per capita* (CMH3).

Caveats

Some important caveats apply to the results presented here. First, the estimates refer to the dollar

[4] The model also assumes that if there were no NCDs in a given time frame, there would be no rise in deaths from other causes.

[5] The EPIC model is only calibrated for 101 countries. For the purposes of the exercises reported in Bloom *et al.* (2011b), further calibration was done for 68 countries.

[6] The original EPIC model accommodates diabetes, ischemic heart disease, cerebrovascular disease, chronic obstructive pulmonary disease, and breast cancer. This study uses EPIC to generate results for these five conditions, and then scales up to derive figures for the larger NCD categories.

[7] The VSL estimates that appear here are used as primary data.

[8] The VSL data are taken to be the value of life of a representative median-aged member of the corresponding national population. For example, consider a population in which life expectancy at birth is 75, median age is 25, and VSL is US$1 million. Suppose further that a 50-year-old dies unexpectedly and suddenly. This death contributes 25 DALYs, and an economic loss of US$500,000 (= [25/(75–25)] *US$1 million). The CMH1, CMH3, and VSL figures reported herein may be interpreted as the total future cost of incident NCD cases in 2010 (2030). The implicit assumption is that the value of a life-year is not a function of age.

impact of all future NCDs, *not* the cost of inaction, nor the cost of preventable disease burden only. Expressing the cost of NCD prevalence in dollar terms is meant to garner the attention of economic policy-makers, and perhaps to spur them to action. Second, all of the methods used by these studies are sub-optimal: they all rely on assumptions that are less than ideal and on data that are far from perfect. Third, the set of NCDs studied is not comprehensive; not included, for example are vision and hearing disorders, digestive diseases, and musculoskeletal diseases. And, fourth, the various methods used in the report (COI, value of lost output, and VSL) are sufficiently disparate that their results cannot be compared with each other. The VSL estimates are drawn from only ten countries, of which only one (India) is a low- and middle-income country (Viscusi and Aldy, 2003). Finally, there is uncertainty in the causes of death given low levels of medical certification of adult deaths world-wide (RGI/CGHR, 2009). However, the magnitude of the major causes of death is such that it exceeds greatly the uncertainty in the point estimates. Indeed, the major uncertainty is in the size and shape of the future tobacco hazards which make several of the chronic diseases more common (Jha, 2009). The estimates are simply intended to provide a ballpark idea of the economic cost at the macro level of NCDs, to complement estimates of their impact on morbidity and mortality. Estimates of cost at the micro level (on households and individuals) for specific populations have been published elsewhere (Suhrcke *et al.*, 2006; IOM, 2010). Better data and further refinement of analytical techniques will yield more accurate estimates.

COI estimates

- Cancer: *The 13.3 million new cases of cancer world-wide in 2010 were estimated to cost US$290 billion.* Medical costs accounted for the greatest share at US$154 billion (53 percent of the total), while non-medical costs and income losses accounted for US$67 billion, and US$69 billion, respectively. *The total costs are expected to rise to US$458 billion in the year 2030.*
- CVD: *In 2010, the global cost of CVD was estimated at US$863 billion (an average* per capita *cost of US$125), and it is estimated to rise to US$1,044 billion in 2030 – an increase of 22 percent.* Overall, the cost for CVD could be as high as US$20 trillion over the twenty-year period (an average *per capita* cost of nearly US$3,000). Currently about US$474 billion (55 percent) is due to direct health care costs and the remaining 45 percent to productivity loss from disability or premature death, or time lost from work because of illness or the need to seek care.
- Chronic obstructive pulmonary disease (COPD): *The global cost of illness for COPD is projected to rise from US$2.1 trillion in 2010 to US$4.8 trillion in 2030.* Approximately half of all global costs for COPD arise in developing countries.
- Diabetes: *Diabetes cost the global economy nearly US$500 billion in 2010. That figure is projected to rise to at least US$745 billion in 2030,* with developing countries increasingly taking on a much greater share of the outlay.
- Mental health conditions: *The global cost of mental health conditions in 2010 was estimated at US$2.5 trillion, with the cost projected to surge to US$6.0 trillion by 2030.* About two-thirds of the total cost comes from indirect costs and the remainder from direct costs. Currently, high-income countries shoulder about 65 percent of the burden, which is not expected to change over the next twenty years.

Value of lost output

Over the period 2011–2030, the total lost output from the five NCD conditions (including mental health) is projected to be nearly US$47 trillion (see Table 3.3). On a per year basis, this loss is equivalent to about 5 percent of global GDP in 2010. For every country income group, CVDs and mental illnesses each account for approximately one-third of the total loss. High-income countries, which currently account for only 16 percent of world population, are slated to absorb 55 percent of the loss, largely because their economic output *per capita* is high. That is, when a high-income worker stops working because of an NCD, the lost economic output is much greater than in a country where economically measured output is lower. Conversely, lower- and middle-income countries, which together currently account for only 25 percent of world income, are projected to experience

Table 3.3 Economic burden of NCDs, 2011–2030 (2010 of US$ trillion), based on EPIC model

Country income group	Share of world economic losses from NCDs	Share of world population, 2010	Share of world mortality, 2008	Share of world income, 2010 (constant 2000 US$)	Total loss	CVD	Cancers	CRD	Diabetes	Mental illness
Low (L)	0.02	0.12	0.43	0.01	0.9	0.3	0.1	0.1	0.0	0.3
Lower-middle (LM)	0.12	0.37	0.32	0.05	5.4	2.0	0.5	0.9	0.2	1.9
Upper-middle (UM)	0.32	0.36	0.10	0.19	14.9	4.8	2.3	2.2	0.6	5.1
High	0.55	0.16	0.14	0.75	25.5	8.5	5.4	1.6	1.0	9.0
L + LM + UM	*0.45*	*0.84*	*0.85*	*0.25*	*21.2*	*7.1*	*2.9*	*3.2*	*0.8*	*7.3*
World					46.7	15.6	8.3	4.8	1.7	16.3

Notes: CVD = cardiovascular disease; CRD-chronic respiratory disease.

45 percent of the losses. Upper-middle-income countries will experience nearly one-third of the cost of NCDs over the period 2011–2030, even though their share of world mortality is currently only 10 percent.

Tobacco use is unique in its scale of contribution to these costs, as it increases the number of deaths from vascular disease, cancers and chronic respiratory disease, which together account for about US$28.7 trillion (or about 60 percent of the total loss for all chronic diseases). Conservatively estimating that tobacco is a cause of about 30 percent of the vascular disease, 50 percent of the cancers, and 60 percent of chronic respiratory diseases (Peto *et al.*, 2006; Jha, 2009), we estimate a total economic loss from tobacco of about US$12.7 trillion (Table 3.4). This corresponds approximately to about 1.3 percent of GDP on annual basis, or roughly US$0.9 trillion in 2010 terms.

Table 3.4 Economic burden of tobacco, 2011–2030 (2010 US$ trillion), based on EPIC model

Country income group	Total due to vascular disease, cancers, and CRD	Tobacco attributable loss
High	15.5	6.6
Lower and middle	13.2	6.0
World	28.7	12.7

Source: Author calculations.

VSL approach

The VSL approach leads to economic burden estimates that vary, depending on which assumption is used, by a factor of more than 6 – from 2010 US$3.6 to 22.8 trillion in 2010, and from 2010 US$6.7 to 43.4 trillion in 2030 (see Table 3.5). The upper end of these estimates looms exceedingly large, representing a notable and growing fraction of GDP, but even at the lower end these estimates for 2010 and 2030 are sizable. All three methods used in this approach show that high-income countries currently bear the greatest burden. But all three methods also show that in 2030 upper-middle-income countries will approach high-income countries in the burden borne.

Conclusions of costing studies

Three main messages from the economic analyses can now be summarized. First, NCDs already pose a substantial economic burden, and this burden will evolve into a staggering one over the next two decades, particularly from tobacco use. Second, although high-income countries currently bear the biggest economic burden of NCDs, the developing world, especially middle-income countries, is

Table 3.5 VLL due to NCDs, by estimation method and income group (2010 US$ trillion)

Country income group	2010 total (CMH1)	2030 total (CMH1)	2010 total (CMH3)	2030 US$ total (CMH3)	2010 total (VSL)	2030 total (VSL)
Low (L)	0.0	0.1	0.1	0.2	0.5	1.0
Lower-middle (LM)	0.2	0.6	0.6	1.9	2.4	5.3
Upper-middle (UM)	0.7	2.6	2.1	7.8	5.1	17.4
High	2.7	3.4	8.0	10.3	14.8	19.7
L + LM + UM						
World	3.6	6.7	10.7	20.2	22.8	43.4

Notes: The table incorporates losses from all five categories of NCDs; CMH1 = DALYs valued at 1 × GDP/capita; CMH3 = DALYs valued at 3 × GDP/capita.

expected to assume an ever-larger share as its economies and populations grow, and third, CVD and mental health conditions are the dominant contributors to the global economic burden of NCDs.

The above estimates on the economic costs of chronic diseases are consistent with earlier studies of economic losses due to medical costs and productivity losses of poor health (WHO, 2001) including from more extreme changes in adult mortality arising from advanced HIV/AIDS epidemics (CMH, 2002). Moreover, earlier work by Jamison *et al.* (2002) examined the contribution of improvements in adult survival to economic growth in the former socialist economies. Among fifty-two countries, adult male survival between ages 15 to 60 (45p15) rose from 70 percent to 80 percent between 1965 and 1990. This better survival raised income growth by 0.23 p.a. between 1965 and 1990, after adjustment for changes in physical capital, education, fertility, economic openness, and technical progress. Between 1960 and 1990 there was a sharp divergence in the survival probability of males between the former socialist economies (FSE) in Eastern and Central Europe and those in the OECD. Much, but not all of this 1960–1990 difference was attributable to the markedly higher rates of tobacco-attributable mortality in the FSE (Peto *et al.*, 2006; Zatonski and Jha, 2002). However the dramatic worsening of adult mortality in many FSE countries, particularly Russia, after 1990 is due to binge alcohol drinking (Zaridze *et al.*, 2009). Jamison *et al.* (2002) estimated that were adult male survival in FSE at the levels in OECD countries, annual growth rates over the last three decades would have been about 1.4 percent versus 1 percent. This would have meant that the 1990 *per capita* income would have been $3,000 versus the actual of $2,700, or about 12 percent higher or $140 billion greater.

Murphy and Topol (2006) estimated that in the United States gains in longevity between 1970 and 1990 (using WTP to avoid death) amounted to $57 trillion or over 50 percent of the average of GDP per year during the period. About half of the gain was from reduction in CVD alone. They further estimate that elimination of CVD and cancer would generate about $47 and $48 trillion in economic value, respectively. They further find, consistent with the Hum *et al.* (2013) analysis, that there are increasing returns in health improvements.

Given the enormous health and economic burden of chronic diseases, we next turn to the criteria to assess which of the numerous interventions might be used to reduce disease.

Major criteria to assess priority interventions

Chronic disease and poverty

A starting point for cost-effectiveness analysis is to observe that health systems have two objectives: (a) to improve the level and distribution of health outcomes in the population and (b) to protect individuals from financial risks that are often very

Table 3.6 Post-heart-attack mortality by income, Indian males

	Rich	Upper-mid	Lower-mid	Poor	*P* for trend
Death rate (unadjusted)	*5.5*	*5.9*	*6.5*	*8.2*	<0.0001
Death rate (adjusted for RFs)	*5.1* 1.0	*5.9* 1.16 (0.83,1.63)	*6.7* 1.32 (0.96, 1.82)	*7.8* 1.57 (1.12, 2.20)	0.0093
Death rate (adjusted for RF+Trt)	*6.9* 1.0	*7.0* 1.01 (0.50, 2.02)	*6.5* 0.94 (0.48, 1.84)	*6.7* 0.96 (0.46, 2.01)	0.9487

Notes: RF = Risk factors such as age sex, previous heart attack, diabetes, hypertension, smoking, heart rate, body mass index (BMI), and stage of heart attack. Treatment = Trtm: type of hospital, time to hospital, use of in-hospital drugs, interventions.
Source: Xavier *et al.* (2008).
Risk ratios of the highest socio-economic group are taken as the baseline and plotted as a value of 1.0.

substantial and that are frequent causes of poverty (WHO, 2000). Financial risk results from illness-related loss of income as well as expenditures on care; the loss can be ameliorated by preventing illness or its progression and by using appropriate financial architecture for the system.

The distribution of chronic diseases has often been assumed to be one that falls mostly on affluent, more educated, and urban adults in low- and middle-income countries (LMICs). A variety of recent epidemiological data, including from the ongoing Indian "Million Death Study," finds that the highest burdens of cancer, stroke, and heart attacks are in the least educated and in the rural areas (RGI/CGHR, 2009). For example, the age-standardized cancer mortality rates were surprisingly similar in rural and urban areas, and were twofold higher in the least-educated compared to the most-educated adults (Dikshit *et al.*, 2012). While this pattern is not universally true in LMICs, a growing body of literature points toward NCDs becoming associated with lower socio-economic status (SES). For example, in high-income countries, risk factors such as smoking and high intakes of saturated animal fat were first observed in higher-income groups, but migrated over time to become more common in lower SES groups (Popkin *et al.*, 1996).

Most LMICs lack universal health coverage and safety nets to prevent large expenditures on out-of-pocket spending during illness. In many of these settings, chronic disease can thus cause households to fall into poverty. Work by Reddy *et al.* (2007) found that risk factors for heart attacks and acute heart attacks and their associated treatment costs were a major source of distressed selling of household assets or severe debt. Similar work by John *et al.* (2011) found that tobacco use is a major source of households falling below the poverty line in India. Conversely, new evidence by Xavier *et al.* (2008) found that the risk of death after a heart attack was notably higher in the lowest socio-economic group (Table 3.6). However, upon adjustment for the access to treatments, including heart attack "clot"-busting drugs and adjustment for the higher levels of smoking and other risk factors in the poor, these marked differences in death rates disappeared.

Demands of intervention on health systems

The literature on the economic evaluation of health projects typically reports the cost per unit of achieving some measure of health outcome – QALYs, or DALYs, or deaths averted – and at times addresses how that cost varies with the level of intervention and other factors. Cost-effectiveness calculations provide important insights into the economic attractiveness of an intervention, but other considerations – such as consequences for financial protection and demands on health system capacity – need to be borne in mind.

We can consider two classes of resources to be available: financial resources and health system capacity. To implement an intervention in a population, the system uses some of each resource. Just as some interventions have higher dollar costs than others, some interventions are more demanding of system capacity than others. In countries with limited health system capacity, it is clearly important to select interventions that require relatively little of such capacity. Human resource capacity constitutes a particularly important aspect of system capacity, discussed in a report of the Joint Learning Initiative (Gostin *et al.*, 2011). Jamison *et al.* (2008) provides a more extended discussion.

Although in the very short run little trade-off may exist between dollars and human resources or system capacity more generally, investing in the development of such capacity can help make more of that resource available in the future. Mills *et al.* (2006) discuss different types of health system capacity and intervention complexity and point to the potential for responding to low capacity by selecting interventions that are less demanding of capacity and by simplifying interventions. Mills *et al.* (2006) also explore the extent to which financial resources can substitute for different aspects of system capacity (see also Gericke *et al.*, 2003). An important mechanism for strengthening capacity, inherent in highly outcome-oriented programs, may simply be to use it successfully – learning by doing. Re-orientation of system capacity might also hold the potential to deliver interventions for chronic conditions in a more cost-effective manner than currently implied. Health system capacity in LMICs may be ill suited to respond to chronic conditions in particular, which demand long-term, sustained care, close monitoring, and specialized knowledge following the care model used in high-income countries. Even in some high-income countries, current chronic disease management schemes are perceived to be unsustainable due to increasing caseload, cost, and sub-optimal outcomes related to the low quality of care.

Increased costs of chronic disease in developing countries are fueling experimentation in the field of chronic care delivery models. This conversation is taking place in the context of efforts to strengthen developing country health systems to manage a broader array of health conditions and achieve better outcomes. It is conceivable that experimentation in LMICs to identify and scale up affordable prevention and treatment of chronic conditions may fuel reverse technology transfer that could slow the rise of health costs in developed countries.

In the traditional (Western) health care model, the primary care provider (usually a physician) manages chronic illness, with input from specialist physicians and ancillary services such as pharmacists. More recently, there has been a turn towards more collaborative models that shift tasks and give patients more responsibility over their own care. The following types of programs have recently been promoted, particularly in the United States and United Kingdom: the "Chronic Care Model" (or CCM) (Pearson *et al.*, 2005), peer support programs, self-management interventions, and "full self-management" (van Olmen, 2011). Aside from full self-management, these strategies have been trialed and their cost-effectiveness estimated in limited settings, as discussed below.

Collaborative care strategies have been recognized for over a decade, and the best-known example is the CCM, which expands team-based primary care disease management. Several studies from the United States and other countries show immediate improvement in process outcomes (e.g. percentage of diabetics screened), as well as delayed improvements in intermediate outcomes (e.g. changes in average plasma glucose concentration) (Coleman, 2009). More recently, evidence has emerged of cost-effective reductions in adverse events and mortality from a societal perspective (Huang *et al.*, 2007). The CCM is a complex intervention, however, and its cost-effectiveness as a whole model has not been established (Coleman, 2009); therefore, it is perhaps more salient for developing regions to examine its individual components, since the CCM is highly resource-intensive and would be difficult to scale to less developed health systems (van Olmen, 2011). The WHO has developed the Innovative Care for Chronic Conditions (ICCC) model, which is meant to scale CCM-based principles to resource-limited settings (WHO, 2002). Unfortunately, rigorous trials of this program have not yet been conducted in developing countries.

Some of the components of the CCM and ICCC have undergone economic assessment. These include case management, peer support, and self-care. Shifting to lower-level providers and caregivers for on-going patient support shows promise for achieving good outcomes at lower cost in a developed country setting. Protocols of nurse-led diabetes case management have been cost-effective in low-income American populations, with incremental cost-effectiveness ratios (ICERs) approximately US$10,000 per QALY (Gilmer *et al.*, 2007). Similarly, multi-disciplinary home-based care for chronic heart failure is cost-saving in South Australia and markedly improves survival (Inglis *et al.*, 2006). Peer support, or "lay-led" programs make use of highly knowledgeable patients with chronic diseases to be community spokespersons for behavior change or self-management. Peer support for diabetes (Lujan *et al.*, 2007) and tobacco addiction (Woodruff, 2002) were highly cost-effective, with results driven by the size of the potential gain from the healthy behavior that is being promoted – whether changing diet, quitting tobacco, or adhering to a complicated regimen of medication (Carr *et al.*, 2011). These findings were echoed by an earlier meta-analysis demonstrating that behavior change (in the context of a self-management program) can lead to clinically meaningful reductions in blood pressure and glycemic control (Chodosh *et al.*, 2005). One study of peer programs in Cambodia combined individual clinic counseling and peer support for patients with diabetes, hypertension, and HIV/AIDS (Janssens *et al.*, 2007). Cost-effectiveness was not assessed.

A final component of "collaborative care" relates to tools for self-care and self-management (SMS) without explicit peer assistance. Many of these programs use internet- or mobile phone-based technology to educate patients and improve adherence. Overall, the literature on self-management interventions shows mixed results, depending on the condition and type of intervention. Examples of effective interventions include SMS-based diabetes self-care (Liang *et al.*, 2011), and interactive health education software developed for various chronic diseases (Murray *et al.*, 2005). World-wide cell phone usage is expected to reach about 5 billion in the 2010s, and as such offers a novel platform for information and delivery of services. In the near term, limits on technology and connectivity beyond simple mobile phone and SMS technology are likely to deter broader applications for disease management.

Cost-benefit methodology

This section explicitly builds on the CBA framework in the 2008 Copenhagen Consensus paper on disease control (Jamison *et al.*, 2008a). The basic approach to CBA used in this chapter is to start with the cost-effectiveness results from the extensive comparative analyses reported in DCP2 (Jamison *et al.*, 2006; Laxminarayan *et al.*, 2006). These results are expressed as the cost of buying a DALY, a summary measure involving mortality change and a valuation of disability change that can be considered to have been generated by calibration against mortality change.

The next subsection describes an idealized version of our approach to cost-effectiveness – idealized in the sense that it seeks to explicitly call attention to the value of financial protection and non-financial costs (e.g. use of limited system capacity). The point is to serve as a reminder in drawing conclusions of some important considerations that go beyond the cost-effectiveness ratios reported. The next subsection discusses DALYs. The next subsection draws on the discussion on p. 144 to assign, very conservatively, dollar values to DALYs for the subsequent CBA. The final subsection summarizes this chapter's approach to costing.

Cost-effectiveness analysis broadly and narrowly construed

As mentioned on pp. 145–8, a starting point for cost-effectiveness analysis broadly construed is to observe that health systems have two objectives: (a) to improve the level and distribution of health outcomes in the population and (b) to protect individuals from financial risks that are often very substantial and that are frequent causes of poverty (WHO, 2000). Financial risk results from illness-related loss of income as well as expenditures on care; the loss can be ameliorated by preventing illness or its progression and by using an appropriate financial architecture for the system.

The literature on the economic evaluation of health projects typically reports the cost per unit of achieving some measure of health outcome – QALYs, or DALYs, or deaths averted – and at times addresses how that cost varies with the level of intervention and other factors. Pritchard (2004) provides a valuable introduction to this literature. DCP1 reported such cost-effectiveness findings for about seventy interventions; DCP2 does so as well, in the end providing evidence on about 315 interventions. The DCP2 authors were asked to use the methods described in Jamison *et al.* (2006a).

Defining and redefining DALYs

The DALY family of indicators measures the disease burden from the age of onset of a condition by summing an indicator of YLL due to the condition and an indicator of YLL due to disability (YLD) resulting from the condition. DALYs due to a condition are the sum of the relevant YLLs and YLDs.

DALYs generate a measure of the disease burden resulting from premature mortality by integrating a discounted, potentially age-weighted, disability-adjusted stream of life years from the age of incidence of the condition to infinity using a survival curve based on the otherwise expected age of death. The formulation within the family of DALYs previously used to empirically assess the global burden of disease specifies a constant discount rate of 3 percent p.a. and an age-weighting function that gives low weight to a year lived in early childhood and older ages and greater weight to middle ages. The current global burden of disease estimates are generated with the 3 percent discount rate but uniform age weights (Lopez *et al.*, 2006a). Mathers *et al.* (2006) provide an extensive exploration of the uncertainty and sensitivity inherent in disease burden assessment, including the results of differing assumptions about age weighting and discount rates.

To be clear about the particular form of DALY being used, the terminology from Mathers *et al.* (2006) is employed. DALYs(r, K) are DALYs constructed using a discount rate of r percent per year and an amount of age weighting indexed by a parameter K. DALYs(3,1) are DALYs generated with a discount rate of 3 percent per year and with full age weighting, that is, $K = 1$. DALYs (3,0) are DALYs generated with a discount rate of 3 percent per year and with no age weighting, that is, $K = 0$. Mathers *et al.* (2006) present results concerning the burden of disease based on DALYs (3,0); Ezzati *et al.* (2006) present estimates of the burden of major risk factors. Their chapter is based on DALYs (3,0).

The value of a DALY

The VSL estimates discussed on p. 144 yield a range of values for a statistical life – from around 100 to almost 200 times *per capita* income. Very approximately this can be translated to a value for a statistical life year in the range of 2 to 4 times *per capita* income. Tolley *et al.* (1994) provide a valuable overview of relevant estimates, including estimates of the value of preventing disability. The emphasis in the latter paper is on low-income countries defined by the World Bank for 2001 as countries with *per capita* incomes of less than $745. The World Bank's estimate of the average income of people living in low-income countries is $430 per year (World Bank, 2003: Table 1.1). Choosing a value for a statistical life year near the low end of the range (a little above 2) would give a convenient value of $1,000, which is what this chapter uses in its main calculations as the value of a DALY. We explore the sensitivity of our results to these assumptions by using a DALY value of $5,000.

The cost of a DALY

The cost of buying a DALY with different interventions was calculated, in DCP2, by combining "typical" prices for a geographical region (Mulligan *et al.*, 2003) with input quantities estimated from clinical and public health experience and case studies in the literature. For internationally traded inputs, prices were the same for all regions. (Because of tiered pricing, off-patent drugs were *not* considered to be internationally traded.) For local costs, regional estimates were used. Intervention costs, therefore, are *not* expressed in PPP dollars. The reason for this is that local costs present decision-makers with the appropriate numbers for budgeting and for comparing interventions in the context where they are working. The estimates of DALY benefits from various interventions were

Table 3.7 Chronic disease control: key investment priorities

Priority area	Indicative BCR	Level of capacity required[a]	Financial risk protection provided[a]	Relevance for development assistance[a]	Annual costs ($ billion)	Annual benefits[b]
1. Cancer, heart disease, other : tobacco taxation	40:1	L	H	H	0.5	1 million deaths averted or 20 million DALYs
2. Heart attacks (acute myocardial infarction, AMI): acute management with low-cost drugs	25:1	H	H	H	0.2	300,000 heart attack deaths averted each year or 4.5 million DALYs
3. Heart disease, strokes: salt reduction	20:1	M	H	H	1	1.3 million deaths averted or 20 million DALYs
4. Hepatitis B immunization	10:1	H	H	H	0.1	150,000 deaths averted or 3 million DALYs
5. Heart attacks and strokes: secondary prevention with 3–4 drugs in a "generic risk pill"	4:1	H	H	H	32	1.6 million deaths averted or 118 million DALYs averted

Notes:

[a] Level of capacity required, extent of financial risk protection provided, and relevance for development assistance, are judged by the authors to be high (H), medium (M), or low (L).

[b] In the formulation of DALYs, the benefits of averting a death in a given year all accrue in that year and are calculated as the PV (at a 3 percent discount rate) of the future stream of life years that would have occurred if the death had been prevented.

provided by each DCP2 author team, and do vary across disease groupings.

Opportunities for controlling chronic diseases

This section provides a specific overview of the most cost-beneficial interventions, including considerations of their system demands, risk protection, and other metrics described above. It then goes on to discuss briefly examples of prevention and treatment of chronic diseases.

Cost benefits of selected interventions

The DCP2 experience shows that there is a broad range of reasonable estimates of the cost-effectiveness of most interventions. This results partly from (often highly) incomplete information and uncertainty. It results also, and even more importantly, from the responsiveness of the cost-effectiveness function to variations in prices, in the scale of the intervention (and of its substitutes and complements), and in the epidemiological environment.

Given these often broad ranges in cost-effectiveness ratios, and hence in BCRs, it makes little sense to conclude with precise estimates or with attempts to quantify statistical uncertainty around the point estimates. Rather, we have identified major opportunities for investment in interventions that address a large disease burden highly cost-effectively (Table 3.7). Even valuing DALYs at a conservative $1,000 the BCRs associated with investing in these opportunities is enormously high. The appendix (pp. 161–2) provides a brief assessment of the sensitivity of our findings to key assumptions. Overall this suggests that the conclusions in Table 3.7 are conservative.

Table 3.7 lists the main health outcomes influenced by the five interventions that were selected for their high BCRs. Calculations were derived from reliable estimates of the adult mortality (age 30–69) for the world arising from those health conditions. Benefits were valued at $1,000 per death following the VSL approach discussed above. The costs of each intervention were taken from experience or published estimates to depict as closely as possible the full social costs of intervening but, absent social values in most instances, the costs reflect financial estimates. An indicative BCR is calculated.

Table 3.7 orders opportunities by BCR – from 40:1 for tobacco taxation to 4:1 for the "generic risk pill." Every opportunity in the table has not only a high estimated BCR but also addresses a major disease burden. For example, despite the considerable cost of $32 billion a year, secondary management with the "generic risk pill" would treat over 320 million adults, and avoid annually about 16 million heart attacks and strokes (of which a significant number would be fatal).

Table 3.7 also provides a "dashboard" of indicators that can be used as selection criteria for interventions provided by a public health system and/or development assistance. These include the demands placed on health system capacity, the degree of financial protection afforded, and the relevance to donors of each of the interventions selected for this analysis. The ratings of level of capacity required are, admittedly, speculative, and are drawn mostly from the author's experience and feedback from the DCP2 authors (Laxminarayan *et al.*, 2006a). Thus, they use only a qualitative ranking of high capacity (meaning substantial transaction and organizational costs) to low capacity (meaning much less administrative and organizational effort to implement the intervention). Experience with implementation of heart attack treatment and, to a lesser extent, tobacco taxation and salt reduction, is much more limited in low-income countries. There is a strong case for early, large-scale implementation trials in each of these three areas, and correspondingly strong arguments for international development assistance to finance these trials and learn from their results.

The opportunities identified do not explicitly address the strengthening of health system capacity. It will be important to ensure that implementation includes related investments in human resources and institutions, with "related" broadly defined. In the cases of tobacco taxation and salt reduction, this could include public sector capacity to impose change on the private sector. One might consider there to be two broad approaches to strengthening health systems. One involves relatively nonspecific investments in capacity and reforms of process. The second involves creating specific capacity to deliver priority services in volume and with high quality. In the second model capacity strengthening spreads out from high-performing initial nodes. The approach that this chapter implicitly advocates is very much in the latter spirit.

These analyses are consistent with a WHO report (WHO, 2012) that examined both population-wide and individual-focused measures that LMICs can take to reduce the burden of chronic diseases. The study finds that "best-buy" interventions are relatively inexpensive, and further, evaluates interventions on the basis of other criteria including system capacity. For US$2 billion per year (less than US$0.40 per person) LMICs can adopt a set of feasible population-based measures that can reduce the burdens imposed, including those by tobacco, unhealthy diet, and lack of physical activity. Adding interventions that focus on individuals would result in a total cost of US$11.4 billion, implying an annual *per capita* investment of less than US$1 in low-income countries and approximately US$3 in upper-middle-income countries.

Reducing tobacco use

In most low-income countries, death in middle age increases in relative importance as the effects of smoking increase. Most adult deaths world-wide involve vascular, neoplastic, and respiratory disease and smoking makes each of these more common. However, tobacco kills differently in different parts of the world. In China, the leading causes of death from smoking are chronic lung disease (CLD) and lung cancer, with a noted excess also of TB deaths but much lower CVD (Liu *et al.*, 1998). In India, the leading causes of death from smoking are TB and CVD, with relatively less lung cancer (Jha and Chen, 2007). In 2001, the number of tobacco-related deaths in developing countries was

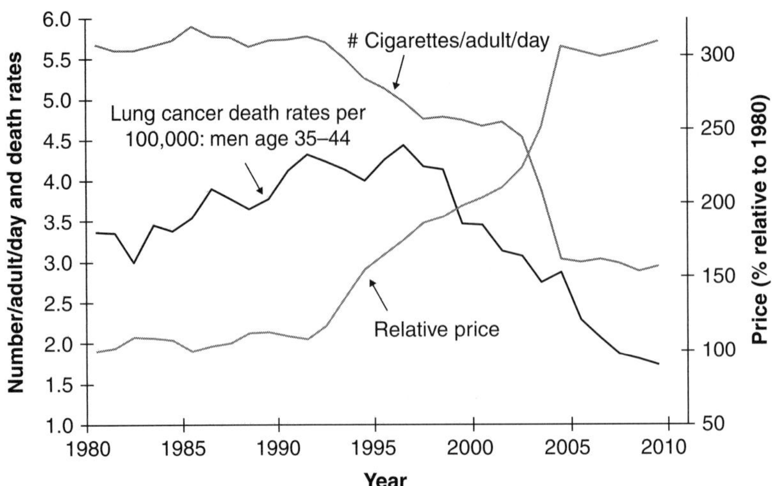

Figure 3.2 *France: smoking, tax and male lung cancer*, 1981–2009*

Note: Lung cancer rates shown at ages 35–44 are divided by 4.
Source: Jha (2009); Hill, (2010).

estimated to be 3.34 million, or about 9 percent of deaths over age 5 in these countries (Jha, 2009b). But if current patterns continue, tobacco use may account for some 10 million deaths per year by 2030, with most of these occurring in LMICs. In total, some 1 billion tobacco deaths might occur this century, in contrast to 100 million in the twentieth century. Unless there is widespread cessation of smoking, some 100 million of China's 200 million young male smokers and about 40 million of India's 100 million young male smokers will eventually die from tobacco-related causes. Smoking is already more common among poor (uneducated) males than among richer (educated) males, and smoking mortality accounts for about half of the difference in mortality risk between rich and poor men in Western countries (Jha *et al.*, 2006b).

Per adult consumption of cigarettes (cigarettes smoked, divided by the population of smokers and non-smokers) has more than halved in the last three decades in the United States, United Kingdom, Canada, France, and other high-income countries (Forey *et al.*, 2009). In contrast, male smoking has risen sharply in many LMICs such as China and Indonesia (Jha, 2009). Indian smoking is mostly in the form of bidis, which are smaller than cigarettes and typically contain only about a quarter as much tobacco, wrapped in the leaf of another plant. Bidis account for approximately 85 percent of total smoked tobacco consumption in India, although cigarettes appear to be displacing bidis among younger males over the last twelve years (Joseph *et al.*, 2011). Brazil, exceptionally, has recorded decreases in the prevalence of adult smoking (Monteiro *et al.*, 2007).

Preventing the initiation of smoking is important because addiction to tobacco makes smoking cessation very difficult, even for the numerous individuals who would like to do so. However, helping people to quit smoking is at least as important as preventing initiation. Far more lives could be saved between now and 2050 with successful efforts to help people stop smoking than with efforts to keep them from starting. Reducing smoking levels is demonstrated to be well within the control of public policy. Indeed, many OECD countries have seen substantial declines in smoking deaths over the past two decades; for example, lung cancer deaths among young men 30–44 years of age have fallen by nearly 80 percent in the United Kingdom (Peto *et al.*, 2006), a change attributable chiefly to marked increases in cessation. Also, in OECD countries more than 30 percent of the adult population are ex-smokers, in contrast to only 2–5 percent in India, 9 percent in China, and 15 percent in Thailand (Jha *et al.*, 2006a). Tobacco tax increases, dissemination of information about the health risks of smoking, restrictions on smoking in public and work places, comprehensive bans on advertising and promotion, and increased access to cessation therapies are effective in reducing tobacco use and its consequences (Jha *et al.*, 2006a). Of these, tobacco taxation is particularly effective – with a 10 percent increase in price leading to a 4–8 percent drop in consumption (roughly equally split between cessation and changes in power initiation). Young people and the poor are particularly more responsive to price (Jha and Chaloupka, 2000a). Because the poor in many countries are more responsive to price than higher-income groups, tax increases might not be as regressive financially as might be believed. Analyses of the US federal excise tax increase of $0.53 in 2009 suggests that Americans below the poverty line bore 12 percent of the marginal higher tax, with Americans having income at twice or more of the poverty line bearing 67 percent of the increase. In contrast, the health benefits were very progressive – with nearly half of the reduced deaths arising in those below the poverty line (Chaloupka *et al.*, 2012). Indeed, in Canada, aggressive tobacco control and use of higher taxes has led to greater absolute declines in tobacco deaths among the lowest income group than in the highest income group of men (Singhal *et al.*, 2012).

Powerful policy interventions to tax and regulate consumption and to inform consumers of health risks have reduced consumption in most high-income countries (Jha and Chaloupka, 1999; Molarius, *et al.*, 2001; Forey *et al.*, 2009). The United States and United Kingdom each took about thirty-five years and Canada about twenty-five years to halve per adult cigarette consumption (from about ten per adult per day to about five) (Forey *et al.*, 2009). However, France took only fifteen years (Hill and Laplanche, 2003). France's uptake of smoking was chiefly after the Second World War and its prevalence rose until the mid 1980s. From 1990 to 2005, cigarette consumption fell from about six cigarettes per adult per day (which is comparable to the *per capita* adult male consumption in India today) to three cigarettes (Figure 3.2, p. 152). This decline was mostly due to a sharp increase in tobacco taxation starting in 1990 under the then President Jacques Chirac. These price increases raised the inflation-adjusted price threefold. Among men, the corresponding lung cancer rates at ages 35–44 fell sharply from 1997 onward. During this period, revenues in real terms rose from about 6 to 12 billion euros (Hill, 2003). The stagnation in tax levels from 2004 onward when Nicolas Sarkozy became Finance Minister has also led to stagnation in *per capita* cigarette consumption. The decline in lung cancer was also due, more controversially, to the replacement of high-tar with lower-tar cigarettes (Jha and Chaloupka, 1999).

High specific excise duties are far more likely to discourage switching between different types of tobacco products, are much easier to administer, and produce a much steadier stream of revenue (WHO, 2010). The exact impact of this excise duty structure would depend, of course, on market conditions, industry efforts to counter the tax hike, and large-scale tax avoidance. The use of excise duty also would decrease the difference between higher- and lower-priced cigarettes, effectively increasing the public health impact. In India, higher taxes on all lengths of cigarettes would slow the growth of the lower-length cigarettes that appear to be displacing bidi sales (Joseph *et al.*, 2011). The main weakness is that such excise duties need to adjust periodically for inflation, which is much higher in developing than in developed countries. Thus a complementary strategy is to raise the excise duty every year, in line with overall inflation and preferably in excess of inflation, such that the number of ex-smokers increases every year. Australia and New Zealand have opted to raise tax rates above inflation automatically, rather than necessitating annual increases through the usual channels (WHO, 2010). France pursued such an objective from 1991, and increased cigarette prices by 5 percent or more in excess of inflation (Recours 1999; see p. 152). In high-inflation settings, it might make sense to focus on affordability, in which case tobacco taxes would be increased by enough to raise prices above income growth so as to reduce affordability (Blecher and van Walbeek, 2004).

An increase in cigarette taxes of 10 percent globally would raise cigarette tax revenues by nearly

7 percent as the fall in demand is less than proportional to the price increase in most countries (Jha and Chaloupka, 1999). However, taxes are underused in most developing countries (Guindon and Bettcher, 2001; Blecher and van Walbeek, 2004). Taxes tend to be absolutely higher and account for a greater share of the retail price (71 percent as of 2006) in high-income countries. In LMICs, taxes account for 54 percent of the final price of cigarettes (Jha and Chaloupka, 1999). In South Africa, tax as a percentage of retail price fell to about 20 percent around 1990, but has subsequently risen to nearly 40 percent (Jha and Chaloupka, 1999). As a result, consumption fell from about four cigarettes per adult per day to two over a decade (van Walbeek, 2005). Poland's 2011 tax increases doubled the real price of cigarettes and lowered consumption (Ciecierski, 2003). Mauritius and Mexico raised taxes by about 30 percent in 2012, which has already reduced consumption.

A tax increase needed to raise the street prices of cigarettes by 70 percent would involve a 2.0–2.8fold increase across countries (Jha, 2009). The increase would raise the street price from about \$0.7 to \$1.3 in low-income countries, from about \$1.3 to \$2.3 in middle-income countries, and from about \$3.7 to \$6.3 in high-income countries. Such increases, while large, have been achieved in numerous countries, including Canada, France, Poland, and South Africa and within various US states. Indeed, price elasticity studies (Tauras and Chaloupka, 2004) suggest that the 2.5fold increase in the US federal cigarette tax in 2009 (rising by 62 cents to \$1.01/pack) might get about 1 million Americans to quit smoking and deter another 2 million youth from starting, thus saving over 1 million lives.

Tobacco use is substantially different than other health challenges as it involves a consumer good, with presumed economic benefits from that consumption. This has led to criticisms that tobacco control ignores the welfare benefits of smoking (Wolf, 2006). Given that smoking is addictive and that most smoking starts early in life when youths are short-sighted, the calculation of welfare benefits is tricky (meaning that these benefits are simply the costs of withdrawal from smoking). In countries with good information, the vast majority of smokers themselves support much higher taxation on tobacco products (WHO, 2010). Moreover, the nature of the tobacco industry's manufacturing process of cigarettes is to spike cigarettes with nicotine in ways that increase the addictive power of tobacco (US DHSS, 2001). This is not to argue that cessation is not possible, as large numbers of adults in the United States and other high-income countries have quit smoking in recent decades (Jha, 2009). But the presence of information gaps, the strong addictive properties of consumption, and the considerable costs of quitting smoking on physical and mental health mean that defining the welfare benefits which would normally be calculated against the costs of illnesses (shown on p. 144 to be quite sizable at about 1.3 percent of global GDP) might well be zero. Hu and colleagues (Hu *et al.*, 1998) examined deadweight losses in China and noted that these varied greatly from quite small to actual deadweight gains from reduced smoking, depending on the assumptions used.

The biggest cost of smoking is the value of life forgone among smokers who wish to quit, but struggle against the strongly addictive properties of tobacco. Putting addiction into a cost-benefit framework is equally tricky. Peck *et al.* (2000) built on an earlier framework by Barnum (1994) by comparing the consumer and producer surplus of tobacco (based on price and supply elasticities) to the VSL (conservatively valued as 1 times *per capita* GDP) weighted by tobacco-related mortality and the degree to which health smoking risks are known. They conclude that if a typical smoker underestimates his or her own health costs by 3–23 percent, then the net benefits of consumption are zero. Similarly, the marginal costs of a 10 percent higher price due to taxation have net welfare gains as long as 3 percent of smokers or more underestimate their health risks of smoking. Gruber and Mullainathan (2002) have conducted economic work that incorporates addiction into consumption choices and conclude that higher taxes increase welfare because the health costs to smokers are huge (even though the external costs to others might be small). The same work finds that higher cigarette taxes do not hurt the poor (since the self-control value of higher taxes helps the poor more).

In sum, it might suffice to say that the tobacco market suffers from three major market failures, thus justifying a public response. Two market failures relate to lack of sufficient information for consumers to make a rational decision about tobacco use: (i) most consumers do not have full knowledge of the risks associated with the consumption of tobacco, and (ii) consumers, especially young smokers, underestimate the risk of addiction to tobacco. In India, few smokers know that 70 percent of smoking deaths occur during productive middle age or that the average YLL from smoking is as great as ten years, and fewer than 50 percent know that smoking is a cause of stroke (Government of India – IIPS, 2011). In China fully 61 percent of smokers thought tobacco did them no or little harm (Chinese Academy of Preventative Medicine, 1997). The lack of information on the full risks of smoking, paired with the strongly addictive nature of manufactured smoked tobacco, results in smokers facing high costs (withdrawal symptoms and physical distress) if they try to quit. In high-income countries with good information on smoking hazards, over 80 percent of adult smokers wish they had never started. Thus, there is no comparable consumer product that carries such severe health risks from continued use, causes regret among informed consumers, and has high costs from the withdrawal of its use. Moreover, the tobacco industry specifically engineers cigarettes to be addictive, and designs reinforcing media messages and consumer signals to maintain this addiction (US DHHS, 2001).

The third market failure arises from health externalities from exposure to tobacco smoke and some financial externalities due to public spending to treat diseases caused by smoking. The costs of exposure to second-hand smoke have not been well studied in developing countries. However, 6–15 percent of health spending were estimated to go toward tobacco-related diseases in other developing countries (Lightwood *et al.*, 2000). The direct cost of treating four major tobacco-related diseases in India amounted to US$1.2 billion, or 4.7 percent of India's national health care expenditure in 2004 (John *et al.*, 2004). Of course, the adage that the cheapest patient is a dead patient also applies to smoking-related deaths, and indeed some have argued that the death of a smoker saves money for others in pension schemes (Raynauld, 1992). However, this argument relies on the false assumption that smokers are fully informed about their consumption choices. Moreover, the costs to households who lack formal insurance schemes or pensions and in whom smoking-related diseases leads to poverty or borrowing to treat the sick and loss of intergenerational wealth transfers is likely to be large. A study found that after accounting for direct expenditure on tobacco by Indian households in 2004, tobacco consumption in India impoverished roughly 15 million people (John *et al.*, 2004). Households with a smoker have worse child health outcomes, including lower immunization rates in children (Rani *et al.*, 2003).

While acknowledging the importance of attempts to estimate welfare losses associated with tobacco use and cessation, our approach in this chapter is simpler. We use published estimates of the costs of mounting a comprehensive tobacco control program (analogous to the "combination prevention" approach to HIV/AIDS transmission). The Center for Disease Control and Prevention (CDC) has recommended expenditures of $1–4 *per capita* but some US states have done well with less. Estimates for India from DCP2 are for about $80 million per year. This figure includes the costs of mobilizing public support, anti-smoking advertising and promotion, support for cessation programs, and tax administration costs. (Proposed levels of taxation are revenue-enhancing for governments relative to the overall cost of comprehensive anti-smoking program, but our CBA is based on social costs.) In light of the range of published program cost we use $0.5 billion per year as a reasonable estimate of the cost of comprehensive programs in LMICs. Indeed, this is the amount of tobacco control funding pledged from the philanthropic foundations of Bill and Melinda Gates and of Michael Bloomberg. Our specific estimates of mortality reduction are based on the effect of a 33 percent price rise (about a 50 percent increase in tax) on demand with a price elasticity of 0.4 percent (i.e. a 10 percent increase leads to about a 4 percent reduction in demand, of which about half is on current consumption), and assume a total of 1 million deaths (or 20 million DALYs) averted annually. Jha *et al.* (2006a) reported that, over fifty years, world-wide, among smokers alive today, a 33 percent price increase would yield a reduction of 22–66 million deaths. This BCR of 40:1 is reported in Table 3.7 (p. 150).

Management of acute and chronic vascular diseases

CVDs in LMICs result in about 13 million deaths each year, over a quarter of all deaths in those countries. Most CVD deaths result from ischemic heart disease (5.7 million) or cerebrovascular disease (4.6 million). A potentially substantial fraction of the heart disease deaths may result from congestive heart failure. In both high-income countries and LMICs, these deaths occur at older ages than do infectious conditions and thus account for a substantially smaller fraction of the total disease burden in DALYs – 12.9 percent – than they do of deaths. However, a far greater proportion of the CVD deaths in LMICs occurs in middle age (30–69) than the proportion of these diseases in high-income countries, where they are concentrated at older ages.

The main risk factors for CVD account for very large fractions of the deaths (and even more of the burden) from those diseases. For ischemic heart disease, they collectively account for 78 percent of deaths in LMICs; for stroke, they account for 61 percent (Ezzati *et al.*, 2006). Measures to reduce the levels of those risk factors – high blood pressure, high intake of saturated animal fat, smoking, obesity, binge drinking of alcohol, physical inactivity, and low fruit and vegetable consumption – are needed for prevention. Unlike experience with controlling tobacco use, there have been far fewer attempts to change the behaviors leading to obesity, hypertension, adverse lipid profiles, or physical activity, and there are few examples of success at a population level. Notable exceptions are the remarkable decline of 25 percent in vascular mortality in the 1990s in Poland, which appears to be due to macroeconomic reforms that effectively removed the government subsidy for butter overnight, and simultaneously opened up markets from Western Europe of fresh fruits and vegetables as well as products with lower amounts of saturated fat (Zatonski and Jha, 2002), and the Finnish experience of reducing vascular mortality first in North Karelia and then country-wide, with an aggressive population-based program of interventions. Common sense suggests that they should be initiated even while more systematic efforts to develop and evaluate behavior-change packages are ramped up.

Low-cost generic risk pills for vascular disease

Despite the uncertainty in effective interventions to prevent elevated blood pressure, blood lipids, and diabetes, there is considerable evidence that a simple combination of cheap drugs can be highly effective at reducing mortality among the millions of adults in South and East Asia who have some existing vascular disease or diabetes (Gaziano *et al.*, 2006; Peto, 2006; Rodgers *et al.*, 2006). Consider the following: in the absence of any drug therapy, adults with previous stroke, heart attack, diabetes or any other evidence of some serious vascular disease have about a 7 percent annual risk of either dying or being re-hospitalized with a recurrence. If they take an aspirin a day, that risk drops to 5 percent; if they add two more drugs to reduce blood pressure and blood lipids, it drops to 2 percent. The exact sequence of drugs matters little, but being on three or four drugs (aspirin, a blood pressure pill or two, and a statin drug to lower cholesterol) daily versus none means a ten-year risk of death or re-hospitalization of about 50 percent untreated versus 16 percent on treatment. All these drugs are low-cost, and thus could be easily packaged into "polypills" or generic risk pills for widespread use (Peto, 2006). Indeed, China's success in widely accessible TB therapy with several drugs (Dye and Floyd, 2006) serves as a model on which simple drug therapy for vascular disease could be introduced in the region.

Provision of a generic risk pill to adults could be cost-effective. We consider a cohort of about 400 million adults to have some indication of existing vascular disease (typically by a physician diagnosis or earlier clinical event). Of these, using Indian registry data, about 20 percent of them will already be on treatment (80 million adults, Xavier *et al.*, 2008) therefore 80 percent (320 million adults) would see the benefits of the pill. Without treatment, about 5 percent would have a stroke or heart attack

(16 million events) and 10 percent of these events will be fatal, as acute management of these is uncommon in most developing countries (a total of 1.6 million deaths or 24 million DALYs if one assumes 15 DALYs per death averted). The rest (90 percent, or 14.4 million adults) will have disability (disability weight of 0.437, Lopez *et al.*, 2006a), which leads to about 94 million DALYs. Hence, the intervention would avert a total of 1.6 million deaths (or 118 million DALYs) annually. If the cost per adult patient were $100, the total cost would then be $32 billion per year, hence a BCR of 118/32 ~ 4:1 (Table 3.7, p. 150).

Pharmaceutical interventions to manage two major components of cardiovascular risk – hypertension and high cholesterol levels – are well established and are highly cost-effective for individuals at high risk of a stroke or heart attack. Adding aspirin to the list of pharmaceutical interventions can reduce risk significantly further. From at least the time of publication of DCP1, researchers have recognized that the low cost and high effectiveness of drugs to prevent the reoccurrence of a cardiovascular event made their long-term use potentially cost-effective in low-income environments. Even if sustained behavior change proves difficult to achieve, medication has the potential to reduce CVD risks by 50 percent or more. Gaziano *et al.* (2006) and Rodgers *et al.* (2006) develop the current evidence on that point. A key problem, however, concerns the health care personnel and systems requirements associated with the need for lifelong medication, a problem also facing antiretroviral therapy for HIV/AIDS and the use of medication to target several major psychiatric disorders. Adherence to drugs is a key issue, but unlike the challenge with HIV/AIDS drugs, resistance to the polypill drugs are unlikely, and their costs are quite low. Uncertainty about adherence is one of the prompts for exploration of alternative chronic care, discussed on pp. 146–8.

Aside from the lifelong requirement for drug use associated with CVD risk reduction in high-risk individuals, treatment of acute heart attacks with inexpensive drugs is slightly less demanding of system resources and also cost-effective (Gaziano *et al.*, 2006). Given the high incidence of these problems, system-wide efforts to achieve high rates of appropriate drug use in response to acute heart disease are a high priority. As identified by Jamison *et al.* (2008) and reported in Table 3.7, acute management of heart attacks with low-cost drugs can prevent 300,000 heart attack deaths (4.5 million DALYs) at a cost of $200 million annually (Jamison *et al.*, 2008). This produces a BCR of 25:1.

Prevention of obesity and diabetes

Obesity and lack of physical activity are clear risk factors for development of diabetes, which can be further compounded by raised blood pressure and lipid imbalances, such as elevated "bad" cholesterol (PSC Collaborators, 1995). These factors work together, so only careful epidemiological studies can tease out which contributes to eventual mortality from vascular disease, and to a less clear extent from selected cancers. It is clear that diabetes rates are markedly increasing with urbanization: in China and India, diabetes prevalence among urban adults is nearly ten times that of their rural counterparts (Jha and Anderson, 2007). However, the contribution of body mass to premature mortality in developing countries such as India and China may well be different, for reasons that are not well understood. A ten-year prospective study of 220,000 men in urban China found higher risks of vascular deaths among those with an elevated body mass index (BMI), but also excess risk at low BMI levels. Indeed, the excess risk at lower BMI persisted after restricting analysis to never-smokers or excluding the first three years of follow-up, and became about twice as great after allowing for blood pressure (Chen *et al.*, 2006). In Mumbai (formerly Bombay), elevated as well as low BMI were noted; thinness was more common among illiterate men, and was associated with smoking and chewing tobacco, whereas higher education was associated with raised BMI (Gupta and Mehta, 2000; Shukla *et al.*, 2002). Interventions to reduce obesity, aside from the general recommendations to increase physical activity, are not yet widely practicable. Better public information on risks, including more widespread communication of emerging scientific findings for large, reliable studies, is likely to influence both individual behavior by adults, and

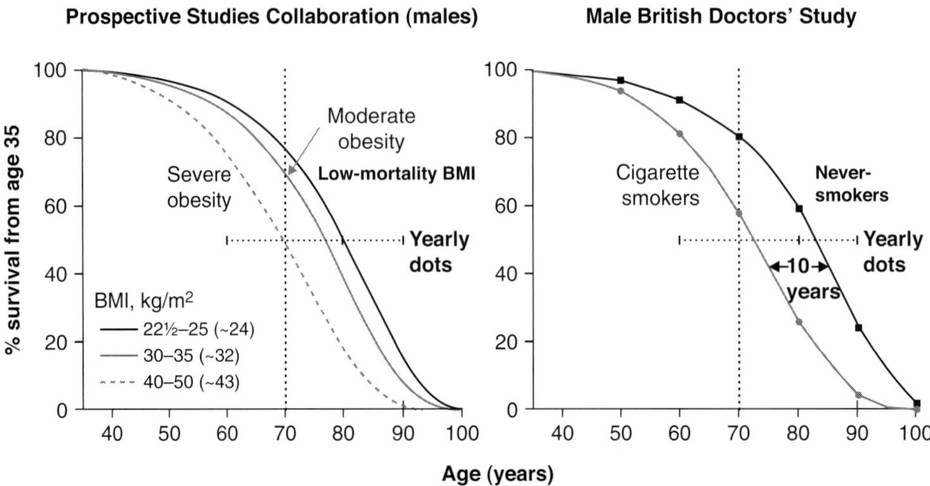

Figure 3.3 *Mortality risks from smoking and obesity*

Note: Life expectancy loss of three years with moderate obesity and 10 years with smoking.
Male survival, ages 35–100: severe obesity and cigarette smoking each shorten life expectancy by ~10 years, and moderate obesity shortens it by ~3 years; so, 2 kg/m^2 extra BMI (if overweight) or a 10 percent prevalence of smoking shortens it by ~1 year. Left: PSC analyses of BMI among males; effects among females are not greater (Peto *et al.*, 1995). Right: Analyses of persistent cigarette smoking among male British doctors (Doll *et al.*, 2004).
Source: Peto et al. (2010).

lead to further public demand for control of risk factors.

Comparison of smoking and obesity risks

Studies of tens of thousands of deaths have reliably assessed mortality from adult obesity and from persistent smoking in developed countries (Peto *et al.*, 2010). In the PSC Collaborators study (PSC Collaborators, 1995) of 70,000 deaths in 900,000 adults, an increase of 2 units in the BMI (the weight in kg divided by the square of the height in mt) among men who were overweight reduced life span by one year (mostly from an increase in vascular disease death rates). This loss of one year of life was comparable to the reduction in life span from an increase of 10 percent in the prevalence of smoking seen among UK doctors (Doll *et al.*, 2004; Figure 3.3, p. 158). Moderate obesity (overweight, defined as BMI range 30–35, mean 32) shortens life expectancy by approximately three years. Only among the small minority of adults with severe obesity (BMI range 40–50, mean 43) was the loss of life comparable to the ten years lost for being a lifelong smoker. Thus, stopping smoking (which is widely practicable) can lead to a gain of about ten years in life expectancy, far more than smokers could expect from weight control (which is currently far less practicable).

Salt reduction

High blood pressure is a significant chronic disease risk factor, responsible for at least 50 percent of CVD, particularly stroke and ischemic heart disease. Reduction in salt intake is a key factor in reducing hypertension. Moderate salt reduction can lower systolic blood pressure by small (1.7–3.4 mm Hg) but meaningful amounts (He and MacGregor, 2004; Hooper *et al.*, 2004).

Salt reduction was identified by the WHO as a "best buy" for NCD prevention and control (WHO, 2011) and attention is turning to finding the most effective methods to achieve it. Depending on the diet composition in a population, a greater effect may occur through interventions to reduce salt in food processing or at the cooking or eating stages. The former approach is being tried in Latin America, where Brazil, Argentina, and Chile are among the countries with industry agreements to reduce salt in processing. The main limitation in salt reduction strategies is the unproven impact on changing behavior when salt is mostly added at the table, often as a sole condiment to food. This is the dietary pattern in much of India and Asia, for example.

Increasing numbers of countries are implementing national policies to reduce salt consumption. Population-based interventions to achieve salt reduction include information and behavior change to reduce use at the point of cooking and eating and changes by manufacturers in processed product formulation and food preservation through regulatory or voluntary steps. Studies of consumer acceptance of reduced salt from developing countries have not yet been done, but experience in the United States and other developed countries suggest that a substantial reduction from current levels is feasible with little or no consumer resistance. Selecting the appropriate level of intervention to achieve the greatest possible reduction in salt intake requires understanding local consumption habits and food systems. For instance, Argentina and South Africa are focusing on salt reduction in bread (Rubinstein *et al.*, 2010; Bertram *et al.*, 2012). Reducing salt in bread has been found to be very cost-effective in Argentina with an ICER of (2007) I$1,407 or a savings of US$703 per DALY gained. The cost-effectiveness of 15–30 percent reduction in salt intake in Mexico through the two channels of voluntary and legislated manufacturing changes and labeling was modeled. The average cost-effectiveness across the population was US$286 (in 2005 US$) per DALY gained (Salomon *et al.*, 2012).

Asaria *et al.* (2007) estimated the cost-effectiveness of interventions to achieve lower systolic blood pressure for age groups and sex across twenty-three LMICs, which account for 65 percent of the global population. They describe a combined population-level intervention to reduce salt intake through voluntary manufacturing changes, behavior change using mass media, and other awareness-raising campaigns. As pointed out in DCP2, the cost-effectiveness of public information efforts through mass media or other campaigns varies widely depending on the population reached and assumptions about their responsiveness to information. Large reductions in salt intake – up to 30 percent of average daily intake – are achievable through changed table and cooking behavior, but depend on context. Population-level manufacturing changes have become a favored intervention in recent years because they appear to reduce this uncertainty.

Over a ten-year period (2006–2015), Asaria *et al.* (2007) estimate that a 15 percent reduction in salt consumption in twenty-three LMICs would avert 8.5 million deaths. This is achieved through lowering blood pressure by 1.24 to 3.46 mm Hg (depending on age) at an average cost of US$0.14 *per capita*. Our analysis uses this figure as the basis for *per capita* program costs. The salt reduction intervention is most cost-effective in countries with a high average salt intake, such as China and the Philippines.

The twenty-three countries from the Asaria *et al.* (2007) list count 2.1 billion adults over age 30; the total world population counts about 3.3 billion people (UN, 2009). If one were to scale the intervention presented by Asaria *et al.* (2007) to the global level, potentially, this intervention would save 13 million deaths over ten years (~ 200 million DALYs assuming that 1 death averted corresponds to 15 DALYs). At a tentative cost of $0.3 per adult p.a., the total costs of the intervention would be $10 billion over ten years. Hence, the BCR would be 20:1.

Hepatitis B vaccination

Hepatitis B is a viral infection that attacks the liver and can cause acute and chronic disease (WHO, 2012). It is transmitted through contact with body fluids, especially blood, of a person infected (WHO, 2012). In high-income countries, hepatitis B transmission occurs mostly during adolescence or at the early adulthood, with the onset of sexual activity and drug abuse involving the unsafe reuse of needles (Brenzel *et al.*, 2006). In LMICs, such as in SSA and South Asia, hepatitis B transmission occurs mostly at early childhood through contact with infectious body fluids and unsafe injections, and through mother-to-infant transmission (Brenzel *et al.*, 2006).

About 2 billion people world-wide have been infected with hepatitis B and about 350 million live with chronic infection (WHO, 2012). An estimated 600,000 persons die each year due to the consequences of hepatitis B (WHO, 2012). For those who are already infected, strategies to reduce co-factors, such as exposure to aflatoxins and alcohol, are required.

Hepatitis B is preventable with a safe and very effective vaccine of 75–95 percent efficacy (Brenzel *et al.*, 2006). Current global immunization coverage with hepatitis B vaccine is high, at 75 percent (WHO, 2011a). The cost per child vaccinated with hepatitis B monovalent vaccine (birth dose) is up to US$ 2–4 (Brenzel *et al.*, 2006). The cost of India's hepatitis B immunization program, vaccinating about 37 percent of the Indian birth cohort (about 10 million children) is 1.8 billion Indian Rupees (US$36 million) (Jha and Laxminarayan, 2009), leading to a cost per vaccinated child of about US$3.6.

Most vaccine-preventable diseases result in deaths occurring at an early age, usually shortly after vaccination. Conversely, deaths from hepatitis B happen many years into the future. Therefore, countries and immunization programs that introduce hepatitis B vaccination today will not see most of the health benefits for many years. A one-, five- or ten-year time period into the future is too short to accumulate the total health benefits (deaths averted) resulting from universal hepatitis B immunization today, as deaths from liver cancer or liver cirrhosis occur at older ages (Brenzel *et al.*, 2006).

Universal immunization with hepatitis B vaccine is highly cost-effective. Consider aiming for universal immunization of the world birth cohort (~ about 136 million children, UN, 2009), which corresponds to raising the immunization coverage from 75 percent to 100 percent. Take a cost of $3.6 per child vaccinated. The total annual cost would be $122 million (or about US$0.1 billion, Table 3.7, p. 150). If we assume that this 25 percent incremental coverage raise would avert 25 percent of the 600,000 annual deaths forty years into the future (about 150,000 deaths or 3 million DALYs – assuming 1 death averted corresponds to 20 DALYs averted – Table 3.7), then the undiscounted BCR would be 30:1. Discounting health benefits to PV at a 3 percent discount rate would yield a BCR of about 10:1.

This calculation evidently presents limitations in terms of the dynamic modeling of transmission, including herd immunity as well as a potential exogenously-driven decline of hepatitis B-related mortality and morbidity because of other behavioral or dietary interventions in the future.

Implications for development assistance for health

The spreading awareness of changing health needs in developing countries to include chronic disease has not translated into major shifts in resources from international donors or governments in affected countries. The donor role in addressing specific global health conditions is important for several reasons. First, poor countries face severe resource constraints and have little to no latitude to add services, especially for seemingly less urgent needs. Second, donors provide global public goods in the form of research. Third, donor priorities influence their own resource allocations for health conditions, as well as provide a signaling effect to LMICs.

According to a review of donor health funding, chronic disease receives the smallest amount of donor assistance of all health conditions, having lost ground since 1990 relative to infectious diseases (IHME, 2010a) Donor assistance for health (DAH) was estimated at almost $26 billion in 2009. The amount allocated to chronic disease was $270 million, or about 1 percent of the total (IHME 2010a). An earlier, more comprehensive, measure of global health funding for chronic diseases that includes corporate philanthropic contributions and research funding shows $750 million dedicated to chronic diseases in 2008, or less than 3 percent of the total external assistance for health (Nugent and Feigl, 2010). In relation to the burden of disease, donors and other funders provided about $0.76/DALY lost due to chronic diseases in developing countries, compared to $12.5/DALY lost due to all infectious diseases (Nugent and Feigl, 2010).

The costs of chronic diseases on a global basis have been estimated for specific diseases and regions of the world as consuming significant GDP shares (these estimates were discussed on p. 143).

The picture of donor involvement in chronic diseases is not entirely bleak. Narrowly defined NCD donor funding rose from $30 million in 1990 to $270 million in 2009 (IHME, 2010). This translates into a ninefold rise over the period. The largest share of the increase in NCD funds for developing countries comes from private, non-profit donors, and there is evidence of accelerating interest from public donors (Nugent and Feigl, 2010).

The above findings on large and growing costs of chronic diseases, escalating costs to achieve maximal survival, and the growing tobacco and obesity epidemics, all suggest that a more fundamental re-alignment of developmental assistance is required. While such major changes may not be politically feasible in the short or even medium term, we pose them nonetheless. The main requirement might well be to substantially re-engineer developmental assistance, particularly from bilateral agencies, to solve the intervention, delivery, and implementation challenges of chronic disease control. Specifically, households in LMICs already spend considerable sums on adult clinical services (such as those for acute or chronic management of heart attacks). Thus, the key issue is to ensure that the spending is as effective and cost-effective as possible. Borrowing from the success in reducing childhood mortality, the requirement for improved adult health would see a considerable scale up and change in traditional development assistance to focus on research of new interventions as well as operational research and modules to deliver these at low cost.

While such a substantial shift in the nature of developmental assistance may be feasible even without substantial increases in overall funding if cost-saving or low-cost interventions are prioritized, the longer-term prospect is that health services will need to shift substantially toward chronic care and disease management. Hum *et al.* (2013) suggest that the marginal costs of increasing longevity are rising. The logic is that chronic diseases consume a substantial amount of adult disposable income, pose considerable risk to the economic growth prospects of LMICs, and governments in such require more know-how and intervention strategies and tools, including operational tools, to tackle chronic diseases. Thus, the requirement is less to finance these services directly, but rather to conduct research which makes the marginal costs of them affordable. As with the development of cheaper and widely available technologies for the prevention and treatment of undernutrition and infectious diseases, this implies the need for greater R&D for technology, but also investment in both implementation science and in closing the "know–do" gap. Specific examples might well be to permit more rapid licensing and approval of generic drug risk combinations, and perhaps even to think of global subsidies to alter risk behaviors, along the lines of the AmFM. Also needed is a substantial scale up of mortality statistics and risk-factor information on chronic diseases, perhaps based on the WHO data (WHO Ad Hoc Committee, 1997).

Over the past few decades, the development of new technologies (drugs, vaccines, policies) has focused mostly on childhood and infectious diseases, with fewer world-wide investments in R&D for adult chronic diseases. Thus the longer-term trajectory of critical incomes for adult survival might well depend on the development of newer interventions, as well as more widespread application of interventions already proven to be cost-effective.

Appendix: sensitivity analysis

The analysis upon which we based the conclusions reported in Table 3.7 were undertaken with the following assumptions:

1 The discount rate is 3 percent per year and the version of the DALY that was used was based on this 3 percent and *no age weighting*. These are the assumptions used in the most recent presentation of methods, data sources, and results on the 2001 global burden of disease (Lopez *et al.*, 2006a, 2006b).
2 In an attempt to include relevant health systems costs and to take a long-run view, cost estimates in this chapter are based on long-run average costs (at least in principle, as there is some variation in actual costing methods).

3 The chapter assumes the value of a DALY to be $1,000.
4 The chapter assumes zero deadweight loss from taxation.

We proceeded in a sensitivity analysis of our findings while examining three dimensions of sensitivity:

(i) A change in the discount rate from 3 percent to 5 percent per year

We then moved from the use of DALYs (3,0) to the use of DALYs (5,0). Therefore, thirty YLL discounted at 3 percent (~ 20 DALYs), when discounted at 5 percent amounted to 15 DALYs: in this case, all health benefits and BCRs were divided by 4/3. In the same way, twenty YLL discounted at 3 percent (~ 15 DALYs), when discounted at 5 percent, amounted to 12 DALYs: in this case, all health benefits and BCRs were divided by 5/4.

The ensuing BCRs become: 30:1 (tobacco taxation), 20:1 (acute management with low-cost drugs), 16:1 (salt reduction); 3:1 (hepatitis B immunization), and 3:1 (generic risk pill).

(ii) Inclusion of the underestimation of ex ante *costs*

Since *ex ante* costs are often substantially underestimated, we multiplied all costs by 3 consistently with Jamison *et al.* (2008). Therefore, all BCRs are divided by 3.

(iii) A change in the value of a DALY to $5,000 rather than $1,000

All health benefits are multiplied by 5, and therefore all the BCRs become multiplied by 5.

The most optimistic alternative assumption of (i)–(iii) increases all BCRs by a factor of 5. The most pessimistic alternative assumption of (i)–(iii) decreases all BCRs by 4, and the BCR for hepatitis B immunization becomes about 1:1 (when both (i) and (ii) are applied).

Without discounting its future health benefits, the BCR for hepatitis B immunization would rise to 30:1.

Bibliography

Ad Hoc Committee on Health Research Relating to Future Intervention Options, & World Health Organization, 1996: *Investing in Health Research and Development: Report of the AD Hoc Committee on Health Research Relating to Future Intervention Options*, Convened Under the Auspices of the World Health Organization, Geneva

Asaria R., D. Chisholm, C. Mathers, M. Ezzati, and R. Beaghole, 2007: Chronic disease prevention: health effects and financial costs of strategies to reduce salt intake and control tobacco use, *Lancet* **370**, 2044–63

Ballard, C., J. Shoven, and J. Whalley, 1985: General equilibrium computations of the marginal welfare costs of taxes in the United States, *American Economic Review* **74**, 128–38

Barnum, H., 1994: The economic burden of the global trade in tobacco, *Tobacco Control* **3**, 358–61

Behrman, J. R., H. Alderman, and J. Hoddinott, 2007: Hunger and malnutrition, Paper Prepared for 2008 Copenhagen Consensus

Bertram, M., K. Steyn, E. Wentzel-Viljoen, S. Tollman, and K. Hofman, 2012: Reducing the sodium content of high-salt foods: effect on cardiovascular disease in South Africa, *South African Medical Journal* **102**, 743–5

Blecher, E. H. and C. P. van Walbeek, 2004: An international analysis of cigarette affordability, *Tobacco Control* **13**, 339–46

Bloom, D. E. and D. Canning, 2006: Booms, busts and echoes: how the biggest demographic upheaval in history is affecting global development, *Finance and Development* **43**, 8–13

Bloom, D. E., D. Canning, and D. T. Jamison, 2004: Health, wealth and welfare, *Finance and Development*, **41**, 10–15

Bloom, D. E., E. T. Cafiero, E. Jané-Llopis, S. Abrahams-Gessel, L. R. Bloom, S. Fathima, A. B. Feigl, T. Gaziano, M. Mowafi, A. Pandya, K. Prettner, L. Rosenberg, B. Seligman, A. Z. Stein, and C. Weinstein, 2011a: The Global economic burden of non-communicable diseases, World Economic Forum, Geneva, www.weforum.org/economicsofncd

Bloom, D. E., D. Chisholm, E. Jané-Llopis, K. Prettner, A. Stein, and A. Feigl, 2011b: From burden to "Best buys": reducing the economic impact of non-communicable diseases in low- and middle-income countries, World Health Organization and World Economic Forum, Geneva

Brenzel B., L. J. Wolfson, J. Fox–Rushby, M. Miller, and N. A. Halsey, 2006: Vaccine–preventable diseases, in D. T. Jamison, A. R. Measham, J. B. Bremen *et al.* (eds.), *Disease Control Priorities in Developing Countries*, 2nd edn, Oxford University Press New York, 389–412

Carr, S. M. *et al.*, 2011: An evidence synthesis of qualitative and quantitative research on component intervention techniques, effectiveness, cost-effectiveness, equity and acceptability of different versions of health-related lifestyle advisor roles in improving health, *Health Technology Assessment* **15**(9), iii–iv, 1–284

Center for Disease Control and Prevention (CDC), 1997: *Unrealized Prevention Opportunities: Reducing the Health and Economic Burden of Chronic Disease* CDC, Atlanta, GA

Chaloupka, F. K., Yurekli, A., and Fong, G. T., 2012: Tobacco taxes as a tobacco control strategy, *Tobacco Control* **21**, 172–80

Chen Z., G. Yang, M. Zhou, M. Smith, A. Offer, J. Ma, L. Wang, H. Pan, G. Whitlock, R. Collins, S. Niu, and R. Peto, 2006: Body mass index and mortality from ischaemic heart disease in a lean population: 10 year prospective study of 220 000 adult men, *International Journal of Epidemiology* **35**, 141–50

Chinese Academy of Preventative Medicine (CAPM), 1997: *Smoking in China: 1996 National Prevalence Survey of Smoking Pattern*, China Science and Technology Press, Beijing

Chodosh, J. *et al.*, 2005: Meta-analysis: chronic disease self-management programs for older adults, *Annals of Internal Medicine* **143**, 427–38

Ciecierski, C., 2003: Tobacco control and economics in Poland, in 12th World Conference on Tobacco or Health: Global Action for a Tobacco Free Future, Helsinki

Coleman, K., B. T. Austin, C. Brach, and E. H. Wagner, 2009: Evidence on the chronic care model in the new millennium, *Health Affairs* **28**, 75–85

Cutler, D., A. Deaton, and A. Lleras-Muney, 2006: The determinants of mortality, *Journal of Economic Perspectives* **20**, 97–120

Daar, A., P. Singer, D. Persad, S. Pramming, D. Matthews, R. Beaglehole, A. Bernstein *et al.*, 2007: Grand challenges in chronic non-communicable diseases, *Nature* **450**, 494–6

Dikshit, R., P. Gupta, C. Ramasundarahettige, 2012: Cancer mortality in India: a nationally representative survey, *Lancet* **6736**, 60358–4

Doll, R. and R. Peto, 1981: The causes of cancer: quantitative estimates of avoidable risks of cancer in the United States today, *Journal of the National Cancer Institute* **66**, 1191–308

Doll, R., R. Peto, J. Boreham, and I. Sutherland, 2004: Mortality in relation to smoking: 50 years' observations on male British doctors, *British Medical Journal* **328**, 1519–28

Dye, C. and K. Floyd, 2006: Tuberculosis, in D. T. Jamison, A. R. Measham, J. B. Breman *et al.* (eds.), *Disease Control Priorities in Developing Countries*, 2nd edn. Oxford University Press, New York, 289–309

Ezzati, M., S. Vander Hoorn, A. D. Lopez, G. Ganaei, A. Rodgers, C. D. Mathers, and C. J. L. Murray, 2006: Comparative quantification of mortality and burden of disease attributable to selected risk factors, in A. D. Lopez, C. D. Mathers, M. Ezzati, D. T. Jamison, and C. J. L. Murray (eds.), *Global Burden of Disease and Risk Factors*, Oxford University Press, New York, 241–396

Forey, B., J. Hamling, and P. Lee, 2009: *International Smoking Statistics: A Collection of Historical Data from 30 Economically Developed Countries*, Oxford University Press, New York

Gakidou, E., M. Hogan, and A. D. Lopez, 2004: Adult mortality: time for a reappraisal, *International Journal of Epidemiology* **33**, 710–17

Gaziano, T., K. S. Reddy, F. Paccaud, S. Horton, and V. Chaturvedi, 2006: Cardiovascular disease, in D. T. Jamison, J. Breman *et al.* (eds.), *Disease Control Priorities in Developing Countries*, 2nd edn., Oxford University Press, New York, 645–62

Gericke, C. A., C. Kurowski, M. K. Ranson, and A. Mills, 2003: Feasibility of scaling-up interventions: the role of interventions design, *Working Paper* **13**, Disease Control Priorities Project, Bethesda, MD

Gilmer, T. P. *et al.*, 2007: Cost-effectiveness of diabetes case management for low-income populations, *Health Services Research* **5**, 1943–59

Global IDEA Scientific Advisory Committee, 2004: Health and economic benefits of an accelerated program of research to combat global infectious diseases, *Canadian Medical Association Journal* **171**(10), 1203–8

Gostin, L. O., E. A. Friedman, G. Ooms, T. Gebauer, N. Gupta, D. Sridhar, W. Chenguang, J. A. Røttingen, and D. Sanders, 2011: The joint action and learning initiative: towards a global agreement on national and global responsibilities for health, *PLoS Med*, **8**

Government of India – IIPS, 2011: *Global Adult Tobacco Survey: India*, Government of India, MOHFW, New Delhi

Gruber, J. and S. Mullainathan, 2002: Do cigarette taxes make smokers happier?, *NBER Working Paper* **8872**, NBER, Cambridge, MA

Guindon, E. and D. Bettcher, 2001: Tobacco control in tobacco-producing countries, *Bulletin, World Health Organization* **79**, 1086

Gupta, P. C. and H. C. Mehta, 2000: Cohort study of all-cause mortality among tobacco users in Mumbai, India, *Bulletin, World Health Organization* **78**, 877–83

He, F. J. and G. A. MacGregor, 2004: Effects of longer-term modest salt reduction on blood pressure, Cochrane Database of Systematic Reviews **1**, CD004937

Hill, C., 2003: *Le tabac en France les vrais chiffres*, La Documentation Française, Paris

Hill, C. and A. Laplanche, 2003: *Le tabac en France les vrais chiffres*, La Documentation Française, Paris

Hoddinott, J., M. Rosegrant, and M. Torero, 2012: Investments to reduce hunger and undernutrition, Paper prepared for 2012 Copenhagen Consensus, see Chapter 6 in this volume

Hooper, L., C. Barlett, G. D. Smith, and S. Ebrahim, 2004: Advice to reduce dietary salt for prevention of cardiovascular disease, Cochrane Database of Systematic Reviews **1**, CD003656

Hu, T., X. P. Xu, and T. Keeler, 1998: Earmarked tobacco taxes: lessons learned, in I. Abedian, R. van der Merwe, N. Wilkins, and P. Jha (eds.), *The Economics of Tobacco Control: Towards an Optimal Policy Mix*, University of Cape Town 102–18

Huang, E. S. *et al.*, 2007: The cost-effectiveness of improving diabetes care in US federally qualified community health centers, *Health Services Research* **6**, 2174–93

Hum, R. J., P. Jha, A. M. McGahan, and Y. L. Cheng, 2013: Global divergence in critical income for adult and childhood survival: analyses of mortality using Michaelis–Menten, eLife Sciences 1:e00051

Inglis, S. C. *et al.*, 2006: Extending the horizon in chronic heart failure: effects of multidisciplinary, home-based intervention relative to usual care, *Circulation* **144**, 2466–73

Institute for Health Metrics and Evaluation (IHME), 2010a: *Financing Global Health 2010: Development Assistance and Country Spending in Economic Uncertainty*, Institute for Health Metrics and Evaluation, Seattle

2010b: *Adult Mortality Estimates by Country 1970–2010*, Institute for Health Metrics and Evaluation, Seattle

Institute of Medicine (IOM), 1985: *New Vaccine Development: Establishing Priorities*, Vol. 1 of *Diseases of Importance in the United States*, National Academies Press, Washington, DC

2010: *Promoting Cardiovascular Health in the Developing World*, V. Fuster and Br. B. Kelly (eds.), National Academies Press, Washington, DC

International Diabetes Federation (IDF), 2010: *International Diabetes Atlas*, Brussels

Jamison, D. T., 2006a: Investing in health, in D. T. Jamison, J. Breman, A. Measham *et al.* (eds.), *Disease Control Priorities in Developing Countries*, 2nd edn, Oxford University Press, New York, 3–34

2006b: The neglected problems of stillbirths and neonatal deaths, Paper prepared for the Global Forum on Health Research, 10th Meeting, Cairo

Jamison, D. T. and S. Radelet, 2005: Making aid smarter, *Finance and Development* **42**(2), 42–6

Jamison, D. T., J. Sachs, and J. Wang, 2001: The effect of the AIDS epidemic on economic welfare in Sub-Saharan Africa, *CMH Working Paper* **WG1:13**, Commission on Macroeconomics and Health, World Health Organization, Geneva

Jamison, D. T., P. Jha, and W. Zatonski, 2002: The effect of the tobacco and chronic disease on economic welfare in former socialist economies, Poland Health Foundation Annual Meeting, Warsaw

Jamison, D. T., E. A. Jamison, and J. D. Sachs, 2003: Assessing the determinants of growth when health is explicitly included in the measure of economic welfare, Paper presented at the 4th World Congress of the International Health Economics Association, San Francisco

Jamison, D. T., M. E. Sandbu, and J. Wang, 2004: Why has infant mortality decreased at such different rates in different countries? *Working Paper* **21**, Disease Control Priorities Project, Bethesda, MD

Jamison, D. T., J. Breman, A. R. Measham *et al.* (eds.), 2006a: *Disease Control Priorities in Developing Countries*, 2nd edn. Oxford University Press, New York

Jamison, D. T., S. Shahid-Salles, J. S. Jamison, J. Lawn, and J. Zupan, 2006b: Incorporating deaths near the time of birth into estimates of the global burden of disease, in A. D. Lopez, C. D. Mathers, M. Ezzati, D. T. Jamison, and C. J. L. Murray (eds.), *Global Burden of Disease and Risk Factors*, Oxford University Press, New York, 427–62

Jamison, E. A., D. T. Jamison, and E. A. Hanushek, 2007: The effects of education quality on income growth and mortality decline, *Economics of Education Review* **26**, 772–89

Jamison, D. T., P. Jha, and D. E. Bloom, 2008: *Disease Control*, Paper prepared for 2008 Copenhagen Consensus, www.cc08.org

Jamison, D. T., P. Jha, V. Malhotra, and S. Verguet, 2012a: *The 20th Century Transformation of Human Health: Its Magnitude and Value*, Copenhagen Consensus Center, Manuscript in press, to be published in *How Much Have Global Problems Cost the World? A Scorecard from 1900 to 2050*, Cambridge University Press

Jamison, D. T., S. M. Murphy, M. E. Sandbu, and J. Wang, 2012b: Why has under-five mortality decreased at such different rates in different countries?, Unpublished manuscript

Jamison, D. T., P. Jha, R. Laxminarayan, and T. Ord, 2012c: Infectious disease, injury and reproductive health, Paper prepared for 2012 Copenhagen Consensus Chapter 7 in this volume

Janssens, B. *et al.*, 2007: Offering integrated care for HIV/AIDS, diabetes and hypertension within chronic disease clinics in Cambodia, *Bulletin, World Health Organization* **85**, 880–5

Jeemon, P. and K. S. Reddy, 2010: Social determinant of cardiovascular disease outcomes in Indians, *Indian Journal of Medical Research* **132**, 617–22

Jha, P., 2009a: Avoidable global cancer deaths and total deaths from smoking, *Nature Reviews Cancer* **9**, 655–64

2009b: Avoidance of worldwide cancer mortality and total mortality from smoking, *Nature Reviews Cancer* **9**, 655–64

Jha, P. and I. Anderson, 2007: Reducing adult deaths from chronic diseases in Asia: evidence and opportunities, in D. T. Jamison, R. Measham, J. B. Breman *et al.* (eds.), *Disease Control Priorities in Developing Countries*, 2nd edn., Oxford University Press, New York

Jha, P. and F. J. Chaloupka, 1999: *Curbing the Epidemic: Governments and the Economics of Tobacco Control*, The World Bank, Washington, DC

2000a: The economics of global tobacco control, *British Medical Journal* **321**, 358–61

2000b: *Tobacco Control in Developing Countries*, Oxford University Press

Jha, P. and Z. Chen, 2007: Poverty and chronic diseases in Asia: challenges and opportunities, *Canadian Medical Association Journal* **177**(9), 1059–62

Jha, P. and R. Laxminarayan, 2009: *Choosing Health: An Entitlement for all Indians*, CGHR, University of Toronto, Toronto and New Delhi, http://cghr.org/wordpress/wp-content/uploads/2011/06/Choosing-Health-report-FINAL.pdf

Jha, P. and A. Mills, 2002: *Improving Health of the Global Poor. The Report of Working Group 5 of the Commission on Macroeconomics and Health*, Organization, Geneva

Jha, P., R. Peto, and W. Zatonski, 2006b: Social inequalities in male mortality, and in male mortality from smoking: indirect estimation from national death rates in England and Wales, Poland, and North America, *Lancet* **368**, 367–70

Jha, P., A. Mills, K. Hanson, L. Kumaranayake *et al.*, 2002: Improving the health of the global poor, *Science* **295**(5562), 2036–9

Jha, P., F. J. Chaloupka, J. Moore, V. Gajalakshmi, P. C. Gupta, R. Peck, S. Asma, and W. Zatonski, 2006a: Tobacco addiction, in D. T. Jamison, R. Measham, J. B. Breman *et al.* (eds.), *Disease Control Priorities in Developing Countries*, 2nd edn., Oxford University Press, New York, 869–86

John, R. M., H.-Y. Sung, and W. B. Max, 2004: Economic cost of tobacco use in India, *Tobacco Control* **18**, 138–43

John, R. M., H. Y. Sung, W. B. Max, and H. Ross, 2011: Counting 15 million more poor in India, thanks to tobacco, *Tobacco Control* **20**, 349–52

Joseph, R. *et al.*, 2011: Male smoking in India: trend analysis from 1998–2010, *British Medical Journal* Open 2013, in press

Kohler, H.-P., 2012: Population growth, Paper prepared for 2012 Copenhagen Consensus, Chapter 9 in this volume

Larsen, B., G. Hutton, and N. Khanna, 2008: Air pollution, Paper prepared for 2008 Copenhagen Consensus

Laxminarayan, R., J. Chow, and S. A. Shahid-Salles, 2006a: Intervention cost-effectiveness: overview of main messages, in D. T. Jamison, A. Measham, J. B. Breman *et al.* (eds.), *Disease Control Priorities in Developing Countries*, 2nd edn., Oxford University Press, New York, 35–86

Laxminarayan, R., A. J. Mills, J. G. Breman, A. R. Measham, G. Alleyne, M. Claeson, P. Jha, P. Musgrove, J. Chow, S. A. Shahid-Salles, and D. T. Jamison, 2006b: Advancement of global health: key messages from the disease control priorities project, *Lancet* **367**, 1193–208

Liang, X. *et al.*, 2011: Effect of mobile phone intervention for diabetics on glycemic control: a meta-anyalsis, *Diabetic Medicine* **28**, 455–63

Lightwood, J., D. Collins, H. Lapsley, and T. E. Novotny, 2000: Estimating the costs of tobacco use, in P. Jha and F. J. Chaloupka (eds.), *Tobacco Control in Developing Countries* Oxford University Press, New York, 63–103

Lim, S. S. *et al.*, 2010: A comparative risk assessment of the burden of disease and injury attributable to 67 risk factors and risk factor clusters in 21 regions, 1990–2010: a systematic analysis for the Global Burden of Disease Study 2010, *Lancet* **380**, 2224–60, doi: 10.1016/SO140-6736(12)61766-8

Liu, B. Q., R. Peto, Z. M. Chen *et al.*, 1998: Emerging tobacco hazards in China: 1. retrospective proportional mortality study of one million deaths, *British Medical Journal* **317**, 1411–22

Lopez, A. D., S. Begg, and E. Bos, 2006a: Demographic and epidemiological characteristics of major regions of the world, 1990 and 2001, in A. D. Lopez, C. D. Mathers, M. Ezzati, D. T. Jamison, and C. J .L. Murray (eds.), *Global Burden of Disease and Risk Factors*, Oxford University Press, New York, 17–44

Lopez, A. D., C. D. Mathers, M. Ezzati, D. T. Jamison, and C. J. L. Murray (eds.), 2006b: *Global Burden of Disease and Risk Factors*, Oxford University Press, New York

2006c: Global and regional burden of disease and risk factors, 2001: systematic analysis of population health data, *Lancet* **367**, 1747–57

Lopez-Casasnovas, G., B. Rivera, and L. Currais (eds.), 2005: *Health and Economic Growth: Findings and Policy Implications*, MIT Press, Cambridge, MA

Lujan, J., S. T. Ostwald, and M. Ortiz, 2007: Promoting diabetes intervention for Mexican Americans, *Diabetes Education* **33**, 660–70

Mathers, C. D., C. J. L. Murray, and A. D. Lopez, 2006: The burden of disease and mortality by condition: data, methods and results for the year 2001, in A. D. Lopez, C. D. Mathers, M. Ezzati, D. T. Jamison, and C. J. L. Murray (eds.), *Global Burden of Disease and Risk Factors*, Oxford University Press, New York, 45–240

Measham, A. R., K. D. Rao, D. T. Jamison, J. Wang, and A. Singh, 2003: The performance of India and Indian states in reducing infant mortality and fertility, 1975–1990, *Economic and Political Weekly* **34**, 1359–67

Mills, A. and S. Shillcutt, 2004: Communicable diseases, in B. Lomborg (ed.), *Global Crises, Global Solutions*, Cambridge University Press, 62–114

Mills, A., F. Rasheed, and S. Toilman, 2006: Strengthening health systems, in D. T. Jamison, A. Measham, J. B. Breman *et al.* (eds.), *Disease Control Priorities in Developing Countries*, 2nd edn., Oxford University Press, New York, 87–102

Molarius, A. *et al.*, 2001: Trends in cigarette smoking in 36 populations from the early 1980s to the mid-1990s: findings from the WHO MONICA Project, *American Journal of Public Health* **91**, 206–12

Monteiro, C. A., T. M. Cavalcante, E. C. Moura, R. M Claro, and C. L. Szwarcwald, 2007: Population-based evidence of a strong decline in the prevalence of smokers in Brazil (1989–2003), *Bulletin, World Health Organization* **85**, 527–34

Mulligan, J., J. A. Fox-Rushby, T. Adam, B. Johns, and A. Mills, 2003: Unit costs of health care inputs in low and middle income regions, Fogarty International Center, National Institutes of Health, Disease Control Priorities, *Project Working Paper* **9**, Bethesda, MD

Murphy, K. M. and R. H. Topel, 2006: The value of health and longevity, *Journal of Political Economy* **114**, 871–904

Murray, E., J. Burns, S. See Tai, R. Lai, and I. Nazareth, 2005: Interactive health communication applications for people with chronic disease, *Cochrane Database of Systematic Reviews*, 4. Art

Nugent, R. and A. Feigl, 2010: Where have all the donors gone? Scarce donor funding for non-communicable diseases, Center for Global Development, *Working Paper* **228**

Orazem, P. F., 2012: The case for improving school quality and student health as a development strategy, Paper prepared for 2012 Copenhagen Consensus, Chapter 5 in this volume

Orazem, P. F., P. Glewwe, and H. Patrinos, 2008: The challenge of education, Paper prepared for 2008 Copenhagen Consensus

Peabody, J. W., M. M. Taguiwalo, D. A. Robalino, and J. Frenk, 2006: Improving the quality of care in developing countries, in D. T. Jamison, A. Measham, J. B. Breman *et al.* (eds.), *Disease Control Priorities in Developing Countries*, 2nd edn., Oxford University Press, New York, 1293–1308

Pearson, M. L. *et al.*, 2005: Assessing the implementation of the chronic care model in quality improvement collaboratives, *Health Services Research* **40**, 978–96

Peck, R., F. J. Chaloupka, P. Jha, and J. Lightwood, 2000: Welfare analyses of tobacco, in P. Jha and F. J. Chaloupka (eds.), *Tobacco Control in Developing Countries*, Oxford University Press, 131–52

Peto, R., 2006: Noncommunicable diseases, Paper delivered at Disease Control Priorities Project Launch and 2nd Global Meeting of the Inter-Academy Medical Panel, Beijing

Peto, R. and C. Baigent, 1998: Trials: the next 50 years. Large scale randomised evidence of moderate benefits, *British Medical Journal* **317**, 1170–1

Peto, R., R. Collins, S. Parish *et al.*, 1995: Cholesterol, diastolic blood pressure, and stroke: 13,000 strokes in 450,000 people in 45 prospective cohorts, Prospective Studies Collaboration, *Lancet* **346**, 1647–53

Peto, R., A. D. Lopez, and J. Boreham 2006: *Mortality from Smoking in Developed Countries, 1950–2000*, 2nd edn., Oxford, Clinical Trial Service Unit www.ctsu.ox.ac.uk/~tobacco/, accessed September 24, 2007

Peto, R., G. Whitlock, and P. Jha, 2010: Effects of obesity and smoking on US Life expectancy, *New England Journal of Medicine* **362**, 855–7

Popkin, B. M., A. M. Siega-Riz, and P. S. Haines, 1996: A comparison of dietary trends among racial and socioeconomic groups in the United States, *New England Journal of Medicine* **335**(10), 716–20

Preston, S. H., 1975: The changing relation between mortality and level of economic development, *Population Studies* **29**, 231–48

Pritchard, C., 2004: Developments in economic evaluation in health care: a review of HEED, *OHE Briefing* **40**, Office of Health Economics, London, March

PSC Collaborators, 1995: Cholesterol, diastolic blood pressure, and stroke: 13,000 strokes in 450,000 people in 45 prospective cohorts. Prospective studies collaboration, *Lancet* **346**, 1647–53

Rajaratnam, J. K. *et al.*, 2010a: Worldwide mortality in men and women aged 15–59 years from 1970 to 2010: a systematic analysis, *Lancet* **375**, 1704–20

2010b: Neonatal, postneonatal, childhood, and under-5 mortality for 187 countries, 1970–2010: a systematic analysis of progress towards Millennium Development Goal 4, *Lancet* **375**, 1988–2008

Rani, M. *et al.*, 2003: Tobacco use in India: prevalence and predictors of smoking and chewing in a national cross sectional household survey, *Tobacco Control* **12**(4), 1–8

Raynauld, A., 1992: Smokers' burden on society: myth and reality in Canada, *Canadian Public Policy* **18**(3), 300–17

Recours, A., 1999: Politique de santé et Fiscalité du tabac: Rapport à Monsieur le Premier Ministre, September

Reddy, K. S., D. Prabhakaran, P. Jeemon, K. R. Thankappan, P. Joshi, V. Chaturvedi, L. Ramakrishnan, and F. Ahmed, 2007: Educational status and cardiovascular risk profile in Indians, *Proceedings of the Natural Academy of Sciences USA* **104**(41), 16263–8

RGI/CGHR, 2009: Causes of death in India: results from the Million Death Study, Registrar General, New Delhi

Richardson, G. *et al.*, 2008: Cost-effectiveness of the expert patients programme (EPP) for patients with chronic conditions, *Journal of Epidemiology and Community Health* **62**, 361–7

Rijsberman, F. and A. P. Zwane, 2012: Sanitation and water challenge paper, Paper prepared for 2012 Copenhagen Consensus, Chapter 10 in this volume

Rodgers, A., C. M. M. Lawes, T. Gaziano, and T. Vos, 2006: The growing burden of risk from high blood pressure, cholesterol, and bodyweight, in D. T. Jamison, A. R. Measham, J. B. Breman *et al.* (eds.), *Disease Control Priorities in Developing Countries*, 2nd edn., Oxford University Press, New York, 851–68

Rubinstein, A., L. Colantonio, A. Bardach *et al.*, 2010: Estimation of the burden of cardiovascular disease attributable to modifiable risk factors and cost-effectiveness of preventative interventions to reduce this burden in Argentina, *BMC Public Health* **10**, 627

Rousson, V. and F. Paccaud, 2010: A set of indicators for decomposing the secular increase of life expectancy, *Population Health Metrics* **8**, a–d

Salomon, J. A., N. Carvalho, C. Gutiérrez-Delgado, R. Orozco, A. Mancuso *et al.*, 2012: Interventions to reduce the burden of non-communicable diseases in Mexico: cost effectiveness analysis, *British Medical Journal*, 344:e355

Singhal, S., P. C. Gupta, R. Dikshit, and P. Jha, 2012: Increased risk of coronary heart disease in female smokers, *Lancet* **379**, 802

Shukla, H. C., P. C. Gupta, H. C. Mehta, and J. R. Hebert, 2002: Descriptive epidemiology of body mass index of an urban adult population in western India, *Journal of Epidemiol Community Health* **56**, 876–80

Suhrcke, M., R. Nugent, D. Stuckler, and I. Rocco, 2006: *Chronic Disease: An Economic Perspective*, Oxford Health Alliance, London

Tauras, J. A. and F. J. Chaloupka, 2004: Impact of tobacco control spending and tobacco control policies on adolescents' attitudes and beliefs about cigarette smoking, *Evidence Based Prevention Medicine* **1**, 111–20

Tolley, G., D. Kenkel, and R. Fabian, 1994: *Valuing Health for Policy: An Economic Approach*, University of Chicago Press

United Nations (UN), 2009: Department of Economic and Social Affairs, Population Division, *World Population Prospects: The 2008 Revision*, Geneva

US DHHS, 2001: *The Health Consequences of Smoking: The Changing Cigarette*, Report of the Surgeon General, US DHHS, Center for Disease Control and Prevention, Washington, DC

Van Olmen, J. *et al.*, 2011: The growing caseload of chronic life-long conditions calls for a move towards full self-management in low income countries, *Globalization and Health* **7**, 1–10

Van Walbeek, C., 2005: Tobacco control in South Africa, *International Journal of Health Promotion and Education*, Suppl. **4**, 25–8

Viscusi, W. K. and J. E. Aldy, 2003: The value of a statistical life: a critical review of market estimates throughout the world, *NBER Working Paper* **9487**, National Bureau of Economic Research, Cambridge, MA

Wagner, E. H., B. T. Austin, and M. Von Korff, 1996: Organizing care for patients with chronic illness, *Milbank Quarterly* **74**, 511–44

Weatherall, D., B. Greenwood, H. L. Chee, and P. Wasi, 2006: Science and technology for disease control: past, present, and future, in D. T. Jamison, A. R. Measham, J. B. Breman *et al.* (eds.), *Disease Control Priorities in Developing Countries*, 2nd edn., Oxford University Press, New York, 119–38

Wolf, M., 2006: The absurdities of a ban on smoking, *Financial Times*, June 22

Woodruff, S. I., 2002: Evaluation of a culturally-appropriate smoking cessation intervention for Latinos, *Tobacco Control*, **11**, 361–7

World Bank, 1993: *World Development Report: Investing in Health*, Oxford University Press, New York

2003: *World Development Indicators*, World Bank, Washington, DC

World Economic Forum (WEF), 2008: *Tackling Tuberculosis: The Business Response*, The World Economic Forum, Davos

World Health Organization (WHO), 2000: *World Health Report: Health Systems*, Geneva

2001: Commission on Macroeconomics and Health, *Macroeconomics and Health: Investing in Health for Economic Development*, WHO, Geneva

2002: Innovative care for chronic conditions: building blocks for action, www.who.int/diabetes/publications/icccreport/en/index.html, accessed February 12, 2012

2010: *WHO Technical Manual on Tobacco Tax Administration*, Geneva
2011a: Global routine vaccination coverage, 2010, Weekly epidemiological record **46**, 509–20
2011b: Scaling up action against non-communicable diseases: how much will it cost, http://whqlibdoc.who.int/publications/2011/9789241502313_eng,pdf accessed February 26, 2013
2012: Hepatitis B, www.who.int/mediacentre/factsheets/fs204/en/, accessed March 9, 2012
Xavier, D., P. Pais, P. J. Devereaux, C. Xie, D. Prabhakaran, K. S. Reddy, R. Gupta, P. Joshi, P. Kerkar, S. Thanikachalam, K. K. Haridas, T. M. Jaison, S. Naik, A. K. Maity, and S. Yusuf, 2008: CREATE registry investigators: treatment and outcomes of acute coronary syndromes in India (CREATE). A prospective analysis of registry data, *Lancet* **371**(9622), 1435–42
Zaridze, D., P. Brennan, J. Boreham, A. Boroda, R. Karpov, A. Lazarev, I. Konobeevskaya, V. Igitov, T. Terechova, P. Boffetta, and R. Peto, 2009: Alcohol and cause-specific mortality in Russia: a retrospective case-control study of 48,557 adult deaths, *Lancet* **373**(9682), 2201–14
Zatonski, W. and P. Jha, 2002: The health status of Central and Eastern European after 1990: a second look, *Health Development in Central and Eastern Europe after Transition*. Warsaw, 2000

3.1 Chronic Disease

Alternative Perspective

JULIA FOX-RUSHBY

Introduction

Chapter 3 by Jha and his colleagues introduces the case for increased funding of five health interventions to control chronic disease in low-and middle-income countries (LMICs): a 33 percent tax on tobacco; acute management of heart attacks with low-cost drugs; prevention of heart attacks and stroke through salt reduction by a mix of voluntary manufacturing changes, behavior change using mass media and other awareness-raising campaigns; prevention of hepatitis B through immunization; and secondary prevention of heart attacks and stroke through a combination of three–four drugs in a "generic risk" pill.[1] The BCRs range, in order, from 40:1 to 4:1.

The determination of priorities begins with a focus on the current and expected future burden of disease, as measured by deaths, avoidable mortality, and cost of illness. The "very approximate" (Jha *et al.*, 2012) discounted BCRs are based on comparing a monetized value of a DALY with intervention cost. Evidence on interventions draws largely from the second Disease Control Priorities Project (DCP 2) (Jamison *et al.*, 2006), the 2008 Copenhagen Consensus paper on disease control (Jamison *et al.*, 2008), and selected other literature with a statement that the investments proposed reflect views of other similar exercises. The five BCRs are subject to sensitivity analyses of single and combined changes in the following assumptions; changing the discount rate from 3 percent to 5 percent, increasing all costs by 300 percent, and increasing the value of a DALY from $1,000 to $5,000.

The BCRs are supplemented, to indicate a move to an "idealized" version, by "accounting" for the value of financial protection and non-financial costs (e.g. transaction, organizational and administrative efforts to implement the intervention). The "accounting" is a categorization that relies on: a literature review of various aspects of health system capacity and; a review of the (limited) evidence on the costs and effects of the Chronic Care Model (CCM) and its very limited adapted application to low-resource settings. This, at least partly, influences the qualitative ratings based on the "speculative" judgment of financial protection and "non-financial" costs by the authors. All interventions are argued to offer high financial protection with only the impact of "capacity" differentiating the proposed interventions; tobacco taxation is considered to have low-capacity requirements, a salt-reduction program to have medium-capacity requirements, and the others to have high-capacity requirements.

The chapter ends by calling for an increased role for donor assistance in controlling chronic diseases, despite a concern that this "may not be politically feasible in the short or even medium term." This role is also charged to "conduct research which makes the marginal costs of [interventions] affordable" and includes both more research and development of relevant health technologies as well as implementation research to close the gap between knowledge and action.

There is a real challenge in drawing together a justified list of priorities for funding in an area which is recognized as being short of evidence both in terms of geographical coverage and range of

* This paper was prepared with a small grant from the Copenhagen Consensus Center.

[1] E.g. use of aspirin, a statin, and an anti-hypertensive drug (Jamison *et al.*, 2008).

interventions evaluated (Suhrcke *et al.*, 2012) and hampered by poor-quality studies (Mulligan *et al.*, 2006). The chapter by Jha and his colleagues is therefore a valiant effort to put forward the case for investment in an area of human life that has a worrying future health and economic impact.

This Alternative Perspective chapter considers whether the best interventions for investing in the improvement of chronic disease are presented in the Challenge Paper. It considers the influence that of burden of illness analysis might have had and should have; the construction and testing of BCRs for the five interventions selected; and the approach taken to reflecting uncertainty. The chapter ends by suggesting alternative interventions for the Expert Panel to consider.

Questioning the influence of the burden of illness

Chapter 3 appears to reflect the premise that the decision problem should be framed in terms of the burden of disease and, having accounted for the size of the burden, focus on the set of cost-effective interventions to reduce it. The evidence presented points to mental health conditions having the highest economic burden using the cost-of-illness (COI) method and the second largest using the value of lost output (VOL) method. However, no interventions are proposed for addressing this burden. By implication, the authors may have applied a burden of disease approach inconsistently, adopted a very restricted definition of the burden of disease, or considered the evidence on BCRs for all mental health interventions to be less than 4:1. These possibilities are considered below.

It is not clear how the estimates of burden in the Challenge Paper have been used in practice to narrow down towards the selected interventions. For example, a burden of illness approach based on mortality rates in Table 3.1 (p. 138) would suggest that ischemic and hypertensive heart disease should be the focus of all interventions. However, this is not the case as the selected interventions aim at alleviating heart disease, stroke, and cancer.[2] The use of avoidable mortality might explain the discrepancy but these data are not provided by disease and therefore the potential influence of this approach is unclear. Two further possibilities are that either the burden of disease approach has been applied inconsistently or it has not been the lens through which the cost-effective interventions are selected. However, if the burden of disease is not the original frame it does not explain why so much information on the burden of disease is presented without reference to the impact of health interventions.

Perhaps interventions to improve mental health are absent because the impact on mortality is comparatively low. There is a notable absence of cause of death attributed directly to mental health in Table 3.1 and a statement that "we focus chiefly here on changes in mortality . . . simply because it is far less likely to be misclassified than are the more subjective measures of disability." The valuation of health benefits in the BCR therefore only appear to account for disability averted when tied to cases of premature mortality. This suggests first that the burden and impact of chronic disease is massively underestimated, as highly morbid low-mortality chronic diseases will be missing from any estimate of the burden presented here. Indeed the co-authors of the Challenge Paper conclude elsewhere (Bloom *et al.*, 2011) that CVD and mental health conditions are the dominant contributors to the global economic burden of NCDs. Secondly, it implies a further restriction imposed by the particular burden of disease approach adopted in the Challenge Paper – that the cost-effective interventions aimed at alleviating conditions with lower mortality rates are highly unlikely to be recommended regardless of their cost-effectiveness. For a proposal focused on "best buys" for reducing chronic disease, this seems somewhat limited and means that the investment proposals presented are unlikely to reflect the best-possible investment possibilities for reducing chronic disease.

The possibility that the BCRs for all mental health interventions are less than 4:1 is a moot point and the authors provide no evidence to support or refute this position. However, evidence from DCP2 (Jamison *et al.*, 2006: 40), on which Chapter 3 itself

[2] Given an assumption that mortality gains from the tobacco tax are split equally between cancer and heart disease.

draws, supports the case that interventions to reduce mental health are valid contenders to the proposals offered in Chapter 3.

Evidence from DCP2 (Jamison *et al.*, 2006: 40) indicates that cost-effectiveness ratios for mental health interventions in the area of alcohol abuse are around \$600–800/DALY averted, and that treatment for depression by drugs with episodic or maintenance psycho-social treatment) is roughly \$900–3000/DALY averted. The detailed DCP2 chapter by Hymen *et al.* (2006) suggested that treatment of depression with episodic treatment using older tricyclic anti-depressants ranged (by World Bank region) between \$478–1,288/DALY averted. More recent evidence suggests that several mental health interventions could be provided for under \$1,000/DALY averted in both SSA and South East Asia. These include a bundle aimed at alcohol reduction (including tax increases, reduced access, and tax enforcement), episodic treatment of depression with newer anti-depressants (selective serotonin reuptake inhibitors), and treatment of epilepsy with older anti-epileptics at 80 percent coverage (Chisholm *et al.*, 2012).

Evidence presented in Jamison *et al.* (2006: 41) for the five selected interventions suggests that interventions to improve mental health compare well. For example, legislation with public education to reduce salt content was shown to have a cost/DALY averted of around \$2,000 and secondary treatment of AMI and stroke with a polypill to be around \$700/DALY averted. It is likely, therefore, that BCRs of 4:1 or greater for mental health interventions may exist and be on a par with several of the interventions proposed. This is particularly likely because the Challenge Paper converts DALYs lost to a monetary value to estimate BCRs without accounting for other non-money values.

While the absence of interventions for improving mental health may be of concern, it is only an example and many other cost-effective interventions could be missing. Of particular concern, given the lack of clarity in the use of the burden of disease estimates in selecting interventions in this case, is that the proposals could be systematically biased against recommending the most cost-effective interventions. Why are some potentially cost-effective treatments of chronic diseases missing? Some justification of interventions narrowly missing inclusion (e.g. in terms of BCRs or the other criteria) would have helped illuminate the authors' approach more clearly.

While there is unease with the mechanics of using the burden of illness approach adopted here, of much greater concern is why a burden of illness approach is used to structure the decision problem. Counting the size of the epidemiologic or economic problem may indicate challenges for which there are no solutions and could lead to distorted priorities as more cost-beneficial interventions might never even be considered (Wiseman and Mooney, 1998; Williams, 1999). Beginning with BCRs first is more appropriate as it is a solution-focused approach. It allows a fuller range of potential interventions to be considered regardless of the focus of disease. It is possible that the most cost-beneficial intervention would also address the disease of highest burden, but not necessarily.

It is important to recognize that the Challenge Paper authors were limited to recommending a maximum of five interventions. In this case it is not unreasonable to consider the burden of disease estimates in order to benefit from more of the set budget of \$75 billion. However, to provide the "best buy" would require considering BCRs *before* considering the burden of disease. As the methods of combining information on the disease burden and BCRs are not clear, it is possible this was done, but this would be important to see.

Construction and sensitivity of the BCRs

"Indicative" BCRs are presented in Table 3.7 of the Challenge Paper (p. 150), with details of calculation presented in the text and sensitivity analysis in the Appendix. Reflecting past research on immunization for hepatitis B (Sanderson, 2005; Brenzel *et al.*, 2006), I opted to replicate and reconsider one of the options, using the approach presented in Chapter 3. Column 2 of Table 3.1.2 shows the replication. This indicates a 7:1 ratio which, through the rounding in Table 3.7 and further recalculation to

Table 3.1.1 Alternative assumptions

For achieving more favorable BCRs	For achieving less favorable BCRs
1. Mean cost from Brenzel *et al.* (2006) referenced in the Challenge Paper (range \$2.02–\$2.37) and inflated to the publication year for Indian cost data used in the base case. The new cost was \$2.7 per vaccinated child.	1. Doubled cost of achieving last 10%-point increase in coverage to achieve 100%[a] from \$3.6 to \$7.2 per child vaccinated for (the effective average cost increased to \$5.04 from 75–100% coverage).
2. No amendment made for avoidable mortality as assumptions already appeared favorable (future burden likely to decline given increasing hepatitis B vaccination rates and assumption of 100% efficacy).	2. Used assumptions on avoidable mortality from Brenzel *et al.* (2006).
3. Used a slightly older coverage rate of 64% vaccine coverage from Duclos *et al.* (2009). While out of date, the % reflects the position for some countries.	3. Assumed increase of 3% in global coverage rates since 2010.
4. Assumed benefits occurred in thirty rather than forty years.	4. Assumed benefits occurred in fifty rather than forty years.

[a] Johns and Baltussen (2004) showed that marginal costs rose by 70–100% roughly double for achieving the last 10% coverage of a hygiene outreach program.

reflect the rounding was increased by the chapter authors to 10:1 (Verguet, personal communication). The replication therefore satisfactorily reflects the assumptions of Chapter 3.

The assumptions specific to the hepatitis B vaccination option were:

(a) Cost per vaccinated child was \$3.6, reflecting a study of India's national hepatitis B vaccination program
(b) All benefits would occur forty years after immunisation
(c) Of the 600,000 annual deaths from hepatitis B reported by the WHO, a quarter were considered avoidable by increasing global vaccination rates from 75 percent to 100 percent.

While vaccine effectiveness was referred to as 75 percent and 95 percent, the increase from 75–100 percent coverage appears to implicitly assume 100 percent effectiveness, as all 150,000 deaths were considered avertable. All other assumptions (e.g. value of a DALY averted, discount rate, DALYs lost per death) were constant across investment options.

In reviewing the benefit-cost calculations, three questions arose: Why were particular data and assumptions adopted? How valuable were the sensitivity analyses in exploring these issues? What is the potential impact of adopting different assumptions?

Little justification was provided for the hepatitis B vaccination-specific parameter values. As the sensitivity analyses only evaluated generic assumptions across all options, no sensitivity analysis considered the impact of option-specific assumptions. Therefore little consideration was given to the possibility that the BCRs might change in relation to each other. If one (or more) intervention could move significantly closer to another, differences between options would diminish and this could be of decisional importance. As it is relatively easy to choose alternative assumptions to effect change in these BCRs, the reasoning for choosing alternative values is important. Therefore this quick re-analysis reflects sources the authors have cited, and applies health sector-specific evidence to well-versed economic arguments (i.e. rising marginal cost to achieve maximum coverage) to support four cumulative analyses (Table 3.1.1).

Results for the final cumulative step are given in Table 3.1.2. The more favorable assumptions move the BCR from 7:1 to 9:1 and 13:1. The less favorable assumptions move the BCR from 7:1 to 5:1 to 4:1, and finally to 3:1, which is on a par with the "generic risk" pill. Further investigation of the impact of alternative option-specific assumptions for the four other interventions may reveal a credible alternative positioning of BCRs in both absolute and relative terms.

Table 3.1.2 Replication and extension of the Jha *et al.* estimate for hepatitis B vaccination

	Jha *et al.* estimates	Less favorable assumptions	More favorable assumptions
(1)	(2)	(3)	(4)
Birth cohort	136,000,000	136,000,000	136,000,000
Average cost vaccination	3.6	4.6	2.7
Annual cost of vaccinating all children	489,600,000	625,600,000	367,200,000
Proportion vaccinated	0.75	0.64	0.75
New proportion to be vaccinated	1	1	1
1 percent linear cost	4,896,000	6,256,000	3,672,000
Extra percent coverage re expected cost	122,400,000	225,216,000	91,800,000
Deaths from Hepatitis B	600,000	1,400,000	600,000
Deaths assumed potentially savable from (HBV) given current and future vaccination coverage	150,000	176,400	150,000
DALYs lost per death	20	20	20
DALYs	3,000,000	3,528,000	3,000,000
Value of death/DALY averted	1,000	1,000	1,000
Value of death averted	150,000,000	176,400,000	150,000,000
Value of DALY averted	3,000,000,000	3,528,000,000	3,000,000,000
Undiscounted BCR (death)	1	1	2
Undiscounted BCR (DALYs)	25	16	33
Discounted deaths (3%, 40 years)	45,179	39,360	60,985
Discounted DALYs	903,583	787,203	1,219,709
Discounted value deaths	45,179,132	39,360,160	60,985,449
Discounted value DALYs	903,582,636	787,203,205	1,219,708,979
Discounted BCR deaths	0	0	1
Discounted BCR DALYs	7	3	13

Treatment of uncertainty

The Challenge Paper refers to uncertainty[3] in a number of ways: the size and shape of the future tobacco hazards; greater misclassification of morbidity compared with mortality statistics; methodological uncertainty about the completeness of data, age weighting, and discount rates; effectiveness of the interventions to prevent elevated blood pressure, blood lipids, and diabetes; and adherence to the polypill. To reflect this, the benefit-cost estimates are referred to as "indicative" and parameters to being a "ballpark idea" (e.g. of the economic cost at the macro level). In each case further information on these issues would reduce uncertainty and provide more precise estimates.

Chapter 3 judges that, given the "often broad ranges in CE ratios, and hence in BCRs, it makes little sense to conclude with precise estimates or with attempts to quantify statistical uncertainty around

[3] This should be distinguished from variation for which further information could not increase precision as heterogeneity in patient (e.g. age, severity of disease, health outcomes) or health system (e.g. price) characteristics refers to real differences. Chapter 3 mentions additionally variation in prices, scale of the intervention, and epidemiological environment.

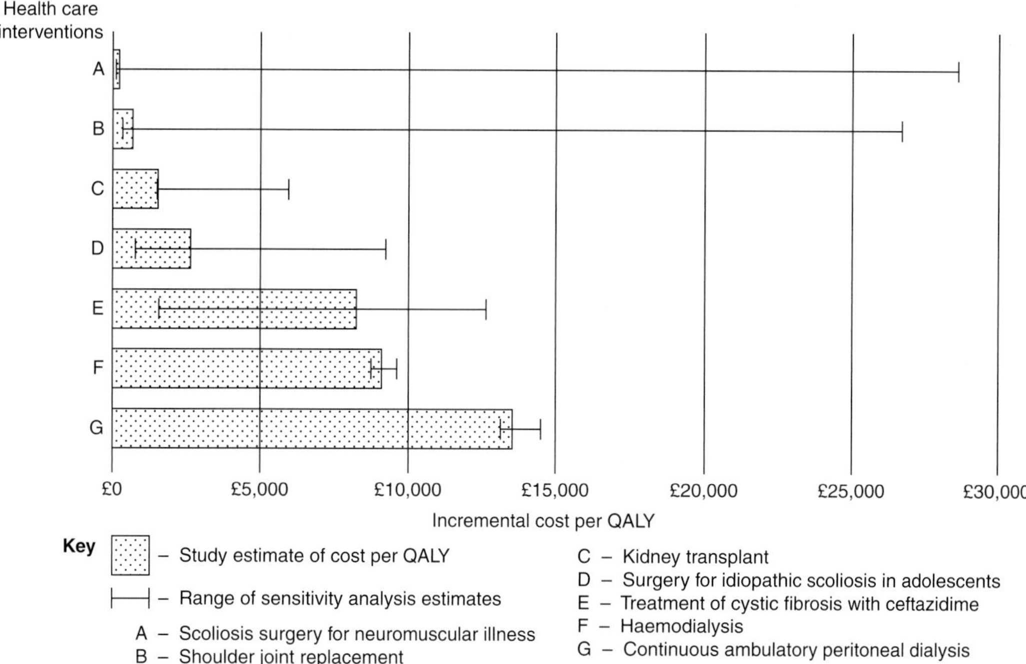

Figure 3.1.1 *Variability in point estimates of incremental cost-effectiveness following sensitivity analysis*

Source: Briggs (1995).

the point estimates." While there may be little possibility, given the uncertainties noted, of providing precise estimates, the conclusion that quantification of uncertainty should therefore be avoided is a little hasty. Indeed, its avoidance may result in inappropriate recommendations.

Briggs (1995) showed clearly that knowing the precision of an incremental cost-effectiveness ratio can affect the decision about which intervention to implement, and indicated that choices may differ from that implied by point estimates alone. For example, in Figure 3.1.1 a decision-maker with a WTP of £10,000 per QALY might justifiably prefer intervention C above intervention A or B, because it is a more precise estimate of the incremental cost-effectiveness ratio, even though the point estimate of the cost per QALY is higher. Since this work, much progress has been made in defining, measuring, and interpreting uncertainty in the context of using economic evaluation to aid both investment adoption decisions as well as defining the need for further research. It has also led to much greater emphasis on the systematic search and review of evidence, as well as methods for eliciting expert opinion and analysis of evidence that can influence the choice of parameter estimates in economic evaluations of health interventions (Griffin and Claxton, 2011).

As uncertainty in both costs and effects can vary by intervention (e.g. Sassi *et al.*, 2009) it is possible that the BCRs presented in Chapter 3 could be differentially affected by uncertainty. While it is unusual for uncertainty to be reflected in BCRs, the analysis of benefit by Jha and his colleagues relies heavily on the value of DALYs averted and is not intrinsically different from the majority of economic evaluations presented in the health sector. Therefore analysis of uncertainty could be expected and decisions made without reference to it could badly mislead understanding of the likelihood of future costs and benefits.

Evidence to substantiate, refute, and counter the priorities recommended

Two exercises designed to help encourage and guide investment decisions for controlling chronic disease have now been published. The WHO produced three related reports (WHO, 2011a, 2011b, 2011c) outlining the "best buys" for controlling chronic disease and detailing the costs of scaling up the proposed interventions (to a level where 80 percent coverage is achieved within fifteen years). A "best buy" was considered to be an intervention that averts 1 DALY for less than the average annual income *per capita* but is also considered "cheap, feasible and culturally acceptable to implement."[4]

As Chapter 3 states, all five interventions proposed are, at least partially, reflected in the listing of "best buys." While this is important corroboration of the value of their investment proposal, there are two important caveats to accepting this as sufficient validation. First, further inspection of the "best buys" indicates that several other interventions could have been selected, but Chapter 3 is silent on both their non-selection and the reasons for their non-selection.[5] The missing interventions include entire areas, such as controlling alcohol,[6] as well as competing and complementary interventions for the risk factors addressed.[7] Secondly, the reference point for the WHO reports was a focus on "four diseases; cardiovascular disease, cancer, diabetes and chronic respiratory disease . . . [which are] largely caused by four shared behavioural risk factors: tobacco use, harmful alcohol use, physical inactivity, and unhealthy diet" (WHO, 2011c: 10). Therefore, confirmation is less convincing as a case for accepting that the best investments have been presented in the Challenge Paper, as good alternatives may exist outside of these disease areas.

A second exercise conducted by the WHO focused on the cost-effectiveness of over 500 single or combined interventions for the prevention and control of NCDs and injuries in countries in SSA and South East Asia that have high adult and child mortality (Baltussen and Smith, 2012; Chisholm and Saxena, 2012; Chisholm *et al.*, 2012; Ginsberg *et al.*, 2012; Ortegón *et al.*, 2012a; Ortegón *et al.*, 2012b). This is interesting for a number of reasons: the analysis extends beyond the disease areas of the Challenge Paper and the "best buy" analysis, including road traffic injuries, mental health, and sensory loss disorders; it provides a more accountable and direct comparison of a broader range of interventions; and, for the interventions that are not dominated[8] (within disease clusters), a probabilistic cost-effectiveness analysis indicates some degree of the uncertainty. However, there are still limitations with using this analysis as a full critique or validation of investment options presented in the Challenge Paper. For example, the analysis is restricted to two WHO regions, one intervention proposed by Jha and his colleagues is excluded entirely (hepatitis B vaccination[9]), and the drug-based interventions proposed in Chapter 3 are potentially grouped slightly differently.[10]

The second exercise, led by Chisholm, provides strong support for increasing tobacco tax as it

[4] This contrasts with "good buys" which are other interventions that may cost more or generate less health gain but are still considered to provide good value for money.

[5] The need to select is, however, clear as the total cost of the package was expected to be $170 billion with an average annual cost of $11.4 billion per year.

[6] This included restricting access, enforcing bans on advertising, raising taxes on alcohol, monitoring, advocacy/support. The authors explained (personal communication) that, while excess deaths in Russia can be linked clearly to binge drinking, the net effect in other populations is less clear. However, this decision also appears to be another impact of linking morbidity only to cases of mortality.

[7] For diet, these include promoting public awareness about diet and physical activity, and replacing trans fat with polyunsaturated fat. For tobacco it includes smoke-free indoor work places and public places, health information and warning, bans on advertising, promotion and sponsorship. Other possibilities to reduce CVD and cancer risks not presented include: screening in primary care for CVD risk; counseling and multi-drug therapy for individuals with >30 CVD risk; prevention of cervical cancer through screening and lesion removal.

[8] An intervention is "dominated" if it is more costly and/or less effective than other (more efficient) interventions

[9] Because treatment of liver disease was considered not to have strong evidence of effectiveness and aspects of prevention of hepatitis B and cirrhosis were "covered" already in some of the alcohol interventions evaluated (Ginsberg *et al.*, 2012).

[10] This isn't entirely clear, as the WHO-based analysis does allow combinations of therapies.

Table 3.1.3 Costs and effects of a 50% increase in tobacco tax (from 40–60%)

	WHO Africa region	WHO South East Asia region
Annual DALYs saved per million population	687	3,043
Annual cost *per capita* (Int$)	0.31	0.27
Average cost-effectiveness ratio (Int$)	448	87
Incremental cost-effectiveness ratio (Int$)	448	87
Sensitivity	Horizontal ellipse stretching from roughly Int$0.1–0.7 *per capita* and 200–1,200 DALYS averted per year per million population (i.e. most uncertainty with effectiveness)	Horizontal ellipse stretching from roughly Int$0.1–0.9 *per capita* and 1,200–5,500 DALYS averted per year per million population (i.e. most uncertainty with effectiveness)

Source: Ortegón *et al.* (2012).

Table 3.1.4 Costs and effects of two alternative interventions for investment

	WHO Africa region	WHO South East Asia region
Costs and effects of achieving 95% coverage of cataract, extracapsular cataract extraction with posterior chamber lens implant (CAT-6)		
Annual DALYs saved per million population	6,281	6,447
Annual cost *per capita* (Int$)	0.73	0.63
Average cost-effectiveness ratio (Int$)	116	97
Incremental cost-effectiveness ratio (Int$)	117	97
Sensitivity	Not possible to read from graph	Horizontal ellipse from (roughly 1,800–10,800 DALYs and Int$0.1–1.0 *per capita*
Treatment based on absolute risk of a cardiovascular event in next ten years with statin, diuretic, beta blocker, and aspirin for cardiovascular risk of 5% (CVD-11)		
Annual DALYs saved per million population	3,163	2,984
Annual cost *per capita* (Int$)	0.33	0.41
Average cost-effectiveness ratio (Int$)	104	138
Incremental cost-effectiveness ratio (Int$)	104	146
Sensitivity	Horizontal ellipse from (roughly) 800–5,200 DALYs lost per million population and (roughly) $0.2 to 0.5 *per capita*	Horizontal ellipse from (roughly) 1,000–5,000 DALYs lost per million population and (roughly) $0.2 to 0.5 *per capita*

Note: CAT-6 = Extracapsular cataract extraction with posterior chamber lens implant (95 percent coverage).
CVD-11 = Statin, diuretic, β blocker + aspirin for CVD risk of 5 percent.
Sources: Baltussen and Smith (2012); Ortegón *et al.* (2012).

is a particularly cost-effective intervention for both WHO regions (see Table 3.1.3). However, salt-reduction and all salt-based interventions were dominated by other options (within their disease/risk factor cluster), as was the treatment of AMI with aspirin, ace inhibitors, and beta blockers and all of the drug therapy-based secondary/tertiary prevention of myocardial infarction. This indicates that other interventions could achieve greater DALY gain per dollar spent.

Chisholm *et al.* (2012) note that, compared with all other interventions for controlling chronic disease, "antibiotic treatment of chronic otitis media (a persistent inflammation of the middle ear) is the most cost-effective intervention in the two regions (<$Int 100/DALY saved), while extraction of cataracts and proactive screening for hearing loss are among the biggest contributors to population health gain." The detailed results are provided in Table 3.1.4, and it can be seen that, even in comparison with tax increases for tobacco, these interventions are more cost-effective. However, with a population of 2 million needing cataract surgery in Africa and 4.2 million in South East Asia (Baltussen and Smith, 2012), the annual treatment is unlikely make a significant dent in the hypothetical budget facing the Copenhagen Consensus Expert Panel given that the number of interventions selected are restricted to five. However, this is unlikely to be the case for an intervention such as treatment based on absolute risk of a cardiovascular event in next ten years with a statin, diuretic, beta blocker, and aspirin for cardiovascular risk of 5 percent (CVD-11). In this case, the annual DALYs saved per million population is 3,163 at a cost of Int$0.33 *per capita* and both an average and incremental cost-effectiveness ratio of Int$104 per DALY averted.

Conclusion

Whether an additional investment of up to $75 billion should comprise the five interventions proposed by Jha and his colleagues is questionable. The initial filtering through calculations of the disease burden combined with a lack of accounting for uncertainty and a sensitivity analysis that did not question the relative rankings of interventions suggests that the "best buys" are unlikely to be presented. Other evidence suggests that alternative interventions could indeed provide a better return on investment. Examples include cataract surgery, antibiotic treatment for otitis media, and primary prevention of CVD. However, the cost-effectiveness analysis on which the latter suggestions are made do not account for the level of health system support needed. Jha and his colleagues do discuss this at length and it would have been interesting to see both a quantification of the health system support needed for the proposed interventions in the Challenge Paper as well as understanding why this would not support the range of alternative interventions highlighted in the recent series of papers in the *British Medical Journal* (Chisholm *et al.*, 2012).

Bibliography

Baltussen, R. and A. Smith, 2012: Cost effectiveness of interventions to combat vision and hearing loss in sub-Saharan Africa and South East Asia: mathematical modelling study, *British Medical Journal* **344**, e615

Bloom, D. E. *et al.*, 2011: *The Global Economic Burden of Non-Communicable Diseases*, World Economic Forum, Geneva

Brenzel, L., L. Wolfson, J. Fox-Rushby, M. Miller, and N. Halsey, 2006: Vaccine preventable diseases, in D. Jamison, G. Alleyne, J. Breman, M. Claeson, D. Evans, P. Jha, A. Measham, A. Mills, and P. Musgrove (eds.), *Disease Control Priorities in Developing Countries*, 2nd edn., Oxford

Briggs, A., 1995: Sensitivity analysis in economic evaluation, *Office of Health Economics Briefing Paper* **32**, September

Briggs, A., M. Sculpher, and K. Claxton, 2006: *Decision Modelling for Health Economic Evaluation*, Oxford University Press

Cecchini, M. *et al.*, 2010: Tackling of unhealthy diets, physical inactivity, and obesity: health effects and cost-effectiveness, *Lancet* **376**, 1775–84

Chisholm, D. and S. Saxena, 2012: Cost effectiveness of strategies to combat neuropsychiatric conditions in sub-Saharan Africa and South East Asia: mathematical modelling study, *British Medical Journal* **344**, e609 doi: 10.1136/bmj.e609

Chisholm, D., C. Lund, and S. Saxena, 2007: Cost of scaling up mental healthcare in low- and middle-income countries, *British Journal of Psychiatry* **191**, 528–35

Chisholm, D., R. Baltussen, D. Evans, G. Ginsberg, J. Lauer, S. Lim, M. Ortegón, J. Salomon, A. Stanciole, and T. Tan-Torres, 2012: What are the priorities for prevention and control of non-communicable diseases and injuries in sub-Saharan Africa and South East Asia?, *BMJ* **344**, e586

Duclos, P., J. M. Okwo-Bele, M. Gacic-Dobo, and T. Cherian, 2009: Global immunization: status, progress, challenges and future, *BMC International Health and Human Rights* **9**(Suppl 1), S2

Ginsberg, G., J. A. Lauer, S. Zelle, S. Baeten, and R. Baltussen, 2012: Cost effectiveness of strategies to combat breast, cervical, and colorectal cancer in sub-Saharan Africa and South East Asia: mathematical modelling study, *British Medical Journal* **344**, e614

Griffin, S. and K. Claxton, 2011: Analysing uncertainty in cost-effectiveness analysis for decision-making, in S. Glied and P. C. Smith (eds.), *The Oxford Handbook of Health Economics*, Oxford University Press

Hyman, S. *et al.*, 2006: Mental disorders, in D. T. Jamison *et al.* (eds.), *Disease Control Priorities in Developing Countries*, Oxford University Press, New york, 605–12

Jamison, D. T. *et al.* (eds.), 2006: *Disease Control Priorities in Developing Countries*, Oxford University Press, New York

Jamison, D. T., P. Jha, and D. E. Bloom, 2008: Disease control, Paper Prepared for 2008 Copenhagen Consensus

Jha, P. *et al.*, 2012: Chronic disease, Paper prepared for 2012 Copenhagen Consensus, Chapter 3 in this volume

Johns, B. and R. Baltussen, 2004: Accounting for the cost of scaling-up health interventions, *Health Economics* **13**, 1117–24

Mulligan, J., D. Walker, and J. Fox-Rushby, 2006: Economic evaluations of non-communicable disease interventions in developing countries: a critical review of the evidence base, *Cost Effectiveness and Resource Allocation* **4**

Ortegón, M., S. Lim, D. Chisholm, and S. Mendis, 2012: Cost-effectiveness of strategies to combat cardiovascular disease, diabetes, and tobacco use in sub-Saharan Africa and South East Asia: mathematical modelling study, *British Medical Journal* **344**, e607

Sanderson, C. *et al.*, 2005: *Modelling the Impact and Incremental Cost-Effectiveness in Bangladesh and Peru of Introducing Vaccines Against hepatitis B, Haemophilus influenzae type b, and rotavirus into Routine Infant Immunisation Programs, and of Modifications to Current Programs with a Particular Focus on the Measles and Pertussis Components*, Department of International Development, London

Sassi, F. *et al.*, 2009: *Improving Lifestyles, Tackling Obesity: The Health and Economic Impact of Prevention Strategies* (Online), *OECD Health Working Papers Series* **48**, http://dx.doi.org/10.1787/220087432153, Accessed April 30, 2012

Suhrcke, M., T. Boluarte, and L. Niessen, 2012: A systematic review of economic evaluations of interventions to tackle cardiovascular disease in low- and middle-income countries, *BMC Public Health*, **12**, doi: 10.1186/1471-2458-12-2

Williams, A., 1999: Calculating the global burden of disease: time for a strategic re-appraisal, *Health Economics* **8**, 1–8

Wiseman, V. and G. Mooney, 1998: Burden of illness estimates for priority setting: a debate revisited, *Health Policy* **43**, 243–51

World Health Organization (WHO), 2011a: *From Burden to "Best Buys": Reducing Economic Impact of Non-Communicable Disease in Low and Middle-Income Countries*, World Health Organization, Geneva

2011b: *Global Status Report on Non-Communicable Diseases 2010*, World Health Organization, Geneva

2011c: *Scaling up Action against Non-Communicable Diseases: How Much will it Cost?*, World Health Organization, Geneva

3.2 Chronic Disease

Alternative Perspective

MARC SUHRCKE

The Challenge Paper by Jha and his colleagues (Chapter 3) provides a comprehensive perspective on a range of relevant health and economic issues around chronic diseases in developing countries. In particular, the authors propose the following five interventions, due to their highly favorable BCRs (1) tobacco taxation, (2) acute management of heart attacks with low-cost drugs, (3) heart disease and strokes with salt reduction, (4) hepatitis B immunization, and (5) secondary prevention of heart attacks and strokes with three–four drugs in a "generic risk pill."

In my review I focus on three principal issues that may affect either the basic rationale for intervention and/or the size of the BCRs.

Value of a statistical life year (VSL)

Jha and his colleagues use the VSL concept to value the benefits of their proposed interventions. Given the persistent lack of VSL estimates in developing countries, this does require strong assumptions. The authors acknowledge and take account of the uncertainty around what could be the true VSL in low-income countries by using a very wide range of VSL estimates. In the VSL estimates used for the calculation of the economic burden of chronic disease, the highest VSL estimate (and hence the overall cost estimates) is 6.3 times the value of the lowest VSL estimate, while in the VSL estimates used in the benefit valuation of the intervention this difference is fivefold.

The authors' strategy to foresee such wide intervals is to be commended. Yet the question arises whether it is possible to narrow down the VSL estimates to what might be the most likely "true" value? If that was possible, the overall BCRs of the recommended interventions might be easier to compare to BCRs in the other policy areas covered by the Copenhagen Consensus.

A common way of "transferring" VSL estimates from countries that have VSL estimates to those (typically low-income ones) that do not is by using the income elasticities of VSL coming from meta-analytical studies. This is also the approach used by (Chapter 3) for part of the estimates, at least when calculating the economic burden of chronic disease. In particular, Jha *et al.* use the parameter estimates (associated with GDP *per capita* and life expectancy) from the landmark review and meta-analysis of VSL studies by Viscusi and Aldy (2003), who had included about fifty studies from ten countries, all but one from high-income countries. While there exists no perfect way of transferring VSL figures, this is arguably a less ad hoc approach than the rule-of-thumb employed by the Commission on Macroeconomics and Health (CMH), i.e. that of using a value that is equal to 1–3 times the value of the country's *per capita* income. Hence it should in principle deliver more reliable VSL estimates, if and only if the assumed income elasticity is the correct one.

Jha *et al.* do not give the VSL estimate they obtain from applying this procedure but since the income elasticity in the Viscusi and Aldy study ranges from 0.46–0.60 – meaning that as *per capita* national income grows by 1 percent, the VSL will grow by about half that – one can roughly estimate the VSL for an average low-income country by applying the simplified[1] formula:

$$VSL_b = FSL_a \times (\, per\_capita\_income_b / per\_capita\_income_a)^{elasticity}$$

[1] The key critical assumption is that elasticity is constant over the income levels of concern.

Here, *a* denotes the country for which a VSL estimate does exist (e.g. the United States) and *b* stands for the country for which a VSL is to be estimated.

Using a VSL for the United States of USD 6.3 million (which is the VSL that Robinson, 2008, suggests for the United States in 2007), the 2007 value of national GNI *per capita* of $46,900 (according to World Bank Development Indicators World Bank, 2012), an income elasticity of 0.5, and an average *per capita* GNI of a low-income country in the same year ($395), this gives a VSL for the low-income country of $578,166. To compare this figure to the estimates of the CMH approach (which are given in terms of the value of a statistical life *year*, VSLY), we need to transform this VSL figure into the corresponding figure for a life year. Again, using simplifying assumptions, this results in a VSLY of $27,074 for the low-income country – and $295,012 for the United States.

Comparing these figures to the national *per capita* GNI gives some idea of its dimension: for a low-income country, the VSLY is 68 times bigger than its GNI *per capita*, while for the United States the difference is sixfold. It may be unrealistic to assume that the average individual in low-income countries would indeed be willing to dedicate such a large amount for a relatively limited mortality risk reduction, not least due to the need to fund basic necessities (Hammitt and Robinson, 2011).

Obviously, the relatively large VSLY in the low-income country (as a share of its GNI *per capita*) is driven by the low income elasticity found in the Viscusi and Aldy study. The lower (higher) the income elasticity, the higher (lower) will be the resulting estimated VSL in a low-income country, derived from that elasticity.

While the debate is far from settled, there may reason to believe that the income elasticity of VSL is closer to 1 or maybe even higher. Table 3.2.1 gives a (non-exhaustive) overview of comparable meta-analytical studies that have come up with estimates of VSL income elasticities.

Without entering into the details of the differences between these studies, it is of note that at least three of the six studies have produced higher income elasticity estimates, and only one has produced a lower estimate.

Table 3.2.1 Other meta-analysis findings on income elasticity of VSL

Study	Income elasticity of VSL
Mrozek and Taylor (2002)	0.46–0.49
Liu *et al.* (1997)	0.53
De Blaeij *et al.* (2003)	0.5
Miller (2000)	0.85–1.00
Bellavance *et al.* (2009)	0.84–1.08
Bowland and Beghin (2001)	1.7–2.3

The possibility that income elasticity may be closer to or even above 1 is further strengthened by evidence from longitudinal studies – e.g. Hammitt *et al.* (2000) estimate the relationship between wages and job-related risks for each year from 1982 to 1997 in Taiwan in times of fast economic growth, and they find income elasticities ranging from 2.0 to 3.0. Costa and Kahn (2004) consider changes in the wage–risk relationship between 1940 and 1980 in the United States, finding elasticity estimates in the area of 1.5 to 1.7.

We may thus tentatively assume that the Viscusi and Aldy income elasticity could be too low, and we might therefore be able to exclude some of the higher ranges of the VSL estimates. This applies to both the VSL estimates in the economic burden section and in the Benefit-Cost estimates, where the upper-boundary VSLY estimate ($5,000) corresponded to a more than eleven times higher figure than national *per capita* GNP in low-income countries.

A more realistic assumption might be that of an income elasticity closer to 1 or beyond, though of course there is no way of being certain about this. By way of illustration, what would be the effect of, say, an income elasticity of 1 or even 1.2 on the VSLY estimates in low-income countries? This would produce a VSLY of $2,485 for a unitary elasticity and VSLY of $956 for an income elasticity of 1.2, corresponding to, respectively, 6.3 times and 2.6 times the GNI *per capita*. Hence, if income elasticity was about 1.2 or higher, then even the lower boundary of the VSLY used by Jha *et al.* would be too high an estimate.

A further issue relates to the within-country distribution of VSL – a consideration not explicitly taken into account in Chapter 3. If VSL varies with income across countries, it will also vary with personal incomes within countries. If it is the case that the beneficiaries of the selected interventions are the less wealthy members of society, who likely have a lower WTP to (marginally) reduce mortality risks, and hence lower VSLs, then this would tend to reduce the expected benefit of the intervention, compared to a scenario in which the population on average would benefit.[2] The section on chronic diseases and poverty (pp. 145–6) appears to suggest that chronic diseases may well be to a large extent a problem of the poor within developing countries, and that hence the benefits might well occur primarily among the lower socio-economic groups. The truth is, however, probably more nuanced than this, not least because we are dealing with various and very different chronic disease conditions. For instance, it is fairly uncontroversial to assume that tobacco consumption is disproportionately a problem of the poor within low-income countries (as opposed to the better off in those countries). Taken together with the observation that smokers in lower socio-economic groups are more responsive to tobacco price increases, one could expect that the health benefits from the proposed tobacco taxation are primarily incurred by the poor within countries, and hence that the VSL might need to be corrected downwards.

By contrast, the distribution of other risk factors, e.g. obesity, is decidedly different from smoking, in that the shift of the obesity burden from the rich to the poor (within countries) has not yet progressed to the extent we see in the case of smoking – certainly not among men at least (Monteiro *et al.*, 2004; Dinsa *et al.*, 2012). If this is an indication of the socio-economic distribution of heart attacks and stroke, this would suggest that the parts of the population that stand to benefit from the recommended drug treatment and prevention are either of an average or of a higher level of economic wealth. As a result, using an average VSL for one country may underestimate the benefit of the intervention in this case.

Some discussion of the potential variation in the likely beneficiaries by socio-economic status across the different interventions may have been worthwhile, even though there is preciously little hard evidence on the distributional effects of the interventions, especially in low-income countries.

The (non-)consideration of the economic burden estimates in the benefit-cost analysis

While part of the above comments suggest that the higher boundaries of the VSL estimates (and hence of the benefit estimates associated with the interventions) may indeed be too large, there are also reasons to think that the benefit provided by Jha *et al.* could be underestimates. This is because while the authors have discussed at some length the existing economic costs associated with chronic diseases (especially the COI and the value of lost output), when Jha *et al.* turned to estimating the benefits of the interventions, none of the previous "economic burden" estimates are factored into their BCRs. The authors present extensive data on the costs of chronic diseases, using the COI approach, and based on the impact of health on growth. To the extent that the authors are confident about these findings, one might have expected them to reflect at least part of those in their benefit-cost estimates.

That said, personally I would have some concerns about part of the economic burden results presented on pp. 143–4. In particular the value of lost output approach rests on the WHO's EPIC model, which in turn rests on the assumption that there is a harmful effect of health on economic growth, and in particular a harmful effect of chronic disease mortality on growth. These two critical assumptions might deserve some discussion in light of the influential Acemoglu and Johnson (2007) finding that improvements in life expectancy mainly trigger faster population growth, but have a negative causal effect on income *per capita*, at least over an adjustment period (which can last several decades). They regress income growth on the increase in life expectancy between 1940 and 1980, and instrument for the growth in life expectancy by exploiting the wave of health innovations that occurred in the

[2] This assumption could be seen as implicit in the use of an average VSL for the country as a whole.

1950s and affected all countries world-wide: they use the pre-intervention distribution of mortality from fifteen diseases and the dates of global interventions to construct a country-varying instrument for life expectancy.

These findings appear to have spurred an interest among economists to reconsider the relationship between health and growth. Some studies have indeed found opposing results to Acemoglu and Johnson, (see, e.g. Aghion *et al.*, 2011), and Cervellati and Sunde, 2011).[3] Most of the existing studies have, however, not paid specific attention to the effect of growth on chronic diseases. It may well be that the effect of chronic diseases on growth is different from that of infectious diseases or malnutrition. After all, they tend to affect very different segments of the population – i.e. chiefly elderly people in the case of chronic diseases. Depending on the demographic profile of the population, if the reduction of chronic diseases as a result of the proposed interventions occurs only among those already near or beyond retirement age, then it is conceivable that the economic growth impact will be minimal, and may even be negative. On the other hand, reductions in chronic disease risk may have less of a population-augmenting effect compared to infectious disease risk reductions. (The population-enhancing effect of health improvements was the main driver of the negative growth effects of life expectancy improvements in the Acemoglu and Johnson study.)

To the best of our knowledge only one study has looked specifically at the growth impact of chronic diseases (Suhrcke and Urban, 2010), finding that reductions in CVD mortality in adults can significantly reduce subsequent *per capita* income growth. However, this finding applied only to the high-income countries, not to the LMICs. (This may however also be explained by data deficits in these countries.)

The mixed evidence on the macroeconomic growth impact is in contrast to the fairly reliable impact of health (including chronic disease) on individual-level economic outcomes, such as labor market earnings, labor market participation, etc. (Suhrcke *et al.*, 2006). Jha *et al.* have, however, not considered the latter aspect. The microeconomic effect might have been a useful additional input into the CBA, even though there are no consensus estimates on the magnitude of such effects.

On balance, and given the substantial variation and challenges in the current economic cost evidence – and those challenges might be larger than Jha *et al.* have acknowledged – it is probably understandable that they decided not to include the COI and VOL estimates into their benefit-cost estimates.

Economic rationales for public policy investment

In the context of tobacco taxation, there is some discussion of what the market failures might be that could justify public policy intervention in this particular area. Jha *et al.* mention two information imperfections (about health risks and about the consequences of the addictive properties of smoking) and one on externalities. While the latter market failure could justify tobacco taxation as a direct response, tobacco taxation would not – from an economic perspective – be the first response to the presence of information imperfections. The first recommendation, if those were the main market failures, would be to run information campaigns.[4]

Further economic rationales could be brought to bear in the context of tobacco, i.e. the existence of less than perfectly rational decisions made by individuals trading off the long-term "pleasure" of consumption now with the adverse health effects a (too long) time in the future: the idea of time-inconsistent preferences. If this was an empirically proven point, then there might be a rationale for the state to help the individuals make "better" decisions – better in the sense of "in people's long term self-interest" (which is seen to be in conflict with the immediate self-interest). It is, however, important to bear in mind that the welfare economic implications of behavioral economics are complex,

[3] See also Lorentzen *et al.* (2008) for a careful study on the growth-enhancing effects of adult mortality reductions.

[4] The evidence for information campaigns to be effective in changing health behaviors in general, and in tobacco in particular, is very poor.

and public policy intervention cannot always unambiguously be inferred (Sugden, 2009).

There is no discussion in the chapter on what the market failures might be underlying the other interventions. The rationale for salt regulation may not be too dissimilar from that for tobacco, though arguably the addictive properties of the latter are far greater than of the former. Consumers have little choice in the amount of sodium they consume every day, as most of it is already inside the food products purchased and/or consumed. It may also be difficult to understand how much sodium is in a given food. The latter may represent an imperfect information the direct response to which would be information campaigns (though this would likely be an ineffective response). Excessive salt consumption may also exert external costs if the treatment costs for heart diseases, etc. that result are being co-financed by others in society (if there is collective insurance financing).

The second recommended intervention – acute management of heart attacks with low-cost drugs – is estimated to provided a BCR of 25:1 – which is a very high return on investment, which makes one wonder why the individual does not pay himself or herself to fund an intervention that is low cost and entails such huge benefits. It could be a problem of poverty – i.e. the low cost of the drugs is not low enough for them to be truly affordable. Or the cash needed to pay is not available to the individual and capital markets do not function well enough to allow for borrowing. In any case, some discussion of the potential market failure and how it relates (or not) to the recommended intervention would be of use.

Bibliography

Acemoglu, D. and S. Johnson, 2007: Disease and development: the effect of life expectancy on economic growth, *Journal of Political Economy* **115**, 925–85

Aghion, P., P. Howitt, and F. Murtin, 2011: The relationship between health and growth: when Lucas meets Nelson-Phelps, *Review of Economics and Institutions* **2**, 1–24

Bellavance, F., G. Dionne, and M. Lebeau, 2009: The value of a statistical life: a meta-analysis with a mixed effects regression model, *Journal of Health Economics* **28**, 444–64

Bowland, B. J. and J. C. Beghin, 2001: Robust estimates of value of a statistical life for developing economies, *Journal of Policy Modeling* **23**, 385–96

Cervellati, M. and U. Sunde, 2011: Life expectancy and economic growth: the role of the demographic transition, *Journal of Economic Growth* **16**, 99–133

Costa, D. L. and M. E. Kahn, 2004: Changes in the value of life, 1940–1980, *Journal of Risk and Uncertainty* **29**, 159–80

De Blaeij, A., R. J. G. M. Florax, P. Rietveld, and E. Verhoef, 2003: The value of statistical life in road safety: a meta-analysis, *Accident Analysis and Prevention* **35**, 973–86

Dinsa, G. D., Y. Goryakin, E. Fumagalli, and M. Suhrcke, 2012: Obesity and socio-economic status in developing countries: a systematic review, *Obesity Reviews* **13**, 1067–79

Hammitt, J. K. and L. A. Robinson, 2011: The income elasticity of the value per statistical life: transferring estimates between high and low income populations, *Journal of Benefit-Cost Analysis* **2**, DOI: 10.2202/2152–2812.1009

Hammitt, J. K., J.-T. Liu, and J.-L. Liu, 2000: *Survival is a Luxury Good: The Increasing Value of a Statistical Life*, Paper prepared for the NBER Summer Institute Workshop on Public Policy and the Environment

Liu, J.-T., J. K. Hammitt, and J.-L. Liu, 1997: Estimated hedonic wage function and value of life in a developing country, *Economic Letters* **57**, 353–8

Lorentzen, P., J. McMillan, and R. Wacziarg, 2008: Death and development, *Journal of Economic Growth* **13**, 81–124

Miller, T. R., 2000: Variations between countries in values of statistical life, *Journal of Transport Economics and Safety* **34**, 169–88

Monteiro, C. A., E. C. Moura, W. L. Conde, and B. M. Popkin, 2004: Socioeconomic status and obesity in adult populations of developing countries: a review, *Bulletin of the World Health Organization* **82**, 940–6

Mrozek, J. R. and L. O. Taylor, 2002: What determines the value of life? A meta-analysis, *Journal of Policy Analysis and Management* **21**, 253–70

Robinson, L. A., 2008: *Valuing Mortality Risk Reductions in Homeland Security Regulatory*

Analyses, report prepared for US Customs and Border Protection, Department of Homeland Security, under subcontract to Industrial Economics, Inc.

Sugden, R., 2009: On nudging: a review of "Nudge: Improving decisions about health, wealth, and happiness", by Richard H. Thaler and Cass R. Sunstein, *International Journal of the Economics of Business* **16**, 365–73

Suhrcke, M., R. Nugent, D. Stuckler, and Rocco, 2006: *Chronic Disease: An Economic Perspective*, Oxford Health Alliance, London

Suhrcke, M. and D. Urban, 2010: Are cardiovascular diseases bad for economic growth?, *Health Economics* **19**, 1478–96

Viscusi, W. K. and J. E. Aldy, 2003: The value of a statistical life: a critical review of market estimates throughout the world, *Journal of Risk and Uncertainty* **27**, 5–76

World Bank, 2012: *World Bank Development Indicators*, http://data.worldbank.org/data-catalog/world-development-indicators

CHAPTER 4 Climate Change

This Challenge Paper consists of four separate contributions, updating key research papers from the 2010 Copenhagen Consensus on Climate Change project:

- An Updated Analysis of CO_2 Emission Abatement as a Response to Climate Change, Richard S. J. Tol
- A Technology-led Climate Policy in a Changing Landscape, Isabel Galiana and Christopher Green
- Climate Change: Climate Engineering Research, J. Eric Bickel and Lee Lane
- Market and Policy-Driven Adaptation, Francesco Bosello, Carlo Carraro, and Enrica De Cian

CO_2 ABATEMENT

Richard S. J. Tol

Introduction

In the 2010 Copenhagen Consensus on Climate Change (Lomborg, 2010), reduction of carbon dioxide (CO_2) emissions received a low priority. This follows from the particularities of the *Gedankenexperiment* that is at the core of all Copenhagen Consensus exercises: there is a finite budget, that needs to be spent, on a separate project, informed by disjoint CBAs.

Climate policy does not fit in that mold, and CO_2 emission reduction fits least of all.

Climate change is a big problem. In order to halt anthropogenic climate change, the atmospheric concentrations of GHGs need to be stabilized. For that, CO_2 emissions need to be reduced to zero. This requires a complete overhaul of the energy sector. That is a big job. It should be done as long as the benefits exceed the costs. If it does not fit in the budget of the Copenhagen Consensus, then more money should be raised. Indeed, it would be profitable to borrow money if the BCR is greater than 1.

There is wide agreement in the economic literature that GHG emission reduction is best done through a carbon tax. A uniform carbon tax implies equimarginal abatement costs. Climate change is a stock problem, so a price instrument is more robust to uncertainty than a quantity instrument. Taxes properly incentivize R&D. That is, climate policy is not about spending money: it is about raising money (and, of course, about finding the best way to spend the revenues raised through a carbon tax.)

Drastic reduction of CO_2 emissions would be very expensive with current technologies; R&D is a critical part of CO_2 abatement policy. However, most of that R&D is innovation and diffusion, rather than invention. Grants are suitable for invention. For innovation and diffusion, the regulator should create a credible promise of a future market: in this case, the promise of an emission reduction target or, better, a carbon tax in the future. The best way to give a credible signal is to start now – which has an additional advantage because the regulator does not know how close to market renewable energy technologies really are. That is, R&D and CO_2 abatement are complements, not substitutes.

CBA, the purported aim of the Copenhagen Consensus, is an analysis of efficiency. Cost-efficacy is a precondition for efficiency. Cost-efficacy requires that all alternative solutions to a problem – CO_2 emission reduction, reduction of other GHGs, carbon capture and storage, and indeed R&D and geoengineering – are priced equally at the appropriate margin. It is inconceivable that a CBA would conclude that climate change is a problem that should be addressed through one channel – say, geo-engineering – but not through other channels, provided that those channels are complements and their marginal cost curves go through the origin.

Geo-engineering indeed is a complement to CO_2 emission reduction. Geo-engineering addresses warming, a subset of climate change, whereas CO_2 emission reduction addresses the whole of climate change as well as ocean acidification. Geo-engineering is a transient, end-of-pipe solution to climate change whereas CO_2 emission reduction is a permanent, structural solution. Geo-engineering may have a place in an optimal portfolio of climate policy because CO_2 emission reduction will take considerable time to create an effect, but it cannot dominate the portfolio.

The 2010 Copenhagen Consensus on Climate Change overlooks these issues. Its conclusions are therefore unsupported.

Costs and benefits of climate policy: an update

My contribution to the 2010 Copenhagen Consensus came in five parts. I here briefly summarize each of these parts and offer the latest insights.

Impacts of climate change

In Tol (2010), I survey the literature on the total economic impact of climate change. No new studies have been published since. The bottom-line conclusions are therefore still the same:

- The net impact of climate change is probably positive for moderate climate change, but turns negative at some point in the twenty-first century. The incremental impact becomes negative well within the committed warming. The net benefits are sunk benefits.
- The best estimates of the global average impact of a century of climate change are of the same order of magnitude as annual economic growth rates, and the impacts of centennial climate change are unlikely to exceed decadal growth rates.
- National average impacts may be much larger than global average impacts. Poor countries in the tropics are particularly vulnerable to climate change.
- Impact estimates are very uncertain. Negative surprises are more likely than positive surprises. Primary estimates are available for global warming up to 3°C; beyond that, impact estimates are largely speculative.

In Tol (2010), I surveyed the literature on the social cost of carbon or the marginal impacts of climate change. I then counted 232 published estimates. Since then, more than 100 new estimates have been published (Tol, 2011). Despite the large increase in the number of estimates, the results are similar:

- The social cost of carbon is most likely positive. That is, GHG emissions are a negative externality that should be taxed or otherwise regulated.
- The social cost of carbon strongly depends on the parameters of the welfare function, notably the pure rate of time preference and the rate of risk aversion.
- Estimates of the social cost of carbon are highly uncertain, and the uncertainty is right-skewed, possibly with a fat tail.

Table 4.1.1 shows the results of (Tol, 2011), and emphasizes three things. The right tail is heavy, perhaps fat. The discount rate is crucial. Impacts fall disproportionally on the poor, so that equity-weighted impacts are much larger than risk-neutral impacts.

Impacts of GHG emission reduction

New estimates of the costs of GHG emission reduction are published regularly, but as they add to an already large body of work, overall conclusions change only slowly. The following lessons can be drawn:

- Deep cuts in GHG emissions are technically feasible.
- The costs of deep emission cuts are relatively small if
  - emission reduction targets are lenient at first, but accelerate over time.
  - All emitting sectors are regulated and marginal abatement costs are the same.
  - All gases are regulated and priced uniformly.

Table 4.1.1 The social cost of carbon ($/tC); sample statistics and characteristics of the Fisher–Tippett distribution fitted to 311 published estimates, and to three alternative ways to split the sample[a]

		PRTP			Equity		Uncertainty	
	All	0%	1%	3%	Yes	No	Best	Mean
Mean	177	276	84	19	168	177	206	68
SD	293	258	93	18	200	316	332	93
Mode	49	126	48	10	65	44	55	23
P(SCC) < 0	25%	10%	17%	11%	16%	27%	25%	22%
33%	35	125	35	8	59	26	40	19
50%	116	212	71	15	117	112	135	49
67%	213	339	112	23	189	213	250	86
90%	487	646	204	44	478	489	573	177
95%	669	749	252	52	614	690	777	233
99%	1602	966	359	68	789	1684	1676	422
N	311	53	76	84	102	209	242	69

Note:
[a] PRTP = Pure rate of time preference; Equity = equity-weighted; Uncertainty = best guess or mean value.

  - All countries reduce emissions, and marginal costs are equal.
  - Climate policy is coordinated with other policies.
- The costs of emission reduction rapidly escalate if the above rules are violated.

Since the publication of (Tol, 2010), progress has been made in alternative energy technologies, notably in bio-energy and solar power. On the other hand, nuclear power has fallen out of favor. It is also increasingly clear that governments have great difficulty in delivering emission reduction programs that are least-cost.

Scenarios

2010 Copenhagen Consensus

In (Tol, 2010), $250 billion p.a. was spent for a decade, which is equivalent to a budget with an NPV of $2 trillion at a 5 percent money discount rate. I considered five scenarios:

(1) A carbon tax is levied in the countries of the OECD for ten years. The carbon tax rises with the rate of discount until 2020, and then falls to zero. The initial level of the carbon tax is such that the net present welfare loss is $2 trillion.
(2) A carbon tax is levied in all countries for ten years. The carbon tax rises with the rate of discount until 2020, and then falls to zero. The initial level of the carbon tax is such that the net present welfare loss is $2 trillion.
(3) A carbon tax is levied in all countries. The carbon tax rises with the rate of discount. The level of the carbon tax is the same as in Scenario (2), but continues rising after 2020.
(4) A carbon tax is levied in all countries. The carbon tax rises with the rate of discount. The initial level of the carbon tax is such that the net present welfare loss is $2 trillion.
(5) A carbon tax is levied in all countries. The carbon tax rises with the rate of discount. The initial level of the carbon tax is set equal to the social cost of carbon.

Scenarios (1) and (2) are for diagnostic purposes only, illustrating (a) that it is pointless to have a climate policy for ten years only and (b) that it is largely ineffective and needlessly expensive to limit CO_2 emission reduction to OECD countries. The BCR is less than 1.

Scenario (3) roughly corresponds to the long-term target of the European Union: the atmospheric concentration of CO_2 stays well below 450 ppm. But because other GHGs are uncontrolled (because of the silly rules of the Copenhagen Consensus), the global mean temperature continues to rise above 2°C warming. This scenario violates the budget constraint of the Copenhagen Consensus, and its BCR is 2.

Scenario (4) spends all the Copenhagen money on CO_2 emission reduction. I argue above that this would be unwise: other GHGs should be reduced, too. CO_2 emissions begin to fall around 2055. The BCR is 26 – ignoring uncertainty and equity.

Scenario (5) spends a fraction (5 percent) of the Copenhagen budget on CO_2 emission reduction. CO_2 emissions begin to fall around 2090. The BCR is 151 – again ignoring uncertainty and equity.

Scenarios (3)–(5) illustrate the fact that an economic case can be made for CO_2 emission reduction, even under conservative assumptions. The analysis ignores the large and right-skewed uncertainty about climate change and its impacts, and also ignores the fact that the impacts of climate change would fall disproportionally on the global poor. At the same time, Scenarios (3)–(5) illustrate that while some CO_2 emission reduction is justified, there are limits to the desired stringency of climate policy.

2012 Copenhagen Consensus

The main difference between the current and the previous round of the Copenhagen Consensus is that the budget is much smaller: $75 billion for a period of four years, with an NPV of $70 billion. This is less than the budget of the cheapest Scenario (5) above, so that all those scenarios are impermissible for the current edition of the Copenhagen Consensus for Climate.

Figure 4.1.1 shows the net present welfare loss, the BCR, the peak year of emissions, and the CO_2 concentration in 2100, each as a function of the initial carbon tax for Scenarios (3)–(5) (see also Table 4.1.2). I add, by interpolation, Scenario (6): a carbon tax of $3/tC is levied on all emissions of CO_2 from fossil fuel combustion and industrial processes from all sectors in all countries in 2010; the carbon tax increases with the rate of discount to $242/tC in 2100.

For such a tax, the net present welfare loss is $280 billion, which exceeds the Copenhagen budget. Emissions peak around 2080, and the atmospheric CO_2 concentration in 2100 is 815 ppm. The BCR is 1.02. This project is worthwhile, albeit only just so.

I add a Scenario (7) by infrapolation. The initial tax is $1.8/tC. Emissions peak around 2090 (as in Scenario (5)) but the CO_2 concentration rises to 875 ppm. The NPV of the emission reduction costs is $70 billion, equal to the Copenhagen Consensus budget. The BCR is 1.56.

Biased BCRs?

Table 4.1.2 shows the BCR for Scenarios (1)–(5). There are several biases in the results. First, the benefits are taken from the FUND model, which estimates a social cost of carbon of $2/tC for the 5 percent discount rate. A comparison with Table 4.1.1 (Tol, 2011) reveals that the average in the literature for that discount rate is $10/tC – I therefore multiply the benefits by five. Second, the benefits are not equity-weighted – that is, the analysis assumes that a dollar to a poor woman is worth the same as a dollar to a rich woman. Table 4.1.1 reveals that the social cost of carbon increases by a factor of 1.5 if equity-weighted. Third, the analysis ignores uncertainty. Table 4.1.1 suggests that the social cost of carbon decreases by a factor of 0.4 if the expected benefits are considered rather than the best guesses.[1] Fourth, that factor of 2.4 only considers within-model uncertainty. Table 4.1.1 suggests that, for a discount rate of about 5 percent, the social cost of carbon increases by a factor of 1.9 if between-model uncertainty is included, too. Put together, Table 4.1.1 underestimates the benefits by a factor of 33.6.[2]

[1] This is counterintuitive. The explanation is that only the more sophisticated analyses include uncertainty, and more sophisticated analyses tend to be less pessimistic about climate change and its impacts.

[2] There are, of course, different ways of navigating through Table 4.1.1. If, for instance, we evaluate the equity bias and the within-model bias at the mean rather than the mode, then the total bias would be 3.0. Time did not permit us going

Table 4.1.2 Selected characteristics of the scenarios: initial carbon tax, peak year of CO_2 emissions, atmospheric concentration of CO_2 in 2100, NPV of the costs of emission reduction, BCR

Scenario	Tax	Peak year	Concentration	NPV costs	BCR
7	$1.8/tC	2090	875	$70 10^9	1.56
5	$2/tC	2090	850	$100 10^9	1.51
6	$3/tC	2080	815	$280 10^9	1.02
4	$12/tC	2055	675	$2,000 10^9	0.26
3	$250/tC	2010	425	$47,600 10^9	0.02

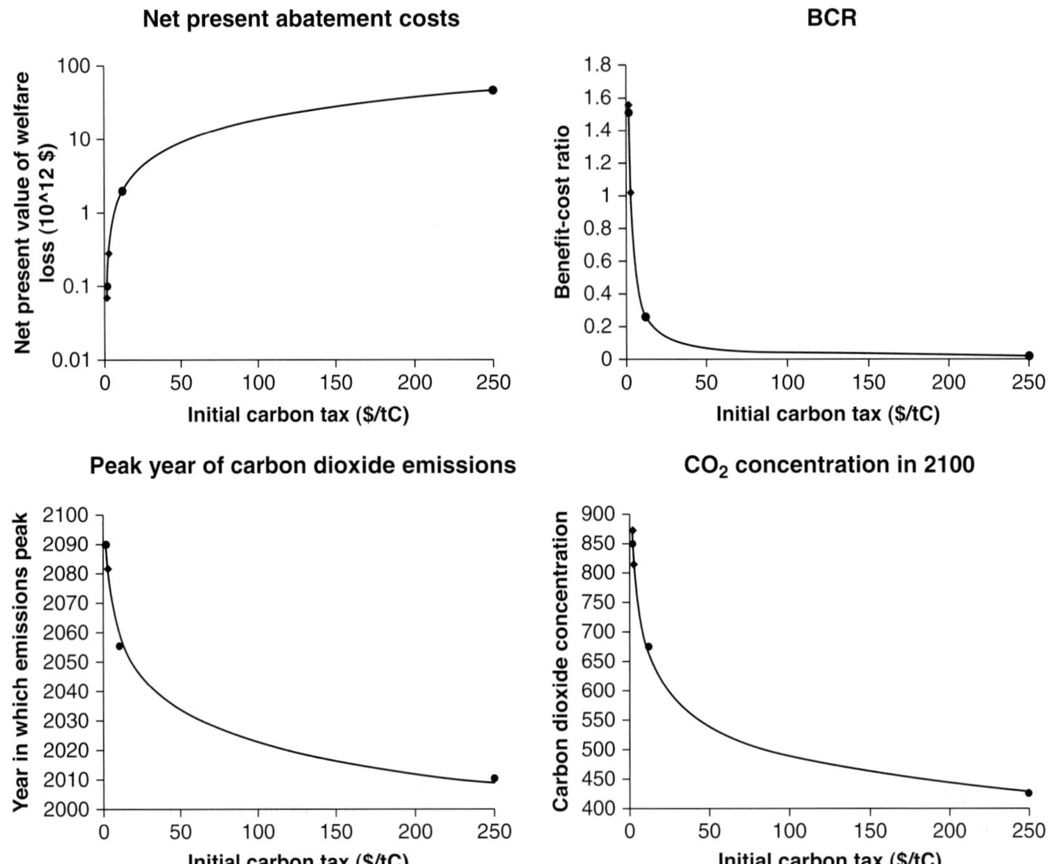

Figure 4.1.1 *Selected characteristics of the scenarios as a function of the initial carbon tax; dots are taken from (Tol, 2010), triangles are interpolated*

Table 4.1.3 shows the corrected BCRs. The low carbon taxes ($2/tC and $3/tC) could already be justified with conservative assumptions, and look very attractive if equity, uncertainty, and model bias are corrected. The $12/tC tax can also be justified, but the assumptions of Table 4.1.2 need to be stretched further. The $250/tC is unjustifiable.

back to the data underlying Table 4.1.1 and further refining the analysis.

Table 4.1.3 Corrected BCRs

Scenario	7	5	6	4	3	Factor
Tax	$1.8/tC	$2/tC	$3/tC	$12/tC	$250/tC	
Table 4.1.2	1.56	1.51	1.02	0.26	0.02	–
Equity weighting	2.30	2.23	1.50	0.38	0.03	1.5
Between-model uncertainty	2.96	2.87	1.93	0.49	0.04	1.9
Within-model uncertainty	0.65	0.63	0.43	0.11	0.01	0.4
Multi-model	7.78	7.55	5.09	1.30	0.10	5.0
All of the above	9.14	8.86	5.98	1.53	0.12	5.9

Table 4.1.3 does not correct all biases. One could argue that the cost estimates suffer from similar biases. However, the uncertainty about the costs of emission abatement is more symmetric, the costs are more equitably spread over countries, and FUND tends be closer to the middle of the model distribution, albeit a bit on the expensive side. The bias correction factor would thus be smaller. As the (incomplete) results in Table 4.1.3 are so robust, it is not likely that further bias corrections would qualitatively change the conclusion.

Conclusion

In this chapter, I revisit the scenarios of the 2010 Copenhagen Consensus. I argue that the format of the Copenhagen Consensus is ill suited for a problem like climate change, and that it is inappropriate for evaluating the different aspect of climate policy. Climate policy is a long program, not a short project, and revenue should be raised through a carbon tax, rather than spent by a blue-ribbon panel. Climate policy is a portfolio of adaptation, abatement of various gases, R&D, and perhaps geoengineering. Ignoring the complementarity of these options is silly.

I re-assess the estimates of the costs and benefits of CO_2 emission reduction, and find that no reason has arisen in the last two years to radically change the numbers published in 2010.

I re-evaluate the scenarios of the 2010 project, and add two new scenarios, one that fits the revised budget, and one that is the most stringent justifiable policy. Based on conservative assumptions, modest CO_2 emission reduction can be justified. If this does not fit within the budget of the Copenhagen Consensus, then money should be borrowed. The analysis above reveals that the Copenhagen Consensus budget is indeed inadequate for a problem like climate change.

Properly accounting for uncertainty and equity, modest emission reduction appears to be a very lucrative proposition and more stringent emission reduction can readily be justified.

Very stringent emission reduction targets, in line with the long-term goals of the European Union, do not pass the benefit-cost test, however.

Bibliography

Lomborg, B. (ed.), 2010: *Smart Solutions to Climate Change – Comparing Costs and Benefits*, Cambridge University Press

Tol, R. S. J., 2010: An analysis of mitigation as a response to climate change, in B. Lomborg (ed.), *Smart Solutions to Climate Change – Comparing Costs and Benefits*, Cambridge University Press

2011: The social cost of carbon, *Annual Review of Resource Economics* **3**, 419–43

TECHNOLOGY-LED MITIGATION

Isabel Galiana and
Christopher Green

Introduction

In 2009 (Galiana and Green, 2009; Galiana and Green 2010) proposed a technology-led climate policy. Specifically, we proposed that on average \$100 billion be spent globally on basic R&D, the testing and demonstration of low-carbon energy technologies plus the required infrastructure support. The expenditure would be supported by a low-carbon tax (we suggested \$5.00/tCO_2), the revenues from which would be placed in dedicated trust funds in each participating country. Over time, the carbon price would rise gradually (we suggested a doubling every ten years), thereby sending a forward price signal to commercialize and deploy scalable, cost-effective energy technologies as they became available.

There are several reasons for proposing a technology-led climate policy. Five stand out, and each was elaborated on in some depth in Galiana and Green (2010). First, we demonstrated that the size of the energy-technology challenge to "stabilizing climate" is huge, and that it has been seriously understated by those who use the IPCC emission scenarios as baselines for estimating the size and cost of that challenge. Second, we examined the low-carbon energy sources and found a current lack of technological readiness and scalability. Third, we explained why we cannot depend on carbon pricing to generate the necessary long-term investments in *basic* R&D, the fruits of which may not prove successful and, if successful, may take decades rather than years to prove so, and even then may generate benefits that are not appropriable. Fourth, we showed that a "brute-force" approach to reducing GHG emissions in the absence of technological readiness could generate economic costs an order of magnitude or more, greater than the GDP cost estimates presented by the IPCC. Finally, we calculated that an effective technology-led policy would pass a benefit-cost test by wide margins.

Here, we undertake an update of our proposal:

(1) Is it as compelling as it was three years ago?
(2) Would it continue to pass a benefit-cost test with high marks?
(3) Is there anything important that has changed or has occurred that should be considered in a re-evaluation of the proposal?

Our answers to the three questions are: *yes* to compelling; *still high* to the benefit-cost test; and *yes indeed* to whether the landscape has changed and there is new information to consider. It is the last of these that is the chief focus of this update.

What has changed?

Receptivity to the idea

When we began our analysis of a technology-led policy just prior to Conference of the Parties (COP 15) in Copenhagen, target-based climate policies were the only game in town. COP 15 was hailed as the last chance to halt climate change by negotiating a second Kyoto commitment period. Three COPs have since passed. The first was Copenhagen, which resulted in a non-legally binding document that recognizes that actions should be taken to keep any temperature increases to 2 °C. The second, COP 16 in Cancún gave us the Green Climate Fund and a Technology Mechanism. While this defection from emission targets as the main tool for climate policy was promising, the third COP 17 in Durban has unfortunately extended the life of the Kyoto Protocol for at least five years and the period for negotiating a new global emission reduction agreement to 2015. At best, the so-called "Durban Platform" serves to distract from the pressing need to develop fundamentally new technologies. At worst, we could end up with an agreement that focuses on emission reduction *ends* and overlooks the technological *means* to achieve them.

Nonetheless, it is our impression that there is now widespread acknowledgment that energy technologies are at the core of any serious attempt to stem the growth and begin to substantially reduce *global* emissions. We are less likely to hear that energy efficiency, conservation, and changed lifestyles will largely do the trick. Perhaps this is a reflection of the growing appreciation that the lion's share of emissions now and in the future will come from the developing world, in particular the newly "emerging" economies such as China, India, Korea, Indonesia, and Brazil. In fact, we would go so far as to suggest that it is in the "emerging" economies that there is receptivity to a technology-based stance to climate policy. This is particularly evident in the case of China.

In the West the technology response has been more tentative. In some respects, it has also been perverse. As a result of the financial crash of 2008 and the deep recession and continuing slump some governments, particularly the US, saw spending on (including investment in) "green technologies" as a means to a "green recovery." The American Recovery and Reinvestment Act of 2009 dedicated $112 billion (threefold the budget of these programs) to climate initiatives, largely related to energy efficiency and renewables. The result is technology promotion largely in the form of subsidies to production and deployment. Such a response is perverse because it generates waste and leads to spurious levels of progress without really solving the basic impediments to scalability and cost-effectiveness of low-carbon technologies. Subsidies and other inducements, such as FITs and renewable portfolio standards (RPSs), have been shown to be extremely cost-ineffective and have not impacted emissions as hoped. In the United States, under RPSs, utilities are being forced to adopt gerrymandered systems in order to find some way to smooth out and provide a modicum of storage for the intermittent, non-dispatchable energies, primarily solar and wind, that they are forced to take on. The case for FITs in Europe looks no better. The UK-based Renewable Energy Foundation (REF) finds the cost of abatement under FITs to be between £174 and £800 per tonne of CO_2 (Constable, 2011). In Spain, FITs have led to a record deficit of US$8.3 billion for a total five-year deficit of about US$20 billion.[1]

Moreover, subsidies have an important Achilles heel. They are prone to stop-and-go financing in the short term and rapidly rising budgetary costs in the long run, as the number of green energy suppliers and customers rise. For example, Victor and Yanosek (2011) point out that investors "flock to clean energy projects that are quick and easy to build rather than invest in more innovative technologies that could stand a better chance of competing with conventional energy sources over the long haul."

In the meantime, funds for basic R&D, testing, and demonstration have been limited and increasingly subject to budget cuts. Yet without the technology breakthroughs that innovation funding may bring, there is little hope of increasing the scalability and cost-effectiveness of most low-carbon technologies. A series of reports (CATF, 2009; AEBB, 2010; AEIC, 2010; AH, 2011; Anadon *et al.*, 2011; ITIF, 2011) and commentaries (Gates 2011; Hoffert 2011) have recognized the need for much greater support for energy-technology innovation. Significantly, none of these advocates subsidies to clean energy manufacturing and deployment. And some reports, such as AEBB and AH, pointedly deplore the penchant for granting downstream subsidies while skimping on support for energy innovation. There has yet to be a righting of the balance.

In testimony before the US Congress Joint Economic Committe (JEC), Michael Greenstone, Professor of Economics at MIT, discussed the importance of clean energy R&D (July 27, 2010):

> The bottom line is that for a substantial period of time, developing countries are likely to be . . . focused on increasing their incomes and using the cheapest energy sources available to do so. Without a change [in] the cost of low-carbon fuels, this will mean increased demand for fossil fuels.

Greenstone's recommendations include increased federal funding that is focused not only on basic R&D but also on demonstration. Furthermore he goes on to say that "demonstration should not be expanded to include the deployment of new technologies." This view, which coincides perfectly with our own, has yet to be widely adopted, as is evident by the growth in FITs and RPSs.

The appearance of numerous studies on the importance of combining environmental policy

[1] www.economist.com/node/21524449.

with R&D subsidies is encouraging. Acemoglu *et al.* (2012) find that the optimal policy mix includes both a carbon tax and R&D subsidies. In late 2009, a group of thirty-four US Nobel Laureates wrote a letter[2] to urge Congress to include an R&D fund of $150 billion over ten years in climate legislation, the primary argument being the need for stable funding to induce the necessary progress. The European Commission proposed that global public support for energy R&D should at least double by 2012 and quadruple from 2020 (European Commission, 2009). In the United States, the recent creation of ARPA-E (Advanced Research Projects Agency – Energy) shows some promise but its 2011 budget was only $300 million, which is approximately 1 percent of the National Institute of Health (NIH) budget.

The American Energy Innovation Council (AEIC), made up of representatives of the largest US corporations, acknowledges the underinvestment of the private sector in energy R&D and calls for, among other things, the support of "innovation hubs" and increased funding for ARPA-E.

Harvard University's Belfer Center for Science and International Affairs released a report entitled *Transforming US Energy Innovation* (Anadon, *et al.*, 2011) based on a three-year project primarily involving industry surveys and case studies. The report recommends doubling government funding for energy research, development, and demonstration (RD&D) to about $US10 billion per year. The Belfer survey suggests that government-funded RD&D in the United States beyond $10 billion p.a. may have decreasing marginal returns. As the United States emits 18 percent of global emissions, scaling up the Belfer estimate superficially implies spending *globally* $55 billion p.a. on energy R&D. Taken at face value, the $55 billion p.a. is just a little over half the $100 billion p.a. we indicated in our 2010 Copenhagen Consensus papter (Galiana and Green, 2010). But Belfer's $10 billion p.a. R&D estimate for the United States is supplemented by a huge carbon tax, which reaches $300/tCO_2$ to meet the Obama Administration's 2050 target of an 80 percent reduction in emissions.

The Belfer survey's need for a high and rapidly rising carbon price to induce the commercialization and development of low-carbon energy technologies suggests a lack of confidence that R&D alone can sufficiently reduce the cost of low-carbon technologies. In our view, this result is a direct consequence of a stringent emissions target whose time frame (83 percent reduction from 2005 by 2050) does not necessarily coincide with the development of scalable technologies. In our 2010 paper we implied that if the R&D commitment was strong enough, not only could sufficient scalable technologies be developed but they could be made cost-effective with a low, slowly rising carbon tax. To use a metaphor from our paper (Galiana and Green, 2010: 310–11), where we put the technology chicken ahead of the carbon price egg, Belfer more or less does the opposite by allowing an emission target to dictate the appropriate carbon price.

We think it revealing that Belfer does not say what would happen to global emissions if the United States placed a high and rising price on carbon, but the rest of the world did not. As we note on pp. 197–8, and is indicated in Figures 4.2.1 and 4.2.2, since the adoption of the non-globally harmonized Kyoto Protocol, the West has transferred a substantial portion of its emission responsibilities to developing countries/emerging economies, especially in the Far East. Significantly, a study in *Science* (Williams *et al.*, 2012) analyzes the technologies required to meet California's emission reduction target of 80 percent below 1990 by 2050. It finds not only a large gap between those technologies currently "commercialized" and scalable and those required, but its results depend on the crucial and unrealistic assumption that neighboring states would harmonize policy such that the carbon intensity of their energy production would be similar to that of California's.

In sum, although there is much more talk about technology in the context of climate policy, progress in adopting a technology-led policy as envisioned in Galiana and Green (2009, 2010) has been limited and slow. Worse, for political and other reasons the increasing interest in low-carbon

[2] www.fas.org/press/_docs/Nobelist%20Letter%20-%2007162009.pdf.

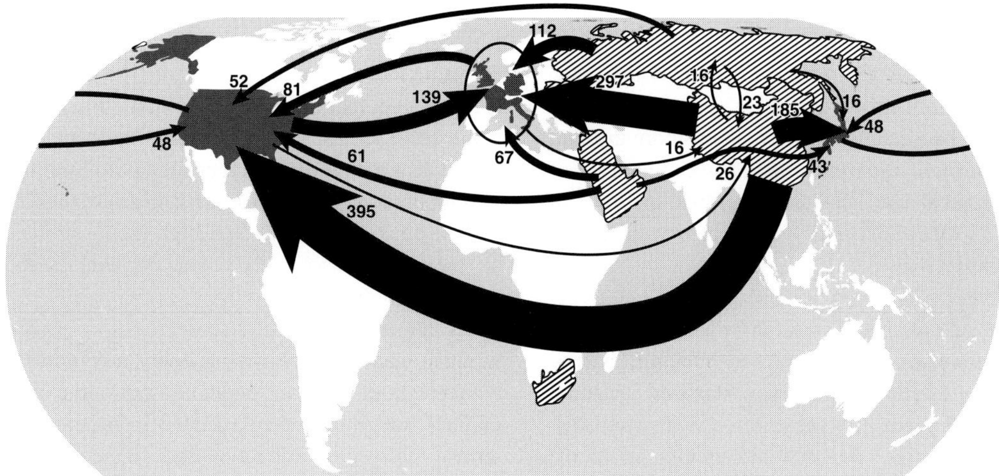

Figure 4.2.1 *Largest interregional fluxes of emissions embodied in trade (Mt CO_2 y − 1) from dominant net exporting countries (latched) to the dominant net importing countries (shaded)*

Fluxes to and from Western Europe are aggregated to include the United Kingdom, France, Germany, Switzerland, Italy, Spain, Luxembourg, the Netherlands, and Sweden.
Source: Davis and Caldeira (2010).

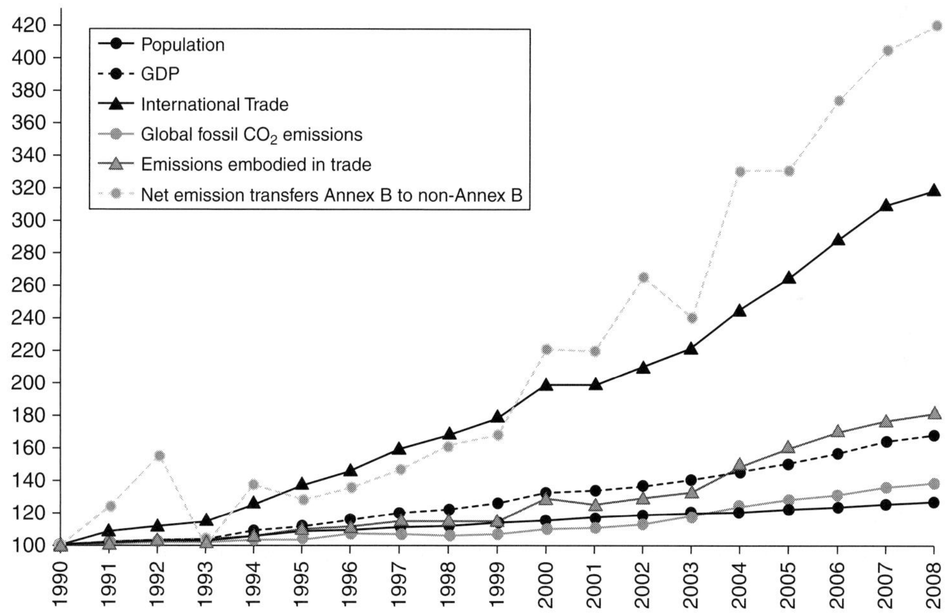

Figure 4.2.2 *Development of Various global macrovariables indexed to 1990 BCRs from 2009 Copenhagen Consensus (3 percent discount rate)*

energy technologies has been used opportunistically, and in the process has probably generated considerable waste and few tangible benefits. We did not envision this occurrence in 2009.

Technology developments

In 2009, we seemed to be on the cusp of a nuclear renaissance. While Fukushima has not put an end to nuclear development, it has slowed it, certainly when measured in global terms. As a result, a slower pace of deployment of a technology crucial to the gradual displacement of fossil fuels over the next half-century could make it more difficult to achieve the rapid decline in carbon intensity of output needed to substantially reduce the level of *global* GHG emissions by mid-century, or shortly thereafter.

An even more significant development is the emergence of shale gas as an important source of energy. Hydraulic fracturing, or "fracking," has the potential to produce large new supplies of natural gas, thus allowing for substitution away from coal, increasing energy security, and creating additional competition for and (thus slowing the entry of) intermittent renewables. The success of "fracking" seems likely to accelerate the transition away from coal while decelerating the move towards renewables. However, the combination of impacts, while perhaps mitigating short-term emission growth, may have less impact on temperature change than expected. Wigley (2011) shows that if natural gas leakage cannot be kept at a very low level, and if the switch to natural gas hastens the elimination of sulfur dioxide emissions, the transition from coal to gas by itself may not alter the trajectory of global average temperature change. An additional concern, not taken up here, is that "fracking" may pose water and other environmental-resource issues (Zoback *et al.*, 2010; Wood *et al.*, 2011).

There is another aspect of "fracking" which is changing the landscape. Not only has the combination of horizontal drilling and "fracking" teamed up to greatly increase the available reserves of natural gas, the same thing is now beginning to occur in the oil industry. Accessible reserves of oil in the United States have jumped substantially as a result of "fracking." Moreover, US reliance on overseas oil is declining. If reports are to be believed, it is no longer far-fetched that the United States, or at least North America, will once more be self-sufficient in petroleum (oil and natural gas). If so, the implications could be far-reaching, including geo-political ones.

There are potentially important ramifications if "fracking" makes possible US (or North American) *energy security*. In an uncertain and dangerous world, placing a value on energy security increases the social value of petroleum (oil and gas) above the value individuals place on them. The increased social value makes it all the more difficult for *low*-carbon energies to outcompete fossil fuels. It would also render policies that attempt to limit the development of the oil and gas industries, such as carbon emission permits and high carbon prices, all the more anathema to voters as well as the petroleum industry.

To put it another way, an increase in energy security made possible by abundant new domestic fossil fuel reserves implicitly raises the cost of CO_2 mitigation when assessed in benefit-cost terms. A key new mitigation-cost element is the lost user value of oil petroleum that is *artificially* priced out of the market or subjected to production constraints. In a world that depends so heavily on energy, and in which security has taken on new and important dimensions, it would be a hard sell to trade-off energy security/reliability for environmental health.

While "fracking" has made possible the addition of abundant previously inaccessible gas and oil reserves, efforts to capture emissions from stationary sources that use fossil fuels and store them in the ground (CCS) has progressed much more slowly. There are to be sure a large number of pilot projects around the world[3] and a small number of industrial operations actually using CCS. But it has yet to be shown that the 3.5–4.0 $MtCO_2$ emissions from a moderate-sized (400 GW, net energy) coal-fired plant can be captured and stored safely and economically, even with a price placed on carbon of \$40/t CO_2 (equivalent to \$110/t coal – or almost a 200 percent tax on coal used in electricity generation). From the accounts that we have seen, there continue to be unpredictable technological complications which have slowed the development of CCS, and almost surely have delayed the date at which any substantial fraction of power plant or mining operation emissions can be sequestered.

One thing that has not changed is the race to install wind turbines and solar arrays. This race is on-going in the absence of utility-scale storage,

[3] http://sequestration.mit.edu/tools/projects/index.html, accessed in late 2012.

necessary to handling more than a small amount of these intermittent and variable energy sources. The result is that while wind and solar energy capacity increase rapidly, the contribution of these sources to energy consumption remains very small. Solar and wind energies perhaps best illustrate the need for drastic technological breakthroughs if most low-carbon sources are to make more than a niche contribution to global energy consumption. An important article on battery research (Dunn *et al.*, 2011) and a *New York Times* report (October 2011) on a wind turbine farm in West Virginia that combined 1.3 million C and D batteries at a cost of $28 million to provide just 15 minutes of back-up aptly demonstrate the need for basic scientific R&D in energy technologies.

Despite some changes in the energy-technology landscape, we have barely scratched the surface of the huge energy-technology challenge to climate stabilization. Perhaps as a result there is a lingering concern among some that a concerted R&D effort to fill the gap will "crowd out" other worthwhile R&D investments. In our 2009 report (Galiana and Green, 2010: 321) we addressed these concerns noting (i) the decline in energy R&D in the past quarter-century; (ii) the long-term nature of a technology-led policy, which allows plenty of time to develop requisite resources; and (iii) the increasing elasticity of supply of potential R&D resources as a result of a growing and more educated global population. Indeed the evidence indicates globally a continued growth in science and engineering personnel and peer-reviewed articles in scientific journals. In the United States alone, over 5 million persons are employed in science and engineering occupations; fragmentary data indicate that the US world share continues to decline (National Science Foundation, 2010).

The real problem is not "crowding out": it is misspending scarce financial resources on subsidies to manufacturing and deployment. The failure here is one of implementation. As we emphasized (Galiana and Green, 2010: 316–17), an incentive compatible technology-led policy is self-funding (we proposed a low-carbon tax/fee) with revenues placed in a dedicated trust fund administered by public and private sector officials, as independent from political influence as possible, with allocations made by a panel of experts, perhaps modeled along the lines of the Bill and Melinda Gates Fund. In our view "crowding out" is a "straw man"; incentive compatible implementation is a very serious, and largely overlooked, concern.

Emission responsibility

In assigning national emission responsibilities, the Kyoto Protocol followed the International Energy Agency (IEA) and the US Energy Information Agency (EIA) in using estimates of emissions produced at home. Against claims that a production-based standard might induce energy-(and emission)-intensive activity to move to locations without emission controls, analysts, including the IPCC, have contended that the resultant "carbon leakage" would be small. Be that as it may, there is growing evidence of emission transfer from the European Union and the United States to developing and emerging economies especially in the Far East (Davis and Caldeira, 2010; Peters *et al.*, 2011). Moreover, individual country studies indicate the potential for large differences in emission responsibility between emissions *produced* on the one hand and emissions embedded in goods and services *consumed* on the other. For example, a UK study in 2005 indicated that while measured on a production basis the United Kingdom had reduced emissions by 11 percent from 1990, its emissions had increased 14 percent on a consumption basis (Helm *et al.*, 2007). In contrast, China's emissions would be an estimated 20 percent lower if they were measured on a consumption rather than a production basis (Yan and Yang, 2010).

The path-breaking research of Davis and Caldeira (2010), and Peters *et al.* (2011) suggests that the *global* emissions picture is a good deal more complicated than the production-based statistics would suggest. Important processes related to the interconnection between international trade and the economic transformation occurring in developing and emerging economies are driving a wedge between emission responsibilities based on production and those based on consumption. Thus, as evidenced by the examples given above, a country's *responsibility* for emissions looks quite different when measured in terms of emissions embedded in the goods and services a nation consumes than in terms of those produced by a nation's activities. Figures 4.2.1 and 4.2.2, drawn from the Davis and Caldeira (2010) and Peters *et al.* (2011) papers, indicate that via international trade the West is transferring responsibility for a substantial amount of global emissions to the developing world, especially "emerging" economies in the Far East. The drastic increase, since 1990, in emissions produced in Annex B countries and consumed in non-Annex B countries exposes a fundamental flaw in production-based emission-target policies (Figure 4.2.1).

It is, of course, still a matter of debate what are the relative roles of increased trade (globalization) on the one hand and climate policy-induced "leakage" on the other in increasing the discrepancy between emissions *produced* and emissions *consumed*. Either way, the wedge cannot be ignored and it is growing, as Figure 4.2.2 indicates. For at least some countries that wedge makes all the more difficult to accept, much less defend, a *global* climate policy that has been based on the assignment of *national production* rather than *consumption* responsibilities. Moreover, the likelihood that the wedge is at least partly attributable to climate policy-induced leakage is another reason why a technology-led climate policy is preferable to high carbon prices, especially *non*-harmonized ones.

Adaptations, infrastructure, and energy

The continued build-up of GHGs in the atmosphere, the growing awareness, if not incidence of, extreme weather events, and the increasingly extended timetable for deep reductions in global emissions (due in part to a failed climate policy), has accented the role of adaptation. In the past few years, and particularly since the Copenhagen conference in December 2009, adaptation has been given greater attention by climate policy and science. And the reasons are clear: in the circumstances in which mitigation will be slow and the climate effects of mitigation far slower, humans and other species will have to *adapt* to whatever changes occur.

In most cases, human adaptation can be left to individual, group, and private sector efforts. But in two essential respects there are "public good" aspects of adaptation. First, one can think of infrastructure investments that whether financed publicly or privately convey benefits that aid in adaptive efforts. These include transportation systems, irrigation, desalinization plants, food technologies, ecosystem strengthening, Noah's Ark rules to limit species extinction, energy systems (whatever the energy source – preferably concentrated), and advanced warning systems. Second, investment in rapid emergency-response systems and teams can play an essential role in reducing the costs associated with natural disasters that may, or may not, have anything to do with climate change. These investments are variously capital and "know-how"-intensive. But they all have one thing in common: they are likely to have *ancillary* benefits. It is likely that some of the research funded through a technology-led policy will come in the form of adaptation technologies and not necessarily low-carbon technologies.

They also are likely to be energy-using. Thus a second common denominator is energy. It is impossible to envision adaptation and infrastructure without energy. But, in the long run, the kind of energy matters greatly. Ultimately, curbing GHG emissions will require a lot of energy that is not carbon-emitting. That requires an energy-technology revolution, which brings us back to a technology-led climate policy.

New views about a "level playing field"

Another thing that may have changed is the view of just what a "level playing field" is. In the case of mitigation the *sine qua non* for economists is a globally harmonized price for carbon. In fact, one might claim that climate policy has proceeded on the premise that we should at least "level the playing field" between carbon-free energy and fossil-energy sources, if not tilt toward the former. A theoretical justification for leveling the playing field is that carbon energy produces a large externality in the form of heat-trapping gases that can alter climate and threaten undesirable consequences, albeit that these are uncertain in nature or magnitude. For economists, an efficient means of leveling the playing field is through Pigovian taxes in the form of a price for carbon. The CBA that underlies the

Pigovian tax price weighs climate damages avoided against the cost of mitigation.

As a practical matter, such a tax price is further away from realization than ever. But there is also some reason to believe that the economist's version of a "level playing field" may not be as compelling as once seemed. Here is why. What is the cost of mitigation? In the standard analysis it is the cost associated with a higher price for the energy input and/or the *policy*-induced limitations on the use of fossil fuels. But is this all? What of the oil and the gas left in the ground? Should not the lost value of mineral wealth "shut in" by environmental policy be recognized as a "cost" in a CBA?

A so-called "Green Paradox" debate (Grafton *et al.*, 2010; Van der Ploeg *et al.*, 2010) has recently attracted a good deal of economists' attention. It recognizes how the threat of an alternative technology, or future limitations on petroleum use, could lead petroleum suppliers/exporters to step up production now in order to gain something from their mineral wealth. In prosaic terms it is a matter of "use it or lose it." That point may not yet have been reached. However, we have witnessed how fear of lost economic rents from their oil wealth has made oil exporters, especially Saudi Arabia, strong opponents of UN climate treaties. Although the United States is unlikely to ever again become a net oil exporter (it once was sixty+ years ago), could new-found petroleum energy self-sufficiency produce similar reactions?

But let us leave aside the politics and return to the economic question. Should the PV of the economic rents lost be accounted for in a benefit-cost assessment of policies designed to permanently curtail the use of fossil fuel wealth? Perhaps taking a totally global view of the issue might suggest not. But if the assessment is from a national viewpoint, it seems to us that on economic grounds the wealth loss should enter into the CBA calculus alongside other mitigation costs, to be weighed against the prospective environmental benefits.

We raise the "playing field" question in part to draw attention to some recent statements made by Bill Gates concerning energy technologies. At the beginning of his review of Daniel Yergin's new book, "The Quest: Energy, Security, and the Remaking of the Modern World" (Yergin, 2011), Zakaria (2011) draws attention to Bill Gates' "energy miracle" wish. If Gates were allowed only one wish "to improve humanity's lot," it would be a new carbon-free technology that produced huge amounts of energy at half the price of coal. As it happens, Gates' miracle energy technology would solve the economic rent–playing field issue discussed above.

If the Gates technology is as scalable and reliable, as it must be to displace fossil fuels, and if it is at half the cost of coal, it would, in open competition, destroy the economic rents associated with petroleum wealth, whether fracking-generated or not. With a Gates' miracle technology, no artificial price or quantity restraint on fossil fuel use is needed. Also there is no rent loss that needs to be tallied. The issue of rents lost as a cost in a CBA becomes moot. Gates' miracle wish avoids any problem of assessing the economic or environmental desirability of the new technology, even if in the time between invention and deployment it may prompt some "Green Paradox" behavior. Gates' miracles wish ideal implicitly helps make the case for a technology-led policy.

Reassessing benefits and costs

Climate change is too important to ignore. At the same time climate policy should reflect what *can* be done in real-world circumstances, not what ought to be done. Ideally, if the requisite low-carbon energy technologies were at hand, a focus on rapid mitigation could be both timely and inexpensive. Realistically, however, that is simply not the case – far from it. Lacking the requisite low-carbon energy technologies, difficult-to-achieve emission-reduction policies are both expensive and destined to failure (Table 4.2.1).

In 2009, our proposal for a technology-led climate policy made sense. It still does! This brings us finally to the quintessential Copenhagen Consensus concern: BCRs. In 2009 (Galiana and Green, 2010: 322–9), we used three different approaches to calculate BCRs for the technology-led policy we proposed. All produced BCRs greater than 1. For 2010–2100 the BCRs relative to BAU ranged from 1.36 to 7.56, with the lowest (highest) ratios

Table 4.2.1 DICE model results from 2009 Copenhagen Consensus (3% discount rate)

	Early return to R&D	Mid return to R&D	Late return to R&D
2010–2110	3.64	3.31	2.23
2010–2200	11.66	10.95	8.59

when we use a 4 percent (1.4 percent) rather than a 3 percent discount rate.

When compared to the alternative, a "brute-force" target-based mitigation policy, our BCRs were 10 or higher regardless of discount rate. In Table 4.2.1 we summarize the DICE model results from our 2009 analysis for a 3 percent discount rate. Note that the BCRs are always higher for the long term (2010–2200). This is due to the fact that the greatest benefits of a technology-led policy are derived once the innovations have been deployed on a large scale. While a technology-led policy does not generate immediate benefits in terms of emission reductions, over the long term the induced transitions to a "low-carbon" economy more than offsets the initial climate damages. It is this characteristic of a technology-led policy that allows the CBAs to remain high, despite a slight delay in its implementation.

For the 2012 Copenhagen Consensus CBA, we need to answer two questions:

(1) Has "landscape" change substantially altered the BCRs calculated for the 2009 Copenhagen Consensus assessment?
(2) Does it matter for the BCRs we calculated in 2009 that the initial 2012 Copenhagen Consensus budget is much smaller than in 2009? For 2012, our charge is to address in a qualitative manner whether the BCRs out to 2100 and 2200 are much affected if the total budget for the first four years is $75 billion ($18.75 p.a.)

We address each of these questions in turn.

Landscape changes

We do not think that the changes in the landscape we have described will have much effect on the range of BCRs we calculated in 2009. We acknowledge that delays in adopting a technology-led policy to date may lower the BCRs somewhat when compared to damages avoided in the DICE model – although not with respect to "brute-force" mitigation. Fortunately, we may be able to buy some time if non-CO_2 GHGs (soot, methane, and ozone) are reduced substantially in the next few decades. Shindell *et al.* (2012) demonstrate that technologically achievable reductions in these short-lived emissions, with non-climate (air quality, and health) as well as climate-related benefits that substantially outweigh their mitigation costs, could slow the rise in global average temperature by 0.5°C out to 2050. We therefore remain confident that a long-term commitment to a technology-led policy will produce fruits – and will generate benefits – that far outweigh the costs. We feel certain that where CO_2 mitigation is concerned the technology-led policy continues to dominate – and probably by a wide margin. It would be an even more compelling policy if it were combined with adaptation-easing infrastructure investment.

Budget constraint change

We do not think the altered budget constraint in the first four years makes much difference to the BCRs we calculated in 2009. A technology-led policy is a long-run policy. What matters is not how much is spent initially but whether (i) continued funding can be counted upon, and (ii) that rising levels of R&D, testing, and demonstration (R&DTD) receive the support needed to bring about an energy-technology revolution. In this regard, we wish to underline the importance that we placed in Galiana and Green (2010) on a low, dedicated carbon fee/tax that provides a regular source of revenue to finance R&DTD. Although in Galiana and Green (2009, 2010) we used a constant level of R&DTD of $100 billion annually over a ninety-year (2010–2100) period (easily financed by a $5.00/t$CO_2$ fee), we were cognisant that as a practical matter spending would start lower and rise over time.

We are confident that an initial amount of $75 billion spent over the first four years would do no harm, and in fact could improve the CBA, for two reasons. First, the lower initial investment reduces our costs significantly in the CBA. Second, it is likely that, in the near-term, investments beyond

$75 billion have decreasing returns, thus minimally affecting our benefits. Both the Belfer report and the Nobel laureates' letter to the US Congress have suggested annual US expenditure on R&D of $10 billion and $15 billion, respectively. What is vital for a technology-led policy to be effective is a stable source of R&DTD funds that rises very substantially in succeeding years.

Bibliography

Acemoglu, D. *et al.*, 2012: The environment and directed technical change, *American Economic Review* **102**, 131–66

AEBB (American Enterprise Institute-Brookings Institution–Breakthrough Institute), 2010: *Post Partisan Power*, Washington, DC

AEIC (American Energy Innovation Council), 2010: *A Business Plan for America's Energy Future*, http://americanenergyinnovalion.org/wp-content/uploads/2012/04/AEIC The Business Plan 2010.pdf

AH (American Hartwell), 2011: *Climate Pragmatism*, Breakthrough Institute, San Francisco, CA

Anadon, L. D., M. Bunn *et al.*, 2011: *Transforming US Energy Innovation*, Report for Energy Technology Innovation Policy research groups, Belfer Center for Science and International Affairs, Harvard Kennedy School, Cambridge, MA, November

CATF (National Commission on Energy Policy and Clean Air Task Force), 2009: *Innovation Policy for Climate Change*, Washington, DC

Constable, J., 2011: *The Green Mirage: Why a Low-Carbon Economy May Be Further Off than We Think*, Civitas, London

Davis, S. J. and K. Caldeira, 2010: Consumption-based accounting of CO_2 emissions, *Proceedings of the National Academy of Sciences of the United States of America* **107**, 5687–92

Dunn, B., H. Kamath *et al.*, 2011: Electrical energy storage for the grid: a battery of choices, *Science* **334**, 928–35

European Commission, 2009: *Towards a Comprehensive Climate Change Agreement in Copenhagen*, COM, 2009, 39/3

Galiana, I. and C. Green, 2009: Let the global technology race begin, *Nature* **462**, 570–1

2010: Technology-led climate policy, in B. Lomborg (ed.), *Smart Solutions to Climate Change*, Cambridge University Press, 292–339

Gates, B., 2011: The energy research imperative, *Science* **334**, 877

Grafton, R. Q., T. Kompas *et al.*, 2010: *Biofuels Subsidies and the Green Paradox*, CESifo, Center for Economic Studies & Ifo Institute for Economic Research, Munich

Greenstone, M., 2010: The importance of research and development (R&D) for US competitiveness and a clean energy future, testimony to Congress, Joint Economic Committee Hearing on Promoting a Clean Energy Economy, July 27

Helm, D., R. Smale, and J. Phillips, 2007: Too good to be true? The UK's climate change record, www.dieterhelm.co.uk

Hoffert, M., 2011: Governments must pay for clean-energy innovation, *Nature* **472**, 137

ITIF (Information Technology and Innovation Foundation), 2011: *A Model for Innovation: ARPA-E Merits Full Funding*, Washington, DC

National Science Foundation, S&E Indicators, www.nsf.gov/statistics/seind10/pdf/seind10.pdf

Peters, G. P., J. C. Minx *et al.*, 2011: Growth in emission transfers via international trade from 1990 to 2008, *Proceedings of the National Academy of Sciences of the United States of America* **108**, 8903–8

Shindell, D. *et al.*, 2012: Simultaneously mitigating near-term climate change and improving human health and food security, *Science* **335**, 183–9

Van der Ploeg, F., C. Withagen *et al.*, 2010: *Is there really a Green Paradox?*, CESifo, Munich

Victor, D. and K. Yanosek, 2011: The crisis in clean energy, *Foreign Affairs* **July–August**, 112–20

Wigley, T. M. L., 2011: Coal to gas: the influence of methane leakage, *Climatic Change* **108**, 601–8

Williams, J. H. *et al.*, 2012: The technology path to deep greenhouse gas emissions cuts by 2050: the pivotal role of electricity, *Science* **35**, 53–9

Wood, R., P. Gilbert *et al.*, 2011: Shale gas: a provisional assessment of climate change and environmental impacts, Tyndall Center for Climate Change Research, University of East Anglia

Yan, Y.F. and L. K. Yang, 2010: China's foreign trade and climate change: a case study of CO_2 emissions, *Energy Policy*, **38**, 350–6

Yergin, D., 2011: *The Quest: Energy, Security and the Remaking of the Modern World*, Penguin New York

Zakaria, F., 2011: Review of *The Quest*, *New York Times*, September 27

Zoback, M., S. Kitasei *et al.*, 2010: Addressing the environmental risks from shale gas development, Natural Gas and Sustainable Energy Initiative, Worldwatch Institute, Washington, DC

CLIMATE-ENGINEERING R&D

J. Eric Bickel and
Lee Lane*

Introduction

This subchapter seeks to answer a question that has been posed as part of the 2012 Copenhagen Consensus exploration of global policy. That question is:

> If the global community wants to spend up to, say, $75 billion over the next four years to do most good for the world, which solutions would yield the greatest net benefits?

To address this question, we agreed to update our 2009 Copenhagen Consensus chapter (Bickel and Lane, 2010), hereafter **BL10**. That chapter estimated the net benefit of an R&D program to explore the safety and efficacy of climate engineering (CE). The current subchapter extends those estimates. **BL10** considered two different CE approaches, solar radiation management (SRM) and air capture (AC); in this subchapter, however, we restrict our attention to SRM. The chapter is intended to be self-contained. The interested reader will, however, find many supporting details and further discussion in **BL10**.

We begin by first acknowledging that the potential benefit of SRM is so obvious that one hardly needs a formal economic assessment to prove that researching its merits could pay large dividends. The logic is simple: if global warming will cause large damages and require costly abatement measures, then having a relatively low-cost SRM technique to offset warming, even partially, would pay large dividends. Furthermore, initial studies estimate the cost of an SRM R&D program as being on the order of $1 billion. This sum is a small fraction of the 2012 Copenhagen Consensus budget. It is an even smaller fraction of what the United States alone is spending on climate-change research each year.

Thus, we believe that the case for including SRM R&D in a portfolio of responses to climate change is strong. Others, such as the Royal Society, agree (Royal Society, 2009). Yet, the 2012 Copenhagen Consensus process requires numeric BCR estimates. A truly comprehensive CBA of R&D into SRM would require quantifying many factors that are highly uncertain. Such an analysis might create the illusion of rigor, but its extreme complexity would be more likely to obscure the policy choices at hand than to clarify them. We have therefore not carried out the most technically detailed analysis that we could imagine. In fact, as discussed below, we decided not to perform a "value of information" (VoI) or an "options analysis." We made this choice precisely because we believe that given the current state of knowledge, such an analysis would have offered very little in the way of additional insight. Thus, our SRM R&D BCR estimates are necessarily incomplete. We offer them in hopes that initial R&D will produce the new knowledge needed for more refined analysis.

While R&D into SRM might produce some useful spinoffs, its main value clearly depends on the possibility that SRM might actually be deployed. Thus, our BCRs necessarily depend on the estimated benefits of using SRM. These estimates, in turn, hinge upon the way in which SRM may be used and on how events might unfold were no SRM capability developed. Certainty about such matters is impossible; hence we explore the benefits and costs of using SRM across a number of disparate policy options and climate futures.

BL10 looked at the impacts of deploying SRM with economically efficient GHG controls, no controls, controls aimed at achieving a temperature cap of 2°C, and Stern Report-like controls. It also compared the impacts of earlier and later deployment of SRM.

This subchapter broadens **BL10** in two important ways. First, it extends our modification of the DICE-2007 model (Nordhaus, 2008) to include the possibility of SRM-caused climate damages and determine how large these damages would have to be for SRM deployment to incur net costs. Second, we focus on using SRM to avoid severe harm

* The authors thank Kasper Anderskov, Samuel Fankhauser, and Anil Markandya, for their comments on an earlier draft of this chapter.

from climate change. As a framework for this analysis, we assume that states might use SRM in conjunction with GHG controls to limit temperature changes to no more than 2°C.

Thus, between the two studies, we have used a widely cited integrated-assessment model to examine futures in which climate policy, climate change damage, discount rates, SRM start dates, and SRM side effects all vary. Across these diverse scenarios, one finding remains constant: a workable SRM option would produce very large net benefits.

Summary of findings

We continue to support the creation of a formal SRM R&D program, endorsed by the 2009 Copenhagen Consensus Expert Panel (Stokey *et al.*, 2010). We roughly estimate that the BCR of such R&D is on the order of 1,000 : 1. The following findings support this recommendation:

(1) SRM holds the potential of reducing the economic damages caused by both warming and costly abatement measures. The early costs of GHG controls tend to be higher than those of climate change; so by lessening the stringency of controls, SRM may provide *near-term benefits* – compared to strategies relying exclusively on either emissions reductions or unchecked climate change.

(2) Current climate policy efforts and existing R&D programs fail to address directly the single largest risk we face: uncertainty about climate sensitivity. Indeed, our current plan seems to be one of hoping that emissions can be reduced and praying the climate sensitivity is not too large. This approach is worrisome. The uncertainty surrounding this parameter is almost an order of magnitude (IPCC, 2007). This large range of uncertainty implies, on, the one hand, a risk of paying too much for GHG abatement should actual climate sensitivity be on the low end of the possible range. On the other hand, it implies high climate damages and maybe large abatement costs should actual sensitivity be high. In fact, SRM appears to be the *only technology that could quickly cool the Earth* should the need arise to do so. This feature would allow it to *play an important risk management role* despite this so far intractable source of uncertainty.

(3) SRM use may cause climate damages but, in order to negate its benefits, these damages would need to be at least as costly, and potentially twice as costly, as those from unchecked climate change. In other words, *SRM need not be damage-free* because its use could possibly offset climate damages and abatement costs. The latter are also not damage-free.

(4) *Relatively small amounts of SRM appear to be able* to meet the 2°C increase target. To meet this goal, SRM need not be deployed until 2075. Through the end of this century, SRM would require less than about 1.4 Watts per square meter (W m^{-2}), or 0.75 terragrams of sulfur (Tg S) per year. As a point of reference, the IPCC (IPCC, 2007) estimates that aerosols are *currently* offsetting about 1.2 W m^{-2} of the forcing caused by the increase in GHG concentrations; this amounts to about a 40 percent reduction in forcing. In addition, human activity presently injects about 55 Tg S per year into the atmosphere (Stern, 2005).

(5) The *net benefit of SRM*, even after accounting for possible damages, is on the same order as a technology that *could costlessly eliminate all CO2 emissions over eighty years.* Given that annual "clean energy R&D," currently totals about $15 billion globally (Chiavari and Tam, 2011), it seems reasonable to believe that SRM deserves some modest formal research funding.

The remainder of this subchapter expands upon these findings. It is organized as follows. In the next section, we discuss the rationale for and possible necessity of climate engineering. We then briefly summarize the most recognized SRM technologies. After that, we discuss the feasibility and potential cost of a climate-engineering research program. With this background, we then frame the SRM R&D decision, and compute the possible net benefits of SRM deployment and the possible returns to R&D investment. Finally, we discuss our results and conclude.

The need for climate engineering research

The GHGs in the Earth's atmosphere, such as CO_2, methane, and water vapor, cause the planet's surface to be about 30°C warmer than would otherwise be the case (Stocker, 2003). All else being equal, although all else may not be equal, higher GHG concentrations will raise global mean temperatures (IPCC, 2007). Higher temperatures, and the climate changes that may follow in their wake, are likely to lead to a mix of costs and benefits. As warming proceeds, its net effects will grow more negative.

CO_2, once in the atmosphere, will remain there for a century or more. Attempts to abate GHG emissions are also subject to long time lags. They will, for one thing, demand far-reaching changes in technology. Developing much of that technology, according to former US Secretary of Energy Steven Chu, must await the appearance of multiple major break-throughs in basic science (Broder and Wald, 2009).

Galiana and Green (2010) argue convincingly that the IPCC has underestimated the scale of this challenge. Pielke *et al.* (2008) show that the IPCC's GHG emissions scenarios assume major reductions in carbon emissions, absent any climate policy. By doing so, they understate the scale of the changes that must occur. For example:

> The median of the reference scenarios considered by the IPCC AR4 requires 2,011 gigatonnes of carbon in cumulative emissions reductions to stabilize atmospheric carbon-dioxide concentrations at around 500 parts per million... *This scenario also assumes that 77% of this reduction occurs spontaneously*, while the remaining 25% would require explicit policies focused on decarbonization (emphasis added).

Such major technological changes are often slow to mature, and they can take much longer still to disseminate globally (Edgerton, 2007). Electrification of the global economy has been in train for over 100 years, and it is still incomplete. That process, moreover, has advanced because large net benefits accrued to those who invested in it. Most low-GHG technologies cost more than those that they seek to replace. Government action will be required to spur their adoption.

Effective GHG controls, moreover, will require that the policy changes be nearly world-wide (Jacoby *et al.*, 2008). GHG control requires many states to cooperate. Each of them must take costly affirmative steps, and collective action problems of this type often defeat attempts to solve them (Barrett, 2003). Little wonder, then, that the UN talks have gone on now for twenty years without yielding a tangible fall in GHG emissions. Where emissions have from time to time declined, "underlying changes in economic structure may have played a bigger role than climate policy" (Lane and Montgomery, 2008). Neither the UN climate talks in Durban, South Africa, nor trends in the major emitters seem to presage any near-term change in this pattern.

Thus, a serious accord on GHG control is, as yet, nowhere in sight. Even if it were, a great deal of time is certain to separate the onset of serious GHG controls and climate stabilization. The slow speed with which GHG controls can take effect adds to the risk posed by rapid climate change. Should such change appear, speeding up GHG cuts would carry a hefty cost penalty (Richels *et al.*, 2004). Even then, controls might do little to stabilize the situation.

Climate engineering

With these challenges as a backdrop, it is easy to understand why proposals to more intensively study climate engineering are gaining adherents. Both the National Academy of Sciences in the United States and the Royal Society in Britain have explored the concept. After considering potential benefits and highlighting significant unknowns, the Royal Society recommended a formal research program be undertaken (Royal Society, 2009).

CE is composed of two distinct technology families: AC and SRM. We briefly cover each of the concepts here, and the reader is directed to **BL10** for additional detail and discussion.

AC

AC removes CO_2 from ambient air and sequesters it away from the atmosphere. The primary attractions of AC are that it (1) separates CO_2 production from capture, adding flexibility and reduced CO_2 transportation costs and (2) it might reverse the rise in CO_2 concentrations. AC, however, currently suffers from two major defects. These flaws also affect GHG controls, but they do so to a lesser degree. The first is cost. Pielke (2009) estimates that the cost to reduce CO_2 concentrations by 1 ppm is on the order of $1 trillion. The second is the fact that CO_2 removal may not be able to act upon the climate system as quickly as may be required. As Blackstock *et al.* (2009), hereafter **B09**, note:

> Significant technical difficulties are associated with rapidly removing large quantities of CO_2 from the atmosphere. Proposed approaches for removing carbon dioxide from the atmosphere include concepts such as enhancing biological uptake through fertilization or chemical removal and sequestration with engineered systems. However, even if such efforts were to become economically competitive with low-carbon energy systems, the scale required to make a significant impact on the existing stock of carbon in the surface ocean–atmosphere system is so large that reducing the atmospheric carbon dioxide concentration by a significant amount more quickly than several decades is essentially impossible.

Recognizing this issue, the 2009 Copenhagen Consensus Expert Panel (Stokey *et al.*, 2010) gave research into AC a middling rating. For purposes of the 2012 Copenhagen Consesus effort, research into AC more closely resembles research into carbon capture and storage, and for this reason could be considered part of an energy R&D program. We will, therefore, focus the rest of this subchapter on SRM.

SRM

SRM aims at offsetting the warming caused by the build-up of man-made GHGs in the atmosphere by reducing the amount of solar energy absorbed by the Earth. At least some of the risks of global warming can, thereby, be counteracted (Lenton and Vaughan, 2009). SRM would leave the GHGs themselves in the atmosphere. **B09**, which details the possible structure of an SRM R&D program, summarizes the concept as follows:

> The basic concept of [SRM] is to reduce the shortwave radiation absorbed [by the Earth] by reflecting more of it back to space (~30 percent is already reflected by the natural constituents of Earth's atmosphere and surface.) Basic considerations show that an additional 1–2% of reflectivity would balance, in net energy terms, the additional heating caused by a doubling of atmospheric CO_2 concentration. The globally average long-wave radiative forcing due to a doubling of atmospheric CO_2 is approximately 4 W/m^2. As the globally averaged shortwave solar energy reaching the Earth is roughly 342 W/m^2, the reflection of an additional ~1 percent by [SRM] would roughly restore the energy balance.

Scattering this amount of sunlight appears to be possible. As **B09** further notes: "basic technical analyses suggest that the scale of the required reduction would be within our current technological capabilities."

For example, as mentioned on p. 204, the IPCC (2007) estimates that aerosols currently provide about 1.2 W m^{-2} of negative forcing. Past volcanic eruptions have shown that injecting relatively small volumes of matter into the stratosphere can cause discernible cooling. The 1991 eruption of Mount Pinatubo reduced global mean temperature by about 0.5°C (Lane *et al.*, 2007; **B09**).

A unique feature of SRM is that it holds the potential of acting on the climate system on a time scale that might prevent abrupt harmful changes (see **B09**). In fact, SRM may be the only human action that can cool the planet in an emergency. As Lenton and Vaughan (2009) note:

> It would appear that only rapid, repeated, large-scale deployment of potent shortwave geoengineering options (e.g. stratospheric aerosols) could conceivably cool the climate to near its preindustrial state on the 2050 timescale.

As detailed in **BL10**, several concepts have been proposed for accomplishing SRM. We briefly summarize the most promising here: the interested reader may wish to consult **BL10** for more detail.

Stratospheric aerosol injection

Paul Crutzen, a Nobel Laureate in Chemistry, has suggested research into stratospheric aerosol injection (SAI) (Crutzen, 2000). With SAI, a precursor of sulfur dioxide (SO_2) would be (continuously) injected into the stratosphere. There, it would add to the layer of sulfuric acid that is already present in the lower stratosphere (Pope *et al.*, 2012). This layer would reflect sunlight. The amount of sulfur required to offset global warming is on the order of 2 percent of the sulfur that humans already inject into the atmosphere. (Today's injections occur mostly in the troposphere via the burning of fossil fuels.)

Marine cloud whitening

Marine cloud whitening was suggested by Steven Salter and John Latham (Latham *et al.*, 2008; Salter *et al.*, 2008). This technique would inject seawater, in the form of a sea-salt aerosol, into marine clouds. The aerosol would cause more water droplets and/or ice crystals to form in the clouds. The clouds would, therefore, become whiter and more reflective.

Climate engineering research and development

While SRM appears feasible and potentially promising, many important uncertainties remain about it. **B09** note that:

> Climate engineering science and technology are in their infancy. [SRM] investigations to date have been limited to speculation, paper studies, and preliminary climate simulations of uniform [SRM] with coarse-resolution models. Targeted and directed investigations across a wide range of subjects – from basic climate science to intervention system engineering – could significantly improve our understanding and reduce uncertainty in the climate response to a given [SRM] intervention.
>
> Basic understanding is sufficient to conclude that a simple decrease of the solar constant can compensate for the increase in global average temperature caused by anthropogenic GHG emissions, but would not fully eliminate all impacts of climate change. For instance, temperature compensation at the regional scale would not be perfect, and other climate parameters currently perturbed by atmospheric GHGs – most notably ocean acidity – would remain largely unaffected. But beyond these basic observations, we know essentially nothing about the net combined impacts of shortwave climate engineering and elevated GHGs on a wide range of other climate and ecological parameters (e.g. regional precipitation, atmospheric and oceanic circulation, patterns of interannual variability, net ecological productivity, etc) or about the extent to which various [SRM] concepts might be optimized to address them.

In particular, as **B09** shows, the simple considerations discussed on p. 206 regarding the Earth's energy balance and the globally uniform implementation of SRM

> ignore the distribution of energy within the climate system. As the incoming shortwave and outgoing longwave energies have different spatial and temporal distributions, the net impact of [greenhouse gases and SRM] on the climate system would not be zero. Climate features such as regional temperatures and precipitation levels, interannual variability, ecological productivity, and many others could all remain impacted. Scientific investigations of these distributional issues using observation of natural experiments, climate modeling, and potentially even field testing of [SRM] are needed to provide insight.

Research agenda

To address this lack of understanding, **B09** laid out a ten-year R&D program. It was divided into two phases: (1) non-invasive laboratory and computational research and (2) field experiments. After the successful completion of Phase 2, presuming the decision to deploy was made, a third phase would follow. It would consist of monitored deployment. *Phase (1)* would consist of laboratory experiments and computational modeling. Its goal would be to explore the climate response to differing levels of SRM intervention. This phase would not include any direct intervention in the actual climate. *Phase (2)* would begin intentional interventions into the climate system. These interventions would be limited in their duration, magnitude, and/or spatial range. They would not aim to offset increased GHG concentrations; rather, they would seek to understand SRM's efficacy. **B09** estimated that elements of Phase 1 would take place over the entire ten-year period, but that field experiments would only begin in year five (see Figure 5 in **B09**, p. 41).

An R&D effort would seek to answer questions in three research streams. One such stream would be engineering-intervention system deployment. The second would be climate science, modeling, and experimenting to understand and articulate impacts. The third would be climate monitoring, detecting and assessing the actual impacts of the intervention. It is important to stress that neither we nor **B09** envision this R&D effort as only focusing upon a single SRM technology. To the contrary, an important aspect of the research program would be to explore a range of SRM solutions.

A successful R&D program would enable scientists and engineers to specify four critical components of the SRM system. One of these is the material composition of aerosol particles. (For instance, making the cross-section of the particles longer than the light-wave lengths used in photosynthesis may limit SRM's impact on plant life.) A second system component is the amount dispersed. A third is the geographic and vertical locations of aerosol dispersion. The fourth key component is the temporal sequencing of aerosol dispersion.

SRM R&D should also entail policy research. Such research should consider how the use of SRM might affect other major policy goals. It should encompass the effects of choices of SRM technology and the timing and extent of its use. It should study effects of disparate national preferences on the timing and use of SRM.

Regime-building is a standard response to the challenge of cooperation among states (Keohane, 1984). SRM policy research, therefore, should explore options for structuring an SRM regime. This research should be forward-looking. That is, it should explore likely future trends in SRM technology, major states' preferences over climate, and global power balances. Such research should seek to define the conditions under which SRM deployment would align with the incentives of the ruling coalitions of the major world powers. Of course, this same question should also be posed with regard to all policies that require the participation, or at least the acquiescence, of many states.

Cost of an R&D program

B09 did not estimate the cost of their proposed R&D program. However, two of that study's coauthors, Ken Caldeira and David Keith, have made such estimates (Caldeira and Keith, 2010). They estimate that Phase (1) would start at $5 million p.a. and would gradually ramp up to $30 million p.a. Phase (2) would begin at $30 million p.a. and would ramp up to $100 million p.a. as initial field tests began. The program's total, undiscounted, expenditure would be about $500 million. For comparison, today, the US federal government is spending about $16 billion p.a. on climate-change science and related technologies (Higgins, 2011). Caldeira and Keith's estimates of early spending slightly exceed those made by a 2001 George W. Bush Administration interagency panel on R&D for CE. That panel devised a plan based on a gradually rising budget with a total five-year cost of $98 million (US DOE 2002). This program was not funded.

Given the roughness of these estimates, and erring on the side of conservatism, we assume in this chapter that SRM R&D might require a total ten-year R&D investment of $5 billion – ten times the amount estimated by Caldeira and Keith. This cost increase could be seen as compensating for potential cost overruns, the R&D program running for longer than ten years, or the fact that SRM R&D might "crowd out" other productive research (Nordhaus, 2002; Popp, 2004). In any case, as the reader will see, the potential net benefits of an SRM capability are about 1,000 times greater than our R&D estimate. Thus, our cost estimates play almost no role in determining SRM's net benefit.

The challenge of assessing the returns to SRM R&D

Five major uncertainties cloud estimates of CE's BCR. These uncertainties are as follows: first, how will R&D spending affect the capabilities of a future SRM option? Success in this context means that R&D would develop a functional SRM system that society would be willing to deploy. Second, how would SRM be deployed? Some proposals envision global systems, some only in the Arctic, and many other options are possible. Third, what will be the future state of the climate, both with SRM and without it? Four, how does warming relate to damages? Five, what action, or inaction, will take place if no SRM R&D is done?

Dealing with all these factors in a meaningful way is a severe challenge. One could attempt to create a detailed "value of information" (VoI) or an "option valuation" model (Bickel, 2008). A 2009 Copenhagen Consensus Alternative Perspective Paper (Smith 2010) suggested this approach. At this point, the uncertainties that surround CE are so deep that we believe such an analysis does little more than formalize our perplexity. Yet governments will decide on whether to undertake R&D on CE, and they will do so despite the uncertainties.

CE is, in this regard, hardly a unique problem. Estimating the returns to R&D investment is difficult even in well-defined areas. Arrow (1962) raised the crucial issue:

> The central economic fact about the processes of invention and research is that they are devoted to the production of information. By the very definition of information, invention must be a risky process, in that the output (information obtained) can never be predicted perfectly from the inputs.

Attempts to quantify the value of R&D in the area of climate change have highlighted the risky nature of R&D and the challenge that it poses to CBA. For example, Baker *et al.* (2009) asked three experts to assess the likelihood that R&D investments in advanced solar technologies would succeed. The assessed probabilities among the three experts differed by a minimum of 2 times to a maximum of 640 times. For example, when considering investment in new inorganic solar-cell technologies, one expert assessed the chance of success at 0.001, while another thought it was 0.64. In the case of purely organic solar cells, one expert assessed the chance of R&D success at 0.01; another believed the chance as being 0.34. Similar divergences were observed in assessments regarding the chance of R&D success in the areas of carbon capture and storage and advanced nuclear power technologies (Baker and Peng, 2012). This is not a criticism. It simply acknowledges the point made by Arrow and others: uncertainty is inherent in invention. We suspect that the results would be much the same were one to poll experts regarding the likely success of a large-scale SRM R&D program.

Before a technical problem has, in fact, been solved, one cannot know how difficult its solution will be (Nelson and Winter, 1977). Nonetheless, Hecht *et al.* (2011), in assessing the BCR of R&D into an AIDS vaccine, assumed, with probability 1, that current R&D spending will lead to a vaccine, and that additional spending would advance the date of discovery. In a similar vein, 2009 Copenhagen Consensus authors Galiana and Green (2010) recognize this problem in their assessment of the BCR of energy-technology R&D. And they express the hope that a diversified enough R&D portfolio will lessen the uncertainties. They assumed that R&D spending of $100 billion p.a. for the next 100 years, more than a sixfold increase from current spending levels, would accelerate the decarbonization of the global economy via the development carbon-free energy sources (e.g. carbon capture and storage, nuclear fusion, breeder reactors, deep geothermal energy, etc.) and equated benefits with reduced climate damages. They assumed that the R&D would call forth technologies attractive enough to penetrate markets without the benefit of any but very mild GHG control policies.

In reality, many innovations that at first seem promising fail to pan out. In other cases, unwanted side effects erode the benefits of otherwise appealing options. One thinks of nuclear power and proliferation risks. Bio-fuels have worsened global food shortages just as SRM entails some risks of unwanted effects. In all these cases, the value of the innovation cannot be known without reference to the scale of the risks it poses.

Framing the SRM R&D decision

This section will describe the scenarios that we have analyzed. The reader should not take our focus on

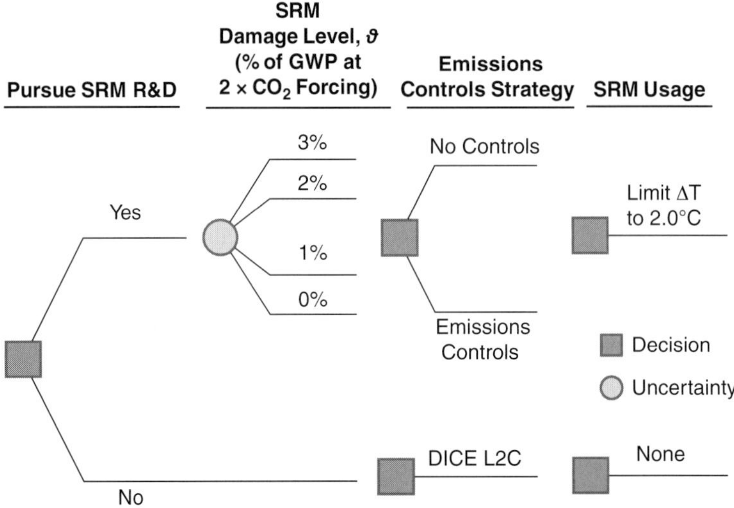

Figure 4.3.1 *Framing of SRM R&D decision*

the two scenarios that we are about to describe as a statement that we believe either of them to be very desirable. Still less do we regard them as realistic projections of the future. Rather, the analysis shows that across a very broad spectrum of GHG control policies, climate sensitivities, and assumptions about SRM side effects an SRM option would have the potential to yield very large net benefits.

Figure 4.3.1 describes the analysis performed in this subchapter. In it, we assume that key governments' overarching goal is to limit temperature change to no more than 2°C. Galiana and Green (2010) also measure the benefit of their emissions reduction strategy by this standard, and our adopting it here helps make our results more comparable.

Our analysis begins with the decision (represented with a square) about whether or not to conduct R&D on SRM. If SRM R&D is not performed, we assume that SRM is unavailable. In that case, governments enact the most cost-effective emissions controls able to achieve the 2°C temperature increase target. We refer to this emissions control regime as Limit to 2°C (L2C). As we stated in **BL10**, we believe it is unlikely that SRM would ever be used without development and testing. True, we might face a climate emergency that brings calls for deployment, but this possibility is currently believed to be low, but not zero. Furthermore, recognizing that we are facing an emergency is likely to be difficult. Or obvious emergency situations, such as the rapid disintegration of the West Antarctic Ice Sheet, may come with the realization that it is too late to deploy SRM (see **B09**). Allowing for the possibility that an unproven SRM system could be deployed would only amplify our conclusion that research is likely to pay large dividends.

If SRM R&D is pursued, we assume that the uncertainty (represented in Figure 4.3.1 with a circle) regarding SRM's damages is resolved. For the sake of simplicity, we assume damages will be either 0 percent, 1 percent, 2 percent, or 3 percent of gross world product (GWP), at an offsetting SRM forcing equivalent to a doubling of CO_2, concentrations. After the damages have been revealed, society implements a less stringent emissions control regime. To make the situation concrete, we investigate either a policy of *no controls* (NC) or some *emissions controls* (EC). As a point of reference, and to maintain simplicity, our emissions control policy is the same as the economically efficient policy that Nordhaus (2008) refers to as *optimal controls* (OC). The level of emissions controls under EC and L2C are shown in Figure 4.3.2.

After selecting either NC or EC, government next deploys a level of SRM that holds temperature change to no more than 2°C, which we refer to as SRM2C. The ability to manage the climate system in this way would require deploying a monitoring

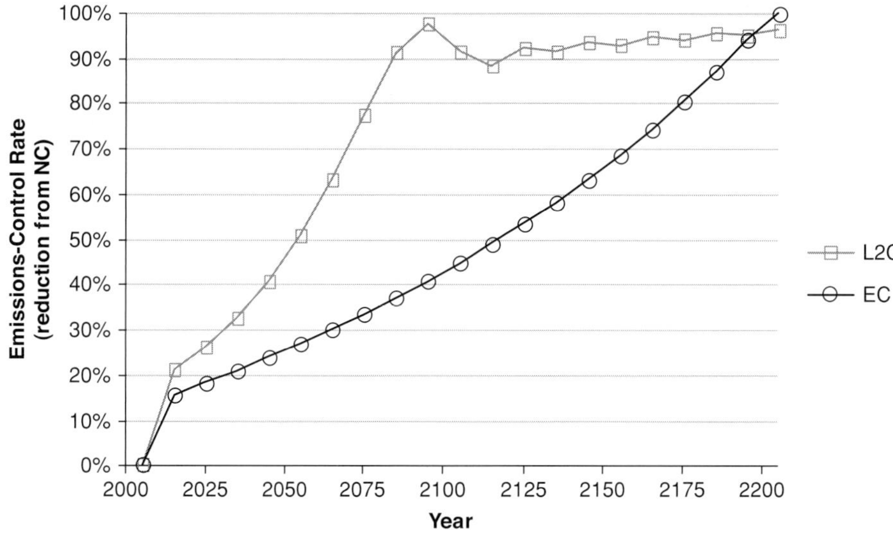

Figure 4.3.2 *Emissions-control rates under EC and L2C*

system that could observe the Earth's energy balance. Developing such a system, therefore, would be part of an R&D program (see **B09**).

It is important to note that by EC we do not mean the level of emissions controls that would be optimal given an SRM capability. We take this approach for two reasons. First, we believe it is much too early to determine the "optimal" use of SRM and the degree to which it should substitute for emissions reductions. Such an analysis would require an estimate of the damage SRM would cause for different levels of usage. Understanding this relationship would be a fundamental part of an R&D program. Second, in this subchapter, we treat SRM damage as a variable to which we test sensitivity. Thus, the reader should envision EC as a possible emissions control scenario, in much the same way that the IPCC considers emission controls scenarios, without claiming that these scenarios are in some sense optimal.

As we show in Figure 4.3.1, for the sake of simplicity, we assume that SRM R&D will lead to the development of an SRM capability and resolve any uncertainty regarding the level of damages. The reality is certainly more complex and it is possible that SRM R&D may fail. Again, as we stressed on p. 209, previous Copenhagen Cosensus authors (Galiana and Green, 2010; Hecht *et al.*, 2011) also assume that R&D will produce results. If the reader prefers to allow for some probability p that SRM R&D will succeed, then they can determine the expected net benefits for their preferred scenario by multiplying the estimates we present below by p. Of course, if one believes that SRM R&D will fail ($p = 0$) then SRM R&D would be worthless; one does not need a model to understand this fact. While we do not attempt to estimate the chance of success, we do not believe it to be so low as to negate the value of R&D. After all, as **B09** noted, "basic technical analyses suggest that [SRM] would be within our current technological capabilities (p. 4)." The primary uncertainty is the degree of damage that would attend SRM's use.

The model

As in **BL10**, we use the DICE-2007 model Nordhaus (2008) to examine the economics of climate change and the possible use of SRM. As before, we use DICE's endogenously determined discount rate to calculate PVs. This has the following benefits. First, it facilitates the comparison of our results with those of Nordhaus (2008). Second, using a different discount rate would be internally inconsistent with the DICE model. While our real discount

Table 4.3.1 Performance characteristics of considered emissions controls regimes (2005 $ trillion)

Emissions control regime	Years to phase out CO_2 emissions	Max. temp. change (by 2205) (°C)	Years above 2°C (by 2205)	Climate damages ($)	Abatement costs ($)	Total damages ($)
No Controls (NC)	NA	5.2	140	22.5	0.0	22.5
Emissions Controls (EC)	185	3.5	130	17.4	2.1	19.5
Limit 2°C (L2C)	80	2.0	0	13.4	11.8	25.2

rate varies, it averages about 4 percent over our 200-year study period (2005 through 2205). Investigating other discount rates, such as 3 percent or 5 percent, would not materially change our results, while doubling the number of cases we need to consider, which could obfuscate our results and reasoning.

Table 4.3.1 summarizes the performance of the emissions control regimes we consider here. The maximum temperature change by 2205 under a policy of NC is 5.2°C and it is above 2°C for 140 years. Total damages, which are comprised solely of climate damages, are $22.5 trillion (2005$). Under EC, temperature change is above 2°C for 130 years and reaches a maximum of 3.5°C. Total damages in this case total $19.5 trillion, almost 90 percent of which are in the form of climate damage. Thus, economically efficient emission controls regimes are structured to accept significant climate damages. Climate damages are reduced to $13.4 trillion by limiting temperature change to 2°C, but the increase in abatement costs leads to about $2.7 trillion more damage than under a policy of NC.

Changes made to DICE

To estimate the benefits of SRM we modify a few of DICE's features. As detailed in **BL10**, these include changes to DICE's radiative forcing equation, given in (1). $F(t)$ is the increase in radiative forcing at the tropopause at the beginning of period t (decades), measured in W m^{-2}.

$$F(t) = \eta \log_2 \left[\frac{M_{AT}(t)}{M_{AT}(1750)} \right] + F_{EX}(t) - SRM(t) \quad (1)$$

η is the increase in radiative forcing due to a doubling of CO_2 concentrations, assumed to be 3.8 W m^{-2}. $M_{AT}(t)$ is the mass of carbon in the atmosphere at the beginning of period t. $M_{AT}(1750)$ is the pre-industrial concentration of atmospheric CO_2, which is defined as the concentration in 1750 (280 ppm). When the ratio of $M_{AT}(t)$ to $M_{AT}(1750)$ is 2 the log-base-2 term will evaluate to 1. $F_{EX}(t)$ is the external forcing of non-CO_2 GHGs and the negative forcing of aerosols. $SRM(t)$ is the negative forcing created by an SRM program. Our treatment of aerosol forcing is consistent with DICE's own modeling of aerosols and the work of other researchers (Andronova and Schlesinges, 2001; Bickel and Agrawal, 2012; Goes *et al.*, 2011). We emphasize, however, and as noted by **B09**, that this global and uniform treatment of SRM is done for reasons of convenience. It may not be feasible or desirable to implement SRM in this way.

This subchapter further modifies DICE to account for the damages that SRM might cause. To do so, following Bickel and Agrawal (2012), and Goes *et al.* (2011), we introduce a parameter θ that is the damage caused by SRM, as a percentage of GWP, when SRM offsets radiative forcing equal to a doubling of CO_2 concentrations ($\eta = 3.8$ Wm^{-2}). Specifically, the modified damage function, as a percentage of GWP, is given in (2). $T_{AT}(t)$ is the global mean temperature of the

$$D(t) = \psi_1 T_{AT}(t) + \psi_2 T_{AT}(t)^2 + \theta \frac{SRM(t)}{\eta} \quad (2)$$

atmosphere in period t. ψ_1 and ψ_2 are parameters chosen to match the literature regarding climate impacts (Nordhaus, 2008). As mentioned on p. 210 we investigate four values for θ, equal to 0 percent, 1 percent, 2 percent, and 3 percent.

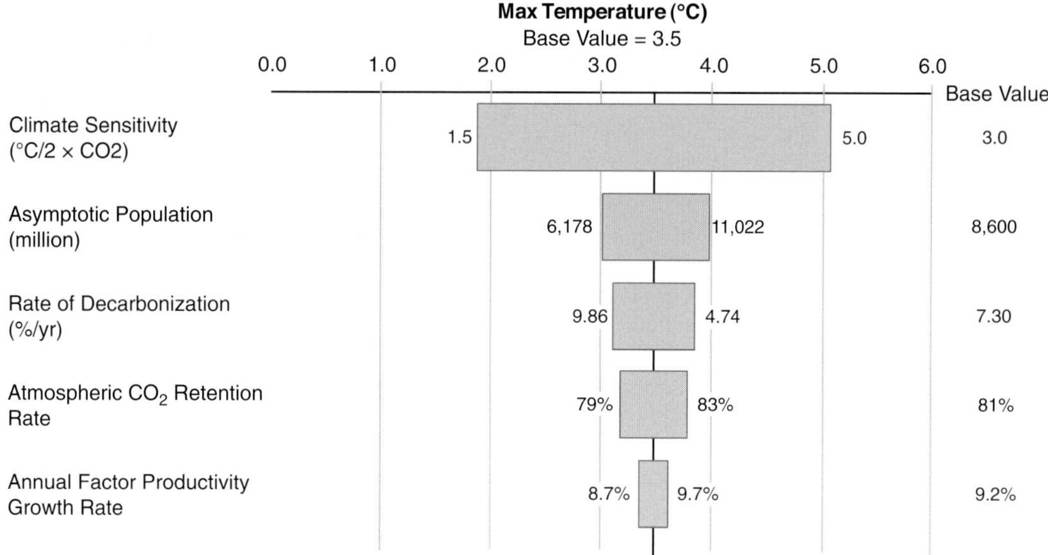

Figure 4.3.3 *Sensitivity of maximum temperature change under EC to key model inputs*

Net benefit of SRM R&D

This section estimates the net benefit of using SRM to hold temperature changes below 2°C. It begins, however, by highlighting the most significant risk driver: the climate sensitivity.

Climate sensitivity

The values given in Table 4.3.1 are based on a single set of deterministic model assumptions. Of course, key model inputs are in fact uncertain. For example, regarding the climate sensitivity, the IPCC (2007) states:

> The equilibrium climate sensitivity . . . is likely to be between 2°C and 4.5°C, with a best estimate of 3°C and it is very unlikely to be less than 1.5°C. Values substantially higher than 4.5°C cannot be excluded, but agreement of models with observations is not as good for those values.

The IPCC defines *likely* as greater than a 66 percent probability and *very unlikely* as less than a 10 percent probability (IPCC, 2005). Bickel (2013) found that a log-normal distribution with a mean of 3.0°C and standard deviation of 1.5°C represented this uncertainty well. This, in turn, implies that there is about a 10 percent chance that the climate sensitivity is below 1.5°C and a 10 percent chance it is above 5.0°C.

Figure 4.3.3 details how uncertainty in the climate sensitivity propagates to uncertainty in the maximum temperature change under EC. In the base case, the climate sensitivity is 3.0°C and the maximum temperature change is 3.5°C. If the climate sensitivity was, on the other hand, 1.5°C, then the maximum temperature change would be 1.9°C. If the climate sensitivity was 5.0°C, the maximum temperature change would be 5.1°C.

High climate sensitivities are all the more troubling when one notes that scientists warn that the climate may contain "tipping points." Crossing these points may trigger large changes in the Earth's system. These may include loss of Arctic sea ice, melting of the Greenland and Antarctic Ice Sheets, irreversible loss of the Amazon rain forest, and abrupt changes in the Indian and African monsoons (Meehl *et al.*, 2007). Lenton *et al.* (2008) augment the work of the IPCC and prioritize these tipping points in terms of their likelihood and proximity. They are particularly concerned about the loss of Arctic sea ice and melting of the Greenland Ice Sheet. As Arctic sea ice melts, it exposes the darker ocean waters. The change leads to additional warming, a positive feedback. Scientists have not identified the critical tipping point temperature, but Lenton *et al.* (2008) conclude that "a summer ice-loss threshold, if not already passed may be very close and a transition could occur well within this century."

Nordhaus (2008) provided uncertainty ranges for a set of uncertainties that he found to be the most critical. In addition to the climate sensitivity, these included the rate of growth in TFP, the rate the economy can be decarbonized, the asymptotic global population, and the rate at which CO_2 is retained in the atmosphere. Figure 4.3.3 displays the 80 percent probability interval for each of these uncertainties. It shows that, in terms of potential warming, that the climate sensitivity is far and away the largest risk-driver. Other uncertainties, such as the speed with which the economy can be decarbonized, play a much more modest role. This fact is not surprising. Even if emissions reductions do begin, it will take many, possibly hundreds of years for the climate to stabilize. This simple fact has significant implications for climate policy and research. For example, current global "clean energy R&D," which is focused on decarbonizing the economy (the third bar in Figure 4.3.3) totals over $15 billion p.a. (Chiavari and Tam, 2011). Yet, no formal research program supports SRM even though it is the only technology that may be able to address the single largest risk factor, the climate sensitivity. Indeed, some environmentalists wish to declare it off-limits (ETC Group, 2010). This hardly seems a prudent course of action.

Direct cost estimates

SRM includes a range of technologies. These have included options from marine cloud whitening to mirrors in space. For simplicity, this chapter focuses on SAI, and bases its direct cost estimates on this approach. Using published studies, including the NAS (1992) report, **BL10** estimated that the cost to inject aerosols into the stratosphere would be $40 per kg (2005$), or $40 billion per Tg (1 Tg = 1 trillion grams = 1 million metric tons). The required mass depends upon the efficiency of aerosol forcing, the residence time of these aerosols, and the aerosol precursor. Following Crutzen (2006), we assume an efficiency of -0.75 W m^{-2} per Tg S.[1] We assume a residence time of 2.5 years based on Rasch *et al.* (2008). As in **BL10**, we assume hydrogen sulfide (H_2S) as a precursor. As a point of comparison, based on these assumptions, offsetting 1 W m^{-2} would require the injection about 0.57 Tg H_2S per year, costing $0.023 trillion. These costs are a very small fraction of the potential benefits (reduced climate damages and avoided abatement costs). Therefore, our direct cost estimates play an inconsequential role in our results.

SRM net benefit

Table 4.3.2 presents the net benefits of SRM as a function of SRM damages. These benefit estimates include the direct costs to deploy SRM and the indirect climate damages attributable to it. The first row repeats the total damages (climate and abatement) under the L2C policy; these damages are not a function of the damage caused by SRM, since no SRM is used in this case.

Total damages under a policy of NC, with SRM used to hold temperature change below 2°C, are shown in the second row. If, for example, SRM causes no damage ($\theta = 0$ percent) then total damages would be $14.7 trillion, yielding a net SRM benefit of $10.5 trillion ($25.2 – $14.7). If SRM causes damages equal to 1 percent, 2 percent, or 3 percent of GWP at a forcing of 3.8 W m^{-2}, equivalent to a doubling of CO_2 concentrations ($2 \times CO_2$), then the benefit of SRM is reduced to $7.5, $4.4, or $1.2 trillion, respectively. Thus, under NC, every percentage point increase in SRM damages lowers the net benefit of SRM by about $3 trillion. SRM would provide no net benefit if SRM damages were about 3.4 percent of GWP at a $2 \times CO_2$ forcing.

Under a policy of EC with SRM2C, a damage-free version of SRM would be worth about $9.2 trillion. This value declines by about $1.6 trillion for every percentage-point increase in SRM damages and would equal about $4.5 trillion at 3 percent SRM damage. The net benefit of SRM would be negative in this case if SRM damages were greater

[1] At this rate, 1 g of S offsets about 320,000 g (0.32 MT) of CO_2. Or, every Tg of S offsets about 40 ppm of CO_2, which is about twenty years of global emissions.

Table 4.3.2 Net benefit of SRM under no controls and emissions controls (2005$ trillion)

	SRM damages (θ)			
	0% ($)	1% ($)	2% ($)	3% ($)
Limit 2°C (L2C)	25.2	25.2	25.2	25.2
No controls + SRM2C	14.7	17.7	20.8	24.0
NC SRM2C benefit	10.5	7.5	4.4	1.2
Emissions controls + SRM2C	16.0	17.6	19.1	20.7
EC SRM2C benefit	9.2	7.7	6.1	4.5

than about 5.7 percent at a forcing of 3.8 W m^{-2} (2 × CO_2 forcing).

Some observers have claimed that DICE understates the marginal damage from climate change. In fact, estimates of marginal damage vary widely (Tol, 2008). In any case, SRM both lessens climate damage and permits lower GHG control costs. Should the climate change prove either more harmful than DICE assumes, or less, added gains in one class of benefits will offset at least part of the shortfall in the other. The adjustments are not likely to change the finding of large and robust net benefits.

According to Table 4.3.2, SRM has a positive net benefit for all the SRM damage levels depicted in Figure 4.3.1. Thus, society would still gain by deploying SRM, even were SRM to cause damages equivalent to 3 percent of GWP at a 2 × CO_2 forcing. How can this be?

The damages caused by GHGs and policies to address them come in two forms: climate damages and abatement costs. Figure 4.3.4 displays these components for L2C and EC. L2C incurs substantial abatement costs, which results in total damages under this policy exceeding those of EC until about 2125. In fact, damages under L2C exceed those of NC (shown in Figure 4.3.5) through 2105. As mentioned earlier, it is also clear than the economically efficient policy of EC would still accept substantial climate damages.

A successful SRM program would offset both of these costs, not just climate damages. The question, of course, is whether or not the damages caused by SRM would exceed the sum of climate damages *and* the abatement costs that SRM is intended to offset. Figure 4.3.5 compares total damages under L2C to EC with SRM2C; NC is shown as a point of reference. Total damages, when using SRM2C, begin to diverge from those of EC in 2075. Given DICE's assumptions, 2075 is the first year in which temperatures without SRM would exceed 2°C. Hence, it is the first year in which SRM would be deployed. If SRM causes no damage ($\theta = 0$ percent) then total damages are substantially reduced and below those of L2C until about 2205. Allowing for SRM damages increases total damages, but they are still below L2C until the next century. In fact, even if SRM caused 3 percent damages, it would still be less damaging than attempting to limit temperature changes to 2°C based solely on emissions reductions.

Just how damaging SRM might be is a question for an R&D program, but we offer two points of reference. First, unabated climate change is projected by DICE to cause damages of about 1.4 percent of GWP in 2065, which is the year in which CO_2 concentrations are doubled. Thus, the SRM damage scenarios we investigate here range from an assumption that SRM is about as damaging as the climate change itself (1 percent) to one that SRM is more than twice as damaging as climate change (3 percent). Second, as discussed on p. 204, the IPCC (2007) estimates that aerosols are currently providing negative forcing of 1.2 W m^{-2}, which is equivalent to about 32 percent of the forcing we expect for a doubling of CO_2. Current emissions are primarily into the troposphere, whereas most SAI concepts envision injection taking place in the stratosphere. However, as a very rough estimate, SRM damages of 1 percent, 2 percent, or 3 percent at a forcing equivalent to a doubling of CO_2 concentrations would equate to GWP reductions of 0.32 percent (32 percent of 1 percent), 0.64 percent, or 0.96 percent, respectively.

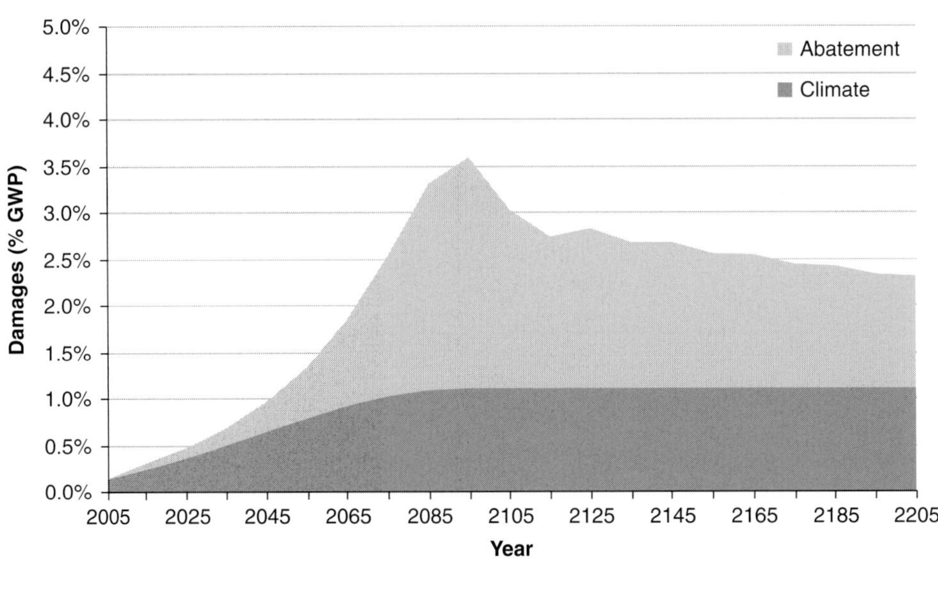

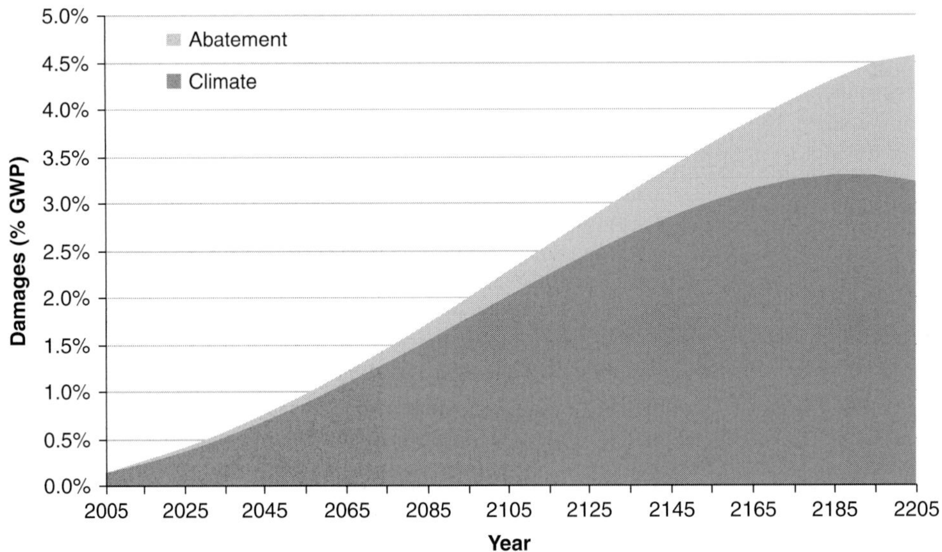

Figure 4.3.4 *Components of total damages for L2C (top) and EC (bottom)*

Net benefit for differing climate sensitivities

The preceding section's analysis assumed that the climate sensitivity was 3.0°C. Figure 4.3.6 presents the net benefits of SRM under NC (top) and EC (bottom) for climate sensitivities of 1.5°C, 3.0°C, and 5.0°C, as a function of the damage caused by SRM. The lines labeled 3.0°C match the net benefits given in Table 4.3.2. At a climate sensitivity of 1.5°C the net benefit of SRM changes very little under NC and not at all under EC. This occurs because little (NC) or no (EC) SRM is needed in this case. Under EC, the benefit attributable to SRM, about $8 trillion, is comprised solely of the fact that with an SRM capability society has the option

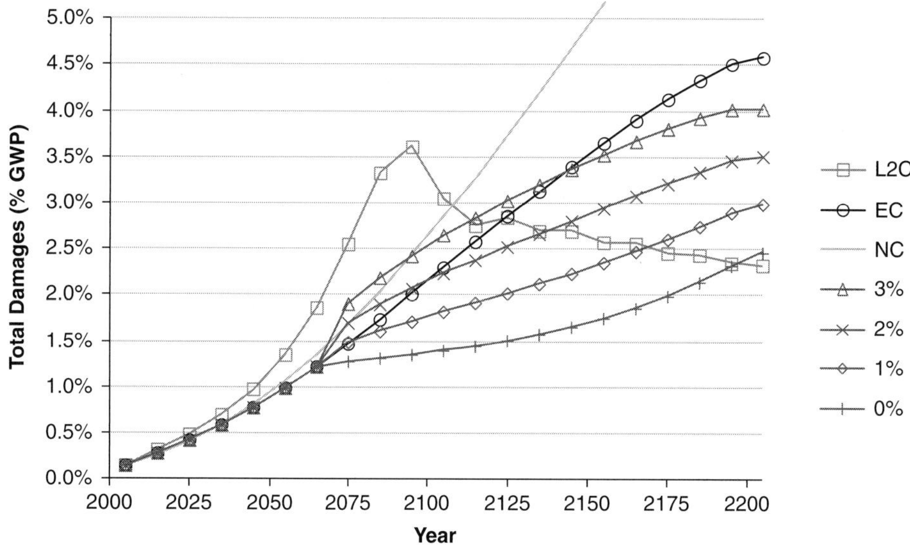

Figure 4.3.5 *Comparison of total damages under L2C to EC with SRM2C, as a function of the damages caused by SRM (0 percent, 1 percent, 2 percent, or 3 percent)*

of choosing a less stringent emissions control policy. This pays off in the case of a 1.5°C climate sensitivity because temperatures would not have reached 2.0°C under EC in any event and, thus, the stricter and more costly controls were not needed. A 5.0°C climate sensitivity tends to increase the value of SRM. However, this value decreases more rapidly with the SRM damage level because the intensity of SRM usage is greater. At a damage level of 3 percent and a 5.0°C climate sensitivity, SRM would cause net damages under NC.

Level of SRM usage

Figure 4.3.7 displays the level of SRM usage required to hold temperature change under 2.0°C for NC (top) and EC (bottom) as a function of the climate sensitivity. SRM usage intensity is measured in W m^{-2} (left-hand axis) and Tg S p.a. (right-hand axis), assuming a forcing efficiency of −0.75 W m^{-2} per Tg S and a residence time of 2.5 years. As discussed on p. 216, under EC and with a climate sensitivity of 1.5°C, SRM is not required. If the climate sensitivity is 3.0°C, then SRM is first deployed in 2075 and reaches about 1.4 W m^{-2} (about 0.75 Tg S p.a.) by 2100. SRM usage in this case does not exceed 2.0 W m^{-2} until 2100. To place this intervention in perspective, consider four comparisons:

(1) 2 W m^{-2} is about 0.6 percent of the incoming solar radiation of 341 W m^{-2} (Trenberth *et al.*, 2009)
(2) Anthropogenic aerosol emissions currently provide negative forcing of 1.2 W m^{-2} (IPCC, 2007)
(3) Anthropogenic emissions of sulfur total 55 Tg per year (Stern, 2005)
(4) Mount Pinatubo injected 10 Tg of sulfur into the stratosphere (Crutzen, 2006).

Under NC, with a 3.0°C climate sensitivity, SRM is deployed in 2065 and exceeds about 2.5 W m^{-2} (1.3 Tg S) by the end of the century. If the climate sensitivity was 1.5°C, SRM would not be deployed until the next century and would not exceed 2.0 W m^{-2} until 2165. A sensitivity of 5.0°C would bring increased usage, but the SRM intervention would remain below 3 W m^{-2} until 2095. In all cases, SRM is deployed at earliest in 2045, which would seem to provide ample time for a well-designed R&D program.

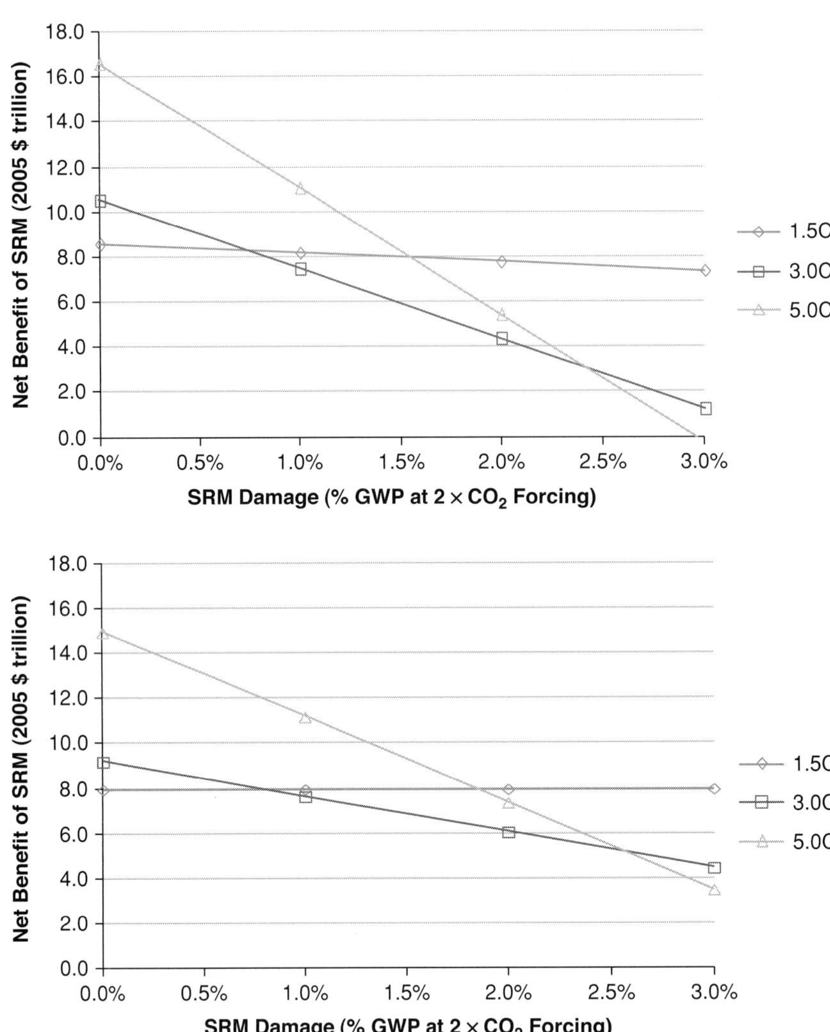

Figure 4.3.6 *Sensitivity of SRM net benefits to the climate sensitivity under NC (top) and EC (bottom)*

Thus, deploying SRM is not on its face infeasible. Further, as its use is considered here, the magnitude of the intervention may be within that which the climate system currently experiences. The interventions considered in this analysis are a fraction of those that humans are currently making. They are an even smaller fraction of natural events such as volcanic eruptions. Even so, the sustained forcing that SAI would cause would differ fundamentally from the impulse disturbances produced by volcanoes (see **B09**). We conclude that SRM should not be deployed given the current uncertainties, nor could it be. At the same time, SRM cannot be dismissed out of hand, and research should be conducted to learn more about the range of possible impacts.

Comparison to emissions reductions

Since the 2012 Copenhagen Consensus Expert Panel is tasked, in part, with ranking differing, but not necessarily exclusive, approaches to climate change, we now compare the net benefit of

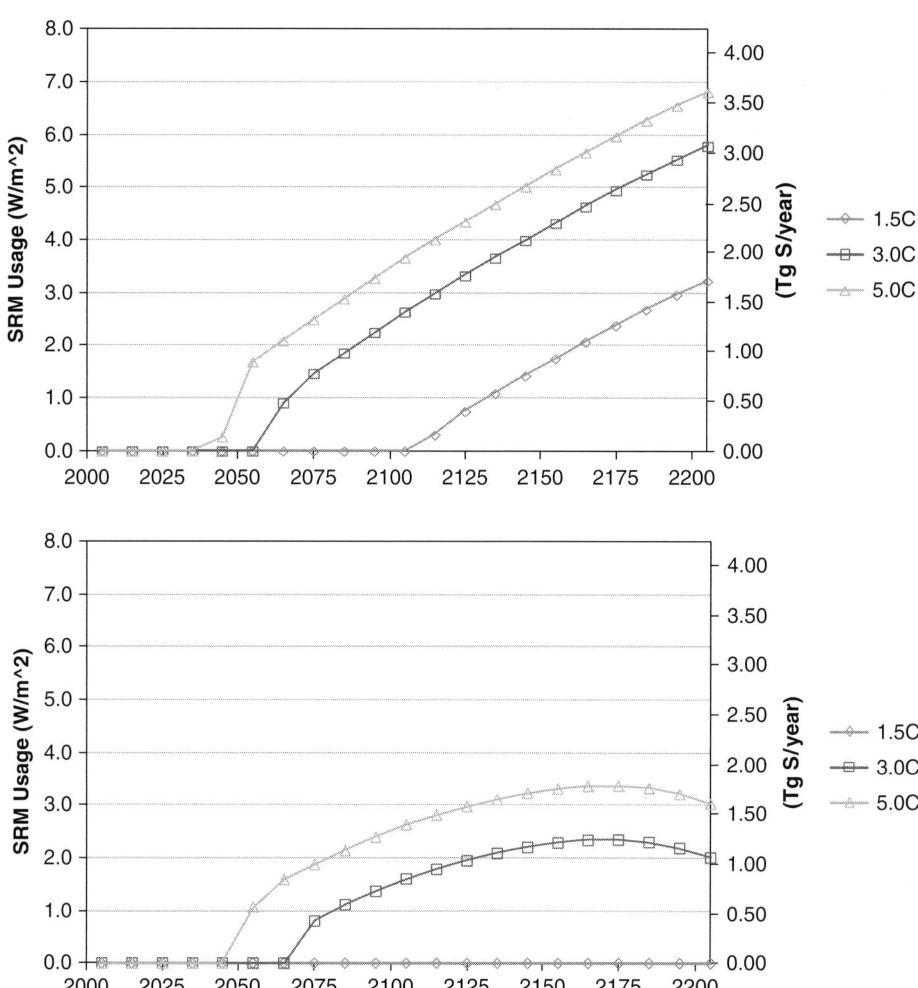

Figure 4.3.7 *Level of SRM usage under NC (top) and EC (bottom) for differing climate sensitivities*

Table 4.3.3 Net benefit of costless and complete CO_2 emissions reductions beginning in 2025 ($2005 trillion)

Years to phase out all CO_2 emissions	Climate sensitivity		
	1.5°C	3.0°C	5.0°C
40	4.1	10.5	18.2
80	3.0	7.7	13.5
120	2.3	5.8	10.1

SRM to *costless* emissions reductions. This comparison is helpful since estimates of both benefits are performed within the same model. Table 4.3.3 presents the benefit of a technology (or technologies), to be deployed in 2025, that could costlessly (and linearly) eliminate all CO_2 emissions within either 40, 80, or 120 years for differing climate sensitivities. Phasing out CO_2 emissions, in this way, over 80 years brings a benefit of between $3.0 and $13.5 trillion, depending upon the climate sensitivity. A, very rapid, 40-year phase out is worth between $4.1 and $18.2 trillion.

The values presented in Table 4.3.3 are on the same order as the benefit of SRM, even accounting for the fact that SRM is not costless and may incur damages (compare Table 4.3.3 to Table 4.3.2 and Figure 4.3.6). This occurs because even if CO_2

Table 4.3.4 BCR of SRM R&D under no controls and emissions controls

	SRM damages (θ)			
	0%	1%	2%	3%
NC SRM2C	2,107	1,497	877	247
EC SRM2C	1,844	1,530	1,214	895

emissions begin in 2025, the CO_2 that is currently in the atmosphere, and that which would be emitted during the phase-out period, will take many, possibly hundreds of years to fade away. This, in conjunction with thermal capacity of the oceans, means that some warming will be unavoidable – unavoidable that is, if one does not consider the use of SRM. This highlights another important policy issue regarding the use of SRM: SRM's performance characteristics differ completely from those of emissions reductions. While SRM may not be well suited to substitute for emissions reductions in the long term, emissions reductions are certainly not suited to provide benefits in the near term. This suggests a blended strategy, where SRM might be used to lessen warming and risk in the near term, while emission reductions address long-term risks.

BCR of SRM R&D

With the results of the previous section, we can now estimate the BCR of SRM R&D. Following Galiana and Green (2010), we define the BCR of R&D as

$$BCR = \frac{\text{Present Value of Net Benefits}}{\text{Present Value of R\&D Expenditures}} \quad (3)$$

Assuming that an SRM R&D program would require a total investment of \$5 billion, as we detailed earlier in the chapter, and using the net benefit assessments contained in Table 4.3.2, we obtain the BCR estimates shown in Table 4.3.4.

Thus, we believe the BCR for SRM R&D is large: possibly between about 250 : 1 and 2,000 : 1. The actual BCR depends on the damages caused by SRM. As a rough estimate, though, we might say the BCR is 1,000 : 1. Again, these results assume that an SRM R&D program would be successful. But the very large net benefits that would flow from the success of SRM argue that R&D is a very good investment. *Even a 10 percent chance of success will result in an expected BCR of 100 : 1.*

Discussion and conclusion

As discussed at the outset, the results of this chapter are hardly surprising and the logic is easy to follow: if one believes that climate change will result in significant damages either due the warming itself or the costs imposed by abatement measures, then the ability to reduce warming at low cost will accrue substantial benefits. Given that the technology to achieve these benefits does not exist and might itself cause damage, research is likely to pay large dividends.

Funding request

The 2012 Copenhagen Consensus Expert Panel is tasked with allocating a total budget of \$75 billion over the next four years. The analysis presented above details the BCR of a complete, ten-year, R&D program. We do not attempt to compute the BCR of only the first four years of research. Had we done so, the values are likely to be even greater than those shown in Table 4.3.4 for at least two reasons. First, the required investment for Phase (1), of the R&D program consists almost entirely of laboratory experimentation and computational modeling. It is, therefore, only about 12 percent of the total ten-year requirement. Second, much is likely to be learned during the initial research.

Caldeira and Keith's R&D cost estimates (Caldeira and Keith, 2010) imply spending of about \$60 million over the first four years. We multiplied these estimates by 10 and thus request \$600 million (\$0.6 billion) or 0.8 percent of the 2012 Copenhagen Consensus budget be allocated to climate engineering R&D. In all likelihood, this funding request is too large but, again, we have tried to err on the side of underestimating the BCRs.

Climate engineering R&D: why not?

We believe the analysis outlined in this subchapter makes a compelling case for CE research. Why, then, do some oppose it? What is the case against *research*? There are five primary arguments:

(1) The climate system's complexity is beyond our capacity to understand and therefore any intervention is fraught with risk and should be considered unsafe (Cicerone, 2006).
(2) SRM will be perceived as a substitute for GHG controls and therefore society will lose its will to implement emission controls (Cicerone, 2006).
(3) SRM treats the symptoms of man-made climate change rather than removing its root cause (Tetlock and Oppenheimer, 2008).
(4) The development of technology to reduce warming may trigger international tensions and even conflict as countries vie for the right to choose the optimal climate (Victor *et al.*, 2009).
(5) SRM is inherently unjust because (i) its benefits and costs will not be uniform, (ii) it places future generations at risk, and (iii) it is inexpensive and thus could be implemented unilaterally (Svoboda *et al.*, 2011).
(6) Once started, it might be stopped prematurely resulting in rapid warming and increased damages (Goes *et al.*, 2011).

Addressing all of these concerns in detail is beyond the scope of our current effort. However, we would like to offer a few thoughts, which we number in accordance with the list above.

(1) **Complexity** First, the complexity of the climate system also makes it difficult to know the degree to which increased GHG concentrations will cause harmful climate change. Second, ignorance is in any case an argument for research rather than one against it.
(2) **Substitution** One might argue that SRM should only be deployed as a "last resort." While this is easy to say and might allow one to discuss SRM without controversy, we do not subscribe to this view. First, how do we define "last resort"? Even if the answer were clear, will we be able to tell that such a moment has arisen? Second, it may indeed be economic to replace some degree of emissions reductions with SRM. Substitution might well lessen both climate damages and the costs of GHG controls. We are not aware of any proof that such a blended strategy is clearly suboptimal. What valid reason, then, could warrant suppressing a welfare-enhancing policy option, and, absent an order of Platonic guardians, on what authority would it be done?
(3) **Treating symptoms** This approach is often the most cost-effective available response: "Typically in an attempt to find a solution to a problem people look to its causes, or yet more fatuously, to its *root* causes. However, there need be no logical connection between the cause of a problem and appropriate or even feasible solutions" (Collier, 2010, emphasis in the original). Thus, in economics, medicine, and politics treating symptoms often lowers total costs. The high institutional hurdles to curbing GHG emissions suggest that, with climate change too, treating symptoms may offer great benefits.
(4) **Conflict** Except for purely domestic adaptation, all steps to cope with climate change are likely to trigger some level of conflict. Efforts to control emissions certainly have. Growing global interdependence strengthens all states' incentives to cooperate. Yet the interests of major states often conflict. States build regimes such as the World Trade Organization (WTO) to lower the transaction costs of cooperating on the issues on which they have some interests in common and some in conflict (Keohane, 1984). Experienced diplomats expect that, were SRM to be deployed, the major powers would form a regime to govern its use (Benedick, 2011).
(5) **Justice** No action we may take in response to climate change will result in uniform costs/benefits and remove all risk from future generations. In fact, a failure to research and deploy SRM would be unjust by this standard because it moves future generations towards a climate tipping point.
(6) **Termination** For two reasons, once SRM starts, there will be strong incentives to continue it. First, termination would be unlikely just because it would be costly. Second, as interest groups organize around existing programs, government policy often develops strong path dependence. Further, the validity of the case against a start-and-stop use of SRM depends heavily on what will happen if SRM is not used. Bickel and Agrawal (2011) detail many cases

where SRM would produce net benefits even if it was aborted.

In sum, SRM is a family of technologies that could offer immense benefits. The proposed research program is inexpensive, a small fraction of current climate science R&D spending and the 2012 Copenhagen Consensus budget. The time has come to begin formally researching this approach to dealing with climate change.

Bibliography

Andronova, N. G. and M. E. Schlesinger, 2001: Objective estimation of the probability density function for climate sensitivity, *Journal of Geophysical Research* **106**, 22605–11

Arrow, K. J., 1962: Economic welfare and the allocation of resources for invention, in R. Nelson (ed.), *The Rate and Direction of Inventive Activity: Economic and Social Factors*, Princeton University Press

Baker, E. and Y. Peng, 2012: The value of better information on technology R&D programs in response to climate change, *Environment Modeling and Assessment* 17, 107–21

Baker, E., H. Chon, and J. Keisler, 2009: Advancing solar R&D: combining economic analysis with expert elicitations to inform climate policy, *Energy Economics* **31**, S37–S49

Barrett, S., 2003: *Environment and Statecraft: The Strategy of Environmental Treaty-Making*, Oxford University Press New York

Benedick, R. E., 2011: Considerations on governance for climate remediation technologies: lessons from the "ozone hole," *Stanford Journal of Law, Science & Policy* **4**, 6–9

Bickel, J. E., 2008: The relationship between perfect and imperfect information in a risk-sensitive two-action problem, *Decision Analysis* **5**, 116–28

2013: Climate engineering and tipping point scenarios, *Economic Systems and Decisions*, DOI 10.1007/S10669-013-9435-8

Bickel, J. E. and S. Agarwal, 2012: Reexamining the economics of aerosol geoengineering, *Climatic Change*, DOI 10.1007/S10584-00-0619-x

Bickel, J. E. and L. Lane, 2010: Climate engineering, in B. Lomborg (ed.), *Smart Solutions to Climate Change: Comparing Costs and Benefits*, Cambridge University Press, 9–51

Blackstock, J. J., D. S. Battisti, K. Caldeira, D. M. Eardley, J. I. Katz, D. W. Keith, A. A. N. Patrinos, D. P. Schrag, R. H. Socolow, and S. E. Koonin, 2009: *Climate Engineering Responses to Climate Emergencies*, archived online at: http://arxiv.org/pdf/0907.5140

Broder, J. M. and M. L. Wald, 2009: Big science role is seen in global warming cure, *New York Times*, 12 February, A24

Caldeira, K. and D. E. Keith, 2010: The need for climate engineering research, *Issues in Science and Technology* **27**, 57–62

Chiavari, J. and C. Tam, 2011: *Good Practice Policy Framework for Energy Technology Research, Development and Demonstration (RD&D)*, International Energy Agency, Paris

Cicerone, R. J., 2006: Geoengineering: encouraging research and overseeing implementation, *Climatic Change* **77**, 221–6

Collier, P., 2010: *The Plundered Planet: Why We Must – and How We Can – Manage Nature for Global Prosperity*, Oxford University Press, New York

Crutzen, P. J., 2006: Albedo enhancement by stratospheric sulfur injections: a contribution to resolve a policy dilemma?, *Climatic Change* **77**, 211–20

Edgerton, D., 2007: *The Shock of the Old: Technology and Global History since 1900*, Oxford University Press, New York

ETC Group, 2010: *Geopiracy: The Case Against Geoengineering*, Ottawa

Galiana, I. and C. Green, 2010: Technology-led climate policy, in B. Lomborg (ed.), *Smart Solutions to Climate Change: Comparing Costs and Benefits*, Cambridge University Press, 292–339

Goes, M., N. Tuana, and K. Keller, 2011: The economics (or lack thereof) of aerosol geoengineering, *Climatic Change* 109, 719–44

Hecht, R., D. T. Jamison, J. Augenstein, G. Patridge, and K. Thorien, 2011: *Vaccine Research and Development*, Copenhagen Consensus Center and Rush Foundation

Higgins, Paul A. T., 2011: Climate change in the FY 2011 budget, *AAAS Report XXXV: Research and Development FY 2011*, Washington, DC

IPCC, 2005: *Guidance notes for lead authors of the IPCC Fourth Assessment Report on addressing uncertainties*, New York

2007: Summary for policymakers, in S. Solomon, D. Qin, M. Manning, Z. Chen, M. Marquis *et al.*

(eds.), *Climate Change 2007: The Physical Science Basis. Contribution of Working Group 1 to the Fourth Assessment Report of the Intergovernmental Panel on Climate Change*, Cambridge University Press, New York

Jacoby, H. D., M. H. Babiker, S. Paltsev, and J. M. Reilly, 2008: Sharing the Burden of GHG reductions, *MIT Joint Program on the Science and Policy of Global Change*, Report **167**

Keohane, R. O., 1984: *After Hegemony: Cooperation and Discord in the World Political Economy*, Princeton University Press

Lane, L. and D. Montgomery, 2008: Political institutions and greenhouse gas controls, AEI Center for Regulatory and Market Studies, Related Publication **08–09**

Lane, L., K. Caldeira, R. Chatfield, and S. Langhoff, 2007: *Workshop Report on Managing Solar Radiation*, NASA Ames Research Center, Carnegie Institute of Washington Department of Global Ecology, **NASA/CP-2007–214558**

Latham, J., P. J. Rasch, C. C. Chen, L. Kettles, A. Gadian, A. Gettleman, H. Morrison, K. Bower, and T. Choularton, 2008: Global temperature stabilization via controlled albedo enhancement of low-level maritime clouds, *Philosophical Transactions of The Royal Society A* **366**, 3969–87

Lenton, T. M. and N. E. Vaughan, 2009: The radiative forcing potential of different climate geoengineering options, *Atmospheric Chemistry and Physics Discussions* **9**, 2559–2608

Lenton, T. M., H. Held, E. Kriegler *et al.*, 2008: Tipping elements in the Earth's climate system, *PNAS* **105**, 1786–93

Meehl, G. A., T. F. Stocker, W. D. Collins *et al.*, 2007: Global climate projections, in S. Solomon, D. Qin, M. Manning, Z. Chen, M. Marquis *et al.* (eds.), *Climate Change 2007: The Physical Science Basis. Contribution of Working Group 1 to the Fourth Assessment Report on the Intergovernmental Panel on Climate Change*, Cambridge University Press, New York

National Academy of Sciences (NAS), 1992: *Policy Implications of Greenhouse Warming: Mitigation, Adaptation, and the Science Base*, National Academy Press, Washington, DC

Nelson, R. R. and S. G. Winter, 1977: in search of a useful theory of innovation, *Research Policy* **6**, 36–76

Nordhaus, W. D., 2002: Modeling induced innovation in climate change policy, in A. Grubler, N. Nakicenovic, and W.D. Nordhaus (eds.), *Modeling Induced Innovation in Climate Change Policy*, Resources for the Future Press, Washington, DC

2008: *A Question of Balance: Weighing the Options on Global Warming Policies*, Yale University Press, New Haven, CT

Pielke, Jr., R. A., 2009: An idealized assessment of the economics of air capture of carbon dioxide in mitigation policy, *Environmental Science & Policy* **12**, 216–25

Pielke, Jr., R. A., T. M. L. Wigley, and C. Green, 2008: Dangerous assumptions, *Nature* **452**, 531–2

Popp, D., 2004: ENTICE: endogenous technological change in the DICE model of global warming, *Journal of Environmental Economics and Management* **48**, 742–68

Rasch, P. J., P. J. Crutzen, and D. B. Coleman, 2008: Exploring the geoengineering of climate using stratospheric sulfate aerosols: the role of particle size, *Geophysical Research Letters* **35**, L02809

Richels, R.G., A. S. Manne, and T. M. L. Wigley, 2004: Moving beyond concentrations: the challenge of limiting temperature change, AEI-Brookings Joint Center for Regulatory Studies, *Working Paper* **04–11**

Royal Society, 2009: Geoengineering the climate: science, governance and uncertainty, Royal Society, London

Salter, S., G. Sortino, and J. Latham, 2008: Sea-going hardware for the cloud albedo method of reversing global warming, *Philosophical Transactions of The Royal Society A* **366**, 3989–4006

Smith, A. E., 2010: Climate engineering, Alternative Perspective Paper, in B. Lomborg (ed.), *Smart Solutions to Climate Change: Comparing Costs and Benefits*, Cambridge University Press, 62–73

Stern, D. I., 2005: Global sulfur emissions from 1850 to 2000, *Chemosphere* **58**, 163–75

Stocker, T. F., 2003: Changes in the global carbon cycle and ocean circulation on the millennial time scale, in X. Rodó and F. A. Comín (eds.), *Global Climate: Current Research and Uncertainties in the Climate System*, Springer-Verlag, Berlin

Stokey, N. L., V. L. Smith, T. C. Schelling, F. E. Kydland, and J. N. Bhagwati, 2010: Expert

Panel Ranking, in B. Lomborg (ed.), *Smart Solutions to Climate Change: Comparing Costs and Benefits*, Cambridge University Press, 381–93

Svoboda, T., K. Keller, M. Goes, and N. Thana, 2011: Sulfate aerosol geoengineering: the question of justice, *Public Affairs Quarterly* **25**, 157–80

Tetlock, P. E. and M. Oppenheimer, 2008: The boundaries of the thinkable, *Daedalus* **137**, 59–70

Tol, R. S. J., 2008: The social cost of carbon: trends, outliers and catastrophes, *Economics: The Open-Access, Open-Assessment E-Journal* **2**, 1–22

Trenberth, K. E., J. T. Fasullo, and J. T. Kiehl, 2009: Earth's global energy budget, *Bulletin of the American Meteorological Society* **90**, 311–23

United States Department of Energy (US DOE), 2002: *Response Options to Limit Rapid or Severe Climate Change: Assessment of Research Needs*, National Climate Change Technology Initiative, Washington, DC

Victor, D. G., M. G. Morgan, J. Apt, J. Steinbruner, and K. Ricke, 2009: The geoengineering option: a last resort against global warming?, *Foreign Affairs*, **88**, 64–76

CLIMATE-CHANGE ADAPTATION

Francesco Bosello, Carlo Carraro, and Enrica De Cian*

Introduction

The 2011 climate talks in Durban, by postponing negotiations on future commitments to 2015, are likely to increase the risk of exceeding the 2°C target and to make the pathway towards 2.5–3.5°C a likely outcome of global economic development.[1] After the Copenhagen Conference of Parties (COP 15), a number of studies made the point that the outcome of COP 15 was inconsistent with the 2°C temperature target re-stated in the Copenhagen Accord.[2] At that time, it was already clear that stabilizing global warming below what is commonly considered a "dangerous" level was a very difficult task. After Durban, this is even more true. The unspoken implication is that adaptation to climate change becomes even more necessary. Additional effort and resources should then be devoted to narrowing the gap between what needed to be done and what would be done to adapt to future climate change.

However, adaptation should not be considered as a substitute for mitigation. The ultimate question that interests policy-makers is how to reduce the climate-change vulnerability of socio-economic systems in the most cost-effective way. This objective needs to be achieved with both mitigation and adaptation policies. What, therefore, is the optimal balance of mitigation and adaptation? What is the regional distribution of this policy mix? How should adaptation and mitigation be allocated over time? To address these questions requires, on the one hand, a thorough knowledge of the size and the regional distribution of climate-related damages and, on the other, a precise assessment of the costs and benefits of alternative policy mixes.

Given its local- and project-specific nature, the CBA of adaptation strategies has been treated within a micro-perspective. Although this approach can inform about the economic performance of specific projects, it lacks a broader perspective on the interactions with other economic activities. Adaptation is only one of the possible responses to global warming within a range of possible options. In order to maximize the benefit from a portfolio of alternatives, a joint analysis of different measures is certainly more informative.

If an extended literature has investigated the different dimensions of mitigation strategies and their interactions with economic development, much less can be found on adaptation. Even less attention has been paid to the interactions between adaptation and mitigation. At the same time, the interest in defining their strategic complementarity or trade-off in a macroeconomic cost-benefit context has constantly risen. This is witnessed by an increasing number of research efforts and publications. A survey of these contributions is provided by Agrawala *et al.* (2011a), while Agrawala *et al.* (2011b) contains the first comparison of model results on adaptation and mitigation costs.

Nonetheless, many questions concerning the design of an optimal mix of mitigation and adaptation measures, the BCR of different adaptation/mitigation options, and their regional distribution, are still unanswered. Following the outcome of the Copenhagen and Durban Conferences, a renewed interest on how to spend the money that will be disbursed through the Green Climate Fund (this fund, reaching US$100 billion in 2020, is meant to finance mitigation and adaptation in developing countries) has emerged. Historically, the majority of climate funding (US$93 billion out

* This subchapter of Chapter 4 was originally prepared for the 2009 Copenhagen Consensus (see Bosello *et al.*, 2010a). This version is a revised and updated version prepared for the 2012 Copenhagen Consensus and further summarized for this book. AD-WITCH, the model used in this study, has been developed by FEEM in cooperation with the OECD. The authors gratefully acknowledge their financial support. They are also grateful to Shardul Agrawala, Rob Dellink, Kelly de Bruin and Richard Tol for helpful comments. Nonetheless, the views expressed in this subchapter are the authors' sole responsibility. Finally, the contribution of all colleagues who worked to the development of the original WITCH model – in particular Valentina Bosetti, Emanuele Massetti, and Massimo Tavoni – is gratefully acknowledged.

1 http://climateactiontracker.org/news/last amended November 30, 2012.

2 Carraro and Massetti 2010a, 2010b.

of US$97 billion) has been used for mitigation, with adaptation receiving only US$4.4 billion. Most of the current adaptation financing comes from bilateral accords between countries, whereas dedicated funds, such as the Adaptation Fund, play only a minor role (Buchner *et al.*, 2011). The question arising is whether this uneven allocation of short-term climate funds is justified or whether more resources should be devoted to adaptation, given the low BCR of many mitigation measures and given the complementarity of adaptation expenses with development goals, which increases their BCR.

This subchapter addresses the question of how resources for climate change should be allocated between adaptation, mitigation, and residual damage from climate change. The study adopts a macro-angle and uses the AD-WITCH model, an Integrated Assessment Model (IAM) that has been developed for the joint analysis of adaptation and mitigation.[3] With respect to the existing studies in the field (de Bruin *et al.*, 2009a, 2009b, Hof *et al.*, 2009, 2010; Bahn *et al.*, 2010; Bosello *et al.*, 2010b) the proposed modeling framework provides a novel characterization of the adaptation process, which includes not only anticipatory and reactive adaptation, but also adaptation-specific technological change. This enables us to:

- Analyze adaptation to climate change both in isolation and jointly with mitigation strategies
- Provide a comparative CBA of both adaptation and mitigation
- Assess the marginal contribution to the BCR of different adaptation modes
- Emphasize the region-specific characteristics of climate policy.

The study is organized as follows. First we present a CBA of macro-, policy-driven responses to climate change – namely, adaptation, mitigation, and joint adaptation and mitigation. By narrowing down the focus on policy-driven adaptation, we will then compute the BCRs of three macro-adaptation strategies (reactive, anticipatory or proactive, and knowledge adaptation).

A second novel contribution of this subchapter is the assessment of the market potential to adjust to climate change and to reduce the vulnerability of economic systems to it. To some extent, adaptation will occur without any policy intervention, as a reactive response to changes in climate, driven by market-price signals. Although market-driven adaptation has a strong damage-smoothing potential at the global level, we show that damages are likely to remain significant, especially in developing countries. We therefore compute and discuss the BCRs of different policy-driven adaptation strategies net of market-driven, autonomous adaptation to climate change.

AD-WITCH, the model used to carry out most of the analysis, is an optimal growth IAM endowed with an adaptation module to compute the costs and benefits of policy-driven mitigation and adaptation strategies. Given the game theoretic and regional structure of AD-WITCH (see Bosello *et al.*, 2010a), both first-best and second-best climate policies can be computed. In this study, we focus on a first-best world in which all externalities are internalized. The social planner implements the optimal levels of adaptation and mitigation, namely the level that equalizes marginal costs and benefits.

To account for both market-driven and policy-driven adaptation, two different modeling tools have been used. The ICES model, which is a highly disaggregated CGE model, has been used to identify the effects of market–driven adaptation. ICES and AD-WITCH have then been integrated to provide a full assessment of both market- and policy-driven adaptation. More precisely, the effects of market-driven adaptation on regional climate damages have been estimated using the ICES model. These estimates have been used to modify all regional climate-change damage functions in the WITCH model to compute climate damages net of market-driven adaptation.

The final part of this subchapter describes specific adaptation proposals. These are consistent with the analysis carried out in the first part of the subchapter, and build upon existing estimates of costs and benefits of specific adaptation strategies.

[3] The model has been developed by FEEM in cooperation with the OECD team led by Shardul Agrawala.

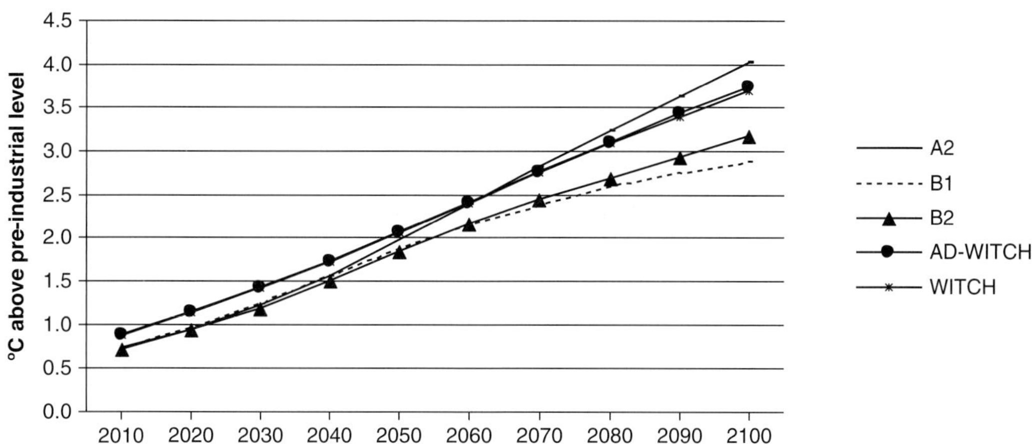

Figure 4.4.1 *Temperature estimates of the IPCC SRES (IIASA), the WITCH model (Bosetti* et al.*, 2006, and the AD-WITCH baseline scenario used in this study*

Note: Available at: www.iiasa.ac.at/Research/GGI/DB/.
Source: Our elaboration.

Background concepts

In this subchapter, "climate change" is defined as a set of alterations in the average weather caused by global warming, which is due to emissions of GHGs. Climate change affects not only average surface temperature, but also involves other physical modifications, such as changes in precipitations, intensity and frequency of storms, and the occurrence of droughts and floods.

Average temperature is already 0.7°C above pre-industrial level and further warming might be substantial if no immediate global action is undertaken. Even if all radiative forcing agents were held constant at the 2000 level, a further warming would be observed due to the inertia of the oceans. According to the main IPCC scenarios,[4] world-average temperature is likely to increase in the BAU scenarios, as shown in Figure 4.4.1, which also shows the expected pathways produced by AD-WITCH. Projected global temperature increases above pre-industrial levels range between 2.8° and 4°C.

Anthropogenic climate change, accelerating the natural trend, will induce a series of impacts on natural and social ecosystems with potentially both negative and positive consequences on human well-being. As highlighted in the IPCC Fourth Assessment Report (Parry *et al.*, 2007), already a moderate warming produces negative consequences: increasing number of people exposed to water stresses; extinction of species and ecosystems; decreases in cereal productivity at low latitudes; land loss due to sea-level rise in coastal areas; increases in mortality and morbidity associated to change in the incidence of vector-borne diseases or to increased frequency and intensity of heat waves; infrastructural disruption and mortality increase due to more frequent and intense extreme weather-event occurrence.

A first classification of climate change impacts distinguishes between market and non-market impacts. Market effects can be valued using prices and observed changes in demand and supply, whereas non-market effects have no observable prices and therefore require other methods such as valuations based on WTP.

The recent literature points to the large potential damages from climate change, especially in developing countries and non-market sectors (Stern,

[4] The SRES scenarios A2, B1, and B2 are from www.iiasa.ac.at/Research/GGI/DB/.

2006; Parry *et al.*, 2007). In particular, important non-market impacts are those on health. Current estimates are largely incomplete and most assessments have looked at specific diseases (vector-borne diseases, CVD and respiratory diseases) and do not consider other adaptation costs, such as those relating to building the required infrastructure that will be particularly needed in developing countries. Nonetheless, for the United States only, Hanemann (2008) estimates large impacts on health, reporting a loss of 1990 $US 10 billion p.a. against the $US 2 billion reported in Nordhaus and Boyer (2000).

Climate change can lead to a significant rise in sea level and catastrophic events with implications on migrations and the stock of capital. Insurance companies are an important source of information regarding estimates of capital losses due to climate change impacts. UNFCCC (2007) reports a cost of protecting infrastructure from climate change in North America between 1990 $US 4 and 64 billion already in 2030, when temperature increase is likely to be far below 2°C.

The Munich Re insurance company has developed a database which catalogs great natural catastrophes that have had severe impacts on the economic system. Such a database underestimates damages from climate, because only large events are included. Yet estimated losses are in the order of 0.5 percent of current world GDP, and damages are increasing at a rate of 6 percent a year in real terms. Using this information and adjusting for the under-reporting of other minor impacts, UNFCCC (2007) extrapolated a cost between 1 and 1.5 percent of world GDP in 2030, which corresponds to 1990 $US850–1,350 billion. Nordhaus and Boyer (2000) reported similar figures for total impacts, and for a temperature increase of 2.5°C, which is likely to occur at least several decades after 2030.

For a temperature increase above 2.5°C, the majority of Impact Assessment (IA) models currently used to evaluate the full cost of climate change, forecast net losses from climatic changes ranging roughly around 2 percent of world GDP

Should global warming exceed the 3°C above pre-industrial, climate-change impacts are likely to be more drastic and move to a higher level of risk. The probability of the so-called climate "tipping points" increases non-linearly when certain temperature thresholds are crossed. Zickfeld *et al.* (2007) reports probability estimates for the shutdown of Atlantic meridional overturning circulation until 2100. It ranges between 0–0.2 percent for low temperature increases (2°C), but it increases significantly (0–0.6 percent) for medium level of global warming (2–4°C).

Climate change is not uniform over the world though, moreover impacts are diverse and highly differentiated by regions. Regions themselves differ for their intrinsic adaptive capacity. These dimensions – i.e. exposure, sensitivity and autonomous adaptive capacity – determine a highly differentiated regional vulnerability to climate change. Accordingly, the global picture can provide only a very partial and potentially misleading insight into the true economic cost of climate change. As a general rule, developing countries will be more affected than their developed counterparts.

Among rich countries, Europe is estimated to suffer most from climate change, because of the assumption of high vulnerability to catastrophic events. Among developing regions, Africa and India face larger climate damages due to impacts on health and catastrophic events, respectively. It is worth noticing that sea-level rise constitutes a higher share of damages in developed than in developing countries. However, the aggregated data hide important hotspots for vulnerability to sea floods in developing regions. In these regions, densely populated urban areas are often located in river deltas particularly exposed to sea-level rise (e.g. the Ganges, Mekong, Niger, Nile, etc.). Impacts on agriculture vary a lot with the climatic conditions of the region and become positive for cold or mild regions (e.g. Russia, China). A similar pattern can be identified for impacts on energy use, with cold regions being more positively affected (Russia).

In the light of this, and as stressed by the EU White Paper on Adaptation (EC, 2009) and the European strategy on adaptation (EEA, 2010), mitigation needs to be coupled with adaptation actions to cope with unavoidable climate-change impacts that mitigation cannot eliminate.

Defining adaptation: a multi-dimensional concept

Adaptation to climate change has received a wide set of definitions, by both the scientific and the policy environments. Among the first group, see e.g. Burton (1992); Smit (1993); Smithers and Smit (1997); Smit *et al.* (2000). Among the second group, see e.g. EEA (2005); Lim and Spanger-Siegfred (2005); UNFCCC, 2007. The large number of not always coincident definitions already highlights a specific problem concerning adaptation: it is a process that can take the most diverse forms depending on where and when it occurs, and on who is adapting to what.

Indeed, probably the most comprehensive, known, and widely accepted definition of adaptation is the one provided by the IPCC Third Assessment Report, which states that *adaptation* is any "adjustment in ecological, social, or economic systems in response to actual or expected climatic stimuli, and their effects or impacts. This term refers to changes in processes, practices or structures to moderate or offset potential damages or to take advantages of opportunities associated with changes in climate" (McCarthy *et al.*, 2001), which is general enough to encompass the widest spectrum of options.

Adaptation can be identified along three dimensions:

- the subject of adaptation (*who* or *what* adapts)
- the object of adaptation (*what* they adapt *to*)
- the way in which adaptation takes place (*how* they adapt).

This last dimension includes what resources are used, when and how they are used, and with which results (Wheaton and Maciver, 1999).

The subject of adaptation: who or what adapts

Adaptation materializes in changes in ecological, social, and/or economic systems. These changes can be the result of natural responses and in this case they usually involve organisms or species, or socio-economic or institutional reactions, in which case they are undertaken by individual or collective actors, private or public agents.

Table 4.4.1 Adaptation: possible criteria for classification

Concept or attribute	
Purposefulness	Autonomous → Planned
Timing	Anticipatory → Reactive, Responsive
Temporal scope	Short-term → Long-term
Spatial scope	Localized → Widespread
Function/Effects	Retreat – Accommodate – Protect – Prevent
Form	Structural – Legal – Institutional
Valuation of performance	Effectiveness–Efficiency–Equity–Feasibility

Source: Our adaptation from Smit *et al.* (1999).

The object of adaptation: what they adapt to

In the case of climate change, adaptive responses can be induced either by changes in average conditions or by changes in the variability of extreme events. While in the first case the change is slow and usually falls within the coping range of systems, in the second case changes are abrupt and outside this coping range (Smit and Pilifosova, 2001).

How adaptation occurs: modes, resources and results

The existing literature (see e.g. Klein and Tol, 1997; Fankhauser *et al.*, 1999; Smit *et al.*, 1999; McCarthy *et al.*, 2001) proposes several criteria that can be used to identify the different adaptation processes. Table 4.4.1 offers a tentative summary of this classification based upon spatial and temporal aspects, forms and evaluation of performances.

This subchapter focuses on a different way of classifying adaptation to climate change, by distinguishing between autonomous or market-driven and planned or policy-driven adaptation. Within policy-driven adaptation, we will distinguish between anticipatory or proactive and responsive or reactive adaptation.

The IPCC Third Assessment Report defines *autonomous adaptation* as "adaptation that does not constitute a conscious response to climatic stimuli but is triggered by ecological changes in natural systems and by market or welfare changes in human systems" and *planned adaptation* as: "adaptation that is the result of a deliberate policy decision based on an awareness that conditions have changed or are about to change and that action is required to return to, maintain, or achieve a desired state" (McCarthy *et al.*, 2001).

This apparently clear distinction may originate some confusion when adaptation involves socio-economic agents. Indeed, climate change may induce market- or welfare-effect-triggering reactions in private agents without the necessity of a planned strategy designed by a public agency, but just as a response to scarcity signals provided by changes in relative prices. A typical example of this is the effect of climate change on crop productivity. This has both physical effects (changing yields) and economic effects (changing agricultural goods prices) that can induce farmers to some adaptation (for example, changes in the cultivation type or timing). This form of private socio-economic adaptation, even though responding to a plan and originated by (rational) economic decisions, is considered autonomous or market-driven (see e.g. Smit, 1993; Leary, 1999). On the contrary, the term "planned adaptation" is reserved to public interventions by governments or agencies.[5]

Another important distinction is that based on the timing of adaptation actions which distinguishes between *anticipatory* or proactive adaptation and *reactive* or responsive adaptation. They are defined by the IPCC Third Assessment Report (McCarthy *et al.*, 2001) as: "adaptation that takes place before and after impacts of climate change are observed," respectively. There can be circumstances when an anticipatory intervention is less costly and more effective than a reactive action (a typical example is that of flood or coastal protection), and this is particularly relevant for planned adaptation. Reactive adaptation is a major characteristic of an unmanaged natural system and of the autonomous adaptation reactions of social economic systems.

The temporal scope defines long-term and short-term adaptation. This distinction can also be referred to "tactical" as opposed to "strategic," or to "instantaneous" versus "cumulative." In the natural hazards field it is adjustment versus adaptation (Smit *et al.*, 2000).

For the sake of completeness, let us mention other classifications of adaptation. Based on spatial scope, adaptation can be localized or widespread, even though it is noted that it can have an intrinsic local nature (Füssel and Klein, 2006). Several attributes can also characterize the effects of adaptation. According to Smit (1993) they can be: accommodate, retreat, protect, prevent, tolerate, etc. Based on the form adaptations can take they can be distinguished according to whether they are primarily technological, behavioral, financial, institutional, or informational.

Finally the performance of adaptation processes can be evaluated according to the generic principles of policy appraisal: cost-efficiency,[6] cost-effectiveness, administrative feasibility, and equity. As noted by Adger *et al.* (2005), in such appraisal effectiveness has to be considered *lato sensu*. Indeed, it is important to account for the spatial and temporal spillovers of adaptation measures. Basically, a locally effective adaptation policy may negatively affect neighboring regions, and a temporary successful adaptation policy can weaken vulnerability in the longer term; both constitute examples of maladaptation. By the same token efficiency, effectiveness, and equity are not absolute, but context-specific, varying between countries, sectors within countries, actors engaged in adaptation processes.

[5] The IPCC (McCarthy *et al.*, 2001) also provides the definition of *private adaptation*: "adaptation that is initiated and implemented by individuals, households or private companies. Private adaptation is usually in the actors' rational self interest" and of *public adaptation*: "adaptation that is initiated and implemented by governments at all levels. Public adaptation is usually directed at collective needs."

[6] The concept of cost-efficiency implies that resources are used in the best possible way, cost-effectiveness that resources to reach a given target – that can be suboptimal – are used in the best possible way. The practical implementation of both concepts requires that actions respond to some kind of cost-benefit criterion.

Mitigation and adaptation as a single integrated policy process

Adaptation and mitigation are both viable strategies to combat damages due to climate change. However they tackle the problem from completely different angles.

Mitigation and adaptation work on different spatial and time scales. Mitigation is global and long-term while adaptation is local and short-term (Klein *et al.*, 2003; Ingham *et al.*, 2005; Tol, 2005; Wilbanks, 2005; Füssel and Klein, 2006). This has several important implications.

Firstly, mitigation can be considered as a *permanent* solution to anthropogenic climate change. Indeed, once abated, 1 ton of, say, CO_2 cannot produce damage any longer (unless its removal is temporary as in the case of carbon capture (cc) and sequestration provided by forests or agricultural land). In contrast, adaptation is more temporary as it typically addresses *current* or *expected* damages. It may require adjustments, if climate-change damage varies or if it is substantially different from what was originally expected.

Secondly, the effects of mitigation and adaptation occur at different times (Klein *et al.*, 2003; Wilbanks, 2005; Füssel and Klein, 2006). Mitigation is constrained by long-term climatic inertia, adaptation by a shorter-term, social-economic inertia. In other words, emission reductions today will translate in a lower temperature increase and ultimately lower damage only in the (far) future, whereas adaptation measures, once implemented, are immediately effective in reducing the damage.[7] This differentiation is particularly relevant from the perspective of policy-makers. The stronger reason for the lower appeal of mitigation policies is probably their certain and present costs and future and uncertain benefits.[8] This issue is less problematic for adaptation. Moreover the different intertemporal characteristics tend to expose mitigation more than adaptation to subjective assumptions in policy decision-making, like the choice of discount rates. It can be expected that a lower discount rate, putting more weight on future damages, will increase the appeal of mitigation with respect to adaptation.

Thirdly, mitigation provides a global good, whereas adaptation is a local response to anthropogenic climate change. The benefits induced by 1 ton of carbon abated are experienced irrespectively of where this ton has been abated. Adaptation entails measures implemented locally whose benefits advantage primarily the local communities targeted. The global public good nature of emissions reduction creates the well-known incentive to free ride. This is one of the biggest problems in reaching a large and sustainable international mitigation agreement (Carraro and Siniscalco, 1998; Bosetti *et al.*, 2009). Again, this should be less of a problem in the case of adaptation policies.

It is worth mentioning that mitigation involves decision-making at the highest level, such as national governments. Mitigation is implemented at the country level (Tol, 2005) and it concerns large, highly concentrated sectors – for example, energy and energy-intensive industries (Klein *et al.*, 2003). Adaptation needs to be implemented at an atomistic level, involving a much larger number of stakeholders. Thus, at least in principle, the design of an international policy effort could be easier and the related coordination and transaction costs lower.

In the absence of international coordination, substantial unilateral mitigation actions are unlikely to occur. Here the concern is twofold. On the one hand, the environmental effectiveness of unilateral action is likely to be small. On the other, the national goods and services of the abating country can lose competitiveness in international markets if their prices incorporate the cost of the tighter emission standards. This is not necessarily true with adaptation. Its smaller-scale, and the excludability of its benefits can make unilateral effort a viable choice.

The different regional effectiveness of adaptation and mitigation is also relevant in the light of the spatial uncertainty of climate-change damages

[7] It has to be stressed that economic inertias can be long as well – e.g. implementing coastal protection interventions can take many years (or even decades) and that adaptation may not be immediately effective, as it is the case for anticipatory adaptation.

[8] Füssel and Klein (2006) note that monitoring mitigation-effectiveness is easier than monitoring adaptation. They refer to the fact that it is easier to measure emission reduction than quantify the avoided climate-change damage due to adaptation. They do not refer to the quantification of the avoided future damage due to emission reduction.

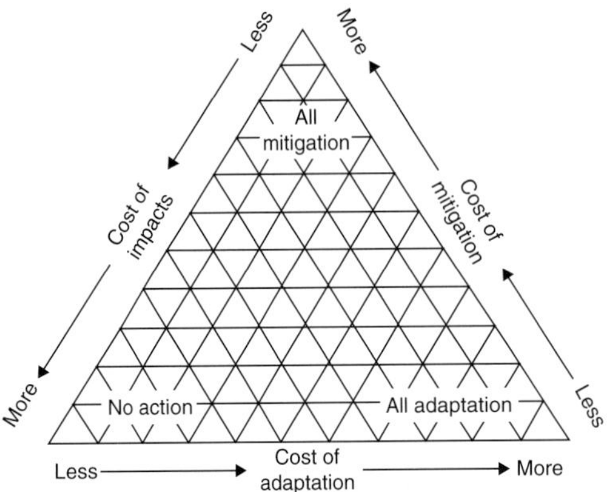

Figure 4.4.2 *Mitigation adaptation and impacts: a schematic "decision space"*

Source: Klein *et al.* (2007).

(Lecoq and Shalizi, 2007). Since we do not know exactly where and with what intensity negative climatic impacts are going to hit, policy decisions should be biased toward mitigation which is globally effective. On the contrary, adaptation should be used to deal with reasonably well understood local phenomena.

Finally, there is an equity dimension. Mitigation intrinsically endorses the polluter-pays principle (PPP). Each one abates her own emissions (directly or indirectly, if flexibility is allowed).[9] This is not necessarily the case with adaptation. It can well alleviate damages which are not directly provoked by the affected community. This is particularly important for international (especially North/South) climate negotiations. Indeed adaptation is particularly needed in developing countries which are either more exposed or vulnerable (higher sensitivity, lower capacity to adapt) to climate change (Watson *et al.*, 1995; McCarthy *et al.*, 2001; Parry *et al.*, 2007), while historically they contributed relatively less to the problem. Adaptation in developing countries thus calls objectively for strong international support.

Following a widely accepted efficiency principle according to which a wider portfolio of options should be preferred to a narrower one, the integration of mitigation and adaptation should increase the cost-effectiveness of a policy aimed at facing climate change (Kane and Yohe, 2000; Parry *et al.*, 2001; Ingham *et al.*, 2005). This is particularly true in light of the overall uncertainty that still surrounds our understanding of climatic, environmental, and social-economic processes, which ultimately determines the uncertainty in the assessment of the costs and benefits of climate-change policy. In an uncertain framework, a precautionary policy would avoid the extremes of both total inaction and of drastic immediate mitigation. The optimal strategy would be a combination of mitigation and adaptation measures (Kane and Shogren, 2000; McKibbin and Wilcoxen, 2004). In other words, the decision-maker needs to place herself somewhere inside the decision space represented by the triangle of Figure 4.4.2. Vertexes are possible, but unlikely.

How should mitigation and adaptation be combined? This intuitively depends on their degree of substitutability or complementarity. Kane and Shogren (2000) analyze this issue in the context of the economic theory of endogenous risk. They demonstrate that when both adaptation and mitigation reduce the risk of adverse effects of climate change, they are used by agents until expected marginal benefits and costs are equated across strategies. Corner solutions (adaptation- or mitigation-only outcomes) are also discussed as theoretical possibilities. They could occur if, for instance, an international mitigation agreement failed to be signed, making agents aware of the practical ineffectiveness of (unilateral) mitigation action or if, conversely, the climate regime is so strict as to eliminate the necessity to adapt to any climate-change damage. The analysis of agents' response to increased climate-change risk is more complex. It depends on two effects: a direct effect of risk on the marginal productivity of a strategy and an indirect effect of risk which is determined by risk impacts on the other strategy and by the relationship between the two. The indirect effect amplifies (dampens) the direct effect if the marginal productivity of one strategy increases (decreases) and the two strategies are complements (substitutes) or if marginal productivity decreases (increases) and the strategies are substitutes (complements). Kane and Shogren (2000) suggest that the actual relationship

[9] Again, this is not necessarily so in the case of sequestration activities.

between adaptation and mitigation strategies is an empirical matter.

Buob and Stephan (2011) found similar results. They investigate the problem in a non-cooperative game theoretical setting showing that adaptation-only and mitigation-only equilibria are possible only when the two are perfect substitutes. The strategy that exhibits the lower discounted marginal costs will prevail. This reflects the fact that if there are two almost equally effective ways to improve a region's environmental quality, the decision to mitigate or to adapt in the end depends on their intertemporal cost-effectiveness. On the contrary, when the strategies are complements, an equilibrium in which all regions invest in mitigation and adaptation from the outset can exist.

In this vein, Antweiler (2011) stresses the role of the shape of mitigation and adaptation costs in driving the final outcome. If they are quasi-linear, mitigation-only and adaptation-only outcomes can be expected. Which of the two prevails depends straightforwardly on the mitigation–adaptation cost ratio. The higher it is the more likely adaptation will prevail, and vice versa. With quasi-quadratic costs, mixed strategic outcomes can be observed. An interesting point stressed by Antweiler (2011) is that, in the quasi-quadratic case, when the temperature (and, accordingly, damages) are increasing more rapidly, both mitigation and adaptation increase, but mitigation relatively more than adaptation. A final insight regards the role of country heterogeneity: a country with a high emission share is shown to have a higher mitigation–adaptation ratio than a country with a small emission share. As small emitters will tend to prefer adaptation over mitigation, which reduces the potential for the efficacy of mitigation, Antweiler (2011) concludes that coordination on mitigation policies is very unlikely.

Finally, Bréchet *et al.* (2010) builds on a Solow–Swan growth set-up endowing a central planner with the possibility to decide how much to invest in mitigation and adaptation. In their comparative static analysis, they show that the ratio between adaptation and mitigation crucially depends on the stage of development of the economy. In richer, developed, and more productive economic systems, it is worth investing in adaptation, whereas in developing, poorer, weakly efficient economies the opportunity cost of adaptation can be too high, thus inducing zero adaptation. Unlike adaptation, some level of mitigation is always optimal. The consequence is a bell-shaped behavior of the mitigation–adaptation ratio. Before a given development level is reached, no adaptation is undertaken and only mitigation takes place. With economic growth, adaptation increases to a maximum level, after which adaptation investment starts to decline. This is driven by the specific modeling of adaptation: it is a cumulative stock with declining marginal productivity. Therefore, when almost full protection is reached, the value of additional adaptation investment is very small and it becomes more efficient to invest in productive capital.

In the light of this, it is then crucial to assess the exact nature of the relationship between mitigation and adaptation. However, the literature on this topic, either that focusing on the general characteristics of mitigation and adaptation or that proposing specific case studies, does not seem to converge on a consistent characterization of the trade-off between the two climate policy measures.

According to Klein *et al.* (2003) complementarity can be invoked, as important synergies can be created between the two strategies when measures that control GHG concentration also reduce the adverse effects of climate change, or vice versa. In addition, there is the possibility that many adaptation measures implemented specifically in developing countries may also promote the sustainability of their development (see e.g. Dang *et al.*, 2003; Huq *et al.*, 2003).

Parry *et al.* (2001) highlight that mitigation delaying climate change impacts can buy more time to reduce vulnerability through adaptation (the converse is more controversial, see Klein *et al.*, 2007). Symmetrically, adaptation can raise thresholds which need to be avoided by mitigation (Yohe and Strzepek, 2007). Consequently there is an intuitive appeal to exploit and foster synergies by integrating mitigation and adaptation.

An excessive *emphasis on* synergies can present some risks as well (Dang *et al.*, 2003; Klein *et al.*, 2003, 2007; Tol, 2005). Adaptation measures could pose institutional or coordination difficulties, especially at the international level, and these may be transmitted to the implementation of mitigation measures if the two are conceived as tightly linked. Synergetic interventions can be less cost-effective than separate mitigation, adaptation, and especially (sustainable) development interventions.

There are finally trade-offs between mitigation and adaptation (Tol, 2005; Bosello 2010; de Bruin *et al.*, 2009a). Resources are scarce. If some of them are used for mitigation, fewer are available for adaptation, and vice versa. This point is clarified by Ingham *et al.*, (2007), who demonstrate that mitigation and adaptation are substitutes in economic terms, implying that if the cost of mitigation falls agents' optimal response would be to increase mitigation and decrease adaptation.

It is worth noting that substitutability is not in contradiction with the fact that mitigation and adaptation should be both used in climate-change policies. Substitutability justifies an integrated approach because either mitigation or adaptation alone cannot optimally deal with climate change (Watson *et al.*, 1995; Pielke, 1998). The point is that an increase in climate-related damage costs would increase both mitigation and adaptation efforts, which is the typical income effect with normal goods. Finally, as noted by Tol (2005), if adaptation is successful, a lower need to mitigate could be perceived.

The above considerations can also be of practical relevance for the analysis of international environmental negotiations. Even though the literature is still in its early stages, results show that the joint presence of mitigation and adaptation, depending on their assumed degree of substitutability, can indeed influence participation in an environmental climate agreement. Barrett (2010), for instance, demonstrates that if more adaptation implies less mitigation, adaptation can enlarge participation to a mitigation agreement in a non-cooperative game theoretical set-up. Enlargement occurs because adaptation decreases the need to mitigate, thus pushing the environmental-effectiveness and costs of the agreement closer to a non-cooperative effort.

Auerswald *et al.* (2011) show that in a leader–follower game, early-adaptation commitment from a group of countries can be used as credible signal of low engagement in mitigation. This would induce other countries to increase their abatement effort. Total abatement effort can then increase or decrease, depending on the shape of the respective reaction functions.

An interesting perspective encompassing both Barrett (2010) and Auerswald *et al.* (2011) is provided by Marrouch and Chauduri (2011). They show that, at given conditions, the presence of adaptation can enlarge the size of a mitigation coalition. Moreover, if the coalition acts as a Stackelberg leader, total emissions can decrease. The intuition behind this is as follows: unlike a no-adaptation case, if a country can also adapt it may respond with higher adaptation and lower abatement (thus higher emissions) to higher emissions from another country. On the one hand, this lowers the incentive to free-ride on a mitigation agreement and could enlarge participation. On the other hand, if the coalition acts as leader, it may be induced to lower its emissions to lower the emissions in non-participatory countries.

More pessimistic results can be found in Buob and Stephan (2008): in a non-cooperative setting, they show that in principle rich countries can fund adaptation in poor countries to foster their abatement effort as well as global mitigation when mitigation and adaptation are complements. Nonetheless, they also show that the additional abatement costs in developing countries are typically higher than the adaptation aids. Consequently, developing countries will not be willing to accept such an agreement.

Turning to more case-specific examples, Klein *et al.* (2007) discuss many circumstances in which mitigation and adaptation can complement (facilitate) or substitute (conflict with) each other. In general, each time adaptation implies an increased energy use from fossil sources, emissions will increase and mitigation become more costly. This is the case, for instance, of adaptation to changing hydrological regimes and water scarcity. This form of adaptation takes place through increasing reuse of wastewater and the associated treatment, deep-well pumping, and especially large-scale desalination. These adaptation measures increase energy use in the water sector, leading to increased emissions and mitigation costs (Boutkan and Stikker, 2004, quoted by Klein *et al.*, 2007). Another example is the case of indoor cooling, which is proposed as a typical adaptation in a warming world (Smith and Tirpak, 1989, quoted by Klein *et al.*, 2007).

However, there are also adaptation practices that decrease energy use and thus facilitate mitigation. For instance, the new design principles for commercial and residential buildings could simultaneously reduce vulnerability to extreme weather events and energy needs for heating and/or cooling. Carbon sequestration in agricultural soils also highlights a positive link from mitigation to adaptation. It creates an economic commodity for farmers (sequestered carbon) and it makes the land more valuable, by improving soil and water conservation. In this way, it enhances both the economic and environmental components of adaptive capacity (Butt and McCarl, 2004; Klein *et al.*, 2007).

There are finally ambiguous cases. For instance, avoided forest degradation implies in most cases an increased adaptive capacity of ecosystems through biodiversity preservation and climate benefits. However, if incentives to sequester carbon by afforestation and reforestation spur an overplantation of fast-growing alien species, biodiversity can be harmed (Caparrós and Jacquemont, 2003) and the natural system can become less adaptable.

These examples demonstrate the intricate interrelationships between mitigation and adaptation, and also the links with other environmental concerns, such as water resources and bio-diversity, with profound policy implications.

Adaptation strategies and macro-, policy-driven, integrated measures

Given the multi-faceted features of adaptation, and the difficulty of comparing the very different adaptation actions or even the same adaptation strategy in different locations, the choice of this subchapters is to aggregate adaptation responses into three main categories: anticipatory adaptation, reactive adaptation, and adaptation R&D.

Anticipatory adaptation implies building a stock of defensive capital that must be ready when the damage materializes. It is subject to economic inertia: investment in defensive capital translates into protection capital after some years. Hence, it needs to be undertaken before the damage occurs.

Reactive adaptation is represented by all those actions that need to be undertaken every period in response to those climate-change damages that cannot be or were not accommodated by anticipatory adaptation. They usually need to be constantly adjusted to changes in climatic conditions. Examples of these actions are energy expenditures for air conditioning or farmers' yearly changes in the seasonal crop mix.

Investing in R&D and knowledge can be seen as a peculiar form of anticipatory adaptation. Innovation activity in adaptation or simply knowledge adaptation is represented by all those R&D activities and investments that make adaptation responses more effective. These are especially important in sectors such as agriculture and health, where the discovery of new crops and vaccines is crucial to reduce vulnerability to climate change (Barrett, 2008).[10]

These three groups of adaptation measures will be contrasted one against the other and with mitigation in a CBA in both a non-cooperative and cooperative (first-best) setting. The analysis will be conducted with the AD-WITCH model (see Appendix I in Bosello *et al.*, 2010a for more information). AD-WITCH is a climate-economic, dynamic-optimization, IAM that can be solved under two alternative game theoretic scenarios:

- In a non-cooperative scenario, each of the twelve regions in which the world is disaggregated maximizes its own private welfare (defined as the PV of the logarithm of *per capita* consumption), taking other regions' choices as given. This yields a Nash equilibrium, which is also chosen as the baseline. In this context, externalities are not internalized.
- In a cooperative scenario, a social planner maximizes global welfare and takes into account the full social cost of climate change. In this

[10] To test the generality of results, Appendix III in Bosello *et al.* (2010a) proposes an alternative specification in which R&D contributes to build adaptive capacity that improves the effectiveness of all adaptation actions, be they proactive or reactive.

scenario, the first-best cooperative outcome in which all externalities are internalized can be achieved.

The climate-change damage function used by the AD-WITCH model includes a reduced-form relationship between temperature and gross world product which follows closely Nordhaus and Boyer (2000), in both the functional form and the parameter values. Higher losses are estimated in developing countries, in South Asia (including India) and SSA, especially because of higher damages in agriculture, from vector-borne diseases, and because of catastrophic climate impacts.

Damage estimates in agriculture, coastal settlements, and catastrophic climate impacts are significant in Western Europe, resulting in higher damages than in other developed regions. In China, Eastern EU countries, non-EU Eastern European countries (including Russia), and Japan–Korea, climate change up to 2.5°C would bring small benefits, essentially because of a reduction in energy demand for heating purposes (non-EU Eastern European countries including Russia) or positive effects on agricultural productivity (China).

Nonetheless recent evidence – an important contribution on this is the 2007 Stern Review (Stern, 2007), but also UNFCCC (2007) and the IPCC Fourth Assessment Report (Parry *et al.*, 2007) – suggests that climate-change damages may be higher than the values proposed in the RICE model by Nordhaus and Boyer (2000). Probably, the most important reason is that RICE, as well as AD-WITCH and many other IAMs, only partially captures non-market impacts, which are confined to the recreational value of leisure. Important climate-related impacts on bio-diversity and ecosystem losses or on cultural heritage are not part of the damage assessment.

Secondly the model abstracts from very rapid warming and large-scale changes of the climate system (system surprises). As a consequence, AD-WITCH yields climate-related impacts that, on average, are smaller than those described in studies like the 2007 Stern Review or the UNFCCC (2007) report, which do consider the possibility of abrupt climate changes.

Thirdly, the time horizon considered in this subchapters also plays a role. The longer it is, the larger the observed damages from climate change, as temperature is projected to keep an increasing trend. Like most IAMs, AD-WITCH considers the dynamics of economic and climatic variables up to 2150 while, for instance, the Stern Review reaches the year 2200.

Finally, the AD-WITCH model was partly based on out-of-date evidence, as many regional estimates contained in Nordhaus and Boyer (2000) are extrapolations from studies that have been carried out for one or two regions, typically the United States.

In order to account for new evidence on climate-related damages and economic impacts, the CBA of adaptation has been performed under two different specifications of the damage functions. The standard one, based on the assessments contained in Nordhaus and Boyer (2000), and a new one, characterized by a much higher damage from climate change, about twice the standard one. This new specification of the damage function yields values of damages larger than those contained in UNFCCC (2007) and closer to those in Stern (2007).

As suggested by Stern (2007), we have also assessed the BCRs of adaptation under two possible values of the pure rate of time preference. The standard one, again based on Nordhaus and Boyer (2000), is equal to 3 percent declining. The new one is much lower and equal to 0.1 percent, as in Stern (2007). Still the AD-WITCH model does not perform a risk assessment on threshold effects or on discontinuous low-probability, high-damage impacts, which go beyond the scope of this subchapter.[11]

Summing up, four cases will be considered when analyzing the costs and benefits of mitigation, adaptation and of different types of adaptation:

[11] However, it is likely that the general conclusions of the present subchapters would not change. What can change is the relative weight of mitigation and adaptation in the optimal policy mix. As adaptation to catastrophic events can only be partial, and given that the probability of their occurrence can be lowered only by reducing temperature increase, mitigation could become more appealing than adaptation when the occurrence of catastrophic events is accounted for.

1. **LDAM_HDR** : low damage–high discount rate. This is the baseline scenario with a discount rate set initially at 3 percent and then declining over time, as in WITCH, DICE, and RICE (see Nordhaus and Boyer, 2000).
2. **LDAM_LDR**: low damage–low discount rate. The damage is the same as in the baseline; the discount rate is 0.1 percent and then declining over time, as in Stern (2007).
3. **HDAM_LDR**: high damage–low discount rate. The damage is about twice the damage in the baseline; the discount rate is 0.1 percent and then declining over time, as Stern (2007).
4. **HDAM_HDR**: high damage–high discount rate. The damage is about twice the damage in the baseline; the discount rate is 3 percent and then declining over time, as in WITCH, DICE, and RICE.

Optimal integrated climate-change strategy in a non-cooperative setting

The main strategic difference between the mitigation and adaptation responses to global warming can be summarized as follows. Mitigation provides a public good that can be enjoyed globally, while adaptation provides private or club goods. Mitigation is thus affected by the well-known free-riding curse, while this is much less of an issue for adaptation.

In the absence of climate change international cooperation, climate-change policies at the regional level are chosen to equalize marginal private benefits and marginal private costs, without internalizing negative externalities imposed globally. Because of the free-riding incentive, little mitigation effort is thus undertaken.

In the absence of any policy the total climate-change damage (residual damages + adaptation expenditure) amounts to an annual average of US$584 billion already in 2035, and increases exponentially over time. Adaptation reduces substantively residual damages (see Figure 4.4.3), up to 55 percent in 2100. Adaptation starts slowly. Consistently with the AD-WITCH damage function, damages from climate change are indeed low in the first two decades. Hence, adaptation, typically addressing current and near-term damages, is only marginally needed. This applies also to anticipatory adaptation. Economic inertia in the model is about five years. As a consequence, adaptation investments do not need to start too far in advance. When considering higher damages and higher preferences for the future (the high-damage–low-discount rate case), adaptation starts earlier – already in 2020 US$60 billion are allocated to the reduction of damage. Hence, total damage reduction increases – it amounts to more than 70 percent in 2100 (see Figure 4.4.4).

The BCRs of adaptation, measured as the discounted sum of avoided damages over the discounted sum of total adaptation expenditures, are reported in Table 4.4.2. On a sufficiently long-term perspective, they are larger than 1. Had we chosen a longer time period they could have been even higher, as in the model benefits increase more than costs, due to the stronger convexity of the damage function with respect to the adaptation cost function.[12]

Table 4.4.2 also shows that adaptation BCRs increase more when climate damage increases than when the discount rate decreases. When damages become more relevant all along the simulation period and not only at its later stages, adaptation becomes relatively more useful.

Our results confirm the theoretical insight[13] that, in a non-cooperative setting, adaptation is the main climate policy tool. Mitigation is negligible at the non-cooperative equilibrium. As a consequence, adaptation investments are high and increasing over time. Most importantly, the BCR is larger than 1. Higher emissions in the presence of adaptation, and the relatively higher sensitivity of adaptation to the level of climate damages, already highlight the potential strategic complementarity between mitigation and adaptation. This issue will be addressed more deeply in the following sections.

[12] This result is driven by our model assumptions, which are anchored on calibration data.

[13] There is an extensive literature on international environmental agreements showing that the non-cooperative abatement level is negligible at the equilibrium. Therefore, adaptation remains the only option to reduce climate damages.

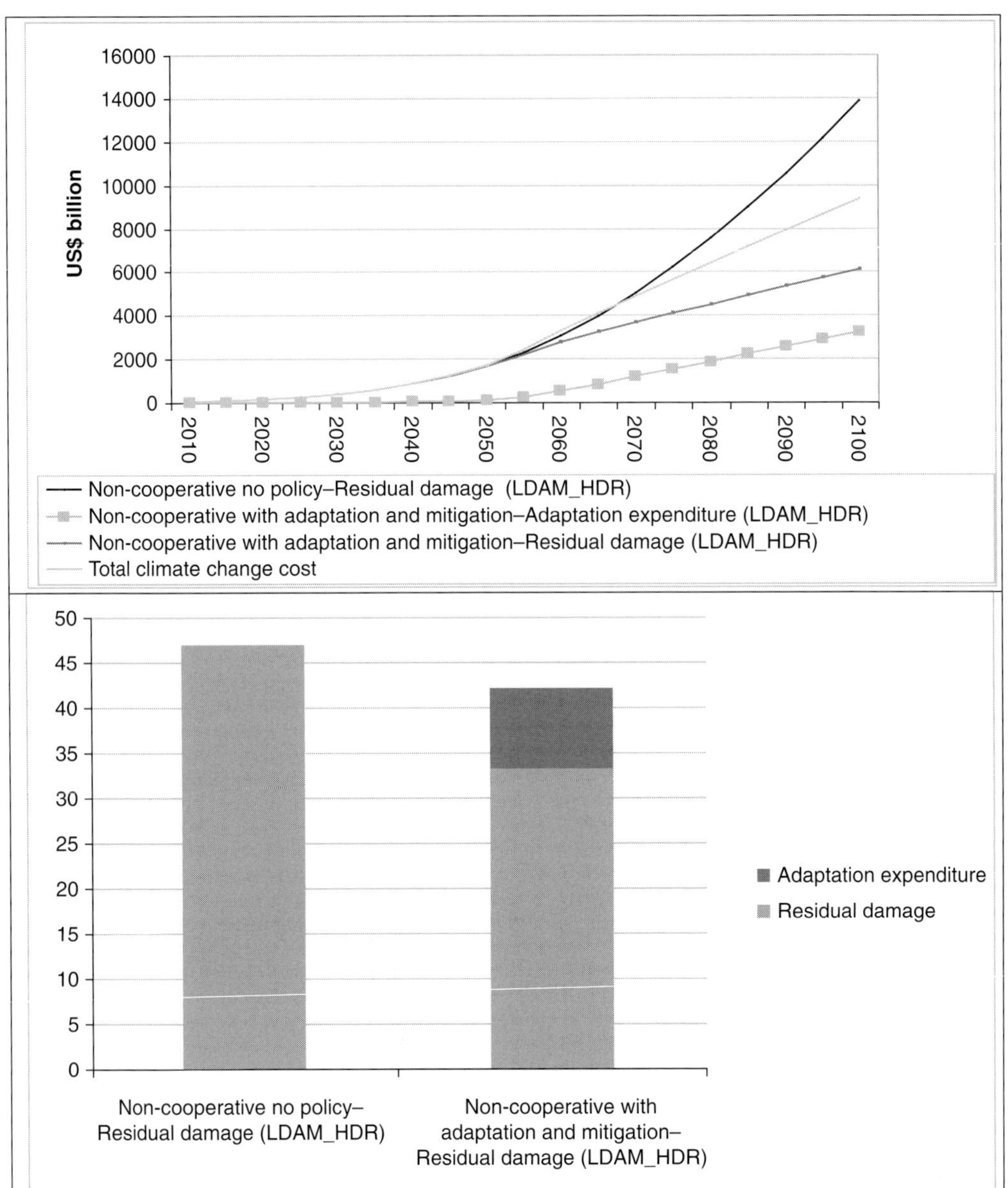

Figure 4.4.3 *Residual damage and adaptation expenditure in the non-cooperative scenario: LDAM_HDR. On the lower panel, discounted values are at a 3 percent discount rate, US$ 2005 trillion*

An optimal integrated climate-change strategy in a cooperative scenario

In a cooperative scenario, all externalities originated by emissions are internalized. Accordingly, emission abatement (mitigation) is considerably higher than in the non-cooperative scenario. Adaptation is still undertaken, but slightly less than in the non-cooperative case. Higher cooperative mitigation efforts reduce the need to adapt with respect to the non-cooperative scenario (Figure 4.4.5). At the same time, adaptation reduces the need to

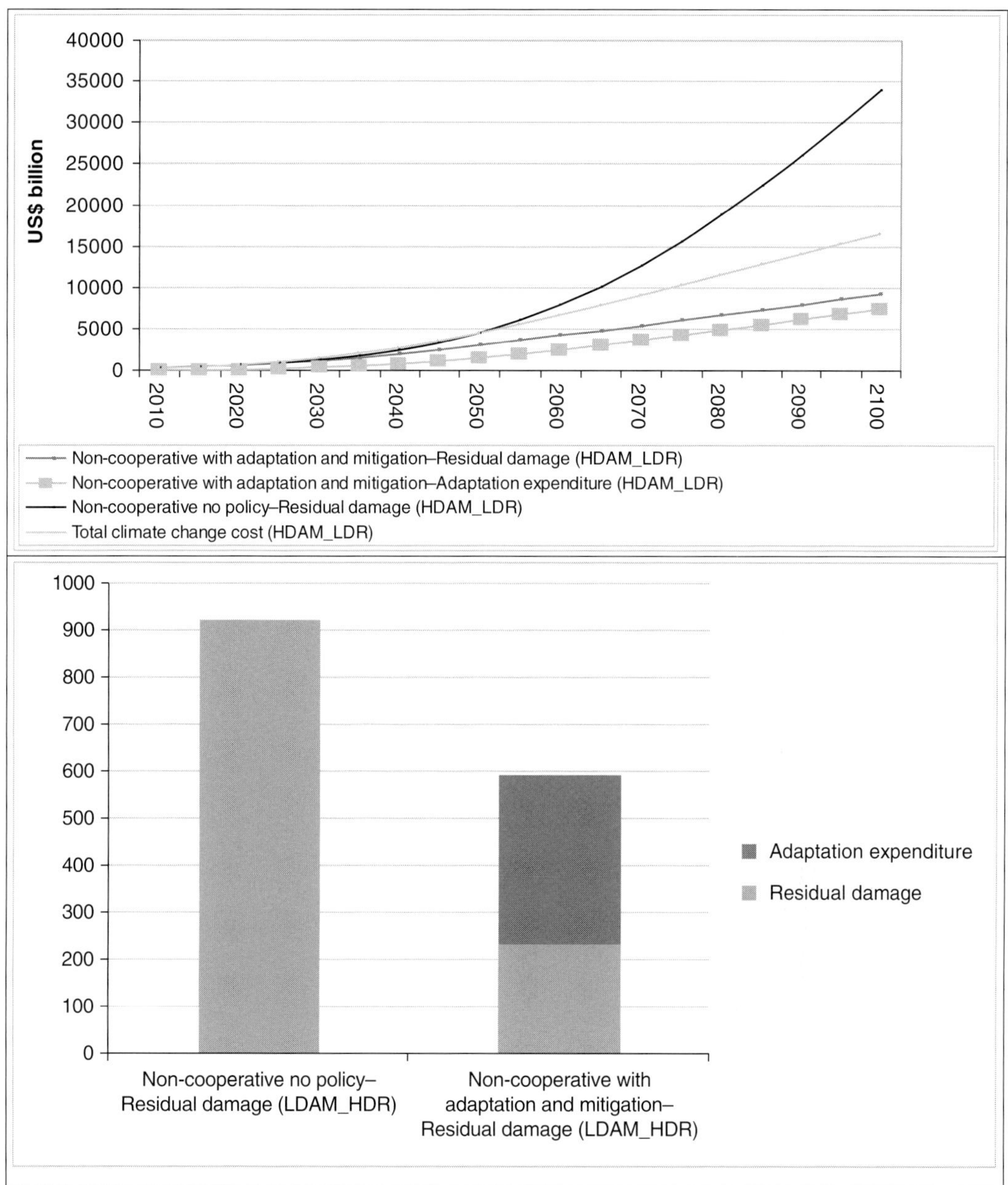

Figure 4.4.4 *Residual damage and adaptation expenditure in the non-cooperative scenario: HDAM_LDR. On the right panel, discounted values are at a 0.1 percent discount rate, US$ 2005 trillion*

mitigate, i.e. cooperative emissions in the presence of adaptation are higher (Figure 4.4.6).

Table 4.4.3 highlights another important difference between mitigation and adaptation: their timing. Mitigation starts well in advance with respect to adaptation. Abatement is substantial when adaptation expenditure is still low. Mitigation needs to be implemented earlier than adaptation; it works through carbon cycle inertia. Accordingly action needs to start soon to grasp some benefits in

Table 4.4.2 BCRs of adaptation in four scenarios (non-cooperative scenario with adaptation and mitigation)

Trillion US$ 2005 Discounted values over 2010–2105	LDAM_HDR	HDAM_HDR	LDAM_LDR	HDAM_LDR
Benefits[a]	16	62	227	695
Costs[b]	10	25	134	270
BCR	1.67	2.41	1.69	2.57

Notes:

[a] Benefits are measured as total discounted avoided damages compared to the non-cooperative no-policy case.

[b] Costs are measured as total discounted expenditures on adaptation. Values are discounted using a 3 percent discount rate in the LDAM_HDR and HDAM_HDR cases and 0.1 percent discount rate in the LDAM_LDR and HDAM_LDR cases.

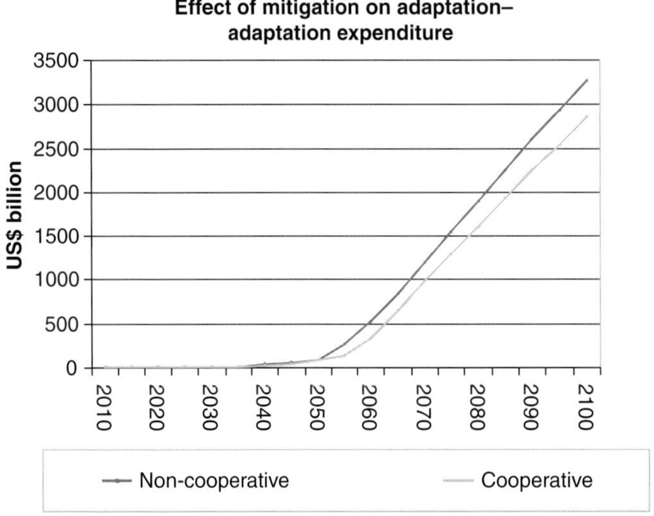

Figure 4.4.5 *Optimal adaptation in a cooperative scenario*

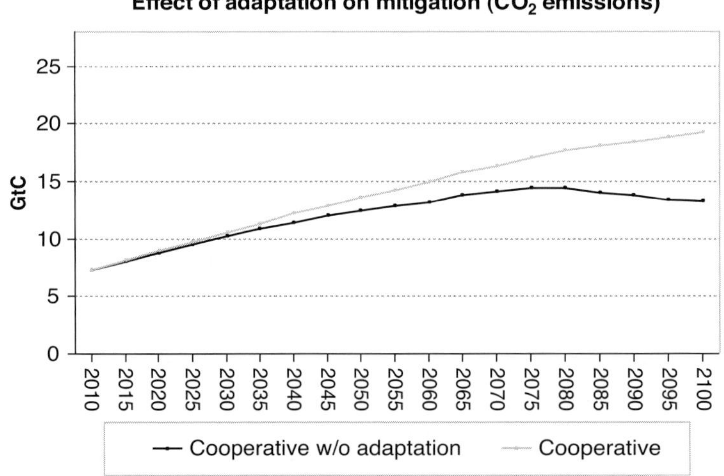

Figure 4.4.6 *CO_2 emissions*

Table 4.4.3 Timing of adaptation and mitigation in a cooperative scenario, 2035–2100

	2035	2050	2100
Adaptation (Total protection costs – billion US$ 2005)	2	78	2838
Mitigation (emission % wrt BAU)	−18.8%	−18.7%	−15.1%

Note:
wrt = with respect to.

Table 4.4.4 BCR of adaptation and of joint adaptation and mitigation

Discounted values over 2010–2105	BCR adaptation		BCR joint adaptation and mitigation
	Non-cooperative	Cooperative	Cooperative
Benefits[a]	16	14	19
Costs[b]	10	8	9
BCR	1.67	1.73	2.11

Notes:
[a] Benefits are measured as discounted avoided damages compared to the non-cooperative no-policy case.
[b] Adaptation costs are measured as discounted expenditures on adaptation.
Mitigation costs are measured as additional investments in carbon-free technologies and energy efficiency compared to the non-cooperative no-policy case.

the future. By contrast, adaptation measures work through the much shorter economic inertia, and can thus be implemented when relevant damages occur, which is from the third decade of the century.

Table 4.4.4 shows the BCR of adaptation in the non-cooperative and in the cooperative scenarios. The BCR of adaptation improves when it is optimally complemented by mitigation.[14] This is another way of expressing the rule that two instruments are better than one instrument at the first best, i.e. (net) welfare can be enhanced by increasing the degrees of freedom of the policy-maker. When combined, both mitigation and adaptation can better be used than in isolation, i.e. with a higher BCR.

The sensitivity analysis reported in Table 4.4.5 highlights the fact that adaptation becomes more profitable when climate-related damages increase. Indeed, compared to mitigation, which reduces mainly future damages, adaptation is more rapidly effective in contrasting future and present damages. Accordingly, in a high-damage world (but without climate catastrophes), adaptation becomes the preferred strategy and this is reflected in an increasing BCR. When the discount rate declines, the opposite occurs: future damages become more relevant; mitigation is thus preferred; the BCR of adaptation declines. With low discounting, a larger share of damage reduction is achieved with mitigation. Similar results hold also when adaptation and mitigation are implemented jointly.

Summing up, mitigation and adaptation are strategic complements. Therefore, they should be integrated in a welfare-maximizing climate policy. It is worth stressing again that the possibility to mitigate (adapt) reduces, but does not eliminate, the need to adapt (mitigate). The optimal climate policy mix is composed by both mitigation and adaptation measures. The BCR of a policy mix where mitigation and adaptation are optimally integrated is larger than the one in which mitigation and adaptation are implemented alone.

Unraveling the optimal adaptation strategy mix

The analysis performed so far does not disentangle the role of different adaptation strategies. This is the aim of this section. Let us consider first the relationship between proactive (anticipatory) and reactive adaptation. As shown by Table 4.4.6, the non-cooperative and the cooperative scenarios highlight the same qualitative behavior: not surprisingly anticipatory adaptation is undertaken in advance with respect to reactive adaptation.

Consequently, until 2085 the bulk of adaptation expenditure is devoted to anticipatory measures; reactive adaptation becomes the major budget item afterwards. This is the optimal response to climate-damage dynamics. When it is sufficiently low, it is worth preparing to face future damages. When eventually it becomes high and increasing, a larger amount of resources will need to be invested in

[14] This also happens to mitigation, not shown.

Table 4.4.5 Sensitivity analysis: BCR of adaptation and of joint adaptation and mitigation in a cooperative scenario

Discounted values over 2010–2105[a]	LDAM_HDR	HDAM_HDR	LDAM_LDR	HDAM_LDR
Adaptation				
Benefits	14	55	99	337
Costs	8	21	65	144
BCR	1.73	2.63	1.52	2.33
Joint adaptation and mitigation				
Benefits	19	67	294	811
Costs	10	24	266	347
BCR	1.93	2.82	1.10	2.34

Note:
[a] Values are discounted using a 3 percent discount rate in the LDAM_HDR and HDAM_HDR cases and a 0.1 percent discount rate in the LDAM_LDR and HDAM_LDR cases.

Table 4.4.6 Expenditure composition of the adaptation mix

	Non-cooperative setting (%)	Cooperative setting (%)
2035		
Reactive adaptation	0.2	0.6
Anticipatory adaptation	99.6	99.1
Knowledge adaptation	0.2	0.2
2050		
Reactive adaptation	19.5	17.2
Anticipatory adaptation	80.3	82.6
Knowledge adaptation	0.2	0.2
2100		
Reactive adaptation	56.8	55.8
Anticipatory adaptation	42.7	43.8
Knowledge adaptation	0.5	0.5

reactive interventions, coping with what cannot be accommodated *ex ante*.

Notice that investments in adaptation R&D show a behavior similar to anticipatory adaptation, but the scale of dedicated resources is much smaller. This result depends on the calibration data: we relied on quantitative estimates provided by UNFCCC (2007) on the aggregate amount of money that could be spent on R&D in agriculture, which is estimated to be around US$7 billion in 2060, a very tiny amount compared to world GDP.[15]

The results shown in Table 4.4.6 are based on the full availability of resources and political consensus to implement the optimal policy mix. What happens when first-best options are not available? In other words, what kind of adaptation strategy should a decision-maker prefer were she forced to make a choice between different adaptation measures because of resource scarcity? The answer to this question is summarized by Table 4.4.7. It reports the BCR when either one of the three options is forgone.

If just only one adaptation strategy were to be chosen, reactive adaptation should be privileged. Indeed, the non-implementation of reactive adaptation would induce a worsening of the BCR of the whole climate-change strategy by 41 percent (and by 45 percent in welfare terms). By contrast, the impossibility of using anticipatory adaptation

[15] UNFCCC (2007) provides estimates for 2030. We scale this number up proportionally to the temperature gap between 2030 and our reference 2.5°C, which is our calibration point.

Table 4.4.7 BCR of the adaptation strategy mix in a cooperative scenario

Option excluded from the optimal mix			
Discounted values over 2010–2105	Reactive adaptation	Anticipatory Adaptation	Knowledge Adaptation
Benefits	789	7.4	13657
Costs	771	5.7	7938
BCR	1.02	1.30	1.72

would decrease the BCR by 24 percent (33 percent in welfare terms).

R&D adaptation appears to be the less crucial adaptation option, but this depends on the way it is modeled. R&D adaptation improves the productivity of reactive adaptation. Hence, its elimination does not impair excessively reactive adaptation itself. Appendix III in Bosello *et al.* (2010a) illustrates an alternative formulation in which R&D augments the productivity of both proactive and reactive adaptation and in which the adaptation R&D investments are therefore much larger. Nonetheless, all other conclusions are robust to changes in the model specification as described in Appendix III.

Regional analysis

In order to provide insights on regional specificities, this section disaggregates the above results between developed and developing countries. Even this broad disaggregation is sufficient to highlight substantial differences.

Not surprisingly, non-OECD countries spend a higher share of their GDP on adaptation than OECD countries. This is driven by their higher damages – by the end of the century, also in absolute terms, optimal adaptation expenditure is nearly 5 times higher in non-OECD than in OECD countries – and by their lower GDP.

It is also worth noting the different composition and timing of the optimal adaptation mix between the two regions. Non-OECD countries rely mainly on reactive measures, which in 2100 contribute to 65 percent of their total adaptation expenditure, whereas OECD countries focus on anticipatory measures, which constitute 85 percent of their total expenditure on adaptation. As for the timing, adaptation in non-OECD is undertaken much earlier than in OECD regions.

The different composition of adaptation responses depends upon two facts:[16] firstly, the regional characteristics of climate vulnerability. In OECD countries, the higher share of climate-change damages originates from loss of infrastructures and coastal areas, whose protection requires a form of adaptation that is largely anticipatory. In non-OECD countries, a higher share of damages originates from agriculture, health, and the energy sectors (space heating and cooling). These damages can be accommodated more effectively through reactive measures.

Secondly, OECD countries are richer. Thus, they can give up relatively more easily their present consumption to invest in adaptation measures that will become productive in the future. By contrast, non-OECD countries are compelled by resource scarcity to act in an emergency.

Only the expenditure on adaptation R&D is higher in OECD countries than in non-OECD countries. Data on R&D and innovation aimed at improving the effectiveness of adaptation are very scarce. Starting from UNFCCC (2007), we decided to distribute adaptation R&D to different regions on the basis of current expenditure on total R&D, which is concentrated in OECD countries. This explains why adaptation R&D investments in developing countries in 2100 are roughly 1/10 and 1/5 of that of developed regions – as a share of their GDP and in absolute terms, respectively.

Tables 4.4.8 and 4.4.9 show the BCR of adaptation, and of mitigation and adaptation jointly. In non-OECD countries, the combination of the two strategies always shows a higher BCR than adaptation alone (Table 4.4.9). By contrast, in OECD regions (Table 4.4.8) this remains true only with a high discount rate. With a lower discounting, mitigation increases its weight in the policy mix. The additional effort undertaken by OECD countries, which is the group of countries investing more in low-carbon technologies, benefits mostly

[16] More on the calibration procedure can be found in Appendix I of Bosello *et al.* (2010a) and in another Annex available upon request.

Table 4.4.8 Sensitivity analysis: BCR of adaptation and of joint adaptation and mitigation in a cooperative scenario – OECD regions

Discounted values over 2010–2105[a]	LDAM_HDR	HDAM_HDR	LDAM_LDR	HDAM_LDR
Adaptation				
Benefits	2.2	16	14	93
Costs	1.5	5.9	12	39
BCR	1.45	2.64	1.12	2.38
Joint adaptation and mitigation				
Benefits	4.2	21	68	238
Costs	1.8	6.6	146	164
BCR	2.23	3.17	0.46	1.45

Note:
[a] Values are discounted using a 3 percent discount rate in the LDAM_HDR and HDAM_HDR cases and a 0.1 percent discount rate in the LDAM_LDR and HDAM_LDR cases.

Table 4.4.9 Sensitivity analysis: BCR of adaptation and of joint adaptation and mitigation in a cooperative scenario – non-OECD regions

Discounted values over 2010–2105[a]	LDAM_HDR	HDAM_HDR	LDAM_LDR	HDAM_LDR
Adaptation				
Benefits	11	40	86	243
Costs	6	15	53	105
BCR	1.79	2.63	1.61	2.31
Joint adaptation and mitigation				
Benefits	15	46	226	573
Costs	6.9	16	128	183
BCR	2.11	2.85	1.77	3.13

Note:
[a] Values are discounted using a 3 percent discount rate in the LDAM_HDR and HDAM_HDR cases and a 0.1 percent discount rate in the LDAM_LDR and HDAM_LDR cases.

non-OECD regions. In other words, in a cooperative setting OECD countries are called to abate partly on behalf of non-OECD countries. For example, consider the low-damage–low-discount case (LDAM_LDR). Global benefits of joint mitigation and adaptation amount to US$294 trillion (see Table 4.4.5); 75 percent of these benefits occur in non-OECD countries, for a total benefit of US$226 trillion, whereas OECD countries receive the remaining 25 percent (US$68 trillion), though they bear slightly higher costs.

Again, what happens if first-best options are not fully available? If just only one adaptation strategy were to be chosen, anticipatory adaptation should be privileged by OECD countries, whereas non-OECD countries should prioritize expenditure on reactive adaptation (see Table 4.4.10).

Indeed, the elimination of anticipatory adaptation from the adaptation option basket of OECD countries induces a worsening of the BCR of the whole climate-change strategy equal to 72 percent. The impossibility of using reactive adaptation in

Table 4.4.10 Marginal contribution of specific policy-driven strategies

	WORLD (%)	OECD (%)	Non-OECD (%)
Reactive adaptation	–41	–29	–48
Anticipatory adaptation	–24	–72	–24
Knowledge adaptation	–0.36	–2	–0.1

non-OECD countries reduces the overall BCR by 48 percent (Table 4.4.10).

The difference between developing and developed regions is notable. Forgoing reactive adaptation is much more damaging for developing than for developed countries, consistently with what has been observed about the regional structure of damages and adaptation expenditure, whereas the opposite holds for anticipatory adaptation. Again, R&D adaptation appears to be the adaptation option one can give up less regretfully.

These results, although driven by our model specification and calibration, contain three preliminary policy implications:

- OECD countries invest heavily in anticipatory adaptation measures. This depends on their damage structure. Planned anticipatory adaptation is particularly suited to cope with sea-level rise, but also with hydro geological risks induced by more frequent and intense extreme events, which are a major source of negative impacts in the developed economies. Thus, it is more convenient to act *ex ante* rather than *ex post* in OECD countries.
- In non-OECD countries, climate-change adaptation needs are presently relatively low, but will rise dramatically after the mid century, as long as climate-change damages increase. In 2050, they could amount to US$ 78 billion, in 2065 they will be above US$ 500 billion to peak to more than US$ 2 trillion by the end of the century. It is sufficient to recall that in 2007 total overseas development aid (ODA) was slightly above US$ 100 billion to understand by how much climate change can stress adaptive capacity in the developing world. Non-OECD countries are unlikely to have the resources to meet their adaptation needs, which calls for international aid and cooperation on adaptation to climate change.
- At the equilibrium, non-OECD countries place little effort on adaptation R&D and rely primarily on reactive adaptation. This outcome, however, depends on the particular structure of non-OECD economic systems. Being poor, other forms of adaptation expenditures, more rapidly effective, mainly of the reactive type, are to be preferred. This suggests that richer countries can also help developing countries by supporting their adaptation R&D (e.g. by technology transfers) and their adaptation planning.

A comparison with the existing modeling literature

The modeling literature that analyzes the optimal investments in adaptation, their time profile, and the trade-off between mitigation and adaptation is rapidly increasing, but is still in its infancy and is for the larger part confined to the gray area (see Agrawala *et al.*, 2011a for a review).

Such literature started with the pioneering PAGE model (Hope *et al.*, 1993, then updated in Hope 2006) where adaptive policies operate in three ways: they increase the slope of the tolerable temperature profile, increase its plateau, and finally decrease the adverse impact of climate change when the temperature eventually exceeds the tolerable threshold. The default adaptation strategy has a cost in the EU of US$3, 12, and 25 billion p.a. (minimum, mode, and maximum respectively) to achieve an increase of 1°C of temperature tolerability and of an additional US$0.4, 1.6, 3.2 billion p.a. to achieve a 1 percent reduction in climate-change impacts. At the world level, this implies, at a discount rate of 3 percent declining, a cost of nearly US$3 trillion to achieve a damage reduction of roughly US$35 trillion within the period 2000–2200. Impact reduction ranges from 90 percent in the OECD to 50 percent elsewhere.

With the given assumptions, the PAGE model could easily justify aggressive adaptation policies (see e.g. Hope *et al.*, 1993), implicitly decreasing the appeal of mitigation. However, in all its versions the PAGE model treats adaptation as exogenous or a scenario variable decided at the outset. As a consequence, the model cannot endogenously determine the optimal characteristics of a mitigation and adaptation policy portfolio.

Adaptation is treated as an explicit control variable by a more recently developed group of models – FEEM-RICE (Bosello, 2010), AD-DICE (De Bruin *et al.*, 2009a; Agrawala *et al.*, 2011b), AD-RICE (De Bruin *et al.*, 2009b; Agrawala *et al.*, 2011b), AD-FAIR (Hof *et al.*, 2009, 2010), Ada-BaHaMa (Bahn *et al.*, 2010).

All these models build on the economic core offered by the RICE–DICE model family (Nordhaus, 1994; Nordhaus and Boyer, 2000), where a single world or multiple regional social planners choose between current consumption, investment in productive capital, and emissions reduction balancing a climatic-damage component. This is represented by global or regional damage functions that depend on the temperature increase compared to 1900 levels.

In De Bruin *et al.* (2009a) adaptation is a flow variable: it needs to be adjusted period by period, but also, once adopted in one period, it does not affect damages in the next. The authors show that mitigation and adaptation are strategic complements: optimal policy consists of a mix of adaptation measures and investments in mitigation. Adaptation is the main climate-change cost-reducer until 2100, whereas mitigation prevails afterwards. In addition, it is shown that benefits of adaptation are higher than those of mitigation until 2130.

The authors highlight the trade-off between the two strategies: the introduction of mitigation decreases the need to adapt, and vice versa. However, the second effect is notably stronger than the first. Indeed, mitigation only slightly lowers climate-related damages, especially in the short–medium term. Therefore, it does little to decrease the need to adapt, particularly during the first decades.

Sensitivity over the discount rate highlights the fact that mitigation becomes relatively more preferable as the discount rate becomes lower. Intuitively, mitigation reduces long-term climatic damages: thus, it becomes the preferred policy instrument as these damages become more relevant.

All these results are consolidated in De Bruin *et al.* (2009b), which repeats the analysis with an updated calibration of adaptation costs and benefits and also proposes regional results. They show that in terms of utility for a low level of damages that adapting-only is preferable than mitigating-only. However, the relationship is reversed when climate damages increase.

Stock adaptation is introduced by Bosello (2010) in the FEEM-RICE model (Buonanno *et al.*, 2000), a modified version of Nordhaus' with RICE model endogenous technical progress, and by Bahn *et al.* (2010) in a DICE-type model which distinguishes a fossil fuel-based and a carbon-free sector. Modeling adaptation as a stock of defensive capital cumulating in a periodical protection investment instead of a flow has two main consequences. Both studies show that mitigation should be optimally implemented in early periods, whereas adaptation should be postponed to later stages. Accordingly – and this is the first key qualitative difference with studies modeling adaptation as a flow – the main damage-reducer is mitigation and not adaptation, at least in the first decades. Secondly, while "stock-and-flow" approaches agree that a lower discount rate tends to favor mitigation, when adaptation is a stock, both mitigation and adaptation increase, but mitigation is used more intensively in relative terms; when adaptation is only a flow expenditure, it is substituted by mitigation. Other findings are robust across the two approaches, especially the trade-off between the two strategies. Bahn *et al.* (2010) also demonstrate that a particularly effective adaptation, by shielding the economy from climate-change damages, can delay the transition towards a cleaner economy, leading to very high GHG concentrations at the end of the century.

All these papers adopt a cost-benefit perspective: they aim at determining the first-best balance between mitigation and adaptation, given the respective costs and benefits. Three studies – Hof *et al.* (2009, 2010), Agrawala *et al.* (2011a), and

Bosello *et al.* (2011) – propose instead a cost-effectiveness approach: having set a mitigation policy target, they investigate the optimal adaptation effort and its feedback on the mitigation policy. In Hof *et al.* (2009) mitigation lowers baseline adaptation costs in 2100 from 1 percent to 0.4 percent in the case of a 3°C target, and to approximately 0.1 percent in the case of a 2°C target.

In Agrawala *et al.* (2011a) and Bosello *et al.* (2011) mitigation to stabilize CO_2 concentration at 550 ppm lowers the need to adapt and crowds out adaptation expenditure. The crowding out is particularly prominent after the mid century, when it reaches about 50 percent. Nonetheless, adaptation remains substantial and it still exceeds US$1 trillion in 2100. Interestingly, unlike Hof *et al.* (2009), adaptation slightly increases mitigation costs. Indeed, the possibility to adapt increases the amount of damage that can be endured, and thus the level of tolerable emissions. Therefore, reaching the GHG concentrations target requires a slightly higher abatement effort. According to both studies, adaptation efforts remain far from negligible anyway, and particularly so in developing countries.

In Hof *et al.* (2010), the cost-effectiveness analysis of the 2°C and 3°C targets is enriched by the regional picture and by the implications of different allocation schemes for emission rights. The study flags the high distributional implications triggered by both the stringency of the policies and the allocation rules. In terms of total discounted climate-change costs, the 3°C policy costs half the 2°C policy (1 percent versus 2 percent of global GDP). The lower residual damages and adaptation costs are more than compensated by the higher mitigation costs. Nonetheless at the regional level a 2°C policy implies lower costs for Western Africa and South Asia, with the policy burden sustained by all the other regions. It is also shown that the differences between the regimes are considerable in the short–medium term, but they all move in the same direction in the long term. A contraction and convergence regime would provide the higher benefits for the poorer regions in the short term, but the highest in the long term. A multi-stage approach creates exactly the opposite. Finally, and in accordance with our results, with both policies, but especially with the 3°C one, adaptation costs are higher in the developing countries and concentrated in the second half of the century. Therefore, financing adaptation in developing countries will become a more and more pressing issue over time.

In their critical review of modeling climate-change adaptation, Fisher-Vanden *et al.* (2011) identify five characteristics that an ideal IAM of adaptation should possess:

(1) It should combine regional and sectoral resolution for impacts and adaptation strategies.
(2) It should represent the different types of adaptation – market-driven adjustments, proactive, and reactive adaptation.
(3) It should allow for intertemporal decision-making under uncertainty.
(4) It should account for induced innovation in adaptation-related technologies; and
(5) It should be connect with empirical work on impacts and adaptation.

The model used for the present analysis includes all the characteristics just mentioned. What is missing is an explicit treatment of uncertainty with a probabilistic representation of different states of the world. This would make intertemporal optimization computationally difficult and would require some new techniques to keep the problem tractable.

Finally, the quantitative results of the modeling exercise proposed in this subchapter crucially hinge on the empirical estimates of climate-change impacts and adaptation costs. Two types of issues arise. First, there can be a lack of sound empirical evidence. This is the main obstacle in modeling adaptation knowledge and R&D. The lack of empirical studies restricts our ability to calibrate changes in adaptation technology. Second, although some empirical evidence does exist, the linkage between bottom-up, impact-specific studies and the top-down framework adopted in this subchapter is not always straightforward. Judgments and assumptions are needed in order to translate the empirical information and data into calibrated impacts and adaptation cost curves.

Assessing the role of market-driven adaptation

The analysis conducted so far abstracted from any role potentially played by market-driven adaptation. In other words, either the economic impact assessment or the design of the optimal mix between mitigation and adaptation strategies are based on damage functions not accounting for behavioral changes induced by market or welfare changes in human systems.

Modeling and then quantifying market-driven adaptation is extremely challenging. In economic terms, this means representing supply and demand reactions to scarcity signals conveyed by prices and triggered by climate-related impacts. Even assuming a satisfactory knowledge of these impacts, this requires assessing substitution elasticities in consumers' preferences and transformation elasticities in production functions for all goods and services. Most studies use applied or CGE models (see, for example, Darwin and Tol, 2001; Deke *et al.*, 2001; Bosello *et al.*, 2006; Aaheim *et al.*, 2010; Ciscar *et al.*, 2012).

Initially, CGE models were developed mainly to analyze international trade policies and, partially, public sector economic issues (e.g. fiscal policies). Soon, because of their great flexibility, they became a common tool for economists to investigate the consequences of the most diverse economic perturbations, including those provoked by climate change. Indeed, notwithstanding their complexity, as long as climate-related physical impacts can be translated into a change in productivity, production, or demand for the different inputs and outputs of the model, their GDP implications can be determined by a CGE model.[17]

In this study, the ICES model replicates more or less the same geographical disaggregation as the WITCH and AD-WITCH models. Our main results can be summarized as follows. Socio-economic systems share a great potential to adapt to climate change. Figure 4.4.7 shows the difference between the direct cost of climate-change impacts (all jointly considered) and the final impact on regional GDP after sectoral and international adjustments have taken place. Resource re-allocation smooths initial direct costs in some cases turning them into gains. Nevertheless, it is worth highlighting that in some regions (SASIA, EASIA and CHINA) the final costs are very close to the direct costs and in China they are *higher*. This means that some market-adjustment mechanisms, primarily international capital flows and terms-of-trade effect, can exacerbate initial impacts.[18]

Interactions among impacts are also relevant. In general, the costs of impacts together are higher than the sum of the cost associated with each single impact. This also provides an important justification for performing a joint-impact analysis instead of collecting the results provided by a set of single-impact studies.

Finally, climate-change impacts at the world level induce costs, even when market-driven adaptation is accounted for. Impacts and adaptive capacity are highly differentiated, though – i.e. a relatively small loss at the world level may hide large regional losses. In particular, developing countries remain the most vulnerable to climate change especially because of the adverse impacts on the agricultural sector and food production.

Let us underline that these results have been computed only for a subset of potential adverse effects of climate change (possible consequences of increased intensity and frequency of extreme

[17] In principle, the CGE models also offer the possibility to measure welfare changes captured by changes in indicators other than GDP, like the Hicksian equivalent variation or consumers' surplus from a pre- to a post-perturbation state. However, great care should be placed on their interpretation. Here it is sufficient to mention that CGE models only partially capture changes in stock values (like property), and that they usually miss non-market aspects to understand the important limitation of these assessments. Nevertheless a CGE approach has the merit of depicting explicitly resource relocation, a crucial aspect of which is international trade, which is not captured by traditional direct-costing methodologies.

[18] In principle, some adverse market effects could be controlled by a clairvoyant decision-maker. Some restrictions could, for instance, be imposed on trade or international capital movement to offset negative terms-of-trade effects. In practice, this is extremely difficult: on the one hand, these controls are hardly accepted by the international community, on the other, and most importantly, this would require us to isolate the climate-change influence on world trade, by country and commodity, which is an almost impossible task.

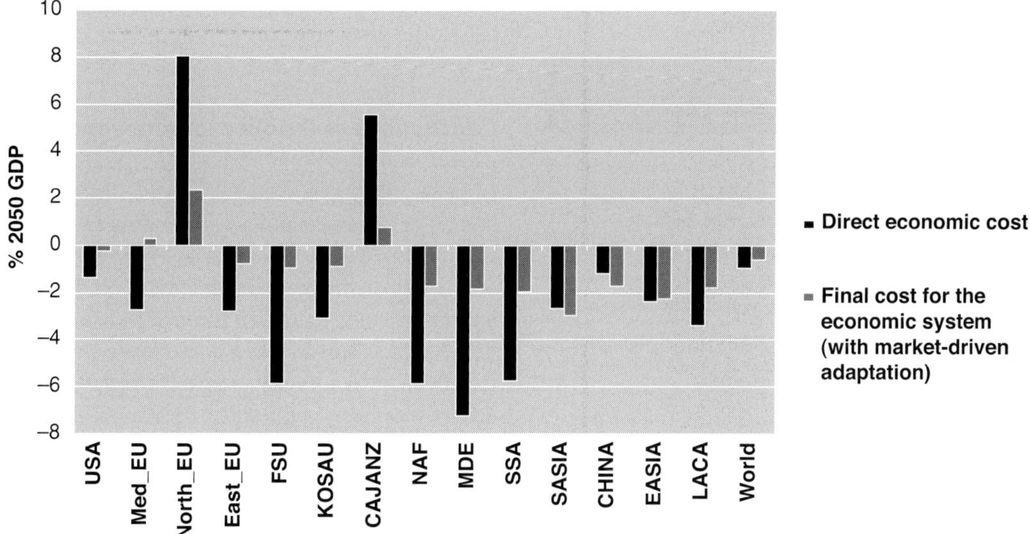

Figure 4.4.7 *Direct versus final climate-change costs as percentage of regional GDP (in 2050 for a temperature increase of 3°C wrt 2000)*

weather events and of bio-diversity losses, for instance, are not included). Irreversibilities or abrupt climate and catastrophic changes to which adaptation can be only limited are neglected. Then, the model assumes costless adjustments and no frictions. Finally, the world is currently on an emission path leading to higher temperature increases than the ones consistent with the A2 scenario (IPCC SRES, 2000). Hence, for these four reasons, our analysis is likely to yield a lower bound of climate-change costs. It can be considered as optimistic and cautious at the same time. Nonetheless, the main conclusion can be phrased as follows.

Despite its impact-smoothing potential, market-driven adaptation cannot be the solution to the climate-change problem. The distributional and scale implications of climate-related economic impacts need to be addressed by adequate policy-driven mitigation and adaptation strategies.

Our study of market-driven adaptation enabled us to recompute the damage functions for the different regions modeled in WITCH. We have been able to compute the residual damage after market-driven adaptation has displayed its effects and a new equilibrium has been reached in the economic systems. The new damage functions can be used to recompute the BCRs of different policy-driven mitigation and adaptation strategies.

Re-examining policy-driven adaptation: the effects of including market adjustments

In this last section, the previous results obtained with the AD-WITCH model are re-examined by accounting for the contribution of market-driven adaptation. To do so, firstly the AD-WITCH climate-damage function has been recalibrated in order to replicate the regional damage patterns estimated by the ICES model. Then, optimal mitigation and adaptation strategies have been recomputed.

The first clear insight is that market-driven adaptation has a strong damage-smoothing potential at the global level. This result hides some important distributional changes. Market-driven adaptation re-ranks winners and losers. In particular, the main OECD countries are likely to gain from climate change, while all non-OECD countries still lose (even though less than with previous estimates of climate damages). It also hides the fact that

Table 4.4.11 BCR of policy-driven adaptation in the presence of market-driven adaptation

Discounted values over 2010–2105 (billion US$ 2005)	With market-driven adaptation		
	World	OECD	Non-OECD
Benefits	5,282	202	5,079
Costs	3,123	164	2,959
BCR	1.69	1.24	1.72
Discounted values over 2010–2105 (trillion US$ 2005)	Without market-driven adaptation		
	World	OECD	Non-OECD
Benefits	14	2.2	11.5
Costs	8	1.5	6.4
BCR	1.73	1.45	1.79

a positive effect can be the sum of positive and negative impacts. Accordingly the need to adapt can persist even in the presence of a net gain from climate change.

The policy implications are relevant. Non-OECD countries still face positive damages, but smaller than in the absence of market-driven adaptation, thus also leading to lower adaptation spending in these countries. Accordingly, optimal mitigation and policy-driven adaptation expenditures are smaller. In particular, by the end of the century, adaptation expenditure is half of what it would have been in the absence of market-driven adaptation, even though adaptation expenditure reaches the remarkable amount of US$1.5 trillion anyway. Almost all this expenditure is concentrated in developing countries.

As a consequence, BCRs are slightly lower than in the absence of market-driven adaptation, both regionally and globally. The upper part of Table 4.4.11 shows the global and regional BCRs of adaptation, in comparison with those obtained without accounting for market-driven adaptation (lower part). The largest difference can be seen in OECD regions, where aggregate regional damages have turned positive (overall, they have a benefit). Only a few OECD regions still face negative damages, and therefore find it optimal to spend resources on adaptation. The BCRs are also lower in developing regions (non-OECD), reflecting the fact that market-driven adaptation can reduce overall climate-change impacts.

Conclusions and policy implications

Climate policy is a complex process. Many economic, environmental, and social dimensions are strictly interrelated. The focus on mitigation efforts seems outdated; recent international negotiations and the on-going policy decisions give increasingly more emphasis to adaptation to climate change. It then becomes necessary to provide policy-makers and governments with some indications on how to allocate climate-related funding wisely and efficiently between the alternatives available to cope with present and expected climate-change impacts.

In particular, it becomes relevant to understand to what extent market-driven adaptation can reduce climate-change damages. Should short-run funds go to mitigation policies? Or should we postpone action by focusing more on policy-driven adaptation? Is there an optimal level of adaptation and mitigation? Let us summarize the main conclusions contained in this chapter.

Firstly, markets cannot deal with all climate damages. Even under the optimistic assumptions of this subchapter, market-driven adaptation can attenuate the total damage from climate change, but not fully eliminate it. The global, direct impacts of climate change would lead to a loss of about 1.55 percent of GWP in 2050. Market-driven adaptation reduces this loss to 1.1 percent of GWP. However, although market-driven adaptation has a strong damage-smoothing potential, still global damage remain significant, especially in some LDCs. The challenge for adaptation, therefore, lies in tackling climate-change impacts in developing countries. Here, policy interventions are needed, beyond what market-driven adaptation can deliver.

Second, under a social optimum perspective (global cooperation to internalize the social cost of climate change), the optimal strategy to deal with climate change includes both mitigation and adaptation measures. Mitigation is always needed to avoid irreversible and potentially unmanageable consequences, whereas adaptation is necessary to address unavoidable climate-change damages. The optimal mix of these two strategies has been shown to be welfare-improving. At the global level, their joint implementation increases the BCR of each of them.

Third, there is a trade-off between mitigation and adaptation. The use of mitigation (adaptation) decreases the need to adapt (mitigate). In addition, resources are scarce. If some resources are used for mitigation (adaptation), fewer are available for adaptation (mitigation). Nonetheless, in the optimal policy mix, the possibility to abate never eliminates the need to adapt, and vice versa.

Fourth, in terms of timing, mitigation, if needed, should be carried out earlier, because of its delayed effects driven by environmental inertia, while adaptation can be postponed until damages are effectively higher. Were damages considerable in earlier period, adaptation would also be carried out earlier.

Fifth, both higher damages and lower discount rates foster mitigation and adaptation efforts. However, in the first case, adaptation expenditures increase more than mitigation ones, while in the second mitigation becomes relatively more important. The intuition goes as follows. If present and future damages increase uniformly, adaptation, which deals effectively with both, is to be preferred. If future damages increase relatively more (because of a lower discounting), mitigation, which is more effective in the distant future, is to be preferred.

Sixth, OECD countries should invest heavily in anticipatory adaptation measures. This depends on their damage structure. Planned anticipatory adaptation is particularly suited to cope with sea-level rise, but also with the hydro geological risks induced by more frequent and intense extreme events, which are a major source of negative impacts in the developed economies. Thus, in OECD countries it would be more convenient to act *ex ante* rather than *ex post*.

In non-OECD countries, the climate-change adaptation needs are estimated to be relatively low in the short run, US$30 billion at most in 2030.[19] However, they will rise dramatically as the economic impacts of climate change increase over time. In 2050, they will amount to US$78 billion, in 2065 they will be above US$500 billion, to peak to more than US$2 trillion by the end of the century. Non-OECD countries are unlikely to have the resources to meet their adaptation needs, which call for international aid and cooperation on adaptation and adaptation planning. In light of the current development deficit of developing countries, these resources are to be considered additional to the development aids required to fill this gap. They can also offer an additional opportunity to foster development itself when they take the form of educational programs, easier access to bank credit for dedicated projects, etc.

Non-OECD countries place little effort on adaptation R&D and rely primarily on reactive adaptation. This outcome, however, depends on the particular structure of non-OECD economic systems. Being poor, other forms of adaptation expenditures, more rapidly effective and mainly of the reactive type, are to be preferred. This suggests that richer countries can help developing countries also by supporting their adaptation R&D (e.g. by technology transfer). The success of this policy is crucially dependent on the design of the technology transfer program that must take into account the absorptive capacity of the developing country.

As shown by our sensitivity analysis, these results are robust to different model specifications and parameterizations.

There is a final important issue to be emphasized. We have shown that both mitigation and adaptation belong to the optimal policy mix to deal with climate change, even though with different timing (mitigation comes first) and different distribution across world regions (more mitigation in developed countries, more adaptation in developing countries). In this policy mix, the optimal balance between adaptation and mitigation depends on the discount rate and the level of damages. This is clearly shown by Table 4.4.12. With low discounting, a larger share of damage reduction is achieved with mitigation. With high damage, a larger share of damage reduction is achieved with adaptation.

What are the environmental implications of the optimal policy mix? Figure 4.4.8 shows the global average temperature increase above pre-industrial level, ranging between 2.5 and 3°C.

[19] These are the estimated adaptation costs under the high-damage–low-discount rate case.

Table 4.4.12 Share of damage reduction in the optimal policy mix

	Total damage reduction (Undiscounted cumulative sum 2010–2100) (%)	Adaptation (%)	Mitigation (%)
LDAM_HDR	44	77	23
HDAM_LDR	73	41	59
LDAM_LDR	60	33	67
HDAM_HDR	62	85	15

Figure 4.4.9 shows the significant effectiveness of adaptation on reducing residual damages, which are between 1 and 2 percent of GWP.

What, then, are the implications for climate finance? Our analysis suggests that the optimal strategy is to undertake mitigation first to control the most dangerous future damages from climate change – i.e. to stabilize them to a level that future damages can be dealt with through adaptation. Then, adaptation, if well prepared in advance, will protect our socio-economic systems from climate change. In terms of climate funds allocation, this implies that funding mitigation is more urgently needed than adaptation and fast-start investments should address mitigation, even though the targets should not be too ambitious. It is important to stress, however, that achieving less ambitious stabilization targets will still require important financial resources. Bastianin *et al.* (2009) estimate that changing the energy infrastructure to manage a 550CO_2-eq stabilization target will require US$600 billion of energy investments in 2030.

Figure 4.4.10 shows the differential in climate investments between the two extreme cases shown in Figure 4.4.8, HDAM_LDR and LDAM_HDR. It highlights that in order to reduce global average warming by 1°C, investments in energy R&D, renewables, and nuclear power need to be scaled up by at least US$200 billion between 2015 and 2030. In contrast, adaptation expenditure would be negligible until 2020, but become substantial after 2030.

Short-term international cooperation on adaptation should mostly address "soft" adaptation measures, including infrastructure development and some degree of cooperation on adaptation R&D. This is in line with what Fankhauser and Burton (2010) argue would be a good way to use money for adaptation. They advise financing soft, or less tangible, development activities that increase overall adaptive capacity.

To conclude, it is worth stressing again the important qualifications of our findings. Firstly, the

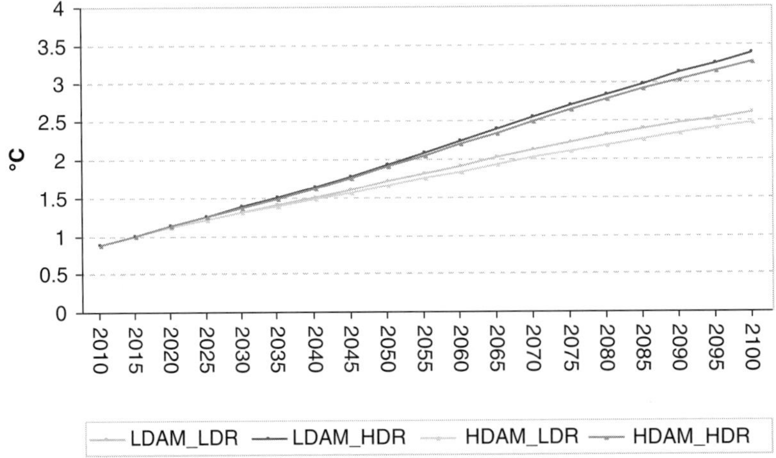

Figure 4.4.8 *Temperature change in the four scenarios*

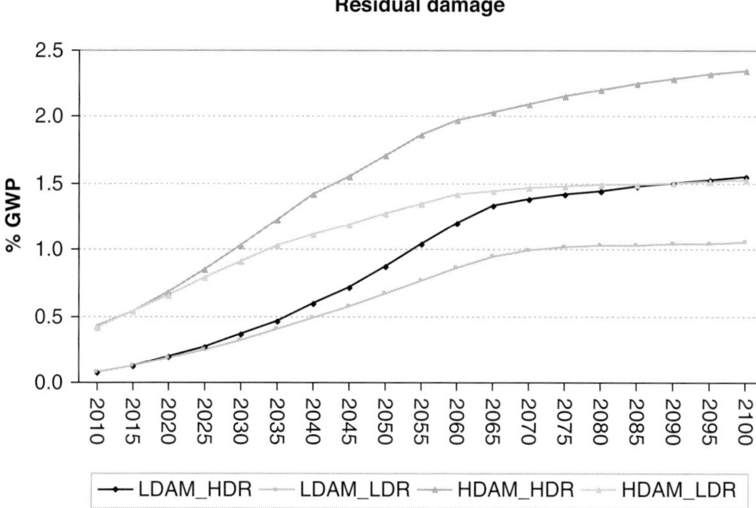

Figure 4.4.9 *Residual damages from climate change in the four scenarios*

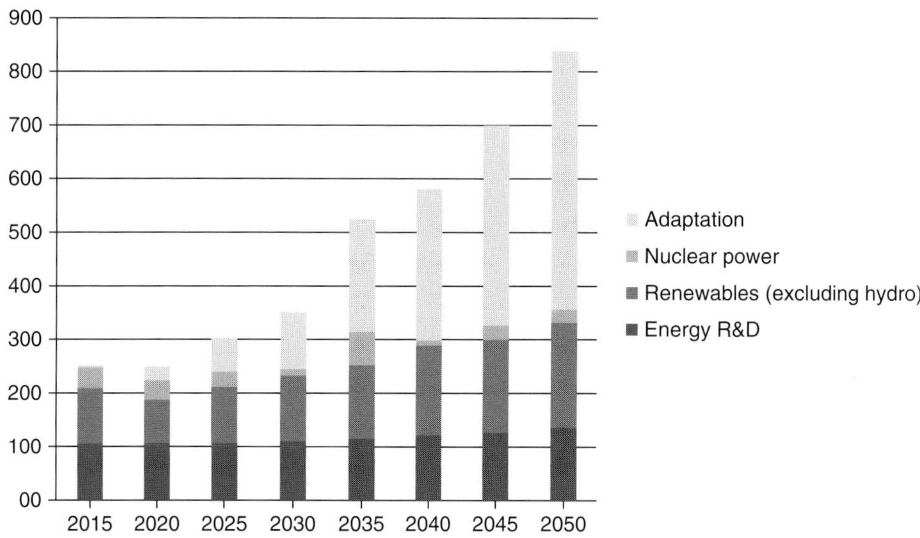

Figure 4.4.10 *Global investments in mitigation and adaptation (US$ billion): additional spending in the HDAM_LDR case compared to the LDAM_HDR case*

damage function used in AD-WITCH is highly stylized. The aggregation of different damage categories hides the existence of hotspots at the sectoral level, with the risk of underestimating adaptation needs. Second, this subchapter only partially considers non-market impacts. Third, this subchapter refers to a "smooth" world. It considers neither irreversibility and tipping points nor extreme temperature scenarios. Fourth, a perfect-information world in which uncertainty does not play a role is assumed. These introduce another downward bias to mitigation needs and adaptation anticipatory strategies, which are mainly driven by precautionary motives.

Bibliography

Aaheim, A., T. Dokken, S. Hochrainer, A. Hof, E. Jochem, R. Mechler, and D. P. van Vuuren, 2010: National responsibilities for adaptation strategies: lessons from four modelling frameworks, in M. Hulme and H. Neufeldt (eds.), *Making Climate Change Work for US: European Perspectives on Adaptation and Mitigation Strategies,* Cambridge University Press, 87–112

Adams, R. M., L. L. Houston, and B. A. McCarl, 2000: The benefits to Mexican agriculture of an El Niño-southern oscillation (ENSO) early warning system, *Agricultural and Forest Meteorology* **115**, 183–94

Adger, N. W., N. W. Arnell, and E. L. Thompkins, 2005: Successful adaptation to climate change across scales, *Global Environmental Change* **15**, 77–86

Agrawala, S. and S. Fankhauser (eds.), 2008: *Economics Aspects of Adaptation to Climate Change: Costs, Benefits and Policy Instruments*, OECD, Paris

Agrawala, S. F., C. Bosello, E. Carraro, De Cian and Elisa Lanzi, 2011a: Adapting to climate change: costs, benefits, and modelling approaches, *International Review of Environmental and Resource Economics* 245–84

Agrawala, S., F. C. Bosello, E. Carraro, E. De Cian, E. Lanzi, K. De Bruin, and R. Dellink, 2011b: PLAN or REACT? Analysis of adaptation costs and benefits using Integrated Assessment Models, *Climate Change Economics* **2**, 1–36

Antweiler, W., 2011: Mitigation + adaptation: what is the optimal climate change policy mix?, University of British Columbia, http://ssrn.com/abstract=1802857, accessed December 22, 2010

Association of British Insurers (ABI), 2005: *Financial Risk of Climate Change*: Summary Report, London

Auerswald, H., K. A. Konrad, and T. P. Marcel, 2011: Adaptation, mitigation and risk-taking in climate. *CESifo Working Paper Series* 3320

Bahn, O., M. Chesney, and J. Gheyssens, 2010: The effect of adaptation measures on the adoption of clean technologies, Paper presented at the WCERE Congress, Montreal, accessed December 22, 2010

Barrett, S., 2008: A portfolio system of climate treaties, *Discussion Paper* **08–13**, The Harvard Project on International Climate Change Agreements

Barrett, S., 2010: *Climate Change and International Trade: Lessons on their Linkage from International Environmental Agreements*, Paper prepared for Conference on Climate Change, Trade and Competitiveness: Issues for the WTO, World Trade Organization, Geneva, 16–18 June

Bastianin, A., A. Favero, and E. Massetti, 2009: Investments and financial flows induced by climate mitigation policies, *FEEM Working Paper* 0913

Bettina, M. and K. L. Ebi (eds.), 2006: *Climate Change and Adaptation Strategies for Human Health*, Steinkopff Verlag, Dresden

Bosello, F., 2010: Adaptation, mitigation and green R&D to combat global climate change: insights from an empirical integrated assessment exercise, *FEEM Working Paper* **22**

Bosello, F., C. Carraro, and E. De Cian, 2010a: Market and policy driven adaptation, in B. Lomborg (ed.), *Smart Solutions to Climate Change: Comparing Costs and Benefits*, Cambridge University Press, New York, 222–91

2010b: Climate policy and the optimal balance between mitigation, adaptation and unavoided damage, *Climate Change Economics* **1**, 71–92

2011: Adaptation can help mitigation: an integrated approach to post-2012 climate policy, *FEEM Working Paper* **1169**

Bosello, F., R. Roson, and R. S. J. Tol, 2006: Economy wide estimates of the implication of climate change: human health, *Ecological Economics* **58**, 579–91

Bosello, F., E. De Cian, F. Eboli, and R. Parrado, 2009: Macro-economic assessment of climate change impacts: a regional and sectoral perspective, in *Impacts of Climate Change and Biodiversity Effects*, Final Report of the CLIBIO project, European Investment Bank, University Research Sponsorship Program, Brussels

Bosetti, V., E. Massetti, and M. Tavoni, 2007: The WITCH model: structure, baseline, solutions, *FEEM Working Paper* **10–2007**

Bosetti, V., C. Carraro, R. Duval, A. Sgobbi, and M. Tavoni, 2009: The role of R&D and technology diffusion in climate change mitigation: new perspectives using the WITCH model, *OECD Working Paper* **664**

Bosetti, V., C. Carraro, M. Galeotti, E. Massetti, and M. Tavoni, 2006: WITCH: a world induced technical change hybrid model, *The Energy Journal, Special Issue on Hybrid Modeling of Energy–Environment Policies: Reconciling Bottom-up and Top-down*, 13–38

Bosetti, V., C. Carraro, E. De Cian, R. Duval, E. Massetti, and M. Tavoni, 2009: The incentives to participate in and the stability of international climate coalitions: a game-theoretic approach using the WITCH Model, *OECD Working Paper* **702**

Boutkan, E. and A. Stikker, 2004: Enhanced water resource base for sustainable integrated water resource management, *Natural Resources Forum* **28**, 150–4

Bréchet, T., N. Hritonenko, and Y. Yatsenko, 2010: Adaptation and mitigation in long-term climate policies, *Core Discussion Paper* **4/2010.65**

Buchner, B., A. Falconer, M. Hervé-Mignucci, C. Trabacchi, and M. Brinkman, 2011: The landscape of climate finance, *CPI Report*, Venice

Buob S. and G. Stephan, 2008: Global climate change and the funding of adaptation, *Bern University Discussion Papers* **08–04**

2011: To mitigate or to adapt: how to confront global climate change, *European Journal of Political Economy* **27**, 1–16

Buonanno, P., C. Carraro, E. Castelnuovo, and M. Galeotti, 2000: Efficiency and equity of emission trading with endogenous environmental technical change, in C. Carraro (ed.), *Efficiency and Equity of Climate Change Policy*, Kluwer Academic Publishers, Dordrecht

Burton, I., 1992: *Adapt and Thrive*, Unpublished manuscript, Canadian Climate Centre, Downsview

Butt, T. A. and B. A. McCarl, 2004: Farm and forest carbon sequestration: can producers employ it to make some money?, *Choices* **19**, 3–11

Callaway, J. M., D. B. Louw, J. C. Nkomo, E. M. Hellmuth, and D. A. Sparks, 2006: The Berg River dynamic spatial equilibrium model: a new tool for assessing the benefits and costs of alternatives for coping with water demand growth, climate variability, and climate change in the Western Cape, *AIACC Working Paper* **31**, Washington, DC, 41, www.aiaccproject.org

Caparrós, A. and F. Jacquemont, 2003: Conflicts between biodiversity and carbon offset programs: economic and legal implications, *Ecological Economics* **46**, 143–57

Carrarro, C. and E. Massetti, 2010a: Two good news from Copenhagen?, www.climatescienceandpolicy.eu/2010/01/two-good-news-from-copenhagen/

2010b: Adding up the numbers: mitigation pledges under the Copenhagen Accord, www.pewclimate.org/docUploads/copenhagen-accord-adding-up-mitigation-pledges.pdf

Carraro, C. and D. Siniscalco, 1998: International environmental agreements: incentives and political economy, *European Economic Review* **42**, 561–72

Ciscar J. C., L. Szabó, D. van Regemorter, and A. Soria, 2012: The integration of PESETA sectoral economic impacts into the GEM-E3 Europe model: methodology and results, *Climatic Change* **112**, 127–42

Dang, H. H., A. Michaelowa, and D. D. Tuan, 2003: Synergy of adaptation and mitigation strategies in the context of sustainable development: the case of Vietnam, *Climate Policy* **3**, S81–S96

Darwin, R. and R. S. J. Tol, 2001: Estimates of the economic effects of sea level rise, *Environmental and Resource Economics* **19**, 113–29

De Bruin K. C., R. B. Dellink, and S. Agrawala, 2009a: Economic aspects of adaptation to climate change: integrated assessment modelling of adaptation costs and benefits, *OECD Working Paper* **6**

De Bruin K. C., R. B. Dellink, and R. S. J. Tol, 2009b: AD-DICE: an implementation of adaptation in the DICE model, *Climatic Change* **95**, 63–81

Deke, O., K. G. Hooss, C. Kasten, G. Klepper, and K. Springer, 2001: Economic impact of climate change: simulations with a regionalized climate-economy model, *Kiel Working Paper* **1065**

Ebi, K. L., 2008: Adaptation costs for climate change cases of diarrhoeal disease, malnutrition and malaria in 2030, *Globalization and Health 2008* **4**, 1–9

EIA, 2008: *Annual Energy Outlook. Energy Information Administration*, Washington, DC

European Commission (EC), 2005: *Winning the Battle Against Global Climate Change* **COM/2005/0035**, Brussels

2007: *Limiting Global Climate Change to 2 degrees Celsius – The Way Ahead for 2020 and Beyond* **COM2007/0002**, Brussels

2007a: *Green Paper from the Commission to the Council, the European Parliament, the European Economic and Social Committee and the Committee of the Regions* **COM2007/0354**, Brussels

European Environment Agency (EEA), 2005: Vulnerability and adaptation to climate change in Europe, *EEA Technical Report* **7/2005**

2007: Climate change: the cost of inaction and the cost of adaptation, *EEA Technical Report* **13/2007**

2009: *White Paper – Adapting to Climate Change: Towards a European Framework for Action* **COM/2009/0147**, Brussels

2010: Adapting to climate change – SOER 2010 thematic assessment, European Environmental Agency, November

2011: *Energy Roadmap* **COM(2011) 885/2**, Brussels

Fankhauser, S. and I. Burton, 2010: Spending adaptation money wisely, Grantham Research Institute on Climate Change and the Environment, *Working Paper* **37**

Fankhauser, S. and R. S. J. Tol, 1996: The social costs of climate change, the IPCC Assessment Report and beyond, *Mitigation and Adaptation Strategies for Global Change* **1**, 386–403

Fankhauser, S., J. B. Smith, and R. S. J. Tol, 1999: Weathering climate change: some simple rules to guide adaptation decisions, *Ecological Economics* **30**, 67–78

Farrell A. E. and A. R. Brandt, 2005: Risks of the oil transition, *Environmental Research Letters*, **1**, 1–6

Fisher-Vanden, K., I. Sue Wing, E. Lanzi, and D. C. Popp, 2011: *Modeling Climate Change Adaptation: Challenges, Recent Developments and Future Directions*, http://people.bu.edu/isw/

Füssel H. M. and R. J. T. Klein, 2006: Climate change vulnerability assessments: an evolution of conceptual thinking, *Climatic Change* **75**, 301–29

Hanemann, W. M., 2008: What is the cost of climate change?, *CUDARE Working Paper* **1027**, University of California, Berkeley, CA

Hof, A. F., M. G. J. den Elzen, and D. P. van Vuuren, 2010: Including adaptation costs and climate change damages in evaluating post-2012 burden-sharing regimes, *Mitigation and Adaptation Strategies for Global Change* **15**, 19–40

Hof, A. F., K. C. de Bruin, R. B. Dellink, M. G. J. den Elzen, and D. P. van Vuuren, 2009: The effect of different mitigation strategies on international financing of adaptation, *Environmental Science and Policy* **12**, 832–43

Hope, C., 2003: The marginal impacts of CO_2, CH_4 and SF_6 emissions, *Judge Institute of Management Research Paper* **2003/10**, Cambridge

Hope, C. and D. Newbery, 2007: Calculating the social cost of carbon, *Electricity Policy Research Group Working Papers* **EPRG 07/20**, Cambridge

Hope, C., J. Anderson, and P. Wenman, 1993: Policy analysis of the greenhouse effect: an application of the PAGE model, *Energy Policy* **21**, 327–38

Hope, C. W., 2006: The marginal impact of CO_2 from PAGE2002: an integrated assessment model incorporating the IPCC's five reasons for concern, *The Integrated Assessment Journal* **6**, 19–56

Huq, S., A. Rahman, M. Konate, Y. Sokona, and H. Reid, 2003: *Mainstreaming Adaptation to Climate Change in Least Developed Countries (LDCs)*, IIED, London

IEA, 2007: *World Energy Outlook 2007*, OECD/IEA, Paris

Ingham, A., J. Ma, and A. M. Ulph, 2005: Can adaptation and mitigation be complements?, *Working Paper* **79**, Tyndall Centre for Climate Change Research, University of East Anglia

2007: Climate change, mitigation and adaptation with uncertainty and learning, *Energy Policy* **35**, 5354–69

IPCC SRES, 2000: N. Nakićenović and R. Swart (ed.), *Special Report on Emissions Scenarios: A Special Report of Working Group III of the Intergovernmental Panel on Climate Change*, Cambridge University Press

Jamison, D. T., A. R. Measham, J. G. Breman *et al.* (eds.), 2006: *Disease Control Priorities in Developing Countries*, 2nd edn., World Bank, Washington, DC

Kane, S. and J. Shogren, 2000: Linking adaptation and mitigation in climate change policy, *Climatic Change* **45**, 75–102

Kane, S. and G. Yohe, 2000: Societal adaptation to climate variability and change: an introduction, *Climatic Change* **45**, 1–4

Kirch, W., B. Menne, and R. Bertollini (eds.), 2005: *Extreme Weather Events and Public Health Responses*, Springer Verlag, Berlin

Kirshen, P., 2007: *Adaptation Options and Cost of Water Supply*, Tuft University, Boston, MA

Kirshen, P., M. Ruth, and W. Anderson, 2006: Climate's long-term impacts on urban infrastructures and services: the case of metro Boston, in M. Ruth (ed.), *Regional Climate Change and Variability: Local Impacts and Responses*, Edward Elgar, Cheltenham

Klein, R. J. T. and R. S. J. Tol, 1997: Adaptation to climate change: options and technologies – an overview paper, *Technical Paper* **FCCC/TP/1997/3**, United Nations Framework Convention on Climate Change Secretariat, Bonn

Klein, R. J. T., E. L. Schipper, and S. Dessai, 2003: Integrating mitigation and adaptation into climate and development policy: three research questions, *Working Paper* **40**, Tyndall Centre for Climate Change Research, University of East Anglia

Klein, R. J. T., S. Huq, F. Denton, T. E. Downing, R. G. Richels, J. B. Robinson, and F. L. Toth, 2007: Inter-relationships between adaptation and mitigation, in M. O. Parry, J. Canziani, J. Palutikof, P. J. van der Linden, and C. Hanson (eds.), *Contribution of Working Group II to the Fourth Assessment Report of the Intergovernmental Panel on Climate Change*, Cambridge University Press, 745–77

Kouvaritakis, N., A. Soria, and S. Isoard, 2000: Endogenous learning in world post-Kyoto scenarios: application of the POLES model under adaptive expectations, *International Journal of Global Energy Issues* **14**, 228–48

Kurukulasuriya, P. and R. Mendelsohn, 2008: How will climate change shift agro-ecological zones and impact African agriculture?, *Policy Research Working Paper* **WPS4717**, World Bank, Washington, DC

Kypreos, S., 2007: A MERGE model with endogenous technical change and the cost of carbon stabilization, *Energy Policy* **35**, 5327–36

Leary, N. A., 1999: A framework for benefit-cost analysis of adaptation to climate change and climate variability, *Mitigation and Adaptation Strategies for Global Change* **4**, 307–18

Lecoq, F. and Z. Shalizi, 2007: Balancing expenditures on mitigation and adaptation to climate change: an explorations of issues relevant for developing countries, *World Bank Policy Research Working Paper* **4299**

Lim, B. and E. Spanger-Siegfred (eds.), 2005: *Adaptation Policy Framework for Climate Change: Developing Policies Strategies and Measures*, Cambridge University Press

Marrouch, W. and A. R. Chaudhuri, 2011: International environmental agreements in the presence of adaptation, *Working Papers* **2011.35**, Fondazione Eni Enrico Mattei

McCarthy, J. J., O. F. Canziani, N. A. Leary, D. J. Dokken, and K. S. White (eds.), 2001: *Climate Change 2001: Impacts, Adaptation and Vulnerability. Contribution of Working Group II to the Third Assessment Report of the Intergovernmental Panel on Climate Change*, Cambridge University Press

McKibbin, W. J. and P. J. Wilcoxen, 2004: Climate policy and uncertainty: the roles of adaptation versus mitigation, *Brookings Discussion Papers in International Economics* **161**

McKinsey & Co., 2009: *Pathways to a Low-Carbon Economy: Version 2 of the Global Greenhouse Gas Abatement Curve*, New York

Mendelsohn, R. O., W. N. Morrison, M. E. Schlesinger, and N. G. Andronova, 2000: Country-specific market impacts of climate change, *Climatic Change* **45**, 553–69

Metz, B., O. R. Davidson, P. R. Bosch, R. Dave, and L. A. Meyer (eds.), 2007: *Climate Change 2007: Mitigation of Climate Change. Contribution of Working Group III to the Fourth Assessment Report of the Intergovernmental Panel on Climate Change*, Cambridge University Press

Nemet, G. F., 2006: Beyond the learning curve: factors influencing cost reductions in photovoltaics, *Energy Policy* **34**, 3218–32

Nicholls, R. J., 2004: Coastal flooding and wetland loss in the 21st Century: changes under the SRES climate and socio-economic scenarios, *Global Environmental Change* **14**, 69–86

Nicholls, R. J. and R. J. T. Klein, 2003: Climate change and coastal management on Europe's Coast, *EVA Working Paper* **3**

Nicholls, R. J. and R. S. J. Tol, 2006: Impacts and responses to sea-level rise: a global analysis of the SRES scenarios over the twenty-first century, *Philosophical Transactions of the Royal Society* A **364**, 1073–95

Nicholls, R. J., S. Brown, S. Hanson, and J. Hinkel, 2010: Economics of coastal zone adaptation to climate change, *Discussion Paper* **10**, World Bank, Washington, DC

Nordhaus, W. D., 1994: *Managing the Global Commons: The Economics of the Greenhouse Effect*, MIT Press, Cambridge, MA

Nordhaus, W. D. and J. G. Boyer, 2000: *Warming the World: The Economics of the Greenhouse Effect*, MIT Press, Cambridge, MA

Palutikof, J., M. Parry, O. Canziani, J. P. J. van der Linden, and C. E. Hanson (eds.), 2007: *Climate Change 2007: Impacts, Adaptation and Vulnerability. Contribution of Working Group II to the Fourth Assessment Report of the Intergovernmental Panel on Climate Change*, Cambridge University Press, 745–77

Parry, M., 2009: Closing the loop between mitigation, impacts and adaptation, *Climatic Change* **96**, 23–7

Parry, M., O. Canziani, J. Palutikof, P. van der Linden, and C. Hanson (eds.), 2007: *Contribution of Working Group II to the Fourth Assessment Report on Climate Change*, Cambridge University Press

Parry, M., N. Arnell, T. McMichael, R. Nicholls, P. Martens, S. Kovats, M. Livermore, C. Rosenzweig, A. Iglesias, and G. Fischer, 2001: Millions at risk: defining critical climate change threats and targets, *Global Environmental Change* **11**, 181–3

Pearce, D. W., W. R. Cline, A. N. Achanta, S. Fankhauser, R. K. Pachauri, R. S. J. Tol, and P. Vellinga, 1996: The social costs of climate change: greenhouse damage and the benefits of control, in J. P. Bruce, H. Lee, and E. F. Haites (eds.), *Climate Change 1995: Economic and Social Dimensions. Contribution of Working Group III to the Second Assessment Report on Climate Change*, Cambridge University Press

Pielke, R. A., 1998: Rethinking the role of adaptation in climate policies, *Global Environmental Change* **8**, 159–70

Smit, B. (ed.), 1993: *Adaptation to Climatic Variability and Change*, Environment Canada, Guelph

Smit, B. and O. Pilifosova, 2001: Adaptation to climate change in the context of sustainable development and equity, in *Climate Change 2001: Contribution of Working Group II to the Third Assessment Report on Climate Change*, Cambridge University Press, 877–912

Smit, B., I. Burton, R. J. T. Klein, and R. Street, 1999: The science of adaptation: a framework for assessment, *Mitigation and Adaptation Strategies for Global Change* **4**, 199–213

Smit, B., I. Burton, J. T. Klein, and J. Wandel, 2000: An anatomy of adaptation to climate change and variability, *Climatic Change* **45**, 223–51

Smith, J. B. and J. K. Lazo, 2001: A summary of climate change impact assessments from the US Country Studies Program, *Climatic Change* **50**, 1–29

Smith, J. B. and D. A. Tirpak (eds.), 1989: *The Potential Effects of Global Climate Change on the United States. Executive Summary*, US Environmental Protection Agency, Washington, DC

Smithers, J. and B. Smit, 1997: Human adaptation to climatic variability and change, *Global Environmental Change* **7**, 129–46

Solomon, S., D. Qin, M. Manning, Z. Chen, M. Marquis, K. B. Averyt, M. Tignor, and H. L. Miller (eds.), 2007: *Climate Change 2007: The Physical Science Basis. Contribution of Working Group I to the Fourth Assessment Report of the Intergovernmental Panel on Climate Change*, Cambridge University Press

Solow, R., 1956: A contribution to the theory of economic growth, *Quarterly Journal of Economics* **10**, 373–431

Stern, N., 2006: *The Economics of Climate Change: The Stern Review*, Cambridge University Press

Swan, T. W., 1956: Economic growth and capital accumulation, *Economic Record* **66**, 334–61

Tol, R. S. J., 2005: Emission abatement versus development as strategies to reduce vulnerability to climate change: an application of FUND, *Environment and Development Economics* **10**, 615–29

UNFCCC, 2007: *Investments and Financial Flows to Address Climate Change*, Climate Change Secreteriat, Bonn

Watson, R. T., M. C. Zinyowera, Richard H. Moss, and D. J. Dokken (eds.), 1995: *Climate Change, 1995: Impacts, Adaptations, and Mitigation of Climate Change: Scientific-Technical Analyses. Contribution of Working Group II to the Second Assessment Report of the Intergovernmental Panel on Climate Change*, Cambridge University Press

Wheaton, E. E. and D. C. Maciver, 1999: A framework and key questions for adapting to climate variability and change, *Mitigation and Adaptation Strategies for Global Change* **4**, 215–25

Wilbanks, T. J., 2005: Issues in developing a capacity for integrated analysis of mitigation and adaptation, *Environmental Science & Policy* **8**, 541–7

World Bank, 2006: *Clean Energy and Development: Towards an Investment Framework*, World Bank, Washington, DC

2010: *Economics of Adaptation to Climate Change: Synthesis Report*, The International Bank for Reconstruction and Development/The World Bank, Washington, DC

Yohe, G. and K. Strzepek, 2007: Adaptation and mitigation as complementary tools for reducing the risk of climate impacts, *Mitigation and Adaptation Strategies for Global Change*, **12**: 727–39

Zickfeld, K. *et al.*, 2007: Expert judgments on the response of the Atlantic meridional overturning circulation to climate change, *Climatic Change* **82**, 235–65

Climate Change

Alternative Perspective

SAMUEL FANKHAUSER*

Introduction

This chapter offers a broader perspective on climate change to complement the four Challenge Papers on the topic. The Challenge Papers cover most of the policy options that are available to combat climate change, that is:

- Constraining emissions through a carbon price (Tol, 2012)
- Promoting low-carbon technology (Galiana and Green, 2012)
- Adapting to the consequences of climate change (Bosello *et al.*, 2012)
- Exploring climate engineering solutions (Bickel and Lane, 2012).

The only generic option that is missing is the pursuit of energy efficiency. It is a surprising omission, given that energy efficiency improvements are one of the cheapest ways to reduce GHG emissions. Perhaps it was assumed that a carbon price would take care of these opportunities. A price on carbon is certainly important, but the empirical evidence has identified wider market imperfections and behavioral barriers that have to be tackled separately (de Canio, 1998; de Canio and Watkins, 1998; Martin *et al.*, 2011; Sanstad and Howarth, 1994).

The subchapters that comprise Chapter 4 give a fair assessment of the pros and cons of the four options considered. I will offer a few technical comments in passing, but my main concern is not the technical merit of the chapters. Instead I make two more fundamental observations.

My first observation is that ***the four chapters understate the case for tackling climate change***. This is mostly due to the way in which the Copenhagen Consensus experiment is set up, rather than misrepresentations in the chapters themselves. By exploring individual response options separately, the chapters inevitably focus on the relative merit of one option over the others (carbon taxes versus technology, etc.). None of the chapters explicitly makes the overall case for climate change action, which entails a smart combination of all four measures. I will address this omission in the next section.

My second observation is that ***the four chapters could be grounded better in the emerging empirical evidence***. Most of the conclusions are derived from high-level simulation models. Although these models represent the state of the art in climate change economics, they are too stylized to base policy decisions exclusively on their outputs. Where possible, additional empirical evidence should be mustered to reinforce their conclusions. Such evidence is beginning to emerge from the practical experience with climate policy in countries like the United Kingdom. Although still sketchy, it can help to inform the Copenhagen Consensus. I will summarize this experience in the final section of this chapter.

The economic case for climate change action

It is worth recapitulating the overall case for climate change intervention before reviewing the relative merit of different climate policies. The subchapters by (Tol, 2012) and (Bosello *et al.*, 2012) implicitly look at the question, but it is not explicitly addressed as an issue in the Consensus exercise.

* The Grantham Research Institute is supported financially by the Grantham Foundation for the Protection of the Environment and through the center for climate change Economics and Policy (CCCEP) by the UK Economic and Social Research Council (ESRC) and Munich Re.

Both Tol and Bosello *et al.* base their arguments on a cost-benefit rationale. That is, the aggregate (world-wide) costs of climate action are compared with the aggregate (world-wide) benefits, which take the form of avoided climate change damages. This is an intuitive way for economists to think about the problem, although most economists (including Tol and Bosello *et al.*) would agree that climate change is too complex to lend itself to simple CBA. Complicating factors include tough questions about intergenerational and intragenerational equity and the fact that climate change poses an existential threat to some unique natural and social systems.

However, the main complication is risk. Stern (2006) and Weitzman (2011) argue convincingly that climate change is primarily an issue of risk management. Unabated climate change would expose the world to climate regimes not experienced for millions of years. No climate model can offer assurances that these fundamental changes will not turn out to be calamitous. In fact most models suggest that they might be.

Tol (2012) gives a sense of the broad range of damage cost (or social cost) estimates. He notes that the probability distribution is skewed, with the possibility of a fat tail at the catastrophic end, and acknowledges that even his wide range may not cover the full set of possible outcomes. His subsequent analysis is based on a much narrower range of numbers, though, and this needs to be borne in mind when interpreting his results. His main case, in particular, is based on a marginal damage value that is in no way representative of the underlying probability distribution.

An alternative way of thinking about the problem is to ask what an acceptable insurance premium might be to mitigate the worst (but by no means all) risks of dangerous climate change. Two areas of risk-averse societal behavior may shed light on this question:

- People in industrialized countries spend the equivalent of about 5 percent of GDP on life insurance. In emerging markets, the corresponding sum is close to 2 percent of GDP (Swiss Re, 2011).
- Most nations spend at least around 1 percent of GDP on military defense, and often a lot more. This is true even for countries with explicitly defensive armies and no immediate threats from neighbors, such as Austria, Germany, and Switzerland.[1]

There is a clear parallel with climate risks, although it is not perfect. In both examples significant sums of money are spent to reduce a threat that is relatively remote but devastating if it does occur. How do these sums compare to the expected cost of climate change insurance?

The order of magnitude is similar. Energy-economy models suggest that limiting the atmospheric concentration of GHGs to around 450 ppm might cost between 1 and 3 percent of GDP over the next forty years, although achieving this would require near-perfect policy coordination (Clarke *et al.*, 2009; Edenhofer *et al.* 2010). That is, GDP in 2050 would be 1–3 percent lower than would otherwise be the case. In return, the probability of a risky climate change outcome – say of warming in excess of 4°C – would be reduced to perhaps 1 percent (Committee on Climate Change, 2008).

While not based on careful integrated modeling, the above line of argument suggests that limiting atmospheric GHG concentrations to around 450 ppm is a rational precaution and the ensuing costs are a reasonable insurance premium to pay. It still leaves open the question about the appropriate mix of policies – that is, the choice between pricing carbon, promoting technology, adapting, and climate engineering. I turn to this next.

Empirical evidence on the choice of climate policies

As more and more countries begin to address climate change it becomes possible to complement the top-down simulation results in the four subchapters with empirical insights from actual climate change policy. Townshend *et al.* (2011) count no fewer than 286 climate-change or climate-change-related

[1] http://data.worldbank.org/indicator/MS.MIL.XPND.GD.ZS.

laws in a survey of thirty-three economies. Many of these laws have been in place for several years.

The analysis and evaluation of existing climate policies is only just beginning, but it can add important empirical credibility to the climate change story. Models like DICE (used in Bickel and Lane, 2012), FUND (Tol, 2012), and WITCH (Bosello *et al.*, 2012) are excellent tools to describe high-level trends, but they are much too stylized to offer firm evidence on how policies work on the ground. They do not have the same level of detail and richness as the models used to inform decisions in Ministries of Finance and Central Banks, for example.

A good place from which to distil policy lessons is the United Kingdom, although there is also evidence from many other places. The climate change debate in Britain is fairly advanced, with a strong legal basis for climate action, ambitious targets, and sophisticated institutional arrangements (Fankhauser, 2012). Through a combination of dedicated policies and serendipity the United Kingdom has succeeded in reducing its carbon emissions by about 25 percent between 1990 and 2010, and by about 12 percent since 2007. The policy mix features carbon pricing, technology support, and adaptation (although not climate engineering). The main planks of the low-carbon policy are:

- A price on carbon, primarily through the EU Emissions Trading Scheme (EU ETS), which covers about half of Britain's carbon emissions. This is flanked by a climate change levy on firms outside the EU ETS, and soon to be by a carbon price "underpin" to prop up the ETS price.
- Support for low-carbon technologies, through a mix of supply-push (e.g. demonstration projects, a new Green Investment Bank) and demand-pull measures (a renewable energy obligation and feed-in tariffs (FITs) for small-scale renewables and renewable heat).
- Measures to address barriers to energy efficiency, an area that is not covered by the subchapters but which receives much policy attention. There is a bewildering range of mostly regulatory measures (such as obligations on energy suppliers) to facilitate the uptake of energy efficiency.

Evidence on the effectiveness of these policies comes in the form of empirical policy evaluations, independent monitoring reports, and the detailed modeling of policy choices.

An econometric analysis by Martin *et al.* (2009) finds that Britain's climate-change levy – a carbon-cum-energy tax – has reduced the energy intensity particularly of larger and more energy-intensive plants. The authors find no statistically significant impacts of the tax on employment, gross output, total factor productivity or (TFP), firm exit.

The EU ETS has helped to curtail European carbon emissions, although the amount of abatement has been modest (Ellerman and Buchner, 2008; Ellerman *et al.*, 2010). There is as yet no evidence that the scheme has triggered much low-carbon innovation (Calel and Dechezleprêtre, 2012), although innovation effects associated with pricing policies are documented elsewhere in the literature (Popp, 2002). This suggests that additional, technology-oriented policies will be needed, as suggested by Galiana and Green (2012).

The fact that the United Kingdom is reducing emissions faster than some of its economic competitors is having a surprisingly small impact on British industry. The sectors for which loss of competitiveness is an issue are those where high trade exposure goes together with high carbon compliance costs (such as aluminium or steel). They account for less than one percent of UK GDP and UK jobs, although this result will obviously be different in countries with a stronger industrial base (Carbon Trust, 2008). In fact, many firms have benefitted from the EU ETS: they are allocated free emissions permits, the opportunity cost of which they are able to pass on to consumers. This is a distributional feature the European Commission is now trying to address.

The Committee on Climate Change (2011) finds that low-carbon policies have added 12.5 percent, in nominal terms, to the typical household energy bill since 2004. Over the same period, fuel price shifts have added 63 percent to the typical bill. The general level of inflation was 16 percent (reflecting, among other factors, the hike in energy prices). The Committee anticipates that the effect of tighter policies between now and 2020 will be roughly offset by the effect of energy-efficiency measures. The overall resource cost of Britain's commitment to reduce GHG emissions by 50 percent by 2027 is estimated to be less than 1 percent of GDP (Committee on Climate Change, 2010). The estimate is based on fairly detailed sector-by-sector modeling, although it is a bottom-up estimate and does not include indirect general equilibrium effects.

Despite their small economic impact there has been opposition to Britain's carbon policies from vested interests. Such lobbying is normal, of course, and there are also business interests that have seized the low-carbon opportunities and are pushing for tighter targets (as well as better policies). There is some apprehension in the Treasury about pursuing low-carbon polices at a time of austerity and low growth, but there are also compelling arguments that low-carbon investment is no worse, and arguably better, at kick-starting a flagging economy than other forms of support (Bowen and Stern 2011; Zenghelis, 2011).

The UK policy framework recognizes the need for both adaptation and mitigation. Although the United Kingdom is fairly well adapted to the current climate, a closer look (ASC, 2011) identified a number of low-cost options that have attractive BCRs even before taking climate change into account (see also Swiss Re, 2009). Their short-term benefits in terms of current climate resilience, water efficiency, or other concerns are up to five times higher than the initial outlay. The list is similar to that reviewed in Bosello *et al.* (2012), and includes:

- Improvements in residential water efficiency, such as low-flow taps, showers and toilets, which could reduce water use by up to a third.
- Flood-protection measures in buildings, such as airbrick covers, door-guards, repointing of walls, drainage bungs, and non-return valves.
- Measures to avoid overheating in buildings, such as energy-efficient appliances to reduce waste heat and increased window-shading.
- Improved flood-risk management, including awareness campaigns for local residents (such as risk profiles for individual homes) and improved emergency response training.

A rational adaptation policy would focus on such win–win options. They also feature prominently in low-income countries, where there are strong overlaps between adaptation and development (Fankhauser and Burton, 2011).

In addition, a rational adaptation policy would begin to incorporate adaptation into strategic long-term decisions on zone planning (e.g. on building in hazard zones like flood plains and coastal zones), infrastructure development, and building design, where cheap adjustments today can save potentially large sums of money later. The proposal is not to automatically climate-proof all these investments, but to invest into an informed decision-making process that factors in future climate risks and prevents the need for costly retrofits later.

There are no policy frameworks, in the United Kingdom or elsewhere, that include climate engineering. However, Bickel and Lane (2012) are right that research into geo-engineering is an important insurance policy to complement the other climate measures. Given the early stage of this research, it seems sensible to cast the net more widely than Bickel and Lane suggest, and explore air capture as well as solar radiation management. Climate engineering raises important ethical and regulatory issues, as well as questions of technical feasibility and environmental side effects. For example:

- Which organization should provide the global public good "climate stabilization"?
- How would that organization be regulated?
- How would the optimal level of climate stabilization be determined?
- How would potential liabilities be apportioned if something goes wrong?
- How would unilateral action by rogue states be prevented?

These questions are crucial and need to be part of the research effort into climate engineering. Demonstrating technical feasibility and environmental acceptability alone is not enough.

Conclusions

This Perspective Paper complements the subchapters on climate change by offering a broader viewpoint on the merits of climate-change policy. It makes two key points.

First, spending money to deal with climate change is a worthwhile investment. There is strong scientific evidence about the downside risks from climate change. The "insurance premium" society would have to pay to mitigate these risks is not dissimilar to the premiums paid for other threats to life and territorial integrity. Initial evidence from the United Kingdom suggests that early emissions reductions can be achieved at a relatively low cost to the economy.

This risk-based argumentation is different from the straight benefit-cost calculus applied elsewhere in the Copenhagen Consensus. However, it is arguably more appropriate given the levels of risk and uncertainty involved.

Second, a rational response to climate change should combine all the four options put forward in the subchapters. The main thrust should be to reduce emissions through a combination of carbon pricing (either a tax or trading scheme), the promotion of low-carbon technologies and measures to unlock energy efficiency improvements. We are starting to see evidence from countries like the United Kingdom that ambitious decarbonization policies are technologically and economically feasible. As in other areas of public policy, the challenge is competent implementation.

Some climate change is now unavoidable, and measures to adapt to these residual risks are important. Adaptation can be timed, given the gradual onset of climate change, but there are measures that ought to be considered now. They include decisions with long-term consequences, such as infrastructure investments and spatial planning, and decisions with early side benefits – for example in terms of economic development, resource efficiency, and poverty alleviation. It is worth spending money on ensuring that climate change is properly factored into these decisions.

Climate-engineering solutions play a role as a last-resort option to guard against adverse surprises. They are worth spending some research money on, including on work to understand their environmental side effects and the regulatory, governance, and institutional implications of this option.

Bibliography

ASC, 2011: *Adapting to Climate Change in the UK. Measuring Progress*, UK Adaptation Sub-Committee, London

Bickel, E. and L. Lane, 2012: *Climate-Engineering R&D*, Challenge Paper, Copenhagen Consensus, March, see p. 203 in this volume

Bosello, F., C. Carraro, and E. De Cian, 2012: *Climate-Change Adaptation*, Challenge Paper, Copenhagen Consensus, March, see p. 225 in this volume

Bowen, A. and N. Stern, 2011: Environmental policy and the economic downturn, *Oxford Review of Economic Policy* **26**, 137–63

Calel, R. and A. Dechezleprêtre, 2012: *Environmental Policy and Directed Technological Change: Evidence from the European Carbon Market*, Grantham Research Institute, London School of Economics, February, mimeo

Carbon Trust, 2008: *EU ETS Impacts on Profitability and Trade*, Carbon Trust, London

Clarke, L., J. Edmonds, V. Krey, R. Richels, S. Rose, and M. Tavoni, 2009: International climate policy architectures: overview of the EMF 22 International Scenarios, *Energy Economics* **31**, S64–S81

Committee on Climate Change, 2008: *Building a Low-Carbon Economy: The UK's Contribution to Tackling Climate Change*, December

2010: *The Fourth Carbon Budget – Reducing Emissions through the 2020's*, December

2011: *Household Energy Bills: Impact of Meeting Carbon Budgets*, December

De Canio, S. J., 1998: The efficiency paradox: bureaucratic and organizational barriers to profitable energy-saving investments, *Energy Policy* **26**, 441–54

De Canio, S. J. and W. E. Watkins, 1998: Investments in energy efficiency: do the characteristics of firms matter?, *Review of Economics and Statistics* **80**, 95–107

Edenhofer, O., B. Knopf, T. Barker, L. Baumstark, E. Bellevrat, B. Chateau, P. Criqui, M. Isaac, A. Kitous, S. Kypreos, M. Leimbach, K. Lessmann, B. Magné, S. Scrieciu, H. Turton, and D. Van Vuuren, 2010: The economics of Low stabilization: model comparison of mitigation strategies and costs, *Energy Journal* **31**, 11–48

Ellerman, A. and B. Buchner, 2008: Over-allocation or abatement? A preliminary analysis of the EU ETS based on the 2005–06 emissions data, *Environmental and Resource Economics* **41**, 267–87

Ellerman, D., F. Convery, C. de Perthuis, and E. Alberola, 2010: *Pricing Carbon: The European Union Emissions Trading Scheme*, Cambridge University Press

Fankhauser, S., 2012: *A practitioner's guide to a* low-carbon economy: lessons from the UK, *Climate Policy*, doi:10.1080/14693062.2013.749124

Fankhauser, S. and I. Burton, 2011: Spending adaptation money wisely, *Climate Policy* **11**, 1–13

Galiana, I. and C. Green, 2012: *A Technology-Led Mitigation*, Challenge Paper, Copenhagen Consensus, February, see pp. 192–202 in this volume

Martin, R., L. de Preux and U. Wagner, 2009: *The Impacts of the Climate Change Levy on Business: Evidence from Microdata*, Working Paper **6**, Grantham Research Institute, London School of Economics

Martin, R., M. Muûls, L. de Preux, and U. Wagner, 2011: Anatomy of a paradox: management practices, organizational structure and energy efficiency, *Journal of Environmental Economics and Management* doi 10.1016/j.jeem.2011.08.003

Popp, D., 2002: Induced innovation and energy prices, *American Economic Review* **92**, 160–80

Sanstad, A. and R. Howarth, 1994: Normal markets, market imperfections and energy efficiency, *Energy Policy* **22**, 811–18

Stern, N., 2006: *The Economics of Climate Change: The Stern Review*, Cambridge University Press

Swiss Re, 2009: *Shaping Climate Resilient Development*, Economics of Adaptation Working Group, www.swissre.com/rethinking/what_does_economics_of_climate_adaptation_mean_for_insurance.html, accessed 13 February, 2013

2011: *Insurance in Emerging Markets: Growth Drivers and Profitability*, Sigma 5/11, Zürich

Tol, R., 2012: *Carbon Dioxide Abatement*, Challenge Paper, Copenhagen Consensus, March, see pp. 187–91 in this volume

Townshend, T., S. Fankhauser, R. Aybar, M. Collins, T. Landesman, M. Nachmany, and C. Parvese, 2013: *The Globe Climate Legislation Study*, 3rd edn., Globe International and Grantham Research Institute, London School of Economics, London

Weitzman, M., 2011: Fat-tailed uncertainty in the economics of climate change, *Review of Environmental Economic Policy* **5**, 275–92

Zenghelis, D., 2011: *A Macro-Economic Plan for a Green Recovery*, Policy Brief, Grantham Research Institute, London School of Economics, March

4.2 Climate Change

Alternative Perspective

ANIL MARKANDYA

Background

The four subchapters that comprise Chapter 4 provide a valuable discussion of the options for addressing climate change. Tol (p. 186) examines the possible role of economic instruments such as carbon taxes; Galiana and Green (p. 192) emphasize the importance of measures to promote the development of technological low-carbon solutions; Bosello *et al.* (p. 225) look at the balance between adaptation and mitigation, and Bickel and Lane (p. 203) make a case for investing in finding out more about geo-engineering.

I review each of these subchapters briefly and in the final section I give my overall assessment of how well they cover the issues that arise when formulating climate policy.

Review of Chapter 4

Co₂ abatement

Tol provides an excellent review of the state of knowledge on climate economics and notes that the most efficient economic instrument to reduce GHGs is a carbon tax. Some might argue that emissions trading is equally good, if not better (Aldy and Stavins, 2008), and politically has a better chance of being implemented, so perhaps the case for a carbon tax is not so clear.

The subchapter surveys the literature on the economic impacts of climate change very well indeed and rightly concludes that: (a) these vary a lot from country to country, with negative impacts falling disproportionally on the poor and (b) there is still a great deal of uncertainty about the numbers. On the costs of mitigation Tol is also right to note that deep cuts are possible and the costs of making these cuts are not that high if the reductions are made progressively, starting from a low base.

The subchapter then goes on to consider different carbon tax profiles, with a cost in welfare terms of \$75 billion over four years. These give rise to different concentrations of GHGs in 2100. Tol's calculations show a BCR of over 1 for the tax scenarios that are very low in the initial year (less than \$3/ton carbon). However these scenarios result in concentrations that are well above the current consensus level of 450 ppm, while the tax scenario needed to get to that level involves a tax of around \$250/ton of carbon and has a BCR of only 0.2.

There are several problems with the analysis, and the author is aware of them. First it ignores the equity and uncertainty aspects of the problem, taking point estimates of damages through the social costs of carbon. Moreover the estimates Tol takes (from the FUND model) are on the low side from the range that exists in the literature.

The subchapter does try to allow for the equity and uncertainty aspects in a modified set of calculations, which could justify an initial tax of around \$12/ton of carbon, with a resulting concentration in 2100 of around 675 ppm, but no higher tax is justified. It is not clear how the uncertainty is accounted for in these calculations. The devil really is in the detail here, and we need to know the basis of that analysis.

Finally the assumption that the tax will be imposed only for four years and then stopped does not make sense: again, the author is aware of that but feels he had to work within such a structure because that is what the Copenhagen Consensus framework required. Climate change is a longer-term problem and short-term analyses are not the right way to decide on policy.

A technology-led mitigation

Galiana and Green propose a policy for climate change based exclusively on a carbon tax that is used to fund R&D in new low-carbon technologies. The tax starts out at a modest level but increases over time. They claim that this one measure is enough and that there is no need for any targets for reductions in emissions or for any other measures to increase existing carbon efficiencies.

The authors had put forward five arguments for this approach in earlier work. First they state that the challenge of stabilizing climate requires innovation and development of new technologies to an extent that has been underestimated. Second the current level of technology is not able to cope with the scale of the transformation in low-carbon use that is required. Third, subsidies to R&D are required because the incentive from a carbon tax or other measure is not enough to provide enough resources to this activity. Fourth the costs of reducing emissions from current technologies are underestimated. And, finally, their proposed program has a very high BCR.

In this subchapter they claim the case is as strong as it was before, perhaps even more so given some changes in the landscape for policy-making in this area. The changes they cite are: (a) the continuing focus on targets to reduce emissions as a distraction from technology-led solutions, (b) the fact that emerging economies see technology as the "way forward," and (c) the adoption of low-carbon options from existing technologies is hampered by the development of indigenous gas and oil from "fracking" that provide energy security at an affordable cost.

There is general agreement that innovation has an important role in the package of instruments to achieve the required transition and most of the serious applied and theoretical work has recognized the need for some subsidies to R&D in this area. Where a number of researchers would disagree with the subchapter is on the exclusive dependence on this instrument. Here are the main reasons:

(a) Some existing low-carbon technologies are becoming competitive with fossil fuels, as a result of learning-by-doing and by increasing production. The problems alluded to of energy storage are being addressed in technologies such as solar thermal, for example, and will be more effectively resolved through the implementation and trial and error with existing plants. The log-linear relationship between unit cost and cumulative production of a good applies to these areas and we can only move down the curve if more plants are installed. This requires some incentives to overcome these learning-by-doing constraints and spillover externalities. Since a carbon tax is unlikely to be implemented in many countries (in the United States it can hardly be mentioned in political circles), other instruments are needed to make progress in this direction.

(b) A sharp increase in government funding for any good or service generally results, in the short term, in an increase in the price of that good or service, more than an increase in the output. The same applies to R&D. If you push for major increases in R&D, the first thing that will happen is an increase in the salaries of researchers and not an increase in the total output. Programs that seek to increase R&D have to be introduced over time to avoid this impact.

(c) The authors are too dismissive of the range of measures introduced so far to promote low-carbon energy. Even the Kyoto Protocol resulted in an increase in innovations. The different programs for promoting energy efficiency have resulted in gains and some countries have increased their non-carbon energy shares. One has to compare the present emissions of CO_2 against the counterfactual of what they would have been without any of the measures being introduced, not against what they were twenty years ago.

(d) A carbon tax is probably the best measure to address climate change (although some analysts prefer emissions trading – see my comment on the previous paper[1]). Models that seek to achieve targets based on existing technology *plus* likely developments in technology

[1] If emissions are auctioned, the revenues could be used to support R&D research, so the desired program could be financed in that way,

suggest slightly higher rates than this subchapter – e.g. the POLES model comes up with around \$8/ton CO_2 in 2010, \$35 in 2020 and \$110 in 2030: Criqui *et al.* (1999); EC (2003). This is similar to the tax quoted in the study from the Harvard Belfer Centre on which the authors state:

> The Belfer survey's need for a high and rapidly rising carbon price to induce the commercialization and development of low carbon energy technologies suggests a lack of confidence that R&D alone can sufficiently reduce the cost of low carbon technologies. In our view, this result is a direct consequence of a stringent emissions target whose timeframe (83 percent reduction from 2005 by 2050) does not necessarily coincide with the development of scalable technologies.

I do not think that is right. Certainly in the POLES model (and from what I could see also in the Belfer model) new and unproven technologies are assumed to come in. The fact that there are stringent targets implies that in their absence, and with the taxes the authors propose (they start at \$5/ton of CO_2 in 2010, they would go up to \$20 in 2020 and \$40 in 2030), we would get much lower levels of emissions reduction. This would then result in not meeting a stabilization target that is widely regarded as desirable.

(e) To summarize, the authors are more optimistic about the power of the tax and indifferent to meeting any kind of target. This is a risk many of us are not willing to take. In the meantime, given that such taxes are not on the cards, we need to use other instruments, and in this regard some are better than others.

Specific comments

(a) On the issue of the oil in the ground, I believe that optimal growth models such as DICE do take account of this. The optimization is carried out subject to the available resources and fossil resources such as oil are included. The estimate social cost of carbon from the model is therefore calculated based on an optimal extraction of remaining stocks.
(b) The discussion on adaptation is rather casual. In what ways would R&D contribute to the infrastructure solution to adaptation? So far, it is not new technologies that are the problem but the uncertainty in knowing when to implement the technologies we have.
(c) I do agree that a consumption-based calculation of emissions is the better method of making any national allocations, and we should move to that basis.

Climate change adaptation

Bosello *et al.* is very comprehensive and wide-ranging, covering the relative roles of mitigation and adaptation policies to address climate change. It is not so much a case for spending a given amount to achieve the highest return as an exploration of the factors that determine the forms of intervention for climate policy. Some BCRs are presented, but these are not really returns on a given expenditure over a short period of time; rather, they report the discounted PV of reduced damages following a long-term investment program. In the case of adaptation, much of the investment will be made much later, as the subchapter rightly concludes.

I broadly agree with most of its conclusions. To summarize, they are:

(a) The optimal response to climate change is a combination of mitigation and adaptation – there are no "corner" solutions.
(b) Market-induced adaptation can ease the burden of public adaptation, but it will not eliminate it.
(c) The burden of adaptation will fall more heavily in developing countries.
(d) In most cases, mitigation actions need to be undertaken earlier and adaptation can be undertaken later. This does not apply to all areas of adaptation, however.

I am not convinced of the conclusion that developed countries should undertake more anticipatory adaptation and developing countries more reactive adaptation. One of the reasons given is that:

> OECD countries are richer. Thus they can give up relatively more easily their present consumption to invest in adaptation measures that will become productive in the future. By contrast non-OECD countries are compelled by resource scarcity to act in [an] emergency

If the solution being sought is a global cooperative equilibrium, it should not matter how poor or rich a country is. The solution should be determined by where the net benefits are greatest.

The modeling of mitigation and adaptation is impressive. Yet there are questions that remain to be addressed at different levels. I will comment on some of these and indicate where I think we need to go to help answer them:

(a) *Modeling adaptation impacts* It is now common practice to assume an "adaptation function" linking the reduction in damages to expenditure and AD-WITCH using a nested CES, with components consisting of reactive and anticipatory adaptation. Yet the empirical basis for the parameters of this function is very weak. We are highly uncertain about the damages caused by climate change in the first place, and we compound that uncertainty when we deal with the changes in damages following any given level of adaptation expenditure. These uncertainties cannot be ignored; they are at the heart of the problem and although they are briefly mentioned in the subchapter they are not directly addressed.[2] There are some attempts in the literature to address them. For example, see the chapter by Chris Hope on the use of the Page model in Parry *et al.* (2009), in which he looks at adaptation benefits using probability distributions, which is helpful. The authors criticize the Page model on the grounds that the adaptation is not endogenous to the solution in his model. However, the version referred to above does look at the optimal level of adaptation for different mitigation policies and while this does not give an optimal solution to both it does show the trade-offs quite well. If I had to pick between shedding more light on the uncertainties and going for a full optimal control model, I would go for the former.

(b) The timing issue is important for the reasons given, but also because of a changing knowledge base. As noted, most of the adaptation can be left to later because the lag between the timing of the investment and the impacts is measured in years and not in decades. This also allows us to take advantage of the fact that more information will be forthcoming. The analysis presented here does not build in that aspect. Were it to do so I suspect it would make it even more desirable to go for the low-regret options now and postpone action by "buying" an option to act more aggressively in the future. Some work has already pointed in that direction (Ranger *et al.*, 2010).

(c) One area where early adaptation action is warranted is land use planning. The model and analysis cannot show that (although the authors do pick this up based on their good common sense). It should be possible to show formally that not addressing this issue now will create patterns of land use in areas more prone to flooding and extreme events, which in turn will entail significantly higher adaptation costs in the future.

(d) Returning to the issue of detailed impacts at the sectoral level, a CGE model (ICES) is used to allow for market-driven adaptation, which is a valuable contribution to the assessment of climate policies. The results, however, are highly dependent on the structure of that model (many of the parameters of which we do not know) and on the evolution of future trade regimes. The work of Parry and others emphasizes how much these scenarios matter (Parry, 2007). Broadly speaking I would expect that a world with a more liberalized trade regime would allow for a higher level of effective market-driven adaptation and therefore place a lower overall burden. The distributional effects, however, could be more severe in some regions. In general, more information on the ICES model and how it links to AD-WITCH would be helpful.

(e) Another important aspect of adaptation expenditures is equity. We may not be able to justify some proposed actions on benefit-cost grounds, but failure to act to address agricultural yield losses in some places could, for example, leave some vulnerable people in a state of destitution. Should this not be taken into account?

[2] The authors made some additions in response to comments I sent, including addressing this issue, but I could only find a short comment.

Specific comments

(i) In the adaptation versus mitigation debate, a question that comes up is: how much effect does an effective adaptation program have on the desired mitigation program? If we institute the optimal adaptation plans it should allow us to be more lenient on the GHG reduction targets. Figure 4.4.10 shows the difference in future emissions with and without adaptation: up to 2030 there is little difference but after that the "with-adaptation" program allows emissions to rise more so that by 2100 they are about 7 gigatons higher. It would be of considerable interest to see the implications of these differences in terms of CO_2 stabilization targets and projected temperature increases.

(ii) With coastal zones adaptation, the central issues are timing of the investment and uncertainty.

(iii) Sea-level rise is an important factor in several developing countries.

(iv) In the case of health adaptation, cost-effectiveness analysis is used, partly because it is the preferred tool for health sector decisions.

(v) The agricultural adaptation choices are very much influenced by global trade scenarios. These effects need to be studied further.

Climate engineering R&D

Bickel and Lane make a cogent case for climate engineering as part of the solution for global warming. Paradoxically a strong part of the case is based on the fact that, even though its success is highly uncertain, it can help improve the outcome of an emissions reductions program when climate sensitivity is high (i.e. when the climate outcomes are at their outlying extremes).

The problem with the assessment is that we are dealing with a very uncertain technology, with significant risks. The authors reject the option of evaluating an R&D program to find out more about its potential by using a value of information (VoI) approach (probably rightly). Instead, they assume that investment to scope out one of the climate engineering options (solar radiation management, or SRM) will generate a workable technology after ten years. The technology may turn out to have risks and damages, but these can be summarized as amounting to damages in the range of 0–3 percent of the world's GDP. The technology is then included in the Integrated Assessment Model (DICE) to see how it affects the optimal solution. The conclusions are that including SRM reduces the cost of the "consensus" solution of stabilization at 2°C considerably. It does this by reducing the costs of abatement (fewer emissions reductions are needed), while implementing it is relatively a low-cost option.

Yet there are unanswered questions that need to be considered. Here are some of them:

(a) The R&D program for SRM may conclude that it is not a viable option. This may be for technical reasons or for global institutional ones. In that event, the investment will have no return and this has not been taken into account.

(b) Likewise it may take longer to establish SRM as feasible, in which case its implementation may be delayed. This possibility will reduce the rate of return on the investment.

(c) An important factor to consider is the fact that such injections of sulfur would need global agreement. Given the difficulty we are having on reducing GHGs emissions, it is fanciful to think the political issues could be resolved for an unknown technology such as SRM.

Specific comments

(a) DICE is not a bad model to use for the comparison but it is conservative in its damage estimates: it does not take account of regional differences and it ends up with less control on radiative forcing and a global higher temperature profile than other Integrated Assessment Models.[3] These will affect the base values for a 2°C stabilization and then the additional gains

[3] See, for example, a recent model; this is DICER, based on DICE, but more disaggregated and more accurate in its modeling of radiative forcing and emissions. See Ortiz *et al.* (2012).

from SRM, but they should still show that SRM reduces abatement costs.

(b) I would not refer to the final column of Tables 4.3.1 and 4.3.2 as "Total Damages," but rather as "Net Damages," since the abatement costs are undertaken as a policy to reduce the total damages.

(c) It may be worth looking at SRM as an option, which you are buying through the investment proposed, and then evaluate its benefit in the case where traditional technologies and prospective innovations do not deliver. This sees SRM as a "last-resort" solution, which may be politically more feasible. This would require a different kind of analysis than the ones conducted here.

Conclusions

These four subchapters enrich our understanding of the options for addressing the climate change challenge and cover the main forms of intervention. Their main shortcoming is their failure to address two of the most important aspects: public concern about possible major negative impacts and the fact that even modest damages would have serious consequences for the vulnerable and poor members of society. CBA has always tended to be weak on these issues of uncertainty and equity, yet tools have been developed to address them; but these tools have either not been used in the subchapters or, if they have, their treatment is unclear.

The consensus for a target stabilization of GHGs at 450 ppm is largely based on the precautionary principle – this is the level at which the risks of major damage are kept low while the costs of the target are not unduly high. That was the argument in the Stern Report (Stern, 2006), for example, and I do not see the subchapters rebutting it. Tol assumes damage levels that are too low and does not give enough importance to the equity and uncertainty issues. Galiana and Green focus on an important instrument for reducing GHGs but focus exclusively on R&D and do not pay enough attention to the role of incentives in reducing emissions from energy-efficiency improvement and the risk that the technologies may take longer to come up with the required solutions. Bickel and Lane make a case for R&D on climate engineering but the assessment does not allow enough for the risks that the investment will produce a non-viable technology. Finally Bosello *et al.* do not take account of the poor state of knowledge on the returns to investment in both adaption and mitigation.

Knowledge on impacts is improving, and when we appraise the introduction of new policies and measures, it would be worth our while to see what we can learn from the success and failure of the instruments that are currently being implemented, instruments such as carbon taxes and emissions trading schemes, R&D subsidies, non-economic measures to promote energy efficiency, and the like. They will not work equally well or badly in all places where they are tried, and details of how they are implemented will influence the estimated BCRs.

Bibliography

Aldy, J. E. and R. N. Stavins, 2008: Introduction: international policy architecture for global climate change, in J. E. Aldy and R. N. Stavins (eds.), *Architectures for Agreement: Addressing Global Climate Change in the Post-Kyoto World*, Cambridge University Press, New York

Criqui, P., S. Mima, and L. Viguier, 1999: Marginal abatement costs of CO_2 emission reductions, geographical flexibility and concrete ceilings: an assessment using the POLES model, *Energy Policy* **27**, 585–601

EC, 2003: *World Energy, Technology, and Climate Policy Outlook: WETO 2030*, EUR 20366, Directorate General for Research, European Commission, Brussels

Ortiz, R. A., A. Golub, A. Markandya, O. Lugovoy, and J. Wang, 2012: DICER: a tool for analyzing uncertainties in climate policy analysis, *Energy Economics*

Parry, M., 2007: The implications of climate change for crop yields, global food supply and risk of hunger, SAT eJournal | ejournal.icrisat.org, **4**, 1–44

Parry, M., N. Arnell, P. Berry, D. Dodman, S. Fankhauser, C. Hope, S. Kovats, R. Nicholls, D. Satterthwaite, R. Tiffin, and T. Wheeler, 2009:

Assessing the Costs of Adaptation to Climate Change: A Review of the UNFCC and Other Recent Estimates, International Institute for Environment and Development and Grantham Institute for Climate Change, London School of Economics, London

Ranger, N., A. Millner, S. Dietz, S. Fankhauser, A. Lopez, and G. Ruta, 2010: *Adaptation in the UK: A Decision-Making Process*, Policy Brief, September 2010, International Institute for Environment and Development and Grantham Institute for Climate Change, London School of Economics, London

Stern, N., 2006: *The Economics of Climate Change: The Stern Review*, Cambridge University Press

CHAPTER 5

Education

PETER F. ORAZEM*

Introduction

The World Bank's first effort to spur educational investments in children was in Tunisia in 1962. At that time, 41 percent of the world's children aged 6–11 were not in school.[1] In SSA, only 25 percent of primary-aged children were in school, while enrollment rates in the Arab States (39 percent) and South Asia (44 percent) were only modestly better. Their parents were not in a position to produce the education in the home – only one-third of the adult population in low-income countries were literate and the average adult education level was 1.6 years. Even in middle-income countries, about 20 percent of the primary-aged children were not in school, and one-third of their parents were illiterate with an average education level of 2.8 years. Given the overwhelming evidence that literacy and schooling can improve health and economic outcomes, the World Bank's focus was on expanding the supply of available schools and qualified teachers.

Over the next forty-nine years, the World Bank has invested $69 billion around the world to increase schooling outcomes in developing countries. Schooling outcomes have improved dramatically in the developing world over that time. Only 10 percent of primary-aged children are not in school. The enrollment rates in the Arab States (86 percent) and South Asia (91 percent) are more than double the rates in 1960. Of the primary-aged children out of school in these regions, just over half will never attend school while the rest have either dropped out after attending for at least some years or will enter eventually. Consequently, primary completion rates are approaching 90 percent or more in these areas, as they are in the world as a whole.

Current children in low-income countries had the added benefit of more literate parents: now 61 percent of adults in low-income countries can read and write. In middle-income countries, 83 percent of parents are literate. As the children currently in school become adults, they will continue the process of making schooling investments self-sustaining. The link between the education of parents and their children is strong in every country, whether through the added income that schooling generates or through the added appreciation for schooling among literate adults. Consequently, the cost of inducing parents to send their children to school declines as education becomes more widespread in the adult population.

Nevertheless, progress on school enrollment is quite uneven. In SSA, 23 percent of primary-aged children are not in school. This is an improvement from 1960 to be sure, but still a disturbingly high level in a world where universal completion of primary schooling by 2015 is one of the UN MDGs. But even in SSA, the problem is not common across all countries. Over 30 percent of primary-aged children are not in school in Equatorial Guinea (46 percent); Côte d'Ivoire (43 percent); Niger (41 percent); Nigeria (37 percent); Burkina Faso (36 percent), and the Central African Republic (CAR) (31 percent).[2] In South Asia, where progress toward schooling for all has been impressive in general,

* I thank Yiting Li and Claudio Montenegro for helping me locate critical data for the report, Beth King for providing background information, and Lant Pritchett, George Psacharopoulos, and the staff at Copenhagen Consensus for helpful comments on earlier drafts.

[1] These are UNESCO and UNICEF data compiled in Bellamy (1999).

[2] Data are from UNESCO (2011).

Pakistan still has 34 percent of its primary-aged children out of school. The source of these weakest educational outcomes in South Asia and SSA seems to reside outside the school system, however. All of these countries rank among the poorest governed according to the Fund for Peace Failed States index.

The interactions between incentives to invest time in schooling and the economic and political climate in which the schools reside are critically important if we are to make progress on universal primary education. To capture a return on investments in schooling, individuals have to have the expectation that the government can insure them from the threat of expropriation of life, liberty, or property. And given that security, the rewards are greatest if the government provides sufficient mobility so that each individual can allocate their skills to the sector that offers the greatest reward. As shown in King *et al.* (2012), the highest returns to schooling in the developing world are found in countries that score highest in economic freedom. It is in those countries that demand for schooling will be greatest and where progress toward schooling for all will be most easily made. Of course children can be compelled to attend school, but absent the freedom to use their skills, both the individual's and the country's returns will be small.[3]

This brief summary of the world's success in getting children into school suggests that the vast majority of children in even the poorest countries attend school and most now complete the primary cycle. Any effort to move children never in school to enroll will have to target children in failed states: the countries that now produce most of the exceptions to this general trend of rising enrollments. These are the countries that fail to provide many other public services besides education; that cannot provide their citizens the benefit of the rule of law; and whose governments are themselves ridden with corruption and criminality. Such countries are not good candidates for schooling investments. Rampant corruption means that any international transfer of funds directed to education in the country will likely be subject to large leakages to other purposes. Even if the funds go to their intended ends, parents will be unlikely to respond because there is little perceived return to human capital in countries that do not protect property rights, enforce contracts, or protect life. Even if the children go to school, the public and private returns will be lower because the child is less likely to have a long productive work life and because the skills learned in school will not be used for their most productive ends. Perhaps one could justify schooling investments in such countries on strictly moral grounds, but the investments cannot be justified using a cost-benefit criteria such as that underlying the Copenhagen Consensus.

I should note that in his Alternative Perspective Paper on this topic (Chapter 5.2), George Psacharopoulos argues that we should not ignore the failed states on both expected returns and on equity grounds, and he makes a strong case in support of his view. While I am not persuaded that the returns are higher on that margin than the ones I propose, other readers will be, and so I encourage you to examine his case as well.[4]

My assessment is that the more plausible returns come from schooling investments in developing countries whose market and political institutions instill confidence that schooling investments will be rewarded. Because these countries already have most of their children in school for at least some period of time, the investments' possibilities will

[3] An example is Cuba, where schooling rates and test scores are the highest in Latin America but the country remains much poorer than countries with lower levels of schooling but greater freedom to apply skills to their most productive ends.

[4] George Psacharopoulos reports that returns to schooling in twenty-one of the sixty countries designated as failed states have returns to schooling that are as large as returns in more functional countries. My concern is that estimated returns are lacking in thirty-nine of the sixty states. I suspect that estimated returns are lacking because it is not safe to conduct a survey, which is also why returns to human capital investments are likely to be low in these states. In the remaining twenty-one failed states, I suspect that the surveys are confined to subregions where data is safe to collect. However, even if these estimates are accurate for children who receive schooling, one must ask why the other children are not in school. My assessment is that it is not because schools are unavailable, but rather that factors associated with the failed state (insecurity, corruption, discrimination, ethnic conflict) are constraining enrollment. If so, enrollments will not increase until the government establishes legitimacy.

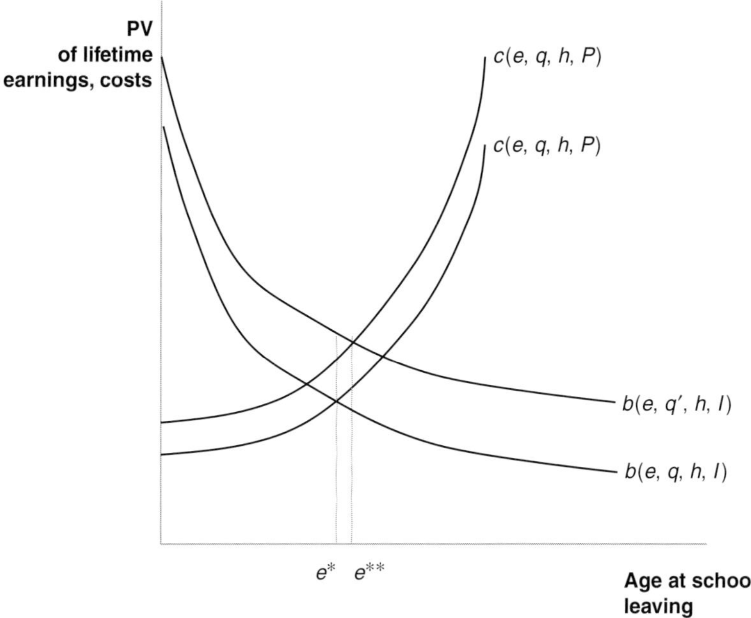

Figure 5.1 *Marginal cost and benefit of schooling*

be either to increase the number of years of schooling or to increase learning p.a. of schooling. In the next section, we examine which of those options is more likely to capture a large return.

Why school quality improvements are the dominant strategy in theory

Our theoretical presentation is an adaptation of the framework developed by Bleakley (2010b). For a given country i in year t, the anticipated PV of devoting e_{it} years of life to schooling is given by $b(e_{it}, q_{it}, \boldsymbol{h}_{it}, l_{it})$. The benefit is presumed to decline in years of schooling due to the diminishing marginal productivity of schooling. School quality, q_{it}, and a health index, $\boldsymbol{h}_{it}$, both raise the marginal benefit of schooling. Higher-quality schooling increases the marginal increment in skills from a year of schooling, skills that raise wages every year after leaving school. Better health raises the ability to learn while in school and raises the productivity of skills after leaving school.[5] Finally, better economic institutions, I_{it}, that improve the climate for applying skills to sectors freely without fear of expropriation also raise the efficient allocation of skills to tasks and hence raise returns to schooling.[6] The presumed shape of the marginal schooling benefit relationship is shown in Figure 5.1.

The parents' discounted cost of investing in an additional year of schooling is given by $c(e_{it}, q_{it}, \boldsymbol{h}_{it}, P_{it})$. The primary source of these costs is the opportunity cost of time, which rises with years of schooling and past human capital accumulations. We would also expect that higher school quality raises past skill attainment for every year of schooling, and so the opportunity costs of

[5] See Bleakley (2010b) for a comprehensive review of the evidence supporting the role of improved health on earnings and education.

[6] Murphy *et al.* (1991, 1993) provide theoretical and empirical arguments explaining why free and open economic institutions are conducive to growth. Acemoglu and Johnson (2005) and Acemoglu *et al.* (2001) show how the protection of property rights and the rule of law benefit growth. Acemoglu and Robinson (2005) also argue that more democratic political institutions benefit growth. King *et al.* (2012) show that these same factors raise the returns to human capital.

Table 5.1 Change in the percentage of primary-aged children in school after fee elimination in SSA

Country	Year fees eliminated	% enrolled before elimination (year)	% enrolled 2009	% change in enrollment rate
Cameroon	2000	69.5 (1991)	91.6	31.8
Ethiopia	1994	20.3 (1994)	82.7	307.4
Ghana	2005	59.5 (1999)	75.9	27.6
Kenya	2003	62.4 (1999)	82.1	31.6
Lesotho	2000	57.3 (1999)	73.1	27.6
Mozambique	2004–2006	52.4 (1999)	90.6	72.9
Tanzania	2001	49.3 (1999)	96.4	95.5
Zambia	2002	69.3 (1999)	90.7	30.9
Malawi	1994		90.8	49[a]
Uganda	1997		92.2	68[a]
Other SSA	Reference	62 (1999)	77	24

Note: [a] Estimated by Kattan (2006) from changes in gross primary enrollment rates.
Sources: Kattan (2006); World Bank (2009); Author's computation of *World Development Indicators*.

schooling also rise in q_{it}. Greater health makes anyone more productive in the labor market, and so opportunity costs also rise in $\boldsymbol{h}_{it}$. The direct costs of schooling are given by P_{it}, which includes the distance to school and the fees or material costs charged to parents. The presumed shape of the marginal cost of schooling is also demonstrated in Figure 5.1. Parents evaluate the benefits and costs of the schooling opportunities afforded their children and decide to keep their children in school through age e^*.

There are several mechanisms that the government has at its disposal to influence parental schooling investment. These include building more schools, eliminating school fees, improving school quality, improving the provision of government services that complement schooling such as public health, or improving economic institutions to enhance the market return on human capital investments. The relative returns to these policies depends on the country's current level of schooling investment and the fraction of children already in school.

When a country has a large share of its children out of school, so that schooling costs exceed the benefits at all positive values of e, policies that shift the cost function downward are most effective. These would include building more schools to lower the travel costs of attendance or lowering fees. This could also involve tying school attendance to transfers to the household, whether in kind (meals or health services provided at the school) or in cash transfers. Programs that shift schooling investments from 0 to some positive level will capture returns equal to the area under the marginal benefit curve in Figure 5.1. Because the highest marginal benefits are at the lowest levels of schooling, such strategies can capture substantial returns. However, these policies will have much smaller returns if a substantial portion of the school-aged population is already in school.

It is apparent that households can be quite sensitive to changes in schooling fees. Several African countries have eliminated fees over the past fifteen years. The increase in the proportion of primary-aged children attending school is often dramatic, as shown in Table 5.1. Countries that have eliminated fees have experienced much larger increases in school enrollment than their neighboring countries that continued to charge fees. Furthermore, several studies have shown that the dramatic increase in school enrollments has not seriously eroded school quality and may even be accompanied by improvements in test scores.[7] Nevertheless, these policies are only cost-effective when a large number of

[7] See the reviews by Kattan (2006) and the World Bank (2009).

parents are withholding children from school because of the fees. As indicated on p. 274, the remaining countries with substantial proportions of children being withheld from school tend to be ones with poor prospects for a return to investments in schooling.

Consequently, our better strategy is to focus on policies that will raise returns in countries that already have their children in school. In such countries, a policy that moves average years of schooling from e^* to e^{**}, as in Figure 5.1, will have only a modest return. Instead, policies should focus on shifting the entire schedule of marginal benefits upward through improved economic institutions, improving child health, or providing higher-quality schools.

The least expensive of these options is to improve the climate for economic freedom. King *et al.* (2012) showed that countries with low costs of establishing a business, strong protection for property rights, and a low tax burden for supporting the government had significantly higher returns to schooling than did similar countries with more restrictive economic climates. The improved marginal benefit from these institutions are substantial. An additional year of schooling increased annual income by 9.7 percent in developing countries in the upper quartile of the Heritage Foundation's Economic Freedom Index, but only 6.3 percent for developing countries in the bottom quartile. In other words, a country can increase the returns to schooling by a third by making it easier for their population to pursue entrepreneurial ventures and by insuring that the gains to success will not be expropriated by the government or by criminals. While the cost of these reforms is low in one sense, it often requires a complete reorientation of the economy and the government to a market system. The experience of the transition to market in the former Soviet states suggests that the cost of the conversion can be substantial, even if the benefits once the transition is completed are also substantial.

The theoretical effect of improvements in school quality are similar to the theoretical effects of improved health – both will shift up the marginal benefit curve and both will increase the cost of additional schooling because of added opportunity costs. In Figure 5.1 we demonstrate the theoretical effects of an improvement in school quality from a level q_{it} to a level q'_{it}. Notice first that because both marginal benefits and marginal costs rise, the effect of improved school quality on years of schooling is ambiguous. Children may actually spend less time in school when school quality improves, although in our example, we let years of schooling rise modestly as a particular example.[8] What is unambiguous is that the PV of any given year of additional schooling rises with school quality.

Not shown in Figure 5.1 is that an improvement in health from a level $\boldsymbol{h}_{it}$ to $\boldsymbol{h}'_{it}$ will shift the marginal benefit and marginal costs curves in the same direction as an improvement in school quality. Improved health will raise the PV of schooling in any given year, but it may cause years of schooling to decrease.

The other important implication is that the gains from an increase in q_{it} or h_{it} come mainly from their effect on increased productivity of schooling for years 0 through e^*, and not from any induced change in years of schooling. As school quality rises from q_{it} to q'_{it}, or as health rises from $\boldsymbol{h}_{it}$ to $\boldsymbol{h}'_{it}$, the value of the induced increase in schooling productivity is the change in the area under the two marginal benefit curves as the school leaving age increases from 0 to e^*. The gain attributable to the induced increase in years of schooling is the area below $b(e_{it}, q'_{it}, h_{it}, l_{it})$ between e^* and e^{**}. Of course, it is possible that the age of school leaving actually declines as school quality or health improve, which implies that all of the gain from improved school quality or health comes from the increased efficiency of producing human capital per year of schooling.

This chapter is supposed to evaluate alternative development strategies for the education sector. Now that the vast majority of children in developing countries are in school or else in a country where education investments hold little value, the best option is to try to bump up the marginal benefit per year of schooling in countries where children are already in school rather than to add additional years of schooling. As this section demonstrates,

[8] Cross-country analysis by Castelló-Climent and Hidalgo-Cabrillana (2012) is consistent with modest increases in attendance as school quality improves.

investments in health behave much like investments in school quality. Therefore, it is useful to compare the case for improving school quality versus an alternative use of the funds: to invest in child health. If education investments are to meet the Copenhagen Consensus cost-benefit bar, they must hold greater promise than investments in health, an issue we will address in the last section.

The World Bank's education strategy, *Learning for All* (World Bank, 2011) also focuses on school quality as the preferred mechanism to stimulate human capital development in LDCs. The World Bank's rationale for focusing on learning rather than years in school is quite different from the theoretical argument presented on pp. 275–7. The World Bank's strategy is predicated on the perception that many schools in developing countries are of poor quality. As evidence, the report cites findings that school achievement in developing countries lags that in developed countries for similar years of schooling and that children often complete the primary cycle unable to read and write. Indeed, studies show that cognitive attainment is more highly correlated with economic growth and *per capita* income than is years in school. But that finding is hardly surprising when we consider the implications of Figure 5.1. Cross-country variation in years of schooling has to explain less of the variation in *per capita* incomes than would direct measures of schooling outcomes such as test scores: Better schools and better complementary inputs such as health do not necessarily raise years in school but they do raise schooling outcomes. However, we do not know how much of the higher test scores in developed countries are attributable to better schools and how much to better complementary inputs such as better child health.

Focusing on school quality makes sense because the returns from expanding access to schools have been exhausted and not because the schools in developing countries are poor. The schools have always been poor, but they were better than no schools. We should now focus on the quality of schooling offered to those already in school, because the return from getting the last 5 percent of children never attending school to enter a school is outweighed by the cost.

There are several options that have been proposed to improve school quality in developing countries. The three that I will review in detail here include efforts to improve school management through decentralizing decision-making or increasing parental involvement; increasing the quality of teacher–student interactions through incentive programs or greater accountability that increase teacher effort; and efforts to increase the quality of child effort in school. These three strategies will be evaluated with respect to the quality of our current knowledge of their effectiveness, their costs of implementation, and how easily strategies that prove effective in a local area can be generalized to the country level or to other countries. I will then compare the potential benefits of these three options to a like-sized investment in child health.

Do investments in child health contribute to economic growth?

Maddison (2001) developed series of world populations and output that spanned 2,000 years. His data provide a useful perspective from which to judge the role of health and nutrition on growth. At the time of the first Roman Census, there were 231 million world inhabitants. By the cusp of the Industrial Revolution in 1700, the world population was 603 million – a net increase of 0.06 percent per year. Labor productivity grew at an even slower pace of 0.02 percent per year, so that a worker in 1700 was only 1.4 times more productive than a worker in year 0.

In the subsequent 300 years, the world population increased tenfold, a rate of 0.8 percent per year. Even so, the average person was becoming better off because labor productivity was also rising at 0.8 percent per year. As a result, living conditions improved rapidly along almost any metric. Life expectancy in England stood at thirty-two years at the start of the industrial revolution, and rose to forty-eight by 1900. Similar gains occurred elsewhere in Europe (Fogel, 2004).

One key factor was rising scientific knowledge, that led to improved sanitary and health conditions for peoples living in close proximity to one another, and a rising literacy base that enabled individuals to learn about how to avoid disease. But none of that would have been possible, as persuasively argued by Fogel (2004), without the dramatic improvement in agricultural technology that led to a rising nutritional status of the average citizen, the freeing up of rural labor for industry, and the rising purchasing power of urban wages due to cheaper food. The role of the agricultural revolution in setting the stage for rising living standards is so important that Huffman and Orazem (2007) could point to only two cases – Hong Kong and Singapore – where growth had occurred without a dramatic increase in agricultural yields. In those two cases, the city states were able to trade their way into the agricultural revolutions occurring elsewhere.

Before 1700, the Malthusian prediction that the population expanded to consume any available increases in food production was essentially correct, as evidenced by the absence of appreciable growth in *per capita* output. During those 1,700 stagnant years, *per capita* food production was too low to energize the labor force for hard work. Fogel (2004) estimated that at least 2,000 calories per person would be necessary to support a full day of productive work. In the late 1700s, about 40 percent of the French males and 20 percent of the British males did not attain this minimal level of nutrition, meaning that they were too undernourished to perform a full day of work. Because the location of crop failures and food shortages varied from year to year, even those who attained the minimal level of nutrition on average were so stunted that they were at substantially higher risk of incurring chronic health conditions and of premature mortality. Only after the improvements in fertilizers, animal husbandry, plant and animal breeding, transportation, storage, and sanitation were the populations of Europe sufficiently nourished to do the work of the Industrial Revolution. Only with the resulting rise in life expectancy did the average citizen have an incentive to acquire added skills, including literacy and numeracy. Only then was there a critical mass of educated citizenry necessary to spur the technological revolutions that followed.

Applying Pritchett's (1997) estimate of the minimum income necessary to attain nutritional subsistence to Maddison's (2001) estimates of GDP *per capita*, we know that most of the world's population in 1700 was too malnourished to perform significant work. In much of SSA, diets today are comparable to the diets available to the OECD countries at the start of the Industrial Revolution. It is doubtful that we will see dramatic growth in *per capita* incomes in Africa without the same attainment of nutritional adequacy that has pre-dated the industrial revolutions on all the other populated continents.

UNICEF compilations indicate that 28 percent of children in developing countries are moderately or severely undernourished. In areas where malnutrition is common, nutritional supplements and/or treatments for intestinal diseases or parasites offer an inexpensive way to raise school attendance and physical and mental capacity. The earliest efforts to use nutrition as a development tool date back to the 1969 intervention designed by the Institute of Nutrition of Central America and Panama (INCAP) in Guatemala. Researchers provided food supplements to pregnant women and young children in four villages. Two villages were given a high-protein, high-energy drink and two were provided a no-protein, low-energy drink. Both supplements contained vitamins and minerals. For seven years, information was collected on physical growth, mental development, school attendance, and morbidity along with information on nutrient intake and on characteristics of the family.[9] Because the assessment reflects a comparison of two nutritional supplements that differ only in protein, the effects understate the benefits of more general improved nutrition that would include vitamins and minerals. Nevertheless, the effects were quite impressive. Taking the more complete dietary supplement led to increased birthweights, lower infant mortality, and faster physical growth through the first three years. Thereafter, both groups of children grew at rates comparable to those of well-nourished children.

[9] Summaries of the study design and findings can be found in Martorell (1995) and Martorell *et al.* (1995). Behrman (2009) provides a comprehensive review of the short- and long-term studies from an economic perspective.

However, the more impressive results came from a follow-up survey of the children when they reached 25–42 years of age. Both boys and girls who received the high protein-high energy drink demonstrated better cognitive abilities. The males were able to engage in more physical labor and they earned a third more than comparable males in the control villages. The young women who took the more nutritious drink were taller and had lower body fat. The boys did not attend school longer, but they learned more. The girls attended school 1.4 years longer, and learned more. While there are weaknesses in the study's design that might give us pause, the weight of the evidence that improving nutrition improves human capital outcomes is quite impressive.

A key advantage of these nutritional supplement interventions is their modest cost. Damon and Glewwe (2009) estimated that the program cost $23.25 per year per child including a $5 annual cost for medical care. There are additional efficiencies from distributing these supplements at school which limits costs of transportation and storage. One could even consider making the supplement conditional on child attendance, although that seems unnecessary. Parents who value the supplement may end up sending their children to school longer even if attendance is not required, as was true in the INCAP case for girls. Furthermore, if the treatment is not for nutrition but for disease prevention or eradication, as with vaccinations or treatments for intestinal worms, broader distribution increases the effectiveness of the treatment by lowering the number of children in the area who are at risk for contracting and spreading the disease.

Improved health increases the efficiency of child time in school through several avenues. Properly nourished children can better concentrate on school work. Moreover, brain development is adversely affected by nutrient deficiencies so that supplements of micronutrients such as iodine, zinc or iron or additional calories available from school meals can improve cognitive ability (Zimmerman *et al.*, 2006; Horton *et al.*, 2009). As shown in the INCAP study, these nutrient advantages even pass from mother to child, as children undernourished *in utero* are also disadvantaged in cognitive development (Doblhammer *et al.*, 2011; Zimmerman, 2009) and infant health. Finally, if the nutrients are made available at the school, there is an additional reason for the parents to send their children to school.

Just as there is evidence that improving nutrition can have lifetime benefits, there is also evidence that malnutrition during a child's formative years compromises both cognitive and physical development later in life. Glewwe *et al.* (2001) found that, controlling for other household background measures, children who were malnourished early in life start school later, complete fewer years of schooling, and learn less per year of schooling. In a series of studies examining the role of armed conflicts on child welfare, Richard Akresh and his colleagues[10] demonstrated that crop failures and disruptions in food supply consistently led to stunting of young children and to decreased completed years of schooling which would permanently lower lifetime earnings.

There are strong theoretical reasons why interventions aimed at raising human capital accumulations should occur early in life. Examination of Figure 5.1 shows that an early intervention with persistent effects can raise the marginal benefit curve at every stage of life, but waiting limits the benefits to whatever length of life is left. James Heckman and his colleagues have argued in a series of studies that it is the earliest interventions in schooling that are the least costly and most effective.[11] Indeed, there is ample evidence that early nutrition interventions are successful and can have favorable lifetime impacts in both developed and developing countries. In the United States, Bhattacharya *et al.* (2006) found that recipients of school breakfast programs built better eating habits by reducing the percentage of calories from fat and increasing fiber intake. Recipients also had fewer deficiencies in vitamin C, vitamin E, folate, potassium, and iron, all of which have important implications for improved health or cognitive development.

In Bolivia, Behrman *et al.* (2004) conducted an experimental evaluation of the *Proyecto Integral*

[10] See Akresh and de Walque (2011), and Bundervoet *et al.* (2009, 2011).

[11] See Heckman and Masterov (2009) for a review of this literature.

de Desarrollo Infantil (PIDI) program in Bolivia. This program provides daycare, nutritional inputs, and pre-school activities for low-income children aged 6–72 months. For children exposed to the program for periods exceeding 1 year, the authors report permanent gains in cognitive development and fine motor skills. Grantham-McGregor *et al.* (1991) report comparable findings for a similar program aimed at stunted infants in Jamaica, as do Armecin *et al.* (2006) for low-income rural households in the Philippines.

Nevertheless, nutritional interventions can still be cost-effective later in life, even if they would have been even more effective had they been implemented earlier. The benefits are not confined to early childhood interventions. McGuire (1996) reports that giving iron supplements to secondary school age children (13–15 years) in a low-income country can raise cognitive abilities by 5–25 percent or the equivalent of 0.5 years of schooling. These nutrients can even improve cognitive abilities in adults, as was demonstrated by Brown *et al.* (2006), who found that Indian textile workers became more productive after being given inexpensive iron supplements and treatments for intestinal parasites.

Parasitic infestations can rob a child of necessary nutrients even when the child has enough food. Worm infestations cause symptoms ranging from chronic fatigue and weakness to protein malnutrition, abdominal pains, and anemia. Malaria is a parasitic invasion of the bloodstream that can result in recurring bouts of chills, sweats, nausea, aches, and fatigue in the milder cases to seizures, kidney and liver disease, and death in the more severe cases. Numerous studies have shown that children exposed to intestinal worms or malaria miss significantly more days of school (Miguel and Kremer, 2004; Bobonis *et al.*, 2006; Bleakley, 2010a).

Protection from the worms is amazingly inexpensive. A 20 cent pill provides protection for four months with 99 percent efficacy, meaning that less than $1 a year can protect 99 percent of the children from the disease. Because the disease is spread by fecal contamination of water or soil by infected people, as the number of infected people decreases the probability of infection falls even for people who are not treated. Therefore there is a significant external benefit to untreated people from treating a subset of the population.

Miguel and Kremer (2004) examined the effects of an intervention in which a subset of schools received treatments and a second set of schools were excluded. The cost of the program, including the pills along with the costs of distribution and administration, came to $3.50 per student. As expected, infection rates were cut in half in treated schools. However, student absenteeism in treated schools fell 25 percent. Follow-up surveys of the children who were exposed to the program early on worked 13 percent more hours and earned 20–29 percent more than did the children in the control schools who were not exposed to treatment until two–three years later (Karlan and Appel, 2011).

Bobonis *et al.* (2006) repeated the intervention for a sample of pre-school students in Delhi. Treated children received deworming medicine along with iron and vitamin A supplements. Attendance increased 20 percent.

By now, we can have a high confidence that nutritional supplements and treatments for parasites can make children healthier and increase the productivity of the time spent in school, at least in experimental settings. We also have strong evidence that protracted interventions on a broader scale have significant positive effects on student time in school, learning, and lifetime earnings. Bleakley (2007) studied the impacts on health, education, and income from a large-scale hookworm eradication program that was initiated in the Southern United States in 1910. Infection rates were 30–40 percent. Children who grew up in the areas where the eradication campaign was focused most intensively increased school attendance and literacy attainment significantly. The estimated impacts on adult income suggest that going from an area with 100 percent probability of infection to 0 raises adult income by 43 percent.

Bleakley (2010a) performed a similar analysis of the effects of growing up in an area that experienced malaria eradication in Brazil, Colombia, Mexico, and the United States. Children growing up in areas with successful eradication were much more likely to attain literacy and had significantly higher incomes later in life: from 12 percent higher in the United States to 40 percent higher in Latin America.

In short, there is substantial evidence from small-scale experiments to large-scale parasitic eradication and nutrition programs that children can gain lifetime benefits from improvements in their nutritional health. These interventions are frequently of modest cost compared to other programs aimed at raising human capital development. They also have substantial external benefits in that even untreated recipients can benefit, whether *in utero* children are born healthier when their mother receives nutrient supplements or untreated children face lower risk of infection because their friends are receiving deworming medicine. It is against this backdrop that other programs aimed at improving schooling outcomes must be judged for cost-effectiveness. For children who start school malnourished, stunted, and deprived of nutrients necessary for proper cognitive development, no improvement in school quality will improve the child's lifetime prospects more than addressing the malnutrition at an early age.

Do school investments contribute to economic growth?

Years of schooling

Before embarking on strategies expending public funds for schooling, we have to establish whether such investments contribute to the public good. Human capital has played a prominent role in explanations of economic growth since the time of Adam Smith (Smith, 1776), who pointed to the ability to specialize according to skill as the source of increasing labor productivity. Schultz (1975) emphasized the ability to combine managerial skills with other inputs as a source of increasing returns to scale that is essential to economic growth. Lucas (2002) saw spillover benefits from placing educated peoples in the presence of other educated peoples. All of these ideas suggest that investments in education make the individual more productive but make other workers and other factor inputs more productive as well.

Given the prominence of human capital in theoretical explanations of economic growth, the empirical evidence supporting the existence of spillover benefits from private educational investments is decidedly mixed. Punctuating that view are three reviews of social returns to schooling in developing countries, all basing their conclusions using a different approach to comparable cross-country data sets and all using the level or growth of output per worker as the dependent variable. Patrinos and Psacharopoulos (2011) found large positive spillover benefits that were much larger than private returns to schooling. Lange and Topel (2006) concluded that social returns were no smaller than private returns, but were not much larger. Pritchett (2006) concluded that there was no evidence of spillover benefits.[12]

It is tempting to dismiss these macroeconometric studies of the role of educational attainment on the productive capacity of an economy, given the lack of agreement on how to properly specify empirical formulations of economic growth. Durlauf *et al.* (2005) reported that across over 400 studies, 145 different variables had been shown to explain the cross-country pattern of growth in at least one analysis. Consequently, it is not surprising that schooling has been shown by some to be critical to economic growth while others conclude that it lacks any social benefit beyond the private return earned by those receiving the schooling. Nevertheless, this research has played a significant role in the debate on public support for schooling, including in 2004 and 2008 Copenhagen Consensus Challenge Papers, and so I provide my assessment of this research.

One reason for the lack of consensus on the magnitude of social returns to schooling investments is that the presence of these spillover benefits depends critically on the ability for individuals to apply their human capital to productive ends. Countries that protect property rights and allow individuals to apply their skills to their highest rewards

[12] Cohen and Soto (2007), Barro and Lee (2010) and Breton (2012) present evidence that when additional data, alternate measures of education, or alternative specifications are used, macroeconometric estimates of the effect of schooling on output per worker are similar to the returns to schooling estimated from microeconometric Mincerian earnings functions. However, they are not larger than the private returns, as would be required if education had substantial external benefits.

Table 5.2A Random effects estimation of the effect of changes in level and average schooling on ten-year labor productivity growth

Exogenous Variable	1	2	3
S_{it}	0.023** (2.35)	– 0.134** (2.41)	– 0.132** (2.37)
S_{it*} *Heritage*		0.0025** (2.48)	0.0024** (2.41)
S_{it*} *Polity*		0.0027 (0.79)	0.0028 (0.81)
K_{it}	– 0.032** (2.46)	0.183** (1.95)	0.24** (2.34)
K_{it*} *Heritage*		– 0.0029* (1.75)	– 0.004** (2.11)
K_{it*} *Polity*		– 0.0136** (2.24)	– 0.014** (2.32)
$(S_{it} - S_{it-10})$			– 0.263 (1.37)
$(S_\downarrow it - S_\downarrow(it - 10))$**Heritage*			0.004 (1.15)
$[\![(S]\!]_{it} - S_{it-10}) * Polity$			0.008 (0.69)
Trend	– 0.0025** (2.3)	– 0.0027 (1.30)	– 0.0024** (2.14)
Constant	5.22** (2.47)	4.23* (1.86)	3.42 (1.42)
R–squared	0.022	0.056	0.064
N	309	309	309

Notes:
t-statistics in parentheses.
Dependent variable: $[\ln(y_{it}) - \ln(y_{it-10})]$, where y_{it} is GDP per worker in country *i* in year *t*.
S_{it}: average years of schooling for the population aged 25 and over in country *i* in year *t*.
K_{it}: capital per worker in constant 2005 dollars in country *i* and year *t*.
Heritage: Heritage Foundation Index of Economic Freedom, with higher values being freer in the base year *t*.
Polity: Freedom House Imputed Polity Index, with higher values being more Democratic in the base year *t*.
Regressions also included uninteracted Heritage and Polity effects which were significant and positive in all regressions.

will encourage the types of productive contracting that Schultz (1975) and Lucas (2002) argued would generate spillover benefits. Schultz (1975) went further, to explain that managerial skills are most productive in the face of rapidly changing technologies and market conditions, but that human capital has little value in economies where traditional technologies are used. On the other hand, corrupt political institutions encourage unproductive applications of skills where the most able try to extract resources from their neighbors (Murphy *et al.*, 1991, 1993). Studies that fail to control for the economic environment in which the educational investments occur will have trouble identifying spillovers.

We can illustrate the importance of economic and political institutions by replicating the specifications used by Lange and Topel (2006) and Pritchett (2006) with a dataset composed solely of developing countries over the period 1960–2010. The growth in GDP per worker is regressed on initial levels and changes in average years of schooling, holding fixed capital per worker and a trend measure. The results are shown in Table 5.2A. Column (1) shows that starting a decade with an additional year of average schooling leads to 2.3 percent faster productivity growth over the next ten years. While the effect is statistically significant, it is quite small in magnitude and does not suggest large external benefits from schooling, consistent with the Topel–Lange and Pritchett conclusions. Column (2) adds interaction terms with measures of economic and political freedom. Column (3) adds terms in the change in years of schooling over the decade as well as the start-of-period level of schooling. The change in years of schooling does not add significantly to our ability to explain labor productivity growth, so we will focus on the results in column (2).

The level effect of years of schooling on growth turns out to be negative – implying literally that a country that has no democracy and no economic freedom loses 13.4 percent of its productivity over ten years per year of schooling. Counteracting that

Table 5.2B Implied impact of schooling level and economic and political freedom on ten-year growth in labor productivity

	Schooling quartile (average years of schooling in year *t*)		
Freedom quartile	25 %ile (1.9 years)	Median (3.6 years)	75 %ile (6.1 years)
25 %ile	0.004	0.007	0.012
Median	0.03	0.058	0.098
75 %ile	0.068	0.130	0.220

effect is the finding that as the country moves up the distribution of economic and political freedom, the returns to schooling in the form of productivity growth turn positive. While the coefficient on the interaction between *Polity* and years of schooling is not significant, the joint effect of schooling including the interactions with *Polity* and *Heritage* were significant.

In Table 5.2B, we simulate the effect of rising schooling and rising economic and political freedom on labor productivity growth. At the lowest freedom quartile, being in the upper quartile of years of schooling only raises ten-year productivity growth by 1.2 percent. In contrast, the same level of schooling in a country at the upper quartile of economic and political freedom will experience 22 percent labor productivity growth over the next ten years. In effect, if a country wishes to reap a reward from its schooling investments, it needs to provide its citizens sufficient freedom to apply their human capital. King *et al.* (2012) found corroborating evidence that it is the freest societies that have the highest returns to schooling.

There is also more consistent corroborating evidence of the existence of educational spillovers in microeconomic datasets. Moretti (2004a, 2004b) showed that workers and firms gain productivity when they are in markets with greater concentrations of educated workers. Nor are the benefits confined to economic returns. Lochner and Moretti (2004) showed that education lowers incidence of crime. Currie and Moretti (2003) showed that higher maternal education increases infant health and lowers the probability that the child will have only one parent or will be exposed to second-hand smoke. Grossman (2006) provides a comprehensive review of studies that demonstrate that higher levels of education lower population growth, raise child health and education, and improve individual health as an adult. These benefits provide additional social returns beyond the estimated improvements in labor productivity above any private gain.

Two further studies provide a historical context that further demonstrates why education still remains a compelling strategy for economic development. Becker and Woessmann (2009) show that the spread of the Protestant Reformation and its emphasis on reading scripture led to a more literate work force. Counties closer to Wittenberg, the home of Martin Luther, experienced more rapid income growth and a more rapid path to industrialization. Given the improvements in employment opportunities for low-skilled labor and gains in life expectancy and nutritional status associated with the industrial revolution (Fogel, 2004), it seems apparent that the gains in average literacy benefitted not only those who acquired literacy but the population as a whole.

Aaronson and Mazumder (2011) evaluated the impact of a philanthropic effort to add schooling options and improve school quality for black children in the American South. The Rosenwald Rural School Building Program to educate Southern black children added almost 5,000 schools between 1913 and 1931. Because the program was not evenly distributed throughout the South, we can assess how exposure affected years of schooling, cognitive attainment, and geographic mobility of these children when they reached adulthood. Children exposed to the program had significantly improved human capital and mobility outcomes compared to those who did not grow up in close proximity to a Rosenwald school. The estimated rate of return in the form of enhanced earnings potential of recipients relative to the cost of the schooling investment was between 7–9 percent, well in excess of returns to bonds at the time. That the program served a social desire to equalize economic opportunity for a population that was inefficiently excluded from the opportunity to acquire human capital means that there was an additional social return beyond the private return going to the recipients.

My assessment of the most recent macroeconometric evidence supports the view that increased years of schooling can yield significant social returns, but only if the country has economic and political institutions that complement schooling. That still leaves open the issue of how one can increase schooling investments most efficiently.

School quality

A second series of papers has argued that it is school quality and not years of schooling that matters for economic growth. The empirical evidence advanced to support this conclusion involves findings that direct measures of human capital outperform years of schooling in explaining various measures of labor productivity. Microeconometric studies that have information on both years of schooling and measures of cognitive attainment typically find that it is the latter that raises earnings (Glewwe, 2002). A similar result holds in studies of economic growth. When both measures of average years of schooling and average cognitive attainment are included as variables explaining growth in output *per capita*, it is the cognitive attainment that more strongly affects growth (Hanushek and Kimko, 2000; Hanushek and Woessman, 2008).[13] These studies treat higher average cognitive attainment as indicative of better school quality.[14]

While countries that have higher test scores at the same years of schooling may have higher school quality, that is not the only possible interpretation. It is possible that greater cognitive attainment is due to factors separate from the school but that complement educational production. Countries with higher tests scores at a given level of schooling may have higher parental inputs into their children's human capital production; greater endowments of child health; more favorable community support for education; or any number of other factors that could affect child learning. It is also possible that cognitive attainment and years of schooling are alternative measures of human capital attainment, but that the latter measure is subject to more random error. The greater weight placed on cognitive attainment could be a simple artifact of measurement error.

An additional concern is that there are relatively few developing countries that have participated in the international tests used to measure relative cognitive attainment by country. Of the sixty-two countries that participated in the PISA test, only four are LMICs and none are poorer than that. As a result, the conclusion that it is cognitive scores and not years of schooling that is critical to economic growth is based disproportionately on the experience of developed countries.

The World Bank strategy to focus on school quality rather than expanding enrollment was heavily influenced by the finding that measured school output dominates measured time in school as a predictor of economic growth or individual earnings. Nevertheless, it is important to understand that the studies cited in this section only demonstrate that cognitive attainment matters for growth, but they do not necessarily show that it is improved school quality that generates the improvements in cognition. We will return to that point in the next section, after defining the educational production process more rigorously.

How is school quality produced?

Educational production

A tremendous amount of work has been expended trying to identify what inputs or strategies make schools more efficient at generating human capital. A review by Glewwe *et al.* (2011) reported that there had been over 9,000 studies completed since 1990! And yet we have few concrete findings that would guide a strategy using school quality as a way to foster economic development. It is useful

[13] Breton (2011) argued that when correct empirical specifications and properly timed measures of school quality are used in the estimation, both quality and quantity of schooling matter for explaining economic growth.

[14] Castelló-Climent and Hidalgo-Cabrillana (2012) provide a different argument: that school quality raises the return to schooling and is the cause for rising quantity of schooling.

to review a simple model of the educational production process that explains why research on this topic has proven so frustrating.

The process of education involves a cooperative venture between teacher and student to produce educational outcomes, B.[15] The value of B can be viewed as the area under the marginal benefit curve in Figure 5.1: the PV of all skills produced in school over the years the child is in school. Both teachers and students get utility from higher levels of B, and so they have an incentive to cooperate to produce more skill. The key cooperative element is the willingness of the teacher and the child to allocate time to the school. The proportion of time that the teacher attends school is e_T and the proportion of time the child attends is e_C. Attendance varies between 0 and 1, with 0 meaning never attending and 1 meaning attending full-time. The teacher and child time interact with school and home inputs to produce B according to

$$B = \gamma(q_T e_T^{\rho} + q_C e_C^{\rho})^{\frac{1}{\rho}} \tag{1}$$

where q_T and q_C are the quality of school inputs attached to the teacher and the child. The teacher's input quality will depend on the school attributes X and the teacher's own attributes, μ_T: $q_T = q(X, \mu_T)$. The child's input quality will also depend on the school attributes and the child's attributes, μ_C: $q_C = q(X, \mu_C)$. Relevant teacher attributes include ability, training, and socio-economic background. Relevant child attributes include ability, health, and socio-economic background. The parameter γ is a measure of school efficiency in converting inputs into cognitive skills and can be viewed as a measure of administrative skills available in the school. The parameter ρ is a measure of increases in the substitutability of teacher and student inputs in the production of cognitive skills.

This simple model of educational production makes it clear why the evidence that cognitive skills are more closely tied to growth in earnings or labor productivity does not imply that length of time in school is less valuable than school quality. Cognitive skills are a direct measure of school output B while time in school (e_C) is just one of several inputs into the production of B. Children with identical school effort will nevertheless have very different values of B depending on the levels of e_T, μ_T, μ_C, X, and γ. In addition, one cannot take a high realization of B and presume to know which one of the inputs e_T, e_C, μ_T, μ_C, X, or γ is responsible. Presumably, the most productive schools have high values of all of these inputs.

(1) also explains why despite the 9,000 studies of the educational production process reviewed by Glewwe *et al.* (2011) and the thousands that were produced before 1990,[16] we have no confidence regarding which school inputs are the key ones to produce quality. The production process is driven by unobservable teacher and child attributes μ_T, and μ_C, that are offered to the process subject to the parents' and teachers' assessments of the production process. The time in school e_T, and e_C, is observed on attendance registers, but the actual effort expended in learning and teaching is not. Furthermore, levels of e_T and e_C are themselves chosen based on the expectations of both parties. Consequently, schools with the same attributes X can produce dramatically different levels of skill B depending on the effort expended by teachers and students (e_T and e_C) and depending on the quality of complementary backgrounds that teachers and students bring to school (μ_T and μ_C). Even the various school inputs X are subject to choice because their use depends on the children's capacity to learn and the teachers' ability to teach.[17]

The most important element of school quality is undoubtedly the teacher. An early project by Murnane (1975) showed that certain teachers in inner-city schools consistently produced classes of high-achieving students while their colleagues consistently produced inferior results. Thirty years later, Rivkin *et al.* (2005) found the same results in Texas. And yet the teachers were indistinguishable in terms of education, experience, pay, and

[15] This model is based on Banerjee *et al.* (2012), who present a more detailed version of the joint-attendance decisions of teachers and students. Note that one could also couch this model as a bargain between schools and households, but the discussion is more straightforward when we focus on teacher and child.

[16] See reviews by Hanushek (1986, 1997) for earlier studies of the education production process.

[17] In Pakistan, I visited a school with classroom closets full of textbooks left in their original paper wrappers while the children were left without books. The teachers did not want the books to be damaged.

in-service training. Good teachers had high levels of unobserved attributes μ_T and effort e_T, and they inspired their students to apply high levels of their own unobserved attributes μ_C and effort e_C, and yet the source of the persistent quality was not identifiable by either the econometricians conducting the analysis or the administrators setting the compensation policy.

The most comparable example from a developing-country perspective is the study of middle-school test performance in China by Lai *et al.* (2011). Again, there were large differences in student performance across schools that appear driven by teacher abilities. However, the key observable teacher attribute was the teacher's rank, which is set by an evaluation process. Students taught by higher-ranked teachers performed better, but there were no significant relationships between student performance and university-educated teachers, teachers who undertook informal pedagogical training, or teachers' years of experience. We are left with the circular result that higher-ranked teachers teach better, and that teacher ranking is based on their ability to teach.

Any effort to raise school quality has to confront the decisions that set levels of the key inputs, e_T, e_C, μ_T, μ_C, X, and γ. The challenge is that most of the relevant variation in these inputs across schools is not measured by administrative data. Schools and teachers with outstanding levels of cognitive attainment B will look identical on paper to schools and teachers with mediocre results.

Incentives and effort

A common problem in developing countries is that the teachers shirk their responsibilities. Teacher absenteeism averages 19 percent in developing countries compared to 5 percent in developed countries (Chaudhury *et al.*, 2006; Das *et al.*, 2007). Moreover, substitute teachers available in developed countries are largely absent in developing countries. Improving school quality in developing countries has to confront the problem of shirking teachers.

Teachers are paid w_T as long as they are not caught shirking. The probability of being caught shirking and then being fired is α, $\alpha \in [0, 1]$. The teacher can also earn an alternative wage outside their teaching obligations, w_{0T}. Therefore the teacher faces a budget constraint composed of what they can earn in and out of school:

$$W_T = (1 - \alpha(1 - e_T))w_T + (1 - e_T)w_{0T} \qquad (2)$$

If teachers get utility from the attainment of their students and they take the child's attendance as determined, their attendance decision is governed by

$$U_T'(B)\left(q_T e_T^{\rho} + q_C e_C^{\rho}\right)^{\frac{1}{\rho}-1} q_T e_T^{\rho-1} = U_T'(b)\frac{\partial B}{\partial e_T} = w_{0T} - \alpha w_T \qquad (3)$$

The left-hand side of (3) is the marginal utility the teacher gets from spending additional time in school and producing added cognitive attainment in the child and the right-hand side is the amount the teacher could earn if that same time were instead spent in an alternative activity net of any expected lost earnings from teaching if caught shirking. The condition encapsulates many of the issues surrounding the debate on school quality in both developing and developed countries. If teachers are held responsible for shirking (α is set at a high level, so the expected penalty from poor performance is high), then teachers will attend more regularly. On the other hand, teachers will also attend more regularly if they are paid more (w_T is set at a high level). Teachers also attend more regularly if the school offers high-quality inputs (high levels of X), or if the teacher values child learning highly (high level of $U_T'(B)$). But the other implication of (3) is that *anything that raises child attendance will cause teachers to attend more regularly as well.*

The child's decisions are symmetric. The child can earn a wage w_{0C}(B) if the child works rather than attending school, where the child labor wage is conditional on the child's cognitive attainment to date. The condition setting how much time the child will attend is:

$$U_C'(B)\frac{\partial B}{\partial e_C} = w_{0C} - \frac{(1 - e_C)\partial w_{0C}}{\partial B}\frac{\partial B}{\partial e_C} \qquad (4)$$

The left-hand side of (4) is the marginal utility from additional cognitive attainment from spending more time in school, while the right-hand side is the earnings from spending time in the child labor market net of the lost opportunity to raise the opportunity wage even more by spending additional time in school. The child attends more regularly if child labor is prohibited and if cognitive attainment is highly valued. High-quality school and teacher inputs raise the marginal product of child time in school, which both increases the utility from time in school and lowers the value of time in child labor which increases child attendance. In particular, *anything that raises teacher attendance will raise child attendance as well.*

We can now summarize the options available to policy-makers trying to improve school quality. Those include:

- Improve school inputs, X
- Improve school efficiency, γ
- Raise teacher attendance, e_T, by raising wages, w_T, or by increasing monitoring for shirking, α
- Raise child attendance, e_C, by lowering child opportunity wage, w_{OC}, or by raising the anticipated return to schooling, $\frac{\partial B}{\partial e_C}$
- Improve child health or other elements of socio-economic background, μ_C.

We will review the prospects for cost-effective interventions for each of these in turn.

What are the prospects for getting a reasonable return from improving school quality?

Investing in improved school characteristics, X

Perhaps because countries attempt to standardize the inputs they allocate to schools, there is not much evidence that variation in school characteristics alter learning outcomes to a significant degree. By and large, schools have the same textbooks and materials, classroom buildings, and curricula, at least on paper. That lack of variation makes it difficult to evaluate whether changes in the input mix would affect learning outcomes. Glewwe *et al.* (2011) concluded that children perform better in schools with adequate desks and a permanent structure as compared to sitting on mats in the open air, but most children already have access to those minimal school attributes. Glewwe and Kremer (2006) did suggest that developing countries probably underinvested in schooling compared to developed countries, but they did not have strong suggestions for how additional monies might be spent.

In times past when there were many underserved children lacking access to a nearby school, the case for large public building efforts may have been more compelling. That was the case with the Rosenwald schools. That was also the case in Indonesia in the 1970s, where Duflo (2001) showed that a major effort to expand primary-school access in Indonesia had a large impact on enrollments and, over time, a modest but significant impact on earnings as well. As we showed on p. 273, however, the vast majority of children in the world have access to a school and spend at least some time in it. Even if we had better understanding of the productivity of various inputs, it is doubtful that we would get sufficient improvements in learning outcomes to pay back the costs of further investments in school infrastructure.

Improving school quality by improving school management, γ

As early as 1962, international agencies such as the United Nations and the World Bank were advising that the decentralization of public service delivery could serve as a development strategy. The move toward more local control is motivated by the belief that decentralized control will result in better school outcomes, holding constant the level of resources devoted to the school. Local decision-makers should have more information on local needs and conditions, and could adjust resource allocations accordingly. Central dictates that are aimed at maximizing welfare on average may over-supply the service in some areas and undersupply it in others. Local officials should better respond to local needs because they are more exposed to pressure from constituents and because they may use quality public services to attract or retain residents.

Tempting as it is to assume that we can spend the same amount on schooling and get better outcomes if we only managed schools better, evidence that we can raise γ by shifting responsibility from the Ministry of Education to local school managers is decidedly mixed. In the case of schooling outcomes, even the most supportive studies tend to argue that decentralization helps some schools but not others. There are numerous reasons why local control may yield poor outcomes. Bardhan (2005) and Bardhan and Mookherjee (2006) argue that autonomous decisions are particularly prone to fail in developing countries. First, populations may not be mobile, and so households may not move because of poor-quality public services. Second, local officials may be subjected to undue influence by prominent local families seeking to divert public resources towards their private needs. A related problem is that there may be no tradition of monitoring of local officials by local residents, so presumptions of greater accountability with local control may not hold in fact. Finally, local officials may lack the necessary experience or skills to manage resources in countries with few well-educated professionals. Any one of these problems could create difficulties for decentralized school systems.

A more fundamental concern is that any effort to devolve authority to the local school level will require that local school principals, teachers, parents, or community leaders choose to exert effort to manage the school. This point was driven home by Gunnarsson *et al.* (2009), who found that most of the variation in school autonomy was within countries and not between countries. Even supposedly centrally managed school systems have some degree of local participation while supposedly locally managed systems often have decisions dictated by central authorities. As a result, localities only participate actively in decentralization initiatives if it is in their interest to do so. In Latin America, more local authority was exercised by schools in localities with more-educated parents and more-remote locations (Gunnarsson *et al.*, 2009). In Argentina, the best outcomes from a decentralization initiative were in districts that responded quickest and were in wealthier areas Galiani *et al.*, 2008). In El Salvador, benefits of decentralization were found in the schools that took up an offer of greater autonomy, but not all schools opted in (King and Ozler, 2001).

The key benefit of decentralization is supposed to be that resources will be used more efficiently. However, that requires both capable and ethical public servants at all levels of the government. Unethical local authorities may take advantage of their increased freedom to transfer resources away from their efficient uses. In Uganda, only 13 percent of bloc funding for decentralized schools ended up at the schools while the rest disappeared in the bureaucratic maze (Reinikka and Svensson, 2004).

Hanushek *et al.* (2011) examined the role of decentralization on student outcomes across forty-two countries that participated in the PISA international tests. They conclude that decentralization increases test scores in developed countries and countries with well-developed managerial capacity in education. However, decentralization lowers student outcomes in poorer countries and countries that lack institutional capacity to manage schools. Their cross-country results are consistent with the findings within countries that decentralization works best in the best-managed and most-educated communities. Losers tend to be the districts with the weakest managerial capacity and the poorest and least-educated parents.

These findings suggest that decentralization ought to be offered but not mandated. Only those communities or districts that expect to benefit will participate. The poorest and least-educated communities will opt not to participate, the communities that would be harmed if the decentralization were mandated by the central authority. Because I can not advocate a universal move toward increased local autonomy, I do not believe that this option would pass muster on a global benefit–cost criterion.

Raising teacher attendance by improving compensation (w_T) or increasing monitoring (α)

We know that teachers are important for school quality and that teacher absenteeism is a common problem in developing countries. A naïve view would be to contend that if teachers are paid to teach, then public expenditures are already in place and one need only compel the teachers to show up for work. But teacher absenteeism has been recognized as a problem for decades, and yet it persists. Governments either lack the will to enforce contractual obligations; or they lack the resources to monitor teacher performance; or they view teacher postings more as investments in political patronage than human capital development. It seems clear that the solution to teacher absenteeism will not be found by asking governments to continue doing what they are currently doing, but with more diligence.

Several efforts have attempted to improve the monitoring of teacher attendance. Duflo *et al.* (2010) report on an experiment where teachers in a one-teacher school were asked to have a student take a picture with a date stamped on the photo. Teachers were paid a bonus depending on how many days they attended. Absenteeism was 44 percent before the program was instituted and fell to 21 percent afterward while remaining above 40 percent in a set of control schools. The improvement persisted over time, increasing the time students had access to a present teacher by 30 percent. Student performance was 0.17 standard deviations higher in the schools with the cameras than in the control schools.

Unfortunately this solution has only limited application. It works in cases in remote schools where monitoring teacher attendance is costly. It is also important to note that these teachers were not part of the government system where bureaucratic rules would undoubtedly conspire to restrict its use. Indeed the authors also followed a similar scheme used to monitor the absenteeism of government nurses. At first, nurses' absenteeism fell by half, similar to the finding for the teachers. But soon the government began allowing exceptions to the monitoring program and lax enforcement caused a reversal of the initial improvements.

This divergence of outcomes between similar interventions applied to teachers in government postings versus teachers hired outside the civil service bureaucracy is a recurring theme in the development literature. Teacher attendance in private schools is much more regular than in government schools despite higher pay in government schools. Duflo *et al.* (2009) report on Kenya's Extra Teacher Program, which provided funds to hire additional teachers on a contract basis to be used in grades 1 and 2. Despite the reduced class size, children assigned to civil servant teachers in the schools receiving extra teachers scored no better than those in schools without the additional teachers. The apparent reason is that from an already abysmal attendance rate of 58 percent, civil service teachers reduced their attendance an additional 13 percentage points in schools that received extra teachers. Meanwhile, the contract teachers attended more frequently than civil service teachers despite being paid 25 percent of the civil service rate. Students taught by the contract teachers attended more frequently and scored 0.23 standard deviations higher on tests than did students taught by the civil service teachers in the same schools.

A similar program was instituted in Andhra Pradesh province in India (Muralidharan and Sundararaman, 2010). Teachers on fixed term, renewable contracts lacking the professional training normally required for a civil service posting were hired and randomly posted to 100 government schools. Pay was on a par with private school salaries, but only one-fifth the pay of the civil service teachers. Nevertheless, attendance by contract teachers was significantly higher than for civil service teachers (84 percent versus 73 percent). Students in schools receiving the extra teacher performed significantly better in tests of mathematics and language. An earlier study by Banerjee *et al.* (2007) found that contract teachers who provided tutoring to weak students significantly raised the performance of those children in the current year and the effect remained significant but smaller once the tutoring ended. A third study in Uttar Pradesh and Bihar by Atherton and Kingdon (2010) also found that contract teachers attended more regularly, performed better, and at a third of the civil service pay standard.

The Indian cases demonstrate a significant challenge to school reformers. In private schools, teacher performance is closely tied to pay, but not in government schools (Kingdon and Teal, 2007). In private schools, teacher attributes such as tenure on the job, scores on tests, and pedagogical methods affect students' performance, but not so in government schools (Aslam and Kingdon, 2011). Unionized teachers are paid more, but perform worse in the classroom (Kingdon and Teal, 2010). Why then would a move toward contract teachers not be warranted?

There are two main concerns that suggest that the use of contract teachers will only be a short-term solution. First, it is not sustainable to maintain two teaching cadres, one that is highly paid, enjoys job security, and has no expectation of performance and a second that is poorly paid, has no job security, and is expected to make up for the failings of the first group. At some point, one would have to ask why the government continues to employ the civil service teaching cadre. If the contract teachers become a threat, the civil service teachers will press to have the system disabled.[18] Replacing the civil service teachers with contract teachers is a political impossibility

The second concern is that if the contract system becomes regularized so that there are two teaching systems, the contract system will eventually adopt the rules that have made the civil service system non-functioning. Once contract teachers become regular teachers, why would their performance not revert to the civil service standard? In fact, the superior performance of contract teachers may be a transitory phenomenon if the contract teachers ultimately expect to become civil service teachers. If contract teachers discover they will never gain a permanent posting, would their superior performance continue?

Nor does decentralized control of the schools appear to offer a solution to civil service teacher absenteeism. Banerjee *et al.* (2010) review a series of efforts in India designed to improve community monitoring of schools and teachers in the village. Village Education Committees (VEC) composed of parents, the village head, and the head teacher are empowered to monitor teacher performance and to request school resources from the education district. The experiments attempted to improve the capacity of the VEC to manage the schools. One intervention was aimed at informing the village about the function and power of the VEC to manage the school. A second added training in administering and interpreting literacy tests that would give the village an independent assessment of children's progress in the school. The third added an additional component that trained volunteers to provide supplemental reading instruction after school. None of the interventions significantly affected teacher attendance. Children who attended the afterschool reading classes did improve their reading skills, but there were no apparent enhanced learning outcomes related to the teacher's actions. These disappointing outcomes mirror the findings from efforts to decentralize discussed in the previous section: local control is difficult to foster in areas that lack managerial capacity and educated parents.[19]

The most plausible solution is to tie teacher pay to performance, the subject of an experimental evaluation conducted by Muralidharan and Sundararaman (2011a) in Andhra Pradesh province, India. The program offered a bonus averaging 3 percent of annual pay to civil service teachers based on the average improvement of their students' test scores in an independently administered exam. Despite the modest cost increment, student performance was 0.27 standard deviations higher in mathematics and 0.17 standard deviations higher in languages compared to students in schools without the bonus. In addition, students performed better in sciences and social studies. The gains came despite the fact that teacher attendance was no higher in the bonus schools. On the other hand, teachers apparently used their in-class time more effectively and their students were given more out-of-class assignments to work at home or in teacher-administered supplementary sessions. Furthermore, teachers appear to have been accepting of the bonus payment system, especially younger teachers who had lower initial pay. Interestingly, teachers who expressed the greatest support *ex ante* were the ones whose students performed the best *ex post*, suggesting that the most able teachers are the ones who are comfortable with performance pay.

This most favorable outcome serves as a counterpoint to a similar experiment attempted in Kenya (Glewwe *et al.*, 2010). Teachers were offered a reward amounting to 2–4 percent of annual pay

18 In both Kenya and Andhra Pradesh, the perceived need to add teachers led to proposals to expand the civil service ranks substantially, so the policy was to expand the underperforming ranks while limiting the size of the contract teacher program.

19 An expert on educational decentralization confided to me that, in his experience, every successful effort to foster parental control over local schools involved support of the parents' activities by an NGO commissioned to carry out the project. Once the project ended and the NGO exited, the parental control would fall apart, suggesting that it was the NGO that had effectively exerted authority over the local school.

based on their students' test scores, with penalties applied if students did not take the exam. Performance on the exam increased, but performance on other exams showed no improvement. Performance did not persist beyond the current school year. Neither teacher nor student attendance was affected. The one significant behavioral change was that time spent preparing for the incentivized exam increased in 88 percent of the schools where bonuses were offered.

It is tempting to use the Indian case to support a move toward bonus pay. The cost was modest compared to the benefits of increased cognitive development. However the Kenya experience suggests that the case for a broad-based adoption of performance-based pay is premature.

This is the stage where Lant Pritchett departs from my suggested strategy, arguing in his Alternative Perspective Paper (Chapter 5.1) that the case for improvements in school management and improved teacher incentives promise the highest returns. We differ in our assessment of whether the current state of evidence is sufficiently strong to advocate a general move toward strategies such as those summarized on pp. 288–91. I encourage readers to examine his arguments advocating a focus on improving school quality, in both Chapter 5.1 and in his forthcoming book on the subject (Pritchett, 2013).[20]

Lowering child opportunity wage (w_{OC}), raising the return to schooling $\left(\frac{\partial B}{\partial e_C}\right)$, or improving the child's socio-economic status (μ_C)

Providing information on the true returns to schooling

One of the barriers to schooling is that parents and children do not have a grasp of the true returns to education. This is particularly true in rural or remotely sited schools where it is more difficult to observe how education can raise lifetime earnings. As Schultz argued in his essay on the role of human capital in disequilibria (Schultz, 1975), traditional farm households are efficient given what they know about their markets and technologies, but they are poor because those traditional markets and methods do not allow for much more than subsistence. A production analysis confirms that formal schooling does not have a return in traditional rural households (Fafchamps and Quisumbing, 1999) tied to migration to an urban market where skills and specialization are rewarded.

Supportive evidence is found in the fact that rural enrollments react positively to the possibility of migrating to nearby urban markets (Tansel, 2002) or to higher observed returns in those markets (Kochar, 2004). Boucher *et al.* (2005) found that rising returns to education in Mexico following the installation of the PROGRESA rural conditional cash-transfer (CCT) program (discussed on p. 293) is largely attributed to the migration of the more-educated rural workers to urban markets. It seems that knowledge of returns to schooling in other markets and the ability and willingness to commute to those markets is critical to school enrollments and attendance in more remote locations.

Orazem and Tesfatsion (1997) demonstrated that when children based their expectations of returns to schooling on their parents' experiences rather than global information on returns to schooling, inefficient human capital investments resulted. In developed countries, the empirical research on impacts of neighborhoods on schooling decisions of disadvantaged youth is mixed at best (Oreopoulos, 2003; Lang, 2007). However, information on returns to schooling are easily observed in developed countries, but less so in developing countries. An inexpensive way to increase child attendance may be to provide children and their parents with accurate information about the value of education.

Jensen (2010) found that 8th-grade boys had a very low subjective estimate of the returns to schooling in the Dominican Republic. A random sample of these boys were given correct information on returns. The result was a significant

[20] My quibble with a key argument advanced by Pritchett concerns the exercise whereby cognitive attainment by children in the poorest-performing schools is compared to their attainment had they learned at the pace of the children in the best-performing schools. Pritchett argues that the source of the gap is due to underperformance of the schools, and he may be correct. But it is also possible that the children perform poorly in the "bad" schools because they lack the inputs that complement schooling such as adequate nutrition, health, or family support of schooling, in which case they would still under perform in the "good" school.

increase in persistence to graduation from high school of 9 percentage points for those whose subjective returns were increased to the true rate of return. Nguyen (2008) conducted a similar experiment on primary students in Madagascar. Grade 4 students in schools where they and their parents were given information on the returns to schooling increased their attendance by 3.5 percentage points and increased their test scores by 0.2 standard deviations.

With only limited experience with these interventions, it is premature to propose a global program of informing parents and children about the true returns to schooling. And yet it would be difficult to devise a less-expensive intervention and one with virtually no chance of unintended consequences. In the Madagascar case, Nguyen reported that the cost was just 8 cents per student! If children increase their intensity of effort in school as a result of being told the best estimates of the true returns in the local and more remote labor markets, it would have to meet a benefit-cost criteria.

CCTs for school attendance

The most widely studied development intervention over the past fifteen years has been to tie desired household behaviors to the receipt of cash or in-kind transfers from the government. Fiszbein *et al.* (2009) listed twenty-eight countries that had initiated at least a pilot program since 1997 including virtually all Latin American countries, four in Africa, six in Asia, and two in the Middle East. The programs are targeted to households in the lowest socio-economic strata. In most cases, coverage includes 20 percent or less of the country's population. The targeting is pragmatic as the countries cannot afford to extend the benefits to all. The poorest are the group that is most likely to underinvest in their children's schooling because of liquidity constraints, and the amount of the transfer necessary to induce the desired behavior will be smallest in households with the lowest opportunity costs of time. Perhaps because the programs focus so intensively on the poorest social strata, benefits have shown little evidence of leakage to the non-poor.

The CCT programs typically require that child attendance in school meet a threshold level of 80 percent per month or more. They may also require that the children receive periodic health assessments at a local clinic and receive timely vaccinations, that the mothers receive training in nutrition and health, and that the mothers participate in perinatal care and receive training in early childhood development. As a result, the CCTs become an "umbrella program" aimed at incentivizing a broad array of desired behaviors believed to improve private and social outcomes. The transfers themselves are aimed at lowering the incidence of poverty and inequality in the society.

Few interventions have been subjected to so many rigorous evaluations that allow us to evaluate the outcomes relative to a baseline collected before the conditional transfers were implemented and that include randomized participants and controls. As such, the evidence of the outcomes of these programs should be particularly reliable for assessing whether further expansion is warranted.

First, the program has been applied to some of the poorest countries (Bangladesh, Burkina Faso) as well as countries that are relatively well off (Chile, Argentina). The transfers are typically modest, representing 10 percent of pre-transfer household consumption levels or less.[21] Median administrative costs including management, monitoring, and evaluation across ten programs evaluated by Grosh *et al.* (2008) came to 8 percent of the total costs which was lower than the administrative costs for other social assistance programs. The programs' transfer mechanisms have been adaptable to the level of financial sophistication in the country – from the use of debit cards readable at ATMs in Brazil to payments distributed through the post office or through village leadership. In short, CCTs have been quite flexibly applied to countries at all stages of development.

The Fiszbein *et al.* (2009) review summarizes how households have responded to these incentives. First, the transfers raised *per capita* consumption in all the countries evaluated, the primary aim of the poverty alleviation aspect of the program. In four of five countries with necessary data, expenditure shares on food rose significantly, suggesting that the transfers helped households meet their basic

21 The highest transfers were in Mexico and Nicaragua, averaging about one-third of pre-transfer consumption.

Table 5.3 Estimated short-run effect of CTTs on child time in school, by country

Country	Age/Grade	Impact (%)[a]	Transfer (%)
Bangladesh	11–18 (girls)	**27**	0.6
Cambodia	Grade 7–9	**33**	2.5
Chile	Age 6–15	**12**	7
Colombia	Age 8–13	**2**	17
	Age 14–17	**9**	17
Ecuador	Age 6–17	**14**	10
Honduras	Age 6–13	**5**	9
Jamaica	Age 7–17	**3**	10
Mexico	Grade 0–5	2	20
	Grade 6	**19**	20
	Grade 7–9	1	20
Nicaragua	Age 7–13	**18**	27
Pakistan	Primary girls	**38**	3
Turkey	Primary	–3	6
	Secondary	13	6

Note: [a] **Bold** values are significant at the 10% level or more.
Source: Authors' compilation of results reported in Table 5.1 of Fiszbein *et al.* (2009).

needs. In most countries, the incidence of health care visits and vaccinations for children in recipient households increased significantly. These results are important because they suggest that even before we consider child time in school, CCTs improve child health, nutrition, and socio-economic status. We learned on pp. 275–7 that these are factors that increase returns to schooling, at least in theory.

As for time in school, the evidence consistently supports the view that CCTs increase time in school. The short-term effects of the program are summarized for eleven countries in Table 5.3. In almost all cases, households increase their children's time in school in response to the CCT. Within countries, the largest impacts are found among the poorest households that are the most likely to face liquidity constraints that would inefficiently limit the time their children spend in school. Larger effects are found in rural areas where children face the highest opportunity cost of time in school. Consistently where evaluated, we find that the increased child time in school is accompanied by a reduced incidence of child labor. In one case in Brazil, the biggest decline was in the most hazardous forms of child labor (Yap *et al.*, 2009).

The Brazil case is useful because it is the largest CCT program. It also began as a municipality-led innovation and so it was implemented only gradually over time until it became a national plan. While it was not subject to an experimental design, Glewwe and Kassouf (2012) were able to evaluate its impacts on student outcomes by exploiting variation across municipalities in the timing of its implementation and program expansion. The program significantly reduced dropout, raised the promotion rate, and increased primary enrollment by 6 percent.

Less certain is whether more time in school results in better cognitive development. Few studies have examined the effect of receiving a CCT on test scores. Ponce and Bedi (2008) found no difference in 2nd-grade test scores between recipient and non-recipient children in Ecuador, but it is not clear that differences would show up that early in the primary cycle. More importantly, the test score is administered to children in school which means that time in school is held constant for recipient and non-recipient children. If CCTs increase cognitive attainment by increasing time in school, this study would fail to capture any effect. A study of adolescent girls who were exposed to a CCT program in Malawi (Baird *et al.*, 2011) found significantly higher performance in tests of English, mathematics, and cognitive attainment. It is plausible that the more positive evidence of cognitive improvements in Malawi are due to their inclusion of girls out of school as well as those still in school into the study. The girls receiving CCTs had more time in school relative to the control girls, and that additional time may be responsible for their higher test scores. Furthermore, by middle school, differences in academic attainment are easier to measure than they are in the 2nd grade.

The only long-term experimental measure of the effects of conditional transfers was reported by Behrman *et al.* (2011) for the PROGRESA/Oportunidades program in Mexico. Youths aged 9–15 when first exposed to the CCT program were aged 15–21 when an evaluation was made of their labor market and educational outcomes. Boys who were exposed to the program at age 9 ended up completing a year more of schooling than did boys without the program. The magnitude of the effect decreases as the length of exposure decreases. Girls exposed to the program earliest received 0.7 more years of schooling while girls exposed at older ages experienced no difference in schooling. Child labor decreased significantly for boys but not girls after exposure to the program. Exposure to the program significantly lowered the probability of working in agriculture, meaning that the additional schooling encouraged migration out of traditional employment. This is consistent with the role Schultz (1975) proposed for education of rural peoples – to allow them to adapt to changing economic opportunities – and is consistent with the Boucher *et al.* (2005) finding that the most educated rural youth are moving to urban markets.

What does the CCT have to do with school quality? Child attendance complements other school inputs, and so child cognitive attainment should be enhanced by more regular attendance. In addition, as shown in (3), teacher attendance will also increase with child attendance to the extent that teachers view cognitive attainment as a shared good with their students. Unfortunately, we do not have any studies that have examined what happens to teacher attendance in the presence of a CCT program aimed at their students, and so that link between child and teacher attendance must remain conjectural.[22]

It is important to note that the substantial increases in attendance related to the elimination of school fees reported in Table 5.1 did not erode learning outcomes in Africa, even when class sizes rose substantially. One would have expected that the addition of more children to existing schools would disadvantage those already in school, but that does not appear to have happened. One would also expect that the added children disproportionately come from more disadvantaged backgrounds and so they should underperform those who would have attended without an intervention, but that does not appear to be the case. Government schools were apparently able to adapt to the rising demand, even if resources were not added proportional to the increased enrollments. Similarly, rising demand for schooling induced by CCT programs or by improved information on returns to schooling do not appear to have lessened school quality. These results are consistent with a model where teachers respond positively to an increased demand for their services, but actual proof will require further study.

Benefit-cost comparisons of the most promising strategies

We can now return to the initial challenge posed on p. 278: do any of these interventions dominate a competing strategy aimed at improving child health? The answer is almost certainly no. Health interventions undertaken before schooling age, whether nutritional supplements, anti-parasitics, anti-microbials, or vaccinations, can insure the proper brain development necessary to optimize time in school. The cost of such programs is often quite modest and the gains last a lifetime. One could pair these interventions with schooling as the child ages by tying their distribution to the school. I would hesitate to suggest withholding the treatments only to regular attendees of the school, however, as the benefits of the health improvement alone is adequate justification for the treatment, independent of the complementary effects on schooling. Nevertheless, a program that combines CCTs for student attendance with improved information on the returns to schooling and school-based health programs represents a compelling package of complementary interventions that simultaneously address current poverty, health, nutrition, and human capital development. If the resulting boost to attendance results in a complementary increase in the quality of schooling provided by teachers who attend more regularly, the BCR becomes that much more attractive.

In Table 5.4, I present the benefits and costs of the three strategies that I believe offer the best evidence of success to date – nutrition supplements, offering information on returns to schooling, and

[22] An exception is Banerjee *et al.* (2012), who find that the single most important factor explaining primary-teacher attendance in the Northwest Frontier Province of Pakistan is the attendance of their pupils.

Table 5.4 BCRs from various interventions affecting schooling

	Low-discount (3%)			High-discount (5%)		
	Benefit[a] ($)	Cost[b] ($)	BCR	Benefit ($)	Cost ($)	BCR
Health and nutrition programs						
Bolivia pre-school (Behrman *et al.*, 2004)	5,107	1,394	3.7	3,230	1,301	2.5
Kenya worms (Miguel and Kremer, 2004)	1,560	3.5	445.7	646	3.5	184.6
Kenya pre-school (Vermeersch and Kremer, 2005)	1,560	29.1	53.6	646	28.6	22.6
Iron supplements (Knowles and Behrman, 2005)	474	10.5	45.1	330	10.3	32.0
India worms (Bobonis *et al.*, 2006)	2,201	112.0	19.7	868	112.0	7.8
Guatemala (Damon and Glewwe, 2009)	622	52	12.0	301	51	5.9
Information on returns						
Madagascar (Nguyen, 2008)	3,349	2.30	1456	1,455	2.30	632.6
Dominican Republic (Jensen, 2010)	7734	417	18.6	3356	417	8.1
CCTs						
Mexico (Behrman *et al.*, 2011)	2,679	500	5.4	1,082	390	2.8
Nicaragua (Maluccio, 2009)	6,003	1,574	3.8	4,412	1574	2.8
Honduras (Glewwe *et al.*, 2004)	9,178	266	34.5	4,064	219	18.6
Colombia (Attanasio *et al.*, 2005)						
Urban ages 8–13	9395	1,916	4.9	3168	1898	1.7
Urban ages 14–17	9395	767	12.2	5,957	759	7.8
Rural ages 8–13	9395	767	12.2	3168	759	4.2
Rural ages 14–17	9395	479	19.6	5,957	474	12.6
Ecuador (Schady and Araujo, 2008)	9100	572	15.9	4665	572	8.2
Chile (Galasso, 2011)						
Urban ages 6–15	0–21504[c]	542	0–39.7[c]	0–9903[c]	446	0–22.2[c]
Rural ages 6–15	0[c]	542	0.0	0[c]	446	0.0
Cambodia (Filmer and Schady, 2009)	1,849	709	2.6	939	709	1.3

Notes:
[a] Benefits are the PV from an additional year of schooling evaluated over a forty-year work career, evaluated at the average annual wage in the country.
[b] Costs are the PV of inducing 1 additional year of schooling.
[c] Estimated impact of schooling was not significantly different form 0 in some specifications. Estimates in rural areas were insignificant or negative.

CCTs. All have been shown to succeed with benefits that dominate costs.

Interested readers can request my detailed computations. My strategy was to first compute the cost of inducing an added year of schooling. These were discounted back to the first period of the intervention. I then imputed the PV of an added year of schooling over a forty-year work career. For very early interventions such as those in pre-school or primary grades, I assumed that the work career began at age 15. For the others, I assumed it began at the end of the intervention. Returns to induced schooling were computed using the returns to schooling for each country that were estimated for the King *et al.* (2012) study. Average wages in the country were computed using those same datasets. Therefore, the stream of returns from the intervention reflects the imputed gain from a worker

Table 5.5 Incidence of malnutrition, by region and income level, most recent measure available

	% of infants born with low birthweight	% of children under 5 who are malnourished[a]	% of population undernourished	% of households that use iodized salt
Region				
East Asia/Pacific	6.0	19.3	10.6	86.8
Latin America/Caribbean	8.4	2.0	8.9	
South Asia	27.3	47.5	20.3	
SSA	13.7	41.8	22.2	52.3
Middle East/North Africa	10.4	23.2		68.9
Income level				
Low-income	15.4	44.5	29.5	62.8
LMIC	21.0	41.8	16.5	54.2
Middle-income	15.2	30.4	12.5	72.3
Upper-middle-income	5.4	12.6	8.5	91.4
World	15.2	31.8	12.9	70.7

Note: [a] Measured by height for age.
Source: World Bank, *World Development Indicators and Global Development Finance*, http://data.worldbank.org/data-catalog/world-development-indicators.

having one more year of schooling compared to the average worker in the country.

There are several caveats to this procedure. First, not all papers reported increases in years of schooling as a result of the intervention, and so I had to generate an implied gain in years of schooling from reported increases in enrollment or attendance rates. Second, this method assumes that all returns come from increased years of schooling, but we know from p. 275 that the larger gains may come from increased human capital produced per year of schooling. As a result, these estimated returns are likely to be overly conservative as they ignore gains in the pace of cognitive development of the children while in school. Also, I do not add in likely external benefits from increased schooling in the form of reduced incidence of early pregnancy, lower incidence of criminal activity, improved health, or improved mobility of labor.

Several general findings are apparent. First, the climate for these interventions are better in economies with strong returns to schooling than in those where returns to schooling are depressed by poor government institutions. Therefore, the best places to try these interventions are countries that protect individual economic and political freedoms. Of course those countries would also have the better capacity to implement an intervention, whether distributing medication, CCTs, or information on the returns to schooling. Therefore my earlier comments regarding failed states apply to these interventions as well. Perhaps there is a menu of interventions one could apply to failed states, but it is unlikely to involve a coordinated government effort to improve schooling outcomes.

Second, nutrition or health interventions are much less expensive than are CCT programs. Perhaps that is why the CCT programs are concentrated in wealthier countries while the nutrition programs typically focus on the poorest. In fact, CCT programs require at least some minimum level of development to be feasible because they require a large enough population of the relatively well-off to subsidize those at the bottom of the income distribution. If the entire population is poor, redistribution is impossible (Table 5.5).

Related to that is that the requirement that benefits outweigh costs requires that the more expensive interventions be applied in relatively more developed economies. Returns come from induced returns to additional years of schooling. As thousands of Mincerian earnings function studies have found, log-wages are approximately linear in years of schooling, and so wage levels rise at an increasing rate as years of schooling increase. That means that increasing schooling by one year in a country where average schooling is at the primary level or less will generate a relatively small stream of benefits compared to an added year of schooling in a country where average schooling is at the secondary level. Only relatively inexpensive interventions can be tried in the poorest and least-developed countries.

Finally, the appropriateness of one type of intervention versus another also reflects the proximate cause for poor educational outcomes in the area. Not surprisingly, micro-nutrient interventions and deworming strategies will be most effective where those problems are most severe. As shown in Table 5.4, that would be in the poorest countries and in South Asia and SSA. Those interventions also tend to have the largest benefits relative to costs. That is to be expected. Provision of nutrient supplements and anti-parasitic medicines are very inexpensive and they can be delivered to children very early in life where they can make a lifetime of difference. Insuring proper nutrition at the time when brain development is occurring, whether before birth by insuring maternal nutritional health, in infancy, or in pre-school can both shift up and out the marginal return to schooling in Figure 5.1. It would be very difficult to design an intervention in these poorest countries that would dominate the BCRs of these nutritional interventions.

That said, the two studies that have explored the benefits of providing accurate information on the returns to schooling suggest that, for older children, a very inexpensive intervention with very large returns is just to provide children and their parents with accurate information on the value of schooling. Such an intervention could be easily built into the standard curriculum at low cost and has the potential of increasing academic effort while in school as well as increasing years of schooling.

Finally we have the CCT programs that have been popular in Latin America. Most but not all have been cost-effective. They are most effective when targeted at child ages where dropout begins, and so transfer programs aimed at younger children tend to fail the benefit-cost criteria.

These programs are most cost-effective when there is already a pre-existing CCT program aimed at helping the poor. These tend to be the more developed countries among the ones we have examined. In such circumstances, the marginal cost of taking an existing CCT program and adding conditions for its receipt is relatively low. It is unlikely that a country that has an insufficient upper class that could afford a CCT program or that does not have a pre-existing tax/transfer program would find such a program feasible on a national scale.

To that end, Behrman *et al.* (2011) present estimates of the benefits and costs of Mexico's PROGRESA/Oportunidades program which I reproduce in Table 5.4. Including possible costs of distortionary taxes and the opportunity cost of child time out of school as well as the costs of administering the program, the benefits of induced increased earnings easily outpace the costs of the program. However, they do not also add in the costs of the transfer itself, arguing that the transfer comes at no real cost to the country. While I appreciate the public finance argument underlying this stance, I do not believe it applies as well when one is first implementing a CCT program where the opportunity cost of scarce government funds may be very high. It is not obvious that if the transfer comes at the expense of government programs to provide security, rule of law, infrastructure, or other fundamental government services that the transfers come at zero cost to the country. In Mexico, where such transfers have been in place for many years, the opportunity cost of such funds can be more plausibly argued to be negligible.

Summary and recommendations

Now that most children in developing countries enroll in school, economic development strategies have shifted to enhancing their learning while in school. This has led to a focus on improvements in school quality. While such improvements should increase lifetime returns to schooling in a comparable fashion to improvements in child health, investments in school quality have some important disadvantages to health interventions in a benefit-cost sense. On the cost side, these interventions are typically more expensive per recipient than are nutrition supplements or preventive health. On the benefit side, the link between investment and resulting human capital acquisition is weaker than that between treatment and desired health outcomes. Our knowledge of which inputs generate quality schooling outcomes is very weak, and additional investments in school inputs are unlikely to generate the desired learning response. There is widespread acknowledgement that resources are used inefficiently, but efforts to improve resource management by devolving authority to local jurisdictions are as likely to fail as succeed. There is ample evidence of shirking by government teachers but efforts to increase monitoring have been disappointing. Use of alternative teachers, whether contract teachers or tutors, are often successful, but their use begs the question of why they must be hired when civil service teachers appear to be underperforming. In addition, if these teachers will be converted into permanent government employees eventually, we must presume that the benefits of using contract teachers or tutors will be fleeting. Tying teacher bonus payments to student performance on exams shows some promise, but there are too few studies to justify firm support for that option. Increasing years of schooling simply by providing accurate information on the returns to schooling is also quite promising and an inexpensive intervention, but again there are too few studies upon which to base a world strategy.

The most consistent evidence of success from schooling interventions in recent years comes from transfer payments targeted to the poorest segments of society conditional on the children attending school. These programs have consistently increased child attendance, even when the transfer is of modest size. Program administration costs have been lower than those of other social interventions. In addition to the positive schooling outcomes, these transfers have lowered the poverty rate, improved the nutritional status of poor households, and have increased the fraction of children receiving vaccinations and other health services. Even the most expensive and comprehensive of these programs, the Mexican PROGRESA/Oportunidades program, have met the benefit-cost criteria. Because the programs increase the intensity of child investment in school as well as increasing child time in school, they help to break the cycle of poverty whereby poor parents underinvest in their children's schooling and doom their children to poverty as well. And by increasing child attendance, we should see a concomitant increase in teacher attendance which will increase the quality of schooling offered to the poorest children in the country.

Nevertheless, these programs can only succeed in relatively developed countries where the government institutions necessary to identify the poorest households, manage a large CCT program, and monitor child attendance are well developed. That would suggest the prospects for using CCTs would be best in countries in South or East Asia or in the more advanced countries of Africa. Caldès *et al.* (2006) report that the per child cost of three CCTs programs in Latin America ranged from $468 to $514 in 2012 dollars. At $468/child, using CCTs for the poorest decile of all the children in South Asia would cost $7.8 billion, while targeting 10 percent of the children in East Asia would cost $6.7 billion. As a particular example, the annual cost of a CCT program would be $320 million in Vietnam and $221 million in Thailand.

In the poorer countries, programs aimed at improving the nutrient health of children are less expensive and can meet benefit-cost criteria despite the lower potential returns to human capital in such countries. Such programs can target very young children, taking advantage of potential increasing returns from interventions that bump up the marginal benefit from schooling. One could address the needs of all 175 million malnourished children in the developing world under age 6 at a cost of roughly $5 billion per year using estimates provided by John Hoddinott *et al.* in their Challenge Paper (Chapter 6).

All countries could benefit from improved information on the true returns from schooling. Although only two studies have buttressed that recommendation, the costs are very low and the potential benefits are quite promising. If one used the Madagascar estimates of 8 cents per child (Nguyen, 2008), one could address all 670 million school-aged children for $54 million, which is just implausibly low. However, there is certainly a case for applying the strategy in more piloted cases with rigorous evaluations so that we can get a better grasp of how best to transfer information on the benefits of schooling to children and their parents. The cost of a few more studies would be modest, and we would be ready to scale up four years from now once broader evidence is available.

Bibliography

Aaronson, D. and B. Mazumder, 2011: The impact of Rosenwald Schools on black achievement, *Journal of Political Economy* **119**, 821–88

Acemoglu, D. and S. Johnson, 2005: Unbundling Institutions, *Journal of Political Economy* **113**, 949–95

Acemoglu, D. and J. A. Robinson, 2005: *Economic Origins of Dictatorship and Democracy*, Cambridge University Press

Acemoglu, D., S. Johnson, and J. A. Robinson, 2001: The colonial origins of comparative development: an empirical investigation, *American Economic Review* **91**, 1369–1401

Akresh, R. and D. de Walque, 2011: Armed conflict and schooling: evidence from the 1994 Rwandan genocide, *World Bank Policy Research Working Paper* 4606, World Bank, Washington, DC

Alderman, H., 2001: Multi-tier targeting of social assistance: the role of intergovernmental transfers, *World Bank Economic Review* **15**, 33–53

Armecin G., J. Behrman, P. Duazo, S. Ghuman, S. Gultiano, E. King, and N. Lee, 2006: Early childhood development programs and children's development: evidence from the Philippines, *World Bank Policy Research Working Paper* 3922, World Bank, Washington, DC

Aslam, M. and G. Kingdon, 2011: What can teachers do to raise pupil achievement?, *Economics of Education Review* **30**, 559–74

Atherton, P. and G. Kingdon, 2010: The relative effectiveness and costs of contract and regular teachers in India, *CSAE Working Paper* 2010–15

Attanasio, O., E. Fitzsimmons, and A. Gomez, 2005: The impact of a conditional education subsidy on school enrollment in Colombia, *IFS Report Summary Familias 01*

Baird, S., C. McIntosh, and B. Ozler, 2011: Cash or condition? Evidence from a randomized cash transfer experiment, *Quarterly Journal of Economics* **126**, 1709–53

Banerjee, A., R. Banerji, E. Duflo, R. Glennerster, and S. Khemani, 2010: Pitfalls of participatory programs: evidence from a randomized evaluation in education in India, *American Economic Journal: Economic Policy* **2**, 1–30

Banerjee, A., S. Cole, E. Duflo, and L. Linden, 2007: Remedying education: evidence from two randomized experiments in India, *Quarterly Journal of Economics* **122**, 1235–64

Banerjee, R., E. M. King, P. F. Orazem, and E. M. Paterno, 2012: Student and teacher attendance: the role of shared goods in reducing absenteeism, *Economics of Education Review*, **31**, 563–74

Bardhan, P., 2005: *Scarcity, Conflicts and Coooperation: Essays in the Political and Institutional Economics of Development.* MIT Press, Cambridge, MA

Bardhan, P. and D. Mookherjee, 2006: Decentralisation and accountability in infrastructure delivery in developing countries, *Economic Journal* **116**, 101–27

Barro, R. J. and J.-W. Lee, 2010: A new data set of educational attainment in the world, 1950–2010, *NBER Working Paper* 15902, NBER, Cambridge, MA

Becker, S. O. and L. Woessmann, 2009: Was Weber wrong? A human capital theory of Protestant economic history, *Quarterly Journal of Economics* **124**, 531–96

Behrman, J. R., 2009: Early life nutrition and subsequent education, health, wage and intergenerational effects, in M. Spence and M. Lewis (eds.), *Health and Growth*, World Bank, Washington, DC

Behrman, J. R., Y. Cheng, and P. E. Todd, 2004: Evaluating pre-school programs when length of exposure to the program varies: a nonparametric approach, *Review of Economics and Statistics* **86**, 108–32

Behrman, J. R., P. E. Todd, and S. Parker, 2011: Do conditional cash transfers for schooling generate lasting benefits? A five-year followup of PROGRESA/Oportunidades, *Journal of Human Resources* **46**, 93–122

Bellamy, C., 1999: *The State of the World's Children, 1999*, UNICEF, New York

Bhattacharya, J., J. Currie, and S. J. Haider, 2006: Breakfast of champions? The school breakfast program and the nutrition of children, *Journal of Human Resources* **41**, 445–66

Bleakley, H., 2007: Disease and development: evidence from hookworm eradication in the

American South, *Quarterly Journal of Economics* **122**, 73–117

2010a: Malaria in the Americas: a retrospective analysis of childhood exposure, *American Economic Journal: Applied Economics* **2**, 1–45

2010b: Health, human capital, and development, *Annual Review of Economics* **2**, 283–310

Bobonis, G. J., E. Miguel, and C. P. Sharma, 2006: Anemia and school participation, *Journal of Human Resources* **41**, 692–721

Boucher, S., O. Stark, and J. E. Taylor, 2005: A gain with a drain? Evidence from rural Mexico on the new economics of the brain drain, University of California, Davis, mimeo

Breton, T. R., 2011: The quality vs. the quantity of schooling: what drives economic growth?, *Economics of Education Review* **30**, 765–73

2012: Were Mankiw, Romer and Weill right? A reconsideration of the micro and macro effects of schooling on income, *Macroeconomic Dynamics*

Brown, D., T. Downes, K. N. Eggleston, and R. Kumari, 2006: "Human resource management technology diffusion through global supply chains: productivity and workplace based health care, *Tufts University Department of Economics Discussion Papers* 616, Medford, MA

Bundervoet, T., P. Verwimp, and R. Akresh, 2009: Health and civil war in rural Burundi, *Journal of Human Resources* **44**, 536–63

2011: Civil war, crop failure and child stunting in Rwanda, *Economic Development and Cultural Change* **59**, 777–810

Caldès, N., D. Coady, and J. Malluccio, 2006: The cost of poverty alleviation transfer programs: a comparative analysis of three programs in Latin America, *World Development* **34**, 818–37

Castelló-Climent, A. and A. Hidalgo-Cabrillana, 2012: The role of educational quality and quantity in the process of economic development, *Economics of Education Review*, **31**, 391–409

Chaudhury, N., J. Hammer, M. Kremer, K. Muralidharan, and H. F. Rogers, 2006: Missing in action: teacher and health worker absence in developing countries, *Journal of Economic Perspectives* **20**, 91–116

Cohen, D. and M. Soto, 2007: Growth and human capital: good data, good results, *Journal of Economic Growth* **12**, 51–76

Currie, J. and E. Moretti, 2003: Mother's education and the intergenerational transmission of human capital: evidence from college openings, *Quarterly Journal of Economics* **118**, 1495–1532

Damon, A. L. and P. Glewwe, 2009: Three proposals to improve education in the LAC region: estimates of the costs and benefits of each strategy, in B. Lomborg (ed.), *Latin American Development Priorities*, Cambridge University Press, New York

Das, J., S. Dercon, J. Habyarimana, and P. Krishnan, 2007: Teacher shocks and student learning: evidence from Zambia, *Journal of Human Resources* **42**, 820–62

Doblhammer, G., G. J. van den Berg, and T. Fritze, 2011: Economic conditions at the time of birth and cognitive abilities late in life: evidence from eleven European countries, *IZA, Bonn Discussion Papers* 5940

Duflo, E., 2001: Schooling and labor market consequences of school construction in Indonesia: evidence from an unusual policy experiment, *American Economic Review* **91**, 795–813

Duflo, E., P. Dupas, and M. Kremer, 2009: Peer effects, pupil–teacher ratios, and teacher incentives: evidence from a randomized evaluation in Kenya, Unpublished manuscript, Massachusetts Institute of Technology, Cambridge, MA

Duflo, E., R. Hanna, and S. Ryan, 2010: Incentives work: getting teachers to come to school, *American Economic Review*, forthcoming

Durlauf, S. N., P. A. Johnson, and J. R. W. Temple, 2005: Growth econometrics, In P. Aghion and S. N. Durlauf (eds.), *Handbook of Economic Growth*, Vol. **1A**, North-Holland, Amsterdam

Fafchamps, M. and A. Quisumbing, 1999: Human capital, productivity, and labor allocation in rural Pakistan, *Journal of Human Resources* **34**, 369–406

Faguet, J.-P., 2004: Does decentralization increase responsiveness to local needs? Evidence from Bolivia, *Journal of Public Economics* **88**, 867–94

Filmer, D. and N. Schady, 2009: School enrollment, selection, and test scores, *Policy Research Working Paper* **4998**, World Bank, Washington, DC

Fiszbein, A. and N. Schady with F. H. G. Ferreira, M. Grosh, N. Kelleher, P. Olinto, and E. Skoufias, 2009: *Conditional Cash Transfers: Reducing*

Current and Future Poverty, World Bank, Washington, DC
Fogel, R., 2004: *The Escape from Hunger and Premature Death, 1700–2100: Europe, America, and the Third World*, Cambridge University Press
Galasso, E., 2011: Alleviating extreme poverty in Chile: the short term effects of Chile Solidario, *Estudios de Economia* **38**, 101–27
Galasso, E. and M. Ravallion, 2005: Decentralized targeting of an anti-poverty program, *Journal of Public Economics* **89**, 705–27
Galiani, S., P. Gertler, and E. Schargrodsky, 2008: School decentralization: helping the good get better, but leaving the poor behind, *Journal of Public Economics* **92**, 2106–20
Glewwe, P., 2002: Schools and skills in developing countries: education policies and socioeconomic outcomes, *Journal of Economic Literature* **40**, 436–83
Glewwe, P. and A. L. Kassouf, 2012: The impact of the *Bolsa Escola/Familia* conditional cash transfer program on enrollment, dropout rates and grade promotion in Brazil, *Journal of Development Economics* **97**, 505–17
Glewwe, P. and M. Kremer, 2006: Schools, teachers and educational outcomes in developing countries, in E. Hanushek and F. Welch (eds.), *Handbook of the Economics of Education*, Vol. **2**, North-Holland, Amsterdam
Glewwe, P., N. Ilias, and M. Kremer, 2010: Teacher incentives *American Economic Journal: Applied Economics* **2**, 205–27
Glewwe, P., H. G. Jacoby, and E. M King, 2001: Early childhood nutrition and academic achievement: a longitudinal analysis, *Journal of Public Economics* **81**, 345–68
Glewwe, P., P. Olinto, and P. de Souza, 2004: Evaluating the impacts of conditional cash transfers on schooling in Honduras: an experimental approach, unpublished manuscript, University of Minnesota
Glewwe, P., E. A. Hanushek, S. Humpage, and R. Ravina, 2011: School resources and educational outcomes in developing countries: a review of the literature from 1990 to 2010, University of Minnesota, mimeo
Godoy, R., D. S. Karlan, S. Rabindran, and T. Huanca, 2005: Do modern forms of human capital matter in primitive economies? Comparative evidence from Bolivia, *Economics of Education Review* **24**, 45–53
Grantham-McGregor, S. M., C. A. Powell, S. P. Walker, and J. H. Himes, 1991: Nutritional supplementation, psychosocial stimulation, and mental development of stunted children: the Jamaican study, *Lancet* **338**, 1–5
Grosh, M. E., C. del Ninno, E. Tesliuc, and A. Oeughi, with A. Milazzo and C. Weigand, 2008: *For Protection and Promotion: The Design and Implementation of Effective Safety Nets*, World Bank, Washington, DC
Grossman, M., 2006: Education and nonmarket outcomes, in E. Hanushek and F. Welch (eds.), *Handbook of the Economics of Education*, Vol. **1**, Elsevier North-Holland, Amsterdam
Gunnarsson, V., P. F. Orazem, M. Sanchez, and A. Verdisco, 2009: Does local school control raise student outcomes?: Evidence on the roles of school autonomy and parental participation, *Economic Development and Cultural Change* **58**, 25–52
Hanushek, E. A., 1986: The economics of schooling, *Journal of Economic Literature* **49**, 1141–77
1997: Assessing the effects of school resources on student performance: an update, *Education Evaluation and Policy Analysis* **19**, 141–64
Hanushek, E. A. and D. D. Kimko, 2000: Schooling, labor force quality, and the growth of nations, *American Economic Review* **90**, 1184–1208
Hanushek, E. A. and L. Woessmann, 2008: The role of cognitive skills in economic development, *Journal of Economic Literature* **46**, 607–68
Hanushek, E. A., S. Link, and L. Woessmann, 2011: Does school autonomy make sense everywhere? Panel estimates from PISA, *IZA Discussion Papers* 6185, Bonn
Heckman, J. J. and D. V. Masterov, 2009: The productivity argument for investing in young children, *Review of Agricultural Economics* **29**, 446–93
Horton, S., H. Alderman, and J. R. Dommarco, 2009: Hunger and malnutrition, in B. Lomborg (ed.), *Global Crises, Global Solutions: Costs and Benefits*, Cambridge University Press
Huffman, W. E. and P. F. Orazem, 2007: Agriculture and human capital in economic growth: farmers, schooling and health, in R. E. Evenson and P. Pingali (eds.), *Handbook of Agricultural Economics*, Vol. **3**, North-Holland, Amsterdam
Jensen, R., 2010: The (perceived) returns to education and the demand for schooling, *Quarterly Journal of Economics* **125**, 515–48

Karlan, D. and J. Appel, 2011: *More than Good Intentions: How a New Economics is Helping to Solve Global Poverty*, Dutton, New York

Kattan, R. B., 2006: Implementation of free basic education policy, *Education Working Paper Series* 7, World Bank, Washington, DC

Kaufmann, K. M. 2008: Understanding the income gradient in college attendance in Mexico: the role of heterogeneity in expected returns to college, Department of Economics, Stanford University

King, E. M. and B. Ozler, 2001: What's decentralization got to do with learning? Endogenous school quality and student performance in Nicaragua, Development Research Group Project, World Bank, Washington, DC

King, E. M., C. Montenegro, and P. F. Orazem, 2012: Economic freedom, human rights, and the returns to human capital: an evaluation of the Schultz hypothesis, *Economic Development and Cultural Change*, 61, 39–72

Kingdon, G. and F. Teal, 2007: Does performance related pay for teachers improve student performance? Some evidence for India, *Economics of Education Review* **26**, 473–86

2010: Teacher unions, teacher pay and student performance in India: a pupil fixed effects approach, *Journal of Development Economics* **91**, 278–88

Knowles, J. C. and J. R. Behrman, 2005: Assessing the economic returns to investing in youth in developing countries, in C. B. Lloyd, J. R. Behrman, N. P. Stromquist, and B. Cohen (eds.), *The Changing Transitions to Adulthood in Developing Countries: Selected Studies*, National Academies Press, Washington, DC

Kochar, A., 2004: Urban influences on rural schooling in India, *Journal of Development Economics* **74**, 113–36

Lai, F., E. Sadoulet, and A. de Janvry, 2011: Do school characteristics and teacher quality affect student performance? Evidence from a natural experiment in Beijing middle schools, *Journal of Human Resources* **46**, 123–53

Lang, K., 2007: *Poverty and Discrimination*, Princeton University Press

Lange, F. and R. Topel, 2006: The social value of education and human capital, in E. Hanushek and F. Welch (eds.), *Handbook of the Economics of Education*, Vol. **1**. Elsevier North-Holland, Amsterdam

Lochner, L. and E. Moretti, 2004: The effect of education on crime: evidence from prison inmates, arrests, and self-reports, *American Economic Review* **94**, 155–89

Lucas, Jr., R. E., 2002: *Lectures on Economic Growth*, Harvard University Press, Cambridge, MA

Maddison, A., 2001: *The World Economy: A Millennial Perspective*, OECD, Paris

Maluccio, J., 2009: Education and child labor: experimental evidence from a Nicaraguan conditional cash transfer program, in P. Orazem, G. Sedlacek, and Z. Tzannatos (eds.), *Child Labor and Education in Latin America: An Economic Perspective*, Palgrave Macmillan, New York

Martorell, R., 1995: Results and implications of the INCAP follow-up study, *Journal of Nutrition* **125**, 1127S–1138S

Martorell, R., J.-P. Habicht, and J. A. Rivera, 1995: History and design of the INCAP longitudinal study (1969–1977) and its follow-up (1988–89), *Journal of Nutrition* **125**, 1027S–1041S

McGuire, J. S., 1996: The payoff from improving nutrition, The World Bank, Washington, DC, unpublished manuscript

Miguel, E. and M. Kremer, 2004: Worms: identifying impacts on education and health in the presence of treatment externalities, *Econometrica* **72**, 159–217

Moretti, E., 2004a: Workers' education, spillovers, and productivity: evidence from plant-level production functions, *American Economic Review* **94**, 656–90

2004b: Estimating the social return to higher education: evidence from longitudinal and repeated cross-sectional data, *Journal of Econometrics* **121**, 175–212

Muralidharan, K. and V. Sundararaman, 2010: Contract teachers: experimental evidence from India, University of California, San Diego, unpublished manuscript

2011a: Teacher performance pay: experimental evidence from India, *Journal of Political Economy* **119**, 39–77

2011b: Teacher opinions on performance pay: evidence from India, *Economics of Education Review* **30**, 394–403

Murnane, R. J., 1975: *Impact of School Resources on the Learning of Inner City Children*, Ballinger, Cambridge, MA

Murphy, K. M., A. Schleifer, and R. W. Vishny, 1991: The allocation of talent: implications for growth, *Quarterly Journal of Economics* **116**, 503–30

1993: Why is rent-seeking so costly to growth?, *American Economic Review* **83**, 409–14

Nguyen, T., 2008: Information, role models and perceived returns to education: experimental evidence from Madagascar, MIT, Cambridge, MA, unpublished manuscript

Orazem, P. F. and L. Tesfatsion, 1997: Macrodynamic implications of income transfer policies for human capital investment and school effort, *Journal of Economic Growth* **2**, 305–29

Orazem, P. F., P. Glewwe, and H. Patrinos, 2009: The benefits and costs of alternative strategies to improve educational outcomes, in B. Lomborg (ed.), *Global Crises, Global Solutions*, 2nd edn., Cambridge University Press

Oreopoulos, P., 2003: The long-run consequences of living in a poor neighborhood, *Quarterly Journal of Economics* **118**, 1533–75

Patrinos, H. A. and G. Psacharopoulos, 2011: Education: past, present and future global challenges, *World Bank Policy Research Working Paper* 5616, World Bank, Washington, DC

Ponce, J. and A. S. Bedi, 2010: The impact of a cash transfer program on cognitive achievement: the Bono de Desarrollo Humano of Ecuador, *Economics of Education Review* **29**, 116–25

Pritchett, L., 1997: Divergence, big time, *Journal of Economic Perspectives* **11**, 3–17

2006: Does learning to add up add up? The return to schooling in aggregate data, in E. Hanushek and F. Welch (eds.), *Handbook of the Economics of Education*, Vol. **1** Elsevier North-Holland, Amsterdam

2013: The Rebirth of Education: From *Universal Schooling to Universal Learning*

Reinikka, R. and J. Svensson, 2004: Local capture: evidence from a central government transfer program in Uganda, *Quarterly Journal of Economics* **119**, 679–705

Rivkin, S. G., E. A. Hanushek, and J. F. Kain, 2005: Teachers, schools, and academic achievement, *Econometrica* **73**, 417–58

Schady, N. and M. Caridad Araujo, 2008: Cash transfers, conditions, and school enrollment in Ecuador, *Economía* **8**, 43–77

Schultz, T. W., 1975: The value of ability to deal with disequilibria, *Journal of Economic Literature* **13**, 827–46

Smith, A., 1776: *An Inquiry into the Nature and Causes of the Wealth of Nations*, W. Strahan and T. Cadell, London

Tansel, A., 2002: Determinants of school attainment of boys and girls in Turkey: individual, household and community factors, *Economics of Education Review* **21**, 455–70

UNESCO, 2005: *Children out of School: Measuring Exclusion from Primary Education*, UNESCO Institute for Statistics, Montreal

2011: *Out of School Children: New Data Reveal Persistent Challenges*, UNESCO Institute for Statistics, Montreal, mimeo, www.uis.unesco.org/FactSheets/Documents/FS12_2011_OOSC_EN.pdf

Vermeersch, C. and M. Kremer, 2005: School meals, educational achievement and school competition: evidence from a randomized evaluation, Harvard University, mimeo, Cambridge, MA

World Bank, 2009: *Abolishing School Fees in Africa: Lessons from Ethiopia, Ghana, Kenya, Malawi, and Mozambique*, International Bank for Reconstruction and Development, Washington, DC

2011: *Learning for All: Investing in People's Knowledge and Skills to Promote Development*, International Bank for Reconstruction and Development, Washington, DC

Yap, Y.-T., G. Sedlacek, and P. F. Orazem, 2009: Limiting child labor through behavior-based income transfers: an experimental evaluation of the PETI program in rural Brazil, in P. Orazem, G. Sedlacek, and Z. Tzannatos (eds.), *Child Labor and Education in Latin America: An Economic Perspective*, Palgrave Macmillan, New York

Zimmermann, M. B., 2009: Iodine deficiency in pregnancy and the effects of maternal iodine supplementation on the offspring: a review, *American Journal of Clinical Nutrition* **89**, 668S–672S

Zimmermann, M. B., K. J. Connolly, M. Bozo, J. Bridson, F. Rohner, and L. Grimci, 2006: Iodine supplementation improves cognition in iodine-deficient schoolchildren in Albania: a randomized, controlled, double-blind study, *American Journal of Clinical Nutrition* **83**, 108–14

5.1 Education

Alternative Perspective

LANT PRITCHETT

Peter Orazem's Challenge Paper on Education (Chapter 5) has the big picture exactly right. At this juncture, the most productive investments will be those that increase the learning of children per year of school. Currently nearly all children do attend at least some school, but are often getting very little out of it and, at least in part because of this, do not attend and/or drop out early. Therefore investments in getting marginal children into school, while perhaps justified on moral grounds of a drive to universal schooling, are not particularly high.

However, this conclusion – that the focus on learning is the right approach – leads into the difficulty of the question: "how should resources be spent?" From a purely economic perspective many of the "investment" possibilities are in fact "win–win" – *cheaper* and *produce better learning outcomes*. Activities that are "win–win" have essentially infinite economic returns. This leads directly to the puzzle of why they are not adopted – as it must mean that some relevant cost to some relevant decision-maker is not being taken into account. This makes the question of how to spend resources even more difficult as perhaps rather than thinking of logistical tasks by existing actors at existing institutions and incentives the highest returns are to changing ideas and institutions.

Infinite returns available in schooling and what they imply about "opportunities"

Let me give two examples of "win–win" policies that have ample evidence that they work at scale. This leads to some reflection on what an "opportunity" is and suggest that the current exercise, while headed in the right direction, is not bold enough.

Contract teachers

An extreme illustration of the infinite economic returns comes from recent research (Kingdon and Atherton, 2012) in two states of India, Uttar Pradesh and Bihar, with large samples of students and with repeated measurements of student learning across grades. Their estimates of learning gains, which are plausibly identified even if not experimental, show that contract teachers, hired on one-year contracts and hence subject to at least some sorts of "high-powered" incentives in Uttar Pradesh produced roughly twice the learning gain per year of the regular, civil service, teachers. That is, students learned in one year with a contract teacher the equivalent of two years' worth of gain of students with civil servant teachers. In 2009 the contract teachers were making roughly 3,000 Indian Rupees a month whereas the regular teachers were making around 11,000 Indian Rupees a month.

What is the cost-benefit of replacing civil service teachers with contract teachers in this case? Crude calculations (which suffice for this purpose) suggest that the savings would be roughly $1 *billion* (around 600,000 primary and upper-primary teachers × 8,000 rupees monthly wage differential (11,000 less 3,000) × 12 months ÷ by 45 rupees/$). And for this $1 billion in cost savings, learning per year would double. At the margin the BCR of hiring a teacher on contract instead of via the civil service is infinitely large as benefits go up and costs go down (even over the very short run, as this is a feasible option even with no incremental training or recruitment costs).

What did the government of Uttar Pradesh actually do? Of course they *raised* the wages of civil service teachers (as part of an overall pay hike to government workers in the Sixth Pay Commission) and hired *more* of them. Kingdon's current calculations, updated from 2009, suggest that the replacement of civil service with contract teachers would save the state $8 billion, not just $1 billion.

This finding of infinite returns with contract teachers in India is not a fluke of this particular study or its methodology. (Muralidharan and Subrararaman, 2010) evaluate experimentally the impact on learning of an extra contract teacher in Andhra Pradesh (in assessing the relevance of evidence from states of India that Andhra Pradesh is larger in population than Germany) and find that an extra contract teacher raises learning by 0.1 to 0.13 effect sizes (student standard deviations). Moreover, when they evaluate the gains to contract teachers compared to regular teachers they find that the gain is roughly the same (usually slightly higher for contract teachers, but not statistically significantly so). In their experiment the contract teachers made *one-fifth* the pay of regular teachers.

Again, on a CBR there is an infinitely high return at the margin of hiring a contract teacher over a regular teacher as the output is the same or higher and the cost is much less (and not just on salaries, as the contract teachers have less education and less training, both of which are costly, and still do as well).

These findings are perhaps a bit specific to India (and similar South Asian countries) since (a) the wage gaps between regular teachers and the market wage for equally capable teachers have reached such astronomic proportions and (b) the dysfunction of the civil service cadre has reached such dispiriting levels (evidenced by high absenteeism and lack of effort).

But evidence on contract teachers in Kenya finds similar results (Duflo *et al.*, 2009). Here the contract teachers were of the same qualifications and paid the same as regular teachers and hence just their contractual status varied. In this case, the learning gains were much larger for students exposed to contract teachers than to regular teachers. In fact, in assessments a year after the intervention (to account for learning "depreciation") the students who were randomly assigned an extra contract teacher had learning 0.19 student standard deviations higher than the control group while those assigned a civil service teacher were 0.011 units *lower* (obviously not statistically significant). Amazingly (and not amazingly if one is cynical enough), the addition of an extra teacher caused the existing civil service teachers to attend *less* so that the net teaching from an additional teacher was much less than the net impact of adding a teacher.

Again, at the margin, the return to contract teachers (with big learning effects) over civil service teachers (with zero learning effects) at the same economic cost is *infinitely large*.

Turning back to India, not only are these returns infinitely high at the margin but they are also massive in total. Suppose, that spending on education in India is 4 percent of GDP and primary education is 40 percent of that and teacher wages are 80 percent of spending, then teacher wages in primary schools are roughly 1.25 percent of GDP. If these costs could be reduced by a factor of 4 with no reduction in quality then there is a full 1 percent of GDP to be saved. Suppose this is in India alone, this is still a saving of $*18 billion* – with no loss in learning or educational output.

Private schooling in Pakistan (and elsewhere)

A team of researchers has done a massive exercise in studying education in Punjab, Pakistan, tracking students and schools over several years. One of the main things to emerge from this study (Andrabi *et al.* 2009) is that low-cost private schools are both much *cheaper* in terms of total expenditures per child per year of schooling (the costs in private schools were about half that of government schools) *and* provide massively more learning per child than government schools (on reasonably, if not experimentally, identified causal estimates) – by 07 of a student standard deviation in maths, for instance (Andrabi *et al.*, 2009).

Already parents are voluntarily switching from public to private schools (and there is higher reported parental satisfaction with private schools over government schools). At the margin even small incentives would be sufficient to move children from public to private schools. Suppose the government took the Pakistani Rupees 2000 it was spending to educate a child in a public school and instead paid a voucher that covered the average cost of a private school (Pakistani Rupees 1,000 in the Learning and Education Achievement in Pakistani Schools (LEAPS) sample). This would have the effect of *reducing* costs and *increasing* learning substantially.

Again, at the margin this has an *infinite* rate of return as costs go down and learning goes up as the private sector spends Pakistani Rupees 1 per percent correct while the public sector spends Pakistani Rupees 3.

While the "global" literature on the causal impact of private schools is "mixed" (meaning that in well-functioning and high-state capability countries like the United States, the gains are small) there is little doubt that in countries with poorly functioning states there has been a massively voluntary shift into private schools even with no policy encouragement, which is suggestive of much higher quality. Evidence from India is consistent with large learning gains from shifting to the private sector with plausible identification – especially in the low-performing states of India.

But suppose that even just in Pakistan and India (over 1.2 billion people) one could reduce costs of primary schooling by half and have equal or better outcomes. The cost savings alone exceed the wildest hypothetical of what would be the additional money the world would spend on addressing "global problems." That is, back to our earlier calculation of what could be saved, between just India and Pakistan about $30 billion. This is not additional expenses but *savings*. Given that one way of expressing the 2008 goal of the Copenhagen Consensus was "how to spend an additional 50 billion" across all global problems, in the education area in just two countries we can identify *savings* of $30 billion with equal (likely much better) outcomes.

How to "cost" opportunities

The difficulty, of course, is in deciding what is an "opportunity"? In education it is always politically feasible to do incrementally more of the same. Especially if governments are provided with more money for it they will build more schools, hire more teachers, buy more chalk and textbooks, train more teachers. That is, they will willingly do BAUWMM – "business as usual with more money" – and it is an interesting conjecture to ask whether if among the clearly politically feasible opportunities in the BAUWMM set some have higher impacts (in enrollments or learning) than others.

But if one is imagining spending $50 billion to improve the human condition, why take current politics and hence existing political feasibility as a "hard" constraint? Spending money on advocacy that creates new political possibilities might well be fantastically more cost-effective than anything in the BAUWMM set. Imagine what I could do with $1 billion spaced over ten years ($100 million a year) just to promote the idea and hence raise the political feasibility of contract teachers or private schools or other cost-saving/learning achievement-raising win–win options. I could set up institutes around the world to do more research, I could promote the research findings in popular media, I could hold conferences with policy-makers, I could fund exemplars around the world, I could do lots of things. Maybe I would succeed, maybe I would not.

Suppose one does the rate of return to spending $1 billion for policy advocacy for contract teachers in India over ten years followed by, after ten years, some probability of success, which would mean $18 billion in gains for each of the next thirty years (relative to the counterfactual). If this would work for sure the internal rate of return (IRR) is 68 percent. But, suppose the odds are only 50 percent it would work, the IRR is still 57 percent (because after all we are still only investing $100 million a year to then get $9 billion a year). Even if the probability of the success of the advocacy falls to just 1 in 10 that spending $1 billion on advocacy will reach the goal, the IRR on such advocacy in expected value is still 34 percent.

The problem is that there are two separate domains: "what will get done" and "what the impact on outcomes of what gets done will be." Right now there is seemingly more and more attention being paid to the latter. There is a drive for more rigorous evidence about cause-and-effect relationships between programs/projects/policies and outcomes. But it is not at all obvious to me, or any careful observer, that the latter plays an important role (or much of any role at all) in the former.

Advocacy seems to play a much larger role in what gets done, particularly in the development sphere, than evidence. For instance, there was a massive expansion of US foreign assistance under President George Bush – most of which was accounted for by a $15 billion program over five years devoted to HIV/AIDS. While this may have been the optimal allocation of resources as measured by some objective metric of improved human well-being per dollar, it also may not have been. But importantly, no one really cared. The decision was not made on the basis of evidence about the relative merits of investments in health versus education versus roads, nor even on the evidence of the relative merits of investments in health between vaccinations, clean water, prenatal care, smoking prevention, and HIV/AIDS, nor even on the evidence of the relative merits of spending on prevention versus treatment. This is not to say that there were not some kinds of evidence on these various topics put forward, just to say in no one's causal narrative of "what got done" was compelling evidence the operative explanation.

This is not to mention the rise of many other issues in the development agenda – e.g. the environment, gender – or even how some issues come, go, and then come back – like the importance of "infrastructure." There is no question that advocacy plays a role in what gets advanced and hence "what gets done" on the international agenda, by creating persuasive cases to core constituencies and stakeholders. The question is the relationship between "persuasive" and "evidence."

In part because I am so well trained at the production and evaluation of evidence as construed by a particular academic discipline it has taken me a long time to escape from the myth that what I am good at is also important. That there is no (reputable) "science" or "discipline" of "what gets done" does not mean that there is not a way in which things get done. Moreover, it does not mean that there are people out there engaged in getting things done and that those people are often better funded, cleverer, and overall just better at getting things done than are academic experts.

This also means that, potentially, the highest return activity could be the creation of a persuasive case for the adoption of good "policies" or good "programs" – knowing that "persuasive" and "evidence-based" need not be the same thing. There are "successful failures" in which it is possible to get something done politically even though its cause-and-effect efficacy and accomplishing the putative objectives is zero. Prohibition in the United States in the early twentieth century is a great example. Its advocates were massively successful in doing what is extremely difficult: amending the US Constitution. However, they wanted Prohibition because they believed that the *impact* of Prohibition would be certain desirable goals – like stronger families, or less domestic violence. However, they proved to be much better at advocacy than at social science and their means did not accomplish their ends, which led to the end of Prohibition by re-amending the US Constitution.

But there are also successful successes, and it only takes a few successful successes to justify enormous amounts of spending. For instance, Orazem suggests that reforms in the economic climate in which education was used would have enormous returns. This again falls into the space of the "political feasibility" assessment. If these reforms are "win–win" – good for the country's economic growth and also good for raising returns to schooling – why have they not already been adopted? The answer is, tautologically, because the people who have the power to adopt them have not done so and, only slightly less tautologically, have not done so either because (a) they are ignorant (e.g. are unaware of means-to-ends actions that would promote their own interests) or (b) it is not in their interests. Rather than glossing over this as Orazem does as a kind of a result to be pointed out, but not really an "opportunity," let us ask what it would be cost-effective to do to achieve this result.

Take the case of the economic reform in India in the early 1990s. India had been growing rapidly in the 1980s but, like many other countries, hit an impasse in 1990–1991 as a delayed devaluation combined with a controlled, anti-competitive,

Table 5.1.1 Gains from return to rapid growth after the crisis in India in 1991 versus downside scenarios

	GDP *per capita* at 0 ppa growth since 1991	GDP *per capita* growth at 2.2 ppa growth since 1991
GDP *per capita* in PPP in 2007 (actual): 3,826	1,964	2,782
Loss in total annual GDP in 2007 from slower growth since 1991 in PPP$ trillion	2.10	1.18
Gains adjusted for higher marginal utility of consumption with log-utility (coefficient 1)	20.64	11.57
Coefficient 2	202.48	113.49

Note: USGDP in 2007: $14 trillon
Source: Author's calculations using *Penn World Tables* 6.3 data for GDP *per capita*.

anti-outward-oriented economy took the country into a potentially severe macroeconomic crisis. The Latin American countries which hit a similar crisis after decades of growth in the early 1980s saw their growth drop to near zero for a decade or more. In India, this incipient crisis was used as an opportunity and the macro-aspects were handled well (a devaluation restored external balance very quickly), and in addition a set of reforms in trade (lowered barriers in the most restrictive import regime in the world at that time), regulation, and in the financial sector were implemented. Of course one can debate cause and effect, but the fact of the matter is that after these reforms the economy quickly returned to a rapid growth path and has persisted in rapid growth (accelerating even further prior to the global crisis of 2008) until today (maybe that would have happened anyway, but maybe not).

Let us do the simple calculation of the gains of some simple counterfactuals about Indian growth. What if a poor handling of the macro-crisis had led to stagnation in growth? Or, more modestly, if India had returned to its 1970s level of growth? Table 5.1.1 shows the resulting PPP$ GDP *per capita* from the actual trajectory up until 2007 versus the counterfactuals of zero growth or 2.2 ppa growth since 1991. The simple math is that at 2.2 ppa p.a. growth GDP *per capita* would be roughly 1,000 PPP$ *per capita* lower, and India has roughly a billion people, so total GDP would be *1$ trillion* lower p.a. If mishandling of the crisis has led to zero growth, as in the Latin American experience, then GDP would be lower by *$2 trillion* p.a.

If we are thinking about global welfare and well-being then it is perfectly legitimate to adjust those gains to OECD-equivalent dollars by adjusting for declining marginal utility as the average GDP *per capita* in India over this period was 2,600 PPP$ compared to 26,000 PPP$ in the OECD. If we adjust for marginal utility at log-utility, this means that the welfare gains from the difference in the actual growth rate compared to the downside counterfactual of zero growth are larger than US GDP – $20 trillion.

International organizations like the World Bank and private foundations were supporting think-tanks that brought together economists and supported them in the research and advocacy to create the intellectual climate in which the costs and benefits of alternative growth strategies – including more market-oriented ones – were debated. This small group, challenging the conventional wisdom at the time of state-led growth, eventually got more and more intellectual traction. I do not want to tell any simplistic cause-and-effect story that this "caused" the reforms in India, but it is hard to believe that it played no role. Moreover, many of the key actors responsible for the reforms spent significant time in these organizations and think-tanks, essentially preparing themselves for the time when the opportunity would come. Let us suppose that all this contributed only 1 percent to the reforms and suppose (I agree, debatably, but suppose) that the reforms accounted for sustained growth versus reversion to mean growth of 2.2 percent. How much would it have been optimal to invest in this research and advocacy for economic policy change *ex ante?* Even 1 percent of $11 trillion (welfare gains at log-utility by 2007) is $110 billion p.a. In the 1980s the *total* operating budget of the World Bank was on the order of $1 billion p.a. – obviously even if *all* of that had been spent on nothing but creating the possibility of reform in India this would have been dramatically underinvesting in the creation of conditions propitious for successful handling of the crisis.

One might think that I have wandered far from the economics of the opportunities in education – but I have not. The point is that if "opportunities" are defined as "incremental ways of spending money that are currently politically feasible" then one will get a certain array of mostly programmatic answers – e.g. nutrition programs, CCTs, targeted inputs (e.g. girls' toilets). One could ask which of these is the most cost-effective and hence what fraction of some incremental available resources should be devoted to that – and come up with numbers in the, say, few $ billion.

Total education spending by developing country governments around the world is now on the order of $800 billion. There is no question that much of this money is spent in extremely inefficient, if not absolutely wasteful or counter-productive ways. Suppose, that through some combination of new information, research, and advocacy one could expand the set of the politically and administratively feasible ways to do education that improved the effectiveness of existing spending by, say, a tiny fraction, say 1 percent. That is an equivalent of $8 billion in gains p.a. What is the "opportunity" there?

Of course, one could say, "we have a science of 'what works' but do not have a science of 'what gets done' and hence we should stick to science." That is true if one's objective is exclusively science for its own sake. But in terms of improving the human condition this is the classic response of the drunk searching under the streetlight. So far, economists have been very stubborn drunks.

Minor quibbles with Chapter 5

I wish to make three technical comments:

First, I am glad that Orazem was clear about "CCTs" as an *education* intervention. If the government is *already* making a cash transfer (CT) the incremental costs and benefits of making that CT conditional on school attendance are almost certainly worth it as the *incremental* cost is only the cost of adding the "C" to the "CT," and the bulk of the cost of the "CT" is "sunk" in this calculation.

However, if one does a CCT and includes the entire cost of the CT itself then I do not think that in most circumstances this makes for an attractive education intervention as the cost per additional enrolled student is very high. For instance, take the Colombia results in Table 5.3 (p. 294). Households received 17 percent of pre-transfer income as the transfer at child time in school for ages 8–12 went up 2 percent. There is just no way this works out to be cost-effect compared to other interventions in the education sector as nearly all of the CT went to infra-marginal households (that is, households that would have had their children in school anyway). In my mind a CT has to be mostly justified on its CT merits (e.g. transferring purchasing power to people with low incomes) and the "C" in the "CT" against the incremental cost benefit of adding the "C."

Second, I disagree with Orazem's evaluation of fee elimination in SSA, particularly with the view that it did not decrease quality. This all depends on what was done with the fees before their elimination. The only empirical evaluation I have seen of the impact of fee elimination on quality is for Kenya, and there the evidence is pretty compelling that fee elimination led to massive deteriorations in, at the very least, parental perceptions of school quality. In Kenya the fees had been locally collected and controlled and used at the school level. Their elimination plus replacement with a central transfer was by and large a disaster. As Bold *et al.* (2011) show, Kenya eliminated fees in primary but not secondary schools and nearly all of the incremental enrollment in primary schools happened in *private* schools while most of the incremental enrollment in secondary schools was in *government* schools. This "differences in differences" seems pretty compelling that abolishing fees led to a massive flight out of public schools even though their money price had fallen, which is only consistent with a very substantial reduction in perceived quality.

Several of the countries on the list in Table 5.1 (p. 276) of having eliminated fees have also been participating in the Southern and Eastern African Consortium for Measuring Education Quality

Table 5.1.2 Secondary school scores in Tanzania, 2007–2011

Registered for Certificate of Secondary Education Examination (CSEE)	Sat CSEE	Scores in Divisions 1–3	Share of exam-takers getting divisions 1–3	Year
199,283	189,398	44,567	23.5%	2007
241,472	233,848	41,915	17.9%	2008
351,152	339,925	42,790	12.6%	2009
458,114	441,426	40,807	9.2%	2010
450,324	426,314	33,869	7.9%	2011

Source: Author's calculations based on CSEE results from *Tanzania Ministry of Education and Vocational Training* (2012).

(SACMEQ) testing and show pretty substantial deteriorations in learning achievement at grade 6. For instance on a SACMEQ norm of 500 Mozambique fell from 516 in 2000 to 476 in 2007, Malawi fell from 462 in 1995 to 433 in 2007. Of course we don't know cause and effect and this could just be compositional shifts as less-prepared students come in – but the case that this does not deteriorate quality has to be made case by case.

Table 5.1.2 is pretty sobering. In Tanzania (reported as eliminating fees in 2001) the number registering for the secondary school leaving test from 2007 to 2011 more than doubled, but the absolute number getting division 1 to 3 marks actually *fell* by more than 10,000 students (almost a quarter of the baseline total) as the percentage of exam-takers getting good marks fell by a third. It is hard to say what is test comparability, cause and effect, and so on, but when only 8 percent are passing the leaver's exam it is hard to be sanguine about quality or the impact of increased enrollments on quality.

Third, and much more minor, is the fact that the assessment of whether or not there are "positive externalities" to schooling has to be balanced against the fact that nearly everywhere and always schooling is massively subsidized already. So the standard welfare calculation of an *increase* in the subsidy for schooling has to be based on an assessment that currently at the margin the externalities exceed the existing subsidy. So while the academic debate is about whether there are positive growth externalities *at all* (and both Orazem (Table 5.2, pp. 283–4) and I find that in the median country there are not) the policy question is about *increasing* the subsidy from its already massive level of typically providing school free of charge already.

An actual proposal on teachers

In comments on an earlier version of Orazem's Chapter 5 I emphasized the infinite returns to contract teachers; he made my point by invoking otherwise unspecified "political" constraints to argue: (a) that contract teachers and regular teachers cannot work side by side over the long term as eventually they will be regularized and (b) that whatever the long-term arrangement for regularizing teachers it will then just produce the same outcome as for regular teachers. The most obvious response to that is that one should still use contract teachers whenever one can (where they are win–win on learning and cost) for as long as one can and if it is not "sustainable" one still gets the gains as long as they last so what is the harm from a rate of return (ROR) sense?

On a deeper level I have thought of, and thought through, all of Orazem's objections to why "contract teachers" are not a viable proposal for education. In a paper some years ago (Pritchett and Murgai, 2007) we laid out a plan that tried to get the benefits of contract teachers on to a sustainable basis. The basics of the plan were:

- The old cadre of the "regular" civil service teachers would be eliminated so that no more appointments could be made under those employment conditions (of course all existing teachers were grandfathered).

- The new cadre of teachers had an entirely different system of compensation and, importantly, assignment, which had four features:
  - A long probationary period of wages equivalent to those of contract teachers. So, rather than beginning at a wage that is fivefold the market wage from day one all teachers have to be "apprentice" teachers at the much lower wage for an extended period (five–to seven years).
  - Confirmation as a "tenured" teacher in the new cadre came only after a threefold criterion was met: (a) a local school had to demand you as a teacher, (b) your performance as a teacher had to be documented administratively (e.g. attendance, training, etc.), and (c) a peer review had to certify your quality as a teacher.
  - At tenure the wage went up substantially so that over a life-course teaching was an attractive occupation.
  - The new process separated "hiring" from "assignment" so that to be appointed as a teacher in any school required that one met the eligibility criterion but to be in a classroom the local school committee had to approve your appointment. That is, the *assignment* of teachers is controlled at the local level not at the bureaucratic level. During their probationary period teachers not assigned did not get paid (essentially the contract teacher model). So you could only get "tenure" after *X* years of teaching but you could only teach if you could find an assignment (over which local committees hold veto power). The assignment of teachers with tenure was more complicated since after tenure the district had an obligation to pay irrespective of assignment, but tenured teachers got multiple chances at assignment until their pay was gradually reduced if they were not teaching.

This has several advantages as (a) the gains to lower pay and higher accountability are in full force for all non-tenured teachers and (b) those who make it through to tenure are likely to be those more likely to comply even once the "high-powered" threats are removed. With "normal" turnover patterns for teaching most teachers will be in the "probationary" period and if the filters work well only "good-type" teachers will make it through to the tenured condition. This gives time for the "norms" of performance to change.

Something very much like this plan was adopted in Bihar, India, and the same evaluation quoted above for Uttar Pradesh also found that the "apprentice" teachers in this new plan were both cheaper (though not as much cheaper as pure contract teachers, unfortunately due to political pressures) and their students had higher learning than regular teachers (though not as much, as the "high-powered" threat was apparently less high-powered). While it is still too early to tell if in the long run this reverts to the norms of non-compliance it is at least an administratively and politically feasible plan that simultaneously lowers costs and raises performance. At the margin the returns are infinite (compared to the counterfactual of hiring regular teachers).

Of course the total gains depend on how much the system is expanding and how much turnover there is in the teaching force. In mature systems with little turnover obviously the incremental gains are small as all teachers have to be grandfathered so even though the marginal returns are high the total gains are low. But in expanding systems or systems with turnover the move to a newly designed system of teacher compensation and assignment (and the assignment bit is key as it creates local accountability) can produce both high marginal and large total returns.

Bibliography

Andrabi, T., J. Das, A. Khwaja, and T. Zajonc, 2009a: Do value added estimates add value? Accounting for learning dynamics, *American Economic Journal: Applied Economics* **3**, 29–54

Andrabi, T., J. Das, A. Khwaja, T. Viswanath, and T. Zajonc, 2009b: *Pakistan: Learning Achievement in Punjab Schools*, World Bank, Washington, DC

Bold, T., M. Kimenyi, G. Mwabu, and J. Sandefur, 2011: Did abolishing school fees reduce quality? Evidence from Kenya, *Center for Study of African Economics (CSAE) Working Paper WPS/2011-04*

Duflo, E., P. Dupas, and M. Kremer, 2012: School governance, teacher incentives and pupil-teacher ratios: experimental evidence from Kenyan primary schools, *NBER Working Paper* **17939**

Kingdon, G. and P. Atherton, 2010: The relative effectiveness and costs of contract and regular teachers in India, *Center for the Study of African Economies (CSAE) Working Paper WPS/2010–15*

2012: The relative effectiveness and costs of contract and regular teachers in India, *Economics of Education Review*, 1–15

Muralidharan, K. and V. Subrararaman, 2010: *Contract Teachers: Experimental Evidence from India*, www.fas.nus.edn.sg/es/events/seminar/seminar-papers/31Aug10.pdf

Pritchett, L. and R. Murgai, 2007: *Teacher Compensation: Can Decentralization to Local Bodies Take India from the Perfect Storm Through Troubled Waters to Clear Sailing*?, India Policy Forum **3**, 123–68

5.2 Education

Alternative Perspective

GEORGE PSACHAROPOULOS

Essence of the challenge

The Challenge Paper (Chapter 5) is thought-provoking and will serve well the purpose for which it has been written. Its line of argument goes as follows:

- There has been a lot of progress world-wide regarding education quantity (e.g. coverage), hence the policy frontier today lies in improving education quality.
- Investments in education quantity or quality are likely to yield returns only in non-failed states because the lack of basic institutions in failed states dampens the incentives to invest in education.
- Complementary inputs, such as health, raise the marginal product of schooling.
- In theory, the PV of any given year of additional schooling rises unambiguously with school quality.
- In theory, improvements in school quality have an ambiguous effect on years of schooling but must raise the PV of lifetime earnings.
- The evidence on the contribution of years of schooling or education quality on economic growth is mixed.
- Focusing on school quality makes sense because the returns from expanding access to schools have been exhausted.
- The policy focus should be on the quality of schooling offered to those already in school, because the return from getting the last 5 percent of children never attending school to enter a school is outweighed by the cost.

Three options are reviewed to improve school quality:

- Decentralizing educational management
- Offering teachers' incentives
- Lowering the opportunity cost of attending school.

After reviewing the empirical evidence on these options, CCTS are the only intervention that exhibit an acceptable BCR.

Adding perspective to the Challenge

In what follows I offer a series of remarks on the theoretical, empirical, and policy sections of Chapter 5. I list a number of additional references that could be considered in refining the challenge. I produce additional cost-benefit evidence on some of the key issues raised, and in doing so I take the liberty of broadening the challenge and proposing new real solutions.

The thrust of my perspective is that expanding education quantity is a necessary condition for quality improvements to be enacted, and that the BCRs of investment in human capital in poor countries pass the Copenhagen Consensus test. Perhaps it is in the so-called "failed states" (dismissed in Chapter 5 as candidates for human capital investments) that such investment should take place as a matter of priority.

Theory

The supply and demand model underpinning Figure 5.1 provides a nice framework for disentangling the education quantity/quality quandary. The way the relative shifts of the marginal product and marginal cost curves are drawn results in an ambiguous effect of enhanced

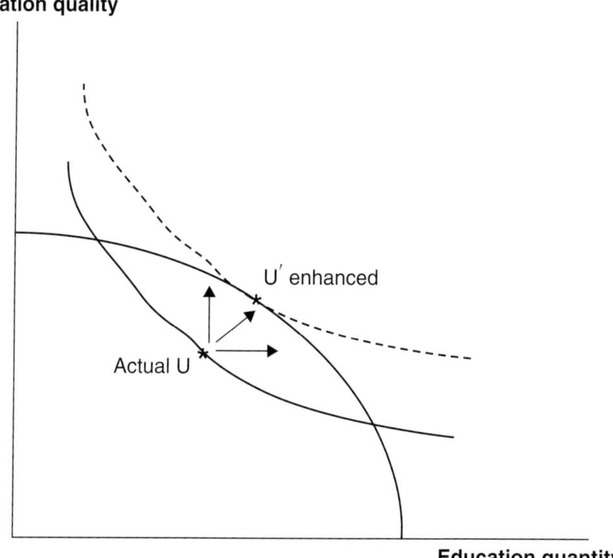

Figure 5.2.1 *Education quantity and quality combinations*

school quality on years of schooling but an unambiguous positive effect on the PV of any given year of schooling. Of course what matters for policy purposes is the *net* PV of quality enhancements. Thus, in theory, costly quality interventions might not pass a cost-benefit test.

A complementary way at looking at the problem is to use an equally simplified supply and demand framework depicted in Figure 5.2.1. Country resources allow different mixes of quantity and quality of schooling along a production transformation curve that is concave to the origin. Superimposed are indifference curves convex to the origin representing levels of utility derived by the beneficiaries of education or society as a whole. In any given country, rich or poor, the actual situation must be at utility level U – i.e. inside the production possibility curve (PPC) due to inefficiencies of various kinds. Removing such inefficiencies would mean a higher level of utility, perhaps never reaching the optimal U^*. The model predicts that it is possible to achieve a higher level of utility (e.g. *per capita* income) by raising *either* education quantity or quality. Whether the move would be more quantity-oriented or quality-oriented, depicted by the arrows, is again an empirical matter depending on the CBA of the various options.

The most critical statistic for the position taken in Chapter 5 is the BCRs for education quantity versus quality improvements. Chapter 5 does not present any BCRs of improving school quality, apparently because such analyses do not exist. The only BCRs in the chapter refer to CCTs that are designed to bring or keep children in school – i.e. they refer to education quantity.[1]

Educational development frontiers in the world today

The frontier of a country's state of education is a function of the level of economic development. Thus in poor countries the challenge is at

[1] Regarding CCTs the chapter could use the published version of Behrman *et al.* (2011). Regarding the role of parents the chapter could consider a paper, Gertler *et al.* (2012) regarding the AGE program in Mexico that reduced grade failure and repetition.

Table 5.2.1 Countries with over 1 million children out of school, 2009

Country	Children out of school
Nigeria	8,650,000
Pakistan	7,300,000
India	3,852,000
Ethiopia	2,184,000
Bangladesh	1,835,000
Côte d'Ivoire	1,384,000
Niger	1,073,000
Kenya	1,059,000
Yemen	1,037,000

Source: UNESCO (2011: 3).

least to enroll all children in primary school,[2] and in advanced countries to have no students dropping out before completing secondary education.[3] In both country settings, an additional challenge is to improve the quality of any given level of schooling.[4]

Education quantity issues

Out-of-school children in developing countries

According to the latest Unesco data (UNESCO, 2011), there are today 67 million children out of school. The majority of these children are in the so-called failed states cited in Chapter 5 (Table 5.2.1).

Enrolling all children in school has been a moving target of governments and international organizations for a very long time. In 1990 "Education for All" by 2000 was proclaimed by UNDP, UNESCO, UNICEF, and the World Bank (UNDP *et al.*, 1990). Yet this target has been shifting every five years or so, and the prospects are that the latest 2015 target will be missed as well (UNESCO, 2011). The latest World Bank education strategy shifted the emphasis to "Learning for All" (World Bank, 2011).

The role of international organizations in building human capital in developing countries might not be as significant as one might think. For example, the first World Bank loan for education in Tunisia cited in the chapter (World Bank, 1962) was not exactly aimed at bringing more children to school. In 1962 only about half of children aged 6–14 were in school in Tunisia, yet the Bank opted to expand secondary education. The reason mentioned in the Bank's appraisal report was to meet manpower requirements, a discredited Bank policy that carried on into the late 1980s. Also, Bank loans for improving education quality – e.g. by diversifying the secondary curriculum and injecting a degree of vocationalization – did not have the expected effects according to the Bank's own evaluations (Psacharopoulos and Loxley, 1985). Given this state of education enrollments in poor countries, the case for expanding the quantity of education cannot be dismissed that easily.

Azariadis and Drazen (1990), using a model that allows for multiple equilibria, suggest that "once ... the stock of knowledge surpass[es] certain critical values, aggregate production possibilities may expand especially rapidly." As depicted in Figure 5.2.2, a country is trapped in a low-returns equilibrium (AA′) until the level of human capital accumulation rises, say, when the mean years of schooling of the population exceeds six years. Once the threshold is passed, the country rides on a higher returns-growth path (BB′). An empirical test of this theory found that the threshold might be early literacy.

Others have found that there might be a threshold in terms of human capital accumulation before a country can reap growth benefits (Anderson and Bowman, 1963; Easterlin, 1981). Lau *et al.* (1996) using data from Brazil, found a threshold effect of education on output between three and four years of schooling (see also Jamison and Lau, 1982). In other words, a country must have a critical mass of basic education before the returns to education manifest themselves. This finding is consistent with Romer's hypothesis (Romer, 1986) that there exist increasing returns to intangible capital. Regarding the effect of education on economic growth in Sri Lanka the chapter could use the findings of Ganedodage and Rambaldi (2011).

Glaeser (1994) used the Mincerian earnings function in a country cross-section to decompose

2 UNDP *et al.* (1990).
3 E.g. European Commission (2006).
4 E.g. World Bank (2011).

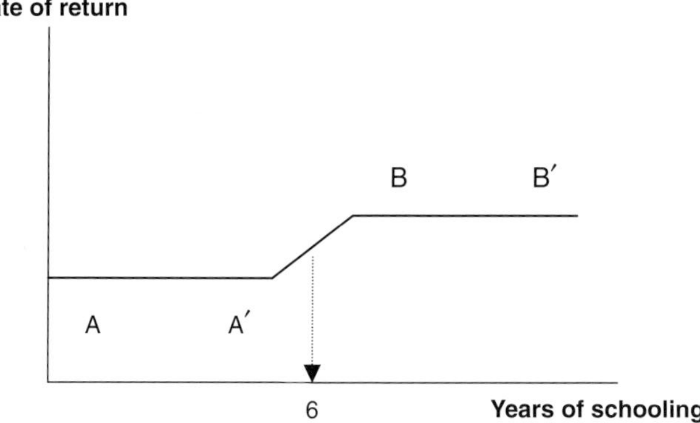

Figure 5.2.2 *A critical level of education quantity*

the effect of education on growth into (a) an effect of the changed returns to education over time, (b) an indirect effect of schooling's positive effect on schooling growth, and (c) a direct effect of education raising income, holding education growth constant. He found that the indirect schooling-to-schooling effect had the greatest impact in the decomposition. This finding is in the spirit of Becker and Murphy (1992), suggesting that earlier human capital creates later human capital, linking to the new growth literature on increasing returns to scale. Several other studies have found that parental education is a strong determinant of children's school participation and eventual educational attainment (e.g. Birdsall, 1985 on Brazil).

It is well known that micro- and macro-estimates of the effect of human capital on growth are often at odds. Breton (2012) finds that for thirty-six countries the (macro-) marginal product of human capital accruing to workers is consistent with estimates of the (micro-) marginal return on investment in schooling in workers' earnings studies. Regarding the effect of education quality on economic growth the chapter could use the findings of Castelló-Climent and Hidalgo-Cabrillana (2011).

Advanced countries

Turning to advanced countries, the frontier of the education quantity problem is secondary school graduation. In 2000 the European Union defined the dimension of the school failure problem as: "The number of 18 to 24 year olds with only lower-secondary level education who are not in further education and training." An EU benchmark was set that the proportion of early school leavers should not be more than 10 percent by 2010 (European Commission, 2006).

According to the latest Eurostat data (Eurostat, 2012), 15 percent of secondary school students fail to complete the upper-secondary cycle and receive no further training. As shown in Table 5.2.2, twenty-two European countries register a dropout rate above the 10 percent target.

There have been several studies assessing the costs and benefits of avoiding secondary school failure. The most comprehensive study refers to the United States, where three out of ten students do not graduate on time in the public school system (Levin, 2005; Levin *et al.*, 2006, 2007a, 2007b).

Based on labor market, health,[5] crime, welfare expenditures and taxes, and the cost of interventions to keep students in school, Levin reports NPVs of each intervention ranging from $65,500 to $150,100 per high-school graduate and CBRs ranging from 1.5 to 3.5 – i.e. the benefits far exceed the costs of the intervention in all cases. If the number of high-school dropouts were reduced by half through teacher salary increases, the NPV of the economic benefits would be $45 billion per year.

[5] Notwithstanding Sansani's (2011) findings inverting the causation – i.e. education quality affecting health.

Table 5.2.2 Secondary-school dropouts[a] in advanced countries

Country	Early leavers (%)
Malta	36.9
Portugal	28.7
Spain	28.4
Iceland	22.6
Italy	18.8
Romania	18.4
Norway	17.4
FRY.	15.5
United Kingdom	14.9
Bulgaria	13.9
Greece	13.7
Latvia	13.3
France	12.6
Cyprus	12.6
Belgium	11.9
Germany	11.9
Estonia	11.6
Denmark	10.7
Ireland	10.5
Hungary	10.5
Finland	10.3
Netherlands	10.1

Notes: [a] Percentage of the population aged 18–24 with at most lower secondary education and not in further education or training. FRY = Former Republic of Yugoslavia.
Source: Eurostat (2012).

In a related subanalysis of minorities, Levin *et al.* (2007b) calculated the public savings (financial benefits) from greater public investments in the education of African American males among whom over one-fifth do not graduate from high school. Based on a number of interventions, they calculated the lifetime public benefits in terms of increased tax revenues and lower spending on health and crime. In terms of PVs for a black male aged 20, these public benefits amount to $256,700 per new graduate, while the median intervention would cost only $90,700. Taking into account the increased tax revenues, health cost savings, and crime cost savings, and comparing these benefits to the cost of the five interventions, they came up with the BCR reported in Table 5.2.3. If the high-school graduation rate of black males were equalized to that of white males, the net public benefit would range from $3.3 to $4.7 billion for a single cohort of 20-year-olds. Levin (2005) reports a 7:1 BCR of pre-school programs in terms of reduced costs of crime, drug use, and teen parenting.

Table 5.2.4 BCRs closing the high-school gap for Blacks and Hispanics

Location	Public[a]	Societal[b]
California	2.4	4.6
Rest of the United States	3.3	5.7

Notes:
[a] The "public" ratio includes the savings in public expenditures and the increase in tax revenues.
[b] The "societal" ratio includes these two public benefits plus the increase in private disposable income.
Source: Vernez *et al.* (1999: Table 5.2).

A Rand Corporation study (Vernez *et al.*, 1999) found BCRs ranging from 2.4 to 5.7 for keeping minorities in school (Table 5.2.4).

There also exist similar studies in Australia reporting high NPVs and BCRs for interventions to reduce secondary-school dropouts – Applied

Table 5.2.3 Costs and benefits of education for interventions for Blacks

Intervention	First Things First	Chicago Parent–Child	Perry Pre-school	Class-size reduction	Teacher-salary increase
NPV	$197,599	$188,951	$165,971	$159,292	$136,427
BCR	4.4	3.8	2.8	2.6	2.1
Total economic effect of equal graduation rates for black and white males	$4.74 billion	$4.53 billion	$3.98 billion	$3.82 billion	$3.27 billion

Source: Levin *et al.* (2007a: Table 4).

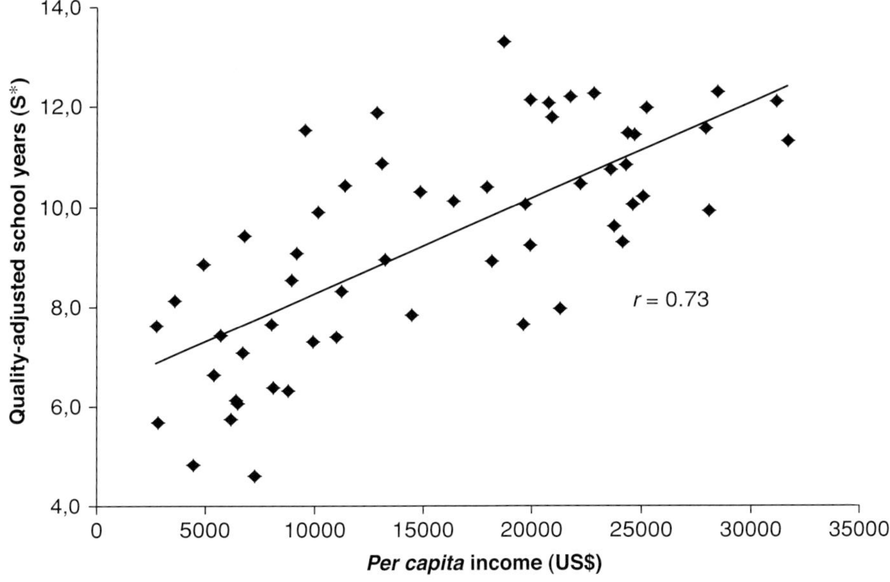

Figure 5.2.3 *Quality-adjusted schooling and* per capita *income*

Source: Based on Table A5.2.5 (p. 328).

Economics (2002); Allen Consulting Group (2003); Access Economics Pty Ltd (2005).

Quality state

Whereas education quantity is typically measured by years of schooling or highest degree obtained, education quality is measured by student performance at cognitive achievement tests, such as IEA's TIMMS[6] or OECD's PISA.[7] It has been a great conceptual and empirical advance to measure education quality by such output, rather than the older cost-based input method (e.g. expenditure per student).

The good called education (E) can be expressed as a function of both the quantity of schooling measured, say in years (S), and the quality of each year of schooling, say measured by the PISA score (Q):

$$E = f(S, Q)$$

A simple way to specify the above function is multiplicative:

$$E = SQ$$

where E is expressed as quality-adjusted years of schooling, a good proxy for a country's level of educational development (Figure 5.2.3). Based on matched data on the quantity and the quality of schooling in fifty-eight countries (Appendix Table A5.2.5), there is a strong positive correlation between economic and educational development.

Cost-benefit tests

How does the expansion of education or improvements in its quality fare on a cost-benefit scrutiny?

Chapter 5 reviews a vast set of literature on this subject and presents only one set of BCRs related to CCTs designed to keep children in school. This type of evidence refers more to the quantity than the quality of education. This paucity is understandable given the scarcity of CBAs of education quality interventions. On the other hand, the literature is very rich on the CBA of investments in the quantity of education.

[6] http://timssandpirls.bc.edu/timss2011/frameworks.html.

[7] www.oecd.org/dataoecd/34/60/46619703.pdf.

Table 5.2.5 Mean returns to investment in education, by country type (%)

	Private returns (%)			Social returns (%)			
Country type	Prim.	Sec.	Higher	Prim.	Sec.	Higher	No. of obs.
Failed states	29.3	21.4	24.5	20.2	17.1	12.1	21
Non-failed states	25.5	15.6	17.0	18.2	11.6	10.4	62

Source: Table A5.2.5 (pp. 328–9).

I review below the evidence on improvements in the quantity of education relative to the two policy frontiers identified above – i.e. expanding primary school coverage in developing countries, especially the "failed" ones; and policies on reducing secondary-education dropouts in high-income countries.

Table 5.2.6 NPVs and returns to investment in upper-secondary education completion, OECD average

Cost-benefit type	NVP per person ($US)	RoR (%)
Private	77,604	11.4
Social	36,302	7.7

Source: Appendix Table 5A.2.4.

Returns to education in failed and other states

The Fund for Peace, a think-tank based in Washington, DC, publishes an annual "Failed States Index" (Foreign Policy, 2011). The Index is based on a series of indicators such as weak central government, non-provision of public services, widespread corruption, criminality, and sharp economic decline: 60 countries (out of the UN 193 countries) are classified as failed (Appendix Table A5.2.1, pp. 323–4).

It so happens there exists evidence on the returns to investment in education in twenty-one of the failed countries (Appendix Table A5.2.2, p. 323) that can be compared to the returns in non-failed countries (Appendix Table A5.2.3, p. 324).

The returns to investment in education are estimated using a common methodology by comparing the PV of benefits of education to the cost of obtaining a given level of education. The benefits are typically earnings differentials between adjacent levels of education, before tax in the private calculation and after tax in the social calculation. The cost refers to what the individual forgos in terms of lost earnings and incidental schooling expenses in the private calculation, and the full resource cost of education in the social calculation.

As shown in Table 5.2.5, the RoR of investment in any level of education is higher in the failed states relative to the rest. It is true that in some rural areas and in failed states the returns obtained by local surveys may be lower than those in Table 5.2.5. But this does not seem to apply using data for a country as a whole from national household surveys that tacitly incorporate the effect of corruption and other barriers.

It should not be surprising that the pay-off of educational investment is higher in failed states, in the sense that the poorer the country the higher the returns to investment in education because of the relative scarcity of human capital.[8] And it so happens that the failed countries are also very poor.

Turning to the research frontier in advanced economies, the OECD (2011) reports NPVs and returns to completing upper-secondary education in a large number of countries (Appendix Table A5.2.4, p. 327). The reference to advanced countries demonstrates that even in these countries attention to the quantity of schooling is important in the sense that it yields high returns and BCRs.

As shown in Table 5.2.6, both private and social NPVs are positive at the OECD's 3 percent discount rate, implying a BCR well above unity. In other words, investments in completing upper-secondary

[8] This is a kind of the law of diminishing returns in operation, extensively documented since the beginning of the literature on the subject (e.g. Psacharopoulos, 1973).

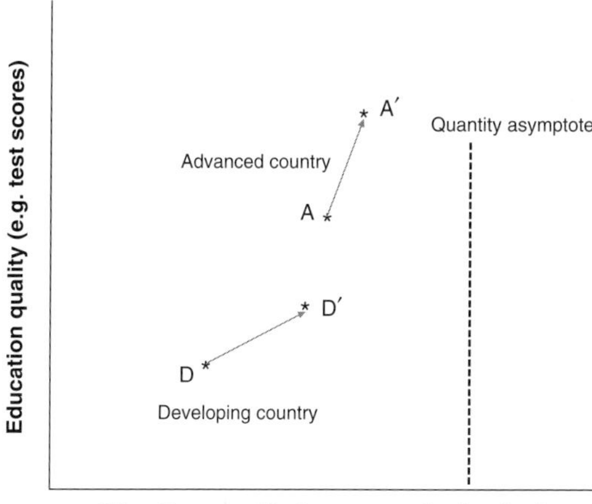

Figure 5.2.4 *Alternative education quantity and quality paths*

education pass the Copenhagen Consensus benefit-cost test.

Broadening the challenge

Educational development has been associated with a large number of benefits, both private and social. Educational development can be brought about by expanding the quantity of schooling and/or improving its quality. Given budgetary constraints governments and international donors alike face the difficult task of allocating resources towards expanding education places and/or improving education quality.

The relative mix of education quantity and quality is a function of the country's level of economic development (Figure 5.2.4). In developing countries the mix is bound to be quantity-biased (DD path) – i.e. the main challenge being how to bring more children to school, while of course trying to improve the quality of any given level of schooling.[9] The desirability of such a mix is supported by extensive evidence regarding the profitability of investment in expanding education coverage. Advanced countries sooner or later face an asymptote regarding how many years an individual can stay in education, so the challenge is to improve the quality of schooling (AA′ path).

Heckman and his colleagues are now pointing to high returns to interventions *before* children are in the formal school system. Evaluations of the *HighScope Perry Pre-school program* found that adults at age 40 who had the pre-school program had higher earnings, were more likely to hold a job, had committed fewer crimes, and were more likely to have graduated from high school than adults who did not have a pre-school program.

Similar evaluations exist for the Chicago Child Parent Centers that provide services to pre-school children and their parents who live in low-income areas. Comparing the costs of these programs to their long-term benefits yield BCRs of the order of 8–9 (Cunha *et al.*, 2006). Heckman's conclusion (Heckman, 2008) is that interventions targeted to the earliest years exhibit the highest social return (Figure 5.2.5).

As shown in Table 5.2.7 there exist several estimates of BCRs ratios for early interventions in developing countries ranging from 2 to 700.

Summing up

Beyond moral grounds, to be financially sustainable education investments must pass the Copenhagen Consensus cost-benefit test. Given the available evidence reviewed above, we are very confident that expanding education quantity passes this test, especially in poor countries. The test is positive even in failed states.[10]

Unfortunately, we are not yet on such solid ground regarding investments in school quality (Glewwe *et al.*, 2011). In addition, Hanushek and Woessmann's widely cited finding that it is the quality and not the quantity of schooling that determines economic growth (Hanushek and Woessmann, 2008) has been recently challenged. Breton (2011) claims that the statistical analysis underpinning their finding is flawed. He shows that when

[9] Regarding school quality and student attendance, see Marshall (2011).

[10] Of course, there is the risk that educating people in failed states may have the adverse effect of making more educated persons more efficient in exploiting the corruptive system. But such a possibility must be diluted in the overall beneficial effect of education on society.

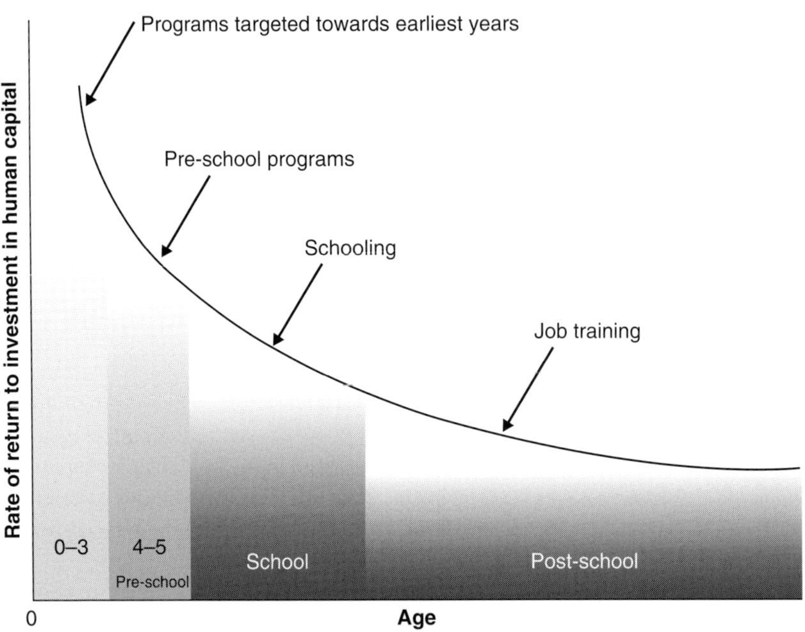

Figure 5.2.5 *Returns to investment in human capital, by age*

Source: Heckman (2008).

Table 5.2.7 BCRs of early interventions in developing countries

Country	Intervention	BcR [a]
India	Tutorial program	711.0
Kenya	Deworming	642.0
Kenya	Pre-school and nutrition	77.0
Kenya	Iron supplements	45.2
Pakistan	Urban girls' scholarship	36.3
Uganda	Free primary	26.3
Pakistan	Rural girls' scholarship	10.1
Mexico	PROGRESA transfers	6.8
Nicaragua	RED social protection	3.8
Bolivia	Pre-school and nutrition	3.7
Philippines	Pre-school	3.0
Colombia	School voucher	2.5
Egypt	Pre-school	2.3
Brazil	Pre-school	2.1

Note: [a] All BCRs are estimated using a 3% discount rate.
Source: Bolivia, Kenya, Pakistan, India, Uganda, Colombia, Mexico, and Nicaragua from Orazem *et al.* (2008: Table 4). Brazil, Egypt, and the Philippines from Patrinos (2007: Table 2).

a country's average test scores and average schooling attainment are included in a national income model, both measures explain income differences, but schooling attainment has greater statistical significance. The high correlation between a nation's average schooling attainment, cumulative investment in schooling, and average tests scores indicates that average schooling attainment implicitly measures the quality as well as the quantity of schooling.

Given state budgets, countries face a trade-off between investing in the extensive (quantity) or extensive (quality) margin. The quality challenge might be more appropriate in advanced countries. The challenge could be split by the level of a country's economic development where improvements in quantity might be more relevant for low-income countries and quality improvements more relevant for high-income countries. Regarding failed states, it might be that these countries would exhibit the highest BCRs by bringing children to school, let alone the fact that educating those out of school now is certainly bound to help such states exit the failed list.

Table 5.2.8 Broadening the challenge

	Chapter 5 position		Alternative Perspective Paper position	
Country type	Ed. quantity	Ed. quality	Ed. quantity	Ed. quality
Failed			XXX	X
Not failed		XXX	X	XX

Note: Shaded area: No feasible solution, no action needed. Cross-hatched area: Feasible solution, priority action needed. Number of X-marks: relative action importance.

Table 5.2.8 gives an illustrative summary of the positions in Chapter 5 and the two Alternative Perspective Papers.

Appendix

Table A5.2.1 Failed countries' index and education characteristics

Country	Failure index	Years of schooling S
Afghanistan	108	4.3
Angola	85	
Bangladesh	94	5.8
Bhutan	85	
Bolivia	83	9.9
Burkina Faso	89	
Burma	98	4.8
Burundi	99	3.3
Cambodia	89	6.0
Cameroon	95	6.1
Central African Rep.	105	3.6
Chad	110	
Colombia	87	7.7
Comoros	84	
Djibouti	82.6	
DRC	108	3.5
East Timor	95	
Egypt	87	7.1

Real solutions?

Based on the evidence presented in this Alternative Perspective the 2012 Copenhagen Consensus may consider prioritizing two real solutions for addressing the global challenge of education:

- Real solution 1 : Expand basic education capacity in developing countries, especially in failed states.
- Real solution 2 : Expand pre-school interventions in developing countries, especially in failed states.

It is beyond the scope of this chapter to provide a fully fledged Copenhagen Consensus CBA of the above solutions. The Expert Panel, however, may judge that the evidence presented above is sufficient to give serious consideration of these solutions.

Table A5.2.1 ***(cont.)***

Country	Failure index	Years of schooling S
Equatorial Guinea	88	
Eritrea	94	
Ethiopia	98	
Georgia	86	
Guinea	103	
Guinea–Bissau	98	
Haiti	108	5.2
Iran	90	8.1
Iraq	105	5.9
Israel/West Bank	84	
Ivory Coast	103	3.7
Kenya	99	7.3
Kyrgyzstan	92	8.7
Laos	87	5.1
Lebanon	88	
Liberia	94	5.4
Madagascar	83	
Malawi	91	4.7

(cont.)

Table A5.2.1 (*cont.*)

Country	Failure index	Years of schooling S
Mauritania	88	4.6
Mozambique	84	1.8
Nepal	94	
Niger	99	1.8
Nigeria	100	
North Korea	96	
Pakistan	102	5.6
Papua New Guinea	84	4.8
Philippines	85	9.0
Rep. of Congo	91	6.0
Rwanda	91	4.0
Sierra Leone	92	3.4
Solomon Islands	86	

Table A5.2.1 (*cont.*)

Country	Failure index	Years of schooling S
Somalia	113	
Sri Lanka	93	8.5
Sudan	109	3.3
Syria	86	5.3
Tajikistan	88	9.3
Togo	89	5.9
Uganda	96	5.4
Uzbekistan	88	
Yemen	100	3.7
Zambia	84	6.7
Zimbabwe	108	7.7
Mean years of schooling		5.6

Sources: Failure index from Foreign Policy (2011);) years of schooling from Barro and Lee (2010).

Table A5.2.2 Returns to investment in education in failed states (%)

	Private			Social		
Country	Prim.	Sec.	Higher	Prim.	Sec.	Higher
Bolivia	20.0	6.0	19.0	13.0	6.0	13.0
Burkina Faso				20.1	14.9	21.3
Colombia	27.7	14.7	21.7	20.0	11.4	14.0
Ethiopia	24.7	24.2	26.6	14.9	14.4	11.9
Iran		21.2	18.5	15.2	17.6	13.6
Ivory Coast	25.7	30.7	25.1			
Kenya		16.0			10.0	
Liberia	99.0	30.5	17.0	41.0	17.0	8.0
Malawi	15.7	16.8	46.6	14.7	15.2	11.5
Nepal	16.6	8.5	12.0	15.7	8.1	9.1
Nigeria	30.0	14.0	34.0	23.0	12.8	17.0
Pakistan	8.4	13.7	31.2			
Papua New Guinea	37.2	41.6	23.0	12.8	19.4	8.4
Philippines	18.3	10.5	11.6	13.3	8.9	10.5
Sierra Leone				20.0	22.0	9.5
Somalia	59.9	13.0	33.2	20.6	10.4	19.9
Sri Lanka		12.6	16.1			
Uganda				66	28.6	12
Yemen	10.0	41.0	56.0	2.0	26.0	24.0
Zambia			19.2			5.7
Zimbabwe	16.6	48.5	5.1	11.2	47.6	-4.3
Mean	29.3	21.4	24.5	20.2	17.1	12.1

Sources: Based on Psacharopoulos and Patrinos (2004: Table A-1); failed classification from Foreign Policy (2011).

Table A5.2.3 Returns to investment in education in non-failed states (%)

	Private			Social		
Country	Prim.	Sec.	Higher	Prim.	Sec.	Higher
Argentina	10.1	14.2	14.9	8.4	7.1	7.6
Australia		8.1	21.1			16.3
Austria		11.3	4.2			
Bahamas		26.1			20.6	
Belgium		21.2	8.7		17.1	6.7
Botswana	99	76	38	42	41	15
Brazil	36.6	5.1	28.2	35.6	5.1	21.4
Canada		7.8	13			
Chile	9.7	12.9	20.7	8.1	11.1	14
China	18	13.4	15.1	14.4	12.9	11.3
Costa Rica	12.2	17.6	12.9	11.2	14.4	9
Cyprus	15.4	7	5.6	7.7	6.8	7.6
Denmark			10			7.8
Dominican Republic	85.1	15.1	19.4			
Ecuador	17.1	17.2	12.7	14.7	12.7	9.9
El Salvador	18.9	14.5	9.5	16.4	13.3	8
Estonia				14	2.2	10.3
France		14.8	20			
Germany		6.5	10.5			
Ghana	24.5	17	37	18	13	16.5
Greece		8.3	8.1		6.5	5.7
Guatemala	33.8	17.9	22.2			
Honduras	20.8	23.3	25.9	18.2	19.7	18.9
Hong Kong		18.5	25.2		15	12.4
Hungary		8.2	13.4		6	2.6
India	2.6	17.6	18.2			
Indonesia					11	5
Israel	27	6.9	8	16.5	6.9	6.6
Italy		17.3	18.3			
Jamaica	20.4	15.7		17.7	7.9	
Japan	13.4	10.4	8.8	9.6	8.6	6.9
Korea		10.1	17.9		8.8	15.5
Lesotho	15.5	26.7	36.5	10.7	18.6	10.2
Malaysia		32.6	34.5			
Mexico	18.9	20.1	15.7	11.8	14.6	11.1
Morocco				50.5	10	13
Netherlands		8.5	10.4		5.2	5.5
New Zealand		13.8	11.9		12.4	9.5

(*cont.*)

Table A5.2.3 (*cont.*)

Country	Private			Social		
	Prim.	Sec.	Higher	Prim.	Sec.	Higher
Nicaragua				13.6	10.4	14.7
Norway		7.4	7.7		7.2	7.5
Panama	5.7	21	21			
Paraguay	23.7	14.6	13.7	20.3	12.7	10.8
Peru	13.2	6.6	40			
Puerto Rico	68.2	52.1	29	24	34.1	15.5
Senegal	33.7	21.3		23	8.9	
Singapore	22.2	12.9	18.7	16.7	10.1	13.9
South Africa				22.1	17.7	11.8
Spain				7.4	8.5	13.5
Sudan		13	15		8	4
Sweden			10.3		10.5	9.2
Taiwan	50	12.7	15.8	27	12.3	17.7
Tanzania	7.9	8.8				
Thailand	16	12.9	11.8			
The Gambia	37.1	12.7		33.5	12.1	
Tunisia		13	27			
Turkey	1.9	8.6	16.2			8.5
United Kingdom				8.6	7.5	6.5
United States					10	12
Uruguay	27.8	10.3	12.8	21.6	8.1	10.3
Venezuela	36.3	14.6	11	23.4	10.2	6.2
Vietnam	10.8	3.8	3	13.5	4.5	6.2
Yugoslavia	14.6	3.1	5.3	3.3	2.3	3.1
Mean	25.5	15.6	17.0	18.2	11.6	10.4

Sources: Based on Psacharopoulos and Patrinos (2004): Table A-1); failed classification from Foreign Policy (2011).

Table A5.2.4 Cost-benefit values of investment in upper-secondary-school completion

Country	Private			Social		
	Total benefits ($US 2007)	NPV[a]	RoR (%)	Total benefits ($US 2007)	NPV[a]	RoR (%)
Australia	110,032	84,479	14.4	46,632	27,518	8.6
Austria	166,386	123,931	12.3	128,205	79,637	8.7
Canada	116,248	85,382	12.2	51,178	28,204	7.1
Czech Rep.	118,224	90,722	14.3	47,037	21,927	6.7
Denmark	90,497	61,352	13.3	99,870	59,089	8.7
Finland	57,009	27,416	7.5	40,991	18,362	7.6
France	75,341	44,544	8.7	32,221	−2,501	2.7
Germany	74,370	37,908	7.4	88,089	56,680	15.6
Hungary	54,225	35,808	10.9	53,507	32,938	8.3
Ireland	104,166	75,191	9.6	71,408	43,624	7.1
Italy	110,497	71,717	7.2	81,343	42,162	5.7
New Zealand	107,081	72,251	9.0	54,096	33,553	8.0
Norway	153,566	111,251	13.2	91,904	46,711	7.7
Poland	51,207	34,910	10.6	26,050	6,010	4.4
Portugal	133,074	109,618	11.5	76,420	52,629	7.7
Slovenia	82,381	61,921	12.1	48,543	22,981	6.2
Spain	67,913	52,987	9.5	26,317	7,738	4.3
Sweden	87,328	60,477	11.7	64,944	31,056	9.7
Turkey	46,637	35,082	9.5	20,699	11,371	6.4
United Kingdom	189,781	150,982	13.5	91,815	72,161	10.1
United States	228,142	201,745	21.4	102,029	70,497	10.4
OECD mean	105,910	77,604	11.4	63,967	36,302	7.7

Note: [a] NPV using OECD's 3% discount rate.
Source: OECD (2011: Tables A.9.1 and A.9.2).

Table A5.2.5 Education quantity, quality, and *per capita* income

Country	Years of schooling S	School quality (mean PISA) Q	Quality-adjusted years of schooling S*	per capita income ($US) Y
(1)	(2)	(3)	(4)	(5)
China[a]	8.2	577	9.4	6,725
Hong Kong	10.4	546	11.3	31,704
Finland	10.0	543	10.8	24,344
Singapore	9.1	543	9.9	28,107
Korea	7.1	541	7.6	19,614
Japan	11.6	529	12.3	22,816
Canada	11.4	527	12.0	25,267
New Zealand	12.7	524	13.3	18,653
Taiwan	11.3	520	11.8	20,926
Australia	11.8	519	12.2	21,732
Netherlands	11.0	519	11.4	24,695
Switzerland	9.9	517	10.2	25,104
Estonia	11.8	514	12.1	19,951
Germany	11.8	510	12.1	20,801
Belgium	10.5	509	10.7	23,655
Poland	9.9	501	9.9	10,160
Norway	12.3	500	12.3	28,500
United Kingdom	9.6	500	9.6	23,742
Denmark	10.1	499	10.0	24,621
Slovenia	8.9	499	8.9	18,170
Ireland	11.6	497	11.6	27,898
France	10.5	497	10.5	22,223
United States	12.2	496	12.1	31,178
Hungary	11.7	496	11.5	9,500
Sweden	11.6	496	11.5	24,409
Czech Rep.	12.1	490	11.9	12,868
Portugal	8.0	490	7.8	14,436
Slovak Rep.	11.2	488	10.9	13,033
Austria	9.5	487	9.3	24,131
Latvia	10.6	487	10.3	14,816
Italy	9.5	486	9.2	19,909
Spain	10.4	484	10.1	19,706
Lithuania	10.9	479	10.4	11,342
Croatia	9.0	474	8.5	8,904
Greece	10.7	473	10.1	16,362
Russian Fed.	9.7	469	9.1	9,111
Israel	11.3	459	10.4	17,937

Table A5.2.5 (*cont.*)

Country	Years of schooling S	School quality (mean PISA) Q	Quality-adjusted years of schooling S^*	*per capita* income ($US) Y
(1)	(2)	(3)	(4)	(5)
Turkey	7.0	455	6.4	8,066
Serbia	9.2	442	8.1	3,620
Chile	10.2	439	8.9	13,185
Bulgaria	9.9	432	8.5	8,886
Uruguay	8.6	427	7.3	9,893
Romania	10.4	427	8.8	4,895
Thailand	7.5	422	6.3	8,750
Mexico	9.1	420	7.7	7,979
Trinidad & Tobago	9.6	414	8.0	21,314
Jordan	9.2	402	7.4	5,702
Brazil	7.5	401	6.0	6,429
Colombia	7.7	399	6.1	6,330
Kazakhstan	10.4	399	8.3	11,245
Argentina	9.3	396	7.4	10,995
Tunisia	7.3	392	5.7	61,03
Indonesia	6.2	385	4.8	44,28
Albania	9.9	384	7.6	2,741
Qatar	6.1	373	4.6	7,179
Panama	9.6	369	7.1	6,675
Peru	9.0	368	6.6	5,388
Kyrgyzstan	8.7	325	5.7	2,835

Note: [a] China PISA score refers to Shanghai.
Sources: Col. (2) from Barro and Lee (2010).
Col. (3) based on OECD (2010). Mean 2009 PISA score on reading, mathematics, and science.
Col. (4) = [Col. (2) × Col. (3)] / 500.
Col. (5), from Maddison (2010).

Bibliography

Access Economics Pty Ltd, 2005: *The Economic Benefit of Increased Participation in Education and Training*, Dusseldorp Skills Forum, Sydney

Allen Consulting Group, 2003: *The Economy-Wide Benefits of Increasing the Proportion of Students Achieving Year 12 Equivalent Education: Modelling Results*, Sydney

Anderson, C. A. and M. J. Bowman, 1963: Concerning the role of education in development, in C. Geertz (ed.), *Old Societies and New States: The Quest for Modernity in Asia and Africa*, Collier Macmillan, London, 247–79

Applied Economics, 2002: *Realising Australia's Commitment to Young People. Scope, Benefits, Cost, Evaluation & Implementation*, Dusseldorp Skills Forum, Sydney

Azariadis, C. and A. Drazen, 1990: Threshold externalities in economic development, *Quarterly Journal of Economics* **105**, 501–26

Barro, R. J. and J.-W. Lee, 2010: A new data set of educational attainment in the World, 1950–2010, *NBER Working Paper* **15902**, NBER, Cambridge, MA

Becker, G. S. and K. M. Murphy, 1992: The division of labor, coordination costs, and knowledge,

Quarterly Journal of Economics **107**, 1137–60

Behrman, J. R., S. W. Parker, and P. E. Todd, 2011: Do conditional cash transfers for schooling generate lasting benefits?: a five-year followup of PROGRESA/Oportunidades, *Journal of Human Resources* **46**, 93–122

Birdsall, N., 1985: Public inputs and child schooling in Brazil, *Journal of Development Economics* **18**, 67–86

Breton, T. R., 2011: The quality vs. the quantity of schooling: what drives economic growth?, *Economics of Education Review* **30**, 765–773

2012: Were Mankiw, Romer, and Weil right? A reconcilation of the micro and macro effects of schooling on income, *Macroeconomic Dynamics* **31**, 391–409

Castelló-Climent, A. and A. Hidalgo-Cabrillana, 2012: The role of educational quality and quantity in the process of economic development, *Economics of Education Review* **31**, 391–409

Cunha, F., J. J., Heckman, L. Lochner, and D. V. Masterov, 2006: Interpreting the evidence on life cycle skill formation, in E. A. Hanushek and F. Welch (eds.), *Handbook of the Economics of Education*, North-Holland, Amsterdam

Easterlin, R., 1981: Why isn't the whole world developed?, *Journal of Economic History* **41**, 1–19

European Commission, 2006: *Detailed Analysis of Progress towards the Lisbon Objectives in Education and Training: Analysis of Benchmarks and Indicators* (Annex), European Commission, Brussels

Eurostat, 2012: *Early school leavers*, http://epp.eurostat.ec.europa.eu/tgm/download.do?tab=table&plugin=1&language=en&pcode=tsisc060, accessed February 3, 2012

Foreign Policy, 2011: foreignpolicy.com/articles/2011/06/17/2011_failed_states_index_interactive_map_and_rankings

Ganegodage, K. R. and A. N. Rambaldi, 2011: The impact of education investment on Sri Lankan economic growth, *Economics of Education Review* **30**, 1491–1502

Gertler, P. J., H. A. Patrinos, and M. Rubio-Codina, 2012: Empowering parents to improve education: evidence from rural Mexico, *Journal of Development Economics* **99**, 68–29

Glaeser, E. L., 1994: Why does schooling generate economic growth?, *Economics Letters* **44**, 333–7

Glewwe, P., E. A. Hanushek, S. Humpage, and R. Ravina, 2011: *School resources and educational outcomes in developing countries: a review of the literature from 1990 to 2010*, University of Minnesota, mimeo

Hanushek, E. A. and L. Woessmann, 2008: The role of cognitive skills in economic development, *Journal of Economic Literature* **46**, 607–68

Heckman, J. J., 2008: Schools, skills, and synapses, *IZA Discussion Paper* 3515 http://ftp.iza.org/dp3515.pdf

Jamison, D. T. and L. Lau, 1982: *Farmer Education and Farm Efficiency*, Johns Hopkins University Press, Baltimore, MD

Lau, L. J., D. T. Jamison, S. Liu, and S. Rivlin, 1996: Education and economic growth: some cross-sectional evidence, in N. Birdsall and R. H. Sabot (eds.), *Education in Brazil*, Inter-American Development Bank, Washington, DC and Johns Hopkins University Press, Baltimore, MD, 83–116

Levin, H. M., 2005: *The Social Costs of Inadequate Education*, A Summary of the First Annual Teachers' College Symposium on Educational Equity, October 24–26, Teachers' College, Columbia University

Levin, H. M., C. R. Belfield, P. Muennig, and C. E. Rouse, 2006: *The Costs and Benefits of an Excellent Education for America's Children – Technical Appendix*, Teachers' College, Columbia University

2007a: *The Costs and Benefits of an Excellent Education for America's Children – Overview*, Teachers' College, Columbia University

2007b: The public returns to public educational investments in African American males, *Economics of Education Review* **26**, 699–708

Maddison, A., 2010: Historical statistics of the world economy: 1–2008 AD, www.ggdc.net/Maddison/Historical_Statistics/horizontal-file_02--2010.xls

Marshall, J. H., 2011: School quality and learning gains in rural Guatemala, *Economics of Education Review* **28**, 207–16

OECD, 2010: *PISA 2009 Results: What Students Know and Can Do: Student Performance in Reading, Mathematics and Science*, Vol. 1, OECD, Paris

2011: *Education at a Glance 2011*, OECD, Paris

Orazem, P., P. Glewwe, and H. Patrinos, 2008: The Challenge of Education, Paper Prepared for 2008 Copenhagen Consensus

Patrinos, H., 2007: Living conditions of children, in B. Lomborg (ed.), *Solutions for the World's Biggest Problems: Costs and Benefits*, Cambridge University Press, 358–75

Psacharopoulos, G., 1973: *Returns to Education: An International Comparison*, Elsevier, Amsterdam

Psacharopoulos, G. and W. Loxley, 1985: *Diversified Secondary Education and Development: Evidence from Colombia and Tanzania*, Johns Hopkins University Press, Baltimore MD

Psacharopoulos, G. and H. Patrinos, 2004: Returns to investment in education: a further update, *Education Economics* **12**, 111–35

Romer, P., 1986: Increasing returns and long-run growth, *Journal of Political Economy* **94**, 1002–37

Sansani, S., 2011: The effects of school quality on long-term health, *Economics of Education Review* **30**, 1320–33

UNDP, UNESCO, UNICEF and the World Bank 1990: *Meeting Basic Learning Needs: A Vision for the 1990s*, UNICEF, New York

UNESCO, 2011: *Out of School Children: New Data Reveal Persistent Challenges*, UNESCO Institute for Statistics, Montreal, www.uis.unesco.org/FactSheets/Documents/FS12_2011_OOSC_EN.pdf

Vernez, G., R. Krop, and C. P. Rydell, 1999: *Closing the Education Gap – Benefits and Costs*, RAND Corporation, New York

World Bank, 1962: Tunisia Education Project Appraisal Report, www-wds.worldbank.org/external/default/WDSContentServer/WDSP/IB/2002/07/25/000178830_98101903465813/Rendered/PDF/multi0page.pdf

2011: *Learning for All: Investing in People's Knowledge and Skills to Promote Development*, World Bank, Washington, DC

Hunger and Malnutrition

JOHN HODDINOTT, MARK ROSEGRANT, AND MAXIMO TORERO

Introduction: the challenge of hunger and undernutrition

Current estimates suggest that there are approximately 925 million hungry people in the world. Just under 180 million pre-school children are stunted – that is, they are the victims of chronic undernutrition. This deprivation is not because of insufficient food production. Approximately 2,100 kcal/person/day, provides sufficient energy for most daily activities; current *per capita* global food production, at 2,796 kcal/person/day, is well in excess of this requirement. Given that there is more than enough food in the world to feed its inhabitants, global hunger is not an insoluble problem.

Deprivation in a world of plenty is an intrinsic rationale for investments that reduce hunger and undernutrition; our focus in this chapter, as with previous Copenhagen Consensus papers on this topic, Behrman *et al.* (2004) and Horton *et al.* (2008), is on the instrumental case for doing so. In its simplest form, the central argument of this chapter is that these investments are simply good economics. Our solutions, however, represent a partial departure from those earlier Copenhagen Consensus papers. First, we re-introduce attention to solutions to hunger with a focus on investments that will increase global food production. This might seem strange given our observation that global food production exceeds global food needs. But as we argue in this chapter, these investments are needed for two reasons: to lower prices so as to make food more affordable; and because, given the consequences of climate change, there can be no complacency regarding global food production. Second, previous Copenhagen Consensus papers on hunger and undernutrition have considered very specific interventions that focus on single dimensions of undernutrition. In this chapter, we examine the economic case for bundling these. Our proposed investments are:

- *Investment 1*: Accelerating yield enhancements
- *Investment 2*: Market innovations that reduce hunger
- *Investment 3*: Interventions that reduce the micronutrient malnutrition and reduce the prevalence of stunting

We begin with background material that contextualizes our proposed solutions:

- What are the causes of hunger?
- How many hungry and undernourished people are there in the world?
- And what are the likely trends in hunger over the next twenty-five–thirty-five years?

We then describe our three proposed investments, explaining how each addresses the problems of hunger and undernutrition and describing their costs and benefits. Caveats and cautions are noted in the third section and our concluding section summarizes the case for these investments.

Understanding global hunger

This section provides background material that contextualizes our proposed solutions. We cover the following topics:

* We thank Derek Headey, Finn Kydland, Bjørn Lomborg, Henrik Meyer, Robert Mundell, Thomas Schelling, Vernon Smith, and Nancy Stokey for comments on earlier versions of this chapter. Financial support for the preparation of this chapter was provided by the Copenhagen Consensus Center and by the Department for International Development (UK) through its funding of the Transform Nutrition Consortium.

- What are the causes of hunger? Here, we present a conceptual model that identifies the causes of hunger. We do so in a largely non-technical way, though we will also briefly explain how this can be derived formally. We place our proposed solutions within this causal framework.
- How many hungry people are there in the world, and where do they live?
- What are the likely trends in hunger over the next twenty-five–thirty-five years?

What are the causes of hunger?

Definitions

We begin with three definitions: food security, hunger, and nutritional status.

The concept of *food security* has spatial and temporal dimensions. The spatial dimension refers to the degree of aggregation at which food security is being considered. It is possible to analyze food security at the global, continental, national, subnational, village, household, or individual level. The temporal dimension refers to the time frame over which food security is being considered. A distinction is often made between chronic food insecurity – the inability to meet food needs on an ongoing basis – and transitory food insecurity, when the inability to meet food needs is of a temporary nature (Maxwell and Frankenberger, 1992). Transitory food insecurity is sometimes divided into two subcategories: *cyclical*, where there is a regular pattern to food insecurity, such as the "lean season" that occurs in the period just before harvest; and *temporary*, which is the result of a short-term, exogenous shock such as a drought or flood (Hoddinott, 2001). Mindful of these dimensions, we follow the current, standard definition of food security:

> Food security exists when all people, at all times, have physical, social and economic access to sufficient, safe and nutritious food which meets their dietary needs and food preferences for an active and healthy life. Household food security is the application of this concept to the family level, with individuals within households as the focus of concern . . . Food insecurity exists when people do not have adequate physical, social or economic access to food as defined above. (FAO, 2010: 8)

Hunger is "A condition, in which people lack the basic food intake to provide them with the energy and nutrients for fully productive lives" (Hunger Task Force, 2003: 33). Hunger and food security are related, but are not synonymous. An absence of hunger does not imply food security and, particularly in times of stress, households and individuals may go hungry in order to safeguard longer-term food security.

Nutrients provided by food combine with other factors, including the health state of the person consuming the food, to produce "nutritional status." Some forms of poor nutritional status often described as undernutrition reflect an absence of macronutrients or micronutrients which may be exacerbated by debilitating health stresses such as parasites.[1] Undernutrition with regard to macronutrients and micronutrients continues to be the dominant nutritional problem in most developing countries. Other forms of malnutrition, sometimes inelegantly termed overnutrition, result from the excessive caloric intake, exacerbated by diseases such as diabetes and low levels of physical activity, are of considerable concern in upper- and many middle-income countries. We do not consider overnutrition further.

A conceptual framework

Food security, hunger, and undernutrition reflect the purposive actions of individuals given preferences and constraints. Our conceptual framework for thinking about these has four components: settings, resources, activities, and outcomes.[2]

[1] Somewhat confusingly, FAO uses the word "undernourishment" but in a manner that is different from undernutrition. FAO defines undernourishment to exist when caloric intake is below the minimum dietary energy requirement (MDER) (FAO, 2010). The MDER is the amount of energy needed for light activity and to maintain a minimum acceptable weight for attained height. It varies by country and from year to year depending on the gender and age structure of the population.

[2] There are many good conceptual frameworks for food security and nutrition, and in setting this out we do not privilege ours over these others. We note that what we present here attempts to encompass approaches found in development economics, the food security literature, development discourse, and nutrition. What we describe here can be readily recast as an agricultural household model (Singh *et al.*, 1986) extended to incorporate health and nutrition (as in

"Settings" refers to the broader environment in which a household is situated and which creates both opportunities and constraints on the actions of both households and individuals. We describe these in terms of five categories: physical, social, legal, governance, and economic.

The physical setting refers to the natural and man-made environment. It includes the level and variability of rainfall, access to irrigation, availability of common property resources such as grazing land, forests and fishery resources, elevation, soil fertility, the extent of environmental degradation, exposure to rapid-onset natural disasters, distances to markets, and the availability and quality of infrastructure – health clinics, schools, roads, markets, and telecommunications. The physical environment also incorporates phenomena that affect human health – temperature; rainfall; access to safe water; the presence of communicable human and zoonotic diseases all being examples.

The social setting captures such factors as the existence of trust, reciprocity, social cohesion, and strife. The existence of ethnic tensions and conflicts, conflicts between other groups (e.g. the landless and the landed), gender relations and norms regarding gender roles, the presence (or absence) of civil society organizations are also part of the social setting. Norms of gender roles, of "correct" behaviors and folk wisdom – for example, what type of foods mothers "should" feed their children – are also part of the social setting.

The legal setting can be thought of as the "rules of the game" under which economic exchange takes place. As such, it affects agriculture through the restrictions and opportunities it creates for the production and sale of different foods, the regulation of labor, capital, and food markets. This setting includes the formal and informal rules regarding the ownership and use of assets, political freedoms such as the right of expression and restrictions on personal liberties. The legal setting is linked, but is distinct from, the governance setting.

The governance setting captures how rules are developed, implemented, and enforced. This includes the political processes which create rules – for example, centralized or decentralized decision-making, dictatorial or democratic, and so on – and the implementation of these rules through bureaucracies, parastatals, and third-party organizations.

Finally, the economic setting captures policies that affect the level, returns, and variability of returns on assets and, as such, influence choices regarding the productive activities undertaken by individuals, firms, and households. In our setup, this has two principal components. There are macro-level considerations: economic policy (fiscal and monetary); balance of payments; exchange rates; foreign exchange reserves; opportunities and constraints for economic growth; and trends in growth and employment. There are meso-level or market-level considerations that capture their structure, conduct, and performance as measured by price levels, variability, and trends as well as government policies towards them. While many markets affect the livelihoods and well-being of poor people, of particular importance here is the functioning of the market for food. Relevant considerations include the contestability of such markets, the extent of domestic, regional, and international market integration and the presence and level of duties or quantitative restrictions (such as quotas) on internal and external trade.

Households have resources. They can be divided into two broad categories: time (or labor power) and capital. Time refers to the availability of physical labor for work. We divide capital into three categories. One is assets such as land, tools, and equipment used for agricultural or non-agricultural production, livestock, social capital, and financial resources that, when combined with labor, produce income. A second is human capital, in the form of formal schooling and knowledge. Knowledge includes how to recognize and treat illness, and how to maintain good health. It also includes knowledge of good nutrition practices such as appropriate

Behrman and Deolalikar, 1988; Behrman and Hoddinott, 2005; Strauss and Thomas, 1995), extended to capture intrahousehold and gender allocation issues (Pitt *et al.*, 1990; Haddad *et al.*, 1997), and dynamics of health and nutrition (Hoddinott and Kinsey, 2001). It can also be seen as an elaboration of Sen's entitlement theory of famine (Sen, 1981a, 1981b). The discussion of resources bears similarity to components of the Sustainable Livelihoods approaches (DfID, 1999). For children, the discussion of nutritional outcomes bears similarities to UNICEF's Causal Framework of Malnutrition (Maxwell and Frankenberger, 1992: 25). This exposition builds on ideas found in Baulch and Hoddinott (2000); Hoddinott and Quisumbing (2010); and Hoddinott (2012).

complementary foods and the frequency of feeding of young children. The final resource is human capital, in the form of health and nutrition status – specifically, the physical capacity to do work. Some household resources, such as health and schooling, are always held by individuals while others, such as land and financial capital, may be held individually (for example, men and women may not pool their land holdings) or collectively owned.

Households allocate these resources to different types of livelihood strategies or activities. These activities can be divided in any number of ways, for example agricultural activities; wage work outside the household; and non-agricultural own-business activities. Some of these are a direct source of food while others generate cash. In addition, households may obtain food or cash income from transfers received in the form of remittances or gifts from other community members or from the community itself, or through government interventions. Conditional on the resources available to the household, the choice of a particular set of activities is affected by perceptions of the level and variability of returns to each activity, the time period over which these returns are earned, and the correlation of returns across activities. For example, the household may decide to grow a mix of crops that embodies differing levels of susceptibility to climatic shocks and returns.

These activities generate income. But the relationship between these allocations and outcomes such as food security, hunger, or nutrition is not deterministic. First, random events or "shocks" can, and indeed do, occur. Different environmental, economic, governance, social, and legal settings will produce different combinations of possible shocks. These can affect the stock of assets, the returns to these assets in different activities, and the relationship between income generated and consumption or other measures of well-being. Second, households allocate income to goods that affect food security and nutritional status, other goods, and savings. The choices made reflect the preferences of households (either expressed collectively or as the outcome of bargaining among individual members), the prices of all goods that they face, and the settings in which they find themselves. Goods that affect food security include food consumption at the household level (referred to as "food access" in much of the food security literature); goods directly related to health care, such as medicines; and goods that affect the health environment, such as shelter, sanitation, and water. These three goods, together with knowledge and practice of good nutritional and health practices (called "care behaviors") and the public health environment (for example, the availability of publicly provided potable water), affect illness and individual food intake, which in turn generate nutritional status or food utilization. Individual intakes are a reflection in part of individual needs, which themselves will vary by age and sex, by household choices such as decisions to protect the most vulnerable members in times of stress or to allocate calories to those with the highest work-related caloric needs, by norms regarding intra-household food allocation (for example, a norm that men eat before women or one where protein-rich foods are given to higher-status household members) and, in the case of very young children, caregiver practices relating to the frequency with which infants are fed.

Global estimates of the prevalence of hunger and undernutrition

Hunger

From our discussion of definitions and our conceptual framework, there are a number of concepts that we could consider measuring: food security; hunger; household food acquisition; food intake; and nutritional status. While individual studies provide many measures of these, at the global level, information is limited to a specific measure of hunger and of elements of nutritional status. There are no estimates of the number of people who are food insecure. There are no *direct* estimates of the extent of the hungry. That is, there are no direct estimates based on a comparison of measured intakes and minimum dietary requirements. Instead, the most widely cited data on the number of persons considered hungry come from the UN Food and Agriculture Organization (FAO). FAO constructs an indirect measure of the following form:

> [FAO] estimates the prevalence of undernourishment [or hunger] . . . as the proportion of the population in the Country with a level of Dietary Energy

Consumption (DEC) lower than the Dietary Energy Requirements (DER). (Cafiero and Gennari, 2011)

The calculation of DER begins with country-level census data on population size, disaggregated by age and sex. The disaggregated data are needed because basal metabolic rates – which account for a large fraction of energy requirements for bodies at rest – differ by both age and sex. This is then adjusted for a minimal Physical Activity Level (PAL) "compatible with a healthy life" (Cafiero and Gennari, 2011: 17) and with an allowance for the fact that a certain percentage of the female population will be pregnant in any given year (FAO, 2008).

DEC is based on combining two items of information. On an ongoing basis, FAO constructs estimates of mean *per capita* dietary energy supply (production + stocks – post-harvest losses + commercial imports + food aid – exports) into what is called a "food balance sheet." When calculating the number of undernourished people, it takes a three-year average of these data. It then imposes a distribution on this supply. The distribution is often, but not always, taken from a household budget survey from which estimates of household caloric acquisition are derived.

Apart from the reliability of census data, the construction of country-level DERs is relatively unproblematic. Other elements, however, are more controversial. Dietary energy supply is not measured directly and so any errors in its components, such as feed and stock estimates, both of which are notoriously difficult to measure, are transmitted to it (Jacobs and Sumner, 2002). Of even greater concern is the construction of an assumed distribution of caloric intakes. Consider, for example, the distribution derived in the illustrative example from a "recent National Household Budget Survey conducted in the hypothetical country" (FAO, 2008: 6). This shows that for the poorest decile, average DEC is 1,554 kcal/person/day. For the second richest decile, it is 3,093, and for the richest decile, it is 3,373. Both are problematic. The DEC figure for the poorest decile is nearly identical to the diet administered to volunteers during the Minnesota Starvation Experiment, an intake level which, had it continued for more than the twenty-four weeks of

Table 6.1 Global estimates of undernourishment (hunger), 1969–2010

Period	No. of undernourished (million)	Prevalence (%)
1969–1971	875	33
1979–1981	850	25
1990–1992	848	16
1995–1997	792	14
2000–2002	836	14
2006–2008	850	13
2009	1023	18
2010	925	16

Source: FAO (2010) (for 1969–1971 and 1979–1981) and spreadsheet downloaded from FAO for all others. Data for 2009 and 2010 are FAO extrapolations based on US Department of Agriculture projections.

the experiment would have likely led to the deaths of the participants (Keys *et al.*, 1950). At the other end of the distribution, the rising levels of DEC are inconsistent with the microeconometric evidence of Hoddinott *et al.* (2000) and others that shows that caloric-income elasticities are virtually zero in relatively wealthy households. A second example is found in the technical appendix to FAO (2010). This shows that updating the distributional data for India reduced the estimated number of hungry people by 31 million people in 2005–2007 and 57 million people in 2000–2002.

While debates over this methodology continue, the numbers produced by FAO remain the most frequently quoted in discussions surrounding global hunger.[3,4] Table 6.1 provides these estimates for the periods 1969–1971 to 2010. These show a slow

[3] FAO's website notes, "During its meeting in 2010, the Committee on World Food Security (CFS) asked FAO to review its methodology for estimating undernourishment in order to provide more timely updates and incorporate all relevant information, including analysis of the large number of household surveys that have become available in recent years. Therefore, no updated estimates for the number of undernourished people in 2009 and 2010 are reported, nor has an estimate been made for 2011" (FAO, 2012).

[4] Headey (2011) provides a detailed critique of FAO methodology. He notes that in the Gallup World Poll, respondents are asked "Have there been times in the past 12 months when you or your family have gone hungry?" and that this provides an alternative way of estimating global hunger.

Table 6.2 Regional estimates of undernourishment, 1990–2008

	1990–1992	1995–1997	2000–2002	2006–2008
Africa	170.9	193.6	203.3	223.6
Northern Africa	*5.0*	*5.4*	*5.6*	*6.1*
SSA	*165.9*	*188.2*	*197.7*	*217.5*
Latin America and the Caribbean	54.4	53.4	50.8	47.0
Asia	607.1	526.2	565.7	567.8
Oceania	0.7	0.8	1.0	1.0

Source: Spreadsheet downloaded from FAO.

drift down in absolute numbers between 1969–1971 and 1995–1997. The number of undernourished remains relatively unchanged over the 2000s before first spiking up, then down, following the 2008 food price crisis. The global prevalence of hunger drops from 33 to 14 percent between 1969–1971 and 2000–2002, rising to 18 percent in 2009.

Table 6.2 provides a breakdown by the number of people considered undernourished by region.[5] The hungry are found predominantly in Asia (567 million) and secondarily in SSA (217 million); these two regions account for more than 90 percent of the world's hungry. Unfortunately, even this regional disaggregation is not especially helpful. Six countries – China, India, Bangladesh, Pakistan, Ethiopia, and the DRC accounted for 62 percent of the global hungry in 2006–2008. Estimated changes in these countries dominate the "headline" changes in global estimates of hunger. For example, between 1990–1992 and 2005–2007, the number of hungry people fell by 80 million in China but rose by 65 million in India and 14 million in Pakistan. In SSA, the number of hungry rose by 32 million in the DRC and this accounted for 60 percent of the continent's increase in undernourishment between 1990–1992 and 2005–2007.

Two further limitations should be noted. None of these estimates gives us any sense as to the severity of hunger. They make no distinction between someone with a DEC just slightly below the DER and someone whose DEC is 20 or 30 percent below this cutoff, even though hunger for the latter person is significantly more severe and more debilitating. Second, they give no sense where the hungry are found within individual countries. Behrman *et al.* (2004) cited statistics from the UN's Hunger Task Force (Hunger Task Force, 2003) that suggested that approximately 50 percent of those who are hungry globally are in farm households, 22 percent are the rural landless, 20 percent live in urban areas, and 8 percent are resource-dependent (pastoralists, fishers, etc). Unfortunately, there have been no updates of these data.

Undernutrition

In contrast to the somewhat messy approaches to defining and measuring hunger and food insecurity, a considerable body of knowledge exists surrounding the measurement of undernutrition.

Linear (height) growth failure is widespread in poor countries. An estimated 175 million or more pre-school children are stunted, meaning that their height given their age is more than 2 standard deviations below that of the international reference standard (Black *et al.*, 2008; UNSCN, 2010). Table 6.3 provides data on the regional distribution of stunting along with trends in prevalences since 1990. In brief, the prevalence of stunting has been falling globally since 1990, but the regional distributional of this trend is uneven, with rapid falls being observed in eastern Asia, a more gradual decline in Latin America and the Caribbean, and no change in SSA. The greatest concentration of stunted children is found in south central Asia. Table 6.4 provides comparable statistics on the prevalence of low weight-for-age, a MDG indicator. These show a similar pattern of change over time.

[5] Regional breakdowns are not available after 2006–2008.

Table 6.3 Global and regional prevalences of stunting, 1990–2007

	Prevalence (%)					No. (million)
	1990	1995	2000	2005	2007	2005
Africa	40.3	39.8	39.3	38.8	38.5	56.9
Eastern	48.1	47.4	46.7	46	45.7	
Middle	45.3	43.8	42.3	40.8	40.3	
Northern	29.4	27.4	25.5	23.7	23.0	
Southern	35.4	34.7	34.1	33.5	33.3	
Western	38.1	38.1	38.1	38.1	38.1	
Asia	48.6	43.1	37.7	32.6	30.6	111.6
Eastern	35.9	28.2	21.7	16.3	14.4	
South-central	60.7	54.6	48.4	42.3	39.9	
South-eastern	47.0	41.5	36.2	31.3	29.4	
Western	28.2	25.9	23.7	21.6	20.9	
Latin America and the Caribbean	23.7	20.9	18.1	15.7	14.8	9.2
Caribbean	15.0	12.0	9.6	7.5	6.9	
Central America	32.5	28.6	25.1	21.8	20.6	
South America	20.9	18.3	16	13.9	13.1	
Oceania		39.8	39.1	38.5	38.2	
All developing countries	44.4	40.1	36.1	32.5	31.2	177.7

Source: Black *et al.* (2008); UNSCN (2010).

The physical and neurological consequences of growth failure arising from chronic undernourishment are increasingly well understood. Chronic nutrient depletion, resulting from inadequate nutrient intake, infection, or both, leads to retardation of skeletal growth in children and to a loss of, or failure to accumulate, muscle mass and fat (Morris, 2001); this lost linear growth is never fully regained (Stein *et al.*, 2010). Chronic undernutrition has neurological consequences, adversely affecting the hippocampus, damaging the chemical processes associated with spatial navigation and memory formation, and reducing myelination of axon fibers; see Hoddinott *et al.* (2011) for further discussion and references.

Micronutrient deficiencies are another important component of undernutrition. These are discussed at length in Behrman *et al.* (2004) and Horton *et al.* (2008), so our treatment here is brief. The greatest concern lies with deficiencies in Vitamin A, iron, iodine, and zinc. Vitamin A deficiencies are associated with increased risk of infant and child mortality; Black *et al.* (2005) estimate that they account for just over 650,000 deaths annually in children under 5. Currently, approximately 163 million pre-school children are Vitamin A deficient, with the highest prevalences found in central and south Asia (including India) and central and west Africa. Iodine deficiency adversely affects development of the central nervous system, leading to mental retardation and stunted growth (UNSCN, 2010). While increased availability of iodized salt has reduced iodine deficiencies, UNSCN (2010) estimates that 1.8 billion people are iodine deficient as measured by low urinary iodine. The vast majority of these people – 1.3 billion – are found in Asia.

Anemia is widespread in the developing world. In women, this leads to increased risk of maternal mortality and ill-health and low maternal iron availability leads to reduced iron stores in newborns (UNSCN, 2010). Iron deficiency in children constrains cognitive development (UNSCN, 2010). World-wide, more than 40 percent of pregnant

Table 6.4 Global and regional prevalences of underweight, 1990–2007

	Prevalence (%)					No. (million)
	1990	1995	2000	2005	2007	2005
Africa	21.5	21.1	20.5	19.9	19.6	31.1
Eastern	25.6	24.6	23.6	22.7	22.3	
Middle	24.3	23.3	22.3	21.4	21	
Northern	10.8	10	9.2	8.5	8.2	
Southern	11.7	12.1	12.5	13	13.2	
Western	25.1	24.4	23.6	22.8	22.5	
Asia	33.8	30	26.4	23	21.6	78.6
Eastern	16.2	11.5	8.1	5.6	4.8	
South-central	49.9	44.6	39.4	34.4	32.5	
South-eastern	30.6	26.6	22.9	19.6	18.3	
Western	12.8	10.7	9	7.5	7	
Latin America and the Caribbean	7.5	6.2	5	4.1	3.8	2.7
Caribbean	8.4	6.8	5.5	4.5	4.1	
Central America	10.6	8.5	6.8	5.4	4.9	
South America	6.1	5.1	4.2	3.5	3.2	
Oceania		18.5	17.3	16.2	15.8	
All developing countries	28.7	25.7	22.8	20.3	19.3	112.4

Source: Black *et al.* (2008); UNSCN (2010).

women are iron-deficient, as are 47 percent of preschool children (Black *et al.*, 2008). Unlike Vitamin A and iodine deficiencies, these prevalences have remained stubbornly high over the last ten years. Zinc deficiency affects children's physical growth and leads to increased susceptibility to a number of infections, including diarrhea and pneumonia (Brown *et al.*, 2009). Currently, there are no global estimates of zinc deficiency.

The IMPACT model

In this section, we provide an application of the model described on pp. 333–5 to two outcome measures described on pp. 335–7, the number of undernourished people in the world and the number of undernourished children as measured by weight-for-age. We do so using the International Model for Policy Analysis of Agricultural Commodity and Trade (IMPACT) model. IMPACT is a partial equilibrium, multi-commodity, multi-country model.

IMPACT covers over forty-six crops and livestock commodities including cereals, soybeans, roots and tubers, meats, milk, eggs, oilseeds, oilcakes, sugar, and fruits and vegetables. It includes a set of 115 countries/regions where each country is linked to the rest of the world through international trade and 281 food-producing units (grouped according to political boundaries and major river basins) (Rosegrant *et al.*, 2008). It starts with assumptions about specific aspects of the settings described on pp. 333–9. These include assumptions about population growth,[6] urbanization, and the rate of income growth. Note that the extensive degree of geographic disaggregation in the IMPACT model means that individual country-level variations in these assumptions typically have little impact on global-level projections. IMPACT

[6] Population projections are the "Medium" variant population growth rate projections from the Population Statistics division of the United Nations and income projections are estimated by the authors, drawing upon Millennium Ecosystem Assessment (2005).

also makes assumptions about international trade regimes for both agricultural and non-agricultural commodities; it is possible, however, to relax these. For example, Rosegrant (2008) describes the consequences for global food prices of trade-distorting subsidies to biofuels. Crucially, however, IMPACT does not take one dimension of the physical setting – water availability and use – as given but instead models this explicitly.

In IMPACT, agricultural activities are carefully modeled. Growth in crop production in each country is determined by crop and input prices, exogenous rates of productivity growth and area expansion, investment in irrigation, and water availability. Other sources of income are, in IMPACT, assumed to follow from the World Bank's EACC study (Margulis *et al.*, 2010), updated for SSA and south Asian countries. Demand for agricultural commodities is a function of prices, income, and population growth. Four categories of commodity demand are included: food, feed, biofuels, feedstock and other uses. As a partial equilibrium model, demands for non-food-related goods are not considered. The model links countries and regions through international trade, using a series of linear and non-linear equations to approximate the underlying production and demand relationships. World agricultural commodity prices are determined annually at levels that clear international markets (Table 6.5). IMPACT is designed to recognize that there are interlinkages within the agricultural sector and that exogenous changes can play out in complex ways. For example, urbanization and income growth mean that meat and dairy consumption are likely to grow rapidly as better-off consumers diversify diets. While this means that the consumption of cereals *per capita* will decline, some of this decline is offset by increased demand for animal feeds. For a detailed description of the IMPACT methodology, see Rosegrant *et al.* (2008).

IMPACT generates long-term projections of food supply, demand, trade, and prices that enable us to estimate the trends in global food security between now and 2050 (Table 6.5). These can be thought as "BAU" scenarios that would prevail in the absence of the investments we describe on pp. 342–9. These baseline scenarios do not consider the consequences for agricultural production of climate change; we return to these on p. 349. With this in mind, we begin with projections for world prices of major agricultural commodities. These are presented in Table 6.6.

Table 6.5 Projected change in world commodity prices presented as the percentage change between baseline 2010 and baseline 2050

Commodity	World commodity prices (% change)
Beef	20
Pork	55
Lamb	2
Poultry	47
Milk	8
Rice	34
Wheat	40
Maize	56
Millet	12
Sorghum	32
Other grains	14
Soybean	24
Soybean oil	51
Rapeseed	47
Rapeseed oil	92

Source: IFPRI IMPACT projections (2011).

Prices increase for all major agricultural commodities between 2010 and 2050. This is a result of significant rise in demand despite the increase in production and also due to constraints on crop productivity and area. Prices increases significantly, with highest price increase in rapeseed oil followed by maize, wheat, and rice. Rapeseed oil and soybean oil price increases are because of biofuel initiatives by the European Union and United States that increase demand for these oils. With the increase in demand for livestock and the rise in feedstock prices, large price increases are seen in livestock sector, particularly for pork and poultry. The price of pork increases by 55 percent and poultry by 47 percent between 2010 and 2050.

Baseline results are shown in Table 6.7. Globally, IMPACT predicts that under BAU, there is

Table 6.6 Baseline projections for people at risk of hunger, 2010, 2025, and 2050

	People at risk of hunger (million)		
Region	2010	2025	2050
East Asia and Pacific	177	131	122
Europe and Central Asia	23	23	21
Latin America and the Caribbean	60	61	45
Middle East and North Africa	17	21	24
South Asia	318	310	235
SSA	240	275	268
Developing	835	821	716
Developed	49	50	50
World	884	870	766

Source: IFPRI IMPACT projections (2011).

Table 6.7 Baseline projections for number of malnourished children, 2010, 2025, and 2050

	No. of malnourished children (million)		
Region	2010	2025	2050
East Asia and Pacific	20	13	8
Europe and Central Asia	4	3	3
Latin America and the Caribbean	8	7	4
Middle East and North Africa	4	3	2
South Asia	74	65	50
SSA	41	44	39
Developing	150	135	106
Developed	12	12	12
World	163	147	118

Source: IFPRI IMPACT projections (2011).

essentially no change in the number of hungry people in the world in 2025 and only a modest decline, from 884 to 776 million, by 2050. Given a predicted global population of 9.3 billion by 2050, this projection implies a decline in the prevalence of hunger from 16 to 8.2 percent. There are also significant regional variations in the distribution of hunger. In Latin America and the Caribbean there is a 24 percent decline in the population at risk of hunger between 2010 and 2050. South Asia, which has the largest share of population at risk in 2010, only has a 26 percent decline, which is slightly higher than that seen in Latin America and the Caribbean. On the other hand, the share increases by significant amounts in the Middle East and North Africa and SSA between 2010 and 2050.

IMPACT uses approximations of care behaviors, the household health environment, and food intake to project the number of children that will be underweight in 2050. It uses elasticities of relationships between female education (where female secondary enrollment rates serve as a proxy for improved care behaviors), access to health and sanitation (where life expectancy and access to safe water are used as proxies), and changes in food availability (a crude proxy for food intake) taken from a cross-country study by Smith and Haddad (2000).[7] The number of underweight children slowly drifts lower, from 163 million in 2010 to 147 million in 2025 and 118 million by 2050. Over this period, the distribution of underweight children becomes increasingly concentrated in two regions, South Asia and SSA. By 2050, 84 percent of all undernourished children reside in these regions.

Solutions to global hunger and undernutrition

In this section, we describe three solutions to reducing global hunger and undernutrition:

- *Investment 1*: Accelerating yield enhancements
- *Investment 2*: Market innovations that reduce hunger
- *Investment 3*: Interventions reduce micronutrient malnutrition and reduce the prevalence of stunting

[7] The data used to make this calculation are obtained from the WHO Global Database on Child Growth Malnutrition, the UN Administrative Committee on Coordination – Subcommittee on Nutrition, the World Bank *World Development Indicators*, the FAO FAOSTAT database, and the UNESCO UNESCOSTAT database.

Accelerating yield enhancements

Basic calculations

We consider the impact on our baseline projections of additional R&D investments in agricultural yield enhancements. We construct an alternative scenario that assumes significant, but plausible, increases in these investments, with resulting increases in crop and livestock yields. These include research that enhances drought, heat, and salt tolerance, identifying and disseminating varieties with enhanced yield potential, addressing virulent wheat rust, developing resistance to cattle diseases such as East Coast Fever (which would increase milk yields), and soil diagnostics that would permit optimal combinations of organic and inorganic fertilizers.[8] Specifically, the baseline IMPACT model assumes annual global public investment in agricultural R&D of $5 billion per year. In our alternative scenario, we increase this annual investment by $8 billion to $13 billion.

This investment increases productivity; it can be thought of as a means by which, for a given set of inputs (the assets and labor described on pp. 333–5), output increases. Specifically, we estimate that this investment increases the yield growth rate for crops yields by 0.40 for all crops and the livestock yield growth by 0.20. The impact of higher research investment on yield growth rates is estimated by using the elasticity of yields with respect to research expenditures. The elasticitites are synthesized from the literature, including Fan *et al.* (1998); Schimmelpfenig and Thirtle (1999); Thirtle *et al.* (2003); Kiani *et al.* (2008); and Alene and Coulibaly (2009).

Yield growth has both income and price effects. The increase in productivity also generates increases in agricultural GDP growth, which leads to total GDP growth averaging 0.25 percentage points higher in the world as a whole. The impact of agricultural R&D-induced crop and livestock productivity growth on GDP growth is derived by linked analysis using ABARE's CGE model GTEM. GTEM (Ahammad and Mi, 2005) is a multi-region, multi-sector, dynamic, general equilibrium model of the global economy. GTEM provides projections for a host of variables including GRP (a GDP equivalent for GTEM regional economies). The GDP variables from GTEM were used to validate the GDP (and population) input data to achieve cross-sectoral consistency with the partial general equilibrium agricultural sector IMPACT model through soft-linking. Once consistent GDP growth rates have been established, the GDP impacts of increased agricultural productivity growth can be estimated for any specified increase in productivity.

Table 6.8 Projected change in world commodity prices presented as the percentage change between baseline and alternative scenario 2050

Commodity	World commodity prices (% change)
Beef	−11
Pork	−12
Lamb	−12
Poultry	−12
Milk	−9
Rice	−22
Wheat	−18
Maize	−16
Millet	−20
Sorghum	−18
Other grains	−16
Soybean	−18
Soybean oil	−18
Rapeseed	−18
Rapeseed oil	−68

Source: IFPRI IMPACT projections (2011).

Table 6.8 shows the percentage change in the world commodity prices between the baseline and the alternative scenario for 2050. As a result of higher yields that increases production, the prices for almost all the commodities decrease from the baseline. The largest decline in world prices is 68 percent for rapeseed oil, followed by 22 percent for rice between the baseline and the alternative scenario. If we look at livestock, lower feedstock costs lower costs of production, leading to an expansion in production and therefore lower prices. The prices of livestock decline by 11 percent–12 percent

[8] Von Braun *et al.* (2008) describe these in further detail.

Table 6.9 Projected change in people at risk of hunger presented as the percentage change between baseline and alternative scenario for 2050

Region	Share at risk of hunger (million)		
	2050 baseline	2050 scenario	% change
East Asia and Pacific	122	103	−15
Europe and Central Asia	21	21	−4
Latin America and the Caribbean	45	36	−20
Middle East and North Africa	24	20	−18
South Asia	235	152	−35
SSA	268	175	−35
Developing	716	507	−29
Developed	50	49	−1
World	766	556	−27

Source: IFPRI IMPACT projections (2011).

Table 6.10 Projected change in number of malnourished children presented as the percentage change between baseline and alternative scenario 2050

Region	No. of malnourished children (million)		
	2050 baseline	2050 scenario	% change
East Asia and Pacific	8	7	−12
Europe and Central Asia	3	2	−15
Latin America and the Caribbean	4	4	−18
Middle East and North Africa	2	1	−19
South Asia	50	48	−6
SSA	39	33	−13
Developing	106	96	−10
Developed	12	11	−7
World	118	106	−10

Source: IFPRI IMPACT projections (2011).

between the baseline and the alternative scenario for 2050. Therefore, with the increase in productivity of both crop and livestock, prices are lower in the alternative scenario than the baseline in 2050.

Table 6.9 shows IMPACT's projections of the effect of this investment on the number of people projected to be hungry in 2050. The global number of hungry falls from 766 to 556 million people, a decline of 27 percent. With an estimated global population of 9.3 billion by 2050, this implies a global prevalence of hunger of 5.9 percent, meaning that prevalence would be 63 percent less (5.9 versus 16) in 2050 than it was in 2010. Table 6.9 also shows that this reduction is most pronounced in the two parts of the world where hunger remains most virulent. In this alternative scenario, both south Asia and SSA have a 35 percent decline between the baseline and the alternative scenario. Other regions like Latin America and the Caribbean, the Middle East and North Africa, and East Asia and Pacific also make significant reduction from the baseline.

Recall that in the IMPACT model, these improvements in production feed through to lower numbers of underweight children through increased food availability, one input into child nutritional status. The results are shown in Table 6.10. There is a reduction in the number of children predicted to be underweight, with this figure falling from 118 to 112 million, with half of this reduction, 6 million children, coming in SSA. By contrast, the reduction in underweight prevalence in south Asia is only 2 million children, a fall of only 6 percent. This demonstrates the need to complement these investments with those that attack other causes of undernutrition.

Under this scenario of increased investments in agricultural R&D, an additional $8 billion dollar per year would, by 2050, reduce the number of hungry people in the world by 210 million and the number of underweight children by 10 million. But while impressive numbers, these do not necessarily privilege these investments over others being considered under the 2012 Copenhagen Consensus. Mindful of this, we now construct a BCR for these investments.

Cost estimates are straightforward. Using a 5 percent discount rate, the net present cost of this additional investment between 2010 and 2050 is $154 billion. We also estimated the welfare impacts of agricultural research investments, using a high discount rate where we double the discount rate to

10 percent and a low discount rate of 3 percent. The net present cost between 2010 and 2050 is reduced to $87 billion when the high discount rate is used and is increased to $214 billion with the application of the 3 percent discount rate.

There are five potential benefit streams: (i) increases in welfare gains resulting from lower prices faced by consumers; (ii) welfare gains from reduced yield volatility; (iii) the option value of reduced yield volatility resulting from climate change; (iv) productivity gains derived from the impact of increased caloric consumption on worker productivity; and (v) the income gains in adulthood resulting from reduced undernutrition in early life. We consider (i) and (ii) here, and the remaining points in the subsections that follow.

We estimate welfare gains by calculating the changes in consumer surplus, producer surplus, and net surplus arising from the investment-induced changes in crop yields, production, and food prices. The BCR is then computed as the ratio of the NPV of the net surplus to the NPV of the investment costs. The welfare component of the calculations follows a traditional economic welfare analysis approach to estimate the benefits to society on the consumer and producer side. On the consumer side this is straightforward, as the IMPACT model has demand curves with demand elasticities, which allow us to calculate the consumer surplus. On the producer side, it is not as straightforward, as the quantity supplied of each commodity is an area-yield equation, and does not represent the traditional supply curve that reflects the producer's marginal cost curve. Therefore, we have synthesized supply curves by land-type for each activity from the area and yield functions, calculated the producer surplus for each of these supply curves, and then aggregated to the national level. The total changes in consumer and producer surplus, when combined, provide us with a benefit flow, which we then use in a CBA, to compare a technology's overall impact in the agriculture sector.

Because crop and livestock prices decline by more than the increases in productivity growth, there is a 3.87 percent decline in producer surplus. By contrast, consumer surplus rises substantially, by 16.91 percent. Thus, consumers (including net-consuming farmers in developing countries) gain substantially due to the lower prices and higher consumption in the high productivity scenario. Globally, this additional investment in agricultural R&D raises total welfare by 4.06 percent, and with a 5 percent discount rate yields an NPV of benefits of $2475 billion (see Table 6.11). The IRR to increased investments is 61 percent with a BCR of 16.1 indicating the high returns to expanded investment in agricultural R&D.

Table 6.11 Percentage change in producer surplus, consumer surplus, and welfare between baseline and alternative scenario

	Base (billion)	Alternative scenario with 5 percent discount rate (billion)	% change
Producer surplus	40,011	38,461	−3.87
Consumer surplus	24,716	28,895	16.91
Welfare	64,727	67,357	4.06

Source: IFPRI IMPACT projections (2011).

We assess these BCRs under two additional discount rates (Table 6.12). In the high-discount rate scenario, where the discount rate is set to 10 percent, producer surplus declines by 2.42 percent and the consumer surplus increases by 10.38 percent compared to 16.91 percent in the alternative scenario. In the low-discount rate scenario, where the discount rate is set to 5 percent, producer surplus declines by 4.67 percent and the consumer surplus increases by a significant 20.47 percent. The total welfare using the high discount rate increases by 2.41 percent giving an NPV of benefits of $702 billion, which is about one-third the value of net benefits in the alternative scenario. But even with this reduction in benefits due to the high discount rate, the BCR remains high at 8.07 (see Table 6.16, p. 347). On the other hand, when a discount rate of 3 percent is used, total welfare increases by 5 percent, giving a net benefit of $4561 billion, almost twice the amount as seen with the 5 percent discount rate. Using the 3 percent discount rate, we obtain a high BCR of 21.31. These high rates of return to agricultural research are consistent with a large literature estimating the returns to agricultural research (Alston *et al.*, 2009).

Table 6.12 Change in producer surplus, consumer surplus, and welfare with different discount rates

	5 percent discount rate (billion)	High-discount rate scenario (10 percent discount rate) (billion)	Low-discount rate scenario (3 percent discount rate) (billion)
Producer surplus change	−1,550	−493	−2,750
Consumer surplus change	4,179	1,282	7,525
Welfare change	2,629	789	4,775

Source: IFPRI IMPACT projections (2011).

Table 6.13 Change in producer surplus, consumer surplus, and welfare using a 5 percent discount rate, by region

	(billion)			
Region	Producer surplus change	Consumer surplus change	Welfare change	Share of welfare change (%)
East Asia and Pacific	−483	1332	850	32.3
Europe and Central Asia	−153	317	164	6.2
Latin America and the Caribbean	−176	465	289	11.0
Middle East and North Africa	−61	233	172	6.5
South Asia	−193	623	430	16.4
SSA	−111	455	344	13.1
Developing	−1,179	3,438	2,259	85.9
Developed	−370	741	371	14.1
World	−1,550	4,179	2,629	

Source: IFPRI IMPACT projections (2011).

These investments in new crop varieties and livestock technologies are not country-specific. An innovation that raises rice productivity can be readily transferred to Bangladesh or Thailand. For this reason, it does not make sense to try to disaggregate the costs of these increased investments by country or region. This means that we cannot calculate regional-specific BCRs. But absent any sort of disaggregation, our results are open to the criticism that we do not say anything about the distribution of benefits. Is it the case, for example, that the increased consumer surplus is dominated by gains to Western consumers? We can calculate changes in producer surplus, consumer surplus and welfare in different regions using different discount rates as shown in Tables 6.13, 6.14, and 6.15. These show clearly that welfare gains are dominated by benefits accruing to developing countries.

These BCRs omit the fact that these investments are also variability-reducing. Prior to the early 2000s, progress on this had been relatively slow. However, new research in the last ten years by both private and public sector actors has demonstrated that for rice (Pray *et al.*, 2011; Serraj *et al.*, 2011), maize and wheat (Kostandini *et al.*, 2009), it is possible to breed varieties that are both higher yielding and also less susceptible to drought and other climatic stresses (Table 6.16). For example, Kostandini *et al.* (2009) model the benefits associated with investments that increase drought tolerance in rice, maize, and wheat while also achieving the yield gains described above. Specifically they measure the benefits of yield-variance reductions as the money value of reduced variability in incomes to producers and reduced price variability to consumers. Calculating the value of these is complex. For producers, they need to

Table 6.14 Change in producer surplus, consumer surplus, and welfare using a 10 percent discount rate, by region

Region	(billion) Producer surplus change	Consumer surplus change	Welfare change	Share of welfare change (%)
East Asia and Pacific	−157	415	258	32.7
Europe and Central Asia	−51	104	54	6.8
Latin America and the Caribbean	−54	144	90	11.4
Middle East and North Africa	−19	68	49	6.2
South Asia	−63	186	123	15.6
SSA	−33	124	91	11.5
Developing	−377	1,045	668	84.7
Developed	−116	238	122	15.5
World	−493	1,282	789	

Source: IFPRI IMPACT projections (2011).

Table 6.15 Change in producer surplus, consumer surplus, and welfare using a 3 percent discount rate, by region

Region	(billion) Producer surplus change	Consumer Surplus change	Welfare change	Share of welfare change (%)
East Asia and Pacific	−849	2383	1534	32.1
Europe and Central Asia	−294	616	323	6.8
Latin America and the Caribbean	−317	834	517	10.8
Middle East and North Africa	−109	428	319	6.7
South Asia	−337	1,119	783	16.4
SSA	−203	859	656	13.7
Developing	−2,089	6,214	4,125	86.4
Developed	−661	1311	650	13.6
World	−2,750	7,525	4,775	

Source: IFPRI IMPACT projections (2011).

account for the share of income derived from these crops, the size of the reduction in yield variability, elasticities of supply, adoption rates of these new technologies, and risk preferences. For consumers, they need to account for price elasticities of demand, the share of expenditures that go to these staples, and risk preferences. A number of these variables, such as the reduction in yield variability, are location-specific and, Kostandini *et al.* restrict their calculations to eight countries: Bangladesh, Ethiopia, India, Indonesia, Kenya, Nigeria, the Philippines, and South Africa. They estimate that yield-variance reductions generate annual benefits to these eight countries of \$569 million – \$256 million to producers and \$313 million to consumers.[9]

The Kostandini *et al.* calculations suggest that our BCRs are underestimates because the benefits of reduced yield variability are underestimated. As an order of magnitude exercise, consider the following. Suppose that these drought-resistant varieties are made available on a wide scale, starting in 2025. The PV of the stream of benefits from reduced yield

9 They conduct sensitivity analyses, noting that these findings are sensitive to the extent to which supply shocks induce price volatility.

Table 6.16 BCRs of investments that increase yields

	Discount rate		
	3 percent	5 percent	5 percent
Benefits derived from yield enhancement (billion USD)	4,561	2,475	702
Cost (billion USD)	214	154	87
BCR	21.31	16.07	8.07

Source: Authors' calculations.

volatility in these eight countries is $7,807 million, $5,280 million, and $2,213 million under 3, 5, and 10 percent discount rates, respectively. This is a conservative assumption given that large-scale trials of drought-resistant maize are already under way and that these benefits are calculated for only eight countries.

Accounting for climate change

The Fourth Assessment Report of the IPCC (IPCC, 2007) concluded that the evidence supporting global warming in unequivocal and that this is very likely to be a consequence of increased human GHG concentrations. The extent of this warming is subject to uncertainty, depending on assumptions about income and population growth, land use changes, and technological progress. The IPCC constructs a set of "Special Reports on Emissions Scenarios" (SRES) that show that, by 2050, global mean temperatures will rise by about 1°C under most scenarios but that further rises are expected after that time, with the magnitude of those rises being scenario-dependent. How do the implications of climate change affect our proposed investments in yield enhancement?

Nelson *et al.* (2010) provide a detailed assessment of the consequences of these climate-change scenarios on global food supply, food prices, the prevalence of hunger, and undernutrition in 2050. They do so by linking IFPRI's IMPACT model with the Decision Support System for Agrotechnology Transfer (DSSAT) crop model suite. DSSAT takes into account location-specific information on climate, soils, and nitrogen application to simulate multi-year outcomes based on crop-management strategies, varietal improvements, changes in soil fertility, and changes in weather.[10] Nelson *et al.* note that "The modeling methodology reconciles the limited spatial resolution of macro-level economic models that operate through equilibrium-driven relationships at a national level with detailed models of biophysical processes at high spatial resolution" (Nelson *et al.*, 2010: 6). This allows them to take into account location-specific effects of climate change in terms of its impact on temperature, precipitation, and increases in atmospheric concentrations of CO_2.[11] These impacts are used to model consequences for crop productivity. In turn:

> The climate-change-driven productivity effects are incorporated into the hydrology and economic elements of the IMPACT model to assess the combined effects of economic, population, and climate scenarios. The process of modeling agricultural futures proceeds roughly as follows. Supply is determined at the food production unit (FPU) level by farmer responses to prices, conditioned by assumptions about exogenously determined area (AGRs) and yield growth rates (IPRs) as well as assumptions regarding climate productivity effects on irrigated and rainfed crops. Demand is determined at the national level by consumer responses to changes in national income and prices. When supply is greater than demand, exports occur. For the world, net trade in a commodity must be zero. World prices are adjusted to ensure this outcome for a year. This process is repeated for each year through to 2050. (Nelson *et al.*, 2010: 20)

[10] DSSAT is underpinned by detailed data inputs and modeling work: "Crop models require daily weather data, soil surface and profile information, and detailed crop management as input. Crop genetic information is defined in a crop species file that is provided by DSSAT and cultivar or variety information that . . . [is] . . . provided by the user. Simulations are initiated either at planting or prior to planting through the simulation of a bare fallow period. These simulations are conducted at a daily step and, in some cases, at an hourly time step depending on the process and the crop model. At the end of the day the plant and soil water, nitrogen and carbon balances are updated, as well as the crop's vegetative and reproductive development stage" (DSSAT, 2012).

[11] Specifically, Nelson *et al.* (2010) use version 4.5 of DSSAT, with atmospheric concentration of CO_2 in 2050 set at 369 ppm (see Nelson *et al.*, 2010: 14–18, for further explanation).

Table 6.17 Predicted impact of climate change on production of maize, rice, and wheat

		Developed	Developing	World
Maize	Predicted output under climate change (mmt)	454.8	629.7	1084.5
	Predicted output with perfect mitigation (mmt)	525	612.1	1137.1
	Predicted loss under climate change (mmt)	−70.2	17.6	−52.6
	Percentage loss due to climate change	−13	3	−5
Rice	Predicted output under climate change (mmt)	17.6	398.1	415.7
	Predicted output with perfect mitigation (mmt)	19.9	433.4	453.3
	Predicted loss under climate change (mmt)	−2.3	−35.3	−37.6
	Percentage loss due to climate change	−12	−8	−8
Wheat	Predicted output under climate change (mmt)	243.2	598.8	842
	Predicted output with perfect mitigation (mmt)	261.3	647.4	908.7
	Predicted loss under climate change (mmt)	−18.1	−48.6	−66.7
	Percentage loss due to climate change	−7	−8	−7

Note: mmt = Million metric tons.
Source: Authors' calculations based on figures found in Nelson *et al.* (2010: Table 2.5).

Nelson *et al.* (2010) model these climate-driven productivity changes under three income and population growth scenarios.[12] Table 6.17 shows baseline scenarios for the production of three crops – maize, rice, and wheat. Compared to "perfect mitigation" – investments that would ensure that atmospheric concentration of CO_2 in 2050 were the same as those in 2010 – climate change reduces maize production by 52.6 million metric tonnes, rice production by 37.6 million metric tonnes, and wheat production by 66.7 million metric tonnes. Linking these changes in agricultural production to the prevalence of child underweight, Nelson *et al.* show that under their baseline scenario, absent perfect mitigation, child underweight would be 9.8 percent higher in 2050. This is an increase of 11.5 million in the number of undernourished children.

Having undertaken these calculations, Nelson *et al.* simulate the impact of a number of investments that would offset the malign impacts of climate change on production. These include boosting productivity growth in a variety of crops and improvements in irrigation efficiency. The following example gives a flavor of these. Suppose that additional spending is undertaken that raises productivity growth in wheat production by 2 percent p.a. in seven developing countries that account for about 40 percent of global wheat production.[13] These investments reduce expected increases in wheat prices by just under 50 percent. It reduces the number of underweight children by 3.3 million, with most of this reduction occurring in middle-income developing countries. In so doing, it offsets 29 percent (3.3/11.5) of the predicted increase in children's undernutrition.

Nelson *et al.* (2010) also note that climate change may well result in increased frequency of extreme weather events, such as extended droughts. They give the example of a failure of the monsoon rains between 2030 and 2035 as an example. Were this to occur, their modeling suggests that global prices would rise as reduced supply from south Asia would not be offset by increased production elsewhere. Over the period 2030–2040, prices would first rise, peaking in 2035 at increases of 43 percent (wheat), 16 percent (rice), and 67 percent (maize) over trend before falling back to trend by 2040. In addition, this extended drought would increase the number of underweight children by around 900,000.

Moving from examples such as these to the calculation of BCRs is enormously difficult. As Nelson *et al.* carefully explain, different climate models produce different predictions of the geographic

[12] These are: baseline (World Bank projections for global income growth and UN medium-variant population projections); pessimistic (low income growth rates and UN medium-variant population projections); and optimistic (high income growth rates and UN low-variant population projections) (see Nelson *et al.*, 2010: Table 1.1, for further details).

[13] These are Argentina, China, India, Iran, Kazakhstan, Pakistan, and Ukraine.

distribution of the impacts of climate change – impacts that are amplified by different assumptions regarding global income and population growth which affect the predicted trajectory of global food prices. In turn, this affects the benefits associated with investments in productivity-enhancing investments in different crops and in different countries. They also note that climate change is expected to increase the frequency of severe weather events such as droughts but it is not possible to predict where and when these will occur, and they note that their south Asia example is meant to be illustrative.

In light of all this, we do not calculate formal BCRs of agricultural investments that mitigate the impact of climate change on yield levels and variability. Instead, we argue that the changes induced by climate change imply that there is an option value to investments in agriculture. To see this, consider the following. We take the predicted changes in price trajectories between 2030 and 2040 that an extended drought in south Asia between 2030 and 2035 would induce. We calculate the cost to consumers of this higher price based on current consumption levels for these three staples. The present value of this global cost is $247 billion. Based on the patterns we see in Tables 6.13, 6.14, and 6.15, we assume that a third of this cost is transferred to producers, so the next welfare cost is $165 billion. We further assume that the probability of an event of this magnitude occurring is 25 percent and so the NPV of this cost – excluding the costs created by higher price variability that might occur and the costs associated with increased child undernutrition – is $41 billion. The option value of agricultural investments that mitigate the impact of climate change on yield levels and variability is the amount of money that one would be willing to pay now to reduce the costs of such extreme weather events in the future. Assuming that this option value is positive, it is a further stream of benefits in addition to those described above.

Calorie productivity and undernutrition benefits

At least since the late 1950s, economists have hypothesized a link between caloric intake and worker productivity (Leibenstein, 1957), a link sometimes referred to as the "wage-efficiency hypothesis." In its simplest form, the argument is that individuals with very low caloric intakes, possibly exacerbated by low body mass, have insufficient energy to undertake remunerative labor. Dasgupta (1993) provides more detail, noting that under this hypothesis low caloric intakes are both a consequence and cause of poverty. Teasing out these links, however, is enormously complicated. The data demands are high, requiring detailed individual-level information on intakes and physical activities as well as data that allow the analyst to account for the fact that, in econometric terms, both are endogenous. Given these data requirements, the empirical literature is not surprisingly scant. Carefully executed studies provide some evidence supporting the wage-efficiency hypothesis, but this evidence tends to be locationally, temporally (e.g. harvest, season of peak labor demand, Behrman and Deolalikar, 1989), and sex-specific (Pitt *et al.*, 1990). Given this heterogeneity, we do not calculate the additional benefit stream derived from the impact of increased caloric consumption on worker productivity. Instead, we note the important implication that the existence of these additional benefit streams implies that our BCRs are conservative.

Lastly, Behrman *et al.* (2004) and Horton *et al.* (2008) have stressed that investments that reduce undernutrition in pre-school children provide considerable economic benefits. As discussed above, investments in agricultural R&D do reduce undernutrition, but the magnitude of this change is relatively small.

Market innovations that reduce hunger

The conceptual model described on pp. 333–5 placed particular emphasis on the economic setting in which a household finds itself. We described the economic setting as capturing policies that affect the level, returns, and variability of returns on assets and, as such, influencing choices regarding productive activities undertaken by individuals, firms, and households. We noted that this included meso-level considerations that captured food market structure, conduct, and performance as measured by price levels, variability, and trends as well as government policies towards them. Roughly 80 percent of the global hungry and 75 percent of the world's poor live in rural areas and half the global hungry are smallholders (Hunger Task Force, 2003). Given all this, are there investments that can improve these settings for smallholders – for example, by linking "farms to markets," reducing transaction cost or reducing risk? In this section, we consider two (i) the provision of market information through cellular phones; and (ii) reducing barriers to fertilizer access.

Information and communication technologies

Models of perfect competition predict the maximization of social welfare. However, this prediction relies on a set of critical assumptions. One of these key conditions is the prevalence of perfect information. Since the publication of Stigler's seminal work (Stigler, 1961), such assumptions have been contested. Imperfect information is pervasive in many agricultural markets in developing countries, a consequence of remoteness, poor infrastructure, and thin markets. The deployment of information and communication technologies (ICTs) can remedy some of the dimensions of imperfect information. Jensen (2010) demonstrates some of the main gains of information in agricultural markets:

- *Information, arbitrage and efficiency*: price differentials (in excess of transportation costs) can signal agents to re-allocate their production towards higher-profit markets. In doing so, there are potential gains to aggregate welfare.
- *Information, market power and welfare transfers*: by lowering search costs, phones enable producers to research sales opportunities in more markets and to obtain better prices for their products. This argument also holds when farmers do not sell directly in markets. Even in the presence of monopsonistic middlemen, if farmers have better information traders may need to offer higher prices to prevent farmers from selling their products directly in other markets. This argument also applies to input and transport costs as the following anecdote illustrates:

> I was in process to transport my produce of (approx 1,000 boxes in 2 trucks) to Delhi when I got an SMS through RML (Renters Marker Light) that the freight rate from Kotgarh to Delhi is Rs 41.07 per box. I showed this message to the truck operator, who till then was citing a rate of Rs 44 per box. Following this I was able to settle the transporting deal at Rs. 41.07, finally saving around 3,000 rupees (Reuters, 2012).

- *Reduced price variability*: when there is no information (and limited arbitrage), prices tend to vary with local supply. However, when information is widespread (and there is more arbitrage), price fluctuations are related to aggregate supply.
- *Production patterns*: information can also affect land use patterns, where households can shift towards more profitable crops.

A small number of studies examine the impact of improved information flows on the dimensions of smallholder welfare. These typically exploit the existence of natural experiments, such as the roll-out of cellular phone services or access to radio broadcasts. They provide a range of estimates. Some, such as those in the Svensson and Yanagizawa (2009) study of the impact of price dissemination via radio, found large income gains through higher realized prices, on the order of an increase of 15 percent in maize income. Similarly large effects were found in Peru (Chong *et al.*, 2005; Beuerman, 2011) and the Philippines (Labonne and Chase, 2009). Others find much smaller effects (1–6 percent impacts on soya bean income in Madhya Pradesh, India) (Goyal, 2010) or no effects at all (Mitra *et al.*, 2011; Fafchamps and Minten, 2012). The literature is suggestive of the possibility that gains to improved information flows are larger in SSA than south Asia, and that these are larger where products are more perishable.

Mindful of these variations in impacts, consider the following investment that increased farmers' access to market information through mobile phones. Our model here is RML Program which is widely available in India (Reuters, 2012). Under RML, for a monthly fee, farmers receive crop advisory SMS text messages. These are tailored to specific points in the crop cycle, including location-specific information on weather forecasts, local market price information, and local and international commodity information. Users can configure these messages so that the farmers only receive the information most relevant to them in their language of choice. In India, the monthly cost of this service is $1.50. We assume that the messages are needed for six months and we convert this US$ cost into PPP$ so as to apply it across a number of countries. In our base model, the annual cost is PPP$21.92 per household or, assuming household sizes of 5.5 persons, PPP$3.98 *per capita*. We also undertake an alternative calculation where, perhaps because of scale economies, this cost is reduced by 50 percent. We assume that beneficiaries are responsible for the purchase of handsets. This can be thought of as a commitment device that self-selects those households who intend to use this information.[14]

In our base case, we take the simple averages of four African studies on the impacts of improved market information (results in parentheses): Svensson and Yanagizawa (2009) (15 percent); Futch and McIntosh (2009) (no effect); Aker and Fafchamps (2010) (no effect); and Muto and Yamano (2009) (positive impacts for bananas but no impact on maize). We then assume that the average impact is a 3.75 percent increase in agricultural incomes through higher prices. Four papers presented evidence from south Asia: Mitra *et al.* (2011) (no effect); Goyal (2010) (1.6 percent); Fafchamps and Minten (2012) (no effect); and Jensen (2007) (8 percent). The simple average of their estimated impacts is a 2.4 percent increase in agricultural incomes. We consider two alternatives to this: (i) one where we assume benefits are lower,[15] a 1 percent increase in south Asian countries and a 2 percent increase in Africa; and (ii) one where the base case benefits are doubled (4.8 percent for south Asia and 7.5 percent for Africa). To calculate benefit streams and the total value of benefits obtained, we consider two south Asian countries (Bangladesh and India), and four African countries (Senegal, Ghana, Kenya, and Tanzania). To make these results comparable across countries, calculations for all scenarios are based on the following five assumptions:

- We consider the *per capita* household expenditures in rural areas as a proxy for income. We use the most recent household survey available for each of these countries. Data sources are the following:
  - *Bangladesh*: mean *per capita* expenditure in rural areas from the Household Income and Expenditure Survey (HIES) of 2005.[16]
  - *India*: mean *per capita* expenditure in rural areas from the 66th round of the National Sample Survey (NSS) (2009–2010).[17]
  - *Tanzania*: mean *per capita* expenditure in rural areas from the 2007 Household Budget Survey (HBS).
  - *Kenya*: average *per capita* expenditure of the fifth decile from the Kenya Integrated Household Budget Survey (KIHBS, 2005–2006).[18]
  - *Senegal*: average rural *per capita* expenditure from the Enquête Sénégalaise Auprés des Ménages (ESAM-II).[19]
  - *Ghana*: average rural *per capita* household expenditure from the Fifth Round of the Ghana Living Standards Survey (GLSS5).
- we also adjust household expenditures for inflation and for PPP, using the *World Bank Development Indicators*.[20] Thus, all our estimations are comparable across countries and expressed in 2010 PPP$.
- The share of crop sales in total income is a rough estimate (40 percent in Asia and 30 percent in Africa).
- The poverty elasticity of income is based on international experience (–2), taking into account that the base is rural income.

[14] If we included handsets as part of the investment, there would be a risk of beneficiaries choosing to participate solely to receive the phone. Basic mobile phones in south Asia and much of Africa are cheap (around $15), and there is no reason why small groups of households could not pool their resources to purchase them.

[15] This is based on the fact that Fafchamps and Minten (2012) and Mitra *et al.* (2011) find no significant effect for some ICT interventions in India while Goyal's (Goyal, 2010) estimates suggest a 1 percent lower bound for the impact.

[16] http://siteresources.worldbank.org/BANGLADESHEXTN/Resources/295759–1240185591585/BanglaPD.pdf.

[17] http://mospi.nic.in/mospi_new/upload/Press%20Release%20KI-HCE-66th_8july11.pdf.

[18] http://siteresources.worldbank.org/INTAFRREGTOPGENDER/Resources/PAKENYA.pdf.

[19] http://ns.ansd.sn/nada/site_enquete/CD_ESAM2/survey0/data/Rapport%20Esam2.pdf.

[20] http://data.worldbank.org/data-catalog/world-development-indicators.

Table 6.18 General assumptions used to calculate benefits and costs of ICT intervention

	Bangladesh	India	Kenya	Ghana	Senegal	Tanzania
PC rural income (LCU)	13,236	12,636	17,496	458	127,340	197,016
Source	HIES	NSS	KIHBS	GLSS 5	ESAM II	HBS
Year	2005	2009/10	2005/06	2005/06	2001	2007
CPI index survey year	100.0	143.8	114.5	105.5	95.7	114.8
CPI index 2010	144.6	151.9	180.1	188.9	114.5	150.8
PC HH income LCU 2010	19,140.1	13,351.3	27,529.9	820.5	152,376.5	258,753.5
Exchange rate (LCU/$PPP) 2010	28.14	17.95	37.28	1.12	264.90	518.23
Rural HH PC annual income ($PPP)	680.1	743.8	738.4	731.6	575.2	499.3
Proportion of ag income	40%	40%	30%	30%	30%	30%
Rural HH PC ag exp – annual ($PPP)	272.0	297.5	221.5	219.5	172.6	149.8
Cost per year						
Conservative cost ($PPP)						
Household	21.92	21.92	21.92	21.92	21.92	21.92
Per capita	3.98	3.98	3.98	3.98	3.98	3.98
Optimist cost						
Household	10.96	10.96	10.96	10.96	10.96	10.96
Per capita	1.99	1.99	1.99	1.99	1.99	1.99
Affected population (000)	1,000	2,000	995	585	280	1,195

Notes: PA = *per capita*; LCU = Local currency units; HH = Households.
Source: Authors' calculations.

- The affected population is assumed to be 2 million households in India, and 1 million in Bangladesh. In Africa, the affected population is assumed to be 5 percent of the rural population.

These basic data are summarized in Table 6.18 and our results are reported in Table 6.19.

Under scenario 1 – with our base assumptions about benefits and costs – this investment always generates a positive rate of return. Across these six countries, the BCRs lie between 1.41 (Tanzania) and 2.09 (Kenya). If we are very pessimistic about the benefits and if we believe that it is not possible to reduce costs (an especially strong assumption), then the BCRs are only high enough to justify this investment in Kenya and Ghana. But under any other set of assumptions, these BCRs exceed 1 and in some cases they do so by a considerable margin. For example, under the high-benefit, reduced-cost scenario, these range from 5.64 to 8.35.

Investments that increase competition in the fertilizer market

It is well established that low adoption of improved land management practices is one of the main factors behind lagging agricultural productivity in many developing countries. Although an increase in fertilizer use is not the only solution to this problem, countries that have increased their agricultural productivity have also considerably increased their use of fertilizer. Several regional and local policies have been promoted to stimulate sustainable fertilizer use, with mixed results, but not much has been said about the high and increasing dependence of developing regions on imported fertilizer, which is a highly concentrated industry at the global level. As shown in Table 6.20, a small number of countries control most of the production capacity for the main nitrogen, phosphate, and potash fertilizers. The top five countries control more than half of the world's production capacity for all major fertilizer products. Similarly, except for China, the industry shows a high level of concentration among

Table 6.19 Estimates of impacts and BCRs of ICT intervention under different benefit and cost scenarios

	Bangladesh	India	Kenya	Ghana	Senegal	Tanzania
Scenario 1: base benefits, base costs						
Increase in income (%)	2.40	2.40	3.75	3.75	3.75	3.75
Reduction in poverty (%)	1.9	1.9	2.3	2.3	2.3	2.3
Increase in income ($PPP)	6.53	7.14	8.31	8.23	6.47	5.62
Net benefit PC	2.55	3.16	4.33	4.25	2.49	1.64
BCR	1.64	1.79	2.09	2.07	1.63	1.41
Scenario 2: conservative benefits, base costs						
Increase in income (%)	1.0	1.0	2.0	2.0	2.0	2.0
Reduction in poverty (%)	0.8	0.8	1.2	1.2	1.2	1.2
Increase in income ($PPP)	2.72	2.98	4.43	4.39	3.45	3.00
Net benefit PC	−1.26	−1.00	0.45	0.41	−0.53	−0.99
BCR	0.68	0.75	1.11	1.10	0.87	0.75
Scenario 3: high benefits, base costs						
Increase in income (%)	4.80	4.80	7.50	7.50	7.50	7.50
Reduction in poverty (%)	3.8	3.8	4.5	4.5	4.5	4.5
Increase in income ($PPP)	13.06	14.28	16.61	16.46	12.94	11.23
Net benefit PC	9.08	10.3	12.63	12.48	8.96	7.25
BCR	3.28	3.59	4.17	4.14	3.25	2.82
Scenario 4: base benefits, reduced costs						
Increase in income (%)	2.40	2.40	3.75	3.75	3.75	3.75
Reduction in poverty (%)	1.9	1.9	2.3	2.3	2.3	2.3
Increase in income ($PPP)	6.53	7.14	8.31	8.23	6.47	5.62
Net benefit PC	4.54	5.15	6.32	6.24	4.48	3.63
BCR	3.28	3.59	4.18	4.14	3.25	2.82
Scenario 5: conservative benefits, reduced costs						
Increase in income (%)	1	1	2	2	2	2
Reduction in poverty (%)	0.8	0.8	1.2	1.2	1.2	1.2
Increase in income ($PPP)	2.72	2.98	4.43	4.39	3.45	3.00
Net benefit PC	0.73	0.99	2.44	2.4	1.46	1.01
BCR	1.37	1.50	2.23	2.21	1.73	1.51
Scenario 6: high benefits, reduced costs						
Increase in income (%)	4.80	4.80	7.50	7.50	7.50	7.50
Reduction in poverty (%)	3.8	3.8	4.5	4.5	4.5	4.5
Increase in income ($PPP)	13.06	14.28	16.61	16.46	12.94	11.23
Net benefit PC	11.07	12.29	14.62	14.47	10.95	9.24
BCR	6.56	7.18	8.35	8.27	6.50	5.64

Note: PC = *per capita*.
Source: Authors' calculations.

firms within each main producing country. In most cases, the top four firms control more than half of each country's production capacity.

The high levels of concentration in the fertilizer industry mainly result both from the high requirements of raw materials, which are not available world-wide, and from potential economies of scale in production, which result in cost efficiencies. However, high concentration in an industry may also result in market-power exertion and tacit collusion among firms, which may allow a few companies to take full advantage, for example, of international price spikes in energy and grain markets to the detriment of farmers' wealth. Consider Figure 6.1. This shows that during the food crisis of 2008, where oil and agricultural prices drastically increased, ammonia and urea prices exhibited even higher price spikes. By mid 2008, when the crisis was felt most, ammonia and urea prices were 2–3 times larger than in mid 2007; oil and corn prices, in turn, were 1.5–1.9 times larger. The market-power effects could be outweighing the cost-efficiency effects in this highly concentrated industry.

Table 6.20 Concentration of world fertilizer production capacity, 2008–2009

Fertilizer	Top-5 countries (% of world in parenthesis)	Top-5 Capacity (000 MT)	Top-5 Share (% of world)
Ammonia	China (22.8), India (8.9), Russia (8.5), United States (6.5) and Indonesia (3.9)	84,183	50.6
Urea	China (33.1), India (13.1), and Indonesia (5.4) Russia (4.2) and United States (4.1)	95,802	59.9
DAP/MAP	China (23.3), United States (21.2), and India (11.4), Russia (6) and Morocco (4)	22,896	65.9
Phosphoric Acid	United States (20.9), China (19.3), Morocco (9.6), Russia (6.2), and India (5.3)	28,274	61.3
Potash	Canada (37.6), Russia (13.2), and Belarus (9.9), Germany (8.2) and China (7.7)	39,687	76.7
NPK	China (29.3), India (8.2), Russia (6), France (4), and Turkey (3).	47,186	50.4

Notes: DAP/MAP = Diammonium phosphate/MAP = Monoammonium phosphate, the most commonly used phosphate-based fertilizers; NPK = nitrogen, phosphorus, and potassium, the three nutrients that compose complete fertilizers.
Source: IFDC Worldwide Fertilizer Capacity Listing, by Plant.

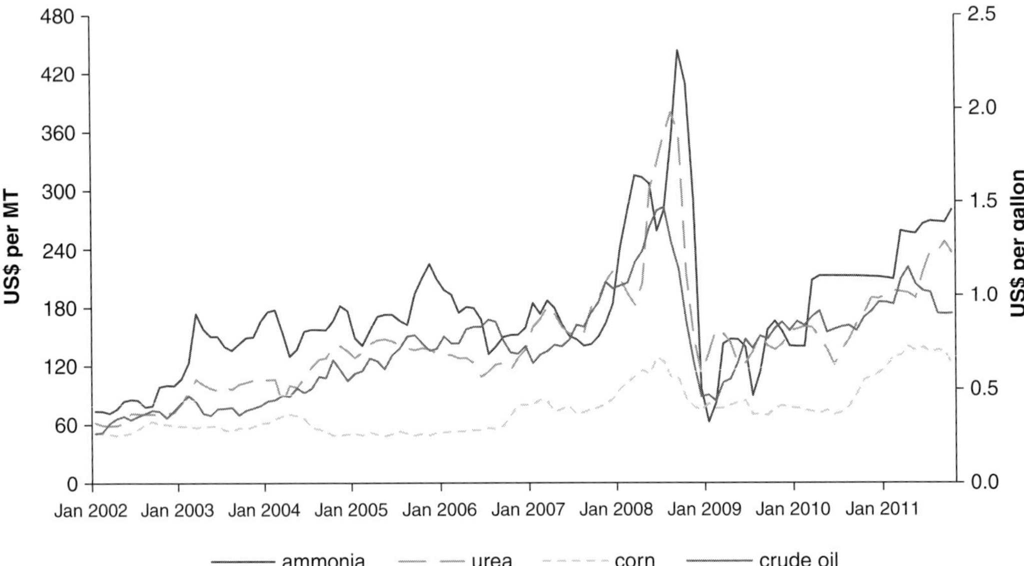

Figure 6.1 *Real monthly ammonia, urea, corn, and crude oil prices, 2002–2011*

Note: Prices deflated by CPI, 1982–1984 = 100. The prices correspond to Ammonia US Gulf barge, Urea US Gulf prill import, No. 2 yellow corn FOB US Gulf, and Oklahoma crude oil FOB spot price.
Source: Green Markets, Energy Information Administration, and FAOSTAT.

Hernandez and Torero (2011) analyze this issue formally. Specifically, they examine the relationship between fertilizer (urea) prices and market concentration in the fertilizer industry using annual data from a panel of thirty-eight countries. Concentration is measured as the top-4 concentration ratio (CR4), the sum of the market shares of the four largest firms operating in the market. The shares are measured in terms of both production capacity and number of plants. The analysis accounts for the relative importance of fertilizer imports on use in each country. The estimation results indicate a positive correlation between prices and market concentration. A 10 percent decrease in the CR4 using production capacity to measure market share leads, on average, to an 8.2 percent decrease in fertilizer prices, while a 10 percent decrease in the CR4 using number of plants leads to an 11.6 percent decrease in prices.

This evidence suggests that there could be considerable welfare gains if this concentration could be reduced. One option could be the forcible break-up of this concentrated industry. But it is not immediately obvious that this is a good idea. Quite apart from the disruption this would cause, it could well lead to a loss of economies of scale. Regulation is another possibility but imposing price restrictions, as well as regulations governing exports might well lead to unproductive rent seeking.

Another alternative is to invest in the construction of new production capacity. The underlying logic for this investment is that private sector actors are deterred from entering these markets by the joint existence of high fixed costs and strategic pricing behavior by incumbents. Here, we consider the case of public investment in production capacity, with the understanding that the operation of the facility would be turned over to the private sector. Based on the Hernandez and Torero (2011) study, we take the impact of increased competition on prices and use this to estimate its impact on fertilizer intake and crop production. From this, we calculate costs and benefits over a forty-year time horizon (2010–2050) for the same six countries that we considered for ICT investment – Bangladesh, Ghana, India, Kenya, Senegal, and Tanzania. We also estimate impact on poverty.

We start with the Hernandez and Torero findings; an 8.2 percent decrease in prices could be considered as a conservative scenario while an 11.6 percent decrease could be regarded as an optimistic scenario. Gruhn *et al.* (1995) report an average elasticity of fertilizer demand with respect to prices of around –1.62 based on work by David and Otsuka (1994) in Asia. Similarly, Bumb *et al.* (2011) assume that the elasticity of crop production with respect to fertilizer use is 0.25. With these elasticities, an estimated impact of the change in prices on both fertilizer intake and crop production can be derived, as shown in Table 6.21. A 10 percent increase in competition in the fertilizer industry will increase crop production by 3.3 percent in the conservative scenario and by 4.7 percent in the optimistic scenario.

Table 6.21 Impact of increased competition on fertilizer intake and crop production

	Conservative	Optimistic
Decrease in fertilizer prices (%)	8.2	11.6
Elasticity of fertilizer demand to prices	−1.62	−1.62
Increase in fertilizer use (%)	13.3	18.8
Elasticity of crop production to fertilizer use	0.25	0.25
Increase in crop production (%)	3.3	4.7

Source: Gruhn *et al.* (1995); Bumb *et al.* (2011).

The simulated effect on crop production, assuming a conservative scenario, can be used to approximate the impact on poverty reduction using some countries in south Asia (India and Bangladesh) and Africa (Ghana, Kenya, Senegal, and Tanzania) as examples. A poverty elasticity of income of –2.0 is assumed based on international experience. The share of crop sales in total income is assumed to be 40 percent in south Asia and 30 percent in Africa. Based on these calculations, a 10 percent decrease in the level of concentration in the fertilizer industry reduces poverty by 2.6 percent in the south Asian countries and by 2 percent in the African countries. This is equivalent to 20.1 million people in India, 2.7 million in Bangladesh, 100,000 in Senegal, 200,000 in Ghana, 400,000 in Kenya, and half a million in Tanzania. Overall, there will be a total poverty reduction of 24 million people in the six countries (Table 6.22).

In order to decrease the CR4 in south Asia and Africa by 10 percent, it is necessary to build a fertilizer plant in each region with a corresponding annual production capacity of 1.2 million metric tons (MT) and 0.7 million MT (recall that in the conservative simulation analysis above, the concentration measure is based on production

Table 6.22 Impact of increased competition on poverty reduction (conservative scenario)

	India	Bangladesh	Senegal	Ghana	Kenya	Tanzania
Decrease in global concentration (%)	10	10	10	10	10	10
Decrease in global fertilizer prices (%)	8.2	8.2	8.2	8.2	8.2	8.2
Increase in crop production (%)	3.3	3.3	3.3	3.3	3.3	3.3
Crop sales as % of income	40	40	30	30	30	30
Increase in average rural income (%)	1.3	1.3	1	1	1	1
Poverty elasticity of income (%)	−2.0	−2.0	−2.0	−2.0	−2.0	−2.0
Poverty reduction (%)	2.6	2.6	2	2	2	2
Total rural population (million) (%)	772	105	5.6	11.7	19.9	23.9
Poverty reduction (million) (%)	20.1	2.7	0.1	0.2	0.4	0.5

Source: Authors' calculations.

capacity).[21] The new plant will absorb this share-reduction of the top-4 firms in each market and will not be large enough to be among the top-4 producers in each region. We assume that the cost of building a 1.2 million MT plant in South Asia would roughly equal around US$1.2 billion and the cost of building a 0.7 million MT plant in Africa would roughly equal around US$700 million.[22] For the purpose of our CBA, these investment costs are prorated based on the relative amount of (nitrogen) fertilizers consumed by each country. For example, India accounts for 93 percent of the total fertilizer used between India and Bangladesh, so we ascribe 93 percent of the building costs of the plant in south Asia (around US$1,111 million) to India. We assume that the cost per MT of (nitrogen) fertilizer production is US$130 for a plant size over 1,000 MT of capacity per day, see Kim *et al.* (2001).

We assume that only 20 percent of the rural population in each country will experience an effective increase in their income (an increase of 1.3 percent in South Asian countries and of 1 percent in African countries, based on the simulation above). This (conservative) scenario accounts for the fact that some farmers may already be using the optimal amount of fertilizer while the increase in fertilizer use for several others may still not reach a certain level which results in higher income. As with our work on ICTs, *per capita* household expenditure in rural areas is used as a proxy for rural income using the most recent household surveys in each country.

The results are given in Table 6.23. These show that at both 3 and 5 percent discount rates, the NPVs of these investments are positive for all countries except Kenya.

The total NPV of such a policy over a time horizon of 2012–2050 (thirty-nine years) will be equal to US$20.4 billion, assuming an annual discount rate of 3 percent, and to US$12.5 billion, assuming an annual discount rate of 5 percent.

Bundling interventions that reduce micronutrient deficiencies and reduce the prevalence of stunting

In Behrman *et al.* (2004), Copenhagen Consensus solutions to undernutrition covered a range of interventions including those relating to low birthweight, improving infant and child nutrition in populations with high prevalence of child malnutrition, addressing micronutrient deficiencies, and new investments in agricultural technologies. Two of these – addressing micronutrient deficiencies and new investments in agricultural technologies – were ranked highly by the 2004 Copenhagen Consensus panel while efforts to reduced low birthweights and

[21] These numbers are equivalent to 10 percent of the annual production capacity reported by the top-4 firms in each region, according to IFDC Worldwide Fertilizer Capacity Listing by Plant.

[22] These cost estimates are based on the estimated cost of a nitrogen fertilizer plant currently under construction in the Delta and Lagos States of Nigeria.

Table 6.23 CBA of investments

	India	Bangladesh	Senegal	Ghana	Kenya	Tanzania
Rural income						
Rural *per capita* annual income in $PPP	743.8	680.1	575.2	731.6	738.4	499.3
Rural affected population (million)	154	21	1	2	4	5
Annual income of affected population in $PPP million	114,836	14,282	644	1,712	2,939	2,387
Fertilizer use						
Country consumption of nitrogen fertilizers in 000 MT	39,972	3,198	128	256	896	512
Increase in fertilizer consumption (=)	13.3	13.3	13.3	13.3	13.3	13.3
Increase in consumption of nitrogen fertilizers in 000 MT	5,316	425	17	34	119	68
Change in income						
Increase in average rural income (%)	1.3	1.3	1.0	1.0	1.0	1.0
Total increase in annual income for affected population in $PPP million	1,493	186	6	17	29	24
Change in costs						
Cost of building plant in region (prorated) in $PPP million	1,111	89	50	100	350	200
Variable cost per MT in US$	130	130	130	130	130	130
Total variable annual costs for increased fertilizer use in $PPP million	691	55	2	4	15	9
NPV at 3% discount rate (2012–2050) in $PPP million	17,176	2,885	46	190	−33	142
NPV at 5% discount rate (2012–2050) in $PPP million	12,532	2,130	22	116	−113	56

Note: MT = Million tons.
Source: Author's calculations.

improving infant and child nutrition were seen as "Fair" investments. The 2008 Copenhagen Consensus, based on the paper by Horton *et al.* (2008), continued to rate micronutrient interventions highly with vitamin A and zinc supplements for children ranked first, iron and iodine fortificants third, and biofortification fifth. One component relevant to stunting, community based nutrition programs, was ranked ninth.

In this section, we do the following. For highly ranked micronutrient interventions (vitamin A, zinc, iron, and iodine) we update the BCRs based on new studies published since 2008. Second, since the publication of those earlier Copenhagen Consensus papers, there have been two major developments in the evidence base related to interventions that will reduce the prevalence of growth failure. These are: the work by Bhutta *et al.* (2008), on establishing which interventions have been demonstrated to have the most powerful effects on reducing stunted linear growth, and the monograph by Horton *et al.* (2010), that provided detailed costings on these interventions. These new sources provide the basis for our second set of investments related to undernutrition: a package of interventions that will reduce stunting.

Updated estimates of highly ranked micronutrient interventions

We update the BCRs for vitamin A, iodine, iron, and zinc. All of these are described by Bhutta *et al.* (2008) as having sufficient evidence of benefits to support their widespread implementation. We note

Table 6.24 BCRs of micronutrient interventions

		2004/2008 Copenhagen Consensus estimates		New estimates			Current estimates of cost per beneficiary
Micronutrient	Intervention	BAH	HAR	Rajkumar	Horton	Other	
Iodine	Salt-iodization	15–520	30	81			$0.05 (HAR)
Iodine and iron	Doubly-fortified salt			2.5	2–5		$0.25 (Horton)
Iron	Supplements, mothers and children 6–24 months			23.8			$0.96 (Rajkumar)
	Supplements, pregnant mothers	82–140		8.1			$2.00 (Horton 2010)
	Fortification, general		7.8				
	Fortification of wheat flour				9.1	6.7 (Casey, 2011)	$0.17 (Horton)
	Home fortification				37		$1.20 (Horton)
	Biofortification	11.6–19	16.7				< $0.01 (Horton)
Vitamin A	Supplement	4.3–43	6.1–250	12.5			$0.29 (Rajkumar)
Zinc	Supplement			2.85			$1.26 (Rajkumar)

Notes: BAH = Behrman *et al.* (2004). HAR = Horton *et al.* (2008). Horton = Horton *et al.* (2011). Rajkumar *et al.* (2012).
Source: Authors' compilation.

that we now have BCR estimates of a novel delivery form – doubly fortified salt, fortified with both iodine and iron. In Table 6.24, we summarize the principal BCRs from previous Copenhagen Consensus estimates, as well as new results that have emerged since 2008.

Several results emerge. First, the BCRs for iodized salt continue to be overwhelmingly high, with the most recent calculations from the work of Rajkumar *et al.* (2012) in Ethiopia suggesting that this is 81, a ratio higher than that reported by Horton *et al.* (2008) but within the range suggested by Behrman *et al.* (2004). Second, the most recent BCRs for Vitamin A supplementation lie towards the bottom end of earlier estimates but this appears to be an artifact of a much lower monetary valuation of averted mortality. While the Behrman *et al.* (2004) initial BCR for iron supplementation for pregnant mothers now looks far too high, several studies provide estimates for a range of delivery mechanisms for iron between 6.7 and 23.8. Horton *et al.* (2011) note that the figure of 37 for home fortification is probably too high, because the study on which it is based assumes far lower distribution costs than those found in other papers. We now also have a stand-alone estimate for zinc supplements for children, 2.85.

Investments that reduce the prevalence of stunting

Recall that in our conceptual framework the proximate determinants of nutritional status were health status and individual food intake which themselves were a consequence of good nutritional and health practices, the health environment, and food availability at the household level. Bhutta *et al.* (2008) undertake a systematic review identifying those interventions for which there is compelling evidence of their impact on mortality and stunting between birth and 36 months.[23] They argue that there exists rigorous evidence to support the large-scale implementation of the following interventions:

23 The methods they use to establish their criteria of compelling evidence are carefully detailed in their paper.

- *Interventions that improve the health of mothers*: this includes iron fortification of staples, universal salt iodization and iron–folic acid supplementation for mothers during pregnancy.
- *Interventions aimed at improving care behaviors*: this includes community-based nutrition programs that provide information on breastfeeding and complementary feeding. It also includes dissemination of change behaviors that increase the frequency and effectiveness of hand washing. Bhutta *et al.*'s pooled analysis of six studies of hand washing counseling reduces the risk of diarrhea by 30 percent.
- *Interventions that address ill-health-related causes of poor pre-school nutrition*: Vitamin A is important for the immune system. Bhutta *et al.* report pooled analyses of trials of Vitamin A supplementation showing that mortality in children aged 6 to 59 months declines by 24 percent; however, there is no impact on anthropometric measures. Therapeutic zinc supplementation reduces the duration of diarrhea by 15–24 percent. Finally, deworming has small effects on linear growth but in areas with high rates of intestinal helminthiasis can reduce anemia by 5–10 percent.
- *Interventions that improve the quantity and quality of a child's diet*: Bhutta *et al.*'s analysis of seven interventions where children aged 6 to 23 months received food supplements showed that these increased height-for-age by 0.41 standard deviations – a large increase – in food insecure populations. Further, they find that the application of WHO guidelines for the treatment of children with severe acute malnutrition (which includes ready-to-use therapeutic foods) reduces mortality by 45 percent.

Having identified these interventions, Bhutta *et al.* construct a cohort model that assesses the cumulative impact of these interventions in the thirty-six countries which collectively account for 90 percent of the moderately or severely stunted children world-wide.[24] They find that these would reduce stunting at age 36 months by 36 percent and mortality by 25 percent.

Horton *et al.* (2010) estimate the budgetary costs of scaling up these nutrition interventions in these high-burden countries. Their cost estimates are based on what is called the "program experience" approach. Under this approach, per unit costs are derived from actual program experiences operating these interventions in poor countries. The context from which these have been taken – whether they are part of outreach programs, stand-alone interventions or components of primary health services – is considered, as is the collective packaging of these interventions. As Horton *et al.* (2010: 10) stress, an attraction of this approach is that it produces more conservative estimates of costs because, unlike other costing methods, it takes into account the fact that interventions may well not operate at maximum efficiency. They account for differences in costs across countries (see Horton *et al.*, 2010: Table 2.2) and assume, as do Bhutta *et al.* (2008), that it may not be possible to reach all children; in fact Horton *et al.*'s cost estimates are based on 80 percent coverage. Per child costs of these interventions are given in Table 6.25. In SSA and south Asia, the total cost per child is $96.10 with nearly 60 percent accounted for by the provision of complementary foods. In India, where the cost of supplementary feeding is higher, the per child cost is $111.62.

We now consider estimates of the *economic* benefits of implementing this package of interventions. We begin with stunting. In Behrman *et al.* (2004), the benefits of reduced prevalence of stunting were constructed by stitching together estimates of the impact of linear growth failure on attained height and then monetizing this impact by applying estimates of the impact of height on earnings derived from wage regressions where height appears as an argument; and on grade attainment and cognitive skills, again monetizing this impact by applying estimates of the impact of schooling or cognitive skills on earnings derived from wage regressions where these education-related outcomes appear as arguments. More recently,

[24] These countries are: Afghanistan, Angola, Bangladesh, Burkina Faso, Burundi, Cambodia, Cameroon, Congo (DR), Côte d'Ivoire, Egypt, Ethiopia, Ghana, Guatemala, India, Indonesia, Iraq, Kenya, Madagascar, Malawi, Mali, Mozambique, Myanmar, Nepal, Niger, Nigeria, Pakistan, Peru, Philippines, South Africa, Sudan, Tanzania, Turkey, Uganda, Vietnam, Yemen, and Zambia.

Table 6.25 Per child costs of interventions to reduce stunting and mortality at age 36 months

Intervention	Child age range (months)	Cost per unit ($)	Total cost per child ($)
Community-based nutrition programs that provide information on breastfeeding, complementary feeding, hand washing and distribute micronutrient powders and iron-folate supplements	0–59	7.50 per child	7.50
Vitamin A supplementation	6–59	1.20 p.a.	4.80
Therapeutic zinc supplementation for management of diarrhea	6–59	1.00 p.a. (assumes two or three treatments p.a.)	4.00
Multiple micronutrient powders	6–23	3.60 per course; three courses recommended	10.80
Deworming	12–59	0.25 per round; one round recommended p.a.	1.00
Iron-folic acid supplementation for mothers during pregnancy		2.00 per pregnancy	2.00
Iron-fortification of staples	12–59	0.20 p.a.	0.80
Universal salt-iodization	12–59	0.05 p.a.	0.20
Providing complementary foods to 80 percent of children in south Asia, 50 percent in Africa and East Asia, 10 percent elsewhere	6–23	0.11 per day 0.14 per day in India	56.88
Community-based management of severe acute malnutrition	6–59		8.13*

* This is calculated by taking the per child cost of community management of severe acute malnutrition ($200 per treated child) and multiplying it by the prevalence of severe acute malnutrition.
Source: Horton *et al.* (2010).

Hoddinott *et al.* (2011) provide direct estimates of the impact of stunting in early life on later life outcomes. Specifically, they follow up on a group of approximately 2,300 individuals who participated in a nutritional supplementation trial in Guatemala in the late 1960s and early–mid 1970s. These persons were traced as adults, aged somewhere between 25 and 42 at the time of interview, and data obtained on their schooling, marriage and fertility histories, earnings, health, and consumption levels. Hoddinott *et al.* find that multiple malign effects of growth failure persist into adulthood including, *inter alia*, lower levels of *per capita* consumption. Treating stunting as endogenous, Hoddinott *et al.* find that stunting reduces *per capita* consumption by a massive 66 percent. They emphasize that stunting carries such high costs because it has a large impact on cognitive skills and that these skills have high returns in the labor market.

We use this information as follows. Suppose that, starting in 2015, the full package of interventions described above is implemented. This benefits a cohort of individuals born in 2015 whom we assume enter the labor market at age 21. We treat an increase in *per capita* consumption due to moving one of these individuals from being stunted to not-stunted as equivalent to an increase in *per capita* permanent income. We multiply the point estimate, 0.66, by 0.36 in recognition of Bhutta *et al.'s* estimate that this package of interventions will reduce stunting by 36 percent. We apply this predicted increase in income – 23.8 percent – to predicted *per capita* incomes of four countries where stunting is widespread and which represent a range of income levels – Bangladesh, Ethiopia, India, and Kenya – for the period 2036–2050, that is, the first fifteen years of their working lives. Using both a 3 and a 5 percent discount rate, we construct the NPV of these increased earnings. We replicate this exercise

Table 6.26 BCR estimates of investments that reduce stunting

		23.8% income increase		15% income increase	
		Discount rate		Discount rate	
		5 percent	3 percent	5 percent	3 percent
Bangladesh	Increased income, NPV	3,647	7,165	2,303	4,523
	Cost	96.1	96.1	96.1	96.1
	BCR	38.0	74.6	24.0	47.1
Ethiopia	Increased income, NPV	2,289	4,496	1,445	2,838
	Cost	96.1	96.1	96.1	96.1
	BCR	23.8	46.8	15.0	29.5
Kenya	Increased income, NPV	3713	7295	2344	4605
	Cost	96.1	96.1	96.1	96.1
	BCR	38.6	75.9	24.4	47.9
India	Increased income, NPV	7875	15470	4972	9767
	Cost	111.62	111.62	111.62	111.62
	BCR	70.6	138.6	44.5	87.5

Source: Authors' calculations.

making an even more conservative estimate of the increment in income, 15 percent.

The results are reported in Table 6.26. Using the most conservative assumptions – a 15 percent increase in income, a 5 percent discount rate, and data from Ethiopia – yields a BCR of 15.0. Relaxing these conservative assumptions, either by using a 3 percent discount rate or our point estimate of the predicted increase in income, yields BCRs between 23.8 and 138.6. These vary across countries because of pre-existing differences in income levels and predicted growth rates.

Note that at least in two other ways these BCRs are conservative. First, some of these interventions – such as salt-iodization and iron-fortification of staples – convey benefits to all, not just pregnant women and young children. Second, these estimates do not account for the reduction in child mortality which we know to be substantive. Black *et al.* (2008) indicate that "Maternal and child undernutrition is the underlying cause of 3·5 million deaths, 35 percent of the disease burden in children younger than 5 years and 11 percent of total global DALYs." Ascribing a monetary benefit to this is difficult as it entails ascribing a monetary value to a lost life, an exercise that, as Behrman *et al.* (2004) describe in detail, has myriad pitfalls. Given these significant challenges, we do not calculate such a benefit stream, instead noting that the additional benefits of reduced mortality likely mean that our BCRs are underestimates.

Desiderata and caveats

In undertaking these calculations, we are aware of a number of important desiderata and caveats. We note four here: issues relating to measurement and discounting; global trade regimes; gender; and responses to the most virulent forms of hunger, famine.

Behrman *et al.* (2004) provide an exhaustive review of measurement and discounting issues as they relate to the calculations for Copenhagen Consensus-type exercises. Rather than recount all this in detail, we remind the reader of several important points. First, the investments being considered here convey benefits many of which are obtained well into the future – for example, investments made to reduce stunting do not begin to generate monetary benefits until 2036. This makes them especially sensitive to the choice of discount rate. As Behrman *et al.* note, the present discounted value of $100 received fifty years later is $608.04 with a discount rate of 1 percent but only $8.52 with a discount rate of 10 percent and so, in their words, "whether an investment is a great choice or a lousy choice" depends critically on the discount rate used. Second, our cost estimates are based on the marginal public costs of undertaking these investments. They exclude any private costs associated with these, such as the time costs incurred by mothers in taking their children to clinics to receive therapeutic zinc supplements when they have diarrhea. They also exclude the distortionary or deadweight costs associated with raising public funds for these investments. Finally, where there are diseconomies of scale associated with program implementation, costs may be underestimated. That all said, we note that for a number of our BCR estimates, we use multiple discount rates and, where possible, actual program costs as a guide to the cost estimates given here. And of course these considerations apply to all investments being considered by the Copenhagen Consensus, not just those presented here.

We began the substantive discussion with a conceptual framework that noted that hunger and undernutrition reflect the purposive actions of individuals given preferences and constraints. The settings in which our investments are placed offer both opportunities and threats to the reduction of hunger and undernutrition, global climate change being an excellent example of the latter. Here we note that all our BCR estimates rely on *ceteris paribus* assumptions regarding these settings. Improvements in settings which, for example, increase returns to human capital, would increase our estimates of benefits from investments that reduce stunting. The discussion of benefits from investments in yield enhancements relies critically on assumptions regarding the global trade regime for agricultural commodities. This is especially important when we consider the impact of climate change on global food prices. As Nelson *et al.* (2010) make clear, the consequences of climate change for crop production are unevenly distributed across the globe. Global trade reduces the adverse impact of lowered production in some regions because it permits consumers in those adversely affected localities to access production from other parts of the world less badly affected. We have not explicitly assessed the consequences of both climate change and a breakdown in global agricultural trade; suffice it to say that if this were to occur, that the welfare costs – for example, in terms of the number of children undernourished – would likely be significantly higher.

Investments aimed at reducing hunger and undernutrition cannot be gender blind. Gender considerations enter into our investments in two ways.

(1) *Gendered investments in agriculture*: we can think of no better statement of the importance of this than the following:

> The rationale for considering gender in agricultural research relates to agricultural productivity, food security, nutrition, poverty reduction and empowerment. In all of these, women play a critical but often under-recognized role and face greater constraints than men. (Meinzen-Dick *et al.*, 2011)

(2) *Women's education*: as noted in Behrman *et al.* (2007), there are many studies showing strong correlations between maternal education and reductions in undernutrition among pre-school children. With the caveat that some of these correlations may reflect unobserved characteristics such as family background, increasing women's education is likely to produce benefits in terms of reduced undernutrition.

Behrman *et al.* (2004) noted as part of their desiderata that improvements in infrastructure – specifically communication and transportation – would reduce the possibilities of famine. Since 2004, there have been considerable investments (both private and public) in infrastructure, particularly in SSA. Despite these, was a minor famine in 2005 in Niger in which poor communication played a role, and a major famine in 2011 in Somalia, where it is estimated that tens of thousands of people, many of them pre-school children, died. What does this tell us about investments to prevent famine? Here, we note the following.

The last twenty years have seen considerable public investment in early-warning systems, most notably in the Famine Early Warning Systems Network (FEWS NET).[25] FEWS NET combines agro-climatic monitoring data largely derived from meteorological satellites with information on crop and

[25] See www.fews.net for further details.

livestock production, food market flows, geographically disaggregated price data, and information on households' livelihoods (information which is not dissimilar to our description of the "activities" found on pp. 333–5). FEWS NET combines information from these disparate sources to place localities within an Integrated Food Security Phase Classification (IPC). The IPC "is a standardized scale that integrates food security, nutrition, and livelihood information into a common classification of the severity of acute food insecurity outcomes" (FEWS NET, 2012) The IPC ranges from Phase 1 ("No Acute Food Insecurity") to Phase 5 ("Catastrophe"). FEWS NET issued a warning in November 2010 noting that rainfall would be below average in southern Somalia and that, "Pre-emptive livelihood support could mitigate likely La Niña impacts in the eastern Horn" (FEWS NET, 2011) followed by an update in March 2011 indicating that food insecurity was reaching extreme levels in some parts of Somalia. Despite these warnings, international requests for assistance were not made until June 2011. This suggests that, at least in terms of eliminating the most catastrophic aspects of famine conditions, that the problem lies not so much with communications and information flows than with international decision-making in response to this information. One way in which this could be addressed is through the creation of a rapid response draw-down fund where donor countries pre-commit a certain level of funds that could be automatically drawn on in response to movements along the IPC scale.

Conclusions

In our introduction, we noted that deprivation in a world of plenty is an intrinsic rationale for investments that reduce hunger and undernutrition. This paper argues, as did the 2004 and 2008 Copenhagen Consensus papers by Behrman *et al.* (2004) and Horton *et al.* (2008) that in addition to this intrinsic rationale, these investments are simply good economics.

Unlike those earlier papers, we have put greater emphasis on solutions which focus on agriculture. Investments that enhance crop and livestock productivity and that reduce yield losses given climatic stresses have a BCR of 16.07 when we use a 5 percent discount rate. This figure is much higher than that reported in previous Copenhagen Consensus estimates. Note that it does not account for productivity effects associated with higher caloric consumption in poor countries or the benefits accrued through reduced child undernutrition. Further, in a world where climate change is occurring but the severity and distribution of that change is uncertain, investments that increase yield productivity have a significant option value. While everyone benefits from these investments, they are especially valuable to the approximately 925 million people who are hungry. An additional $8 billion per year would, by 2050, reduce the number of hungry people in the world by 210 million and the number of underweight children by 10 million.

We consider two market interventions that can increase rural incomes while reducing hunger and poverty. These are expenditures that improve access to market information through SMS messaging and interventions that reduce concentration in fertilizer markets. Across the countries and scenarios we consider, SMS messaging appears particularly promising. It has a modal BCR around 4 going as high as 8.35. This intervention is relatively cheap to provide, costing in our base case, PPP$ 3.98 *per capita*. We suspect that as these technologies continue to develop, scale economies will drive costs down further while movement by smallholders out of staples into higher-value, perishable products, will increase benefits.

We update previous Copenhagen Consensus estimates of the BCRs associated with reducing vitamin A, iodine, iron, and zinc deficiencies. Based on current estimates that there are approximately 163 million pre-school children who are vitamin A deficient, an annual investment of $50 million would eliminate this deficiency in this age group using the cost estimates from Rajkumar *et al.* (2012). If instead we use the higher cost estimate provided in Horton *et al.* (2010) ($1.20 per year) and apply this to children aged 6–24 months (so that the total cost per child is $2.40) – the annual cost would be $391 million dollars. Iodine deficiencies are widespread but the cost of iodizing salt is cheap ($0.05 per person p.a.). An investment of

$100 million p.a. would eliminate the iodine deficiencies affecting 1.8 billion people. Annually, there are approximately 200 million pregnancies in the world and approximately 40 percent of these pregnant women are anemic. The annual cost of eliminating maternal anemia during pregnancy, assuming that supplements could be provided during ante-natal visits, is $160 million.

A novel estimate that we provide is for investments that will allow the scale-up of a bundled set of interventions that reduces the prevalence of stunting. Under the most conservative assumptions that we consider, these yield a BCR of 15. If we relax these, the BCR rises to somewhere between 23.8 and 138.6. In the country with the largest number of undernourished children in the world, India, these BCRs lie between 44 and 138.6. Note that these calculations do not explicitly account for the benefits from salt-iodization and iron-fortification of staples that will accrue more widely across populations and which previous Copenhagen Consensuses have perceived to be very promising investments. Nor do they place a monetary value on the additional benefits that this bundle of investments will have through reduced child mortality. Figures from Horton *et al.* (2010) indicate that a $3 billion investment per year would provide this bundle of interventions to 100 million children.[26]

As with all calculations of BCRs, there are caveats and desiderata. Salient ones here include the mechanics underlying the calculation of PVs, assumptions made about the global trade regime, the salience of gender, and the need to improve the speed with which international resources are deployed to combat famine. Mindful of these, investments to reduce hunger and undernutrition would appear to have powerful positive benefits, both intrinsically and instrumentally.

Bibliography

Ahammad, H. and R. Mi, 2005: Land use change modeling in GTEM: accounting for forest sinks. Australian Bureau of Agricultural and Resource Economics (ABARE) Conference Paper 05.13, presented at the workshop, Energy Modeling Forum 22: Climate Change Control Scenarios, 25–27 May, Stanford University

Aker, J. C., 2008a: Does digital divide or provide? The impact of cell phones on grain markets in Niger, Center for Global Development, Washington, DC

2008b: Can you hear me now? How cell phones are transforming markets in Sub-Saharan Africa, Center for Global Development, Washington, DC

Aker, J. C. and M. Fafchamps, 2010: How does mobile phones coverage affect farm-gate prices? Evidence from West Africa, Paper presented at the Allied Social Science Association Meeting, Denver, CO, 2011

Aker, J. C. and I. M. Mbiti, 2010: Mobile phones and economic development in Africa, Center for Global Development, Washington, DC, *Working Paper* 211

Alene, A. D. and O. Coulibaly, 2009: The impact of agricultural research on productivity and poverty in sub-Saharan Africa, *Food Policy* **34**, 198–209

Alston, J., P. Pardey, J. James, and M. Andersen, 2009: The economics of agricultural R&D, *Annual Review of Resource Economics* **1**, 537–66

Baulch, B. and J. Hoddinott, 2000: Economic mobility and poverty dynamics in developing countries, *Journal of Development Studies* **36**, 1–24

Behrman, J. R. and A. Deolalikar, 1988: Health and nutrition, in H. B. Chenery and T. N. Srinivasan (eds.), *Handbook on Economic Development*, Vol. 1, North-Holland, Amsterdam, 631–711

1989: Agricultural wages in India: the role of health, nutrition and seasonality, in D. E. Sahn (ed.), *Seasonal Variability in Third World Agriculture: The Consequences for Food Security*, Johns Hopkins University Press, Baltimore, MD

Behrman, J. and J. Hoddinott, 2005: Program evaluation with unobserved heterogeneity and selective implementation: the Mexican *Progresa* impact on child nutrition, *Oxford Bulletin of Economics and Statistics*, **67**, 547–69

Behrman, J., H. Alderman, and J. Hoddinott, 2004: Hunger and malnutrition, in B. Lomborg (ed.), *Global Crises, Global Solutions*, Cambridge University Press

[26] Globally, there are approximately 356 million children under the age of 5.

Beuerman, D., 2011: Telecommunication technologies, agricultural productivity and child labor in rural Peru, University of Maryland, unpublished manuscript

Bhutta, Z., T. Ahmed, R. Black, S. Cousens, K. Dewey, E. Giugliani, B. Haider, B. Kirkwood, S. Morris, H. Sachdev, and M. Shekar, 2008: What works? Interventions for maternal and child undernutrition and survival, *Lancet* **371**, 417–40

Black R. E., L. H. Allen, Z. A. Bhutta, L. Caulfield, M. de Onis, M. Ezzati, C. Mathers, and J. Rivera, 2008: Maternal and child undernutrition: global and regional exposures and health consequences, *Lancet* **371**, 243–60

von Braun, J., S. Fan, R. Meinzen-Dick, M. Rosegrant, and A. Pratt, 2008: *What to Expect from Scaling Up CGIAR Investments and "Best Bet" Programs*, International Food Policy Research Institute, Washington, DC

Brown, K., J. Peerson, S. Baker, K. Shawn, and S. Hess, 2009: Preventive zinc supplementation among infants, preschoolers, and older prepubertal children, *Food and Nutrition Bulletin* **30**, 12S–40S

Bumb, B. L., M. E. Johnson, and P. A. Fuentes, 2011: Policy options for improving regional fertilizer markets in West Africa, *IFPRI Discussion Paper* **1084**, IFPRI, Washington, DC

Cafiero, C. and P. Gennari, 2011: The FAO indicator of the prevalence of undernourishment, Food and Agriculture Organization, Rome, mimeo

Casey, G. J., D. Sartori, S. E. Horton, T. Q. Phuc, L. B. Phu *et al.*, 2011: Weekly iron-folic acid supplementation with regular deworming is cost-effective in preventing anaemia in women of reproductive age in Vietnam, *PLoS ONE* **6**, 23723. doi:10.1371/journal.pone.0023723

Chong, A., V. Galdo, and M. Torero, 2005: Does privatization deliver? Access to telephone and household income in poor rural areas using a quasi-natural experiment in Peru, Inter American Development Bank, Washington, DC

Dasgupta, P., 1993: *An Enquiry into Well-Being and Destitution*, Clarendon Press, Oxford

David, C. and K. Otsuka, 1994: *Modern Rice Technology and Income Distribution in Asia*, International Rice Research Institute, Los Banos

Department for International Development (DfID), 1999: *Sustainable Livelihoods Guidance Sheets*, London

DSSAT, 2012: http://dssat.net/, accessed February 28, 2013

Fafchamps, M. and B. Minten, 2012: The impact of SMS-based agricultural information on indian farmers, *World Bank Economic Review* **26**, 383–414

Fan, S., P. Hazell, and S. Thorat, 1998: Government spending, growth and poverty: an analysis of interlinkages in rural India, Environment and Production Technology Division *Discussion Paper* **33**

FAO, 2008: *FAO Methodology for the Measurement of Food Deprivation: Updating the Minimum Dietary Energy Requirements*, FAO, Rome

2010: *The State of Food Insecurity in the World: Addressing Food Insecurity in Protracted Crises*, FAO, Rome

2012: Why are no hunger statistics produced for 2011?, www.fao.org/hunger/en/, accessed February 20, 2012

FEWS NET, 2011: EAST AFRICA Food Security Alert, www.fews.net/docs/Publications/EA_Regional%20Alert%20Oct%202010_Final.pdf, November 2, 2010

2012: IPC Acute Food Insecurity Reference Table for Household Groups, www.fews.net/ml/en/info/pages/scale.aspx, accessed February 2012

Futch, M. D. and C. T. McIntosh, 2009: Tracking the introduction of the village phone product in Rwanda, *Information Technologies and International Development* **5**, 54–81

Goyal, A., 2010: Information, direct access to farmers, and rural market performance in Central India, *American Economic Journal: Applied Economics* **2**, 22–45

Gruhn, P., F. Goletti, and R. N. Roy, 1995: *Proceedings of the IFPRI/FAO Workshop on Plant Nutrient Management, Food Security and Sustainable Agriculture: The Future through 2020*, Viterbo, Italy

Haddad, L., J. Hoddinott, and H. Alderman (eds.), 1997: *Intrahousehold Resource Allocation in Developing Countries: Models, Methods and Policy*, Johns Hopkins University Press, Baltimore, MD

Headey, D., 2011: Was the global food crisis really a crisis? Simulations versus self-reporting, *IFPRI Discussion Paper* **1087**, IFPRI, Washington, DC

Hernandez, M. and M. Torero, 2011: Fertilizer market situation: market structure, consumption and trade patterns, and pricing behavior, *IFPRI Discussion Paper* **1058**, IFPRI, Washington, DC

Hoddinott, J., 2001: Introduction, in J. Hoddinott (ed.), *Food Security in Practice: Methods for Rural Development Projects*, IFPRI, Washington, DC

2012: Agriculture, health, and nutrition: toward conceptualizing the linkages, in S. Fan and R. Pandya-Lorch (eds.), *Reshaping Agriculture for Nutrition and Health*, IFPRI, Washington, DC

Hoddinott, J. and B. Kinsey, 2001: Child growth in the time of drought, *Oxford Bulletin of Economics and Statistics* **63**, 409–36

Hoddinott, J. and A. Quisumbing, 2010: Methods for microeconometric risk and vulnerability assessment, in R. Fuentes-Nieva and P. Seck (eds.), *Risk, Vulnerability and Human Development: On the Brink*, Palgrave Macmillan–United Nations Development Programme, London

Hoddinott, J., E. Skoufias, and R. Washburn, 2000: The impact of PROGRESA on consumption: report submitted to PROGRESA, IFPRI, Washington, DC, mimeo

Hoddinott, J., J. Maluccio, J. Behrman, R. Martorell, P. Melgar, A. Quisumbing, M. Ramirez-Zea, A. Stein, and K. Yount, 2011: The consequences of early childhood growth failure over the life course, IFPRI, Washington, DC, mimeo

Horton, S., H. Alderman, and J. Rivera, 2008: Hunger and malnutrition 2008. Copenhagen Consensus Challenge Paper

Horton, S., A. Wesley, and M. G. Venkatesh Mannar, 2011: Double-fortified salt reduces anemia, benefit:cost ratio is modestly favorable, *Food Policy* **36**, 581–7

Horton, S., M. Shekar, C. McDonald, A. Mahal, and J. Brooks, 2010: *Scaling up Nutrition: What Will it Cost?*, World Bank, Washington, DC

Hunger Task Force, 2003: *Halving Hunger by 2015: A Framework for Action*, Interim Report, Millennium Project, UNDP, New York

Intergovernmental Panel on Climate Change (IPCC), 2007: *Climate Change 2007: The Physical Science Basis*, Working Group I Contribution to the Fourth Assessment Report of the Intergovernmental Panel on Climate Change, Figure 104, Cambridge University Press

Jacobs, K. and D. Sumner, 2002: The food balance sheets of the Food and Agriculture Organization: a review of potential ways to broaden the appropriate uses of the Data, Department of Economics, University of California, Davis, mimeo

Jensen, R. T., 2007: The digital provide: information (technology), market performance and welfare in the South Indian fisheries sector, *Quarterly Journal of Economics* **122**, 879–924

2010: Information, efficiency and welfare in agricultural markets, *Agricultural Economics* **41**(S1), 203–16

Keys, A., J. Brožek, A. Henschel, O. Mickelsen, and H. L. Taylor, 1950: *The Biology of Human Starvation*, University of Minnesota Press, Minneapolis, 2 vols.

Kiani, A. K., M. Iqbal, and T. Javed, 2008: Total factor productivity and agricultural research relationship: evidence from crops sub-sector of Pakistan's Punjab, *European Journal of Scientific Research* **23**, 87–97

Kim, C. S., H. Taylor, C. B. Hallahan and G. D. Schaible, 2001: *Economic Analysis of the Changing Structure of US Fertilizer Industry*, ERS-USDA,

Kostandini, G., B. F. Mills, S. W. Omamo, and S. Wood, 2009: *Ex ante* analysis of the benefits of transgenic drought tolerance research on cereal crops in low-income countries, *Agricultural Economics* **40**, 477–92

Labonne, J. and R. Chase, 2009: The power of information: the impact of mobile phones on farmers' welfare in the Philippines, *The World Bank Working Paper* **4996**

Leibenstein, H., 1957: *Economic Backwardness and Economic Growth*, Wiley, New York

Margulis, S., U. Narain, P. Chinowsky, L. Cretegny, G. Hughes, P. Kirshen, A. Kuriakose *et al.*, 2010: *Cost to Developing Countries of Adapting to Climate Change: New Methods and Estimates*, World Bank, Washington, DC

Maxwell, S. and T. Frankenberger, 1992: Household food security: concepts, indicators, measurements, IFAD, Rome

Meinzen-Dick, R., A. Quisumbing, J. Behrman, P. Biermayr-Jenzano, V. Wilde, M. Noordeloos, C. Ragasa, and N. Beintema, 2011: Engendering agricultural research, development and extension, *IFPRI Research Monograph*, IFPRI, Washington, DC

Millennium Ecosystem Assessment, 2005: *Ecosystems and Human Well-Being, Vol. II: Scenarios*, Island Press, Washington, DC

Mitra, S., D. Mookherkee, M. Torero, and V. Sujara, 2011: Asymmetric information and middleman margins: an experiment with potato farmers, Boston University

Morris, S., 2001: Measuring nutritional dimensions of household food security, in J. Hoddinott (ed.), *Food security in practice: Methods for Rural Development Projects*, International Food Policy Research Institute, Washington, DC

Muto, M. and T. Yamano, 2009: The impact of mobile phone coverage expansion on market participation: panel data evidence from Uganda, *World Development* **37**, 1887–96

Nelson, G., M. Rosegrant, A. Palazzo, I. Gray, C. Ingersoll, R. Robertson, S. Tokgoz, T. Zhu, T. Sulser, C. Ringler, S. Msangi, and L. You, 2010: Food security, farming and climate change to 2050, *IFPRI Research Monograph* **172**, IFPRI, Washington, DC

Orden, D., M. Torero, and A. Gulati, 2004: Agricultural markets and the rural poor, Background paper for workshop of the Poverty Reduction Network, March 5, Markets, Trade and Institutions Division, IFPRI, Washington, DC

Pitt, M. M., M. R. Rosenzweig, and M. N. Hassan, 1990: Productivity, health and inequality in the intrahousehold distribution of food in low-income countries, *American Economic Review* **80**, 1139–56

Pray, C., L. Nagarajan, L. Li, J. Huang, R. Hu, K. N. Selvaraj, O. Napasintuwong, and R. Chandra Babu, 2011: Potential impact of biotechnology on adaption of agriculture to climate change: the case of drought tolerant rice breeding in Asia, *Sustainability* **3**, 1723–41

Rajkumar, A. S., C. Gaukler, and J. Tilahun, 2012: *Combating Malnutrition in Ethiopia: An Evidence-Based Approach for Sustained Results*, World Bank: Washington, DC

Reuters, 2012: Reuters Market Light: impacts. www.reutersmarketlight.com/impact.php, accessed March 28, 2012

Rosegrant, M. W., 2008: *Biofuels and Grain Prices: Impacts and Policy Responses*, Testimony for the US Senate Committee on Homeland Security and Governmental Affairs, Washington, DC

Rosegrant, M. W., C. Ringler, S. Msangi, T. B. Sulser, T. Zhu, and S. A. Cline, 2008: International Model for Policy Analysis of Agricultural Commodities and Trade (IMPACT): model description, IFPRI, Washington, DC, www.ifpri.org/sites/default/files/publications/impactwater.pdf

Schimmelpfenig, D. and C. Thirtle, 1999: The internationalization of agricultural technology: patents, R&D spillovers, and their effects on productivity in the European Union and United States, *Contemporary Economic Policy* **17**, 457–68

Sen, A., 1981a: *Poverty and Famines*, Oxford University Press

1981b: Ingredients of famine analysis: availability and entitlements, *Quarterly Journal of Economics* **96**, 433–64

Serraj, R., K. L. McNally, I. Slamet-Loedin, A. Kohli, S. M. Haefele, G. Atlin, and A. Kumar, 2011: Drought resistance improvement in rice: an integrated genetic and resource management strategy, *Plant Production Science* **14**, 1–14

Singh, I., L. Squire, and J. Strauss (eds), 1986: *Agricultural Household Models, Extensions, Applications and Policy*, Johns Hopkins University Press, Baltimore, MD

Smith, L. and L. Haddad, 2000: Explaining child malnutrition in developing countries, *IFPRI Research Monograph* **111**, IFPRI, Washington, DC

Stein A. D., W. Wang, R. Martorell, S. A. Norris, L. Adair, I. Bas, H. S. Sachdev, S. K. Bhargava, C. H. D. Fall, D. Gigante, and C. Victora, 2010: Consortium on Health Orientated Research in Transitional Societies Group, 2010: growth patterns in early childhood and final attained stature: data from five birth cohorts from low and middle-income countries, *American Journal of Human Biology* **22**, 353–9

Stigler, G. J., 1961: The economics of information, *Journal of Political Economy* **69**, 213–25

Strauss, J. and D. Thomas, 1995: Human resources: empirical modeling of household and family decisions, in J. Behrman and T. N. Srinivasan (eds.), *Handbook of Development Economics*, Vol. 3A, North–Holland, Amsterdam

Svensson, J. and D. Yanagizawa, 2009: Getting prices right: the impact of the Market Information Service in Uganda, *Journal of the European Economic Association* **7**, 435–45

Thirtle, C, Lin, L., and J. Piesse, 2003: The impact of research-led agricultural productivity growth on poverty reduction in Africa, Asia and Latin America, *World Development* **31**, 1959–75

United Nations Standing Committee on Nutrition (UNSCN), 2010: *6th Report on the World Nutrition Situation*, Geneva

Hunger and Malnutrition

Alternative Perspective

ANIL B. DEOLALIKAR

Introduction

The Challenge Paper on Hunger and Nutrition (Chapter 6) is novel both in the nutrition literature as well as in the Copenhagen Consensus series in that it looks beyond the traditional nutritional interventions for solutions to the problem of hunger and malnutrition. It focuses on agricultural interventions, most notably on increasing crop yields and agricultural market innovations (e.g. use of cell phone technologies for better price information), as a means of reducing hunger. (The chapter also considers traditional micronutrient and nutritional supplementation interventions to reduce the prevalence of stunting.) As I argue in this Alternative Perspective Paper, while the focus on agriculture is a refreshing and important change, it comes with some risks of its own.

One of the main tools used by Chapter 6 is a partial equilibrium model (called the IMPACT model) to generate long-term projections of food supply, demand, trade, and prices based on a number of different factors. The model is disaggregated across forty-six crops, with growth in crop production in each country being determined by crop and input prices, exogenous rates of productivity growth and area expansion, investment in irrigation, and water availability. The demand for agricultural commodities is modeled as a function of prices, income, and population growth. Rates of hunger and child underweight are also modeled as functions of food and calorie consumption. Using this model, the chapter calculates the impact of alternative agricultural (and micronutrient supplementation) interventions on both the number of hungry persons and the rate of child malnutrition. It also computes the BCRs of the agricultural and nutritional interventions.

There are three problems in particular on which I wish to focus. First, considering interventions outside a particular sector (e.g. nutrition) as a means of influencing outcomes in that sector (e.g. hunger and malnutrition) opens up a Pandora's box. This is particularly true of such broad goals as enhancing agricultural productivity and making agricultural markets more efficient. I would consider these to be overarching systemic (i.e. development) goals, not really narrowly defined interventions. In this case, why stop at improving productivity in agriculture and making it more efficient? Why not also consider the effects on hunger and malnutrition of other system changes, such as better transport infrastructure, more education (for women), higher-quality and more accessible health care services, universal health coverage for children, and the like. Perhaps, the BCRs of these economy-wide interventions could be even larger than those of the agricultural interventions considered by the chapter.

Second, the problem with considering broad systemic changes is that these often have multiple outputs, and it is extremely difficult to calculate BCRs for interventions that have multiple outputs and outcomes. Reducing hunger and malnutrition is only one of several goals of agricultural development; as the five-decade-old literature on economic development has argued, agricultural productivity growth has numerous other broad-based benefits. Indeed, productivity growth in agriculture is a *sine qua non* of sustained industrialization and of economic development itself (Southworth and Johnston, 1967; Timmer, 1988). How does one value all of these other benefits of agricultural productivity growth? Surely, the BCRs of agricultural interventions calculated by the authors are probably underestimated relative to the BCRs of the micronutrient

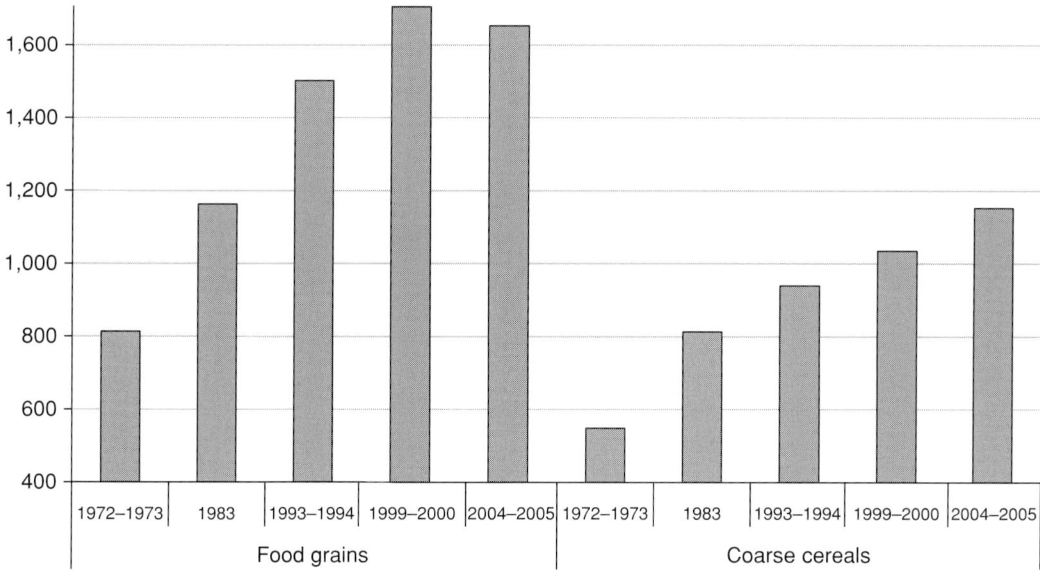

Figure 6.1.1 *Average crop yields (kg/ha) of all food grains and coarse cereals, India, 1972–1973 to 2004–2005*

Source: Indiastat.com.

supplementation interventions. In fact, the two sets of estimates are really not comparable, since most micronutrient interventions typically only have one output/outcome while agricultural development has numerous outputs and outcomes. This is not a shortcoming of the chapter, but of the BCR methodology itself.

The third problem is more specific. Improvements in agricultural productivity are likely to affect hunger and malnutrition in two ways: by reducing food prices and by increasing household incomes in the rural areas. But the evidence linking agricultural productivity growth to reductions in hunger and malnutrition is elusive and ambiguous at best. Indeed, there is a strong disconnect between agricultural productivity growth and reductions in hunger and child malnutrition throughout the world, but particularly in south Asia, which has the largest number of underweight and stunted children of any region in the world. Even as agricultural productivity and rural incomes have increased sharply in countries such as India, mean calorie intake has actually fallen and the proportion of children who are underweight and stunted has remained stubbornly high. Across Indian states, there appears to be very little, if any, correlation between agricultural productivity growth and the reduction of child malnutrition. This casts considerable doubt on the assertion that agricultural productivity growth will significantly reduce hunger and malnutrition rates around the world.

Agricultural productivity and calorie intake in India

India provides an interesting example of the disconnect between agricultural productivity growth and reduction of hunger. As Figure 6.1.1 shows, crop yields in India increased dramatically over the thirty-two years between 1972–1973 and 2004–2005. For food grains as a whole, crop yields almost exactly doubled over the period and they more than doubled in the case of "coarse cereals" (maize, sorghum, and pearl millet), which are traditionally the main components of the food basket of the poor in India. Because these rates of productivity

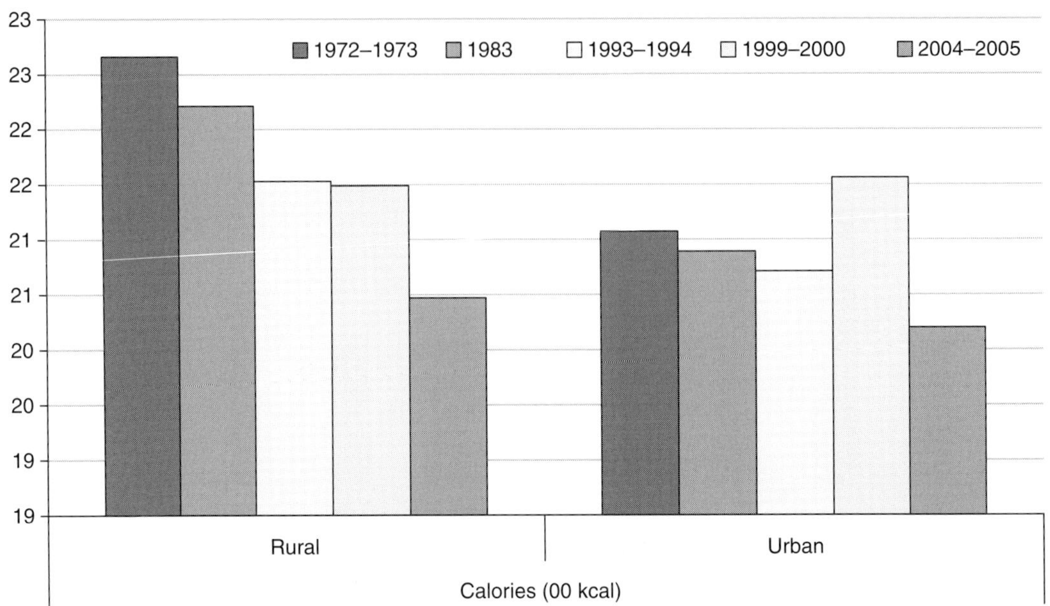

Figure 6.1.2 *Calorie intake per person per day, by rural/urban residence, India, 1972–1973 to 2004–2005 (00 calories)*

Source: Author's calculations from NSS unit record data.

growth, averaging about 2.5 percent per year over thirty-two years, would have significantly increased rural incomes and lowered food prices, the IMPACT model used in the chapter would likely have predicted that mean calorie intake would have increased – and both hunger and child underweight rates would have fallen – over this period.

But Figure 6.1.2 shows exactly the opposite. In fact, over this time period, mean calorie intake actually fell – by about 10 percent in the rural areas and 4 percent in the urban areas. If calorie requirements were unchanged over the period, the proportion of individuals considered hungry would have increased. Certainly, *prima facie*, there appears to be a weak link between agricultural productivity growth and calorie consumption in India.

Deaton and Drèze (2009) have noted the near-secular in calorie consumption in India over the last few decades. They, too, regard it as a puzzle, especially given that incomes have increased significantly – and relative food prices have fallen – over this period. A possible explanation they offer for this drift is that calorie requirements have declined due to better health conditions (e.g. greater availability of safe drinking water and higher vaccination rates) and lower physical activity levels (arising in turn due to changes in the occupational structure as well as expanded ownership of various effort-saving durables). However, there is really no strong evidence for this hypothesis, and the assertion is speculative at best.

Figure 6.1.3 plots changes in mean calorie consumption between 1993–1994 and 2004–2005 against percentage changes in *kharif* (summer) crop yields between 1991–1992 and 2000–2001 across fifteen major Indian states. There does not seem to be any association between the two variables. Similar results are obtained for the *rabi* (winter) crop yields. Thus, the connection between crop yield growth and improvements in calorie intake appears weak to non-existent across states in India.

The Asian enigma

The "Asian enigma" is a term that is often used to denote the failure, especially in the south Asian countries, of high rates of economic growth and poverty reduction translating into sharply falling rates of child malnutrition. The region fares much

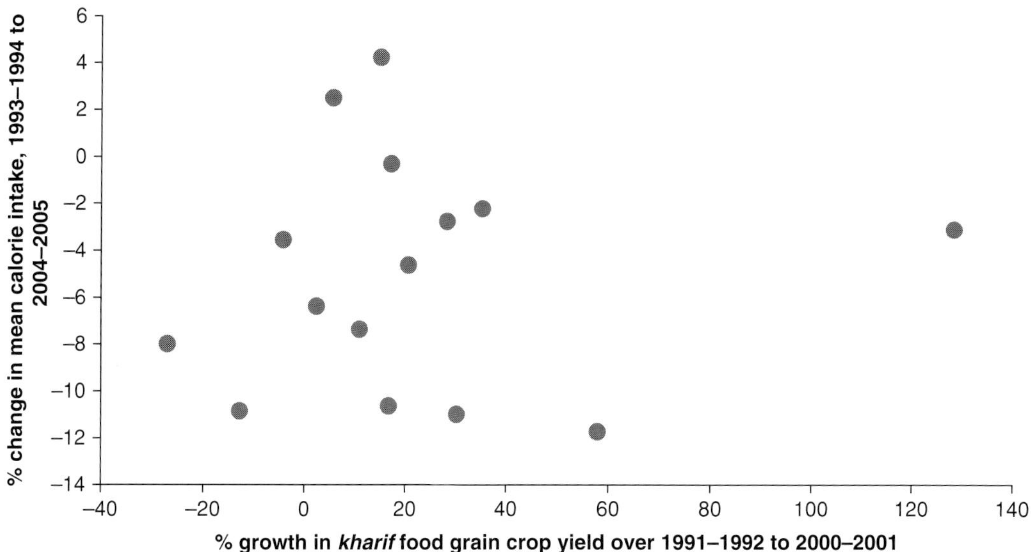

Figure 6.1.3 *Percentage change in mean calorie intake from 1993–1994 to 2004–2005, in comparison to crop yield growth (*kharif *food grains) over 1991–1992 to 2000–2001, across Indian states*

Source: NSS unit record data and indiastat.com.

worse than any other world region, including SSA, in terms of child malnutrition.

India has one of the highest rates of child malnutrition in the world, with nearly half of all children under 3 years of age being either underweight or stunted. Further, the incidence of child malnutrition has remained stubbornly high even after nearly two decades of economic and agricultural productivity growth in the country (Figure 6.1.4).

Figure 6.1.5 plots the changes in child underweight rates against changes in *kharif* crop yields across the major twelve Indian states for which data are available. Again, as with *per capita* calorie consumption, no association is observed between the two variables. For instance, the child malnutrition rate in Rajasthan, which saw the most rapid growth of crop yields during the 1990s, barely budged between 1992–1993 and 2005–2006. In contrast, West Bengal, which saw virtually no growth in *kharif* crop yields over the period, experienced a decline of about 21 percent in the proportion of underweight children. The results are largely unchanged if one uses *rabi* crop yields (instead of *kharif*) or the rate of stunting (instead of the rate of underweight children).

That child malnutrition is weakly correlated with income is additionally borne out by the findings (from the third round of the National Family Health Survey (NFHS)) that a quarter of Indian children of mothers with ten or more years of schooling – and an equivalent proportion of children from the top wealth quintile – were underweight in India in 2005–2006. These children are very unlikely to have faced food insecurity. Even in a relatively prosperous and dynamic state like Gujarat, child malnutrition rates have been stagnant over the past decade.

The "Asian enigma" throws up many interesting questions – is it culture and dietary habits (e.g. extensive vegetarianism) that account for high rates of child malnutrition in South Asia? Is it the poor nutritional status of mothers and their low weight gain during pregnancy that lead to low birthweight babies who grow on to become malnourished children? Is it poor breast-feeding practices in infancy that set children on the path of malnutrition very early in life?

Reasons for the agriculture–nutrition disconnect

The point of the above discussion is that the connection between agricultural productivity growth

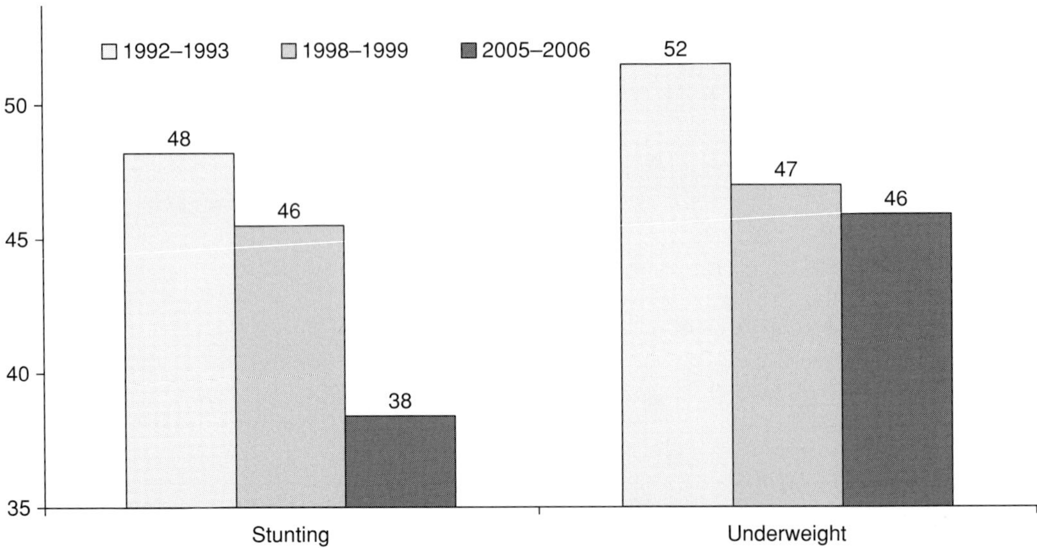

Figure 6.1.4 *Percentage of children under 3 years who are underweight or stunted, India, 1992–1993 to 2005–2006*

Source: nfhsindia.org.

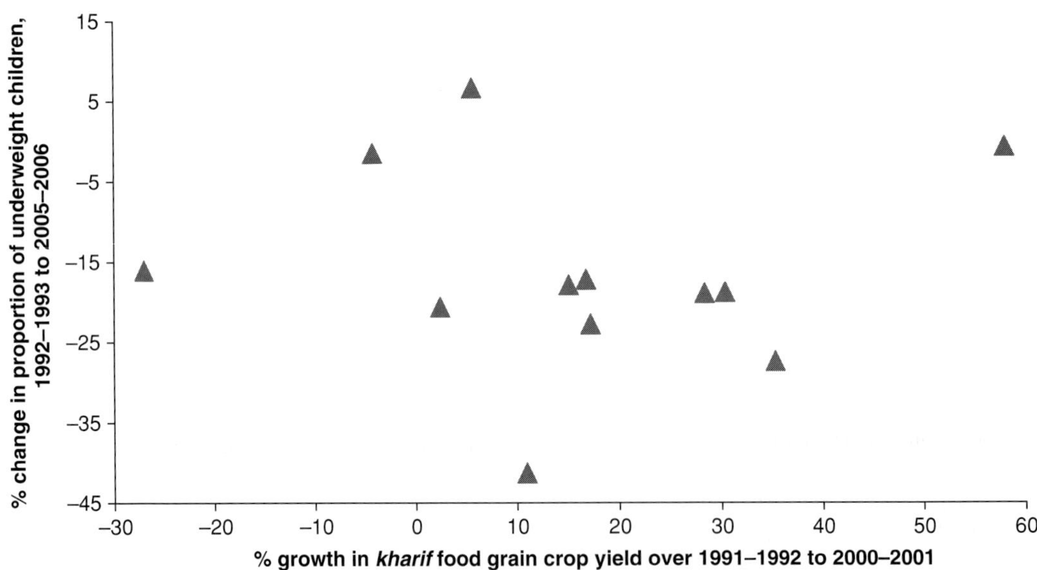

Figure 6.1.5 *Percentage change in the proportion of underweight children under 3 years of age from 1992–1993 to 2005–2006, in comparison to crop yield growth (*kharif *food grains) over 1991–1992 to 2000–2001, across Indian states*

Source: nfhsindia.org and indiastat.com.

and nutritional improvements is by no means established. If anything, there is a lot of evidence to suggest that improvements in agriculture do not always translate into better nutritional intake, less hunger, and less child malnutrition. By using a simulation model in which changes in agricultural productivity deterministically improve nutrition (via food price and household-income effects), the chapter oversimplifies the problem of combating malnutrition.

It is not that the existing literature has completely ignored the possible disconnect between agriculture and nutrition. But the chapter does not refer to this literature. For instance (pp. 333–5), the chapter presents a discussion of the conceptual framework, as well as a discussion of what constitutes hunger, without citing any prior studies in this area. There is a rather large literature that has analyzed the socioeconomic determinants of nutrient intake and nutritional status in developing countries. These studies have often found that the relationship between nutrient intake/outcomes and household-level factors, such as household income and assets, is not straightforward.

The fact is that researchers do not have a good handle on how households make food and nutritional choices. The old adage of whether people eat to live or live to eat is very relevant here. Food is a fuel for the human body, and therefore its demand is partly based on the caloric needs and requirements of the human body. But it does not typically take very much to satisfy these basic caloric demands of the body, even in a poor country. A very large portion of the demand for food is thus based on the non-nutritive attributes of food, such as taste, aroma, variety, and status. This means that increases in household income do not always translate into improvements in calorie consumption. Behrman and Deolalikar (1987) noted this twenty-five years ago; they found that even in one of the poorest regions of India (the semi-arid villages of Andhra Pradesh and Maharashtra), the income gradient of calorie intake was essentially flat, even after controlling for unobserved heterogeneity. This did not mean that household food consumption was not elastic with respect to household income; indeed, expenditure on food was highly responsive to income changes. What was occurring was that as incomes increased, households – even very poor households that were presumably (according to most external observers' standards) "hungry" and undernourished – changed the composition of their food consumption away from energy-efficient (i.e. low-price per calorie) staples, such as sorghum and millet, to less energy-efficient (higher-price per calorie) foods, such as rice, vegetables, and sugar. In some cases, the shift was even more subtle, such as the shift from short-grain, broken rice to long-grain rice. This shift in consumption accounted for the larger expenditures on food, but unchanged energy intakes, with increasing income.

In another paper, Behrman and Deolalikar (1989) found, in a cross-section of developing and developed countries, that the demand for food variety was very strongly responsive to rising incomes and food budgets. Interestingly, one implication of their results is that "if the food-nutrient choices of individuals are informed choices, the low income elasticities of calories and the relatively high income elasticities of food variety . . . suggest that, even in relatively poor populations, individuals do not perceive inadequate calorie intakes to be as high a priority problem as many outside observers have suggested."

Banerjee and Duflo (2011) make essentially the same point:

> In Udaipur, India, for example, we find that the typical poor household could spend up to 30 percent more on food, if it completely cut expenditures on alcohol, tobacco, and festivals. The poor seem to have many choices, and they don't choose to spend as much as they can on food. Equally remarkable is that even the money that people do spend on food is not spent to maximize the intake of calories or micronutrients. Studies have shown that when very poor people get a chance to spend a little bit more on food, they don't put everything into getting more calories. Instead, they buy better-tasting, more expensive calories. (2011: 23)

They go on to conclude that "all told, many poor people might eat fewer calories than we – or the FAO – think is appropriate. But this does not seem to be because they have no other choice; rather, they are not hungry enough to seize every opportunity to eat more. So perhaps there aren't a billion 'hungry' people in the world after all."

Conclusions

Chapter 6 is novel in that it goes beyond traditional nutritional interventions and focuses on agricultural interventions as a means of combating the global challenge of hunger and malnutrition. But such an approach relies too much on an assumed connection between increases in agricultural productivity and calorie consumption. It is not clear from the chapter what coefficients of calorie responsiveness to income and food prices are used in the simulation model. Naturally, these coefficients are critical to the simulated impacts of agricultural interventions on the number of hungry people and the extent of child malnutrition. Given the considerable uncertainty about how calorie consumption and child malnutrition actually respond to household income and food prices, one should be wary of simulation models that simply assume this relationship. Indeed, it could be argued that the concept of hungry people is itself somewhat problematic.

Perhaps, it is best to end with a quote from Deaton and Drèze (2009):

> The limitations of intake-focused nutritional assessments reinforce the case for supplementing intake data with outcome-focused indicators, such as anthropometric measurements. However, anthropometric data have some limitations too. For one thing, there are unresolved puzzles about anthropometric indicators in India, such as the high prevalence of stunting among privileged children (which is seemingly at variance with the premises of accepted "growth standards"). For another, there are inconsistencies between different sources of anthropometric data, as well as puzzling contrasts between nutrition trends based on different anthropometric indicators, such as height-for-age and weight-for-height. While broad, long-term trends are reasonably clear, there is some confusion about recent changes . . . the nutrition situation in India is full of puzzles. (2009: 63)

Bibliography

Banerjee, A. and E. Duflo, 2011: *Poor Economics: A Radical Rethinking of the Way to Fight Global Poverty*, Public Affairs, New York

Behrman, J. R. and A. B. Deolalikar, 1987: Will developing country nutrition improve with income? A case study for rural South India, *Journal of Political Economy* **95**, 492–507

1989: Is variety the spice of life? Implications for calorie responses to income, *The Review of Economics and Statistics* **71**, 666–72

Deaton, A. and J. Drèze, 2009: Food and nutrition in India: facts and interpretations, *Economic and Political Weekly* **54**, 42–65

Southworth, H. M. and B. F. Johnston, 1967: *Agricultural Development and Economic Growth*, Cornell University Press, Ithaca, NY

Timmer, C. P., 1988: The agricultural transformation, in H. Chenery and T. N. Srinivasan (eds.), *Handbook of Development Economics*, Vol. 1, Elsevier, Amsterdam, 275–331

Hunger and Malnutrition

Alternative Perspective

BEATRICE LORGE ROGERS*

Introduction

This Alternative Perspective Paper is a response to the Challenge Paper (Chapter 6) prepared by Hoddinott, Rosegrant, and Torero on recommendations to address hunger and malnutrition. The suggestions made in the chapter are comprehensive in crossing multiple sectors: agricultural research, marketing, and direct health/nutrition interventions. The present chapter strongly supports the proposed interventions, and particularly the approach of treating hunger and malnutrition as problems requiring a multi-sectoral response. The causal pathways leading to malnutrition lie in many sectors – health, agriculture, water and sanitation, food systems, and economic development – and sustainable improvements in nutrition and food security may often require interventions in all of them.

Implementing multi-sectoral interventions poses a challenge to the estimation of BCRs. Quantifying the costs of nutritional insult – whether stunting and wasting, specific micronutrient deficiencies, or nutrition-related chronic disease – is perhaps more straightforward than identifying and attributing the costs of a particular component in a package of interventions to an impact which is the result of the interaction of several actions working together. This is especially relevant in cases where multiple interventions are required for any one of them to achieve its potential impact – as is the case, for example, with improving food consumption and reducing exposure to infection as means to address child growth retardation. In cases where the sequencing of interventions is critical, the same approach may be effective or ineffective depending on whether critical preconditions for success have been put in place, so attributing a given impact to the later intervention alone may be misleading. It is noted on p. 378 that improved agricultural productivity and smallholder income may be a prerequisite for increasing the quality and quantity of food consumed in the household, but explicit interventions focused on behavior change are necessary in order to realize the potential nutritional effects of these improvements in resources. This argues for a flexible approach to benefit-cost estimation, with a focus on addressing the most urgent and costly problems and, through implementing and evaluating the best available interventions, building the evidence base for selecting the most effective and cost-effective combined multi-sectoral approaches.

The intervention package proposed in the chapter is well justified. Nonetheless, there are additional elements that could well be included. The chapter explicitly rejects consideration of what is commonly (and misleadingly) called "overnutrition" – that is, the rising problem in the developing world of nutrition-related chronic diseases linked to overweight, obesity, and physical inactivity. These chronic diseases are increasing in prevalence among poor populations in low-income countries and CMICs, and their high cost in terms of lost productivity and increased demand for health care poses a threat to economic progress. Further, there are strong reasons to link approaches to addressing undernutrition with those to address chronic disease: the demonstrated relationship between early nutritional deprivation and later susceptibility to obesity and chronic disease, and the fact that increasing access to health care and capacity in the health care system will benefit both sets of health issues.

* Thanks for helpful comments from Will Masters, Brooke Colaiezzi, and Amelia Fischer.

This chapter elaborates on these points, with the goal of complementing the suggestions incorporated in Chaper 6 and contributing an additional perspective to the process of identifying priority actions to promote economic development and the improved well-being of poor and vulnerable populations.

Combining and sequencing interventions

Chapter 6 makes an important contribution in proposing a combination of interventions to improve health and reduce undernutrition. It seems intuitively obvious that addressing the multiple constraints to nutrition and food security will be more successful than dealing with single approaches or single nutrients. BCR estimates are difficult enough for single interventions, but such an estimation for combined interventions is much more so. If a combined intervention is effective, and in the absence of full-factorial experimental designs to test all possible combinations, attribution of a benefit to one or another component is not difficult, but impossible. (IFPRI's evaluations of CCTs in Nicaragua did in fact implement a full-factorial design, testing combinations of "supply-side" – improving the quality of service – and "demand-side" – providing a CT – for the relative contribution of each to the overall goals of the program (Maluccio and Flores, 2005). Such studies are very useful, but also costly and therefore rare.) This is in no way an argument for implementing only isolated, unitary nutrition interventions; bundling interventions for maximum impact is quite valuable – essential, in fact – but the CBAs will generally have to be for the combined intervention rather than for each individual element. Webb and Block (2010) rightly argue for the development of new measures to account for the interactive and cumulative effect of multiple policies, to go beyond techniques that link single policies to unitary outcomes.

There are two ways to think about combining interventions. One is to consider that each intervention by itself may be necessary, but not sufficient to achieve the nutrition, health, or economic benefit anticipated. A good example of this would be the provision of supplementary food to children to promote linear growth and prevent stunting in the absence of complementary interventions to improve household hygiene practices and environmental sanitation, including access to adequate and safe water. In a food-scarce environment, either one alone may be insufficient to prevent, much less reverse, stunting. A second is to recognize that there are interventions that depend for their effectiveness on certain preconditions being in place; the example given here is the uptake of agricultural improvements before the establishment of agricultural markets that create the potential for farmers to benefit from them.

Combining food access with safe water and sanitation

The evidence to support the provision of food supplements to pregnant and lactating women and children up to the age of 2 in order to prevent growth retardation is strong, but the evidence for the potential for catch-up growth after that age is mixed. Martorell *et al.* (1990, 1994) argue that there is very limited potential for catch-up growth after the age of 2, but Golden (1994) holds that the reason that catch-up growth is not observed is that the conditions that led to early childhood stunting are rarely changed. It has been suggested (Solomons *et al.*, 1993; McKay *et al.*, 2010; Kau *et al.*, 2011) that a major cause of impaired linear growth in children is the presence of low-level infection: environmental stress on the immune system produces pro-inflammatory cytokines that impair the metabolic pathways that promote bone growth. It is also argued that asymptomatic gastrointestinal enteropathies can cause gut abnormalities and impair nutrient absorption, leading to growth failure (Lunn, 2002; Guerrant *et al.*, 2008; Humphrey, 2009).

It is well recognized that frequent diarrheal infections are an independent risk factor for child undernutrition (Brown, 2003). A multi-country study by Checkley *et al.* (2008) showed a dose-response relationship between diarrheal disease burden and subsequent growth faltering: the odds of being stunted at 24 months increased significantly with each additional episode of diarrhea prior to that age. Humphrey (2009), however, argues that tropical enteropathies significantly outweigh diarrhea as a cause of growth retardation, and suggests that an exclusive focus on diarrhea results in underestimation of the contribution of improved water and sanitation to child growth. Further, she suggests, these conditions explain why food supplementation does not fully achieve adequate growth in malnourished children (Dewey and Adu-Afarunah, 2008).

Whatever the mechanism, the association of water and sanitation with malnutrition is clear. Studies by Merchant *et al.* (2003) and Checkley *et al.* (2004) demonstrate the contribution of access to safe water and sanitation to reductions in child stunting. Initial access to safe water and the change in access to safe water over time were found to be significant predictors of improvements in stunting prevalence after controlling for a wide range of factors including household food supply in a cross-country, longitudinal analysis (Milman *et al.*, 2005). The effectiveness of food supplementation is compromised by infection; to reach his/her growth potential, a child needs both adequate food *and* protection from infectious disease.

Estimates of the cost-effectiveness of improved water and sanitation are mixed (Ahuja *et al.*, 2010), in part because the measures of these interventions vary widely. Access to piped water (a measure of achievement of the MDG for water) does not by itself assure that the water is microbiologically safe (Kayser, 2011). Both water quality and environmental sanitation contribute to diarrheal disease incidence (Fewtrell *et al.*, 2005). Still, the evidence is very strong that *safe* water is strongly associated with reduced diarrheal disease (Clasen *et al.*, 2007; Ahuja *et al.*, 2010), which may be a marker for other infections as well; such infection in turn is associated with inadequate child growth.

These studies taken together argue that in the absence of significant improvement in water quality and sanitation, food supplements will not be able to achieve adequate growth, much less catch-up growth in settings where sanitation, and water quality are poor. Therefore, the two interventions – one addressing inadequate diet and another addressing water, sanitation and hygiene – need to be implemented together for either one to have a substantial impact on child stunting. This means that BCR estimation for one intervention may be misleading, making it seem less effective than its potential would be if other constraints on adequate growth were addressed.

This further suggests that the critical contribution of water and sanitation interventions to achieving reductions in child undernutrition is underemphasized in Chapter 6. Along with interventions to improve food consumption, parallel efforts to increase access to safe water and improve sanitation should be included in the "bundle" of interventions proposed in order to achieve the desired reductions in childhood stunting.

Establishing the conditions for uptake of agricultural improvements

A second aspect of the proposal to implement combined interventions has to do with their appropriate sequencing. An example here is the development of improved seeds (higher-yielding, drought- and salt-tolerant, adapted to the local conditions of smallholders in target regions) and the promotion of demand for fertilizer through a reduction in price. Demand for fertilizer among smallholder farmers may indeed be constrained by price and access (including access to credit), but in the short run it is conditioned more on farmers' perception of the marginal benefit of using such inputs (Byerlee and de Polanco, 1986; Lindert, 2000). The adoption of new seeds that are responsive to fertilizer should eventually result in demand for fertilizer, especially if farmers are at the same time linked to markets, so that their increased production can be translated into increased income, providing the resources to purchase inputs; but response to a lower fertilizer price may be disappointing if adoption of improved seed varieties does not precede it.

Similarly, the ability of the proposed interventions – improved seeds (appropriate to the crops and context of smallholder farmers), cheaper fertilizer, better market information – to improve household income, and thereby at least potentially the nutritional status of children, depends on having a functioning market at the regional and national level. Continued use of improved seeds and purchased agricultural inputs depends on commercialization of these crops, so that sales can fund future purchases of inputs. To benefit sustainably from the proposed package of agricultural interventions, farmers must be able to gain access to a functioning market. This is not only a matter of sequencing interventions; it is equally a matter of institutional and economic context. Factors such as market infrastructure, marketing and trade regimes, and small-farmer integration into regional, national, or international markets (individually or as part of a farmers' organization) will affect the success of interventions aimed at smallholders.

The proposed package of interventions for reducing stunting and micronutrient deficiencies includes elements known to be both effective in addressing undernutrition and cost-effective in terms of expected impact on economic growth (Bhutta *et al.*, 2008). Direct provision of food supplements to pregnant/lactating women and children aged 6–23 months has been demonstrated to be effective in reducing rates of stunting, especially if given preventively (that is, provided to at-risk populations, not conditional on being stunted or wasted before receiving the supplement) (Ruel *et al.*, 2008). Nonetheless, in contexts where absolute food scarcity is not a constraint, behavior-change strategies that promote the appropriate use of locally available (purchased or home-produced) foods for complementary feeding of weanlings may be a cost-effective option. This is a case where, again, sequencing may be critical: increased agricultural productivity, more food available in the household, and increased income to permit food purchases are likely to be essential precursors to the promotion of the use of local food as a substitute for the direct provision of supplementary food to prevent stunting and wasting. (Clearly, this argument does not apply to therapeutic food in emergencies or for the treatment of acute malnutrition, where immediate provision of nutrient-dense food is critical to assuring rapid recovery and avoiding the high risk of mortality.)

Finally, the BCR estimates incorporated into the IMPACT model analysis need to take account of the non-linear relationship between cost and benefit. As a higher percentage of the target group is reached, it becomes more costly to reach the remaining 10 or 20 percent. This non-linearity has been explicitly recognized in the BCR estimates associated with the "Scaling up Nutrition" initiative to bring nutrition interventions to low-income populations (Horton *et al.*, 2010). Ecker *et al.* (2012) note, for example, that malnutrition is less responsive to economic growth as its prevalence declines. The reasons are twofold: presumably it is the remote, hard-to reach populations that will be the last to benefit from any intervention and the most costly to reach due to their remoteness; but it is also likely that the causal pathways underlying nutritional outcomes may be different, perhaps more intractable, but in any case possibly requiring different approaches to benefit that small remaining percentage.

Strengthening agriculture: nutrition linkages

Hoddinott (2011), in his introduction to the Delhi conference on Agriculture–Nutrition Linkages, lays out a rich and comprehensive set of pathways by which improved agricultural productivity might affect the nutritional status of farm household members, especially children. These pathways are entirely plausible, and some have been documented in particular settings. But while agricultural development may play a key role in improving child nutrition status through increasing rural household income and crop productivity, increased food production does not necessarily nor automatically lead to improved nutrition outcomes. Furthermore, these pathways and linkages are culturally and geographically diverse. The impact of similar agricultural programs on nutritional outcomes may vary by context. The relationship between production, income, and nutrition is neither direct nor simple, and depends on social and economic factors specific to the geographic context (Marsh 1998; von Braun 2002).

A review of the links between agricultural interventions and nutrition outcomes (Berti *et al.*, 2003) found mixed evidence of direct benefits on children's or adults' anthropometric status, although most had significant impacts on household food production. Home gardens were more consistently associated with nutritional improvement, presumably because these interventions were typically implemented in the context of explicitly nutrition-focused programs that included other components such as behavior-change communication. The review found that when agricultural interventions were combined with nutrition education, dietary improvement was more likely, but also found that changing household diets did not always correlate closely with anthropometric status. They conclude that health and nutritional status are not consistently responsive to agricultural interventions without complementary efforts focused explicitly on nutritional outcomes.

A simulation of agricultural investment strategies in Tanzania (Pauw and Thurlow, 2012) similarly concluded that agricultural growth had inconsistent impacts on poverty, calorie insufficiency, and undernutrition; the effects were dependent on growth in the agricultural sectors where smallholders are concentrated: production of staple crops such as maize, root crops, oil seeds, and pulses, since these are produced by low-income farmers, and their increased production (in the simulation) lowered prices for these foods, which are disproportionately consumed by the poor. This suggests that yield improvements in the right crops have the potential to affect food consumption of the poor, but there is still an intra-household process by which household food consumption translates into the nutritional status of its members.

These observations suggest that agricultural interventions need to be designed with local context in mind in order to produce nutritional benefits, and underline the importance of ensuring that the proposed agricultural strategies end up reaching the smallholder farmers who are the presumed beneficiaries, and to integrate improvements in agricultural production and marketing with explicit nutrition programs that translate production and income gains into nutritional benefit.

Addressing the rising problem of overweight/obesity and chronic disease

Childhood undernutrition is without a doubt the most pressing nutrition priority for global development. According to UNICEF's most recent statistics (UNICEF, 2012), sixty-six countries in the world have a prevalence of childhood stunting of 25 percent or more, and thirty-one countries have prevalence over 40 percent. There are twenty-seven countries with a 10 percent or higher prevalence of wasting among children below 5 years of age. The average prevalence of childhood stunting is 39 percent in SSA, and reaches 47 percent in south Asia (34 percent for Asia as a whole); comparable figures for wasting are 9 percent for SSA and 19 percent for South Asia. The problems of micronutrient deficiency highlighted in earlier Copenhagen Consensus papers are far from eliminated. These statistics are unarguable and compel continued attention to these issues.

Nonetheless, the time has passed when it is reasonable to ignore the rising prevalence of overweight and obesity and associated chronic disease in the developing world. Rates of overweight and obesity in low-income countries have reached levels comparable to those of high-income countries (Beaglehole *et al.*, 2007), and the incidence of non-communicable chronic diseases (NCCDs), including coronary heart disease and stroke, diabetes, chronic pulmonary disease, and cancer, is rising rapidly (Beaglehole *et al.*, 2007). Deaths and DALYs from NCCDs in low-income countries are projected to exceed, by a wide margin, deaths from undernutrition and infectious disease by 2015, and to increase sharply by 2030 (WHO, 2008). Developing countries including India, Indonesia, and Pakistan, as well as China and Brazil, are among the top ten countries for prevalence of diabetes (IDB, 2009). Previous Copenhagen Consensus papers have rightly focused on the nutritional status of children at risk of undernutrition. Global efforts on "Scaling Up Nutrition" similarly focus primarily on the needs of young children at risk, based on recognition of the critical importance of the "first 1,000 days" in determining the health of a child into adulthood (Horton *et al.*, 2010; Shekar *et al.*, 2011). Chronic disease, of course, primarily affects adults, although adults under 60 in low-income countries are far more likely to suffer morbidity and mortality from chronic disease than those in developed countries (Nugent, 2008).

Given the current significance and rapidly rising burden of chronic disease in CMICs, addressing them is justified as a priority for investment in economic development for several reasons. First, the economic cost of these diseases is substantial. Costs to the existing health care system are significant, but in low-income countries, where much of the population does not have access to high-quality health care, the major cost is from lost economic contributions due to disability and premature death (Abegunde *et al.*, 2007b). Further, it is no longer the case (if it ever was) that chronic disease can be considered a "disease of affluence." It is true that wasting and stunting fall and obesity rises with GDP growth and the population shift out of agriculture – an increase of 4.4 percent for every 10 percent increase in GDP (Webb and Block, 2010). But overweight, obesity, and chronic disease are rising rapidly in the poorest countries (WHO/FAO, 2002; Popkin, 2009; Finucane *et al.*, 2011). The "double burden" of undernutrition and infectious disease, along with overweight/obesity and chronic disease, is posing serious challenges to the health care systems and to prospects for continued economic development in many LMICs, including India and China as well as those in SSA – regions that are the target of the interventions proposed in Chapter 6 (as well as "Scaling Up Nutrition" efforts).

Second, the evidence is strong that the risk of chronic disease in adulthood is related to health and nutritional status in early childhood (Hales *et al.*, 1991; Barker *et al.*, 1993; Joseph and Kramer, 1996; Prentice and Moore, 2005; Calkins and Devaskar, 2011) – in the "first 1,000 days" – which suggests that the benefits of improving nutrition in early childhood include a reduction in chronic disease in later life. The arguments for investing in childhood undernutrition and for investing in the prevention and control of chronic disease converge in this case.

A third argument for investing in the prevention and control of chronic diseases is that even beyond the protective effect of early-child nutrition, there is likely significant overlap, and large potential synergy, between interventions aimed at children and those aimed at adults at risk. Among the priority interventions recommended in the *Lancet* series on Chronic Disease (Beaglehole *et al.*, 2007) and by the WHO Task Force on Chronic Disease (WEF/WHO, 2011), strengthening the primary health care system and increasing access to it in order to permit behavior-change communication, screening, and the distribution of medications to those at highest risk (or already suffering from chronic disease) again converges with the priorities for reaching undernourished children and their mothers with growth monitoring, primary care, and the provision of micronutrient and food supplements. It is very much in the spirit of Chapter 6 to emphasize potential synergies in the proposed interventions between agricultural and targeted nutrition interventions; addressing chronic disease adds another layer of potential benefit to these health interventions.

Finally, there have been few documented successes in reversing the trend toward higher prevalence of overweight and obesity through changes in diet and physical activity. WHO (2009) identifies characteristics of successful efforts to promote physical activity; these are largely modifications in the built environment and local services (sidewalks, amenities within walking distance, recreational facilities). But overweight and obesity continue to rise in the developing world (Popkin, 2009), and there is little evidence of a potential to reverse the trend. Chronic disease prevalence continues to rise as well, although the rate of increase in adult BMI appears to slow at higher incomes (Nugent, 2008). Interventions that focus on prevention may possibly have a higher likelihood of success than interventions to reverse the process once it is far advanced.

Chronic disease as a health and development priority

The "double burden" of malnutrition – that is, the coexistence in a single country of high rates of child undernutrition and infectious disease along with high and rising rates of overweight, obesity, and chronic disease, has been documented in developing countries in all regions of the world (FAO, 2006). According to WHO (2009), chronic disease risk factors (high blood pressure, high blood glucose, physical inactivity, tobacco and indoor smoke exposure, and high cholesterol) account for almost 28 percent of attributable mortality in low-income countries, compared to 7.8 percent of deaths due to child undernutrition and another 3.4 percent due to poor breast-feeding practices.

(Infectious disease does not make it into the top ten risk factors, though unsafe water, sanitation, and hygiene add 6.1 percent to attributable mortality.) The Institute of Medicine (IoM) finds that CVD accounts for 30 percent of all mortality in LMICs (Fuster and Kelley, 2011). High cholesterol and blood glucose, high blood pressure, and physical inactivity together account for 19.6 percent of deaths in low-income countries. In middle-income countries, over 45 percent of deaths are due to these four factors plus poor diet (low fruit/vegetable intake). The picture is reversed for DALYs, with child underweight and micronutrient deficiencies accounting for more attributable DALYs than chronic disease risk factors: 18.1 percent compared with 8.1 percent for chronic disease risk factors (counting only those in the top ten risk factors). Nonetheless, chronic diseases are associated with significantly lower life expectancy (WHO, 2009) and a long period of disability before death.

More than 84 percent of diseases associated with chronic disease risk factors occur in LMICs (WHO, 2009; WEF/HSPH, 2011). Only in south Asia and SSA, the two regions with the highest prevalence of child undernutrition, are risk factors for chronic disease present in less than 50 percent of the adult population (Nugent, 2008), but rates there are rising, and the rate of increase in factors such as overweight and physical inactivity appears to become greater as prevalence rises (Martorell *et al.*, 2000). CVD is now the second leading cause of adult death in SSA (FAO, 2006); rates of diabetes in that region doubled between 1994 and 2010 (FAO, 2006). Rates in Latin America are similarly projected to rise (Kain *et al.*, 2003).

The economic cost of chronic disease in low-income countries is high and rising. Nugent (2008) reports WHO estimates that the annual cost of chronic disease in twenty-three developing countries will reach $84 billion in the ten years to 2015 (Abegunde *et al.*, 2007b). Other estimates put the economic cost for low-income countries at $310 million, and for LMICs at $1.85 trillion over the period 2011–2025 (Abegunde and Stanciole, 2006). The cost in terms of lost GDP in LMICs has been estimated as being as high as 4 percent (WEF/WHO, 2011). It has been estimated that each 10 percent rise in chronic disease mortality slows economic growth by 0.5 percent in LMICs (Stuckler *et al.*, 2010). Thus chronic disease poses a serious threat to the pace of economic development (WHO, 2004a). WHO has also identified NCCDs as a significant barrier to achievement of the MDGs (WHO, 2008a), since chronic disease results in disability and death that can precipitate a fall into poverty due to both medical costs and lost earnings (as demonstrated by Mahal *et al.*, 2010, for India).

Chronic disease is now recognized as an important health issue in LMICs. The UN World Health Assembly, convened in 2004, adopted a Global Strategy on Diet, Physical Activity and Health, and in 2005 WHO developed the Framework Convention on Tobacco Control (Uauy and Kain 2002; Beaglehole *et al.*, 2007). An influential series published in *Lancet* (*Lancet* 370, 2007) drew attention to the problem of chronic disease in the developing world, and provided estimates of the economic and health burden, with recommendations and cost estimates for interventions to address the risk factors. A subsequent series published in 2010 (*Lancet* 376) provided more detailed assessments of the health and economic costs, and the effectiveness and cost of possible interventions. The UN High Level Meeting on Non-Communicable Diseases, convened in September 2011, represented a convergence of opinion on the importance of these diseases, and provided an opportunity to promote coordinated national and global action to address them.

Clearly, it is time to consider chronic disease, along with undernutrition, as a challenge to economic progress that should not be ignored.

Links of chronic disease with poverty and undernutrition

The rise of chronic disease in the developing world is linked to lifestyle changes that are occurring rapidly in low-income countries: increased access to supermarkets (Reardon *et al.*, 2003; Witherspoon and Reardon, 2003) and other sources of refined foods high in fat, salt, and sugar (Popkin and Nielsen, 2003; Popkin, 2006); availability of mechanized transportation, and mechanization of labor (Webb and Block, 2010). Many researchers cite urbanization as a factor in the disease process (WEF/WHO, 2011), but there is evidence that the same process is operating in both rural and urban areas (Popkin and Gordon-Larsen, 2004; Mendez *et al.*, 2005), suggesting the possibility of similar interventions in both areas, though the challenge of delivering services in rural areas is likely to be higher.

Low-income populations exposed to nutritional deprivation *in utero* or in the first two years of life are at higher risk of chronic disease if, in later life, they have access to a more abundant, calorie-dense diet (Barker *et al.*, 1993; Joseph and Kramer, 1996; Prentice and Moore, 2005), consistent with the hypothesis advanced by Barker and his colleagues in 1986 (Barker and Osmond, 1986; Barker *et al.*, 1989; see also Erikkson *et al.*, 1999). There is evidence that in children born with intrauterine growth restriction (IUGR), rapid growth up to the age of 2 results in accumulation of lean body mass and has positive health benefits, while rapid growth in stunted children after the age of 2 risks accretion of adiposity, with consequent health risks including hormone-related cancers (breast, prostate) as well as CVD (Newsome *et al.*, 2003; Sachdev *et al.*, 2005; Wells *et al.*, 2005; Victora *et al.*, 2007; Victora *et al.*, 2008). Investing in prevention of chronic disease starts with addressing undernutrition in children, and a corollary is that obesity prevention is an especially high priority for those undernourished in early life.

Beyond childhood, chronic disease risk factors are no longer characteristic of those with higher income. The poorest populations in the poorest nations have high rates of obesity, and the burden of obesity is shifting to the poor in these countries (Popkin, 2009). In thirty-six low-income countries, overweight exceeds underweight in both rural and urban areas (Mendez *et al.*, 2005). Monteiro *et al.* (2004a, 2004b) have estimated that overweight and obesity become problems of lower-income populations within a given country at a *per capita* GDP around $2,500, a relatively high level when compared with the incomes of the countries with the highest burden of childhood undernutrition (*Lancet* 371 countries). But overweight and obesity represent only one of many risk factors for chronic disease; the prevalence of NCCDs is greater than that of overweight/obesity, and is more skewed toward the poorer populations even in low-income countries (Popkin, 2009); and the poor are less likely to receive treatment for NCCDs due to lack of access and affordability of preventive health care (Nugent, 2008). Furthermore, resource-constrained governments are more apt to fund basic health services, as outlined in the UN MDGs, rather than the prevention and treatment of NCCDs (WEF/HSPH, 2011) although, as noted above, extending the reach and capacity of basic health services contributes to addressing chronic disease as well as infectious disease and maternal and child health.

Chronic disease priorities for intervention, their cost and effectiveness

As already noted, the United Nations convened a High Level Meeting on Non-Communicable Diseases in September 2011 to focus attention on the importance of implementing cost-effective, achievable interventions to prevent and treat NCCDs in LMICs. The meeting built on the work of the World Economic Forum and Harvard School of Public Health to identify priority actions for reducing the impact of chronic disease (WEF/HSPH, 2011). The actions, defined as "Best Buys," were recommended based on three factors: (a) feasibility; (b) reasonable cost; (c) demonstrated effectiveness. The aggregated cost of these interventions was estimated in this study at about $500 billion a year, or 4 percent of the combined annual output of the LMICs considered in the analysis.

Not all the interventions recommended at the Meeting relate to nutrition. Their recommendations for top-five priorities for addressing chronic disease are: reducing the use of tobacco to a target level of 4 percent; reducing the consumption of salt; improving dietary quality (increased fruit and vegetable consumption, reduced consumption of sugar, saturated, and trans fats) and increasing physical activity; reducing abuse of alcohol; and, finally, targeted counseling and medical intervention for individuals at high risk or already suffering from chronic disease (CVD, cancer, diabetes, chronic respiratory disease).

The first four are addressed at the population level, through a combination of taxes, regulation, and communication strategies. The last is targeted at individuals and makes use of the primary health care system to screen, counsel, and prescribe medications for high-risk patients. The WEF/HSPH study estimated costs and benefits for this set of interventions in the forty-two LMICs that represent 90 percent of the chronic disease burden. As would be expected, population-based strategies are far less costly than those targeted at individuals. The total package of "Best-Buy" interventions is estimated to cost $11.4 billion per year, of which only $2 billion is for the population-based interventions, and about $2 billion represent private costs (cost to patients of participating in screening and treatment). However, as Nugent (2008) points out, the evidence base for the effectiveness of population-based measures is weak, and even more so in LMICs.

The preventive strategies proposed by WHO include taxing and regulating access to tobacco and alcohol; work place interventions to reduce smoking; health information campaigns; and restrictions on advertising these products. Dietary interventions include working with the food industry to reduce salt and replace saturated and trans fats with healthier fats, as well as advertising and mass media campaigns to promote healthier diets and physical activity. The targeted strategies delivered through the health care system include screening for CVD and diabetes risk, and provision of a multi-drug regimen targeting blood pressure and cholesterol and including aspirin, as well as immunizing for hepatitis B. These cost estimates have a time horizon of fifteen years, from 2011–2025, and are based on a target of 80 percent population coverage.

The authors recognize that time is required to develop sufficient reach and capacity in the primary health care system, but may be optimistic in assuming only a one-year lag compared with the implementation of population-based interventions. Direct treatment need not depend only on doctors, but could be incorporated into the work of community-based health workers, allowing for greater coverage at lower cost (Abegunde *et al.*, 2007a), but still would require training and capacity-building as well as expanded outreach.

This package of interventions is viewed as having a highly favorable BCR. For example, the WEF/HSPH report estimates that achieving a 10 percent reduction in CVD would reduce economic losses by $25 billion annually, about three times the estimated cost of the interventions. However the basis for the 10 percent figure for expected impact is not given.

Cecchini *et al.* (2010), in a simulation analysis of six countries, find that price interventions (taxation) produce the most rapid gains. The most cost-effective measures in their analysis include taxes, regulation (restricting access to tobacco and alcohol), and work place interventions. They note that obesity, diet quality, and physical activity are targeted by similar interventions, and suggest that all the proposed interventions have synergies in addressing multiple chronic diseases, improving the benefit cost picture.

Beaglehole *et al.* (2007) estimated the annual cost of interventions proposed by the Chronic Disease Action Group to cost $5.8 billion a year in the twenty-three highest-burden countries (2005$), again with a highly favorable BCR. Similar to the WEF/HSPH study, they find population-based interventions to be less costly: $1.1 billion p.a. for the twenty-three countries, compared with $4.7 billion for individual medical attention. Their estimate is that an achievable reduction in salt consumption of 15 percent would avert 13.8 million deaths between 2006 and 2015 at a cost of $1 billion p.a.; individual screening and multi-drug treatment could avert 17.9 million deaths over the same period at a cost of $4.7 billion.

Meanwhile, the IOM report on cardiovascular health emphasizes that chronic disease requires a multi-sectoral, coordinated approach that involves agricultural policy, urban planning, and transportation policy to promote physical activity, taxes and regulations to affect the food supply as well as access to tobacco and alcohol, and mass media campaigns and capacity-building within the public health system (Fuster and Kelly, 2011). Such coordinated and potentially synergistic approaches are exceedingly difficult to cost, but most of the literature recognizes the need to move beyond unitary to multi-sectoral approaches.

Many of these estimates are based on simulation models that have significant error associated with them. Good empirical information on the costs and effectiveness of interventions is lacking, and (as mentioned earlier), BCR estimates are typically unable to account for potential synergies (for example, other benefits from improving access to the primary health system; multiple benefits from single public health campaigns) or diseconomies. Nonetheless there is little question that investment in the prevention and treatment of chronic disease in LMICs, including those suffering from the "double burden" of undernutrition and chronic disease, can have significant pay-offs for health and well-being as well as for poverty reduction and economic development through more years of healthy life.

The policies proposed by the UN Task Force incorporate exercise and dietary modification, on the assumption that both of these approaches would address the calorie imbalance between intake and expenditure that is at the root of obesity. Some analysts lay the blame for the obesity epidemic in the developed world on the productivity of agriculture and the ready availability of abundant and cheap food (Schoonover and Muller, 2006; Bleich *et al.*, 2007), but in countries facing the "double burden," it is a policy challenge to devise policies that address undernutrition while not exacerbating the problems of excess. Price policies need to be carefully framed, and feeding programs carefully designed to promote healthy consumption and discourage unhealthy consumption without jeopardizing their ability to address nutritional insufficiency.

Future research needs

The BCR estimates incorporated into these figures are based on assumptions about the presumed potential effect of regulations, labeling, mass media campaigns, and work place interventions on outcomes such as salt consumption, tobacco and alcohol use, diet and physical activity, but empirical support for the effectiveness of specific interventions in developing country contexts is sparse at best. Many of the action plans described above rightly call for more rigorous assessment and recommend allocating substantial resources to developing the evidence base for designing effective and cost-effective programs, and to incorporate assessment of coordinated multiple interventions. There can be no question that chronic disease is emerging as a major threat to health and well-being, and to poverty reduction and economic growth, but estimating the cost associated with this burden is more straightforward than assessing the potential impacts and BCRs of specific programs.

Given the need for individual medical intervention, research into better and lower-cost methods of screening would also be a useful target for future research.

Nonetheless, action should not be conditioned on such studies; rather, action on this front will provide the basis for future evaluation and the design of more effective and cost-effective means to reduce the spread of chronic disease risk.

Summary and conclusions

This chapter has suggested some additional considerations to complement the proposals in Chapter 6. These points are summarized below.

- The effectiveness of multiple interventions depends on their appropriate combination and sequencing; the effectiveness of some of the suggested interventions, policies, and programs depends on others already being in place.
- In addition to the sectors mentioned, water and sanitation may be critical inputs into the prevention of child growth retardation.
- Assessing the BCRs of combined, multi-sectoral interventions is far more challenging than calculating such ratios for one single intervention at a time; estimates of the cost-effectiveness of the contribution of individual components of an integrated package of different interventions may in many cases not be realistic to achieve.
- This in no way argues against implementing combined and multi-sectoral interventions; indeed, such packages of interventions have a higher likelihood of sustainable success than isolated interventions. Implementing multi-sectoral activities with the explicit goal of evaluation can

contribute to the empirical basis for choosing interventions.

- It is critical to recognize that improvements in agricultural productivity, even if targeted appropriately to poor smallholder farmers, will not automatically translate into improvement in the diet, and thus the nutritional status, of vulnerable household members. Explicit nutrition-focused efforts are needed to ensure that the potential nutritional impact of these improvements is realized.
- The rapidly rising prevalence of risk factors for NCCDs (including overweight/obesity and physical inactivity) in low-income countries and LMICs, and of the NCCDs themselves, constitutes a serious threat to the health and well-being of poor populations in poor countries, and a challenge to their economic progress. These conditions are costly in terms of lost income due to DALYs and premature death as well as health care, and efforts to prevent them are likely to be cost-effective.
- Dietary and epidemiologic transitions exacerbate the threat of childhood undernutrition because of the relationship between early-life undernutrition and increased risk of overweight/obesity and chronic disease later in life.
- Investment in improved access to health care and in interventions to prevent and treat both undernutrition in early life and chronic disease risks in older children and adults represents a convergence of goals.
- Research is needed on effective interventions to prevent and reverse the rise of NCCDs and their risk factors, and on methods of assessing their BCRs, but action should not be delayed on this account; rather, action to address these problems can provide the basis for expanding the evidence base for future actions.

Bibliography

Abegunde, D. and A. Stanciole, 2006: An estimation of the economic impact of chronic noncommunicable diseases in selected countries, *WHO Working Paper, Department of Chronic Diseases and Health Promotion (CHP)*

Abegunde, D. O., C. D. Mathers, T. Adam, M. Ortegon, and K. Strong, 2007b: The burden and costs of chronic diseases in low-income and middle-income countries, *Lancet* **370**, 1929–38

Abegunde, D. O., B. Shengelia, A. Luyten *et al.*, 2007a: Can non-physician health-care workers assess and manage cardiovascular risk in primary care?, *Bulletin of the World Health Organization* **85**, 432–40

Ahuja, A., M. Kremer, and A. Peterson Zwane, 2010: Providing safe water: evidence from randomized evaluations, *Annual Review of Resource Economics* **2**, 237–56

Alwan, A., D. R. MacLean, L. M. Riley *et al.*, 2010: Monitoring and surveillance of chronic non-communicable diseases: progress and capacity in high burden countries, *Lancet* **376**, 1861–8

Asaria, P., D. Chisholm, C. Mathers, M. Ezzati, and R. Beaglehole, 2007: Chronic disease prevention: health effects and financial costs of strategies to reduce salt intake and control tobacco use, *Lancet* **370**, 2044–53

Barker, D. J. and C. Osmond, 1986: Infant mortality, childhood nutrition, and ischaemic heart disease in England and Wales, *Lancet* **1**, 1077–81

Barker, D., C. Osmond, J. Golding, D. Kuh, and M. E. Wadsworth, 1989: Growth in utero, blood pressure in childhood and adult life, and mortality from cardiovascular disease, *British Medical Journal* **298**, 564–7

Barker, D. J., P. D. Gluckman, K. M. Godfrey, J. E. Harding, J. A. Owens, and J. S. Robinson, 1993: Fetal nutrition and cardiovascular disease in adult life, *Lancet* **341**, 938–41

Beaglehole, R., S. Ebrahim, S. Reddy *et al.*, 2007: Prevention of chronic disease: a call to action, *Lancet* **370**, 2152–7

Berti, P. R., J. Krasavec, and S. FitzGerald, 2003: A review of the effectiveness of agriculture interventions in improving nutrition outcomes, *Public Health Nutrition* **7**, 599–609

Bhutta, Z. A., T. Ahmed, R. E. Black *et al.*, 2008: What works? Interventions for maternal and child undernutrition and survival, *Lancet* **371**, 417–40

Bleich, S., D. Cutler, C. Murray, and A. Adams, 2007: Why is the developed world obese? *National Bureau of Economic Research Working Paper No.* **12954**, Cambridge, MA

Briend, A., 1990: Is diarrhoea a major cause of malnutrition among the under-fives in developing countries? A review of available evidence, *European Journal of Clinical Nutrition* **44**, 611–28

Brown, K., 2003: Diarrhea and malnutrition, *Journal of Nutrition*, **133**, 328S–332S

Byerlee, D. and E. Hesse de Polanco, 1986: Farmers' stepwise adoption of technological packages: evidence from the Mexican Altiplano, *American Journal of Agricultural Economics* **68**, 519–27

Calkins, K. and S. U. Devaskar, 2011: Fetal origins of adult disease, *Current Problems in Pediatric and Adolescent Health Care* **41**, 158–76

Cecchini, M., F. Sassi, J. A. Lauer *et al.*, 2010: Talking of unhealthy diets, physical inactivity, and obesity: health effects and cost effectiveness, *Lancet* **376**, 1775–84

Checkley, W., R. H. Gilman, R. E. Black, L. D. Epstein, L. Cabrera, C. R. Sterling, and L. H. Moulton, 2004: Effect of water and sanitation on childhood health in a poor Peruvian peri-urban community, *Lancet* **363**, 112–18

Checkley, W., G. Buckley, R. H. Gilman, A. M. Assis, R. L. Guerrant, S. S. Morris, K. Molbak, P. Valentiner-Branth, and R. E. Black, 2008: Multi-country analysis of the effects of diarrhoea on childhood stunting, *International Journal of Epidemiology* **37**, 816–30

Chow, C. K., K. Lock, K. Teo, S. V. Subramanian, M. McKee, and S. Yusuf, 2009: Environmental and societal influences acting on cardiovascular risk factors and disease at a population level: a review, *International Journal of Epidemiology* **38**, 1580–94

Clasen, T., I. Roberts, T. Rabie, W. Schmidt, and S. Cairncross, 2007: Interventions to improve water quality for preventing diarrhea: systematic review and meta-analysis, *British Medical Journal* **334**, 755–6

Dewey, K. G. and S. Adu-Afarwuah, 2008: Systematic review of the efficacy and effectiveness of complementary feeding interventions in developing countries, in *Maternal and Child Nutrition*. Blackwell, Oxford, Program in International and Community Nutrition, University of California, Davis, CA, 24–85

Dillingham, R. and R. L. Guerrant, 2004: Childhood stunting: measuring and stemming the staggering costs of inadequate water and sanitation, *Lancet* **363**, 94–5

Du, S., T. A. Mroz, F. Zhai, and B. M. Popkin, 2004: Rapid income growth adversely affects diet quality in China – particularly for the poor! *Social Science Medicine* **59**, 1505–15

Ecker, O. L., C. Breisinger, and K. Pauw, 2012: Reshaping agriculture, in S. Fan and R. Pandya-Lorch (eds.), *Reshaping Agriculture for Nutrition and Health*, IFPRI, Washington, DC

Eriksson, J. G., *et al.*, 1999: Catch-up growth in childhood and death from coronary heart disease: a longitudinal study, *British Medical Journal* **318.7181** (1999), 427–31

Fewtrell, L., R. Kaufman, D. Kay, W. Enanoria, L. Haller, and J. Colford, 2005: Water, sanitation, and hygiene intervention to reduce diarrhea in less developed countries: a systematic review and meta-analysis, *Lancet: Infectious Disease* **5**, 42–52

Finucane, M. M., G. A. Stevens, M. J. Cowan, G. Danaei, J. K. Lin, C. J. Paciorek, and M. Ezzati, 2011: National, regional, and global trends in body-mass index since 1980: systematic analysis of health examination surveys and epidemiological studies with 960 country-years and 9.1 million participants, *Lancet*, **377**, 557–67

Food and Agricultural Organization (FAO), 2006: *The Double Burden of Malnutrition: Case Studies from Six Developing Countries*. FAO, Rome

Fuster, A. and C. Kelly, 2011: Summary of IOM Report 'Promoting Cardiovascular Health in the Developing World', *Global Heart* **6**, 4

Gaziano, T. A., G. Galea, and K. S. Reddy, 2007: Scaling up interventions for chronic disease prevention: the evidence, *Lancet* **370**, 1939–46

Gluckman, P. and M. Hanson, 2006: *Mismatch: Why Our World no Longer Fits Our Bodies*, Oxford University Press

Golden, M. H. N., 1994: Is complete catch-up possible for stunted malnourished children?, *European Journal of Clinical Nutrition* **48**, S45–S57

Guerrant, R. L., R. B. Oriá, S. R. Moore, M. O. Oriá, and A. A. Lima, 2008: Malnutrition as an enteric infectious disease with long-term effects on child development, *Nutrition Review* **66**, 487–505

Hales, C. N., D. J. P. Barker, P. M. S. Clark, L. J. Cox, C. Fall, C. Osmond, and P. D. Winter, 1991: Fetal and infant growth and impaired glucose tolerance at age 64 years, *British Medical Journal* **3003**, 1019–22

Hoddinott, J., 2011: Agriculture, health, and nutrition, in *Toward Conceptualizing the Linkages. Leveraging Agriculture for Improving Nutrition and Health, 2020 Conference Paper*, Vol. **2**

Horton, S., M. Shekar, C. McDonald, A. Mahal, J. K. Brooks, 2010: *Scaling Up Nutrition: What Will It Cost?*, World Bank, Washington, DC

Humphrey, J., 2009: Child undernutrition, tropical enteropathy, toilets, and handwashing, *Lancet* **374**, 1032–5

International Diabetes Federation (IDB), 2009: *The Diabetes Atlas*, 4th edn., International Diabetes Federation, Brussels

Jamison, D. T., J. G. Breman, A. R. Measham *et al.*, 2006: *Disease Control Priorities in Developing Countries*, 2nd edn., Oxford University Press and World Bank, Washington, DC

Joseph, K. S. and M. S. Kramer, 1996: Review of the evidence on fetal and early childhood antecedents of adult chronic disease, *Epidemiology Review* **18**, 158–74

Kain, J., F. Vio, and C. Albala, 2003: *Obesity Trends and Determinant Factors in Latin America, Cad. Saúde Pública* **19**, S77–S86

Kau, A. L., P. Ahern, N. W. Griffin, A. L. Goodman, and J. I. Gordon, 2011: Human nutrition, the gut microbiome, and the immune system, *Nature* **474**, 327–36

Kayser, G., 2011: Moving beyond the Millennium Development Goal for water: testing the safety and sustainability of drinking water solutions in Honduras and El Salvador, Fletcher School, Tufts University, Medford, MA, unpublished doctoral dissertation

Lim, S. S., T. A. Gaziano, E. Gakidou *et al.*, 2007: Prevention of cardiovascular disease in high-risk individuals in low-income and middle-income countries: health effects and costs, *Lancet* **370**, 2054–62

Lindert, P., 2000: *Shifting Ground: The Changing Agricultural Soils of China and Indonesia*, MIT Press, Cambridge, MA

Lock, K., J. Pomerleau, L. Causer, D. R. Altmann, and M. McKee, 2005: The global burden of disease due to low fruit and vegetable consumption: implications for the global strategy on diet, *Bulletin of the WHO* **83**, 100–8

Lopez, A. D., C. D. Mathers, and M. Ezzati *et al.*, 2006: *Global Burden of Disease and Risk Factors*, World Bank, Washington, DC

Lunn, P. G., 2002: Growth retardation and stunting of children in developing countries: invited commentary, *British Journal of Nutrition* **88**, 109–10

Mahal, A., A. Karan, and M. Engelau, 2010: *Economic Implications of Non-Communicable Diseases for India*. World Bank, Washington, DC

Maluccio, J. and R. Flores, 2005: Impact evaluation of a conditional cash transfer program: the Nicaraguan Red de Protección Social, *IFPRI Research Report* **141**, IFPRI, Washington, DC

Marsh, R., 1998: Building on traditional gardening to improve household food security, *Food Nutrition and Agriculture* **4**,

Martorell, R., 2005: The policy and program implications of research on the long-term consequences of early childhood nutrition: lessons from the INCAP follow-up study, Pan American Health Organization, Washington, DC

et al., 2000: Obesity in women from developing countries, *European Journal of Clinical Nutrition* **54**, 247–52

Martorell, R., L. Kettel Khan, and D. G. Schroeder, 1994: Reversibility of stunting: epidemiological findings in children from developing countries, *European Journal of Clinical Nutrition* **48**, S45–S57

Martorell, R., J. Rivera, and H. Kaplowitz, 1990: Consequences of stunting in early childhood for adult body size in rural Guatemala, *Annales Nestle* **48**, 85–92

Matsudo, S. M., V. R. Matsudo, T. L. Araujo, D. R. Andrade, E. L. Andrade, L. C. de Oliveira, and G. F. Braggion, 2003: The Agita São Paulo Program as a model for using physical activity to promote health, *Revista Panamericana de Salud Pública*, **14**, 265–72

McKay, S., E. Gaudier, D. I. Campbell, A. M. Prentice, and R. Albers, 2010: Environmental enteropathy: new targets for nutritional interventions, *International Health* **2010**(2), 172–80

Mendez, M. A., C. A. Monteiro, and B. M. Popkin, 2005: Overweight exceeds underweight among women in most developing countries, *American Journal of Clinical Nutrition* **81**, 714–21

Merchant, A. T., C. Jones, A. Kiure, G. Fitzmaurice, M. G. Herrera, and W. W. Fawsi, 2003: Water and sanitation associated with improved child growth, *European Journal of Clinical Nutrition* **57**, 1562–8

Milman, A., E. A. Frongillo, M. de Onis, and J.-Y. Huang, 2005: Differential improvement among countries in child stunting with associated long term development and specific interventions, *Journal of Nutrition* **135**, 1415–22

Monteiro, C. A., E. C. Moura, W. L. Conde, and B. M. Popkin, 2004a: Socioeconomic status and obesity in adult populations of developing countries: a review, *Bulletin of the World Health Organization* **82**, 940–6

2004b: Obesity and inequities in health in the developing world, *International Journal of Obesity* **28**, 1181–6

Newsome, C. A., A. W. Shiell, C. H. Fall, D. I. Phillips, R. Shier, and C. M. Law, 2003: Is birth weight related to later glucose and insulin metabolism? – A systematic review, *Diabetic Medicine* **20**, 339–48

Nielsen, S. J. and B. M. Popkin, 2003: Patterns and trends in food portion sizes, 1977–1998, *JAMA: The Journal of the American Medical Association* **289**, 450–3

Norgan, N. G., 2000: Long-term physiological and economic consequences of growth retardation in children and adolescents, *Proceedings of the Nutrition Society* **59**, 245–56

Nugent, R., 2008: Chronic diseases in developing countries: health and economic burdens, *Annals of the New York Academy of Sciences* **1136**, 70–9

Pauw, K. and J. Thurlow, 2012: The role of agricultural growth in reducing poverty and hunger, in S. Fan and R. Pandya-Lorch (eds.), *Reshaping Agriculture for Nutrition and Health*, IFPRI, Washington, DC

Popkin, B., 2006: Global nutrition dynamics: the world is shifting rapidly toward a diet linked with noncommunicable diseases, *American Journal of Clinical Nutrition* **82**, 289–98

2009: *The World Is Fat: The Fads, Trends, Policies, and Products That Are Fattening the Human Race*, Penguin Books, London

Popkin, B. M. and P. Gordon-Larsen, 2004: The nutrition transition: worldwide obesity dynamics and their determinants, *International Journal of Obesity and Related Metabolic Disorders* **28**, S2–S9

Popkin, B. M. and S. J. Nielsen, 2003: The sweetening of the world's diet, *Obesity Research* **11**, 1325–32, doi: 10.1038/oby.2003.179

Prentice, A. M., 2006: The emerging epidemic of obesity in developing countries, *International Journal of Epidemiology* **35**, 93–9

Prentice, A. M. and S. E. Moore, 2005: Early programming of adult diseases in resource poor countries, *Archives of Diseases in Childhood* **90**, 429–32

Reardon, T., P. C. Timmer, and J. A. Berdegue, 2003: Supermarket expansion in Latin America and Asia: implications for food marketing systems, New Directions in Global Food Markets/AIB-**794**, Economic Research Service/USDA, Washington, DC

Ruel, M. T., P. Menon, J. P. Habicht, C. Loechl, G. Bergeron, G. Pelto, M. Arimond, J. Maluccio, L. Michaud, and B. Hankebo, 2008: Age-based preventive targeting of food assistance and behaviour change and communication for reduction of childhood undernutrition in Haiti: a cluster randomised trial, *Lancet*, **371**, 588–95

Sachdev, H. S., C. H. Fall, C. Osmond *et al.*, 2005: Anthropometric indicators of body composition in young adults: relation to size at birth and serial measurements of body mass index in childhood in the New Delhi birth cohort, *American Journal of Clinical Nutrition* **82**, 456–66

Sassi, F., M. Cecchini, J. Lauer, and D. Chisholm, 2009: Improving lifestyles, tackling obesity: the health and economic impact of prevention strategies, *OECD Health Working Paper* **48**, OECD, Paris, www.who.int/choice/publications/d_OECD_prevention_report.pdf, accessed May 26, 2012

Schoonover, H. and M. Muller, 2006: Food without thought: How US farm policy contributes to obesity, Institute for Agriculture and Trade Policy, Minneapolis

Shekar *et al.*, 2011: *Scaling Up Nutrition: A Framework for Action*, World Bank, Washington, DC

Solomons, N. W. Shekar, M. Mazariegos, K. H. Brown, and K. Klasing, 1993: The underprivileged, developing country child: environmental contamination and growth failure revisited, *Nutrition Review*, **51**, 327–32

Stuckler, P. S., M. Basu, and M. McKee, 2010: Drivers of Inequalities in MDG Progress: a statistical analysis, *PLoS Medicine* 7e100241
Uauy, R. and J. Kain, 2002: The epidemiological transition: need to incorporate obesity prevention into nutrition programmes, *Public Health Nutrition* **5**, 223–9
UNICEF, 2012: ChildInfo: Monitoring the Situation of Children and Women, www.childinfo.org/undernutrition_nutritional_status.php, accessed May 3 2012
Victora, C., L. Adair, C. Fall, P. C. Hallal, R. Martorell, L. Richter, and H. S. Sachdev, 2008: Maternal and child undernutrition: consequences for adult health and human capital, *Lancet* **371**, 340
Victora, C. G., D. Sibbritt, B. L. Horta, R. C. Lima, T. J. Cole, and J. Wells, 2007: Weight gain in childhood and body composition at 18 years of age in Brazilian males, *Acta Paediatrica* **96**, 296–300
Von Braun, D., 2002: Is globalization taking a pause? Implications for international agriculture and food security policy, *Quarterly Journal of International Agriculture* **41**, 187–90
Waage, J. *et al.*, 2010: The MDGs: a cross-sectoral analysis and principles for goal setting after 2015, *Lancet* **376**, 991–1023
Webb, P. and S. Block, 2010: Support for agriculture during economic transformation: impacts on poverty and undernutrition, PNAS, www.pnas.org/cgi/doi/10.1073/pnas.0913334108, accessed May 25, 2012
Wells, J. C., P. C. Hallal, A. Wright, A. Singhal, and C. G. Victora, 2005: Fetal, infant and childhood growth: relationships with body composition in Brazilian boys aged 9 years, *International Journal of Obesity (London)* **29**, 1192–8
Witherspoon, D. D. and T. Reardon, 2003: The rise of supermarkets in Africa: implications for agrifood systems and the rural poor, *Development Policy Review* **21**, 333–55
World Economic Forum and Harvard School of Public Health (WEF/HSPH), 2011: *The Global Economic Burden of Non-Communicable Diseases*, www.weforum.org/EconomicsOfNCD, accessed May 25, 2012
2004a: Global strategy on diet, physical activity and health, World Health Organization, Geneva, www.who.int/dietphysicalactivity/strategy/eb11344/strategy_english_web.pdf, accessed May 25, 2012
2004b: *Global Strategy on Diet, Physical Activity and Health*, World Health Organization, Geneva
2008a: World Health Organization Commission on Social Determinants of Health, World Health Organization, Geneva
2008b: *World Health Statistics*, World Health Organization, Geneva
2008c: *2008–2013 Action Plan for the Global Strategy for the Prevention and Control of Non-communicable Diseases*, World Health Organization, Geneva
World Health Organization (WHO), 2009a: *Global Health Risks: Mortality and Burden of Disease Attributable to Selected Major Risks*, World Health Organization, Geneva
2009b: *Interventions on Diet and Physical Activity: What Work*, World Health Organization, Geneva
2011: Scaling up action against noncommunicable diseases: How much will it cost?, www.who.int/nmh/publications, accessed May 25, 2012
World Health Organization and Food and Agriculture Organization (WHO/FAO), 2002: *Report of the Joint WHO/FAO Expert Consultation on Diet, Nutrition and the Prevention of Chronic Diseases*, World Health Organization, Geneva
World Economic Forum and World Health Organization (WEF/WHO), 2011: From Burden to "Best Buys": Reducing the Economic Impact of Non-Communicable Diseases in Low- and Middle-Income Countries, World Economic Forum, Geneva
Younger, M., H. Morrow-Almeida, S. Vindigni, and A. Dannenberg, 2008: The built environment, climate change, and health: opportunities and co-benefits, *American Journal of Preventative Medicine* **35**, 517–26

Infectious Disease, Injury, and Reproductive Health

DEAN T. JAMISON, PRABHAT JHA, RAMANAN LAXMINARAYAN, AND TOBY ORD*

This chapter identifies key priorities for the control of infectious disease, injury, and reproductive health problems for the 2012 Copenhagen Consensus. It draws directly upon the disease control paper (Jamison *et al.*, 2008) from the 2008 Copenhagen Consensus 2008 and the AIDS vaccine paper for the 2011 Copenhagen Consensus RethinkHIV project (Hecht and Jamison, 2012). This chapter updates the evidence and adjusts the conclusions of the previous work in light of subsequent research and experience. For the 2012 Copenhagen Consensus NCDs are being treated in a separate paper (Jha *et al.*, 2012, Chapter 3 in this volume) that complements this one. This chapter's conclusions emphasize investments in control of infection. That said, one of the six investment areas advanced – essential surgery – addresses both the complications of childbirth and injury, and points to the potential for substantial disease burden reduction in these domains.

All this work builds on the results of the Disease Control Priorities Project (DCPP).[1] The DCPP engaged over 350 authors and estimated the cost-effectiveness of 315 interventions. These estimates vary a good deal in their thoroughness and in the extent to which they provide regionally-specific estimates of both cost and effectiveness. Taken as a whole, however, they represent a comprehensive canvas of disease control opportunities.[2] We will combine this body of knowledge with the results from research and operational experience in the subsequent four years.

The DCPP concluded that some interventions are clearly low priority. Others are worth doing, but either address only a relatively small proportion of disease burden or simply prove less attractive than a few key interventions. This chapter identifies six key interventions in terms of their cost-effectiveness, the size of the disease burden they address, the amount of financial protection they provide, their feasibility of implementation, and their relevance for development assistance budgets. The resulting "dashboard" of indicators underpins overall judgments of priority. Separate but related papers for the 2012 Copenhagen Consensus deal with malnutrition (Hoddinott *et al.*, 2012, Chapter 6 in this volume), with water and sanitation (Rijsberman and Zwane, 2012, Chapter 10 in this volume), with population growth (Kohler, 2012, Chapter 9 in this volume), and with education (Orazem, 2012, Chapter 5 in this volume).

Before turning to the substance of the chapter it is worth briefly stating our perspectives on the roles of the state and of international development assistance in financing health interventions. There are major positive externalities associated with control of many infections and there are important public goods aspects to health education and R&D. On one view, the rationale for state finance is to address these market failures and the needs of vulnerable groups. Our view is rather different.

Among the high-income OECD countries, only the United States focuses public finance on vulnerable groups – the poor and the elderly. Other OECD countries provide universal public finance for the

* This chapter was prepared with partial support from the Disease Control Priorities Network Project (DCPNP) funded by the Bill and Melinda Gates Foundation. The authors thank Ms Brianne Adderley for valuable assistance.

[1] The DCPP was a joint effort, extending over four years, of the Fogarty International Center of the US National Institutes of Health, the World Bank, and the WHO, with financial support from the Bill and Melinda Gates Foundation. While the views and conclusions expressed in this chapter draw principally on the DCPP, others might draw different broad conclusions. In particular, the views expressed in this chapter are not necessarily those of any of the sponsoring organizations.

[2] See Jamison *et al.* (2006) and Laxminarayan *et al.* (2006b).

(generally comprehensive) set of health interventions that the public sector finances at all. Private finance is explicitly crowded out by public action, even for purely private clinical services (such as setting fractures) which most individuals would be willing and able to pay for themselves (perhaps with privately financed insurance). Arrow's classic paper (Arrow, 1963) points to potential theoretical justifications for choosing universal public finance. The poor outcomes of the US system with respect to health indicators, financial protection, and total costs (and even with respect to public sector expenditures as a percentage of GDP) provide empirical evidence suggestive of the merits of universal public finance.[3]

The perspective of this chapter is that of universal public finance adopted by the non-US OECD countries.[4] From this perspective, one is seeking to maximize health gains (or a broader objective function) subject to a public sector budget constraint without regard for the presence of public goods or externalities (except insofar as they affect aggregate health) and by addressing the needs of the poor through selecting interventions for universal finance that are of particular importance to them. No costs then accrue to targeting and no disincentives to work effort result from the potential loss of income-related health benefits. We further view the political economy of universalism as enhancing sustainability. Reasonable people may disagree, however, on the merits of universal public finance but even in that case private purchasers of health or health insurance may find cost–benefit information relevant to choice.

Our view of the role of international development assistance in health does, in contrast, centrally involve externalities and international public goods. Cross-border transmission of infection or drug resistance involves important negative externalities and R&D constitutes a public good that has been enormously important in health. Two of our six priorities reflect those concerns. Likewise, facilitating diffusion of best practice through development assistance or price incentives can be viewed as correction of temporary price distortions and hence a reasonable purpose of aid. (Foreign direct investment (FDI) in the private sector provides an analogy, whereby international investors bring best practices along with their financial investments.) When we discuss the "best buys" in health we do so principally from the perspective of national authorities, but for interventions that may be of importance to development assistance beyond their importance from a national perspective we point to the role of development assistance.

The chapter begins by documenting the enormous success in much of the world in the past forty years in improving health in LMICs. Its conclusion is that future investments can build on past successes – increasing confidence in the practical feasibility of major additional gains in disease control. The next section summarizes evidence that health gains have had major economic and welfare impact, and the next section uses this economic context to describe the methods used for the CBAs reported. The next three sections discuss problems and opportunities in reproductive and child health, HIV/AIDS, and TB, respectively. The final section concludes by identifying the six most attractive solutions and presenting (very approximate) CBAs for them. Our BCR estimates are placed on a "dashboard" including other information relevant for priority-setting. This chapter emphasizes, although not exclusively, opportunities relevant to low-income countries.

Progress and challenges

Health conditions improved markedly throughout the world during most of the second half of the twentieth century and this section begins by highlighting those achievements. Nonetheless major problems remain in the early twenty-first century. Parts of the world have failed to keep up with the remarkable progress in others; declines in mortality and fertility had led to an increasing importance of NCDs; and the now maturing problem of HIV/AIDS rapidly became prominent in many countries. Addressing these problems within highly constrained budgets will require hard choices, even in the current era of

[3] See Barr (2001) and Lindert (2004) for more extended discussions.

[4] If implemented, the 2012 Obama health care reform will align the US system much more closely with those of other high-income countries.

Table 7.1 Levels and rates of change in life expectancy, 1960–2010, by UN region

	Life expectancy (years)			Rate of change (years per decade)	
	1960	2000	2010	1960–1999	2000–2009
World	52	66	69	3.5	2.4
China	50	72	74	5.4	2.3
India	44	62	65	4.4	3.2
SSA	42	50	53	2.3	2.7
More-developed regions	70	76	78	1.6	2.0
Less-developed regions	48	64	67	4.2	2.6

Source: United Nations (2009).

expanding domestic health spending and overseas development assistance (ODA) on health. This section concludes by reviewing these challenges.

Progress

Table 7.1 shows progress in life expectancy, by UN region, between 1960 and 2010. For the first three decades of this period, progress was remarkably fast – a gain of 4.2 years in life expectancy per decade on average, in the LDCs, albeit with substantial regional variation. Progress continued between 2000 and 2010, but at a slower pace. In addition to overall progress, since 1950 life expectancy in the median country has steadily converged toward the (steadily growing) maximum across all countries and cross-country differences have decreased markedly (Oeppen and Vaupel, 2002; Vallin and Mesle, 2010). This reduction in inequality in health contrasts with long-term *increases* in income inequality between and within countries. Yet despite the magnitude of global improvements, many countries and populations have failed to share in the overall gains, or have even fallen behind. Some countries – for example, Sierra Leone – remain far behind. China's interior provinces lag behind the more advantaged coastal regions. Indigenous people everywhere lead far less healthy lives than do others in their respective countries, although confirmatory data are scant.

Much of the variation in country outcomes appears to result from the very substantial cross-country variation in the rate of diffusion of appropriate health technologies (or "technical progress"). Countries range from having essentially no decline in the infant mortality rate (IMR) caused by technical progress to reductions of up to 5 percent per year (Jamison *et al.*, forthcoming). Measham *et al.* (2003) reached a similar conclusion concerning the variation in IMR decline across the states of India. Cutler *et al.* (2006) provide a complementary and extended discussion of the importance of technological diffusion for improvements in health. Consider, for example, the 8 million child deaths that occur currently each year. If child death rates were those seen in OECD countries, fewer than 1 million child deaths would occur each year. Conversely, if child death rates were those in OECD countries just 100 years ago, there would be 30 million child deaths a year. The key difference between now and then is not income but technical knowledge – on disease causation, interventions, and their application.

Consider the remarkable declines in infectious disease, excepting HIV/AIDS, world-wide. It is difficult to overstate how much infectious disease control improved the human condition in the twentieth century. For comparison, the average annual death rate from all acts of war, genocide and murder in the twentieth century (including non-combatants) was approximately 2 million deaths p.a. Yet reasonable estimates suggest that improved immunization saves more lives p.a. than would be saved by world peace. The same can be said for each of three other areas: smallpox eradication, diarrhea treatment, and malaria treatment. The development of improved environmental living conditions combined with vaccination, anti-microbial chemotherapy, and the ability to identify new microbes has been central to the more than 90 percent reduction in communicable disease mortality in Canada and the United States (US Centers for Disease Control and Prevention, 1999). Today more than thirty common infectious diseases are controllable with vaccines. In 1970, only 5 percent of the world's children under 5 were immunized against measles, tetanus, pertussis, diphtheria, and polio. The Expanded Program on Immunization has raised this to about 75 percent of children by 1990, saving perhaps 3 million lives a year (England *et al.*, 2001). The clearest success in immunization is the WHO-led eradication of smallpox, which culminated in the eradication of smallpox in human populations by 1979. WHO is engaged in an ongoing effort to eradicate poliomyelitis, which is more difficult technically than smallpox eradication. Nonetheless, the effort has reduced polio cases by more than 99 percent to fewer than 1,000 per year.

Prior to 1950, the only major antibiotics were sulphonamides and penicillin. Subsequently, there has been remarkable growth in discovery and use of anti-microbial agents effective against bacteria, fungi, viruses, protozoa, and helminths. Delivery of a combination of anti-TB drugs with direct observation (or DOTS, described on p. 415) has lowered case-fatality rates from well over 60 percent to 5 percent, and also decreased transmission. The percentage of the world's TB cases treated with DOTS has risen from 11 percent to about 53 percent (Dye and Floyd, 2006), which points to the practical possibility of still further gains. Research into HIV/AIDS and related diseases is providing a better understanding of the internal structure of retroviruses, and is accelerating the number of antiviral agents. Sustained investment in HIV/AIDS vaccine development is, very recently, beginning to bear fruit (Maurice, 2011). This chapter argues that investments to advance the time to availability of a vaccine would be highly attractive. Similarly, there is increasing knowledge of the modes of action of anti-fungal and anti-parasitic agents (Weatherall *et al.*, 2006). Large-scale studies have been able to identify smoking as a major cause of tuberculosis mortality world-wide (Bates *et al.*, 2007) but especially in India (Gajalakshmi *et al.*, 2003). Finally, large-scale randomized trials have been increasingly used to establish widely practicable therapies, especially when modest, but important treatment benefits are sought (Peto and Baigent, 2003). Advances in computing and statistics have led to more robust mathematical models of understanding infectious disease spread (Nagelkerke *et al.*, 2002), and a new chapter is the development of molecular biology and recombinant DNA technology since the second half of the twentieth century. The benefits of DNA science to global health are as yet limited but could be extraordinary (see Weatherall *et al.*, 2006, in DCP2).

Factors from outside the health sector also affect the pace of health improvement: education levels of populations appear quite important although the level and growth rate of income appear much less so. Of course, the importance of technical progress and diffusion should be viewed in a larger context. Expanded education improves the coverage and efficiency of disease control, as in the case of maternal education improving child health. Indeed, rapid economic growth in many parts of the world, especially in China and India, might well mean that some can buy their way into better health, but this chapter argues there will be far more benefit if expanded public coffers are used on a relatively limited set of highly effective public health and clinical interventions. This point bears reiterating in a slightly different way: income growth is neither necessary nor sufficient for sustained improvements in health. Today's tools for improving health are so powerful and inexpensive that health conditions can be reasonably good even in countries with low incomes.

Reasons for remaining health inequalities thus lie only partially in poverty or income inequality: the experiences of China, Costa Rica, Cuba, Sri Lanka, and Kerala state in India, among others, conclusively show that dramatic improvements in health can occur without high or rapidly growing incomes. The experiences of countries in Europe in the late nineteenth and early twentieth centuries similarly show that health conditions can improve without prior or concomitant increases in income (Easterlin, 1996). One review has identified many specific examples of low-cost interventions leading to large and carefully documented health improvements (Levine and the What Works Working Group, 2007). The public sector initiated and financed virtually all of these interventions.

The goal of this chapter is to assist decision-makers – particularly those in the public sector – to identify the highest-priority low-cost interventions to rapidly improve population health and welfare where the needs are greatest.

Remaining challenges

Three central challenges for health policy ensue from the pace and unevenness of the progress just summarized and from the evolving nature of microbial threats to human health.

Unequal progress

The initial challenge results from continued high levels of inequality in health conditions across and within countries. Bourguignon and Morrisson (2002) have stressed that global inequalities are declining if one properly accounts for convergence across countries in health conditions, which more than compensates for income divergence. However, in far too many countries health conditions remain unacceptably – and unnecessarily – poor. This reality remains a source of grief and misery, and it is a brake on economic growth and poverty reduction. From 1990 to 2001, for example, the under-5 mortality rate remained stagnant or increased in twenty-three countries. In another fifty-three countries (including China), the rate of decline in under-5 mortality in this period was less than half of the 4.3 percent per year required to reach MDG-4. Meeting the MDG for under-5 mortality reduction by 2015 is not remotely possible for these countries.[5]

Yet the examples of many other countries, often quite poor, show that with the right policies dramatic reductions in mortality are possible. A major goal of this chapter is to identify strategies for implementing interventions that are known to be highly cost-effective for dealing with the health problems of countries remaining behind – for example, treatment for diarrhea, pneumonia, TB, and malaria; immunization; and other preventive measures to reduce stillbirths and neonatal deaths. About 7.2 million of the 49 million deaths in LMICs occur in children between birth and age 5.[6] Table 7.2 summarizes what is known about the causes of deaths under the age of 5, and under the age of 28 days, in 2010; these proportions are unlikely to have changed substantially. Table 7.2 also includes an estimate on the number of stillbirths. About half of all deaths under the age of 5 (including stillbirths) occur in the first 28 days, indicating the importance of addressing conditions related to this period. Table 7.3 shows also that there are marked gender disparities in child mortality, for example in India, where death rates from pneumonia and diarrhea are fourfold to fivefold higher in girls in one region than in boys in other regions.

Epidemiological transition

A second challenge lies in NCDs. The next two decades will see the continuation of rising trends resulting from dramatic fertility declines (and consequent population aging) in recent decades, as well as change in patterns of risk factors. The companion 2012 Copenhagen Consensus paper (Jha *et al.*, 2012, Chapter 3 in this volume) discusses these matters further.

The combination of an aging population with increases in smoking and other lifestyle changes mean that the major NCDs – circulatory system diseases, cancers, respiratory disease, and major psychiatric disorders – are fast replacing (or adding to) the traditional scourges – particularly infectious diseases and undernutrition in children. Additionally, injuries resulting from road traffic are replacing more traditional forms of injury. Responding to this epidemiological transition within sharply constrained resources is a key challenge since NCD disease already accounts for two-thirds of all deaths over age 5 in these countries, although nearly 22 percent of deaths continue to be from infection, undernutrition, and maternal conditions, creating a "dual burden" that Julio Frenk and his colleagues have noted (Bobadilla *et al.*, 1993).

[5] See Lopez *et al.* (2006a), for country-specific estimates of child and adult mortality rates in 1990 and 2001 that were generated in a consistent way over time and across countries, and Liu *et al.* (2012) for estimates of these rates of decline between 2000 and 2010.

[6] See Lozano *et al.* (2011).

Table 7.2 Causes of under-5 mortality, world-wide, 2010,[a] estimates from Child Health Epidemiology Reference Group (000)

Cause Days 0–27 (Neonatal)	No. (000)
Pneumonia	325
Pre-term birth complications	1,078
Intrapartum-related events	717
Sepsis/meningitis/tetanus	451
Other conditions	181
Congenital abnormalities	270
Diarrhea	54
All causes	3,072
1–59 months	
Diarrhea	751
Measles	114
Injury	354
Malaria	564
HIV/AIDS	159
Meningitis	180
Other conditions	1,356
Pneumonia	1,071
All causes	4,550
All Children 0–59 months	7,622
Stillbirths (2001 estimate)[b]	3,274

Source: Liu *et al.* (2012).
Notes:
[a] Of the estimated 7.6 million under-5 deaths in 2010 less than 0.5% occurred in high-income countries. Thus the cause distribution of deaths in this table is essentially that of LMICs countries.
[b] "Stillbirths" are defined as fetal loss in the third trimester of pregnancy. About 33 percent of stillbirths occur after labor has begun – so-called intrapartum stillbirths. No good estimates exist for stillbirths by cause, but some of the cause categories (e.g. birth asphyxia, birth trauma, congenital anomalies) are the same as for age 0–4, so part of what is categorized as "other conditions" in the total row will be distributed among the other existing rows when estimates are available. Note that these estimates use 2001 data from the *Global Burden of Disease* study (Jamison *et al.*, 2006; Mathers *et al.*, 2006) and have not yet been updated for 2010. The proportion of neonatal to total child deaths was 36 percent in 2001, but rose to 40% by 2010 (even though overall child deaths fell from about 13.8 to 7.6 million over the decade). Thus as stillbirths approximately track neonatal mortality, the absolute number in 2010 should be somewhat lower than the 2001 stillbirth totals.

Table 7.3 Gender variation in child mortality at ages 1–59 months, by cause in parts of India, 2005

Cause	Mortality rate per 1,000 live births
Pneumonia	
Girls in Central India	21
Boys in South India	4
Diarrhea	
Girls in Central India	18
Boys in West India	4

Source: Million Death Study Collaborators (2010).

HIV/AIDS epidemic

A third key challenge is the HIV/AIDS epidemic. Control efforts and successes have been very real in high- and middle-income countries but are not yet widespread in low-income countries. As we outline below, the HIV/AIDS epidemic is best viewed as a set of diverse epidemics in regions or subregions, but with the dominant focus in Africa. Each scenario demands understanding the reasons for HIV/AIDS growth, appropriate interventions to decrease transmission to uninfected populations, and clinical care with life-prolonging drugs for those already infected. Recent data suggest that growth of HIV/AIDS is slowing in large parts of Asia, Latin America, and elsewhere, and that such reductions might be due to a (very uneven) increase in prevention programs. The 2011 Copenhagen Consensus's RethinkHIV effort reviews priorities for addressing AIDS in Africa and placed accelerated work on development of a vaccine as the top priority.

The economic benefits of better health

On the global scale, the dramatic health improvements during the twentieth century arguably contributed as much or more to improvements in overall well-being as did the equally dramatic improvements in the availability of material goods and services. Through their substantial effects on reducing morbidity and mortality, the economic welfare returns to health investments are likely to be exceptional and positive – with only partially recognized implications for public sector resource allocation. The purpose of this section is to motivate the high values this chapter (and other 2012 Copenhagen Consensus papers) place on mortality reduction in its CBAs. Returns to better health go far beyond the contribution better health makes to per person income, which itself appears substantial (see Bloom *et al.*, 2004; Lopez-Casasnovas *et al.*, 2005). This section first summarizes the evidence concerning the effect of health on per person income and then turns to more recent literature concerning the effect of health changes on a broader measure of economic well-being than per person income.

Health and income

How does health influence income per person? One obvious linkage is that healthy workers are more productive than workers who are similar but not healthy. Supporting evidence for this comes from studies that link investments in health and nutrition of the young to adult wages (Strauss and Thomas, 1998). Better health also raises *per capita* income through a number of other channels. One involves altering decisions about expenditures and savings over the lifecycle. The idea of planning for retirement occurs only when mortality rates become low enough for retirement to be a realistic prospect. Rising longevity in developing countries has opened a new incentive for the current generation to invest in physical capital and in education – an incentive that can dramatically affect national saving rates. Although this saving boom lasts for only one generation and is offset by the needs of the elderly after population aging occurs, it can substantially boost investment and economic growth rates while it lasts.

Encouraging FDI is another channel: investors shun environments in which the labor force suffers a heavy disease burden and where they may themselves be at risk. Endemic diseases can also deny humans access to land or other natural resources, as occurred in much of West Africa before the successful control of river blindness. Boosting education is yet another channel. Healthier children attend school, and learn more while they are there.

Demographic channels also play an important role. Lower infant mortality initially creates a "baby-boom" cohort and leads to a subsequent reduction in the birth rates as families choose to have fewer children in the new low-mortality regime. A baby-boom cohort thereby affects the economy profoundly as its members enter the educational system, find employment, save for retirement, and finally leave the labor market. The cohorts before and after a baby boom are much smaller; hence, for a substantial transition period, this cohort creates a large labor force relative to overall population size and the potential for accelerated economic growth (Bloom and Canning, 2006).

If better health improves the productive potential of individuals, good health should accompany higher levels of national income in the long run, although as Acemoglu and Johnson (2007) suggest, effects or per person income may also be adversely affected by health-related population increases. Bloom *et al.* (forthcoming) argue that a failure to consider lags between health improvements and economic gains led Acemoglu and Johnson to underestimate the net effect of health improvements on *per capita* income. Countries that have high levels of health but low levels of income tend to experience relatively faster economic growth as their income adjusts. How big an overall contribution does better health make to economic growth? Evidence from cross-country growth regressions suggests the contribution is consistently substantial. Indeed, the initial health of a population has been identified as one of the most robust drivers of economic growth – among such well-established influences as the initial level of income *per capita*, geographic location, and institutional and economic policy environment. Bloom *et al.* (2004) found that one extra year of life expectancy raises GDP per person by about 4 percent in the long run. Jamison *et al.* (2005) estimated that reductions in adult mortality explain 10–15 percent of the economic growth that occurred from 1960 to 1990. Although attribution of causality remains equivocal in analyses like these, household-level evidence also points consistently to a likely causal effect of health on income.

Health declines can precipitate downward spirals, setting off impoverishment and further ill health. For example, the effect of HIV/AIDS on *per capita* GDP could prove devastating in the long run. The IMF has published a collection of important studies of the multiple mechanisms through which a major HIV/AIDS epidemic can be expected to affect national economies (Haacker, 2004).

Health and economic welfare

Judging countries' economic performance by GDP per person fails to take sufficient account of health: a country whose citizens enjoy long and healthy lives clearly outperforms another with the same GDP per person but whose citizens suffer much illness and die sooner. Schelling (1968) initiated efforts to assign economic value to changes in mortality probability and Johannson (1995) and Viscusi and Aldy (2003) provide more recent explications of the theory. Individual willingness to forgo income to work in safer environments and social WTP for health-enhancing safety and environmental regulations provide measures, albeit approximate, of the value of differences in mortality rates. Many such WTP studies have been undertaken in recent decades, and their results are typically summarized as the *value of a statistical life* (VSL).

Although the national income and product accounts include the value of inputs into health care (such as drugs and physician time), standard procedures do not incorporate information on the value of changes in longevity. In a seminal paper, Usher (1973) first brought estimates of VSL into national income accounting. He did this by generating estimates of the growth in what Becker *et al.* (2003) later called *full income* – a concept that captures the value of changes in life expectancy by including them in an assessment of economic welfare. Estimates of changes in full income are typically generated by adding the value of changes in annual mortality rates (calculated using VSL figures) to changes in annual GDP per person. These estimates of change in full income are conservative in that they incorporate only the value of mortality changes and do not account for the total value of changes in health status.

This chapter will later use a DALY measure, that includes disability as well as premature mortality in a way that calibrates disability weight in terms of mortality changes. Valuation of changes in mortality, it should be noted, is only one element – albeit a quantitatively important one – of potentially feasible additions to national accounts to deal with non-market outcomes. The US National Academy of Sciences has proposed broad changes for the United States that would include but go beyond valuation of mortality change (Abraham and Mackie, 2005). The Sarkozy Commission in France (Stiglitz *et al.*, 2009) reached similar conclusions. Of specific relevance to recent economic evaluations of health interventions is the economic welfare value of reductions in financial risk potentially associated either with a health intervention – typically prevention or early treatment – or with a risk-pooled way of financing it.

For many years, little further work was done on the effects of mortality change on full income although, as Viscusi and Aldy (2003) document, the number of carefully constructed estimates of VSLs increased enormously. Bourguignon and Morrisson (2002) address the long-term evolution of inequality among world citizens, starting from the premise that a "comprehensive definition of economic well-being would consider individuals over their lifetime." Their conclusion is that rapid increases in life expectancy in poorer countries have resulted in declines in inequality (broadly defined to reflect the distributions of both mortality and income) beginning some time after 1950, even though income inequality continued to rise.

In another important paper, Nordhaus (2003) assessed the growth of full income *per capita* in the United States in the twentieth century. He concluded that more than half of the growth in full income in the first half of the century – and somewhat less than half in the second half of the century – had resulted from mortality decline. In this period, real income in the United States increased sixfold and life expectancy increased by more than twenty-five years.

Three lines of work extend those methods to the interpretation of the economic performance of developing countries. All reach conclusions that differ substantially from analyses based on GDP alone. Two of those studies – one undertaken for the Commission on Macroeconomics and Health

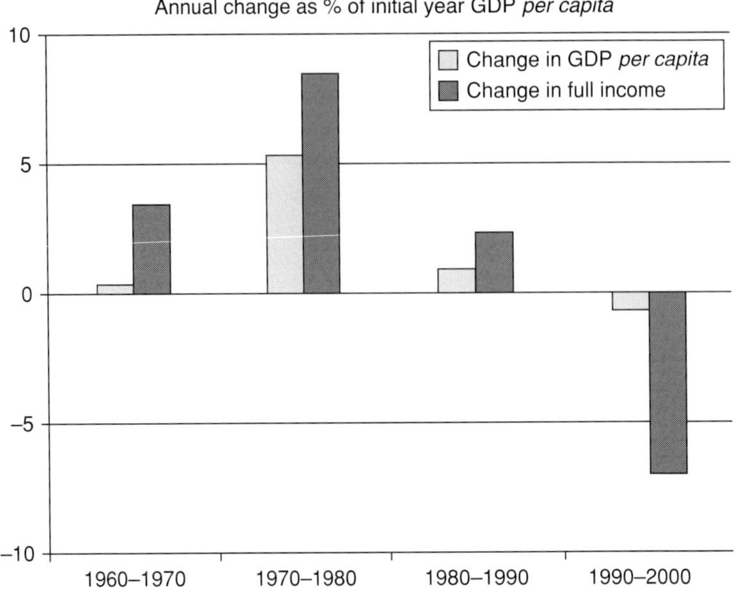

Figure 7.1 *Changes in GDP and full income, Kenya, 1960–2000*

(CMH) of WHO (Jamison *et al.*, 2001) and the other at the IMF (Crafts and Haacker, 2004) – assessed the impact of the HIV/AIDS epidemic on full income. Both studies conclude that the HIV/AIDS epidemic in the 1990s had far more adverse economic consequences than previous estimates of effects on per person GDP growth would suggest. The benefit estimates used in this chapter for successful interventions against HIV/AIDS are consistent with these findings from the CMH and IMF.

Accounting for mortality decline in Africa before the 1990s, on the other hand, leads to estimates of much more favorable overall economic performance than does the trend in GDP per person. Figure 7.1 shows that in Kenya, for example, full income grew more rapidly than did GDP per person before 1990 (and far more rapidly in the 1960s). After 1990 the mounting death toll from HIV/AIDS appears to have only a modest effect on GDP per person but a dramatically adverse impact on changes in full income. Becker *et al.* (2003) confirmed and extended the earlier work of Bourguignon and Morrisson (2002) in finding strong absolute convergence in full income across countries over time, in contrast to the standard finding of continued divergence (increased inequality) of GDP per person. Finally, Jamison *et al.* (2003) have adapted standard cross-country growth regressions to model determinants of full income (rather than GDP per person). Like Bourguignon and Morrisson (2002), they concluded that inequalities have been decreasing.

The dramatic mortality declines of the past 150 years – and their reversal in parts of Africa by HIV/AIDS subsequent to 1990 – have had major economic consequences. The effect of health on GDP is substantial. The intrinsic value of mortality changes – measured in terms of VSL – is even more so. What are the implications of these findings for development strategy and for CBAs of public sector investment options? Using full income in CBAs of investments in health (and in health-related sectors such as education, water supply and sanitation, and targeted food transfers) would markedly increase estimates of net benefits or rates of return. A major purpose of the Copenhagen Consensus process is to undertake intersectoral comparisons of investment priorities by utilizing this "full benefit" approach.

Cost-benefit methodology

The basic approach to CBA used for most of the solutions is to start with the cost-effectiveness results from the extensive comparative analyses reported in DCP2 (Jamison *et al.*, 2006a; Laxminarayan *et al.*, 2006a). These results are expressed as the cost of buying a DALY, a summary measure involving mortality change and a valuation of disability change that can be considered to have been generated by calibration against mortality change.

The next subsection describes an idealized version of our approach to cost-effectiveness – idealized in the sense that it seeks to explicitly call attention to the value of financial protection and non-financial costs (e.g. use of limited system capacity). The point is to serve as a reminder in drawing conclusions of some specific important considerations that go beyond the cost-effectiveness ratios reported, considerations that appear in our "dashboard" reporting of results. The next subsection discusses DALYs and explicitly argues for a change in the way DALYs associated with deaths under the age of 5 are calculated. This change, which is adopted in our CBAs, reduces the DALY cost of a typical death under the age of 5 by about 50 percent while leaving the construction of DALYs for older ages unchanged. The next subsection draws on the earlier discussion to assign, very conservatively, dollar values to DALYs for the subsequent CBA. The final subsection summarizes this chapter's approach to costing.

Canning (2009) provides a valuable critique of aspects of this approach to valuing DALYs for a CBA. He points to a potentially lower dollar valuation of mortality reduction both in poorer countries and among the poor in a given country. This issue cuts across the 2012 Copenhagen Consensus analyses. Our view is that $1,000/DALY is a reasonable lower bound independent of the process of getting to the number.

Cost-effectiveness analysis broadly and narrowly construed

A starting point for cost-effectiveness analysis broadly construed is to observe that health systems have two objectives: (a) to improve the level and distribution of health outcomes in the population and (b) to protect individuals from financial risks that are often very substantial and that are frequent causes of poverty (WHO, 1999, 2000). Financial risk results from illness-related loss of income as well as expenditures on care; the loss can be ameliorated by preventing illness or its progression, by using an appropriate financial architecture for the system, and by improving access to capital markets or social insurance.

We can also consider two classes of resources to be available: financial resources and health system capacity. To implement an intervention in a population, the system uses some of each resource. Just as some interventions have higher dollar costs than others, some interventions are more demanding of system capacity than others. In countries with limited health system capacity, it is clearly important to select interventions that require relatively little of such capacity. Human resource capacity constitutes a particularly important aspect of system capacity, discussed in a report of the Joint Learning Initiative (2004). Figure 7.2 illustrates this broadly construed vision of cost-effectiveness and, in its shaded region, the more narrow (standard) approach for which quantitative estimates are available. Jamison (2008) provides a more extended discussion.

Although in the very short run little trade-off may exist between dollars and human resources or system capacity more generally, investing in the development of such capacity can help make more of that resource available in the future. Mills *et al.* (2006) discuss different types of health system capacity and intervention complexity and point to the potential for responding to low capacity by selecting interventions that are less demanding of capacity and by simplifying interventions. Mills *et al.* (2006) also explore the extent to which financial resources can substitute for different aspects of system capacity (see also Gericke *et al.*, 2003). An important mechanism for strengthening capacity, inherent in highly outcome-oriented programs, may simply be to use it successfully – learning by doing.

The literature on the economic evaluation of health projects typically reports the cost per unit of achieving some measure of health outcome – QALYs, or DALYs, or deaths averted – and

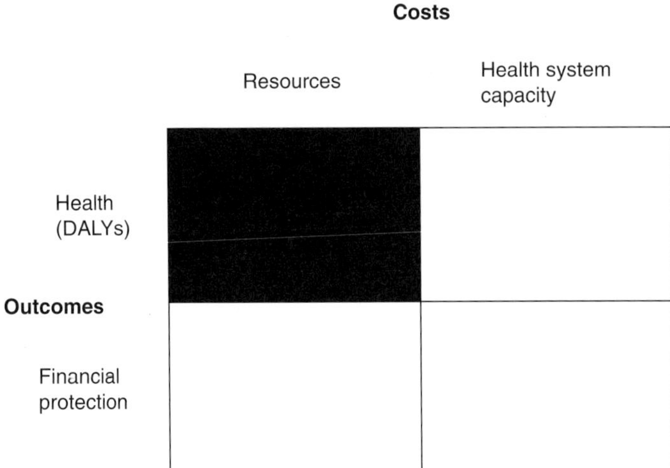

Figure 7.2 *Intervention costs and effects: a more general view*

Note: The black box represents the domain of traditional cost-effectiveness analysis.

at times addresses how that cost varies with the level of intervention and other factors. Pritchard (2004) provides a valuable introduction to this literature. DCP1 reported such cost-effectiveness findings for about seventy interventions; DCP2 does so as well, in the end providing evidence on about 315 interventions. DCP2 authors were asked to use the methods described in Jamison (2003). Cost-effectiveness calculations provide important insights into the economic attractiveness of an intervention, but other considerations – such as the consequences for financial protection and the demands on health system capacity – need to be borne in mind. Even if factors such as system capacity remain difficult to quantify it may be useful to include a subjective judgment, for each intervention, of the extent of its demand on system capacity. We complement our quantitative (if imprecise) benefit-cost estimates with subjective judgments of this type in a "dashboard" comparison of interventions.

Defining and redefining DALYs

The DALY family of indicators measures the disease burden from the age of onset of a condition by combining an indicator of years of life lost (YLL) due to the condition with an indicator of years of life lost due to disability (YLD) resulting from the condition. DALYs due to a condition are the sum of the relevant YLLs and YLDs.

DALYs generate a measure of the disease burden resulting from premature mortality by integrating a potentially discounted, potentially age-weighted, disability-adjusted stream of life years from the age of incidence of the condition to infinity using a survival curve based on the otherwise expected age of death. The formulation within the family of DALYs previously used to empirically assess the global burden of disease specifies a constant discount rate of 3 percent per year and an age-weighting function that gives low weight to a year lived in early childhood and older ages and greater weight to middle ages. The current comprehensive volume on burden of disease reports global burden of disease (GBD) estimates generated with the 3 percent discount rate but uniform age weights (Lopez *et al.*, 2006b). Mathers *et al.* (2006) provide an extensive exploration of the uncertainty and sensitivity inherent in disease burden assessment, including the results of differing assumptions about age-weighting and discount rates. (A major revision and update of the *Global Burden of Disease* (GBD) is now nearing completion for publication later in 2012. Its headline reporting of results uses uniform age-weighting and a zero discount rate. The practical effect is to increase markedly (and, in our view, implausibly) the relative importance of deaths in childhood relative to earlier publications.)

To be clear about the particular form of DALY being used, the terminology from Mathers *et al.* (2006) is employed. DALYs(r,K) are DALYs constructed using a discount rate of r percent per year and an amount of age-weighting indexed by a parameter K. DALYs(3,1) are DALYs generated with a discount rate of 3 percent per year and with full age-weighting, that is, $K = 1$. DALYs(3,0) are DALYs generated with a discount rate of 3 percent per year and with no age-weighting, that is, $K = 0$. Mathers *et al.* (2006) present results concerning the burden of disease based on DALYs(3,0); Ezzati *et al.* (2006) present estimates of the burden of major risk factors. This chapter is based on DALYs (3,0), but slightly generalized.

A serious problem for the standard conception of DALYs concerns death near the time of birth. The DALY measure suffers from a discontinuity at this time, with a death seconds before birth counting for 0 DALYs and a death seconds after counting for more than 30 (at 3 percent discounting). However, while there is serious disagreement about the ethics of the beginning of life, there are very few advocates of such a discontinuous jump in moral status at the exact moment of birth.

The DALY framework can be extended to smooth out this discontinuity. This can be done using a method from Jamison *et al.* (2006a), which introduces a concept called the "acquisition of life potential" (ALP). The idea is that instead of instantaneously gaining full moral weight, the fetus begins acquiring it at some stage before birth, and gradually acquires full status by some stage after birth. To calculate the DALYs due to death of a fetus or infant, one multiplies the DALYs as calculated by the standard approach by a number between 0 and 1 which represents the current level of "life potential."

Operationalizing this concept involves introducing a parameter, A, that indicates the speed of ALP (see Jamison *et al.*, 2006a for precise definitions and assessments of the burden of disease that result). A is constructed so that for the fastest possible speed of ALP, namely, instantaneous ALP, $A = 1$. A is bounded below by 0. This chapter extends the notation DALYs(r,K) in two ways. First, it explicitly indicates the level of A by extending the DALY nomenclature to DALYs(r,K,A). Thus using this nomenclature, DALYs(3,0) become DALYs(3,0,1), because the standard DALY is the special case with instantaneous ALP. Second, when stillbirths are included in the range of events to be measured in the GBD, this is explicitly noted in the DALY nomenclature as DALYsSB(r,K,A). Notation around YLL is similarly extended.

Explicit modeling of ALP permits three instrumentally useful improvements to the previous DALYs formulation:

- The ALP formulation allows, but does not require, the discontinuity in DALY loss at the time of birth to be avoided.
- The ALP formulation allows, but does not require, a positive DALY loss associated with stillbirths.
- The ratio of the DALY loss from a death at age 20, say, to that at birth is close to 1 for any reasonable set of parameter values in the previous DALY formulation. However, many people's ethical judgments would give this ratio a value substantially greater than 1. The ALP formulation allows, but does not require, these judgments.

Only a limited number of empirical studies have attempted to assess directly the views of individuals concerning deaths at different ages. In an important early study, Crawford *et al.* (1989) relate grief from a death to the concept of reproductive potential in population biology. They conclude that for several diverse human groups the relationship shows grief to be closely related to prehistoric reproductive value. An Institute of Medicine review of vaccine development priorities (IOM, 1985) uses infant mortality equivalence in cost-effectiveness calculations. The committee members preparing the report collectively judged that the loss from a death at age 20 should be about twice that from an infant death. However, some preliminary trade-off studies suggest a value closer to three or four times. All three lines of evidence point to gradual rather than instantaneous ALP. What is clear, however, is that no completely defensible estimate (or even range) is currently available, and hence the numbers used in Jamison *et al.* (2006b) should be viewed as only

Table 7.4 Discounted YLL at different ages of death for several DALY formulations

Age group	Representative age of death (years)	YLL(3,1)	YLL(3,0)	$YLL_{SB}(3,0, 0.54)$
Antepartum	–0.080	0	0	4.95
Intrapartum	–0.001	0	0	9.13
Neonatal	0.020	33.09	30.42	9.40
Infant	0.300	33.36	30.40	12.95
Postneonatal infant	0.500	33.56	30.39	15.42
Child	2.000	34.81	30.28	26.40

Note: YLL(3,1), YLL(3,0), and $YLL_{SB}(3,0,1)$ assume instantaneous acquisition of life potential, ALP ($A = 1$). YLL(3,1) assumes full age-weighting ($K = 1$); the other three formulations assume uniform age weights ($K = 0$). $YLL_{SB}(3,0,0.54)$ assumes gradual acquisition of life potential ($A = 0.54$). The subscript SB refers to formulations that do not give stillbirths zero weight.
Source: Jamison *et al.* (2006b: Table 6.6).

suggestive. Table 7.4 shows the YLLs associated with deaths at different young ages for alternative formulations of the DALY, including one with their preferred value of $A = 0.54$. This final column reports several estimates. (It is important to note the DALYs and YLLs for deaths above age 5 are unaffected by introduction of ALP.) *Weighting the YLLs at different ages by the relative frequency of deaths at those ages gives a $DALY_{SB}$ (3,0, 0.54) loss of 16.4 DALYs for a typical under-5 death, about half what is typically used.* Our analyses use this figure.

The value of a DALY

The VSL estimates discussed on p. 397 yield a range of values for a statistical life – from around 100 to almost 200 times *per capita* income. Very approximately, this can be translated to a value for a statistical life *year* in the range of 2–4 times *per capita* income. Tolley *et al.* (1994) provide a valuable overview of relevant estimates, including estimates of the value of preventing disability.

However, this does not answer the question of which income level we should use to set the value of a DALY. The answer to this question is highly dependent upon what the cost-benefit calculation is being used for. For example, if Uganda is deciding whether to publicly finance a disease control program, the money raised for this would come from the Ugandan people. Their nominal GNI *per capita* is about $500, so the above method would suggest that the Ugandans would value a DALY as much as a sum of money between $1,000 and $2,000. Thus it would be counter-productive for their government to spend more than $2,000 to provide a DALY. In this usage case, where a country is spending its own money to help its own citizens, we need to use each country's GNI to determine their dollar value of a DALY and hence their BCRs. It is irrelevant to the Ugandans that the Nigerians have a GNI *per capita* of approximately $1,180 and would thus value a DALY at more than twice as many dollars.

In contrast, if we are trying to produce a global prioritization, there are strong ethical reasons for using a single dollar value for DALYs (or VSLs), no matter which country they occur in. Otherwise we would be failing to value all people equally and would end up grossly neglecting death and disability in poorer countries. Since the interventions in this chapter affect people in relatively poor countries, this effect is limited but could still be as much as a factor of 10 or 20. However, if we wanted to compare these interventions with interventions that affected people in high-income countries, then the effect could rise to a factor of 100, with a DALY being valued at $100,000–$200,000 in the United States. While there are no health interventions for US citizens discussed here, the problem could come up for any type of benefit for members of high- or middle-income countries calculated from their WTP.

For the reasons above, there cannot be a single dollar value that we can place on a DALY or a

VSL to take account of the different ways in which people might wish to use it. The best compromise that we have been able to find is to use a single figure based on the average income in our target countries. The emphasis in this chapter is on low-income countries, defined by the World Bank for 2001 as countries with *per capita* incomes of less than $1,005 (exchange rate). The World Bank's estimate of the average income of people living in low-income countries is $509 per year (World Bank, 2011: Table 1.1). Choosing a value for a statistical life year near the low end of the range (a little above 2) would give a convenient value of $1,000, which is what this chapter uses in its main calculations as the value of a DALY. (Note that, for the reasons discussed on p. 419, the DALY loss from a death under age 5 – and hence the benefit from preventing it – is about half that used in standard DALYs.)

Note that health programs in poor countries should adjust this number according to their own national incomes, as mentioned in the sensitivity analysis in the Appendix (p. 419). Furthermore, comparisons between this chapter and any CBA where WTP has been calculated based on the preferences of people in a richer country will need to scale up these ratios accordingly. For example, while our recommended TB program has an indicative BCR of 20:1, the BCR of the program should be thought of as 2000:1 if it were being compared to interventions that benefited people in the United States and used American willingness to pay estimates.

We explore the sensitivity of our results to these effects in the Appendix, as well as considering a DALY value of $5,000 for low-income countries and the standard DALYs (DALYs (3,0)) for child deaths.

The cost of a DALY

The cost of buying a DALY with different interventions was calculated, in DCP2, by combining "typical" prices for a geographical region (Mulligan *et al.*, 2003) with input quantities estimated from clinical and public health experience and case studies in the literature. Because the solutions being considered usually involve substantial increments from the status quo, long-term average costs were used. For internationally traded inputs, prices were the same for all regions.[7] For local costs regional estimates were used. Intervention costs, therefore, are *not* expressed in PPP$. The reason for this is that local costs present decision-makers with the appropriate numbers for budgeting and for comparing interventions in the context where they are working. Regional costs are taken to be a better approximation of these local costs than global costs would be. On this point the methods of this chapter differ from those of the 2004 Copenhagen Consensus (Mills and Shilcutt, 2004).

Child health

A small number of conditions account for most of the large differences in health between the poor and the not so poor. For example, less than 1 percent of all deaths from AIDS, TB, and malaria occur in the high-income countries. Available technical options – exemplified by but going well beyond immunization – can address most of the conditions that affect children, and can do so with great efficacy and at modest cost. That short list of conditions, including undernutrition, relates directly to achieving the MDGs for health. The section begins by discussing intervention to address under-5 mortality. It then turns to the problem of the world's most prevalent infections, intestinal worm infections, and the relatively straightforward approach to dealing with those in schoolchildren. The final subsection discusses delivery and includes two of our solutions for the 2012 Copenhagen Consensus pricing mechanisms to facilitate uptake of appropriate anti-malarials and the essential surgical platform.

Under-5 health problems and intervention priorities

The MDG for under-5 mortality (MDG-4) (reducing its level in 2015 by two-thirds relative to what

[7] Because of tiered pricing, on-patent drugs were *not* considered to be internationally traded.

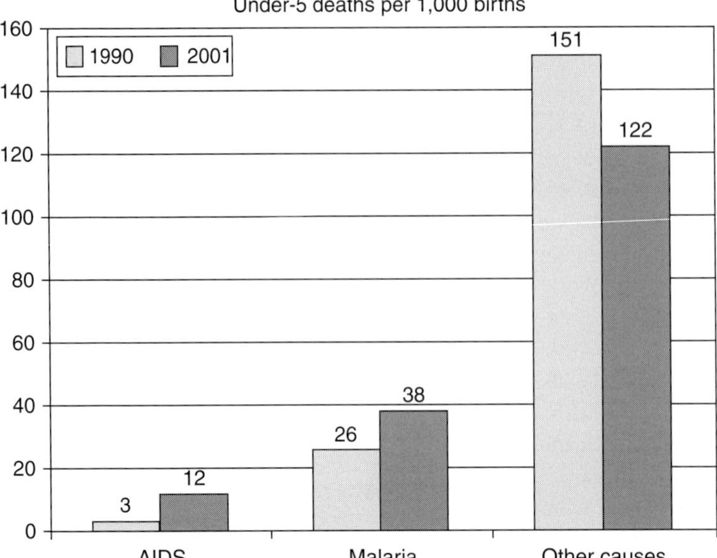

Figure 7.3 *Under-5 deaths from AIDS, malaria, and other causes, per 000 births, SSA, 1990 and 2001*

it was in 1990) is highly ambitious. Yet its implication of an average 4.3 percent per year decline is well within recent experience. In the first half of the MDG period (1990–2002), forty-six countries achieved rates of decline in under-5 mortality greater than 4.3 percent per year (Lopez *et al.*, 2006a).

Basic knowledge about the power and the cost-effectiveness of interventions to address maternal and child health has been available for many decades. DCP2's work makes four important and relatively new points. First, major declines in childhood mortality could well be accelerated with expanded case management of acutely ill children and with the addition of several new antigens to routine vaccination. These include *Haemophilus influenza* type b (Hib) and *Streptococcus pneumonia* which are common causes of childhood pneumonia; hepatitis B which protects against liver cancer; and newer rotavirus and shigella vaccines against diarrhea (England *et al.*, 2001). The Global Alliance for Vaccines and Immunization (GAVI) estimates that the addition of Hib and pneumococcal vaccines to vaccination programs could save 800,000 lives a year by 2010. Further GAVI estimates suggest that rotavirus and shigella vaccines might save 600,000 lives a year by 2010.

Second, about 40 percent of under-5 deaths (excluding stillbirths) occur at ages less than 28 days (Liu *et al.*, 2012), when the substantial but usually neglected problem of stillbirth is considered. DCP2 identifies some highly cost-effective approaches to intervention against stillbirth and neonatal death (Lawn *et al.*, 2006). These include increased reliance on delivery in facilities with surgical capacity to deal with complex obstetric emergencies, which are life-threatening for both mother and for child.

Third, there is a rapid spread of resistance of the malaria parasite to chloroquine and to sulfadoxine-pyrimethamine (SP). These inexpensive, highly effective, widely available drugs provided an important partial check on the high levels of malaria deaths in Africa, which are concentrated particularly in children. Their loss is leading to a rise in malaria mortality and morbidity that could be substantial. Figure 7.3 illustrates increases in malaria death rates and decreases in death rates from other causes except HIV/AIDS in under-5 children in SSA in the period from 1990 to 2001. This death rate increase results in hundreds of thousands of deaths more than would otherwise have occurred. (With malaria, however, there is increasing evidence that widespread use of bednets and better treatment is partially reversing the adverse trend prior to 2011, see WHO, 2011.) The design of instruments for financing a rapid transition to effective new treatments – artemisinin combination therapies (ACTs) – is a high priority. Kenneth Arrow chaired a committee of the US IOM to design appropriate financial instruments (IOM, 2004; Arrow *et al.*, 2005). This resulted in creation of the Affordable Medicines Facility-malaria (AMFm), which would reduce the relative prices which public or private sector providers face for ACTs rather than increasing their budgets for purchasing them. This effort is now under way and early results indicate that the mechanism has been successful in lowering the price of ACTs in eight pilot countries. Fourth, although education interventions are considered in a separate paper for CC12 (Orazem, 2012), it is worth noting here that improvements in the quality of basic education can plausibly have BCRs as high as for many health interventions – even if no benefits of education other than mortality reduction are included. In a recent paper, Jamison *et al.* (2007) estimate that the effect of a 1 standard deviation improvement in quality[8] would increase the annual rate of decline of infant mortality by about 0.6 percent leading, after twenty years, to something over a 10 percent reduction in IMR relative to what it would otherwise have been. They estimate that this effect could be achieved for on the order of 10 percent of the cost of a year of schooling, which is likely to be less than $100 per student per year in a low-income country.

If the total fertility rate is 3 and the base level of IMR is 70 per 1,000 then education quality improvement is likely to result in a cost per (undiscounted) child death averted of around $1,000. Assuming (as this chapter does) a low DALY loss per child death of about 16 and the value of a DALY in low-income countries of $1,000, then the BCR will be about 13. Discounting the benefits at 5 percent would give a BCR of 4, again ignoring any other benefits from education. Increasing the value of a DALY from $1,000 to $5,000 would increase the BCR to 20 even with 5 percent discounting. In our next subsection we turn to a mechanism through which health intervention – deworming – can contribute to increasing both the quantity and quality of education, with benefits through the mechanism reviewed here, on the next generation.

In addition to the above, other intervention priorities for addressing under-5 mortality are for the most part familiar:

- Exclusive early breast-feeding, which has increased widely in all parts of the world over the last few years.
- Expanding immunization coverage of the current set of antigens in the Expanded Program on Immunization (EPI), as well as addition HiB, hepatitis B, rotavirus, and streptococcus.
- Expanding the use of the simple and low-cost but highly effective treatments for diarrhea and child pneumonia through integrated management of childhood illness or other mechanisms.
- Preventing transmission of malaria by expanding coverage of insecticide-treated bednets; by expanding use of intermittent preventive treatment for pregnant women; and by use of indoor residual spraying with DDT.
- Enabling the use of effective anti-malarial medication, and preventing the development of resistance to it by subsidizing its price to make it affordable and to crowd out counterfeits and monotherapies that will speed resistance. The AMFm has been successful in doing this in its initial year. Its continuation and expansion is one of the five priorities this chapter recommends, in part because it addresses the externality associated with monotherapy-induced antibiotic resistance.
- Ensuring the widespread distribution of key micronutrients, most notably Vitamin A, zinc, and iron. (See Hoddinott *et al.*, 2012, Chapter 6 in this volume)
- Expanding the use of anti-retrovirals and breast-feeding substitutes to prevent mother-to-child transmission of HIV/AIDS.

Worm infections in school-age children

In addition to interventions to reduce under-5 mortality, one other priority is increasingly

[8] As measured by scores on internationally standardized achievement tests (SATS), particularly those in mathematics.

clear. The world's most prevalent infections are intestinal helminth (worm) infections, and children of all ages are among the most heavily affected. Hotez *et al.* (2006) discuss these infections, which a low-cost drug (albendazole), taken every six months to a year, can control effectively. The Bundy *et al.* (2006) discussion of school health services points to both the importance to children's school progress of taking albendazole where needed and the potential efficacy of school health programs as a vehicle for delivery. Canning (2009) emphasized that standard health-related cost-effectiveness assessments (CEAs) fail to capture the importance (and feasibility) of deworming and the 2008 Copenhagen Consensus overall ranking for deworming was number 6 out of 30 (Bhagwati *et al.*, 2009). In the long run, improved sanitation and water supplies will prevent transmission of worm infections. Use of albendazole is only an interim solution until development-driven sanitation improvements take over, but it is one that may be required for decades if the experience of the currently high-income countries is relevant.

Worms remain a neglected infection despite the high prevalence and the low cost of treatment (Bundy *et al.*, 2006). Regions such as SSA, Southeast Asia and parts of Latin America are disproportionally affected by worms due to poor and unsanitary living conditions and personal hygiene (Hall and Horton, 2009). Human behavior, climate, and overcrowding can all contribute to the survival and transmission of worms. From complications with digestion to difficulty absorbing nutrients, worms can be detrimental to a person's overall well-being, including productivity, appetite, fitness, and growth (Stephenson, 1987; Bundy *et al.*, 2004). Children are at greater risk of infection than adults and will suffer more severe, lifelong complications if worms are left untreated. Children who do experience worm infection often live in poor communities and need a sustainable treatment plan to remedy any loss in education, nutrition, and intellectual development they may experience. The behavioral patterns of children put them at greater risk of serious infection than other age groups.

Currently there is much literature suggesting that deworming programs are extremely cost-effective. According to Deworm the World, a joint initiative launched in 2007 by the WEF, deworming programs are one of the most cost-effective health interventions in the world (Deworm the World, 2009). It is helpful in analyzing the educational consequences of deworming programs to consider more explicitly than is typical for education administrators the relation between system capacity and system utilization. The number of student places needed to serve a catchment area is simply the population size in the relevant age cohort, here ages 5–14, times the percentage of that cohort that would ideally be in school (for this age group, it would be 100 percent). Each student place requires (given local policies on class size) a certain amount of physical plant, teacher availability, and so forth; the level of those resources actually available determines the number of student places installed. Enrolment will typically be less, perhaps substantially less, than the number of places installed due to dropouts and repetitions leaving upper-grade classrooms only partially filled; similarly, student absences on any given day will leave classrooms only partially utilized. The ratio of utilization to capacity provides, we suggest, the appropriate measure of the quantitative efficiency of a school system. (The concept of qualitative efficiency, which relates the rate of learning to the expenditure per student-year of actual attendance, is more frequently discussed in the literature.) Miguel and Kremer (2004) find the major effect of deworming in Kenya to be on quantitative efficiency: treated children ended up acquiring 0.15 additional years of school, at only the cost of deworming because capacity limits had not been met. Orazem *et al.* (2009) stress the importance of explicit attention to these limits, which suggest corresponding limits on extent of potential impact of deworming absent complementary investments in educational infrastructure.

The preceding discussion has provided a structure for deworming in the context of interventions to affect educational outcomes. The examples developed by Jamison and Leslie (1990), and Horton and Hall (2009) and the Kenya work of Miguel and Kremer (2004) all point to the potential for *highly* attractive cost-effectiveness or BCRs from deworming's effect through school. In the 2008 Copenhagen Consensus assessment of educational priorities deworming ranked high (Orazem *et al.*, 2009) as it also did in the context of assessing nutritional priorities (Horton *et al.*, 2008). And, as previously noted, the 2008 Copenhagen Consensus Expert Panel of distinguished economists (Bhagwati *et al.*, 2009) ranked school-based deworming number 6 in its assessment of 30 development priorities.

When turning to the health dimension of outcomes and cost-effectiveness there has been substantial recent controversy. The non-profit charity evaluator GiveWell, in its review of DCP2's estimates of cost per DALY found (in collaboration with the DCP2 authors) important errors that suggest (from a health perspective) that deworming may be far less cost-effective than thought. A major problem was an error in WHO's published disability weights for helminthic infection.[9]

Two related issues arise in trying to express health loss from worm infections in an aggregate measure like the DALY. The first is that the DALY loss from these infections is very little in mortality (YLLs) and very substantial in disability (YLDs). The effective disability weights are small but multiplied by an enormous number of infections. Whether the product is large or small depends entirely on the disability weights and we would assert that *estimating these small disability weights with any accuracy is far beyond the state of the art*. A second related problem is that the distribution of intensity of worm infections is highly "overdispersed," i.e. only a few people harbor most worms (Bundy *et al.*, 2004; Hall and Horton, 2009). Defining who is sick, and how sick, becomes rather arbitrary even though the definitions may be quite clear. We suggest that any discussion of the health-related cost-effectiveness for deworming not use DALYs and focus instead on costs per "real" outcome: person treated; infected person treated; "diseased" person treated (at greater than or equal to 10 worms, etc.). Hall and Horton (2009) provides an excellent example.

Delivering reproductive and child health interventions

The list of potential interventions is far from exhaustive and different regions, countries, and communities will face different mixes of the problems that these interventions address. However, there can be little dispute that any short list of intervention priorities for under-5 mortality in LMICs would include many on the list in the preceding sections. Why not, then, simply put money into scaling up these known interventions to a satisfactory level? In this section we first discuss constraints to scaling up and approaches to overcoming them. We next discuss a specific financial mechanism – the AMFm – in detail and conclude that its continuation and expansion is a high priority. Finally we discuss the neglected priority often accorded to the platform of essential surgery. Much of what surgical intervention addresses deals with complicated delivery, contraception (vasectomy, tubal ligation and subdermal hormones), and injury.

Overcoming implementation constraints

To greatly oversimplify – and these issues are discussed more substantially in Mills *et al.* (2006) – two schools of thought exist. One line of thinking – often ascribed to the macroeconomist Jeffrey Sachs and his work as chair of the WHO CMH – concludes that more money and focused effort *are* the solutions. Although acknowledging dual constraints – of money and of health system capacity – Sachs and his colleagues (WHO CMH, 2001; Sachs, 2005) contend that money can buy (or develop, or both) relevant system capacity even over a period as short as five years. Major gains are affordable and health system capacity constraints can be overcome. Immunization provides an example of where, even in the short term, money can substitute for system capacity. Adding newer antigens to the immunization schedule is costly (although still cost-effective). In some environments, however, it proves less demanding of system capacity than expanding coverage does. Money can be effectively spent by adding antigens at the same time as investing in the capacity to extend coverage.

A second school of thought acknowledges the need for more money but asserts that health system capacity is often a binding short- to medium-term

[9] See http://blog.givewell.org/2011/09/29/errors-in-dcp2-cost-effectiveness-estimate-for-deworming/.

constraint on substantial scaling up of interventions. Van der Gaag (2004) emphasized this point in his critique of an earlier Copenhagen Consensus paper on health. Critical priorities are, therefore, system reform and strengthening while ensuring that such reforms focus clearly on achieving improved health outcomes and financial protection.

This chapter's perspective is closer to that of Sachs than of Van der Gaag while emphasizing the need (on p. 400) to be explicit about intervention costs that are non-financial. This points both to the need for considering how to relax these constraints and to selecting interventions in part on the extent to which they are less demanding of non-financial inputs. Frenk *et al.* (2006) and Sepúlveda *et al.* (2006) have described a "diagonal" approach being used in Mexico where systems are strengthened while focusing on specific disease outcomes. Experience suggests that while such an approach demands considerable management, it is highly effective.

Against a backdrop of low immunization coverage in Africa, Malawi, one of the poorest countries in the world, has succeeded in boosting immunization coverage against measles from only 50 percent in 1980 to almost 90 percent today. Malawi undertook a program to raise routine measles immunizations, including campaigns to catch children missed out by routine efforts. As a result, the number of reported cases and deaths has fallen dramatically. During 1999, only two laboratory-confirmed cases were reported and, for the first time ever, no measles deaths. Yet only two years earlier, almost 7,000 measles cases were reported and 267 deaths (both of which are likely to be undercounts). This was achieved despite one in five of the population not having access to health services, fever than 50 percent having access to safe water, and only 3 percent having access to adequate sanitation (Jha and Mills, 2002).

Mills *et al.* (2006), as indicated, discussed these issues further in the context of all the problems facing a health system. From an individual country's perspective, however, if financial resources are available, the question is very much an empirical one: to what extent can those resources be effectively deployed in buying in interventions, in buying out of prevailing system constraints, and in investing in relevant system capacity for the future? Accumulating experience suggests that, to be successful, these choices will involve sustained funding to achieve specific outcomes (Jha *et al.*, 2002; Crogan *et al.*, 2006).

The AMFm

Innovations in financing and delivery have been a key feature of global health investments during the past decade. The number of privately initiated, publicly funded innovative financing mechanisms includes GAVI (for vaccines), the Global Fund for AIDS, TB, and malaria (for anti-retrovirals, TB drugs and diagnostics, bednets and drugs for malaria), Advance Market Commitments (for pneumococcal and other vaccines), and, more recently, the AMFm. The AMFm was created in 2010 as a separate arm of the Global Fund to implement the pilot phase of a high-level subsidy for ACTs in eight countries in SSA. The original idea of AMFm was mooted by the IOM committee as a response to the problem of growing artemisinin monotherapy use in the retail shops where treatment for malaria is most frequently obtained. And artemisinin monotherapy could increase the likelihood of parasite resistance to artemisinins, the last major class of compounds that are still effective against malaria parasites. ACTs were available in some public sector facilities through donor financing and in the private sector at a cost of between $8 and $12, which is out of the reach of all but the wealthiest section of the population in malaria-endemic countries. Artemisinin monotherapies, and monotherapies of the drugs used to protect artemisinin in ACTs, were typically available at far lower prices, with the obvious behavioral consequences.

A high-level subsidy for quality ACTs, it was argued, would crowd out monotherapies from the informal private sector, increase access to these drugs in both public and private sectors, lower ACT prices by ensuring stable and high demand, and lower incentives for sales of counterfeit and expired artemisinin drugs. Since the cost of delivering the drugs would be borne largely by private sector supply chains, the donor cost of the subsidy would be restricted to the difference between the unsubsidized wholesaler price and the subsidized price.

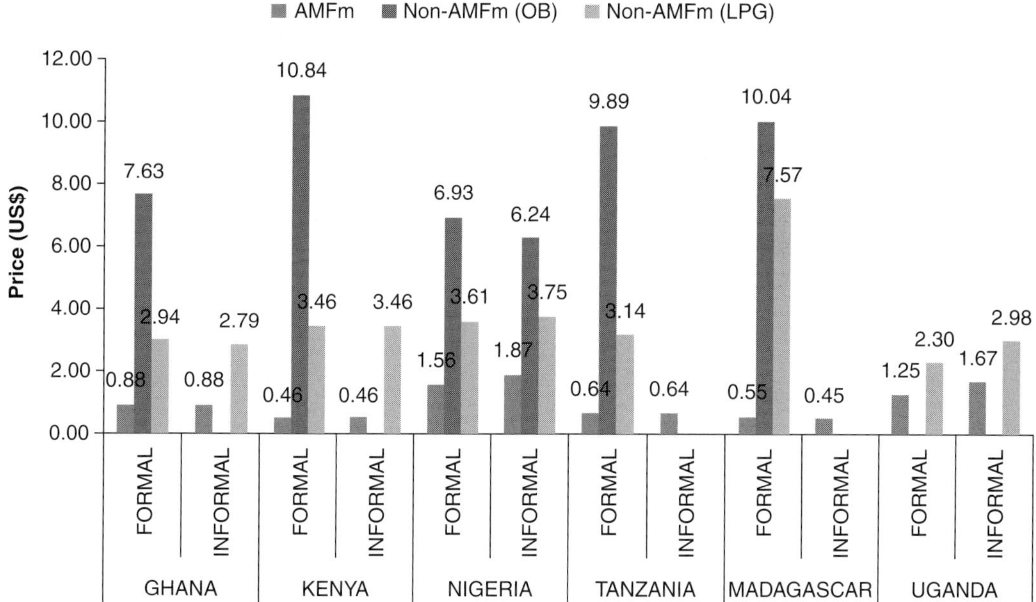

Figure 7.4 *Median prices of AL 20/120 mg (pack size 6 × 4), by country: AMFm versus non AMFm*

Note: OB: Other brands; LPG: Lowest-priced generic

Early cost-effectiveness estimates based on sophisticated mathematical models of malaria transmission and resistance indicated that a child death could be averted at roughly $1,000 (Laxminarayan *et al.*, 2006c). Similar estimates are obtained through back-of-the-envelope calculations. US$1 million spent on a subsidy would expand access to 300,000 more children with malaria (based on 67 percent of AMFm ACTs being pediatric formulations), treat 20,000 severe malaria cases, and avert roughly 1,000 child deaths. This calculation does not include the benefits associated with averted resistance because of crowding out artemisinin monotherapy, the benefits of lower counterfeit drugs use, or of price reductions because of stabilized demand for ACTs. According to one model-based study, the discounted externality benefits of resistance reduction including (a) the reduction in malaria transmission from infected to susceptible individuals due to increased overall drug treatment and (b) the increase in average drug effectiveness, which benefits treated patients themselves as well as reducing infection transmission from them to other individuals; and less the discounted gross distortionary cost of the subsidy, is about 6:1 (Laxminarayan *et al.*, 2010).

Early evidence from the AMFm pilot indicates that the goal of lowering ACT prices relative to other drugs in the retail sector has been achieved in nearly all AMFm countries (see Figure 7.4). The ratio of the price of a full course of AMFm-subsidized ACTs to the price of a full course of the lowest-priced generic ranges from 1:2 in Nigeria and Uganda to 1:14 in Madagascar. The ratios are even more stark when the price of AMFm drugs is compared to the price of non-AMFm branded drugs, and range from 1:3 in Nigeria to 1:23 in the Kenyan formal sector. A full independent evaluation of the AMFm pilot has been commissioned by the Global Fund board and is expected in September 2012. This should shed more light on the utility of this novel market-based mechanism in drug delivery, and inform a future course of action once the large-scale pilot funding runs out in December 2012. One of our 2012 Copenhagen Consensus solutions is that continued funding for AMFm should claim high priority.

Essential surgery

Almost one in ten pregnancies in developing countries result in deliveries with major complications – heavy bleeding, torn tissues, or obstruction to the child's passage, that leads to days of extreme pain and often death for the mother and child. Dealing with these problems usually requires surgical intervention (although not necessarily by a board-certified surgeon or obstetrician.) A range of correctable problems of the very young also require surgical intervention and the global community has advanced "safe motherhood" initiatives to strengthen the national capacity to deal with these problems. The same skill sets – surgery, anesthesia, nursing – that can respond to complications of pregnancy can also respond to a range of other problems, most prominently trauma including burns but also a range of abdominal problems and suppurative infections common in developing countries (see Mock *et al.* (2009) for a discussion of priority areas for essential surgery).

Debas *et al.* (2006) in DCP2 decided to undertake a CEA of a modest district hospital (100-bed) with some degree of surgical capacity rather than to look at the cost-effectiveness just of obstetric or other specific surgical interventions. The reasoning is that investment in expanding capacity or improving quality are, at this *platform* level, a platform that responds to multiple and diverse problems. For undertaking a CEA they assessed all the costs of operating the district hospital surgical platform for a year. For effectiveness they looked, in different epidemiological environments, at the annual mix of admissions and at the consequences (using best judgment to apportion part of the consequence to surgical intervention). An early example of this platform analysis comes from Bangladesh, where low costs and substantial numbers of (probably) obstetric deaths averted led to highly favorable cost-effectiveness estimates. (McCord and Chowdhury, 2003). The best estimates of cost per DALY for what we might call "essential surgery" range across geographical regions from $40–$100, with their high estimates at about twice their best estimates (Debas *et al.*, 2006).

Why might such surgery appear so cost-effective? Like the drugs for malaria, TB, HIV/AIDS pneumonia, and other infectious killers, a one- or two-hour surgical procedure can change outcomes decisively: from death to a four-week recovery or from being seriously crippled for life to having a mild limp. Very basic surgery can achieve these outcome changes at modest cost.

HIV/AIDS

For dozens of countries around the world – including several of the most populous – the HIV/AIDS epidemic threatens every aspect of development. No other threat comes close, with the possible exceptions of use of nuclear weapons in densely populated areas or a devastating global pandemic similar to the 1917–1918 influenza episode. Most governments of affected LMICs and most providers of development assistance have only recently begun to respond more than minimally at the beginning of the twenty-first century. The creation of the Global Fund to Fight AIDS, Tuberculosis, and Malaria can be viewed as an attempt of the world's top political leaders to improve on the records of existing institutions. The Global Fund's initial years have seen substantial success, but as this volume goes to press that success is being undermined by sharp constraints on resource availability, as was foreseen by Bezanson (2005).

Thirty years have passed since the recognition of the infectious disease now named acquired immune deficiency syndrome (AIDS). In that relatively short time HIV/AIDS has killed over 30 million individuals, and an additional 33.3 million people are now living with the infection. Africa shoulders the burden of the epidemic: UNAIDS estimates that in 2009 1.3 million people died from AIDS in Africa, 22.5 million were living with the infection, and a further 1.5 million acquired the infection during the year. Even though prevention and treatment programs are expanding, the epidemic is holding its ground. Only two out of every five people requiring anti-retroviral therapy currently have access to treatment – and this number is threatened by financial pressures. Though universal access to treatment is a morally compelling goal, the high costs associated with treatment argue for a strategy that emphasizes prevention (See Hecht *et al.*, 2010; UNAIDS *et al.*, 2010).

In contrast to the initially slow programmatic movement of most national leaders and international institutions, the R&D community – public and private – has made rapid progress in developing tools to control the HIV/AIDS epidemic. Sensitive, specific, and inexpensive diagnostics are available; means of prevention have been developed and tested; modes of transmission are well understood; and increasingly powerful drugs for controlling the viral load allow radical slowing of disease progression. Tools for dealing with HIV/AIDS are thus available: Bertozzi *et al.* (2006) emphasized that a number of countries have shown by example that those tools can be put to effective use. Most of the high-income countries have done so, and Brazil, Mexico, and Thailand provide examples of upper-middle-income countries that have forestalled potentially serious epidemics (del Rio and Sepúlveda, 2002).

This section first discusses behavioral prevention and medical then vaccine development. It closes with a discussion of anti-retroviral therapy. It draws importantly on papers prepared for the 2011 Copenhagen Consensus RethinkAIDS exercise.

Prevention of HIV transmission

The reasons for the variations in prevalence between countries are not entirely clear despite substantial research. It is now established that high levels of male circumcision protect against HIV/AIDS transmission at the population and individual level (Abdool Karim, 2007). High levels of genital ulcer disease and low levels of male circumcision may help to explain the high levels of HIV/AIDS infection seen in southern and eastern Africa. These conditions also include high levels of paid sex and partner change, common sexually transmitted infections (STIs), low condom use rates, male mobility and migration, and low rates of male circumcision. These points suggest the opportunities for preventive intervention.

The key challenge for HIV/AIDS policy is to prevent HIV transmission. In the absence of a vaccine, several interventions are of key importance. For the Copenhagen Consensus effort Rethink HIV, Bollinger (2012) reviews the benefits and costs of options for presenting non-sexual transmission, and Behrman and Kohler (2010) assess sexual transmission. The most clearly effective preventive interventions against HIV/AIDS are those targeting groups that – because of high rates of partner change, increased susceptibility to infection, or both – are highly vulnerable. Peer interventions among sex workers teach them high levels of condom use, control of STIs, and client negotiation skills that appear highly effective. Sex workers and their clients represent an important vulnerable group who are central to the spread of HIV/AIDS in most populations, including in Africa, and vulnerable groups might even be important in early as well as late stages of the epidemic (Chen *et al.*, 2007). In some contexts fewer than one sex worker would need to be covered in a program for one year to prevent one infection (Jha *et al.*, 2001).

A few countries in Asia with conditions for rapid growth in HIV/AIDS infections acted early by scaling up vulnerable group interventions. Their common principles were to work with the commercial sex industry, map where it occurs, aim for high coverage, and base action on solid epidemiological information. The results are impressive. Thailand is the most famous example, where HIV/AIDS peaked in the early 1990s and has stayed at below 2 percent seroprevalence since. Less known are Mexico (del Rio and Sepúlveda, 2002) and Cambodia, which copied the Thai "100 percent condom" program in commercial sex in 1997 in one state, and has shown impressive declines in HIV/AIDS. More recent evidence from the four southern states of India suggest that new HIV/AIDS infections might have dropped by 30 percent, probably due to change in sex workers (either the proportion using condoms or men going less often to sex workers, Kumar *et al.*, 2006).

Other measures that complement vulnerable group interventions are effective. Despite controversy about the evidence, the best judgment is that STIs remain important as risk markers and risk factors for HIV/AIDS spread. STI treatment for vulnerable and general populations is probably effective for HIV/AIDS control. Voluntary counseling and testing has led to some reduction in unsafe behavior in some studies, though the duration of the change is not clear. However, such testing is not necessarily a cost-effective form of prevention in all or even most settings, especially where prevalence is low. Voluntary testing is, however, a necessary prerequisite to some forms of treatment.

Although the transmission of HIV/AIDS from mother to child is not of great epidemiological importance, since the infected children are very unlikely to transmit the disease, it is a mode of transmission that can be blocked. Short courses of single anti-retrovirals can halve the transmission risk from about 40 percent to 20 percent. To be fully effective, replacement feeding is also required, given that breast milk is a source of transmission. Finally, needle exchange and blood safety programs can reduce these less common modes of transmission.

More broadly, prevention efforts appear to work best when there is national leadership and simultaneous, sustained investment in multiple approaches to prevention, including efforts to reduce the stigmatization of vulnerable groups. Increasing the availability of condoms for the wider population can be enabling of more focused action. For example, the proportion of Senegalese women easily able to procure condoms rose from below 30 percent to 80 percent between 1992 and 1997. Focused information campaigns aimed at building public support and awareness are also seen to be important, although these are not likely to change behavior by themselves, but reinforce the message of simultaneous use of multiple interventions.

In those SSA countries with generalized epidemics that have spread far beyond vulnerable groups, a national approach is a necessity. The reasons for the sharp decline in HIV/AIDS prevalence in Uganda, from about 20 percent in 1990 to 10 percent in 1999, are widely debated. It may be due, at least in part, to a broad-based prevention strategy addressed at the population as a whole, or due simply to the fact that high death rates among the most susceptible helped the epidemic to decline (James, 2005). The replicability of the Ugandan experience to lower-prevalence settings has not been established.

Bertozzi *et al.* (2006) point out that even by 2003 fewer than one in five people at high risk of infection had access to the most basic preventive services. In much of the world, little has been spent on prevention, and little has been achieved. In addition, fundamentalist factions in both national governments and the development assistance community may be partially responsible for discouraging condom use in some countries and in stigmatizing and alienating commercial sex workers who are particular priorities for prevention programs. Despite those problems, the potential for prevention is very real, and a number of successful countries have shown the possibility of using that potential well. While evaluations of single interventions have often failed to find an impact, the countries that have mounted major programs of "combination prevention" have often achieved substantial success. The ingredients in the combination cocktail will vary by location, but Peter Piot has argued that there is now reasonable evidence for its general success (Piot *et al.*, 2008). Combination prevention was on the solution list for the 2008 Copenhagen Consensus.

AIDS vaccine development

An AIDS vaccine[10] is the ultimate preventative tool – vaccination would provide a manageable and affordable way to confer protection against HIV infection. When fully developed and licensed, an AIDS vaccine could have a powerful and immediate impact; the International AIDS Vaccine Initiative (IAVI) estimates that an AIDS vaccine of 50 percent efficacy given to just 30 percent of the population could reduce the number of new infections in the developing world by 24 percent in 15 years (IAVI, 2009). Yet AIDS vaccine development is proving to be enormously expensive. Is the perhaps $15–20 billion of additional resources that it may cost the world to develop an AIDS vaccine worth it?

[10] We use the term "AIDS vaccine" to denote the probable set of vaccines that could emerge from ongoing development efforts. Hypothetical values of vaccine cost and efficacy in this chapter are for the best (mix) to emerge over time, and in a more extended assessment the sensitivity of the CBA results to these parameters would be evaluated. We limit our discussion in this chapter to vaccines that prevent infection, but it is important to note that efforts are also under way to develop vaccines that strengthen the immune system's response to established disease. Animal trials have generated hope for the prospects of this type of vaccine (Maurice, 2011).

One of the papers in the 2011 RethinkHIV project addressed the potential returns to expanding the technological base through development, manufacture, and utilization of a vaccine to prevent HIV infection (Hecht and Jamison, 2012). That paper did not argue for investment in vaccine development at the expense of ongoing HIV prevention or treatment interventions. Rather, it examined the proposition that accelerated investment in AIDS vaccine development would have high benefit relative to cost – and hence justify diversion of resources from less productive development assistance investments.

The current and likely future sources of funding for vaccine development come from parts of the public sector that differ from those that fund AIDS control. Private sector product development funds likewise do not come at the cost of control money. Only in foundations is there likely to be genuine fungibility between product development resources and control sources. In this environment the role of the 2012 Copenhagen Consensus is perhaps not that of trading-off vaccine development resources with resources for attractive control options. Rather, a conclusion that the economic attractiveness of a continued vaccine development effort is high relative to other development assistance options would be *signaled* by perhaps modest allocation of control resources to vaccine development by the Expert Panel. That new products such as potential AIDS vaccines constitute international public goods – unlikely to be domestically financed by developing countries – is an additional factor. The RethinkHIV paper compared continued vaccine development efforts to a base scenario of discontinued funding and it also estimated what the benefits would be if additional funding were to reduce the time until a vaccine becomes available. The RethinkHIV Panel placed accelerated vaccine development at the top of its list of priorities, and this Challenge Paper places it on the short list of six solutions, replacing the expansion of combinations of existing means of prevention.

Hecht and Jamison (2012) assessed the consequences of scaling up funding to reduce the amount of time it takes to develop an AIDS vaccine. They assumed modest but real time savings from an additional $100 million dollar expenditure p.a. (over the approximately $900 million p.a. current rate of expenditure). The $100 million figure was based on interviews with vaccine experts, who argued that the award of five–ten packages of $10–20 million a year over a decade to carefully selected research consortia would substantially accelerate progress. They assumed that an 11 percent increase in vaccine R&D ($100 million more each year) would correspond to a shortened time to product launch of 0.4–1.0 years (with much uncertainty). Assuming first a 1.0-year gain, the time to vaccine approval would be eighteen years as opposed to nineteen years in the base scenario. This implies that an additional $100 million dollar expenditure p.a. would increase the total discounted funding requirement from $13.9 billion to $15.4 billion. However, shortening the time to approval would also decrease proportionally the number of years in which one would have to pay development costs. Because of this shortened period of expenditure, the (discounted) funding requirement would result in a net increase to $14.6 billion. The calculation of discounted R&D financing for accelerating vaccine development by 0.42 of a year follows the same steps as those outlined above.

What would be the benefits of such accelerated vaccine development? To calculate this, Heent and Jamison used the estimated benefits from receiving the vaccine in 2030 (or in 2040, under alternative assumptions about product launch), then calculated the incremental benefit associated with accelerating the time to vaccine development by 1.0 or 0.4 years. They found that for a $5,000 VSLY and a 5 percent discount rate, the benefits of advancing the approval time by 1.0 years is $73.5 billion (or $29.3 billion when the time gain is 0.4 years). From there, we estimate the BCR with sensitivity analyses around the VSLY and the discount rate. Even in the most conservative case of a $1,000 VSLY, a 3 percent discount rate, and a 0.4 year advance, the BCR exceeds 6:1. Table 7.5 showns the BCR of accelerating vaccine development under alternative assumptions. These findings make a strong case for increased funding to AIDS vaccine R&D, even though there is great sensitivity in benefit-cost to the underlying assumptions. For the 2012 Copenhagen Consensus we assume a $1,000 VSLY, a 5 percent discount rate, and an intermediate

Table 7.5 Hypothetical BCRs from advancing time of vaccine availability

Value of statistical life year (VSLY) ($)	Discount rate p.a. (%)	Years sooner that vaccine is available	
		1.0	0.4
1,000	3	26:1	6:1
1,000	5	18:1	4:1
5,000	3	106:1	22:1
5,000	5	71:1	16:1

Note: Entries in the table are BCRs.
Source: Hecht and Jamison (2012).

reduction in time to vaccine availability implying a BCR of 11:1.

Anti-retroviral treatment of AIDS

A primary focus on prevention strategies in the global response to HIV/AIDS reflects the fact that the future of the pandemic lies with those not yet infected. However, this cannot be taken as a reason to neglect the 33 million people currently living with the infection, two-thirds of them in Africa. Prophylaxis or treatments for some of the opportunistic infections that contribute to HIV/AIDS mortality are cost-effective (most notably antibiotics effective against TB). Since 1996, highly active anti-retroviral therapy has increased the life expectancy of people on treatment considerably. In developed countries, anti-retroviral therapy has dramatically reduced but not eliminated AIDS mortality. Reduction in the viral load slows or halts the progression of AIDS and can return individuals from serious illness to reasonable health. Available drugs leave a residual population of HIV in the body, however, and this population grows if the drugs stop. At present, the drugs must be taken for life. Widespread use of these drugs in high-income (and some middle-income) countries has transformed the life prospects of HIV-infected individuals and the RethinkHIV paper on treatment (Over and Garnett, 2011) found an attractive BCR for expanded treatment.

Early-generation anti-retroviral drugs suffered notable shortcomings: they were enormously costly; regimens for their use were complicated, making adherence difficult; their use generated unpleasant side effects; and rapid evolution of HIV led to resistant mutants that undermined the efficacy of therapy. In a remarkably short time scientific advances have substantially attenuated those problems, making feasible, at least in principle, anti-retroviral therapy in low-income settings. WHO's "3 by 5" program had as its objective, for example, to reach 3 million people in LMICs with anti-retroviral therapy by 2005. That goal was met (by 2007) and the global effort to make treatment widely available is well under way. An important contributor has been the Clinton Foundation's effort to negotiate reductions in the prices of first-line and, more recently, second-line drugs.

Despite the indicated progress against the problems with anti-retroviral drugs, challenges to their effective use in low-income environments remain formidable. The complexity of patient management is very real. Management requires high levels of human resources and other capacities in many of the countries where those capacities need to be most carefully rationed. Perhaps in consequence, achieving effective implementation has been difficult on even a limited scale. Bertozzi *et al.* (2006) review those problems and how they might be addressed.

Three points concerning widespread anti-retroviral drug use are particularly noteworthy:

- Poor implementation (low adherence, development of resistance, interruptions in drug supplies) is likely to lead to very limited health gains, even for individuals on therapy. (This outcome is unlike that of a weak immunization program in which health gains still exist in the fraction of the population that is immunized.) Poorly implemented anti-retroviral drug delivery programs could divert substantial resources from prevention or from other high-pay-off activities in the health sector. Even worse, they could lead to a false sense of complacency in affected populations: evidence from some countries suggests that treatment availability has led to riskier sexual behavior and increased HIV transmission.

The injunction to "do no harm" holds particular salience.

- Unless systematic efforts are made to acquire hard knowledge about which approaches work and which do not, the likelihood exists that unsuccessful implementation efforts will be continued without the appropriate reallocation of resources to successful approaches. Learning what works will require major variations in approach and careful evaluation of effects. Failing to learn will lead to large numbers of needless deaths. Most efforts to scale up anti-retroviral therapy unconscionably fail to commit the substantial resources required for evaluation of effects. Such evaluations are essential if ineffective programs are to be halted or effective ones are to receive more resources. While this point about learning from evaluation applies more generally, it is particularly salient for HIV/AIDS treatment.
- Many programs rely exclusively on the cheapest possible drugs, thereby risking problems with toxicity, adherence, and drug resistance. From the outset a broader range of drug regimens needs to be tested.

Use of anti-retrovirals is likely to have a BCR greater than 1 in many circumstances. However if it competes with other highly attractive health investments in environments with limited human and financial resources, widespread adoption needs to be carefully sequenced.

Control of TB

TB is the leading cause of adult death from infectious disease after HIV/AIDS. Nearly 9 million new cases and perhaps 1.6 million deaths were caused by TB globally in 2003, with over 90 percent of these in LMICs. TB, like HIV/AIDS, causes deaths in productive working age, and can thus be a trigger into household poverty. Only a small percentage of those infected with the TB bacillus go onto to active disease such as pulmonary TB. Key risk factors for active TB include poverty, household crowding, and smoking (Pai *et al.*, 2006).

TB can be controlled by preventing infection, by stopping progression from infection to active disease, and by treating active disease. The principal intervention is the "directly observed therapy, short-course" (DOTS) strategy and its variations, centered on the diagnosis and observed treatment of the most severe and most infectious (smear-positive) forms of TB but including treatment for smear-negative and extra-pulmonary cases as well. Anti-TB drugs can also be used to treat latent infection and active TB in patients with HIV coinfection. The widely used BCG vaccine prevents severe forms of TB in childhood (Dye and Floyd, 2006).

The cornerstone of TB control is the prompt treatment of active cases using first-line drugs, administered through the DOTS strategy which has five elements: (i) political commitment; (ii) diagnosis primarily by sputum-smear microscopy among patients attending health facilities; (iii) short-course chemotherapy with three–four drugs including effective case management (including direct observation of treatment); (iv) a regular drug supply; and (v) systematic monitoring to evaluate the outcomes of every patient started on treatment.

The MDGs call for halting and beginning to reverse new cases of TB by 2015 and the Stop TB Partnership calls for halving prevalence and deaths by 2015 relative to 1990 rates. It has been estimated that these goals can be reached if 70 percent of new infectious (smear-positive) cases world-wide are detected and 8 percent of those cases are treated successfully with the DOTS regime.

WHO and others have focused their operational efforts in high-burden countries, and progress has been impressive. The case-detection rates has increased from 11 percent globally in 1996 to 53 percent in 2004 and over 21 million TB patients have been treated in DOTS programs in the decade since 1994. China and India have been noted as having particularly strong programs – although rigorous evaluation of the mortality impact of TB programs awaits. Key challenges remain the spread of HIV/AIDS infection in parts of Africa and drug resistance, especially in Eastern Europe. This suggests that DOTS alone might not be able to bring TB under control, especially in Africa and in the countries of the FSU.

The cost-effectiveness of TB control has been well established (summarized in Dye and Floyd, 2006), but more recently Laxminarayan *et al.* (2007) have calculated the cost-benefit of the WHO DOTS strategy at current levels relative to having no program in place. This finds that using VSL of roughly 100 times *per capita* GDP, the net gain is about $1.7 trillion versus program costs of $18.3 billion in the twenty-two high-burden countries. The ratio of the marginal benefits of implementing a global plan for DOTS to their costs were a factor over 15 in the twenty-two high-burden countries, and a factor of 9 in the Africa region. These estimates are thus in the plausible range with the values shown on p. 418.

The minor change in the 2012 Copenhagen Consensus recommendation on TB relative to CC08 lies in an explicit concern for dealing with multi-drug-resistant (MDR) TB as an integral part of an overall control strategy. This helps preserve available drugs for continued use and provides (partial) insurance against a disastrous breakout of MDR TB. However, addressing resistance increases costs, despite the long-term insurance value, and the short-term benefits in averted deaths are limited. Although TB treatment remains on our solutions list it appears slightly less attractive than before for reason of cost.

Opportunities for disease control

The preceding three sections identified a range of attractive options for disease control based, for the most part, on the 315 interventions that DCP2 reviewed (Jamison *et al.*, 2006b). Laxminarayan *et al.* (2006a) summarized DCP2's main findings on cost-effectiveness which form the basis for the CBAs reported here. One thing that is clear in the summarization of the cost-effectiveness information is that there is a broad range of reasonable estimates for most interventions. This is partly due to incomplete information and uncertainty. Even more importantly, it is also due to the responsiveness of the cost-effectiveness function to variations in prices, to the scale of application of the intervention (and of its substitutes and complements), and to the epidemiological environment.

Given these often broad ranges in cost-effectiveness ratios, and hence in BCRs, it makes little sense to conclude with precise estimates of uncertainty or effect size. Rather we have identified six solutions for investment in interventions that address a large disease burden highly cost-effectively even granted substantial uncertainty and variability in the underlying estimates. Even valuing DALYs at a conservative $1,000 and, again conservatively, reducing by 50 percent the DALY loss associated with an under-5 death (this affects the malaria and immunization numbers) the BCRs associated with investing in these opportunities is enormously high. In the Appendix we provide a brief assessment of the sensitivity of our findings to key assumptions.

This concluding section provides three summarizing tables on our six solutions. Table 7.6 summarizes what the solutions consist of and the sources of our economic evaluations. Table 7.7 summarizes our results in a simple "dashboard" and Table 7.8 relates our conclusions to the conclusions in the related areas of the 2008 Copenhagen Consensus.

Table 7.6 presents our solutions. Three are interventions in the traditional sense (those dealing with TB, immunization, and deworming). One is a pricing policy instrument (AMFm), one is a product development investment (HIV vaccines), and one is a platform carrying multiple, diverse interventions (essential surgery). All promise extraordinary benefit for cost. Two of the six solutions are preventive (the two dealing with vaccines) and the other four provide treatments.

Table 7.7 is presents a "dashboard" rather than a league table to summarize our solutions. Every opportunity in the table has not only a very high estimated BCR but also addresses a major disease burden. The interventions that would address the most DALYs are TB treatment (1) and district hospital surgery (5). Both would provide relatively a high degree of financial protection to populations.

Table 7.8 compares the results in Table 7.7 to those of CC08 and shows substantial carryover. The early success of the AMFm and increasing signs of promise in AIDS vaccine development led to their inclusion for CC12.

With the exception of surgery in the district hospital, the opportunities identified do not

Table 7.6 Summary of solutions

Solution	Economic evaluation
1. Tuberculosis treatment This solution involves expansion of coverage of the WHO-recommended treatment algorithm, directly observed therapy, short course (DOTS). Despite the label "short course" treatment requires six months of observed drug use with concomitant expense, but DOTS has proved highly effective in practice in reducing mortality. For CC12 we include attention to dealing with multi-drug resistance TB (MDR-TB).	Cost-effectiveness numbers are drawn from DCP2 (Jamison *et al.*, 2006a). The resulting cost per DALY is converted to a BCR by valuing a DALY at $1,000 (or $5,000). See also Laxminarayan *et al.* (2007a).
2. Malaria: support for AMFm The two previous mainline anti-malarial drugs, chloroquine and SP, lost efficacy in much of the world in the 1990s because of resistance. Both drugs were highly efficacious and inexpensive, whereas artemisinin derivatives, although effective, are far more expensive. The AMFm operates from the Global Fund to provide manufacturers' subsidies for artemesinin in combination with another drug in order to provide access to the effective treatment while undercutting prices of monotherapies.	CBAs match total costs, including subsidies, against the DALY gains (drawing on DCP2) then convert to dollar benefits at $1,000/DALY. See also Laxminarayan *et al.* (2010).
3. Childhood immunization This solution involves increased coverage of the six vaccines in the WHO-designated "Expanded Program on Immunization"	CBAs are based on DCP2 cost-effectiveness analyses with DALYs valued at $1,000. The estimates here are broadly consistent with assessments of the economic value of ongoing global immunization programs (Ozawa *et al.*, 2011; Stack *et al.*, 2011).
4. HIV: accelerated vaccine development This solution involves increasing the rate of expenditure on HIV vaccine development from about $500 million per year to about $1 billion per year.	The CBA was undertaken for the Copenhagen Consensus RethinkHIV project using methods like those of CC12.
5. Essential surgery This solution involves strengthening surgical capacity at the district hospital to better deal with trauma or obstructed labor.	CBAs are based on DCP2 cost-effectiveness analyses with DALYs valued at $1,000.
6. Deworming schoolchildren Over a billion individuals are infected by intestinal worms for which there is inexpensive, highly effective drug treatment. Children are the worst affected. Reinfection entails the need for continual deworming at a rate of once or twice a year. Great heterogeneity in the intensity of infection implies similar heterogeneity in the benefits, which are here measured in increased quantity of schooling valued in terms of its impact on subsequent earnings.	CBAs for deworming are drawn but (subjectively) modified from those of CC08. The CC08 education paper (Orazem *et al.*, 2009) assessed deworming schoolchildren and the malnutrition paper (Horton *et al.*, 2008) assessed both school-based and community-based (for younger children) deworming. Numbers here follow the nutrition paper more closely.

explicitly address the strengthening of health system capacity. (Option 2, support for the AMFm, can in part be viewed as a substitute for strengthening capacity.) It will be important to ensure that implementation includes related investments in personnel and institutions, with "related" broadly defined. (By using long-term average costs for the cost-effectiveness analysis, these issues were implicitly, although mechanically, dealt with.) One might consider there to be two broad approaches to strengthening health systems. One involves relatively non-specific investments in capacity and reforms of process. The second relies on learning by successfully doing and involves creating specific capacity to deliver priority services in volume and with high quality. In Option 2, capacity-strengthening spreads out from high-performing initial nodes. The approach that this chapter implicitly advocates is very much in the spirit of the latter.

From national perspectives the interventions on TB, on essential surgery, and on immunization and

Table 7.7 Disease control: investment solutions[a]

Solution	Indicative BCR	Level of capacity required	Financial risk protection provided	Relevance for development assistance	Annual costs ($ billion)	Annual benefits
1. Tuberculosis: appropriate case finding and treatment, including dealing with MDR-TB	15:1	M	H	M	1.5	1 million adult deaths averted or 30 million DALYs
2. Malaria: subsidy for appropriate treatment via AMFm	35:1	L	M	H	0.3	300,000 (mostly child) deaths averted or 10.5 million DALYs
3. Childhood diseases: expanded immunization coverage	20:1	L	L	L	1	1 million child deaths averted or 20 million DALYs
4. HIV: accelerated vaccine development	11:1	L	H	H	0.1	24% reduction in HIV/AIDS incidence fifteen years after introduction
5. Essential surgery: to address difficult childbirth, trauma and other	10:1	H	H	H	3	30 million DALYs
6. Deworming schoolchildren	10:1	L	L	L	0.3	About 300 million children dewormed

Note:
[a] This refers to level of capacity required for implementation in a developing country. While HIV vaccine development, for example, requires enormous scientific capacity, that capacity is functionary already where the development work would be undertaken.

malaria treatment appear as very high priorities. Given that, for whatever reason, these interventions remain underfunded, there is a reasonable argument that development assistance funds should address these needs and to an important extent they do (through the very substantial resources of GAVI and the Global Fund Against AIDS, Tuberculosis and Malaria).

Most valuable interventions are familiar interventions with only modest international externalities. There is a reasonable argument that development assistance should finance international public goods such as R&D (e.g. AIDS vaccine development) and help reduce the risks of adopting new areas of public investment (e.g. essential surgery in many countries). Development of resistance to effective drugs in one country generates very substantial negative externalities affecting all the others. AMFm, proposed by an IOM committee Kenneth Arrow, explicitly addresses these negative externalities through pricing mechanisms that work through both the public and private sector. International support for TB control indirectly addresses these negative externalities by attempting to diffuse appropriate drug use protocol.

In the 2008 Copenhagen Consensus, TB treatment stood out as perhaps the most important investment on grounds of its high BCR, its high level of financial risk protection, its moderate systemic requirements, and in the size of disease burden potentially averted. Because of the explicit recognition in the 2012 Consensus of the costs of dealing with MDR TB we now list it overall on a par with the other five. Each of the other solutions have advantages and disadvantages relative to each other and different individuals might well order them differently. Our most general conclusion, however, is that even if all costs were increased by a factor of, say, 3 there is a substantial and very specific list of major and highly attractive investment

Table 7.8 Infectious disease, injury, and reproductive health: solutions in 2008 and 2012 Copenhagen Consensus exercises

Solution in CC08	Expert Panel ranking in 2008 Copenhagen Consensus (out of 30)	Related solution in the 2012 Copenhagen Consensus, Infectious diseases, reproductive health and injury chapters
1. TB treatment	13	Very similar but with more explicit emphasis on the need to treat multi-drug resistant (MDR-) TB as part of the treatment package H.
2. Malaria: package of treatment and preventative measures	12	The 2012 solution provides a much more focused malaria recommendation: financial support for the AMFm, which provides manufacturer-level subsidies for ACTs. By reducing the price of a resistance-postponing combination therapy the AMFm makes effective treatment affordable and undercuts prices of resistance-inducing monotherapies.
3. Childhood immunization	14	No change
4. HIV: combination prevention package	19	Proposes the rate of expenditure on HIV vaccine development. This recommendation was ranked number 1 by the CC Rethink HIV Expert Panel.
5. Injury, difficult childbirth: invest in surgical capacity at district hospital	21	No change except to be relabeled as "essential surgery" to reflect current nomenclature.
6. Deworming children at schools[a]	6	Little changed

Note:
[a] The deworming solutions proposed for 2012 were addressed in both the education and the nutrition Challenge Papers. The decision was made to have deworming addressed by this Challenge Paper.

opportunities for dealing with infectious disease, reproduction health, and injury. Table 7.8 compares the solutions proposed for the 2012 with those proposed for 2008 Consensus.

Appendix: sensitivity analysis

The analysis upon which we based the conclusions reported in Table 7.8 were undertaken under the following assumptions:

(1) The discount rate is 3 percent per year and the version of the DALY that was used is based on this 3 percent and no age-weighting. These are the assumptions used in the most recent presentation of methods, data sources, and results on the global burden of disease (Lopez *et al.*, 2006b, 2006c). Earlier tabulations of the disease burden used age-weighted DALYs which give broadly similar results except that somewhat more weight is given to conditions of middle age (TB, maternal deaths, trauma, psychiatric illness).

(2) Jamison *et al.* (2006) of (Chapter 6 in Lopez *et al.* (2006b)) points to the mathematical impossibility of having the standard formulation of a DALY give a loss from a death at age 25 that is more than 20 percent greater than the loss from a death at age 1 day. An alternative version of the DALY is proposed there [DALY (3,0, 0.54)] and used in this chapter. The effect is to reduce the DALY loss of a death under age 5 by about 50 percent without changing the DALY loss from deaths at older ages.

(3) In an attempt to include relevant health systems costs and to take a long-run view, cost estimates in this chapter are based on long-run average costs (at least in principle, as there is some variation in actual costing methods).

(4) Cost analyses in this chapter assumes 0 deadweight losses from taxation, but the analyses in this Appendix explore sensitivity to their valuation

Table A7.1 Sensitivity analysis

Change in assumption	Consequence
1. Change the discount rate from 3% to 6% p.a., i.e. change to DALYs (6, 0, 0.54)	The number of DALYs gained from each of the interventions and hence the BCR will decline by about 50%.
2. Change from DALYs (3, 0, 0.54) to DALYs (3,0)	The number of DALYs gained from immunization and from malaria control will approximately double, as will the BCR for the related interventions.
3. Since *ex ante* costs are typically underestimated, often substantially, multiply all costs by 3	The BCR will decline to one-third of its otherwise estimated value for all interventions.
4. The deadweight loss from taxation is increased from 0 to 50% of the revenue raised (Ballard *et al.*, 1985, provide estimates in this range).	The BCR value declines by one-third.
5. The value of a DALY is $5,000 rather than $1,000.	The BCR values go up by a factor of 5.

5. The chapter assumes the value of a DALY or of a VSLY to be $1,000.

Appendix Table A7.1 reports assessments of the robustness of our conclusions with respect to changes in these assumptions. On the most optimistic alternative assumption of Appendix Table A7.1 the BCR for immunization and for malaria would increase by a factor of 10; for the other interventions the factor is 5. Taking the least optimistic assumptions the BCR of all interventions would decline by a factor of 10.

If the BCR is being used by a government to decide whether to fund the relevant health program compared with other programs or saving the money, it should adjust the value of a DALY in line with its GNI *per capita*. To do so, it should multiply it by its GNI *per capita* and divide by 500. The BCR will move by the same factor.

If the BCR is being used to compare the interventions in this chapter with interventions that affect people in richer countries, it needs to be significantly increased to avoid discounting the value of the health effects just because they accrue to the world's poorest people. To do so, multiply the BCR by the GNI *per capita* of the country for whose citizens the WTP of the other interventions was estimated and then divide by 500. This could increase these ratios by as much as a factor of 100. Note that the "500" in each of these is because that is the current implicit estimate of the country's GNI *per capita*, so if you change the $1,000 per DALY figure, you would want to adjust these proportionally – e.g. if you use $1,500 per DALY, then make these 750.

Bibliography

Abdool Karim, Q., 2007: Prevention of HIV by male circumcision, *British Medical Journal* **335**, 4–5

Abraham, K. G. and C. Mackie (eds.), 2005: *Beyond the Market: Designing Nonmarket Accounts for the United States*, The National Academies Press, Washington, DC

Acemoglu, D. and S. Johnson, 2007: Disease and development: the effect of life expectancy on economic growth, *Journal of Political Economy* **115**, 925–86

Aids2031 Costs and Financing Working Group, 2010: *The Long Term Fight Against AIDS*, Results for Development Institute, Washington, DC

Aral, S. O., M. Over, L. Manhart, and K. K. Holmes, 2006: Sexually transmitted infections, in A. R. Measham, D. T. Jamison, J. Breman *et al.* (eds.), *Disease Control Priorities in Developing Countries*, 2nd edn.

Arrow, K. J., 1963: Uncertainty and the welfare economics of medical care, *American Economic Review* **53**, 851–83

Arrow, K. J., H. Gelband, and D. T. Jamison, 2005: Making antimalarial agents available in Africa, *New England Journal of Medicine* **353**, 333–35

Bailey, R. C., S. Moses, C. B. Parker, K. Agot, I. Maclean, J. N. Kreiger, C. F. M. Williams, R. T. Campbell, and J. O. Ndina-Achola, 2007: Male circumcision for HIV prevention in young men in Kisumu, Kenya: a randomised controlled trial, *Lancet* **369**, 643–56

Ballard, C., J. Shoven, and J. Whalley, 1985: General equilibrium computations of the marginal welfare costs of taxes in the United States, *American Economic Review* **74**, 128–38

Barr, N., 2001: *The Welfare State as Piggy Bank: Information, Risk, Uncertainty, and the Role of the State*, Oxford University Press

Bates, M. N., A. Khalakdina, M. Pai, L. Chang, F. Lessa, and K. R. Smith, 2007: Risk of tuberculosis from exposure to tobacco smoke: a systematic review and meta-analysis, *Archives International Medicine* **167**, 335–42

Becker, G. S., T. J. Philipson, and R. R. Soares, 2003: The quantity and quality of life and the evolution of world inequality, *American Economic Review* **95**, 277–91

Behrman, J. R. and H. P. Kohler, 2010: Assessment Paper, Sexual Transmission of HIV, Copenhagen Consensus on RethinkHIV

Bertozzi, S., N. S. Padian, J. Wegbreit, L. M. DeMaria, B. Feldman, H. Gayle, J. Gold, R. Grant, and M. T. Isbell, 2006: HIV/AIDS prevention and treatment, in D. T. Jamison, A. R. Measham, J. Berman *et al.* (eds.), *Disease Control Priorities in Developing Countries*, 2nd edn.

Bezanson, K., 2005: *Replenishing the Global Fund: An Independent Assessment*, Global Fund, Geneva, 35

Bhagwati, J., F. Bourgignon, F. Kydland, R. Mundell, D. North, T. Schelling, V. Smith, and N. Stokey, 2009: Expert Panel Ranking, in B. Lomborg (ed.), *Global Crises, Global Solutions*, 2nd edn., Cambridge University Press, 657–79

Bloom, D. E. and D. Canning, 2006: Booms, busts and echoes: how the biggest demographic upheaval in history is affecting global development, *Finance and Development*, **43**, 8–13

Bloom, D. E., D. Canning, and G. Fink, forthcoming: Comment on Acemoglu and Johnson, *Journal of Political Economy*

Bloom, D. E., D. Canning, and D. T. Jamison, 2004: Health, wealth and welfare, *Finance and Development* **41**, 10–15

Bloom, D. E., D. Canning, and J. P. Serilla, 2004: The effect of health on economic growth: a production function approach, *World Development* **32**, 1–13

Bollinger, L., 2012: Assessment Paper on prevention of non-sexual transmission of HIV, Copenhagen Consensus on RethinkHIV

Bourguignon, F. and C. Morrisson, 2002: Inequality among world citizens: 1820–1992, *American Economic Review* **92**, 727–44

Breman, J. G., A. Mills, R. W. Snow, J. Mulligan, C. Lengeler, K. Mendis, B. Sharp, C. Morel, P. Marchesini, N. J. White, R. W. Steketee, and O. K. Doumbo, 2006: Conquering malaria, in D. T. Jamison, J. Breman, A. Measham, G. Alleyne, M. Claeson, D. Evans, P. Jha, A. Mills, and P. Musgrove (eds.), *Disease Control Priorities in Developing Countries*, 2nd edn., Oxford University Press, New York, 413–32

Brenzel, L., L. J. Wolfson, J. Fox-Rushby, M. Miller, and N. A. Halsey, 2006: Vaccine-preventable diseases, in D. T. Jamison, J. Breman, A. Measham, G. Alleyne, M. Claeson, D. Evans, P. Jha, A. Mills, and P. Musgrove (eds.), *Disease Control Priorities in Developing Countries*, 2nd edn., Oxford University Press, New York, 389–412

Bundy, D. A. P., M. S. Chan, G. F. Medley, D. Jamison, and L. Savioli, 2004: Intestinal nematode infections, in C. J. L. Murray, A. D. Lopez, and C. D. Mathers (eds.), *The Global Epidemiology of Infectious Disease*, World Health Organization, Global Burden of Disease and Injury Series, Vol. **IV**, Geneva, 243–300

Bundy, D. A. P., S. Shaeffer, M. Jukes, K. Beegle, A. Gillespie, L. Drake, S. F. Lee, A. M. Hoffman, J. Jones, A. Mitchell, D. Barcelona, B. Camara, C. Golmar, L. Savioli, M. Sembene, T. Takeuchi, and C. Wright, 2006: School-based health and nutrition programs, in D. Jamison, A. R. Measham, J. G. Breman *et al.* (eds.), *Disease Control Priorities in Developing Countries*, 2nd edn., Oxford University Press, New York, 1091–1108

Canning, D., 2009: Perspective Paper 3.1 on disease control, in B. Lomborg (ed.), *Global Crises, Global Solutions*, 2nd edn., Cambridge University Press, 164–71

Chen, L., P. Jha, B. Stirling, S. K. Sgaier, T. Daid *et al.*, 2007: Sexual risk factors for HIV infection in early and advanced HIV epidemics in Sub-Saharan Africa: systematic overview of 68 epidemiological studies, *PLoS ONE* **2**(10), e1001 doi:10.1371/journal.pone.0001001

Claeson, M., D. Evans, P. Jha, A. Mills, and P. Musgrove, Oxford University Press, New York, 331–70

Clemens, M., S. Radelet, and R. Bhavnani, 2004: Counting chickens when they hatch: the short-term effect of aid on growth, *Working Paper* **44**, Center for Global Development, Washington, DC

Crafts, N. and M. Haacker, 2004: Welfare implications of HIV/AIDS, in M. Haacker (ed.), *The Macroeconomics of HIV/AIDS*, International Monetary Fund, Washington, DC, 182–97

Crawford, C. B., B. E. Salter, and K. L. Jang, 1989: Human grief: is its intensity related to the reproductive value of the deceased?, *Ethology and Sociobiology* **10**, 297–307

Crogan, T. W., A. Beatty, and A. Ron, 2006: Routes to better health for children in four developing countries, *The Milbank Quarterly* **84**, 333–58

Cutler, D., A. Deaton, and A. Lleras-Muney, 2006: The determinants of mortality, *Journal of Economic Perspectives*, **20**, 97–120

Davis, K., 1956: The amazing decline of mortality in underdeveloped areas, *American Economic Review* (*Papers and Proceedings*) **46**, 305–18

Debas, H. T., R. Gosselin, C. McCord, and A. Thind, 2006: Surgery, in D. T. Jamison, A. R. Measham, J. Breman *et al.* (eds.), *Disease Control Priorities in Developing Countries*, 2nd edn., Oxford University Press, New York, 1245–60

de Savigny, D., H. Kasale, C. Mbuya, and G. Reid, 2004: *Fixing Health Systems*, International Development Research Centre, Ottawa

Del Rio, C. and J. Sepúlveda, 2002: AIDS in Mexico: lessons learned and implications for developing countries, *AIDS* **16**, 1445–57

Deworm the World, 2009: *Annual Report: Increasing Access to Education by Expanding School-Based Deworming*, www.dewormtheworld.org/sites/default/files/pdf/DtW_AnnualReport_2009.pdf

Dye, C. and K. Floyd, 2006: Tuberculosis, in D. T. Jamison, A. R. Measham, J. Breman *et al.*, (eds.), *Disease Control Priorities in Developing Countries*, 2nd edn., Oxford University Press, New York, 289–310

Easterlin, R. A., 1996: *Growth Triumphant: The Twenty-First Century in Historical Perspective*, University of Michigan Press, Ann Arbor MI

England, S., B. Loevinsohn, B. Melgaard, U. Kou, and P. Jha, 2001: The evidence base for interventions to reduce mortality from vaccine-preventable diseases in low and middle-income countries, *CMH Working Paper Series* **WG5 10**, www.cmhealth.org/docs/wg5_paper10.pdf

Ezzati, M. *et al.*, 2006: Comparative quantification of mortality and burden of disease attributable to selected risk factors, in A. D. Lopez *et al.*, *Global Burden of Disease and Risk Factors*, Oxford University Press, 241–396

Feachem, R. G. A., T. Kjellstrom, C. J. L. Murray, M. Over, and M. Phillips (eds.), 1992: *Health of Adults in the Developing World*, Oxford University Press, New York

Frenk, J. *et al.*, 2006: Bridging the divide: global lessons from evidence based health policy in Mexico, *Lancet* **368**, 954–61

Gajalakshmi, V. *et al.*, 2003: Smoking and mortality from tuberculosis and other diseases in India: retrospective study of 43,000 adult male deaths and 35,000 controls, *Lancet* **362**, 501–15

Gericke, C. A., C. Kurowski, M. K. Ranson, and A. Mills, 2003: Feasibility of scaling-up interventions: the role of interventions design, *Working Paper* **13**, Disease Control Priorities Project, Bethesda, MD

Graham, W. J., J. Cairns, S. Bhattacharya, C. H. W. Bullough, Z. Quayyum, and K. Rogo, 2006: Maternal and perinatal conditions, in D. T. Jamison, A. R. Measham, J. Breman *et al.* (eds.), *Disease Control Priorities in Developing Countries*, 2nd edn., Oxford University Press, New York, 499–530

Global IDEA Scientific Advisory Committee, 2004: Health and economic benefits of an accelerated program of research to combat global infectious diseases, *Canadian Medical American Journal* **171**,

Haacker, M. (ed.), 2004: *The Macroeconomics of HIV/AIDS*, International Monetary Fund, Washington, DC

Hall, A. and S. Horton, 2009: Best practice paper: new advice from CC08 – deworming, Paper prepared for the 2008 Copenhagen Consensus www.copenhagenconsensus.com/Admin/Public/DWSDownload.aspx?File=%2fFiles%2fFiler%2fCCC%2fBest±Practice±Papers%2fdeworming . . . .pdf

Hecht, R. J. and D. Jamison, 2012: Vaccine research and development, in B. Lomborg (ed.), *Rethink HIV*, Cambridge University Press

Hecht, R. J., J. Stover, L. Bollinger, F. Muhib, K. Case, and D. de Ferranti, 2010: Financing of

HIV/AIDS programme scale-up in low-income and middle-income countries, 2009–2031, *Lancet* **376**, 1254–60

Hoddinott, J. *et al.*, 2012: Chapter 6 in this volume

Horton, S., H. Alderman, and J. A. Rivera, 2008: Hunger and malnutrition, in B. Lomborg (ed.), *Global Crisis, Global Solutions*, 2nd edn., Cambridge University Press, 305–33

Hotez, P. *et al.*, 2006: Helminth infections: soil-transmitted helminth infections and schistomiasis, in D. T. Jamison *et al.*, *Disease Control Priorities in Developing Countries*, 2nd edn., Oxford University, Press, 467–82

Institute of Medicine (IOM), 1985: *New Vaccine Development: Establishing Priorities*. Vol. **1** of *Diseases of Importance in the United States* National Academies Press, Washington, DC

International AIDS Vaccine Initiative (IAVI), 2009: Estimating the potential impact of an AIDS vaccine in developing countries, IAVI, New York

James, J. S., 2005: Uganda study found that death reduced HIV prevalence: did the public take home the wrong message?, *AIDS Treat News*, February 25, 5–6

Jamison, D. T., 2006: Investing in health, in D. T. Jamison, A. R. Measham, J. Breman *et al.* (eds.), *Disease Control Priorities in Developing Countries*, 2nd edn., Oxford University Press, New York, 3–34

2008: Priority setting in health, Presentation at the Institution for Health Metrics and Evaluation-*Lancet* Conference on Global Metrics and Evaluation, Current State and Future Directions, Seattle, Washington

Jamison, D. T., L. J. Lau, and J. Wang, 2005: Health's contribution to economic growth in an environment of partially endogenous technical progress, in G. Lopez-casasnovas *et al.* (eds.), *Health and Economic Growth*, MIT Press, Cambridge, MA, 67–91

Jamison, D. T. and J. Leslie, 1990: Health and nutrition considerations in educational planning II: the cost and effectiveness of school-based interventions, *Food and Nutrition Bulletin* **12**, 204–14

Jamison, D. T. and S. Radelet, 2005: Making aid smarter, *Finance and Development* **42**, 42–6

Jamison, D. T., J. Sachs, and J. Wang, 2001: The effect of the AIDS epidemic on economic welfare in Sub-Saharan Africa, *CMH Working Paper* **WG1:13**, Commission on Macroeconomics and Health, World Health Organization, Geneva

Jamison, D. T., E. A. Jamison, and J. D. Sachs, 2003: Assessing the determinants of growth when health is explicitly included in the measure of economic welfare, Paper presented at the 4th World Congress of the International Health Economics Association, San Francisco, June

Jamison, D. T., M. Sandbu, and J. Wang, 2004: Why has infant mortality decreased at such different rates in different countries?, *Working Paper* **21**, Disease Control Priorities Project, Bethesda, MD

Jamison, D. T., A. R. Measham, J. Breman *et al.* (eds.), 2006a: *Disease Control Priorities in Developing Countries*, 2nd edn., Oxford University Press, New York

Jamison, D. T., S. A. Shahid-Salles, J. Jamison, J. E. Lawn, and J. Zupan, 2006b: Incorporating deaths near time of birth into estimates of the global burden of disease, in A. D. Lopez, C. D. Mathers, M. Ezzati, D. T. Jamison, and C. J. L. Murray (eds.), *Global Burden of Disease and Risk Factors*, Oxford University Press, New York, 427–62

Jamison, E. A., D. T. Jamison, and E. A. Hanushek, 2007: The effects of education quality on income growth and mortality decline, *Economics of Education Review* **26**, 771–88

Jamison, D. T., P. Jha, and D. E. Bloom, 2008: Disease Control, in B. Lomborg (ed.), *Global Crisis, Global Solutions: Costs and Benefits*, Cambridge University Press, New York, 126–63

Jamison, D. T., P. Jha, V. Malhotra, and S. Verguet, 2012: The 20th century transformation of human health: its magnitude and value, in B. Lomborg (ed.), Cambridge University Press

Jha, P. and Z. Chen, 2007: Poverty and chronic diseases in Asia: challenges and opportunities, *Canadian Medical Association Journal* **177**, 1059–62

Jha, P. and A. Mills, 2002: Improving health of the global poor: The Report of Working Group 5 of the Commission on Macroeconomics and Health, World Health Organization, Geneva

Jha, P., A. Mills, K. Hanson, L. Kumaranayake *et al.*, 2002: Improving the health of the global poor, *Science* **295**, 2036–9

Jha, P., N. J. D. Nagelkerke, E. Ngugi, B. Wilbond, J. V. R. Prasada-Rao, S. Moses, F. A. Plummer, 2001: Reducing HIV transmission in developing countries, *Science* **292**, 224–5

Jha, P., R. Nugent, S. Verguet, D. Bloom, and R. Hum, 2012: Chapter 3 in this volume

Jha, P., D. Brown, N. Nagelkerke, A. S. Slutsky, and D. T. Jamison, 2005: Health and economic benefits of an accelerated program of research to combat global infections, *Canadian Medical Association Journial*, 172–6

Johansson, P. O., 1995: *Evaluating Health Risks*, Cambridge University Press

Joint Learning Initiative, 2004: *Human Resources for Health: Overcoming the Crisis*, Harvard University Press, Cambridge, MA

Kanbur, R. and T. Sandler, 1999: *The Future of Development Assistance: Common Pools and International Public Goods*, Overseas Development Council, Washington, DC

Keusch, G. T., O. Fontaine, A. Bhargava, C. Boschi-Pinto, Z. A. Bhutta, E. Gotuzzo, J. A. Rivera, J. Chow, S. A. Shahid-Salles, and R. Laxminarayan, 2006: Diarrheal diseases, in D. T. Jamison, A. R. Measham, J. Breman *et al.* (eds.), *Disease Control Priorities in Developing Countries*, 2nd edn., Oxford University Press, New York, 371–88

Kohler, A.-P., 2012: Chapter 9 in this volume

Kumar, D. *et al.*, 2006: Trends in HIV-1 in young adults in South India from 2000 to 2004: a prevalence study, *Lancet* **367**, 1164–72

Lawn, J. E., J. Zupan, G. Begkoyian, and R. Knippenberg, 2006: Newborn survival, in D. T. Jamison, A. R. Measham, J. Breman *et al.* (eds.), *Disease Control Priorities in Developing Countries*, 2nd edn., Oxford University Press, New York, 531–50

Laxminarayan, R., J. Chow, and S. A. Shahid-Salles, 2006a: Intervention cost-effectiveness: overview of main messages, in D. T. Jamison, A. R. Measham, J. Breman *et al.* (eds.), *Disease Control Priorities in Developing Countries*, 2nd edn., Oxford University Press, New York, 35–86

Laxminarayan, R., E. Kelin, C. Dye, K. Floyd, S. Darly, and O. Adeyi, 2007: Economic benefit of tuberculosis control, *Resource for the Future Working Paper*

Laxminarayan, R., A. J. Mills, J. G. Breman, A. R. Measham, G. Alleyne, M. Claeson, P. Jha, P. Musgrove, J. Chow, S. Shahid-Salles, and D. T. Jamison, 2006b: Advancement of global health: key messages from the Disease Control Priorities Project, *Lancet* **367**, 1193–208

Laxminarayan, R. *et al.*, 2006: Will a global subsidy of new antimalarials delay the emergence of resistance and save lives? *Health Affairs* **25**, 325–36

Laxminarayan, R., I. W. H. Parry, E. Klein, and D. L. Smith, 2010: Should new antimalarial drugs be subsidized?, *Journal of Health Economics* **29**, 445–56

Levine, R. and the What Works Working Group, 2007: *Millions Saved: Proven Successes in Global Health*, Jones & Bartlett, Sudbury, MA

Lindert, P. H., 2004: *Growing Public: Social Spending and Economic Growth since the Eighteenth Century*, Vol. **1**, Cambridge University Press

Liu, L., H. L. Johnson, and S. Cousens, 2012: Global, regional, and national causes of child mortality: an updated systematic analysis for 2010 with time trends since 2000, *Lancet* **379**, 2151–61, Epub May 11

Lomborg, B. (ed.), 2004: *Global Crises, Global Solutions*, Cambridge University Press

2006: *How to Spend $50 Billion to Make the World a Better Place*, Cambridge University Press

Lopez, A. D., S. Begg, and E. Bos, 2006a: Demographic and epidemiological characteristics of major regions of the world, 1990 and 2001, in A. D. Lopez, C. D. Mathers, M. Ezzati, D. T. Jamison, and C. J .L. Murray (eds.), *Global Burden of Disease and Risk Factors*, Oxford University Press, New York, 17–44

Lopez, A. D., C. D. Mathers, M. Ezzati, D. T. Jamison, and C. J. L. Murray (eds.), 2006b: *Global Burden of Disease and Risk Factors*, Oxford University Press, New York

2006c: Global and regional burden of disease and risk factors, 2001: systematic analysis of population health data, *Lancet* **367**, 1747–57

Lopez-Casasnovas, G., B. Rivera, and L. Currais (eds.), 2005: *Health and Economic Growth: Findings and Policy Implications*, MIT Press, Cambridge, MA

Lozano, R., H. Wang, K. J. Foreman, J. Knoll Rajaratnam, M. Naghavi, J. R. Marcus, L. Dwyer-Lindgren, K. T. Lofgren, D. Phillips, C. Atkinson, A. D. Lopez, and C. J. L. Murray, 2011: Progress toward Millennium Development Goals 4 and 5 on maternal and child mortality: an updated systematic analysis, *Lancet* **378**, 1139–65

Mathers, C. D., C. J. L. Murray, and A. D. Lopez, 2006: The burden of disease and mortality by condition: data, methods and results for the year 2001, in A. D. Lopez, C. D. Mathers, M. Ezzati, D. T. Jamison, and C. J. L. Murray (eds.), *Global Burden of Disease and Risk Factors*, Oxford University Press, New York, 45–240

Maurice, J., 2011: Quest for an effective AIDS vaccine takes a new tack, *Lancet* **378**, 213–14

McCord, C. and Q. Chowdhury, 2003: A cost-effective small hospital in Bangladesh: what it can mean for emergency obstetric care, *International Journal of Gynecology and Obstetrics* **81**, 83–92

Measham, A. R., K. D. Rao, D. T. Jamison, J. Wang, and A. Singh, 1999: The performance of India and Indian states in reducing infant mortality and fertility, 1975–1990, *Economic and Political Weekly* **34**, 1359–67

Meltzer, D., 2006: Economic approaches to valuing global health research, in D. T. Jamison, A. R. Measham, J. Breman *et al.* (eds.), *Disease Control Priorities in Developing Countries*, 2nd edn., Oxford University Press, New York, 157–64

Million Death Study Collaborators, 2010: Causes of child and neonatal mortality in India: nationally-representative mortality survey, *Lancet* **376**, 1853–6

Mills, A. and S. Shillcutt, 2004: Communicable diseases, in B. Lomborg (ed.), *Global Crises, Global Solutions*, Cambridge University Press, 62–114

Mills, A. *et al.*, 2006: Strengthening health systems, in D. T. Jamison *et al.*, *Disease Control Priorities in Developing Countries*, 2nd edn., Oxford University Press

Mock, C., M. Cherian, C. Julliard, P. Donker, S. Bickler, D. Jamison, and K. McQueen, 2009: Developing priorities for addressing surgical conditions globally: furthering the link between surgery and public health policy, *World Journal of Surgery* **34**, 381–5

Mulligan, J. A., J. A. Fox-Rushby, T. Adams, and A. Mills, 2003, revised 2005: Unit costs of health care inputs in low and middle income countries, *Disease Control Priorities Paper Working Paper* 9, http://dcp2.org/file/24/wpg.pdf

Nagelkerke, N. J., P. Jha, S. J. de Vlas, E. L. Korenromp, S. Moses, J. F. Blanchard, and F. A. Plummer, 2002: Modelling HIV/AIDS epidemics in Botswana and India: impact of interventions to prevent transmission, *Bulletin of the World Health Organization* **80**, 89–96

Nordhaus, W., 2003: The health of nations: the contributions of improved health to living standards, in K. M. Murphy and R. H. Topel (eds.), *Measuring the Gains from Health Research: An Economic Approach*, University of Chicago Press, 9–40

Oeppen, J. and J. W. Vaupel, 2002: Demography, broken limits to life expectancy, *Science* **296**, 1029–31

Orazem, P., 2012: Chapter 5 in this volume

Orazem, P., P. Glewwe, and H. Patrinos, 2009: The benefits and costs of alternative strategies to improve educational outcomes, in B. Lomborg (ed.), *Global Crisis, Global Solutions*, 2nd edn., Cambridge University Press, 657–79

Over, M., 2011: *Achieving an AIDS Transition*, Brookings Institution Press, Baltimore

Over, M. and G. Garnett, 2011: Assessment paper on treatment. Rethink HIV, Copenhagen Consensus on RethinkHIV

Ozawa, S., M. L. Stack, D. M. Bishai, A. Mirelman, I. K. Friberg, L. Niessen, D. G. Walker, and O. S. Levine, 2011: During the "decade of vaccines," the lives of 6.4 million children valued at $231 billion could be saved, *Health Affairs* **30**, 1010–20

Pai, M. *et al.*, 2006: Lethal interaction: the colliding epidemics of tobacco and tuberculosis, *Expert-Review of Anti Infective Therapy* **5**, 385–91

Peabody, J. W., M. M. Taguiwalo, D. A. Robalino, and J. Frenk, 2006: Improving the quality of care in developing countries, in D. T. Jamison, A. R. Measham, J. Breman *et al.* (eds.), *Disease Control Priorities in Developing Countries*, 2nd edn., Oxford University Press, New York, 1293–308

Piot, P., M. Banton, H. Larson, D. Zewdie, and P. Mane, 2008: Coming to terms with complexity: a call to action for HIV prevention, *Lancet* **372**, 845–59

Preston, S. H., 1975: The changing relation between mortality and level of economic development, *Population Studies* **29**, 231–48

1980: Causes and consequences of mortality declines in less developed countries during the twentieth century, in R. Easterlin (ed.),

Population and Economic Change in Developing Countries, University of Chicago Press, 289–360

Pritchard, C., 2004: Developments in economic evaluation in health care: a review of HEED, *OHE Briefing* **40**, Office of Health Economics, London, March

Radelet, S., 2003: *Challenging Foreign Aid*, Center for Global Development, Washington, DC

Rijsberman, F. and A. P. Zwane, 2012: Chapter 10 in this volume

Schelling, T., 1968: The life you save may be your own, in S. B. Chase, Jr. (ed.), *Problems in Public Expenditure Analysis*, Brookings Institution, Washington, D.C

Sepúlveda, J. *et al.*, 2006: Improvement of child survival in Mexico: the diagonal approach, *Lancet* **368**, 2017–27

Simoes, E. A. F., T. Cherian, J. Chow, S. A. Shahid-Salles, R. Laxminarayan, and T. J. John, 2006: Acute respiratory infections in children, in D. T. Jamison, A. R. Measham, J. Breman *et al.* (eds.), *Disease Control Priorities in Developing Countries*, 2nd edn., Oxford University Press, New York, 483–98

Stack, M., S. Ozawa, D. M. Bishai, A. Mirelman, Y. Tam, L. Niessan, D. G. Walker, and O. Levine, 2011: Estimated economic benefits during the "decade of vaccines" include treatment savings, gains in labor productivity, *Health Affairs* **30**,

Stephenson, L. S., 1987: *Impact of Helminth Infections on Human Nutrition: Schistosomes and Soil Transmitted Helminths*, Taylor & Francis, New York

Stiglitz, J., A. Sen, and J. P. Fitoussi, 2009: *Report of the Commission on the Measurement of Economic Performance and Social Progress*, Paris, www.stiglitz-sen-fitoussi.fr

Strauss, J. and D. Thomas, 1998: Health, nutrition and economic development, *Journal of Economic Literature* **36**, 251–86

Tolley, G., D. Kenkel, and R. Fabian, 1994: State of the art health values, in G. Tolley, D. Kenkel, and R. Fabian (eds.), *Valuing Health for Policy: An Economic Approach*, University of Chicago Press, 323–44

UNAIDS *et al.*, 2010: *Report on the global AIDS epidemic*, UNAIDS, Geneva, www.unaids.org/globalreport/global_report.htm

United Nations, 2009: UN Population Division, *World Population Prospects* (2008 revision), 28 June

US Centers for Disease Control, 1999: Achievements in public health, 1900–1999: changes in the public health system, *Morbidity and Mortality Weekly Report (MMWR)* **48**, www.cdc.gov/mmwr/PDF/wk/mm4850.pdf

Usher, D., 1973: An imputation to the measure of economic growth for changes in life expectancy, in M. Moss (ed.), *Measurement of Economic and Social Performance*, Columbia University Press for the National Bureau of Economic Research, New York

Vallin, J. and F. Meslé, 2010: Will life expectancy increase indefinitely by three months every year?, *Population & Societies* **473**, 1–4

Viscusi, W. K. and I. E. Aldy, 2003: The value of a statistical life: a critical review of market estimates throughout the world. *Journal of Risk and Uncertainty* **27**, 5–76

Weatherall, D., B. Greenwood, H. L. Chee, and P. Wasi, 2006: Science and technology for disease control: past, present, and future, In D. T. Jamison, A. R. Measham, J. Breman *et al.* (eds.), *Disease Control Priorities in Developing Countries*, 2nd edn., Oxford University Press, New York, 119–38

Wolf, M., 2006: The absurdities of a ban on smoking, *Financial Times*, June 22

World Bank, 1993: *World Development Report: Investing in Health*, Oxford University Press, New York

2003: *World Development Indicators*, World Bank, Washington, DC

2011: World Development Indicators, World Bank, Washington, DC

WHO CMH, 2001: *Report on the Commission on Macroeconomics and Health*, WHO, Geneva

World Economic Forum (WEF), 2008: *Tackling Tuberculosis: The Business Response*, World Economic Forum, Davos

World Health Organization (WHO), 1999: *World Health Report*, WHO, Geneva

2000: *World Health Report*, WHO, Geneva

2011: *World Health Report*, WHO, Geneva

Yamey, G., 2007: Which single intervention would do the most to improve the health of those living on less than $1 per day?, *PLoS Med.* **4**,

Infectious Disease, Injury, and Reproductive Health

Alternative Perspective

TILL BÄRNIGHAUSEN, DAVID BLOOM, AND SALAL HUMAIR

Introduction

In the 2012 Copenhagen Consensus Challenge Paper "Infectious disease, injury, and reproductive health" (Chapter 7) Jamison *et al.* (2012) select six "investment solutions" to address infectious-disease, injury and reproductive-health burdens in low-income countries. We discuss the issues of the approach the authors follow in selecting these six "investment solutions," focusing on the multi-criteria decision-making process they have chosen and on uncertainty, risk attitudes, and evaluation time horizons.

Multi-criteria decision-making

Using the tools of economic evaluation to inform the selection of health interventions for funding and implementation can be a useful exercise, because it allows systematic comparison of interventions accounting for benefits and costs (in the case of CBAs) or for health outcomes and costs (in the case of cost-effectiveness analysis, CEAs). The economic evaluation process can be broken down into four steps:

(1) Defining the universe of possible interventions
(2) Estimating the BCRs for a CBA, or cost-effectiveness ratios (CERs) for a CEA, for all individual interventions (or combinations thereof)
(3) Ranking the interventions by their BCR or CER in a league table
(4) Selecting the interventions for implementation. We can do this in two ways:

  (a) When the available budget is unlimited, we use a fixed threshold value for the BCR or CER to separate the interventions that should be funded from those that should not. In a CBA, all interventions with a BCR > 1 are worthwhile doing. (In the case of a CBA that has taken into account all social benefits and all social costs, all interventions with a BCR > 1 are *socially* worthwhile doing.) In a CEA, we do not have an internal threshold value that divides those interventions that are worthwhile doing from those that are not. The CER threshold value must thus come from sources external to the analysis – e.g. a political decision.
  (b) When the available budget is limited, we start by selecting the intervention that has the most favorable BCR or CER, then the one that has the second most favorable ratio, and so on, until either the available budget is exhausted or the threshold values for the ratios has been passed. In a CBA, the threshold value is always unity. In a CEA, such a threshold value may or may not exist before the intervention selection exercise. If it does not exist, it will be determined during the exercise and represent the budget limit rather than (and unlike the BCR threshold in a CBA) carry any normative meaning about the social net benefit of the intervention.

Step (1) in this evaluation process will usually include defining the boundaries of the universe of interventions to be considered for the analysis through explicit inclusion and exclusion criteria. Given the title of Chapter 7, "Infectious disease, injury, and reproductive health," the boundary definition could have, for instance, excluded all health interventions that do not address an infectious disease, injury, or reproductive health burden. The result of the selection process summarized in steps (1)–(4) will be that, given a certain budget limit, the implementation of the selected interventions will maximize the benefits that can be achieved with the interventions included in the universe of possible interventions. For instance, in the case of a CBA conducted from the social perspective (i.e. incorporating all social benefits and all social costs), the net benefits to society due to the interventions will be maximized.

The CBA that Jamison *et al.* consider has been conducted from the social perspective. All of the six "investment solutions" that they select for funding have BCRs that are far greater than unity, implying that their implementation will confer positive social benefits. However, Jamison *et al.* do not present the BCRs of those interventions that were not selected as "investment solutions." The absence of BCRs of interventions that were part of the initial universe of possible interventions but are not part of the six "investment solutions" could imply that all other possible interventions in the initial universe have BCRs that are smaller than those of the six "investment solutions." However, judging from the description of the approach that Jamison *et al.* have taken in selecting the six "investment solutions," the reason for the absence of other BCRs is a different one. The authors do not follow the four-step process outlined above but instead select the six "investment solutions" based on a range of arguments (described on pp. 403–16 of the chapter) including the BCRs, which is required to indicate that the "investment solutions" are "highly cost-effective" (or rather highly cost-beneficial) (Jamison *et al.*, 2012): "we have identified six solutions for investment in interventions that address a large disease burden highly cost effectively."

The authors do not, therefore, adhere to the standard algorithm for selecting the six "investment solutions." Their approach deviates from standard economic evaluation in two important respects: first, they do not necessarily maximize the benefits given the universe of possible interventions and a budget constraint; and, second, they use multiple criteria for the selection of the interventions instead of the single criterion BCR (or CER). Rather than selecting the *most* cost-effective (cost-beneficial) interventions based on economic evaluation results covering the universe of possible interventions, Jamison *et al.* select the interventions based on a range of criteria, including some threshold of "high cost-effectiveness" whose precise value remains unspecified (Jamison *et al.*, 2012):

> Cost-effectiveness calculations provide important insights into the economic attractiveness of an intervention, but other considerations – such as consequences for financial protection and demands on health system capacity – need to be borne in mind. Even if factors such as system capacity remain difficult to quantify it may be useful to include a subjective judgment, for each intervention, of the extent of its demand on system capacity. We complement our quantitative (if imprecise) BCR estimates with subjective judgments of this type in a "dashboard" comparison of interventions.

This selection process may reflect the experience of the author team, "realism," or an underlying theory of decision-making. It is important to note in this context, however, that the Copenhagen Consensus explicitly endorses an economic evaluation approach choosing "*the most* cost-effective" investment solutions rather than merely "*highly* cost-effective" ones (our emphasis) (Copenhagen Consensus Center, 2012):

> After deliberations, the Expert Panel's task is to create a prioritized list of solutions to the ten challenges, showing the most cost-effective investments.

Of course, the fact that the Copenhagen Consensus combines economic evaluation with deliberations of Expert Panels might be seen to indicate that in addition to the single criterion of maximizing effects or benefits given a budget constraint, the Consensus implicitly endorses the inclusion of other criteria in decision-making. It then would remain to be clarified whether the selection and application of these additional criteria in the process of the Copenhagen Consensus is intended to be left to the deliberations of the Expert Panel, or whether it should already take place in the earlier stages of the work for the Challenge Papers.

In addition to the intentions of the Copenhagen Consensus, we have a number of concerns related to the particular multi-criterion selection process used by Jamison *et al.* (as described in Chapter 7).

First, the reasons for choosing a multi-criterion process of selecting the "investment solutions" are not explained. Do the authors believe that economic evaluation cannot capture some of the criteria they consider in the multi-criterion process (Baltussen *et al.*, 2006)? Or do they want to ensure that criteria, which could theoretically be incorporated in economic evaluations, are considered separately, to emphasize that they are indeed considered? Or do they want to ensure that policy-makers do not only learn which interventions should be prioritized, but also for which particular reasons these interventions should be prioritized?

Second, it remains unclear how the authors used the multiple criteria in selecting the "investment solutions." How did they trade the different criteria off against each other, when in the comparison of two interventions one scores higher on some criteria than the other but lower on other criteria? For instance, the intervention "Childhood diseases: expanded immunization coverage" scores lower on the "financial risk protection" criterion and the "relevance for development assistance" criterion than the intervention "HIV: accelerated vaccine development," but the former has a more favorable BCR than the latter. If we could only fund one of these two interventions, which one would we choose?

Third, while the authors provide some explanations why they included the five criteria in the selection process, in addition to cost-effectiveness, they do not explain why they did not include yet other criteria in the process. One meaningful additional criterion could have been whether existing organizations are already committed to supporting a particular intervention or not. It could, for instance, be argued that the intervention "Childhood diseases: expanded immunization coverage" is already sufficiently supported by the GAVI Alliance and thus does not need to be considered in the set of interventions for selection for future funding commitments. The distribution of benefits across populations in LMICs could have been another criterion (Baltussen and Niessen, 2006). For instance, on normative grounds, we might argue that, all else equal, we should prefer an intervention that benefits primarily poor populations in these countries over one that benefits primarily the wealthy. The probability that an intervention would cause unintended consequences (Bärnighausen *et al.*, 2011a), and the severity of such consequences should they occur, might be yet other criteria that could have been justified to be included in the set of criteria used to select the "investment solutions." For instance, efforts by the AMFm to reduce prices for anti-malarial medicines through negotiations with private sector pharmaceutical manufacturers may in the long run reduce research investment in new anti-malarial medicines and thus decrease our future ability to successfully treat malaria patients.

Regarding the selection of multiple criteria for multi-criterion decision-making, it is important to note that in past applications of such approaches for selecting interventions to address infectious disease burdens, the criteria, and their relative weights have commonly been based on empirically elicited stakeholder or community preferences (Youngkong *et al.*, 2009; Youngkong *et al.*, 2010; Youngkong *et al.*, 2012), rather than on expert choice, as in this chapter.

Fourth, the possible reasons for including at least one of the criteria, "size of the disease burden," do not seem convincing. There are two possible reasons for a small disease burden. First, only a few people suffer from it; and, second, many people suffer from it but the per person disease burden is on average small. In the first case, because an intervention addresses a rare disease it should not, in our opinion, be excluded from funding. Some characteristics of rare diseases, such as difficulty in identifying the people suffering from the disease, are indeed important, but can be captured in other criteria, such as the cost-effectiveness (it will be more costly to find those who suffer from the disease), the feasibility criterion (it might not be possible to identify them at all), or the relevance for development assistance criterion (particular funders may not be interested in funding interventions that benefit only a few, for one reason or another). However, given that the BCR is favorable and the intervention possible and relevant for donor assistance, we see no reason why an intervention that improves the health of only a few people should not be implemented.

Given a favorable BCR, an implementation reaching a large proportion of the people suffering from the rare disease will not be expensive compared to the implementation of an intervention that benefits many, leaving most of the budget available for other funding opportunities. A similar argument can be made for the case of a disease that affects many but causes only comparatively little suffering in each person who has the disease. In this case, a favorable BCR implies low costs per person and implementing the intervention, so that it reaches a large proportion of the sufferers, will not be expensive. Of course, in this second case, we might be opposed to the funding for yet other reasons, such as a belief that funding of interventions that avert or successfully treat small individual disease burdens should be left to the individual sufferers. But this would be a different criterion than "size of the disease burden."

One argument for the "size of the disease burden" criterion could be that we would want to consider the disease-burden size in prioritizing R&D investments. However, the BCR for such investment decisions – e.g. investment in HIV vaccination research – already incorporates the size of the disease burden in the estimation of the potential benefits of the investments and thus does not need to be considered separately.

Fifth, it remains unclear how the authors derived the scores for the different interventions on the five criteria. Some of the scores lack face validity. For instance, it seems surprising to us that the intervention "Childhood diseases: expanded immunization coverage" scores low ("L") on the criterion "Financial risk protection provided" (Table 7.8, p. 419). Some childhood diseases, such as measles or *Haemophilus influenzae* type B infection can lead to sequelae that severely impede children's physical or cognitive development and school attainment (Bärnighausen *et al.*, 2011b), which will tend to diminish the children's potential productivity and income as an adult and thus render them and their families financially vulnerable.

In sum, while a case could theoretically be made that instead of the single-criterion decision-making of economic evaluation a multi-criterion decision-making process should be followed, such a process would need to be aligned with the intentions and the existing process of the Copenhagen Consensus – i.e. selection of "the most cost-effective" investments after the deliberations of an Expert Panel. The particular multi-criterion decision-making process needs further clarification and justification in terms of the choice of the process, the selection of the multiple criteria and how they are jointly used in decision-making, and the scoring of interventions on each of the criteria.

Uncertainty, risk attitudes, and time horizons

Jamison *et al.* take the following approach to dealing with uncertainty in their economic evaluation results (Jamison *et al.*, 2012):

> Given these often broad ranges in cost-effectiveness ratios, and hence in BCRs, it makes little sense to conclude with precise estimates of uncertainty or effect size. Rather we have identified six solutions for investment in interventions that address a large disease burden highly cost-effectively, even granted substantial uncertainty and variability in the underlying estimates.

This approach introduces yet another criterion for decision-making: robustness of the economic evaluation results to changing parameter estimates. While robustness checks are sensible, the particular approach the authors use to test robustness does not account for differential uncertainty between the different interventions selected as "investment solutions" and between the selected interventions and interventions that were not chosen or considered as priorities.

Ignoring differential uncertainty is justified for government decision-making, if the benefits and losses of all interventions are spread widely and evenly across a population. However, as has been noted elsewhere, this prerequisite for justifying risk-indifferent decision-making in public investment is commonly violated in infectious disease prevention and control, because the diseases and the results of the prevention efforts affect different individuals very differently (Dijkhuizen *et al.*, 1994). HIV, TB, and malaria are no exceptions to this rule, as they have widely varying effects on different population subgroups. For these diseases – and for others that share the distributional characteristic – national policy-makers and international donors should arguably behave risk-aversely to arrive at the best public investment decisions. Risk-aversion, however, implies that the degree of uncertainty in results will matter in addition to the expected value of the results: it will be worthwhile to trade off some expected value against reductions in uncertainty.

Jamison *et al.* do not account for differential uncertainty in their economic evaluations of "investment solutions" – at the same time, the interventions they select are likely to differ widely in terms of the variance of their potential impacts. At one end of the spectrum is investment in research to develop an HIV vaccination, with extremely high levels of uncertainty about success; at the other end are the delivery of interventions with well-established efficacy and effectiveness, such as childhood vaccinations and deworming. It is possible that the BCR ranking of "HIV: accelerated vaccine development" (BCR 11:1) and "Deworming schoolchildren" (BCR 10:1) will be reversed once the different levels of uncertainty in the results of these two investments is taken into account by risk-averse decision-makers.

It is similarly likely that investment in the scale-up of medical male circumcision (MMC), an intervention with well-established efficacy and effectiveness in reducing HIV acquisition, would have outperformed investment in HIV vaccine development, had the authors taken uncertainty into account in their economic evaluations. MMC is equivalent to a vaccination with about 60 percent efficacy in reducing HIV acquisition in men (Auvert *et al.*, 2005; Bailey *et al.*, 2007; Gray *et al.*, 2007; Newell and Bärnighausen 2007). Jamison *et al.* state that "[s]ustained investment in HIV vaccine development is, very recently, beginning to bear fruit" (Jamison *et al.*, 2012). We do not necessarily agree with this assertion: thirty years of research to develop an HIV vaccine have not produced a convincing vaccine candidate, and the only vaccine that did show some promise in randomized controlled trials did not reach the efficacy levels of circumcision (Rerks-Ngarm *et al.*, 2009).

Another issue that could affect BCR rankings is the choice of time horizon in economic evaluation. The time horizon – i.e. the date in the future beyond which all benefits and costs of an intervention are ignored (Sugden, 1978) – should be chosen such that it captures all meaningful and relevant differences in benefits and costs between the interventions that are compared in the evaluation (Philips *et al.*, 2004). It seems likely that in the comparison of the six "investment solutions" the time horizon should matter significantly. This is because the benefit and cost streams of the different solutions are likely to follow very different patterns. The solution "HIV: accelerate vaccine development" requires upfront investment but promises returns without a time limit and without additional spending on R&D, once an effective HIV vaccination has become available. In contrast, the solution "Childhood diseases: expanded immunization coverage" will lead to benefits lasting many years and sometimes entire lifetimes – but never indefinitely – for the initial investment in vaccination. And the solution "Tuberculosis: appropriate case finding and treatment including dealing with MDR-TB" will lead to pay-offs shortly after the intervention spending but these benefits will not last for long after the spending has stopped.

Because of these different patterns of benefits and cost streams across the different "investment solutions" it seems plausible that the ranking of their BCRs, and the comparison to interventions not included in the solution set, is not robust to changing evaluation time-horizons. Time-horizon effects should thus be systematically examined in the analysis and, if possible, relatively long time horizons should be chosen for the baseline evaluation. However, a longer time horizon is not always better in economic evaluation, because the assumptions used in predicting future benefit and cost streams of an intervention become increasingly uncertain as the evaluation time horizon is moved further into the future. For instance, assumptions about the costs of medical products, such as drugs and vaccines, may be relatively accurate for a few years but are very unlikely to represent these costs twenty or thirty years into the future with reasonable accuracy, as pharmaceutical firms merge and change ownership and new products become available.

Conclusion

In this Perspective Paper our analysis suggests the following three options for improving the process of selecting interventions for investment:

(1) The multi-criteria decision-making approach could be replaced by a traditional economic evaluation process, coupled with clearly defined criteria for the initial selection of possible interventions into the choice set, or universe, of possible interventions.
(2) The multi-criteria decision-making approach could be improved by clearly justifying (i) the selection of the different criteria, (ii) the approach to scoring the criteria, and (iii) the approach to trade the different criteria off against each other in selecting the "investment solutions." Such justifications could come from theory or empirical work – e.g. eliciting the preferences of relevant stakeholders.
(3) The economic evaluations should incorporate uncertainty estimates into the comparison of the different interventions and a wide range of time horizons should be considered in the analysis.

Bibliography

Auvert, B. *et al.*, 2005: Randomized, controlled intervention trial of male circumcision for reduction of HIV infection risk: the ANRS 1265 Trial, *PLoS Medicine* **2**, e298

Bailey, R. C. *et al.*, 2007: Male circumcision for HIV prevention in young men in Kisumu, Kenya: a randomised controlled trial, *Lancet* **369**, 643–56

Baltussen, R. and L. Niessen, 2006: Priority setting of health interventions: the need for multi-criteria decision analysis, *Cost Efficient Resource Allocation* **4**, 14

Baltussen, R. *et al.*, 2006: Towards a multi-criteria approach for priority setting: an application to Ghana, *Health Economics* **15**, 689–96

Bärnighausen, T., D. E. Bloom, and S. Humair, 2011a: *Strengthening Health Systems: Perspectives for Economic Evaluation*, Copenhagen Consensus Center, Copenhagen

Bärnighausen, T. *et al.*, 2011b: Rethinking the benefits and costs of childhood vaccination: the example of the Haemophilus influenzae type b vaccine, *Vaccine* **29**, 2371–80

Copenhagen Consensus Center, 2012: Copenhagen Consenus background, www.copenhagenconsensus.com/Projects/CC12/Background.aspx, accessed April 12, 2012

Dijkhuizen, A., R. Hardaker, and R. Huirne, 1994: Risk attitude and decision making in contagious disease control, *Preventive Veterinary Medicine* **18**, 203–12

Gray, R. H. *et al.*, 2007: Male circumcision for HIV prevention in men in Rakai, Uganda: a randomised trial, *Lancet* **369**, 657–66

Jamison, D. *et al.*, 2012: Copenhagen Consensus 2012 Challenge Paper: Infectious disease, injury, and reproductive health, Draft

Newell, M. L. and T. Bärnighausen, 2007: Male circumcision to cut HIV risk in the general population, *Lancet* **369**, 617–19

Philips, Z. *et al.*, 2004: Review of guidelines for good practice in decision-analytic modelling in health technology assessment, *Health Technology Assessment* **8**, iii–iv, ix–xi, 1–158

Rerks-Ngarm, S. *et al.*, 2009: Vaccination with ALVAC and AIDSVAX to prevent HIV-1 infection in Thailand, *New England Journal of Medicine* **361**, 2209–20

Sugden, R., 1978: *The Principles of Practical Cost-Benefit Analysis*, Oxford University Press

Youngkong, S. L., Kapiriri, and R. Baltussen, 2009: Setting priorities for health interventions in developing countries: a review of empirical studies, *Tropical Medicine and International Health* **14**, 930–9

Youngkong, S. *et al.*, 2010: Criteria for priority setting of HIV/AIDS interventions in Thailand: a discrete choice experiment, *BMC Health Services Research* **10**, 197

2012: Multi-criteria decision analysis for setting priorities on HIV/AIDS interventions in Thailand, *Health Research Policy and Systems* **10**, 6

Infectious Disease, Injury, and Reproductive Health

Alternative Perspective

DAVID CANNING

Introduction

Chapter 6, "Infectious disease, injury, and reproductive health by Jamison *et al.* puts forward a case for high BCRs for a set of targeted health interventions in developing countries. These are TB treatment, the prevention and treatment of malaria, immunization against childhood diseases, development of an HIV vaccine, surgical treatment of injuries and difficulties in childbirth, and the deworming of children in schools.

My overall view is that the high BCRs the authors ascribe to these interventions based on health benefits are warranted, though with a number of caveats. These caveats on measurement of costs and benefits are discussed in detail in Canning (2009), and are re-examined on pp. 434–5 for the six interventions that are recommended in the chapter. While I think all of the proposed interventions are individually desirable I particularly welcome the inclusion of deworming of children as a priority health intervention. While the effect of these worm infections on children's mortality is low they can have serious consequences for education and learning and adult productivity. The use of health interventions for benefits not only in health outcomes but in education and worker productivity is an important example of intersectoral thinking, and is to be encouraged.

While the interventions being recommended have high BCRs a number of health interventions arguably have even greater effectiveness but did not make the recommended list in the chapter. A major change in its recommendations from the 2009 and 2008 rounds of the Copenhagen Consensus (Jamison *et al.*, 2009) is a shift from an emphasis on implementation of existing known interventions that affect risky behaviors and the transmission of infections to prevent the spread of HIV/AIDS to funding the development of a new vaccine for HIV. While a vaccine is clearly desirable, its development will take many years, and is subject to great risk. Given this, it is not at all clear to me that the emphasis on vaccine development over implantation of existing prevention strategies is justified. This issue is considered in more detail on pp. 435–43.

An additional case as a potential priority health intervention is tobacco control. Evidence from the chapter on disease control in the 2008 Copenhagen Consensus (Jamison *et al.*, 2009), gives figures for the BCRs for this intervention that are substantially higher than some of the interventions being recommended in the current chapter. It would have been very useful to have discussion of why this intervention has been dropped from consideration. Is the BCR now thought to be lower, or are other considerations in play in the setting health priorities?

Another issue is that many of the interventions recommended are disease-specific, and lend themselves to vertical interventions that target these diseases without the need for broad improvements in the overall health system. To some extent this is aimed at overcoming capacity constraints in health systems in developing countries and focusing financial resources where they have the biggest health benefits. An alternative approach would be for a broad expansion of health care resources, coupled with universal health care though public provision or national insurance, to ensure access to a broad range of services. It would be interesting to see what the BCR of this more ambitious approach would be, even if it were subsequently rejected as a priority intervention. These alternative interventions are discussed on pp. 435–6.

The one major issue that creates a worry about the high BCRs found for recommended interventions is the lack of any estimate of the effect of saving lives on income levels through population growth. To the extent that the health benefits are about preventing illness and morbidity, which may be particularly true of surgical treatment and deworming, this is not an issue. However to the extent that the health interventions save lives, which is in most cases the key argument for their health benefits, there will be more rapid population growth. This will have economic effects due to fixed resource constraints, particularly land availability, capital per worker, and the population age structure. The negative effects of population growth on income levels are potentially very large, and should not be ignored.

A key issue is the extent to which reductions in mortality, particularly child mortality, affect fertility decisions. If fertility falls in response to lower child mortality, due to a desired family size being achievable with fewer births in a low-mortality environment, these negative population growth effects will be reduced or eliminated. However, achieving lower fertility requires the provision of family planning services and it may be that the health benefits outlined in the chapter will be undone by population growth unless these services are in place. This is discussed on p. 437, where I advocate the addition of the provision of family planning services as a necessary complement to the health interventions recommended in the chapter.

The cost–benefit estimates

One of the main issues in the BCR calculation is the money value of health gains. Health gains are measured in DALYs and these health benefits are then translated into money units by using estimates of the value of a statistical life (VSL) and value of disability estimates. A key issue is the assumption that the value of a statistical life and a DALY varies with the level of income. The approach taken in the chapter is based on the idea that the value of a year of disability-free life is about three times national income *per capita*. It is argued that this view has empirical support based on the work of Viscusi and Aldy (2003) though the authors argue that the WTP for a life year may increase less than proportionately with income.

The rationale for different values of life is that the WTP for a life year is lower in poor than rich countries. However there is some unease that the life of a person in a poor country is intrinsically worth less than that of a person in a rich country, and most analysis of the health sector has used CEA, rather than CBA, where the benefits are kept in health units (DALYs) rather than converted into money terms at different rates for different people. The difficulty with assuming that lives are equally valuable in all countries is that this would imply high valuations of lives in poor countries, which is not reflected in their WTP.

The chapter makes a distinction between projects funded from a developing country's own resources, when a low money value of life, based on the WTP for a life year within the country, should be used, and projects funded from international sources when a higher value of life, based on the money value of life in developed countries, should be used. This seems inconsistent – the value of life should be the same no matter the source of the funds. In addition once the international funds are in country, and if they can in principle be used for other purposes, would not the optimum now be for a developing country not to undertake the health intervention if the BCR is low from its point of view? This appears to create a time-consistency problem if funds for a health intervention from an international source are channeled through national governments.

An alternative approach, which I think is more logically consistent, is to say that life is intrinsically equally valuable in all countries. However the low WTP money for life in developing countries implies that in these countries money is very valuable (measured in life years). On the other hand in rich countries the high WTP money for life years means that money has low value (measured in life years). This means that the value of life is the same everywhere, but there would be a welfare gain from taking money from the rich, who put little value on it, and giving it to the poor, who value it highly.

While I think this is more logically consistent it implies that a simple redistribution of money from rich to poor countries will be welfare-improving and will have a high BCR (measured in life year equivalents). Using money as the measuring rod for welfare, as in a CBA, means that money is equally valuable for each person, which rules out this kind of redistribution-improving welfare. However the implication of this is that poor peoples' lives are of less value than rich peoples', which is ethically troubling.

The chapter takes proper account of the fact that health interventions have spillover effects into educational outcomes, particularly in the inclusion of deworming as a priority. Work in Kenya has shown that children who were treated as part of a deworming experiment not only had greater educational attainment but also higher wages when they entered the work force (Baird *et al.*, 2011). The large returns to health investments in the children in the form of better educational outcomes and eventual worker productivity (Bleakley, 2007; Canning *et al.*, 2011) could mean that the BCRs for childhood immunization and malaria prevention and treatment may be larger than those reported in the chapter, which focuses mainly on health benefits. There is increasing evidence that these early childhood investments in health and nutrition, *in utero* and in the first few years of life, have large effects on both physical and cognitive development and educational outcomes and eventually income as an adult (Schultz, 2005); this means that there is a strong case for concentrating heath interventions on children to reap these productivity gains as well as the direct health gains.

In addition to the more conceptual issues discussed above there are the practical problems of measuring the benefits and costs of health interventions. However for most of the interventions discussed in the chapter there is evidence from developing countries of both benefits and costs, which avoids the problem of trying to use data from developed countries to estimate values for developing countries where the setting may be very different. Average rather than marginal costs are used in the analysis, which seems appropriate given the large scale of the proposed interventions.

A recurring issue with such high BCRs is why, if the benefits are so large relative to costs, people do not finance these interventions themselves. Even in poor countries an action that produces a benefit that is ten times larger than a cost should be very attractive. The answer for TB treatment, the prevention and treatment of malaria, immunization against childhood diseases, HIV/AIDS prevention, and the deworming of children in schools, is that these all attack infectious disease. With infectious disease there is a large negative externality when one person infects another. The social benefits to these interventions may be much larger than the private benefit to the individual who receives a vaccine or treatment. This produces a clear case for governments or international agencies to intervene.

The case for surgical interventions is quite different. The benefits from essential surgery accrue directly to the patient with no infectious disease agent to cause an externality. If surgery has such a high private BCR, should it not be financed by the individuals affected themselves? Here the case is really the failure of health care markets, health insurance markets, or finance markets for borrowing, which mean that poor people cannot finance even highly beneficial health care. Rather than improve access just to essential surgery there is a case for a broader intervention that improves access to a range of health care services that may be highly beneficial to poor people. This is addressed in the next section, when I discuss universal access to health care.

Alternative cost-effective health interventions

Chapter 6 makes a strong case for six interventions. However there are other health interventions that might be ranked even higher than these. One is in the area of HIV/AIDS prevention. I agree with the view that while treatment with anti-retroviral therapy is probably cost-effective, particularly in light of the high labor productivity and earnings of those in treatment (Thirumurthy *et al.*, 2005) its BCR is not exceptionally high. On the other hand prevention efforts, particularly interventions aimed at behavioral change in high-risk populations and that reduce the likelihood of virus transmission, are highly cost-effective (Canning, 2006). The BCR of these behavioral preventive intervention has been estimated at 12:1 (Jamison *et al.*, 2009).

However the chapter instead highlights investment in the development of a new vaccine to prevent HIV as the priority in this area. This development activity is very risky; it is difficult to know what effect the spending will have on time to development of the vaccine. Also the benefits are well in the future, perhaps twenty years, which means we must apply a discount rate over a long period of time. We also have the issue of whether we should use a low value of life based on the low WTP for a life year in the mainly poor countries affected by HIV/AIDS or a higher valuation of life based on WTP in rich countries, since the funding will be from international sources. Different assumptions about the effect on vaccine development, discounting and the value of life in Table 7.6 (p. 417) produce a range of BCRs from 4:1 to 72:1. They assume an expected ratio of 11:1 to justify making this research funding a priority health intervention.

It is difficult to justify putting vaccine development with an 11:1 BCR, ahead of implementing existing prevention strategies at a BCR of 12:1, especially given the very wide uncertainty about the effect of funding on the chances of vaccine development. An argument given in the chapter is that a decision for funding development of a HIV vaccine would signal the importance of the issue to other players in the development arena. However, it could equally well be argued that such a decision would signal a lack of emphasis on implementing prevention strategies based on changing behaviors and preventing transmission using existing technologies. Given the risks associated with development of an HIV vaccine, and the high BCRs of existing prevention interventions, I think it is very difficult to justify HIV vaccine development as a higher priority. To do this would I think require an additional justification based on prevention using existing methods not being feasible, but the evidence appears to be that it is, if carried out in a systematic way (Piot *et al.*, 2008).

In addition to HIV prevention there are two other health interventions that deserve attention. One is tobacco control through high taxation. This has a very high BCR and would have significant effects on adult health in developing countries. Smoking has important effects on cancer and heart disease, and reducing smoking rates would substantially reduce illness and mortality from these diseases.

One argument against tobacco control is that aside from the externality of second-hand smoke, smoking is a voluntary decision and that people should be expected to take into account the health costs of smoking in their decision-making. This does not allow for the established prevalence of short-term decision-making, or hyperbolic discounting, by consumers where they discount more heavily than rational future benefits relative to current benefits. The addictive nature of smoking means there is a public welfare benefit from preventing the initiation of smoking and encouraging cessation. That a majority of current smokers support tobacco tax increases if the proceeds are used to help smokers quit (Wilson *et al.*, 2010) suggest that there is a serious self-control problem in smoking. Despite its voluntary nature there may still be a large welfare benefit from measures to reduce tobacco use given that the behavior of smokers is non-rational.

The disease-specific nature of most of the interventions in the chapter is somewhat troubling given that the delivery of the interventions will largely be through a common health system infrastructure. Rather than focus on particular interventions, an alternative approach would be to emphasize the provision of health care, particularly preventive care, and cost-effective treatments, using a system based on universal access. One striking feature of the last decade in Africa is a move away from user fees when accessing health care (Yates, 2009) to public provision or national health insurance. India has increased access to health care through its National Rural Health Mission (NRHM) while China has developed the New Cooperative Medical Scheme (NCMS) to provide health insurance to the rural poor (Yip and Mahal, 2008). These changes to the health system are aimed at providing greater access to a broad range of essential health care services for the poor. I am unaware of any benefit-cost figures for these type of reforms, but it would be useful to examine the benefits and costs of this type of policy aimed at extending access to a broad range of services. While foreign donors may emphasize highly cost-effective vertical health interventions targeted as specific diseases, the developing countries themselves seem to be placing greater emphasis on creating universal access to a broad range of health care services.

Population growth and access to family planning services

A serious potential problem with large-scale health interventions is that the result will be larger population numbers. In the simplest sense this is exactly the health benefit we want – it is the survival of greater number of people that provides the bulk of the welfare gain from the health interventions. However, the survival of a greater number of people may have negative effects on income *per capita* due to the effects of population growth on land and capital *per capita*.

Acemoglu and Johnson (2007), in a cross-country study find that improvements in health tend to lead to reductions in income *per capita*, and argue that the mechanism is that while better health may mean improved worker productivity, the larger population numbers may put pressure on scarce resources and reduce income *per capita*. Ashraf *et al.* (2008) use a simulation model to show that the effect of improvements of child health through a malaria intervention may lower GDP *per capita* for three decades, due to increased child survival and population pressure, before the productivity benefits occur as the healthier children enter the work force. Similarly Young (2005) argues that HIV/AIDS has raised income *per capita* in many African countries due to a high death rate and lower population growth.

The population growth that results from mortality reductions is not inevitable. One of the major determinants of fertility is child mortality. When child mortality rates fall, women can achieve their desired family size with fewer births. A reduction in child mortality usually sets off a decline in fertility, leading to a demographic transition (Dyson, 2010). Without this accompanying decline in fertility the population pressure associated with health improvements may have a negative effect on human welfare.

An important factor allowing women to achieve their desired level of fertility is the provision of family planning services. A reproductive health, child health, and family planning intervention in Matlab, Bangladesh, in the 1980s, and a similar intervention in Navrongo, Ghana, in the 1990s, both led to a reduction in total fertility rates of about one child per woman in the treatment areas compared to the control areas (Debpuur *et al.* (2002); Joshi and Schultz, 2007).

The lower fertility allowed by family planning programs plays a central role in preventing a Malthusian trap occurring when child mortality declines. Improvements in reproductive health and access to family planning can also have health benefits. Chapter 6 highlights surgical interventions for complications in pregnancy. Other forms of ante-natal and post-natal care can improve the health of both mothers and children. Access to family planning can not only lead to lower total fertility but can also reduce high-risk births for very young women, and for women at high parities. It can also lead to improved birth spacing. This improved timing of childbirth can again improve the health of mothers and children, reducing maternal and child mortality (Cleland *et al.*, 2012). Fewer children also allow increased parental investment per child in health, nutrition, and education (Joshi and Schultz, 2007).

Bibliography

Acemoglu, D. and S. Johnson, 2007: Disease and development: the effect of life expectancy on economic growth, *Journal of Political Economy* **115**, 925–85

Ashraf, Q., A. Lester *et al.*, 2008: When does improving health raise GDP?, *NBER Working Paper Series* **W1444**

Baird, S., J. H. Hicks *et al.*, 2011: Worms at work: long-run impacts of child health gains, http://elsa.berkeley.edu/~emiguel/pdfs/miguel_wormsatwork.pdf

Bleakley, H., 2007: Disease and development: evidence from hookworm eradication in the American South, *Quarterly Journal of Economics* **122**, 73–117

Canning, D., 2006: The economics of HIV/AIDS in low-income countries: the case for prevention, *Journal of Economic Perspectives* **20**, 121–42

2009: Disease control: alternative perspectives, in B. Lomborg (ed.), *Global Crises, Global Solutions*, Cambridge University Press, 164–71

Canning, D., A. Razzaque *et al.*, 2011: The effect of maternal tetanus immunization on children's schooling attainment in Matlab, Bangladesh: follow-up of a randomized trial, *Social Science and Medicine* **79**, 1429–36

Cleland, J., A. Conde-Agudelo *et al.*, 2012: Contraception and health, *Lancet* **380**, 149–56

Debpuur, C., J. F. Phillips *et al.*, 2002: The impact of the Navrongo Project on contraceptive knowledge and use, reproductive preferences, and fertility, *Studies in Family Planning* **33**, 141–64

Dyson, T., 2010: *Population and Development: The Demographic Transition*, Zed Books, London

Jamison, D. T., P. Jha *et al.*, 2009: Disease control, in B. Lomborg (ed.), *Global Crises, Global Solutions*, Cambridge University Press, 126–63

Joshi, S. and T. P. Schultz, 2007: Family planning as an investment in development: evaluation of a program's consequences in Matlab, Bangladesh, *Working Papers* **951**, Economic Growth Center, Yale University

Piot, P., M. Bartos *et al.*, 2008: Coming to terms with complexity: a call to action for HIV prevention, *Lancet* **372**, 845–59

Schultz, T. P, 2005: Productive benefits of health: evidence from low income countries, in G. Lopez-Casasnovas, B. Riveras, and L. Currais (eds.), *Health and Economic Growth: Findings and Policy Implications*, MIT Press, Cambridge, MA

Thirumurthy, H., J. Graff-Zivin *et al.*, 2005: The economic impact of aids treatment: labor supply in Western Kenya, *National Bureau of Economic Research, Working Paper* **11871**

Viscusi, W. K. and J. E. Aldy, 2003: The value of a statistical life: a critical review of market estimates from around the world, *Journal of Risk and Uncertainty* **27**, 5–76

Wilson, N., D. Weerasekera *et al.*, 2010: Characteristics of smoker support for increasing a dedicated tobacco tax: national survey data from New Zealand, *Nicotine & Tobacco Research* **12**, 168–73

Yates, R., 2009: Universal health care and the removal of user fees, *Lancet* **373**, 2078–81

Yip, W. and A. Mahal, 2008: The health care systems of China and India: performance and future challenges, *Health Affairs* **27**, 921–32

Young, A., 2005: The gift of the dying: the tragedy of AIDS and the welfare of future African generations, *Quarterly Journal of Economics* **120**, 423–66

CHAPTER 8

Natural Disasters

HOWARD KUNREUTHER AND ERWANN MICHEL-KERJAN*

Introduction

Thirty years ago, large-scale natural disasters were considered to be low-probability, high-consequence events. Between 1970 and the mid 1980s, annual insured losses from natural disasters world-wide (including forest fires) were only in the $3–$4 billion range. Hurricane Hugo, which made landfall in Charleston, South Carolina, on September 22, 1989, was the first natural disaster in the United States to inflict more than $1 billion of insured losses. Times have changed.

Economic and insured losses from great natural catastrophes such as earthquakes, hurricanes, and floods have increased significantly in recent years. According to Munich Re (2013), economic losses from natural catastrophes increased from $528 billion (1981–1990), to $1,197 billion (1991–2000), to $1,213 billion (2001–2010). During the past ten years, the losses were principally due to hurricanes and resulting storm surge occurring in 2004, 2005, and 2008. Figure 8.1 depicts the evolution of the direct economic losses and the insured portion from great natural disasters over the period 1980–2012.[1] Given the massive economic losses from the March 2011 earthquake and resulting tsunami in Japan, the year 2011 was the most costly year on record for disasters globally: $370 billion (Swiss Re, 2011).

One measure of the economic impact of natural disasters on those suffering damage is the ratio of *total losses* to *insured losses* (L/I). When there is a limited insurance market, as is the case in most low and middle-income countries (LMICs), the value of L/I will normally be very high. For example, in 1996, major floods in China inflicted about US$24 billion in economic losses, less than US$500 million of which was covered by insurance, so that the L/I ratio was greater than 50. In 2010, China suffered its most devastating flood in a decade, which cost about US$50 billion in direct economic losses, with US$1 billion covered by insurance so the L/I ratio was 50 (Michel-Kerjan and Kunreuther, 2011).

Even in developed countries, such as Japan, the L/I ratio from a disaster can be high. The large-scale earthquake that devastated Kobe, Japan, in 1995 cost US$110 billion (L), only US$3 billion of which was covered by insurance (I), resulting in an L/I of 36.7. In the United States, the L/I ratio has been much lower (ranging from 2 to 4) due to higher insurance coverage. In the cases of Hurricane Andrew (1992 prices), the Northridge earthquake (1994 prices), and Hurricane Katrina (2005 prices) the L/I ratios were about 1.5 (26/17), 2.8 (44/15.5) and 3 (150/45), respectively.

* Wharton School, University of Pennsylvania. Emails: kunreuther@wharton.upenn.edu; erwannmk@wharton.upenn.edu.

We thank Kasper Thede Anderskov, Benjamin Collier, Stephâne Hallegatte, Bjorn Lomborg, Roland Mathiasson, Henrik Meyer, Ilan Noy, and Members of the Expert Panel at the Copenhagen Consensus 2012: Finn E. Kydland, Robert Mundell, Thomas C. Schelling, Vernon Smith, Nancy Stokey for insightful comments on an earlier version of this work. Excellent research assistance was provided by Peter Eschenbrenner and Christina Zima. Financial support for this project was provided by the Copenhagen Consensus, the Center for Risk and Economic Analysis of Terrorism Events (CREATE), at USC, the Center for Research on Environmental Decisions (CRED; NSF Cooperative Agreement SES-0345840 to Columbia University), the Travelers Foundation, and the Wharton Risk Management and Decision Processes Center of the University of Pennsylvania.

[1] Catastrophes are classified as "great" if the ability of the region to help itself is overtaxed, making interregional or international assistance necessary. This is normally the case when thousands of people are killed, hundreds of thousands made homeless, or when a country suffers substantial economic loss.

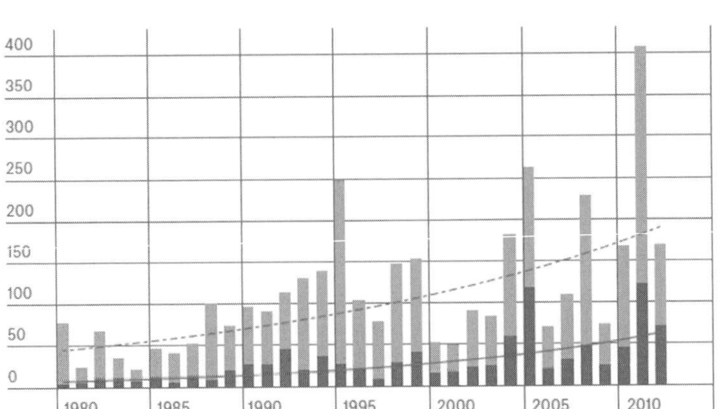

Figure 8.1 *Overall and insured losses with trend, 1980–2012 (US$ billion)*

Source: Munich Re (2013).

Impact on GDP

At a more aggregate level, one can estimate the economic impact of disasters by determining the losses in relation to the country's annual GDP. A major flood in the United States or a large European country will have much less of an impact on GDP than a similar event occurring in a developing country. In the United States, where the GDP is nearly US$15 trillion (as of 2013), even a US$250 billion loss due to a series of major disasters will have an impact on GDP that is less than 2 percent. In Myanmar, a 2 percent GDP loss would mean a loss of approximately US$1.8 billion. Natural disasters have had a long-enduring impact on small islands, with economic losses from major natural disasters representing several times the annual GDP, compared to losses in developed countries where damage is a very small percentage of annual GDP, as shown in Table 8.1.

Larger countries also often have a greater geographical spread of their economic assets relative to the spatial impact of disasters, and can therefore avoid more direct losses while minimizing indirect and downstream losses. Smaller countries like island nations can also face increased disaster risks not only by having a smaller economy, but by also having a larger proportion of their total land exposed to hazard (UNDP, 2004).

Using annual GDP to measure the relative economic impact of a disaster does not necessarily reveal the impact of the disaster on the affected region, however; property damage, business interruption, real estate prices, and tax revenue could be very severe locally but not large enough to have an impact on GDP.[2] The long-term effects of disasters on a country's GDP can also vary based on the state of development of the country, the size of the event, and the overall economic vulnerability of the country. Potentially negative long-term economic effects after a disaster include increase in the public deficit and worsening of the trade balance (demand for imports increase and exports decrease). For example, after Hurricane Mitch in 1998, Honduras experienced total direct and indirect losses that were 80 percent of its GDP (Mechler, 2003).

Fatalities

Natural disasters in developing countries also have a devastating human impact. The Bhola cyclone in the Ganges Delta in 1970 killed an estimated 500,000 in East Pakistan (now Bangladesh) and is classified as one of the deadliest natural disasters in history. In recent years, the 2004 tsunami in Southeast Asia killed between 225,000 and

[2] Six years after Hurricane Katrina struck New Orleans, the population was estimated to be 361,000, just over two-thirds of the size that it was before the disaster in 2005. It is very likely that this loss of residents will be permanent.

Table 8.1 Examples of disasters and damages as percentage of GDP

Year	Natural disaster	Country	Region	Damage (US$ million)	Damage (% of GDP)
Large economies					
2005	Hurricane (Katrina)	USA	North America	125,000	1.1
1995	Earthquake	Japan	East Asia	100,000	3.2
1998	Flood	China	East Asia	30,000	0.7
2004	Earthquake	Japan	East Asia	28,000	0.8
1992	Hurricane (Andrew)	USA	North America	26,500	0.4
Small island economies					
1988	Hurricane (Gilbert)	St. Lucia	Caribbean	1,000	365
1991	Cyclone (Val and Wasa)	Samoa	Oceana	278	248
2004	Hurricane (Ivan)	Grenada	Caribbean	889	203
1990	Cyclone (Ofa)	Samoa	Oceana	200	178
1985	Cyclone (Eric and Nigel)	Vanuatu	Oceana	173	143

Source: World Bank (2008).

275,000; the earthquake in Haiti in 2010 killed approximately 230,000 (CBC News, 2010). The historic floods in Pakistan in the summer of 2010 killed 2,000 and affected 20 million people. It is a challenge to think about how to address a large-scale crisis where one-fifth of the entire country's land is under water and 20 million are displaced for weeks (Michel-Kerjan and Slovic, 2010). These fatalities have a long-term impact on the development potential for a country. A population weakened by a natural disaster can often lack the organizational capacity to maintain social assets (sanitation, education, health care, housing, etc.), further crippling an already affected nation (UNISDR/World Bank, 2011).

Reasons for concern

The main drivers of these increasing losses from natural disasters are two socio-economic factors which directly influence the level of economic damage: *degree of urbanization* and *value at risk*. In 1950, about 30 percent of the world's population (2.5 billion people) lived in cities. In 2000, about 50 percent of the world's population (6 billion) lived in cities. Projections by the United Nations show that by 2025, this figure will have increased up to 60 percent as the population reaches 8.3 billion people. A direct consequence of this trend is the increasing number of so-called mega-cities with population above 10 million. In 1950, New York City was the only such mega-city. In 1990, there were twelve such cities. By 2015, there are estimated to be twenty-six, including Tokyo (29 million), Shanghai (18 million), New York (17.6 million), and Los Angeles (14.2 million) (Crossett *et al.*, 2004).

With respect to the developing world, Istanbul, a city subject to losses from earthquakes, has significantly increased in population over the past sixty years from less than 1 million in 1950 to more than 13 million by the end of 2010. This makes the Istanbul metropolitan area the third largest in Europe after London and Moscow. In India, about 48 percent of the land is prone to cyclones, 68 percent to droughts, and more than 40 million (nearly one-eighth of India) to floods (Government of India, 2004). Ten of the most deadly disasters since 1970 occurred in this country. Furthermore, several large cities in India subject to natural disasters are very densely populated. Mumbai (20 million people) has a population density of over 20,000 inhabitants per km^2. More than 3,300 people were killed in the monsoons in the summer of 2007; the overall loss is estimated at US$750 million. Delhi, which is also prone to major floods, has seen its population increase from 2 million in 1950 to over 16.7 million in 2011. Its population density is also very high.[3]

Many urban centers in India and other countries have large informal settlements and slums, with a population that is now over 1 billion people. The poor construction standards and land use strategies, overcrowding, and location in often significantly hazard-prone areas (for example, low-lying areas or riverbanks) compounds disaster risk for these populations (Wilton Park Conference Report, 2010).

The trend toward much larger populations in disaster-prone locations does not seem to be reversing. Quite the opposite: in the next ten to fifteen years there will be an additional billion people on planet Earth, after 1 billion had already been added in the previous decade. Most of those people will live in developing countries, a large portion in urban zones located in hazard-prone areas. So we can expect disasters to become more devastating in the coming ten years, unless we become more proactive in creating resilient communities.

Disasters in low-income countries: a vicious cycle creates poverty traps

As discussed above, disasters are known to have enduring negative effects on less-developed countries because of the magnitude of the damage relative to their GDP (Gurenko, 2004; Linnerooth-Bayer *et al.*, 2005; UNISDR/World Bank, 2011). The macroeconomic status of developing countries has also been shown to be an important factor in how they respond to disasters (Hallegatte and Ghil, 2008; Hallegatte and Dumas, 2009). One other major challenge in developing countries is that disasters not only destroy physical infrastructure on a large scale, but also affect a disproportionally high number of individuals, compared to OECD countries. Finally, many residents in developing countries do not undertake appropriate risk-reduction measures nor do they purchase adequate insurance to protect themselves against the economic consequences of future catastrophes.

When one combines all these elements that characterize the situation in a number of low-income countries, a vicious cycle emerges. When disasters occur, the countries may have a difficult time achieving sustainable economic development if those disasters repetitively destroy crops, infrastructure, and services. Any previous development gains can also be wiped out. As a result, the reconstruction process will be slow and during that time financial and human capital will be allocated to rebuilding the country, rather than being used for development. Another disaster is likely to occur before the region has had the time to fully recover from the previous one. And so on – repeated disasters in these countries are poverty traps.

More frequent and relatively localized disasters thus take a toll on the development potential of a country. The frequency of these events can deplete resources and favor the adoption of unsustainable coping mechanisms, which can increase the vulnerability of the environment and livelihoods of the population. If the economy is also relatively lacking in diversification, a disaster can have an increased economic impact (UNDP, 2004). This raises the question as to the appropriate private and public sector strategies to encourage individuals and communities in these countries to undertake measures that improve human well-being and social equity (UNEP, 2010).

A key challenge facing developing countries – as well as many nations in the developed world – is constructing buildings that can withstand the impacts of severe natural disasters such as earthquakes, floods, and tropical cyclones/hurricanes. Many countries do not have building codes in place today. In hazard-prone areas where codes exist, the empirical evidence suggests that they are often not enforced. When the next disaster hits these areas, the property damage can be severe and will likely result in many fatalities due to individuals trapped inside these buildings.

To address this problem we will undertake a cost–benefit analysis (CBA) of allocating $75 billion to retrofit schools in seismically active

[3] In the United States, New York City has the highest population density of all American cities with 10,500; Los Angeles is three times less densely populated. As a reference point, the population density of the city of New Orleans is only 1,000 inhabitants per km^2.

developing countries to withstand damage from severe earthquakes and to residential structures in areas that are subject to severe flooding and tropical cyclones. The Alternative Pespective papers on natural hazards will suggest complementary strategies for reducing the economic and human impacts of disasters: early-warning systems (EWS) (Chapter 8.1 by Stéphane Hallegatte) and macroeconomic policies (Chapter 8.2 by Ilan Noy).

Four proposals for reducing disaster losses

We introduce four proposals for significantly reducing damage and human deaths from earthquakes, floods, and cyclones/hurricanes/storms, and calculate the benefit generated by spending $75 billion on these proposals. We vary the discount rate (d) (3 percent and 5 percent) and value of life (VoL) ($40,000/ $200,000/$1.5 million/$6 million) to show how the benefit–cost ratios (BCRs) change and their impact on expected benefits for a given cost.

- **Proposal I retrofits schools in seismically active countries in the developing world so they are earthquake-resistant.** It would cost approximately $300 billion to retrofit all the schools in the thirty-five most exposed countries we studied, saving the lives of 250,000 individuals over the next fifty years. With a VoL of $40,000, only several countries exhibit a BCR greater than 1. As the VoL increases, the BCR exceeds 1 for an increasing number of countries. More specifically, using a discount rate of 3 percent and a VoL = $1.5 million, thirteen countries have a BCR higher than 1. An expenditure of $75 billion on retrofitting schools in the twelve countries with the highest BCRs, would save more than 135,000 lives over the next fifty years.
- **Proposal II examines two measures for reducing losses from severe flooding: (a) constructing a 1 m high wall to protect homes in communities subject to flooding; (b) elevating each of these houses by 1 m.** We find that it would cost nearly $940 billion to undertake the community-based disaster risk-reduction (DRR) measure of building walls around the affected communities, and $5.2 trillion to elevate all houses exposed to floods in the thirty-four most exposed countries. Undertaking either of these measures will save 61,000 lives over the next fifty years. Investing $75 billion to construct 1 m high walls surrounding communities would provide estimated benefits of $4.5 trillion with an average BCR = 60. Elevating homes would yield estimated benefits of $1.1 trillion and an average BCR = 14.5 for {d = 0.03 VoL = $40,000}.
- **Proposal III improves roof protection of homes to reduce losses in areas subject to cyclones, hurricanes, and storms.** We estimate that it would cost $951 billion to undertake this loss-reduction measure in the thirty-four countries most exposed to severe wind damage; all of them exhibit a BCR > 1. Doing so could save 65,700 lives over the next fifty years. If investment were limited to $75 billion in countries with the highest BCR, then the expected benefit will be $168 billion for {d = 0.03 VoL = $40,000}.
- **Proposal IV introduces early-warning systems in advance of the onset of floods, tropical cyclones, and storm-related disasters to improve emergency actions and save lives.** We discuss several CBAs that have been published in the literature that exhibit significant BCRs.

Framework for analysis

This section develops a framework for evaluating the costs and benefits of alternative programs and policies for reducing future damages and fatalities from natural disasters, and facilitating the recovery process. Engineering and the natural sciences provide data on the nature of the risks associated with disasters of different magnitudes and the uncertainties surrounding them (risk assessment). Geography, organizational theory, psychology, sociology, and other social sciences provide insights into how individuals, groups, organizations, and nations perceive risks and make decisions (risk perception and choice). Economics and policy analysis examine various strategies for reducing future losses as well as dealing with recovery (risk management).

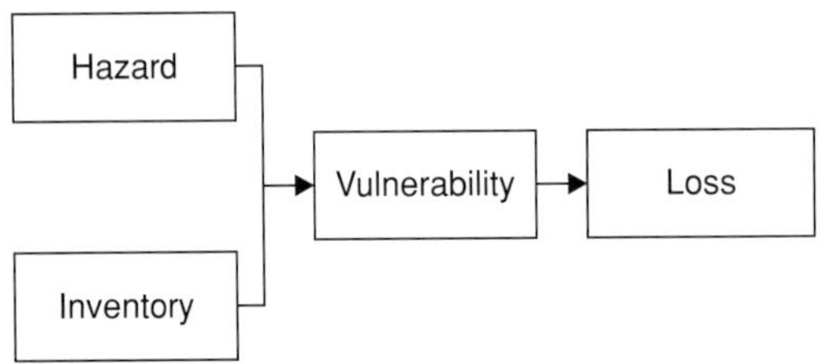

Figure 8.2 *Elements of the risk assessment process model*

Risk assessment

The science of estimating the chances of specific extreme events occurring and their potential consequences originates in the field of property insurance and the science of natural hazards. In the 1800s, residential insurers managed their risk by "mapping" the structures that they covered, pinning tacks onto a wall map to display the degree of physical concentration of exposure. Now, Geographic Information Systems (GIS) software and other digital products address this issue with far more extensive data and sophisticated technologies (Kozlowski and Mathewson, 1995).

Four basic elements for assessing risk – hazard, inventory, vulnerability, and loss – are depicted in Figure 8.2. The first element focuses on the risk of a *hazard*. For example, an earthquake hazard is characterized by its likely epicenter location and magnitude, along with other significant parameters. A hurricane is distinguished by its projected path and wind speed. The hazard can also be usefully characterized as a range of potential scenarios. For example, what is the likelihood that a hurricane of category 3, 4, or 5 on the Saffir–Simpson scale could cause damage if it struck the Miami, Florida area in 2014?

The risk assessment process model's second element identifies the *inventory* of properties, humans, and the physical environment at risk. To inventory structures, for instance, would require evaluation of their location, physical dimensions, and construction quality. Taken together, the hazard and inventory elements enable a calculation of the model's third element, the *vulnerability* of the structures or people at risk. And from the measure of vulnerability, the human and property *loss*, the fourth element, can be evaluated.

In working with catastrophes in this model, it is also useful to distinguish between *direct* and *indirect* losses. Direct losses include injuries, fatalities, financial losses, and the cost to repair or replace a structure, and restore a service. Indirect losses include future forgone income, slower growth, and other longer-term consequences of evacuation costs, disrupted schooling, and company bankruptcies.

Risk perception and choice

While risk assessment focuses on objective losses such as financial costs, *risk perception* is concerned with the psychological and emotional factors associated with risk. Research has demonstrated that the perception of risk has an enormous impact on behavior, regardless of the objective conditions.

In a set of path-breaking studies begun in the 1970s, decision scientists and psychologists such as University of Oregon's Paul Slovic, Carnegie Mellon University's Baruch Fischhoff, and others began studying people's concerns about various types of risks. They found that people viewed hazards with which they had little personal knowledge and experience as highly risky and especially dreaded their possible occurrence. In the case of unfamiliar technologies with catastrophic potential, such as nuclear power, people perceived the risks as much higher than did the experts (Slovic, 2000).

Research also found that people often perceive low-probability, high-consequence events quite differently from experts, and that this impacts on their decision-making process and choice behavior. In recent years, the scientific and engineering communities have devoted attention to the psychological factors that impact on how individuals make decisions with respect to risks from natural and technological hazards.

Researchers have discovered that people are generally not well prepared to interpret low probabilities when reaching decisions about unlikely events. In fact, evidence suggests that people may not even want data on the likelihood of a disastrous event when the information is available to them. If people do not think probabilistically, how then do they make their choices in the face of risk? Extensive research on decision-making now confirms that individuals' risk perceptions are affected by judgmental biases and the use of simplified decision rules (Kahneman *et al.*, 1982; Kahneman, 2011; Kunreuther *et al.*, 2013a). We will discuss below the way decision-makers process information and make choices.

Risk management strategies

In developing effective risk management strategies for reducing losses from natural disasters, leaders of public agencies and private and non-profit organizations will want to appreciate the findings of risk assessment studies and the factors that influence risk perception and choice. A coherent strategy should build on the following four elements.

Mitigation measures

A key challenge is to encourage those at risk from natural hazards to invest in cost-effective loss-reduction measures (called *mitigation* in the disaster literature).[4] Property owners can invest in measures that will reduce losses from future disasters (for example, elevating their residence or business so it is less prone to flood damage; making their property more earthquake-resistant). Mitigation can also be undertaken by the public sector through investments in structural measures such as sea walls, dams and levées that protect communities and regions from damage from disasters such as floods, cyclones or hurricanes.

The core of our analysis will focus on determining the potential benefit of investing in protective actions in low-income and developing countries. But as we will show, there are several factors that discourage decision-makers from investing in these measures. In addition to undertaking CBA, one needs to understand the role of incentive mechanisms and public policies in fostering the adoption of specific loss-reduction measures. In this regard, well-enforced regulations and standards can play a key role in encouraging those at risk to undertake mitigation measures. Well-enforced building codes will encourage property owners and developers to make sure that the structure is well designed against disasters. For these regulations to be effective there is a need for third-party inspections to ensure that the property meets the code, and sufficiently high penalties for those who do not adhere to the standard.

Insurance

Insurance can encourage the adoption of mitigation measures by offering premium reductions to reflect the reduced losses that would result from these investments. Should a disaster occur, insurance can facilitate the recovery process through claim payments to cover some of the resulting damages and losses. For insurance to play this dual role and address distributional issues, we propose the following two guiding principles discussed in more detail in Kunreuther and Michel-Kerjan (2013) and Kunreuther *et al.* (2013):

- *Principle 1: Premiums should reflect risk.* Insurance premiums should be based on risk in order to provide signals to individuals about the hazards they face and to encourage them to engage in cost-effective mitigation measures that reduce their vulnerability to catastrophes. Risk-based premiums should also reflect the cost of capital that insurers must integrate into their pricing in order to ensure adequate return to their investors.
- *Principle 2: Equity and affordability issues should be addressed.* Any special treatment given to home owners currently residing in hazard-prone areas (e.g. low-income uninsured or inadequately insured homeowners) should be funded through general public funding and not through insurance premium subsidies. (In the case of low-income countries, international donors such as European Commission, USAID, and the World Bank could also provide insurance vouchers.) This principle reflects a concern for low-income residents in high-hazard areas who will be faced with large premium increases if insurers adhere to Principle 1. Owners of newly acquired property will be charged premiums reflecting the risk.

[4] Note that in the climate-change literature, "mitigation" refers to reducing green house gas (GHG) emissions and "adaptation" to what can be done to avoid or limit the consequences of a changing climate (see Chapter 4 in this volume).

Early Warning Systems (EWS)

As we discuss in more detail later in the chapter, investment in EWS can be extremely important in reducing human harm and damage from disasters. Advance knowledge of an oncoming hurricane, tsunami, or tornado enables residents to leave the threatened area. The large number of lives taken by the 2004 tsunami because of the inadequate warning system was a wake-up call for the international community in that regard. The potential savings in loss of life and serious injury from a well-publicized and timely warning can be significant. An advance warning can also enable home owners and businesses to take steps to reduce damage to their property and contents. For example, valuable contents could be moved to higher floors to avoid destruction from flooding or storm surge from hurricanes. Residents could sandbag levees to reduce the likelihood that these protective structures would be breached.

Pre-disaster assistance

One also needs to consider the costs and benefits of programs to aid those who cannot afford to undertake mitigation measures or purchase insurance at premiums reflecting risk. This type of assistance can be in the form of low-interest loans for investing in loss-reduction measures or grants such as vouchers to purchase disaster insurance. If these programs are effective then the damage and losses from natural disasters will be considerably reduced over time so that less post-disaster assistance will be required.

These elements constitute the prongs of a more comprehensive strategy for disaster risk reduction and recovery. Mitigation programs are unlikely to be successful without a well-designed insurance program. EWS can be combined with mitigation programs and pre-disaster assistance programs.

A methodological approach to evaluate the economic costs and benefits of disaster risk-reduction measures

Anecdotal evidence and retrospective analyses show large benefits of disaster risk reduction in many developed and developing country contexts. Examining investments in 4,000 mitigation programs, including retrofitting buildings against seismic risk and structural flood defense measures, the US Federal Emergency Management Agency (FEMA) found an average BCR = 4 (MMC, 2005). In developing countries, a review of twenty-one studies on investments as diverse as planting mango forests to protect against tsunamis, and relocating schools out of high-hazard areas demonstrated, with few exceptions, equally high BCRs (Mechler, 2005).

Despite high returns, relatively few people engage in disaster prevention measures. In the United States, several studies show that only about 10 percent of households in earthquake- and flood-prone areas have adopted loss-reduction measures (hereafter referred to as mitigation measures). Kunreuther *et al.* (2013a) attribute this lack of interest to myopia: the upfront costs of the investment in mitigation loom large relative to its perceived benefits over time.

In the absence of concrete information on net economic and social benefits, and faced with limited budgetary resources, many policy-makers are reluctant to commit significant funds for risk reduction. However, when a disaster occurs they then are pressured into providing funds to assist victims and aid the recovery process (Benson and Twigg, 2004; Michel-Kerjan and Volkman Wise, 2011). This may be especially true for development and donor organizations. According to some estimates, bilateral and multilateral donors currently allocate 98 percent of their disaster-management funds to relief and reconstruction, and only 2 percent to proactive disaster risk management (Mechler, 2005). Individuals, governments, and the donor community have begun to encourage pre-disaster, proactive disaster investment and planning to redress this imbalance and reduce the overall costs of disaster management (Kreimer and Arnold, 2000; Gurenko, 2004; Linnerooth-Bayer *et al.*, 2005; UNISDR/World Bank, 2011).

More complete knowledge about the cost and benefits of disaster risk-reduction measures to be implemented *before* a disaster hits is thus critical. In this section we will focus on three types of natural hazards – earthquakes, hurricanes, and floods – and use a CBA methodology to evaluate several physical risk-reduction measures to decrease the consequences of untoward events. There is a substantial literature on the use of CBAs to evaluate risk-reduction investments, but surprisingly few applications in developing countries (Penning-Rowsell *et al.*, 1996; Benson and Twigg, 2004; Smyth *et al.*, 2004; Benson *et al.*, 2007; Dixit *et al.*, 2009; Mechler, 2009; Moench *et al.*, 2009).

Building on ongoing research programs by the Wharton Risk Management Center, Risk Management Solutions (RMS), and IIASA, we examine the benefits and costs of improving or retrofitting residential structures in highly exposed developing countries so that they are less vulnerable to hazards during their lifetime.[5]

In order to provide a diversified portfolio, we selected locations in three different parts of the world: the Caribbean Islands, Indonesia, and Turkey. We also selected three different types of natural disasters: hurricanes, floods, and earthquakes. The structures and risks chosen for this study are typical for many low- and middle-income persons residing throughout these parts of the world.

The methodology developed here could be applied to any location and any type of hazard, provided that good-quality data are available. After undertaking these three individual cases and selecting the most cost-effective measures, we will scale up the investment in those disaster risk-reduction measures across different countries, focusing on where the BCR is the most attractive.

Methodology

The basic measure for assessing the catastrophe exposure of a house, city, or any portfolio of assets is called the *exceedance probability (EP) curve*. An EP curve is basically the mathematical tool used to summarize, for a given location/infrastructure/hazard, all the possible events that can occur and the probability associated with them. More precisely, the EP curve indicates the probability p that *at least* \$$X$ (or lives) is lost in a given year for a given location and type of risk. A typical EP curve can be constructed as depicted in Figure 8.3, where the likelihood that losses will exceed L_i is given by p_i, that is, the x-axis shows the magnitude of the loss in US\$, and the y-axis depicts the annual probability that losses will exceed this

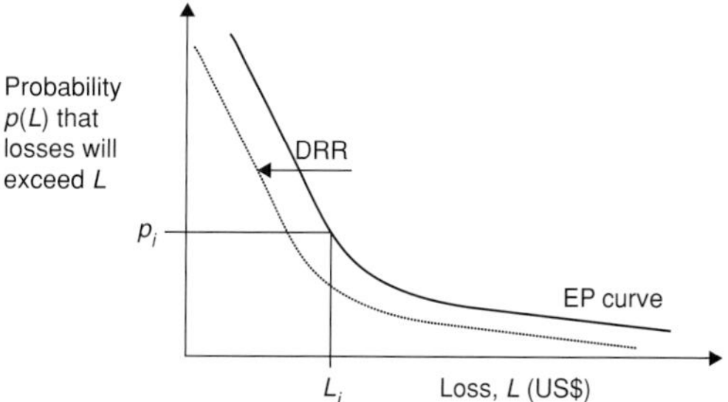

Figure 8.3 *Example of an EP curve and DRR effect*

level. (See for example, Grossi and Kunreuther, 2005 for details on constructing EP curves in the context of catastrophe models.)

One of the advantages of using such a tool is that the area under the EP curve is the average annual loss (AAL). As the term implies, the AAL means that over a long period of time this location should expect to lose this amount, on average, every year. Of course, in some years no disasters occur, while in other years there can be massive losses, hence the concept of averaging the expected yearly losses over a long period of time.[6]

Structural DRR measures typically decrease the vulnerability of the building and therefore reduce the expected loss. Implementing effective DRRs in buildings and infrastructure in the area under study would shift the EP curve to the left in Figure 8.3 and reduce the AAL value. Note that the tail of the curve (the right part of it) would also be diminished, thus reducing the likelihood of suffering catastrophic losses.

For each of our three case studies we select measures for reducing losses from each type of disaster. We then construct EP curves for a representative house or houses with and without the DRR measure in place. Benefits are quantified through reductions in the AAL after measures have been applied to a structure and discounted over the relevant time horizon (e.g. five, ten, twenty years). Cost estimates of each DRR measure are derived from various sources. Combining these

[5] The analysis and results in this section are based on Michel-Kerjan *et al.* (2012).

[6] Assuming everything else being equal; the addition of new construction and population in that location would require one to calculate the curve again.

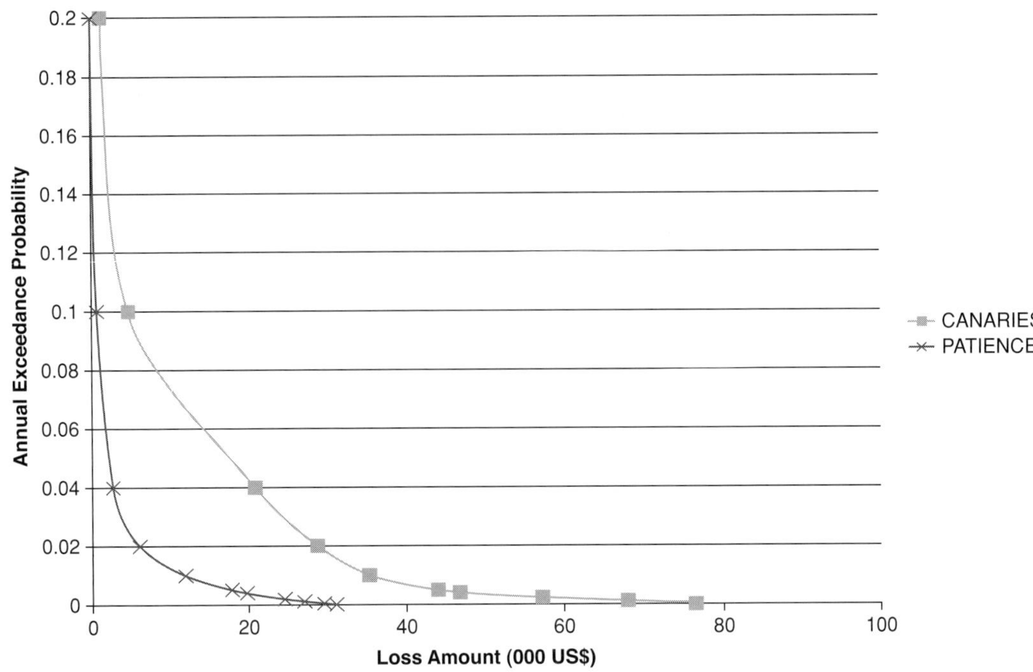

Figure 8.4 *Hurricane risk in St. Lucia: EP curves with no DRR*

estimates, we compute a BCR.[7] The most attractive DRR measure from an economic standpoint is the one with the highest BCR, assuming that there are no budget constraints with respect to the cost of the investment. (Typically, for a specific DRR project in a given location, the analysis will be extended to integrate budget constraints and willingness to pay (WTP).)

From each case study we will select the disaster-reduction measure that offers the highest BCR and use it when we scale up our analysis to other countries.

Case study I: Hurricane risk in St. Lucia (Caribbean island state)

St. Lucia is a small Caribbean island highly prone to hurricane risks. The frequency and magnitude of hurricanes are above what is usual in the region. While a large portion of the population is classified as below the poverty level, there is a growing middle class. The coastline of St. Lucia generally has a sharp topography and although there are locations that can experience significant flooding, experts agree that a storm does not create a significant loss potential. Hence, this analysis focuses only on wind damage to housing structures.

Over 70 percent of residential buildings are constructed using concrete blocks (i.e. masonry structures) or have wooden outer walls such as plywood and wood/timber walls (Kairi, Consultants Ltd 2007). It is assumed that the replacement value of the houses is $100,000. These representative houses are located in the higher- and lower-risk cities of Canaries and Patience, respectively.

For our analysis (see Proposals, pp. 462–464) we will focus on masonry homes. In the absence of DRR measures, the EP curves for a representative residential structure in the two cities are shown in Figure 8.4.

Three DRR measures were examined for reducing hurricane risk to the representative masonry homes in Canary and Patience. The DRR costs for the homes have been developed based on a survey

[7] Using the BCR as the metric captures the concept of the complex interactions of three main components that affect the final decision: vulnerability of the building, the hazard level of the area, and the cost of the measure discussed.

Table 8.2 Hurricane risk in St. Lucia: summary of selected benefit–cost ratios (BCRs)
(BCRs greater than 1 in **bold**)

		Masonry			
		Canaries (Max hazard)		Patience (Min hazard)	
		Discount rate (%)		Discount rate (%)	
DRR measure	Time horizon (years)	5	12	5	12
Roof upgrade	10	0.75	0.55	0.16	0.11
	25	**1.37**	0.76	0.29	0.16
Opening protection	10	0.62	0.46	0.09	0.07
	25	**1.14**	0.63	0.17	0.09
Combined roof upgrade and opening protection	10	0.59	0.44	0.11	0.08
	25	**1.09**	0.60	0.20	0.11

by Risk Management Solutions (RMS) survey of DRR costs and from roofing costs reports (Louis, 2004):

- **Measure 1:** ***Roof upgrade***. This includes the replacement of the roof material with thicker sheeting and tighter screw spacing as well as the use of roof anchors. The total cost of this measure is estimated to be $9,200.
- **Measure 2:** ***Opening protection***. This includes strengthening the resistance of windows and doors against wind and heavy pressure. The total costs are estimated to be $6,720.
- **Measure 3:** ***Roof upgrade and opening protection***. Measures 1 and 2 can be combined to provide a more comprehensive level of protection for the structure. The cost for both is estimated at $15,920.

Table 8.2 shows the results of the BCR calculations for the three measures. Not surprisingly, the results are highly sensitive to the choice of the discount rate, the assumed length of life of the residential structure, and the hazard level. The results in Table 8.2 are based on discount rates of 5 percent and 12 percent[8] and an expected life of the structure of ten and twenty-five years.

The highest BCR occurs in the maximum-hazard location (Canaries) for the roof upgrade measure as highlighted by the shaded area. *We will thus use this roof upgrade measure (replacement of the roof material with thicker sheeting and tighter screw spacing as well as the use of roof anchors) in our global analysis.*

Case study II: Flood risk in Jakarta (Indonesia)

Jakarta is the capital of Indonesia with about 8.5 million inhabitants. Severe flooding is frequent and closely linked to extreme rainfall events. This case study focuses on the region around the Ciliwung River in central East Jakarta, a densely populated and economically important part of the city where flooding occurs most frequently. Jakarta has a wide variety of buildings, from very modern skyscrapers to informal settlements erected on wooden stilts.

We focus our study of individual homes on residential properties in East Jakarta, which make up about 60 percent of the city's structures. Images from Google Earth suggest that most buildings outside of the commercial center are two- or three-story masonry residential homes (typically occupied by persons of high and medium wealth).

We selected two representative housing types: a high-value home constructed with brick walls, concrete floor, and clay roof (referred to as *masonry*) and a middle-income home constructed with mixed wall, concrete floor, and asbestos roof (referred to as *mixed wall*). The replacement value of each of the representative houses is assumed to be $19,200 (based on estimates from Silver, 2007).

Given very limited flood-hazard data for Jakarta, we base our EP estimation on approximate flood-extent maps and limited depth estimates for the two past floods in January/February 2002 and February

[8] These are typical low and high annual discount rates used for evaluating development projects. For more details see Mechler (2004).

Table 8.3 Flood risk in Jakarta: summary of selected benefit–cost ratios (BCRs)
(BCRs greater than 1 in **bold**)

		Masonry				Mixed wall			
		Min hazard		Max hazard		Min hazard		Max hazard	
		Discount rate (%)		Discount rate (%)		Discount rate (%)		Discount rate (%)	
DRR measure	Time horizon (years)	5	12	5	12	5	12	5	12
Improve flood resilience	10	0.49	0.36	0.63	0.46	0.10	0.07	0.11	0.08
	25	0.90	0.50	**1.16**	0.64	0.18	0.10	0.21	0.11
1 m elevation	10	0.83	0.61	**1.18**	0.86	**2.06**	**1.51**	**3.69**	**2.70**
	25	**1.51**	0.84	**2.15**	**1.20**	**3.77**	**2.10**	**6.73**	**3.75**

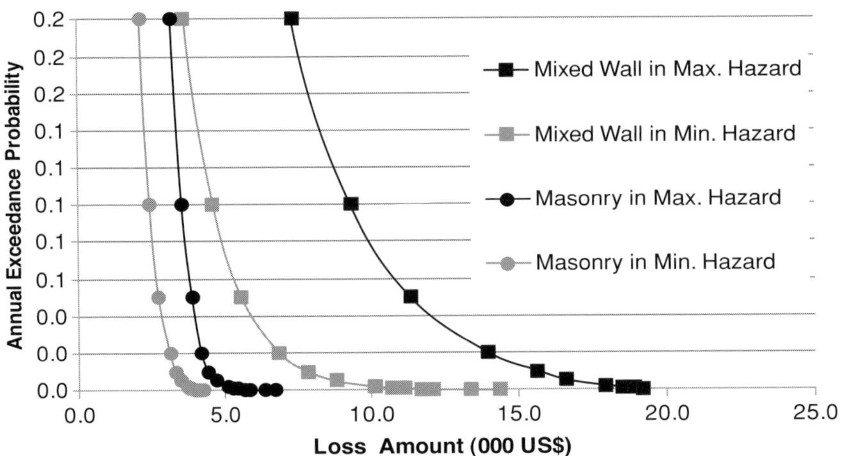

Figure 8.5 *Flood risk in Jakarta: EP curves for two baseline structures in two different hazard locations with no DRR*

2007 (Dartmouth Flood Observatory, 2008). Our hazard analysis also uses a thirty-year monthly rainfall time series, observed at the Jakarta Observatory (NOAA global database) within the catchment of the Ciliwung River and an elevation map based on data from the NASA Shuttle Radar Topography Mission. Based on these inputs, two probabilistic flood depth curves are generated, representing a higher ("max hazard") and lower ("min hazard") hazard location. Using two EP curves we can test the sensitivity of findings to the hazard approximation. Figure 8.5 depicts these EP curves for masonry and mixed-wall structures.

Two individual DRR measures are selected for reducing flood risks to the masonry and mixed-wall dwellings. The cost estimates are based on data from FEMA, adapted to account for labor cost differences in the United States (Teicholz, 1998; Davis, 2002):

- *Measure 1*: Improve flood resilience and resistance of the property. Approximate cost is $3,100 for the typical home.
- *Measure 2*: Elevate the property by 1 m. Costs are estimated to be $9,345.

Cost–benefit calculations

Using data on AAL and estimates of AAL reductions resulting from the application of each aforementioned measure, Table 8.3 shows the results of

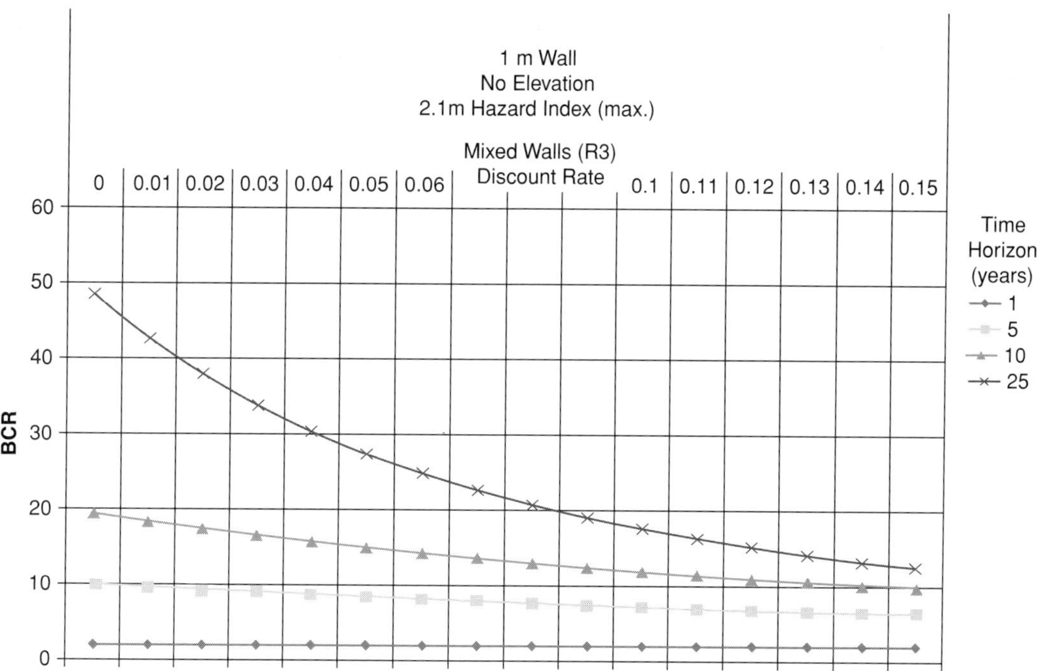

Figure 8.6 *BCR for collective flood-mitigation measure (1 m wall) for different discount rates and time horizons*

the cost-benefit calculations for the two options. As in the case of St. Lucia, the results are highly sensitive to the choice of discount rate, assumed length of life of the residential structure and the hazard level. We show the results for discount rates of 5 and 12 percent and for an expected lifetime of the structures of ten and twenty-five years.

The BCRs are substantially higher for *mixed-wall structures* than for masonry structures. Elevating these homes by 1 m is a cost-effective way of reducing future flood damage (BCR > 1); improving flood resilience is not (BCR < 1). *Our global analysis will thus focus on elevating mixed-wall houses by 1 m to reduce damage from flooding in countries subject to this disaster (individual flood protection).*

We also consider building a wall around a community, typically the work of government that undertakes large-scale protection projects. According to US data from New Orleans, such a project is estimated to cost around $2 billion. The number of permanent residences in Jakarta is about 1,152,000 (Silver, 2007); so the cost of this mitigation measure per household is approximated at $1,736.

We find that the construction of a 1 m wall to protect the 1.2 million permanent residences in Jakarta would result in higher BCRs (48.6) relative to elevating property by 1 m, as shown in Figure 8.6 for different discounts and time horizons. We calculate that the benefit for the representative house over twenty-five years would be $84,338 (Wharton–IIASA–RMS, 2009). *We will also use this community-based flood protection measure in our analysis on pp. 460–462 (see Proposal).*

Case study III: Earthquake risk in Istanbul (Turkey)

Istanbul, which has a population of around 11 million people and accounts for about 40 percent of Turkey's GDP, is at high risk of earthquake. (For a comprehensive background on Istanbul's seismic risk, see Smyth *et al.*, 2004.) The *World Housing Encyclopedia* report on Turkey (Gulkan *et al.*, 2002) indicates that approximately 80 percent of

Turkey's urban households live in mid-rise apartment blocks constructed of reinforced concrete with masonry infill. The representative structure selected in this study is a five-story reinforced concrete building with unreinforced masonry infills (similar to the structure analyzed by Smyth *et al.*, 2004), with a replacement value assumed to be $250,000.

The CBA in Istanbul highlights two points that play an important role in our analysis of retrofitting schools against earthquake damage in several countries, described in Proposal I on pp. 455–460:

(1) If one considers only the physical damage to the building, then the BCRs will be considerably less than 1 and the measure will be deemed economically unattractive
(2) When one adds the reduction in fatalities from retrofitting the structure, then this measure is likely to yield BCRs greater than 1 for the VoLs that are considered to be reasonable for Turkey.

We reach similar conclusions in our analysis of retrofitting schools in countries subject to seismic risk. A key issue that we discuss in our analysis is the appropriate VoL to utilize in evaluating alternative measures.

A typical building in Istanbul has ten units per building and five people per unit. In the aftermath of the 1999 Kocaeli earthquake in Turkey, most buildings of this type collapsed because the columns lacked adequate transverse steel reinforcement to resist lateral loads. Many buildings were also designed with an open ground floor to accommodate other uses, such as parking; the soft-story conditions exacerbated the failures (RMS, 2001). Another phenomenon that contributed to the breaking of the columns and possible collapse of the buildings is a gap between the columns and the infill wall, which reduces the effective height of the column (known as *short column, SC*) (Guevara and García, 2005). Two case study sites, Camlibahce and Atakoy, were selected representing high- and low-hazard locations, respectively.

As shown in Table 8.4, we assume that the initial non-mitigated building can be of three types,

Table 8.4 Type of structures for case study: unmitigated attributes

Type	Have soft story (SS)?	Have short column (SC)?	Need structural upgrade?
Type 1	Yes	No	Yes
Type 2	No	Yes	Yes
Type 3	Yes	Yes	Yes

depending on whether it is characterized by soft story, short columns or both. *Soft story* (SS) means that the ground-floor space – a window, garage door – is situated where a wall might otherwise be. *SC* refers to reinforced concrete buildings where the partial-height infill walls are used to provide natural lighting and ventilation. (If the infill walls in the frame of a structure are shorter than the column height and are connected to the column, there is not enough gap between the columns and the infill wall, so that the effective height of the column is reduced.) Type 1 and Type 3 buildings are about 4 percent and 14 percent more vulnerable than Type 2, respectively.

Figure 8.7 illustrates the EP curves for the different building types that are located in Camlibahce (min hazard) as well as Atakoy (max hazard).

Three DRR measures for reducing seismic risk to a representative five-story reinforced concrete building are thus analyzed:

- *Measure 1*: Retrofit short column (SC), and/or soft story (SS) but no shear walls added.
- *Measure 2*: Partial shear walls (PSW) added. Short columns mitigated if applicable.
- *Measure 3*: Full shear walls (FSW) added. Short columns (SC) mitigated if applicable.

Table 8.5 shows the combined cost of different applicable DRR measures for each building type based on Erdik (2003), Burnett (2004), and Smyth *et al.* (2004).

Table 8.6 summarizes the BCRs for the DRR measures shown in Table 8.5 with selected discount rates (5 percent and 12 percent) and time horizons (ten years and twenty-five years).

All the measures considered have a BCR < 1 regardless of the hazard level. They range from

Table 8.5 Costs of alternative DRR measures for each baseline type

DRR option	Costs ($) for Type 1	Costs ($) for Type 2	Costs ($) for Type 3
1 Mitigating SC/Mitigating SS	25,000	40,000	65,000
2 Mitigating SC/Adding PSW	80,000	120,000	120,000
3 Mitigating SC/Adding FSW	135,000	175,000	175,000

Notes: SS = Soft story; SC = Short column; PSW = Partial shear wall; FSW = Full shear wall.

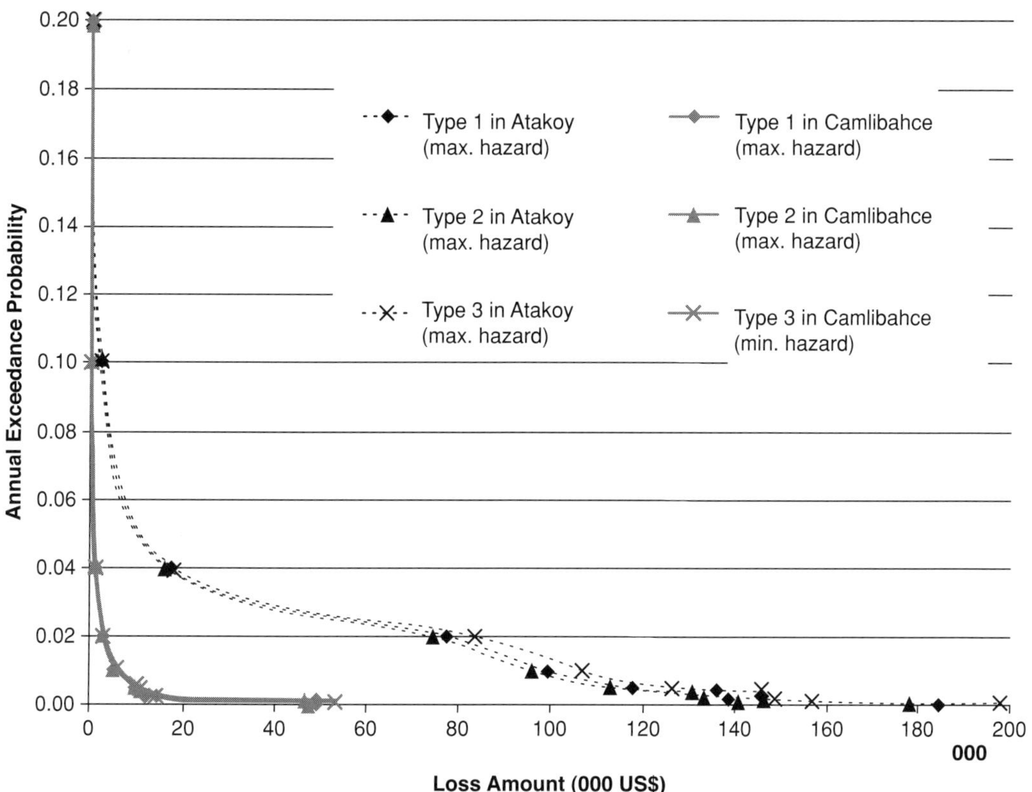

Figure 8.7 *Earthquake risk in Istanbul: EP curves with no DRR*

0 to 0.22, indicating that, from a financial standpoint alone, these measures are not recommended. However, the picture changes when one takes into account the value of reducing risk to human life as shown in the next subsection

Our previous analyses focused only on the direct economic benefits generated by making a construction more disaster-resilient. In reality, there are of course many other benefits beyond the reduction in AAL associated with damage reduction to a given building. The most important additional benefit is the lives that can be saved by making buildings more resistant to catastrophes.

CBAs of projects/investments that save at-risk lives generally make use of a VoL to estimate the benefits and costs – that is, they attempt to associate a monetary value to each life so it is possible to undertake economic comparison (Viscusi, 1993). If a DRR project reduces the probability that an individual dies, conditional on the disaster event

Table 8.6 Earthquake risk in Istanbul: summary of selected BCRs

DRR measure	Time horizon (years)	Type 1				Type 2				Type 3			
		Camlibahce Min hazard		Atakoy Max hazard		Camlibahce Min hazard		Atakoy Max hazard		Camlibahce Min hazard		Atakoy Max hazard	
		Discount rate (%)		Discount rate (%)		Discount rate (%)		Discount rate (%)		Discount rate (%)		Discount rate (%)	
		5	12	5	12	5	12	5	12	5	12	5	12
Mitigating SC/Mitigating SS	10	0.12	0.09	0.01	0.01	0.05	0.04	0.00	0.00	0.08	0.06	0.01	0.00
	25	0.22	0.12	0.02	0.01	0.09	0.05	0.01	0.00	0.14	0.08	0.01	0.01
Mitigating SC/Adding PSW	10	0.12	0.09	0.01	0.01	0.05	0.04	0.00	0.00	0.07	0.05	0.00	0.00
	25	0.22	0.12	0.01	0.01	0.09	0.05	0.01	0.00	0.12	0.07	0.01	0.00
Mitigating SC/Adding FSW	10	0.06	0.05	0.00	0.00	0.03	0.02	0.00	0.00	0.06	0.04	0.00	0.00
	25	0.11	0.06	0.01	0.00	0.06	0.03	0.00	0.00	0.11	0.06	0.01	0.00

Notes: SS = Soft story; SC = Short column; PSW = Partial shear wall; FSW = Full shear wall.

occurring, the project will save a number of *statistical lives* equal to the sum of reductions in the risk of death over the exposed population. We are aware that applying a VoL to a CBA, however, can be controversial since it is ethically difficult to put a price tag on a life.[9] For this reason we do not make use of a point value, but undertake sensitivity analyses using a range of statistical life value estimates.

As an upper bound of the VoL, we take the highest estimate in the United States, $6 million, a figure that is commonly used by the US Environmental Protection Agency (Cropper and Sahin, 2008). As a lower range, we make use of a method suggested by Cropper and Sahin (2008), which scales the VoL (in this case, for Turkey) according to the country's *per capita* income relative to the United States. This method yields a VoL approximately equal to $750,000 in Turkey. We use these figures as the upper and lower range of the VoL for the Istanbul case. We extend the range of VoLs in our global analysis to include $40,000 and $200,000 as suggested by the 2012 Copenhagen Consensus.

In Table 8.7 we show how the BCRs change if we include the value of reducing mortality risk in the Istanbul analysis. We take as an example the case of seismic retrofit using steel metal frames for a Type 1 constructed house in a low-risk area. The BCRs when VoL is not incorporated in the analysis, range from 0.09 to 0.22, depending on the discount rate and time horizon of the building. When lives saved are included in the analysis, the DRR measure becomes attractive assuming a discount rate of 5 percent and a time horizon of twenty-five years, and a VoL of 750,000 or greater.

Table 8.7 Earthquake risk in Istanbul: BCRs taking into account the VoL for baseline Type 1 and measure 1 (BCRs greater than 1 in **bold**)

Analysis	Time horizon (Years)	Camlibahce Min hazard	
		Discount rate (%)	
		5	12
VoL *not* included	10	0.12	0.09
	25	0.22	0.12
VoL = $750,000	10	0.7	0.5
	25	**1.3**	0.7
VoL = $6 million	10	**4.5**	**3.5**
	25	**8.1**	**4.9**

These findings confirm the result by Smyth *et al.* (2004) that only by including the value of lives

[9] At the core of the debate on attributing a monetary value to life is whether a life saved in a rich country should be valued differently than a life saved in a poor country; if so, why and how significant should the difference be? Likewise, should the life of a teenager be valued differently than the life of an elderly person, and why, etc.?

saved do earthquake-strengthening measures for apartment buildings and schools in Turkey pass the benefit-cost test. Our results also show that an international development organization or a donor that made its decision not to provide support for the studied disaster risk reduction program based solely on the CBA for construction would probably be misled – the program would have potentially saved many lives and reduced the economic loss in the city after a massive earthquake, which taken together would have by far offset the cost of the DRR.

Four proposals to reduce economic and human losses from disasters globally

This section generalizes the CBA undertaken in the previous section for a single building to a large number of buildings in countries around the world, following the guidelines provided by the 2012 Copenhagen Consensus.

That is, we will do analyses with an annual discount rate (d) of 3 and 5 percent and value of life (VoL) of \$40,000 and \$200,000 (equivalent to a disability adjusted life year (DALY) of \$1,000 and \$5,000 respectively). In addition we estimate the expected benefits of saving lives by including VoL = \$1.5 million and VoL = \$6 million, values typically used in other studies, as detailed in a comprehensive survey by Viscusi and Aldy (2003).[10]

We focus on three hazards – earthquakes, floods, and cyclones/hurricanes/storms – and for each hazard on thirty to thirty-four countries that are the most exposed to each type of disaster. Our four proposals are as follows:

- Analysis of the cost-effectiveness of retrofitting schools to make them earthquake-proof to reduce the damage and the number of fatalities to children, teachers, and other staff who are in the school at the time of the *earthquake* (*Proposal I*).
- Analysis of the cost-effectiveness of investing in a structural measure (community wall) and elevating residential structures in areas subject to *floods* (*Proposal II*).
- Analysis of the cost-effectiveness of strengthening the resistance of windows and doors against wind and heavy pressure from *cyclones, hurricanes, and storms* (*Proposal III*).
- Analysis of the merits of an early warning system (EWS) (*Proposal IV*).

Proposal I: Designing schools to withstand damage from earthquakes

The damage and number of fatalities from schools impacted by earthquake is highlighted by recent seismic disasters. On October 31 and November 1, 2002, two Mw 5.7 earthquakes struck the rural Molise region in southeastern Italy killing thirty people, twenty-seven of whom were children trapped in the collapse of an elementary school (Maffei and Bazzurro, 2004). Had the earthquake been greater, the damage to schools in the area and the number of fatalities is likely to have been much greater. The Mw 6.4 earthquake that hit the Bingol area in eastern Turkey in May 2003 caused four of the twenty-seven schools in the area to collapse or experience heavy damage and nine others to suffer moderate damage; eighty-four fatalities occurred when a dormitory block collapsed in a boarding school in Celtiksuyu (Ellul and D'Ayala, 2003). In China, after the Sichuan earthquake, more than 7,000 classrooms collapsed. In the provinces of Sichuan and Gansu, more than 12,000 and 6,500 schools respectively, were affected (Reliefweb, 2009).

In the Mw 7.0 earthquake in Haiti in 2010, more than 97 percent of the schools in Port-au-Prince were destroyed. Half of the public schools and the three main universities in the country suffered severe damages (Fierro and Perry, 2010). In a country where 35 percent of the population is under fifteen years of age, the death toll of children constituted a large portion of the 250,000 who died directly or indirectly from the earthquake. Moreover, a study by the Children's Hospital of Los Angeles and the University of Southern California estimated that the number of children injured was 110,000, or roughly half the total number of injuries from the Haiti earthquake (Agence France-Presse, 2010).

[10] In their paper, Viscusi and Aldy point out that the VoL for US labor market studies lies within a range of \$4 million to \$9 million. In developing countries, the VoL presented in the Viscusi and Aldy survey varies from \$750,000 in South Korea to \$4.1 million in India (see Table 4: 27–8).

Table 8.8 Effectiveness of retrofitting schools in Latin America

Country	AAL				% AAL reduction	Retrofitting costs (Million US$)
	Current		Retrofitted			
	Million US$	(‰)	Million US$	(‰)		
(1)	(2)	(3)	(4)	(5)	(6)	(7)
Argentina	7	0.2	3	0.1	57	9,623
Bolivia	6	7.0	3	2.9	50	991
Chile	49	6.4	15	1.9	69	2,750
Columbia	31	2.7	20	1.8	35	5,022
Costa Rica	32	16.4	18	9.1	44	742
Ecuador	33	21.2	29	18.7	12	947
El Salvador	12	24.4	6	11.8	50	263
Guatemala	10	15.1	5	8.0	50	501
Honduras	2	4.6	0	1.5	100	349
Mexico	75	0.8	34	0.4	55	32,354
Nicaragua	5	20.8	3	9.8	40	353
Panama	10	6.4	5	3.3	50	445
Peru	296	33.3	160	18.0	46	4,094
Venezuela	22	0.8	13	0.5	41	5,978
Average	**AAL**					

Source: ERN (2010).

Determining the seismic risk to schools

We were not able to perform a CBA on retrofitting schools in every country that faces a seismic risk, so we utilized data from several sources using the following six-step process:

- *Step 1: Expected reduction in damage from retrofitting schools in Latin America.* A detailed study *Seismic Risk Assessment of Schools in the Andean Region in South America and Central America* (hereafter, SRAS), analyzed the benefits and costs of retrofitting schools in fourteen countries in Latin America, against earthquakes. The study was undertaken by a consortium of experts from Columbia, Spain and Mexico (ERN, 2010) and was included in the World Bank/United Nations *Global Assessment Report on Disaster Risk Reduction 2011* (World Bank, 2011). The study compared the average annual property loss to the buildings and contents with and without retrofitting by undertaking a probabilistic seismic-hazard analysis similar to the one undertaken for apartment buildings in Turkey described on pp. 451–455. EP curves with and without retrofitting are constructed using a structural typology representative of the building stock of schools in each of the countries, ranging from adobe to reinforced masonry and concrete structures. The AAL from earthquakes for the entire portfolio of schools in the country was compared with the reduced AAL if these buildings had been retrofitted, as detailed in Table 8.8.

  It is possible to identify three categories of countries based on the ratio of the AAL to the value of the current portfolio of schools in the country (i.e. Column (3) and Column (5) of Table 8.8). The lowest values of the AAL are found in Argentina, Mexico, and Venezuela. In general, these results reflect a lower concentration of buildings in zones of relative high seismic hazard (in the case of Argentina) as well as the composition of the schools' portfolio by structural typologies of relative low vulnerability such as reinforced concrete and reinforced masonry. The highest values of the AAL are estimated for Peru (33.3 per thousand), El Salvador (24.4 per thousand), Ecuador (21.2 per thousand), Nicaragua (20.8 per thousand), Costa Rica (16.4 per thousand), and Guatemala (15.1 per thousand). These results reflect the composition of the school portfolio by structural typologies of relatively high vulnerability such as unreinforced masonry and adobe, located in zones of relatively high seismic hazard. In the case of Chile, the seismic hazard is relatively high while the school portfolio is composed of structural typologies of relatively low vulnerability, such as reinforced concrete and reinforced masonry (ERN, 2010).

With this analysis it is possible to estimate the expected average annual reduction in property damage from retrofitting schools in country *i*, $[E(AARPD_i)]$, where *i* is one of the fourteen countries in the SRAS study. It varies from a low of 12 percent in Ecuador to a high of virtually 100 percent in Honduras (see column 6 of Table 8.8). We calculate that the average AAL reduction obtained by retrofitting schools across the fourteen countries is 50 percent. We will use this number when extrapolating our analysis to other countries.

- *Step 2: Expected costs of retrofitting schools in Latin America.* The SRAS study also provided data on the costs of retrofitting schools to withstand earthquake damage (shown in column (7) of Table 8.8). These dollar values were obtained by using data on the costs of retrofitting schools of different construction in Bogotá, Columbia and Quito, and Ecuador, and estimating the number of square meters (m^2) of the relevant type of schools. These data enabled the SRAS study to estimate the retrofitting costs in US$/$m^2$ for different construction materials. By combining these data with the distribution of building stock in each country using the structural typology are obtained the costs of retrofitting all schools, is estimated in each of the fourteen Latin American countries in the study. Let the expected upfront cost of retrofitting all schools in country *i* be $E(C_i)$.
- *Step 3: Expected number of fatalities due to earthquakes.* To estimate this figure for each

Table 8.9 Average annual number killed per million as a function of seismic risk class

Class	Relative risk (killed per million per year)	Mid-point of relative risk
9	100–300	200
8	30–100	65
7	10–100	55
6	3–10	6.5
5	1–3	2
4	0.3–1	0.65
3	0.1–0.3	0.2
2	0.03–0.1	0.065
1	>0–0.03	0.015

Source: UNISDR (2010).

country in our analysis, we first approximate the number of schools in each country. To do this we use available data on the number of children ages 0 to 14 years. We then determine the population of this cohort in 2010 for each country in the world that has a significant seismic risk.[11] We then specify the degree of seismic risk for each country in our sample using the classification from the *Global Assessment Report on Disaster Risk Reduction* (UNISDR, 2010). In this study, the United Nations classified all countries according to a mortality risk index from the least prone to earthquakes (Class 1) to those facing the most severe earthquakes (Class 9) [See Table 8.9].

We focused our study on thirty-five countries with an index of Class 5 or higher and eliminated Japan and the United States (Class 6) and Taiwan (Class 7) given their high-income status.[12] Note that all the fourteen countries from Latin America discussed above are in that list. The UNISDR study also provides a range for the number of

[11] See http://data.worldbank.org/indicator/SP.POP.0014.TO.ZS for the specific data we used for each country.

[12] The countries most exposed to earthquakes are in alphabetical order: Afghanistan; Albania; Algeria; Argentina; Armenia; Bolivia; Chile; China; Colombia; Costa Rica; DRC; Ecuador; El Salvador; Guatemala; Honduras; India; Indonesia; Iran; Kyrgyzstan; Mexico; Myanmar; Nepal; Nicaragua; Pakistan; Panama; Peru; Philippines; Romania; Solomon Islands; Sudan; Tajikistan; Turkey; Uganda; Uzbekistan, and Venezuela.

lives lost per million, as shown in Table 8.9 under the column "Relative risk" (defined as the number of people killed per million per year) and the mid-point of the range. Multiplying the mid-point of the range for country i's seismic-risk classification by the number of million people in that country, the resulting figure $E(AAF_i)$ is the average annual number of fatalities (AAF_i) due to earthquakes in country i.

- *Step 4: Expected average annual reduction in fatalities (AARF) from retrofitting schools.* To estimate this figure, $E(AARF_i)$ for country i, we assume that children, teachers and staff are in school 8 hours a day (one-third of a day) and that there is one adult in the building per five children. This means that a school of 1,000 children has 1.2 (1,000) = 1,200 individuals in it. The enrollment rate is estimated to be 70 percent of the eligible population of school-age children based on UNICEF data provided in their Country Profiles.[13] We assumed that retrofitting a school will save the lives of 40 percent of those in the building at the time of the earthquake from what would have occurred if the school had not met the building code standards – the same assumption used in examining the reduction in fatalities in Turkey from reinforcing an apartment building[14] (Smyth *et al.*, 2004). Based on these assumptions, $E(AARF_i) = (1.2) * 1/3 * (0.70)(0.40)E(AAF_i)$ where $E(AAF_i)$ is obtained in Step 3 for each country i.
- *Step 5: Expected BCR for fourteen Latin American countries.* In addition to the annual benefits provided by lowering physical exposure, retrofitting the schools can also save lives. In order to generate an overall BCR (physical and human benefits) one needs to attribute *VoL* saved by retrofitting schools. We estimate schools to last for $T = 50$ years and utilize a discount rate of $d = 0.03$ and 0.05 for converting the expected annual benefits of retrofitting in year $t > 1$ to the present. The expected benefits of retrofitting a structure in country i from the SRAS study for specific values of *VoL* and d are given by:

$$E(B_i) = \sum_{t=1}^{T=50} \frac{\{\text{VoL} * \text{E}(AARF_i) + E(AARPD_i)\}}{(1+\text{d})^t} \quad (1)$$

The BCR for retrofitting schools in country i (BCR_i) is given by

$$BCR_i = E(B_i)/E(C_i)$$

where $E(C_i)$ is obtained from Step 2

- *Step 6: Determining the expected benefits and costs of other countries.* To extrapolate from the expected cost of retrofitting schools in the Latin American countries examined in the SRAS report to other parts of the world that have seismic risks, we need to normalize the benefits and costs. More specifically we need to estimate the expected benefits and costs from retrofitting a school. Recognizing this figure can vary across countries, we assumed that the average number of children per school in any country was 2,000.[15] The expected retrofitting cost per school $[E(SC_i)]$ and retrofitting benefit per school $[E(SB_i)]$ for country i, $i = 1 \ldots 14$ are, respectively, given by:

$$E(SC_i) = E(C_i)/2{,}000 \quad (2)$$

$$E(SB_i) = E(B_i)/2{,}000 \quad (3)$$

To extrapolate the costs and benefits of retrofitting schools in the countries in the SRAS study to other parts of the world, we focus on countries that had mortality index risks in the Class 5–9 range based on the UN's *Global Assessment Report on Disaster Risk Reduction*.[16] We also assumed that there is a constant relationship between GDP *per capita* and both the costs and benefits of retrofitting schools in each country. Using the data from the SRAS study from (2) and (3) for each of the fourteen countries, we estimated the relationship using OLS with

13 Data on the eligible population of school-age children can be found at www.childinfo.org (UNICEF data).

14 A higher protection rate would generate a much higher BCR. We do not undertake a sensitivity analysis on that parameter, though, in this chapter.

15 The number of children in a school will obviously vary from one type of school to another and from one country to another; 2,000 is the average number of children per school discussed in the SRAS analysis undertaken in several Latin American countries.

16 The report can be found at www.preventionweb.net/english/hyogo/gar/report/index.php?id=9413

its intercept at the origin (i.e. the constant term suppressed) to obtain the following regression equation:[17]

$$E(SC_i) = \beta_1.GDP_i$$

Ideally, one should want to consider the nature and enforcement of building codes in each country outside of Latin America with a seismic risk. To the best of our knowledge, such detailed data do not exist on an international scale. We thus assume that the expected benefits for each country i $[E(SB_i)]$ in other parts of the world is 50 percent of the AAL reduction across the fourteen Latin American countries (i.e. $Ave\ \Delta AAL_{14LA}$)[18] normalized by the country's GPD (i.e. GDP_i) in relation to the average GDP of the fourteen Latin American countries (i.e. $Ave\ GDP_{14LA}$). The $E(SB_i)$ is given by the following equation:

$$E(SB_i) = 50\% * (Ave\Delta AAL_{14LA}) * GDP_i/AveGDP_{14LA}$$

The above two equations enabled us to estimate the costs and benefits of retrofitting the schools in twenty-one other countries that have a relatively high seismic risk. We then followed the analysis outlined in Steps 1–5 to determine BCRs for each country given different VoLs and annual discount rates.

Findings for Proposal I

Countries are ranked in descending order based on the BCR determined by the above analysis for different discount rates (d) and value of life (VoL). For each (d, VoL) pair we then calculate the cumulative retrofitting cost and expected benefit (i.e. reduction in physical damage and cumulative number of lives saved across countries multiplied by VoL and properly discounted over time). Our analysis reveals these findings:

- *It would cost about \$300 billion to retrofit all the schools in the thirty-five most exposed countries.* Several highly populated countries would require a large investment to retrofit all schools, for instance, \$32 billion in Mexico, \$65 billion in India, and more than \$100 billion in China.
- *Retrofitting the schools in all thirty-five countries studied here would save the lives of 250,000 individuals over the next fifty years.*

Several of our country-specific findings are highly dependent on the above assumptions made. As the VoL increases, the BCR exceeds 1 for an increasing number of countries. As shown in Table 8.10 for $\{d = 0.03\ VoL = \$1.5 \text{ million}\}$, the BCR > 1 for thirteen countries and the \$75 billion is exhausted with Ecuador, most of the funding going to retrofit schools in India (which has nearly 1.2 billion people).

From Table 8.10 we find that it would cost only \$36 million to retrofit schools in the Solomon Islands. This expenditure would generate a benefit that is more than six times the estimated cost. The costs of retrofitting schools in Afghanistan and Myanmar would be \$698 million and \$1,570 million, and generate high BCRs of 5.11 and 4.65, respectively. By instituting these measures in these three countries, more than 9,500 lives would be saved over the next fifty years, an average of 191 lives per year.

The Appendix shows the results of our analysis for all thirty-five countries, varying the d rate (3 and 5 percent) and the VoL (\$40,000, \$200,000, and \$6 million). For low VoL only a few countries have a BCR > 1. When the VoL is \$6 million and $d = 3$ percent (see Table A8.4), we find that the \$75 billion can best by allocated to retrofitting schools in these countries in the following order, based on their BCRs: Afghanistan, Myanmar, Guatemala, Solomon Islands, Congo, El Salvador, Uzbekistan, Armenia, India, Ecuador, and part of Indonesia. When $d = 5$ percent the expected benefits decrease, as does the BCR, since the retrofitting costs do not change.

[17] An OLS regression with both *GDP* and *RiskClass* as explanatory variables leads to a negative coefficient for *RiskClass* which triggers cost that would be negative for some of these countries, so we use only the *GDP* variable.
[18] Table 8.8 (Col. (4)) shows that mean AAL reduction was estimated to be 50 percent.

Table 8.10 Proposal I: BCA with 3% discount rate and VoL $1.5 million

Country	Final BCR	Cumulative retrofitting cost (Million US$)	Cumulative benefits ($)	Cumulative lives saved
Solomon Islands	6.45	36	235	72
Afghanistan	5.11	698	3,617	4,382
Myanmar	4.65	1,570	7,675	9,548
Guatemala	3.50	2,071	9,428	11,652
Armenia	2.87	2,222	9,863	11,835
El Salvador	2.35	2,485	10,481	12,435
Albania	2.31	2,740	11,070	12,648
Congo	2.02	3,220	12,037	13,880
Uzbekistan	1.66	4,504	14,174	16,416
Peru	1.37	8,598	19,781	19,147
India	1.36	73,923	108,797	134,207
Ecuador	1.26	74,870	109,986	135,614
Indonesia	1.09	89,756	126,175	156,256

Proposal II: Elevating residential structures and building a community wall to reduce losses from floods

We undertook a similar CBA for the thirty-four countries most exposed to flood risk around the world.[19] We analyze the effectiveness of elevating residential structures by 1 m and building a community wall around communities. Those are the two most effective measures revealed by our analysis of Jakarta, which we use here in order to scale up the analysis to a large number of countries.

CBA methodology

We illustrate the methodology here with respect to elevating a residential home. A similar methodology was used for building a community wall around exposed communities in the thirty-four countries:

- *Step 1: Extrapolating the expected reduction in damage from elevating residential homes exposed to flood in Jakarta, Indonesia to other countries.* The Indonesia study provided the average annual property loss to mixed-wall houses before and after they were elevated by 1 m. It is possible to utilize this analysis to extrapolate the average annual reduction in property damage (AARPD) from undertaking this measure in country *i*, $E(AARPD_i)$, where *i* is one of the countries that has a mortality risk index of Class 5 or above from the *Global Assessment Report on Disaster Risk Reduction* (UNISDR, 2010). The AAL extrapolation from Indonesia to another country *i* assumes that homes are elevated by 1 m. Indonesia has a risk class of 5. If a country has a risk class greater than 5 then the reduction in AAL per house is assumed to be 10 percent higher for each risk class (i.e. a country of risk class 7 will have an AAL reduction percentage equal to 120 percent what it is in Indonesia).

  The AAL reduction for that house in country *i* will be:

$$AAL\ Reduction_{Indonesia}$$
$$* (1 + [RiskClass_i - RiskClass_{Indonesia}] * 10\%)$$
$$* GDP_i / GDP_{Indonesia}$$

[19] This list of thirty-four countries for floods is (in alphabetical order): Afghanistan, Algeria, Argentina, Armenia, Bangladesh, Bhutan, Cambodia, CAR, Chad, China, Colombia, Côte d'Ivoire, Democratic People's Republic of Korea, DRC, Egypt, Georgia, India, Indonesia, Iran, Iraq, Kazakhstan, Lao People's Democratic Republic, Myanmar, Nepal, Nigeria, Pakistan, Russian Federation, Somalia, Sudan, Syrian Arab Republic, Thailand, Turkmenistan, Uzbekistan, and Vietnam.

By assuming an average of five individuals living in a house, the number of houses in the country is equal to one-fifth of the country's population. We also assume that 50 percent of the houses in these highly exposed countries are exposed to flood hazard.

The expected benefit of elevating homes in country *i* $E(SB_{ixe})$ is given by:

$$E(SB_i) = \Delta AAL_{Indonesia} * (1+[RiskClass_i - RiskClass_{Indonesia}] * 10\%) * GDP_i/GDP_{Indonesia}) * (Population_i/5) * 0.50$$

- *Step 2: Extrapolating the cost of elevating a house exposed to flood in Jakarta, Indonesia by 1 m to other countries.* The estimated cost of elevating a house in Indonesia was estimated to be \$9,345. Let the expected upfront cost of retrofitting all homes in country *i* be $E(SC_i)$ scaled down appropriately by the ratio of the $GDP_i / GDP_{Indonesia}$ multiplied by the estimated number of homes exposed to flooding in country *i*:

$$E(SC_i) = \$9{,}345 * (GDP_i/GDP_{Indonesia}) * (Population_i/5) * 0.5$$

- *Step 3: Expected number of fatalities due to flooding.* To estimate this figure for each country in our analysis that has a flood risk, we first approximate the number of exposed individuals in each country. To do this we determined the exposed population in 2010 for all countries that have a significant flood risk.[20] We then specify the degree of flood risk for each country in our sample using the classification from the *Global Assessment Report on Disaster Risk Reduction* (UNISDR, 2010). In this study, the United Nations classified all countries from the least prone to flooding (Class 1) to those facing the most severe floods (Class 9). We focused on countries in the mortality index Class 5 or higher. We multiply the mid-point of the range for country *i*'s flood risk classification by the number of people in that country (see Table 8.9)[21] to obtain $E(AAF_i)$, the average annual number of fatalities (*AAF*) due to flooding in country *i*.
- *Step 4: Expected average annual reduction in fatalities from elevating a house exposed to flood.* To estimate this figure, $E(AARF_i)$ for country *i*, we assume that the number of yearly fatalities from flooding will be reduced by 50 percent. The annual fatality figure is determined by multiplying the average fatalities per million per year by the exposed population per million (*total population * % exposed/1 million*). Based on these assumptions:

$$E(AARF_i) = 0.5 * E(AAF_i) * (total\ population * \%\ exposed/1\ million)$$

where $E(AAF_i)$ is obtained in Step 3 for each country *i*.
- *Step 5: Expected BCR for countries prone to flood risk.* Using the same *VoL*, *d*, and time horizons as in the earthquake study, the BCR per country can be determined.

Here, the BCR for elevating homes in country *i* (BCR_i) is given by:

$$BCR_i = E(SB_i)/E(SC_i) \text{ where } E(SB_i) \text{ and } E(SC_i) \text{ are obtained from Steps 1 and 2, respectively}$$

A similar analysis is done for our second mitigation measure: building a 1 m high community wall that will protect all the houses from flood (up to a certain height). Similarly, we used the AAL reduction obtained in our Indonesia study and extrapolated to the other countries under study here.

Findings for Proposal II

- *It would cost \$5.2 trillion to elevate by 1 m all houses exposed to flood in those thirty-four countries* and *nearly \$940 billion to build walls around the affected communities in all thirty-four countries.*

[20] See http://data.worldbank.org/indicator/SP.POP.0014.TO.ZS for the specific data we used for each country. Individual countries' risk profiles are from www.preventionweb.net.

[21] The risk-mortality rate table does not change across hazards; the list of countries of different class for different hazards does. For that reason we do not repeat here in our flood analysis the relative mortality table used for earthquake, since it is similar for flood.

Table 8.11 Proposal II (flood protection) – discount rate 3%; VoL $40,000

Measure	Investment $ billion	Cumulative benefit $ trillion	Lives saved	Average BCR	Countries which will benefit the most[a]
Community wall	75	4.5	19,894	60.1	Cambodia; Laos; Bhutan; Somalia; CAR; Afghanistan; Myanmar; Bangladesh; Korea; Chad; Sudan; Vietnam; India (partially)
Elevating houses	75	1.1	7,195	14.5	Cambodia; Laos; Bhutan; Somalia; CAR; Afghanistan; Myanmar; Bangladesh (partially)

Note: [a] The list of countries for each of the disaster-reduction measures are ordered on the basis of the BCR. (The countries listed first have the highest BCRs.)

- *Undertaking one or both of those measures in all thirty-four countries will save many fewer lives over the next fifty years* than retrofitting schools against earthquake damage.
- Because the reduction in flood damage is so high when collective or individual measures are in place and because fewer lives are saved from such measures than from retrofitting schools against earthquakes, *varying the VoL factor does not change the BCRs very much.*

Table 8.11 summarizes where $75 billion would be best spent for the two measures we consider here. We show the list of countries where the two disaster-reduction measures yield the highest BCR. We find that the cumulative benefit for the community wall will be $4.5 trillion (average BCR = 60 across these countries). Elevating homes will yield a benefit of $1.1 trillion (average BCR = 14.5).

Note that we find a BCR significantly higher than from retrofitting schools for earthquakes as discussed in Proposal I. Furthermore, the community-based disaster protection leads to a much higher BCR than the individual measure. In the case of $\{d = 0.3\ VoL = \$40{,}000\}$, the BCR for elevating houses by 1 m ranges between 11.9 (Russian Federation) and 15.6 (Cambodia). The community wall raises the BCR for the Russian Federation to 50 and for Cambodia to 65.

Proposal III: Designing residential structures to reduce wind losses from cyclones, hurricanes, and storms

Our analysis for cylones/hurricanes/storm follows a similar process as the one just described for flood.

Reducing damage in St. Vincent and the Grenadines and other countries

Here we turn to the case study cited on pp. 448–449 for hurricane risk in St. Lucia. It provided the average annual property loss to masonry houses with and without the *roof upgrade measure* (i.e. replacement of the roof material with thicker sheeting and tighter screw spacing, as well as the use of roof anchors).

Due to its small size, St. Lucia was not on the list of countries with a cyclone risk in the *Global Assessment Report on Disaster Risk Reduction* (UNISDR, 2010). We assumed that the same figures determined from the St. Lucia analysis in the World Bank report would hold true for the nearby Caribbean islands of St. Vincent and the Grenadines, both of which were on the list of countries of Class 5 and above for wind-related disaster,[22] and have relatively similar geography, population, and GDP to St. Lucia.[23] Note that there are thirty-four most exposed countries but many of them are different from the thirty-four countries

[22] The list of countries for cyclones/hurricanes/storms is (in alphabetical order): Antigua and Barbuda, Australia, Bahamas, Bangladesh, Belize, China, Cuba, Dominican Republic, Fiji, Haiti, India, Jamaica, Japan, Lao People's Democratic Republic, Madagascar, Mauritius, Mexico, Micronesia (Federated States of), Mozambique, Myanmar, Netherlands Antilles, New Caledonia, Nicaragua, Northern Mariana Islands, Palau, Philippines, St. Kitts and Nevis, St. Vincent and the Grenadines, Samoa, Solomon Islands, Tonga, Vanuatu, Vietnam, and Zimbabwe.

[23] St. Lucia's population is 176,000; St. Vincent and the Grenadines' population is 110,000. St. Lucia's GDP *per capita* is US $7,200; St. Vincent and the Grenadines' is US $6,300 (2011).

Table 8.12 Proposal III (wind protection against hurricanes, cyclones, and storms): 3% discount rate

VoL $	Investment $ billion	Benefit $ billion	BCR	Lives saved
6 million	75	354	Average: 4.7 Min/Max: 2/18.6	60,761
1.5 million	75	214	Average: 2.8 Min/Max: 2/6.7	60,761
200,000	75	173	Average: 2.3 Min/Max 2/3.3	60,761
40,000	75	168	Average: 2.2 Min/Max: 2/2.9	60,761

we analyzed for flood risk. As we focus only on masonry structures for our CBA, we computed the average percentage of masonry households from the 2010 UN World Population and Housing Census Programme for Belize, India, Jamaica, Mauritius, Philippines, St. Lucia, and Vanuatu – *47.6* percent – and rounded this figure to 50 percent in our analysis.

Every country prone to cyclones/hurricanes/storms in our analysis is assumed to have one-half of their homes built with masonry construction and half of those are exposed to wind damage. As we did for the analysis of elevating houses against flood, we assume that the risk-reduction measure is more effective in a country of higher exposure than St. Vincent and the Grenadines (risk class 5) by 10 percent for each risk class above 5 (that is, 10 percent more effective in a country of risk class 6, 20 percent for risk class 7, 30 percent for risk class 8, etc.).

We follow the same process as before to calculate the reduction in expected number of fatalities due to wind-related damage from cyclones.

The cost of protecting all masonry homes against wind damage in a country i is given by[24]:

$$E(SC_i) = Mitigation\ Cost_{St.\ Lucia} * (GDP_i/GDP_{St.\ Lucia}) * (Population_i/5) * 50\% * 50\%$$

Findings for roof protection against wind-related damage

- *It would cost $951 billion to undertake this DRR measure in all thirty-four countries, each of which has a BCR > 1.*[25]
- *Undertaking this measure will save 65,700 lives over the next fifty years.*

Because cyclones tend to kill large numbers of people in developing countries, our results are significantly affected by the *VoL* figure, as shown in Table 8.12, in which we compare the total benefit of investing $75 billion in countries with the highest BCR and consider four different *VoLs*. We find the highest BCR for Bangladesh (ranging from 2.9 with a *VoL* of $40,000, to 18.6 with a *VoL* of $6 million).

Summary of findings for reducing damage from earthquakes, floods, cyclones, hurricanes, and storms

Our findings with respect to investing in DRR measures to protect buildings and individuals against earthquakes, floods, and wind-related damage from cyclones, hurricanes, and storms can be summarized as follows:

- The most cost-effective measure for reducing future losses would be to invest $75 billion in building flood walls around communities. The cumulative expected benefits would be $4.5 trillon (BCR = 60) (see Table 8.11).
- If the concern is to save lives, then one will want to retrofit schools against earthquake damage. Based on the $40,000 and $200,000 *VoL* figures designated by the Copenhagen Consensus, the proposed risk-reducing measures for

[24] The first 50 percent in the equation comes from our assumption that half of the population is exposed to major wind damage; the second 50 percent comes from our assumption that half of those houses are of the masonry type, on which we focus here.

[25] Note that two-thirds of that amount would go to Australia, China, and Japan.

retrofitting schools are cost-effective for relatively few countries. On the other hand, if we consider $VoL = \$1.5$ million or $VoL = \$6$ million, then retrofitting schools becomes attractive for thirteen and twenty countries, respectively, when the annual discount rate (d) is 3 percent.

- In the case of cyclones, hurricanes, and storms the BCRs > 1 for all thirty-four countries when $VoL = \$40{,}000$ or \$200,000.
- Given the scale of the analyses we undertook (more than thirty countries around the world for each of the three hazards assessed), we had to make simplifying assumptions. In reality, one would want to gather information about the hazard, type of exposure, return period of different events, type of buildings, and their vulnerability to that hazard.

Proposal IV: Saving more lives by investing in effective early warning systems (EWS)

Proposals I–III focus on reducing damage and saving lives by implementing building codes in countries facing earthquakes, floods, and cyclones. As a complement to these measures, Proposal IV examines EWS for reducing fatalities from severe weather events. For example, in the United States, mortality fell by 45 percent and injuries by 40 percent in 15,000 tornadoes from 1986 to 1999 thanks to timely warnings that allowed people to take shelter. Hallegatte (2012) discusses the effectiveness of this proposal in more detail and derives BCRs to highlight the importance of early warnings. Our main purpose here is to indicate the role that EWS can play as part of a comprehensive DRR program. It is unlikely that the investment cost for EWS would be more than several billion dollars so that it can easily complement Proposals I–III.

In order to be effective, EWS must be multifaceted. EWS must monitor the risk as it evolves, disseminate that information, and respond to the event. For example, effective EWS for floods should be able to estimate the risk of flooding in different areas based on historical and topographical data, monitor rainfall levels, predict short-term flooding occurrences based on those levels, alert at-risk communities and the government if necessary, and assist in flood-mitigation methods such as sandbagging or shelter construction. EWS can communicate their messages in many different ways including television, radio, loudspeaker, text message, etc. Currently, EWS exist for floods, heat waves, hurricanes, tornadoes, drought, and other risks in many forms on both a localized and regional/global scale.

EWS can provide a multitude of benefits. These systems reduce loss of life and injuries by giving citizens time to flee and prepare for an impending disaster (for example, getting to a shelter, or higher ground.). Property loss can be avoided depending on the system's disaster lead times. If a lead time of several days or weeks can be given, communities can prepare by securing property, engaging in loss-mitigation measures for crops, and relocating possessions. For example, with a larger lead time on a cyclone, a fisherman could remove his nets and traps, avoiding their destruction. These benefits can be especially evident in low-income countries where disasters can often cripple an unprepared country. Note also that while many other prevention techniques can often marginalize the impoverished by, for example, forcing them to relocate to make way for infrastructure improvements, EWS serve all members of the population equally.

A main challenge that these systems face is balancing the advantages of longer lead times (allowing more property and infrastructure to be protected) with greater accuracy and fewer false alarms (which increase the costs associated with these systems). The benefits relative to the costs of EWS also vary depending on the frequency and severity of the event, and the predictability, with reasonable lead times and accuracy. By coupling these systems with investments in critical infrastructure and environmental buffers, EWS can contribute to an effective disaster-prevention program. However, determining how much to invest in EWS, as well as which systems to invest in, has proven challenging. By utilizing a similar CBA approach as used in previous sections of the chapter, examination of different systems and their effectiveness can be conducted. Since EWS can reduce human casualties, a traditional CBA analysis sometimes has to be modified to take into account the value of lives (as we did in our analysis of earthquake risks in Istanbul). Table 8.13, from a study by Subbiah *et al.* (2008), summarizes several case studies that utilized CBA

Table 8.13 CBA of several EWS projects

Bangladesh: Sidr cyclone case study	• Enhancement of computing resources – i.e. advanced computing equipment, latest numerical weather prediction (NWP) models, trained human resources – in addition to existing level of services in the Bangladesh Meteorological Department, would help increase lead time and accuracy of forecast information. • With additional investment for building capacity for translating, interpreting, and communicating probabilistic forecast information, the case study demonstrates that **for every $1 invested, a return of $40 in benefits over a ten-year period may be realized**.
Sri Lanka: May 2003 floods case study	• Existing NWP models, coupled with use of model outputs from regional and global centers, could help anticipate events such as the extreme floods of May 2003. • CBA reveals that **for every $1 invested, there is a return of only $0.93 in benefits, i.e. the costs outweighs the benefits** since significantly damaging flooding is not very frequent. • In such a case, it makes great sense for such countries to join a collective regional system, due to economies of scale, as demonstrated in the case study on the Regional Integrated Multi-Hazard Early Warning System (RIMES).
Vietnam: 2001–2007 hydro-meteorological hazards case study	• Increased lead time as well as accuracy due to incorporation of the advanced Weather Research Forecasting (WRF) model run at much higher resolutions could help reduce losses and avoidable damages. Due to increased accuracy in predicting the landfall point, as well as associated parameters such as wind speed and rainfall, it would be possible to reduce avoidable responses – such as evacuation across hundreds of km along the coast, as well as disruption of fishing and other marine activities. • **The case study shows that every $1 invested in this EWS will realize a return of $10.4 in benefits**
Indonesia: Seasonal forecasting case study	• The seasonal climate-forecasting model has already been replicated in over fifty districts by the Indonesian government (and is being replicated in other districts). • The case study shows that the indicative value of each seasonal forecast is $1.5 million (currently in fifty districts), and potentially $7.5 million (for 250 districts) per season. The actual one-time investment to produce this forecast is not more than $ 0.25 million, with a marginal recurring cost of $0.05 million per year.

Source: Subbiah *et al.* (2008).

to assess the potential effectiveness of different early warning systems.

Hallegatte (2012) provides a rough calculation of how much it would cost to implement EWS in developing countries and concludes that it would require less than $1 billion a year and would have direct benefits with respect to disaster-loss reductions of between US$1 and 5.5 billion per year, and co-benefits of between US$3 and 30 billion.

The limits of CBA: behavioral economics and disaster management

The CBAs enable one to better appreciate the financial return of several disaster reduction measures. In reality, decision-makers are likely to utilize simplified choice rules, focusing on budget constraints as well as short-run benefits and costs rather than discounting the future exponentially over a fifty-year period, as we have done. They may not even consider probabilities in their decision on whether or not to invest in risk-reduction measures. This behavior needs to be taken into account when designing disaster-management strategies that have a good chance of being implemented. These strategies include land use, enforcement of the most recent international building codes, EWS, economic incentives, and disaster risk-financing mechanisms (e.g. (micro) insurance).

Below we highlight several factors that have been well studied in the behavioral economics literature (see Kunreuther *et al.*, 2013a, for a review).

Budgeting heuristics

The simplest explanation as to why homeowners may fail to invest in flood-mitigation measures is concerns about affordability. If a family has limited disposable income after purchasing necessities, there would be little point in undertaking a CBA as to whether to incur the upfront cost of the new protective measure. If the home owner is focusing on only the next period (i.e. $T = 1$), he may not be able to afford the cost of home improvements.

Budget constraints may extend to higher-income individuals if they set up separate mental accounts for different expenditures (Thaler, 1999). Empirical evidence for this budgeting heuristic comes from a study where many renters indicated no change in their WTP for a dead-bolt lock when the lease for the apartment was extended from one to five years. When asked why, one individual responded by saying: "\$20 is all the dollars I have in the short-run to spend on a lock. If I had more, I would spend more – maybe up to \$50" (Kunreuther *et al*, 1998: 284).

Safety-first behavior

Individuals may utilize a simplified decision rule that determines whether to invest in protective measures only if the probability of the event (p) is above their threshold level of concern (p^*). If the decision-makers perceive $p < p^*$, then they will not undertake any protection. If, on the other hand, $p > p^*$ then they will want to invest in protection.

If there is an opportunity to determine how much to invest in mitigating the consequences of the event, then the decision-maker may utilize a safety-first rule by determining the optimal amount of protection so that $p \leq p^*$. This "safety-first" rule initially proposed by Roy (1952) is utilized by insurers today in determining how much coverage to offer and what premium to charge against extreme events such as hurricane wind damage in hazard-prone areas (Kunreuther *et al.*, 2013b).

Under-weighting the future

There is extensive experimental evidence revealing that human temporal discounting tends to be hyperbolic: temporally distant events are disproportionately discounted relative to immediate ones (Loewenstein and Elster, 1992). The implication of hyperbolic discounting for protective decisions is that home owners might be asked to invest a tangible fixed sum now to achieve a benefit later that they instinctively undervalue. The effect of placing too much weight on immediate considerations is that the upfront costs of protection will loom disproportionately large relative to delayed expected benefits in losses over time.

An extreme form of hyperbolic discounting is when the decision-maker considers the expected benefits from the protective measure only over the next year or two rather than over the life of the equipment. Elected officials may tend to reflect on how their specific decisions are likely to affect their chances of re-election. If the perceived expected benefits from the measure before they start campaigning again are less than the costs of protection, they will very likely oppose the expenditure. They will prefer to allocate funds where they can see an immediate return. The fact that protective measures yield positive returns only when a disaster occurs makes it even more difficult for them to justify these measures. This reluctance to incur upfront costs that do not yield immediate benefits highlights NIMTOF (Not in My Term of Office) behavior.

Underestimation of risk

Another factor that has been shown to suppress investments in protection is underestimation of the likelihood of a hazard – formally, underestimation. There is evidence that people tend to simply ignore risks when the likelihood is small enough. In laboratory experiments on financially protecting themselves against a loss by purchasing insurance or a warranty, many individuals bid 0 for coverage, apparently viewing the probability of a loss as sufficiently small that they were not interested in protecting themselves against it (McClelland *et al.*, 1993; Schade *et al.*, 2011). Many home owners residing in communities that are potential sites for nuclear waste facilities have a tendency to dismiss the risk as negligible (Oberholzer-Gee, 1998).

Even experts in risk disregard some hazards. After the first terrorist attack against the World Trade Center in 1993, terrorism risk continued to be included as an unnamed peril in most US commercial insurance policies. Insurers were thus liable for losses from a terrorist attack without their ever receiving a penny for this coverage (Kunreuther and Michel-Kerjan, 2004). Following the attacks of September 11, 2001, insurers and their reinsurers had to pay over $35 billion in claims due to losses from the terrorist attacks, at that time the most costly event in the history of insurance worldwide, now second only to Hurricane Katrina.

Proposed innovations

We now propose some innovations that could enable countries to be better prepared for future disasters, taking into account the behavior of key decision-makers. Specifically, we will focus on how combining cost-effective risk-reduction measures and risk-financing instruments with economic incentives and well-enforced standards and regulations can significantly reduce future disaster losses. We also discuss several initiatives in developing countries that provide examples of good practices.

Insurance provides assurance of financial protection.[26] When coupled with loans for DRR measures, these two financial products can play a key role in promoting individuals' and businesses' investment. We first discuss an example of financial innovation: index-based insurance in Peru. We then propose that both insurance and loans be issued as *multi-year contracts* to encourage communities and governments to think more long-term. We will also explain how innovative risk-transfer instruments can supplement insurance when losses are truly catastrophic.

Indexed-based insurance in Peru

In a new collaboration between GlobalAgRisk, with the support of the Bill and Melinda Gates Foundation and the UNDP, Peru has initiated a new insurance model to mitigate losses associated with natural events. However, unlike initiatives that use insurance to compensate for losses *after* an event has occurred, Peru has a program that provides payments *before* the event occurs (Cavanaugh *et al.*, 2010).

This program is intended to reduce losses associated with El Niño, an event characterized by the warming of the tropical Pacific Ocean that brings devastating rainfall and flooding to northern Peru, normally occurring with a frequency of once every fifteen years. This event destroys crops, increases water- and pest-relate illnesses, and disrupts supply chains and public utilities. The risk associated with such a disaster limits available credit for farmers. Fortunately, this warming can be predicted months in advance by measuring changes in sea temperatures off the coast of northern Peru. The financial program that has been developed triggers a payment based on the amount the policy holder has chosen to insure whenever an El Niño event is predicted, allowing for the insured to use the payment to mitigate against any losses that would normally occur without the insurance.

There are multiple contract options. To illustrate, purchasers of the insurance pay a relatively small initial premium and receive a payment when sea temperatures are in excess of 24°C between November and December. The payment is a percentage of the total sum insured, and increases in a linear fashion as sea temperatures increase, with 100 percent of the insured sum being paid when the temperature reaches 27°C. This provides a cash infusion to the insured in January, before the serious flooding occurs in February through April. Currently, the insurance is available for purchase by banks and other businesses through La Positiva, a local insurer with the backing of PartnerRe, a global reinsurance company. For banks and large businesses, the insurance allows them to be more prepared for the inevitable increased default rate after the event, to prevent insolvency and transfer the portfolio risks.

This program has led to a change in thinking regarding potential opportunities for "forecast index insurance." There are opportunities to expand coverage to parts of Africa, Asia/Pacific, and the Americas where EI Niño events affect seasonal patterns of rainfall and temperature. This program offers a unique solution to disaster mitigation.

Multi-year insurance and loan programs for communities and governments

Insurance is typically sold as a one-year contract. With respect to investments that have a relatively

[26] Saving accounts and redistributive tax programs are other possible policy tools.

long life, such as DRR systems, there is an opportunity to develop new instruments such as multi-year insurance (MYI) coupled with multi-year loans to encourage these investments.

MYI programs have been proposed to overcome the tendency for individuals to cancel their insurance policies after several years. Even in the United States, where knowledge about flood risk is available to any resident who seeks this information and flood insurance is available at reasonable cost, many residents in hazard-prone areas who purchase flood insurance then cancel their coverage after several years (Michel-Kerjan and Kunreuther, 2011). An MYI contract would increase the likelihood that individuals are protected over time. They will thus be less exposed to severe disaster losses while at the same time benefiting from their investment in risk-reduction measures by paying lower insurance premiums each year. Long-term loans would further encourage investments in cost-effective mitigation by spreading the upfront costs over time. If insurance rates are actuarially based, then the premium reduction from adopting a risk-reduction measure will be greater than the annual loan cost. Well-enforced building codes could ensure that structures are designed to withstand damages from future disasters.

An MYI policy combined with multi-year loans may also encourage communities and national governments in low-income countries to invest in risk-reducing measures such as irrigation systems for reducing the impacts of drought. Here is how the combined insurance–loan system would work:

- The community or government would purchase index-based insurance to protect itself against losses from a disaster. The policy would pay a fixed amount based on certain triggers (e.g. rainfall below a certain amount during a given time period).
- The MYI premium would be based on risk, reviewed every five years to reflect structural alterations such as climate change. The revised premium would be based on a credible index regarding the structural alteration.
- Property owners or farmers would be covered for five consecutive years, making the chances of receiving a claim during this period more likely than if they focused on the annual probability of a disaster occurring.
- The multi-year loan would spread the upfront cost of the investment over a number of years. Local authorities, banks, or institutions (such as the World Bank) could provide the loan.
- The amount of protection against a disaster (for example, drought) required by the community or government would be much lower if they invested in a risk-reducing measure such as an irrigation system.
- The annual premium reduction of the MYI policy when one invested in a risk-reducing measure (for example, an irrigation system) is likely to be greater than the cost of a long-term loan if the measure is a cost-effective one.

MYI policies have been examined by very few pilot studies, with the Peruvian initiative discussed on p. 467 being a notable exception. Since this initiative is so recent there has been little time to examine the effects of tying multi-year loans and insurance policies. With the program's planned expansion into multi-year loans for households, small businesses, and the public sector, there is likely to be an increase in demand, as well as increases in investments in long-term mitigation strategies including irrigation systems (Cavanaugh *et al.*, 2010).

Alternative risk-transfer (ART) instruments for covering catastrophic losses[27]

An MYI and loan program should be a win–win for all interested parties. The farmers would be safer and could generate higher revenue, which in turn would foster economic growth and further investment in innovative technologies. There would be less need for the government and international charities to provide financial assistance and aid to victims of future disasters since the exposure would be reduced by physical investment in risk-reduction measures and by financial protection through insurance.

[27] For a more detailed discussion on the application of ART instruments to developing countries, see Michel-Kerjan *et al.* (2011).

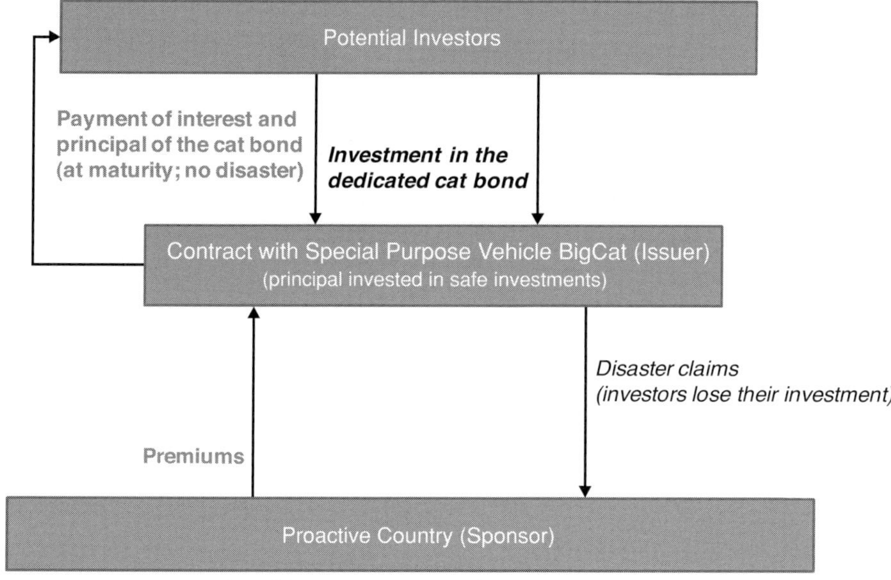

Figure 8.8 *Simplified structure of a government cat bond*

Source: Michel-Kerjan *et al.* (2011).

Still, there is the possibility that a truly devastating disaster could adversely affect a large number of individuals simultaneously even if risk-reduction measures were in place. To deal with a catastrophic loss, governments can use dedicated financial products to supplement traditional insurance and reinsurance products. The development of ART instruments grew out of a series of insurance capacity crises in the 1970s through the 1990s that led purchasers of traditional reinsurance coverage to seek more robust ways to buy protection. Although ART instruments comprise a wide range of products, we focus here on catastrophe bonds that transfer part of the risk exposure directly to investors in the financial markets.[28] This financial instrument has increased in volume in recent years and is likely to continue to grow as the world experiences more costly catastrophes in the coming years.

How do catastrophe bonds work?

Catastrophe bonds ("cat bonds") can enable a country, a company or any organization to access funds from investors if a severe disaster produces large-scale damage. Consider a country, Proactive, which would like to cover part of its exposure against catastrophes. To do so, it creates a company, BigCat, whose only purpose is to finance the disaster costs of Proactive. Notably, BigCat is not a government-run company but an independent company. In that sense, BigCat is a single-purpose insurer (also called a special-purpose vehicle, or SPV) for Proactive. When the insurance contract is signed, the sponsor (Proactive) pays premiums to BigCat. SPV BigCat raises the capital to support its insurance policy by issuing a bond to investors. Premiums collected from Proactive will be used to provide the investors with a high enough interest rate to compensate for a possible loss of their principal should a disaster occur. Figure 8.8 provides the structure of a typical government cat bond.

[28] See Anderson *et al.* (2000) and Cummins and Weiss (2009) for comprehensive journal articles; Lane (2002) and Barrieu and Albertini (2009) for edited volumes; and Michel-Kerjan (2010), OECD (2010), and World Economic Forum (2008) for a more general analysis.

How a government benefits from a cat bond

There are several widely used ways that the payment of a cat bond can be triggered. First, all the stakeholders can agree at the execution of the contract on an external trigger for the insurance payment, independent of the actual level of losses the country has suffered, but easily verifiable, similar to the rainfall trigger on index-based insurance. This is called a *parametric* trigger. The data for this parameter can be collected at multiple reporting stations across a given geographical area. It is also possible to agree on a certain level of the actual economic losses incurred by Proactive from a disaster or series of disasters over the maturity of the cat bond. This is an *indemnity* trigger.[29] The main advantage of an indemnity trigger is that the payment received by Proactive will be much closer to its actual loss. However, it could create a moral-hazard problem by having the country overstate the loss it has incurred. Parametric cat bonds are more transparent and simpler to use and hence have been the preferred type in LDCs.

Advantages of using a cat bond

There are three main advantages of using a cat bond to provide protection against a catastrophic disaster:

(1) *Multi-year coverage and price stability.* Insurance and reinsurance contracts are typically issued for one year and are subject to price increases, particularly after a large-scale disaster.[30] Cat bonds offer an important element of stability for their users by guaranteeing a predefined price over several years. More than 170 catastrophe bonds were issued from 1996 to 2008; their average maturity has been three years with a few bonds being as long as five or ten years. Longer bonds reduce upfront costs by allowing fees to be amortized over a longer period of time (Michel-Kerjan and Morlaye, 2008).

(2) *Guaranteed expedited payment.* Another key advantage of a cat bond is that the money can flow to the government in just a few weeks. By design, the capital of the bond is commonly invested in risk-free assets, such as US Treasury money market funds, so there is limited credit risk.[31]

(3) *Potentially easier to manage politically than a government reserve.* A typical financial policy tool for governments is to build up a reserve of money over time to be used in the case of a catastrophe. However, a catastrophe could occur in the very first years so that the fund simply does not have enough money to pay for the losses. If the country does not suffer major losses for a long period, attention fades and the reserves may be transferred to other programs, particularly when budgets are tight.[32] It is difficult to have a long-term perspective on these issues for reasons discussed above (Michel-Kerjan and Slovic, 2010). Cat bonds overcome these challenges, since the catastrophe portion of the risk is transferred to financial investors who serve as third parties.

[29] This form of cat-bond trigger is more analogous to a traditional insurance policy with its loss-settlement process. Other triggers are *modeled losses* or *industry losses*. For *modeled losses*, instead of dealing with Proactive's actual losses, an exposure portfolio is constructed for use with catastrophe modeling software. When there is a disaster, the event parameters are run against the exposure database in the cat model. If the modeled losses are above a specified threshold, the bond is triggered. For *industry losses*, the cat bond is triggered when the total insurance industry loss from a certain peril in this country reaches a specified threshold.

[30] The Guy Carpenter Rate-on-Line index shows a 30 percent annual volatility over the past ten years. Premiums also differ markedly among perils that increase the concentration of risk to the reinsurers and perils which provide diversification. It is not unusual to see reinsurance prices in a region increase by 20–50 percent after a major disaster. Catastrophe reinsurance prices in Florida increased by nearly 100 percent the year after Hurricane Katrina (Kunreuther and Michel-Kerjan, 2011: Chapter 7).

[31] Note that some reinsurers now provide collateralized reinsurance treaties as well, but those are more expensive than traditional reinsurance treaties.

[32] This was suggested in the United States for the Hurricane Relief Fund in Hawaii in 2009. Another example relates to the US Pension Benefit Guaranty Corporation (PBGC). In the 1990s there were interest groups lobbying the PBGC to reduce premiums because they were "too high," as evidenced by the fact that the Corporation was running a surplus.

Conclusion

During the past few years the world has experienced a series of truly devastating natural disasters that have taken many lives and triggered unprecedented economic losses. Hurricane Katrina in 2005 in the United States, the massive floods in Australia in 2010 and the earthquake/tsunami in Japan in 2011 have demonstrated that even the richest and most prepared countries in the world can experience large-scale damage and destruction. The situation is much worse in low-income countries since they often do not have the financial means to protect their population and economy against catastrophes, or do not consider it a priority. The earthquake in Haiti in 2010 illustrates the challenges for an unprepared and poor country.

Despite this upward trend in catastrophes, knowledge about exposure to natural disasters on an international scale is still rather limited. The development of probabilistic catastrophe models can be of significant help in this regard. This chapter utilizes this methodology to undertake CBAs for disaster-reduction measures by focusing on a single building in the Caribbean (subjected to wind hazard from hurricanes), Indonesia (subjected to flood hazard), and Turkey (subjected to earthquake hazard).

Undertaking a similar CBA for the building portfolio of an entire country is a time-consuming and complex process. It requires a detailed knowledge of the hazard in different parts of the country (down to the local level) and the distribution and location of the entire building portfolio. This portfolio would comprise all residences, commercial and industrial construction, critical infrastructure, and all government buildings. Such a detailed inventory is usually not available in low-income countries, so studies published in the literature have typically focused on one city or part of a community with respect to a specific hazard. A national risk assessment would require knowledge of the vulnerability of the entire portfolio of structures to all the hazards faced by the country. To undertake a CBA, one also needs to determine for each loss-reduction measure under study the cost of raw materials and labor in different parts of the country.

For these reasons, we have undertaken rather preliminary CBAs, building on limited studies that have been undertaken in different parts of the world to reduce losses from natural disasters. For three types of disasters – earthquakes, floods and cyclones/hurricanes/storms – we have focused on residences and schools in more than thirty countries. We have determined the cost of different loss-reduction measures and expected benefits in terms of physical damage reduction and number of lives saved. By design, our CBAs are highly dependent on the very simplified assumptions we had to make. Furthermore, and as expected, the selection of different discount rates, time periods, and VoLs have a significant impact on our findings.

Note, however, that our analysis has not taken into account several additional benefits from these DRR measures in the form of reduction of evacuation costs (from reducing housing damage), lowering the number of injured and possible subsequent health issues, continuity of education (from preserving schools), relieving social stress to individuals and avoiding business interruption (Heinz Center, 2000).

We also discussed the importance of behavioral and economic barriers that prevent people from implementing risk-reduction measures that can appear to be cost-effective. Moreover, in addition to risk assessments and CBAs of specific loss-reduction measures, one needs to design strong risk-financing mechanisms for disaster victims (individuals and firms) so that they can get back on their feet more quickly after a catastrophe rather than relying on uncertain donors' money. Insurance and other alternative risk-transfer instruments can play an important role here. In addition, there is a need for innovations with short-term incentives (such as multi-year contracts) that will be attractive to those living and working in the exposed areas as well as to politicians who are concerned with re-election or staying in power and can grasp the short-term benefits of such innovations.

Finally, the question of *who should pay* for these measures in a real-world setting is an important issue. In this chapter, we have allocated $75 billion that has hypothetically been given to us from some unknown source. If we can convince a panel of our peers that these expenditures have value, we would then have to take our case to those who make decisions where there are scarce resources. We would then have to do the following:

- Convince international donors to start investing more systematically in DRR rather than focusing almost exclusively on post-disaster assistance as they do today.
- Convince NGOs to put their time and energy into reflecting on ways to reduce future losses and fatalities rather than focusing solely on emergency relief.
- Convince more governments in developed countries and multinational corporations (MNCs) to provide some of their funding and technical expertise to assist low-income countries in undertaking these measures.

Our planet is becoming more and more interdependent; a disaster in one part of the world can have ripple effects on many other countries. Stakeholders internationally must recognize that it is in their own best interest to take these steps now rather than procrastinating, because the failure of poor countries can impact on their future as well. If a few key decision-makers, organizations, and countries take the initiative, others may follow suit. As more people work on these questions, economies of scope and scale will likely develop, new technologies will emerge, and the cost of reducing exposure to future disasters will significantly decrease.

Appendix

Analysis for Proposal I (retrofitting schools)

Countries are ranked from the highest BCR to the lowest (see Tables A8.1–A8.4)

Table A8.1 Discount rate 3%; VoL $40,000

Country	BCR	Cumulative retrofitting cost (US$ million)	Cumulative total benefits ($)	Cumulative number of lives saved
Solomon Islands	4.97	36	181	72
Armenia	1.96	188	479	255
Albania	1.69	443	908	468
Peru	0.87	4,537	4,463	3,198
Kyrgyzstan	0.71	4,724	4,595	3,258
El Salvador	0.63	4,987	4,762	3,858
Costa Rica	0.50	5,729	5,130	4,215
Tajikistan	0.41	6,000	5,241	4,320
Romania	0.36	7,906	5,931	5,329
Guatemala	0.34	8,407	6,103	7,434
Chile	0.32	11,157	6,979	7,476
Panama	0.29	11,602	7,108	7,479
Afghanistan	0.22	12,263	7,251	11,789
Myanmar	0.20	13,135	7,428	16,955
Uzbekistan	0.18	14,419	7,660	19,491
Honduras	0.15	14,768	7,712	19,526
Nicaragua	0.15	15,121	7,764	19,533
Ecuador	0.14	16,068	7,895	20,939
Algeria	0.12	19,321	8,295	21,287
Nepal	0.11	19,982	8,368	21,408
DRC	0.09	20,462	8,410	22,640
Sudan	0.09	22,402	8,576	22,794
Bolivia	0.08	23,393	8,654	22,807
Colombia	0.08	28,415	9,035	27,582
Iran	0.07	38,874	9,814	33,169
Uganda	0.07	39,932	9,889	33,362
Turkey	0.06	54,239	10,689	33,595
Indonesia	0.05	69,125	11,370	54,236
India	0.04	134,450	13,939	169,297
Venezuela	0.04	140,428	14,172	169,326
Philippines	0.04	147,466	14,422	170,648
Mexico	0.03	179,820	15,479	170,770
Pakistan	0.02	188,633	15,682	173,194
China	0.02	289,951	17,757	251,800
Argentina	0.01	299,574	17,860	251,812

Table A8.2 Discount rate 3%; VoL $200,000

Country	BCR	Cumulative retrofitting cost (US$ million)	Cumulative total benefits ($)	Number of lives saved
Solomon Islands	5.13	36	187	72
Armenia	2.06	188	500	255
Albania	1.75	443	947	468
Peru	0.92	4,537	4,727	3,198
El Salvador	0.82	4,800	4,943	3,798
Afghanistan	0.75	5,461	5,441	8,108
Kyrgyzstan	0.73	5,648	5,578	8,168
Myanmar	0.69	6,520	6,180	13,334
Guatemala	0.69	7,021	6,526	15,438
Costa Rica	0.53	7,763	6,922	15,795
Tajikistan	0.44	8,035	7,042	15,900
Romania	0.41	9,940	7,816	16,909
Uzbekistan	0.34	11,224	8,256	19,446
Chile	0.32	13,974	9,136	19,488
DRC	0.30	14,454	9,279	20,720
Panama	0.29	14,899	9,408	20,724
Ecuador	0.26	15,846	9,655	22,130
India	0.18	81,170	21,699	137,191
Indonesia	0.16	96,057	24,079	157,832
Honduras	0.16	96,406	24,134	157,867
Colombia	0.15	101,428	24,909	162,642
Nicaragua	0.15	101,781	24,961	162,649
Algeria	0.13	105,034	25,389	162,997
Nepal	0.13	105,695	25,472	163,118
Iran	0.12	116,154	26,711	168,705
Sudan	0.09	118,094	26,890	168,858
Uganda	0.09	119,152	26,981	169,051
China	0.08	220,469	35,528	247,657
Bolivia	0.08	221,460	35,607	247,671
Turkey	0.06	235,767	36,426	247,903
Philippines	0.05	242,805	36,785	249,225
Pakistan	0.05	251,619	37,187	251,649
Venezuela	0.04	257,597	37,422	251,679
Mexico	0.03	289,951	38,489	251,800
Argentina	0.01	299,574	38,593	251,812

Table A8.3 Discount rate 5%; VoL $200,000

Country	BCR	Cumulative retrofitting cost (US$ million)	Total benefits ($)	Cumulative number of lives saved
Solomon Islands	3.64	36	133	72
Armenia	1.46	188	355	255
Albania	1.24	443	672	468
Peru	0.66	4,537	3,354	3,198
El Salvador	0.58	4,800	3,507	3798
Afghanistan	0.53	5,461	3,861	8108
Kyrgyzstan	0.52	5,648	3,958	8168
Myanmar	0.49	6,520	4,385	13,334
Guatemala	0.49	7,021	4,630	15438
Costa Rica	0.38	7,763	4,912	15795
Tajikistan	0.31	8,035	4,997	15900
Romania	0.29	9,940	5,545	16909
Uzbekistan	0.24	11,224	5,858	19446
Chile	0.23	13,974	6,482	19488
DRC	0.21	14,454	6,584	20720
Panama	0.21	14,899	6,675	20724
Ecuador	0.19	15,846	6,851	22130
India	0.13	81,170	15,396	137191
Indonesia	0.11	96,057	17,085	157832
Honduras	0.11	96,406	17,124	157867
Colombia	0.11	101,428	17,673	162642
Nicaragua	0.10	101,781	17,710	162649
Algeria	0.09	105,034	18,014	162997
Nepal	0.09	105,695	18,073	163118
Iran	0.08	116,154	18,952	168705
Sudan	0.07	118,094	19,079	168858
Uganda	0.06	119,152	19,144	169051
China	0.06	220,469	25,208	247657
Bolivia	0.06	221,460	25,264	247671
Turkey	0.04	235,767	25,845	247903
Philippines	0.04	242,805	26,100	249225
Pakistan	0.03	251,619	26,385	251649
Venezuela	0.03	257,597	26,552	251679
Mexico	0.02	289,951	27,309	251800
Argentina	0.01	299,574	27,383	251812

Table A8.4 Discount rate 3%; VoL $6 million

Country	BCR	Cumulative retrofitting cost (US$ million)	Cumulative total benefits ($)	Cumulative number of lives saved
Afghanistan	20.20	661	13,362	4,310
Myanmar	18.37	1,533	29,382	9,476
Guatemala	13.22	2,034	36,008	11,580
Solomon Islands	11.02	2,071	36,410	11,652
DRC	7.96	2,551	40,231	12,884
El Salvador	7.63	2,814	42,239	13,485
Uzbekistan	6.24	4,098	50,249	16,021
Armenia	5.67	4,250	51,108	16,204
India	5.44	69,574	406,567	131,264
Ecuador	4.69	70,521	411,013	132,671
Indonesia	4.30	85,407	475,002	153,312
Albania	4.25	85,662	476,083	153,525
Colombia	2.99	90,684	491,111	158,301
Peru	2.91	94,778	503,040	161,031
China	2.40	196,096	746,200	239,637
Romania	1.99	198,001	749,987	240,647
Costa Rica	1.97	198,743	751,449	241,004
Iran	1.71	209,202	769,364	246,591
Kyrgyzstan	1.69	209,389	769,680	246,651
Tajikistan	1.59	209,660	770,112	246,756
Pakistan	0.87	218,474	777,750	249,180
Nepal	0.67	219,135	778,192	249,300
Uganda	0.63	220,193	778,859	249,493
Philippines	0.61	227,231	783,164	250,815
Honduras	0.45	227,580	783,322	250,850
Algeria	0.45	230,833	784,788	251,198
Chile	0.37	233,583	785,793	251,240
Sudan	0.33	235,523	786,429	251,393
Panama	0.31	235,968	786,569	251,397
Nicaragua	0.21	236,321	786,643	251,404
Bolivia	0.12	237,312	786,761	251,417
Turkey	0.11	251,619	788,273	251,649
Venezuela	0.05	257,597	788,596	251,679
Mexico	0.04	289,951	790,026	251,800
Argentina	0.01	299,574	790,165	251,812

Bibliography

Agence France-Presse, 2010: Almost half Haiti's injured may be children: study, *ReliefWeb*, 28 January, www.reliefweb.int/rw/rwb.nsf/db900sid/SNAA-82587M?OpenDocument&rc=2&emid=EQ-2010–000009-HTI

Anderson, R. R., F. Bendimerad, E. Canabarro, and M. Finkemeier, 2000: Analyzing insurance-linked securities, *Journal of Risk Finance* **1**, 49–78

Barrieu, P. and L. Albertini, 2009: *Handbook of Insurance Linked Securities*, Wiley, Chichester

Benson, C. and J. Twigg, 2004: Measuring mitigation: methodologies for assessing natural hazard risks and the net benefits of mitigation – A scoping study, International Federation of Red Cross and Red Crescent societies/ProVention Consortium, Geneva

Benson, C., J. Twigg, and T. Rossetto, 2007: *Tools for Mainstreaming Disaster Risk Reduction: Guidance Notes for Development Organisations*, ProVention Consortium, Geneva

Burnett, W., 2004: Quake-proof: what S.F. homeowners need to do to be ready for a 7.2 San Andreas shaker, *San Francisco Chronicle*, May 8

Cavanaugh, G., B. Collier, and J. Skees, 2010: Incorporating weather index insurance with territorial approaches to climate change (TACC) in Northern Peru, www.adaptationlearning.net/sites/default/files/GlobalAgRisk_UNDP_Credit%20to%20Households_Report.pdf

CBC News, 2010: The world's worst natural disasters: calamities of the 20th and 21st centuries, August 30

Cropper, M. and S. Sahin, 2008: Valuing mortality and morbidity in the context of disaster risks, Background Paper for the joint World Bank–UN assessment on disaster risk reduction, World Bank, Washington, DC

Crossett, K. M., T. J. Culliton, P. C. Wiley, and T. R. Goodspeed, 2004: *Population Trends Along the Coastal United States: 1980–2008*, National Oceanic and Atmospheric Administration, Silver Spring, MD

Cummins, D. and M. Weiss, 2009: Convergence of insurance and financial markets: hybrid and securitized risk-transfer solutions, *Journal of Risk and Insurance* **76**, 493–545

Dartmouth Flood Observatory, 2008: www.dartmouth.edu/~floods

Davis, L., 2002: *Spon's Asian Cost Construction Handbook*, Taylor and Francis, Abingdon

Dixit, A., A. Pokhrel, and M. Moench, 2009: Qualitative assessment of the costs and benefits of flood mitigation, in M. Moench, E. Fajber, A. Dixit, E. Caspari, and A. Pokhrel (eds.), *Catalyzing Climate and Disaster Resilience*, ISET, Kathmandu

Ellul, F. and D. D'Ayala, 2003: *The Bingol, Turkey Earthquake of the 1st of May 2003*, University of Bath, Architecture and Civil Engineering Department, www.istructe.org/eefit/files/BingolFieldReport.pdf

Erdik, M., 2003: Earthquake vulnerability of buildings and a mitigation strategy: case of Istanbul, World Bank, Washington, DC

Evaluación de Riesgos Naturales (ERN), 2010: *Seismic Risk Assessment of Schools in the Andean Region in South America and Central America*, International Labor Office, www.preventionweb.net/english/hyogo/gar/2011/en/bgdocs/ERN-AL_2010.pdf

Fierro, E. and C. Perry, 2010: *Preliminary Reconnaissance Report: 12 January 2010 Haiti Earthquake*, Reconnaissance and Report partially supported by The Pacific Earthquake Engineering Research Center (PEER), http://peer.berkeley.edu/publications/haiti_2010/documents/Haiti_Reconnaissance.pdf

Government of India, Ministry of Home Affairs, 2004: *Disaster Management of India*, New Delhi

Grossi, P. and H. Kunreuther (eds.), 2005: *Catastrophe Modeling: A New Approach to Managing Risk*, Springer, New York

Guevara, T. L. and L. E. García, 2005: The captive- and short-column effects, *Earthquake Spectra* **21**, 141–60

Gulkan, P., M. Aschheim, and R. Spence, 2002: *Housing Report Reinforced Concrete Frame Buildings with Masonry Infills, Report* **64**, *World Housing Encyclopedia*, EERI/IAEE,

Gurenko, E., 2004: Introduction, in E. Gurenko (ed.), *Catastrophe Risk and Reinsurance: A Country Risk Management Perspective*, Risk Books, London

Hallegatte, S., 2012: A cost effective solution to reduce disaster losses in developing countries: hydro-meteorological services, early warning, and evacuation, Paper prepared for the Copenhagen Consensus Conference, May 7–8

Hallegatte, S. and P. Dumas, 2009: Can natural disasters have positive consequences? Investigating the role of embodied technical change, *Ecological Economics* **62**, 777–86

Hallegatte, S. and M. Ghil, 2008: Natural disasters impacting a macroeconomic model with endogenous dynamics, *Ecological Economics* **68**, 582–92

Heinz, Center, 2000: *The Hidden Costs of Coastal Hazards: Implications For Risk Assessment and Mitigation*, Island Press, Covello, CA

Kahneman, D., 2011: *Thinking Fast and Slow*, Farrar, Strauss & Giroux, New York

Kahneman, D., P. Slovic, and A. Tversky (eds.), 1982: *Judgment under Uncertainty: Heuristics and Biases*, Cambridge University Press, New York

Kairi Consultants Ltd, 2007: Trade adjustment and poverty in St. Lucia 2006/06, *Volume I: Main Report, Submitted to Caribbean Development Bank*, Trinidad, June

Kozlowski, R. T. and S. B. Mathewson, 1995: Measuring and managing catastrophe risk, *Journal of Actuarial Practice* **3**, 211–41

Kreimer, A. and M. Arnold, 2000: World Bank's role in reducing impacts of disasters, *Natural Hazards Review* **1**, 37–42

Kunreuther, H. and E. Michel-Kerjan, 2004: Policy watch: challenges for terrorism risk insurance in the United States, *Journal of Economic Perspectives* **18**

2011: *At War with the Weather*, MIT Press, Cambridge, MA

Kunreuther, H., R. J. Meyer, and E. Michel-Kerjan, 2013a: Overcoming decision biases to reduce losses from natural catastrophes, in E. Shafir (ed.), *Behavioral Foundations of Policy*, Princeton University Press

Kunreuther, H., A. Onculer, and P. Slovic, 1998: Time insensitivity for protective measures, *Journal of Risk and Uncertainty* **16**, 279–99

Kunreuther, H., M. Pauly, and S. McMorrow, 2013, in press: *Insurance and Behavioral Economics: Improving Decisions in the Most Misunderstood Industry*, Cambridge University Press, New York

Lane, M. (ed.), 2002: *Alternative Risk Strategies*, Risk Waters Group, London

Linnerooth-Bayer, J., R. Mechler, and G. Pflug, 2005: Refocusing disaster aid, *Science* **309**, 1044–6

Loewenstein, G. and J. Elster, 1992: *Choice Overtime*. Russell Sage Foundation, 434pp. (ISBN: 9780871545589)

Louis, E., 2004: Damage and needs assessment sub-committee assessed cost of damages caused by Hurricane Ivan, National Emergency Management Organization, September 7, www.reliefweb.int/rw/RWB.NSF/db900SID/SODA-6EM5KB?OpenDocument

Maffei, J. and P. Bazzurro, 2004: The 2002 Molise, Italy, earthquake, *Earthquake Spectra* **20**, S1–S22

McClelland, G., W. Schulze, and D. Coursey, 1993: Insurance for low-probability hazards: a bimodal response to unlikely events, *Journal of Risk and Uncertainty* **7**, 95–116

Mechler, R., 2003: Macroeconomic impacts of natural disasters, http://info.worldbank.org/etools/docs/library/114715/istanbul03/docs/istanbul03/03mechler3-n%5B1%5D.pdf

2004: Natural disaster risk management and financing disaster losses in developing countries, Verlag für Versicherungswirtschaft, Karlsruhe

2005: Cost-benefit analysis of natural disaster risk management in developing countries, Deutsche Gesellschaft für Technische Zusammenarbeit (GTZ), Eschborn

2009: From risk to resilience. The cost-benefit analysis methodology, in M. Moench, E. Fajber, A. Dixit, E. Caspari, and A. Pokhrel (eds.), *Catalyzing Climate and Disaster Resilience*, ISET, Kathmandu

Michel-Kerjan, E., 2010: Catastrophe economics: the national flood insurance program, *Journal of Economic Perspectives* **24**, 165–86

Michel-Kerjan, E. and H. Kunreuther, 2011: Reforming flood insurance, *Science* **333**, 408–9

Michel-Kerjan, E. and F. Morlaye, 2008: Extreme events, global warming, and insurance-linked securities: how to trigger the "Tipping Point", *Geneva Papers on Risk and Insurance* **33**, 153–76

Michel-Kerjan, E. and P. Slovic, 2010: The Collapse of compassion, *The Huffington Post*, October 7

Michel-Kerjan, E. and J. Volkman Wise, 2011: The risk of ever-growing disaster relief expectations, *Wharton Risk Center Working Paper* **2011–09**

Michel-Kerjan, E., I. Zelenko, V. Cárdenas, D. Turgel, 2011: Catastrophe financing for governments: learning from the

2009–2012 MultiCat Program in Mexico, *OECD Working Papers on Finance, Insurance and Private Pensions* **9**

Michel-Kerjan, E., S. Hochrainer-Stigler, H. Kunreuther, J. Linnerooth-Bayer, R. Mechler, R. Muir-Wood, N. Ranger, P. Vaziri, and M. Young, 2013: Catastrophe risk models for evaluating disaster risk reduction investments in developing countries, *Risk Analysis*, **33**(6), 984–99

Moench, M., S. Hochrainer, R. Mechler, D. Kull, J. Linnerooth-Bayer, U. Patnaik, D. Mustafa, S. Opitz-Stapleton, F. Khan, A. Rehman, A. Dixit, A. Pokhrel, M. Upadhya, S. Chopde, P. Singh, S. Tiwari, M. Borgoyary, S. Bose, S. A. Wajih, A. Srivastav, and G. Singh, 2009: Rethinking the costs and benefits of disaster risk reduction under changing climate conditions, in M. Moench, E. Fajber, A. Dixit, E. Caspari, and A. Pokhrel (eds.), *Catalyzing Climate and Disaster Resilience*, ISET, Kathmandu

Multihazard Mitigation Council (MMC), 2005: *Natural Hazard Mitigation Saves: An Independent Study to Assess the Future Savings from Mitigation Activities, Volume 2 – Study Documentation*, Multihazard Mitigation Council, Washington, DC

Munich, Re, 2013: *Topics geo: Natural catastrophes 2012, Analyses, Assessments Position*, Munich Re, Munich

Oberholzer-Gee, F., 1998: Learning to bear the unbearable: towards and explanation of risk ignorance, Wharton School, University of Pennsylvania, Mimeo

OECD, 2010: *Catastrophe-Linked Securities and Capital Markets*, OECD High Level Advisory Board on Financial Management of Large-Scale Catastrophes, Paris

Penning-Rowsell, E., J. Handmer, and S. Tapsell, 1996: Extreme events and climate change: floods, in T. E. Downing, A. A. Olsthoorn, and R. S. J. Tol (eds.), *Climate Change and Extreme Events: Altered Risk, Socio-Economic Impacts and Policy Responses*, Institute for Environmental Studies and Environmental Change Unit Research Report, Vrije Universiteit and University of Oxford, Amsterdam and Oxford, 97–128

Reliefweb, 2009: *China: Sichuan earthquake one year report*, May, http://reliefweb.int/sites/reliefweb.int/files/reliefweb_pdf/node-308366.pdf

Risk Management Solutions (RMS), 2001: *Event Report: Kocaeli, Turkey Earthquake*

Roy, A. D., 1952: Safety first and the holding of assets, *Econometrica* **20**, 431–49

Schade, C., H. Kunreuther, and P. Koellinger, 2012: Protecting against low-probability disasters: the role of worry, *Journal of Behavioral Decision Making* **25**, 534–43

Silver, C., 2007: *Planning the Megacity: Jakarta in the Twentieth Century*, Routledge, London

Slovic, P., 2000: *The Perception of Risk*, Earthscan, London

Smyth, A. W., G. Altay, G. Deodatis, M. Erdik, G. Franco, P. Gülkan, H. Kunreuther, H. Lu, E. Mete, N. Seeber, and Ö. Yüzügüllü, 2004: Probabilistic benefit-cost analysis for earthquake damage mitigation: evaluating measures for apartment houses in Turkey, *Earthquake Spectra* **20**, 171–203

Subbiah, A., L. Bildan, and R. Narasimhan, 2008: *Background Paper on Assessment of the Economics of Early Warning Systems for Disaster Risk Reduction*, World Bank Group for Disaster Reduction and Recovery, http://gfdrr.org/gfdrr/sites/gfdrr.org/files/New%20Folder/Subbiah_EWS.pdf

Swiss, Re, 2011: Press Release: "Sigma – preliminary estimates for 2011: natural catastrophes and man-made disasters caused economic losses of USD 350 billion and cost insurers USD 108 billion." December 15, Zurich, www.swissre.com/media/news_releases/nr_20111215_preliminary_estimates_2011.html

Teicholz, P., 1998: *Labor Productivity Declines in the Construction Industry: Causes and Remedies*, Stanford University Press

Thaler, R., 1999: Mental accounting matters, *Journal of Behavioral Decision Making* **12**, 183–206

United Nations Development Programme (UNDP), 2004: *Bureau for Crisis Prevention and Recovery. A Global Report: Reducing Disaster Risk, A Challenge for Development*, www.undp.org/cpr/whats_new/rdr_english.pdf

United Nations Environment Programme (UNEP), 2010: *Green Economy: Developing Countries Success Stories*

United Nations International Strategy for Disaster Reduction Secretariat (UNISDR), 2010: *Global Assessment Report on Disaster Risk Reduction*, www.preventionweb.net/english/hyogo/gar/report/index.php?id=9413

United Nations International Strategy for Disaster Reduction (UNISDR)/World Bank, 2011: *Global Assessment Report on Disaster Risk Reduction*, www.preventionweb.net/english/hyogo/gar/report/index.php?id=9413

Viscusi, W. K., 1993: The value of risks to life and health, *Journal of Economic Literature* **31**, 1912–46

Viscusi, K. and J. E. Aldy, 2003: The value of a statistical life: a critical review of market estimates throughout the world, *Journal of Risk and Uncertainty* **27**, 5–76

Wharton–IIASA–RMS, 2009: *The Challenges and Importance of Investing in Cost-Effective Measures for Reducing Losses From Natural Disasters in Emerging Economies. Report to the World Bank*, Wharton School, University of Pennsylvania, July

Wilton Park Conference Report, 2010: Urban risks: moving from humanitarian responses to disaster prevention, **WP1059**, November

World Bank, 2008: *Catastrophe Risk Financing in Developing Countries*, World Bank, Washington, DC

World Bank/UN, 2011: *Global Assessment Report on Disaster Risk Reduction 2011*, World Bank, Washington, DC

World Economic Forum, 2008: *Convergence of Insurance and Capital Markets*, World Economic Forum, Geneva

8.1 Natural Disasters

Alternative Perspective

STÉPHANE HALLEGATTE*

A cost-effective solution to reduce disaster losses in developing countries: hydro-meteorological services, early warning, and evacuation

The analysis presented here estimates that, in Europe, hydro-meteorological information and EWS save several hundreds of lives p.a., avoid between 460 million and 2.7 billion Euros of disaster asset losses p.a., and produce between 3.4 and 34 billion of additional benefits p.a. through the optimization of economic production in weather-sensitive sectors (agriculture, energy, etc.).

The potential for similar benefits in the developing world is not only proportional to population, but also to increased hazard risk due to climate and geography, as well as increased exposure to weather due to the state of infrastructure. And as development proceeds, the asset risks will only grow.

This analysis estimates that the potential benefits from upgrading hydro-meteorological information production and early warning capacity in all developing countries include:

- between US$300 million and 2 billion of avoided asset losses p.a. due to natural disasters
- an average of 23,000 saved lives p.a., equivalent to between US$700 million and 3.5 billion p.a. using the 2012 Copenhagen Consensus guidelines
- between US$3 and 30 billion p.a. of additional economic benefits.

The total benefits would reach between US$4 and 36 billion p.a. Because some of the most expensive components of EWS have already been built (e.g. earth observation satellites, global weather forecasts), this analysis estimates that these benefits can be gained with a comparatively small investment of US$1 billion US p.a., reaching BCRs between 4 and 36.

Reaping these benefits would require adding to existing resources (from existing observation networks to satellites) investments in five domains: (1) local observation systems; (2) local forecast capacity; (3) increased capacity to interpret forecasts, and translate them into warnings; (4) communication tools to distribute and disseminate information, data, and warnings; (5) institutional capacity-building and increased decision-making capacity by the users of warnings and hydro-meteorological information.

This chapter starts by investigating benefits from EWS in Europe, in terms of saved lives and reduced disaster asset losses. It then uses this evaluation to estimate the potential benefits of providing similar services in developing countries. The chapter then assesses the other economic benefits that could be derived from the same hydro-meteorological information that is needed for early warning. These benefits are linked to a better optimization of economic production, and can be estimated in Europe to serve as a basis for an estimate for developing countries. The final two sections try to assess the cost of

* The author thanks Ankur Shah and the team of the 2012 Copenhagen Consensus, including Kasper Thede Anderskov, for their comments and suggestions. The chapter also benefited from discussions with Paul Counet, Maryam Golnaraghi, Robert Husband, Kanta Kumari, Vladimir Tsirkunov, and all participants of the 9th International Forum of Meteorology, organized at the World Meteorological Organization (WMO) headquarters in Geneva, March 22, 2012, by "Météo et Climat."

providing this information, and give a CBA of doing so.

The Appendix on pp. 494–6 provides comments on the Challenge Paper by Howard Kunreuther and Erwann Michel-Kerjan (Chapter 8).

Benefits from early warning and preparation measures

This section will investigate the socio-economic benefits from weather forecasts and early warning in Europe, and use it as a benchmark to assess the benefits that could be generated by similar capabilities in developing countries.

Weather forecasts enable the anticipation of, and preparation for, extreme events such as heatwaves, cold spells, windstorms, thunderstorms, and floods. Corresponding benefits accrue in two broad categories: the protection of persons and assets (prevention) and emergency preparation. Early warnings enable the protection of persons in many ways. Individuals can, for instance, avoid road trips when floods are forecast, they can move vehicles out of flood zones and they can implement mitigation actions (e.g. sandbagging). Organizations and businesses can do the same. For instance, schools and businesses can be closed to avoid unnecessary trips and risks. In case of intense events, evacuation is also possible. Asset protection can also offer large benefits. Preparing a house before a hurricane (e.g. by covering windows) can reduce damage by up to 50 percent (Williams, 2002). A study in Germany (Merz *et al.*, 2004) shows that in the residential sector one-third of the damage concerns the non-fixed contents, i.e. the house contents that could be saved, thanks to an early warning, by being moved out of vulnerable places (e.g. moved to the second floor). This proportion is only 10 percent in the infrastructure sector, but it grows to 60 percent in services and 80 percent in the manufacturing sector.

Illustration on Europe

Asset losses

Thieken *et al.* (2005, 2006, 2007) and Kreibich *et al.* (2005) report on the Elbe and Danube the floods in 2002. They show that 31 percent of the population of the flooded areas implemented preventive measures. These measures included moving goods to the second floor of buildings (applied by more than 50 percent of the inhabitants who implemented prevention measures), moving vehicles outside the flood zone (more than 40 percent), protecting important documents and valuables (more than 30 percent), disconnecting electricity and gas supplies and unplugging electric appliances (more than 25 percent), and installing water pumps (between 2 and 10 percent).

Among the inhabitants who did not implement any measure, 65 percent said that they had been informed too late, and about 20 percent said that they were not at home and could not do anything. For this population, it seems that an earlier warning would have allowed a better preparation and lower subsequent damage.

There is also a large potential for businesses. The International Commission for the Protection of the Rhine (2002) estimated that 50 to 75 percent of flood losses could be avoided thanks to emergency preparation measures. For instance, moving toxic materials and chemicals to safe places prevents local pollution (such as observed after Hurricane Katrina flooded New Orleans). Machines and equipment can also be moved to avoid damage. For instance, large savings are possible in the transport sector, through moving transport equipments (trains, buses, etc.) out of dangerous areas. In addition, anticipating transport dislocation reduces the costs and complications of managing passengers blocked during their journey.

However, this potential is not easy to capture, especially because of the difficulties associated with disseminating the warning: according to Kreibich *et al.* (2007), 45 percent of businesses did not receive the warning directly from the authorities before the 2002 flood in Saxony, even though this warning was transmitted 20 hours before the flood.

In spite of this problem, almost 70 percent of all businesses implemented emergency prevention measures, often thanks to informal contacts that helped disseminate the warning. According to the study, 7 percent of all equipment was fully protected, and 75 percent partially protected, thanks to

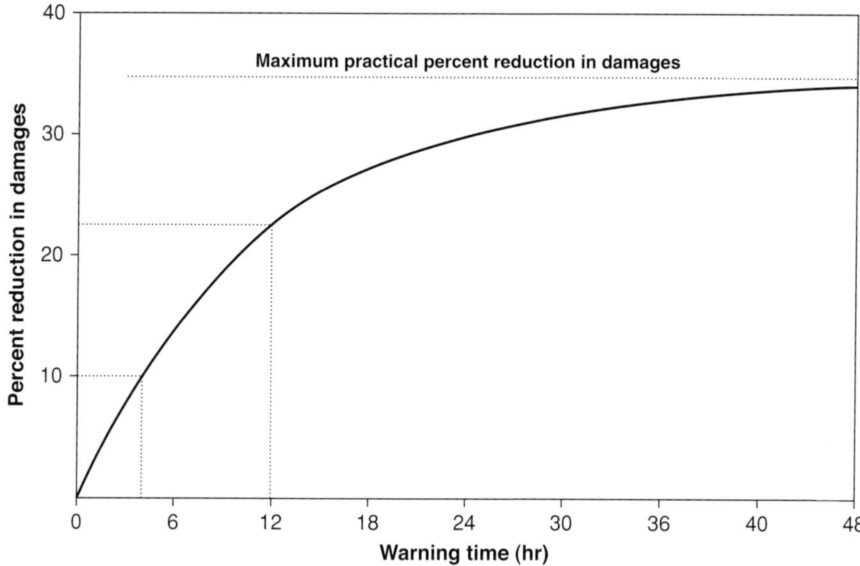

Figure 8.1.1 *Day's curve for damage mitigation as a function of the forecast lead times*

Source: Day *et al.* (1970).

prevention measures. Concerning inventories and production, 10 percent could be fully protected, and 70 percent partially protected. However, Tapsell *et al.* (2008) estimate that the early warning and the subsequent prevention measures reduced flood costs by only 6 percent.

Studies show that the timing of the warning was critical: businesses that protected their equipment or inventories were those that received the warning early enough. This is confirmed by earlier findings by Day (1970), who found that avoided losses grow to near 35 percent when the lead time exceeded 36 hours (see Figure 8.1.1). According to Carsell *et al.* (2004), a warning emitted 48 hours before a flood enables the overall damage to be reduced by more than 50 percent.

Barredo (2009) finds that floods cost on average 4 billion Euros p.a. in Europe (EU27, normalized costs calculated over the 1970–2006 period). Assuming that the warning reduces losses by 10 percent, and if only half of the floods are forecast, the benefits from early warnings could reach 200 million Euros p.a. Using Carsell's estimate, and assuming that 75 percent of the floods can be forecast, the benefits would reach 1,500 million Euros p.a.[1]

According to Swiss Re (2006), storms have cost on average about 2.6 billion euros per year in Europe. If weather forecasts help reduce these losses 10 percent or 50 percent – thanks to the same types of actions than before a flood – the corresponding gains lie between 260 and 1,200 million Euros p.a. For floods and storms, the total could thus lie between 460 million and 2.7 billion Euros p.a. These gains represent between 0.003 percent and 0.017 percent of European GDP.

Human losses

It is more difficult to produce an economic estimate for individual safety. There are many weather-related threats to safety in Europe, such as floods (e.g. le Gars in France in 2002; Lower Silesia in 2005), winter storms (e.g. the storms Lothar and Martin in Franc in 1999; Kyrill in France and Germany in 2011), heatwaves (e.g. the summer of 2003) and cold spells (e.g. 1984–1985 in France;

[1] We assume here that false alarms have no cost, which is not the case, especially in case of large-scale evacuations.

2001 in Hungary; 2010 in Poland), and avalanches (e.g. in les Orres in France in 1998).

In Europe, severe winter storms have a return period of about 10 years and often lead to dozens of casualties. The 2003 heatwave caused about 70,000 deaths in Europe, and the 2006 one led to about 2,000 deaths. Avalanches cause on average thirty-two deaths p.a. in France, for 4.5 million ski tourists.[2]

It is difficult to assess how many lives prevention and early warning save each year, even though local actors consider these tools critical to ensure population safety. Examples of countries where early warning is considered seriously and where prevention emergency actions are well organized (e.g. Cuba) show that casualties can approach zero, apart from really exceptional events.

Other scenarios also need to be considered, such as technological catastrophes (accidents in a chemical or a nuclear plant). In these cases, the capacity to forecast winds, and thus the trajectory of the contamination cloud, can save hundreds of lives. The need to predict the trajectory of radioactive leaks was illustrated in Japan by the March 2011 Fukushima nuclear accident. Even though the likelihood of using this capacity is fortunately very small, the damage avoided can be so large that this possibility needs to be accounted for in the social value of forecast capabilities.

Even in non-extreme situations, hydro-meteorological information plays a large safety role in many outdoor activities (e.g. sailing, hiking, skiing). Specialized services help thousands of people avoid being surprised by a storm at sea. These services have a large audience and probably help avoid hundreds of accidents each year.

Even more important, this information is used for maritime and air traffic.[3] Indeed, these operations depend on detailed weather information and, in the absence of meteorological information it is unlikely that passenger air travel would be safe enough to be commercially viable in its current form.

Another component of forecast value is the ability to prepare the emergency services before an event occurs. During the few hours before an intense weather event much can be done to increase the efficiency of the emergency services. In 2002 during the floods in the Gard, for instance, twenty-two out of the twenty-six French helicopters able to conduct rescue airlifts were pre-positioned in the flood area, thanks to the forecasts. According to local emergency services, this pre-positioning saved about 100 lives, compared with a situation in which it would have taken hours to move helicopters to the affected areas.

It is important to stress that the benefits from forecasts depend largely, and non-linearly, on their accuracy and on the trust of the population. And threshold effects are important. For instance, if it were possible to predict exactly flash-floods, including their location, it would be possible to evacuate the at-risk areas, and reduce human losses to zero without any expensive investment in flood protection. But the decision to evacuate cannot be made if the probability of false alarm is too high (or if the warning area is too large): as, after a few unnecessary evacuations, the trust in the warning system is likely to disappear, and the system becomes useless. This problem is illustrated by the case of New Orleans, which had been unnecessarily evacuated twice (for Hurricanes George in 1998 and Ivan in 2004), making it more difficult to convince inhabitants to leave before Hurricane Katrina. If the risk of false alarm becomes low enough to create and maintain trust and allow for significant prevention measures before disasters, a limited improvement in forecast accuracy can thus lead to a large increase in societal benefits. Trust should also be built through openness and communication from specialists to the public, to explain the limits of forecasts and warning.

Taking into account these numbers, one can assume that hydro-meteorological information saves at least 200 lives p.a. in Europe, which is an extremely conservative estimate. A more likely estimate is about 800 lives.

Using the Copenhagen Consensus value of a human life (i.e. $1,000 and $5,000 DALYs) and the

[2] Dossier d'information "Avalanche" du Ministère de l'Aménagement du Territoire et de l'Environnement, 2000, www.prim.net.fr.

[3] According to the "Bureau Enquête Accident", 7.5 percent of plane accidents have meteorological causes, www.bea-fr.org/etudes/stat9798/stats1997-1998.htm.

global average life expectancy (70 years according to World Bank data in 2009), the value of a life saved at mid-life is between US$35,000 and US$175,000 (i.e. between 26,600 and 133,000 Euros). With these numbers, the annual benefits of EWS in Europe can be estimated between 5 million Euros (200 lives saved, $1,000 DALYs) and 110 million Euros (800 lives saved, $5000 DALYs).

Using standard values of the "statistical value of a human life" from the *Boiteux Report* on the transport sector in France,[4] i.e. 1 million Euros per life, the corresponding benefits can be estimated at between 200 and 800 million Euros p.a.[5]

Potential impact in developing countries

Adding up asset and human losses – using the Copenhagen Consensus numbers only – leads to an estimate of the annual benefits between 470 million and 2.8 billion Euros p.a. from early warning in Europe.

These estimates are useful for our analysis because they provide an illustration of how much can be gained at the global level with current technologies and state-of-the-art modeling and observation systems. Of course, part of the potential benefits from early warning are already realized in the world (especially in developed countries such as Europe, the United States, and Japan). The questions are thus (1) how much of these benefits are already captured at global scale? (2) How much would it cost to capture the full benefit potential?

It is difficult to estimate the existing availability of early warning. Some countries have introduced efficient systems in recent decades (e.g. Bangladesh and its hurricane early warning system). But in other places, the basic observation systems are simply not in place to allow for implementing early warning.

Several institutions (including the WMO, Golnaraghi, 2012) review the ability of national hydro-meteorological services to fulfill their missions. Subbiah *et al.* (2008) distinguish four groups of countries. *Group 1* includes countries with no basic hydro-meteorological services, where the benefits are likely to be close to zero; we assume that only 10 percent of potential benefits are already realized in these countries. *Group 2* includes countries where services exist but are not fully operational; we will assume that these countries realize only 20 percent of the benefits achieved in Europe. *Group 3* includes countries with well-functioning services but with gaps in the chain from data production to EWS; there, we assume that only 50 percent of European benefits are achieved. *Group 4* includes countries where services and EWS are comparable to European ones, and where 100 percent of European-type benefits are achieved.

There is no automatic relationship between these groups and country incomes, but richer countries are more likely to have functioning systems. As a consequence, we will assume that Group 1–4 can be mapped to low-income, low-middle, high-middle, and high-income countries.

Avoided asset losses

Focusing first on asset losses, we assume that all countries face the same level of risk, and that early warning can provide the same relative benefits in terms of avoided disaster losses. In other terms, an-European-like EWS would allow us to reduce disaster-related asset losses in all countries by between 0.003 and 0.017 percent of their GDP. This is conservative, for instance because developing countries are affected by different hazards than industrialized countries (e.g. tropical storms).

The share of losses actually avoided is assumed to depend on the type of country: 10 percent of these benefits in low-income countries; 20 percent in LMIC, 50 percent in upper-middle income, and 100 percent in high-income countries. The difference between the European potential and the share actually avoided provides an estimate of the additional benefits that could be achieved if hydro-meteorological services were upgraded to European standards (see Table 8.1.1).

[4] (Boiteux, 2005).

[5] Another estimate is provided by Viscusi and Aldy (2003), who point out that the VoL for US labor market studies lies within a range of $4 million to $9 million. In developing countries the VoL presented in Viscusi and Aldy varies from $750,000 in South Korea to $4.1 million in India (see Viscusi and Aldy, 2003, Table 4: 27–8).

Table 8.1.1 Potential benefits from avoided asset losses thanks to early warning (with European-standard hydro-meteorological services), and share of these benefits actually realized with current services

	GDP (US$ million)	Potential (European-like) benefits		Ratio of current versus potential benefits (%)	Estimation of actual benefits		Benefits from improved services	
		Low estimate	Likely estimate		Low estimate	Likely estimate	Low estimate	Likely estimate
Low-income	413,000	12	69	10	1	7	11	62
LMIC	4,300,000	122	714	20	24	143	97	572
Upper-middle-income	15,300,000	433	2,542	50	217	1,271	217	1,271
High-income	43,000,000	1,217	7,145	100	1,217	7,145	–	–
Total	63,013 000	1,784	10,470		1,459	8,565	*324*	*1,904*

This estimation suggests thus that generalizing the quality of services and EWS that can be found in developed countries could yield benefits ***in terms of avoided asset losses*** **between US$300 million and 2 billion p.a. in developing countries**, thanks to lower disaster losses.

These values are supposed to increase with economic growth. Some analyses have concluded that disaster-losses' growth is slower than wealth growth (Skidmore and Toya, 2007; Mendelsohn *et al.*, 2012). But in many countries, income growth has also led to increased migrations and investments in at-risk areas, and a simple model shows that this trend may dominate the effect of risk-reduction measures (Hallegatte, 2011, 2012a).

This assessment is probably an underestimation because it does not take into account indirect losses from natural disasters – i.e. the loss in output that results from the loss in assets (see Hallegatte and Przyluski, 2010, on why and how to measure indirect losses). For large-scale disasters, indirect losses can be of the same order of magnitude than direct losses (e.g. Tierney, 1997; Hallegatte, 2008).

This assessment also does not account for the possibility that reduced disaster losses can lead to accelerated economic growth (Hallegatte, 2012b). This is an important assumption, since disasters can have long-lasting consequences on child development (Alderman *et al.*, 2006; Santos, 2007), with large consequences for labor productivity and thus for growth and welfare. Moreover, disasters can lead to significant migrations (e.g. Landry *et al.*, 2007 on Hurricane Katrina in New Orleans). If disasters lead to outmigration, there will be consequences for economic growth, especially if – as suggested by the Katrina case (see Zissimopoulos and Karoly, 2007) – high-skilled, high-productivity workers are more able to migrate than the average population. Strobl (2011) investigates this issue through the impact of hurricane landfall on county-level growth in the United States. He finds that economic growth is reduced on average by 0.79 percent points in countries affected by a hurricane landfall, and increased by only 0.22 percent points the following year, suggesting the existence of long-lasting consequences.

Disaster can also create poverty traps, by destroying assets and wiping out savings. These impacts can push households into situations where productivity is reduced, making it impossible for them to rebuild their savings and assets and return to pre-disaster income levels (Dercon, 2004, 2005; Carter *et al.*, 2007; Lopez and Servén, 2009; Van den Berg, 2010). These poverty traps at the micro-level could even lead to macro-level poverty traps if the investment capacities in a region are insufficient to cope with reconstruction needs (Hallegatte *et al.*, 2007; Hallegatte and Dumas, 2008).

Human losses

In terms of life saved, the calculation is more difficult, because the lower quality of housing and

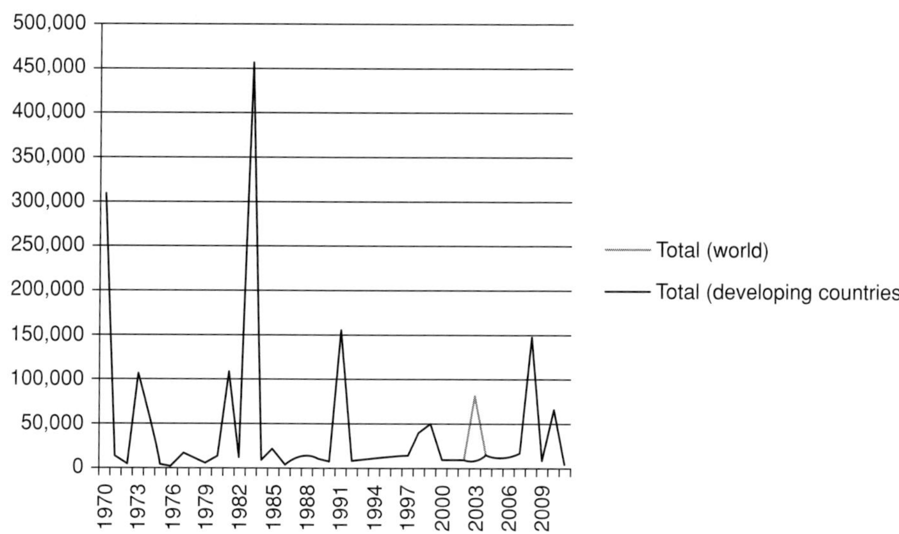

Figure 8.1.2 *Number of people reported killed by weather-related natural disasters (1975–2011), in developing countries and at the world level*

Note: There is no significant trend in these series.
Source: Data from EM-DAT: The OFDA/CRED International Disaster Database.

infrastructure (including coastal and river flood protection) in developing countries means that the role of early warning is even more important than in developed countries.

According to the OFCA/CRED EM-DAT database, extreme weather-related events killed on average 43,000 persons p.a. in developing countries between 1970 and 2011, and there is no visible trend in this figure (see Figure 8.1.2). Since the total population in 2011 in developing countries was approximately 5.7 billion, there is an annual death probability of 7.5 per million due to weather events.

In developed countries, the death toll is 2,500 persons p.a. (mostly from heatwaves). The total population in developed countries is approximately 1.1 billion, and the annual death probability is 2.2 per million inhabitants. The ratio of the death probability in developing countries to the death probability in developed countries is thus 3.4.

This difference is not due only to early warning: housing and infrastructure quality, disaster protection (dikes, drainage systems, etc.) are also important. Differences in climate (e.g. exposure to tropical storms) also make a difference. But early warning plays a huge role, as is illustrated by the case of Bangladesh and coastal floods. Paul (2009) reports on how Hurricane Sidr caused many fewer deaths (about 3,400 deaths in 2007) than other similar storms (such as Cyclone Gorky that killed more than 140,000 people in 1991). The main explanation is the good forecast of the storm, which allowed a warning to be issued early, and the early warning and shelter systems.

According to Paul (2009):

> The Cyclone Preparedness Program (CCP) was established in 1972 and was charged with developing effective cyclone preparedness measures for residents of the Bangladesh coastal areas (Khan and Rahman, 2007). It was jointly set up by the Bangladesh Ministry of Disaster Management and Relief (MDMR) and the Bangladesh Red Crescent Society (BDRCS). CPP activities are centered around three infrastructures: a cyclone early warning system, public cyclone shelters for pre-disaster evacuation, and shelters to provide protection for cattle during storm surges.

The CCP has been reinforced since cyclone Gorky in 1991, with better forecast and warning capacities, and twice as many volunteers involved in the diffusion of warnings and evacuation orders. There is little high technology in the EWS:

> Many Red Crescent volunteers, local government officials, workers from NGOs, and some villagers immediately joined the CCP volunteers. All traveled to threatened communities and disseminated cyclone warning and evacuation orders via megaphones, handheld bullhorns, bicycle-mounted loudspeakers, and house-to-house contacts. They also evacuated people in the path of the cyclone into cyclone shelters. In addition, fishing boats and trawlers over the North Bay of Bengal were instructed to immediately return to inland river ports.

This simple low-technology system saved many lives, in spite of the lack of maintenance of shelters, with only about 60 percent of them being usable. According to field data, more than 85 percent of households were aware of the storm warning and evacuation order in 2007 (versus 60 percent for Cyclone Gorky in 1991), and 40 percent of potentially affected households evacuated (i.e. 3.2 million out of 8 million coastal residents).

It is difficult to generalize the case of Bangladesh at a global scale. Challenges to early warning and evacuation are different depending on the country (e.g. on the existence of transport infrastructure) and on the hazards (e.g. a storm is easier to forecast than the heavy precipitation responsible for the deadly floods in Mumbai in 2005). Here, we will assume that generalizing the early warning and evacuation systems available in developed countries would make the death probability decrease from 7.5 per million to 4 per million (approximately a 50 percent reduction), making it still twice as large as in developed countries.

The number of lives saved every year (with the current population) would be 23,000 deaths p.a. Assuming that each death is equivalent to 30 lost years, and taking the $1,000 and $5,000 values for DALYs, we obtain an annual benefit of US$700 million p.a. or US$3.5 billion p.a. (increasing with population and economic growth). This estimate is conservative, as we do not account for morbidity (injuries and disaster-caused illness), which might play a huge role (according to EM-DAT, more than 1 million persons were injured by weather-related natural disasters between 1988 and 2007, most of them in Asia), and we assume that growth in population and income does not translate into more disaster-related death (which is optimistic, see for instance Kellenberg and Mobarak, 2008).

Overall, the annual benefits of improved hydro-meteorological services and EWS in terms of avoided human losses can thus be estimated at **between US$700 million and 3.5 billion USD p.a.** growing with population and economic growth. Note that this value is highly dependent on the value used for saved lives, and that the $1,000 and $5,000 values used here for DALYs are small, at least for some of the countries that are included in this analysis.

Economic benefits from hydro-meteorological information

Improving services would not only allow for better EWS. In practice, it would also produce economic benefits, in the form of services for industries and businesses and for households and individuals, even in normal conditions (i.e. during non-dangerous times).

In the agriculture sector, weather forecasts are used for planning purposes, e.g. to decide the dates of planting or fertilizer application. A few studies have assessed the productivity gains from short- to medium-term weather forecasts. For instance, Wilks and Wolfe (1998) investigated the use of forecasts to optimize lettuce production in the state of New York, and they found a $900–$1,000 gain per ha and p.a. – i.e. a 10 percent increase in productivity.

In the energy sector, weather forecasts are used to anticipate electricity demand, allowing regions to maximize the use of lower-cost but slowly adjusting production units (e.g. nuclear, coal, or solid biomass) and reduce as much as possible the use of higher-cost production units. But weather forecasts can also be used to manage production. For instance, Roulston *et al.* (2003) estimate the value of weather information to optimize wind power production; they find a doubling in profits thanks to 1- and 2-day forecasts.

In transport, weather forecasts are used to optimize air traffic and ship routes, and to plan road salting and other preventive actions. A study by Leigh (1995) estimates benefits from weather information at Sydney Airport. He finds a benefit of AU$6.9 million p.a., i.e. about US$5 million. In the United Kingdom improved meteorological information services resulted in a 20–25 percent decrease in the use of road salt (Thornes, 1990, cited in Leviäkangas *et al.*, 2007). In Croatia, the socio-economic benefit of hydro-ometeorological information related to the reduced number of accidents was estimated to be 4.3–8.7 million Euros p.a. (Leviäkangas *et al.*, 2007).

In the construction sector, weather forecasts are used to optimize the use of labor resources, and to plan some temperature- or wind-sensitive operations. This avoids accidents (e.g. crane accidents due to high wind) and improves building quality (e.g. by avoiding pouring concrete in very low temperatures).

In the tourism and health sector, weather is a predictor of future activities, useful to plan labor resources and inputs (e.g. anticipating the number of visitors in a tourist site, or the number of customers at a restaurant).

These few examples show a significant impact of weather information on productivity.[6] The use of such forecasts is growing world-wide, with many new businesses specialized in helping other industries to take this information into account. To estimate the orders of magnitude at stake, one can start from the economic value added in the world each year in the sectors considered as sensitive to weather conditions: agriculture: US$2,000 billion; mining and energy: US$7,000 billion; construction: US$3,200 billion; transport: US$4,300 billion. Summing these numbers suggests that these sectors create more than US$ 16,000 billion p.a. of added value – i.e. about 25 percent of world GDP.

Hydro-meteorological information also goes beyond weather forecasts: observations and long data series are useful to design infrastructure, building, or even urban plans. In many countries, new construction is prohibited in flood-prone areas (e.g. the 100-year flood plain in France), but the identification of such zones can be made impossible by the absence of appropriate data (see an illustration on Casablanca and Alexandria in World Bank, 2011). Hydro-meteorological information can also be used to monitor the environment over the long term, detect potentially harmful changes, and anticipate response measures (e.g. detecting as early as possible a change in rainfall to adjust drainage infrastructure, anticipating the arrival of a new pest in the agriculture sector).

Assuming that weather forecasts lead to value-added gains between 0.1 and 1 percent in weather-sensitive sectors, these gains would be approximately equal to between 0.025 and 0.0025 percent of GDP. These estimates are small compared with the sectoral case studies presented above. They are also small compared with estimates from ISDR *et al.* (2008), which propose estimates for seven countries – Albania, Bosnia-Herzegovina, Macedonia, Moldova, Serbia, and Montenegro. In these countries, an economic analysis (carried out by the Technical Research Centre of Finland (VTT), based on available data and detailed surveys in each of the countries) estimated benefits from hydro-meteorological services between 0.09 percent (in Croatia) and 0.35 percent (in Moldova). Our numbers can thus be considered as conservative.

They are also conservative because they do not account for the "small" services that hydro-meteorological information provides to each of us in our daily life. Measuring the value of the private use of forecasts is difficult. It means measuring the willingness of users to pay for the service they get from such information. Knowing if one can go for a picnic without risking heavy rain has a value; being able to decide a few hours in advance if a dinner can be organized outside or inside has a value; deciding whether to take an umbrella when leaving for work in the morning also has a value. Each of

[6] It is important to acknowledge the risk of bias in the literature, published studies being those that find a significant impact of weather information on economic activity. To my knowledge, no paper has been published on *a lack* of such impact.

Table 8.1.2 Potential economic benefits from improved hydro-meteorological services, and share of these benefits actually realized with current services

	GDP (US$ million)	Potential (European-like) benefits		Ratio of current versus potential benefits (%)	Estimation of actual benefits		Benefits from improved services	
		Low estimate	Likely estimate		Low estimate	Likely estimate	Low estimate	Likely estimate
Low-income	413,000	103	1,033	10	10	103	93	929
LMIC	4,300,000	1,075	10,750	20	215	2,150	860	8,600
Upper-middle-income	15,300,000	3,825	38,250	50	1,913	19,125	1,913	19,125
High-income	43,000,000	10,750	107,500	100	10,750	107,500	–	–
Total	63,013,000	15,753	157,533		12,888	128,878	*2,865*	*28,654*

Note: These benefits exclude the benefits from early warning, presented in Table 8.1.1.

these values remains small, but these decisions happen all the time and millions of people are making them; the aggregated value may thus be significant. Lazo *et al.* (2009) conducted a survey of US households to estimate their WTP for the weather information that is currently provided to them, and for potential improvement of this information. The survey focused on normal conditions, and excluded extreme events and safety aspects from the analysis, so there is no double-counting with the previous section. The survey arrived at a median estimate of US$ 280 p.a. and per household, with more than 80 percent of households ready to pay more than US$ 30. Assuming that each European household is ready to pay at least 20 Euros p.a., again a conservative estimate, the societal benefit from weather information would be around 4 billion Euros p.a. With a value of 80 Euros, the estimate reaches 15 billion Euros p.a.

For Europe, it is thus a very conservative estimate to assume that the value of hydro-meteorological information lies between 3.4 and 34 billion Euros p.a. On a global scale, a similarly conservative estimate is that the potential benefits would be between US$16 billion and 160 billion p.a.

As with risk mitigation, part of these benefits has already been realized. Here, we want to assess the additional benefits if the services provided in developed countries were generalized. To do so, we use the same assumption as for risk mitigation, assuming that 10 percent of these benefits are realized in low-income countries, 20 percent in LMICs, 50 percent in upper-middle income, and 100 percent in high-income countries (see Table 8.1.2).

The result is that a generalization of hydro-meteorological services at high-income country levels would generate additional economic benefits ranging between US$3 and 30 billion. This estimate is an underestimation because it does not account for the heavier vulnerability of poor-country economies on environmental stress and weather extreme events.

It is also an underestimation because it does not account for health impacts, and for the fact that higher productivity in agriculture would increase food security, with health and economic benefits.

In that case, therefore, there are probably economic benefits that are even larger than the direct impact of early warning. Economic benefits in normal conditions from hydro-meteorological information developed for disaster mitigation would yield **US$3–30 billion p.a.**

How to improve early warning, and at what cost?

Improving hydro-meteorological services and EWS implies multiple components. Some of the required measures are investments; some are linked to operational expenses and require sustainable funding. Others are linked to the institutional setting and to the training of the producers and of the users of such information.

One important aspect of the production of such information is that all countries do not need to invest in all the components of the forecast chain. Remote-sensing information is provided by satellites that are launched and financed by developed countries (e.g. Meteosat 5 on Africa, operated by EUMETSAT; the Metop system, also operated by EUMETSAT; NOAA 19, financed by the US government). Global modeling is also carried out regularly by many services in the world (e.g. most European services such as Meteo-France and the Met Office, the European Centre for Medium Range Weather Forecasts (ECMWF), US institutions like the National Oceanic and Atmospheric Administration (NOAA)). And even observation can be rationalized thanks to regional integration: a radar network is much less expensive if designed on a regional rather than on a national scale.

What is really needed in developing countries are thus five components:

(1) The local *observation system* – based on ground, in-situ observations, for weather data (e.g. temperature, precipitation), hydrological data (runoff data), topological data (e.g. an elevation database to link runoff forecast with flood extension), and socio-economic data (e.g. population density and transportation capacity to decide on evacuation).
(2) *Forecasting capacity* – i.e. the translation of low-resolution model forecasts into high-resolution forecasts, using statistical downscaling and correction or additional models.
(3) *Interpretation capacity* – to translate model output into actual forecast and warnings, taking into account known model bias and specific local conditions that models cannot integrate.
(4) *Communication tools* – to make sure that the alert reaches the individuals in charge of implementing prevention measures (including the public who are supposed to evacuate), and evacuation and emergency plans.
(5) *Users' decision-making capacities* – to make sure that warnings are actually used (including for evacuation).

The ability to improve forecast capacity, and to provide forecasts that are appropriate and used on the ground, will depend on the local scientific "capacity," including the existence of university and research programs. An example of how capacity can be improved is provided by the program African Monsoon Multi-Disciplinary Analysis (AMMA),[7] an international research program that resulted in (1) better observation systems in Africa; (2) the creation of local research teams on hydrometeorology, health, and agriculture; (3) the creation of new degrees in relevant disciplines in African universities.

Finally, the ability to implement prevention measures will depend on local infrastructure and capacity. Lack of transport capacity (when public transportation is not accessible and poor households do not have individual transport vehicles) can make the entire system less efficient. Hard-protection to windows and cofferdams can be extremely efficient to reduce wind or flood damages to houses and cost only a few dozen US$. They may nevertheless be too expensive to be broadly available in some regions.

The five categories of action may also be designed very differently depending on the local context. For instance, communication through TV, radio, and cell phones can be extremely efficient, but in some countries low-tech options (such as the bicycle-mounted loudspeakers used in Bangladesh) can be a useful complement. When trust does not exist between the population and forecast producers, local contact points (such as Red Cross volunteers) can help in building it.

Here, we focus on the cost of the five elements listed above, without consideration for the more general capacity in the country, assuming that it will not be a constraint to evacuation efficiency (keeping in mind that we still assume that even with early warning and evacuation systems, the death ratio will be twice as large in developing countries as in developed countries, because of the lower building quality and transportation infrastructures).

The cost of strengthening hydro-meteorological service depends on the size of the country, and of

[7] www.amma-international.org.

the context.[8] The range can be from a few million US$ to hundreds of millions. National hydrometeorological services can be as small as five–eight forecasters converting the results of global forecasting centers into national alerts and forecasts supported by very limited infrastructure in the country. In this case the operating costs can be comparable to or exceed the investment costs of setting up the system. This is not a typical case. Usually, in developing countries there are many dozens (or several hundred) low-paid staff dealing with extensive but dilapidated infrastructure (buildings, observation sites, instruments, etc.).

In Russia, the first hydro-meteorological project (WB) invested in was over US$172 million, the second (currently under preparation) is estimated at US$141 million. This is a fraction of the total needs (and real costs). In Mexico, the World Bank is planning to invest US$109 million. Investments in Poland and Turkey have been some US$62 million and 26 million. According to an analysis on South Eastern Europe (ISDR *et al.*, 2008), the estimated financing needed to strengthen national services in seven countries, without regional cooperation and coordination, would be around 90.3 million Euros. With deeper cooperation, the cost is around 63.2 million Euros. This cost includes investment for in-situ measurement, upper-air sounding, radars, communication, and dissemination of data, information, forecasts and warnings. It includes also maintenance over a five-year period.

Moreover, as demonstrated by the case of Bangladesh, forecast capacity is not sufficient and needs to be complemented with decision-making systems to translate a forecast into a warning, and communication tools (possibly with volunteers on the ground to diffuse the evacuation orders).

To be conservative, we will thus assume that the cost of providing appropriate early warning and evacuation orders in developing countries would be equal to about $50 million per country over a five-year period (including maintenance and operational costs). For a set of eighty developing countries, including most of the world population, the cost would be equal to $4 billion over five years, i.e. an annual cost of $800 million p.a.

It is important for hydro-meteorological services to be well connected to their users to ensure that they produce the information that is required for early warning and evacuation (and for operational management). Users of information also need to know how to use it, especially for forecasts that are always uncertain. Deciding when to evacuate a flood-prone area necessitates an analysis of the cost of a false alarm (including the loss of confidence, which can lead the population not to evacuate at the next alert), the cost of missing a dangerous flood, and the probability of error. The easiest way to achieve this is to include hydro-meteorological services in the government services that will use the information and decide on evacuation and preparation measures (e.g. the Ministry of Interior in most countries).

Producing such information and making decisions on when to evacuate and invest in preparation measures requires specific skills that are not always available in developing countries. In addition to investments in hydro-meteorological and risk-management services themselves, it is thus necessary to invest in population skills, for instance through the creation of a specific university program that will train students in information production, risk-management, and decision-making. Training about twenty individuals p.a. in eighty countries would represent 1,600 persons p.a. and would cost less than US$200 million p.a.

Conclusions

This analysis demonstrates the large potential of investments in hydro-meteorological services and early warning and evacuation schemes to reduce the human and economic losses due to natural disasters. It also stresses the existence of significant other socio-economic benefits, which can potentially exceed the benefits in terms of disaster-risk reduction.

A ballpark estimate of how much it would cost the improvement of hydro-meteorological and warning services to make it possible to implement EWS in developing countries is thus lower than **$1 billion a year. With benefits in terms of disaster-risk reduction between US$1 and 5.5 billion p.a.,**

[8] Invaluable information has been provided by Vladimir Vtsirkunov, from World Bank/GFDRR.

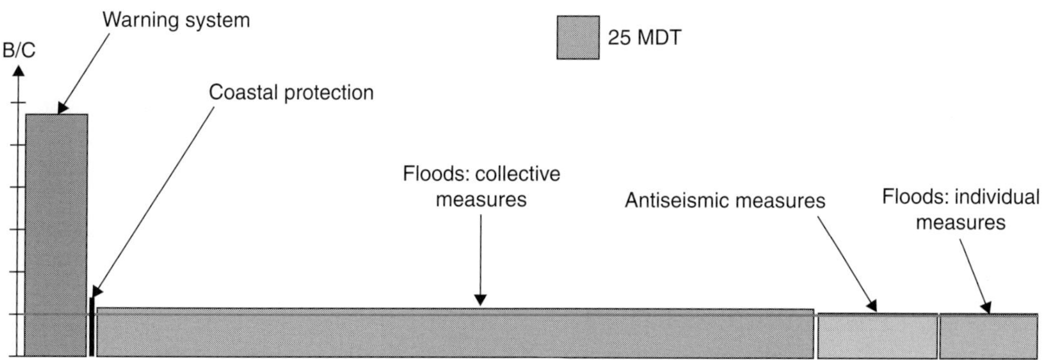

Figure 8.1.3 *BCRs of various risk-mitigation measures in Tunis*

Note: 1 MDT is 1 million Tunisian Dinar (1 DT is worth approximately US$0.66).
Source: World Bank (2011).

and other economic benefits between US$3 and 30 billion, we reach BCRs between 4 and 35 with co-benefits.

Since this analysis compares annual investment and spending to annual benefits, it does not depend on the discount rate. There might however be a several-year delay between an increase in spending and the corresponding increase in benefits. But such a delay should not change the results of the analysis proposed here in a qualitative manner (Table 8.1.3).

This analysis has been done on a global scale, using very simple assumptions that are only capable of providing orders of magnitude. Before real investments are made, local and context-specific analyses are necessary, on a project scale. In some regions, for instance, the main risk is linked to heavy precipitation, and meteorological radars will be extremely useful to provide warning with a lead-time of a few hours. Such radars will be much less necessary where risks are not related to heavy precipitation but (say) to droughts or temperature extremes.

Examples of local-scale case studies

A few project-scale cost-benefits have been made at a local scale, and their results support the global analysis presented here. Subbiah *et al.* (2008) provide, for instance, numbers for Bangladesh, India, Indonesia, Philippines, Sri Lanka, Thailand, and Vietnam. They find that out of the nine case studies they investigate BCRs range from 0.93 to more than 500. Only one project has a BCR below 1. The World Bank conducted an analysis of risk management in Alexandria, Casablanca, and Tunis, and provided cost-benefit analyses of multiple risk-mitigating measures (including seismic risks). In all cases, implementing a warning system was considered as the most (or one of the most) cost-effective measure. In Tunis, for instance, the BCR of such a measure exceeded 5, while hard protection and building retrofit had BCRs between 1 and 2 (see Figure 8.1.3).

Even though the implementation would need to be done country by country – with detailed analyses of each investment – one can make a strong case for **increased investment (and international attention) on EWS to save lives and improve economic efficiency.**

Of course, the benefits from EWS would be maximized if they were designed in conjunction with other disaster-risk management policies and investments, such as those proposed and evaluated in Mechler (2005) or Chapter 8 (Kunreuther and Michel-Kerjan, 2012).

Indeed, there is no single measure that can provide full protection against all natural hazards. The highest and strongest dikes have a failure probability, and risk can never be fully cancelled by any measure and at any cost. Moreover, some approaches are more efficient to cope with frequent, low-intensity events while others are best in managing rare, high-intensity events. For instance, it is

Table 8.1.3 Summary of benefits from and costs of upgraded hydro-meteorological services

Type of benefits	Annual benefits (US$ million) Minimum	Annual benefits (US$ million) Maximum	Annual cost (US$ million)	BCR Minimum	BCR Maximum
Reduced asset losses from disasters	300	2,000	1,000	4	35
Reduced human losses from disasters	700	3,500			
Other economic benefits	3,000	30,000			
Total	4,000	35,500			

easy to avoid the frequent floods that occur in Mumbai almost every year through improvements in the drainage system. But it is almost impossible to prevent floods in the case of exceptional rainfall as in July 2005 (Ranger *et al.*, 2011). To cope with such exceptional events, the early warning and evacuation systems proposed in this chapter can play a very efficient role. But early warning cannot do anything against frequent events: entire parts of Mumbai cannot be evacuated several times every year.

This is why risk management should be done through a policy mix, with several policies targeting different return periods, as suggested in Figure 8.1.4. As stated in Hallegatte and Przyluski (2010), some of these policies will target direct disaster impacts and try to minimize them (DRR actions), while others will target indirect disaster impacts and try to increase resilience (resilience-building actions).

To minimize the cost of risk management, and maximize its benefits, the different policies of the mix should be designed together. With very strong physical protection – as in the Netherlands – there is no need for an evacuation system, an insurance scheme, or specific building norms against floods. Where financial constraints make such protection unaffordable – as in Bangladesh – it is even more critical to implement an efficient early warning and evacuation scheme.

There is thus no "optimal" risk-management policy mix, and different approaches are possible. Rich countries may decide to focus on physical protection, while poor countries may prefer to invest in early warning and evacuation. Depending on which approach is selected, the at-risk areas may be affected more or less often, with more or less damage. As seen with Hurricane Katrina, over-reliance on physical protection and the absence of evacuation can lead to large-scale disasters.

Importantly, a change in one component of the risk management policy mix may require changes in the others. For instance, if the protection level provided by physical infrastructure is reduced by climate change or subsidence, the criteria used to decide when to evacuate at-risk areas may have to be revised; and the financial viability of insurance schemes may be threatened.

In practice, however, developing an integrated risk management strategy is made extremely difficult by institutional fragmentation and coordination issues. Developing such a risk-management package would require in most countries a concerted effort by the ministry in charge of water and coastal management (for the dikes and drainage system), the ministry in charge of land use and urbanization and various local authorities (for land use planning), the Ministry of Interior (often in charge of warning, evacuation, and crisis management), the Ministry of Finance (for insurance and emergency finance), and the Ministry of Foreign Affairs (if external support in case of disasters is concerned). Strong efforts need to be devoted to organizing a dialog of these actors in a constructive way, to make the best use of each DRR action that can proposed – from the improved building norms of Kunreuther and Michel-Kerjan in Chapter 8 to the hydro-meteorological information and EWS proposed here.

Appendix

The proposals made by Kunreuther and Michel-Kerjan in Chapter 8 appear realistic and well

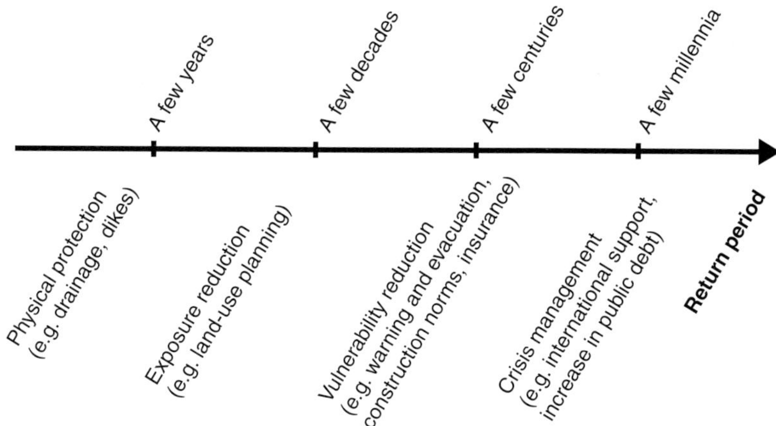

Figure 8.1.4 *Example of risk-management policy mix*

Note: Physical protection avoids frequent events; land use planning limits population and asset exposure if protection is overtopped; early warning, evacuation, and insurance reduce vulnerability, increase resilience, and help affected regions rebound; crisis management and international solidarity help cope with the largest events.

estimated, provided that one agrees on the SVHL that is used in the analysis and follows the Copenhagen Consensus framework.

This is the topic of my first comment. Chapter 8 uses the same SVHL for the different options, including the strengthening of schools and the building of dikes. It could have been possible also to account for the "special case" of schools. First, it would be receivable to attribute a higher value of human life when children are concerned, because they are younger, and for schools, because they represent a public service. France for instance, uses a higher value of a human life in public transportation (1.5 million Euros), than in individual transportation (1 million Euros) (see Boiteux, 2005). This difference is supposed to represent the higher WTP for safety in public transport than in cars (and the difference between chosen risk and imposed risk). In the same way, I guess that many decision-makers and citizen would feel the need to attribute a higher value to the safety of children in schools than to the safety of other people in other places.

Second, school collapses have large indirect costs, which are not considered in Chapter 8. After the Sichuan earthquake in China in 2008, the fact that schools collapsed more than other buildings had a strong impact on population trust in the government, and on social cohesion. Similarly, the collapse of schools in Haiti in 2010 reduced the willingness of parents to send their children to schools (the trust in the government was probably too low already to be affected). These secondary consequences are not negligible – especially if they lead to reduced enrollment numbers – and may provide an additional rationale for investing in safe schools.

My second comment also concerns indirect losses. I was not surprised by the fact that Chapter 8 finds higher benefits for flood-risk mitigation than for earthquake-risk mitigation. Indeed, there is a strong increase in flood-risk world-wide, and floods kill many more than earthquakes. But the difference may be overestimated, because earthquakes are usually much larger events and they affect more individuals at one time (there are some exceptions, such as the Pakistan floods in 2010). Because they are larger events, the indirect consequences are larger for earthquakes than for floods (see, e.g., Hallegatte, 2008, 2012c), and an assessment using only direct losses may shift the balance between earthquake risk and flood risk toward the latter.

More generally, the accounting of indirect losses would increase all BCRs, and make risk-mitigation measures more desirable. Investigating earthquake impact on small business, Tierney (1997) and Kroll *et al.* (1991) show that indirect impacts – in the form of lifeline interruptions and infrastructure problems – cause more dislocation than direct impacts on business equipment or offices. Consistently with modeling exercises (Hallegatte, 2008c, 2012), econometric analyses by Cavallo and Noy (2009) and Loayza *et al.* (2009) suggest that large disasters may have a negative impact on growth while smaller ones sometimes enhance growth through increased demand. On a local scale, Strobl (2011) investigates the impact of hurricane landfall on county-level growth in the United States. He finds that economic growth is reduced on average by 0.79 percent points in counties affected by a hurricane landfall, and increased by only 0.22 percent points the following year.

As already mentioned by Chapter 8, one can also be concerned about poverty traps. Disasters destroy assets and wipe out savings, and can push households into situations where productivity is reduced, making it impossible for them to rebuild their savings and assets (Carter *et al.*, 2007; Dercon, 2004, 2005; Van den Berg, 2010). These poverty traps at the micro-level could lead to macro-level poverty traps, in which entire regions could be affected (Hallegatte *et al.*, 2007; Hallegatte and Dumas, 2008). Reducing direct losses reduces the likelihood of household-scale or regional-scale poverty traps, thereby reducing the total cost of disaster.

A reduction in economic growth could have much large effects than the direct impact of the disaster, both on economic variables (income, etc.), but also on lives saved. Taking into account the positive correlation between health and income, a disaster-caused reduction in income growth may easily have larger consequences on health (morbidity and mortality) than the disaster itself.

My third comment is about what Wiener (1998) calls "countervailing risks" – i.e. the negative implication of risk mitigation on behaviors. Indeed, protecting an area with dikes may lead individuals to disregard flood risks and lead to more risk-taking behaviors. Examples are provided in Glenn *et al.* (1996), and a modeling exercise shows how this effect can make flood risks increase over time (Hallegatte, 2011). This problem is not relevant for strengthening schools or improving robustness of the building. But it is crucial for the proposal based on dikes in Chapter 8. The point is that dikes are useful only when combined with exposure-reducing policies (such as land use plans); they can be very negative if implemented as a stand-alone measure (Burby, 2001). In Chapter 8's proposed analysis, therefore, I would shift the balance toward measures with no or little countervailing risks.

The last point is about the behavioral aspects of risk-taking. Chapter 8 describes well the problems linked to behavioral biases (including discounting and procrastination), but could have been more complete on the policies to deal with it. In particular, an observation of risk-mitigating behavior in different regions shows that information and education play a key role. In French regions with large migration, for instance, newcomers often neglect warnings and have a higher probability of being affected by a flash-flood. Simple and cheap measures based on education in schools (e.g. on what can be done when a warning is issued) can go a long way and be a perfect complement to EWS.

Finally, it is obvious that there are large uncertainties in the assessment the benefits of risk-mitigation measure benefits. Assessments such as the one proposed in Chapter 8 are based on many simple assumptions, which are needed in the low-information and low-data context of developing countries. This chapter is based on the same type of analysis. But both are using conservative assumptions, and what matters are the orders of magnitude, which are large enough to suggest that many risk-mitigation actions would have BCRs largely in excess of 1. A real-world application, however, requires local analyses, and the development of context-specific approaches. There is still a lot to do to move from global analyses and proofs of principle to the implementation on the ground.

Bibliography

Alderman, H., J. Hoddinott, and B. Kinsey, 2006: Long-term consequences of early childhood malnutrition, *Oxford Economic Papers* **58**, 450–74

Barredo, 2009: Normalised flood losses in Europe: 1970–2006, *Natural Hazards Earth Systems Science* **9**, 97–104

Boiteux, X., 2005: Instruction Cadre relative aux méthodes d'évaluation économique des grands projets d'infrastructure, *Rapport du Ministère de l'Equipement*, www.statistiques.equipement.gouv.fr/IMG/pdf/Instruction_cadre_maj_2005_cle147216.pdf

Burby, R. J., 2001: Flood insurance and floodplain management: the US experience, *Environmental Hazards* **3**, 111–22

Carsell, K. M., N. D. Pingel, and D. T. Ford, 2004: Quantifying the benefit of a flood warning system, *Natural Hazards Review* **5**, 131–40

Carter, M., P. D. Little, T. Mogues, and W. Negatu, 2007: Poverty traps and natural disasters in Ethiopia and Honduras, *World Development* **35**, 835–56

Cavallo, E., and I. Noy, 2009: The economics of natural disasters: a survey, *Inter-American Development Bank Working Paper* **124**, IADB, Washington, DC

Day, H. J., 1970: Flood warning benefit evaluation – Susquehanna River Basin (urban residences), *ESSA Technical Memorandum* **WBTM Hydro-10**, National Weather Service, Silver Spring, MD

Dercon, S., 2004: Growth and shocks: evidence from rural Ethiopia, *Journal of Development Economics* **74**, 309–29

2005: Vulnerability: a micro perspective, Paper presented at the Annual Bank Conference on Development Economics, Amsterdam

Glenn, E. P., C. Lee, R. Felger, and S. Zengel, 1996: Effects of water management on the wetlands of the Colorado River delta, Mexico, *Conservation Biology* **10**, 1175–86

Golnaraghi, M., 2012: National hydro and meteorological services, Presentation at the 9th International Forum of Meteorology, Geneva, March 22

Hallegatte, S., 2008: An adaptive regional input-output model and its application to the assessment of the economic cost of Katrina, Risk Analysis **28**, 779–99

2011: How economic growth and rational decisions can make disaster losses grow faster than wealth, *Policy Research Working Paper Series 5617*, World Bank, Washington, DC

2012a: Economics: the rising costs of hurricanes, *Nature Climate Change* **2**, 148–9

2012b: A framework to investigate the economic growth impact of sea level rise, *Environmental Research Letters* **7**, 015604

2012c: Modeling the role of inventories in the assessment of natural disaster economic costs: application on Hurricane Katrina in Louisiana, *Policy Research Working Paper* **6047**, World Bank, Washington, DC

Hallegatte, S. and P. Dumas, 2008: Can natural disasters have positive consequences? Investigating the role of embodied technical change, *Ecological Economics* **68**, 777–86

Hallegatte, S. and V. Przyluski, 2010: The economics of natural disasters: concepts and methods, *Policy Research Working Paper* **5507**, World Bank, Washington, DC

Hallegatte, S., J.-C. Hourcade, and P. Dumas, 2007: Why economic dynamics matter in assessing climate change damages: illustration on extreme events, *Ecological Economics* **62**, 330–40

International Commission for The Protection of the Rhine, 2002: *Non-Structural Flood Plain Management: Measures and Their Effectiveness*, ICPR, Koblenz

ISDR, World Bank, WMO, IMF, 2008: Strengthening the Hydro-Meteorological Services in South Eastern Europe, available on http://www.unisdr.org/we/inform/publications/7650

Katz, R. and A. Murphy (eds.), 1997: *Economic Value of Weather and Climate Forecasts*, Cambridge University Press

Kellenberg, D. K. and A. M. Mobarak, 2008: Does rising income increase or decrease damage risk from natural disasters?, *Journal of Urban Economics* **63**, 788–802

Khan, M. R. and A. Rahman, 2007: Partnership approach to disaster management in Bangladesh: a critical policy assessment, *Natural Hazards* **41**, 359–78

Kreibich, H., M. Muller, A. H. Thieken, and B. Merz, 2007: Flood precaution of companies and their ability to cope with the flood in August

2002 in Saxony, Germany, *Water Resources Research* **43**, 1–15

Kreibich, H., A. H. Thieken, T. H. Petrow, M. Muller, and B. Merz, 2005: Flood loss reduction of private households due to building precautionary measures: lessons learned from the Elbe flood in August 2002, *Natural Hazards and Earth Systems Sciences* **5**, 117–26

Kroll, C. A., J. D. Landis, Q. Shen, and S. Stryker, 1991: Economic impacts of the Loma Prieta earthquake: a focus on small business, *Studies on the Loma Prieta Earthquake*, University of California, Transportation Center, Los Angeles, CA

Kunreuther, H. and E. Michel-Kerjan, 2012: Chapter 8 in this volume

Landry, C. E., O. Bin, P. Hindsley, J. C. Whitehead, and K. Wilson, 2007: Going home: evacuation–migration decisions of Hurricane Katrina survivors, www.ecu.edu/hazards/pdfs/working_papers/Landry etal.pdf

Lazo, J. K., R. E. Morss, and J. L. Demuth, 2009: 300 billion served: sources, perceptions, uses, and values of weather forecasts, *Bulletin of the American Meteorological Society* **90**, 785–98

Leigh, R. J., 1995: Economic benefits of Terminal Aerodrome Forecasts (TAFs) for Sydney Airport, Australia, *Meteorological Applications* **2**, 239–47

Leviäkangas, P., R. Hautala, J. Räsänen, R. Oörni, S. Sonninen, M. Hekkanen, M. Ohlström, A. Venäläinen, and S. Saku, 2007: Benefits of meteorological services in Croatia, *VTT TIEDOTTEITA* **2420**

Loayza, N., E. Olaberria, J. Rigolini, and L. Christiansen, 2009: Natural disasters and growth – going beyond the averages, *World Bank Policy Research Working Paper* **4980**, World Bank, Washington, DC

Lopez, H. and L. Servén, 2009: Too poor to grow, *World Bank Policy Research Working Paper* **5012** World Bank, Washington, DC

Mechler, R., 2005: Cost-benefit analysis of natural disaster risk management in developing countries, Deutsche Gesellschaft für Technische Zusammenarbeit (GTZ), Eschborn

Mendelsohn, R., K. Emanuel, S. Chonabayashi, and L. Bakkensen, 2012: The impact of climate change on global tropical cyclone damage, *Nature Climate Change* **2**, 205–9

Merz, B., H. Kreibich, A. Thieken, and R. Schmidtke, 2004: Estimation uncertainty of direct monetary flood damage to buildings, *Natural Hazards and Earth System Sciences*, **4**, 153–63

Paul, B. K., 2009: Why relatively fewer people died?, The Case of Bangladesh's Cyclone Sidr, *Natural Hazards* **50**, 289–304

Ranger, N., S. Hallegatte, S. Bhattacharya, M. Bachu, S. Priya, K. Dhore, F. Rafique, P. Mathur, N. Naville, F. Henriet, C. Herweijer, S. Pohit, and J. Corfee-Morlot, 2011: A preliminary assessment of the potential impact of climate change on flood risk in Mumbai, *Climatic Change* **104**, 139–67

Roulston, M. S., D. T. Kaplan, J. Hardenberg, and L. A. Smith, 2003: Using medium-range weather forecasts to improve the value of wind energy production, *Renewable Energy* **28**, 585–602

Santos, I., 2007: Disentangling the effects of natural disasters on children: 2001 earthquakes in El Salvador, Doctoral Dissertation, Kennedy School of Government, Harvard University, Cambridge, MA

Skidmore, M. and H. Toya, 2007: Economic development and the impacts of natural disasters, *Economic Letters* **94**, 20–5

Strobl, E., 2011: The economic growth impact of hurricanes: evidence from US coastal counties, *Review of Economics and Statistics* **93**, 575–89

Subbiah, A., L. Bildan, and R. Narasimhan, 2008: *Background Paper on Assessment of the Economics of Early Warning Systems for Disaster Risk Reduction*, World Bank Group for Disaster Reduction and Recovery, http://gfdrr.org/gfdrr/sites/gfdrr.org/files/New%20Folder/Subbiah_EWS.pdf

Swiss, Re, 2006: The effect of climate change: storm damage in Europe on the rise, www.preventionweb.net/files/20629_publ06klimaveraenderungen1.pdf

Tapsell, S. *et al.*, 2008: Modelling the damage reducing effects of flood warnings, Final report of the FLOODsite project, www.floodsite.net

Thieken, A. H., H. Kreibich, M. Muller, and B. Merz, 2007: Coping with floods: preparedness, response and recovery of flood-affected residents in Germany in 2002, *Hydrological Sciences* **52**, 1016–37

Thieken, A. H., M. Muller, H. Kreibich, and B. Merz, 2005: Flood damage and influencing factors: new insights from the August 2002 flood in Germany, *Water Resources Research* **41**, 1–16

Thieken, A. H., Th., Petrow, H. Kreibich, and B. Merz, 2006: Insurability and mitigation of flood losses in private households in Germany, *Risk Analysis* **26**, 383–95

Thornes, J. E., 1990: The development and status of road weather information systems in Europe and North America, Proceedings of the WMO Technical Conference, WMO, Geneva, 204–14

Tierney, K., 1997: Business impacts of the Northridge earthquake, *Journal of Contingencies and Crisis Management* **5**, 87–97

Van den Berg, M., 2010: Household income strategies and natural disasters: dynamic livelihoods in rural Nicaragua, *Ecological Economics* **69**, 592–602

Viscusi, W. Kip, and J. E. Aldy, 2003: The value of a statistical life: a critical review of market estimates throughout the world, *Journal of Risk and Uncertainty* **5**, 5–76

Wiener, J. B., 1998: Managing the iatrogenic risks of risk management, *Risk: Health, Safety and Environment* **9**, 40–82

Wilks, D. S. and D. W. Wolfe, 1998: Optimal use and economic value of weather forecasts for lettuce irrigation in a humid climate, *Agricultural and Forest Meteorology* **89**, 115–30

Williams, B. A., 2002: *Fran, Floyd and Mitigation Policy*, Berry A. Williams and Associates, Inc., Raleigh, NC

World Bank, 2011: *Climate Change Adaptation and Natural Disasters Preparedness in the Coastal Cities of North Africa*, World Bank, Washington, DC

Zissimopoulos, J. and L. A. Karoly, 2007: Employment and self-employment in the wake of Hurricane Katrina, *RAND Working Paper Series* **WR-525**, RAND, Santa Monica, CA

8.2 Natural Disasters

Alternative Perspective

ILAN NOY

Fat tails and extreme disasters

Before analyzing appropriate intervention possibilities, and speculating about the most cost-effective ways of dealing with natural disasters, it is productive to look at the likely risk. Cavallo *et al.* (2010) note that the distribution of disaster damage is highly skewed, with the presence of extreme – "fat-tail" – disasters whose costs (in terms of mortality, morbidity, and/or physical destruction) are vastly larger than the average disaster cost. The Haiti earthquake of January 2010, for example, led to mortality that was 10 standard deviations larger than for similarly strong earthquakes.[1] A 10-sigma event would be associated with extremely small probabilities in "thin-tail" distributions (like the normal distribution). There have been two other 10-sigma earthquake damages in the last forty years (Tangshan, China, in 1976 and Aceh, Indonesia, in 2004).

In elucidating his "dismal theorem" Weitzman (2011) argues that the presence of fat tails in the probability distribution of the likelihood of catastrophic-event scenarios implies that standard CBAs based on means is inappropriate. He argues that the fat-tail risk should dominate all other considerations in evaluating the cost-benefit of interventions. In short, he concludes that catastrophic risks with very small probabilities demand aggressive investment in prevention.[2] Nordhaus (2011) and Pindyck (2011) critically explore the implications of Weitzman's argument.[3] Relevant to our focus here, Pindyck notes that the theorem will apply to any catastrophic event (with a fat-tail distribution associated with either the probability of occurrence, the distribution of impact, or even the estimated probability distribution[4]). Nordhaus notes that the probability distribution of earthquake magnitudes is a classic example of a fat-tail distribution.

Figure 8.2.1, shows the total number of people killed p.a. from natural disasters between 1975 and 2010. The graph is constructed from data available from EM-DAT, the most widely used and publicly available data source about natural disasters. The data clearly demonstrate that the distribution of mortality from disasters is fat-tailed; and a similar conclusion can be drawn when examining disasters' financial damages over time (see Figure 8.1, p. 440, in Chapter 8).

In their critical evaluation of Weitzman's arguments, both Pindyck and Nordhaus essentially conclude that the extreme implications of the "dismal theorem" – that we should invest close to everything in preventing these small-probability catastrophic events – are probably exaggerated (for reasons they explore in detail). Yet, both appear to agree that it is still likely that the fat tails should figure more prominently in discussions of cost-benefits.

[1] Author's calculations, using data from EM-DAT (supported by the Catholic University of Louvain, www.emdat.be). By "similarly" we mean any earthquake whose Richter measure is bigger than 7 (calculated for all earthquakes whose Richter $\geq$7 for 1970–2003. The Haiti earthquake measured as a 7.0–7.1, while the 1976 Tangshan earthquake was 7.8, and the Aceh 2004 event was 9.1–9.3.

[2] Another prominent environmental economist expresses similar concerns (Taylor, 2009).

[3] All three papers were published as a symposium. Weitzman developed his "dismal theorem" in Weitzman (2009).

[4] So that even if the real but unknown probability distribution is thin-tailed, with enough uncertainty about the real parameters of the distribution, the estimated probability distribution will be fat-tailed. Nordhaus (2011), Pindyck (2011), and Weitzman (2011), define more precisely the characteristics of thin- and fat-tailed distributions.

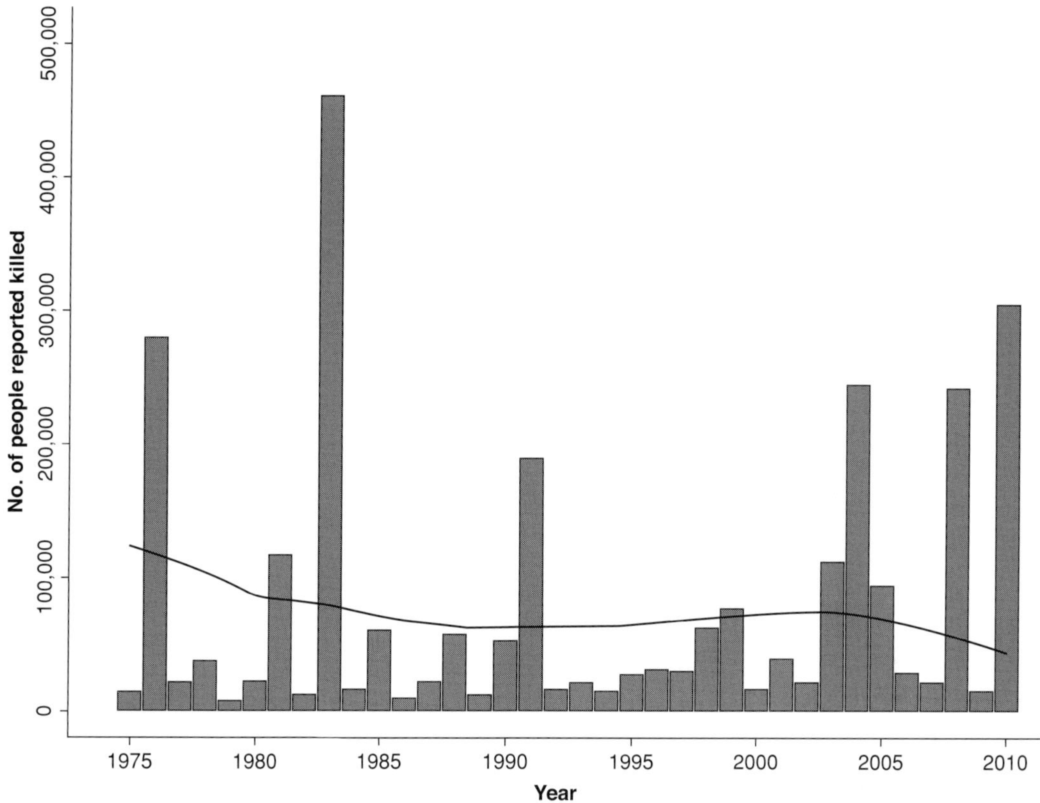

Figure 8.2.1 *Mortality from disasters, 1975–2010*

Source: EM-DAT, The International Disaster Database, www.emdat.be, accessed February 27, 2012.

Cavallo *et al.* (2010) also note that most large disasters (defined as those whose costs are above the mean) are caused by either earthquakes or storms. Therefore, even if Weitzman's extreme and dismal conclusion is not robust – see Millner (2011) for an evaluation of objections and Barrett (2011) for an alternative view of the importance of uncertainty – there is still a case to be made that we are underinvesting in preparing for these low-probability catastrophic earthquakes and tropical storms.

As an illustration, Table 8.2.1 details the cost of catastrophic disasters as measured by mortality and damages, in the last two decades. The table includes the most destructive disaster of recent times, distinguished by the five most common and harmful natural-disaster types (droughts, storms, earthquakes, volcanic activity, and floods). It also

Table 8.2.1 Disasters 1992–2011

	No. Killed
Largest disaster, by type	
Drought (Indonesia, 1997)	672
Earthquake (Haiti, 2010)	222,570
Flood (Venezuela, 1999)	30,000
Storm (Myanmar, 2008)	138,366
Volcanic eruption (Indonesia, 2010)	322
Sum of ten largest disasters, by type	
Drought	1,988
Earthquake	685,127
Flood	50,374
Storm	183,134
Volcanic eruption	775

includes data on the total human cost of the largest ten disasters in each disaster-type category. The information presented demonstrates clearly that, at least according to this metric, earthquakes are by far the most dangerous/damaging, followed by storms. We would arrive at the same conclusion if we focused on monetary damages. Preventing/mitigating the risk of earthquakes and/or storms is thus the most important.

Policy should focus on: (1) the catastrophic low-probability events; and (2) on risks from earthquakes and storms (sudden-onset events). Regionally, the most exposed geographical regions are Central, East and South-East Asia and the Caribbean (for sudden-onset events), and SSA (for slow-onset disasters such as droughts).[5]

In the following sections, I focus on three issues that are, in my view, the most pertinent to addressing the need to deal with catastrophic, low-probability storms and earthquakes (most likely to occur in Asia and/or the Caribbean): (1) the large benefits and BCRs from EWS; (2) the feasibility of an international DRR reduction intervention fund and its guiding principles, and (3) an evaluation of the Copenhagen Consensus methodology that relates to Chapter 8.

EWS

A CBA for prevention and mitigation of future possible events is, of course, inherently inaccurate. As Nordhaus notes: "the data speak softly or not at all about the likelihood of extreme events (2011: 256)," so that any policy-related evaluation will be extremely challenging and fraught with disagreements – all the more so for the rarer still "fat-tail" events. Beyond these obvious and common problems to any CBA, EWS pose two additional problems: Type I and Type II errors, and the temporal nature of the early warning.

A failure to warn against an actual hazard is associated with a serious cost, but also issuing a warning when the hazard does not materialize is costly; these costs include not only the unnecessary evacuations and preparedness measures (which can at times be very costly) but also the damage to the reputation of EWS, that will reduce its future efficacy in decreasing disaster damages.[6] These calculations are further complicated by the dynamic nature of EWS. An earlier forecast of an event is more efficient, as the warning it provides allows people more time to prepare for the hazard (by evacuating, or making changes to protect property and lives) yet more advanced warning is less precise, thus increasing the possibility of inadvertent errors (especially false alarms).

Even though the BCRs for EWS are difficult to construct, the evidence that the easiest prevention and mitigation is achieved by developing effective EWS is overwhelming (see, for example, Chapter 8.1 by Hallegatte in this volume, and the World Bank background papers referred to therein).

Storms warning systems

Storm EWS are straightforward to develop, scientifically feasible, and fairly cheap. The success of both Bangladesh and Cuba, both very poor countries, in developing effective EWS that are connected to a net of public shelters from strong tropical storms clearly demonstrates the cost-effectiveness of this approach. During Tropical Cyclone Sidr (2007), Bangladesh effectively evacuated 3 million people from vulnerable coastal areas. The storm did lead to significant mortality (4,324 people died), and damage. But Cyclone Nargis, that hit nearby in Myanmar the following year, led to 138,366 people losing their lives, after little warning or evacuation, even though Nargis was weaker than Sidr (in terms of measured windspeed).[7] The discussion by Hallegatte in Chapter 8.1, as well as in Rogers and Tsirkunov (2011), elaborates on hydro-meteorological EWS, and concludes that the BCR associated with a universal implementation is very high (in one case, Subbiah

[5] For a discussion about regional exposures and future risks, see Peduzzi *et al.* (2009) and Noy (2012).

[6] Subbiah *et al.* (2008), for example, arbitrarily assume that 1 in 10 warnings are wrong, and that the cost of one misleading warning is exactly equivalent to the benefit from one correct warning, and thus reduces the total benefit calculated for a EWS by 20 percent.

[7] Data in both cases are taken from EM-DAT.

et al., 2008, calculate a BCR for an EWS for storm-induced floods in Bangladesh of 558.87![8]).

Tsunami warning systems

The Pacific already has long had the Pacific Tsunami Warning Centre (PTWC) located in Honolulu, Hawaii, and financed largely by the US government (through NOAA).[9] Following the Aceh tsunami of December 2004, the countries of the Indian Ocean have also started implementing their own mechanism similar to the PTWC. While implementation is not yet complete, the system is operational, and it clearly demonstrates the feasibility of poorer regions developing their own advanced warning systems (with external funding).

The main stumbling block, in terms of costs and institutional feasibility, is not the actual prediction of the tsunami hazard, but developing the decision mechanism to decide on the issuing of tsunami alerts, the transmission of this alert to residents in coastal areas, efficient evacuation and evacuation monitoring – and, in some cases, enforcement. Yet, the development of mass communication in the last decade has enabled a much easier, cheaper, and faster dissemination of alerts. Now, alerts can be transmitted via SMS/text or email to subscribers, universal SMS/text or email to all cell phone/internet users in the hazardous region, TV and radio, social media (services like Facebook and Twitter), and actual sirens located along the coasts.[10]

Evacuating away from tsunamis, moreover, is easier than evacuating away from tropical storms, since only the regions very close to the coast are affected, and a short evacuation upland is generally sufficient. The decision and transmission mechanisms developed for hydro-meteorological hazards can also be used for tsunami alerts. Thus, the cost of developing an effective alert system (assuming the meteorological alert system is already in place) is fairly small but benefits are potentially very large. An effective tsunami alert system in, for example, Sri Lanka, could have saved every single life lost in the tsunami of 2004 (more than 32,000 people lost their lives).

Earthquake warning systems

Earthquake EWS are feasible but are highly local, and can probably best be developed at the national level. There is little scope for international cooperation in developing them, except for sharing of technology. Japan is the only country with a comprehensive EWS (Mexico, Romania, Taiwan, and Turkey have more limited earthquake EWS in place), but these systems only provide advanced warning of a few seconds; the exact timing depends on distance from the epicentre, with locations further away receiving more advance notice (maybe up to a minute).[11] Even this short advance warning, however, enables implementation of many life-saving procedures (stopping trains, shutting down power stations, evacuations of buildings and other vulnerable areas, etc.).

For developing countries, establishing communication systems that can transmit earthquake alerts in the appropriate speed and to a wide enough area is likely to be a difficult undertaking, and its feasibility and associated costs are largely unknown. While we therefore cannot recommend establishing earthquake EWS, given the absence of current knowledge about costs and the difficulty in predicting benefits, this does not preclude future public and international investment in them, especially once the appropriate communication and transmission systems are in place for other types of disaster EWS.

The implementation problems effecting EWS are similar across a large variety of natural disasters. In particular, designing the appropriate decision

[8] Notwithstanding the precision in which this BCR is stated in Subbiah *et al.* (2008), it does rely on very detailed data regarding damages caused by flooding from Cyclone Sidr. Importantly, it does not include the benefits in terms of lives saved or people unharmed, and assumes saving from better warnings that appear understated (10 percent of actual incurred damages to housing and personal property, for example).

[9] The PTWC had already issued Pacific-wide tsunami warnings after the large earthquake in Chile in 1960.

[10] DEWS, a project financed by the European Commission, is developing such multi-channel systems for the Indian Ocean (see Esbrí *et al.*, 2011).

[11] For more detail, see Grasso (2009).

mechanism for issuing alerts, and actual projection of alerts to the appropriate population centers, local government, and households, are all similar. Thus, there are significant economies of scale from developing these capacities. In particular, the design of EWS in developing countries should focus, from the very beginning, on designing systems that can serve as a platform for multiple-hazard EWS, and any explicit CBA of specific EWS should account for this positive externality. It is also important to note that the estimated BCRs of EWS are almost invariably much higher than other mitigation proposals and more so for post-event interventions, which are typically very costly.

Developing DRR policy internationally with a Global Fund for DRR

Why do we need a Global Fund?

If EWS are indeed as cost-effective as we previously claimed, why are they not being implemented wholeheartedly? The answer is most likely political. When facing budgetary choices, between investing in DRR with uncertain and long-horizon pay-offs and other fiscal priorities that can be implemented quickly and benefits accrued immediately, most political systems will prefer myopic policies that invest in the short-term. This, compounded with a "not in my term of office" attitude that discounts the likelihood of catastrophic events in the electorally relevant future is bound to lead to an underinvestment in DRR policies.

Beyond that mismatch between the political and economic horizons, a lack of electoral accountability also does not seem to create the "correct" incentives for preventive DRR measures. Healy and Malhotra (2009), for example, investigate US voter behavior following natural disasters; they argue that voters reward incumbents for post-disaster relief spending, but do not punish them for failure to undertake any preventive measures, even though these measures, according to their calculations, have a BCR of 15. In a follow-up study, Healy and Malhotra (2010) also show that in the United States, incumbents get punished electorally not because of tornado damage, but rather when the government fails to declare the tornado a disaster (and therefore federal assistance is not forthcoming). In a related paper, Garrett and Sobel (2003) document how 50 percent of US Federal Emergency Management Authority (FEMA) payments are guided by political considerations rather than by any CBA, further confirming the Healy–Malhotra description of the electorate. Disasters, in short, are seen as "acts of God," and are thus not widely viewed as preventable.

Cole *et al.* (2012) document very similar incentive structures facing politicians in post-disaster situations in India. Non-democratic governments appear to be even less responsive to DRR opportunities, but are also held accountable for post-disaster assistance. One of the frequently used examples is the mismanagement of foreign aid after the Managua earthquake of 1972 by the Somoza regime, a mismanagement that by all accounts contributed to its downfall. Given this perceived sense of reduced accountability for failure to implement DRR measures, the incentives for DRR policy implementation are limited.

This lack of incentives is apparently also present in the investment made by external organizations and most importantly international non-governmental organizations (I-NGOs). The I-NGOs typically manage to receive most of their revenue through donations in the aftermath of large disasters, and have clear incentives to allocate many resources in the immediate aftermath. Investing in prevention and mitigation, however, is less attractive for fund-raising purposes, and is therefore undertaken much less (see also the discussion in Chapter 8).

In many cases, initiating the development of a DRR policy is clearly needed, and can probably be best developed with external support/incentives from the multilateral organizations. The World Bank, in particular, has been working on this front, but a dedicated fund, a Global Fund for DRR (GF–DRR), that will incentivize and support this work can and should result in the optimal allocation of resources. Many developing countries lack a coherent planning for disaster preparedness and risk reduction, and the knowledge collected by the international organizations (especially the World Bank), together with the funds to support this planning, can lead to a very cost-effective implementation of a much more global DRR policy.

An appropriate DRR policy funded by the GF–DRR may involve funding of EWS, but may also involve other preparatory steps; DRR may mean retrofitting essential infrastructure for earthquakes (especially hospitals and power stations), moving people permanently away from wave-surge-prone coastal regions or river flood-plains, or establishing more robust communication networks that will not collapse in the aftermath of a catastrophic event. The appropriate steps needed depend on the broadly defined institutional details, the current state of the economy, and predictions regarding likely future disaster risks.

Since all three factors (institutions, economy, and disaster risk) are inherently local and widely varying, it would be difficult to attempt to devise a universally appropriate DRR, or to argue for a universal implementation of any specific policy. The degree of involvement of the GF–DRR will also change according to these three factors (i.e. economy, institutions, and risk profile) and the political incentive structure in each country.

For example, the Haiti earthquake of 2010 was unique, in among other characteristics, that it deeply affected a core urban/metropolitan region, unlike most other catastrophic events of the past decade that hit mostly rural areas (the Aceh tsunami of 2004, the Pakistan Kashmir earthquake of 2005, the Sichuan earthquake of 2008, Cyclone Nargis in 2008, or the Tohoku quake and tsunami of 2011[12]). Urban disasters are different, and preparing for them presents unique challenges that are different from preparing to deal with a rural event (Clermont *et al.*, 2011). Each country should evaluate independently the risks facing rural and urban areas, and determine its own policy mix that allows it to implement a DRR plan. There are, however, best practices in DRR and it is undoubtedly true that having a well-rehearsed contingency plan in place (including most crucially logistics and communication planning) is necessary to achieve a dramatic reduction in disaster risk.

Much preparation of DRR is taking place, and that has been the case since antiquity. Much more needs to be done, however, especially since economic conditions are changing, and risk patterns are appearing to change as well. Future economic exposure to tropical storms, for example, is predicted to quadruple by 2100, with roughly half of this increase associated with higher population and property in vulnerable areas and half resulting from changing patterns in terms of new predicted storm tracks and storm intensities (Mendelsohn *et al.*, 2012[13]).

These climatic and demographic changes have of course been occurring for some time, but by all accounts they will likely continue, if not accelerate. As noted by UNISDR, in the past thirty years, the proportion of world population living in flood-prone river basins has already increased by 114 percent, while that living on cyclone-exposed coastlines has grown by 192 percent (UNISDR, 2012).

This chapter eschews recommending specific and concrete action plans because the cost-benefit associated with each specific recommendation for a specific hazard in a well-specified location will necessarily be very different. The investment in quake-proofing schools in developing countries is a case in point. Earthquake hazard is very local and can be very different even within one country. Furthermore, the hazard in urban schools, which would typically be multi-story, is much greater than in rural schools. In countries in which there are two shifts in schools so that the school is occupied for about 12 hours a day (e.g. parts of Argentina), the BCR would necessarily be double that of other areas in which schools only operate with one shift (for maybe 6 hours a day). Equally confounding, an analysis of building schools in Congo will necessarily yield a very high estimate of benefits to costs,

[12] The New Zealand Christchurch earthquake of 2011 is another example of a large urban disaster (the largest in New Zealand history, and one of the most costly in relation to the size of a developed/high-income economy).

[13] The predictions in Mendelsohn *et al.* (2012) do not account for the future impacts on storm damages from predicted sea-level rises, bleaching/destruction of coastal reefs, and drying up of coastal mangrove forests. All of these are likely to increase damages further.

but so would almost any other successful intervention there. The hurdles facing investment in public goods in Congo is not a lack of opportunities with high yields, but the implementation barriers that face any investment in public goods.

Creating the correct incentives for robust DRR plans

The IMF has been involved in post-crisis intervention for several decades. The lessons the IMF learned, in terms of avoiding perverse incentives – e.g. moral hazard and adverse selection – and leading countries to adopt *ex ante* sound policies, are as relevant to natural disasters. In particular, a GF–DRR that operates not unlike the IMF's Flexible Credit Line may create the right incentives for the establishment of a robust DRR policy. Essentially, the idea is that countries will be constantly evaluated for their DRR plans, and given "seals of approval." A country whose plans are favorably evaluated will have access to support for DRR projects from the GF–DRR and in addition will have access to an Emergency Disaster Fund should it be required (as part of the GF–DRR, one can establish triggers that automatically provide affected countries access to pre-specified sums as grants or concessional loans).

Tying a GF–DRR with insurance markets

An additional positive externality would be to enable countries who receive this "seal of approval" for their DRR plans to more easily insure themselves explicitly (with re-insurers), or implicitly by issuing cat bonds, and further enable MYI (see Chapter 8).

While macro-level explicit or implicit insurance has been growing in popularity in the last decade, the vast majority of cat bonds, for example, are still issued by local organizations or specialized insurance companies. Governments, at the local or the national level do not yet appear to avail themselves of these insurance opportunities, and the establishment of a global fund may be the catalyst that will increase utilization of these new financial tools for handling catastrophic risk.

A criticism of the cost-benefit Copenhagen Consensus methodology

Three criticisms of the cost-benefit methodology used by the Copenhagen Consensus can be made: (1) The associated probabilities and uncertainties, especially of fat tails, are not accounted for in a satisfactory way; (2) the decision to use VSL, instead of cost-per-life-saved, and the actual VSL/DALY values being used are very low (though Chapter 8 reports its results using a much higher VSL); (3) the implicit classic utilitarian welfare function is not explicitly stated, and is ethically objectionable.

The "fat-tails" problem has already been discussed; however, it may be beneficial to stress that a feasible and largely acceptable way to treat these fat tail risks in public policy has not yet emerged. My own interpretation of the precautionary principle suggests that we should place a greater weight on these fat-tail events than is currently done and that is implied in the methodology that the Copenhagen Consensus has adopted.

The decision to use VSL essentially puts on an equal footing monetary damages, which are reversible, to life-and-limb damages, which typically are not. It is true that from a consequentialist point of view, monetary damages can also result in irreversible impact on mortality and morbidity.[14] But, under alternative ethical frameworks, direct and indirect impacts may be viewed as very different in their value content and their normative implications. The Copenhagen Consensus ameliorates this problem somewhat by focusing only on developing countries, but this is only a second-best, given the vast differences between these countries.

Kunreuther and Michel-Kerjan already note this in Chapter 8. They point out that when emphasizing mortality (saving lives) their conclusions are different than when they use the total cost calculation that sums up the value of statistical lives with other costs; the former leads them to recommend earthquake-proofing while the latter to recommending the construction of flood defenses. Given the

[14] By "consequentialist" I mean an ethical decision algorithm that examines consequences rather than the process itself, or the procedures that lead to the choice and adoption of that process.

observed correlation between poverty and disaster-related mortality, focusing only on mortality has the additional advantage that it will further emphasize programs that benefit the poor in general and the poorest countries in particular.

The distributional implications of the choice to use cost-per-life calculations rather than VSL in a CBA are also connected to my objection to the utilitarian framework that is being used. While most economists have little objection to consequentialism as a guiding principle in policy evaluation, I disagree with a classic utilitarian framework that ignores distributional concerns or does not prioritize the most vulnerable. Thus, I would have preferred that the Copenhagen Consensus use a procedure that prioritizes assistance to the poorest and the least capable to initiate protection autonomously, rather than just relying on the hope that a CBA will yield such an outcome.

Some comments on Chapter 8

After providing a very useful and insightful summary of the key issues regarding disaster mitigation in developing countries, Chapter 8 examines four proposals: (1) retrofitting schools against earthquakes; (2) constructing dikes or elevating houses to prevent flood damage; (3) strengthening roofs in storm-prone areas; and (4) constructing EWS.

The analysis the authors undertake in estimating the BCRs for Proposals (I)–(III) is ambitious and admirable, and involves the use of very detailed data in constructing both the EP curves and the cost of interventions. They clearly demonstrate that all these will have BCRs that are significantly larger than 1 for higher VSL values and for a fairly large group of countries, and that US$75 billion can easily be spent productively (i.e. with BCR > 1) on each one of these programs. The remaining question that is left unanswered is whether these are the lowest-hanging fruit. Below are a few suggestions that appear to imply that there may be easier fruit to pick.

Retrofitting buildings against earthquake damage is expensive, but since earthquakes cause high mortality, and EWS for them are difficult and expensive to develop, in poor rural areas in particular, this seems to be a valuable strategy to pursue (if indeed EWS are unattainable). While schools are ubiquitous, they are typically only occupied for part of the day (usually around 6–8 hours) so it seems more sensible to invest also in restructuring other public infrastructure that is more continuously occupied, like hospitals or government buildings. Schools should be prioritized only if the lives of children are prioritized – but this is not made explicit in the analysis. The Sichuan earthquake of 2008 demonstrated painfully what are the costs if a destructive earthquake occurs during the school day (2:28 p.m.), but the two 2010 earthquakes that destroyed many buildings: Haiti (4:53 p.m.) and Chile (3:34 a.m.) did not occur during the school day and the high mortality among children in the Haiti case would not have been prevented had schools been more robustly constructed.

Two other proposals, constructing dikes or elevating houses for flood-damage prevention, and improving roofing for wind-damage prevention, deal with natural disasters that usually do not pose a very high mortality risk if EWS are effectively deployed. Given my previous comments, I would have preferred a focus on mortality prevention. In the latter case, tropical storms do pose a very significant mortality risk, as was evident in the aftermath of Cyclone Nargis in 2008, but this risk can be mitigated quite effectively with a combination of appropriate EWS and the provision of storm-resistant public shelters. Schools are often used as public shelters, so constructing schools that are both storm-and earthquake-resistant may actually be, in many cases, a very efficient way of dealing with both storm and earthquake hazards. This strategy would be especially effective in countries that face a high risk for both, as do many of the countries of the Pacific Rim.

Lastly, the difficulty of developing an effective EWS should not be underestimated. On April 11, 2012, a powerful earthquake (8.6 on the Richter scale) occurred not far offshore Banda Aceh, the city that was inundated by the 2004 Boxing Day tsunami with about 25,000 people killed (Doocy *et al.*, 2007). By 2012, there was an EWS in place for tsunami hazard in Aceh, but since everyone attempted to evacuate at the same time, roads became gridlocked very quickly as people were frantically trying to flee (Rondonuwu, 2012). Luckily, no significant tsunami was generated by the earthquake, but the inadequacy of a system developed specifically to prevent mortality if a repeat of the 2004 catastrophe were to occur was quite starkly demonstrated. Investment in effective EWS will thus not be as cheap or easy, as it also needs to secure an effective response to the warnings the system supplies. Yet, the magnitude of benefits, in terms of life saved per dollar spent, are very large if these systems manage to prevent the very catastrophic disasters that occur quite frequently.[15]

As Chapter 8 notes: "Given the scale of the analyses we undertook . . . we had to make very simplifying assumptions. In reality, one would want to gather information about the hazard, type of exposure, return period of different events, type of buildings one consider, their vulnerability to that hazard, etc. (p. 464)" For this reason, I propose the panel recommends the creation of a Global Fund for DRR that will work directly with governments by providing appropriate incentives to emphasize the establishment of EWS, all the while enabling a careful weighting of local circumstances and the most efficient allocation of scarce funds.

Bibliography

Barrett, S., 2011: *Climate Treaties and Approaching Catastrophes*, Columbia University – Earth Institute, New York

Cavallo, E. and I. Noy, 2011: The economics of natural disasters: a survey, *International Review of Environmental and Resource Economics* **5**, 63–102

Cavallo, E., S. Galiani, I. Noy, and J. Pantano, 2013: Catastrophic natural disasters and economic growth, *Review of Economics and Statistics*, forthcoming

Clermont, C., D. Sanderson, A. Sharma, and H. Spraos, 2011: *Urban Disasters: Lessons from Haiti*, Report for the Disasters Emergency Committee (DEC), London

Cole, S., A. Healy, and E. Werker, 2012: Do voters demand responsive governments? Evidence from Indian disaster relief, *Journal of Development Economics* **97**, 167–81

Doocy *et al.*, 2007: Tsunami mortality estimates and vulnerability mapping in Aceh, Indonesia, *American Journal of Public Health* **97**, S146–S151

Esbrí, M. A., J. F. Esteban, M. Hammitzsch, M. Lendholt, and E. Mutafungwa, 2011: *DEWS: Distant Early Warning System: Innovative System for the Early Warning of Tsunamis and Other Hazards*, www.idee.es/resources/presentaciones/JIIDE10/ID409_DEWS_Distant_Early_Warning_System.pdf, accessed March 6, 2013

Garrett, T. and R. Sobel, 2003: The political economy of FEMA disaster payments, *Economic Inquiry* **41**, 496–509

Grasso, V., 2009: *Early Warning Systems: State-of-Art Analysis and Future Directions*, Draft Report, United Nations Environment Programme, Nairobi

Healy, A. and N. Malhotra, 2009: Myopic voters and natural disaster policy, *American Political Science Review* **103**, 387–406

2010: Random events, economic losses, and retrospective voting: implications for democratic competence, *Quarterly Journal of Political Science* **5**, 193–208

Mendelsohn, R., K. Emanuel, S. Chonabayashi, and L. Bakkensen, 2012: The impact of climate change on global tropical cyclone damage, *Nature: Climate Change*, **2**, 205–9

Millner, A., 2011: On welfare frameworks and catastrophic climate risks, University of California, Berkeley, mimeo

Nordhaus, W. D., 2011: The economics of tail events with an application to climate change, *Review of Environmental Economics and Policy* **5**, 240–57

Noy, I., 2012: Natural disasters and economic policy for the pacific Rim, in I. N. Kaur and N. Singh (eds.), *Handbook of the Economies of the Pacific Rim*, Oxford University Press, forthcoming

Peduzzi, P., H. Dao, C. Herold, and F. Mouton, 2009: Assessing global exposure and vulnerability towards natural hazards: the Disaster Risk Index, *Natural Hazards Earth System Science* **9**, 1149–59

Pindyck, R. S., 2011: Fat tails, thin tails, and climate change policy, *Review of Environmental Economics and Policy* **5**, 258–74

Rogers, D. and V. Tsirkunov, 2011: *Costs and Benefits of Early Warning Systems*, Global

[15] In the past decade, there has been about 1 event per year with more than 20,000 deaths.

Assessment Report on Risk Reduction, World Bank, Washington, DC

Rondonuwu, O., 2012: Tsunami alerts pass Indonesia quake test, with luck, Reuters, April 12, www.reuters.com/article/2012/04/12/us-asia-quake-idUSBRE83B09G20120412, accessed March 6, 2013

Subbiah, A. R., L. Bildan, and R. Narasimhan, 2008: *Background Paper on Assessment of the Economics of Early Warning Systems for Disaster Risk Reduction*, World Bank Group's Global Facility for Disaster Reduction and Recovery (GFDRR), Washington, DC

Taylor, M. S., 2009: Environmental crises: past, present and future, *Canadian Journal of Economics*

UNISDR, 2012: *Towards a Post-2015 Framework for Disaster Risk Reduction*, Geneva

Weitzman, M. L., 2009: On modeling and interpreting the economics of catastrophic climate change, *Review of Economics and Statistics* **91**, 1–19

2011: Fat-tailed uncertainty in the economics of catastrophic climate change, *Review of Environmental Economics and Policy* **5**, 275–92

CHAPTER 9 Population growth

HANS-PETER KOHLER*

The challenge of "population growth"

While the majority of the population is now estimated to live in regions with below-replacement fertility, high fertility, poor reproductive health outcomes, and relatively rapid population growth remain an important concern in several low-income countries. International and national spending devoted to family planning, however, has declined significantly in recent years. Recent research has brought about a revision in the understanding of the interactions between population growth and economic development, as well as the effects of family planning programs in terms of reduced fertility, improved reproductive health outcomes, and other lifecycle and intergenerational consequences. This chapter discusses recent evidence about the benefits of family planning programs and the interactions between population growth and developments, and it attempts to estimate BCRs for increased spending on family planning.[1]

The demographic transition: an unfinished success story

The demographic transition in developing countries during the second half of the twentieth century is widely considered a "success story." Between 1950–1955 and 2005–2010, the life expectancy in less-developed countries[2] increased from 42.3 to 66 years (a total gain of 23.7 years, or an average annual gain of 0.43 years), and in least-developed countries it increased from 37.2 to 56.9 (a total gain of 19.7 years, or an average annual gain of 0.37 years). Fertility rates declined from a total fertility rate (TFR) of about 6.1 in less-developed countries in 1950–1955 to 2.7 children per woman in 2005–2010 (an annual decline of about 0.062), and TFR levels declined from 6.5 to 4.4 children per woman in least-developed countries during this time period (an annual decline of about 0.038). Global annual population growth rates declined from a peak of 2.07 percent in 1965–1970 to 1.16 percent in 2005–2010 (Figure 9.1). The growth rate in less-developed countries also peaked during 1965–1970 at about 2.5 percent per year, while growth rates in least-developed countries peaked during 1990–1995 at 2.75 percent. By 2005–2010, the growth rates had declined to 1.33 percent and 2.21 percent, respectively. The majority of the world population is now estimated to live in regions with below-replacement fertility (TFR $\leq$ 2.1) (Wilson, 2004), and the global TFR is projected to

* This chapter is an updated version of the paper distributed during the Copenhagen Consensus Project 2012 Conference in Copenhagen in May 2012. In writing and revising this chapter, I have greatly benefited from the useful and constructive comments by Jere Behrman, John Cleland, Odet Galor, David Lam, Ronald Lee, and James Walker. I gratefully acknowledge the useful feedback from Kasper Thede Anderskov and other members of the Copenhagen Consensus Team, and I have also benefited from discussions with Julio Romero Prieto, Arun Hendi and other students in Demog 796 at the University of Pennsylvania.

[1] Following Bongaarts and Sinding (2011a), "family planning" is used to refer to programs that provide information about contraception, as well as contraceptives themselves and related reproductive health services. Such programs do not generally include abortion, and consensus statements produced by the United Nations explicitly exclude abortion as a method of family planning. However, in some countries where abortion is legal, it is offered alongside contraceptive information and services.

[2] Including least-developed countries; the classification follows the UN Population Division grouping into more-developed countries, less-developed countries, and least-developed countries; where less-developed countries include – unless otherwise noted – the least-developed countries; see for additional information.

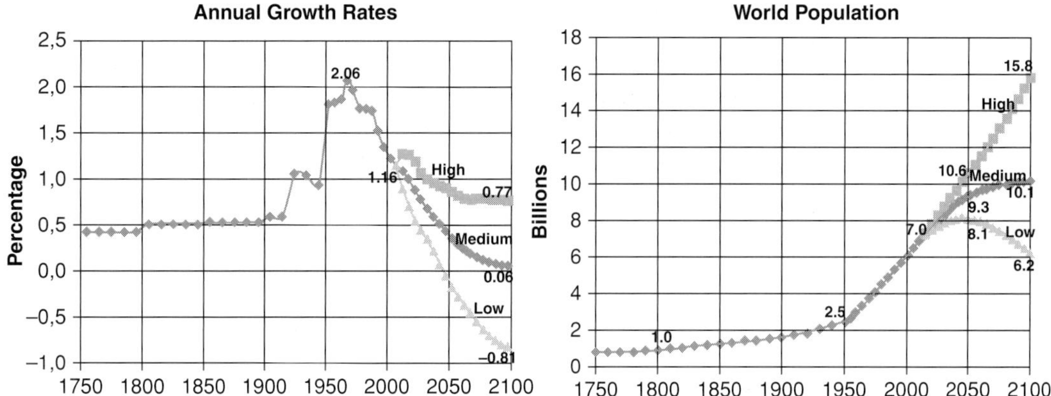

Figure 9.1 *World population and annual growth rates of world population according to different UN projection variants*

Note: The low, medium, and high scenarios assume the same mortality trends, and differ in the level of fertility. After 2010, the fertility levels in the different scenarios converge, and after 2015 the TFR in the high-fertility scenario is 0.5 above that of the medium scenario, and in the low-fertility scenario, the TFR is 0.5 below that of the medium scenario. In the medium scenario, global TFR declines from 2.52 (in 2010) to 2.03 (in 2100).
Source: Global Agenda Council on Population Growth (2012), based on UN Population Division (2010c).

reach 2.1 – the conventional, albeit globally not necessarily correct marker for replacement level fertility (Espenshade *et al.*, 2003; Kohler and Ortega, 2002) – by 2070 (UN median projection, UN Population Division, 2010c). As a result of the increases in life expectancy and reductions in fertility, in many developed countries – and increasingly also in some developing countries – concerns about very low fertility and rapid population aging have emerged as important demographic concerns (Kohler *et al.*, 2002; Lee, 2011), and some scholars have postulated that shrinking families are "the new population problem" (Crouter and Booth, 2005) (Figure 9.2).

In less-developed countries, rapid declines of mortality and fertility have often been associated with rapid economic development. For example, in South Korea during 1950–2010, life expectancy increased from 47.9 to 80 years, fertility (TFR) declined from 5.1 to 1.3 children per woman, and GDP *per capita* grew substantially with a growth rate of more than 5 percent p.a. during 1960–2010. While often seen as a sufficient condition for fertility decline (Figure 9.2), however, rapid economic development is not always a necessary condition: in Bangladesh during 1950–2010, for example, life expectancy increased from 45.3 to 67.8, fertility, (TFR) declined from 6.4 to 2.4 children per woman, and GDP *per capita* grew during 1960–2010 at an average rate of only 1.5 percent p.a. Both India and China saw large fertility declines before the onset of rapid economic growth. Iran holds the record of the most rapid decline in fertility, from 6.5 to 1.8 during the period 1980–2010 when Iran was an Islamic Republic, and average economic growth was relatively modest at around 1.3 percent p.a. (see also Abbasi-Shavazi *et al.*, 2009a, 2009b). During these diverse patterns of demographic transitions that unfolded during the second half of the twentieth century, the world population grew rapidly (Figure 9.1). The world population doubled from 1.5 to 3 billion between the late nineteenth century and 1960, and it doubled again from 3 to 6 billion during 1960–1999. The year 2011 marked the year when the world population reached 7 billion, adding the last seventh billion in a mere twelve years – not unlike the time period it took to add the fifth and sixth billion to the world population.[3] However, despite the rapid

[3] According to UN population estimates, the United Nations estimated that the world population reached 3 billion on October 20, 1959, 4 billion on June 27, 1974, 5 billion on January 21, 1987, 6 billion on December 5, 1998, and

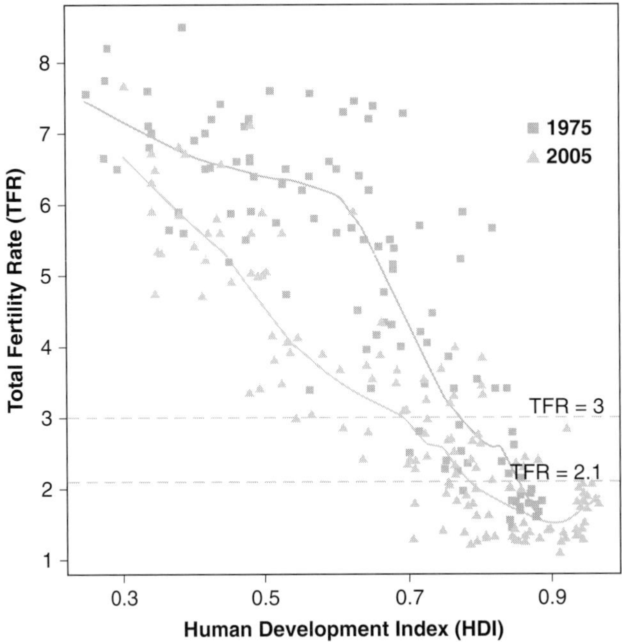

Figure 9.2 *Cross-sectional relationship between the TFR and HDI, 1975 and 2005*

Note: The HDI is the primary index used by the UNDP to monitor and evaluate broadly defined human development, combining with equal-weight indicators of a country's health conditions, living standard, and human capital. The HDI in this figure is recalculated using a time-invariant formula so that it is longitudinally comparable between 1975 and 2005 (for a discussion, see Myrskylä *et al.*, 2009). There is a clear negative association in 1975 and 2005 between the level of human development (as measured by the HDI) and the level of the TFR, with a possible reversal of this correlation occurring in 2005 for the most-developed countries. In addition, there is important heterogeneity in the 2005 fertility rates at the various development stages. On the one hand, low fertility in 2005 is no longer restricted to the most-developed countries: TFR levels of below 2.1 are achieved at 2005 HDI levels as low as 0.7, and TFR levels of below 3.0 are attained by countries at 2005 HDI levels of 0.55. On the other hand, fertility levels vary widely for all but the highest levels of development. For example, countries with a 2005 HDI of 0.4–0.6 exhibit TFR levels ranging from 3 to 7.1 (mean is 4.7), and TFR levels range from 1.2 to 5.9 among countries with a 2005 HDI of 0.6–0.8 (mean is 2.6).
Source: Adapted from Myrskylä *et al.* (2009) and Kohler (2010).

population growth during the last decades, the prominent doomsday prediction from the 1960s and 1970s about the potentially disastrous consequences of rapid population growth did not materialize. Not only did the world avoid the prominent predictions of major food crises and environmental degradation made in books such as *The Population Bomb* or *The Population Explosion* (Ehrlich, 1968; Ehrlich and Ehrlich, 1990), but various measures of individual well-being increased globally – including in both more-developed and less-developed countries: despite rapid population growth during 1960–2010 (Figure 9.1), global GDP *per capita* grew from $2,376 to $5,997 (in constant 2000 US$) (+ 152 percent), life expectancy has increased from 51.2 to 67.9 years (+ 33 percent), infant and maternal death rates have declined substantially, the level of education – and importantly also levels of female schooling – have increased, global *per capita* food production and consumption have risen, and the proportion of the global population living in poverty has declined significantly (Lam, 2011) (Figure 9.3).

7 billion on October 31, 2011 (see http://esa.un.org/wpp/Other-Information/pr_faq.htm); the time it took to add the fourth, fifth, sixth, and seventh billion is therefore 14.7, 12.6, 11.9, and 12.9 years, respectively.

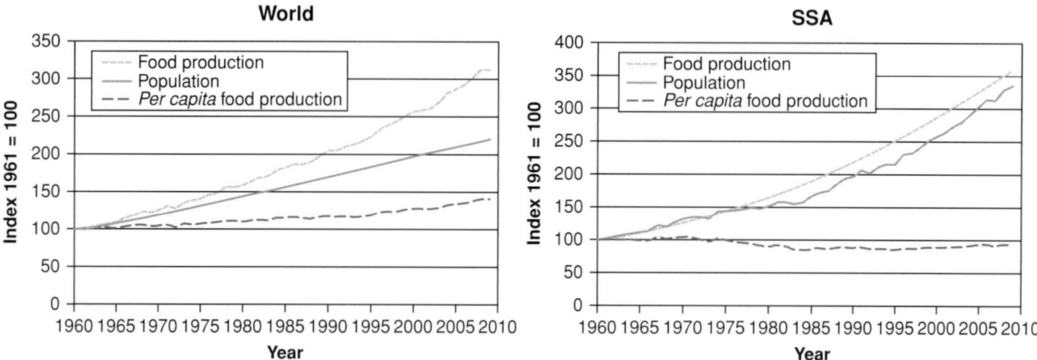

Figure 9.3 *Food production, globally and in SSA, 1961–2009*

Source: Lam (2011), based on data from FAO (2011).

Lam (2011) attributed this accomplishment of increasing well-being despite rapid population growth – which was taken as far from granted several decades ago – to the combined effect of six factors, three of which are economic, three demographic (Lam, 2011):

(1) *Market responses*, causing for instance farmers to grow more food in response to higher food prices or causing individuals to substitute away from scarce resources whose prices increase in response to population pressures
(2) *Innovation*, where population growth increased the incentives (and potentially also the abilities) to develop new technologies and knowledge, such as those underlying the "Green Revolution," that use available resources more efficiently
(3) *Globalization*, resulting in an increased economic integration of countries through international flows of good and capital that improved the efficiency of both production and distribution
(4) *Urbanization*, in which cities absorbed a significant proportion of population growth in recent decades, thereby contributing to innovation, economic growth, and improvements in efficiency that helped to achieve increases in living standards despite growing populations[4]
(5) *Fertility decline*, causing birth rates with some lag to follow declining mortality rates and reducing rates of population growth (Figure 9.1)
(6) *Investments in children and child quality*, resulting in large increases in school enrollment and human capital (for males, and even more so for females), despite rapidly growing cohort sizes, that contributed to reduced fertility, improved own and child health and increased productivities and economic growth.

The chances are that recent decades will remain a unique period in global demographic history: after attaining a doubling of the world population in only thirty-nine years from 3 to 6 billion, the global population is unlikely to double again. In the UN medium projection, the global population will level off at around 10.1 billion in 2100, and even in the high-fertility scenario, the global population will remain below 16 billion. Estimates of the earth's carrying capacity are of little help in assessing if this growth is sustainable and/or compatible with maintaining or even improving living standards (Cohen, 1995a, 1995b). And while adding another 3 billion persons to the global population without undermining past progress in global living standards or measures of well-being – or perhaps even improving upon

[4] Some scholars argue that urbanization in SSA is occurring significantly more slowly than often believed. For example, according to Potts (2012a, Potts, 2012b), very few countries in SSA have been experiencing rapid urbanization, in part because both urban and rural populations are growing rapidly. According to Potts' analyses, many countries in SSA are urbanizing very slowly, and some have even de-urbanized.

them – will remain a challenging task, the tone of the population debate and the perceived urgency of "the population problem" has dramatically changed in recent years. *The Economist*, for example, features major articles with titles such as "Go forth and multiply *a lot less: lower fertility is changing the world for the better*" (Economist, 2009) and "*The world's population will reach 7 billion at the end of October [2011]. Don't panic*" (Economist, 2011a), and while continued challenges of accommodating population growth remain, the most recent press coverage of the seventh billion persons living on earth (Economist, 2011a, 2011b, 2011c; National Geographic Magazine, 2011; Osotimehin, 2011; Roberts, 2011) has been a lot less alarmist than in earlier discussions that echoed the fears expressed in books such as *The Population Bomb* (for analyses of an earlier discussion of these population problem, see Wilmoth and Ball 1992). A possible reason for this shift in perceptions of the problem is that, in many developing countries, as a result of substantial fertility declines any future population growth is much more driven by population momentum – i.e. expected increases in the number of individuals at primary reproductive ages in the next decades that result from young-age distributions and high previous rates of population growth – rather than high current or future levels of fertility for which family planning programs might provide one possibly policy intervention (Figure 9.4).

And yet, despite the undoubted successes of global mortality and fertility declines, and the resulting declines in the rate of global population growth, the demographic transition remains an *unfinished success story*. High fertility and rapid population growth remain important concerns in many least-developed countries that may be most vulnerable to the consequences of population growth (Figure 9.4). For example, because fertility declines in SSA during recent years were less rapid than previously expected earlier (Bongaarts, 2008; Ezeh *et al.*, 2009; Garenne, 2011), the United Nations unexpectedly revised its 2010 forecast for the world population upward to 10 billion, as compared to earlier forecasts predicting a leveling off at 9 billion (UN Population Division, 2010c). A report prepared for the 2012 World Economic Forum (Global Agenda Council on Population Growth, 2012), for example, identifies fifty-eight high-fertility countries, defined as countries with net reproduction rates (NRR) of more than 1.5 (Figure 9.4) that have intrinsic population growth rates of 1.4 percent or higher.[5] The high-fertility countries are concentrated in Africa, where thirty-nine out of the fifty-five countries on the continent have high fertility, but also exist in Asia (nine countries), Oceania (six countries) and Latin America (four countries). Almost two-thirds of these high-fertility countries are classified by the United Nations as least developed, and thirty-eight out of the total of forty-eight countries that are classified as least developed have high-fertility. Most high-fertility countries have current population growth rates of 2.5 percent or higher which, if maintained, would imply a doubling of the population every thirty-five years. Female education levels (as indicated by illiteracy) and contraceptive use tend to be relatively low in the high-fertility countries (Figure 9.5). Despite having currently only about 18 percent of the world population, high-fertility countries account today for about 38 percent of the 78 million persons that are added annually to the world population. Based on UN median population projections, the TFR in high-fertility countries is projected to decline to 2.8 by 2050, and 2.1 by 2100. Despite these projected TFR declines, the current high-fertility countries will make the largest contribution to the annual increment of the world population after 2018, and after 2060 world population is projected to grow exclusively as a result of population growth in the current high-fertility countries (Figure 9.6). During the twenty-first century, therefore, the current high-fertility countries will be the major contributors to continued world population growth. Past and continued progress in reducing mortality, combined

[5] A NRR of more than 1.5 means that more than 1.5 daughters are born to women given 2010 fertility and mortality levels. This implies that the next generation is 50 percent larger than the current generation, and at constant fertility and mortality levels a NRR of 1.5 implies a long-term annual population growth rate of about 1.4 percent. The intrinsic population growth rate is the growth rate that would persist in the long term if current patterns of fertility and mortality were to persist in a population and the population was closed to migration.

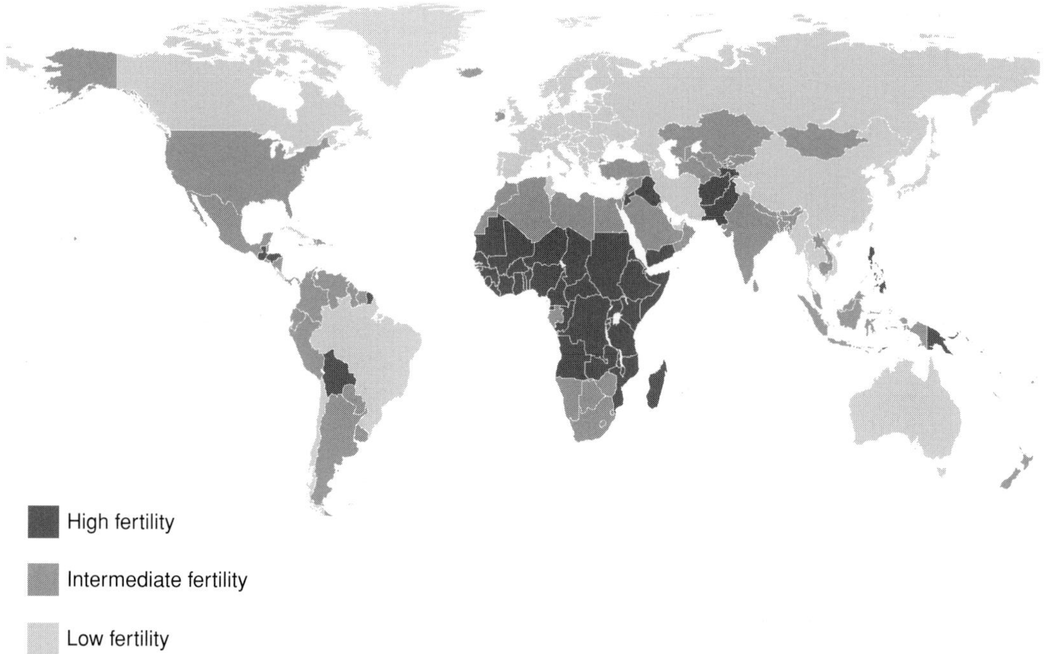

Figure 9.4 *Countries according to fertility level, 2005–2010*

Note: Low-fertility countries: (NRR measured in daughters born per woman) less than 1; intermediate-fertility countries: NRR between 1 and 1.5; high-fertility countries: NRR above 1.5
Source: Global Agenda Council on Population Growth (2012), based on UN Population Division (2010c).

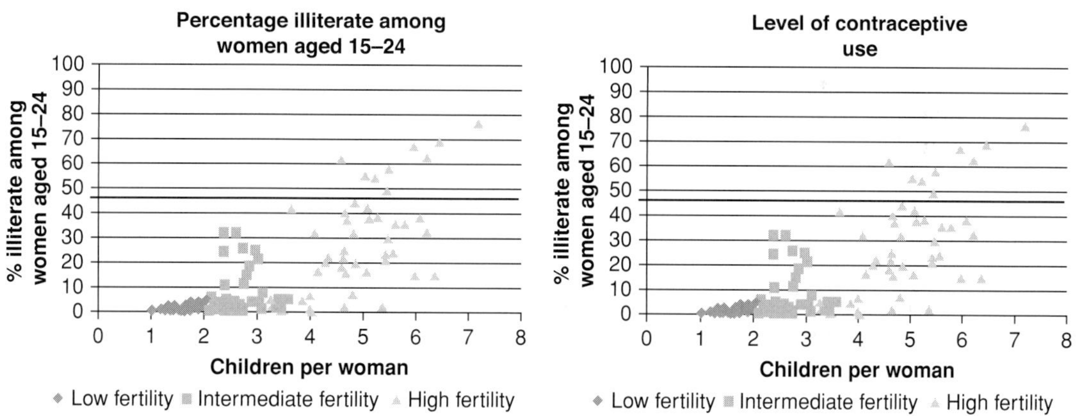

Figure 9.5 *Percentage illiterate among women aged 15–24 and most recent level of contraceptive use, by TFR levels*

Source: Global Agenda Council on Population Growth (2012), based on UN Population Division (2011), UN Statistics Division (2011), and UN Population Division (2010c).

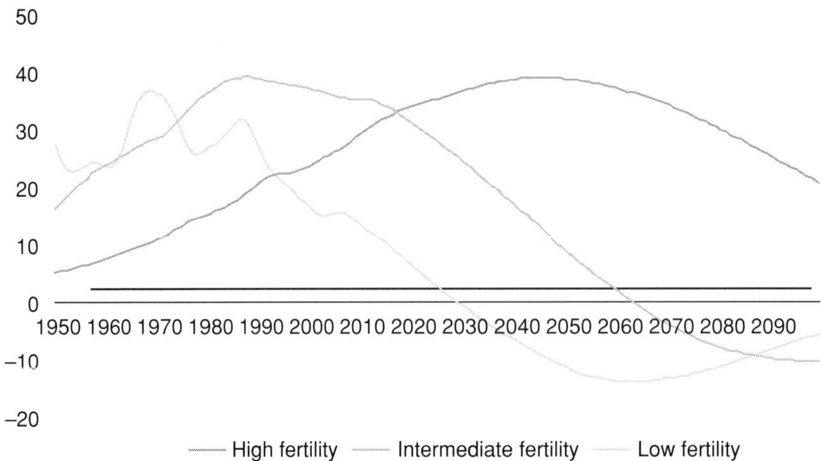

Figure 9.6 *Annual increments of the population in high-fertility countries, intermediate-fertility countries, and low-fertility countries according to the medium-projection variant, 1950–2100 (million)*

Source: Global Agenda Council on Population Growth (2012), based on UN Population Division (2010c).

with sustained above-replacement fertility levels that does not drop to a TFR of 2.1 until 2100 in the UN median projection, will be a primary cause of this rapid population growth, *in addition to* a population momentum that results from the very young age structures in these countries.

The analyses in this chapter will primarily focus on high fertility countries in SSA because this region has the highest concentration of high-fertility countries that make the dominant contribution to the world population growth resulting from such countries (Figure 9.4), and because SSA high-fertility countries belong to the poorest and most vulnerable countries in the world, with often weak institutions and capacities to manage population growth. Figure 9.7 shows the observed and projected (based on UN scenarios) population size, population growth rate, life expectancy at birth, and TFR for the period 1950–2060. The overall SSA population growth rate has peaked in the early 1980s and has been declining from its peak of 2.8 percent in 1980–1985 to 2.5 percent in 2005–2010. It is 110 percent higher than the global population growth rate, resulting in both a projected rapid growth of the population as well as an increasing share of the global population that is in SSA. While mortality has declined, and life expectancy has increased significantly in SSA, progress has lagged behind other developing countries, in part but not only, due to the HIV/AIDS epidemic (Magadi and Agwanda, 2010). For example, the 2005–2010 life expectancy of 52.5 years is 20 percent below the average life expectancy in less-developed countries; infant mortality in SSA is 85 per 1,000, 68 percent higher than the infant mortality rate in all less-developed countries, and the maternal mortality of 640 per 100,000 live births (2008) exceeds that of all less-developed countries by 120 percent (UN Millennium Development Goals, 2011; UN Population Division, 2010c). And while fertility has declined from its peak of 6.71 in 1970–1975, the 2005–2010 TFR levels for SSA of 5.1 exceed that of all less-developed countries by 90 percent. And because more than 42 percent of the SSA population was below the age of 15 in 2010, there is considerable population momentum even if fertility were to decline relatively rapidly.

It is important to emphasize that these averages mask considerable heterogeneity in both fertility and mortality (Table 9.1), with TFR among the ten most populous SSA countries ranging from 2.6 to 6.1, and life expectancy ranging from 48.8 to 62.7. On the one hand, several of these largest SSA countries have experienced substantial declines in fertility. But, on the other hand, these sustained declines in fertility are far from universal in SSA, and many SSA countries continue to have high fertility and rapid population growth rates. The potential

Table 9.1 Population size, TFR, life expectancy, and population growth rate in the ten most populous SSA countries

	Population size (million)		TFR		Life expectancy at birth		Growth rate (%)	
	1980	2010	1980–85	2005–10	1980–85	2005–10	1980–85	2005–10
Nigeria	75.5	158.4	6.8	5.6	45.8	50.3	2.55	2.50
Ethiopia	35.4	82.9	6.9	4.6	43.5	57.2	2.96	2.21
DRC	27.0	66.0	6.7	6.1	46.2	47.4	2.78	2.78
South Africa	29.1	50.1	4.6	2.6	58.4	51.2	2.52	0.96
Tanzania	18.7	44.8	6.6	5.6	50.8	55.4	3.13	2.88
Sudan	20.1	43.6	6.3	4.6	50.2	60.3	3.19	2.51
Kenya	16.3	40.5	7.2	4.8	58.9	55.0	3.78	2.58
Uganda	12.7	33.4	7.1	6.4	49.9	52.2	3.12	3.24
Ghana	10.9	24.4	6.3	4.3	53.8	62.7	3.28	2.39
Mozambique	12.1	23.4	6.4	5.1	42.8	48.8	1.87	2.38

Source: Based on UN median projections (UN Population Division, 2010c).

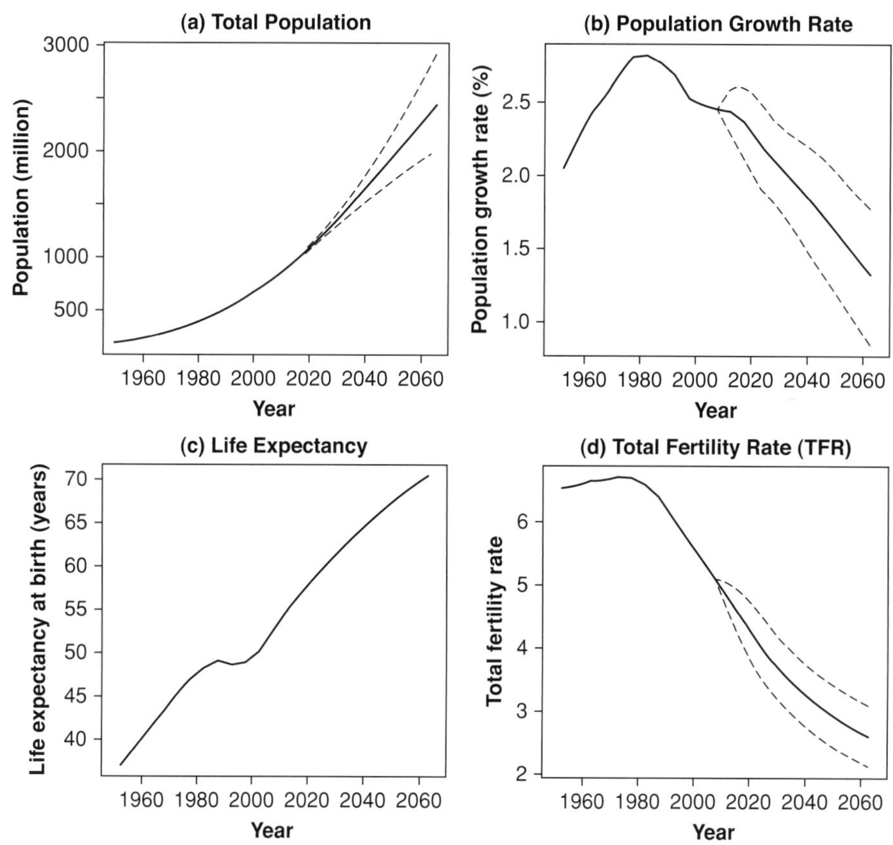

Figure 9.7 *Population size, population growth rate, life expectancy at birth, and TFR for SSA, 1950–2060*

Note: Based on UN median, high and low projections (UN Population Division 2010c). Bold line: median projection. Broken lines: low/high projections. Projected life expectancy is identical across the UN medium, low and high projections.

Table 9.2 SSA countries that are projected to triple their population size during 2010–2060

	Population size (in million)		Ratio 2060 to 2010 population	Projected population growth rate 2010–2060
	2010	2060		
Niger	15.5	70.9	4.57	3.04
Zambia	13.1	59.2	4.52	3.02
Malawi	14.9	63.3	4.25	2.89
Somalia	9.3	36.0	3.85	2.70
Tanzania	44.8	172.2	3.84	2.69
Burkina Faso	16.5	56.8	3.45	2.48
Uganda	33.4	112.6	3.37	2.43
Mali	15.4	50.5	3.29	2.38
Madagascar	20.7	63.2	3.05	2.23
SSA	856.3	2277.3	2.66	1.96

Source: Based on UN median projections (UN Population Division, 2010c).

implications of this are also increasingly being recognized by political leaders. While in 1976 just 38 percent of the governments of countries in Africa viewed fertility as *too high*, 75 percent of them did so by 2009; 68 percent considered the rate of growth of the population as too high, as compared to 35 percent in 1976 (UN Population Division, 2010a).

To illustrate the rapid projected population growth in some SSA countries, Table 9.2 lists nine countries whose population is expected to *triple* between 2010 and 2060 based on the UN medium population projections along with their 2010 and 2060 population size and projected growth rates. The population growth rate in these countries in the next five decades ranges from 2.2–3.0 percent, and is therefore expected to be 14–55 percent higher than the projected SSA average. The relatively high fertility underlying this projected rapid population growth is often attributed to the fact that many high-fertility SSA countries have a considerable – and possibly growing – "*unmet need*" for family planning, where unmet need is a concept used by demographers to measure the number of women who are fecund and sexually active, but are not using any method of contraception, despite the fact that they report not wanting any more children or wanting to delay the next child (Casterline and Sinding, 2000; UN Statistics Division, 2011). The concept of unmet need thus points to a potential gap between women's reproductive intentions and their contraceptive behavior.[6] In high-fertility SSA countries, several studies indicate that a sizable fraction – around 25 percent – of sexually active fecund women who would like to limit their fertility do not use family planning methods and thus have unmet need for family planning

[6] Unmet need has been incorporated into the MDG monitoring, where unmet need is expressed as a percentage of women married and in a union aged 15 to 49 (UN Statistics Division, 2011; Millennium Development Goals Indicators meta-data). Critics of the concept of unmet need point out that this concept implies either a very broad or a very paternalistic notion of "need" (Pritchett, 1994) because it includes not only women who want to use contraception and don't do so because of supply-side restrictions, but also identifies women as "needing" if they require additional motivation before they want to use family planning or are constrained by other than supply-side factors in their contraceptive decision-making; there are hence concerns that unmet need potentially overstates the potential effect of improved contraceptive provision, which modern family planning programs try to address by including also other reproductive health services, behavioral change communication, and interpersonal communication through health workers and community leaders. For a comprehensive discussion of unmet need and its use in discussions of family planning and population policies, see Casterline and Sinding (2000).

(Prata, 2009; UN Population Division, 2009; Darroch and Singh, 2011). Moreover, given the relatively low rates of contraceptive prevalence and weak institutional support of family planning programs, and the significant changes necessary to achieve the fertility decline in the UN median scenario, some scholars consider the UN median scenario as too optimistic in terms of the assumed pace of future fertility decline (Cleland *et al.*, 2011; Eastwood and Lipton 2011) because contraceptive use is unlikely to increase sufficiently fast to achieve these projected TFR declines. Moreover, while global food production has more than kept up with population growth since the 1960 (Figure 9.3), SSA exhibits signs of strain. While food production increased during 1960–2009 by a factor of 3.4 – more than for the world as a whole – the population grew even faster (by a factor of 3.6) in that time period, causing *per capita* food consumption to decline by about 7 percent since 1961 (Lam, 2011) (Table 9.2).[7]

In light of the above trends, a new literature is emerging that emphasizes the "*return of the population growth factor*" (Campbell *et al.*, 2007), the "*unfinished agenda*" of family planning programs (Cleland *et al.*, 2006), or the "*stalls in fertility transitions*" (Bongaarts, 2006, 2008; Ezeh *et al.*, 2009) in SSA. Some analyses have speculated about a "*gift of dying*" in which the HIV/AIDS epidemic enhances the future *per capita* consumption possibilities of the South African economy by reducing fertility, thereby more than compensating for the loss of human capital (Young, 2005). Yet, it is far from clear if such a negative effect of the HIV/AIDS epidemic on fertility exists (Fortson, 2009; Kalemli-Ozcan and Turan, 2011), in which case Young's (2005) argument unravels. And yet, the HIV/AIDS epidemic is not central to the renewed concerns about population growth in SSA since its effect – especially given also the recent expansion of antiretroviral treatment (ART) – on overall population growth trends is relatively modest (UN Population Division, 2010b). Focusing on fertility, therefore, Cleland *et al.* (2006) asked "Can disaster be prevented in Niger?," given Niger's unchanged TFR levels that are among the highest in the world, and "*[Is the] Kenyan success in jeopardy*," given a stalling of the fertility decline in the last decade that has caused the United Nations to revise its median 2050 population projection for Kenya from 44 million (2002 World Population Prospects) to 96.9 million (2010 World Population Prospects). Potts *et al.* (2011) write in an article entitled "Niger: too little, too late" that "the failure to emphasize family planning since 1994 has transformed a serious demographic scenario into a potentially catastrophic one." Campbell (2007) described the silence around population growth as the "perfect storm" that may undermine broader development efforts. Just before the Copenhagen Consensus Project (2012), conference, a theme on population growth in SSA in the *New York Times* included a slide show entitled "*In Nigeria, a preview of an overcrowded planet*" and raised concerns about whether patterns of fertility decline, which have occurred elsewhere in the world and curtailed population growth, will similarly "defuse the population bomb in sub-Saharan Africa [. . .] where the population rise far outstrips economic expansion" (Rosenthal, 2012a, 2012b).

Continued high fertility, such as in Niger or Nigeria, or stalls in fertility declines during the last decade, such as in Kenya, are often attributed to a reduced pace (or lack of) economic development, continued high levels of desired fertility, relatively low levels of contraceptive use (possibly as a result of reduced and/or inadequate resources devoted to family planning programs), and relatively high levels of mortality (in part, but not only, as a result of the HIV/AIDS epidemic) (Bongaarts, 2006, 2008, 2011; Ezeh *et al.*, 2009; Cleland *et al.*, 2011). Many of these analyses call for a renewed emphasis on family planning programs. However, to highlight the potentially broad benefits of reduced fertility and population growth, the contemporary literature arguing for a renewed interest in family planning programs does not view population growth a "problem" in itself, but portrays it as a major threat towards attaining social and economic development, such as for

[7] Lam (2011) also points out that the more recent trend is somewhat more encouraging, given that food production has grown faster than population since about 1995, although not fast enough to completely offset the earlier declines in *per capita* food production.

instance reflected in the MDGs (Cleland *et al.*, 2006; APPG, 2007; Cates *et al.*, 2010). Specifically, the potential adverse effects that are often attributed to rapid population growth include poor health among women and children, slow economic growth and poverty, overcrowded schools and clinics, and an overburdened infrastructure, as well as the depletion of environmental resources (Birdsall *et al.*, 2001). There are also arguments that rapid population growth contributes to high unemployment and inequality among rapidly growing young populations and may contribute to the spread of political violence and civil strife (Cincotta *et al.*, 2003; Goldstone *et al.*, 2012). A recent UK parliamentary report, for example, cites the United Nations Office of the High Representative for the Least Developed Countries as saying "The battle against endemic poverty and chronic hunger, particularly in the world's 50 Least Developed Countries, is made all the more difficult due to their current high rates of population growth" and concludes that "the [MDGs] are difficult or impossible to achieve with current levels of population growth in the least developed countries" (APPG, 2007). Melinda Gates argued at the 2012 TED, Summit "Let's put birth control back on the agenda" (Gates, 2012b), based on the premise that many of the world's pressing social change issues depend on ensuring that women are able to control their rate of having children. In similar vein, Campbell *et al.* (2007) write in a Science Policy Forum: "Decisions made now can influence the growth rate [through lowering fertility]. If the rates are not altered, hundreds of millions of families will suffer from poverty, hunger, inadequate education, and lack of employment opportunities, all of which might otherwise have been avoided."

And yet, despite the rapid population growth and the renewed concerns about social and economic development that are associated with it, the resources devoted to family planning have waned. And while several major foundations – including the Bill and Melinda Gates Foundation and the Hewlett Foundation – have implemented major programs in the area of family planning and are drawing attention to family planning and related needs to invest in reproductive health in developing countries (Gates, 2012a; Hewlett Foundation, 2012), the overall global resources spent on family planning have declined. For example, while funds committed by donors and developing countries to HIV and AIDS increased by nearly 300 percent, funds devoted to family planning declined by some 30 percent (Bongaarts, 2008). In particular, donor funding for family planning peaked in 2002 at US$ 700 million and has since declined to about US$ 400 million (UNFPA, 2010). Given the increase in the number of women of reproductive age, donor funding for family planning *per capita* has declined by more than 50 percent since 1995 in virtually all recipient countries. This relative neglect of family planning programs is arguably due to premature claims of an end to the "population explosion," shifting attention from population growth to the HIV/AIDS epidemic and a consequent reallocation of resources, and growing conservative religious and political opposition (Bongaarts and Sinding, 2011a). These cuts in donor funding are likely to have also contributed to a reduced commitment of developing-country governments to family planning programs and a reduced availability of family planning services today as compared to a decade ago (Bongaarts and Sinding, 2009). Evaluating the progress – or lack of it – in family planning efforts during the recent years, the UK parliamentary report writes that the "The dream of Cairo" (referring to the 1994 UN International Conference on Population and Development (ICPD) in Cairo) has failed, and that the time since has been a "lost decade" for the focus on population and family planning (APPG, 2007).

In light of this mismatch between the declining funding of family planning programs and the reduced international focus on issues related to population growth on the one hand, and the prospect of substantial population growth of some of the world's poorest and most vulnerable populations on the other hand, several scholars have called for a renewed investment in family planning programs, and a reinstatement of these programs as a priority in high-fertility countries, not only to reduce population growth, but also facilitate the achievement of the MDGs (APPG, 2007; Cates *et al.*, 2010; Cleland *et al.*, 2006, 2012). Consistent with this new emphasis on family planning as part of a broader development agenda, the World Bank

(2010) has issued a "reproductive health action plan" that emphasizes reproductive health as a "key facet of human development" and argues that this renewed emphasis on reproductive health offers "an unprecedented opportunity to redress the neglect of the previous decade." And while the tide of the debate might be shifting in the direction of renewed interest in family planning programs, important skepticism about them remains. These critical perspectives on the effectiveness of family planning programs have potentially contributed to the waning support – both financial and otherwise – of these programs. Critics and skeptics, for example (Bongaarts and Sinding, 2009), often claim that family planning programs have little or no effect on fertility levels or the pace of fertility decline (Pritchett, 1994; Connelly, 2008); these programs are no longer necessary since fertility declines are under way globally and will continue even in the absence of such programs (Bongaarts and Watkins, 1996; Eberstadt, 2006); family planning programs are not cost-effective (Pritchett, 1994); the linkage between reduced fertility and slower population growth and economic development is weak (National Research Council, 1986); the reversal of mortality declines as a result of the HIV/AIDS epidemic have made family planning and reduced fertility less important and desirable (Mosher, 2000); and family planning programs have made women the instruments of population control policies, and at worst, have been coercive (Mosher, 2008; Campbell and Bedford, 2009).

The proponents emphasize that many of these criticisms are mistaken (e.g. Bongaarts and Sinding, 2009). Moreover, and potentially more importantly, research on the interactions between population growth and economic developments (Bloom and Canning, 2004; Bloom *et al.*, 1998, 2002, 2007b) and careful evaluations of past family planning programs (Joshi and Schultz, 2007; Schultz, 2009, Joshi, 2011; Mills *et al.*, 2011) have strengthened the case that family planning programs are a good "investment" (Bongaarts and Sinding, 2011b) that not only help to reduce fertility but also facilitate the attainment of a broad set of development goals, such as reduced infant and maternal mortality, increases in schooling and gender equality, and reductions in poverty (Global Aganda Council on Population Growth, 2012). But is this renewed emphasis on population growth and family planning justified given our knowledge about the effects of family planning programs and the current knowledge about the interrelations between population growth and economic development? This chapter therefore revisits the current literature on population growth, the demographic transition and family planning programs, and provides BCRs for investments in family planning programs.

The causes and consequences of the demographic transition

Demographic transitions, including those still in process in the developing world, are frequently perceived as resulting from the economic and technological changes of the modern era that have led to economic development, mass communication, effective programs of public health, availability of contraceptive methods, and related social changes. Before the start of the demographic transition, lives were short (around thirty years), survival at all stages of the life course was relatively uncertain, fertility rates were high (with TFRs around 5–7 children per woman), population growth was slow, and populations were relatively young (Figure 9.8). During the demographic transition, initially mortality and then fertility declines, resulting initially in an increase and then a decline in the population growth rate (Figure 9.8). In addition, the age structure of the population is transformed. Initially, the population grows "younger" as a result of a rapid increase of births and a decline of infant mortality; then, the population grows "older" as a result of smaller birth cohorts, increased longevity, and the aging of the earlier large cohorts. Towards the end of the demographic transition, population growth declines (and potentially ceases or becomes negative), fertility is low, life expectancy is high, with mortality risks being low to very low at young and adult ages and deaths concentrated at older ages, and the population age structure being relatively old (Lee, 2003, 2011). In addition to population size and age structure, family structures, life courses, social and economic contexts are fundamentally

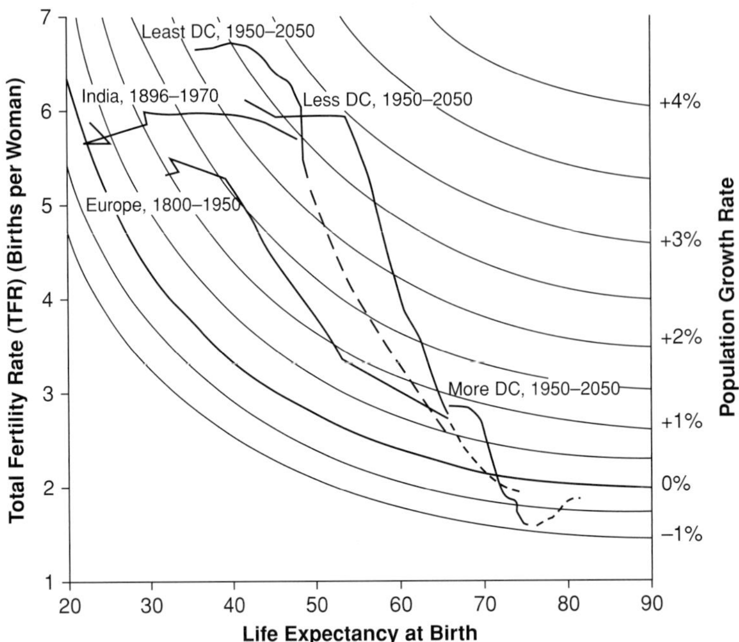

Figure 9.8 *Life expectancy and TFR with population growth isoquants: past and projected trajectories for more-, less-, and least-developed countries*

Note: The horizontal axis of the figure shows life expectancy at birth. The vertical axis shows the TFR. The contours illustrate the steady-state population growth rate corresponding to constant fertility and mortality at the indicated level, where the dark contour represents zero population growth and movement toward the upper right corner indicates increasingly rapid growth. On this graph, the demographic transition will first appear as a move to the right, representing a gain in life expectancy with little change in fertility and a movement to a higher-population growth contour then, as a diagonal downward movement toward the right, reflecting the simultaneous decline in fertility and mortality, recrossing contours toward lower rates of growth.
DC = Developing countries
Source: Lee (2003).

transformed (Lee and Reher 2011), with important implications for social and economic development that may further facilitate the demographic transition (Figure 9.9).

The social context of fertility decisions in pre-transitional populations has varied tremendously over time and space. It changed with trends in culture, religious, and political influences; it was affected by technological progress, innovations, or discoveries; and it evolved through social and cultural adaptation. Despite these variations it is remarkable that population growth rates for most (surviving) societies were relatively modest over much of human history. Preceding the Neolithic Revolution (approximately 10,000 BC) the average long-run net reproduction rate was near unity, to within a few ten-thousandths. Between the Neolithic Revolution and 1750 AD the world population grew from 6 million to 771 million, which implies a very moderate average annual growth rate of 0.04 percent. Short-term fluctuations around this trend are well documented. Yet, the low long-term growth rates, that prevailed despite large variations in reproductive environments and mortality conditions, strongly suggest the existence of an equilibrating mechanism between population size and available resources: population homeostasis. This homeostatic theory was first devised by Malthus (1798) on the strength of the three basic economic relationships he identified in pre-industrial England. On the one hand, when real wages fall below some subsistence level, mortality increases and population growth is curtailed through a positive check on premature mortality. On the other hand,

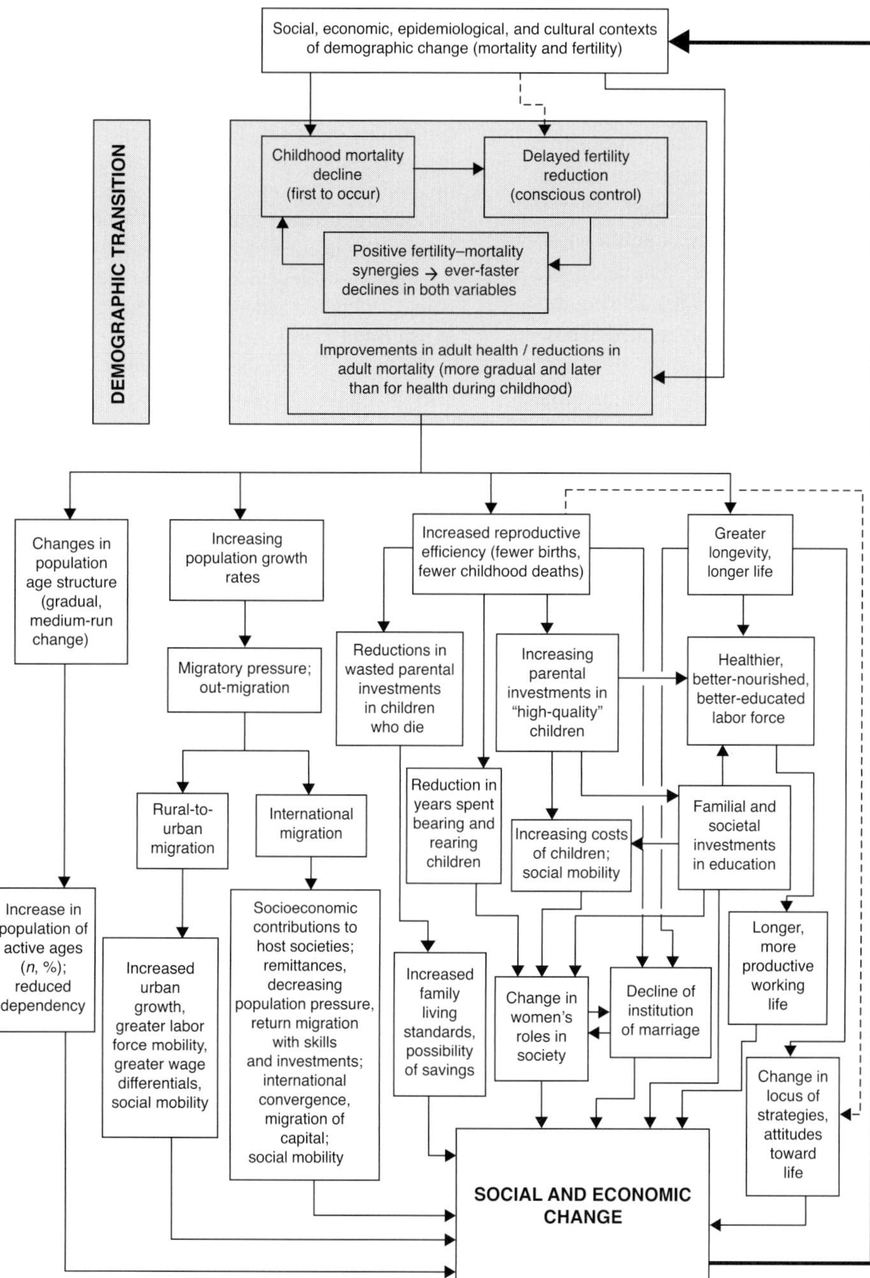

Figure 9.9 *Schematic framework for the demographic transition and associated social and economic changes*

Source: Reher (2011).

when real wages increase, marriage is encouraged. In addition, agricultural production faces diminishing returns to labor. Hence, increases in population size tend to imply lower wages, which in turn will tend to reduce population growth through positive checks (increased mortality) or preventive checks such as abstinence or delayed marriage. Demographic and economic evidence is largely consistent with the homeostatic theory for England from about 1250 to 1700 (Lee, 1973, 1980). During this period, wages were largely inversely related to population size. And despite the frequent association of Malthusianism with a population re-balancing that occurs through increased mortality, even in pre-industrial societies, the preventive check on population growth via fertility occupied a central place, whereas the positive check operated relatively independently of wage rates.

With the beginning of the Industrial Revolution in England these relationships unmistakably altered: population growth initially accelerated as a result of reduced mortality, but wages nonetheless continued to increase. With some delay, fertility started to decline, and so did population growth rates. The occurrence of rapid demographic change during the process of socio-economic modernization led to the formalization of the *demographic transition theory*. The basic idea is that socio-economic development first induces a mortality decline and, with some lag, a decrease in fertility. The easiest way to summarize this theory is to quote from one of its formulators:

> [Premodern birthrates in Europe] . . . were high by present standards. Indeed, they had to be high [in face of the inevitably high mortality] . . . Peasant societies in Europe, and almost universally throughout the world, are organized in ways that bring strong pressures on their members to reproduce. The economic organization of relatively self-sufficient agrarian communities turns almost wholly about the family, and the perpetuation of the family is the main guarantee of support and elemental security . . . In such societies, moreover, there is scant opportunity for women to achieve either economic support or personal prestige outside the roles of wife and mother, and women's economic functions are organized in ways that are compatible with continuous childbearing.
>
> These arrangements, which stood the test of experience throughout the centuries of high mortality, are strongly supported by popular beliefs, formalized in religious doctrine, and enforced by community sanctions. They are deeply woven into the social fabric and are slow to change. Mortality dropped rather promptly in response to external changes because mankind had always coveted health. The decline of fertility, however, awaited the gradual obsolescence of age-old social and economic institutions and the emergence of a new ideal in matters of family size.
>
> The new ideal of the small family arose typically in the urban industrial society . . . Urban life stripped the family of many functions in production, consumption, recreation, and education. In factory employment the individual stood on his own accomplishments. The new mobility of young people and the anonymity of city life reduced the pressures toward traditional behavior exerted by the family and community . . . Education and a rational point of view became increasingly important. As a consequence the cost of child-rearing grew and the possibilities for economic contributions by children declined. Falling death-rates at once increased the size of the family to be supported and lowered the inducements to have many births. Women, moreover, found new independence from household obligations and new economic roles less compatible with childbearing . . . Under these multiple pressures old ideals and beliefs began to weaken, and the new ideal of a small number of children gained strength. (Notestein, 1953: 16–17)

The corpus of this theory is very broad. It entails the central role of norms and their erosion, the emergence of rational fertility decisions, and the changing socio-economic environment. As a descriptive tool, the theory provides a framework to conceptualize demographic change. The question is how well the theory performs as a predictive tool that allows the analysis of fertility behavior in a positive sense, and that establishes a firm link between the causes and consequences of demographic change. Over the past few decades, intensive research on demographic change in historical and contemporary societies has revealed complex patterns that do not fit neatly into the theoretical schema of the demographic transition, including, for instance, the stalled fertility transitions that have occurred in parts of SSA (Bongaarts, 2006, 2008; Ezeh *et al.*, 2009; Garenne, 2011). The transition theory neglected the subtleties and variability of the process, and it became increasingly perceived as being too narrow in terms of the causal mechanisms and factors that are the primary drivers of mortality and fertility change. In particular, observing the fertility transitions during the twentieth century, it is clear that fertility has declined in combination with rapid development, but it has also declined in resource poor countries (e.g. Bangladesh, Vietnam), in countries with low levels of female education (e.g. Cambodia, Haiti), in countries with low levels of female labor force participation (e.g. Egypt, Turkey) and in countries with high levels of gender inequality (e.g. Iran). And yet, the majority of fertility transitions in SSA are still in process, and in some areas a substantial decline in birth and population growth rates is yet to occur (Figure 9.4). Whether the fertility transitions in SSA will follow the pattern of earlier fertility transitions – for instance, those in Latin America and Asia – remains the topic of a controversial debate. And so does the question of whether family planning programs, which may have contributed to the declines of fertility in other contexts, are effective – and possibly cost-effective – programs that can facilitate the decline of fertility and, as a consequence of better fertility control, improvements in health and economic development. To put the discussion of these issues into context, we first review in the following sections the knowledge about the causes of the demographic transition, its implications for economic development, and the role that family planning may have played in facilitating fertility transitions.

Declines in mortality

The decline in mortality is widely perceived to be a prerequisite of sustained fertility decline (Mason, 1997), and population growth during the demographic transition arises due to a lag between declining mortality and fertility rates (Figure 9.8). The decline of mortality therefore deserves some discussion in this chapter, even if it is not the primary focus of the analyses here. In Europe, early declines in mortality during the eighteenth and nineteenth century were importantly driven by improvements in nutrition, sanitation, housing, and transportation (Lee, 2003; Cutler *et al.*, 2006). Knowledge about the germ theory of disease were critical to changing both public health infrastructure and personal behavior. Public health measures played an important role starting in the late nineteenth century, and during the twentieth century medical progress in vaccination and the treatment of infectious and chronic diseases made important contributions to gains in life expectancy. The pace of gains in life expectancy has been remarkably constant, and Oeppen and Vaupel (2002) show that in the 160 years since 1840, life expectancy in the world's leading countries in terms of longevity has increased by three months per calendar year. Improvements in life expectancy in developing countries occurred relatively rapidly compared to the historical gains in Europe. In India and China, for example, life expectancies have risen by nearly thirty years since 1950 and, even in Africa, where there has been much less economic progress, life expectancy rose by more than thirteen years from the early 1950s to the late 1980s, before declining in the face of HIV/AIDS. Reniers *et al.* (2011), for instance, find that declines in adult mortality in SSA during the last few decades have been modest, and in some populations drastic mortality reversals have been recorded. These reversals are primarily driven by the HIV/AIDS epidemic, but the extremely high adult mortality rates in some southeastern African countries are due to the triple burden of infectious and chronic diseases and the relatively high level of deaths due to external injuries.

The rapid decline in mortality after the Second World War in developing countries happened because knowledge and technologies based on 200 years' worth of progress against mortality in the now-rich countries could be used in improving mortality in the rest of the world. Measures such as improvements in water supply, cleansing the environment of disease vectors (like anopheles mosquitoes that carry malaria, or rats that carry lice), the use of antibiotics and the widespread immunization of children – the combined development of which had taken many years in the West – were introduced to the rest of the world over a relatively very short span of time. Preston (1980), for example, attributed about half of the gain in life expectancy in developing countries (excluding China) from the 1930s to the late 1960s to the combined effects of changes in income, literacy, and the supply of calories, and the remaining half to the public health measures newly implemented in these countries. And yet, there is a great deal more to be done before health in poor countries resembles that in rich countries today (Cutler *et al.*, 2006). For many leading causes of death and/or poor health in the least-developed countries, knowledge and technologies about suitable prevention and/or treatments are – at least in principle – relatively inexpensively available. These relatively easily preventable causes of death include, for instance, diarrheal disease and respiratory infections, being respectively the first and fourth leading causes of death world-wide, as well as malaria, tuberculosis, and several infectious children's diseases such as whooping cough, tetanus, polio, diphtheria, and measles. However, in many cases, these available and relatively cheap and easy-to-administer treatments and/or preventive steps continue to be used much less than seems desirable (and beneficial), and specifically in SSA infant, maternal, and adult mortality continue to remain relatively high (Rajaratnam *et al.*, 2010; UN Millennium Development Goals, 2011). Some related Copenhagen Consensus Assessment Papers have addressed some of the benefits and challenges in improving health and mortality through interventions (Behrman *et al.*, 2004; Horton *et al.*, 2009; Jamison *et al.*, 2009, 2012, the former Chapter 7 in this volume; Behrman and Kohler, 2011; Hoddinott *et al.*, 2012, Chapter 6 in this volume; Jha *et al.*, 2012, Chapter 3 in this volume). Efforts to improve health care systems and the utilization of existing technologies, knowledge, and medications are actively promoted in many SSA and other developing countries. In addition, and specifically relevant for SSA, the recent roll-out of anti-retroviral treatment for HIV/AIDS (UNAIDS, 2010, 2011) has started to curtail and possibly reverse the increases in mortality that have occurred since the onset of the HIV/AIDS epidemic (Jahn *et al.*, 2008; Herbst *et al.*, 2009; Bongaarts *et al.*, 2011). Reniers *et al.* (2011) find that the onset of some of these recent declines in adult mortality even preceded the large-scale availability of anti-retroviral therapy.

Why fertility declines

The fertility response to falling infant mortality was often remarkably fast (Mason, 1997), frequently within one generation. Exploiting exogenous variation in the ecology of malaria transmission, McCord *et al.* (2010), for example, estimate that in SSA child mortality is a powerfully robust driver of fertility behavior, and that meeting the MDG of reducing 1990 child mortality rates by 66 percent in SSA would translate into a reduction of total fertility rates from around 6.3 in 1990 to 3.3, more than halfway towards achieving replacement fertility levels of 2.1. The decline of mortality, which initiated the rapid growth of population during the demographic transition, therefore, also contributes to the end of population growth. And while mortality decline is almost always a precondition for sustained fertility decline, the link between patterns of mortality and fertility declines is not very tight (Guinnane, 2011). For example, one of the central challenges to the notion of fertility change as formulated in the demographic transition theory is due to Coale (1973: 65), who concluded, based on analyses of fertility decline in Europe, that "[t]he diversity of circumstances under which marital fertility has declined, and the consequent difficulties of formulating a well-defined threshold, may originate in the existence of more than one broad precondition for a decline." Coale thus identified three preconditions for a major fall in marital fertility: (1) fertility must be within the calculus of conscious choice; (2) reduced fertility must be advantageous; (3) effective techniques of fertility control must be available. These conditions are not so much a predictive tool as an integrative device for discussing the approaches of different behavioral schools. Demand theories, such as the economic approaches to fertility that are often referred to as the "new home economics" (Willis, 1973; Becker, 1991), have traditionally taken conditions (1) and (3) as granted, and analyzed fertility behavior as an adaptation to changing environmental conditions. Ideational and diffusion approaches

(Cleland and Wilson, 1987; Montgomery and Casterline, 1993), on the other hand, emphasize factors (1) and (3). They interpret conscious fertility control within marriage as an innovation and focus on the diffusion or acceptance of this behavior. Supply theories (Easterlin and Crimmins, 1985) emphasize the role of factor (3), the availability of methods to control fertility and the biological context of reproduction.

We focus in this review of fertility theories and the causes of fertility transitions primarily on the economic approach to fertility, which is usually associated with the "new home economics" initiated by Gary Becker (Becker, 1991). The scope of the new economic approach to household behavior reaches far beyond fertility. At the same time, the demand for children and its interaction with related household decisions constitutes a central concern throughout the new home economics literature, and is an important question that continues to stimulate further empirical and theoretical developments. As currently employed, most household models for the demand for children share certain features (Schultz, 1997). First, the traditional money-income budget constraint is replaced by a time budget constraint, and considerable attention is devoted to the allocation of time between market labor supply and non-market activities, especially for women. Second, demographic and economic behaviors depend on the household stocks of human and physical capital, and differences across individuals in their relative advantages of engaging in specific market or non-market activities are an important determinant of a household's time allocation. Third, many models for the demand for children incorporate an explicit lifecycle perspective. Choices of individuals about human capital accumulation, marriage, saving, etc., are therefore considered as interrelated decisions that need to be investigated jointly.

In a simple and commonly used framework of the demand for children, parents are assumed to maximize lifetime utility, which depends for example on the number of children (*quantity* of children), the education and health of the children (often referred to as the *quality* of children), the leisure activities of the husband and wife, and other consumption goods. Each input into the utility function can be thought of as being produced within the home by combining both the non-market time of the household members and the market goods according to a constant returns-to-scale production function. Except for the integrated supply–demand framework by Easterlin and Crimmins (1985), the production function for children in the classic new home economics models does not usually include limitations to the "supply" of children due to fecundity, mortality, and child survival. The allocation of each individual's time is usually mutually exclusive and subject to an overall time budget constraint. Market income is equal to lifetime wage rate, received by each member of the family, times their market labor supply (plus additional non-labor income). The shadow prices of these commodities are then defined as the opportunity costs of market goods and the household member's time inputs used to produce 1 unit of the commodity. In an extension of this framework to overlapping-generations' models, parents exhibit intergenerational altruism and are concerned about the well-being of their children. This leads to a dynastic utility function (Becker and Barro, 1988; Galor and Weil, 1996). The utility of the parents depends on the utility of their immediate offspring, and recursively on all future generations. The head of a dynastic family acts as if she maximizes the dynastic utility subject to a budget constraint that depends on the wealth inherited by the head, the cost of rearing children, and earnings in all future generations. Maximization of the resulting dynastic utility usually implies an arbitrage condition for consumption over generations, and it has important implications for intergenerational relations. According to this model, fertility, but not the growth of consumption per descendant, responds to variations in interest rates and the degree of altruism. More generally, fertility is also related to the growth in net costs between generations, and transfers to children depend on the taxes and production opportunities faced by children in the future (an assumption that has been questioned in more recent studies, e.g. Lee and Kramer, 2002).

The optimal choice of children, consumption, as well as the optimal allocation of time and market goods to the various activities results in the above framework of utility maximization within the time and money-income budget constraint and given the prices and wages faced by the individuals in the household. Within this economic framework, fertility will also be influenced by how economic change influences the costs and benefits of childbearing, and investments in child quality will importantly be influenced by the returns to broadly defined human capital, which in part depends on mortality risks. Given the time intensity of bearing and rearing children, the opportunity costs of time are of particular relevance in determining fertility. Technological progress and increasing physical and human capital make labor more productive, raising the value of time in all activities, which makes children increasingly costly relative to consumption goods. Since women have had primary responsibility for childbearing and rearing, variations in the productivity of women have been particularly important. For example, physical capital may substitute for human strength, reducing or eliminating the productivity differential between male and female labor, and thus raising the opportunity cost of children. Rising incomes have shifted consumption demand toward non-agricultural goods and services, for which educated labor is a more important input. A rise in the return to education then leads to increased investments. Overall, these patterns have several effects: children become more expensive, their economic contributions are diminished by school time and educated parents have a higher value of time, which raises the opportunity costs of childrearing. Furthermore, parents with higher incomes may choose to devote more resources to each child, and since this raises the cost of each child, it also leads to fewer children (Willis, 1973; Becker, 1991). If parents wish to have a certain number of surviving children, rather than births *per se*, then once potential parents recognize an exogenous increase in child survival, fertility should decline. However, interactions between mortality and fertility are potentially important. For example, increased survival raises the return on post-birth investments in children (Kalemli-Ozcan, 2003). Some of the improvement in child survival is itself a response to parental decisions to invest more in the health and welfare of a smaller number of children (Nerlove, 1974). In addition, an increasing marketization of societies and the expansion of government services may imply that governments and/or market services replace many of the important economic functions of the traditional family and household, like risk-sharing, insurance, and the provision of retirement income, further weakening the value of children (Becker, 1991). The extent to which family planning programs and contraceptive technologies affect fertility is hotly debated.

Many of these relationships between fertility and its individual and societal determinants have been extensively studied. One of the strong empirical relationships in developing countries that has received considerable attention from this perspective of how opportunity costs shape fertility outcomes is a negative association between mother's education and children born (Caldwell, 1980; Schultz, 1997; Kravdal, 2002). Using aggregate data in developing countries, for example, Schultz (1997) finds – consistent with the implications of the new home economics – that male education and income from non-human capital sources are associated with higher fertility. Kravdal (2002) also suggests that education effects on fertility exist not only at the individual level, but also at the community level net of urbanization and the mother's own education. Rosenzweig and Wolpin (1980) and Rosenzweig (1990) provide evidence for the quality-quantity trade-off in developing countries by utilizing exogenous variations in the wage of children to infer child costs and the incentives for child quality versus quantity, or using twin births as a natural experiment. Evidence for this trade-off is also found using scholastic performance as an indicator for child quality Hanushek (1992), although some newer studies using gender composition for the first-born children as instruments for overall fertility have found negligible quality–quantity trade-offs in some developed countries (Black *et al.*, 2005). In addition, individual learning about fecundity has been shown as an important factor in its determination (Rosenzweig and Schultz, 1985), and uncertainty about socio-economic conditions during early adulthood has been shown to be an important motivation to delay childbearing (Bernardi *et al.*, 2008; Johnson-Hanks, 2006). Using overlapping generations models, for example, Galor and Weil (1996) suggest that technological progress leads to reduced fertility because it increases the ratio of women's to men's wages, thereby increasing the opportunity costs of children and increasing the motivations to invest in child quality. Manuelli and Seshadri (2009) argue in a study based on an overlapping-generations' model that cross-country differences in productivity and taxes go a long way toward explaining the observed differences in fertility across contemporary developed countries, and Greenwood *et al.* (2005) point to the importance of the relentless rise in real wages during the last 200 years in contributing to increasing the opportunity cost of having children, while at the same time, arguing that the "baby boom" during the 1950–1960s can be explained by an atypical burst of technological progress in the household sector that occurred in the middle of the twentieth century that lowered the cost of having children. Substantial fertility decline has occurred in societies across a broad range of development stages and across the religious spectrum (Rosling, 2012), with Muslim countries exhibiting somewhat higher fertility in a study of thirty contemporary developing countries (Heaton, 2011). This relationship, however, is subject to considerable variability, and interestingly, the Muslim/Christian difference grows wider at higher levels of development and at higher levels of educational achievement. In addition, longstanding differences in norms and beliefs about the appropriate role of women in society, and specifically with respect to the division of labor in the household and female labor force participation, that are not necessarily tied to religion, may have important influences on fertility. For example, Alesina *et al.* (2011a, 2011b) show that the form of agriculture traditionally practiced – intensive-plough agriculture versus shifting-hoe agriculture – affected historic gender norms and perceptions of gender equality, and that these norms and perceptions not only affected historical fertility levels but resulted in long-lasting fertility differences that continue to persist in contemporary contexts around the world today (for related analyses of post-Second World War fertility trends, see Fernández *et al.*, 2004).

Recent economic theories have also developed more explicitly the decision processes within households about fertility and related behaviors. For example, the above models concentrate on a single decision-maker and disregard the fact that household decisions usually involve more than one person who may not agree about the respective factor allocations. Various assumptions, such as Becker's (1974) "Rotten Kid Theorem," establish circumstances under which households act as if they were governed by a single, utility-maximizing decision-maker. Empirical evidence, however, tends to contradict this assumption (Schultz, 1990; Haddad and Hoddinott, 1994), and bargaining theories (Lundberg and Pollak, 1996; Bergstrom, 1997) to provide a sophisticated framework for analyzing this process for fertility and other household decisions. Bargaining between partners (or spouses) can have complex implications for fertility decisions because, among other factors, the ability to dissolve unions, the well-being outside marriage, or the withholding of care or services within a relationship are important determinants of bargaining power in these models. For example, England and Folbre (2002) argue that primary care-givers (usually mothers) usually have less bargaining power than parents whose contributions simply take the form of financial support, and that this weakness in the bargaining process may not be fully compensated by the less tangible, non-pecuniary resources that result from greater physical proximity and stronger emotional connection to the child. Less gender specialization in the form of parental involvement could lead to improved outcomes for children not only by improving mothers' economic position but also by strengthening emotional connections between fathers and children. Using similar views about gender asymmetries in decision-making processes within and outside the family/household, McDonald (2000) argues that an increase in gender equity – and thus more gender-equal bargaining power within families – is a precondition of a rise in fertility from very low levels in developed countries, while at the same time, increased female bargaining power is a necessary condition for achieving lower fertility.

It is well known that the individual decision-making processes that are emphasized in the economic frameworks of fertility do not necessarily result in an optimal fertility level that maximizes some specific indicator of societal well-being like income *per capita* or subjective well-being; or, for that matter, neither do individual decision-making processes necessarily result in a replacement level fertility (for related discussions, see Samuelson, 1975; Lee and Mason, 2012; Strießnig and Lutz, 2012). For example, it is an old observation that individuals' fertility decisions may deviate from the socially perceived optimum level of procreation. Polybius (1927, 36.17.5–7) in the second century BC, for instance, lamented about a decreasing population and a decline of cities because "men had fallen into such a state of pretentiousness, avarice, and indolence that they did not wish to marry, or if they married to rear children born to them, or at most as a rule one or two of them, so as to leave these in affluence." Instead of this concern for underpopulation, recent writers about the divergence between individually and socially desired population growth were primarily concerned with overpopulation. The reasons for this divergence are twofold: the first is that the relative prices of goods and services that households face may simply be "wrong" due to market or policy failures. The second is provided by the ubiquitous phenomenon of externalities. The externalities underlying this divergence of private and social incentives for low fertility are mainly found in three areas. In Malthus' model that emphasizes diminishing returns and the finiteness of space as limits to population increase, the externality is pecuniary and relates to the negative effect of an additional worker on the wage level. Alternative externalities can arise due to public goods or natural resources. An early modern formulation of the "tragedy of the commons" is provided by Hardin (1968). Motivated by this existence of common resources, Demeny (1986) described the population problem as a prisoner's dilemma, in which each couple, acting in their own self-interest, induces suboptimal collective outcomes. The existence of a prisoner's dilemma has been used to advocate population policy and public intervention in individuals' fertility decisions. Yet even if one accepts the relevance of negative externalities, little is known about their magnitude. A study by Lee and Miller (1991) is one of the few attempts to estimate them in the context of developing countries. Contrary to expectations, "[f]or some countries widely viewed as having serious population problems, the net total of these quantifiable externalities was close to zero" (1991: 295). In developed countries where concerns about low fertility are prominent, however, the externalities to childbearing are substantial. Instead of the negative spillovers that dominate the concerns of excessive population growth, these arguments focus primarily on the positive externalities to childbearing resulting from the existence of public transfer and related systems that – in their net effects – transfer resources from the younger to older generations. In addition, as argued by Boserup (1981) and Simon (1981), a larger population could imply a greater probability of increases to knowledge that is a public good (although this positive effect is reduced if knowledge and information are shared relatively easily globally). In this context, children tend to be associated with positive externalities, resulting in lower than socially optimal fertility levels, because the discounted contributions of children to these systems exceed the discounted benefits they receive.

In addition to this focus on economic externalities, fertility models that include social interaction and social learning have emphasized possibly positive externalities – or spillovers – that arise because the adoption of reduced fertility by some parents contributes to the erosion of traditional norms or pressures to conform (e.g. Kohler, 2001). Other forms of social interactions are possible, including also the returns to education or feedbacks affecting the marriage market. For example, these externalities occur because the diffusion of information is a path-dependent process and the choices of early adopters influence the availability of information for later decision-makers (Kohler, 1997).[8] Externalities exist in health behavior due to threshold phenomena in the spread of contagious diseases.

[8] Evidence for relevant social interaction effects on fertility is also provided by Freedman and Takeshita (1969), who report on a controlled experiment in which blocks of neighborhoods in Taichung (Taiwan) were exposed to different information about available family planning services, ranging from no explicit information to mailings and home visits of field representatives. About half of all women who accepted family planning after the initial information campaign, heard about the program from friends, neighbors, and relatives instead of the home visits which provided the second most important source of information.

Alternatively, they emerge in economic development because the return to human capital depends on the average level of education in a community. Or, as Goldin and Katz (2002) argue, during the introduction of the pill that altered women's career decisions through two pathways: a direct pathway that through better fertility control facilitated women to invest in expensive long-duration training without the price of abstinence or a high risk of unwanted fertility, and an indirect pathway in which the resulting delay of marriage increased the size of the marriage pool at older ages, thereby reducing the costs of delaying marriage in terms of the probability of finding an appropriate mate. Alternatively, positive externalities may occur due to increasing informational returns in social learning about contraception and family planning. In particular, because information is to some extent a public good, private providers are not likely to supply it in adequate amounts. This is particularly the case when information (for example, about the possibility of controlling fertility) cannot be easily tied to a specific marketable product. Thus, information about rhythm and withdrawal has no private market, nor does information about the pill in rural areas where there is no real market for private medical services. Yet the welfare gains to individuals from accurate information of this kind may exceed the costs of providing that information (e.g. Behrman and Knowles, 1998).

This information problem may be particularly severe in the context of family planning, where the product is a complex set of ideas and procedures whose benefits are not immediately apparent, but whose perceived risks may be high. In addition, much information – for example, regarding appropriate method and medical contraindications – is client-specific and may be too sensitive and complex for the mass media to convey. Interactions between family planning and other maternal and/or child health programs/policies are also complex, with the benefits of the latter affecting the individual and societal costs and benefits of family planning. The failure of a market for contraceptive information in these contexts is frequently used to motivate family planning programs. These programs use visits by field workers as an adjunct to mass media advertising. Alternatively, they may provide incentives for women to visit a health clinic and acquire information about birth control. This policy intervention is different from many other incentive programs that try to reduce the number of children per couple. Information provision does not affect the desired fertility directly, but rather helps couples to achieve their desired fertility level. Humanitarian or other objections, frequently raised in the context of other population policies, are less severe with respect to pure provision of contraceptive information. Information provided by family planning programs, however, is not the only possibility for women to learn about the availability or the properties of contraceptive methods. The possibility of missing markets and policy failures emphasizes that diffusion of information in social networks may be an important factor in contraceptive choice, and market and/or policy failures provide an economic rationale for the high prevalence of social learning in fertility decisions. A formal model of this diffusion is given in Kohler (1997), and the combination of social learning with family planning efforts in empirical studies may shed light on the different performance of these programs (Kohler *et al.*, 2000). Moreover, social learning implies positive externalities that affect fertility dynamics during the demographic transition. These positive externalities, denoted informational increasing returns, are associated with the adoption of modern contraception because a new user can provide essential information to other women who are uncertain about the costs and benefits of modern family planning and low fertility (Kohler, 2001).

Population growth, demographic dividends, and economic development

Economic development is often seen as a sufficient condition for the decline of fertility as virtually all developed countries have – at least in global comparison (Figure 9.2) – low fertility rates and low intrinsic growth rates (Kohler, 2010), even if among the most advanced societies, fertility may slightly increase with development (Myrskylä *et al.*, 2009). The more interesting – and much more debated – question is if reduced population growth, and the changes in the population age structure that result occur throughout the demographic transition, can possibly facilitate economic growth and development. This debate about the interactions between population growth and economic development has a long history, with influences of these debates on population policy ranging from the pessimistic approaches following Coale and Hoover (1958), to the revisionist views expressed by the National Research Council (1986). The former was decidedly neo-Malthusian and argued that rapid population growth impaired economic development through its negative effects on saving and capital dilution. The latter emphasized the ability of markets and institutions to adjust, and argued that rapid population growth can slow economic development, but only under specific circumstances and generally with limited or weak effects (Kelley, 1988).[9] This report ushered in a period of uncertainty about the priorities that should be given to population policies (Sinding, 2009), as well as what the content of these policies should be – a perspective that arguably fits well with the predispositions of the US Reagan Administration, that announced at the 1984 International Conference on Population in Mexico that "population growth is in and of itself neither good or bad; it is a neutral phenomenon . . . The relationship between population growth and economic development is not necessarily a negative one." In a continuation of this revisionist theme that downplayed concerns about population growth, G. W. Bush declared during the 1991 World Population Week that "every human being represents hands to work, and not just another mouth to feed" (cited in Cohen, 1995a). In perhaps the most optimistic perspective, Simon (1981) wrote in his book on *The Ultimate Resource*, with the "ultimate resource" in the title referring to human ingenuity, that "every trend in material welfare has been improving – and promises to do so indefinitely."[10]

More recently, informed by new theoretical and empirical research in the last two decades, the pendulum in the population and economic development debate has shifted again. A "revisionism revised" perspective emerged (Birdsall *et al.*, 2001; Sinding, 2009) that again re-emphasizes important population–development interactions including, but not only as a result of, the potential "demographic dividends" (Bloom *et al.*, 2002) that can arise during the demographic transition as a result of changes in the age structure after fertility starts to decline (for related reviews, including some specific to the SSA context, see Kelley, 1988; Birdsall *et al.*, 2001; Dyson, 2010; Canning, 2011; Eastwood and Lipton, 2011; Sippel *et al.*, 2011; Teller and Hailemariam, 2011). In addition, on a theoretical level, the "unified growth theory" (Galor, 2005, 2011) has created a new interest in theoretical models integrating demographic change and economic development. After a period where revisionist perspectives have dominated the perceived wisdom on the interaction between population and economic development, the interaction between demographic change and economic development – including the role of family planning programs and reduced fertility for economic growth – has received considerable new attention on both the macro- and micro-level and utilizing both empirical and theoretical approaches.

The Malthusian mechanism by which a high level of population reduces income *per capita* may still be relevant in poor developing countries that have large rural populations dependent on agriculture, as well as in countries that are heavily reliant on mineral or energy exports (Weil and Wilde, 2009). For example, in a provocative simulation work calibrated to SSA contexts, Ashraf *et al.*

[9] For example, the conclusions in National Research Council (1986) state: "On balance, we reach the qualitative conclusion that slower population growth would be beneficial to economic development for most developing countries. A rigorous quantitative assessment of these benefits is difficult and context dependent. Since we have stressed the role of slower population growth in raising *per capita* human and physical capital, it is instructive to use as a benchmark the effects of changes in the ratio of physical capital per person. A simple model suggests that the effect is comparatively modest. Using a typical labor coefficient of 0.5 in estimated production functions, a 1 percent reduction in the rate of labor force growth would boost the growth of *per capita* income by 0.5 percent per year. Thus, after 30 years, a 1 percent reduction in the annual rate of population growth (produced, say, by a decline in the crude birth rate from 37 to 27 per 1,000) will have raised production and income *per capita* to a level 16 percent above what it would otherwise have been. This would be a substantial gain, but by no means enough to vault a typical developing country into the ranks of the developed."

[10] Quoted in Lam (2011).

(2008) study quantitatively the effect of exogenous health improvements – for instance, as a result of policy interventions that target infectious diseases (such as malaria and tuberculosis), or result in improvements of life expectancy through better general health (on output *per capita*, accounting for the effects that these health improvements have towards increasing population growth through the resulting reduction in mortality). (A related study with similar findings is Acemoglu and Johnson, 2007.) The striking finding of Ashraf *et al.* (2008) is that, due to increased rates of population growth that follow from these policies or interventions as a result of reduced mortality, the effects of the resulting health improvements on income *per capita* are found to be substantially lower than those that are often quoted by policy-makers, and may not emerge at all for three decades or more after the initial improvement in health. This emphasis on the Malthusian effects resulting from the more rapid population growth induced by health interventions that reduce mortality is controversial (Bleakley, 2008, 2010; Arndt *et al.*, 2009), and depends critically on the assumptions how fertility and human capital investments respond to health and other societal/technological changes that reduce the relevance of the Malthusian mechanism (see Lam, 2011 and our earlier discussion). Nevertheless, the findings highlight how higher population growth resulting from interventions can potentially reduce the welfare and income gains resulting from improved health, and as a result, the general-equilibrium effect of these policies are less than the partial-equilibrium effects suggested by most micro-studies.

On the other end of the spectrum of the population–development debate, the optimists about the effects of population growth on economic development tend to emphasize the positive contributions of population to innovation, efficiency in use of productive factors, scale economies in transportation and communication, or institutional change. In the view of Boserup (1965, 1981), increases in population density induce shifts to more labor-intensive farming, and the development of new tools and techniques (for example, the plow) permits large increases in productivity. Urbanization has been seen as critical to this process in both historical and contemporary contexts (Jacobs 1969; Glaeser, 2011). In one example documenting these interactions, Kremer (1993) constructs and empirically tests a model of long-run world population growth combining the Malthusian idea that technology limits population with endogenous technological progress. The model predicts that over most of history the population growth rate and the rate of technological progress are proportional to population size. Empirical tests support this prediction and show that historically, among societies with no possibility for technological contact, those with larger initial populations have had faster technological change and population growth. The implication of these models that high population density eventually leads to modernization is qualified by Lee (1986, 1988). The question of institutional adjustment, which weakens the effect of population growth on economic development, is crucially related to the question whether institutional adaptation is a necessary consequence of population pressure. Models with multiple equilibria and possible development traps raise some doubts with respect to this deterministic institutional adjustment (Becker *et al.*, 1990; Galor and Tsiddon, 1991; Dasgupta, 1993). Instead of deterministic long-term modernization, for example, Lee's (1986, 1988) model also exhibits a "Malthusian trap." Depending on the initial combination of technology level and population size, and on the interaction between wages and fertility, the population may either modernize and reach an equilibrium with relatively high income and technology levels, or it may converge to a Malthusian situation where low levels of technology and low wages eventually restrict fertility. This feature of multiple equilibria questions the view of the "pure" optimists that economic modernization is a deterministic consequence of population growth. Arthur and McNicoll (1978), for instance, describe a situation in Bangladesh that seems to fit the description of this trap. They report that peasants "seem quick to sense opportunities for even marginal progress" (1978: 57), but social and economic pressures on families combine to push fertility upward towards a high level, leading to declining wages and severe environmental problems. At the same time, these institutions, such as a lack of political and local organization and a low status of women, seem to be self-enforcing. Although the authors see potential for socio-economic change and modernization, they also question the improvement through induced progress as outlined in the optimists' perspective. More recently, McNicoll (2011) has emphasized the divergent demographic and development paths of two relatively resource-rich countries: Indonesia and Nigeria. A half-century ago, Indonesia and Nigeria appeared to be similarly placed in their development level and both had high fertility and high mortality. In the interim period, however, these countries followed radically different trajectories: Indonesia moved toward an East Asian style of growth accompanied by a progressive reduction of poverty, whereas in Nigeria growth stagnated, the economy became increasingly dominated by oil and natural gas revenues, and poverty remained undiminished. In addition, the demographic transition in these countries unfolded very differently: while Indonesia currently has a life expectancy close to 70 years and fertility averaging little over 2 births per woman, Nigeria's life expectancy is still below 50 and its fertility is above 5. McNicoll (2011) argues that this divergence in demographic and economic trajectories during the last fifty years is due to differences in governance and policy choice, in inherited resources and institutions, and in external conditions. Specifically, with respect to fertility, McNicoll argues that differences in institutional inheritance have been especially important, putting significant obstacles in the way of a Nigerian fertility decline that were not present, or could be fairly readily overcome, in Indonesia.

In a paper addressing the possibilities of a "Malthusian trap" that prevents long-term modernization, Becker *et al.* (1990) combine a theoretical growth model with endogenous fertility choice according to the new home economics. They argue that human capital investments are an important part of modernization, and that parental decisions about these questions are crucial for understanding fertility transitions. The analysis assumes that the rates of return on investments in human capital rise rather than decline as the stock of human capital increases, at least until the stock becomes large. The model exhibits two equilibria, corresponding to undeveloped and developed economies, respectively. The latter are characterized by higher *per capita* human capital and income, and lower fertility. As a result of the multiple equilibria that result from the interaction of individual-level returns to human capital and aggregate levels of human capital, and undeveloped economy can be "stuck" at the high fertility low–development equilibrium unless sufficiently favorable technology becomes available or external shocks disrupt the initial equilibrium. Becker *et al.* (1990) thus conclude that "history and luck are critical determinants of a country's growth experience" and that "[m]any attempts to explain why some countries and continents have had the best economic performance during the past several centuries give too little attention to accidents and good fortune."[11]

The emphasis on initial conditions and exogenous shocks for the selection between equilibria in the above model renders the reader somewhat uncomfortable because it leaves relatively little room for the policy interventions or endogenous social processes that affect the pace of fertility decline and development. Kohler (2000), for example, investigates this selection of equilibria in terms of a *coordination problem*. Expectations emerge in this context as a key determinant of the equilibrium selection. High fertility is rational as long as it is a predominant behavior in the population, and low fertility emerges as a rational choice if a critical mass of other community members follows suit. The main difference is that contemporary or future individual behavior is a potential source of divergence in a society's evolution, and that there is the possibility of self-fulfilling prophecies. An economy may remain undeveloped with high fertility because everyone believes that it will. Institutional contexts, including also the existence of the inclusive or extractive political institutions and elites emphasized in Acemoglu and Robinson (2012), are potentially important determinants of such shared expectations and perceptions. However, if changes in expectations occur, they can imply behavioral changes and may influence the long-term equilibrium selection. Such expectation-driven

[11] For a critical discussion of the Becker *et al.* (1990) model and its ability to describe basic empirical patterns of the onset of the demographic transition, see Galor (2005, 2011).

equilibrium selection is particularly relevant in fertility decisions. Specifically, expectations about future development trajectories and social/economic conditions are important because many externalities associated with fertility decisions are local (Dasgupta, 1993, 1995; Akerlof, 1997). These local externalities pertain either to the return on human capital investments as argued by the literature cited above, or to the social acceptability of contraception, the prevalence of pro-natalist traditional customs, or social norms that affect the status of women. All of these factors are endogenous to the aggregate prevalence of fertility control in the population. They imply that the incentives to reduce fertility depend, at least in part, on the behavior of other community members. A transition from the high-fertility equilibrium towards a persistent fertility decline can be initiated if a coordinated critical mass of behavioral change occurs. This observation provides a theoretical motivation for the "tipping" or "threshold" models suggested by Granovetter (1978) or Schelling (1978).

The unified growth theory (Galor, 2005, 2011) has now elaborated on the above mechanisms and started to provide an integrated perspective on both demographic change and economic development that is consistent with the demographic and economic trends and patterns during the demographic transition. The motivation behind this framework is the claim that the understanding of the contemporary growth process would be limited and distorted unless growth theory were based on microfoundations that reflected the qualitative aspects of the growth process in its entirety. While there remain some controversies about whether the specific mechanisms postulated in these models are consistent with the empirical evidence (Guinnane, 2011), the dynamics of demographic change and economic development – along with the dynamics of changes in technology, human capital levels, fertility, and mortality – are broadly consistent with the observed patterns during the demographic transition. Most importantly for the present discussion, the unified growth theory suggests that the transition from stagnation to growth is an inevitable outcome of the process of development. In the pre-transition Malthusian period, the interaction between the level of technology and the size and the composition of the population accelerated the pace of technological progress, and ultimately raised the importance of human capital in the production process. Technological progress hence becomes sustained and cumulative, and agricultural techniques and the mechanization of agriculture make the fixed factor – land – less important and less of a constraint for population growth and improvements in living standards. Technological progress also leads to new methods of production, and new research methods for producing new technologies, which increase the returns to education. This leads to a quality–quantity trade-off: families choose to have fewer children in order to allow investments in education that will make these children better off. As a result, the rise in the demand for human capital, in the second phase of industrialization, and its impact on the formation of human capital as well as on the onset of the demographic transition, brought about significant technological advancements along with a reduction in fertility rates and population growth, enabling economies to convert a larger share of the fruits of factor accumulation and technological progress into growth of income *per capita*, and paving the way for the emergence of sustained economic growth.

Two aspects of the united growth theory are important for the present discussion about the determinants of the onset and pace of the fertility transition during the demographic transition. First, the fertility transition within the framework of the unified growth theory is triggered by the gradual rise in the demand for human capital that causes parents to shift from child quality to child quantity (Galor, 2011, 2012). Second, the theory argues that international trade was an important reason for the differential timing of the demographic transitions, including those occurring in the second half of the twentieth century in less-developed countries. In particular, contrary to the process occurring in developed countries, international trade in non-industrial economies generated incentives to specialize in the production of unskilled intensive, non-industrial, goods. Hence, the absence of significant demand for human capital reduced the incentives to invest in human capital and child quality, and the gains from trade were utilized primarily for a further increase in the size of the population,

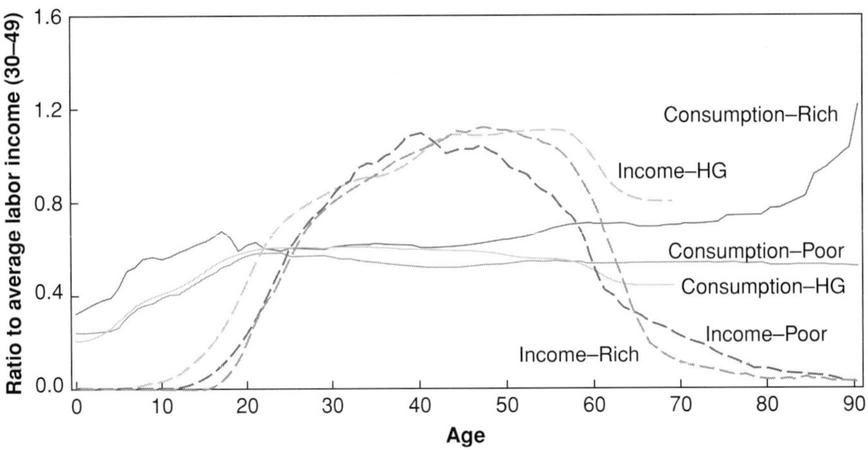

Figure 9.10 *The economic life cycle of hunter-gatherers (HG), poor agricultural populations, and rich industrial populations: consumption and labor income (ratio to average labor income, ages 30–49)*

Source: Lee and Mason (2011).

rather than in the income of the existing population. As a result, the demographic transition in these non-industrial economies has been significantly delayed, increasing further their relative abundance of unskilled labor, enhancing their comparative disadvantage in the production of skilled-intensive goods, and delaying their process of development. International trade therefore reinforced the "great divergence" in income *per capita* across countries during the nineteenth and twentieth centuries, and persistently affected the distribution of population, skills, and technologies in the world economy. And yet, the prediction of the theory is that the demographic transition, and the transition from stagnation to growth, have been merely delayed, and that ultimately the mechanisms and processes emphasized above will result in both demographic and economic change.

A further important contribution that caused the pendulum in the debate about the role of population change and economic development to go into reverse has been made by scholars who have shifted away from focusing on the size of the population and explicitly recognized different stages of the life course and the different economic contributions (positive and negative) to economic growth at different stages of it. Recent years have brought about a hugely improved understanding of the economic lifecycle across time and across different stages of economic development (Lee *et al.*, 2006; Lee and Mason, 2011) (Figure 9.10). These distinct phases of the lifecycle with different patterns of savings, intergenerational transfers, labor force participation, and human capital have received considerable attention as potentially important factors that determine the interactions between population growth and development. In particular, as the population age structure changes during the demographic transition – as is, for instance, illustrated in the recent and projected age structure changes for South Africa and all of SSA combined in Figure 9.11 – the proportion of the population that are children (young dependants), working-age adults (and thus net producers), and elderly individuals (who are net consumers in developed, but not necessarily among the less- and least-developed countries) shifts. Specifically, during the next decades, the proportion of the population that is of working age will increase markedly in countries like South Africa, which has experienced a substantial decline in fertility in recent decades (Table 9.1), as well as to a more modest extent in SSA countries overall where the average pace of fertility decline has been slower (Figure 9.11). This increase in the proportion of the population that is of working age will be least pronounced in the countries that

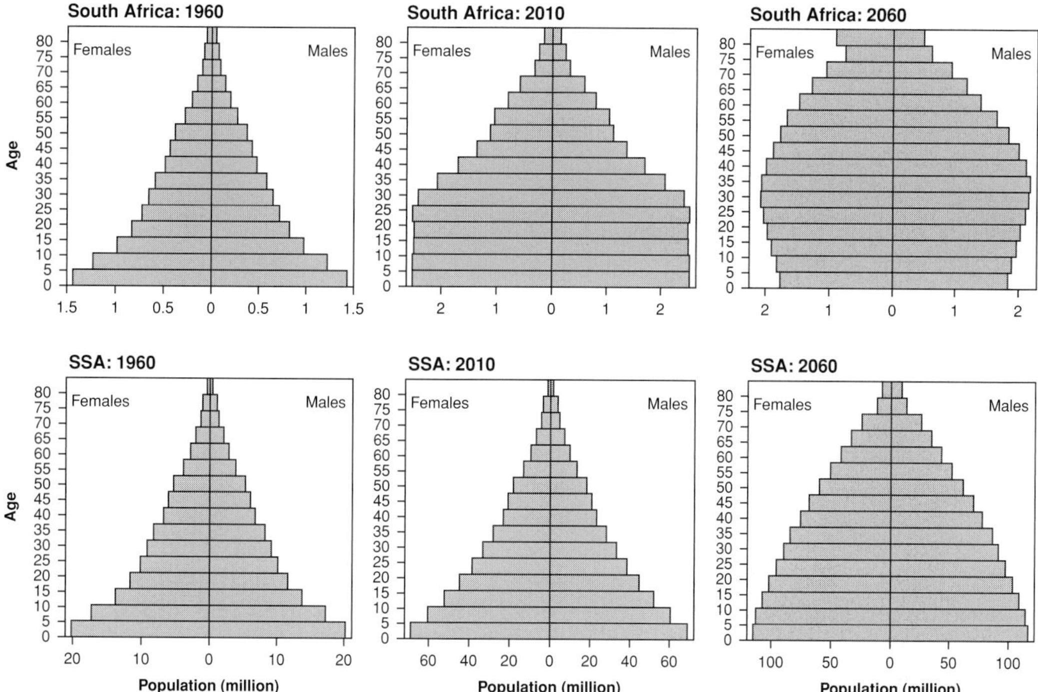

Figure 9.11 *Population age structure in South Africa and SSA, 1960, 2010, and 2060*

Source: Based on UN median projections (UN Population Division, 2010c).

continue to grow rapidly during the next decades, such as the countries included in Table 9.2. Recognizing these shifts in the population-age structure during the demographic transition, several studies have started to investigate the impact on economic growth not only of population growth rates, but also of changing age structures (Bloom and Canning, 2004, 2008; Bloom *et al.*, 2002). This literature hypothesizes that economic growth might benefit from a one-time "demographic dividend" caused by the fact that, as fertility falls, the fraction of the population of working age increases.

Part of this effect of age structure on *per capita* growth is *arithmetic* and follows from the composition $g(Y/N) = g(Y/L) + g(L/WA) + g(WA/N)$, where $g(.)$ denotes the growth rate, Y is output, and N, L, and WA are, respectively, the size of the population, labor force, and working-age population (for simplicity, we assume no unemployment). If productivity per worker (Y/L) and the proportion of the working-age population that is in the labor force (L/WA) are constant, an increasing share of the population that is of working age (i.e. $g(WA/N) = -g(1 + \text{dependency ratio}) > 0$) will necessarily increase the rate of growth of *per capita* income. But the literature on the demographic dividend points out that the effect of changing population age structure may be much stronger than this merely arithmetic effect. For example, a fall in the dependency ratio – especially the fall in the young dependency ratio that a fall in fertility following a decline in mortality will bring about – may well induce more participation of females in the labor force and raise savings. There may also be more investment in child quality as fertility declines, and human capital is likely to increase (most pronounced for women and children). As regards savings, if the population is considered as consisting of dissaving dependants at both ends of the age spectrum plus saving workers in the middle (Figure 9.10), then the early consequences of a fall in fertility will be to raise savings ratios, by reducing the weight of young dissavers in the population. It is also possible that falls in fertility will simultaneously raise females' participation and savings, in which case both financial and labor market conditions will favor the investment that will facilitate gainful employment of the extra labor.

Proponents of the demographic dividend theory argue that these aspects are of considerable importance for understanding the economic development in the context of the demographic transition, and that the age-structure changes during the early stages of the transition, along with the behavioral changes that cause it and result from it, have been an important factor in the rapid growth that have been described as East Asia's "economic miracle" and Ireland's emergence as a "Celtic Tiger." To test this hypothesis about the impact of age-structure changes on economic growth, the literature on the demographic dividend has estimated versions of models of the form $g(Y/N) = \varphi + X\beta + \delta(Y/L) + \gamma g(WA/N)$, where γ indicates the effect of changes in age in the proportion of the population of working age – which tends to increase as fertility declines – on *per capita* income. The arithmetic dividend that follows from only the increase in the proportion of the population that is of working age would imply that $\gamma = 1$. Empirical estimates for γ, however, range from 1.5 to 3.5 – with the higher of these figures obtained for African countries (e.g. Bloom *et al.*, 1998: Table 9.6). These effects therefore suggest that the "demographic dividend" resulting from age structure changes substantially exceeds the arithmetic effect that follows from the compositional change by 50–200 percent, and this additional effect of increases in the fraction of the population in working ages results from changes in fertility, savings, human capital and female labor force participation that occur as part of the demographic transition. Using related analyses that document that higher dependency ratios (including both youth and old-age dependency ratios) have a significant impact on growth, Kelley and Schmidt (2005) conclude that, world-wide, the combined impacts of demographic change have accounted for approximately 20 percent of *per capita* output growth impacts, with larger shares in Asia and Europe.

However, the literature on the demographic dividend also emphasizes that, both theoretically and empirically, the link from demographic change to economic growth is not automatic (Bloom *et al.*, 2002): there is an important role for initial conditions and path dependence (see above). Age-distribution changes merely create the potential for economic growth. Whether or not this potential is captured depends on the policy environment – including, for instance, the quality of governmental institutions, labor legislation, macroeconomic openness to trade, and education policy. According to Bloom and Canning (2008), this is the realm where Latin America stumbled during 1965–1990, and economic performance lagged behind that of East and Southeast Asian countries despite similarly favorable demographic conditions. And the policy and institutional environment is, of course, critical for evaluating the potential of a demographic dividend in SSA (Eastwood and Lipton, 2011; Sippel *et al.*, 2011). While Bloom *et al.* (2007b) find that the relationship between demographic change and economic growth in Africa is much the same as in other regions, primarily those SSA countries with good institutions and an increasing share of the population of working age, who are likely to be the ones that will reap a demographic dividend. However, from the perspective of analysts worried about future population growth, these likely beneficiaries from the demographic dividend are the countries that have already made most progress in reducing fertility and maintaining economic growth. Hence, a more pessimistic assessment about the prospect of a demographic dividend in high-fertility SSA countries is provided by Eastwood and Lipton (2011), who point out that, in comparison with the Asian experience, many SSA countries have been characterized throughout the demographic transition by more rapid population growth and lower savings rates. In particular, while slower population growth will indeed raise sustainable consumption per *capita* by reducing the savings that would be needed to sustain capital *per capita*, this prospect pales into insignificance beside the likelihood that savings will fall far short of the level necessary for sustained growth during the period when demographic conditions provide a context for a demographic dividend. In addition, Eastwood and Lipton (2011) question whether fertility declines – many of which have stalled and/or are progressing slowly (Bongaarts, 2008; Ezeh *et al.*, 2009) – will be sufficiently fast to allow for the changes in dependency ratios that are currently suggested by UN median population projections.

In addition to cross-country and longitudinal country analyses, a related literature that exploits naturally occurring "natural experiments" (Rosenzweig and Wolpin, 2000) has strengthened the case for important interactions between population change and economic and social development. Bleakley and Lange (2009), for example, investigate the eradication of hookworm disease from the American South (c. 1910), arguing that this eradication was principally a shock to the price of child quality because hookworm depresses the return to human capital investment, had a very low case-fatality rate, and had negligible prevalence among adults. Consistent with the quality–quantity trade-off model for fertility, Bleakley and Lange (2009) find that a decline in the hookworm-infection rate from 40 percent to 20 percent was associated with a decline in fertility that amounted to 40 percent of the entire fertility decline observed in the American South between 1910 and 1920; the eradication of hookworm was also associated with a significant increase in school attendance and literacy, and the combined effect of reduced fertility and increased child quality potentially importantly contributed to economic development. Focusing on variation in fertility more directly, Bloom *et al.* (2009a), for example, estimate the effect of fertility on the female labor force participation in a panel of countries using abortion legislation as an instrument for fertility, documenting that removing the legal restrictions on abortion significantly reduces fertility and increases female labor force participation since, on average, a birth reduces a woman's labor supply by almost two years during her reproductive life. As a result, Bloom *et al.* (2009a) argue that behavioral change, in the form of increased female labor supply, contributes significantly to economic growth during the demographic transition when fertility declines. Similarly, using variations in access to abortion as a factor affecting fertility, Pop-Eleches (2006) examines the educational and labor outcomes of children affected by a ban on abortions that was introduced in 1966 in Romania. Birth rates doubled in 1967 because formerly abortion had been the primary method of birth control. Controlling for socio-economic differences in abortion use prior to 1966, the analyses find that children born after the ban on abortions had worse educational and labor market achievements as adults. There is also suggestive evidence that cohorts born after the introduction of the abortion ban had inferior infant outcomes and increased criminal behavior later in life. Acemoglu and Johnson (2007) exploit the large improvements in life expectancy driven by international health interventions, and find that GDP *per capita* and GDP per working-age population show relative declines in countries experiencing large increases in life-expectancy – an effect that is possibly due to the more rapid population growth induced by these life expectancy gains (for a critical perspective on these findings, see Bloom *et al.*, 2009b). Emphasizing these negative effects due to more rapid population growth in response to health interventions in developing countries, Ashraf *et al.* (2008) evaluate changes in the prevalence of malaria and tuberculosis on health, productivity, and population growth, and conclude that the effects of health improvements on income *per capita* are substantially lower than those that are often quoted by policy-makers, and may not emerge at all for three decades or more after the initial improvement in health. Ashraf *et al.* (2008) thus argue that efforts to improve health in developing countries should rely more on humanitarian rather than economic arguments, since the economic growth consequences of such interventions may be small and occurring only after a significant delay.

The role of family planning programs and related policies

In the context of our previous discussions, an obvious question to ask, and yet a complicated question to answer, is whether family planning programs have made important *causal* contributions to declines in fertility, the attainment of other development goals (such as the MDGs), and economic development. And, if so, if these programs are suitable and cost-effective policy instruments to address the concerns about population growth and bring about progress in individual well-being.

In the second half of the twentieth century, family planning programs were the primary approach in developing countries to address rapid population growth, high fertility and unintended childbearing, and poor reproductive health outcomes. The programs tried to help individuals satisfy unmet need by increasing the supply of and access to contraception, as well as reduce other obstacles to contraceptive use such as fears about side effects, husband/familial disapproval, or lack of information/knowledge about contraception and/or the benefits of reduced fertility (see also p. 539). Usually less explicit because of the potential concerns about interfering with an individual's/couple's reproductive decision-making, programs have also tried to affect the level of desired fertility – which the notion of unmet needs takes as a given – through reductions in the costs of fertility regulation, and reforms – such as restrictions on child labor or expansion of required schooling – that affect the costs and/or benefits of children (Schultz, 2007). More recently, programs have also included a broader focus on reproductive and child-health outcomes (Bongaarts and Sinding, 2011a).

The first major family planning program was established in India in 1951, and by 1975 about seventy-four developing countries had established such a program (for reviews of family planning programs and their effectiveness, see Cleland *et al.*, 2006; Seltzer, 2002; Robinson and Ross, 2007; Joshi, 2011; Population Council, 2012; Shiffman and Quissell, 2012; for a more recent broader discussion of population policies, see also Das Gupta *et al.*, 2011; Demeny 2011; May, 2012). During the 1980s, international interest in family planning programs lost momentum, in part as a result of the "revisionist thinking" about population growth and in part in response to criticisms that these programs sometimes had problems in implementation and were unpopular (Seltzer, 2002). In addition, feminist critics argued that these programs were not integrated with a broader reproductive rights-based agenda, as a result of which women paid a high price for population policies since they were often viewed as passive "targets" who had to become "acceptors" of contraception (Dixon-Mueller, 1993), and there was increasing opposition from religious groups (for a response to these criticisms of family planning programs, see Bongaarts and Sinding, 2009). More recently, in light of the demographic trends and newer evidence about the effectiveness of family planning programs reviewed below, family planning programs – especially when they are broad-based, female-focused, voluntary, and respectful of human rights – have regained some of their momentum and are receiving renewed attention (Cleland *et al.*, 2006, 2012; Turner, 2009; Bongaarts and Sinding, 2011a, 2011b). The rationale for these programs in recent discussions is therefore twofold (May, 2012; Shiffman and Quissell, 2012): first, the *reproductive health rights* argument that emphasizes the right of individual women (and couples) to control their reproduction, helping them to attain meaningful and healthy lives; and second, the *ecological* argument that rapid population growth and high fertility imply negative individual-level and societal-level consequences – such as slower economic development, environmental degradation, or poor health outcomes – which could be reduced though family planning programs that help reduce fertility and population growth.

In reviewing the evidence about family planning programs, which is often based on experience in Asia and Latin America, and assessing the applicability of these findings to the current high-fertility countries (Figure 9.4), specifically also those in SSA, it is useful to highlight some of the broad differences in family planning programs across these regions (Joshi, 2011). On the one hand, in Asia (and mainly East and South Asia), most family planning programs aimed specifically at curtailing population growth through explicit policies such as the promotion of contraception and/or incentives for fewer children. On the other hand, in Latin America the programs were mostly promoted with the aim of achieving broader aims such as improving child and maternal health, rather than just reducing fertility. In contrast, African family planning programs were often implemented without explicit population policies, and they were often run by outside donors that were relatively small in scale (Joshi, 2011). Kenya and Ghana, for example, established family planning programs in the late 1960s, and Tanzania did so in 1970. Senegal established an urban family planning program in

1976 and a rural program in 1979. Much of Francophone Africa, however, lagged behind this movement and remained largely untouched by the wave of interest in such programs throughout this period. Even where they were established, programs in Africa often differed from their Asian counterparts. First, the focus was almost entirely on temporary methods, since permanent methods were regarded as culturally unacceptable (Caldwell and Caldwell, 1987); however, establishing of a reliable supply chain and relatively easy access to family planning services proved to be challenging in an African context due to a relatively weak health system infrastructure (Caldwell *et al.*, 1992). Second, African family planning programs were supported by a large number of international donors who rarely coordinated their actions with national governments or even among themselves, resulting in programs that were fragmented, relatively small-scale, and often subject to short-term budget cycles – all of which is in contrast to the Asian and Latin American programs that were typically run by Ministries of Health and backed by long-term budget commitments.

Despite these differences in implementation and design, family planning programs have in common that they emphasize relatively low levels of contraceptive use as a primary proximate determinate of high-fertility. The reasons for not using contraception in high fertility contexts are often thought to include high levels of desired fertility, a lack of knowledge about the existence and availability of contraception, insufficient contraceptive supplies and services, the cost of contraception, an exaggerated fear of side effects, and opposition from spouses and other family member. Family planning programs therefore often go beyond the narrow provision of physical access to contraceptive supplies and services, but also aim at reducing other obstacles to contraceptive use as well – including, for instance, high levels of gender inequality, lack of female autonomy or knowledge about contraception, husbands' opposition or social disapproval of family planning (Cleland *et al.*, 2006). And if the arguments by Ashraf *et al.* (2008) and Acemoglu and Johnson (2007) have merit – that the higher population growth resulting from mortality-reducing health interventions can potentially reduce the welfare and income gains that would otherwise result from improved health – family planning programs should potentially be integrated and jointly implemented with other health interventions that aim at reducing infectious diseases or improving general health (for example, in the context of the 2012 Copenhagen Consensus project, Canning, 2012, Chapter 7.2 in this volume, highlights this point in the discussion of infectious disease interventions).

Family planning programs can affect the costs of reducing fertility, through both subsidizing the cost of contraceptives and making them more readily available, thereby reducing the costs of obtaining/accessing contraceptives. Family planning programs can also increase the information about family planning methods and the potential benefits of reduced fertility, and they can potentially affect preferences for children either directly or through processes such as *social influence* or peer pressures. Family planning programs can thus affect desired fertility, as well as help to reduce unwanted and mistimed births – with the latter representing a significant fraction of births in developing countries. For example, each year about 184 million pregnancies occur in the developing world, and 40 percent of these (74 million) are estimated to be unintended because they occur when women want to avoid or delay pregnancy (Singh *et al.*, 2010). These unintended pregnancies end in abortions (48 percent), unintended births (40 percent), or miscarriages (12 percent) (Bongaarts and Sinding, 2011a).

Proponents of family planning programs have long argued that these programs are effective and made an important contribution to fertility declines during the second half of the twentieth century (Bongaarts *et al.*, 1990; Bongaarts and Sinding, 2011a; Cleland *et al.*, 2006; Lapham and Mauldin, 1985; Turner, 2009). The Population Council (2012: Chapter 2) compares pairs of countries that are relatively similar in terms of social, economic, cultural, and religious characteristics, but where one country implemented a large-scale family planning program and the other did not. Such country-pairs include (with the country with a family planning program in *italics*): *Bangladesh* and Pakistan, *Kenya and Uganda*, *Iran* and Jordan. In all of these pairs, the country with the family planning program (*Bangladesh*, *Kenya*, and *Iran*) experienced more rapid fertility decline after the implementation of the program than the matched-comparison country. While the matching of comparison countries based on characteristics is an advantage of the analyses in Population Council (2012), as compared to earlier studies that related country and/or regional measures of family planning efforts to fertility declines, this line of research is often criticized because it is potentially subject to an endogeneity of family planning program measures that would tend to result in an overestimation of the causal contribution of the program. It is also possible to find counter-examples; as (Lam, 2012) points out, Colombia's fertility decline, which was associated with a very large family planning program, was about the same pace and magnitude as that of Brazil, which had virtually no organized family planning program (see also Potter *et al.*, 2002). In several studies, therefore, after controlling for the possible endogeneity of the program effort, it has been frequently not possible to infer a significant (in a statistical sense) or relevant (in terms of relative magnitude) influence of family planning programs from aggregate country data (Schultz, 1994). In a recent study in Indonesia, McKelvey *et al.* (2012) also question that the use of modern contraception is price-elastic – i.e. is responsive to one important dimension (the price of contraception) that is affected by family planning programs. In particular, McKelvey *et al.* (2012) exploit the substantial variation in prices and incomes that were induced by the economic crisis in the late 1990s and show that monetary costs of contraceptives and levels of family economic resources have a very small (and well-determined) impact on contraceptive use and choice of method – although it is not clear if this finding is specific to the particular Indonesian context.[12] The most prominent critique of family planning programs has been provided by Pritchett (1994), who compared total fertility rates with various measures of wanted or desired fertility to argue that the fertility variation between developing countries was mainly determined by desire for children, with 90 percent of fertility differences between countries being explained by differences in desired fertility, and that the claims that family planning affect fertility levels stem from inferring causation from association. More recent analyses that utilize the more extensive Demographic and Health Survey (DHS) data on wanted fertility (Lam, 2011), which have become available since Pritchett's (1994) work, essentially continue to find the same results: an overwhelming fraction (83 percent) of the cross-country variation in TFR is explained by cross-country variation in wanted fertility. Hence, while unwanted fertility clearly exists in virtually all contexts, the evidence does not suggest that countries with higher levels of fertility have a larger gap between actual and wanted fertility. Based on his analyses (and consistent with the more recent analyses in Lam, 2011), Pritchett (1994) thus concluded that the best way to reduce fertility was to change the economic and social conditions that make large families desirable, rather than investing in family planning programs[13] – a conclusion that caused considerable controversy at the time (Bongaarts, 1994; Knowles *et al.*, 1994). In light of these criticisms, Miller (2010), for instance, summarizes the proponent's view on the effectiveness of family planning programs as "beliefs about the importance of family planning programs are at times stronger than the evidence that supports them."

While significant skepticism prevailed during the 1990s about the effectiveness of family planning programs, a recent literature has begun to shift the evidence about its role. For example, Gertler and Molyneaux (1994) analyzed the contributions of family planning programs, economic development, and women's status to Indonesian fertility decline from 1982 to 1987, and after controlling for the targeted (non-random) placement of family planning program inputs, concluded that 75 percent of the fertility decline resulted from increased contraceptive use, but was induced primarily through economic development and improved education and

[12] For an earlier study of family planning use during the Indonesian financial crisis, see Frankenberg *et al.* (2003) . I am grateful to Lam (2012) for pointing out these Indonesian studies.

[13] Pritchett (1994) points to the fact that family planning programs can improve the timing of first births, with lifelong socio-economic implications for mothers, and that these benefits can provide a better reason for justifying family planning programs rather than declines in fertility *per se*.

economic opportunities for females. And while the direct effect of family planning explained only about 4–8 percent of the decline in fertility, the dramatic impact of the changes in demand-side factors (education and economic development) on contraceptive use and fertility was possible only because, as a result of the established family planning programs in Indonesia, there already existed a highly responsive contraceptive supply delivery system. Montgomery and Casterline (1993) use regional time-series analysis to study the impact of Taiwan's family program. In addition to finding a direct effect of this program on fertility trends, they infer from the positive autoregressive behavior of fertility that there is clear evidence in support of within-township, but only weak evidence for across-township diffusion of fertility control that acts as a *social multiplier* of the direct program effects (see also Rosero-Bixby and Casterline, 1994). Lam (2011) points out that the longitudinal analyses of *changes* in fertility yield a very different picture than the cross-sectional analyses of actual and wanted fertility in Pritchett (1994) (and updated in Lam, 2011). In particular, declines in wanted fertility explain 53 percent of the mean decline in TFR, and the remaining 47 percent of the decline occurs without any change in wanted fertility – suggesting that women have improved their ability to achieve their fertility targets, possibly (in part) as a result of improved access to and/or knowledge about contraception. Miller (2010) studies the regional expansion of the family planning program in Colombia in the 1970s, the timing of which is thought to have been largely determined by exogenous factors. The study finds that exposure of a woman to family planning from age 15 to 44 during the 1970s is associated with a reduction in cumulative fertility in 1993 of 5 percent (about one-third of a child), explaining about 6–7 percent of the fertility decline in Colombia's major population centers during 1964–1993 (and this contribution of family planning is similar to that identified by Gertler and Molyneaux, 1994). Hence, other factors – such as the socio-economic changes occurring during the same period – were more important determinants of the reductions in lifetime fertility. The effect of the family program increases to reductions in lifetime fertility of 10–12 percent for women who started to use contraception as a result of the program in the late 1960s and 1970s. In addition to declines in fertility, exposure to the family planning program when women were teenagers resulted in improvements in educational attainment of 0.05 years, and an increase by 7 percent in the probability of working in the formal sector, an intergenerational increase in children's schooling, and a delay in a child's first birth – the latter potentially being most important for the socio-economic gains resulting from program exposure while a teenager. The study also finds evidence that mothers with longer community exposure to family planning programs are associated with children who are more likely to be attending school, have completed more years of education, are less likely to work in the formal sector, and are less likely to have already had a child of their own by the time of the 1993 census. Similar conclusions are obtained by Pörtner *et al.* (2011), who evaluate the effects of family planning in Ethiopia, using a novel set of instruments that are based on ordinal rankings of area characteristics, motivated by competition for resources between areas. Access to family planning is found to reduce completed fertility by more than 1 child among women without education, while no effect is found among women with some formal schooling. These findings therefore also suggests that family planning and formal education act as substitutes, at least in the low-income, low-growth setting of Ethiopia. Pörtner *et al.* (2011) conclude that these results support the notion that increasing access to family planning can provide an important, complementary entry point to kick-start the process of fertility reduction. Such effects of changes in access to family planning are not restricted to developing countries. Following up on Goldin and Katz's (2002) analyses on the "power of the pill" in the United States, for example, Bailey (2006) use plausibly exogenous variation in state consent laws to evaluate the causal impact of the pill on the timing of first births and extent and intensity of women's labor-force participation. The results suggest that legal access to the pill before the age of 21 significantly reduced the likelihood of a first birth before the age of 22, increased the number of women in the paid labor force, and raised the number of annual hours worked.

Several other studies also point to the broader impacts of family planning programs beyond their effect on fertility. Specifically, cross-sectional analyses suggested that birth to young mothers and births following short birth intervals were associated with elevated mortality risks, and that by reducing these risky births, family planning programs would contribute to declining infant mortality (Bongaarts, 1987). For example, Rosenzweig and Schultz (1982) find that in urban areas in Colombia the availability of medical services – including in particular also family planning activities – in addition to mother's education, are associated with child mortality and fertility within a birth cohort of mothers. The least-educated mothers were the most strongly affected in terms of a reduced fertility and increased child survival by these local urban health programs (similar results are also found by Miller, 2010); no effects of program interventions and medical facilities are found on rural populations, even though both child mortality and fertility are lower for more educated rural women. Rosenzweig and Wolpin (1982) additionally show that services such as governmental health, education, and family planning programs are more effective in shifting resources from increasing family size to augmenting human capital *per capita* when they are provided jointly. In particular, the results show that reductions in the costs of medical services, contraceptives, and schooling and the improvement of water sources are mutually reinforcing alternatives for implementing the joint policy goals of reduced population growth and increased human capital formation. Rosenzweig and Wolpin (1986) find that family planning programs have positive effects on children's health (as measured by child height) in the Philippines, suggesting that family size and child health might be gross substitutes, which might explain why some areas had a family planning clinic but not a health clinic. Do and Phung (2010) also emphasize the potential positive consequences of children being "wanted," which is important as family planning programs are likely to reduce "unwanted" fertility and increase the fraction of children that are wanted by their parents. In particular Do and Phung (2010) exploit the fact that in Vietnam the year of birth is widely believed to determine success. As a result, cohorts born in auspicious years are 12 percent larger, and Do and Phung (2010) argue that this increase is primarily driven by wanted fertility. Comparing siblings with one another, those of auspicious cohorts are found to have two extra months of schooling (despite the larger cohort size in auspicious years), lending support to the conclusion that children benefit from being "wanted" in terms of schooling and possibly other child outcomes (for a related earlier study with similar findings, see Dytrych *et al.*, 1975; David, 2006). Instead of focusing on unwantedness, using twin data and estimates from China, Rosenzweig and Zhang (2009) study the consequences of having an extra child as a result of a twin birth and find that an extra child at parity one or at parity two, net of one component of birth-endowment effects associated with birth weight, significantly decreases schooling progress, expected college enrollment, grades in school, and assessed health of all children in the family. Nevertheless, despite the evident significant trade-off between number of children and child quality in this Chinese context, Rosenzweig and Zhang (2009) conclude that the contribution of the one-child policy in China to the development of its human capital was modest, primarily because the effect of the one-child policy on fertility was assessed to have been relatively small.

All of these studies are potentially affected by the econometric problems that hamper studies relying on observational data and that try to identify causal program effects – if they make any attempt to do so at all – by relying on longitudinal observations that allow controls for fixed effects, and/or instruments that affect family planning programs, and outcomes such as fertility only through their effect of family planning (for a discussion, see Moffitt, 2005, 2009). While not without their own set of limitations (Moffitt, 2005 Duflo *et al.*, 2007; Deaton, 2010), the most convincing evidence about the effects of family planning programs is often thought to be derived from controlled experimental designs that allocated family planning programs across regions or villages in a randomized fashion. Fairly early evidence from such randomized experiments exists showing that family planning programs affect contraceptive uptake, through both direct exposure to the program as well as through social networks. For example, Freedman and Takeshita (1969) report on a controlled experiment in which blocks of neighborhoods in Taichung (Taiwan) were exposed to different information about available family planning services, ranging from no explicit information to mailings and home visits of field representatives. About half of all women who accepted family planning after the initial information campaign heard about the program from friends, neighbors, and relatives instead of the home visits which provided the second most important source of information. Mailings had virtually no effect on increasing women's propensity to adopt family planning. There is also a substantial amount of evidence in the form of responses from women in (focus-group) interviews who state that friends and neighbors were either important sources of information about contraceptive methods, or that the consent of friends was an important factor in their decision to use contraception – which may importantly contribute to the social multiplier effects that have been associated with family planning program efforts (Montgomery and Casterline, 1996; Kohler, 2001). Six months after the program, TFR declined more rapidly in Taichung as compared to other cities – 6.4 versus 3.1 percent. Sunil *et al.* (1999) report on a Ammanpettai Family Welfare Program controlled experiment, which used a monetary incentive program, combined with a motivational program using trained contact persons who visited and followed up eligible women in the program area, to encourage contraceptive use among rural Indian women. While Stevens and Stevens (1992) found that a modest cash incentive for 3–5 months attracted very large numbers of women to a clinic where they learn about and were provided with the pill, condoms, or the IUD, Sunil *et al.* (1999) show that the motivational programs were more likely to improve long-term use of temporary family planning methods than cash incentive programs, suggesting that peer-based family planning education and training in community work to contact persons who make door-to-door visits to promote programs can be an important part of such a strategy.

While these family planning experiments can be used to document the effect of the program on contraceptive uptake, they are not useful for answering the more important questions of whether this update of contraceptive use contributed to declines in fertility and/or if these declines in fertility translated into broader socio-ecomomic gains. Unfortunately, as Schultz (2007) observes:

> Half a century of experience with implementing family planning programs throughout the world has produced few experimental evaluation studies which document the long-term consequences of family planning programs on family welfare. Estimating even the effect of programs on completed fertility of cohorts are rare and instead comparisons of adoption rates of new contraceptive methods or short run period birth rates are reported, few of which are experimentally designed, or statistically matched using propensity score methods or other satisfactory evaluation methods.

One important exception to this statement is the Matlab Family Planning Experiment that was designed as a social experiment in a remote rural area, the Matlab Thana, in Bangladesh.[14] This program was initiated in half of 141 villages for which there was already in place a reliable demographic surveillance system of the population, registering all births, deaths, marriages, and population movements.[15] The family planning program outreach effort was started in October 1977, which contacted in their homes all married women of childbearing age every two weeks, offering them various methods of birth control. The populations were periodically censussed and then randomly sampled in a comprehensive socio-economic survey in 1996. A census in 1974 confirmed that the

[14] The discussion of the Matlab program and its evaluation here follows closely Schultz (2007) and Schultz (2010).

[15] Miller (2010) points to some criticisms that are often raised in the context of the Matlab experiment: (1) there is suggestive evidence that true randomization was not fully achieved (Joshi and Schultz, 2007); (2) the Matlab family planning treatment was often considered too expensive to be financially sustainable without considerable external support – program expenditures per fertile women and per averted birth were roughly 10 percent and 120 percent of *per capita* GDP, respectively (thirty-five times more than mean family planning spending in other Asian countries at the time, Pritchett, 1994); and (3) because health services were integrated into the family planning treatment four years after the experiment began, it is difficult to isolate long-run consequences uniquely attributable to family planning alone (Phillips *et al.*, 1984).

program treatment and comparison villages did not differ significantly three years before the program started in terms of their surviving fertility, approximated by the village ratio of children age 0–4 to women age 15–49. A difference-in-difference change between the program and comparison villages pre-program and post-program indicates that by 1982 surviving fertility was 17 percent lower in the program areas, and remained 16 percent lower in the 1996 survey after the program had been in operation for nearly two decades. Fertility was lower in the program areas only for women less than age 55, presumably because women over 55 were over 37 in 1977 when the program started, and these older women had essentially completed their childbearing at that time and hence their fertility did not respond to the program treatment (Joshi and Schultz, 2007). It is possible to show that, subsequent to the Matlab family planning program, women age 25–55 in 1996 had about 1 child fewer in the program villages compared with the comparison villages. These women in program villages were healthier, measured by their BMI being 1.0–1.5 units higher than in the comparison villages, and their children experienced a death rate by their fifth birthday which was 25 percent lower in the program villages. Moreover, girls age 9–14 and 15–29 had obtained about one-third of a standard deviation more years of schooling for their age and sex in the program areas, whereas the boys had obtained about half a standard deviation more schooling. The estimated program effect on the boy's schooling was statistically significant at the 5 percent level, whereas this schooling effect was not significant for girls. On the other hand, girls age 1–14 were reported to have a significantly higher BMI in the program villages, normalized for age, whereas there was no significant difference in BMI for boys (Joshi and Schultz, 2007). Through the gains in BMI for women, family planning may also contribute to extended benefits in terms of lower mortality for a period of up to twenty years (Menken *et al.*, 2003). Women age 25–54 in 1996 also report monthly earnings a third higher in the program villages compared to the other villages, and the households in which women reside have proportionately more financial, agricultural, non-agricultural, and housing assets, more consumer durables and jewelry, and household tube wells in the program villages (Schultz, 2009). The wages of young men and women, age 15–24, did not decline – as would be predicted by Malthusian diminishing returns – in the program villages despite the tendency for there to be fewer children and they were more likely to attend school. Moreover, the wage rates for adult males age 25–54 are no higher in program areas than in the higher-fertility comparison villages – in contrast to the wages of adult women, that were at least one-third higher. The program also seems to have improved cognitive function at ages 8–14 among children who were eligible for the Matlab child health interventions in early childhood (Barham, 2012).

Schultz (2010) concludes that, based on the study of the long-run consequences of policy-induced voluntary reductions in fertility in the Matlab program:

> in this poor rural South Asian region, a concerted outreach program achieved a significant decline in fertility and sustained lower levels of fertility for two decades, during which fertility has declined substantially in both groups of villages. This policy-induced reduction in fertility is associated with women and children being in better health, sons receiving more schooling, and women earning proportionately more in the paid labor market, and living in households with proportionately greater assets.

These consequences of the program are important, among other reasons, because they have been achieved in a rather impoverished agrarian context with low female education and low female labor-force participation. Of course, based on a single study, it is difficult to assess if similar outcomes would follow from family planning programs in other parts of the world.

The Navrongo project in Ghana provides some evidence that some of the basic conclusions of the Matlab experience will also hold in an SSA context, although it is not yet possible to make inferences about equally long-term effects of the family planning and health programs as for the Matlab project. Like the Matlab project, the Navrongo Community Health and Family Planning project is a quasi-experimental study designed to test the hypothesis that introducing health and family planning services in a traditional African societal setting will introduce reproductive change. At the core of the project is a four-cell study design, where in three randomly assigned regions a new basic primary health care and family planning program were instituted in addition to the standard clinic-based services provided by the Ministry of Health. The fourth region maintained the standard services only and is used as the comparison area for the project. Debpuur *et al.* (2002) show that knowledge of methods and supply sources increased as a result of exposure to project activities and that deployment of nurses to communities was associated with the emergence of preferences to limit childbearing. Fertility impact is evident in all treatment cells, most prominently in areas where nurse-outreach activities are combined with strategies for involving traditional leaders and male volunteers in promoting the program. In this combined cell, the initial three years of project exposure reduced the total fertility rate by one birth, comprising a 15 percent fertility decline relative to fertility levels in comparison communities. In addition, Phillips *et al.* (2006) show that the arm of the experiment that focused exclusively on delivering health services to women and their children succeeded in reducing childhood mortality rates by half, but had a negligible impact on fertility, while the arm that focused on community-mobilization strategies and volunteer outreach led to a 15 percent reduction in fertility. This lends support to the argument that increasing access to contraceptive supplies alone fails to address the social costs of fertility regulation; effective deployment of volunteers and community-mobilization strategies offsets the social constraints on the adoption of contraception. In addition, the Navrongo program – and in particular the provision of convenient and easily accessible nursing care – has also resulted in a significant reduction in infant and child mortality (Pence *et al.*, 2007). As a result, the study claims that affordable and sustainable means of combining nurse services with volunteer action can accelerate attainment of both the International Conference on Population and Development agenda and the MDGs.

In addition, Ashraf *et al.* (2010) emphasize that in an SSA context, intra-household dynamics in contraceptive adoption may be of particular importance in how family planning programs affect contraceptive uptake and fertility, which has important implications for the design of these programs.[16] In particular, Ashraf *et al.* (2010) find that women in Zambia who were given access to birth control individually, rather than in the presence of their husbands, were 23 percent more likely to visit a family planning nurse and 28 percent more likely to receive a concealable form of birth control, leading to a 57 percent reduction in unwanted births. In addition, providing cheaper and more convenient forms of birth control through a voucher program led to a reduction in unwanted births only when women were also given full autonomy over accessing these new methods. Specifically, using comparisons that approximate the impact of lowering barriers to accessing modern contraceptives while maintaining family planning policies that limit women's autonomy over these methods, such as through *de facto* spousal consent requirements that are still in place in much of SSA, Ashraf *et al.* (2010) find higher contraceptive use, but not a decline in unwanted fertility, in response to the program. Hence, it seems that the intervention primarily changed contraceptive use among women who were already fairly successful in preventing unwanted fertility. The findings by Ashraf *et al.* (2010) hence suggest that excess fertility in settings such as Zambia is not necessarily driven by the high cost of birth control; instead, unwanted fertility might be reduced by technologies or policies that shift control of fertility control from men to women.

2012 Copenhagen Consensus: possible solutions for reducing population growth in high-fertility countries

Given the current debate that focuses on the role of family planning programs in addressing concerns about rapid population growth in some of the world's least-developed countries, we focus our benefit-cost calculations on family planning

[16] I am grateful to Lam (2012) for pointing out this study.

programs. In evaluating the benefits of these programs, the discussion in this chapter focuses on the implications of population growth on economic development, the potential effects of family planning programs on development, as well as various measures of individual well-being. It is important to point out that there are several other implications of population growth that are not considered here, including the role of population growth on climate change, political instability, and conflict. While these aspects are potentially importantly related to population change, their evaluation is beyond the scope of this chapter (for a discussion of these issues, suggesting possibly large benefits in terms of environmental sustainability and reduced climate change from slower population growth, see for instance the Royal Society of Science report on *People and the planet* (Sulston *et al.*, 2012), or the analyses of carbon emissions and population growth in O'Neill *et al.*, 2010). The BCRs presented below therefore are likely to be lower bounds to the extent that reduced population growth would result in additional benefits in domains such as climate change, political instability, and conflict.

Challenges of benefit-cost analyses of policies targeted at reducing population growth

Conceptually, a CBA is straightforward. Simply compare the benefits with the costs – if the benefits exceed the costs, or equivalently the BCR exceeds 1, then an intervention is warranted (e.g. Belfield and Levin, 2010). The benefits are simply the sum of the present discounted values (PDVs) of the weighted impacts of the interventions. Likewise the costs are simply the sum of the PDVs of the real resource costs of the intervention. The devil – and the challenges – however, are as usual in the detail. Before embarking on the benefit-cost considerations for family planning programs, therefore, it is important to highlight the challenges in doing so. Our review of the literature has highlighted the many uncertainties in assessing the determinants of fertility decline across a range of very different social and institutional contexts, and in assessing the role of family planning programs in facilitating declines in fertility and the attainment of other development goals. Moreover, the most robust empirical evidence is based on the Asian experience during the second half of the twentieth century and, with respect to family planning programs, the Matlab experiments in particular. The extent to which these findings are applicable to a contemporary SSA context – i.e. the world region with the highest concentration of high-fertility countries (Figure 9.4) – is at least somewhat uncertain. But even after acknowledging the limitations of the empirical evidence for conducting benefit-cost calculations, other problems remain (see also Behrman *et al.*, 2004; Behrman and Kohler, 2011):

Range of impacts

As we have highlighted above, family planning programs and reduced fertility are likely to have a range of impacts. On the micro-level, these impacts are potentially incurred by individuals, their families, and their offspring and/or parents. On the macro-level, these impacts may include economic development, which we will consider as part of the assessments in this chapter, but also aspects such as climate change, political instability, and conflict, which are not considered here due to the lack of detailed empirical studies that could inform benefit-cost evaluations in this domain.

"Prices"

Impacts generally are multiple and measured in different units, but must be combined into the same units (normally monetary units with prices as weights) in order to sum them and to compare them with costs. For some impacts conceptually at least the measurements are relatively straightforward – for instance, market prices for the value of increased labor productivity or reduced use of medical goods and services under the assumption that such prices reflect the true social marginal value of the relevant good or service. But for other impacts, this evaluation is much more challenging. The key example for this project is the value of averting mortality. A range of methods has been proposed in the literature – for example, the lowest-cost alternative means of adverting mortality (Summers, 1992, 1994) and the revealed preference as reflected in wage-risk choices in labor markets (Viscusi, 1993, 2010; Aldy and Viscusi, 2007; Hammitt, 2007; Robinson, 2007). A related question is what prices should be used. For example, should prices (including wages) be used for a poor SSA developing country or for Denmark – under the argument that a life should be valued the same whether it be in a low- or a high-income country? How these questions are answered can make an enormous difference for the present project in which averted mortality is a major impact. For example, Summers (1992) reports that the cost of saving a life through measles immunization was of the order of magnitude of $800 per life saved in the early 1990s or about $1,250 in 2004 (adjusting for inflation and the costs of raising resources, Behrman *et al.*, 2004), while Bartick and Reinhold (2010) use $10.56 million per death in US$2007. For the present project, all of the 2012 Copenhagen Consensus Papers are using the same two alternatives – DALYS of $1,000 per year and $5,000 per year – to assure consistency within the project with regard to this critical assumption.

Range of costs

What is of interest for the costs are the total true resource costs to society. These are not identical to governmental budgetary expenditures, though analysts often seem to assume that they are. On one hand governmental budgetary expenditures in some cases include substantial transfer components (e.g. in CCT programs), which typically involve some but much smaller resource costs than the amount of the fiscal expenditures. On the other hand, private costs and the distortionary costs of raising funds for governmental programs may be considerable. Many programs, for example, may require time inputs from individuals that are not typically covered by governmental expenditures. The Distortion costs of raising resources for governmental expenditures also have been estimated to be of the order of magnitude of 25 percent of those expenditures or more (e.g. Ballard *et al.*, 1985; Feldstein, 1995; Devarajan *et al.*, 1997; Harberger, 1997; Knowles and Behrman, 2003, 2005). Because cost estimates vary considerably, it is important to present estimates that illustrate how robust the BCRs are to different cost estimates.

Discounting

The costs and, probably even more the benefits, may be distributed over a number of years. But the value to society of resources in the future is less than the value of the same resources now because they can be reinvested if they are available now. Therefore future costs and benefits should be discounted to the present for comparability, particularly for costs and benefits that are likely to occur some time into the future. And the discount rate makes a difference. For instance, PDV of $1,000 received in twenty years is $553 if the discount rate is 3 percent, $377 if the discount rate in 5 percent, and $149 if the discount rate is 10 percent (and for forty years, the respective PDVs are $306, $142, and $22). However there is a lack of agreement about what discount rates are appropriate, though rates in the 3 percent–10 percent range are common for the social sectors. For the present project, all of the 2012 Copenhagen Consensus papers are using the same two alternatives – discount rates of 3 percent per year and 5 percent per year – to assure consistency within the project with regard to this critical assumption.

Interactions among policies

Of necessity we consider family planning programs in isolation. But, clearly, these programs are often embedded in other policy interventions (such as programs targeting the HIV/AIDS epidemic in SSA), and even if they are not explicitly integrated in such programs, the impact of family planning programs will likely depend on policies that affect access to health care and/or schooling. The policies will also depend on social and economic institutions, concerning the extent to which such institutions change as a result of either the development process itself or specific policy interventions.

Hence, variation across countries with respect to institutional and policy contexts is likely to have substantial implications on the consequences of scaling up family planning programs – but little systematic knowledge exists that would allow the incorporation of these aspects in the benefit-cost calculations pursued here.

Value of lives not born

Family planning programs, through their effect on fertility, affect the size of the population. This of course gives rise to the question of how to consider the welfare of persons who may not be born as a result of the intervention – a question that has been notoriously difficult to answer and for which no consensus exists in the literature (for discussions of this issue, see for instance Razin and Sadka, 1995; Golosov *et al.*, 2007). In our analyses, we follow Ashraf *et al.* (2011) and related studies and will not consider in the evaluation of family planning programs the welfare of individuals who are not born as part of the program.

Scale

Scale can come into the estimation of BCRs in at least four ways. First, there may be high benefit-cost interventions that are effective for only a small select population, and therefore are not likely to be of interest for the 2012 project with its broad perspective. Second, there may be interventions that have high BCRs on a small scale but that are difficult to scale up because critical dimensions of the small-scale intervention (e.g. high-quality and particularly dedicated staff) cannot be maintained if the intervention is scaled up. Third, there may be important aggregate effects that result from reduced fertility due to family planning programs, including important aggregate impacts on economic growth. Family planning programs that are implemented on a large – possibly national or even regional – scale can potentially affect population dynamics, and through the effects of the reduced population growth and changes in age structure can affect economic development and individual incomes. Programs that are implemented on a smaller scale, however, are unlikely to affect aggregate population dynamics, and any feedback from aggregate population change on the benefits resulting from a family planning program is likely to be absent or minimal. In addition, the effects of reduced fertility on the incentives to invest in child schooling or health may depend on the scale of the program, and the fraction of the population that is reached by it. In our analyses, we will focus on fairly large-scale comprehensive programs that have implications on both the micro- and macro-level. And while detailed analyses of how the scale of programs affects the benefits (and possibly costs) resulting from such programs seem impossible given the state of the literature, it is important to acknowledge the scale of programs in interpreting the results.

Estimation challenges

The estimation challenges for obtaining BCRs are enormous not only for the reasons noted above, but because of the difficulties in obtaining good response estimates due to the endogenous behavioral choices, unobserved variables, selectivity of samples, and different market and policy contexts to which large numbers of academic studies have been devoted. Our review of the literature reflects these uncertainties. For example, for many family planning programs, both program effects and the costs associated with potentially effective programs are difficult to pin down, and scaled up programs may have different effects and be subject to different costs than programs that have been implemented as part of research studies. Moreover, an important body of evidence stems from one specific program, the Matlab family planning experiment in Bangladesh, that was relatively expensive relative to GDP *per capita* and the findings of which may not translate to other contexts. One could therefore conclude that the task of estimating BCRs is so difficult that it would be better to abandon it. But that would leave society with little systematic guidance about policy choices in this important area. Therefore, in hopes of improving the basis for policy guidance, we swallow hard and proceed boldly and hopefully creatively (and hopefully not too foolhardily) to make the best estimates that we can given the present very imperfect information and strong assumptions necessary, with some efforts to explore the sensitivity of our estimates to important alternative assumptions.

Benefit-cost analyses for policies targeted at reducing population growth

Costs of contraception and family planning programs

Several studies have provided estimates of the costs of expanding family planning programs and contraceptive services in developing and high-fertility countries. Evaluations of family planning programs during the 1980s have estimated the costs per averted birth in developing countries ranging from around $45 (Jamaica, Philippines, Sri Lanka, Thailand) to $260 (Latin America and the Caribbean), with some estimates being higher (reported in Pritchett, 1994, and converted to US$2010). Levine *et al.* (2006) estimate costs of birth averted that range from $87 in Latin America and the Caribbean to $131 in SSA and $163 in East Asia and the Pacific (all US$2001).

Because research has demonstrated the broader implication of family planning programs for health and economic outcomes, the literature on family planning de-emphasizes the costs per birth averted and focuses on the costs of service and different health outcomes associated with family planning programs. For example, some estimates of the costs of family planning programs focus on satisfying the demand for contraception as indicated by unmet need. Estimates by the Guttmacher Institute suggest that of the 818 million women who want to avoid a pregnancy (in 2008), 603 million are using modern contraceptives and 215 million are not and are considered as having unmet need (Singh *et al.*, 2010). The majority of women with unmet need are estimated to live in SSA. Figure 9.12, obtained from this Guttmacher Institute report, shows that the current annual cost of providing modern family planning services to 603 million users in the developing world is about $3.1 billion (about $5 per woman using family planning), including the costs of contraceptives and related supplies, the labor costs of health workers and program and other public health systems costs. These services are paid for by a combination of domestic sources including taxes and private sector contributions, employer and employee contributions to health insurance, and out-of-pocket payments by service users. Expanding family planning services to all women with unmet needs – a total of 215 million women – would require an additional annual expenditures of $3.6 billion, bringing the total to $6.7 billion annually, 75 percent of these additional expenses would be required for program and other systems costs related to expanding family planning services, while only 16 percent would be required for the supplies and contraceptive commodities.[17] Based on these estimates, the per person costs of expanding service to women with unmet needs in developing countries is close to $17, more than three times the costs as for current users of family planning services. These costs are broadly consistent with estimates for an SSA context (Kenya) (Figure 9.13) (USAID Health Policy Initiative, 2010) that range from $2.74 (IUD) to $13.42 (implant) per couple–year of protection. Costs at NGO facilities are estimated to be somewhat higher. Increasing the contraceptive prevalence of modern methods by 1 percentage point during one year in Kenya – from 39.5 percent (2008) to 40.4 percent – requires an additional 97,200 users (accounting for population growth) and is estimated to require expenditures of about $1.4 million in terms of commodities and personnel (given current distribution of family planning methods), or about $14 per additional user. The costs are estimated to be considerably higher per additional user if the contraceptive prevalence were to be increased by about 20 percentage points, as such an increase would require substantial additional investments in health service infrastructure that is not required for a more modest increase of only 1 percentage point (for a discussion of the health systems'-strengthening efforts that are required

[17] It is difficult to assess based on Singh *et al.* (2010) and related reports how quickly, if at all, family planning programs could be expanded to reach the unmet need of *all* women in the developing world or SSA, even if the additional funds were provided.

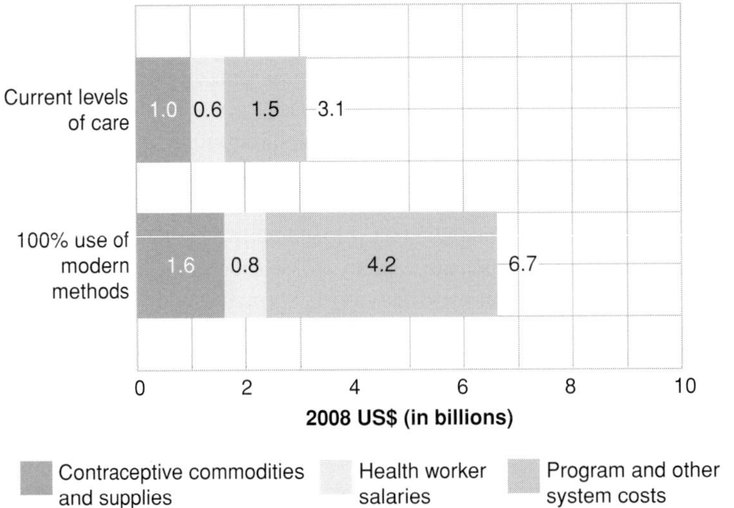

Figure 9.12 *Cost of providing family planning services in developing countries*

Notes: Estimates are for 2008 for all developing countries. Components may not add up to totals because of rounding. "Current levels of care" meet only part (74 percent) of the existing need for modern family planning. "100 percent use of modern methods" meets all existing need for modern family planning. Program and other systems costs include costs for program management, supervision, training of personnel, health education, monitoring and evaluation, advocacy, information systems and commodity supply systems, and costs for maintaining and expanding the physical capacity of health facilities.
Source: Singh *et al.* (2010).

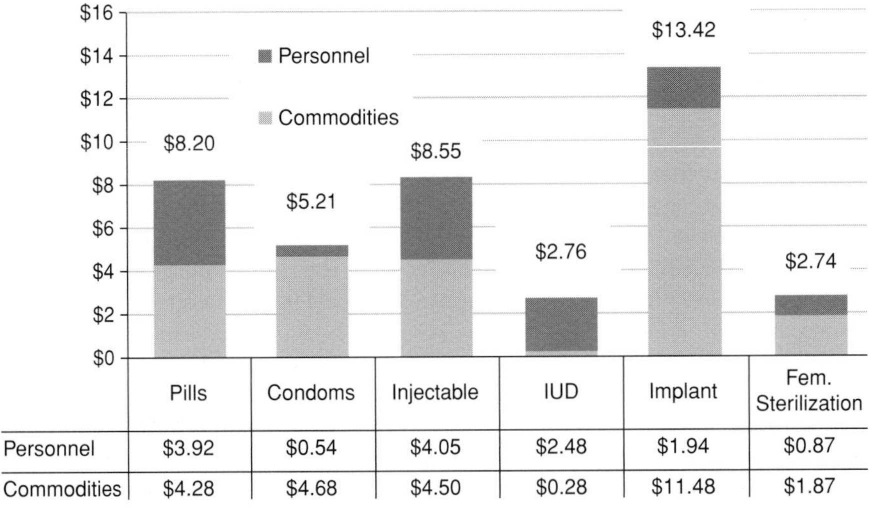

	Pills	Condoms	Injectable	IUD	Implant	Fem. Sterilization
Personnel	$3.92	$0.54	$4.05	$2.48	$1.94	$0.87
Commodities	$4.28	$4.68	$4.50	$0.28	$11.48	$1.87

Figure 9.13 *Cost of providing family planning services in Kenya (government clinics) per couple-year of protection*

Source: USAID Health Policy Initiative (2010).

for the implementation of successful family planning programs, see Population Council 2012: Chapter 3).

It is also important to emphasize that a mere improvement in supply of and access to family planning is unlikely to be adequate to achieve significant changes in family planning use, and the concept of unmet need is correctly criticized for suggesting this (Pritchett, 1994; Bongaarts and Bruce, 1995; Lam, 2012). In addition to supply-side factors, the reasons for the non-use of family planning often include fears about side effects, husband/familial disapproval, or lack of information/knowledge about contraception and/or the benefits of reduced fertility (Sedgh *et al.*, 2007; see also our earlier discussion). Peer pressures and social network influences can also be important factors resulting in non-use (Kohler *et al.*, 2001; Lyngstad and Prskawetz, 2010). And, of course, the level of desired fertility – which the notion of unmet needs takes as a given – can be targeted by policies that affect the costs and/or benefits of children or the costs of fertility regulation (Easterlin and Crimmins, 1985; Pritchett, 1994; Schultz, 2007). Hence, in order to be effective, family planning programs often include *demand generation* through media campaigns and related behavior-change communication in order to stimulate and/or motivate individuals to desire birth spacing or limiting, seek out family planning services, and adopt contraceptive method use (Population Council 2012: Chapter 4). Interpersonal communication through community leaders and health workers has been shown to be an important aspect contributing to the effectiveness of family planning programs (Freedman and Takeshita, 1969; Valente and Saba 1998; Sunil *et al.*, 1999; Arends-Kuenning, 2001; Munshi and Myaux, 2006; Phillips *et al.*, 2006), as are program designs that increase women's autonomy in contraceptive decision-making (Ashraf *et al.*, 2010). Several studies have also documented the effects of media campaigns and related behavioral-change communication on the adoption of contraception and family planning (Freedman, 1997; Valente and Saba, 2001; LaFerrara *et al.*, 2008; Jensen and Oster, 2009), which is expected based on the diffusion of innovation and social interactions (Cleland and Wilson, 1987; Bongaarts and Watkins, 1996; Montgomery and Casterline, 1996; Kohler, 2001). Based on the existing literature, however, the costs of these components of family planning programs are difficult to assess in general and are likely to be relatively country-specific. Rather than trying to account for these costs directly, we conduct in our concluding section sensitivity analyses that document the robustness of our BCRs with respect to a potential underestimation of program costs.

A different approach of assessing the costs of family planning is taken by Moreland *et al.* (2010), who try to estimate the family planning implications of the different UN projection scenarios.[18] The (undiscounted) cumulative family planning costs for the forty-five-year period between 2005–2050 for SSA is estimated to be $178 billion for the median variant (Figure 9.7), with costs ranging from $156 billion for the high-fertility variant and $198 billion for the low-fertility scenario (the PV of family planning costs, discounted at 4 percent, is $60.7 billion (medium variant), $68.4 billion (low-fertility variant) and $52.6 billion (high-fertility variant). The costs include commodities and personnel costs, but not necessarily the costs of scaling up the health systems to facilitate the service provision for these scenarios. Three aspects of these estimates are particularly noteworthy: first, the contraceptive costs of achieving any of the three UN scenarios are fairly substantial, with the discounted family planning costs for the forty-five-year period (excluding health systems cost such as potentially required expansions of the health care system; see Population Council 2012. Chapter 3 for a discussion) corresponding to about 6 percent of the annual SSA GDP. Second, the difference in discounted family planning costs between the UN high and low scenario is about 30 percent, corresponding to a difference in the projected 2050 SSA population of about 478 millions and a difference in the 2005–2050 population growth rate of 0.58 percentage points (between the 2.24 percent growth rate during 2005–2050 in the

[18] Moreland *et al.* (2010) base their calculations on the 2008 version of the UN World Population Prospects, rather than the 2010 version. The differences of assessing the costs of family planning programs between these versions are likely to be minor.

high- and the 1.66 percent growth rate in the low-fertility scenario). Third, based on the difference in UN population projections for 2050, an averted birth during the period 2005–2050 corresponds to family planning costs of $32, and a reduction in the 2050 SSA population of 1 person entails discounted family planning costs of about $33. Or, stated differently, by extrapolating these numbers, a reduction in the population growth rate by 1 percentage point during 2005–2050 would entail discounted family planning costs of about $27 billion (or about 3 percent of current SSA GDP).

Rather than estimating family planning costs based on the commodity and personnel costs required for attaining specific fertility trajectories, such as the UN median scenario, it is also informative to consider the costs of past family planning programs. The Matlab family planning experiment is widely considered to have been fairly expensive (and was thus potentially financially unsustainable), with annual program expenditures of about 10 percent of *per capita* GDP per fertile woman; in contrast, the Profamilia program in Colombia had program costs of about 0.1 percent of GDP *per capita* (or about 1/100th of the Matlab project cost relative to income) (Pritchett, 1994; Miller, 2010). The reasons for these large differences in program costs are not fully transparent; they are possibly related to the fact that the Matlab program was explicitly established to evaluate a best-practice family planning program in a resource-poor context, with considerable resources devoted to program implementation and the development of the relevant infrastructure; the Colombian family planning program, on the other hand, built on existing health infrastructure within a more-developed context (and higher initial *per capita* GDP).

Benefits I: reduced expenditures on health, schooling, etc.

The benefit of family planning programs has often been assessed in terms of savings on social programs as a result of a less-rapidly growing size of birth cohorts, with savings including a reduced need for expanding the school system, providing education, implementing immunization programs, or providing health care for children. Family planning programs also reduce costs of maternal health programs or programs to provide water and sanitation due to less rapid population growth. In a policy brief on "What would it take to accelerate fertility decline in the least developed countries?", the United Nations estimates that "for every dollar spent in family planning, between two and six dollars can be saved in interventions aimed at achieving other development goals" (UN Population Division, 2009, based on calculations in Bernstein, 2006). A related report for Kenya (Figure 9.14), under the heading, *Family Planning is a Good Investment*, estimates that family planning expenditures of $71 million during the period 2005–2015 are associated with social sector cost savings of $271 million – a BCR close to 4:1 (USAID Health Policy Initiative, 2009b). Corresponding estimates in the literature vary widely. For example, due to smaller costs associated with satisfying the demand for unmet needs, USAID Health Policy Initiative (2009b) estimates a ratio of social-cost savings for each dollar spent on family planning of 13 to 1 for El Salvador, and a 1984 study estimated costs savings in government programs of up to $16 for each dollar spend on family planning programs in Thailand for the period 1972–2010 (the ratio is 7:1 for the first nine years of the program) (Chao and Allen, 1984).

Estimates along the above lines are frequently used to argue that "Family planning is a good investment" (UN Population Division, 2009; USAID Health Policy Initiative, 2009b; Bongaarts and Sinding, 2011a) because social-cost savings as a result of reduced fertility and improved health outcomes significantly exceed the expenditures on family planning programs. However, it is important to note that the estimates of these social-cost savings mostly result from "accounting" for lower fertility and improved health outcomes; these estimates generally do not reflect the fact that reduced fertility may results in shifts from child quantity to child quality, which is likely to increase demands for schooling and potentially other health services. Hence, the social costs savings highlighted in Figure 9.14 and related studies may be misleading in terms of reductions in social costs if family

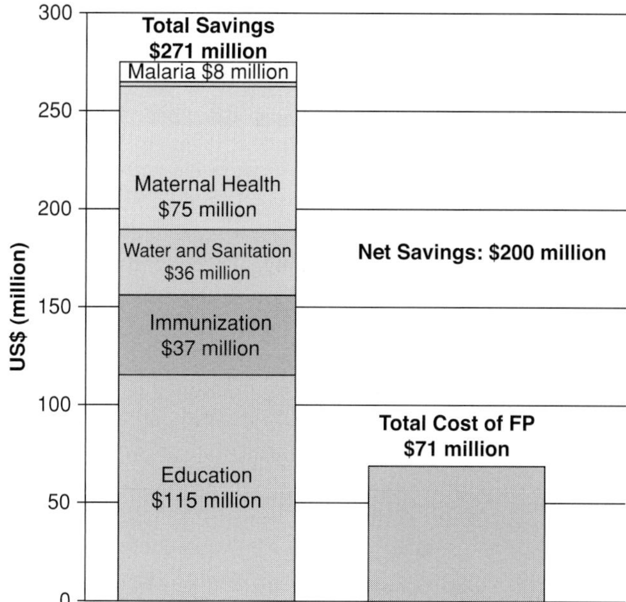

Figure 9.14 *Social sector cost savings and family planning costs in Kenya 2005–2015*

Source: USAID Health Policy Initiative (2009b).

planning programs also result – as is suggested by much of the recent literature – in shifts in the demand for child quality (including for instance, child health and schooling) (see p. 556) (Table 9.3).

Benefits II: evaluating reduced infant and maternal mortality

The research and policy literature on family planning emphasizes the positive reproductive health outcomes associated with increased availability of contraceptives that allow women and couples to satisfy unmet need (Cleland *et al.*, 2012). Table 9.3, for example, reports findings from the Guttmacher Institute report (Singh *et al.*, 2010), arguing that in 2008 modern contraceptive use prevented 188 million unintended pregnancies, 1.2 million newborn deaths, and 230,000 maternal deaths and other negative health outcomes that would have occurred in the absence of any modern method use. According to this report, expanding family planning programs so that (current) unmet need was fulfilled would result in 640,000 fewer newborn deaths, 150,000 fewer maternal deaths (more than 50,000 fewer from unsafe abortion and more than 90,000 fewer from other pregnancy-related causes), and 600,000 fewer children who lose their mother. The report also estimates that satisfying unmet need results in 36 million fewer healthy YLL (12 million fewer among women and 24 million fewer among newborns) (for related analyses, reaching generally similar conclusions, see Ahmed *et al.*, 2012). In a related study, Ross and Blanc (2012) decompose declines in maternal mortality into the contributions resulting from changes in the numbers of women, the number of births, and fertility rates, concluding that declines in fertility averted approximately 1.7 million maternal deaths in developing countries during 1990–2008, corresponding to a 54 percent reduction in the maternal mortality rate. Relating fertility declines to changes in contraceptive use, Cleland *et al.* (2012) argue – with some leap of faith in terms of inferring causal relationships from observed associations – that, because increased contraceptive use accounts for 73 percent of the fertility decline, about 40 percent in the reduction in the maternal mortality rate is

Table 9.3 Benefits resulting from modern contraceptive use among women who want to avoid a pregnancy, according to contraceptive use scenario, 2008

Measure (000)	Current use of modern methods	Fulfillment of unmet need for modern methods	Total
Unintended pregnancies averted	187,800	53,460	241,260
Unplanned births	53,550	21,820	75,370
Abortions	112,310	24,800	137,100
Miscarriages	21,940	6,840	28,780
Deaths averted			
Newborn	1,170	640	1,810
Maternal	230	150	380
Children who would not become orphans	740	600	1,340
DALYs saved			
Women	24,640	12,430	37,070
Newborns	46,350	23,710	70,060
No. contraceptive users	603,090	214,450	817,540

Source: Singh *et al.* (2010).

due to contraception. In analyses that control for potential confounders, Cleland *et al.* (2012) furthermore estimate that for each percentage-point increase in contraceptive use, the maternal mortality rate decreased by 4.3 deaths per 100,000 births. Analyses of demographic and health survey data furthermore suggest that about one-third of maternal deaths in developing countries would be preventable if the unmet need for family planning were satisfied and all women wanting to stop childbearing used effective contraception (Collumbien *et al.*, 2004; Singh *et al.*, 2010). Nevertheless, this progress in reduced maternal mortality – both in terms of risk per birth and the total number of maternal deaths – has occurred relatively unevenly within developed countries. For example, Ross and Blanc (2012) point out that, to date, SSA has experienced minimal declines in maternal deaths, resulting from the combined effect of increases in the number of women at risk and small declines in fertility and mortality. In addition to reducing maternal mortality, increased contraceptive use has been associated with reduced infant mortality, primarily as a result of reducing the frequency of relatively short birth intervals (Hobcraft *et al.*, 1984; Rutstein, 2005) and better child health outcomes (Dewey and Cohen, 2007). Cleland *et al.* (2012) conclude, based on a review of the existing literature, that the infant mortality rate would fall by about 10 percent, and mortality of children aged 1–4 by about 20 percent, if all children were spaced by a gap of at least two years.

Given the fact that some empirical evaluations of family planning programs have documented effects of these programs on infant mortality (e.g. Joshi and Schultz, 2007), but not in all cases where the effect on mortality was investigated (e.g. Miller, 2010), it is difficult to evaluate if these specific assumptions about positive reproductive health outcomes from contraceptive use and satisfying unmet need are realistic and reflect causal estimates of family planning programs rather than merely observed associations. Skeptical readers of the above evidence are likely to be worried that the analyses of the number of maternal and infant/child death averted as a result of increased contraceptive use are overestimates since they are mostly derived from correlational studies that may not necessarily provide estimates of causal effects (for a discussion of these estimation issues, see Schultz, 2010).

Nevertheless, the economic literature on the careful evaluation of family planning programs suggests a relatively convincing basis for concluding that positive health benefits for children and mothers from family planning programs do indeed exist, and that these positive effects persist after controlling for possibly endogeneity of contraceptive use. But these micro-studies are difficult to generalize to SSA or all developing countries for obtaining BCRs. Hence, while acknowledging the potential limitations of these estimates for the benefit-cost analyses in this chapter, we take the estimates in Singh *et al.* (2010) at face value, and evaluate the value of life according to the 2012 Consensus (Copenhagen Consensus Project, 2012) guidelines with $1,000 per DALY, 3 percent discounting and life expectancy at birth (for newborn deaths) and at age 28 (for maternal deaths). In this case, the expansion of family planning programs to cover current unmet need in developing countries results in total benefits of $110 billion. Given the costs of satisfying the current unmet need of $3.6 billion, these calculations suggests a BCR of about 30:1 for the expansion of family planning programs to cover unmet need. This BCR rises to 50:1 if the DALYs saved reported in Table 9.3 are valued at $5,000, and the BCRs would be even higher if the average costs of service provision, rather than the marginal costs of satisfying unmet need, were used in the calculations. However, these BCRs are overestimates to the extent that the causal impacts of family planning programs are less than those estimated in Singh *et al.* (2010) and assumed in the above calculations.

Benefits III: lifecycle, distributional and intergenerational benefits of family planning programs

In addition to the effect of family planning programs towards reducing fertility and reducing maternal/child mortality, these programs have been shown to result in higher levels of female (mother's) education, improvements in women's general health (e.g. as indicated by BMI) and longer-term survival, increases in female labor force participation and earnings, increased child health (up and beyond the effect on reducing child mortality), and increased child human capital (including higher schooling levels) (e.g. Joshi and Schultz, 2007; Schultz, 2009; Miller, 2010). Several of these program effects will affect an individual's well-being because in large-scale family planning programs – the only ones we evaluate here – these effects will make contributions to economic growth, which in turn will affect future income levels. The benefits resulting from increased economic growth – including (at least partially) the effects of improved health, human capital, female labor-force participation, and higher female earnings – will be considered in the next section. In addition, all of the above program effects will generally be considered desirable and beneficial because they reduce inequality, (including gender inequality), contribute to an improved status of women, possibly reduce poverty, and potentially increase subjective well-being among adults (and especially females) and children. Nevertheless, within the current framework and given the available empirical evidence, it will be impossible to explicitly evaluate the benefits of these effects in terms of our benefit-cost calculations up to and beyond their contributions to economic growth that are considered below.

Benefits IV: contributions of reduced fertility on per capita *income growth*

The macro-level interactions between population growth and economic developments are among the key considerations in evaluating the potential benefits of investments in family planning programs. But despite decades of research on this topic with shifting consensus opinions, this aspect remains challenging to evaluate. In this section we review, and then evaluate, some of the prevailing perspectives. It is important to keep in mind that, even if we conclude below that the BCRs of family planning programs are likely to be significantly larger than 1 with respect to contributions to *per capita* income growth, one should not have illusions about the ability of such programs to reduce global inequalities in income levels between developed and developing countries, or even between

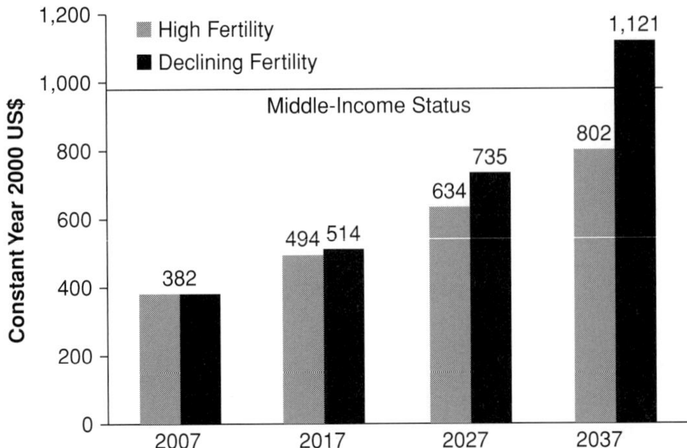

Figure 9.15 *RAPID model simulation: Zambia GDP* per capita *as function of fertility trends based on 6 percent aggregate economic growth rate*

Note: The high-fertility scenario assumes a modest decline of the TFR from 6.2 in 2007 to 5.8 in 2037; the low-fertility scenario assumes a decline to a TFR of 2.2.
Source: Zambia Ministry of Finance and National Planning (2010).

the least- and other less-developed countries. The contribution of reduced population growth to economic growth pales in light of the about twenty-fold differences in income levels that exist in global comparison. Hence, family planning programs are not likely to be a substitute for other development efforts.

To start the discussion of the potential benefits of family planning programs and reduced fertility in terms of economic growth, we initially focus on arguments made by policy-oriented organizations advising SSA governments, NGOs, and international donors such as USAID. For example, to assess the potential contributions of reduced fertility on *per capita* income growth, the USAID-funded Health Policy Initiative (www.healthpolicyinitiative.com/) has developed a computer-based tool RAPID (USAID Health Policy Initiative, 2009c). This tool allows stakeholders to "demonstrate the effect of rapid population growth on different sectors and the benefits of [family planning] programs." The description of the program states:

> The model combines socioeconomic indicators – such as labor force participation, primary school enrollment, and number of nurses *per capita* – with demographic information and population projections to estimate impacts up to 30 years into the future. Different scenarios are projected so that policymakers can compare the consequences if the country/region continues to have high fertility vs. the benefits of reducing fertility, in part, through [family planning] programs.

In recent publications, in collaboration with the respective governments, this model has been used to assess the contributions of population and family planning programs to development in several low-income countries, including Kenya, Malawi, Uganda, and Zambia (Government of Kenya, 2010; Government of Malawi, 2010; Uganda Minstry of Finance, Planning and Economic Development, 2010; Zambia Ministry of Finance and National Planning, 2010). Figure 9.15 illustrates differential *per capita* GDP growth associated with differential fertility rates in the RAPID model, indicating that the low-fertility scenario results in an almost 40 percent higher GDP *per capita* in 2037 as compared to the high-fertility scenario. In the low-fertility scenario, *per capita* GDP grows by 3.6 percent p.a., compared to 2.5 percent in the high-fertility scenario. The per person NPV of this increased *per capita* GDP is close to $1,500, and using earlier estimates of the family planning investments required to achieve the reduced fertility, the BCR is in the order of magnitude of 60:1 as a result of increased GDP *per capita* alone. The USAID Health Policy Initiative report therefore concludes, consistent with these high returns to investments in family planning during the next decades, that "[t]he Zambian vision to become a middle-income country can best be achieved by a combination of fast economic growth and a slower rate of population growth." Very similar conclusions are attained in USAID Health Policy Initiative reports for other higher-fertility low-income countries (Government of Kenya, 2010; Government of Malawi, 2010; Uganda Minstry of Finance, Planning and Economic Development, 2010; Zambia Ministry of Finance and National Planning, 2010).

If the analyses and the interpretation that are illustrated in Figure 9.15 in the case for Zambia are correct, the adoption of a family planning program would result in significant economic gains in terms of a more rapid growth of income resulting from reduced fertility. However, how is this more rapid growth of GDP *per capita* achieved, and is it broadly realistic? Reading the underlying documentation of the RAPID model reveals that:

> The effect of rapid population growth on economic growth depends on a number of factors. It has been difficult for those who study it to find unambiguous connections because many of the factors that influence economic growth vary across countries just as population growth rates do. The variety of issues [has been] examined by the National Research Council in a 1986 study (National Research Council, 1986). [. . .] Since many of these issues are too complex to treat in a short policy presentation, the RAPID model uses only relationships that are well understood and easy to describe. The basic model focuses on three basic concepts: dependency, the requirement for new jobs and *per capita* output. (USAID Health Policy Initiative 2009a: 13)

In terms of modeling assumptions, this implies that the rate of aggregate GDP growth is assumed to be independent of population growth – and set to 6 percent for the calculations shown in Figure 9.15. As a result, reductions in the rate of population growth directly translate into increases *per capita* income, and while GDP *per capita* differs, both fertility scenarios in Figure 9.15 assume an identical aggregate GDP. Moreover, while the documentation reflects the considerable uncertainty surrounding the assumption about the interaction between economic growth and population growth, the above-cited documents targeted at policymakers (Figure 9.15) present a much more clear-cut connection between reduced population growth and more rapid *per capita* income growth.

In light of recent research on the interaction between population growth and economic growth, how realistic are the calculations in Figure 9.15 and related reports about the economic returns (measured in terms of GDP *per capita* growth) of reduced fertility and investments in human capital? Are there reasons to believe that BCRs in the order of 60:1 are realistic in the area of *per capita* GDP growth over several decades?

In order to shed light on this question, the linkages between economic growth and changes in the population size and structure need to be made explicit. One possible approach is provided by Ashraf *et al.* (2011), who revisit the above question about the extent to which economic measures such as GDP *per capita* would change in response to reductions in fertility. Specifically, the model tries to account for different effects through which population size and age structure may affect economic growth. The first two focus on the role of population size: a *Malthusian effect*, reflecting the the congestion of fixed factors, such as land, through population growth; and a *Solow effect*, that captures the capital shallowing resulting from a growth in the labor force. In addition, several channels reflect potential effects of changes in the age structure the population and capture potential demographic dividends: a *dependency effect*, that captures the fact that, in a high-fertility environment, a reduction in fertility leads, at least temporarily, to a higher ratio of working-age adults to dependants and – if income per worker is held constant – mechanically raises income *per capita*; a *lifecycle savings effect*, that captures the fact that a concentration of population in their working years may raise national saving, feeding through to higher capital accumulation and higher output; an *experience effect*, that captures the shift of the working-age population to higher ages – i.e. towards individuals with more experience and potentially higher productivity; a *lifecycle labor supply effect*, that reflects the fact that labor-force participation may increase as a result of differential participation rates when the age structure shifts to older ages, and a *child care effect* that reflects increases in female labor supply as a result of reduced fertility; finally, a *child quality effect*, that reflects the fact that reductions in fertility may result in a quality–quantity trade-off, and increased child quality may foster economic growth. The model does not include one additional potential effect, a *Boserup effect*, that would capture direct effects of the population size on productivity, for instance through economies of scale or induced institutional change.

Figure 9.16 shows the results for the development of GPD *per capita* (light line) along with some related indicators for two scenarios: first, an immediate decline of the TFR by 1 (from 5.32 to 4.32) that is compared to the TFR remaining constant at the 2005 level of 5.3. Second, a future trend of the TFR that follows the UN low-fertility scenario as compared to the medium scenario, resulting in a 12 percent smaller population as compared to the medium scenario. The surprising result from the simulations in Ashraf *et al.* (2011), which are based on an explicit economic model that includes interactions between economic development and the size and age structure of the population – is that the findings are very consistent with the conclusions obtained from the RAPID model reviewed above (see also Figure 9.15). In the top panel of Figure 9.16, GDP *per capita* is about 26 percent higher after fifty years in the scenario where the TFR declines by 1 child as compared to constant fertility. Since the population size is also about 25 percent lower in this case as compared to the constant fertility scenario, over the course of fifty years the more rapid growth in GDP *per capita* after a decline in TFR essentially mirrors the less rapid growth in the size of the population. A similar conclusion follows from the simulations that compare the UN low-fertility scenario with the UN median-fertility scenario. In the low-fertility scenario, the population in 2050 is about 12 percent below that implied by the medium scenario. The simulations in Ashraf *et al.* (2011) associate with this less rapid growth in population a 12 percent higher GDP *per capita* (Figure 9.16, bottom panel). In summary, therefore, the analyses by Ashraf *et al.* (2011) suggest that, across two simulations with very different population and economic growth rates, an approximate calculation in which reductions in population growth rate increase growth in GDP *per capita* almost one-for-one is fairly accurate over a fifty-year horizon.[19] And while the analyses by the USAID Health Policy Initiative using the RAPID model can be correctly criticized for not having an explicit economic model that informs the contribution of demographic changes to economic growth, the conclusions in Figure 9.15 (and related country studies) about the connection between reduced population growth and higher *per capita* GDP are remarkably consistent with the analyses by Ashraf *et al.* (2011) (Figure 9.16). If this were indeed the case, the BCRs in terms of GDP *per capita* would be of the order of magnitude of 60:1 over a fifty-year horizon – as we calculated for Zambia – if reducing the population growth by 1 percent during this period had present *per capita* value costs of around 20–30 percent of *per capita* GDP – an assumption that seems quite plausible given the calculation of family planning program costs above.[20]

In addition to relying on results of simulation models such as in Ashraf *et al.* (2011), we can ask if our knowledge of the interactions between

[19] We emphasize that these calculations are "approximate" in the sense that there is considerable uncertainty about this conclusion. While the model in Ashraf *et al.* (2011) is based on the most recent developments in growth theory that are calibrated to an SSA context, an assessment of the aggregate consequences of fertility declines remains subject to important uncertainties about the parameter values used in the simulation, as well as about the mechanisms for the interactions between population change and economic development that are postulated as part of the model.

[20] The calculation assumes that GDP *per capita* grows at 3–4 percent p.a., and that a reduction in population growth would increase the rate of GDP *per capita* growth by 1 percentage point. The gain in GDP *per capita* is discounted at 3 percent. Even if GDP *per capita* were constant in the presence of more rapid population growth, the BCR would be 60:1 if population growth could be reduced over the fifty-year horizon at a cost of about 10 percent of GDP *per capita*.

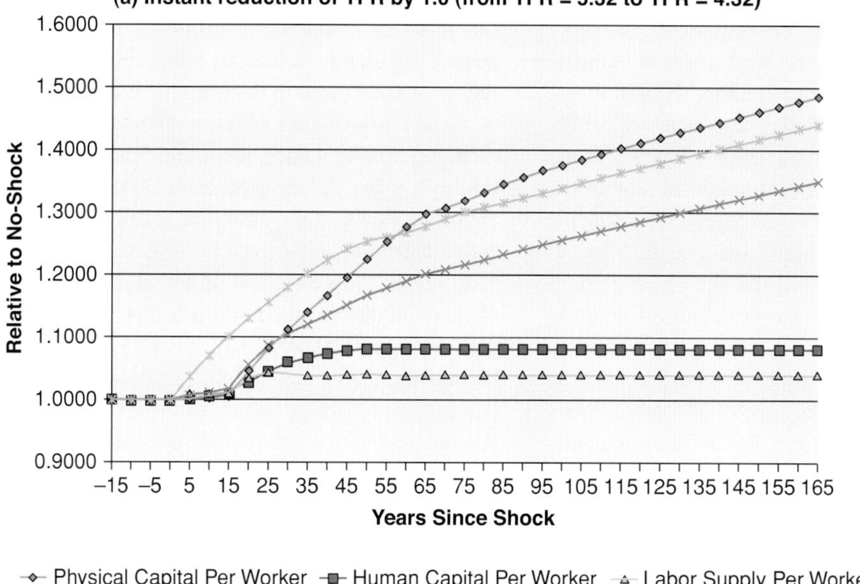

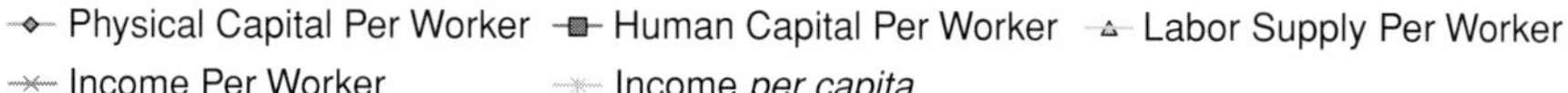

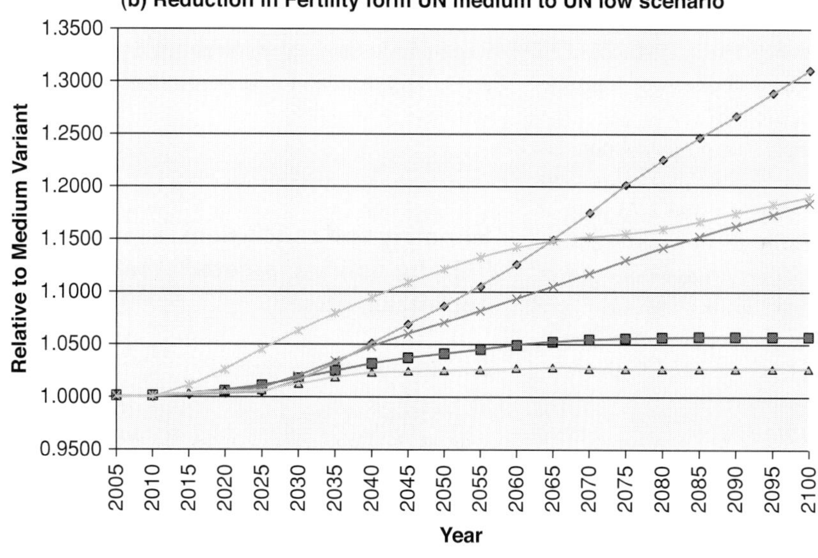

Figure 9.16 *Effect of reduced fertility on economic growth in a unified growth model calibrated to Nigeria*

Notes: Top panel: instant reduction of TFR by 1.0 (from TFR = 5.32 to TFR = 4.32); after fifty years, the population is 25 percent smaller than under constant fertility. Bottom panel: reduction in fertility from UN medium to UN low scenario; by 2050, the population in the low-fertility scenario is 12 percent below that of the medium scenario.
Source: Ashraf *et al.* (2011).

population growth and economic development – and, in particular, our knowledge of the potential impacts of changing ages structures – are consistent with the above interpretations (Bloom *et al.*, 1998, 2007a, 2007b; Kelley and Schmidt, 1995, 2005; Bloom and Canning, 2008). Eastwood and Lipton (2011) provide a detailed discussion of the implications of this literature for understanding the potential of a demographic dividend in SSA. In particular, the literature on the demographic dividend has estimated versions of models of the form $g(Y/N) = \varphi + X\beta + \delta(Y/L) + \gamma g(WA/N)$, where $g(.)$ denotes the growth rate, Y is output, N is the population size, L is the size of the labor force, Y/L is output per worker, (WA) is the population of working age, and WA/N is the fraction of the population of working age. γ indicates the effect of changes in age in the proportion of the population of working age – which tends to increase as fertility declines – on *per capita* income. Estimates for γ range from 1.5 to 3.5, with the higher of these figures obtained for African countries (e.g. Bloom *et al.*, 1998: Table 9.6). Are these estimates possibly consistent with an interpretation such as in Figure 9.15 (and also Figure 9.16) that reduced rates in population growth almost one-for-one translate into increased *per capita* growth?

For Zambia, for example, the projected population growth rate during 2010–2060 is 3.29 percent in the UN high-fertility scenario, and 2.73 percent in the low-fertility scenario; the low-fertility scenario thus implies a 0.56 percentage-point lower growth rate. In the high-fertility scenario, the growth in the fraction of the population of working age (16–65) is 0.121 percent, and in the low-fertility scenario this growth rate increases to 0.292 percent (a difference of 0.171 percentage points). A parameter value of γ of close to 3, which has for instance been estimated for SSA by Bloom *et al.* (1998), would imply that the more rapid growth in the fraction of the population in the low-fertility scenario results in a more rapid growth of GDP *per capita* of about 0.51 percent – a value that corresponds closely to the reduced population growth rate that is implied by the low-fertility scenario as compared to the high-fertility scenario. Very similar results also hold for other high-fertility SSA countries (such as Nigeria).

There is considerable controversy about the validity of the country-level estimates of the demographic dividends – that is, the contribution of changing age structures to economic growth. Some of these concerns are of an econometric nature (Schultz, 2010), while others question the applicability of the Asian experience – which is an important driver of the empirical results – to SSA. Notwithstanding these criticisms, however, if one takes the existing estimates of a demographic dividend (γ in the above notation) at their face value, they are consistent with our earlier discussions of Figures 9.15 and 9.16 and an approximate calculation that reductions in population growth translate one-to-one into increased rates of *per capita* GDP growth. If this is indeed the case, family planning programs are associated with significant BCRs in terms of *per capita* income growth, possibly in the order of magnitude of 60:1 or higher. In interpreting this calculation, however, it is important to emphasize that the evidence underlying such calculations for the effect of family planning programs on increased growth of GPD *per capita* remains tenuous at best, and that there remains considerable uncertainty about the magnitude of these effects that is very difficult to evaluate at this point.

Summary and conclusions: a range of BCRs for policies targeted at reducing population growth

Concerns about continued population growth in some of the least-developed countries are well founded. Current high-fertility countries (Figure 9.4) account currently for about 38 percent of the 78 million persons that are added annually to the world population, despite the fact that they are home to only 18 percent of the current world population. The current high-fertility countries will make the largest contribution to the annual increment of the world population after 2018, and after 2060, world population is projected to grow exclusively as a result of population growth in the current high-fertility countries (Figure 9.6). In the words of Lee (2009), "[it would seem] so obvious: larger, more rapidly growing populations have fewer natural resources per person, less physical capital per worker, more dependents, and greater needs for new social infrastructure. Of course they must be economically worse off." And if this is the case, family planning programs that facilitate a decline in fertility and a reduction in population growth rate would seem potentially highly beneficial interventions that should be expanded. And yet, this conclusion has been the subject of a long-standing and sometimes heated debate, often questioning the basic pillars of the conclusion (Kaiser, 2011): For example, how detrimental, if at all, is population growth for economic development, individual well-being, and the attainment of development indicators such as the MDGs? Do family planning programs have causal effects towards reducing fertility, or would observed declines in family planning program areas also have been observed in the absence of these programs? Is there a window of opportunity in the coming decades in which declines in population growth rates as a result of reduced fertility could provide a "demographic dividend" that would facilitate the social and economic development in some of the world's most underdeveloped countries?

And while research in the last two decades has substantially strengthened the case for family planning programs – documenting, for example, significant effects of these programs towards reducing fertility, increasing female (mother's) education, improving women's general health and longer-term survival, increases in female labor force participation and earnings, increased child health, and increased child human capital – the attempt to obtain reasonably reliable estimates of the benefits, costs, and BCRs of these programs remains very challenging – or possibly almost impossible – given a plethora of estimation problems, a limited knowledge of program costs, and an even more difficult task of assessing the micro- and macro-level benefits of these programs. And, of course, in the implementation of family planning programs many questions related to optimal design are important Prata (2009); Mwaikambo *et al.* (2011); Population Council (2012), including the appropriate integration of family planning programs with other health interventions, the adjustment to specific local contexts, the potential needs for health-systems strengthening, and the combination of family planning programs with information campaigns, behavioral-change communication, and interpersonal counseling. Negotiating population policies within specific political contexts is also non-trivial and can be challenging (Chimbwete *et al.*, 2005; May, 2012; Robinson, 2012). These specific aspects of program implementation and negotiation are beyond the scope of this chapter. Nevertheless, in this section, we attempt to establish benefit-cost considerations based on the existing evidence, and then discuss the sensitivity of these results with respect to several sources of error.

The costs of family planning programs in the past have varied widely, and so have estimates of the costs of expanding family planning services in the current high-fertility countries (Figure 9.4) that have the largest unmet need for such programs. Given the need to expand health systems and related infrastructures, the costs of expanding access to family planning per additional user are thought to exceed – at least in the short-to-medium-term – the average costs per current user in SSA contexts. Recent estimates, for example, suggest that additional annual expenditure of $3.6 billion would allow expansion of family planning services to all women who currently have an unmet need. Arguably most useful for the present benefit-cost calculations are estimates of the family planning costs related to attaining the UN population forecasts (Moreland *et al.* (2010)), which suggest that a reduction in the SSA population growth rate by 1 percentage point during 2005–2050 would entail discounted family planning costs of the order of magnitude of about $27 billion (or about 3 percent of current SSA GDP). These estimates do not consider the potentially necessary expansions of health systems to increase the family planning provisions to the required levels and the possible costs of generating the demand for family planning (Population Council, 2012), and so actual program costs may be significantly higher – however, based on the literature, it is difficult to make precise conclusions about the costs of these additional investments, which are almost certainly context specific and highly variable across countries.

In terms of benefits, our discussion has focused on four categories. First, benefits that result from the fact that family planning programs may reduce expenditures on social programs as a result of a less rapidly growing size of birth cohorts, with savings including a reduced need for expanding the school system, providing education, implementing immunization programs, or providing health care for children. However, these savings are a potentially incorrect estimate of the reductions in social costs, if family planning programs also result – as is suggested by much of the recent literature – in shifts in the demand for child quality (including, for instance, child health and schooling) and increases in female education. Because the net effect is unclear, we do not consider these benefits in our benefit-cost calculations.

Second, the benefits of family planning programs occur because reduced fertility, increased child spacing and possible reductions in unwanted fertility are likely to reduce both infant and maternal mortality. Some recent estimates of the reduction in child and maternal mortality that would result from expanding family planning programs to satisfy current unmet need suggest BCRs in the order of magnitude of 30:1 to 50:1 resulting from the reduction in child and maternal mortality alone. Some caution, however, is necessary in interpreting these numbers since it is not clear to what extent these estimates reflect the causal impact of expanding family planning programs on child/maternal mortality.

Third, our analyses have emphasized that family planning programs – in addition to reducing fertility and related maternal and child mortality – are likely to result in higher levels of female education, improvements in women's general health, increases in female labor-force participation and earnings, increased child health (up and beyond the effect on reducing child mortality), and increased child human capital. Several of these factors will affect economic growth, and will therefore be considered as part of the benefits considered below. And while these consequences are likely to be desirable from a policy perspective up to and beyond their contributions to economic growth, we will not consider these additional lifecycle, distributional, and intergenerational benefits of family planning program due to the difficulties in evaluating them within the framework of this chapter.

Fourth, and finally, benefits of large-scale family planning programs may result from changes in population dynamics – and in particular from reductions in population growth rates, increases in the proportion of the population of working age, and increases in the levels of human capital and female labor-force participation that result from reduced fertility over the coming decades. It is important to emphasize that these aggregate effects of family planning programs – as of many other health interventions (Bleakley, 2010) – are likely to be small in light of the vast differences in income levels among less-developed countries, or between the least-developed and more-developed countries. Some recent discussions of the contribution of demographic change – and specifically declining fertility, age-structure changes, and demographic dividends – to economic development in SSA seem rather optimistic in that regard (Sippel *et al.*, 2011). Nevertheless, our review of the literature suggests that reductions in population growth rates by 1 percentage point in current high-fertility countries may result in increases of the growth rate of *per capita* GDP by approximately 1 percentage point. This effect of reduced population growth on economic development is about twice as large as the effect that was suggested in the National Research Council (1986) report on *Population Growth and Economic Development*.[21] Given the uncertainty in the underlying models, the still limited knowledge about population–development interactions, and the limitations of existing empirical estimates, all of which have been subject to a long and at times

[21] The conclusions in National Research Council (1986) state: "A simple model suggests that the effect is comparatively modest. Using a typical labor coefficient of 0.5 in estimated production functions, a 1 percent reduction in the rate of labor force growth would boost the growth of *per capita* income by 0.5 percent per year." Since the report did not consider age-structure effects, the growth rate of the labor force is equal to that of the population. The report's conclusions therefore continue: "Thus, after 30 years, a 1 percent reduction in the annual rate of population growth (produced, say, by a decline in the crude birth rate from 37 to 27 per 1,000) will have raised production and income *per capita* to a level 16 percent [= exp(0.005 * 30) – 1] above what it would otherwise have been."

Table 9.4 Summary of costs, benefits, and BCRs for family planning programs

Annual net benefits and costs (3 percent discount rate)		Annual benefits	Annual costs of satisfying unmet need in developing countries	BCR
Benefit component:	Assumptions	US$Billion	US$Billion	
Reduced infant and maternal mortality	Low (DALY = 1,000)	110	3.6	30
	High (DALY = 5000)	180		50
Income growth (including life cycle, distributional and intergenerational benefits)	Low	216	3.6	60
	High	360		100
Total, family planning programs (sum)	**Low**	**326**		**90**
	High	**470**	**3.6**	**150**

heated discussion, this finding is hardly more than a rule of thumb or back-of-the-envelope calculation. Nevertheless, if this estimate that reductions in population growth rates by 1 percentage point in current high fertility countries may result in increases of the growth rate of *per capita* GDP by approximately 1 percentage point is broadly accurate, it would suggest substantial BCRs for family planning programs, possibly in the magnitude of 60:1 to 100:1 (or even higher) if the discounted costs of reducing population growth by 1 percentage in SSA are indeed in the order of magnitude of less than 10 percent of current SSA GDP during the next five decades (as is suggested by our discussion of the program costs above). The sizable BCRs essentially result from the fact that reductions in fertility and population growth rates will result in sustained increases in GDP *per capita* over several decades in these calculations, and the costs of achieving these reductions in fertility and population growth are relatively modest when compared to current GDP levels in SSA and other least-developed countries. However, one should not be mistaken about the magnitude of these aggregate economic effects in terms of closing substantially the income gap between the least-developed countries and other developing or even developed countries. While these aggregate effects of family planning programs are likely to contribute substantially and favorably to the BCR of family planning programs, the aggregate effects are too small for these programs to significantly reduce global income inequalities, or to provide a substitute for other development policies. More likely, a convincing case can be made for integrating family planning programs with other development policies (APPG, 2007; Cleland *et al.*, 2006; Wilcher *et al.*, 2009; Eastwood and Lipton, 2011; Sippel *et al.*, 2011; Teller and Hailemariam, 2011; Canning 2012; Global Aganda Council on Population Growth, 2012), including those that target reproductive-health concerns such as HIV/AIDS or other infectious diseases (including specifically also those reducing infant/child mortality) and/or development policies that would help create the institutional environment to capture the demographic dividend from reduced population growth and changes in the population age structure that are likely to occur in the next decades (Table 9.4).

Combining the above estimates of the BCRs for family planning programs in the area of reducing maternal/child mortality and increasing income *per capita* suggest BCRs for investments in family planning programs of 90:1 to 150:1. Table 9.4 summarizes how these BCRs arise from benefits in terms of reduced infant and maternal mortality and income growth. High and low estimates for the former are due to different evaluations of life, and for the latter due to different costs of achieving a specific reduction in fertility and population

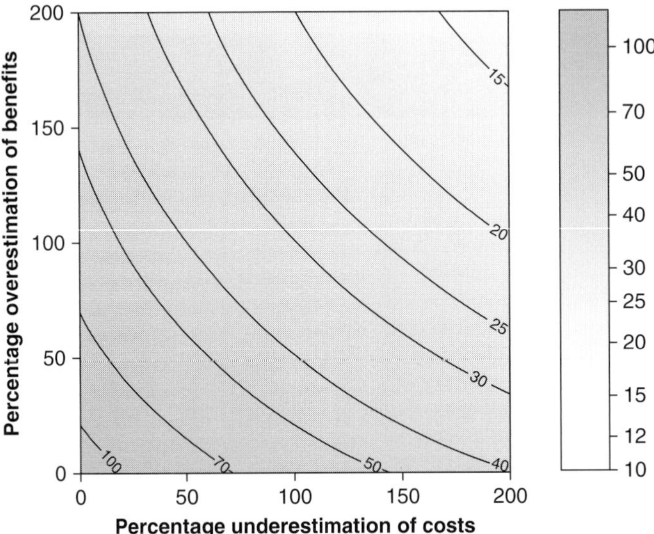

Figure 9.17 *Robustness of benefit-cost calculations: BCR for family planning programs if costs are underestimated and/or benefits are overestimated by a factor of up to 200 percent*

growth rates. Table 9.4 also reports the estimated costs of satisfying the total current unmet need for family planning in developing countries, obtained from Singh *et al.* (2010), as well as the total benefits resulting from this investment in family planning based on the BCRs obtained reported in this table.

Several caveats need to be emphasized when interpreting these favorable BCRs for family planning programs. On the one hand, since there is evidence that family planning programs result in benefits that are not considered here, such as climate change, environmental sustainability, and political stability (Goldstone *et al.*, 2012; O'Neill *et al.*, 2010; Speidel *et al.*, 2009; Sulston *et al.*, 2012), one could argue that the actual BCRs are likely to be higher. On the other hand, we have emphasized throughout this chapter that, despite the progress in the literature during the last two decades, the empirical basis for conducting these benefit-cost calculations remains somewhat weak, and significant uncertainty prevails in both the assessments of the costs of these programs and their expansion, as well as in terms of the causal effects in terms of the range of benefits that these programs will produce. It is easy to argue that the many biases in the existing literature will tend to overstate the benefits resulting from family planning programs and understate the costs of these programs and their expansion. Thus, the above BCRs would tend to be overestimates. Based on the current literature, it is impossible to establish with confidence how large these biases might be. However, in light of the magnitude of the BCRs for family planning programs that emerge from our analyses, and the relatively convincing recent empirical micro- and macro-evidence about the benefits resulting from family planning programs and reductions in fertility, a fairly favorable assessment of family planning programs in terms of their BCRs and cost-effectiveness seems to be justified and relatively robust with respect to measurement errors. For example, Figure 9.17 illustrates how a BCR of 120, which is the average of the high and low overall BCRs reported in Table 9.4, would change if the costs of family planning programs were underestimated, and/or the benefits of these programs were overestimated, by a factor of up to 200 percent (i.e. if the costs were up to three times as high, and/or the benefits were only 1/3 as high as is assumed in the current calculation of the BCRs in Table 9.4). Even in the most pessimistic assumption in Figure 9.17, when the costs are three times as high *and* the benefits are only 1/3 as high as is currently assumed in Table 9.4, the BCRs are fairly favorable and in excess of 13:1; and, of course, the BCRs are higher if the underestimation of the costs and/or the overestimation of the benefits is less pronounced.

In summary, therefore, the conclusion based on this review of the literature and assessment of BCRs for the expansion of family planning programs is quite consistent with several related recent studies that have argued in favor of the expansion of family planning programs (Haveman, 1976; Wulf, 1981; Hubera and Harveya, 1989; Simmons *et al.*, 1991; Chao, 2005; Cleland *et al.*, 2006, 2012; Levine *et al.*, 2006; Joshi and Schultz, 2007; Ashraf *et al.*, 2008; Miller, 2010; USAID Health Policy Initiative 2009b; Babigumira *et al.*, 2012). Our discussion and benefit-cost analyses thus lend support to earlier studies that have argued that family planning programs are a good "economic investment" (Bongaarts and Sinding, 2011b) and the renewed emphasis on family planning programs in light of continued population growth in some of the world's least-developed countries is very much supported by the present analyses. In expanding family planning programs, it is clear – and supported by a fairly broad consensus – that these programs must be voluntary and based on a long-term commitment of resources, and empirical studies suggest that, in order to be effective, such programs should be ideally integrated with other reproductive and child health services, effective community-based programs, and potentially related behavioral-change communication. There is also a rich body of empirical evidence and experience that can inform the important open questions about the optimal design and implementation of these programs. And while the Expert Panel of the 2012 Copenhagen Consensus (Copenhagen Consensus Project, 2012) did not rank family planning programs particularly favorably in comparison with other proposed interventions for confronting ten great contemporary global challenges, the readers of the *Slate Magazine Forum* accompanying the 2012 Copenhagen Consensus ranked population growth and family planning as a top priority (Lomborg, 2012a, 2012b). Based on the evidence reviewed in this chapter, this author tends to agree with the *Slate* readers. Indeed, as stated by Melinda Gates (Gates, 2012b), "Let's put birth control back on the agenda."

Bibliography

Abbasi-Shavazi, M. J., P. McDonald, and M. Hossein-Chavoshi, 2009a: *The Fertility Transition in Iran: Revolution and Reproduction*, Springer, Berlin

Abbasi-Shavazi, M. J., S. P. Morgan, M. Hossein-Chavoshi, and P. McDonald, 2009b: Family change and continuity in Iran: birth control use before first pregnancy, *Journal of Marriage and Family* **71**, 1309–24, doi:10.1111/j.1741–3737.2009.00670.x

Acemoglu, D. and S. Johnson, 2007: Disease and development: the effect of life expectancy on economic growth, *Journal of Political Economy* **115**, 925–85

Acemoglu, D. and J. Robinson, 2012: *Why Nations Fail: The Origins of Power, Prosperity, and Poverty*, Crown Business, New York

Ahmed, S., Q. F. Li, L. Liu, and A. Tsui, 2012: Maternal deaths averted by contraceptive use: an analysis of 172 countries, *Lancet*, preliminary version, http://paa2012.princeton.edu/download.aspx?submissionId=122679

Akerlof, G. A., 1997: Social distance and social decisions, *Econometrica* **65**, 1005–27

Aldy, J. E. and W. K. Viscusi, 2007: Age differences in the value of statistical life: revealed preference evidence, *Review of Environmental Economics and Policy* **1**, 241–60, doi:10.1093/reep/rem014

Alesina, A. F., P. Giuliano, and N. Nunn, 2011a: Fertility and the plough, *American Economic Review* **101**, 499–503, doi:10.1257/aer.101.3.499

2011b: On the origins of gender roles: women and the plough, *NBER Working Paper* **17098**, Cambridge, MA, www.nber.org/papers/w17098

APPG, 2007: Return of the population growth factor: its impact on the Millennium Development Goals, All Party Parliamentary Group on Population Development and Reproductive Health, London, www.appg-popdevrh.org.uk

Arends-Kuenning, M., 2001: How do family planning worker visits affect women's behavior in Bangladesh? *Demography* **38**, 481–96

Arndt, C., S. Jones, and F. Tarp, 2009: Aid and growth: have we come full circle?, University of Copenhagen Department of Economics, *Discussion Paper* **09–22**, http://ssrn.com/abstract=1489392

Arthur, W. B. and G. McNicoll, 1978: An analytical survey of population and development in Bangladesh, *Population and Development Review* **4**, 23–80

Ashraf, N., E. Field, and J. Lee, 2010: Household bargaining and excess fertility: a study in Zambia, Harvard Business School, unpublished manuscript, http://people.hbs.edu/nashraf/papers/Ashraf_Field_Lee_December2010.pdf

Ashraf, Q. H., A. Lester, and D. N. Weil, 2008: When does improving health raise GDP?, *NBER Working Paper* **14449**, Cambridge, MA, www.nber.org/papers/w14449

Ashraf, Q. H., D. N. Weil, and J. Wilde, 2011: The effect of interventions to reduce fertility on economic growth, *NBER Working Paper* **17377**, Cambridge, MA, www.nber.org/papers/w17377

Babigumira, J. B., A. Stergachis, D. L. Veenstra, J. S. Gardner, J. Ngonzi, P. Mukasa-Kivunike, and L. P. Garrison, 2012: Potential cost-effectiveness of universal access to modern contraceptives in Uganda, *PLoS ONE* **7**, e30735–. doi:10.1371/ journal.pone.0030735

Bailey, M. J., 2006: More power to the pill: the impact of contraceptive freedom on women's life cycle labor supply, *Quarterly Journal of Economics* **121**, 289–320

Ballard, C., J. Shoven, and J. Whalley, 1985: General equilibrium computations of the marginal welfare costs of taxes in the United States, *American Economic Review* **75**, 128–38

Barham, T., 2012: Enhancing cognitive functioning: medium-term effects of a health and family planning program in Matlab, *American Economic Journal: Applied Economics* **4**, 245–73, doi:10.1257/app.4.1.245

Bartick, M. and A. Reinhold, 2010: The burden of suboptimal breastfeeding in the United States: a pediatric cost analysis, *Pediatrics* **125**, 1048–58

Becker, G. S., 1974: A theory of social interaction, *Journal of Political Economy* **82**, 1063–93

1991: *A Treatise on the Family*, 2nd edn., Harvard University Press, Cambridge, MA

Becker, G. S. and R. J. Barro, 1988: A reformulation of the economic theory of fertility, *Quarterly Journal of Economics* **103**, 1–25

Becker, G. S., K. M. Murphy, and R. Tamura, 1990: Human capital, fertility, and economic growth, *Journal of Political Economy* **98**, 12–37

Behrman, J. R. and J. C. Knowles, 1998: Population and reproductive health: an economic framework for policy evaluation, *Population and Development Review* **24**, 697–737

Behrman, J. R. and H.-P. Kohler, 2011: Sexual transmission of HIV, Assessment paper for the Copenhagen Consensus Project 2011 on HIV/AIDS in sub-Saharan Africa, www.rethinkHIV.com

Behrman, J. R., H. Alderman, and J. Hoddinott, 2004: Hunger and malnutrition, in B. Lomborg (ed.), *Global Crises, Global Solutions*, Cambridge University Press, 363–420 (see also www.copenhagenconsensus.com)

Belfield, C. and H. Levin, 2010: Cost-benefit analysis and cost-effectiveness analysis, in P. Peterson, E. Baker, and B. McGaw (eds.), *International Encyclopedia of Education*, 3rd edn., Elsevier, Oxford, 199–203, doi:10.1016/B978–0-08–044894-7.01245–8

Bergstrom, T. C., 1997: A survey of theories of the family, in M. A. Rosenzweig and O. Stark (eds.), *Handbook of Population and Family Economics*, North-Holland, Amsterdam

Bernardi, L., A. Klärner, and H. von der Lippe, 2008: Job insecurity and the timing of parenthood: a comparison between eastern and western Germany, *European Journal of Population* **24**, 287–313

Bernstein, S., 2006: Public choices, private decisions: sexual and reproductive health and the Millennium Development Goals, UN Millennium Project, www.unmillenniumproject.org/documents/MP_Sexual_Health_screen-final.pdf

Birdsall N., A. C. Kelley, and S. Sinding (eds.), 2001: *Population Matters: Demographic Change, Economic Growth, and Poverty in the Developing World*, Oxford University Press

Black, S. E., P. J. Devereux, and K. G. Salvanes, 2005: The more the merrier? The effect of family composition on children's education, *Quarterly Journal of Economics* **120**, 669–700, doi:10.1162/0033553053970179

Bleakley, H., 2008: When does improving health raise GDP? Comments on Ashraf, Lester, and Weil (2008), University of Chicago, unpublished manuscript, http://home.uchicago.edu/~bleakley/Bleakley_Comments_ALW.pdf

2010: Health, human capital, and development, *Annual Review of Economics* **2**, 283–310, doi:10.1146/annurev.economics.102308.124436

Bleakley, H. and F. Lange, 2009: Chronic disease burden and the interaction of education, fertility, and growth, *Review of Economics and Statistics* **91**, 52–65, doi:10. 1162/rest.91.1.52

Bloom, D. E. and D. Canning, 2004: Global demographic change: dimensions and economic significance, *NBER Working Paper* **10817**, Cambridge, MA, www.nber.org/papers/w10817

2008: Global demographic change: dimensions and economic significance, *Population and Development Review* **34**(Supplement), 17–51

Bloom, D. E., D. Canning, and G. Fink, 2009b: Disease and development revisited, *NBER Working Paper* **15137**, Cambridge, MA, www.nber.org/papers/w15137

Bloom, D. E., D. Canning, G. Fink, and J. Finlay, 2007a: Does age structure forecast economic growth?, *NBER Working Paper* **13221**, Cambridge, MA, www.nber.org/papers/w13221

2007b: Realizing the demographic dividend: is Africa any different?, Program on the Global Demography of Aging, Harvard University, *PGDA Working Paper* **23**, www.hsph.harvard.edu/pgda/working.htm

2009a: Fertility, female labor force participation, and the demographic dividend, *Journal of Economic Growth* **14**, 79–101, doi:10.1007/s10887–009-9039–9

Bloom, D. E., D. Canning, and J. Sevilla, 2002: *The Demographic Dividend: A New Perspective on the Economic Consequences of Population Change*, RAND Corporation, Santa Monica, CA

Bloom, D. E., J. D. Sachs, P. Collier, and C. Udry, 1998: Geography, demography, and economic growth in Africa, *Brookings Papers on Economic Activity* **1998**(2), 207–95

Bongaarts, J., 1987: Does family planning reduce infant mortality rates?, *Population and Development Review* **13**, 323–34

1994: The impact of population policies: comment, *Population and Development Review* **20**, 616–20

2006: The causes of stalling fertility transitions, *Studies in Family Planning* **37**, 1–16

2008: Fertility transitions in developing countries: progress or stagnation?, *Studies in Family Planning* **39**, 105–10, doi:10.1111/j.1728–4465.2008. 00157.x

2011: Can family planning programs reduce high desired family size in Sub-Saharan Africa?, *International Perspectives on Sexual and Reproductive Health* **37**, 209–16

Bongaarts, J. and J. Bruce, 1995: The causes of unmet need for contraception and the social content of services, *Studies in Family Planning* **26**, 57–75

Bongaarts, J. and S. W. Sinding, 2009: A response to critics of family planning programs, *International Perspectives on Sexual and Reproductive Health* **35**, 153–4

2011a: Population policy in transition in the developing world, *Science* **333**, 574–6, doi:10.1126/science.1207558

2011b: Family planning as an economic investment, *SAIS Review* **31**, 35–44

Bongaarts, J. and S. C. Watkins, 1996: Social interactions and contemporary fertility transitions, *Population and Development Review* **22**, 639–82

Bongaarts, J., W. P. Mauldin, and J. Phillips, 1990: The demographic impact of family planning programs, *Studies in Family Planning* **21**, 299–310

Bongaarts, J. P., F. Pelletier, and P. Gerland, 2011: Global trends in AIDS mortality, in R. G. Rogers and E. M. Crimmins (eds.), *International Handbooks of Population*, vol. 2, Springer, New York, 171–83, doi:10.1007/978–90-481–9996-9_8

Boserup, E., 1965: *The Conditions of Agricultural Growth*, Aldine, New York

1981: *Population and Technological Change: A Study of Long Term Trends*, University of Chicago Press

Caldwell, J. C., 1980: Mass education as a determinant of the timing of fertility decline, *Population and Development Review* **6**, 225–55

Caldwell, J. C. and P. Caldwell, 1987: The cultural context of high fertility in sub-Saharan africa, *Population and Development Review* **13**, 409–37

Caldwell, J. C., P. Caldwell, and I. O. Orubuloye, 1992: The family and sexual networking in sub-Saharan Africa: historical regional differences and present-day implications, *Population Studies* **46**, 385–410

Campbell, M., 2007: Why the silence on population?, *Population & Environment* **28**, 237–46, doi:10.1007/s11111–007-0054–5

Campbell, M. and K. Bedford, 2009: The theoretical and political framing of the population factor in development, *Philosophical Transactions of the Royal Society B: Biological Sciences* **364**, 3093–9, doi:10.1098/rstb.2009.0172

Campbell, M., J. Cleland, A. Ezeh, and N. Prata, 2007: Return of the population growth factor, *Science* **315**, 1501–2, doi:10.1126/science.1140057

Canning, D., 2011: The causes and consequences of demographic transition, *Population Studies* **65**, 353–61, doi:10.1080/00324728.2011.611372

2012: Copenhagen consensus perspective paper on "Infectious Disease", Copenhagen Consensus Project 2012, www.copenhagenconsensus.com

Casterline, J. B. and S. W. Sinding, 2000: Unmet need for family planning in developing countries and implications for population policy, *Population and Development Review* **26**, 691–723, doi:10.1111/j.1728–4457.2000.00691.x

Cates, W., Jr., Q. A. Karim, W. El-Sadr, D. W. Haffner, G. Kalema-Zikusoka, K. Rogo, T. Petruney, and E. M. D. Averill, 2010: Family planning and the Millennium Development Goals, *Science* **329**, 1603, doi:10.1126/science.1197080

Chao, D. N. W., 2005: Family planning in Egypt is a sound financial investment, USAID Health Policy Initiative, www.healthpolicyinitiative.com/index.cfm?ID=publications&get=pubID&pubID=43

Chao, D. N. W. and K. B. Allen, 1984: A cost-benefit analysis of Thailand's family planning program, *International Family Planning Perspectives* **10**, 75–81

Chimbwete, C., E. M. Zulu, and S. C. Watkins, 2005: The evolution of population policies in Kenya and Malawi, *Population Research and Policy Review* **24**, 83–104

Cincotta, R., R. Engelman, and D. Anastasion, 2003: *The Security Demographic: Population and Civil Conflict After the Cold War*, Population Action International, Washington, DC

Cleland, J. G. and C. Wilson, 1987: Demand theories of the fertility transition: an iconoclastic view, *Population Studies* **41**, 5–30

Cleland, J. G., S. Bernstein, A. Ezeh, A. Faundes, A. Glasier, and J. Innis, 2006: Family planning: the unfinished agenda, *Lancet* **368**, 1810–27, doi:10.1016/S0140–6736(06)69480–4

Cleland, J. G., A. Conde-Agudelo, H. Peterson, J. Ross, and A. Tsui, 2012: Contraception and health, *Lancet* **380**, 149–56, doi:10.1016/SO140–6736(12)60609–6

Cleland, J. G., R. P. Ndugwa, and E. M. Zulu, 2011: Family planning in sub-Saharan Africa: progress or stagnation?, *Bulletin of the World Health Organization* **89**, 137–43, doi:10.1590/S0042–96862011000200013

Coale, A. J., 1973: The demographic transition reconsidered, in *International Population Conference, Liège, Vol. 1*, International Union for the Scientific Study of Population, 53–72

Coale, A. J. and E. M. Hoover, 1958: *Population Growth and Economic Development in Low-Income Countries*, Princeton University Press

Cohen, J. E., 1995a: *How Many People Can the Earth Support?*, Norton, New York

1995b: Population growth and earth's human carrying capacity, *Science* **269**, 341–6, doi:10.1126/science.7618100

Collumbien, M., M. Gerressu, and J. G. Cleland, 2004: Non-use and use of ineffective methods of contraception, in M. Ezzati, A. D. Lopez, A. Rogers, and C. J. L. Murray (eds.), *Comparative Quantification of Health Risks, Global and Regional Burden of Disease Attributable to Selected Major Risk Factors*, World Health Organization, Geneva, 1255–320

Connelly, M., 2008: *Fatal Misconception: The Struggle to Control World Population*, Belknap Press of Harvard University Press, Cambridge, MA and London

Copenhagen Consensus Project, 2012: Expert Panel Findings. Copenhagen Consensus Project 2012, Final Outcome Document, www.copenhagenconsensus.com/Default.aspx?ID=1637

Crouter, A. C. and A. Booth (eds.), 2005: *The New Population Problem: Why Families in Developed Counties are Shrinking and What it Means*, Lawrence Erlbaum Associates, Mahwah, NJ

Cutler, D. M., A. S. Deaton, and A. Lleras-Muney, 2006: The determinants of mortality, *Journal of Economic Literature* **20**, 97–120

Darroch, J. and S. Singh, 2011: Adding it up: the costs and benefits of investing in family planning and maternal and newborn health (estimation methodology), Guttmacher Institute Report, Washington, DC, www.guttmacher.org/pubs/AIU-methodology.pdf

Das Gupta, M., J. Bongaarts, and J. C. Cleland, 2011: Population, poverty, and sustainable development: a review of the evidence, *Policy Research Working Paper* **5719**, World Bank, Washington, DC, http://elibrary.worldbank.org/

content/workingpaper/10.1596/1813–9450-5719

Dasgupta, P., 1993: *An Inquiry into Well-Being and Destitution*, Clarendon Press, Oxford

1995: The population problem: theory and evidence, *Journal of Economic Literature* **33**, 1879–902

David, H. P., 2006: Born unwanted, 35 years later: the Prague study, *Reproductive Health Matters* **14**, 181–90, doi:10.1016/S0968–8080(06)27219–7

Deaton, A., 2010: Instruments, randomization, and learning about development, *Journal of Economic Literature* **48**, 424–55, doi:10.1257/jel.48.2.424

Debpuur, C., J. F. Phillips, E. F. Jackson, A. Nazzar, P. Ngom, and F. N. Binka, 2002: The impact of the Navrongo Project on contraceptive knowledge and use, reproductive preferences, and fertility, *Studies in Family Planning* **33**, 141–64, doi:10.1111/j. 1728–4465.2002.00141.x

Demeny, P., 1986: Population and the invisible hand, *Demography* **23**, 473–87

2011: Population policy and the demographic transition: performance, prospects, and options, *Population and Development Review* **37**(Supplement), 249–74, doi:10.1111/j.1728–4457.2011.00386.x

Devarajan, S., L. Squire, and S. Suthiwart-Narueput, 1997: Beyond rate of return: reorienting project appraisal, *World Bank Research Observer* **12**, 35–46

Dewey, K. G. and R. J. Cohen, 2007: Does birth spacing affect maternal or child nutritional status? A systematic literature review, *Maternal & Child Nutrition* **3**, 151–73

Dixon-Mueller, R., 1993: *Population Policy and Women's Rights: Transforming Reproductive Choice*, Praeger, Westport, CT

Do, Q.-T. and T. D. Phung, 2010: The importance of being wanted, *American Economic Journal: Applied Economics* **2**, 236–53, doi:10.1257/app.2.4.236

Duflo, E., R. Glennerster, and M. Kremer, 2007: Using randomization in development economics research: a toolkit, in T. P. Schultz and J. A. Strauss (eds.), *Handbook of Development Economics*, Elsevier, New York, 3895–962; CEPR Discussion Paper **6059**, http://ssrn.com/abstract=997109

Dyson, T., 2010: *Population and Development: The Demographic Transition*, Zed Books, London

Dytrych, Z., Z. Matejcek, V. Schuller, H. David, and H. Friedman, 1975: Children born to women denied abortion, *Family Planning Perspectives* **7**, 165–71

Easterlin, R. A. and E. Crimmins, 1985: *The Fertility Revolution*, University of Chicago Press

Eastwood, R. and M. Lipton, 2011: Demographic transition in sub-Saharan Africa: how big will the economic dividend be?, *Population Studies* **65**, 9–35, doi:10.1080/00324728.2010.547946

Eberstadt, N., 2006: Doom and demography, *Wilson Quarterly* **30**, 27–31

Economist, 2009: Go forth and multiply a lot less: lower fertility is changing the world for the better, The Economist print edition, October 29, www.economist.com/node/14743589

2011a: Demography: a tale of three islands – the world's population will reach 7 billion at the end of October. Don't panic, The Economist print edition, October 22, www.economist.com/node/21533364

2011b: The hopeful continent: Africa rising – after decades of slow growth, Africa has a real chance to follow in the footsteps of Asia, The Economist print edition, December 3, www.economist.com/node/21541015

2011c: World population: now we are seven billion – persuading women to have fewer babies would help in some places, but it is no answer to scarce resources, The Economist print edition, October 22, www.economist.com/node/21533409

Ehrlich, P. R., 1968: *The Population Bomb*, Ballantine, New York

Ehrlich, P. R. and A. H. Ehrlich, 1990: *The Population Explosion*, Simon & Schuster, New York

England, P. and N. Folbre, 2002: Involving dads: parental bargaining and family well-being, in C. S. Tamis-LeMonda and N. Cabrera (eds.), *Handbook of Father Involvement: Multidisciplinary Perspectives*, Lawrence Erlbaum Associates, Mahwah, NJ, 387–408

Espenshade, T. J., J. C. Guzman, and C. F. Westoff, 2003: The surprising global variation in replacement fertility, *Population Research and Policy Review* **22**, 575–83

Ezeh, A. C., B. U. Mberu, and J. O. Emina, 2009: Stall in fertility decline in Eastern African countries: regional analysis of patterns, determinants and implications, *Philosophical Transactions of the Royal Society B: Biological*

Sciences **364**, 2985–90, doi:10.1098/rstb.2009.0137

FAO, 2011: FAOSTAT online database, Food and Agricultural Organization, http://faostat.fao.org, Paris

Feldstein, M., 1995: Tax avoidance and the deadweight loss of the income tax, *NBER Working Paper* **5055**, Cambridge, MA, www.nber.org

Fernández, R., A. Fogli, and C. Olivetti, 2004: Mothers and sons: preference formation and female labor force dynamics, *Quarterly Journal of Economics* **119**, 1249–99

Fortson, J. G., 2009: HIV/AIDS and fertility, *American Economic Journal: Applied Economics* **1**, 170–94

Frankenberg, E., B. Sikoki, and W. Suriastini, 2003: Contraceptive use in a changing service environment: evidence from Indonesia during the economic crisis, *Studies in Family Planning* **34**, 103–16, doi:10.1111/j.1728–4465.2003.00103.x

Freedman, R., 1997: Do family planning programs affect fertility preferences? A literature review, *Studies in Family Planning* **28**, 1–13

Freedman, R. and J. Y. Takeshita, 1969: *Family Planning in Taiwan: An Experiment in Social Change*, Princeton University Press

Galor, O., 2005: From stagnation to growth: unified growth theory, in P. Aghion and S. N. Durlauf (eds.), *Handbook of Economic Growth*, vol. **1**, Part A, Elsevier, Amsterdam, 171–293, doi:10.1016/S1574–0684(05)01004-X

2011: *Unified Growth Theory*, Princeton University Press

2012: The demographic transition: causes and consequences, *IZA Discussion Paper* **6334**, http://ssrn.com/abstract=2003667

Galor, O. and D. Tsiddon, 1991: Technological breakthroughs and development traps, *Economics Letters* **37**, 11–17, doi:10.1016/0165–1765(91)90235-D

Galor, O. and D. N. Weil, 1996: The gender gap, fertility and growth, *American Economic Review* **86**, 374–87

Garenne, M. L., 2011: Testing for fertility stalls in demographic and health surveys, *Population Health Metrics* **1**, 18

Gates, B., 2012a: *2012 Annual Letter From Bill Gates*, Bill and Melinda Gates Foundation, www.gatesfoundation.org/annual-letter/2012

Gates, M., 2012b: Let's put birth control back on the agenda, Presentation at the TED Summit, April, www.ted.com/talks/melinda_gates_let_s_put_birth_control_back_on_the_agenda.html

Gertler, P. J. and J. W. Molyneaux, 1994: How economic development and family planning programs combined to reduce Indonesian fertility, *Demography* **31**, 33–63

Glaeser, E. L., 2011: *Triumph of the City: How Our Greatest Invention Makes Us Richer, Smarter, Greener, Healthier, and Happier*, Penguin, New York

Global Agenda Council on Population Growth, 2012: Seven billion and growing: a 21st century perspective on population, World Economic Forum, Geneva

Goldin, C. and L. F. Katz, 2002: The power of the pill: oral contraceptives and women's career and marriage decisions, *Journal of Political Economy* **110**, 730–70

Goldstone, J. A., E. P. Kaufmann, and M. D. Toft (eds.), 2012: *Political Demography: How Population Changes are Reshaping International Security and National Politics*, Paradigm Publishers, Boulder, CO

Golosov, M., L. E. Jones, and M. Tertilt, 2007: Efficiency with endogenous population growth, *Econometrica* **75**, 1039–71, doi:j.1468–0262.2007.00781.x

Government of Kenya, 2010: *Kenya: Population and Development (RAPID Booklet)*, USAID Health Policy Initiative, Washington, DC, www.healthpolicyinitiative.com/Publications/Documents/1095_1_Kenya_booklet_3_31_10_sglepg_LOW_RES_PDF_for_INTERNET_acc.pdf

Government of Malawi, 2010: *Malawi: Population and Development (RAPID Booklet)*, USAID Health Policy Initiative, Washington, DC, www.healthpolicyinitiative.com/Publications/Documents/1065_1_Malawi_booklet_2_23_10_singlepg_acc.pdf

Granovetter, M. S., 1978: Threshold models of collective behavior, *American Journal of Sociology* **83**, 1420–43

Greenwood, J., A. Seshadri, and G. Vandenbroucke, 2005: The baby boom and baby bust, *American Economic Review* **95**, 183–207

Guinnane, T. W., 2011: The historical fertility transition: a guide for economists, *Journal of Economic Literature* **49**, 589–614, doi:10.1257/jel.49.3.589

Haddad, L. and J. Hoddinott, 1994: Does female income share influence household expenditures? Evidence from Côte-d'Ivoire, *Oxford Bulletin of Economics and Statistics* **57**, 77–96

Hammitt, J. K., 2007: Valuing changes in mortality risk: lives saved versus life years saved, *Review of Environmental Economics and Policy* **1**, 228–40, doi:10.1093/reep/ rem015

Hanushek, E. A., 1992: The trade-off between child quantity and quality, *Journal of Political Economy* **100**, 84–117

Harberger, A., 1997: New frontiers in project evaluation? A comment on Devarajan, Squire and Suthiwart-Narueput, *World Bank Research Observer* **12**, 73–9

Hardin, G., 1968: The tragedy of the commons, *Science* **162**, 1243–8

Haveman, R. H., 1976: Benefit-cost analysis and family planning programs, *Population and Development Review* **2**, 37–64

Heaton, T., 2011: Does religion influence fertility in developing countries?, *Population Research and Policy Review* **30**, 449–65, doi:10.1007/ s11113–010-9196–8

Herbst, A. J., G. S. Cooke, T. Bärnighausen, A. KanyKany, F. Tanser, and M.-L. Newell, 2009: Adult mortality and antiretroviral treatment roll-out in rural KwaZulu-Natal, South Africa, *Bulletin of the World Health Organization* **87**, 754–62, doi:10.1590/S0042–96862009001000011

Hewlett Foundation, 2012: Global development and population program, The William and Flora Hewlett Foundation, www.hewlett.org/ programs/global-development-and-population-program

Hobcraft, J. N., J. W. McDonald, and S. O. Rutstein, 1984: Socio-economic factors in infant and child mortality: a cross-national comparison, *Population Studies* **38**, 193–223

Hoddinott, J., M. Rosegrant, and M. Torero, 2012: Copenhagen consensus challenge paper on "Hunger and Malnutrition" Copenhagen Consensus Project 2012, www. copenhagenconsensus.com

Horton, S., H. Alderman, and J. A. Rivera, 2009: The challenge of hunger and malnutrition, in B. Lomborg (ed.), *Global Crises, Global Solutions*, 2nd edn., Cambridge University Press

Hubera, S. C. and P. D. Harveya, 1989: Family planning programmes in ten developing countries: cost effectiveness by mode of service delivery, *Journal of Biosocial Science* **21**, 267–77, doi:10.1017/S0021932000017971

Jacobs, J., 1969: *The Economy of Cities*, Random House, New York

Jahn, A., S. Floyd, A. C. Crampin, F. Mwaungulu, H. Mvula, F. Munthali, N. McGrath, J. Mwafilaso, V. Mwinuka, B. Mangongo, P. E. M. Fine, B. Zaba, and J. R. Glynn, 2008: Population-level effect of HIV on adult mortality and early evidence of reversal after introduction of antiretroviral therapy in Malawi, *Lancet* **371**, 1603–11, doi:10.1016/S0140–6736(08) 60693–5

Jamison, D. T., P. Jha, and D. Bloom, 2009: The challenge of diseases, in B. Lomborg (ed.), *Global Crises, Global Solutions*, 2nd edn., Cambridge University Press

Jamison, D., P. Jha, R. Laxminarayan, and T. Ord, 2012: Copenhagen consensus challenge paper on "Infectious Disease," Copenhagen Consensus Project 2012, www. copenhagenconsensus.com

Jensen, R. and E. Oster, 2009: The power of TV: cable television and women's status in India, *Quarterly Journal of Economics*

Jha, P., R. Nugent, S. Verguet, and D. Bloom, 2012: Copenhagen consensus challenge paper on "Chronic Disease," Copenhagen Consensus Project 2012, www.copenhagenconsensus.com

Johnson-Hanks, J., 2006: *Uncertain Honor: Modern Motherhood in an African Crisis*, University of Chicago Press

Joshi, S., 2011: How effective are family-planning programs at improving the lives of women? Some perspectives from a vast literature, World Bank, Unpublished manuscript, http:// siteresources.worldbank.org/INTGENDER/ Resources/FPPrograms_Impact_Reviw.pdf

Joshi, S. and T. P. Schultz, 2007: Family planning as an investment in development: evaluation of a program's consequences in Matlab, Bangladesh, Yale University Economic Growth Center *Discussion Paper* **951**, http://ssrn.com/ abstract=962938

Kaiser, J., 2011: Does family planning bring down fertility?, *Science* **333**, 548–9, doi:10.1126/ science.333.6042.548

Kalemli-Ozcan, S., 2003: A stochastic model of mortality, fertility, and human capital investment, *Journal of Development Economics* **70**, 103–18, doi:10.1016/S0304–3878(02) 00089–5

Kalemli-Ozcan, S. and B. Turan, 2011: HIV and fertility revisited, *Journal of Development Economics* **96**, 61–5, doi:10.1016/j.jdeveco.2010.08.001

Kelley, A. C., 1988: Economic consequences of population change in the Third World, *Journal of Economic Literature* **26**, 1685–728

Kelley, A. C. and R. M. Schmidt, 1995: Aggregate population and economic growth correlations: the role of the components of demographic change, *Demography* **32**, 543–55, doi:10.2307/2061674

2005: Evolution of recent economic–demographic modeling: a synthesis, *Journal of Population Economics* **18**, 275–300, doi:10.1007/s00148–005-0222–9

Knowles, J. C. Schmidt, J. S. Akin, and D. K. Guilkey, 1994: The impact of population policies: comment, *Population and Development Review* **20**, 611–15

Knowles, J. C. and J. R. Behrman, 2003: Assessing the economic returns to investing in youth in developing countries, World Bank, Health, Nutrition and Population (HNP) *Discussion Paper* **2888**, www.worldbank.org

2005: Economic returns to investing in youth, in *The Transition to Adulthood in Developing Countries: Selected Studies*, National Academy of Science–National Research Council, Washington, DC, 424–90

Kohler, H.-P., 1997: Learning in social networks and contraceptive choice, *Demography* **34**, 369–83. www.jstor.org/stable/3038290

2000: Fertility decline as a coordination problem, *Journal of Development Economics* **63**, 231–63, doi:10.1016/S0304–3878(00)00118–8

2001: *Fertility and Social Interactions: An Economic Perspective*, Oxford University Press, http://books.google.com/books?id=03WVNSjf1KkC

2010: Fertility and its implications, in Yi Zeng (ed.), *UNESCO-EOLSS Encyclopedia of Life Support Systems: Demography*, Eolss Publishers Co., Ramsey, Isle of Man, www.eolss.net

Kohler, H.-P. and J. A. Ortega, 2002: Fertility, below-replacement, in P. Demeny and G. McNicoll (eds.), *Encyclopedia of Population*, vol. 1, Macmillan, Basingstoke, 405–9, books.google.com/books?id=hFJrPwAACAAJ&pg=PA405

Kohler, H.-P., J. R. Behrman, and S. C. Watkins, 2000: Empirical assessments of social networks, fertility and family planning programs: nonlinearities and their implications, *Demographic Research* **3**, 79–126, doi:10.4054/DemRes.2000.3.7

2001: The density of social networks and fertility decisions: evidence from South Nyanza District, Kenya, *Demography* **38**, 43–58, doi:10.1353/dem.2001.0005, www.jstor.org/stable/3088287

Kohler, H.-P., F. C. Billari, and J. A. Ortega, 2002: The emergence of lowest-low fertility in Europe during the 1990s, *Population and Development Review* **28**, 641–81, www.jstor.org/stable/3092783

Kravdal, Ø., 2002: Education and fertility in sub-Saharan Africa: individual and community effects, *Demography* **39**, 233–50

Kremer, M., 1993: Population growth and technological change: one million BC to 1990, *Quarterly Journal of Economics* **108**, 681–716

LaFerrara, E., A. Chong, and S. Duryea, 2008: Soap operas and fertility: evidence from Brazil, Inter-American Development Bank, Research Department, *RES Working Paper* **4573**, Washington, DC, ideas.repec.org/p/idb/wpaper/4573.html

Lam, D., 2011: How the world survived the population bomb: lessons from 50 years of extraordinary demographic history, *Demography* **48**, 1231–62, doi:10.1007/s13524–011-0070-z

2012: Alternative Perspective Paper 9.2 fw 2012 Copenhagen Consensus, www.copenhagenconsensus.com

Lapham, R. J. and W. P. Mauldin, 1985: Contraceptive prevalence: the influence of organized family planning programs, *Studies in Family Planning* **16**, 117–37

Lee, R. D., 1973: Population in preindustrial England: an econometric analysis, *Quarterly Journal of Economics* **87**, 581–607

1980: A historical perspective on economic aspects of the population explosion: the case of preindustrial England, in R. A. Easterlin (ed.), *Population and Economic Change in Developing Countries*, University of Chicago Press, 517–66

1986: Malthus and Boserup: a dynamic synthesis, in D. Coleman and R. Schofield (eds.), *The State of Population Theory*, Basil Blackwell, Oxford, 96–130

1988: Induced population growth and induced technological progress: their interaction in the

accelerating state, *Mathematical Population Studies* **1**, 265–88
2003: The demographic transition: three centuries of fundamental change, *Journal of Economic Perspectives* **17**, 167–90
2009: New perspectives on population growth and economic development, *Working Paper*, University of California at Berkeley, Center on the Economics and Demography of Aging, www.ceda.berkeley.edu/Publications/pdfs/rlee/UNFPANewPerspectives09.pdf
2011: The outlook for population growth, *Science* **333**, 569–73, doi:10.1126/science.1208859
Lee, R. D. and K. L. Kramer, 2002: Children's economic roles in the Maya family life cycle: Cain, Caldwell, and Chayanov revisited, *Population and Development Review* **28**, 475–99
Lee, R. D. and A. Mason, 2011: Generational economics in a changing world, *Population and Development Review* **37**, 115–42, doi:10.1111/j.1728–4457.2011.00380.x
2012: Low fertility and economic growth, Paper presented at the Annual Meeting of the Population Association of America, San Francisco, May 3–5, http://paa2012.princeton.edu/download.aspx?submissionId=121596
Lee, R. D. and T. Miller, 1991: Population growth, externalities to childbearing, and fertility policy in developing countries, in S. Fischer, D. deTray, and S. Shah (eds.), *Proceedings of the World Bank Annual Conference on Development Economics*, World Bank, New York, S275–S304
Lee, R. D. and D. S. Reher (eds.), 2011: *Demographic Transition and its Consequences*, Wiley–Blackwell, doi:10.1111/j.1728–4457.2011.00374.x, Supplement to *Population and Development Review*
Lee, R. D., S.-H. Lee, and A. Mason, 2006: Charting the economic life cycle, *NBER Working Paper* **12379**, Cambridge, MA
Levine, R., N. Birdsall, G. Matheny, M. Wright, and A. Bayer, 2006: Contraception, in D. T. Jamison, A. R. Measham, J. G. Breman *et al.* (eds.), *Disease Control Priorities in Developing Countries*, 2nd edn., Oxford University Press, 35–86, www.dcp2.org/pubs/DCP
Lomborg, B., 2012a: Family planning, better nutrition, and no more smoking: Slate readers weigh in on their favorite solutions to the world's biggest problems, *Slate Magazine*, Posted Monday, May 7, www.slate.com/articles/technology/copenhagen_consensus_2012/2012/05/copenhagen_consensus_readers_vote_for_family_planning_better_nutrition_and_tobacco_taxes_.html
2012b: Is family planning the most important investment we can make? Slate readers think so, *Slate Magazine*, Posted Friday, May 4, www.slate.com/articles/technology/copenhagen_consensus_2012/2012/05/copenhagen_consensus_readers_say_family_planning_is_the_best_thing_we_can_do_to_help_the_poor_.html
Lundberg, S. and R. A. Pollak, 1996: Bargaining and distribution in marriage, *Journal of Economic Perspectives* **10**(4), 139–58
Lyngstad, T. H. and A. Prskawetz, 2010: Do siblings' fertility decisions influence each other?, *Demography* **47**, 923–34
Magadi, M. A. and A. O. Agwanda, 2010: Investigating the association between HIV/AIDS and recent fertility patterns in Kenya, *Social Science and Medicine* **71**, 335–44, doi:10.1016/j.socscimed.2010.03.040
Malthus, T. R., 1798: *An Essay on the Principles of Population*, 1st edn., J. Johnson, London
Manuelli, R. E. and A. Seshadri, 2009: Explaining international fertility differences, *Quarterly Journal of Economics* **214**, 771–807, doi:10.1162/qjec.2009.124.2.771
Mason, K. O., 1997: Explaining fertility transitions, *Demography* **34**, 443–54
May, J. F., 2012: *World Population Policies: Their Origin, Evolution, and Impact*, Springer, New York
McCord, G. C., D. Conley, and J. D. Sachs, 2010: Improving empirical estimation of demographic drivers: fertility, child mortality and malaria ecology, Columbia university, New York, unpublished manuscript, http://ssrn.com/abstract=1647901
McDonald, P., 2000: Gender equity in theories of fertility transition, *Population and Development Review* **26**, 427–40
McKelvey, C., D. Thomas, and E. Frankenberg, 2012: Fertility regulation in an economic crisis, *Economic Developmemt and Cultural Change*, **61**, 7–38, doi:10.1086/666950
McNicoll, G., 2011: Achievers and laggards in demographic transition: a comparison of Indonesia and Nigeria, *Population and Development Review* **37**(Supplement), 191–214, doi:10.1111/j.1728–4457.2011.00384.x
Menken, J., L. Duffy, and R. Kuhn, 2003: Childbearing and women's survival: new

evidence from rural Bangladesh, *Population and Development Review* **29**, 405–26, doi:10.1111/j.1728–4457.2003.00405.x

Miller, G., 2010: Contraception as development? New evidence from family planning in Colombia, *Economic Journal* **120**, 709–36, doi:10.1111/j.1468–0297.2009.02306.x

Mills, E. J., A. Rammohan, and N. Awofeso, 2011: Ageing faster with AIDS in Africa, *Lancet* **377**, 1131–3, doi:10.1016/S0140–6736(10)62180–0

Moffitt, R. A., 2005: Remarks on the analysis of causal relationships in population research, *Demography* **42**, 91–108

2009: Issues in the estimation of causal effects in population research, with an application to the effects of teenage childbearing, in H. Engelhardt, H.-P. Kohler, and A. Fürnkranz-Prskawetz (eds.), *Causal Analysis in Population Studies*, The Springer Series on Demographic Methods and Population Analysis, Springer Verlag, Berlin, 9–29

Montgomery, M. R. and J. B. Casterline, 1993: The diffusion of fertility control in Taiwan: evidence from pooled cross-section time-series models, *Population Studies* **47**, 457–79

1996: Social learning, social influence, and new models of fertility, *Population and Development Review* **22**(Supplement), 151–75

Moreland, S., E. Smith, and S. Sharma, 2010: World population prospects and unmet need for family planning, The Futures Group, Washington, DC, http://pubs.futuresgroup.com/3571WPP.pdf

Mosher, S., 2000: AIDS and population control in Africa, *Population Research Institute Weekly Briefing* **2**, 1–3

2008: *Population Control: Real Costs, Illusory Benefits*, Transaction Publishers, Edison, NJ

Munshi, K. D. and J. Myaux, 2006: Social norms and the fertility transition, *Journal of Development Economics* **80**, 1–38

Mwaikambo, L., I. S. Speizer, A. Schurmann, G. Morgan, and F. Fikree, 2011: What works in family planning interventions: a systematic review, *Studies in Family Planning* **42**, 67–82, doi:10.1111/j.1728–4465.2011.00267.x

Myrskylä, M., H.-P. Kohler, and F. C. Billari, 2009: Advances in development reverse fertility declines, *Nature* **460**, 741–3, doi:10.1038/nature08230

National Geographic Magazine, 2011: Population 7 billion: there will soon be seven billion people on the planet. By 2045 global population is projected to reach nine billion. Can the planet take the strain?, *National Geographic Magazine*, January (by Robert Kunzig)

National Research Council, 1986: *Population Growth and Economic Development: Policy Questions*, National Academy Press, Washington, DC

Nerlove, M., 1974: Household and economy: toward a new theory of population and economic growth, *Journal of Political Economy* **82**, 200–18

Notestein, F. W., 1953: Economic problems of population change, in *Proceedings of the Eighth International Conference of Agricultural Economists*, Oxford University Press, London, 13–31

Oeppen, J. and J. W. Vaupel, 2002: Broken limits to life expectancy, *Science* **296**, 1029–31

O'Neill, B. C., M. Dalton, R. Fuchs, L. Jiang, S. Pachauri, and K. Zigova, 2010: Global demographic trends and future carbon emissions, *Proceedings of the National Academy of Sciences* **107**, 17521–6, doi:10.1073/pnas.1004581107

Osotimehin, B., 2011: Population and development, *Science* **333**, 499, doi:10.1126/science.1210732

Pence, B. W., P. Nyarko, J. F. Phillips, and C. Debpuur, 2007: The effect of community nurses and health volunteers on child mortality: the Navrongo Community Health and Family Planning Project, *Scandinavian Journal of Public Health* **35**, 599–608, doi:10.1080/14034940701349225

Phillips, J. F., A. A. Bawah, and F. N. Binka, 2006: Accelerating reproductive and child health programme impact with community-based services: the Navrongo experiment in Ghana, *Bulletin of the World Health Organization* **84**, 949–55, doi:10.1590/S0042–96862006001200010

Phillips, J. F., R. Simmons, J. Chakraborty, and A. I. Chowdhury, 1984: Integrating health services into an MCH–FP Program: lessons from Matlab, Bangladesh, *Studies in Family Planning* **15**, 153–61

Polybius, 1927: *The Histories*, trans W. R. Paton, Harvard University Press, Cambridge, MA

Pop-Eleches, C., 2006: The impact of an abortion ban on socioeconomic outcomes of children: evidence from Romania, *Journal of Political Economy* **114**, 744–73

Population Council, 2012: *Family Planning Programs for the 21st Century: Rationale and Design*, The Population Council, New York

Pörtner, C. C., K. Beegle, and L. Christiaensen, 2011: Family planning and fertility: estimating program effects using cross-sectional data, *World Bank Policy Research Working Paper Series* **5812**, http://ssrn.com/paper=1934673

Potter, J., C. Schmertmann, and S. Cavenaghi, 2002: Fertility and development: evidence from Brazil, *Demography* **39**, 739–61

Potts, D., 2012a: Challenging the myths of urban dynamics in sub-Saharan Africa: the evidence from Nigeria, *World Development*, **40**, 1382–93, doi:10.1016/j.worlddev.2011.12.004

2012b: *Whatever Happened to Africa's Rapid Urbanization?*, Africa Research Institute: Counterpoints, ARI, London, www.africaresearchinstitute.org/files/counterpoints/docs/Whatever-happened-to-Africas-rapid-urbanisation-6PZXYPRMW7.pdf

Potts, M., V. Gidi, M. Campbell, and S. Zureick, 2011: Niger: too little, too late, *International Perspectives on Sexual and Reproductive Health* **37**, 95–101

Prata, N., 2009: Making family planning accessible in resource-poor settings, *Philosophical Transactions of the Royal Society B: Biological Sciences* **364**, 3049–65, doi:10.1098/rstb.2009.0162

Preston, S. H., 1980: Causes and consequences of mortality declines in less developed countries during the 20th century, in R. D. Easterlin (ed.), *Population and Economic Change in Developing Countries*, University of Chicago Press, 289–360

Pritchett, L. H., 1994: Desired fertility and the impact of population policy, *Population and Development Review* **20**, 1–55

Rajaratnam, J. K., J. R. Marcus, A. Levin-Rector, A. N. Chalupka, H. Wang, L. Dwyer, M. Costa, A. D. Lopez, and C. J. Murray, 2010: Worldwide mortality in men and women aged 15–59 years from 1970 to 2010: a systematic analysis, *Lancet* **375**, 1704–20, doi:10.1016/S0140–6736(10)60517-X

Razin, A. and E. Sadka, 1995: *Population Economics*, MIT Press, Cambridge, MA

Reher, D. S., 2011: Economic and social implications of the demographic transition, *Population and Development Review* **37**, 11–33, doi:10.1111/j.1728–4457.2011.00376.x

Reniers, G., B. Masquelier, and P. Gerland, 2011: Adult mortality in Africa, in R. G. Rogers and E. M. Crimmins (eds.), *International Handbooks of Population*, vol. 2, Springer, New York, 151–70, doi:10.1007/978–90-481–9996-9_7

Roberts, L., 2011: 9 billion? *Science* **333**, 540–3, doi:10.1126/science.333.6042. 540

Robinson, L. A., 2007: Policy monitor: how US government agencies value mortality risk reductions, *Review of Environmental Economics and Policy* **1**, 283–99, doi:10.1093/reep/rem018

Robinson, R. S., 2012: Negotiating development prescriptions: the case of population policy in Nigeria, *Population Research and Policy Review* **31**, 267–96, doi:10.1007/ s11113–011-9222–5

Robinson, W. C. and J. A. Ross, 2007: *The Global Family Planning Revolution: Three Decades of Population Policies and Programs*, International Bank for Reconstruction and Development and World Bank, Washington, DC, http://siteresources.worldbank.org/INTPRH/Resources/GlobalFamilyPlanningRevolution.pdf

Rosenthal, E., 2012a: Nigeria tested by rapid rise in population, *New York Times* print edition, April 14, www.nytimes.com/2012/04/15/world/africa/in-nigeria-a-preview-of-an-overcrowded-planet.html

2012b: Nigeria's population is soaring in preview of a global problem, *New York Times*, April 15, http://query.nytimes.com/gst/fullpage.html?res=9C04E6D61530F936A25757C0A9649D8B63

Rosenzweig, M. R., 1990: Population growth and human capital investments: theory and evidence, *Journal of Political Economy* **98**, 38–70

Rosenzweig, M. R. and T. Schultz, 1982: Child mortality and fertility in Colombia: individual and community effects, *Health Policy and Education* **2**, 305–48, doi:10.1016/0165–2281(82)90015–7

1985: The demand for and supply of births: fertility and its life cycle consequences, *American Economic Review* **75**, 992–1015

Rosenzweig, M. R. and K. I. Wolpin, 1980: Testing the quantity–quality fertility model: the use of twins as a natural experiment, *Econometrica* **48**, 227–40

1982: Governmental interventions and household behavior in a developing country: anticipating the unanticipated consequences of social programs, *Journal of Development Economics*

10, 209–25, doi:10.1016/0304-3878(82)90017-7
1986: Evaluating the effects of optimally distributed public programs: child health and family planning interventions, *American Economic Review* **76**, 470–82
2000: "Natural experiments" in economics, *Journal of Economic Literature* **38**, 827–74
Rosenzweig, M. R. and J. Zhang, 2009: Do population control policies induce more human capital investment? Twins, birth weight and China's "one-child" policy, *Review of Economic Studies* **76**, 1149–74
Rosero-Bixby, L. and J. B. Casterline, 1994: Interaction diffusion and fertility transition in Costa Rica, *Social Forces* **73**, 435–62
Rosling, H., 2012: Religions and babies, Presentation at the TED Summit, April, www.ted.com/talks/hans_rosling_religions_and_babies.html
Ross, J. and A. Blanc, 2012: Why aren't there more maternal deaths? A decomposition analysis, *Maternal and Child Health Journal* **16**, 456–63, doi:10.1007/s10995-011-0777-x
Rutstein, S., 2005: Effects of preceding birth intervals on neonatal, infant and under-five years mortality and nutritional status in developing countries: evidence from the demographic and health surveys, *International Journal of Gynecology & Obstetrics* **89**(Supplement 1), S7–S24, doi:10.1016/j.ijgo.2004.11.012
Samuelson, P. A., 1975: The optimum growth rate for population, *International Economic Review* **16**, 531–8
Schelling, T. C., 1978: *Micromotives and Macrobehavior*, Norton, New York
Schultz, T. P., 1990: Testing the neoclassical model of family labor supply and fertility, *Journal of Human Resources* **25**, 599–634
1994: Human capital, family planning and their effects on population growth, *American Economic Review* **84**, 255–60
1997: The demand for children in low income countries, in M. R. Rosenzweig and O. Stark (eds.), *Handbook of Population and Family Economics*, North-Holland, Amsterdam, 349–433
2007: Population policies, fertility, women's human capital, and child quality, in T. P. Schultz and J. A. Strauss (eds.), *Handbook of Development Economics*, vol. **4**, Elsevier, Amsterdam, 3249–303, doi:10.1016/S1573-4471(07)04052-1
2009: How does family planning promote development? Evidence from a social experiment in Matlab, Bangladesh: 1977–1996 Yale University, Economic Growth Center, New Haven, CT
2010: Population and health policies, in D. Rodrik and M. Rosenzweig (eds.), *Handbooks in Economics*, vol. **5**, Elsevier, Amsterdam, 4785–881, doi:10.1016/B978-0-444-52944-2.00010-0
Sedgh, G., R. Hussain, A. Bankole, and S. Singh, 2007: Women with an unmet need for contraception in developing countries and their reasons for not using a method, *Occasional Report* **37**, Guttmacher Institute, Washington, DC, www.guttmacher.org/pubs/2007/07/09/or37.pdf
Seltzer, J. R., 2002: *The Origins and Evolution of Family Planning Programs in Developing Countries*, RAND Corporation, Santa Monica, CA
Shiffman, J. and K. Quissell, 2012: Shifting fortunes for family planning/family planning's contentious history, Paper presented at the Annual Meeting of the Population Association of America, San Francisco, CA, May 3–5, http://paa2012.princeton.edu/download.aspx?submissionId=120716
Simmons, G. B., D. Balk, and K. K. Faiz, 1991: Cost-effectiveness analysis of family planning programs in rural Bangladesh: evidence from Matlab, *Studies in Family Planning* **22**, 83–101
Simon, J., 1981: *The Ultimate Resource*, Princeton University Press
Sinding, S. W., 2009: Population, poverty and economic development, *Philosophical Transactions of the Royal Society B: Biological Sciences* **364**, 3023–30, doi:10.1098/rstb.2009.0145
Singh, S., J. Darroch, L. Ashford, and M. Vlassoff, 2010: Adding it up: the costs and benefits of investing in family planning and maternal and newborn health, *Guttmacher Institute Report*, Washington, DC, http://hdl.handle.net/123456789/28189
Sippel, L., T. Kiziak, F. Woellert, and R. Klingholz, 2011: Africa's demographic challenges: how a young population can make development possible, Berlin Institut für Bevölkerung und Entwicklung, Berlin, www.berlin-institut.org/selected-studies/africas-demographic-challenges.html

Speidel, J. J., D. C. Weiss, S. A. Ethelston, and S. M. Gilbert, 2009: Population policies, programmes and the environment, *Philosophical Transactions of the Royal Society B: Biological Sciences* **364**, 3031–47, doi:10.1098/rstb.2009.0156

Stevens, J. R. and C. M. Stevens, 1992: Introductory small cash incentives to promote child spacing in India, *Studies in Family Planning* **23**, 171–86

Strießnig, E. and W. Lutz, 2012: Optimal fertility, Paper presented at the Annual Meeting of the Population Association of America, San Francisco, CA, May 3–5, http://paa2012.princeton.edu/download.aspx?submissionId=121698

Sulston, J. *et al.*, 2012: People and the planet, *Royal Society Science Policy Centre Report* **01/12**, http://royalsociety.org/policy/projects/people-planet/report

Summers, L. H., 1992: Investing in all the people, *Pakistan Development Review* **31**, 367–406

1994: Investing in all the people: educating women in developing countries, *World Bank, Economic Development Institute Seminar Paper* **45**, World Bank, Washington, DC

Sunil, T. S., V. K. Pillai, and A. Pandey, 1999: Do incentives matter? Evaluation of a family planning program in India, *Population Research and Policy Review* **18**, 563–77, doi:10.1023/A:1006386010561

Teller, C. and A. Hailemariam (eds.), 2011: *The Demographic Transition and Development in Africa: The Unique Case of Ethiopia*, Springer, New York

Townsend, J., 2012: Organization and management of the supply of quality services, in J. Bongaarts (ed.), *Family Planning Programs for the 21st Century: Rationale and Design Reconsidered*, Population Council: Report to the World Bank from the Population Council, New York

Turner, A., 2009: Population priorities: the challenge of continued rapid population growth, *Philosophical Transactions of the Royal Society B: Biological Sciences* **364**, 2977–84, doi:10.1098/rstb.2009.0183

Uganda Ministry of Finance, Planning and Economic Development, 2010: Uganda: population factors and national development (RAPID Brief), USAID Health Policy Initiative, www.healthpolicyinitiative.com/index.cfm?ID=publications&get=pubID&pubID=1068

UN Millennium Development Goals, 2011: The Millennium Development Goals Report, United Nations Statistical Division, http://mdgs.un.org/unsd/mdg/Resources/Static/Data/2011%20Stat%20Annex.pdf

UN Population Division, 2009: What would it take to accelerate fertility decline in the least developed countries?, *UN Population Division Policy Brief* **2009/1**, www.un.org/esa/population/publications/UNPD_policybriefs/UNPD_policy_brief1.pdf

2010a: *World Population Policies 2009*, United Nations, Population Division, New York

2010b: World population prospects, the 2010 revision: Aids and no-aids variants, United Nations, Department of Economic and Social Affairs, Population Division, New York, http://esa.un.org/unpd/peps/EXCEL-Data_WPP2010/aids_no-aids_variants.html

2010c: World population prospects, the 2010 revision: standard (median) forecasts, United Nations, Department of Economic and Social Affairs, Population Division, New York, http://esa.un.org/unpd/wpp/

2011: World contraceptive use 2011, United Nations Publication, Sales No. E.11. XIII.2, New York, www.un.org/esa/population/publications/contraceptive2011/contraceptive2011.htm

UN Statistics Division, 2011: Millennium Development Goals Indicators, United Nations: Millennium Development Goals Indicators – The Offical United Nations Site for MDG Indicators, New York, http://mdgs.un.org/unsd/mdg/Data.aspx

UNAIDS, 2010: *Global Report: UNAIDS Report on the Global AIDS Epidemic 2010*, World Health Organization and UNAIDS, New York, www.unaids.org/globalreport/

2011: *AIDS at 30: Nations at the Crossroads*, United Nations Joint Program on AIDS (UNAIDS), New York, www.unaids.org/unaids_resources/aidsat30/aids-at-30.pdf

UNFPA, 2010: Sexual and reproductive health for all, reducing poverty, advancing development and protecting human rights, United Nations Population Fund (UNFPA), New York, www.unfpa.org/public/home/publications/pid/6526

USAID Health Policy Initiative, 2009a: *Documentation: The RAPID Model – An Evidence-based Advocacy Tool to Help Renew Commitment to Family Planning Programs (Spectrum System of Policy Models)*, USAID Health Policy Initiative, Washington, DC, www.healthpolicyinitiative.com/index.cfm?ID=publications&get=pubID&pubID=808

2009b: Family planning and the MDGs: saving lives, saving resources, USAID Health Policy Initiative, Washington, DC, www.healthpolicyinitiative.com/index.cfm?ID=publications&get=pubID&pubID=788

2009c: *The RAPID Model: An Evidence-Based Advocacy Tool to Help Renew Commitment to Family Planning Programs*, USAID Health Policy Initiative, Washington, DC, www.healthpolicyinitiative.com/index.cfm?ID=publications&get=pubID&pubID=808

2010: The cost of family planning in Kenya, USAID Health Policy Initiative, Washington, DC, www.healthpolicyinitiative.com/index.cfm?ID=publications&get=pubID&pubID=1189

Valente, T. W. and W. Saba, 1998: Mass media and interpersonal influence in a reproductive health communication campaign in Bolivia, *Communications Research* **25**, 96–124

2001: Campaign recognition and interpersonal communication as factors in contraceptive use in Bolivia, *Journal of Health Communication* **6**, 1–20

Viscusi, W. K., 1993: The value of risks to life and health, *Journal of Economic Literature* **31**, 1912–46

2010: The heterogeneity of the value of statistical life: introduction and overview, *Journal of Risk and Uncertainty* **40**, 1–13

Weil, D. N. and J. Wilde, 2009: How relevant is Malthus for economic development today? *American Economic Review* **99**, 255–60, doi:10.1257/aer.99.2.255

Wilcher, R., W. Cates, and S. Gregson, 2009: Family planning and HIV: strange bedfellows no longer, *AIDS* **23**, S1–S6, doi:10.1097/01.aids.0000363772.45635.35

Willis, R. J., 1973: A new approach to the economic theory of fertility behaviour, *Journal of Political Economy* **81**, 14–64

Wilmoth, J. R. and P. Ball, 1992: The population debate in American popular magazines, 1946–90, *Population and Development Review* **18**, 631–68

Wilson, C., 2004: Fertility below replacement level, *Science* **304**, 207–9

World Bank, 2010: The World Bank's reproductive health action plan 2010–2015, World Bank, Washington, DC, http://siteresources.worldbank.org/INTPRH/Resources/376374–1261312056980/RHActionPlanFinalMay112010.pdf

Wulf, D., 1981: Cost-benefit and cost-effectiveness analysis for family planning programs, *International Family Planning Perspectives* **7**, 141–4

Young, A., 2005: The gift of the dying: the tragedy of AIDS and the welfare of future African generations, *Quarterly Journal of Economics* **120**, 423–66

Zambia Ministry of Finance and National Planning, 2010: *Zambia: Population and National Development (RAPID Booklet)*, USAID Health Policy Initiative, Washington, DC, www.healthpolicyinitiative.com/index.cfm?ID=publications&get=pubID&pubID=1179

Population Growth

Alternative Perspective

ODED GALOR

Introduction

The demographic transition has swept the world since the end of the nineteenth century. The unprecedented increase in population growth during the Post-Malthusian regime has been ultimately reversed, bringing about significant reductions in fertility rates and population growth in various regions of the world.

The demographic transition has enabled economies to convert a larger portion of the gains from factor accumulation and technological progress into growth of income *per capita*. It enhanced labor productivity and the growth process via three channels. First, the decline in population growth reduced the dilution of the growing stocks of capital and infrastructure, increasing the amount of resources *per capita*. Second, the reduction in fertility rates permitted the reallocation of resources from the quantity of children toward their quality, enhancing human capital formation and labor productivity. Third, the decline in fertility rates affected the age distribution of the population, temporarily increasing the fraction of the labor force in the population and thus mechanically increasing productivity *per capita*.

This chapter examines various mechanisms that have been proposed as possible triggers for the demographic transition and assesses their empirical significance in understanding the transition from stagnation to growth.

- Was the onset of the fertility decline an outcome of the rise in income during the course of industrialization?
- Was it triggered by the reduction in mortality rates?
- Was it fueled by the rise in the relative wages of women?
- Or was it an outcome of the rise in the demand for human capital in the second phase of industrialization?

In addition, the chapter provides some estimates for the effect of the decline in fertility on economic growth.

The rise in the level of income *per capita*

The rise in income *per capita* prior to the decline in fertility has led some researchers to argue that the reduction in fertility was triggered by the rise in income in the process of industrialization. In particular, Becker (1960) advanced the argument that the decline in fertility was a by-product of the rise in income and the associated rise in the opportunity cost of raising children. His thesis suggests that the rise in income induced a fertility decline because the positive income effect on fertility was dominated by a negative substitution effect brought about by the rising opportunity cost of raising children. Similarly, Becker and Lewis (1973) postulated that the income elasticity with respect to investment in children's education was greater than that with respect to the number of children, and hence the rise in income led to a decline in fertility along with an increase in the investment in each child.

However, this preference-based theory is fragile from a theoretical viewpoint. It hinges on the supposition that individuals' preferences reflect an innate bias against child quantity beyond a certain level of income. Most critically, it generates testable predictions that appear inconsistent with the evidence.

The theory appears counterfactual on both counts. The decline in fertility occurred in the same decade across Western European countries that differed significantly in their income *per capita*. The simultaneity of the demographic transition across Western European countries that differed significantly in their incomes *per capita* suggests that the high levels of income reached by these countries in the Post-Malthusian regime played a very limited role, if any, in the onset of the demographic transition, refuting the first testable implication of the Beckerian theory.

Moreover, the evidence presented by Murtin (2009) (based on a panel of countries during 1870–2000) shows that income per worker was positively associated with fertility rates, once controls were introduced for mortality rates and education. Empirical examinations of the various factors that contributed to the demographic transition within an economy also refute the second implication of the Beckerian theory. In particular, cross-sectional evidence from France and England does not lend support to the theory. Murphy (2009) finds, based on panel data from France during 1876–1896, that income *per capita* had a positive effect on fertility rates during France's demographic transition, accounting for education, the gender literacy gap, and mortality rates.

The decline in infant and child mortality

The decline in infant and child mortality that preceded the reduction in fertility and population growth in most advanced economies, with the notable exceptions of France and the United States, has been viewed as a plausible explanation for the onset of the decline in population growth during the demographic transition. Nevertheless, this hypothesis appears to be non-robust theoretically and inconsistent with historical evidence.

The theory suggests that mortality rates have a positive effect on TFRs. Declines in mortality would not lead to a reduction in the number of surviving offspring unless the number of surviving children is uncertain and the following conditions are satisfied: (1) there exists a precautionary demand for children (i.e. individuals are risk-averse with respect to the number of surviving offspring and thus hold a buffer stock of children in a high-mortality environment); (2) risk aversion with respect to consumption is not larger than risk aversion with respect to the number of surviving children; (3) sequential fertility (i.e. replacement of non-surviving children) is modest; (4) parental resources saved from the reduction in the number of children that do not survive to adulthood are not channeled toward childbearing.

While it is plausible that mortality rates were one of the factors that affected the level of fertility throughout human history, historical evidence does not lend credence to the argument that the decline in mortality accounts for the reversal of the positive historical trend between income and fertility and for the decline in population growth (i.e. fertility net of mortality).

The decline in mortality in Western Europe started nearly a century prior to the decline in fertility and was associated initially with increasing fertility rates in some countries. In particular, the decline in mortality started in England in the 1730s and was accompanied by a steady increase in fertility rates until 1800. The sharp decline in fertility in the course of the demographic transition occurred during a period in which income *per capita* maintained its earlier positive trend, while mortality declines maintained the course that had existed in the 140 years preceding the decline in fertility. The sharp reversal in the fertility patterns in Western European countries in the 1870s, in the context of this stable pattern of mortality decline, therefore, suggests that the demographic transition was prompted by a different universal force.

Quantitative and empirical evidence supports the viewpoint that a decline in infant mortality rates was not the trigger for the decline in net fertility during the demographic transition. Doepke (2005), using the mortality and fertility data from England during 1861–1951, finds that in the absence of changes in other factors, the decline in child mortality during this time should have resulted in a rise in net fertility rates, in contrast to the evidence. A similar conclusion about the insignificance of declining mortality for determining the decline in fertility during the demographic transition is reached in the quantitative analysis of Fernández-Villaverde (2001). Moreover, Murphy (2009) suggests, based on his panel data from France, that the mortality rate had no effect on fertility during France's demographic transition, accounting for education, income, and the gender-literacy gap.

Importantly, it is the reduction in net fertility and thus in population growth that is most relevant from the viewpoint of the theory of economic growth. However, in light of the implausible set of conditions that must be met for a decline in mortality rates to generate a decline in net fertility, the observed sharp decline in the number of surviving offspring (i.e. net reproduction rate) during the demographic transition raises further doubts about the significance of mortality declines in triggering the onset of the decline in population growth.

The rise in the demand for human capital

The gradual rise in demand for human capital during the second phase of industrialization and its close association with the timing of the demographic transition has led researchers to argue that the increasing role of human capital in the production process induced households to increase their investment in the human capital of their offspring, leading to the onset of the fertility decline.

Galor and Weil (2000) argue that the acceleration in the rate of technological progress during the second phase of the Industrial Revolution increased the demand for human capital and induced parents to invest more heavily in the human capital of their offspring. This increase in the rate of technological progress and the associated increase in parental income and demand for human capital brought about two effects on population growth. On the one hand, the rise in income eased households' budget constraints and provided more resources for quality as well as quantity of children. On the other hand, it induced a reallocation of these increased resources toward child quality. In the course of transition from the Malthusian epoch, the effect of technological progress on parental income dominated, and population growth as well as the average population quality increased. Ultimately, further increases in the rate of technological progress induced a reduction in fertility, generating a decline in population growth and an increase in the average level of education.

Suppose that individuals generate utility from the quantity and the quality of their children, as well as from their own consumption. They choose the number of children and their quality in the face of a constraint on the total amount of time that can be devoted to childraising and labor market activities. A rise in parental income due to a rise in the demand for parental human capital would generate, in contrast to Becker and Lewis (1973), conflicting income and substitution effects that would not necessarily trigger a decline in fertility. However, the rise in the future demand for the children's human capital would lead to a pure substitution effect, which would induce parents to substitute quality for quantity of children.

Consistent with the theory, the growth rates of income *per capita* among Western European countries were rather similar during their demographic transition, despite large differences in their levels of income *per capita*. The average growth rate among northwestern European countries during this period was 1.3 percent per year – ranging from 1.0 percent per year in the United Kingdom, 1.3 percent in Norway, 1.4 percent in Finland and France, 1.5 percent in Sweden, to 1.6 percent in Germany (Maddison, 2001). Moreover, the adverse effect of an increase in productivity in the advanced stages of development on net fertility has been established by Lehr (2009), using a pooled cross-sectional time series sample during 1960–1999.

Furthermore, evidence from a panel of countries during 1870–2000 demonstrates that investment in education was indeed a dominating force in the decline in fertility. In particular, educational attainment has been negatively associated with fertility, accounting for income per worker and mortality rates (Murtin, 2009). Importantly, cross-sectional evidence from England, France, and Germany supports the hypothesis that the rise in human capital formation has had an adverse effect on fertility. Becker *et al.* (2010) find that education stimulated a decline in fertility in Prussia during the nineteenth century. Similarly, Murphy (2009) finds, based on his panel data from France, that the level of education attainment had an adverse effect on fertility rates during France's demographic transition, accounting for income *per capita*, the gender literacy gap, and mortality rates.

The decline in fertility in England was associated with a significant increase in the investment in child quality as reflected by years of schooling. In particular, Klemp and Weisdorf (2010) establish a causal effect of family sibship size on individual literacy using demographic data for twenty-six English parishes during 1580–1871. Exploiting exogenous variation in sibship size, stemming from parental fecundity, they find that each additional sibling reduces literacy among all family siblings.

A direct test of the effect on fertility of the rise in the return on human capital has been conducted by Bleakley and Lange (2009) in the context of the eradication of hookworm disease in the American South (c. 1910). Noting that the eradication of this disease can be viewed as a positive shock to the return to child quality since (1) it raised the return on human capital investment, (2) it had a very low fatality rate, and (3) it had negligible prevalence among adults, they find that the rise in the return to child quality had a significant adverse effect on fertility rates.

Finally, the prediction of the theory regarding the adverse effect of increased preference for educated offspring on fertility rates is also supported by the empirical evidence (Becker *et al.*, 2010).

The decline in the gender wage gap

The rise in demand for human capital and its impact on the decline in the gender wage gap during the nineteenth and the twentieth centuries have contributed to the onset of the demographic transition. In particular, the rise in women's relative wages during the process of development, its positive impact on female labor force participation, and its adverse effect on fertility rates have been at the center of a complementary theory of the demographic transition that generates the observed hump-shaped relationship between income *per capita* and population growth.

A pattern of rising relative wages for women and declining fertility rates has been observed in a large number of developed and less-developed economies. In addition, the process of development has been associated with a gradual decline in the gender gap in human capital formation. The literacy rate among women in England, which was only 76 percent of that of men in 1840, grew rapidly during the nineteenth century and reached the male level in 1900.

The role that the decline in the gender wage gap played in the onset of the demographic transition has been examined by Galor and Weil (1996). They argue that technological progress and capital accumulation in the process of industrialization increased the relative wages of women and triggered the onset of the demographic transition. They maintain that technological progress, along with physical capital accumulation, complemented mentally intensive tasks more than physically intensive tasks in the production process, raising the return to brain relative to brawn. Thus, in light of the comparative physiological advantage of men in physically intensive tasks and of women in mentally intensive tasks, the demand for women's labor gradually increased in the industrial sector, decreasing the gender wage gap.

In the early stages of industrialization, as long as the rise in women's wages was insufficient to induce a significant increase in women's labor force participation, fertility increased due to the income effect generated by the rise in men's wages in the increasingly more productive industrial sector. Ultimately, however, the rise in women's relative wages was sufficient to induce a significant increase in their labor force participation. This process increased the cost of childrearing proportionately more than the increase in household's income, triggering a fertility decline. Moreover, the rise in demand for human capital in the process of development induced a gradual improvement in women's education. It raised the opportunity cost of raising children more than the increase in household income, and reinforced the fertility decline and the rise in female labor force participation.

Thus, unlike the single-parent model in which an increase in income generates conflicting income and substitution effects that cancel one another if preferences are homothetic, in the two-parent household model, if most of the burden of childrearing is placed on women, a rise in women's relative wages increases the opportunity cost of raising children more than household income, generating a pressure to reduce fertility.

The role of the decline in the gender wage gap in the demographic transition is supported empirically. Schultz (1985) finds that an increase in the relative wages of women played an important role in Sweden's fertility transition, and Murphy (2009) suggests, based on his panel data from France, that a reduction in the gender literacy gap had an adverse effect on fertility during France's demographic transition, accounting for income *per capita*, educational attainment, and mortality rates.

The old-age security hypothesis

The old-age security hypothesis has been proposed as an additional mechanism for the onset of the demographic transition. It suggests that in the absence of capital markets which permit intertemporal lending and borrowing, children serve as an asset that permits parents to transfer income to old age. Hence, the establishment of capital markets in the process of development reduced this motivation for rearing children, contributing to the demographic transition.

Although old-age support is a plausible element that may affect the level of fertility, it appears as a minor force in the context of the demographic transition. First, since there are only rare examples in nature of offspring that support their parents in old age, it appears that old-age support cannot be the prime motivation for childrearing. Second, institutions supporting individuals in their old age were formed well before the demographic transition.

The rise in fertility rates prior to the demographic transition, in a period of improvements in credit markets, raises further doubts about the significance of this mechanism. Moreover, cross-sectional evidence shows that in the pre-demographic transition era wealthier individuals, who presumably had better access to credit markets, had a larger number of surviving offspring, increasing the skepticism about the importance of this hypothesis. Thus the decline in the importance of old-age support is unlikely to be a major force behind the significant reduction in fertility – at a rate of 30–50 percent – that occurred during the demographic transition.

The demographic transition and the origins of modern growth

Unified Growth Theory (Galor, 2011) suggests that the transition from stagnation to growth is an inevitable by-product of the process of development. It argues that the inherent Malthusian interaction between the rate of technological progress and the size and the composition of the population accelerated the pace of technological progress and ultimately raised the importance of human capital in the rapidly changing technological environment. The rise in the demand for human capital and its impact on human capital formation triggered a reduction in fertility rates and population growth and further technological advances. The demographic transition has enabled economies to divert a larger share of the fruits of factor accumulation and technological progress from fueling population growth toward the enhancement of human capital formation and income *per capita*, thus paving the way for the emergence of sustained economic growth.

Thus, Unified Growth Theory suggests that the demographic transition played an important role in the emergence of modern growth. Indeed, cross-country evidence, depicted in Figure 9.1.1, shows that contemporary income *per capita* are significantly and positively associated with the time elapsed since the demographic transition

Estimating the effects of fertility decline on economic growth

Existing estimates of the effects of fertility decline on economic growth are largely imprecise and speculative, since they are based on assumptions that can not be verified about the elasticity of human capital formation and technological progress with respect to fertility. Historic evidence of countries that went through demographic transition earlier could provide some initial conjectures about the

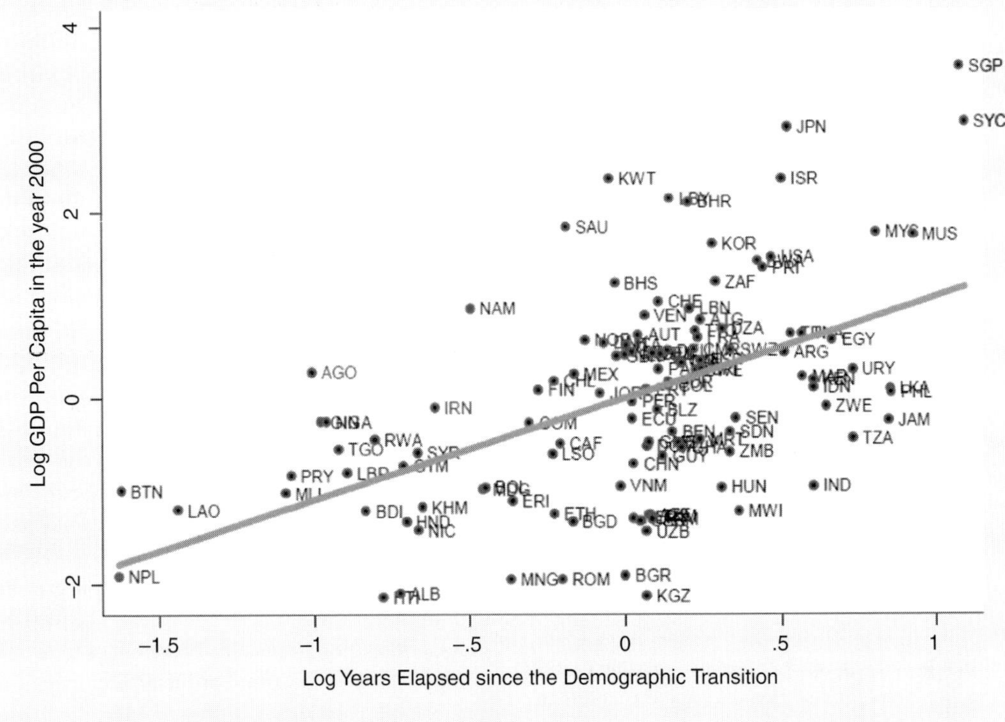

Figure 9.1.1 *Income* per capita*, 2000, and time elapsed since the demographic transition.*

feasible range of these effects in some regions of the world. In particular, the average TFR in SSA was about 5 in 2009. This level corresponds to the TFR of major Western European countries around 1870. From this level, TFR declined to a range of 2–2.5 within a fifty-year period. During this period, enrollment in primary schools increased significantly, ranging from 6 percent in Germany to 45 percent in Finland. In addition, over this period, the growth of *per capita* GDP ranged from 60 percent in countries in the region to 300 percent in Sweden. Moreover, in Western European countries, a decline in TFR by 1 was accompanied by varying increases in the level of *per capita* GDP, from 17 percent in England and Wales to 70 percent in Norway.

Bibliography

Becker, G. S., 1960: An economic analysis of fertility, in G. S. Becker (ed.), *Demographic and Economic Change in Developed Countries*, Princeton University Press, 209–31

Becker, G. S. and H. G. Lewis, 1973: On the interaction between the quantity and quality of children, *Journal of Political Economy* **81**, S279–S288

Becker, S. O., F. Cinnirella, and L. Woessmann, 2010: The trade-off between fertility and education: evidence from before the demographic transition, *Journal of Economic Growth* **15**, 177–204

Bleakley, H. and F. Lange, 2009: Chronic disease burden and the interaction of education, fertility, and growth, *Review of Economics and Statistics* **91**, 52–65

Doepke, M., 2005: Child mortality and fertility decline: does the Barro–Becker model fit the facts?, *Journal of Population Economics* **18**, 337–66

Fernández-Villaverde, J., 2001: Was Malthus right? Economic growth and population dynamics, *Working Paper*, Department of Economics, University of Pennsylvania

Galor, O., 2011: *Unified Growth Theory*, Princeton University Press

Galor, O. and D. N. Weil, 1996: The gender gap, fertility, and growth, *American Economic Review* **86**, 374–87

1999: From Malthusian stagnation to modern growth, *American Economic Review* **89**, 150–4

2000: Population, technology, and growth: from Malthusian stagnation to the demographic transition and beyond, *American Economic Review* **90**, 806–28

Klemp, M. P. B. and J. L. Weisdorf, 2010: The child quantity–quality trade-off: evidence from the population history of England, Department of Economics, University of Copenhagen, mimeo

Lehr, C. S., 2009: Evidence on the demographic transition, *Review of Economics and Statistics* **91**, 871–87

Maddison, A., 2001: *The World Economy: A Millennial Perspective*, OECD, Paris

Murphy, T. E., 2009: Old habits die hard (sometimes): what can département heterogeneity tell us about the French fertility decline?, *Technical Report*, MIMEO, *Working Paper* of Bocconi University, Milan

Murtin, F., 2009: *On the Demographic Transition*, OECD, Paris

Schultz, T. P., 1985: Changing world prices, women's wages, and the fertility transition: Sweden, 1860–1910, *Journal of Political Economy* **93**, 1126–54

Population Growth

Alternative Perspective

DAVID LAM

Introduction

This Alternative Perspective Paper provides reactions to Chapter 9 on population growth prepared by Hans-Peter Kohler for the 2012 Copenhagen Consensus. I begin with some overview comments on Kohler's review of previous literature on population growth and economic development. I then raise some concerns about the estimates of the cost of averting births that are used in his analysis. I also raise concerns over the benefit side of his calculations. My conclusion is that I am quite skeptical of the BCRs of 90:1 to 150:1 provided at the end of his chapter. While family planning may be a good investment, especially in many African countries, I do not think that these estimates provide a sound basis for comparing investments in family planning to other potential investments.

Population growth, the demographic transition, and economic development

One of the great strengths of Kohler's chapter is its comprehensive overview of research on the links between population and development. Kohler provides a very nice summary of the key demographic details, including an overview of the demographic transition and the rapid declines in fertility that have taken place in most parts of the developing world in the last fifty years. As Kohler notes, the big exception to this dramatic fertility decline is SSA, where fertility has fallen much more slowly and where population growth rates are still very high. Kohler provides a good summary of the history of economists' views of the links between population and development. For the most part I agree with his assessment that the consensus view of economists toward family planning has changed somewhat in recent years. While most economists have argued that fertility decline was almost entirely due to changes in the demand for children, with family planning programs facilitating but not driving this decline, more recent evidence has suggested that programs such as the Matlab project in Bangladesh (Joshi and Schultz, 2013) and the family planning program in Colombia (Miller, 2010) have had measurable direct effects on fertility, with resulting indirect effects on outcomes such as health and education.

This comprehensive overview provides a useful background for Kohler's discussion of the costs and benefits of investments in family planning. His analysis concludes that investments in family planning have very large pay-offs. Table 9.4 (p. 565) combines several components of the benefits to come up with a BCR ranging from 90:1 on the low side to 150:1 on the high side. In the end I am not convinced that these are plausible estimates of the BCR, and below I raise some concerns on both the cost and benefit side of his calculations. I expect that the costs of averting births are considerably higher and the benefits considerably lower than Kohler estimates. On the benefit side there are difficult conceptual issues that make it hard to do a careful accounting. Many of the benefits that are included in Kohler's chapter do not seem appropriate for calculating the social benefits of investments in family planning.

The cost of meeting unmet need for family planning

One of the most important components of Kohler's cost-benefit calculations (and indeed any CBA of this kind) is the cost of reducing fertility. Kohler focuses on eliminating "unmet need," an approach that has some appeal since it is arguably the least controversial way to expand family planning services. If we simply make sure that "every birth is a wanted birth" then we do not need to deal with the complicated issue of whether couples' private decisions about fertility deviate from the socially optimal level of fertility. Kohler draws heavily on the Alan Guttmacher Institute's "Adding it Up" Report (Singh *et al.*, 2010), an attempt to estimate the costs and benefits of providing family planning services to the estimated 215 million women with unmet need for modern contraception. While Kohler's chapter is extremely thorough in many dimensions, it gives surprisingly little attention to discussing key concepts such as unmet need and is much too uncritical of the Guttmacher Institute's estimates.

As Kohler points out, the approach in the Guttmacher Report (using the standard approach in the literature) is that "women with unmet need are those who are fecund and sexually active but are not using any method of contraception, and report not wanting any more children or wanting to delay the next child." While this definition seems straightforward, the term has been frequently criticized by economists (e.g. Pritchett, 1994a) and deserves some discussion. The definition assumes that it is lack of access to family planning services that explains why some women who want no more children are not using contraception. While this might be the case, the assumption merits some discussion given the critical role it plays in the cost-benefit calculation. One of the criticisms of the concept of unmet need is that many women who report that they want no more children and are not using contraception in the Demographic and Health Surveys (DHS) go on to report some reason for not using contraception. These reasons include religious reasons, concern over side effects, infrequent sexual activity, opposition from their husband, or some other reason other than lack of availability. In other words, some significant fraction of women seem to choose not to use contraception in spite of its availability. Bongaarts and Bruce (1995) make a similar point, arguing that simply expanding supply may not lead to increased use by many of these women.

The problem can be illustrated in recent DHS data. Figure 9.2.1 shows the reason for not using contraception among women classified as having unmet need for contraception in the 2008 DHS for Ghana, Kenya, and Nigeria. I have classified the reasons into what I call supply issues, demand issues, and health issues (definitions are given below Figure 9.2.1).[1] Health considerations, including fear of side effects, are among the most frequent reasons given. These arguably could be included among demand-side factors, since they prevent women from using contraceptives that may be readily available. A 2007 Guttmacher Report (Sedgh *et al.*, 2007) actually includes them among supply-side factors, on the argument that these are often misplaced fears that can be addressed by effective family planning education. I therefore put them in their own category rather than classifying them as either demand or supply.

Figure 9.2.1 shows that among women classified as having an unmet need in the 2008 Kenya DHS, 12 percent report some kind of supply issue (lack of access, lack of knowledge, or high cost) as the reason for not using contraception, 52 percent give a health reason, and 31 percent give what I call a demand reason (they or their husband are opposed, they have a religious objection, or they have infrequent sex). If we consider the health issues as limiting demand, then 83 percent are not using contraception due to lack of demand. In Nigeria 22 percent give supply-side reasons, 29 percent give health reasons, and 43 percent give demand-side reasons (17 percent say they are opposed to use of contraception, a category that is somewhat difficult to interpret). In Ghana, 13 percent give supply reasons, 42 percent give health reasons, and 29 percent give demand reasons.

The evidence in Figure 9.2.1 suggests that it is questionable to assume that simply scaling up family planning services will cause all women

[1] These are my estimates using DHS sampling weights and using women classified by the DHS as having unmet need for spacing or timing reasons (they either want no more children or do not want any children for the next two years and are not using contraception). Women can list any number of reasons for not using contraception, so the categories are not mutually exclusive.

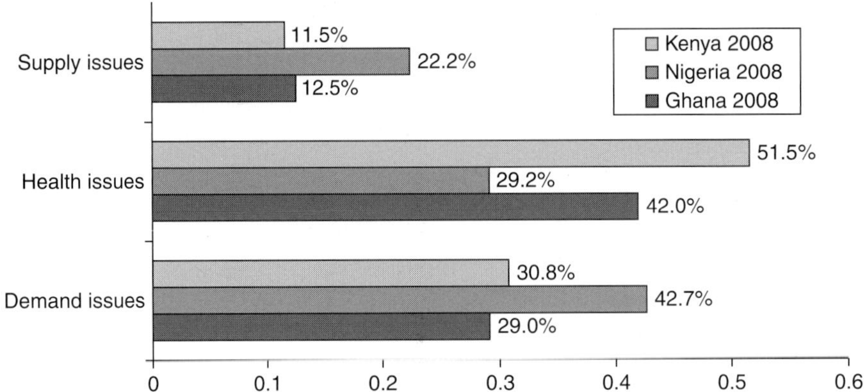

Figure 9.2.1 *Reason for not using contraception among women with unmet need*

Note: Supply issues include: knows no method, knows no source, lack of access, costs too much; Health issues include: health concern, concern over side effects, inconvenient to use, interferes with body processes; Demand issues include: infrequent sex, husband opposed, respondent opposed, religious beliefs. Women could list any number of reasons, so categories are not mutually exclusive.
Source: DHS data.

classified with unmet need to start using contraceptives and have fewer births. The percentage of women who report lack of access is relatively small. Women who report that they or their family members object to using contraceptives (a larger group than those listing supply factors in all three countries) are unlikely to be affected by simply expanding service provision. If we assume that expanded services are no better at dealing with health concerns than are existing services, then there is little reason to think that a simple scaling up will increase utilization among those with health concerns. The bottom line is that the kind of scaling up discussed in the Guttmacher "Adding it Up" report is unlikely to translate into the adoption of contraception among the 215 million women with unmet need.

The issue of supply versus demand determinants of contraceptive use among those classified as having unmet need is not a minor technicality. It is arguably a first-order concern in developing a CBA of the type Kohler provides. Figure 9.2.1 suggests that demand-side issues are several times more important than supply-side issues. If we only take women who explicitly mention issues related to knowledge, access, or cost, the number of women with unmet need in the countries shown might be as low as 12 percent of the total number classified with unmet need. In other words, the Guttmacher Report's estimates of the number of women who would be affected by expansion of supply could plausibly be eight times too large. Of course this means that the cost of expansion might only be 12 percent as large as well, but it is not clear how hard it would be to get services to the particular group of women who give supply-side explanations for their lack of use.

In general, the use of unmet need as measured in surveys like the DHS is probably not the best way to estimate the cost of expanding contraceptive use. Economists are more likely to be convinced by direct evidence that increasing supply actually leads to increased use of contraception. The evidence on this is mixed. Some of this evidence is reported in Kohler's paper and some is not. Miller's study of family planning expansion in Colombia (Miller, 2010) is cited by Kohler as an example of evidence that family planning services do affect fertility. But the impact of Colombia's large family planning program was relatively modest, leading to a decline in fertility of about 1/3 of a child, 6–7 percent of the overall decline in fertility over the 1964–1993 period. While we cannot line these estimates up exactly with what an estimate of unmet need might have been in 1964, such an estimate would have probably been quite high. Given that, an estimate of the impact of the kind of expansion in family planning that Colombia had between 1964 and 1993 would have been considerably larger than 0.3 births. The point isn't simply that other factors were much more important than family planning in driving Colombia's fertility decline. The point is that estimates of unmet need and the cost of meeting that unmet need would almost surely lead to substantial overestimates of the actual impact of expanding family planning on fertility.

Another way to frame the issue is to ask whether an estimate of the cost of averting a birth in a program such as Colombia's can be extrapolated to the cost of averting additional births. In other words, if Colombia had spent twice as much money on its family planning program, would fertility have fallen twice as much? There is good reason to think that the answer is "no." Colombia might have got a bigger and faster decline with a bigger family planning program. But Colombia's fertility decline, which was associated with a very large family planning program, was about the same pace and magnitude as that of Brazil, which had virtually no organized family planning program at all (Lam and Duryea, 1999; Potter *et al.*, 2002). Demand for fertility control was more likely to have been a binding constraint in Colombia than the supply of family planning services, whatever measures of unmet need might have indicated during the period of fertility decline.

An interesting study not mentioned by Kohler is that by McKelvey *et al.* (2012) on the impact of fluctuations in contraceptive prices on demand for contraception in Indonesia. Demand for the pill and IUDs showed little sensitivity to large changes in prices caused by the Indonesian financial crisis. The price of the pill almost doubled between 1998 and 2000, yet there was little change in use of the pill. While this result may be peculiar to the Indonesian setting, with high contraceptive use already in place at the time of the shock, it suggests that a direct experiment in demand sensitivity showed little response of demand to prices.

Another interesting recent study is that by Ashraf *et al.* (2012) of the impact of a randomized family planning intervention in Zambia. The best-known result of this paper is that the take-up rate for the family planning services that were offered was higher when the voucher was given privately to the woman than when the voucher was given to the couple. Another interesting result of the study, however, is the comparison of the couples who were given vouchers (the vouchers provided free guaranteed access to contraceptives and nurses in a setting where wait times are ordinarily long and stockouts are common) to a control group that was only given information about family planning. While the couples that were given vouchers were 18 percentage points more likely than the control group to try a new form of contraception, this did not translate into a reduction in unwanted births 9–14 months after the treatment. The authors interpret this as evidence that "women positioned to take advantage of the more convenient and affordable method were those who were already fairly successful in preventing unwanted births." While women who were given the means to access family planning without the involvement of their husbands did have fewer unwanted births, the otherwise identical program that did not have this provision had no impact on unwanted births. While this is just one study in one particular setting, it is one of the few pieces of direct evidence from a randomized program designed to improve access to family planning in an area with considerable unmet need. It suggests that even a substantial improvement in access may not lead to a decrease in unwanted births.

Estimating the benefits of averted births

The discussion above suggests that the cost of averting births may be greatly understated by estimates such as those in the Guttmacher Report. I turn now to Kohler's estimates of the benefits of averting births. This is a conceptually difficult road to go down, and Kohler has laid out many of the key issues. Some of the challenges are worth highlighting, however, and raise concerns about his cost benefit calculations.

On p. 554 Kohler focuses on the impact of reduced fertility on expenditures on things like schooling and health care for children. While at first glance this seems like a reasonable approach, given the public provision of these services, it is worth thinking about the assumptions required for this to be a good measure of the social benefit of averting births. A useful frame of reference is to consider a regime in which all of the costs of health and education are private costs paid by parents. Most parents would still have children in that case, although they might have fewer children given the increase in their (private) cost. While parents would save the cost of education and child care if they had fewer children, they presumably consider the benefits of children (most of which are non-pecuniary) to be worth the cost for the number of children they choose to have. Starting from this regime, suppose education and health care were to become publicly provided at the same level that was previously chosen by parents. If there were no change in the number of children then it would be odd to argue that the social benefit of averting a birth should now be measured by the public savings in education and health care. Parents were willing to pay that cost when it was up to them, so presumably the socially optimal level of fertility, schooling, and health care are the same as the ones that were chosen privately by parents.

The answer becomes more complicated if parents choose higher fertility when schooling and health care are publicly provided, but it would still be a substantial overstatement to say that the social benefit of reducing fertility is the reduced education and health care expenses. Or, put another way, that calculation ignores the private (and therefore social) benefit of the child. The bottom line is that I do not find the accounting of the benefits of family planning programs on p. 554 to be compelling. For example, Kohler cites an estimate that family planning expenditures of $71 million from 2005–2015 are associated with social sector cost savings of $271 million – "a BCR of 4:1." For any couple the cost of averting a birth is presumably much smaller than the costs of raising a child – it doesn't follow that they should be having fewer children. Just because some costs of children are publicly provided, it does not follow that these should be included in the social benefit of averting a birth. The right counterfactual is to think of what parents would have been willing to pay privately for those costs in order to have a child.

The argument might be more compelling in the case of unwanted births. But even that is not entirely clear. Even if we could identify a birth as an unwanted birth, it is not obvious that we would want to count all the costs that would have been spent on that birth as benefits of averting the birth. Suppose a couple is almost indifferent between having another birth and not having another birth, but on balance reports that they would prefer not to have another birth in the next two years. In the DHS "unmet need" perspective, any birth this couple has within two years is considered an unwanted birth and any couple in this situation that is not using contraception is a case of unmet need. For a proper CBA an economist would like to know the couple's WTP to avert that birth. One of Pritchett's arguments (Pritchett 1994a, 1994b) is that this cost must in many cases be quite low, since many couples seem to be aware of contraceptive methods, could access those methods at some modest cost, but choose not to. If the couple had a birth within two years rather than after two years then they might be very happy to pay the cost of education and health for the child if those costs were private. They might be much happier having the child within two years than not having the child at all. In other words, the fact that they choose not to use contraception suggests that they don't view the costs of having a child as greatly exceeding the benefits. It seems odd, then, that the analysis of the social planner would end up with something like a 50:1 BCR from averting the birth. While it is true that the couple does not bear all the costs of publicly providing education and health, that does not mean that the couple would not have been willing to pay those costs and it does not follow that these costs should be counted as net social benefits of averting a birth.

There is one final point to make about counting the costs of schooling and health care as benefits of averting a birth. If we want to do this kind of calculation then we should evaluate the full set of revenues and expenditures that children will generate over their entire lifetime. Expenditures on schooling and health care should be offset against the tax revenues the child will generate as an adult, along with all other positive and negative public transfers, all discounted back to birth. This is one of the issues that Lee and Mason look at extensively in their National Transfer Accounts (Lee and Mason,

2011). It is a complicated problem both conceptually and empirically. The main point for these purposes is that it is not appropriate to simply pull out one set of expenditures, such as those on health and schooling, and look at them in isolation as a cost of a child that should be put on the benefit ledger of a CBA. Even if we only care about the government budget, which is a very narrow way to think about the problem, this is not a complete accounting of the costs and benefits of a birth. It is not clear exactly how the accounting is done for the estimates that are mentioned by Kohler on p. 554, but it appears that these are based on a very partial accounting.

The discussion on p. 555 looks at benefits from a different perspective, focusing on reduced infant and maternal mortality. I found this section more appealing conceptually, though I was not persuaded by the specific numbers used for the calculations. The estimates once again rely on the assumption that a proportional expansion of family planning services will reduce births based on the estimated unmet need discussed above. The estimates in this section are built around the estimates in the Guttmacher Institute Report that expanding family planning programs to eliminate unmet need would result in 640,000 fewer newborn deaths, 150,000 fewer maternal deaths, and 600,000 fewer children who lose their mother. Given these estimates, Kohler's valuation of these averted deaths is a reasonable application of the Copenhagen Consensus guidelines. But I'm not persuaded that the Guttmacher Institute estimates are reasonable, given the problems with the concept of unmet need.

On p. 557 Kohler looks at contributions of reduced fertility to *per capita* income growth. This is another very tricky conceptual area. It is once again worth thinking about the CBA that couples make on a regular basis when women are in their childbearing years. Most births, even in Africa, are "wanted" births, with couples presumably having decided that the benefits exceeded the costs of having the birth. Yet an additional birth almost surely lowers the *per capita* income of the family for many years, and probably lowers it forever in PDV. So couples seem to routinely reject the maximization of household *per capita* income as a criterion in deciding whether to have another child. Given that, it seems questionable that a social planner should use *per capita* income as a criterion in evaluating the costs and benefits of averting births. Computer simulation programs such as the RAPID program mentioned by Kohler (a program that goes back several decades) have always had the feature that slower population growth produces higher growth of *per capita* income in part simply because the denominator grows more slowly while the growth of the numerator (total GDP) is unaffected. Kohler points out this fundamental feature of these sorts of models, but seems to accept that they may be telling us something useful. I don't think most economists would take these sorts of simulations very seriously as the basis for a CBA of family planning. A model that assumes a constant 6 percent growth rate of aggregate GDP and then looks at how *per capita* income will be affected by different population growth rates cannot be considered a serious economic model of population growth and economic development. Even if we thought it was exactly the way the world works, the logical conclusion of such a model is that we should have the most negative growth rate possible if we want to maximize *per capita* GDP.

It is worth recalling some of the earliest and arguably most influential CBAs of family planning done in the 1960s. The economist Stephen Enke wrote a series of papers analyzing the costs and benefits of family planning (for example, Enke, 1960, 1966, 1971). In his 1960 paper Enke argued "An economy is having too many births for the economic welfare of the existing population if the estimated present value of infants born this year is negative." Enke's approach was to compare the cost of averting a birth, thereby lowering the denominator for *per capita* income, with the return on investments in economic growth that would increase the numerator. He concluded that payments to men to get vasectomies "are several hundred times more effective in raising *per capita* income say over a ten year period than are resources of equal value invested in traditional development projects" (Enke, 1960: 339).

Most economists would find this a questionable way to analyze the costs and benefits of family planning. As Krueger and Sjaastad (1962) wrote in a critique, Enke's assumption of *per capita* income as a social welfare function would imply that all births are suboptimal in any population, even when parents bear all the costs. In his 1966 paper, Enke (1966: 45) provides a more detailed version of his argument. He writes that "output per head (*V/P*) can be increased by investing resources in making the output numerator larger or the population denominator smaller than they would otherwise be in, say, 1975." He then discusses investments that might raise *P* or lower *V*, and concludes "If economic resources of given value were devoted to retarding population growth, rather than accelerating production growth, the former resources could be 100 or so times more effective in raising *per capita* incomes in many L.D.C.s." (Enke, 1966: 56). The logic is essentially the following: if *per capita* income is $5,000, and if the cost of averting a birth is $50, then the BCR of averting a birth is 100:1. Enke's papers were noticed by US Administration officials and were reportedly responsible for President Lyndon Johnson's well-known remark in a speech to the United Nations, "Let us act on the fact that less than $5 invested in population control is worth $100 invested in economic growth," (Johnson, 1965).

Enke's papers, though published in good journals, have not stood the test of time. It is interesting that they are almost never cited in reviews such as Kohler's, in spite of the considerable impact they seem to have had on the large US investment in international family planning programs beginning in the 1960s. Presumably the fact that these papers are rarely cited is because most economists recognize that this is not a serious way to think about the costs and benefits of family planning programs. Enke became involved in the TEMPO program of the General Electric Center for Advanced Studies (described in Enke, 1971). The TEMPO computer simulation model looked at the impact of population growth in a somewhat more complicated way than his earlier work, although Enke's 1971 article makes it clear that the mathematics of rising numerators versus falling denominators still drive the model. USAID's RAPID model, first developed in 1978, drew heavily on the TEMPO models. USAID continues to use the RAPID model to simulate the impact of population growth on economic growth, and Kohler mentions recent versions in his review. While these models may be useful in analyzing the dynamics of population growth, age structure, and dependency ratios, they are not the basis for a theoretically sound analysis of the costs and benefits of family planning. At their heart they are still heavily driven by Enke's original logic that it is cheaper to lower the denominator in *per capita* income than it is to raise the numerator.

More rigorous economic models such as Ashraf *et al.* (2011) deserve much more serious consideration. But these models still raise the question of whether maximizing *per capita* income is an appropriate objective function for thinking about investments in family planning. As noted, couples systematically reject this criterion when making their own fertility decisions, and presumably would do so even if all the costs and benefits of childbearing were entirely private (that is, if there were no implicit subsidies working through publicly provided schooling, etc.). So it is not clear that showing that *per capita* income growth would be 1 percent higher if population growth were 1 percent lower is an adequate basis for evaluating the costs and benefits of family planning. While we might agree that everyone could be better off if *unwanted* births were prevented, these models are not really aimed at addressing the question of averting unwanted births.

Conclusions

My point here is not to argue that a country like Nigeria should not be concerned about its continued high rate of population growth, or that investments in family planning are not worthwhile. My own view is that Nigeria and other African countries should be concerned about high fertility and the consequences of rapid population growth. The countries and their populations will almost surely be better off if Africa makes the same transition toward smaller families with larger investments in children that has occurred in most Asian and Latin American countries. I also agree with the view that providing women the means with which to choose their ideal family size is a high-priority mission for any public health system.

I am skeptical, however, that the BCRs of 90:1 and 150:1 presented in Kohler's conclusions are plausible. I have raised concerns on both the cost and benefit side of the calculations. On the cost side, it is not clear that simply scaling up family planning services will lead to large reductions in fertility. As the DHS data show, many women in these countries have access to family planning services and choose for various reasons not to use them. While more effective service delivery might increase usage, simply expanding services as they currently exist seems unlikely to dramatically lower fertility in the absence of the social and economic changes that would change the demand for children. The estimates of the benefits of family planning also raise a number of issues. Conceptually they seem to include components that I would argue are not appropriate for estimating the benefits of family planning. Counting the costs of health and education, for example, without doing a full calculation of lifetime taxes and benefits, is misleading, even if we accepted the very narrow calculus of evaluating the impact of a child on the public purse. The calculations of the impact of population growth on *per capita* income growth do not seem to be grounded in any theoretical arguments about why private decisions about fertility are suboptimal. Unless there are externalities to childbearing, simply showing that lower fertility would increase *per capita* income is not a sound basis for investing in family planning.

There is almost surely a need for more and better family planning services in many countries, especially in Africa. How to balance this need against the many other needs in these countries is a difficult policy question. If the BCR for investments in family planning is really 90:1 or 150:1 then there are probably few other investments that should come first. Unfortunately I think these estimates are flawed on both the cost and benefit side. As a result I don't think they can really convince us that a marginal dollar spent on family planning has a higher pay-off than a marginal dollar spent on education, malaria eradication, improved sanitation, or the elimination of corruption.

Bibliography

Ashraf, N., E. Field, and J. Lee, 2012: Household bargaining and excess fertility: an experimental study in zambia, Unpublished manuscript

Ashraf, Q. H., D. N. Weil, and J. Wilde, 2011: The effect of interventions to reduce fertility on economic growth, *NBERWorking Paper* **17377**, www.nber.org/papers/w17377

Bongaarts, J. and J. Bruce, 1995: The causes of unmet need for contraception and the social content of services, *Studies in Family Planning* **26**, 57–75

Enke, S., 1960: The economics of government payments to limit population, *Economic Development and Cultural Change* **8**, 339–48

1966: The economic aspects of slowing population growth, *The Economic Journal* **76**, 44–56

1971: Economic consequences of rapid population growth, *The Economic Journal* **81**, 800–11

Johnson, L., 1965: Address in San Francisco at the 20th Anniversary Commemorative Session of the United Nations, June 25, www.presidency.ucsb.edu/ws/index.php?pid=27054#ixzz1siPmMTyN

Joshi, S. and T. P. Schultz, 2013: Family planning and women's and children's health: long-term consequences of an outreach program in Matlab, Bangladesh, *Demography* **50**, 149–80

Krueger, A. and L. Sjaastad, 1962: Some limitations of Enke's economics of population, *Economic Development and Cultural Change* **10**, 423–6

Lam, D., 2011: How the world survived the population bomb: lessons from 50 years of extraordinary demographic history, *Demography* **48**, 1231–62

Lam, D. and S. Duryea, 1999: Effects of schooling on fertility, labor supply, and investments in children, with evidence from Brazil, *Journal of Human Resources* **34**, 160–92

Lee, R. and A. Mason, 2011: *Population Aging and the Generational Economy: A Global Perspective*, Edward Elgar, Cheltenham

McKelvey, C., D. Thomas, and E. Frankenberg, 2012: Fertility regulation in an economic crisis, *Economic Development and Cultural Change* **61**, 7–38

Miller, G., 2010: Contraception as development? New evidence from family planning in Colombia, *Economic Journal* **120**, 709–36

Potter, J., C. Schmertmann, and S. Cavenaghi, 2002: Fertility and development: evidence from Brazil, *Demography* **39**, 739–61

Pritchett, L. H., 1994a: Desired fertility and the impact of population policies, *Population and Development Review* **20**, 1–55

1994b: The impact of population policies – reply, *Population and Development Review* **20**, 621–30

Sedgh, G., R. Hussain, A. Bankole, and S. Singh, 2007: Women with an unmet need for contraception in developing countries and their reasons for not using a method, *Guttmacher Institute Occasional Report* **37**, June, Washington, DC, www.guttmacher.org/pubs/2007/07/09/or37.pdf

Singh, S., J. Darroch, L. Ashford, and M. Vlassoff, 2009: Adding it Up: The Costs and Benefits of Investing in Family Planning and Maternal and Newborn Health, Guttmacher Institute and United Nations Population Fund, www.gultmacher.org/pubs/AddingItUp2009.pdf

Water and Sanitation

FRANK RIJSBERMAN AND ALIX PETERSON ZWANE*

The challenge

The world has met the MDG on water five years early, according to the most recent Joint Monitoring Program update, released in March 2012, but will miss its goal on basic sanitation by almost 1 billion people (WHO/UNICEF, 2012). An astonishing one-third of the world population, 2.5 billion people, does not have access to basic sanitation and over 1 billion people defecate out in the open. In light of the evidence that the world community is making progress in the water sector, and because sanitation is typically the neglected half of the water and sanitation challenge, including in the 2008 Copenhagen Consensus Challenge Paper on water and sanitation (Whittington *et al.*, 2008) this chapter redresses that imbalance and focuses primarily on sanitation and the question of whether and how it would be cost-effective to dramatically change levels of investment to solve this problem.

The benefits of sanitation as a public health solution seem self-evident. Quotations like this from a Lancet editorial are easy to find:

> It is already well known that improved sanitation could prevent 1·5 million deaths from diarrheal illnesses a year, enhances dignity, privacy, and safety, especially for women and girls, benefits the economy – every dollar spent on sanitation generates economic benefits worth around nine more – and is better for the environment. (Lancet, 2008)

In the United States, large public sector investments to provide clean water and sewerage were jointly responsible for most of the rapid decline in the child mortality rate in the early twentieth century (Cutler and Miller, 2005), and more recently for substantial health improvements on Native American Indian reservations (Watson, 2006).

And yet, the continued burden of unsafe and inadequate sanitation is easy to identify. Inadequate sanitation caused a cholera outbreak in Haiti in late 2010 that made half a million people sick and cost some 7,000 lives (McNeil, 2012). Smaller cholera outbreaks are still commonplace during the rainy season in Bangladesh or the low-lying parts of many African cities (Zuckerman *et al.*, 2007). Diarrheal diseases are still a leading cause of death for children under five, second only to respiratory infections (Black *et al.*, 2010). The burden extends beyond health. The 2007 Water and Sanitation Program (WSP) of the World Bank launched a series of national studies to assess the economic impact of poor sanitation. In the Economics of Sanitation Initiative (ESI), a series of reports dating from 2008 to late 2010, WSP concludes that the economic impact of poor sanitation can be as high as 7 percent of GDP for some Asian countries (Bangladesh: 6.3 percent; Cambodia: 7.2 percent; India: 6.4 percent; Lao PDR. 5.6 percent) while it is still of the order of 1–2 percent of GDP for African countries (Benin: 1.5 percent; Burkina Faso: 2 percent; DRC: 1.6 percent; Ghana: 1.6 percent; Kenya: 0.9 percent) and some other Asian countries (Indonesia: 2.3 percent; Philippines: 1.5 percent; Vietnam: 1.3 percent) (Hutton *et al.*, 2008, 2009; Barkat, 2012; Tyagi, 2010; WSP, 2011).

Why has the sanitation challenge proved so elusive for many countries? The simplest answer is the cost of current technologies. For about 200 years the

* We thank Sangeeta Chowdhury, Philip Eckhoff, Doulaye Kone, and Lowell Wood for helpful discussion that informed the development of this chapter. Sarah Herr and Rosalyn Rush provided able research assistance. Kasper Thede Anderskov provided wise advice that strengthened this work considerably, and Guy Hutton and Jan Willem Rosenboom provided helpful comments. All errors and omissions are our own.

water closet – the flush toilet with its smell-limiting water seal that brought the "outhouse" indoors – and the associated sewer networks have been the technology of choice for all who can afford it. The 2008 Copenhagen Consensus sanitation and water paper (Whittington *et al.*, 2008) estimated that the cost of such conventional "modern" water and sanitation systems was of the order of $50–100 per household per month – which puts them squarely out of reach for those living on $1–2 per day.

Faced with such costs and the potential to decouple water and sanitation services, many governments and households have prioritized water over sanitation. Take the cases of China and India: of the 1.8 billion people who gained access to improved drinking water sources between 1990 and 2008, 47 percent lived in China and India alone. Of the 1.3 billion people who gained access to basic sanitation in the same period 38 percent lived in China and India. But while in 2008 88 percent and 89 percent of the population in India and China, respectively, had access to improved water services, only 55 percent and 31 percent had access to basic sanitation (WHO/UNICEF, 2010).

Why does sanitation lag so far behind water? There is a strong *a priori* case to suspect significant disease externalities and intrafamily distributional inequities that would lead to inefficiently low private investment. Standard public finance arguments would thus support public contributions to sanitation. There is also suggestive evidence that improving sanitation presents a coordination failure and that behavioral biases prevent optimal take-up, which also bolsters the case for subsidies (Ban, *et al.*, 2011). Similar arguments have been used to support subsidies for water quality, vaccines, bednets, and primary education in developing countries (Holla and Kremer, 2008; Ahuja *et al.*, 2010).

In addition to these market failures in the sector, the continued focus on water-borne technology compounds the challenges of extending sanitation service to all. Whittington *et al.* (2008) argued that the cost of flush toilets and sewers limits their reach to the top one or two income quintiles. Conventional wastewater treatment plants are not only expensive to construct, but costly to operate because of their high energy requirements. As a consequence, in a SSA typical country, sewers serve only a small core of large cities.

The sanitation that serves those households not in the sewered core is not networked; it is on-site sanitation – i.e. latrines or septic tanks, an investment for which the owner of the house bears primary responsibility. In high-density, low-income urban areas, where one or more families share a single room, finding space for a latrine is problematic and constructing a new latrine when an existing one fills is usually out of the question. Under those conditions latrines have to be emptied and the fecal sludge has to be transported to a place where it can be dumped safely if the health benefits of sanitation are to be realized.

In practice, the urban sanitation service chain often breaks down at the emptying stage to such an extent that the context is one of functional open defecation. This point – that the reality of urban sanitation is a broken service chain that makes health benefits illusive – is central to our argument in this chapter that innovation, not just investment in current technology, is needed if potential health benefits are to be realized.

Some pits and septic tanks are emptied with a vacuum pump truck, which is the standard developed-country solution for emptying septic tanks. Vacuum trucks are expensive and not well suited to empty latrines in high-density low-income urban areas where lanes are small and narrow. An estimated 200 million latrines and septic tanks are emptied manually, by a worker descending into the pit with a bucket and spade. When this approach is taken, the pit contents are generally subsequently dumped or buried in the immediate environment. This reintroduces to the environment pathogens previously contained in the pit or tank. Health costs are also imposed on emptiers. Even when pump trucks are used, in many cities the fecal sludge is not safely disposed, it is dumped in fields or on beaches. The final result is again that the health benefits of sanitation, which assume that fecal matter does not enter the environment, are not realized.[1]

This chapter takes on the question of what it would cost to improve service for both the unserved population in developing countries, those 1 billion

[1] An overview of the situation in five cities is provided by Norman and Parkinson (2011).

or so who must defecate in the open, and what it would cost to improve the quality of service for those people in urban areas who are nominally "served" but struggle to realize the gains from sanitation because of the challenges of emptying and safely disposing of latrine/septic tank contents. We argue that dramatically cutting open defecation rates in rural areas has been shown to be feasible with a reasonable public investment at a scale of tens of millions of people and that it has a positive, though modest, pay-off as measured by a CBA. Our argument on this question is qualitatively similar to that made by Whittington *et al.* (2008). In the case of urban sanitation, which Whittington *et al.* did not consider, we argue that the theoretical benefits of basic on-site sanitation will not be achieved unless specific innovations are put in place. Investments in technological and institutional innovations to reduce the cost and increase the effectiveness of sanitation services to empty and treat human waste collected in latrines and septic tanks would have a very large pay-off. We believe that the innovation required is achievable, as it requires integration and product development rather than blue sky research and discovery. There is credible evidence that the fraction of roll-out costs to achieve adoption that would need to be borne by the public sector is sufficiently small as to make such an investment feasible and attractive. Finally, we argue that there is also a need for radical innovation to "reinvent the toilet." Such radical innovation is indeed high risk, but if successful would lead to very attractive BCRs.

Our approach to making the cost-benefit estimates for sanitation that are the primary focus of this chapter is to build upon the exemplary recent work done by the WSP of the World Bank as part of its ESI. We do not re-visit in detail the ESI calculations and dispute particular parameters; thus we take on the Copenhagen Consensus "challenge" in a way that differs from the tack taken by Whittington *et al.* (2008). There is no need for further detailed calculations when we can build on the ESI work; rather, we accept throughout this chapter the ESI estimates of various levels of total annualized costs of basic sanitation and the associated benefits as appropriate starting points. However, we make arguments that lead us to conclude that the ESI estimates are theoretical maximums and not ratios that could be realized in the world with existing technologies and approaches to service delivery. Under current conditions we argue that the solutions evaluated by ESI suffer from poor adoption as well as poor operation and maintenance, which implies that the health and related water quality assumed by ESI could not be realized.

Indeed, the lack of progress in sanitation relative to water is what economists would call a "revealed preference" argument for this case. If the lost GDP estimated by ESI, and referenced above, were real, then this would be powerful evidence of "dollar bills left on the sidewalk." We do not believe that there are such unrealized gains simply available for the picking. Rather, key investments are needed to create services that people actually want to use, in the case of latrines in rural areas, and that actually result in health benefits, in the case of current non-networked urban sanitation. Adjusting for the implications of these investments for the benefit-cost estimates generated by ESI allows us to implement a straightforward illustrative calculation that we believe creates a powerful rationale for investment in the three sanitation interventions we propose in this paper. The Bill and Melinda Gates Foundation, following the analysis as presented in this chapter, is investing on the order of half a billion dollars in these three interventions in the period 2009–2015.

For completeness, we also consider a rural water-supply intervention that could serve some large fraction of the 770 million people currently lacking access to safe drinking water (WHO/UNICEF, 2012). This is in fact the rural water intervention consisting of boreholes equipped with hand pumps, as analyzed by Whittington *et al.* (2008), contextualized by our interpretation of the data supporting alternative management models for this sort of infrastructure. We accept the conclusion of Whittington *et al.* that this intervention would have a modest, positive BCR, but argue that it is likely to be lower than the 3.4 that is their preferred estimate, because the life of rural water infrastructure is often curtailed in practice.

The remainder of this chapter is organized as follows: the next section summarizes the conventional sanitation solutions that exist to potentially meet the sanitation challenges and provides the specification for a series of innovations that could increase the effectiveness of, or replace, existing solutions. The next section briefly summarizes the methodology used by the ESI and the results of that exercise. The next section builds on the previous information and presents our estimates of the BCR associated with tackling the sanitation challenge. In the next section, we consider the rural water intervention. A final section concludes.

Sanitation solutions

Basic "improved" sanitation

Basic sanitation is the simplest form of sanitation, usually just a latrine that meets the minimum requirements to contain pathogens (such as a latrine cover to keep out flies), but often not pleasant to use. In low-density rural areas, households are expected to have enough space to construct a basic latrine on their plot, at an adequate distance away from their living space and from their water source, and to rebuild a new latrine if the old one fills up. ESI analysis of basic latrines in rural areas in the Philippines and Vietnam shows economic returns with BCRs of 5–8, with annualized costs per household as low as $20.

Smell and flies are key barriers to satisfaction with basic sanitation. There are many latrine designs that attempt to reduce smell and prevent flies from spreading disease through forms of ventilation and systems of double vaults or pits, allowing the waste in one pit to decompose while the other fills up. Generally speaking, the cheapest and affordable forms of these (that cost $30–$100 to construct) tend to be quite unpleasant to use, and the more sophisticated double vault pour-flush latrines or septic tanks are quite expensive to construct ($500–$2,000) and need to be emptied periodically. People have a strong preference for at least a pour-flush latrine, a latrine with a smell-reducing water seal, where users flush urine and excrement with a small amount of water also used for personal hygiene. (Anal cleansing with water rather than paper is the norm in all of Asia and much of Africa.)

Ecological sanitation emphasizes the recycling potential of human waste – i.e. considering urine and feces as a resource that can be made safe to re-use, as an alternative to the emptying and disposal of pit contents or simply leaving full pits undisturbed. In principle, this could increase the benefits associated with rural sanitation. Urine contains significant amounts of nutrients that can be re-used as fertilizer (Esrey *et al.*, 1998; WSP, 2009). Feces have a high energy content that can potentially be recovered for use as fuel. Composting toilets use microbes to decompose human waste and generate compost, but simple models are not that easy to manage and do not effectively remove pathogens; sophisticated ones are not cheap. Biogas toilets also use microbes to decompose waste but capture the methane generated in the process for use as, for example, cooking gas. Some pathogens are particularly difficult to get rid of through these processes. It takes at least six months of composting to remove the large majority of helminth eggs, for example, and some pathogens survive for years in composting-type toilets.

Sewered systems

The conventional solution, the gold standard, and for many governments still the only acceptable long-term solution to the sanitation challenge, is the flush toilet. A toilet is a water closet that is linked to a sewer network that transports human waste diluted in a large volume of clean water to a wastewater treatment plant where it takes considerable energy to remove the waste from that water. Using large volumes of water treated to drinking water quality to flush excrement down expensive pipes in order to spend more money to try to clean that water up again is not necessarily a smart idea anywhere. The ESI estimates the annualized cost per household for sewer networks with wastewater treatment alone for China, Indonesia, the Philippines, and Vietnam to be $100–200. As mentioned before, Whittington *et al.* (2008) estimated that the cost of conventional "modern" water *and* sanitation systems is on the order of $50-100 per household per month.

Though we will not pursue this question further in this chapter, we do note here that there is a potential middle ground between traditional sewerage and the non-networked solutions we discuss. Simplified or low-cost sewer systems, using shallow small-diameter pipes at low gradients at community level, are used in some areas, particularly in Brazil, and may be combined with small-scale decentralized wastewater treatment systems or constructed wetlands (Mara, 2008; Mara and Alabaster, 2008). Particularly in areas with multi-level apartment blocks these systems may have an advantage over latrines but they have not been widely adopted. A challenge for future research might be to estimate carefully the potential market for this approach, barriers to adoption, and potential net benefits.

Fecal sludge management

In urban areas where latrines and septic tanks have to be emptied, and the fecal sludge has to be disposed of safely, its management is a challenge associated with on-site or non-sewered sanitation. In locations where there is a relatively active market for mechanized latrine emptying with vacuum trucks, fecal sludge that is dumped safely is generally kept in large drying beds and left to decompose for at least six months (Klingel *et al.*, 2002; Krekeler, 2008).[2] It is common practice, however, for the sludge trucks to dump their hazardous content directly into agricultural fields, rivers, or on beaches. Certainly, new solutions for fecal sludge management, whether it is technology or business and regulatory models that end such unsafe disposal, are required if hundreds of millions of people are going to be served by non-networked solutions and realize the gains of safe sanitation.

Innovative sanitation solutions

This chatper proposes three novel sanitation solutions for consideration in the 2012 Copenhagen Consensus process as potentially worthy of large-scale investment:

(1) *Community-led total sanitation* (CLTS++): various forms of an approach that emphasizes behavior change, particularly the community's responsibility to share in the creation of open-defecation-free communities, particularly in rural areas.
(2) *Sanitation as a business*: new approaches to on-site sanitation that combine technical innovation to empty latrines and process waste with innovative business or service models to create sustainable sanitation services, particularly in low-income urban areas.
(3) *The reinvented toilet*: efforts to stimulate technical innovation, particularly harnessing advances in physics, chemistry, and engineering, to create a radically reinvented toilet that recycles human waste into re-usable products at the household scale.

Below, we describe these three solutions in some detail, before proceeding with their CBA. A separate section at the end of this chapter (pp. 612–15) includes information on a rural water intervention.

CLTS++

CLTS was developed by Kamal Kar, working with the Bangladeshi NGO, VERC and WaterAid, some ten years ago and has since spread very rapidly, both in its original form and through variations developed by a range of implementing organizations, usually under their own brand names, that collectively we will refer to as CLTS++.

Kar and Milward (2011: 9) describe CLTS as follows:

> CLTS is an innovative approach for empowering communities to completely eliminate open defecation (OD). It focuses on igniting a change in collective sanitation behaviour, which is achieved through a process of collective local action stimulated by facilitators from within or outside the community. The process involves the whole community and emphasises the collective benefit from stopping OD, rather than focusing on individual behaviour or on constructing toilets. People decide together how they will create a clean and hygienic environment that benefits everyone. Certain

[2] Subject to the addition of appropriate amounts of water, sludge can also be introduced to the wastewater treatment system. This is generally how the waste from septic tanks owned by affluent households would be dealt with.

> features have been fundamental to the evolution of CLTS as an approach to sanitation issues. CLTS involves no individual household hardware subsidy and does not prescribe latrine models. Social solidarity, help and cooperation among the households in the community are a common and vital element in CLTS. Other important characteristics are: the spontaneous emergence of natural leaders (NLs) as a community proceeds towards open-defecation-free (ODF) status; local innovation in low-cost toilet models using locally available materials; and community-innovated systems of reward, penalty, spread and scaling up.

CLTS has been very successful in rapidly displacing the previous approach to sanitation of development organizations such as UNICEF, WaterAid, or Plan International (which mostly focused on latrine construction, often through hardware subsidies) and having spread from its original base in Bangladesh to over forty countries by Kar's estimate (Kar and Milward, 2011), with at least five African countries adopting CLTS as the major approach to be used in their national sanitation strategies. UNICEF brands its approach as CATS (Community Approaches to Total Sanitation). The World Bank's WSP calls it TSSM (Total Sanitation and Sanitation Marketing) when combined with some additional supply-side activities, but the core elements of CLTS are more or less common across these "branded" approaches.

The original CLTS approach as championed by Kar focuses purely on facilitating collective action to generate behavior change, assuming that community members have the wherewithal to construct simple latrines if they want to. The CLTS variations used by large implementers such as UNICEF or the government of Indonesia tend to combine the behavior-change elements to stimulate demand with efforts to improve the supply side as well. On the supply side, that usually involves at least training local masons to become sanitation entrepreneurs, offering to construct latrines, and in other cases the development of a network of sanitation shops. We refer to CLTS++ as the intervention we are considering to indicate the collective of CLTS and its variations and derivatives implemented by a range of agencies and actors.

Impressively, CLTS++ programs have reached at least tens of millions of users and are expanding rapidly. Although not all communities in these programs become Open Defecation Free (ODF), assessments show that for some CLTS programs some 25–40 percent of communities do attain ODF status (Otieno *et al.*, 2011) while other programs achieve 30–80 percent ODF communities within three–six months which is a much higher success rate than previous sanitation programs (focusing on simple subsidies in the form of hardware handouts as a means of achieving rapid coverage). CLTS++ is not without its challenges however, particularly:

- Because the latrines constructed through CLTS tend to be of the simplest, sometimes rudimentary, form, user satisfaction tends to be quite low and there is a significant risk of relapse to open defecation.
- Because proper latrine construction does require quite a significant investment by the household, the poorest households in the community are the hardest to reach, particularly without any subsidy (which some CLTS++ programs do in fact employ). This makes achieving ODF communities a challenge, even when significant construction may be observed, unless targeted subsidies are included in the program.
- Rigorous health-impact data of improved sanitation through CLTS++ are still elusive[3] – at least in part because of a lack of an evaluation culture with the implementing organizations, but also likely a result of the limited achievement of ODF status in practice.
- The cost of CLTS++ delivery programs varies from $3–25 per person, which means that while $3 likely yields an attractive BCR and is possibly low enough to enable large scale roll-out, $25 probably is not.

[3] A single recent exception is a randomized-controlled trial of a CLTS campaign in forty villages in Orissa, India. Dickinson and Pattanayak (2011) find that the campaign increased child mid-upper arm circumference (MUAC) *z*-scores by roughly 0.25 standard deviations. The study did not have sufficient power to detect effects on diarrheal disease in children.

The CLTS++ intervention proposed for the 2012 Copenhagen Consensus consideration is a large-scale program, reaching at least hundreds of thousands of people at a one-off delivery cost of $5 per person affected – i.e. a person gaining access to ODF community status, and resulting in the benefits associated with rural sanitation as estimated by the ESI.

Targeted subsidies for the poor can be accommodated at the delivery cost of $5 per person, which we believe is important for achieving sustained ODF status and realizing the associated health gains. When subsidies can be accommodated, the hardware costs can be relatively higher, raising also the total cost of the intervention. Concerns about sustainability with CLTS when implemented as a strictly behavior-change intervention motivate this element of the proposal.

Given the rapid adoption of CLTS++ at a scale of tens of millions of people over the last ten years, and the relatively high rate of success this has in achieving ODF communities, we would consider this to be a comparatively low-risk intervention. Many development organizations and a first cohort of developing-country governments have adopted CLTS++ as best practice for rural sanitation. The Gates Foundation, for example, has committed about $100 million in grant funding to support CLTS++ programs that aim to achieve ODF communities for an additional 20–30 million people over the coming three–five years.

Why are we still proposing CLTS++ as an intervention for the 2012 Copenhagen Consensus, if it is being implemented and adopted quickly and successfully? The primary reason is that while this is a proven solution with an attractive, though modest, BCR, as we will demonstrate later, the observed levels of investment are inadequate to achieve acceptable coverage, as shown by the latest assessment of progress on safe drinking water and sanitation services released by WHO/UNICEF in early March 2012. Development agencies overemphasize safe water projects and underinvest in sanitation. In addition, the lion's share of sanitation investments is still focused on sewer networks and wastewater treatment plants that are largely irrelevant for the low-income part of the population. The sanitation policy of many developing-country governments is still exclusively focused on sanitation through sewer systems. Both lending agencies and developing-country governments tend to focus investment programs on "hardware," or infrastructure, at the expense of soft measures such as behavior-change or demand-creation programs. In short, we are proposing this first intervention primarily as a call to increase investment levels in this relatively new, but tested, solution.

Sanitation as a business

As previously described, a critical bottleneck for the existing over 2 billion latrines and septic tanks in developing countries, affecting particularly the urban poor, is that there are no affordable and sustainable services to effectively and efficiently empty them and process the fecal sludge safely and economically.

While governments tend to consider the supply of drinking water or the construction of sewer networks a public responsibility, servicing latrines and septic tanks, e.g. by having a municipal service similar to garbage collection, is not common. There are exceptions; effective government-run emptying services were organized nation-wide in Malaysia before the sewer network was constructed. The city of Addis Ababa, capital of Ethiopia, runs a fleet of over sixty vacuum trucks that empty latrines and septic tanks at a subsidized rate of $10. More common is a situation like that in Dakar, Senegal, where the government has a few vacuum trucks, but the majority of the service is provided by a fleet of over 100 trucks operated by private businesses, in addition to many individual entrepreneurs who supply manual emptying services. Households that contract with a private emptier using a vacuum truck pay $50–100 for the service. Many of these are owner-operator single-truck businesses that are only profitable by combining latrine-emptying with other seasonal use of their trucks.

Based on a study we undertook in 2011 of the emptying business in thirty cities in ten countries in Africa and Asia (Bill and Melinda Gates Foundation, 2011) we estimate that some 200 million latrines are emptied manually, by workers descending into the pit with a bucket and shovel. The city of Durban, South Africa, is the only place we know that runs a municipal service to empty some 35,000 ventilated improved pit (VIP) latrines manually (but with workers properly protected) at the city's expense.

Urban sanitation is also provided at communal and public toilet "blocks." A well-known organization to provide sanitation services through this model is Sulabh International in India. Sulabh's founder, Bindeshwar Pathak, developed a two-pit pour-flush latrine to avoid manual emptying (or "scavenging" as it is called in India – which is traditionally the work of the lowest caste, now formally illegal but not rooted out) in 1970. Sulabh, the story of which is ably told by George (2008) operates 6,000 communal toilet blocks that serve an estimated 10 million users on a pay-per-use basis, providing caretaker employment to former scavengers. There are other international NGOs and some (social) enterprises that provide mobile or community toilets on a (semi-)commercial basis, but other than Sulabh none of these operates at scale.

The sanitation as a business intervention proposed for the 2012 Copenhagen Consensus is a sanitation service provided by a sanitation entrepreneur at a cost of no more than $10 per household per year and consists of emptying the latrine or septic tank, transporting the fecal sludge to a treatment plant, and treating it to acceptable levels prior to re-use and/or dispersal into the environment. The investment proposed will take the following innovations from early-stage development to demonstrated scale:

- Effective communal toilets: on a pay-per-use basis where high density prevents household or shared toilets – similar to the Sulabh model
- Scheduled desludging: (re-)organization of the latrine-emptying market by municipal governments to enable households to pay an emptying fee as part of their water bill (same as the sewer charge often levied now, even to households not connected to a sewer system) and contracting out regular desludging to municipal services or the private sector
- Privately managed fecal sludge plants: outsourcing management of fecal sludge treatment plants to the private sector to reduce illegal dumping and manage the treatment plants as a business, maximizing revenue from recycled products such as compost
- Innovation in latrine-emptying technology: dedicated mechanized emptying technology that empties latrines effectively and affordably under developing world urban slum conditions
- Innovation in fecal sludge treatment technology: small-scale neighborhood fecal sludge-processing plants that generate biogas, biochar, biodiesel, fertilizer, and/or compost while safely removing all pathogens in small-footprint plants.

While most of these elements have been, or are being, developed and tested individually in a variety of locations, with support from the Bill and Melinda Gates Foundation they have been put together and tested at scale in Dakar, Senegal, at the scale of 1 million people over the next five years. Further development and testing for some 10 million people is proposed for consideration here.

The "reinvented toilet"

Using biological processes to decompose human and animal waste into manure or night soil has been common practice for thousands of years. This is in essence the technology used for composting toilets. "Modern" networked sanitation systems based on sewers have been around for several hundred years. Real investment in innovation over the last several decades has focused almost exclusively on improvement of waste-water treatment – removing nutrients to prevent surface-water pollution such as algae blooms in lakes, and most recently recovery of energy from sewage sludge. The innovations developed for processing or recycling other waste streams, such as gasification, have not yet been applied to human waste.

Early in 2011 the Bill and Melinda Gates Foundation challenged over twenty top universities around the globe to use modern science and engineering to come up with a radically different form of processing and recycling human waste that does not depend on sewer networks and large volumes of water for transportation (Nash, 2012). The challenge was to develop a system that is off the grid, affordable for the poorest members in society (less than $0.05/day), and an aspirational product – something everyone will want to use and that over time will replace the flush toilet as the new gold standard. The foundation awarded eight Reinvent the Toilet Challenge" grants and funded another fifty-seven small grants in 2011 that all aimed to innovate all or part of the non-sewered value chain – from pyrolysis, gasification, hydrothermal carbonation, smoldering and thermo-mechanical treatment processes to microbial fuel cells to nanotechnology-based coatings that would make toilet bowls super-hydrophobic and/or self-disinfecting.

The "reinvented toilet" must overcome at least three principal challenges:

- At its heart it must use one or more processes to dry and heat human waste to safely remove pathogens and recover energy and nutrients in a manner that enables the process to be self-sufficient (carefully managing the energy balance).
- It must miniaturize and automate these processes in a household scale unit that is robust, safe, foolproof, and affordable.
- It must have a user interface that people love to use and that supports a wide range of cultures and customs from sitters to squatters and washers to wipers.

All complete reinvented toilets are currently at the laboratory/proof-of-concept to prototype stage and therefore investments in the development of this solution are high-risk. The Foundation reviewed the first series of prototypes and proof-of-concept results for parts and processes in August 2012. Presuming a reinvented toilet can be successfully developed, and can become an aspirational product – the smartphone of sanitation – the issues of high cost, slow adoption and limited benefits that variously plague the current generation of sanitation technologies will be overcome.

The "reinvented toilet" proposed for the 2012 Copenhagen Consensus as the third sanitation intervention is a household-scale unit that costs less than $0.05 per person per day and that completely and safely recycles the human-waste stream into reusable products or harmless emissions into the atmosphere; an aspirational product that becomes the new gold standard for sanitation.

Rural water services

As a fourth intervention we propose for consideration a standard rural water-supply scheme consisting of borehole wells equipped with handpumps, as described by Whittington *et al.* (2008).

It would also be possible to combine CLTS++ with a water and handwashing or hygiene program to realize the gains of an integrated intervention. However, a paucity of convincing data on the benefits of combined interventions inhibits us from considering seriously an integrated intervention. The WASHBenefits project, ongoing research by the Bill and Melinda Gates Foundation grantee University of California, Berkeley, with fieldwork in Bangladesh and Kenya, seeks to address this gap in the epidemiology literature.

Overview of WSP economics of sanitation initiative CBA

WSP's ESI is the most comprehensive effort to date to assess fully the burden associated with inadequate sanitation using secondary data. For eleven African countries and nine Asian countries,[4] the studies published from 2008–2011 consider health, water, tourism, and other welfare impacts of sanitation. In a follow-up phase published in August 2011 ESI estimated the economic returns to sanitation interventions in Cambodia, China, Indonesia, LAO PDR, Philippines, and Vietnam. They summarized data on costs of infrastructure from actual investments observed in country.

Benefits

The methodology adopted by ESI's studies of the economic impacts of sanitation, such as in India

[4] Africa: Benin, Burkina Faso, DRC, Ghana, Kenya, Madagascar, Mozambique, Niger, Nigeria, Rwanda, Tanzania. Asia: Bangladesh, Cambodia, China, India, Indonesia, Lao PDR, Pakistan, Philippines, Vietnam. More studies are underway in Latin America and the Caribbean.

(Anupam, 2010) included disaggregating the economic impacts of inadequate sanitation into the following categories:

(1) *Health-related impacts*: premature deaths; costs of treating diseases; productive time lost due to people falling ill; time lost by caregivers who look after them.
(2) *Domestic water-related impacts*: household treatment of water; use of bottled water; a portion of costs of obtaining piped water; and time costs of fetching cleaner water from a distance.
(3) *Access-time impacts*: cost of additional time spent for accessing shared toilets or open defecation sites; absence of children (mainly girls) from school and women from their workplaces.
(4) *Tourism impacts*: potential loss of tourism revenues and economic impacts of gastrointestinal illnesses among foreign tourists.

Table 10.1 summarizes the breakdown of benefits between health, water quality, "other welfare" (e.g. time savings and amenity benefits), and tourism, as reported by ESI for several countries. For most countries, the health and water benefits are the greatest fraction of total benefits, between some 70 and 90 percent.

According to Anupam (2010), national data on incidence or actual numbers for the indicators in these subcategories (for example, diarrheal diseases, deaths, and so on) were compiled from secondary data sources (National Family Health Survey 2005–2006; WHO Demographic and Health Surveys; National Sample Surveys; Census of India). Based on the review of scientific literature, attribution factors were used to estimate the populations impacted by inadequate sanitation and, finally, the economic valuation was carried out using costs/prices based on other secondary studies. ESI states that conservative assumptions have been used in economic valuation (e.g. a discount rate of 8 percent and a benefit stream capped at twenty years) and the analysis was done for 2006 for want of comprehensive data for later years.

Health impacts are the most important drivers of costs attributed to inadequate sanitation, and thus uncertainty in this data is an important limitation for the work. This is distinct from the usual controversy associated with monetization of health benefits. For that element of the calculation, ESI take a conservative tack, using the human-capital approach to monetize the costs of premature death. The health gains are a reduction of 36 percent for fecal–oral diseases for basic sanitation and 56 percent for advanced systems. These are based on meta-analyses of sanitation interventions, referenced in the reports. A key issue for assessing whether the ESI numbers can be relied upon for *ex ante* investment planning is the extent to which the interventions in these evaluations compare with the actual-reality cities and the extent to which these analyses accurately capture the causal impacts of sanitation on health.

Table 10.1 ESI estimates of economic impacts of poor sanitation

	Economic losses	
Country and impacts	US$ million	%
Cambodia	448.0	100.0
Health	187.1	41.8
Water	149.0	33.3
Other welfare	38.2	8.5
Tourism	73.7	16.5
Indonesia	6,344.0	100.0
Health	3,350.0	52.8
Water	1,512.0	23.8
Environment	96.0	1.5
Other welfare	1,220.0	19.2
Tourism	166.0	2.6
Philippines	1,412.1	100.0
Health	1,011.1	71.6
Water	323.3	22.9
Other welfare	37.6	2.7
Tourism	40.1	2.8
Vietnam	780.1	100.0
Health	262.4	33.6
Water	287.3	36.8
Environment	118.9	15.2
Other welfare	42.9	5.5
Tourism	68.6	8.8
Total	8,984.2	100.0

The Gates Foundation is supporting additional research on the benefits of sanitation that could be used to refine CBAs three–five years from now. In particular, it is making significant investments in randomized controlled trials in three sites (Bangladesh, Kenya, and Zimbabwe) to assess the "environmental enteropathy" hypothesis.

Nutritionists have hypothesized that reducing a child's fecal bacteria exposure during the first years of life through improved sanitation (and/or handwashing or water treatment) may improve gut function (the ability of the gastro-intestinal tract to absorb nutrients) and subsequent growth (Humphrey, 2009). The pre-natal period and the first two years of life are a critical window for intervention in growth and development: infection and poor nutrition during this window can negatively impact an individual's long-term cognitive development and lifetime physiologic trajectory. Yet, a systematic review of the impacts of complementary feeding and supplementation interventions reports that even the most successful of these interventions cannot eliminate the mean growth deficit for African and Southeast Asian populations. The hypothesis is that nutritional supplementation appears to be necessary but not sufficient to eliminate growth shortfalls because chronic infection and colonization of the gut by fecal bacteria, spread via poor water and sanitation conditions, impedes nutrient absorption and creates low-level immune system stimulation, a condition called environmental enteropathy.

If the environmental enteropathy hypothesis were to be correct, this would significantly alter our understanding of the health benefits associated with sanitation, and increase the estimated cost-effectiveness of these interventions. The change would likely be very large, because of the lifetime gains associated with better nutrition in early childhood (Center for Diarrheal Disease Research, Bangladesh, ICDDR,B) that is the first empirical evidence consistent with the environmental enteropathy hypothesis (personal communication, Dr. Stephen Luby, August 2011). Work at the University of California, Berkeley, and ICDDR,B shows that there are meaningful differences between Bangladeshi children in terms of enteropathy symptoms and stunting, depending on their water, sanitation, and hygiene conditions in the home, even after controlling for sex, age, and socio-economic status. This is suggestive evidence that sanitation may be much more cost-effective as a public health intervention than previously supposed.

The consequences of the environmental enteropathy hypothesis may have implications beyond the sanitation and water sector:

- Reduced gut function may reduce the effectiveness of oral vaccines (e.g. for polio or rotavirus)
- Because reduced gut function reduces nutritional absorptive capacity, an effective nutrition strategy may then require joint action from agriculture, health, and sanitation/water perspectives.

The inclusion of the costs associated with environmental enteropathy could affect the BCRs calculated in the ESI, in the sense that it would significantly increase the benefits associated with sanitation measures.

Costs

ESI has estimated investment and annualized costs – including investment, operation, and maintenance – per household for a range of sanitation interventions in three rural and three urban sites in six South-East Asian countries. The lowest total cost interventions are dry- or wet-pit latrines in rural or urban areas and shared or community toilets in urban areas with annualized cost per household ranging from US$20–50. The highest total-cost interventions are sewerage systems with treatment at an annualized cost per household of US$100–200, with the cost of septic tanks ranging from low, approaching that of latrines (in some countries, without treatment) to high, approaching that of sewerage (in some countries, with treatment).

Table 10.2 summarizes the cost estimates in the ESI for Indonesia as illustrative data. We will use these cost numbers for Indonesia as starting points for our analysis in this chapter. Note that we argue that the simple pit latrines do not provide sufficient aesthetic benefits to ensure sustained use and that rural sanitation interventions must provide a "wet-pit" service, with targeted subsidies for the poor. Based on our experience at the Foundation,

Table 10.2 ESI estimates of average investment cost, by household, for various sanitation technologies: Indonesia

Country	Dry pit	Wet pit	Septic tank	Sewerage with treatment
Indonesia – rural	27	32	82	
Indonesia – urban		37	70	317

programming costs of the order of $5 per person can sustain such interventions.

BCRs

ESI concludes that basic sanitation, dry or wet latrines, and shared or community toilets, have the highest economic return per dollar invested (or BCR) of at least 3 in Cambodia and urban sites in Indonesia, and as high as 5–8 for rural and urban sites in the Philippines and Yunnan Province of China as well as rural sites in Indonesia. Sewers and septic tanks also have a positive, but lower, BCR of around 2.

In our view, the key reasons these ESI BCR estimates are theoretical maxima rather than realistic estimates in practice,[5] particularly for the lower-cost basic-sanitation interventions, are:

- *Low adoption rates*: even though all the interventions described have been available for many years and even if donor agencies or governments heavily subsidize the construction of latrines, or provide hardware free of charge, sustained use and effective operation and maintenance has time and again been lacking (Jenkins and Sugden, 2006). CLTS that results in very low-quality initial investments is also vulnerable to low adoption over the longer run, as the amenity value of the most basic forms of sanitation is so low.
- *Reintroduction of fecal matter into the environment*: when even a small share of all latrines is emptied manually and their content is dumped nearby in the environment, as we estimate to be the practice for some 200 million latrines in urban areas, then the assumed health gains from the meta-analyses cited by ESI will not be realized.

Thus, our approach is to propose means by which these barriers to realizing the ESI benefits can be overcome, illustrate the cost of overcoming those barriers, and revise the relevant BCR calculations. When we argue that health benefits cannot be realized without innovation, as we do in the case of urban sanitation, we ascribe all health and water-quality benefits estimated by ESI to the innovation investment. While this might be an overestimate, if there are indeed some health benefits associated with the broken service chain we described earlier that are different from true open defecation, the excess burden of fecal–oral diseases associated with living in urban areas as opposed to rural ones has been well documented using data such as helminth loads in children (e.g. Garenne, 2010; Penrose *et al.*, 2010; WHO, 2012), and as such this seems a reasonable approximation to make.

CBA of our proposed three sanitation interventions

For our analysis of the economic returns to the three sanitation interventions we propose we use the CBAs developed by ESI as the basis, but we propose additional innovations to realize, and improve on, the benefits as calculated by ESI as explained below.

CLTS++

For sanitation in rural areas we propose CLTS++. The primary impact of CLTS++ as an intervention is that governments or another (development) agency implement a program that creates demand for latrines at the community level, combined with a form of social pressure to motivate late adopters, in order to achieve ODF communities. In terms of our economic analysis it is a one-off additional cost of about $5/person, or $25/household, or an annualized cost of about $6 per household for an assumed wet-pit latrine-life of 10 years and a discount rate of

[5] Another technical issue is that the ESI model uses a discount rate of 8 percent, rather than the 2012 Copenhagen Consensus preferred rate of 3–5 percent. At a lower discount rate, the BCR ratios would be modestly higher than those discussed here.

8 percent – added to the latrine construction, operation, and maintenance as estimated by ESI for wet pits – to be able to realize the benefits estimated by ESI.

That increases the ESI estimated annualized cost of the wet-pit latrine from $32 to $38 per household, and with the same benefits as estimated by ESI, and that reduces the BCR from a range of 5–8 to a range of 4–7. We do not believe that lower-cost-dry-pit latrines provide sufficient amenity benefits to be a sustainable intervention.

The attraction of CLTS++ for investors is that it has shown, in a relatively short period of time since its first development in 2000, to spread and raise adoption, while not to 100 percent then at least to much more respectable rates than anything that came before. As documented by Kar and Milward (2011), this intervention has rapidly spread across Asia, and has become introduced in some forty African countries and adopted as the national approach by at least five. It has become the approach of choice of the key implementing international organizations such as UNICEF, WaterAid, Plan International, and WorldVision in a more or less modified form. Based on assessments of the experience with CLTS in Bangladesh over about ten years (Hanchett *et al.*, 2011) and our experience with a range of implementing organizations, as contained in about ten current contracts (grant agreements negotiated in 2010–2012) we estimate that the Bill and Melinda Gates Foundation investment of US$100 million will increase the number of people living in ODF communities by about 23 million (an estimated adoption rate of about 50 percent).

Extrapolating that experience implies that of the total population in rural areas that does not have access to improved (basic) sanitation of 1.2 billion, about 50 percent, or 600 million people, could be reached by an investment of US$3 billion, at a BCR of 4–7. Note that these numbers are modestly higher than those reported by Whittington *et al.* (2008). Our assessment is that this is due to the updated information available from ESI on actual latrine costs and non-health benefits.

As stated earlier, given that this intervention has been tried and tested at a scale of tens of millions of people in Asia and Africa, we consider this a low-risk, proven intervention.

Sanitation as a business

For urban areas we assume that latrines can be constructed with costs as assessed by ESI, and that these are either private, shared, or community toilets. We will use the ESI cost estimate for the annualized total cost (investment, operation, and maintenance) for a wet-pit latrine in an urban area of US$37, with a BCR of 3.2. (We use the ESI BCR figures for Indonesia in these calculations.) In reality, as we have argued above, such latrines are often emptied by hand, thus these costs understate what would be necessary expenditure for the full health benefits to be achieved. Currently the annual cost of mechanical emptying with a vacuum truck is US$35–91 (Bill and Melinda Gates Foundation, 2011), which reduces the BCR to about 1 if we redo this calculation assuming an annualized total cost of $37 + $60.

Of course, even if a latrine is emptied by truck, the fecal sludge is often dumped illegally, or discharged at a wastewater treatment plant where treatment incurs additional costs. The primary intervention we see as a necessary addition to realize the benefits estimated by ESI is an affordable and effective way to collect and treat the waste – in essence, the equivalent of the sewer and treatment plant for a non-networked system. This is the package of institutional and technological innovations described on pp. 603–4 that we collectively refer to as "Sanitation as a business."

Our assumptions for this intervention are that it is feasible to invest in innovation to achieve the following:

- The current costs of mechanical emptying (with existing technology) are on the order of $35–91 per household in the ten countries studied in Africa and Asia (Bill and Melinda Gates Foundation, 2011). Based on the design of the project we are funding to put in place (for a million people in a low-income part of Dakar, Senegal, a scheduled desludging service, funded on a subscription basis, and outsourced to the private sector through an auction), we estimate that these costs can be brought down to $20 as a result of a more efficient market and more efficient desludging operations.

- We then assume that the cost of mechanical emptying can be brought down further to $10 through improved emptying technology that is currently in the design stage (an ongoing project with prototypes expected to be field-tested in 2013 and 2014). This new emptying technology, replacing the vacuum truck, would also be able to reach 100 percent of low-income urban neighborhoods, including those with streets too narrow for regular trucks. Based on the experience in Addis Ababa, where a government-subsidized mechanical-emptying rate of $10 fully displaced manual emptying, we assume that at this rate we can achieve full mechanical emptying coverage in low income urban areas.
- We finally assume that neighborhood-scale fecal sludge-treatment units can be developed that are cost-neutral – i.e. where the value of the materials recovered from the sludge is at least equal to the cost of processing. We think this can be achieved based on improvements to technology that is currently used to process fecal sludge in Durban (a thermo-mechanical process, the LaDePa sludge-pelletizer), or forms of pyrolizers that are currently used to process wood chips and animal waste.

This Sanitation as a business intervention is clearly more high-risk than the CLTS++ intervention, as several of its elements still have to be developed (such as the improved emptying technology), and the full package of elements still has to be demonstrated to be effective at scale. On the other hand, based on a study that we have commissioned (Bill and Melinda Gates Foundation, 2011) we think that the investment risks associated with this intervention are limited and reasonable because of the evidence that elements of the package have been tried and tested:

- Scheduled latrine desludging, funded through a subscription service, is rare but has been rolled out effectively at national scale in Malaysia.
- We have invested in a project to transform the latrine-emptying market in Dakar, Senegal, for a million people and understand what it costs to implement this innovation.
- Subsidized mechanical latrine-emptying at a $10 price point has been shown to effectively displace manual emptying in Addis Ababa, the capital of Ethiopia, a low-income city.
- Cost-neutral fecal-sludge-processing units at neighborhood scale do not yet exist, but a working "prototype" of such a fecal-sludge-processor (that does not yet recover its full cost) exists in Durban (the LaDePa Pelletizer) and won an IWA Global Project Innovation Award (IWA, 2011). Pyrolizer units that produce biochar from woodchips and animal waste are available in the market (e.g. from Re:Char) but not yet for human waste. We have invested in several projects to develop such fecal-sludge-processor units and have a fair understanding of the cost of this innovation.
- The most risky element of this package is the latrine-emptying technology, which does not yet exist. We have, however, invested in several projects to develop this technology and consider it a project-development-integration challenge, rather than at a research or lab stage. These projects had Critical Design Reviews in April 2012, and were on track to field test prototypes in 2014.

We estimate the total investment cost to develop the latrine-emptying and waste-processing technology into commercial products, and to develop and test the institutional innovations at a scale of a million people, at US$100–120 million; an investment that is part of the sanitation strategy of the Foundation. In addition, to help develop and catalyze a market for Sanitation as a business at scale, we assume it will be necessary to subsidize introduction of these urban sanitation services at US$10 per household for the first 10 million latrines, or households. If we assume a subsidy level of 25 percent borne by the public budget (with the remainder covered by households) of the sanitation service cost for 10 million households for ten years (the life of the latrine) then the NPV of this investment at 5 percent is US$200 million.

We assume that this investment in both the innovation itself (US$120 million) and market development (US$200 million) would result in adoption of these sanitation services for 20 percent, or 40 million, of the urban latrines that are currently emptied manually. Assuming that 80 percent of the ESI-estimated benefits would be realized as a result

Table 10.3 Calculation of BCR for Sanitation as a business

	Parameter	Value	Notes
(1)	ESI estimate of cost of wet-pit latrine	$37/year/hh	
(2)	ESI BCR	3.2	
(3)	Cost of unsafe disposal as currently practiced	$60/year/hh	Source: (Bill and Melinda Gates Foundation, 2011)
(4)	Cost of safe disposal that could displace manual emptying	$10/year/hh	Source: (Bill and Melinda Gates Foundation, 2011); this price in Addis Ababa has ended manual emptying there
(5)	NPV of displacing cost	$77	Ten-year life span; interest rate of 5%
(6)	Illustrative investment in innovation to achieve manual-emptying displacement	$120 million	Foundation-allocated budget (2010–2015)
(7)	Cost to demonstrate technology for 10 million people	$772 million	
(8)	Fraction of cost to be borne by donors/government	25%	Based on Foundation grants in this sector made in 2011
(9)	PV of costs to public budget	$120 million	Ten-year life span; interest rate of 5%
(10)	Pits moved to safe service with technology that displaces manual emptying	40 million	20% adoption rate
(11)	Associated people served	200 million	At hh size of 5
(12)	Annualized marginal net benefits health and water quality	$1.9 billion	80% of total benefits – see Table 10.2
(13)	PV of marginal net benefits	$14.7 billion	Ten-year life span; interest rate of 5%
(14)	Associated BCR–PV marginal net benefits/PV of cost to public budget (9)	47	

Note: hh = Household.

of the Sanitation as a business innovation, as this is about the fraction of benefits associated with health and water quality (see Table 10.1, p. 606), we then calculate a BCR of 46 for this Sanitation as a business intervention of US$320 million, improving sanitation service for 200 million people in low-income urban areas. Table 10.3 lays out the detail of this calculation.

The highest-risk element of the package is the technological innovation related to latrine-emptying (as it does not yet exist). We assess the technical risk related to cost-neutral processing of the waste as "medium," given the extensive experience with biogas installations in China and the current use of a city-scale waste-processor (the LaDePa pelletizer) in Durban. Therefore, the maximum impact of this risk on the BCR occurs if this targeted technology improvement fails to bring the annualized latrine-emptying and processing cost down from $20 to $10 per household. In this case, assuming that the investments are made but the cost reduction is limited to $20, we calculate a reduction in BCR from 47 to 23.

Given that this intervention is an investment in innovation, albeit an investment in product and institutional development rather than research, and that we have evidence of the feasibility for some of the key elements of the innovation package, we consider this a medium-risk intervention.

"Reinvented toilet"

Even though we can reach large numbers of people with the two interventions described above, they would not reach everyone[6] and would still provide a service with pit latrines that people rate

[6] We have assumed 50 percent coverage with basic-sanitation services for the currently unserved in rural areas and 20 percent coverage with safe-sanitation services in low-income urban areas currently emptied manually.

considerably below the unaffordable but gold-standard flush toilet. The "reinvented toilet" we have described on pp. 604–5 would, by definition if successful, provide an affordable new gold-standard service. The risk for this intervention is whether it is possible to develop such a "reinvented toilet" that meets the specifications we outlined above. As this is essentially an investment in research – i.e. in upstream innovation – it is clearly high-risk. If it proves possible to develop such a new aspirational product that provides excellent service at an affordable price, then we can assume that it would enjoy rapid and widespread adoption. For these reasons we have referred to the "reinvented toilet" as the "smartphone of sanitation."

The specification for the developers of the "reinvented toilet" is that it cannot cost more than $0.05 per person per day, or $90 per household per year. Using the same benefits for a wet latrine in an urban setting as estimated by ESI of $115 (a lower boundary given the much better service a "reinvented toilet" would provide), the annual net benefits per toilet would be $25.

We estimate the investment cost of the innovation program (research through product development) to bring one or more models of the toilet to market at $50 million. This investment is part of the Gates Foundation's sanitation strategy. We assume that to gain traction in the market the toilet would have to be marketed (or the market would need to be developed through subsidies, or through partnerships with manufacturers to bring costs down, or via advance market commitments similar to those used to develop the market for vaccines). While clearly we cannot provide a careful estimate of the marketing or market development costs required at this stage, we use an order of magnitude of 25 percent of the cost of the toilet for 1 million households/toilets for three years, which is an estimated $75 million. This brings the total required investment in the "reinvented toilet" to $125 million.

If we assume that this investment would lead to 100 percent coverage for all latrines currently emptied manually, and allocate the net benefits this generates to this $125 million investment, then this would have a BCR of 40, for an investment of $125 million, serving 1 billion people. In addition, if successful, the "reinvented toilet" would serve many more people of the other 3.5 billion people who currently do not have access to a flush toilet – and indeed, over time, would replace the flush toilet itself.

Of course, given that this intervention is an investment in an upstream innovation, a product that is currently under development in the laboratory at the proof-of-concept to prototype stage, we consider this a high-risk intervention.

Rural water services

In this section we consider a rural water intervention. In rural settings, the technologies for bringing safe drinking water to people are well known, similar to the situation in sanitation. The challenges are ones, largely, of sustainability. A rural water intervention like that described here would target the 770 million people in Africa and Asia that currently do not have access to safe water.

To contextualize and value an integrated water intervention, we continue to take the approach used through this chapter and build on excellent work done by others. We are fortunate that Whittington *et al.* (2008) did extensive simulation work to estimate the net benefits of improved rural water service. We reproduce in summary form here that evidence and place this work in context as we did as Perspective Paper authors of the papers for the 2008 Copenhagen Consensus.

Whittington *et al.* found that there were modest positive net benefits associated with rural water service from new borehole wells, with benefits that would be greatest in places where the burden of diarrhea is relatively high and existing water facilities are sparse. Of course, as they point out, such settings may also be those where capital costs are highest, which increases costs as well. The estimated BCR using a base-case set of assumptions about an illustrative investment is 3.4. This is close to our estimate of the BCR for the rural sanitation intervention we consider. Below, we sketch out how Whittington *et al.* arrived at their BCR estimate.

To estimate the economic costs of the installation of a borehole and a public hand pump, Whittington *et al.* used a capital cost estimate of US$6,500 (range US$5,000–8,000). Program overheads that include capacity-building and "software" costs for a large national rural water-supply program were estimated at US$3,500 (range US$2,000–5,000), for a project total of US$10,000. The capital costs were annualized assuming a capital recovery factor of 0.093 (interest rate of 4.5 percent and assuming a life of the infrastructure of fifteen years) which implied annual capital costs of $930. Recurrent expenditures of about $100 per year were also assumed. Using an approach that we critiqued in 2008, and which we say more about below, Whittington *et al.* estimated the labor costs of maintenance at $500 per year, assuming that these costs were implicitly incurred by a well-functioning village water committee in a demand-driven, participatory model. We will come back to this question, but for now accept the estimate for a total annual cost of US$1,530, or about US$128 per month.

The total monthly costs must be divided among the users of a borehole, which of course varies widely in practice. In a reasonable assumption, Whittington *et al.* take as a base case a well used by sixty households. Assuming a family size of five people, the monthly cost per household comes to about US$2.13.

The economic benefits of the borehole and public hand pump described by Whittington *et al.* come from the value of time savings and the monetary value of health benefits. There are other, smaller benefits from "lifestyle and aesthetic" changes that are not directly related to health, in theory, but in practice these are very small. The value of time savings depends critically on the wage rate and the assumed opportunity cost of time.

To illustrate the magnitude of the benefits associated with time savings, Whittington *et al.* begin from an assumption that a new borehole might afford the typical family with 2 m^3 of water per month. The monthly time savings for collection of 2 m^3 of water would be about seventy hours. For purposes of illustration, benefit calculations are made assuming that the local wage for unskilled labor in this rural community is $1.25 per day (US$0.16 per hour) and that the value of the time savings from the new water system is 30 percent of this market wage. The value of aesthetic benefits is also assumed to be linked to the wage rate, and is estimated as 25 percent of the value of the time savings described above. To avoid double counting benefits that are actually related to health, these are further downward corrected, by 25 percent.

To calculate the monetary value of health benefits, the authors assume that the intervention reduces the case fatality rate of diarrhea by 30 percent to 25/10,000. Assuming a base case of the VSL of $30,000, the resulting value of the risk reduction due to the water-supply intervention would then be US$33 per year, or about US$2.7 per household per month. In addition to the mortality benefits, individuals would also receive the economic benefits of not suffering from non-fatal episodes of diarrhea. To estimate these benefits, the authors assume the cost of illness for a case of diarrhea is US$6 (range US$2–10). The US$8.10 cost savings per year from the implementation of the water supply intervention would come to about US$0.68 per month.

Table 10.4 summarizes the data used to calculate the net benefits of the rural water intervention and the steps taken to arrive at a preferred BCR estimate of 3.4. As with the work done by WSP for sanitation, the care and thought put into this exercise is exemplary.

In the 2008 Copenhagen Consensus, we raised concerns about this set of calculations that are similar to those that we have raised about the WSP estimates for sanitation, which have to do with the challenges of bringing estimated BCRs to the reality of the facts on the ground (Rijsberman and Zwane, 2008). In the case of this rural water intervention, our concerns largely center around sustainability. Whittington *et al.* argued that challenges of sustainability and maintenance have been "largely overcome" by the use of participatory demand-driven village water committees for oversight and maintenance. We argued that the data did not in fact support that claim and, thus, the benefits estimates here may be largely overstated. Efforts to assess the functionality of installed handpumps at a large scale as undertaken by WaterAid in Tanzania, Uganda, and Malawi (water-point mapping) show that a large share of the handpumps installed less than five years ago are no longer providing service. We continue to believe that this is the case, and in fact, since 2008, the policy dialog seems to have moved away from voluntary committee-based management models, increasing the role for

Table 10.4 Base-case results: borehole and public hand pump intervention evaluated by Whittington *et al.* (2008)[a]

	Before hand pump + borehole intervention	After hand pump + borehole intervention	Change in physical units	Change in monetary units by discount rate		
Benefits				3%	4.5%	6%
Time spent collecting initial quantity of water (hrs per hh-month) [Value of time savings]	100	30	70	$3.28	$3.28	$3.28
Water use (L per hh-month) [Value of aesthetic and lifestyle benefits from increased water use]	2,000	3,750	1,750	$0.54	$0.54	$0.54
Number of nonfatal cases of diarrhea (per hh-month) [Value of reduction in morbidity]	0.38	0.26	(0.11)	$0.68	$0.68	$0.68
Risk of death from all diarrhea (per 1000 hh-month) [Value of reduction in mortality]	0.30	0.21	(0.09)	$2.70	$2.70	$2.70
Total benefits				$7.19	$7.19	$7.19
Costs						
Expenditures by all parties for new water system (per hh-month)				($2.00)	($2.13)	($2.26)
BCR				3.6	3.4	3.2
Net benefits				$5.20	$5.07	$4.93

Note: [a] For the results reported in this table, all parameters were set at their *base-case* values as described in the text describing the approach used by Whittington *et al.* (2008).
hh = Household; L = Liter.

district governments as service providers. This likely implies higher labor costs for (O&M) than $500 per year, but also increases the probability that the stream of benefits assumed by Whittington *et al.* could be achieved.

Our Perspective Paper for the 2008 Copenhagen Consensus (Rijsberman and Zwane, 2008) also raised the concern that the health benefits of the water intervention may be understated because of a lack of consideration of infectious disease externalities. We also discussed the potential for benefits to be increased by adding source-level community chlorine dispensers, which would have low costs, but the additional benefits associated with the protective effect of chlorine to maintain water quality during transportation and storage. Innovations for Poverty Action estimates that about 150–200 million people would be well served by chlorine dispensers, based on an analysis of populations in areas where the diarrheal disease burden is high and there is reasonable chlorine acceptability (mostly eastern and southern Africa). The number of lives that could be saved each year is up to 30,000 using this conservative estimate of total coverage. The cost per person per year is estimated to be less than $0.5 per person with access per year, and the cost per DALY saved is $25–$35 (Ahuja *et al.*, 2011).

To understand how much it would cost to implement this rural water intervention, we begin with the most recent estimate of the number of unserved. The total number of people left without access to safe water in rural areas, according to the new JMP2012 (WHO/UNICEF Joint Monitoring Program) is 770 million. Given that wells and handpumps are a proven method that would work wherever there is access to groundwater, we assume that the maximum number of people that could be reached through the intervention is 90 percent of those currently not served, or 700 million people. According to Whittington *et al.*, the annualized cost of service per well to serve these people is $1,530 per well (which serves 300 people).

Thus, providing fifteen years of service to all the unserved would cost ($58.9 billion = $1,530 × 15 × 770,000,000/300) or some $4 billion per year, an NPV of a bit over $40 billion (at the same interest rate of 4.5 percent as used above).

To estimate the (external) investment required to achieve the maximum level of coverage (assumed at 90 percent, or 700 million people), the practice is that external donors or the government subsidize most or all of the initial investment cost. In some cases the beneficiaries are asked to contribute part of the initial investment cost, in cash or kind through donated labor, to increase their sense of ownership and increase the likelihood that there is adequate maintenance – which, as we argued above, is a key challenge. That means the external investment ranges, in practice, between 80 percent of the capital costs (estimated as $6,500 per well plus pump, serving 300 people) and 100 percent of the capital plus program costs (estimated at $10,000 per well plus pump serving 300 people), or a total investment covering 700 million people ranging between $12–23 billion.

Conclusions

We have based the calculations in this chapter largely on the extensive cost and benefit data published recently by the very significant ESI of the WSP of the World Bank, resulting from its research undertaken over 2007–2011 on the impacts of sanitation and the economic returns to sanitation interventions in over twenty Asian and African countries. The data this program has generated fill a real gap in knowledge concerning the costs and benefits of basic on-site non-networked sanitation as well as modern networked sewerage and treatment systems. We have generally accepted the cost data for wet and dry latrines in urban and rural areas as realistic and the best available. We have also accepted the benefit estimates of sanitation as the best available.

ESI concludes that basic sanitation, wet and dry latrines, have the highest BCRs of all sanitation interventions, in a range of 5–8. We do not agree that current technology does indeed generate these benefits, both because the adoption rates for dry latrines are low in rural areas and the lack of effective and affordable latrine-emptying and fecal-sludge-treatment services means that particularly in low-income urban areas, the benefits estimated by ESI are not realized.

We propose three sanitation interventions that can potentially help realize the benefits estimated by ESI and have analyzed their BCRs as follows:

(1) CLTS++, a behavior-change program to create demand for sanitation in rural areas: an investment of US$3 billion could serve 600 million people, 50 percent of the rural population currently without basic service, with a BCR of 4–7 at a discount rate of 8 percent. This is a low-risk investment already demonstrated to be effective at a scale of tens of millions of people. Targeted subsidies for the poor will likely be a critical element of a successful program, so that ODF status can be achieved and health gains realized.

(2) Sanitation as a business, latrine-emptying and fecal-sludge-processing services at an annual cost of US$10 per household: an investment of US$320 million ($120 million in technology and institutional innovation, and a further $200 million in market development) could serve 200 million low-income urban people, 20 percent of the latrines currently emptied manually, with a BCR of 23–47. This is a medium-risk investment in a product and development innovation package, key elements of which have already been demonstrated to be feasible.

(3) The "reinvented toilet," an off-the-grid toilet that processes and recycles human waste at household scale and affordably provides an excellent user experience: an investment of US$125 million ($50 million in technology innovation and product development, and a further $75 million in market development) could serve a billion low-income urban people, 100 percent of the latrines currently emptied manually (and potentially many more people) with a BCR of 40. This is a high-risk investment in research, product development, and market development for a product currently at the proof-of-concept/prototype stage.

Table 10.5 Summary of BCR analysis

Intervention	Investment (US$ million)	BCR	People served (million)	Risk
CLTS++	3,000	4–7	600	Low
Sanitation as a business	320	23–47	200	Medium
"Reinvented toilet"	125	40	1000	High
Rural water	12,000–23,000	3.4	700	Low

The fourth intervention we propose is based on the analysis presented in Whittington *et al.* (2008), a rural water intervention which consists of boreholes equipped with handpumps. An investment of $12–23 billion could potentially reach some 700 million people with water services, with a BCR of around 3.4. This is a low-risk investment in proven solutions that are primarily in need of increased levels of resources to roll them out to unserved populations. These results are summarized in Table 10.5.

Bibliography

Ahuja, A., M. Kremer, and A. P. Zwane, 2010: Providing safe water: evidence from randomized evaluations, *Annual Review of Resource Economics* **2**

Anupam, T., 2010: *Economic Impacts of Inadequate Sanitation in India*, World Bank, Water and Sanitation Program, Washington, DC

Ban, R., J. Koola, and A. Zwane, 2011: Dirty work: assessing what works in the sanitation sector, Bill & Melinda Gates Foundation, Seattle, WA, mimeo

Barkat, A., 2012: *Economic Impacts of Inadequate Sanitation in Bangladesh*, World Bank, Water and Sanitation Program, Washington, DC

Bill and Melinda Gates Foundation, 2011: *Landscape Analysis and Business Model Assessment in Fecal Sludge Management*, Bill & Melinda Gates Foundation, Seattle, WA

Black, R., 2012: Global, regional, and national causes of child mortality in 2008: a systematic analysis, *Lancet* **375**, 1969–87

Black, R. E., S. Cousens, H. L. Johnson, J. E. Lawn, I. Rudan *et al.*, 2010: Global, regional, and national causes of child mortality in 2008: a systematic analysis, *Lancet* **375**, 1969–87

Cutler, D. and G. Miller, 2005: The role of public health improvements in health advances: the 20th century United States, *Demography* **42**, 1–22

Dickinson, K. and S. K. Pattanayak, 2011: Open sky latrines: social reinforcing in the case of a (very) impure public good, *Duke University Working Paper*

Esrey, S. A., J. Gough, D. Rapoport, R. Sawyer, M. Simpson-Hébert, J. Vargas, and U. Winblad (eds.), 1998: *Ecological Sanitation*, Sida, Stockholm

Garenne, M., 2010: Urbanisation and child health in resource poor settings with special reference to under-five mortality in Africa, *Archives of Disease in Children* **95**, 464–8

George, R., 2008: *The Big Necessity: The Unmentionable World of Human Waste and Why It Matters*, Metropolitan Books, New York

Hanchett, S., L. Krieger, M. Kahn, C. Kullmann, and R. Ahmed, 2011: Long term sustainability of rural sanitation in Bangladesh, World Bank, Washington, DC

Holla, A. and M. Kremer, 2008: Pricing and access: lessons from randomized evaluation in education and health, Harvard University, Cambridge, MA, mimeo

Humphrey, J. H., 2009: Child undernutrition, tropical enteropathy, toilets, and handwashing, *Lancet* **374**, 1032–5

Hutton, G., B. Larsen, L. Leebouapao, and S. Voladet, 2009: Economic impacts of sanitation in Lao PDR, World Bank, Water and Sanitation Program, Washington, DC

Hutton, G., U. E. Rodriguez, L. Napitupulu, P. Thang, and P. Kov, 2008: *Economic Impacts of Sanitation in Southeast Asia*, World Bank, Water and Sanitation Program, Washington, DC

IWA (International Water Association), 2011: *The 2011 IWA Global Project Innovation Awards–Development: Executive Summaries of Winners and Honour Awards*, London

Jenkins, M. W. and S. Sugden, 2006: *Rethinking Sanitation: Lessons and Innovation for*

Sustainability and Success in the New Millennium, Human Development Report Office Occasional Paper, UNDP, New York

Kar, K. and K. Milward, 2011: *Digging in, Spreading out and Growing up: Introducing CLTS in Africa*, IDS, Brighton

Klingel *et al.*, 2002: *Fecal Sludge Management in Developing Countries: A Planning Manual*, Swiss Federal Institute for Environmental Science (EWAG), Duebendorf

Krekeler, T., 2008: *Decentralised Sanitation and Wastewater Treatment*, Federal Institute for Geosciences and Natural Resources, (BGR), Hannover

Kremer, M., E. Miguel, S. Mullainathan, C. Null, and A. Zwane, 2009: Making water safe: price, persuasion, peers, promoters, or product design? Working Paper, Harvard University, Bookings Institution, and NBER, Cambridge, MA

Lancet, 2008: Editorial: keeping sanitation in the spotlight, *Lancet* **371**, 1045

Mara, D. D., 2008: *Sanitation Now: What is Good Practice and What is Poor Practice?* In: Proceedings of the IWA International Conference 'Sanitation Challenge: New Sanitation and Models of Governance'. IWA International Conference 'Sanitation Challenge: New Sanitation and Models of Governance', 19–21 May 2008, Wageningen, The Netherlands. Wageningen: Sub-department of Environmental Technology, Wageningen University.

Mara, D. and G. Alabaster, 2008: A new paradigm for low-cost urban water supplies and sanitation in developing countries, *Water Policy* 10, 119–29

McNeil, D., 2012: Haiti: cholera epidemic's first victim identified as river bather who forsook clean water, *New York Times*, January 9

Nash, J., 2012: Wasting away: can a Gates Foundation-funded toilet-design initiative end a foul practice in the developing world?, *Scientific American* February 21

Norman, G. and J. Parkinson, 2011: Integrating fecal sludge management into city planning, *WSUP/IWA Discussion Paper* prepared for AfricaSan 3, London

Otieno, P., C. Tiwari, B. Tunsisa *et al.*, 2011: Lukenya notes: taking community led total sanitation to scale with quality CLTS training, triggering and follow-up at scale, *Community Led Total Sanitation*, www.communityledtotalsanitation.org/resource/lukenya-notes-taking-clts-scale-quality, accessed February 23

Penrose, K. *et al.*, 2010: Informal urban settlements and cholera risk in Dar es Salaam, Tanzania, *PLoS Neglected Tropical Diseases* **4**, e631

Rijsberman, F. and A. P. Zwane, 2008: Perspective Paper prepared for the 2008, Copenhagen Consensus

Tyagi, A. and G. Hutton, 2008: Economic impacts of sanitation in India, World Bank, Hanoi

Water and Sanitation Program (WSP), 2009: *Study for Financial and Economic Analysis of Ecological Sanitation in Sub-Saharan Africa*, Final Synthesis Report, Washington, DC

2011: Economic Impact Briefings, for Africa, www.wsp.org/content/africa-economic-impacts-sanitation, accessed March 26, 2013

Watson, T., 2006: Public health investments and the infant mortality gap: evidence from federal sanitation interventions and hospitals on US Indian reservations, *Journal of Public Economics* **90**, 1537–60

Whittington, D. *et al.*, 2008: Copenhagen Consensus 2008 challenge paper: Sanitation and Water

WHO, 2012: Urbanization and health, *Bulletin of the World Health Organization* **88**, 241–32

WHO/UNICEF Joint Monitoring Programme for Water Supply and Sanitation, Washington, DC

WHO/UNICEF, 2010: *Progress on Sanitation and Drinking-Water: 2012 Update*

2012: Progress on Sanitation and Drinking-Water: 2012 Update, WHO/UNICEF Joint Monitoring Programme for Water Supply and Sanitation, Washington, DC

Waterkeyn, J. and S. Cairncross, 2005: Creating demand for sanitation and hygiene through Community Health Clubs: a cost-effective intervention in two districts in Zimbabwe, *Social Science & Medicine* **61**, 1958–70

Zuckerman, J., L. Rombo, and A. Fisc, 2007: The true burden and risk of cholera: implications for prevention and control, *Lancet Infections Diseases* **7**, 521–3

Water and Sanitation

Alternative Perspective

W. MICHAEL HANEMANN

Introduction

The 2012 Copenhagen Consensus Challenge Paper by Rijsberman and Zwane (hereafter, RZ) (Chapter 10) focuses primarily on sanitation and offers three sanitation interventions, characterized as (1) community-led total sanitation (CLTS++); (2) Sanitation as a business; and (3) the "reinvented toilet." In addition, RZ offer a fourth intervention aimed at improving rural water supply consisting of (4) borehole wells equipped with handpumps. As proposed, CLTS++ calls for an investment of US$3 billion that could benefit 600 million people, corresponding to about half of the rural population currently lacking basic sanitation, with a BCR estimated at 4–7, and is characterized as low-risk. Rural water boreholes requires an investment of US$12–23 billion, could potentially reach 700 million people, with a BCR of around 3.4, and is also characterized as low-risk. Sanitation as a business involves an investment of US$320 million, could serve 200 million low-income urban people, with a BCR of 23–47, and is characterized as medium-risk. The "reinvented toilet" involves an investment of $125 million, could serve a billion low-income urban people, with a BCR of 40, and is characterized as high-risk. I certainly believe these interventions are meritorious and deserve support. While RZ are very candid about the assumptions they are making and the limitations of their analysis, I want here to note some of the complications which beset the problem of sanitation.

RZ explain their focus on sanitation by observing that the world has met the MDG on water five years early, but will miss its goal on basic sanitation by almost 1 billion people. As they note, "an astonishing one-third of the world population, 2.5 billion people, does not have access to basic sanitation and over 1 billion people defecate out in the open" (p. 597). This prompts the question: why is there this problem? This is not a new problem, created by some new circumstances, such as the problems of air pollution or climate change. The lack of sanitation is an age-old phenomenon that has stubbornly resisted change. Moreover, as RZ note, the benefits of sanitation seem self-evident. They quote an editorial in the *Lancet* (*Lancet*, 2008): "It is already well known that improved sanitation could prevent 1.5 million deaths from diarrheal illnesses a year, enhance dignity, privacy and safety, especially for women and girls, benefits the economy – every dollar spent on sanitation generates economic benefits worth around nine more – and is better for the environment." If the benefits are self-evident, why is there not more sanitation?

In March 2012, the results of the 2011 Indian Census were released. The Indian Census Commissioner reported that more than half of the population – 53.2 percent – have a mobile phone, and 63.2 percent of homes have a telephone. But only 46.9 percent of India's households have a toilet. The same Census reports that 47.2 percent of Indian households have a television, while only 19.9 percent have a radio.[1] One might ask, why do fewer households in India have a radio than a television, which is presumably more expensive than a radio. A natural answer would be that people in India sometimes value a television more highly than they value a radio. Could the same logic apply to toilets and mobile phones – could people sometimes value a mobile phone more highly than they do a toilet?

While it is easy to understand why a person could value a television more highly than a radio, because

[1] This was reported by BBC News, March 14, 2012, www.bbc.co.uk/news/world-asia-india-17362837.

a television offers more benefits, visual as well as aural, it is not so easy to see why a person could value a mobile phone more highly than a toilet. One possible answer is the following: even without a toilet, everybody has *some* means to deal with defecation, however inconvenient and unpleasant. However, without a mobile phone, not everyone has a means of communicating with other people at a distance. In economic terms, what matters is not the absolute attractiveness of the commodity (toilet or mobile phone) but rather its attractiveness relative to the existing substitutes.

But even with the difference in substitutes, should not a toilet be preferred to a mobile phone given its multiple benefits – health, safety, dignity, privacy, etc? This raises several questions. Just how large are those benefits? The *Lancet* editorial didn't say that improved sanitation *would* prevent 1.5 million deaths, it said "*could* prevent." How much uncertainty is there about the number of deaths that would be prevented? To whom do the benefits accrue, and do they accrue to the same people as those who pay the cost of the improved sanitation? If not, how does the improved sanitation get financed? And, how much do the people to whom the benefits accrue actually value those benefits?

These questions touch on the demand side of the sanitation challenge. While RZ are fully aware of the importance of this, they tend to focus more on the supply side. In response to the question of why the sanitation challenge has proved so elusive, they state "the simplest answer is the cost of current technologies" (p. 597). At least two of their interventions, Sanitation as a business and the "reinvented toilet" are intended, at least in part, to lower the cost of meeting the sanitation challenge.

For a successful solution, *both* sides of the challenge need to be addressed.

Complex pathways of causation

Given the terrible burden of waterborne disease, what is known about sanitation interventions that reduce mortality? RZ cite three papers that use rigorous econometric techniques to demonstrate that an intervention actually reduced mortality. RZ are careful to note that these interventions involved *networked* water and sanitation services. Galiani *et al.* (2005) examined a water privatization reform in Argentina in the 1990s that led to a reduction in child mortality of approximately 8 percent. The privatization was associated with a reduction in deaths from infectious and parasitic diseases, and was uncorrelated with deaths from causes unrelated to water conditions. The causal pathway appears to have been that the privatized utilities significantly increased investment in infrastructure and expanded connections to water service and to sewer services, especially in poor areas that were least served by networked water and sewer services under public ownership. In some cases, the privatized utilities also improved water pressure and service quality. Watson (2006) examined sanitation interventions on US Indian Reservations by the Indian Health Service between 1960 and 1998. She found that a 10 percent point increase in the fraction of homes receiving sanitation improvement reduced Indian infant mortality by 2.5 percent; the reductions in mortality were concentrated in waterborne gastro-intestinal diseases and infectious respiratory diseases. The interventions included both networked services (building or improving water or sewer treatment plants, extending water and sewer lines, connecting individual homes to those lines) and non-networked services (digging wells, providing latrines or septic tanks), and Watson does not distinguish between them. My own understanding, having reviewed water supply and sanitation on some Indian Reservations, is that the main focus of these interventions was on networked services.

The third study cited by RZ is by Cutler and Miller (2005), who found that the introduction of water filtration and chlorination for drinking water led to major reductions in mortality in American cities, explaining nearly half the overall reduction in mortality between 1900 and 1936, and three-quarters of the decline in infant mortality. Cutler and Miller estimate that the rate of return to investment in filtration and chlorination was about 23 to 1. They go on to state: "[I]nexpensive water-disinfection technologies can have enormous health returns – returns that reach beyond reductions in waterborne diseases – even in the absence of adequate sanitation services... [If] only 1 percent of the roughly 1.7 million annual deaths from diarrheal diseases worldwide could be prevented by water disinfection, the corresponding social rate of return for one year alone would be about $160 billion". This is a misleading comparison because the US context in 1900 was significantly different from that in the areas where most of the 1.7 million deaths occur today. By 1900, all of the US urban population was served by a networked water service, and in most cases had been so served for thirty or forty years. In addition, by 1900 over 80 percent of the urban population was served by a networked sewer service. Habits of personal hygiene were well established. The only thing lacking was treatment: there was no treatment of either sewage or drinking water. Sewage was collected and discharged untreated into water bodies that often served as the source of drinking water for other communities. The removal of sewage from places of residence removed the health threat to the people who generated it, but the absence of treatment of the sewage prior to waterborne disposal combined with the absence of treatment of drinking water created a maelstrom of disease downstream. If there had been treatment of drinking water but without networked collection of sewage – which is closer to the situation in some developing countries – there would have been a much larger burden of disease after 1900 than that observed by Cutler and Miller. To make the same point in another way, the efficacy of the investment in the treatment of drinking water after 1900 was boosted by the prior investment in networked sewage collection whose cost was overlooked by Cutler and Miller because it had occurred prior to 1900.

While these studies provide rigorous evidence of the health benefits from investment in a system with networked water and sewage systems, this is hardly of relevance for the populations targeted by RZ's four proposed interventions, which eschew networked systems. This is done with good reason. Jenkins and Sugden (2006) observe that "it is unrealistic to believe that anything but a small percentage of the world's urban poor will be served by sewered systems in the next 20 years. Most of the increases in access to safe excreta disposal over the last decade are due to on-site technologies, not through the expansion of sewer systems and household connections . . . On-site technology should not be regarded as being a sub-standard solution, just a different solution suitable for a different context."[2]

The targets of RZ's interventions are "the rural poor in low income countries . . . and the urban poor in the informal settlements or slums that characterize the places where the underserved live" for whom a "networked service is largely irrelevant"[3]. The evidence for the health impacts of non-networked investments in those locations is more heterogeneous and less clear-cut. For example, a review of the literature on impacts on diarrhea mortality by Cairncross *et al.* (2010) concluded that most of the evidence is of poor quality. Three types of intervention were considered: hand washing with soap; measures to improve the microbial quality of drinking water (for example, household-based point-of-use treatment); and measures to dispose of human excreta so as to reduce direct or indirect human contact (including pit latrines, bucket latrines, hanging toilets, and composting toilets). The evidence was most consistent for hand washing with soap, which was estimated to provide a 48 percent reduction in diarrhea risk. For water-quality improvement some of the studies were problematic; the review assessed a 17 percent reduction in diarrhea risk for this intervention. For excreta disposal, there was very little rigorous evidence of health benefit; the review assessed a 36 percent reduction in diarrhea risk for this intervention.

Two points should be noted about these assessments. First, there is quite a wide dispersion in the results. In the case of hand washing with soap, for example, the 95 percent confidence interval for the reduction in risk was 24–63 percent.[4] Whittington *et al.* (2012) also review studies of hand washing using rates of uptake and usage as metrics of interest. Of the four studies they considered, one involved a usage rate of 79 percent; another involved a usage rate of 60 percent at one location and a usage rate of 88 percent at another; a third

[2] Jenkins and Sugden (2006) point out that 50 percent of households in Japan are not sewered, and there is little intention to get the remainder connected.

[3] Rijsberman and Zwane (2008).

[4] Curtis and Cairncross (2003).

study involved usage rates ranging from 10 percent to 84 percent, depending on gender and age; and the fourth involved a usage rate of 19 percent. Second, in the Cairncross *et al.* (2010) study, the largest impact was associated with a change in behavior (hand washing). The importance of behavioral change has been emphasized by many researchers. For example, Yacoob and Whiteford (1994) state that infrastructure improvements such as the provision of sanitary facilities "rarely result in the anticipated health improvements. Changes in hygiene behavior, that is in the way people utilize their existing resources along with improved infrastructure, are critical to achieving sustained improvements in public health conditions."

The type of excreta handling and disposal envisaged by RZ in connection with Sanitation as a business and with the "reinvented toilet" is considerably more sophisticated than the excreta-disposal interventions considered by Cairncross *et al.* (2010). Therefore, the health benefits that could be attained by RZ's interventions could be substantially larger. Nevertheless, there is a degree of uncertainty at this stage regarding the health outcomes that will be attained through RZ's interventions. The reinvented toilets are currently at an early stage and, as RZ note, investments in the development of this solution are high-risk And, while most of the various elements associated with Sanitation as a business have been, or are being, developed and tested individually in a variety of locations, they are now being put together and tested at scale in Dakar over the next five years with funding from the Gates Foundation. The intervention proposed here would support further development and testing on a larger scale. So, much remains to be learned about the effectiveness of these interventions.

The advantage – in principle – of a networked system of water supply and sewerage is that there are fewer "moving parts" than with a non-networked system – there are fewer separate components that need to be coordinated and kept in sync. With a non-networked system, such as RZ's Sanitation as a business, there are more junctures at which something can go wrong, potentially leading to water contamination and the spread of disease. These include keeping the excreta in an isolated containment, desludging/emptying the container, transporting the effluent, and disposing of it in a safe manner. RZ propose important new technologies to deal with these stages of the system. But, at each stage, there is a substantial human behavioral component. Not only does there need to be a reliable technology but also there needs to be the right incentives – and monitoring – to ensure that it is applied properly and that adverse third-party effects are avoided. RZ point out, correctly, that small-scale private service providers may have a greater incentive than municipal governments to be responsive to the needs of their customers and to service them efficiently. However, without some monitoring and regulation they may not have as strong an incentive to avoid any harmful third-party effects.

The behavioral elements are a fundamental feature of sanitation and disease prevention. They introduce an inherently contingent component into the assessment of outcomes from interventions. Let me illustrate this with an example. As noted earlier, the privatization of municipal water and sewer utilities in Argentina in the 1990s led to an 8 percent reduction in child mortality. How did this come about? According to Galiani *et al.* (2005), the municipally owned utilities were overstaffed and inefficiently operated. The new private owners reduced the overstaffing and improved the efficiency of operations. They invested more in physical infrastructure than the previous management. They restructured the charge for water service, in one case lowering the initial connection fee to one-tenth of the previous level and adding a fixed charge to the water use bills for all customers as a cross-subsidy. And they improved the quality of service.[5] How, then, should one characterize the causal link between privatization and reduced child mortality? Privatization by itself was hardly a sufficient condition for the reduction in mortality. If the privatized owners had operated the system more efficiently but had not invested in new infrastructure, there would not have been the reduction in mortality. If they had invested in infrastructure but had not modified the rate structure, many poorer families would have been unable to afford networked water

[5] Davis *et al.* (2008) and Devoto *et al.* (2011) confirm the importance of financing to overcome the hurdle of the initial connection fee for joining a water and sewer network.

and sewer service, and therefore the health benefits would have been lower. Thus, the health outcome cannot be attributed to privatization alone. If privatization was not a sufficient condition, can we say that it was a necessary condition for the health outcome? Perhaps not – can we be certain that *no* municipally owned utility could invest heavily in physical infrastructure or could restructure rates so as to reduce the initial connection fee?

Similarly with water and sanitation interventions. Having a source of clean water in the home is not a sufficient condition for avoiding illness if one does not practice good personal hygiene. Nor is it a necessary condition since, with good hygiene practices, including boiling water before ingesting it and hand washing, illness can be avoided. The behavioral practices are intertwined with other elements of sanitation interventions in such a manner as to render inaccurate the characterization of a sanitation intervention by itself as a sufficient (or a necessary) condition for reduced morbidity or mortality.[6]

This is worth emphasizing, because the analytical approaches commonly adopted in economic theorizing and, more recently, in econometric modeling specifically represent causal factors as sufficient conditions for the outcome being modeled. This is true of both the conventional production function formalism and also the "treatment effect" approach to program evaluation based on randomized controlled experiments or on quasi-randomization through instrumental variable techniques or natural experiments. As conventionally modeled, adoption of the treatment is interpreted as a sufficient condition for obtaining the average treatment effect. I certainly agree that an experiment where one controls for the factor of interest through the experimental design or through statistical analysis is a desirable source of knowledge regarding which interventions work. But, I do not agree with the tendency to focus on the estimation of the mean impact (the mean treatment effect) as the exclusive object of interest. By way of qualification, if it is the case that there is little variation in the magnitude of the treatment effect across different experiments and different sets of data, then the mean treatment effect becomes of more interest. But, if there is considerable variation in its magnitude, which is typical of water and sanitation interventions in the literature, then just knowing the average treatment effect is not enough. More important is to understand what factors account for the variation in treatment effect, which subpopulations exhibit the greatest (or smallest) effect, and why.[7] The analogy is to know the average reduction in child mortality conditional on the privatization of water supply, without knowing anything about the particular investments and pricing policies adopted by those privatized utilities.

The need to go beyond the average treatment effect is illustrated by the evaluation of piped water for rural households in India by Jalan and Ravallion (2002). They found that the prevalence and duration of diarrhea among children under five were significantly lower on average for families with piped water than for observationally identical households without it. However, they also found that the health gains largely by-passed children in poor families, particularly when the mother was poorly educated. The implication is that unsanitary behaviors in poor households, and especially households where mothers are poorly educated, can nullify the potentially beneficial effect of piped water.

Behavior change

These findings of Jalan and Ravallion (2002) highlight the pivotal role of behavior, and behavior change, in reducing waterborne disease. Our knowledge of what triggers behavior change is woefully limited. Recognizing this, Zwane and Kremer (2007) call for more research targeted at the design of behavioral interventions:

[6] The complexity of the causal pathway connecting health outcomes to water and sanitation interventions is by no means confined to the contemporary experience in developing countries; it is also evident throughout the history of water supply in the United States and Western Europe in the nineteenth century (van Poppel and van der Heijden, 1997).

[7] This point is made by Deaton (2009) and Heckman and Urzua (2009) in the general context of development economics. The unwisdom of relying on a point estimate for a BCR in the context of setting priorities for water and sanitation interventions is forcefully emphasized by Whittington *et al.* (2012).

> Identifying cost-effective ways to facilitate long-term behavior change and technology adoption requires additional research comparing alternative messages and message delivery avenues in several cultural contexts. For example, rigorous evaluations are needed that compare health education messages directed toward women emphasizing family health and those emphasizing children's well-being in particular. The comparative usefulness of positive and negative messages should also be explored, as has been done in other campaigns aimed at inducing behavioral changes in developed countries.

Because human motivation and behavior is multi-faceted, there are numerous potential points of attack. Zwane and Kremer (2007) identify several possibilities – for example, programs working through maternity clinics or schools to provide messaging and education and/or to distribute soap for hand washing. Another possibility is programs targeting community-opinion leaders (most probably males) or targeting women's groups. The point is that behavior change is an exercise in marketing – social marketing – and should be approached in that spirit, using insights from market research. This viewpoint is strongly advocated by Jenkins and Sugden (2006), who characterize the goal as "enhancing the demand for sanitation."

One distinction is between behavior-change programs targeted at individuals and programs targeted at groups of individuals simultaneously. An example of the latter is CLTS, which is one of RZ's proposed interventions. CLTS aims to trigger

> change in collective sanitation behavior, which is achieved through a process of collective local action stimulated by facilitators from within and outside the community. The process involves the whole community and emphasizes the collective benefit from stopping open defecation, rather than focusing on individual behavior or on constructing toilets. People decide together how they will create a clean and hygienic environment that benefits everyone.[8] (p. 601)

It is interesting to contrast this with a program targeted at individuals, the "No Toilet, No Bride" program launched by the Haryana state authorities in India in 2005. The context is the fact that women suffer from widespread and entrenched social constraints and discrimination in rural Haryana, which the state authorities wished to counteract. Roughly 70 percent of rural households in Haryana engaged in open defecation. More than men, women prefer toilets to open defecation because they suffer from male staring and harassment when they urinate, defecate, or attend to menstrual hygiene in the open. For this reason, private latrines generate benefits that accrue disproportionately to women. One time in their lives when women have a degree of power is in the selection of a husband during marriage negotiations. The Haryana state authorities seized on this and mounted an advertising campaign with billboards, posters, and radio advertisements encouraging the families of marriage-age girls to demand that potential suitors' families construct a latrine prior to marriage. "No Toilet, No Bride" and "No Loo, No I do" were slogans used in the advertising campaign. Stopnitzky (2012) analyzed the effects using a comparison of households with and without marriageable boys, and in Haryana versus other states, before and after the campaign. He found that male investment in sanitation increased by 15 percent due to the program. The program effect was four times larger in marriage markets where women were scarce (26 percent) as compared to marriage markets where women were abundant (6 percent).

While "No Toilet, No Bride" is merely one data point, in my mind it raises the question of whether the collective approach represented by RZ's CLTS proposal is adequate as their only intervention focused on behavior change.

There are potentially three steps in motivating behavior change: (1) motivating an individual to stop doing what he or she has typically done; (2) motivating an individual who has decided to make a change to select the targeted alternative as his or her new behavior; and (3) motivating the individual to sustain that change in behavior over time. Sometimes steps (1) and (2) occur at the same time: the decision to make a change occurs simultaneously with the decision to adopt an alternative behavior. Sometimes there is a sufficient degree of commitment that, once the decision in (2) occurs, that in (3) follows automatically. However there are many

[8] Kar and Milward (2011), as quoted by RZ.

examples in the water and sanitation sector where a community initially made a change but later (for example, when a subsidy ended or funds ran out) returned to the former behavior. One factor that can be important in sustaining a behavior change is if there is a shift in expectations or norms: what the person used to accept is now seen as inappropriate or unacceptable. A striking example of a change in behavior sustained by a change in norms is the decline in smoking over the past four decades. In the United States, smoking rates declined from 42 percent of adults in 1965 to 18.5 percent in 2006. While this is a large change in behavior, it certainly did not occur overnight. The question is whether a similar change in attitude with regard to, say, open defecation could occur in developing countries over a similar or longer span of time. And, what would it take to promote such a change in attitude? "No Toilet, No Bride" suggests that empowering women in society is one contributing factor.

Perceived benefits

RZ identify a variety of economic costs from poor sanitation, with corresponding economic benefits from improved sanitation. Following the methodology of the ESI reports, they classify the economic impacts of inadequate sanitation into five categories: (1) *Health-related impacts*, including premature deaths, costs of treating diseases; productive time lost due to people falling ill, and time lost by caregivers who look after them. (2) *Domestic water-related impacts*, including costs of household treatment of water; use of bottled water; a portion of costs of obtaining piped water; and time costs of fetching cleaner water from a distance. (3) *Access time impacts*: cost of additional time spent for accessing shared toilets or open defecation sites; absence of children (mainly girls) from school and women from their workplaces. (4) *Tourism impacts*: potential loss of tourism revenues and economic impacts of gastro-intestinal illnesses among foreign tourists. (5) *Amenity and environmental costs* of water pollution. Categories (1) and (2) account for the lion's share of the impacts. For the four Asian countries listed by RZ, health effects account for 53.5 percent of the economic impact of poor sanitation, and domestic-water effects account for 25.3 percent. Categories (3) – (5) combined account for 21.2 percent of the economic impact.

On the other hand, in a study of why some people want latrines in Benin, Jenkins and Curtis (2005) found that "[h]ealth considerations played only a minor role, and had little if anything to do with preventing fecal-oral disease transmission." Jenkins and Sugden (2006) similarly observe that "overwhelming evidence and common sense have clearly shown that households decide to change their sanitation practices to gain a variety of different benefits, mostly having little to do with avoiding excreta-related diseases." Jenkins and Sugden continue:

> There is a good reason for this. From the perspective of an individual household, changes in illness may be difficult to obtain and impossible to attribute with certainty to sanitation when other fecal–oral transmission routes both inside and outside the home are operating. Thus, the health benefits at the household level tend to be the least reliable to obtain amongst the private benefits of improved sanitation.

Thus, there appears to be some divergence between the benefits of sanitation as seen by the experts, such as are tabulated in the ESI reports, and the benefits as perceived by the people on the ground who actually experience the improvement in sanitation. This raises two questions. First, what is the explanation for the divergence in perceptions – in effect, a divergence between the private and the social benefits of improved sanitation? Second, what is the significance of this divergence – should it be ignored, and should attention be focused solely on the social benefits as perceived by the experts?

RZ are aware of these issues. They identify two factors as explanations for the divergence between private and social perceptions of the benefits of sanitation. One explanation is intra-family distributional inequities, whereby the preferences and interests of women and girls tend to be devalued by males in the household. A second factor is the externality of disease: if a household receives access to improved sanitation, not only is there a reduced burden of disease for the members of the household but, because other people outside the household can be caught in the cycle of disease transmission, there is also a reduced burden of disease for those other people. The disease externality creates a market failure leading to inefficiently low private investment. Both explanations are valid. But, I don't believe that they are the full story. Not only may individuals overlook the health benefits accruing to people outside their family and household, but the findings of Jenkins and Curtis (2005) and Jenkins and Sugden (2006) suggest that people may assess the health benefits to themselves and to their family members as smaller than the health experts would account them.

Against this must be set the fact that the recipients of improved sanitation discern benefits to themselves that the experts usually do not consider. Jenkins and Curtis (2005) group these into three categories: prestige, well-being, and situational goals. *Prestige* includes improved social status, being seen as modern and more urbanized, being able to achieve "the good life," and leaving a lasting monument and legacy to your descendants. *Well-being* includes not only reduced illness, but also increased comfort, increased privacy, increased convenience, increased safety for children and for women, especially at night, and less embarrassment with visitors. *Situational* benefits include reduced conflict with neighbors, help with the restricted mobility that generates physical difficulty with walking to the bush and squatting, increased property value, and increased income from any renters in the house. Jenkins and Curtis note that the weight placed on the non-health motives vary with gender, occupation, life stage, travel experience, education, and wealth.

The fact that the recipients of improved sanitation see the benefits differently than the experts has several important implications. If the prospective recipients of a sanitation improvement project are being asked to pay for it, the benefits that they perceive are a crucial determinant of their WTP, and hence of their uptake of the project. If they perceive the benefits as being low, and less than what they must pay, they will not adopt the project, or they will abandon it as soon as they can. The user perceptions, therefore, provide a roadmap to the successful marketing of sanitation. The challenge is to identify forms of improved sanitation that the recipients see as bringing a benefit to themselves and are willing to pay for.

Not everyone would agree with the last sentence. A common argument is that investment in water and sanitation services should be based on the assessment of their social benefits, not their private benefits. This is a valid argument if water and sanitation are viewed as merit goods, and if there is a funding source, other than the direct beneficiaries, that is available to finance the provision of this merit good. I have no doubt that the provision of some level of water and sanitation service to some people *is* a merit good. But I am not sure that the provision of any level of water and sanitation service to all the people not currently served, for the indefinite future, is a merit good. While there are spillover benefits from disease externalities, as noted above, the enjoyment of water and sanitation is largely a private good, like food, clothing, and housing. It certainly may be appropriate to subsidize water or sanitation during an interim period until there is sufficient economic growth that the recipients would be able and willing to pay for it themselves. It strikes me as less reasonable to commit to financing water and sanitation projects that will have to be subsidized indefinitely because, while there are social benefits, the private benefits are lower than the recipients are willing – now and in the future – to pay for. For this reason, I believe it would be prudent for RZ to give a little more thought to the private benefits of some of the sanitation interventions they propose, to the demand side of sanitation, and to the stimulation of a demand for sanitation among the populations they quite rightly wish to serve.

Bibliography

Cairncross, S., C. Hunt, S. Boisson, K. Bostoen, V. Curtis, I. C. H. Fung, and W.-P. Schmidt, 2010: Water, sanitation and hygiene for the prevention of diarrhoea, *International Journal of Epidemiology* **39**, i193–i205

Curtis, V. and S. Cairncross, 2003: Effect of washing hands with soap on diarrhoea risk in the community: a systemic review, *Lancet Infectious Diseases* **3**, 275–81

Cutler, D. and G. Miller, 2005: The role of public health improvements in health advances: the 20th century United States, *Demography* **42**, 1–22

Davis, J., G. White, S. Damodaron, and R. Thorsten, 2008: Improving access to water supply and sanitation in urban India: microfinance for water and sanitation infrastructure development, *Water Science & Technology* **58**, 887–91

Deaton, A., 2009: Instruments of development: randomization in the tropics, and the search for the elusive keys to economic development, *NBER Working Paper* **14690**, Cambridge, MA

Devoto, F., E. Duflo, P. Dupas, W. Pariente, and V. Pons, 2011: Happiness on tap: piped water adoption in urban Morocco, *NBER Working Paper* **16933**, Cambridge, MA

Galiani, S., P. Gertler, and E. Schargrodsky, 2005: Water for life: the impact of privatization of water services on child mortality, *Journal of Political Economy* **113**, 83–120

Heckman, J. and S. Urzua, 2009: Comparing IV with structural models: what simple IV can and cannot identify, *NBER Working Paper* **14706**, Cambridge, MA

Jalan, J. and M. Ravallion, 2003: Does piped water reduce diarrhea for children in rural India?, *Journal of Econometrics* **112**, 153–73

Jenkins, M. W. and V. Curtis, 2005: Achieving the "good life": why some people want latrines in rural Benin, *Social Science and Medicine* **61**, 2446–59

Jenkins, M. W. and S. Sugden, 2006: *Rethinking Sanitation: Lessons and Innovation for Sustainability and Success in the New Millennium*, UNDP, New York

Kar, K. and K. Milward, 2011: *Digging In, Spreading Out and Growing Up: Introducing CLTS in Africa*, IDS, Brighton

Lancet, 2008: Editorial: Keeping sanitation in the spotlight, *Lancet* **371**, 1045

Rijsberman, F. and A. P. Zwane, 2008: Perspective Paper for the 2008 Copenhagen Consensus

Stopnitzky, Y., 2012: The bargaining power of missing women: evidence from a sanitation campaign in India, *Working Paper*, Department of Economics, Yale University

Van Poppel, F. and C. van der Heijden, 1997: The effects of water supply on infant and childhood mortality: a review of historical evidence, *Health Transition Review* **7**, 113–48

Watson, T., 2006: Public health investments and the infant mortality gap: evidence from federal sanitation interventions and hospitals on US Indian reservations, *Journal of Public Economics* **90**, 1537–60

Whittington, D., M. Jeuland, K. Barker, and Y. Yuen, 2012: Setting priorities, targeting subsidies among water, sanitation and preventive health interventions in developing countries, *World Development* **40**, 1546–68, http://dx.doi.org/10.1016/j.worldder.2012.03.004

Yacoob, M. and L. M. Whiteford, 1994: Behavior in water supply and sanitation, *Human Organization* **53**, 330–5

Zwane, A. P. and M. Kremer, 2007: What works in fighting diarrheal diseases in developing countries? A critical review, Oxford University Press/IBRD

Water and Sanitation

Alternative Perspective

GUY HUTTON

Introduction

According to projections of the latest JMP report – in 2015 the number of people globally without access to improved sanitation (2.4 billion) will exceed those without access to improved drinking-water supply by at least four times (UNICEF/WHO, 2012). Hence, the authors of the Challenge Paper (Chapter 10) rightly focus their assessment on sanitation, one of the most off-track MDG targets. While the sector is indeed redressing the imbalance between water supply and sanitation, it is now widely recognized that increased financing and political attention are not enough: the sector needs successful models of scaling up in order to make a lasting dent on the billions still without basic sanitation. And although risky, as pointed out by the Chapter 10 authors, we do need to identify twenty-first-century solutions to the sanitation challenge, recognizing that managing the wastewater and sewerage of more than 7 billion humans is in dire need of a different approach to that of nineteenth-century engineers.

For some years now, it has been known that both improved drinking-water supply and sanitation offer attractive returns on investment (Hutton and Haller, 2004). BCRs, varying from returns of US$3 to US$34 per dollar invested,[1] have been widely disseminated among the media, at international conferences, and in country dialogues. Recently, more detailed country-level studies have been conducted specifically on sanitation interventions under the ESI.[2] These country studies, which now cover the globe, give sector stakeholders and policy-makers added firepower for arguing for more funds and political support for sanitation, as well as informing selection of efficient and appropriate sanitation technologies.[3] For all three sanitation interventions described in Chapter 10, the authors draw heavily on the ESI datasets and recalculate BCRs and net benefits under different scenarios.

How Chapter 10 used ESI data

Various brief technical responses should be made to the utilization and adjustment of ESI data for the purposes of Chapter 10's three sanitation interventions. On CLTS++, it should be noted that in the two countries where ESI studies evaluated CLTS-type interventions (Cambodia and Indonesia), the program costs of implementing CLTS were included. Indeed, program costs were found to be very high in Cambodia, exceeding by several times the hardware cost of the simple latrines selected by the majority of rural households. Second, BCRs were presented in ESI reports under "ideal" and "actual" scenarios – the former being 100 percent adoption of toilet facilities, and the latter accounting for the fact that a proportion of the targeted households either do not adopt the intervention or, after some time of latrine use, fall back to former practices. These results are presented in detail in the ESI country reports. Third, the reduction in diarrheal disease incidence and mortality used for basic sanitation interventions is 36 percent (from meta-analyses), which is arguably not overly

[1] Depending on which world region or report is cited.

[2] Led by the World Bank Water and Sanitation Program, www.wsp.org.

[3] What have been termed "ESI Phase 1" studies measured the economic impacts of poor sanitation at a national level, while "ESI Phase 2" studies focused on measuring the costs and benefits of alternative sanitation interventions and delivery approaches in selected field sites.

optimistic as claimed by the authors. Hence the thinking behind the adjustments made in Chapter 10 are correct, but the ESI reports have in fact largely accommodated these concerns and issues.

Sanitation as a business is a concept gaining ground within the sector, but still facing many practical challenges. While economic analyses conclude that sanitation is a profitable investment from society's viewpoint, this fact alone does not automatically indicate the existence of a thriving market place, with customers ready and willing to pay for sanitation, and suppliers responding to that demand. Indeed, this is the precise problem of sanitation globally: there is no financially lucrative market in many developing countries because the costs of (off-site) excreta management are perceived by households or local authorities to be greater than the benefits, or simply that individuals and communities lack motivation to change their current habits.

In this respect, it is necessary to distinguish between on-site sanitation whose benefits are mainly to the household and immediate vicinity (containment of unpleasant waste and pathogens, and time savings) versus off-site sanitation whose benefits are to the wider community, especially "downstream" populations (aesthetic and environmental benefits, including pathogen removal). Hence, improved collection, transport, and disposal of excreta have potentially large positive "externalities" and few benefits to the household itself.[4] However, households need to be persuaded to avoid the lower-cost approach of informal self-emptying which is likely to lead to illegal dumping of waste in rivers and elsewhere. Hence, if improved waste management is to become a profitable business, then either the demand of households needs to be stimulated (the "carrot" approach) and/or regulatory measures need to be taken (the "stick" approach). Showing impressive BCRs – as the authors do, of US$47 return per US$1 invested – can inform and motivate these solutions. However, it should be underlined that this figure represents the return to a public or philanthropic budget, which the authors assume to be 25 percent of the total investment required; furthermore, the pit-emptying service claims 80 percent of the health and water quality benefits to sanitation, leaving only 20 percent of the benefits for the latrine intervention itself. Certainly these proportions are debatable, but little empirical evidence exists to date.

The analysis of the third sanitation innovation – reinventing the toilet – is a useful abstraction, asking whether technical innovations could play a role in scaling up sanitation globally. The key question relates to the value-added of such a technical solution: is it cleaner, cheaper, and more environmentally friendly than existing solutions. The analysis relies heavily on the stipulation that the solution should cost less than 5 US cents per day *per capita*, giving roughly US$90 per household per year. Based on the per capita incomes of the lower quintiles in low-income countries, especially subsistence farming households, such a cost will be unaffordable for solving what is only one of many basic needs. It is also unclear whether there can be a universal "reinvented toilet" that will gain 100 percent acceptance among the extremely diverse attitudes around the world that characterize sanitation. Taboos, cultural, and individual preferences abound in relation to sanitation choices, making a single "reinvented toilet" of universal appeal unrealistic.

Omitted benefits

One of the authors' conclusions, that the pay-offs to water and sanitation are "modest," is not supported by their own findings (of BCRs of 3.4–47). Such ratios indicate highly attractive interventions. Neither is this conclusion supported by a series of other benefits of improved sanitation that have been previously evaluated in the same ESI studies, but not referred to in Chapter 10. These include "intangible," environmental, and broader economic benefits.

Due to empirical limitations of doing otherwise, CBAs for water and sanitation have so far focused on evaluating household-level benefits, and to some extent community-level benefits. Some have been easier to quantify than others, such as health and time benefits. Hence any CBA has been partial, and

[4] An exception is that pit or septic tank-emptying allows the household to continue using that facility, rather than constructing a new one.

needs to become broader in the future to highlight some of the other key benefits that may help sell sanitation to both governments and the private sector. The ESI Phase 2 studies have explored some of these issues, and it is hoped will stimulate further research to more fully quantify these benefits.

One key driver of sanitation demand that has largely been ignored in CBAs is the group of benefits known broadly as "intangible" benefits: safety and security, dignity, privacy, and comfort, among others. Some of these benefits are closely linked with the human right to water and sanitation, which was explicitly recognized through resolution 64/292 by the United Nations General Assembly in July 2010. While CLTS++ recognizes and targets aspects related to social values, such as dignity and disgust, there is limited quantification of these aspects so far. In an attempt to raise the profile of these benefits, results on intangible aspects (using ranking scales and focus-group discussions) were presented alongside the BCRs in the ESI Phase 2 reports. In Indonesia, for example, the major intangible benefits cited were convenience (being able to go conveniently at any time, even at night and during the rainy season), ease of accompanying children to the toilet, privacy, pride, reduced risk of accidents, avoided queuing at public toilets, and improved cleanliness and hygiene. Many of these benefits have strong gender dimensions. In marketing sanitation, many populations are more likely to respond to messages based on these intangible benefits than from quantitative "proof" of cost-benefit, which is more the domain of policy-makers.

A second key aspect of sanitation is its link to the environment. Some of the positive benefits have been highlighted in Chapter 10, such as the re-use value of human excreta and related business opportunities. However, the removal of the negative environmental impacts of poor sanitation has been largely omitted in CBAs to date. These are partly broader "intangible" benefits such as the aesthetic value of a clean city environment (without pungent open canals that serve as sewers). Some environmental impacts can in fact be quantified in economic terms, such as the value associated with changes in land use, safeguarding water sources for municipal use, and avoided costs of river clean-up. Such impacts have been captured, although incompletely, in the ESI Phase 1 studies. However, the second phase of the ESI – field-level CBAs – found it methodologically difficult to capture the household cost savings in specific locations as a result of well-managed human excreta. For example, household-level water sourcing and treatment behavior depends on other sources of pollution than just human excreta. Also, many households do not stop taking mitigative measures, such as boiling their drinking water, after water sources become clean. Experience shows that habits are hard to change.

A third key aspect of sanitation brings together intangible and environmental impacts, where sanitation is a driver of the tourism industry and firms' location decisions. To make the point, the argument focuses on foreign rather than domestic[5] tourists and firms, as foreign tourists and firms are likely to be more sensitive to the quality of the environment. While these links are not open to scientific analysis (e.g. randomization) and thus difficult to make empirically, there is clearly a strong association between environmental quality and the attractiveness of locations to foreign visitors and foreign firms (Kirigia *et al.*, 2009). While some firms may be attracted by lax environmental laws (to reduce their own costs), on the other hand international companies seek locations where the local population is healthy for work, where basic infrastructure is available, where water is cheap but can be treated to the quality standards demanded by the production process, and where senior foreign employees are willing to locate to. Hence, governments of developing countries (e.g. Ministers of Finance) may find arguments about sanitation as an engine of economic growth more concrete and convincing than equity and human rights arguments.

"Lining up" the solutions through cost-curve analysis

Chapter 10 has helped understand some of the bottlenecks to scaling up effective sanitation interventions, and the solutions to overcoming them. However, there is a risk that when these solutions are

[5] "Domestic" refers to developing countries.

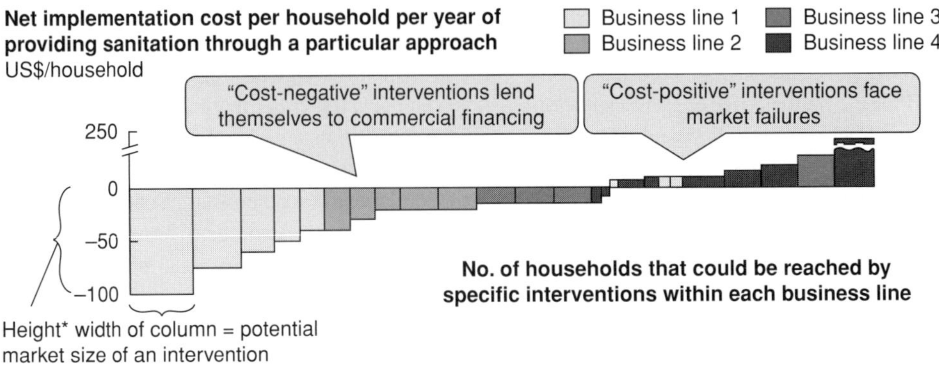

Figure 10.2.1 *Illustrative cost curve for sanitation*

Source: McKinsey & Company.

further developed and "inserted" into development programs, they will continue to operate in isolation from each other. Such fragmentation is common in the water and sanitation sectors of developing countries. The macro-picture on how resources can be best allocated by government, and spent by households, is lost.

It is accepted wisdom in the field of water and sanitation that different technological solutions and management approaches are required for different populations, due to different preferences, different socio-economic backgrounds, different climatic and geographical contexts, and so on. Hence on the demand side, the market is extremely diverse. However, on the supply side, each player implements solutions that are most appropriate to their own organization. Governments are heavily influenced by engineering approaches. The private sector minimizes business risk and targets the majority taste or preference, or the cheapest to reach (e.g. urban areas). There is virtually no pooling of funds to work on common solutions; likewise, pooling of knowledge is limited. Agency-programming cycles, donor-funding cycles, stakeholders' objectives, monitoring and evaluation systems, are not aligned so that sector resources are used in the most efficient way.

Furthermore, as stated in Chapter 10, economic benefits are very rarely fully realized due to market "failure," such as the existence of externalities[6] and inefficiencies in private financing that puts the (rural) masses out of reach of viable micro-credit schemes. A key bottleneck is that the short-term market value (i.e. demand by households and hence return to investors) is below the longer-term economic benefit of declining mortality rates and poverty reduction. Furthermore, the suboptimal rates of latrine adoption in sanitation programmes further reduce their benefits, thus affecting the confidence of funding agencies to support public programmes.

One way to stimulate dialogue and acquire a common understanding of investment options is through a tool that combines the *economic* and *financial* aspects of sanitation, both of which are crucial to the successful functioning of a market "at-scale." The technique, known as the "cost-curve" analysis, was developed by McKinsey & Company and has been applied to the water-resources sector and to GHG abatement (Ankvist *et al.*, 2007; Addams *et al.*, 2009). The cost-curve analysis dissects the market, providing a microeconomic analysis of the cost and potential of a range of existing technical measures to close the projected gap between demand and supply in a given market, whether it be water, carbon, or sanitation. Each of the technical measures is represented as a block on the cost curve (see Figure 10.2.1). The width of the block represents the unit of analysis, whether it is water volume, carbon emissions, or the number of population covered by a sanitation option. The

[6] The health and environmental benefits are not enjoyed by the investing household alone.

height of the block represents its net cost to society: above the horizontal x-axis are interventions that are net positive (i.e. price exceeds production cost – hence with market potential) and below the horizontal x-axis are interventions that are net negative (i.e. production cost exceeds price – hence with need to subsidize this market segment).

The unique feature of the cost-curve analysis is to determine pathways to bring sufficient and appropriate private and social sector solutions as well as finance to significantly impact sanitation coverage. It provides a comprehensive context for investments as well as a prioritization framework for the allocation of funds, by identifying effective, scalable, and sustainable sanitation solutions and their associated financing needs and economic attractiveness. It classifies solutions into "business lines" that can be pursued by different agents according to their expertise and interest.

Three different cost curves can be identified – (1) a (financial) market analysis under the status quo, shown in Figure 10.2.1; (2) an economic analysis that builds on the financial analysis, and incorporates the value provided by positive externalities (if a solution can be provided to capture externalities, such as regulation or financing innovations), and (3) the previous cost curve at scale, where producers and providers exploit economies of scale and innovations that are driven by a larger market potential, thus reducing unit costs. This third scenario would be enabled by improved government policies and large-scale funds from financial markets, attracted by the significant externalities afforded by sanitation. The effect of externalities and interventions at scale is to increase the number of measures (i.e. blocks in Figure 10.2.1) that are net positive – that is, with potential for delivery via the private market.

Such a technical tool has several limitations. First, its findings and hence recommendations are limited by the classifications of population groups, technological options, and geographical locations. Second, robust data are not available for all variables, hence requiring sourcing of second-best data sources or assumptions. Third, the higher the scale (e.g. global or national level), the less specific are the recommendations for lower levels such as districts or communes, where contexts may vary significantly. On the other hand, the cost-curve analysis does not aim to be highly precise; its value lies in providing insights into the range of various solutions, and linkages between solutions, which can address the problem at scale. A larger purpose of the tool is to catalyze dialogue between a range of stakeholders, whose involvement and collaboration is key to the solutions. Case studies are therefore urgently needed to apply the cost-curve approach to sanitation and explore its potential.

Bibliography

Addams, L., G. Boccaletti, M. Kerlin, and M. Stuchtey, 2009: Charting our water future: economic frameworks to inform decision making, 2030 Water Resources Group, with McKinsey & Company, London

Ankvist, P.-A., T. Nauclér, and J. Rodander, 2007: McKinsey's greenhouse gas abatement cost curve, *McKinsey Quarterly* **1**, 35–45

Hutton, G. and L. Haller, 2004: *Evaluation of the Non-Health Costs and Benefits of Water and Sanitation Improvements at Global Level*, World Health Organization, WHO/SDE/WSH/04.04

Kirigia, J., L. Sambo, A. Yokouide, E. Soumbey-Alley, L. Muthuri *et al.*, 2009: Economic burden of cholera in the WHO African region, *BMC International Health and Human Rights* **9**

WHO/UNICEF, 2012: Progress on Sanitation and Drinking-Water: 2012 update, WHO/UNICEF Joint Monitoring Programme for Water Supply and Sanitation, Washington, DC

Corruption and Policy Reform

SUSAN ROSE-ACKERMAN AND RORY TRUEX

Policies designed to improve the quality of life for the poor and to spur economic growth often fail. A program that succeeds in one country or even in one village may not work in another. Promising experiments may not be capable of replication and may be impossible to scale up to cover an entire country. Reformers are told: "One size does not fit all." Yet, problems of poor health, low educational attainment, degraded natural environments, and violence and crime are widespread. Why shouldn't similar policies work in various settings? We argue that, over and above substantive differences, a key reason for cross-country differences in policy efficacy is the quality of government and the ubiquity of corruption and related forms of self-dealing by politicians, civil servants, and the private individuals and business interests with whom they interact. A policy that works quite well in one country may fail or be coopted in another with lower-quality governance.

Understanding the incentives for corruption and self-dealing is a precondition for making progress on the other challenges facing the world. A beautifully designed policy that seems to have high net benefits may fail in the face of weak institutions.[1] One response is to urge a crackdown by law-enforcement authorities, but that strategy will seldom be sufficient. Those seeking to further economic development need to understand the institutional origins of corruption and take them into account in designing policies. Certain policies may simply be infeasible because they are riddled with incentives for illicit self-dealing. Others may need to be combined with programs explicitly designed to reduce the incentives for corruption built into existing institutions.

To set the stage for our analysis, the first section summarizes the macro-data on the overall costs of corruption and then reviews research that illustrates the specific mechanisms by which corruption lowers human welfare. The next section explains how corrupt incentives can arise in a variety of contexts. We outline the basic "corruption calculus" that underlies corrupt behavior. Understanding why people and businesses pay and accept bribes and engage in other forms of malfeasance is a necessary first step towards limiting the damage that corruption causes.

We then discuss six linked types of reforms that each can be part of an overall strategy. The third section discusses solutions that involve external monitoring and enforcement combined with the punishment of wrongdoers. Recognizing the limited impact of such strategies, the fourth section concentrates on bottom-up reforms under which the victims of corruption help to limit its incidence. The fifth section discusses internal controls ranging from reforms in the civil service system to the redesign of programs and service delivery to limit the opportunities for illicit gains. The sixth section moves to the top of the government hierarchy to discuss the control of high-level corruption that distorts infrastructure projects, defense spending, privatization of public assets, and concession contracts. The seventh section locates situations where the private market can substitute for the state to limit corrupt incentives. Even when such opportunities exist, however, the process of shifting assets or services from public to private ownership can itself be corrupted. Sometimes a fall in public corruption simply means a rise in private corruption. Finally, the eighth section discusses a set of new initiatives

[1] In an evaluation of a rice-distribution program in Indonesia, Olken (2006) finds that around 18 percent of the rice was lost from the program due to corruption. Under reasonable assumptions, the welfare losses from the missing rice outweigh the redistributive gains.

Figure 11.1 *Citizens' corruption perceptions, 2010: In the past three years, how has the level of corruption changed?*

Source: Data drawn from TI 2010 *Global Corruption Barometer.*
Note: NIS+ includes Armenia, Azerbaijan, Belarus, Georgia, Moldova, Mongolia, Russia, and Ukraine.

at the international level. We conclude with some reflections on the state of the art of quantitative research on corruption and its reform.

The severity of the problem

Corruption is generally defined as the abuse of public power for private gain. This is an umbrella definition, covering behavior as varied as a head of state embezzling public funds or a police officer extorting bribes in the street. Most cross-country data do not distinguish between varieties of corruption, limiting the relevance of these measures as guides to policy. Nevertheless, research suggests that the many types of corruption are highly correlated so that countries can be characterized as more or less corrupt (Treisman, 2007). In proposing reforms, however, it is important to distinguish between grand and petty corruption, as well as between bureaucratic and political corruption, and to consider reforms that account for the special characteristics of particular sectors.

Citizens perceive that corruption, however defined, is on the rise. According to data from the Transparency International (TI) 2010 *Global Corruption Barometer* (GCB), 56 percent of citizens world-wide believe corruption has increased in the past three years (TI, 2010). Surprisingly, this figure is highest in the European Union, where over 73 percent of respondents perceive that their country has experienced an increase. Such overall attitudes suggest that corruption ought to be an on-going object of study, but they are of little help in assessing the specific impact of different types of corruption on political, economic, and social life (Figure 11.1).

Unfortunately, there has been little systematic data collection on sector-specific corruption, but a cross-national survey conducted by TI permits a preliminary assessment. The 2010–11 version of the GCB polled over 100,000 people in 100 countries on their corruption perceptions and experiences. The survey asked respondents whether they had contact with a government institution and, if so, whether they were asked for a bribe. Experiences were collected for nine different government sectors: health, education, legal, police, registry and permit services, tax collection, utilities, land registries, and customs.

Despite its limitations,[2] the GCB provides a window into the way corruption varies across sectors in different countries. For each country and sector, we can measure bribery rates by dividing the number of respondents asked for bribes by the total number of respondents who had contact with the institution. These rates are a loose proxy for the incidence of corruption. Table 11.1 presents bribery rates by sector for the ninety-eight countries in the GCB where complete data are available.

As expected, corruption is more endemic to some sectors than others (Hunt, 2006). On average, 2–9 percent of respondents faced corruption when interacting with the police, while only 9.7 percent experienced corruption in dealing with utility providers. If we look sector by sector, some countries, such as Cambodia and Burundi, report high rates across all sectors. In others, such as Finland, Norway, and the Netherlands, corruption is very uncommon. Especially interesting from a policy perspective are countries that manage to have several quite clean sectors while at the same time others are quite corrupt. They suggest that progress can be made in some areas of service delivery without solving everything at once. Of course, once the data are disaggregated by sector and country their accuracy diminishes as the sample falls, but Table 11.1 nevertheless suggests the value of reforms that take a sectoral approach. The data, although crude, give a sense of where countries overachieve and underachieve.

For example, the Greek police seem to be performing reasonably well, with only 2.9 percent of police interactions resulting in a bribe request. This relative success is in sharp contrast to corruption in Greek hospitals, where almost 20 percent of users reported some form of bribery. Based on the GCB data, Bolivia seems to have the opposite problem. Doctors and hospitals are relatively clean, only 2.9 percent of interactions involved bribery. In the police sector, Bolivia fares much worse than Greece, with a bribery rate of around 48.9 percent.

Collectively, these different forms of corruption can have crippling effects on development and human welfare. Figure 11.2 illustrates the relationship between the UN's Human Development Index (HDI) and perceived levels of corruption in 2010, as measured by TI's Corruption Perceptions Index (CPI). This correlation is one of the most robust relationships to have emerged out of corruption research.[3] Countries with higher levels of corruption have lower levels of human development. Highly corrupt countries tend to underinvest in human capital by spending less on education, overinvesting in public infrastructure relative to private investment, and degrading environmental quality (Mauro, 1998; Tanzi and

[2] Before engaging in cross-national comparisons using the GCB, it is important to note the limitations of the data. First, the questions only capture low-level petty corruption experiences, not grand corruption by high-level officials. Second, differences in reported bribery rates might be driven in part by cultural differences in respondents' willingness to report illicit behavior. Corruption is more openly discussed in some societies than others. There may also be cultural differences in what constitutes a corrupt transaction: a bribe in one country may be considered a gift in another. Third, government institutions may vary significantly across countries, and "registry and permit services" could represent something quite different in Turkey and Ireland, or in Venezuela and Malaysia. Any cross-national comparison assumes that sector definitions hold relatively constant world-wide.

[3] TI, an international organization that advocates for the control of corruption world-wide, has published cross-country data on corruption since 1995. TI collects data from a number of different surveys that mostly report business and expert perceptions of corruption in various countries. Some of the underlying data sources also include questions concerning the overall business environment – asking about red tape, the quality of the courts, etc. Respondents rank the countries on a scale from "excellent" to "poor." The annual TI indices are a compilation of corruption scores. The CPI is an ordinal ranking and does not provide measures of the volume of bribes, the incidence of corruption, or its impact. The World Bank has made use of most of the underlying indices that make up the TI index and has produced its own "graft" index using a different aggregation method and including more countries. It is highly correlated with the TI index. Most studies use one or the other of these indices. Although some countries change position from index to index and have different rankings in the TI and World Bank data, there is an overall stability to the rankings, even given TI's changed methodology covering the 2011 index. These indices are a rough measure of the difficulties of doing business across countries, but they should not be used to make precise bilateral comparisons between closely ranked countries. See www.transparency.org/policy_research/surveys_indices/cpi/2010.

Table 11.1 Percentage of citizens encountering bribery, by sector, by country, 2010–2011

	Edu.	Legal	Health	Police	Permits	Util.	Tax	Land	Cust.
Global	11.0	22.6	12.1	29.0	17.3	9.7	9.5	19.8	22.7
	–	–	–	–	–	–	–	–	–
Afghanistan	22.0	70.2	21.9	53.2	43.7	26.8	60.7	43.9	67.3
Argentina	0.6	7.2	2.6	21.5	8.7	3.9	3.3	5.5	5.5
Armenia	12.4	16.9	19.4	38.9	17.4	1.6	10.4	17.7	21.1
Australia	1.9	11.4	1.2	3.2	4.7	1.1	1.5	2.3	2.5
Austria	3.8	3.4	6.4	4.3	3.6	4.5	3.3	5.4	–
Azerbaijan	29.8	43.6	46.0	55.7	40.4	7.0	5.9	23.8	44.3
Bangladesh	27.8	63.9	18.1	83.6	48.8	36.0	18.7	47.8	12.4
Belarus	14.5	20.9	22.2	26.6	12.3	2.9	12.7	12.6	30.8
Bolivia	13.3	43.3	2.9	48.9	18.8	1.4	3.5	11.1	38.0
Bosnia and Herzegovina	9.3	10.2	17.3	20.4	9.4	2.2	1.9	11.9	8.9
Brazil	0.5	1.6	1.8	5.7	2.8	3.0	1.5	0.9	–
Bulgaria	3.2	11.4	5.8	16.2	5.8	1.3	1.3	2.7	12.6
Burundi	46.2	41.2	75.3	34.8	49.0	80.9	37.9	39.2	38.9
Cambodia	72.5	79.9	63.2	82.3	77.5	55.0	58.6	68.9	76.2
Cameroon	33.5	48.0	23.8	67.4	30.3	18.6	31.9	27.5	66.3
Canada	2.6	3.6	2.2	2.8	3.2	1.4	2.0	4.9	1.6
Chile	8.0	14.8	12.8	5.4	11.2	10.6	9.9	11.1	10.2
China	3.7	13.9	10.7	9.4	9.8	5.6	7.8	10.3	28.2
Colombia	5.8	18.2	8.7	31.1	17.1	10.5	5.8	11.2	25.0
Croatia	1.1	2.2	4.2	5.1	3.7	1.5	2.2	3.7	–
Czech Republic	3.0	4.1	11.0	7.3	8.9	1.3	1.2	8.9	2.2
Democratic Republic of the Congo	54.0	61.7	21.7	63.6	51.6	42.1	51.6	51.4	48.3
Denmark	0.1	0.6	0.3	–	0.3	0.2	0.3	0.3	–
El Salvador	2.5	8.7	1.0	42.6	14.6	2.3	1.3	4.4	14.5
Ethiopia	8.9	55.1	12.4	43.8	43.3	15.0	40.7	49.6	63.7
Fiji	6.2	7.5	6.2	4.5	7.2	4.4	5.7	9.7	9.8
Finland	1.7	0.8	1.0	0.5	0.5	0.8	0.9	0.9	1.4
France	3.3	2.3	5.1	2.2	3.4	3.6	3.4	8.2	5.4
FYR Macedonia	10.2	20.6	16.2	16.1	7.6	3.9	2.9	9.0	25.8
Georgia	0.9	5.3	2.9	3.2	0.8	1.3	–	–	–
Germany	1.2	0.7	0.7	1.6	1.9	0.9	0.2	0.8	1.1
Ghana	20.2	24.3	10.9	59.1	27.4	11.4	7.6	21.3	56.5
Greece	1.2	1.7	19.9	2.9	4.4	2.1	3.1	4.9	16.9
Hong Kong	2.6	9.3	3.9	6.3	5.2	2.4	2.5	2.5	2.9
Hungary	3.5	1.1	26.2	2.3	3.4	3.6	1.3	3.8	7.2
Iceland	1.9	3.2	1.8	2.7	2.3	1.7	2.4	9.3	2.6
India	22.8	44.8	25.8	63.8	62.3	47.3	50.6	62.5	40.9

(cont.)

Table 11.1 (*cont.*)

	Edu.	Legal	Health	Police	Permits	Util.	Tax	Land	Cust.
Indonesia	2.1	14.3	15.8	10.9	10.2	6.8	7.8	9.1	15.4
Iraq	34.4	49.4	33.4	63.5	54.5	47.2	48.6	50.9	58.6
Ireland	2.1	2.6	2.0	1.7	2.2	2.3	1.4	5.5	2.5
Israel	2.0	2.2	4.0	1.4	2.0	3.0	1.3	3.4	1.2
Italy	5.6	29.6	10.0	3.8	6.4	8.7	6.9	13.0	14.5
Japan	2.3	14.1	7.4	5.5	5.3	8.5	8.6	9.1	–
Kenya	15.1	42.8	15.6	59.3	30.4	9.2	14.0	32.6	24.7
Korea (South)	5.5	7.7	0.7	3.2	1.4	1.2	1.8	2.5	5.3
Kosovo	4.0	9.6	14.1	2.8	7.3	2.2	3.0	1.5	11.9
Latvia	6.1	11.0	15.3	20.9	7.0	1.5	2.9	6.4	5.8
Lebanon	10.9	29.1	12.8	37.9	38.4	13.1	10.5	31.5	46.7
Liberia	75.7	78.3	50.4	86.1	64.6	36.9	62.8	54.5	76.0
Lithuania	9.7	23.4	35.4	32.1	13.9	1.6	3.0	16.2	23.7
Luxembourg	8.7	2.4	12.6	11.1	12.0	9.2	9.1	6.3	3.7
Malawi	26.0	39.4	13.7	56.9	43.8	36.2	11.9	19.4	41.1
Malaysia	1.9	–	1.8	23.9	4.6	3.9	–	12.5	8.0
Maldives	3.0	2.5	2.7	2.0	5.6	5.2	3.4	6.7	8.9
Mexico	9.4	48.5	10.0	50.4	19.3	11.2	9.3	4.9	12.9
Moldova	24.9	32.8	32.9	46.4	17.4	3.9	9.4	23.4	22.8
Mongolia	30.1	40.8	29.2	48.4	28.0	6.3	15.9	42.0	45.5
Mozambique	35.1	20.8	39.4	47.8	34.6	20.8	9.4	21.8	32.5
Nepal	11.8	20.7	9.5	24.5	24.8	9.1	28.9	30.9	45.0
Netherlands	2.0	–	1.4	2.3	3.2	1.1	1.4	–	0.4
New Zealand	2.1	1.7	2.1	3.3	2.8	2.9	1.7	2.5	2.1
Nigeria	33.5	38.8	16.8	78.2	21.8	43.0	38.5	31.3	51.7
Norway	0.5	1.1	0.4	0.4	0.8	0.8	1.2	1.6	1.4
Pakistan	16.5	28.8	20.1	63.5	51.9	49.1	43.4	63.2	49.7
Palestine	26.5	31.1	27.4	28.9	32.0	28.2	26.3	39.4	42.9
Peru	6.2	28.8	4.4	33.0	10.9	3.8	3.0	3.8	17.0
Philippines	7.2	8.8	4.7	32.3	16.6	3.2	10.0	18.7	50.0
Poland	1.8	9.7	16.3	12.5	8.9	1.6	1.5	7.3	5.0
Portugal	0.9	1.9	2.2	2.7	6.3	2.8	1.0	1.0	–
Romania	8.8	13.9	29.5	17.0	11.5	2.6	3.3	6.8	6.6
Russia	18.7	17.9	21.3	28.3	8.7	3.4	6.1	20.3	11.0
Rwanda	14.1	20.9	4.2	42.0	21.5	13.8	15.9	22.8	31.7
Senegal	25.7	47.8	26.6	55.5	49.9	12.3	30.6	46.5	69.9
Serbia	4.3	13.6	13.2	15.1	3.5	2.1	3.1	6.6	12.6
Sierra Leone	57.3	64.5	46.7	75.2	46.5	34.3	27.5	60.2	67.1
Singapore	3.9	18.6	8.3	8.4	8.8	5.2	8.1	17.1	13.1
Slovenia	2.0	4.0	3.3	2.4	1.9	1.3	1.0	2.3	4.3

Table 11.1 (*cont.*)

	Edu.	Legal	Health	Police	Permits	Util.	Tax	Land	Cust.
Solomon Islands	12.1	15.1	9.5	11.2	15.3	8.9	13.8	18.9	10.2
South Africa	7.9	20.5	13.0	44.1	41.4	15.0	4.0	3.8	12.7
Southern Sudan	32.4	43.1	30.9	46.6	45.7	35.1	38.2	41.3	39.2
Spain	2.5	3.1	2.3	3.6	2.7	1.6	1.9	4.3	6.5
Sri Lanka	17.4	19.5	6.2	32.1	15.6	5.3	63.0	30.0	33.3
Sudan	5.0	10.6	7.2	29.2	10.5	6.1	13.7	11.8	23.5
Switzerland	0.3	2.0	0.4	2.1	0.8	1.1	0.4	0.7	4.0
Taiwan	4.0	11.8	7.4	7.6	2.2	2.8	3.3	7.6	11.1
Tanzania	28.9	45.7	32.7	47.5	22.7	24.7	24.9	24.4	39.4
Thailand	7.7	18.8	13.6	15.8	11.6	5.2	14.9	10.1	14.1
Turkey	33.7	26.5	23.3	29.0	31.7	27.7	34.8	32.2	32.4
Uganda	36.1	59.6	50.0	80.8	51.6	40.7	40.5	48.1	45.8
UK	1.4	3.3	0.6	0.9	3.6	0.9	1.2	4.3	4.5
Ukraine	19.8	22.7	33.3	38.5	25.9	8.6	14.2	29.9	29.5
USA	6.5	8.4	3.2	5.7	9.1	4.1	5.6	12.5	18.3
Vanuatu	8.0	8.7	9.4	7.8	9.0	5.8	13.9	7.6	14.0
Venezuela	6.4	20.3	5.1	28.5	25.1	0.9	7.1	16.0	28.3
Vietnam	35.7	16.7	29.4	49.3	22.7	4.2	19.9	25.3	30.8
Yemen	46.6	53.6	31.8	63.7	55.6	25.3	55.0	48.4	67.2
Zambia	21.5	13.1	18.0	38.4	19.7	10.3	6.5	9.1	24.8
Zimbabwe	17.6	31.9	11.1	52.8	38.5	24.2	13.8	14.5	35.8

Source: Transparency International, *Global Corruption Barometer, 2010/2011.*

Davoodi, 2001; Esty and Porter, 2002). However, some countries have managed to have high levels of human development despite high levels of corruption, showing that the relationship is far from deterministic.

In general, richer countries and those with high growth rates have less reported corruption and better functioning governments (Kaufmann, 2003). Estimates of the precise magnitudes of these effects vary. Dreher and Herzfeld (2005) find that an increase of corruption by 1 index point dampens GDP growth by 13 basis points (i.e. 0.13 percentage points) and lowers *per capita* GDP by around $425. Gyimah-Brempong (2002) estimates the effect to be between 75 and 90 basis points or just under 1 percentage point.[4] Aidt (2011) constructs a broader index of sustainable development and shows that corruption, however it is measured, has a detrimental effect. Corruption in Aidt's formulation might spur investment and growth in the short run, but this could have negative effects in the long run if the projects chosen do little to enhance long-term growth and poverty reduction.

Furthermore, the data in Figure 11.3 show that, within countries, low-income respondents tend to experience higher bribery rates than higher-income

[4] There is a fundamental difficulty in using an index of corruption to measure the impact of corruption on growth or GDP. The index is a measure with no obvious physical counterpart and with a minimum and a maximum (or in the World Bank index, a zero mean) determined by the researcher. Thus, it is not clear exactly how to interpret the numbers reported in the text.

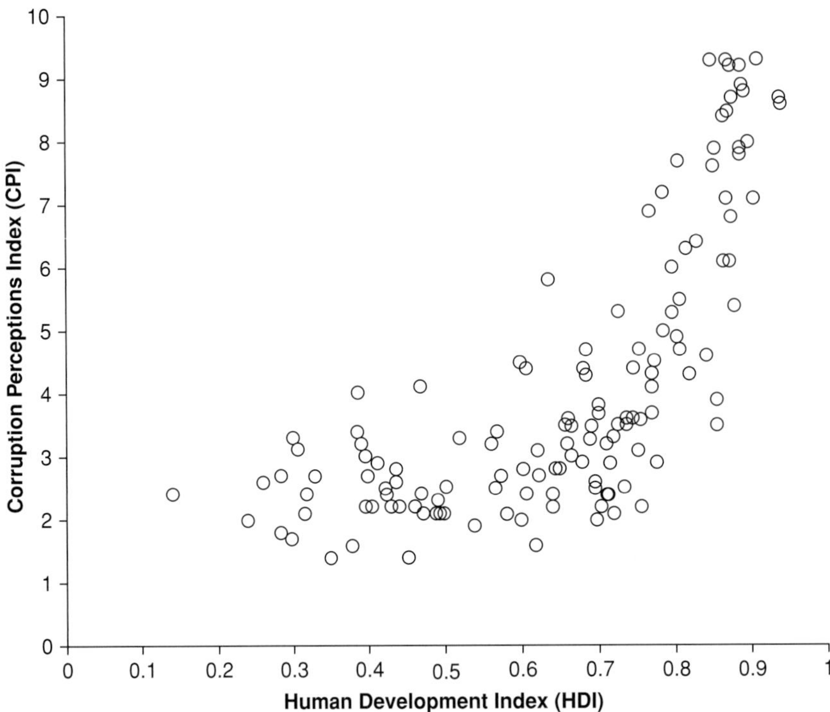

Figure 11.2 *Human development and corruption levels, 2010*

Note: CPI drawn from TI website. HDI drawn from UNDP Human Development Reports website.

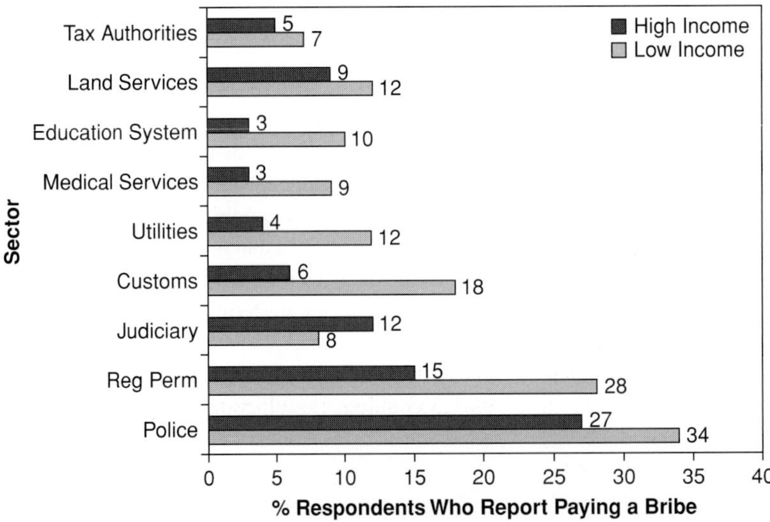

Figure 11.3 *Bribery incidence across income groups, 2010*

Note: Results drawn from TI 2010 *Global Corruption Barometer*. Percentages are weighted and calculated for respondents who came in contact with the services listed. Figures reflect experiences of those people surveyed in the *Barometer*.

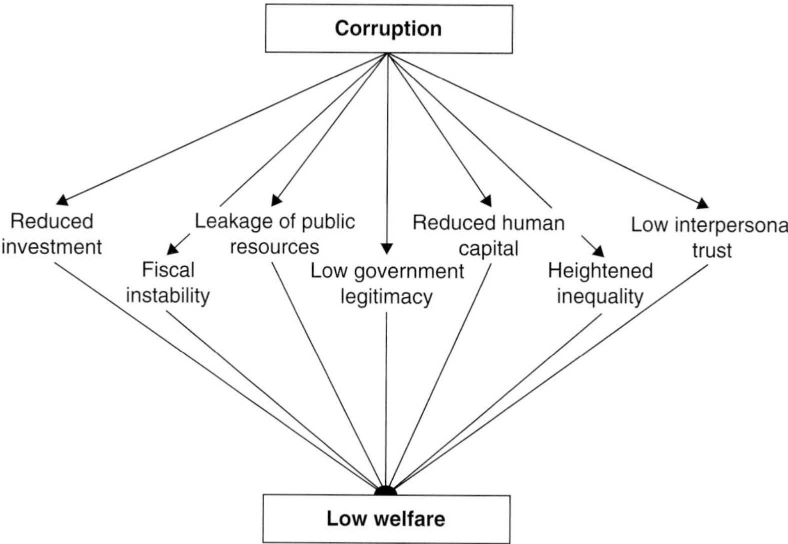

Figure 11.4 *The many consequences of corruption*

individuals. This is true across every government sector except the judiciary.

Much of this work does not deal with the simultaneous-equation nature of the relationship. It leaves unclear whether low levels of income and growth are a consequence or a cause of corruption.[5] Most likely, the causal arrow runs both ways, creating vicious or virtuous spirals (Lambsdorff, 2006; Treisman, 2007). Thus, we must examine more focused research that concentrates on isolating the mechanisms through which corruption reduces growth and human welfare. These links are summarized in Figure 11.4, although more complex interactions are also possible.

First, corruption negatively affects the business and investment climate. Corrupt countries tend to suffer from more bureaucratic red tape, which may be intentionally created by rent-seeking bureaucrats. According to Wei (2000), an increase in the corruption level from relatively clean Singapore to relatively corrupt Mexico is the equivalent of an increase in the tax rate of over 20 percentage points. Lambsdorff (2003a, 2003b) finds that improving Colombia's level of integrity to that of the United Kingdom would increase net yearly capital inflows by 3 percent of GDP. According to World Bank research in Bangladesh, China, India, and Pakistan, firm export levels and foreign investment were higher where hassles and delays were low. To help one understand the magnitude of the effects, the authors report that, "if Calcutta could attain Shanghai's level of investment climate, the share of firms . . . exporting would nearly double from the current 24 percent to 47 percent, comparable to the coastal Chinese cities. Similarly, the share of foreign-invested firms would increase by more than half, from the current 2.5 percent of firms, to 3.9 percent" (Dollar *et al.*, 2006).

There is evidence that corruption distorts firms' production decisions. Thus, Sequeira and Djankov (2010) study bribe payments for cargo passing through customs in ports in Maputo, Mozambique, and Durban, South Africa for a random sample of 1,300 shipments ultimately headed for South Africa. On average, bribes represent 14 percent of

[5] There is also some skepticism over whether the corruption and GDP growth correlation is driven by faulty measurement, specifically the use of perceptions-based corruption measures. Treisman (2007) and Aidt (2009) find no strong relationship between corruption experiences and growth.

the shipping costs for a standard container passing through the port of Maputo and 4 percent of shipping costs for a standard container passing through Durban. They show that some shippers bear higher transport costs in order to ship through the low-bribery jurisdiction and that South African firms are more likely to use domestic suppliers when bribery raises the costs of imports. Corruption in customs creates important distortions in the real economy.

A second mechanism through which corruption dampens development is by inflating the budgetary costs of public goods and services because these costs incorporate kickbacks. Corrupt demands from officials are analogous to a tax on businesses and households, but the consequences are much more pernicious. Bribes are paid to obtain and retain business. Unless the procurement process is very competitive, this means that individual projects and procurement contracts are excessively expensive and unproductive.[6] Cole and Anh (2011) document the magnitude of these costs in an Asian country by examining the account books of two firms. One firm sold industrial parts and reported kickback demands from both private and public buyers, although the level and incidence of kickbacks were higher for government and military sales than for other buyers. They show a statistically significant positive relationship between the profit margin and the size of the pay-off that is almost dollar for dollar. The second firm sold imported pharmaceuticals to public and private hospitals and faced widespread kickback demands from both types. In the former most of the gains flowed to the managers, and in the latter, the hospitals benefitted. Overall pay-offs roughly double the prices of the drugs. If this study can be generalized to other countries and firms, it suggests that the impact of corruption on development is not limited to pay-offs to public officials but extends to private – private dealings as well. It also suggests that if the distortionary effect of kickbacks is not equal across sectors, then that difference will distort the government's programmatic choices. If corrupt officials set priorities, they will set priorities to maximize their pay-offs. If honest officials set priorities, they will use the distorted information on costs that results from the distribution of corrupt kickbacks.

Third, if tax collectors accept pay-offs, the impact on the government budget is direct. One researcher reports that at least half of tax collections are lost to corruption in some countries (Fjeldstad, 2005). In Bolivia, one study estimated that 42 percent of the VAT was lost in 2001; reforms reduced the loss to 29 percent in 2004 (Zuleta *et al.*, 2006). In 2004, Russia reported losing $4.5 billion in duties on goods imported from Europe. Bangladesh in 2000 lost duties equal to 5 percent of GDP, and that figure omits the discouragement of potential investors caused by the corrupt regime (OECD, 2003: 9). Corrupt countries may also be reluctant to balance their budgets during times of financial crises because this would reduce the level of rents available. Using a dataset for twenty-eight OECD countries spanning the period 1978–2007, Peren *et al.* (2011) find that corruption significantly reduces the probability of successful budget consolidation.

In circumstances of low government legitimacy, citizens try to avoid paying taxes, and firms go underground to hide from the burden of bureaucracy. Cole and Anh (2011: 419–24) show how this can be done through the examination of the official and the internal books of an Asian construction firm. In this firm, accounting manipulation to lower taxes mostly involved reporting excess costs for materials and machinery, not labor. High levels of perceived corruption are associated with high levels of tax evasion (Uslaner, 2007). Similarly, Torgler's (2003) study of attitudes toward tax evasion in Central and Eastern Europe (CEE) shows that when individuals perceived that corruption was high, they were less likely to say that people have an obligation to pay taxes. Thus, one indirect impact of corruption is to persuade people that it is acceptable not to pay taxes because the government has been captured by corrupt officials, violating norms of fairness. As a consequence, corrupt governments tend to be smaller than more honest governments,

[6] In a somewhat competitive procurement market, bribes could both reduce firm excess profits and inflate costs. If suppliers collude with each other and corrupt officials to keep prices high, most of the costs of corruption will be shifted to the government budget. See Rose-Ackerman (1978) and Lambert-Mogiliansky (2011).

everything else equal (Friedman *et al.*, 2000; Johnson *et al.*, 2000).

Fourth, corruption negatively affects service delivery and human capital because goods and services leak out of the system before reaching their final recipients. In Uganda, estimates from the 1990s suggested that 40–94 percent of drugs simply disappeared (McPake *et al.*, 1999: 855–6). The Brazilian federal police authorities estimated that embezzlement in the pharmaceutical sector totaled $637 million (Colitt, 2004). In an Indonesian program designed to provide food aid to the poor, at least 18 percent of the rice was lost; in one-third of the villages 43 percent disappeared (Olken, 2006). Ferraz *et al.* (2010) show that students in Brazilian municipalities where corruption was detected in education have test scores that are 0.35 standard deviations lower than those without corruption, as well as higher dropout and failure rates. Teachers in corrupt municipalities are less likely to have a computer or science lab and less likely to have received formal training, presumably because resources have leaked out of the system.

Public Expenditure Tracking Surveys (PETS), a monitoring tool developed by the World Bank, reveal similar estimates of the loss of funds and goods. The first PETS was conducted in Uganda and found that only 13 percent of an annual capitation grant actually reached the intended beneficiary schools (Reinikka and Svennson, 2004). Such leakage undermines the efforts of both governments and donors. In turn, poor service delivery reduces the accumulation of human and physical capital with obvious negative effects on growth. This effect may be particularly acute for the poor because, as we showed above, they tend to report paying bribes more frequently. In a corrupt system the allocation of services will have little to do with need or qualifications, but rather reflects WTP (Bertrand *et al.*, 2007).

Fifth, corruption likely has negative effects on "softer outcomes," such as popular satisfaction with government and democratic legitimacy. Corruption can undermine government competence (Piga, 2011). In a country with high levels of corruption, competence may not be a worthwhile attribute of public officials. Much higher benefits can be obtained through networking activities that give one access to the dominant, corrupt crony- and patronage-dominated environment. The resulting pervasive technical incompetence makes the corrupt system run much more smoothly because of the absence of accurate and precise monitoring and the ease of capture. This interaction, in turn, undermines public trust in government.

Low levels of trust may ultimately contribute to political instability and internal turmoil. Interviews in a range of countries have found widespread popular disapproval of entrenched corruption (Pasuk and Sungsidh, 1994; Anderson *et al.*, 2003). In a study of four Latin American countries, Seligson (2002) finds that citizens who had personally experienced a corrupt act reported lower levels of interpersonal trust and belief in the political system. In Nicaragua, respondents were asked if the payment of bribes "facilitates getting things done in the bureaucracy." Interestingly, those who agreed that corruption gets things done were less likely to believe in the legitimacy of the political system.[7] The corruption–legitimacy finding has been replicated across a number of other countries and contexts (Anderson and Tverdova, 2003; Chang and Chu, 2006).

In short, corruption is a lynchpin problem that both curbs growth and investment and exacerbates other problems associated with weak states and poverty. Efforts to improve educational outcomes will be frustrated by absentee teachers, missing school supplies, and inadequate buildings. Efforts to improve infrastructure will be burdened with nepotism and inflated costs. Efforts to mitigate disease will be thwarted if medical supplies are stolen and sold on the black market.

With this summary as background, the next section outlines the fundamental conditions under

[7] One study of CEE shows that people disapprove of corruption even if they report engaging in it themselves (Miller *et al.*, 2001). Although experience with corruption varied markedly across the countries, the public's underlying values and norms did not differ greatly. A majority in each country expressed strong moral disapproval of pay-offs but, at the same time, a plurality of citizens in every country except the Czech Republic said they would pay a bribe if asked.

which corruption can flourish. That analysis provides a framework on which to build our discussion of efforts, both successful and unsuccessful, to reduce corruption.

The corruption calculus

Corruption is a crime of opportunity. It occurs at the intersection between the public and private sectors (or even entirely within a sector) wherever the opportunity for illicit private economic gain exists. Identifying an act as "corrupt" implies a background standard of acceptable behavior. Thus, its prevalence depends upon the way law and society define the proper scope for public and private action.

A. kleptocracy, cronyism, and corruption

In a state controlled by an autocrat who does not recognize any distinction between public and private funds, bribery, fraud, and other forms of under-the-table pay-offs may be uncommon. The state is simply organized as a personal, kleptocratic fiefdom. It is "corrupt" in the sense that the ruler has no concern for the general welfare. The population is impoverished, and the economy is monopolized by "public" firms controlled by the ruler. Such states, of course, face serious problems of governance, because their rulers do not recognize the distinction between public and private power.[8] It is a sign of progress when those with political power recognize that it is illegitimate for them to use their power to accumulate wealth.

Closely related to such kleptocratic regimes are ones where the state largely serves the interests of a narrow group of business people and politicians, sometimes with criminal elements mixed in. Even if the group with influence changes when the government changes, most of the citizens are left out. In Michael Johnston's taxonomy, the contrast is between "power chasing wealth" and "wealth chasing power" (Johnston, 2005). For example, Russia may be moving from a case where private wealth controlled public power to one where political power dominates private wealth.

In some states where the link between the political and the economic elite is strong, favored firms may not have secure property rights in the legal sense, but they obtain beneficial treatment because of their insider status (Hellman *et al.*, 2003). Political connections can operate much like outright pay-offs to distort investment priorities. In a study of 20,202 publicly traded firms in 467 countries, Faccio (2006) finds that having politicians as board members or substantial shareholders brings a 2.29 percent increase in share value. Political connections may promote short-run economic growth, although it is likely to be unbalanced and inequitable and to limit long-term growth prospects (Rock and Bonnett, 2004; Aidt, 2011). A study of bank loans in Pakistan by Khwaja and Mian (2005) found that firms with a politician on their boards borrow 45 percent more than other firms but have a 50 percent higher default rate on these loans. Because only government-owned banks provide special treatment, the excess defaults are a cost to taxpayers. They estimate the deadweight loss at between 0.15 percent and 0.30 percent of GDP. In addition, many of these bad loans presumably financed projects that did not make economic sense *ex ante*. If so, then Pakistan loses an additional 1.6 percent of GDP per year due to preferential lending.

In such polities the main risk to the economic elite is a change in political leadership. For example, in a study of Indonesia under President Suharto, Fisman (2001) used an index of the political connectedness of firms listed on the Jakarta Stock Exchange, dubbed the "Suharto Dependency Index." He demonstrates that rumors about Suharto's health problems between 1995 and 1997 had a more negative impact on the share prices of firms with high levels of this index and that the differential impact was greater the worse the rumors.[9]

[8] See, for example, some of the cases examined in Barma *et al.* (2011), which discusses the special problems that can arise in natural resource-rich states controlled by a small elite. On the case of Angola, see the reports of the Christian Michelson Institute, Norway, www.cmi.no/angola.

[9] Of course, Suharto did actually resign from office in May 1998 but, as Fisman points out, this is a difficult event to study within his framework because so many other things were happening at the same time: the "event window" was

Sustained corruption can itself undermine political legitimacy, shortening the time horizon of both rulers and investors, and prompting regime change (Rose-Ackerman, 1999: 32). However, the more democratic regimes that emerged in several of the countries studied by Rock and Bonnett (2004: 1101) have had to confront corrupt networks that now work to undermine growth.[10] If top political figures themselves exploit their position for private gain, the effectiveness of government programs and the impact of foreign aid and lending suffers. This inequality of influence can extend beyond special treatment by the executive and the legislature to include the courts as well.

In this chapter we leave to one side such political systems where either regime change or a drastic change of heart at the top is a precondition for reform. We focus, instead, on the structural conditions that create corrupt incentives in states that are nominally organized to benefit their citizens, whether or not they have strong democratic institutions. Thus, we concentrate on situations where private gains are available to officials and to private actors, if they take advantage of the opportunities created by public programs. We recognize that similar conditions may exist entirely within the private sector (Argandona, 2010), especially in large firms, but our focus here is on public sector corruption and its connection with private wealth and public power.

High- and low-level corruption

Corruption can occur when the state engages in large-scale projects that generate massive rents that can be shared between corrupt officials and their private sector counterparts. However, corruption is not just a phenomenon that occurs at the large scale. Although the misallocation of resources may be most dramatic in large projects, day-to-day petty corruption has an immediate impact on people's lives. The basic causes are similar – a scarce public benefit, or one that can be made scarce by corrupt officials – and monitoring difficulties. The gain to the citizen may be access to a public service or the "benefit" of not having the law enforced against her, whether or not she is a lawbreaker. Examples are numerous, but consider just a few. Suppose there are a limited number of places in subsidized housing so that the households that qualify exceed the available apartments. People may pay to be put at the head of the queue, and officials may manage the queue to maximize bribe revenue. Licenses to operate a motor vehicle are not limited in number but are only available to those who qualify. Officials may refuse to award licenses even to those who qualify unless they are paid, and licenses may also be awarded to the unqualified. Tax collectors may accept a pay-off in return for issuing a low tax bill, and inspectors of all kinds can be paid to issue favorable reports. Operators of illegal or unregistered businesses can pay the police to avoid being shut down, and bribes can be levied on ordinary citizens by police to avoid being charged with real or invented offenses (Fried *et al.*, 2009; Peisakhin and Pinto, 2010).

The incidence of both high- and low-level corruption not only depends upon the opportunities available, as determined by the level of rents and the ability to keep pay-offs secret. It also depends upon the effectiveness of measures designed to deter malfeasance. If the law-enforcement system is itself corrupt or simply incompetent, it will not matter much if people know that corruption occurs. Even if the law-enforcement system is honest, it may be understaffed and underfunded. Expected formal punishment is often minimal. However, structural policies can limit corruption even in the face of weak law enforcement, and we outline some of these below. These policies limit the rents in public programs without undermining their basic purposes. They also improve transparency and accountability – both top-down and bottom-up – so

several months long, the successor was a Suharto ally, and trading volumes were exceptionally low by the end of 1997. Perhaps for these reasons, the relationship did not hold in the beginning of 1998 except for steep declines in the shares of firms controlled by Suharto's children. (Fisman, 2001).

[10] See also studies of the former Communist states in Europe and Central Asia. Although administrative corruption is a problem throughout the regions, state capture is a particularly serious problem in the countries of the former Soviet Union (FSU). In such situations the firms that do the capturing perform well, but overall economic growth suffers (Hellman *et al.*, 2003). Fries *et al.* (2003: 31–2) document the differences between "captor" firms with insider status and "non-captor" firms. The former have higher growth rates of fixed capital, revenue, and productivity.

that corruption is exposed and controlled through techniques other than the criminal law. Of course, the criminal law is a necessary background condition, but it will generally be insufficient unless other institutions support the development of honest and effective government (Rose-Ackerman, 2010).

An implication of the above discussion is that the lower the level of rents created by the public sector, the less the incentive for corrupt pay-offs. A highly competitive, open economy where most firms do not earn monopoly rents ought to be less corrupt than a closed, monopolistic one. Indeed, some studies find that trade openness and other measures of competitiveness are associated with less corruption (Ades and Di Tella, 1999, Sandholtz and Koetzle, 2000, Blake and Martin, 2006). However, the direction of causation is unclear. Corrupt officials may create and maintain private monopolies in return for corrupt pay-offs. The causes of corruption may be deeper than the organization of the private sector, which may not be exogenous. Lambsdorff (2003a), for example, finds that weak law and order and insecure property rights encourage corruption that, in turn, discourages foreign capital inflows.

If inequality and poverty lower the level of public oversight, both can contribute to high levels of corruption. In democracies, in particular, inequality is linked to corruption, a result consistent with state-capture. The negative effect of inequality on growth may be the result of its effect on corruption, taken as a proxy for government weakness (You and Khagram, 2005). Here, too, the causal arrow goes both ways. Extreme inequality suggests that a wealthy elite controls the state by paying off officials to provide that elite with benefits.

Corruption and history

Cross-country differences in perceived corruption levels may have historical and social roots. For example, Acemoglu *et al.* (2001) use the mortality rates of European settlers as an instrument for the type of colonial regime put in place by the imperial power and find that it does a good job of predicting expropriation risk (and corruption levels) at the end of the twentieth century. La Porta *et al.* (1999) consider legal origin, religion, ethno-linguistic fractionalization, latitude, and *per capita* income as determinants of a range of features of economic, social, and political life. Corruption and other measures of institutional weakness are worse in countries with higher ethno-linguistic fragmentation, few Protestants, and socialist or French legal origins. (See also Sandholtz and Koetzle, 2000; Treisman, 2000.)

Colonial heritage, legal traditions, religion, and geographical factors seem associated with corruption and other measures of government dysfunction. One can understand why that might be so by studying the different ways that rents are created, maintained, and shared under different systems. However, these factors are not policy variables that present-day reformers can influence. The key issue is whether these historical regularities directly affect government quality or whether they help determine intermediate institutions and attitudes that present-day policies can affect. In La Porta *et al.* (1999), the historical variables are not always significant and become entirely insignificant when their studies include income and latitude as explanatory variables. Historical patterns may operate through their impact on underlying institutional structures, not as direct determinants of corruption. If so, that may be good news for reformers who concentrate on the institutional conditions for corruption and its reform. So long as there are alternative routes to institutional reforms that facilitate economic growth and high income, latitude and history need not be destiny (Rodrik, 2006).

Corruption and democracy

The impact of democracy on corruption is complex. Democracies generally function with higher levels of transparency and public accountability than non-democracies, and that fact should help control corruption. High levels of economic freedom and lower levels of corruption go together, as does an index of democratization (e.g. Sandholtz and Koetzle, 2000; Kunicová and Rose-Ackerman, 2005; Blake and Martin, 2006). Governments with more female participation in politics are less corrupt, and this is consistent with survey evidence suggesting that women are better monitors because, in general, they are more disapproving of corruption than men (Swamy *et al.*, 2001). Within the universe of democracies, elements of constitutional structures – such as presidentialism, closed-list proportional representation, and federalism – facilitate corruption (Treisman, 2000; Kunicová and Rose-Ackerman, 2005).[11] Presidential systems that use proportional representation (PR) to elect their legislature are more corrupt than other types of democracies. Many parliamentary democracies that elect legislatures by plurality rule have a heritage of British colonial rule, and many PR systems had French or Spanish rulers. Present-day levels of freedom also have historical roots. However, if constitutional form, protection of rights, women's rights, and electoral institutions are important determinants in and of themselves, then countries have policy levers available even if their histories led to institutions that favor corruption.

Summing up

To summarize, corruption, like any other crime, occurs when the illicit benefits of malfeasance outweigh the expected costs. However, a distinctive feature of corruption is its two-sided nature. Like any illicit market transaction, both the bribe-payer and the recipient must experience net gains relative to the feasible alternatives. The benefits of corruption to officials include the bribe payment itself as well as the social benefits that come with dealing out illicit favors. Corruption may also allow a bureaucrat or politician to expand his political power. On the cost side of the equation, corrupt officials consider the prospect of formal punishment, as well as the internal moral "psychic costs" of engaging in wrongdoing.[12] If discovered, corrupt officials may also face social opprobrium and the loss of office. On the other side of the transaction, corrupt partners balance the illicit benefits earned through bribery against expected punishments and psychic costs. If officials extort pay-offs by requiring citizens and businesses to pay to get benefits to which they are legally entitled (or to avoid costs), those who pay feel aggrieved, but they are still better off than doing without the benefit (or having a cost imposed on them).

Another distinctive feature of corruption is its tendency to feed on itself (Cadot, 1987, Goel and Rich, 1989; Andvig and Moene, 1990). The more corrupt players there are in the system, the more it pays to be corrupt because the likelihood of both formal and informal punishment is reduced. Bureaucrats who would be honest in Sweden could turn corrupt in Cambodia with no change in their underlying psychology. Conversely, clean governance begets clean governance, as would-be corrupt officials become clean when corrupt networks dry up and self-dealing becomes dangerous and uncouth. The net result of these vicious and virtuous cycles is that countries and sectors can fall into either a high-corruption or a low-corruption equilibrium. And once trapped in a high-corruption equilibrium, a particularly large shock may be needed to shift a country on the path towards good governance. These dynamics are illustrated in Figure 11.5.

The big question facing reformers is how best to produce that shock. The macro-level factors discussed here – inequality, democratic institutions, religion, market structure – are not typically the subject of policy interventions. Reformers need to focus on shifting individual components of the corruption calculus in the right direction, reducing rents, and increasing expected costs. Recent anti-corruption successes seem associated with this sort of "right away and all at once" approach. In Georgia, for example, new leadership embarked on an ambitious large-scale anti-corruption campaign in 2004 – trying high-level corrupt officials, retraining and turning over the bureaucracy, removing bureaucratic discretion, among other things. By 2010, less than 2 percent of citizens had reported paying bribes in the previous year (World Bank, 2012). The column for Georgia in Table 11.1 is consistent with these results. With the right combination of reforms, the corruption calculus can be tipped towards clean governance.

[11] Fjeldstad (2003) reviews the literature on decentralization and corruption and cites studies that contradict the results for federalism found in the sources listed in the text. In any case, it is important to distinguish between federalism and explicit policies designed to empower those at the grassroots.

[12] Recent survey evidence from Nepal suggests that anti-corruption attitudes grow stronger with education (Truex, 2011).

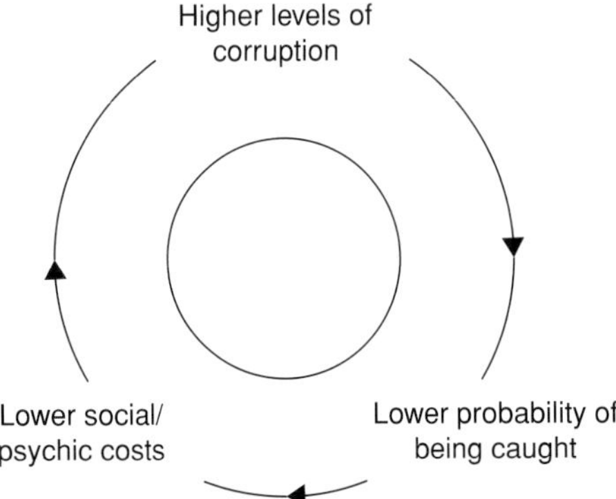

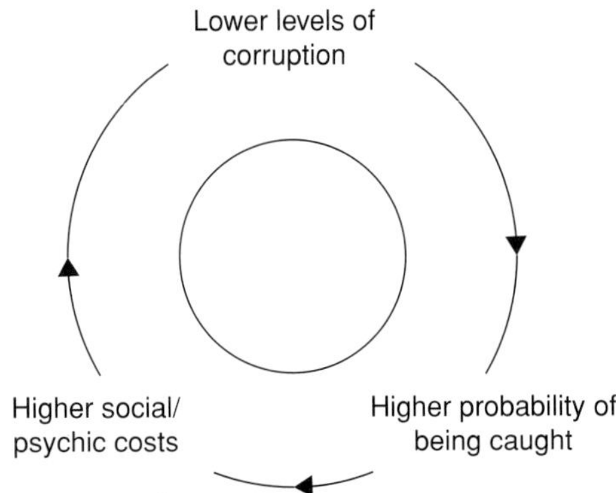

Figure 11.5 *Vicious and virtuous cycles*

Solution 1: external monitoring and punishment

Perhaps the most often prescribed remedy for corruption is to increase top-down monitoring and punishment. The logic is straightforward. Improved monitoring, whether in the form of an external auditor, an anti-corruption agency, or an international oversight body, increases the probability of being caught. Severe punishment also pushes the cost-benefit calculus towards clean government.

There is some evidence that increased monitoring does have positive effects on government performance, reducing the leakage of funds and other forms of malfeasance. In an experiment involving road construction in 608 Indonesian villages, Olken (2007) finds that an increased probability of being audited reduces missing expenditures. At the time the study was initiated, all the villages were in the early stages of building a road as part of a nationwide development effort. A randomly selected subset of villages was told that their projects would be audited by the central government audit agency, effectively increasing the probability of audit from 4 percent (the baseline audit rate) to 100 percent. The results show that the audit treatment reduced missing expenditures by over 8 percent. This translates to a net benefit per village of around $250. Unfortunately, in projects with weak financial controls it may be difficult to establish a cost benchmark, as Olken was able to do in Indonesia. In that case cost overruns can simply lead the recipient country to ask for and obtain more funds.[13]

The relationship between punishment severity and corruption has been more difficult to establish, but there is some evidence here as well. In a laboratory setting, Abbink *et al.* (2002) find that subjects are less likely to engage in bribe-like behaviors if the penalty threat is higher. Different punishment regimes may also have different advantages and disadvantages. Asymmetric punishment regimes – those that grant relative leniency to bribe-givers but not bribe-receivers – can increase the likelihood that citizens will report harassment bribes. Still, this "complaint effect" may go unrealized if surrounding law-enforcement mechanisms are weak (Dufwenberg and Spagnolo, 2011), and granting leniency to bribe-givers has been shown to increase illicit offers (Engel *et al.*, 2012). Other proposals seek to differentiate penalty levels across giving/receiving the bribe and giving/receiving the

[13] Numerous examples can be drawn from the rebuilding experiences in Iraq and Afghanistan. Consult the websites of the Special Inspectors General for Iraq and Afghanistan, www.SIGIR.mil; www.SIGAR.mil.

illicit favor (Lambsdorff and Nell, 2007) but this has yet to see rigorous empirical evaluation.

World Bank researchers are studying the role of anti-corruption authorities (ACAs), an institutionalized form of monitoring and oversight. Since the 1990s, over thirty countries have established ACAs in some form. The success or failure of these institutions depends crucially on the national context. Beyond strong political support, a healthy ACA requires a clear, legally defined mandate, a well-articulated communication strategy, coordination with other agencies, and a clear long-term funding source. Agencies without these agreements end up operating "in an unclear and ineffective legal environment" and accomplish little (Recanatini, 2011).[14]

Some scholars have argued that ACAs and audit mechanisms may grow more effective with time. When they are initiated, the agencies are often small and under-resourced, so that they are barely noticed by bureaucrats and politicians. Over time, as the number of audits and corruption convictions accumulates, officials may take more notice of the agency and adjust their behavior accordingly. Silva (2010) describes this spillover dynamic in a study of a Brazilian anti-corruption program. Beginning in 2003, the national government initiated a program aimed at "naming and shaming" local governments, randomly selecting 4 percent of cities per year for auditing. The analysis suggests that "well-informed" mayors, those in audited cities or in neighboring cities, committed significantly fewer corrupt acts in later periods than those with no proximity to an audit. Silva concludes, "small anti-corruption agencies may become more efficient over time, as their reputation becomes stronger and diffuses amongst the politicians in its jurisdiction."

Increasing audit probabilities, resources for ACAs, and legal penalties will likely reduce corruption, but we should not be overly optimistic about these sorts of interventions. First, although ideally, an ACA or auditing agency is free from political manipulation and staffed with officials willing to punish corruption regardless of the status of the offender, in reality these bodies are often subject to manipulation by those in power. Supposedly random audits and prosecutions may end up being anything but random, as politicians accuse rivals of corruption, veiling political attacks in the guise of good governance. Observers cite instances of well-designed anti-corruption programs that "did not live up to potential" because of political interference (Bryane, 2004; Lawson, 2009). At their worst, these institutions can perpetuate social injustice by allowing a corrupt leader to claim a commitment to anti-corruption while using the agencies themselves for political gain (Shah and Huther, 2000).

Second, there is a risk that external monitoring and punishment may "crowd-out" intrinsic motivations for honest service. When faced with heightened outside control, some officials may perceive such measures as a signal of distrust, an emotive reaction that may counteract the positive monitoring effect. In one laboratory experiment, Schulze and Frank (2003) find that the introduction of monitoring had a deterrent effect, but also destroyed intrinsic honesty norms, thus leaving the net effect on corruption undetermined. High formal penalties may also increase the possibility of collusion between corrupt officials and the judiciary (Kugler *et al.*, 2005). Any anti-corruption reformer aiming to set the level of monitoring must account for these "hidden costs of control" (Falk and Kosfeld, 2006).

Institutions that promote accountability and transparency need more rigorous evaluation. At a theoretical level, their role in promoting anti-corruption and good governance seems clear, but we do not know much about their practical operation or about the conditions required to make them effective. Unfortunately, both country officials and representatives of donor agencies may benefit from the absence of solid data on the effect of good governance programs; this possibility may explain the current lack of information about the efficacy of these institutions. Suppose, for example, that an anti-corruption program involves a series of

[14] The World Bank has also launched a broader Governance and Anti-Corruption (GAC) initiative to promote the demand for good governance, and can point to some positive cases. However, more research is needed both to conceptualize the way accountability institutions operate and to understand how these institutions behave in different national settings, web.worldbank.org/WBSITE/EXTERNAL/TOPICS/EXTSOCIALDEVELOPMENT/0,contentMDK:21211265~pagePK:210058~piPK:210062~theSitePK:244363,00.html.

seminars and workshops for public officials with *per diems* set to encourage attendance. Given the lack of hard measures of corruption, attendance at these events is reported as a measure of success. However, attendance may not translate into concrete achievements, and the seminars themselves, held at attractive locations, can be a kind of perk.[15]

Independent oversight is only as effective as the strength and honesty of the overseer. Furthermore, deeper structural changes may be the only way to improve compliance with the law and the honesty and competence of government. Ironically, countries where corruption programs prove most successful may be the very places where they are needed the least (Truex and Søreide, 2011). Even if the evidence shows that audit agencies and oversight are valuable tools in some settings, one needs to move beyond such policies to consider other interventions.

Solution 2: transparency and bottom-up accountability

The natural complements to external monitoring and punishment by formal organizations are increased transparency and bottom-up accountability. There is substantial variation across countries in the degree of transparency, as well as within countries across different sectors and dimensions. If the processes of government are publicized – budgets posted online, rules/regulations available on notice boards – citizens can hold officials to account if they observe wrongdoing. This punishment may come through complaint procedures, social shunning or, for elected officials, the ballot box. Citizens have an interest in fighting corruption, and if given a voice, they can be a potent force for its reduction.

Transparency and accountability initiatives come in a variety of forms, and a growing body of evidence suggests their beneficial effects. Reinikka and Svennson (2004) demonstrate the power of information in reducing leakage of an education capitation grant. In 2004, the Ugandan government began publishing the details of education-funding processes in local newspapers, allowing citizens and schoolmasters to better monitor the release of funds from higher levels of government. The analysis shows that communities with better access to newspapers, as well as more informed schoolmasters, experienced lower leakage rates, and that the introduction of the newspaper campaign as a whole substantially reduced leakage rates and associated embezzlement.

In general, a free media with active investigative reporting is an aid to anti-corruption efforts (Brunetti and Weder, 2003).[16] If the local media are weak and dependent on either the government or wealthy private interests, outside actors should help to support any independent outlets and engage in reporting activities independent of local entities. These groups might supply well-researched stories to local outlets. They can be a place for whistle-blowers to report and could provide protection to those who reveal corruption if that is a risky activity. They can seek reform in libel laws that make it easy for journalists to "insult" the political and economic elite in ways that "violate national sovereignty" and to be subject to fines and imprisonment. One way to do this is to defend journalists under these laws, publicize cases, and attempt to raise popular awareness of the harm caused by such restrictive laws.[17] International actors may also be able to help local media make effective use of new electronic sources of communication and to help members of the public participate in newsgathering and dissemination. A move away from conventional media to social media leads to what Rusbridger (2010) calls "the mutualization of the news" in ways that can be harnessed to expose corruption and self-dealing.

Good information helps citizens "vote the rascals out" (Adsera *et al.*, 2003). However, even if voters want to punish corruption, they may lack reliable information on politicians' ethics and corrupt behavior. Rumors and whisperings may not be enough to produce coordinated action. In a survey experiment in Brazil, Weitz-Shapiro and Winters (2010) find that respondents who were told of a

[15] For a more extensive discussion of the role of travel perks as a salary supplement and potential source of corruption see Søreide *et al.* (2012).

[16] This section on the media draws heavily on Wrong (2011).

[17] An example here is Reporters without Borders, http://en.rsf.org/.

corrupt act expressed a desire to punish that politician, regardless of the politician's level of performance. De Figueirido *et al.* (2013) go a step further in a randomized field experiment conducted during a Brazilian mayoral election. The authors exploit a situation where both the incumbent and challenger had corruption convictions, randomly informing different blocks of voters about the convictions with 187,177 flyers. The analysis shows that knowledge of corruption can affect vote choices. For one of the candidates, the corruption treatment reduced the vote share by 2.6 percent.

Transparency and citizen-induced mechanisms can be most powerful when combined with external accountability mechanisms. A laboratory experiment on bribery hints at these synergies. Serra (2012) compares an individual's tendency to extort bribes under conventional auditing and a system that allows citizens to trigger audits through complaints with some low probability. He finds that bribery is lowest when external auditing is combined with a citizen-reporting mechanism, suggesting that complaint mechanisms fundamentally change the nature of the official–citizen relationship.

In a non-laboratory setting, Ferraz and Finan (2011) show the interplay between auditing and electoral accountability in Brazil. Starting in 2003, the federal government randomly audited municipalities on the expenditure of transferred funds. The results of the audits were then publicized in local newspapers and on radio programs. The authors compare areas with similar levels of corruption and find that the release of audit results negatively affected the electoral performance of the incumbent. The effect, however, is conditional on the presence of media outlets that released the information, further supporting the Reinikka and Svensson (2011) result on the key role of the media.

Providing information to citizens can reduce corruption and increase the quality of service delivery. Peisakhin and Pinto (2010) find that India's Right to Information Act (RTIA) allows citizens to better access a public service without having to resort to petty bribery. Slum-dwellers in Delhi were randomly assigned to four groups as they applied for ration cards. In the ordinary course of applying for the ration cards, most people made pay-offs, usually to agents who facilitated their applications. The control group applied for the ration card according to the standard legal procedure with no pay-offs. The various treatment groups accompanied their applications with either a RTIA request, a letter of support from a local NGO, or a bribe. Although the bribe proved the most effective tool, those who filed the RTIA request also received their ration cards in a timely manner and at no monetary cost, suggesting the importance of information.

These findings on the efficacy of transparency and accountability reforms are promising, but several caveats are in order. First, as is suggested by some of the research findings, transparency is only as effective as the accompanying punishment mechanisms. If citizens have no way to report their grievances to the authorities, or if officials are never punished for being corrupt, increasing openness and the flow of information may do little to address the problem. Indeed, in many countries, high-level corruption occurs quite openly, suggesting that inadequate information is not the fundamental issue. Transparency can reduce malfeasance through shaming (Masclet *et al.*, 2003), but it seems most effective when complemented by other policies that give these disclosures teeth (Kolstad and Wiig, 2009).

A second caveat concerns the public's monitoring capacity. Although greater information provision is a good in and of itself, one should not overestimate the capacity of the public to digest information and to act accordingly. An international program, the Construction Sector Transparency Initiative (CoST), aims to reduce corruption and increase transparency by making detailed project information publicly available on government websites (Truex and Søreide, 2011). The spirit of the initiative is well taken, but most citizens may be incapable of understanding the nuances of construction contracts, and of those who are, few may take the time to do so. Construction firms may fill the knowledge gap but not if they are directly involved in corruption themselves. Transparency initiatives directed at the general public ought to focus on providing simple pieces of information on topics of direct interest to a large number of citizens.

Solution 3: internal controls and bureaucratic incentives

Solutions 1 and 2 dealt primarily with external forms of accountability, both bottom-up and top-down, but internal bureaucratic organization and the administration of public programs are equally, if not more, important to the anti-corruption calculus. If bureaucrats have easy access to rents, an abundance of corrupt partners, and a low public service ethos, self-dealing is nearly inevitable. Furthermore, even if bribery is limited through harsh penalties, overall governance may remain poor. Internal reforms and program redesign can help ensure that service delivery improves.

Civil service reform

The most common policy remedy is to increase the wages of public servants. In the language of the corruption calculus, higher wages translate to higher expected costs of engaging in malfeasance, as the bureaucrat would be reluctant to put his well-paying job at risk. Conversely, underpaid bureaucrats have a greater incentive to embezzle funds and solicit bribes, as they could easily find a higher wage in the private sector. Generous public pensions that would be lost in the event of corrupt behavior can be a further deterrent (Becker and Stigler, 1974).

There is some evidence that low wages do contribute to high corruption levels although it is largely confined to the laboratory (Azfar and Nelson, 2007). Barr *et al.* (2009) conduct an experiment that mimics an embezzlement opportunity using Ethiopian nursing students as subjects. Subjects were given an opportunity to siphon off a public resource and were also paid a "wage," which was set either high or low. Participants with the higher wage stole fewer public resources. A "natural field experiment" in Burkina Faso, where subjects were not aware they were participating, corroborates these results. Participants each graded an identical set of twenty papers, and the eleventh paper in the set was accompanied by a small bribe. Graders were randomly assigned to high-wage, low-wage, and monitoring treatments (where the quality of their grading was checked), and the graders with higher wages proved less likely to accept the bribe (Armantier and Boly, 2008). Higher salaries seem to yield better political candidates in Brazil – a 20 percent salary increase is associated with an increase in 0.2 years of schooling and a 25 percent increase in the number of bills submitted (Ferraz and Finan, 2010).

This relationship has also been supported at a macro-level using cross-national regressions (van Rijckeghem and Weder, 2001), although the effects of wages on corruption are not particularly impressive. In a cross-section of thirty-one countries, doubling government wages only results in a corruption decrease of 0.5 points on the International Company Risk Guide (ICRG) index – an index that ranges from 1 to 10.

One difficulty with proposals to raise wages is the lack of a clear standard for wage levels. Small changes in wages seem to have little effect, and in many developing countries public servants, especially women, are quite well paid relative to their private sector counterparts (Panizza, 2000; Filmer and Lindauer, 2001; Van Rijckeghem and Weder, 2001). A study of seventeen Latin American countries in the 1990s found that in only three countries were men in the civil service paid lower wages than their private sector counterparts (for one of these, the absolute difference was very small) (Panizza, 2000). For women there was a statistically significant shortfall in only one country. Table 11.2 reports these results. Over and above their wages, civil servants often receive subsidized housing, the use of government vehicles, and foreign travel. Furthermore even if increasing wages curbs corruption, it may at the same time increase inequality in the country and drain government resources. Citizens may especially resent corruption committed by bureaucrats with high wages and generous perks.

Furthermore, above-market public sector wages may simply shift corruption onto the process of selecting applicants for public positions (Patrinos and Kagia, 2006). People may now be required to pay to obtain a scarce government job. In Pakistan, one study reports that teachers commonly paid between $200 and $1,400 for jobs, collected their monthly salaries without actually working, and then paid off their supervisors (Burke, 2000).

Table 11.2 Public sector wages relative to private sector wages, 1990s

	Men	Women
Bolivia	–0.17*	0.01*
Brazil	0.02	–0.08*
Chile	–0.025	0.17
Colombia	0.16	0.27
Costa Rica	0.17	0.47
Ecuador	0.30	0.26
El Salvador	0.27	0.67
Guatemala	–0.045	0.40
Honduras	0.01	0.60
Mexico	0.11	0.23
Nicaragua	–0.02	0.02
Panama	0.11	0.49
Paraguay	0.11	0.28
Peru	0.05	0.11
Dominican Republic	–0.37	0.23
Uruguay	–0.015	–0.04
Venezuela	–0.001	0.27

Note: * = Significant at 1%.
Source: Panizza (2000: Table A2). Surveys from various dates in the 1990s.

The appropriateness of a wage increase is context-specific, but at a minimum it seems prudent to raise wages in instances where public servants are grossly underpaid relative to their counterparts in the private sector and do not value their jobs as a result.

Many corrupt behaviors require partners of some kind, either favor-seeking citizens or co-conspirators in the bureaucracy. The longer a bureaucrat is in his post, the more corrupt relationships he can develop. Many governments, from ancient Chinese dynasties to the current German federal government, employ regular staff rotation as a precautionary measure. To study the effect of this anti-corruption lever, Abbink (2004) conducted a laboratory experiment where pairs of "citizen bribers" and public officials were randomly re-matched after every round, simulating the process of rotation. Compared with the case where the pairs remained fixed, the rotation treatment reduces both the frequency and level of bribes exchanged. There is, however, a downside. In a fully corrupt bureaucratic hierarchy, higher-level officials can use the threat of rotation to a remote and impoverished area as a threat to keep would-be whistleblowers in line and induce them to gather bribes to share with superiors (Rose-Ackerman, 1999). This practice proved common in studies of an irrigation system in India (Wade, 1982) and of police forces in Thailand (Phongpaicht and Piriyarangsan, 1994: 99–120). Furthermore, as we discuss on p. 652, rotation can undermine the impact of another possible option – competition between officials.

A final type of civil service reform seeks to improve meritocratic recruitment practices. Would-be bureaucrats vary widely in their commitment to public service and honest government. Patronage and nepotism can quickly fill the public sector with rent-seekers. Those who paid to obtain public sector jobs will often seek to repay themselves by soliciting bribes. A number of studies have demonstrated a country-level correlation between meritocratic recruiting practices and lower levels of corruption (Rauch and Evans, 2000; Dahlstrom *et al.* 2009). Reform measures include more transparent hiring practices, public job announcements, and independent hiring committees. In Georgia, reform efforts in the tax and police sectors succeeded only after a massive personnel turnover; corrupt bureaucrats were replaced with employees with a better public service ethos (World Bank, 2012).

In theory, civil service reforms, such as wage fairness, staff rotation, and meritocratic recruitment should reduce corruption levels, but the strength of the effects are conditional on the surrounding environment. In the Chinese setting, for example, meritocratic reforms aimed to screen out "shirkers" during a transfer to a new civil service system. However, only 0.3 percent of officials in certain areas ended up failing to make the cut. Interview evidence suggests that local norms of social harmony prevented supervisors from firing lazy subordinates, at the expense of efficiency and anti-corruption (Burns and Wang, 2010). Similar difficulties have been documented in Mexico. According to Laguna (2011), Mexico's civil service reform experience was hampered by the "politico-administrative inheritances that characterize the region" – patronage, corruption, and centralism. Moreover, simpler issues of timing, policy coordination, and resource availability also undermined the reform package. In short, any anti-corruption intervention that targets the rewards and organization of the civil service must consider the full menu of corrupt options and ask if reform in one area will simply transfer corrupt incentives elsewhere.

Competitive service delivery

Under some conditions, bureaucratic competition can reduce the level of rents available. If a citizen who is qualified to receive a benefit can only obtain it from one office or individual, she may be forced to pay a hefty bribe to gain the desired service. If there are multiple bureaucrats, the citizen has more bargaining power, as she can simply move on to the next bureaucrat if she is extorted by the first. This dynamic should reduce the overall level of extortive bribes in the system (Rose-Ackerman, 1978, 1999). For example, in Nepal, traders faced several possible points for passing through customs, and were able to flock to entry points where bribe levels were lowest (Alfiler, 1986: 48). In the study of corruption in the customs services of Maputo, Mozambique, and Durban, South Africa mentioned on pp. 639–40 (Sequeira and Djankov, 2010) shippers sorted themselves between the ports depending upon their vulnerability to high bribes in Maputo and the relative costs of shipping through these ports to buyers in South Africa. This competitive pressure did keep bribes in check in both ports, but it did not equalize them for a range of reasons, including the short time horizon of officials in Maputo. A further reform, presumably designed to limit corruption, rotated officials every six months. This had the effect of leading the officials to extract high bribes in the short run in spite of the fact that their behavior might lead to more cargo being diverted to Durban and lower bribe receipt in the long run. Thus, this study highlights the way in which anti-corruption policies need to consider the broader context in which corruption occurs. Rotation and competition may be incompatible strategies.

Obviously, competitive bureaucracy will not be socially beneficial if citizens are seeking illegal benefits. Bribes may indeed fall, but that will only imply that breaking the law in other ways has become less expensive (Rose-Ackerman, 1978). Increasing the number of bureaucrats with overlapping responsibilities may bring down equilibrium levels of extortion but increase equilibrium levels of bribery. A citizen seeking an undeserved benefit can go to different bureaucrats until she finds a corrupt one willing to accept a bribe (Di Gioacchina and Franzini, 2008). Burgess *et al.* (2011) find evidence of increased bribery with respect to deforestation in Indonesia. Local forestry officials could allow illegal logging in exchange for bribes, and as the number of bureaucratic jurisdictions increased, logging rates increased.

Program redesign to limit corrupt opportunities

One response to corruption is to redesign public programs to reduce the level of rents available to officials and private clients. Rose-Ackerman (1999) provides numerous examples of how this might be done in ways that reduce the discretion and limit the monopoly power of officials. The state can make rules clearer and more transparent; it can increase staffing to reduce delays, or increase supply to reduce scarcity. Many such opportunities are likely to exist in any polity that will be relatively inexpensive to implement. The costs are the loss in discretion that might have been used to sort out the most deserving beneficiaries or to punish only the most harmful behavior. However, if a system is riddled with corruption then discretion is being misused. Hence the losses are likely to be small when an anti-corruption policy is compared with the status quo, not some ideal state of affairs. Many such reforms are thus socially costless, the only losers are those engaged in the corrupt system, who obviously will resist reform. The explanation for the persistence of many corrupt practices is not the high social cost of reform but rather the political power of those engaged in corrupt networks.

Although we lack systematic evidence of the costs and benefits of most programmatic reforms, there is one area where the benefits are particularly easy to measure, and that is tax and customs collection. The evidence suggests that reforms can be very efficacious, although maintaining reform momentum over time can be difficult. The best evidence comes from Latin America since 1990 where there are numerous examples of tax and customs reform (Stein *et al.*, 2005: 186). Most of these reforms consist of a mixture of simplified tax schedules that are affordable to taxpayers and importers, automation of operations, better auditing, and improvements in the training, oversight, and incentives of officials. For example, in Bolivia, where these reforms were combined with overall civil service reforms, corruption and smuggling declined in the customs service, and the proportion of VAT lost went from 42 percent in 2001 to 29 percent in 2004 after the reforms.[18] Gómez Sabaini (2006) reports that tax collections as a share of GDP in Bolivia rose from 8.2 percent in 1990 to 20.5 percent in 2000 to 23.0 percent in 2004. In Peru, total tax revenues increased from 8.4 percent of GDP in 1991 to 12.3 percent in 1998 at the same time as many tax rates were reduced. Taxpayers increased from 895,000 in 1993 to 1,766,000 in 1999. Tariff revenues went from 23 percent of revenues in 1990 to 35 percent in 1996 and increased fourfold in dollar terms despite reductions in duties (OECD, 2003:9).[19] Peru reduced total staff from 4,700 in 1990 to 2,540 in 2002 and increased the share of professionals from 2.5 percent to 60 percent (Goorman, 2004). The average clearance times fell from two days to two hours. In Costa Rica times fell from six days to twelve minutes (OECD, 2003: 22).

A comparison of reforms in Chile and Argentina designed to increase compliance with VAT shows how similar policies can have different results (Bergman, 2003). The average VAT compliance coefficient is 77.6 percent in Chile and 54.3 percent in Argentina. After examining and rejecting other explanations, the author concludes that the difference can be explained by the greater credibility of Chile's reform because the tax agency was stable and had broad autonomy. Hence it was better able to induce voluntary compliance because of its more credible deterrence capacity. However, Chile, with considerable revenue from the copper industry, may simply find tax administration easier because it does not have to tax its citizens as highly. Taxes as a share of GDP were 26.3 percent in 2004 in Argentina and only 17.3 percent in Chile (Gómez-Sabaini, 2006).

These results are consistent with one specific reform that has received detailed study: the creation of a semi-autonomous revenue authority. Taliercio's (2004) study of such authorities in three African and three Latin American countries is broadly favorable. The reforms appear to be very cost-effective. Though some countries had better experiences than others, revenue collection improved. Taliercio points to a range of factors that contributed to increased revenue collection for a modest administrative cost. It is not possible to measure the marginal costs of the reform, but they appear low or even negative. Overall, the cost of revenue collection as a share of revenues collected ranges from 1.7 percent to 2 percent for the Latin American cases. The best performer was Peru whose agency was the most independent from the executive and whose leaders were most able to motivate employees by creating a professional organizational culture. Taliercio does, however, recognize the need for accountability and recommends the Mexican model under which the authority reports to the legislature. Unfortunately, when Taliercio checked to see if the reforms had been sustained over time, he found a disappointing pattern of backsliding in all the cases he studied (Taliercio 2001).[20] He argues that the political coalition in favor of independent revenue authorities is likely to be fragile, and demonstrates that this is so. Officials in the Ministry of Finance oppose the revenue authorities, especially if the authorities seem competent and professional and, as a consequence, seek to be involved in tax policy, not just tax collection. Furthermore, taxpayers may also object. However, at the time of his study, the one bright spot was Peru

[18] Unfortunately, however, smuggling appears to be on the rise (Escobar, 2004; Zuleta *et al.*, 2006).

[19] Including social security contributions, the tax share increased from 11.6 percent in 1990 to 14.0 percent in 2000. However, the share fell between 1995 and 2000 from a high of 15.4 percent (Gómez Sabaini, 2006).

[20] Stein *et al.* (2005: 186, 192) also found that countries, such as Colombia, are forced to pass reform after reform because each gets watered down in the approval process.

where the organized business community supported the independent revenue authority because it was able to collect taxes more evenhandedly from all businesses and because it promised certainty and limited official extortion.

Solution 4: controlling "grand corruption"

So far, our solutions have concentrated on reforms in monitoring, in transparency and accountability, and in the operation of the bureaucracy. We turn now to the special problems that arise when the state carries out large-scale projects, signs contracts, and sells assets. These are usually special-purpose, one-of-a-kind deals so that it is difficult to locate benchmarks to measure excessive costs or to set externally verifiable quality standards. They produce high levels of economic rents (financial gains) that are difficult to monitor. Hence, "grand corruption" may be a serious problem. Although the solutions outlined above have value even here, they are unlikely to be sufficient. They must be supplemented by *ex ante* polices that limit rents up-front. Because of the special-purpose nature of these deals, good statistical evidence is difficult to come by. The broad cross-country indices discussed on pp. 633–8 go some way to capturing this aspect of corruption because they are largely based on the perceptions of international actors. However, those data do not translate easily into policy recommendations. They highlight interstate differences in perceptions of corruption without providing information on the mechanisms at work.

If the state carries out infrastructure-construction projects, privatizes public firms, makes large defense purchases, or allocates concessions to natural resources, these activities are very valuable to the successful private firms and, as one-of-a-kind projects, are difficult to price competitively. Thus, those involved in the government and in the private sector may inflate overall contract values and then struggle over the division of the excess profits. Some of these profits will be provided as bribes or kickbacks; the rest will revert to the contractor with some of the total siphoned off by agents and firm managers. This competition for gains means that the size of the bribe *per se* is not a good measure of the social harm. A very influential private actor may pay only a small bribe in return for a massive gain because of its overwhelming bargaining power.

If corruption is endemic in large public undertakings, it will give officials incentives to create extra unneeded projects to hide monopoly gains to be split between government officials and their private sector counterparts. These projects may be self-consciously designed as special-purpose deals to make monitoring difficult by both insiders and outsiders, such as aid and lending organizations. In such cases the loss to society is not just the bribes paid; it is the total of wasted resources spent on the project.

Corrupt payments and excess profits can be more easily hidden in complex, special-purpose deals. This implies that one anti-corruption strategy is to change the types of things the government buys to favor standardized, off-the-shelf products as much as is feasible. The government would go "shopping." It would, for example, buy standardized fighter jets already in wide use around the world for the air force, purchase ordinary automobiles for the police with special features priced separately and transparently. Government land purchases or sales would be made public and benchmarked in comparison with private sales (Rose-Ackerman, 1999).

If the state cannot go "shopping" but instead needs to sign a special-purpose contract – for example, for a major infrastructure project – the nature of the bidding process is a central concern. The World Bank's most recent standards for International Competitive Bidding, for example, include provisions designed to limit corruption,[21] and the World Bank has begun a more stringent crackdown on corrupt contractors than at any time in its history (Dubois and Nowlan, 2010). However, it is by no means obvious that the Bank has hit upon the optimal formulation. There needs to be a more careful study of the relationship between the bidding and auction processes, on the one hand, and the

[21] See: http://web.worldbank.org/WBSITE/EXTERNAL/PROJECTS/PROCUREMENT/0,contentMDK:20060844~menuPK:93305~pagePK:84269~piPK:84286~theSitePK:84266,00.html.

results, on the other. Such studies would not need to document corruption itself but would instead ask how different procedures perform in terms of the ultimate outcome of concern, be it efficiently provided infrastructure or a privatization process that enhances competition and increases efficiency while bringing revenue to the state.

Procurement

Corruption can occur at many different stages in the procurement process. Before the formal process begins, the government must decide what projects it wants to support and must produce preliminary designs and cost estimates to help it set priorities. Even in the absence of kickbacks and bribes, procurement officials have an incentive to underestimate both costs and technical difficulties and to overestimate benefits (Flyvbjerg *et al.*, 2003; Flyvbjerg and Molloy, 2011). If they compete with others for scarce public funds, they will seek to make "their" projects look better than the competition. Infrastructure projects are usually *de facto* irreversible once begun because governments are likely to be punished politically for leaving big holes in the ground and unfinished buildings to blight the landscape. Because everyone expects everyone else to issue overly optimistic projections, even those who would never think of paying or accepting an outright bribe play along or exit the sector. Because there are no good objective measures of costs and benefits, this opens the door to corrupt operatives who exploit the unreliability of the data to enrich themselves and to further the interest of their firms. If officials, both bureaucrats and politicians, are not held responsible *ex post* for their optimistic projections *ex ante*, they are likely to continue to act in this fashion. Waste and corruption are facilitated by the lack of clear lines of responsibility.

Over and above inflated net-benefit projections, the bidding process itself can be undermined by firms that act as a cartel to share government business. Here, too, corruption can thrive, but in this case as a counterpart of the collusive behavior of the cartel. Thus, Lambert-Mogiliansky (2011) shows how instead of competing with each other in the level of bribe payments, firms may organize a cartel and pay off the procurement official to keep the collusive arrangement operating, giving him a share of the excess profits from the project. If a reform targets kickbacks, the official has less power to extort pay-offs, but the firms may still collude to share the market. If corruption is attacked with no concern for collusion, there may be few social benefits from a crackdown. An anti-corruption drive might simply make the cartel cheaper and more lucrative to organize, so that the firms still present a united front that forces the state to continue overpaying for public projects. Therefore, the state must target the risks of corruption and collusion simultaneously – in both the reform of overall procurement procedures and in the implementation of specific procurement projects. This argument exemplifies a general point about anti-corruption policy. It needs to be developed to fit the context in which it occurs, with account taken of the ways officials and bribers may seek to compensate for any constraints on corrupt deals.

Modern technology can assist in reducing corruption in procurement although these systems cannot address deeper questions about the type of projects that the state sponsors. A number of countries have experimented with procurement reforms designed to limit corruption, and several have proved quite successful and may provide models for other reformers. However, even the most successful are not a sufficient response. The state also needs to confront the issues outlined on p. 654 relating to the choice of public projects and the competitiveness of the private contracting market. The most well-documented examples of e-procurement come from South Korea, Mexico, and Chile.[22] In South Korea, an e-procurement system permits public bodies to shop for standardized goods and services and to manage bidding processes efficiently. The government saved over $2.5 billion in 2002 simply by streamlining bureaucratic procedures. This is a lower bound, however, because the government has not measured the savings in the lower cost of purchased goods and services. It would be valuable to study the impact of the system on prices paid and the number of bidders participating. Has

[22] See Ware *et al.* (2011: 98–9), which provides links to the underlying studies.

private cartel behavior fallen? In Mexico, the government created an e-procurement system, called CompraNet, to deal with corruption and waste. Administrative costs fell by 20 percent as a result of reductions in both paperwork and face-to-face interactions. The system is much more transparent and, therefore, is more easily subject to citizen oversight. The government estimated that every $1 invested in an internet procurement system earned a social return of $4.[23] Chile also streamlined its procurement system and put more material on line. The result was a shorter bid cycle and more competitive processes. The government estimates an annual savings of $70 million from both internal efficiencies and cost savings on contracts. With total procurement totaling about $7 billion per year, however, this is only 1 percent of the budget.

Beyond efforts to streamline the procurement process and make it more competitive, improvements in *ex post* oversight are a second option. Two groups with an incentive to monitor corruption are competitors and newly installed political regimes. These groups may seek redress inside the state, but if the domestic legal system has been coopted by the corrupt elite or is simply weak, international options may have some efficacy as well. The international aid and lending organizations have improved their anti-corruption oversight, and some argue that anti-corruption measures ought to be built into the international arbitration system. We discuss each below, although neither seems a panacea. Domestic reform will remain a priority for the foreseeable future.

Privatization

Privatization raises some similar concerns. One study documents the overall favorable impact of privatization in economic terms at least in Latin America (Chong and López-de-Silanes, 2003), but for public utilities, in particular, the experience has been mixed. For example, in telecommunications privatization has eliminated unmet demand by raising prices so that many households still lack service.[24] Barrera-Osorio and Olivera (2007) find that privatization of water supply in Columbia was beneficial overall; however, the price increases had a strongly negative effect on poor rural households' access to water. Some transfers to private ownership are marred by corruption and patronage, and impose costs on ordinary citizens. The familiar trade-off between maximizing the revenue earned by the government from the sale versus creating a competitive market without monopoly profits is evident in many programs and has often been resolved by giving private firms monopoly power (Manzetti, 1999; Hoffmann, 2007). The most successful cases involved transparent and homogeneous procedures, speed, and limited restructuring prior to privatization (Chong and Lopez-de-Silanes, 2003).

Privatization programs and concession agreements are prime locations for corrupt deals (Manzetti, 1999). This means that privatization is not always a move in the direction of efficiency and good service. Some firms might be better off remaining in public hands; some natural resources might be better exploited by public companies. Case studies from World Bank projects in the water, electricity, and rails sectors illustrate that, compared to private sector alternatives, the performance of public firms varies widely – from bodies that perform well to wasteful, inefficient providers (Vagliasindi, 2011). This variation suggests that privatization is not always indicated, but it also suggests that corruption is a likely problem in the poorly managed state firms. According to Vagliasindi, governance reform should involve a combination of internal incentives, coming from incorporation and strong oversight by the firm's board, and of external checks, such as public-stock listing. Such governance mechanisms improve public firms' performance, in part, by controlling self-dealing by public firm managers and political favoritism. Vagliasindi proposes to align incentives by publicly monitoring the performance of state enterprises through regulatory contracts that are subject to third-party monitoring and scrutiny by the general public.

The privatization process may involve interplay between corruption and competition that can introduce distortions (Auriol and Straub, 2011). First, a

[23] Kossick (2004).

[24] Hoffmann (2007: 10).

corrupt process reduces the price received by the government and leads the privatized firm to set prices and sell quantities that are not socially optimal, perhaps because it has obtained a monopoly franchise. Notice, however, that this monopoly result could arise not only from corruption but also from a revenue-maximizing government that does not factor in the social benefits of competition or of effective natural monopoly regulation (Bjorvatn and Søreide, 2005). Second, government officials may privatize the wrong firms – that is, firms that are operating at a high level as state firms and so appear valuable to private bidders. Very inefficient state-owned enterprises do not produce many corrupt rents to share and may stay in public hands, perhaps as a repository for patronage appointments of incompetent but politically connected people.[25] Once again, pure revenue-maximizers might make the same socially harmful choices as corrupt officials, but the prospect of personal enrichment can be an additional spur to distort the privatization process. Notice that if this dynamic operates, the management problems isolated by Vagliasindi are especially likely to arise. Weak firms stay in state hands because some individuals or groups benefit from their very inefficiency. If an internal reform agenda is pushed too hard, those who benefited from the status quo may switch sides and support privatization because that may allow them to preserve some of their illicit rents.

* * **

This discussion suggests that a range of options exist to control corruption but that all of them need to be put in a larger context of state functioning. We have already shown how reducing corruption along one dimension – say by raising salaries – can increase corruption elsewhere – say, by leading to the sale of civil service jobs. Here we have seen how reductions in corruption need to be combined with efforts to increase the competitiveness of contracting and privatization processes. Otherwise, the result may just be to increase the monopoly rents available to private firms who obtain contracts and government assets. Furthermore, decisions on what to buy and what assets to sell need to be made with an eye to their overall social benefits, not just their impact on the public budget.

Solution 5: shifting service provision to the private sector

If government bodies are riddled with corruption and inefficiency, a final drastic remedy is to remove certain tasks from the public sector completely, moving their provision to the private sector.[26] Firms have taken over basic service provision in parts of India (Bussell, 2012), tax collection in Uganda (Iversen *et al.*, 2006), transportation in Mexico City (Wirth, 1997), and parts of customs inspection in over fifty developing countries (Yang, 2008). Provided there is some market competition, private actors may have a strong incentive to curb malfeasance and promote cost savings. The risk is that private actors lack a "public service ethos," and may ultimately become more corrupt and parasitic than the government bureaucrats they replace. The existing record suggests that privatization is a high-risk, high-reward strategy – some reforms seem to have substantially reduced corruption; others appear to have made the situation worse.

Bussell (2012) studies a unique privatization reform in rural areas of the south Indian state of Karnataka. Starting around 2006, the state government began to create 800 one-stop outsourced service posts called Nemmadi centers in village areas, a substitute for government-run *taluk* offices. A portion of offices were also computerized, allowing the citizen to interact primarily with a computer program. Because of staggered implementation across the state, Bussell was able to evaluate the effects of both privatization and computerization on service delivery. The analysis suggests that privatization reduced corruption – citizens visiting Nemmadi centers reported spending less money overall to access services and faced fewer demands for bribes. Computerization also showed similar positive effects although on a smaller scale than privatization.[27]

[25] See also Shleifer and Vishny (1993), who make a similar point using a different theoretical approach.

[26] Note that this "privatization" refers to services and is distinct from the privatization of state assets.

[27] Interestingly, neither reform resulted in higher levels of reported satisfaction.

Yang (2008) documents similar success in the introduction of privatization reforms in the customs sector. Over the last twenty years, a number of developing countries have hired private firms to conduct pre-shipment inspections (PSIs) of imports that allow for an independent assessment of the value and tariff classification of incoming goods. The evidence suggests that countries adopting these reforms experience substantial increases in import duty collections, as well as decreased import misclassifications.[28] Most importantly, the intervention seems to be cost-effective, with the increase in tax collections representing 2.6 times program costs within the first five years.

Governments also sign contracts with private firms to deliver services such as health care. Here the government funds the program and sets eligibility criteria, but it does not provide the service itself. One option is to use NGOs as service providers. Loevinsohn and Harding (2005) review ten evaluations of contracting-out in the delivery of primary health and nutrition services in developing countries. Compared with government provision, most showed positive results from management contracts, as measured by coverage of the program. The authors conclude that contracting-out should be considered but that rigorous evaluation should go along with experiments. The results suggest the value of combining contracting-out with some type of bottom-up public accountability as discussed above.

Although these successes are encouraging, there are also prominent privatization horror stories, the most prominent being tax privatization in Uganda (Iversen *et al.* 2006). After a fiscal decentralization prompted by the 2001 presidential election, local governments privatized tax collection in hopes of improving both tax yield and efficiency. For a given area, the local government would estimate the revenue potential, otherwise known as the reserve price. Private firms would bid on the right to collect this revenue, as well as a 20 percent margin for cost recovery. Iversen *et al.* (2006) provide an independent estimate of actual tax collections across six sample markets that could be compared to the agreed reserve price. They found that actual collections greatly exceeded the reserve price, even when the 20 percent margin was included. Actual gross margins ranged from 71 percent to 970.1 percent, resulting in "lost revenue" of 25–75 percent across the different markets. The authors conclude that privatization gave local bureaucrats an incentive to underestimate the reserve price, which would allow firms to collect a larger pool of corrupt rents. The reform merely shifted the locus of corruption from the collection point into the bureaucracy and procurement process.

To summarize, current reform experiences suggest that privatization can improve service delivery and reduce corruption, but that reforms must not be implemented without careful planning. Private sector actors engaged in service delivery must be monitored and audited and, in turn, punished for any improprieties. If the threat of losing the public contract is not credible, because either there are no alternative providers or there is no political will, firms once thought to curb corruption may ultimately promote it. The privatization process itself also presents opportunities for collusion in procurement, with bureaucrats and firms working together to create a rent-generating situation at the expense of public welfare. Thus, when a service has some public service characteristics, simply devolving the service to private-firms will not be sufficient. Honest, competent regulation is necessary and should accompany the shift to private firm provision. If such oversight is not possible, it may be better to keep the service inside the public sector.

Solution 6: international efforts

Solutions need to focus not only on controls inside states where corrupt deals occur, but also on international forams. As we have argued, reforms in the former category include both more competitive and transparent bidding processes and careful evaluation of what is being bought and sold *ex ante* to be sure that these choices are not being distorted by self-dealing officials. At the international level, reforms should go beyond the weak enforcement mechanisms in existing treaties and contracts. Initiatives need to stress both transparency *ex ante* and

[28] The growth rate of other tax revenues did not change appreciably, lending greater validity to the results.

a credible threat *ex post*. These efforts will do little to constrain the low-level corruption that affects people's daily lives. However, it has the potential to limit high-level or "grand" corruption, especially when combined with the structural or institutional efforts described on pp. 654–8.

Transparency: from soft to hard law

Voluntary international efforts have concentrated on improvements in transparency. Good examples include the Extractive Industries Transparency Initiative (EITI) and the efforts by TI – UK to compile country-by-country data on defense contracting.

The EITI aims to further greater transparency in corporate/country agreements in the mining, oil, and gas industries.[29] The EITI does not measure corruption directly. The goal is to permit individuals and advocacy groups to monitor the flow of funds with the aim of benefitting the citizens of countries with valuable resources. The effort grew out of the Publish What You Pay initiative that targeted only multinational firms. Under EITI countries can become candidate countries and then must propose plans that are compliant with EITI standards. These standards focus on transparent reporting and auditing of payments from firms to countries. Firms that support the initiative must publish what they pay to compliant countries and submit a self-assessment to EITI.[30] Other organizations may piggyback off the EITI and other ratings in making decisions about funding and other forms of engagement (de Michelle, 2011).

The EITI is moving from soft to hard law in the United States. One section of the US Dodd–Frank Act[31] requires firms in extractive industries to report payments under rules similar to those governing the EITI. It imposes financial disclosure requirements on all resource-extraction companies listed on US stock exchanges.[32] Such resource-extraction issuers must disclose: "(i) the type and total amount of . . . payments made for each project of the resource extraction issuer relating to the commercial development of oil, natural gas, or minerals, and (ii) the type and total amount of such payments made to each government."[33] This statutory provision is unprecedented in requiring disclosure at the project level, as opposed to data aggregated at the country or continent level.[34]

The TI–UK defense industry initiative is an effort to increase disclosure and encourage integrity among defense contractors and government defense ministries.[35] It is at an early stage and has had limited success in obtaining country-level data. For example, it asked countries in the OECD and European Union to supply data on the proportion of defense procurement that was single-source on the grounds that high levels of single-source procurement indicates a corruption risk. To highlight the problems of transparency in defense budgets the project published a report in October 2011 that grouped almost 100 countries by the degree of transparency in their defense budgets. Only about one-third were in the top two categories (TI, Defence and Security Program, October 2011: 6) In spite of the lack of systematic data, the project's reports are full of enlightening case studies and practical suggestions for reducing corruption risks based on the experiences it has documented. The Program hopes that it can have an impact on industry practice by showing how some countries are setting an example of disclosure and some firms are working to curb kickbacks. It is working with a number of large defense contractors to realize the program's aims.

Such pure transparency initiatives are a first step, but they will mean little if they are not combined with follow-up mechanisms that permit those who suspect corruption to initiate complaints and to spur government or international bodies to take action.

[29] See http://eiti.org.

[30] For details, See http://eiti.org/.

[31] §1504, 124 Stat. at 2220.

[32] §1504, 124 Stat. at 2220 (defining a "resource-extraction issuer" as an issuer that "(i) is required to file an annual report with the [Securites and Exhcange Commission] SEC, and (ii) engages in the commercial development of oil, natural gas, or minerals" (internal quotation marks omitted)).

[33] §1504, 124 Stat. at 2221.

[34] EITI, for example, requires "regular publication of all material oil, gas and mining payments by companies to governments," i.e. country-level disclosures *The EITI Principles and Criteria*, http://eiti.org/eiti/principles.

[35] Their informative website is www.ti-defence.org. See especially, TI, Defence and Security Program, April 2010, September 2011, and October 2011, Pyman *et al.* (2009).

Some proposals have been made along those lines, but none is fully operational. Furthermore, measuring their impact will be difficult given the one-of-a-kind nature of many resource deals and the indirect nature of the control mechanism.

Legal remedies: national courts and international forums

In a few cases, the courts of one country, such as the United States can be used to address offenses that occur in countries with weak or corrupt judiciaries. Sometimes foreign courts help with recovery of assets held abroad. Even the Swiss have frozen questionable assets of deposed rulers and have transferred them to incumbents who claim that the funds belong to the state. The World Bank's Stolen Asset Recovery Initiative (StAR) aims to assist countries seeking to recovery illicitly appropriated assets, but the task is difficult.[36] Sophisticated money launderers manage to hide funds in major financial centers, disguising the funds' origin through a chain of shell companies. Although domestic actions can be useful in particular cases, especially when aided by information from banking havens, they hardly represent a general solution.[37]

There are weaknesses on two fronts. First, the treaties and institutions that seek to control international corruption are all voluntary systems in the sense that nation states opt into them only if they are willing to accept the treaties' conditions. Second, domestic courts are seldom willing to take on foreign bribery cases unless they involve domestic firms under the OECD Convention or involve limits on the transfer of assets held in a country's financial institutions. Law-enforcement bodies in one country may extradite accused offenders to face trial, but they do not bring the cases themselves.

That leaves a final set of institutions that may be a future locus of reform – the international arbitration system. That regime is the main international forum for resolving commercial and investor–state disputes. States or state-owned entities are parties to many of these disputes, and corruption has been alleged in a number of cases. However, although recognized as an important issue, corruption remains a vexed and difficult problem for arbitrators, given their insulation from domestic criminal law institutions (Pauwelyn, 2011).[38] Nevertheless, the institutions that organize arbitrations are stepping gingerly into this arena as litigants seek to void contracts tainted by corruption. As Mark Pieth writes, "Arbitration is no longer an exclusive area of party interest, especially as far as large infrastructure projects are involved. It is right to consider corruption an issue of (domestic and international) public interest" (Pieth, 2011).

One study located thirty-eight international arbitration cases that dealt with corruption, but the arbitral system has not yet settled on an appropriate framework (Olaya, 2010; Pauwelyn, 2011). In an ironic twist, the first set of disputes arose between firms and their local intermediaries who allegedly had paid bribes. The firms were seeking to avoid paying their agents on the ground that bribery was illegal, even if they knew that pay-offs were taking place (Meyer, 2013). In such cases, arbitrators generally refuse jurisdiction on the ground that they have no authority to resolve criminal allegations. Going beyond disgruntled intermediaries, the arbitral status of contracts allegedly obtained by corruption is unclear, especially because they are plagued by problems of proof. This is unsatisfactory if the complainant has been harmed by the corrupt nature of the deal and if the domestic law-enforcement system is dysfunctional and even corrupt. Furthermore, in many cases, neither the host state nor the international investor has an interest in raising corruption charges – even if they can be proved. The exception, which has been arisen in a number of cases, is when a new host government introduces evidence of corruption under the previous regime.[39]

[36] See Dubois and Nowlan (2010). More information is available at the website of the World Bank's investigative unit, www.worldbank.org/integrity

[37] On tax havens, see Shaxson (2010).

[38] According to Pauwelyn, the term "corruption" does not appear in the WTO rulebook. He argues that the WTO tribunals could consider corruption to the extent that it affects trade, but its reach would be limited by the fact that only nation-states can bring claims and that it only judges government conduct, not the conduct of private parties. The penalties only involve reciprocal trade restrictions.

[39] An example from ICSID is *World Duty Free Co.* v. *Republic of Kenya*, ICSID Case No. ARB/00/07 (October 4, 2006).

There are two types of forums. One is the private commercial arbitration regime; the second, the World Bank's International Center for the Settlement of Investment Disputes (ICSID), only considers cases where investors sue nation states, usually under the provisions of bilateral investment treaties (BITs). In both cases private firms can initiate the arbitration process, but only if they are parties to the contracts in question. Disappointed bidders, or other outsiders to the contract, have no standing. Pauwelyn (2011) argues that BIT provisions requiring "fair and equitable treatment" could be extended to cover corruption. But so far, no cases have made that connection.

This weaknesses in the present system have led to reform proposals that range from the more explicit incorporation of corruption charges into the arbitral process, to the creation of a separate body, either a formal court or another type of arbitral tribunal, that would explicitly deal with claims that corruption should void a contract or, at least, lead to its renegotiation. Reform may require structural changes. Carrington, for example, argues for a new international forum to hear cases initiated by outsiders to the deal. In the alternative, he suggests an expanded mandate for arbitrators to accept submissions from *amici curiae* that provide evidence of corruption (Carrington, 2007, 2010).

However, even with this reform, arbitrators could not influence state governance structures directly. They would simply invalidate contracts on the basis of evidence that corruption had tainted the original deal. Carrington's ultimate goal is to increase the cost of paying and receiving bribes. Even if a country's criminal justice system is weak or corrupted, an arbitral decision that invalidates a contract, or awards damages to a successor government, ought to deter kickbacks up-front. This deterrent will be most effective in a multi-party democracy or in an autocracy whose leader is aging or losing popular support.

Within existing domestic legal frameworks, corruption charges have been incorporated into the resolution of private-law disputes in different ways (Maeyer, 2013). Litigants can sometimes use the legal system to obtain compensation for their losses, helping to deter corruption in the first place. In the United States they have used private rights of action under US securities and anti-trust laws, as well as fiduciary duty class actions, to seek redress. Losing competitors have also claimed unfair competition or tort damages from firms convicted of overseas bribery in the United States and the European Union.[40] This may be a growth area for anti-corruption efforts if domestic courts in industrialized countries prove ready to accept jurisdiction.[41] Unfortunately, however, the area is so new and so focused on a set of large-scale international deals that we have no data on its potential impact on the global contracting regime. This is an area where fruitful collaborative efforts between international lawyers and empirical social scientists may have large pay-offs.

Conclusion: options and CBA

A weak and corrupted government can undermine efforts to carry out otherwise beneficial policies. Programs designed to help the poor, improve the natural environment, and stimulate economic growth will have little impact and risk inflicting harm.

If possible, the choice of reform options should be driven by data and a thorough CBA.[42]

[40] In the United States see *Boyd et al.*, v. *AWB Ltd. et al.*, 544 F. Supp. 2d 236 (SD NY 2008). In the European Union, see *ADT Projekt Gesellschaft der Arbietisgemeinschaft Deutscher Tierzuchter mbH* v. *Commission of the European Communities*, Case t-145/98 European Court Reports p. II-00387. In South Africa see: *Transnet Ltd* v. *Sechaba Photoscan (Pty) Ltd* 2005 (1) SA 299 (SCA). Abiola Makinwa supplied these citations.

[41] Governments have also sometimes turned to ordinary courts for redress. Thus, in 1999 the Nigerian Government sought to recover the assets of a former President by asking the High Court in London to freeze his assets as a prelude to their repatriation. See also a failed effort by a state-owned Costa Rican company to block Alcatel–Lucent's Foreign Corrupt Practices Act (FCPA) settlement under a US victim's rights law.

[42] The last few years have seen a growth of corruption metrics, ranging from household-bribery-experience surveys to detailed tracking of public expenditures at all stages in the government hierarchy. Such metrics both allow researchers to understand the determinants of corruption and permit reformers to identify particularly problematic sectors or regions. The simple act of publishing corruption measures gives citizens

Information about possible policy initiatives needs to be grounded in valid studies that document the success or failure of policies in a variety of settings. Results in one country can help establish benchmarks for reforms elsewhere. To do this, governments must cooperate with donors in the design of projects that include competent social science evaluations. Unfortunately, evaluation may seem risky both to incumbent politicians who fear objective data and to donors who worry that evidence of failure will undermine their credibility. Even when governments and donors cooperate, studies must comply with social science protocols, including the collection of baseline data, valid-study design, and competent statistical analysis. This will require international institutions to design, carry out, and monitor pilot programs. Providing information on what works and what does not is impossible without hands-on projects in countries at risk of corruption.

There is an on-going debate in economics and political science over the best evaluation methods. Nevertheless, there is widespread agreement on the limitations of many current claims for policy efficacy. International financial institutions (IFIs), possessing staff expertise, need to do more to incorporate evaluation procedures into projects for governance and anti-corruption reform. This may require them to provide some tailored benefits to governments willing to accept evaluation as part of an aid program and to incorporate the stick of reduced funding if they do not. It is not sufficient merely to provide information about on-going projects; the projects themselves must be set up with built-in evaluation processes.

Assuming that these evaluations locate successful interventions, IFI staff should bring these positive cases to the attention of officials in other countries. At a minimum, IFIs should be information banks that public officials world-wide can turn to for help (Rodrik, 2006).[43] IFIs should have a toolkit of options that developing countries can use to develop their domestic strategies. This does not imply that one size fits all. Some countries might well reject particular reforms as incompatible with their own situation, but if they want financial assistance from aid agencies, they should have the burden of explaining why they will not adopt good governance and anti-corruption reforms shown to work elsewhere. The difficulty, of course, is that corrupt officials and contractors will try to neutralize and undermine programs that aim to improve government accountability and transparency. Representatives of donor agencies may be similarly reluctant to support serious and systematic evaluation, especially after working closely with host governments over the years.

At present, we still do not have good data on the relative effectiveness of most reform programs. After fifteen years of effort to promote anti-corruption and good governance, it would be valuable to consolidate experience across projects sponsored by aid and lending organizations – sharing successes, failures, and ambiguous cases. A fundamental problem here concerns public information that names countries and projects. Specific context is needed to decide if a program that worked in one country will succeed elsewhere. Domestic policy-makers need to know how to evaluate programs that worked in other countries in order to generate local buy-in. Yet, country leaders often object to publicizing projects that will put them in a bad light. Alternatively, incumbent politicians may be too eager to flag the malfeasance of the previous government in the hope of assuring their own re-election. Thus, some evaluations will be easier to accomplish than others, and some political contexts will simply be impossible to use as sites for evaluation studies.

Improved metrics will assist policy-makers by estimating the costs and benefits of specific reforms, a task that remains difficult and is rarely undertaken. Unresolved empirical issues limit the value of estimates of the relative cost-effectiveness of different strategies and the ways in which distinct alternatives interact. Cross-country research

and observers the opportunity to name and shame governments that foster the abuse of public power for private gain. This approach can also be employed effectively for subnational units, as evidenced by Vietnam's Public Administration Performance Index (PAPI), http://www.papi.vn, which quantifies government performance at the provincial level, and TI Mexico's National Index of Corruption and Good Governance, http://www.tm.org.mx/c/incio/.

[43] Rodrik stresses the need to present options to developing countries based on individual country experiences, not impose a single "consensus."

suggests that the gains from reducing corruption and improving governance are large. The main problem is tracing specific links from particular, concrete policies to desirable outcomes.[44] Even the World Bank, which has been a leader in quantifying the costs of the corruption, has been unwilling to organize the data in that fashion.

The few studies that do exist suggest a substantial net benefit for the anti-corruption intervention. In the audit study of Indonesia, Olken (2007) finds that the audit treatment produced a net benefit of $245–508 per village, depending on the assumptions being used. The improved road quality, as well as the increased wages received by workers, far outweighed the monetary and opportunity costs of the audit. Yang (2008) finds that privatized pre-shipment inspections increase import duty collections around 15–30 percent. Studies suggest the promise of various impersonal bureaucratic systems of tax collection and service delivery.[45] Even assuming that a country must pay the private firm 1 percent of the value of all imports inspected, the effect of privatization in this sector looks positive – the ratio of import duty improvement to fees paid is around 2.6. The tax and customs reform efforts in several Latin American countries outlined on pp. 652–4 led to substantial increases in revenue at minimal social cost. Online procurement systems are another reform that appears to pay for itself, although it is not a full response to corruption in procurement.

Even without definitive studies, some options look promising because the benefits seem clear and the costs are minimal. Hence, even if the benefits cannot be precisely measured, the rates of return appear large. The release of information to citizens, for example, may require little more than a website or a well-placed newspaper story. And if the estimates from Uganda's newspaper campaign are correct, added citizen accountability could decrease leakage by 60 percentage points in places where embezzlement is particularly endemic (Reinikka and Svennson, 2011). Civil service reforms, with the exception of wage increases, may require little more than a thoughtful reshuffling of personnel and recruitment practices. Audits and heightened monitoring do require resources, but have proven effective in many contexts. These possibilities are summarized in Table 11.3, along with others that ought to receive more systematic study.

Collectively, improving top-down monitoring and punishment, fostering transparency and citizen involvement, adjusting bureaucratic incentives through civil service reforms, improving the competiveness of government asset sales and large purchases, and privatizing certain government services may provide the shock needed to push a country or sector towards a self-fulfilling cycle of good governance. It is likely that these initiatives would prove most effective when bundled together, signaling a firm commitment to anti-corruption for all would-be corrupt officials.

Obviously, individuals and firms, many with political power, benefit from the status quo and will oppose change. A major challenge for governance reform is to overcome or coopt entrenched interests. If there has been one collective lesson from decades of anti-corruption reform, it is that political calculations can derail even the most well-conceived initiatives. Some reforms may be blocked directly, but equally pernicious are corrupt leaders who pose as reformers – expressing a superficial commitment to good governance as they continue to gain at public expense. A crackdown on low-level corruption may just push the illicit rents up the hierarchy where they can be captured by the top officials.

We conclude with a few thoughts about the relationship between these policy proposals and the international environment. Consider aid and lending. Presently there is an on-going debate about the value of conditionality in the provision of aid. "Conditionality" in some broad sense is inevitable. International donors must choose where to put scarce funds, and they will consider where the funds will have some positive payoff. A weak state or one with high levels of corruption will be unlikely to manage aid well and so will get less. A state that does receive aid must comply with financial reporting requirements to assure that the funds are not lost to corruption and waste. Such conditionality, however, is less directly intrusive than aid that

[44] See the similar conclusions of Olken and Pande (2012) after a review of the empirical research.

[45] In addition to the material summarized here, see the ongoing research summarized in Olken and Pande (2012).

Table 11.3 Outline of corruption solutions

Solution	Description	Benefits	Costs	Positive examples	Key lessons/risks
1. External monitoring and punishment	• Increase audit probabilities and strengthen anti-corruption agencies • Increase expected criminal punishments for corruption	• Reduction in all forms of malfeasance, most noticeably embezzlement	• Costs of audits and other monitoring resources • Law-enforcement costs and costs of false accusations	• Missing expenditures reduced by 8% in Indonesia village audit campaign	• Formal accountability mechanisms may be captured by political interests
2. Transparency and bottom-up accountability	• Increase transparency and provide information to citizens on government services • Improve complaint mechanisms	• Reduction in leakage of funds • Heightened citizen involvement in public affairs	• Costs of providing information to citizens and help to organize	• Uganda newspaper campaign reduced capture of educational funds from 80% to 20%	• Efficacy of transparency is conditional on presence of accountability mechanisms • Certain processes may be too complex for citizens to use
3. Internal controls and bureaucratic efficiency	• Meritocratic recruitment • Foster bureaucratic competition where appropriate • Ensure public salaries are competitive, including perks • Consider staff rotation • Reduce rents in public programs	• Reduction in corrupt networks throughout the bureaucracy • Better service delivery and revenue collection	• Higher wage bill • Perhaps some efficiency losses from rotation, bureaucratic competition, and simplification • Risk of sale of offices • Some tax and customs reform are net revenue-raisers	• Chile meritocratic civil service reforms in 2003 • Lower corruption at Durban port compared to competitors • Latin American tax and customs reform	• Wage interventions may not always be appropriate • Bureaucratic competition may cause substitution across different corrupt behaviors • All require on-going oversight to maintain benefits
4. Controlling "Grand corruption" inside states	• Enact procedural reforms to standardize purchases and enhance market competition • Develop e-procurement system on the models of Korea, Mexico, and Chile	• Cheaper and better-quality government purchases and infrastructure • Higher return from privatizations	• Organizing auctions and bidding systems • *Ex post* oversight by states and IFIs • E-procurement likely to pay for itself	• Need better empirical studies, but costs are small and potential benefits very large (Chile, Korea, Mexico)	• Consider links between grand corruption and both the organization of markets and decisions of which firms to privatize and which projects to pursue
5. Shifting service provision to private sector	• Delegate service provision to private firms using open-tender process	• Elimination of bureaucracy for certain aspects of service provision • Efficiency gains from privatization	• Possible loss of service ethos in transfer to private sector • Weaker monitoring	• Privatization of pre-shipment inspection increases tax revenue 2.6 times • India service privatization reduces extortion	• Possibility for corrupt transactions in privatization process • Private contractors must also be monitored
6. International initiatives	• Introduce international checks through stronger enforcement of OECD Convention, more active debarment processes at IFIs	• Better value for money for government projects • More competitive international markets	• Burden on IFIs and international arbitration system, • Costs of new adjudicatory body	• Reforms appear to have potential but generalizations difficult	• Potential for national courts and international arbitration regime to constrain corruption needs to be explored and strengthened

comes with explicit requirements for institutional reform. This latter type of conditionality has not been notably successful. An alternative is to organize projects that are directly focused on improved governance, but experience here is mixed – with some notable failures, such as the effort to control the use of the windfall produced by the discovery of natural gas in Chad.

A related problem arises when aid is tied directly to perceptions-based measures of corruption, as has historically been done by the US Millennium Challenge Corporation (MCC). Such measures rely on expert surveys of the level of corruption in a given country in a given year, which have proven subject to several systematic biases (Treisman, 2007; Kenny, 2006; Seligson, 2006; Olken, 2009).[46] At best, these measures are noisy indicators of the level of corruption, and they may fail to capture important policy changes. For example, if anti-corruption agencies successfully prosecute high-level politicians for corruption in country X, experts may hear of these convictions and perceive that the country has become more corrupt, even though it is on the path towards good governance. Perversely, countries that have actually taken a stand against corruption may take a hit on aid allocation because of the biases in the corruption indices. This problem speaks to the importance of developing richer, more accurate metrics.

We have documented some successes and some failures, but projects that improve governance and oversight should be priorities for IFIs and other international donors to put resources. If they do so, however, they need a plausible exit strategy so that external funds and experts can leave with some assurance that the program will continue. A condition of such projects should be a research component that measures progress (or its opposite) by providing information on background conditions, tracking the design and implementation of the reform, and measuring outputs. Donors and country partners would try to quantify inputs and outputs in terms such as the speed and effectiveness of government activities, the satisfaction of citizens, and the distribution of benefits. Sometimes, as in a tax or procurement reform, one can quantify the benefits in terms of additional dollars collected or cost savings, but in other cases, such as more transparent government, the benefits take the form of greater citizen satisfaction and better government accountability. These factors are valuable in their own right and are associated with higher levels of growth and individual well-being, but the precise links from specific policy interventions to outcomes are not well specified.

Recent discussions of how to allocate foreign assistance to developing countries sometimes conclude that some countries have such poorly functioning institutions that no external aid should be provided because so much of it will be lost. This represents not, as some say, an end to conditionality but is instead conditionality writ large – at the level of the country as a whole, rather than at the level of the program. The best mixture seems to be broad-based decisions about which countries to support with some share of aid taking the form of grants to improve government performance. Outsiders would not micro-manage individual projects – for example, to build roads, support education, or provide health care. Instead, they would supply technical assistance that could involve them quite deeply with the details of government operations. In contrast, policies which try to isolate corrupt countries and individuals from the international community encourage their rulers to descend into paranoia and isolation and are ineffective ways to help the citizens of these countries who are the real victims of corruption. Durable reform requires systemic policy initiatives. Corruption is a problem of institutional failure. A "clean-hands" policy in which wealthy countries hold themselves aloof from tainted countries and individuals without

[46] Examining the relationship between corruption incidence and perception-based data, Treisman (2007) finds that the perceptions-based indices are not as well correlated with incidence as would be expected, and many of the factors that predict high levels of perceived corruption do not explain levels of actual corruption. Other scholars have levied additional critiques. Kenny (2006) argues that TI's CPI as a lagging, not leading, indicator of corruption scandals. Olken (2009) finds that although Indonesian villagers' perceptions of corruption correlated reasonably well with incidence, using perceptions data would give misleading results for the explanatory power of variables like ethnic heterogeneity and social capital. Among other critiques, Seligson (2006) notes that the CPI may be influenced by stereotypes and factors unrelated to corruption, like economic performance.

doing anything actually to address the underlying problems will simply further divide the world into rich and poor blocs.

Bibliography

Abbink, K., 2004: Staff rotation as an anti-corruption policy: an experimental study, *European Journal of Political Economy* **20**, 887–906

Abbink, K., B. Irlenbusch, and E., Renner, 2002: An experimental bribery game, *The Journal of Law, Economics, and Organization* **18**, 428–54

Acemoglu, D., S. Johnson, and J. A. Robinson, 2001: The colonial origins of comparative development: an empirical investigation, *American Economic Review* **91**, 1369–1401

Ades, A. and R. Di Tella, 1999: Rents, competition, and corruption, *The American Economic Review* **89**, 982–93

Adsera, A., C. Boix, and M. Payne, 2003: Are you being served? Political accountability and the quality of government, *Journal of Law, Economics, and Organization* **19**, 445–90

Aidt, T., 2009: Corruption, institutions, and economic development, *Oxford Review of Economic Policy* **25**, 271–91

2011: Corruption and sustainability, in S. Rose-Ackerman and T. Søreide (eds.), *The International Handbook on the Economics of Corruption*, Vol. 2, Edward Elgar, Cheltenham, 3–51

Alfiler, M. C. P., 1986: The process of bureaucratic corruption in Asia: emerging patterns, in L. A. Carino (eds.), *Bureaucratic Competition in Asia: Causes, Consequences and Controls*, JMC Press, Quezon City, 15–68

Anderson, C. J. and Y. V. Tverdova, 2003: Corruption, political allegiances, and attitudes toward government in contemporary democracies, *American Journal of Political Science* **47**, 91–109

Anderson, J., D. Kaufmann, and F. Recanatini, 2003: *Service Delivery, Poverty and Corruption: Common Threads from Diagnostic Surveys*, Background Paper for 2004 World Development Report, World Bank, Washington, DC, June 27, www.worldbank.org/wbi/governance/capacitybuild/d-surveys.html

Andvig, J. C. and K. O. Moene, 1990: How corruption may corrupt, *Journal of Economic Behavior and Organization* **13**, 63–76

Argandona, A., 2010: Private-to-private corruption, *Journal of Business Ethics* **46**, 253–67

Armantier, O. and A. Boly, 2008: Can corruption be studied in the lab? Comparing a field and a lab experiment, *CIRANO – Scientific Publications* **2008s-26**

Auriol, E. and S. Straub, 2011: Privatization of rent-generating industries and corruption, in S. Rose-Ackerman and T. Søreide (eds.), *The International Handbook on the Economics of Corruption*, Vol. 2, Edward Elgar, Cheltenham, 207–30

Azfar, O. and W. Nelson, 2007: Transparency, wages and the separation of powers: an experimental analysis of corruption, *Public Choice* **130**, 471–93

Barma, N., K. Kaiser, T. M. Le, and L. Viñuela, 2011: *Rents to Riches? The Political Economy of Natural Resource-Led Development*, World Bank, Washington, DC

Barr, A., M. Lindelow, and P. Serneels, 2009: Corruption in public service delivery: an experimental analysis, *Journal of Economic Behavior & Organization* **72**, 225–39

Barrera-Osorio, F. and M. Olivera, 2007: Does society win or lose as a result of privatization? Provision of public services and welfare of the poor: the case of water sector privatization in Colombia, *Research Network Working Paper* **R-525**, Inter-American Development Bank, Washington, DC, www.iadb.org/topics/Home.cfm?topicID=RM&parid=2&language=English

Becker, G. and G. J. Stigler, 1974: Law enforcement, malfeasance, and compensation of enforcers, *The Journal of Legal Studies* **3**, 1–18

Bergman, M. S., 2003: Tax reforms and tax compliance: the divergent paths of Chile and Argentina, *Journal of Latin American Studies* **35**, 3–28

Bertrand, M., S. Djankov, R. Hanna, and S. Mullainathan, 2007: Obtaining a driver's license in India: An experimental approach to studying corruption, *Quarterly Journal of Economics* **122**, 1639–76

Bjorvatn, K. and T. Søreide, 2005: Corruption and privatization, *European Journal of Political Economy* **21**, 903–14

Blake, C. H., and C. Martin, 2006: The dynamics of political corruption: re-examining the influence of democracy, *Democratization* **13**, 1–14

Brunetti, A. and B. Weder, 2003: A free press is bad news for corruption, *Journal of Public Economics* **87**, 1801–24

Bryane, M., 2004: Depoliticising anti-corruption in Bolivia: local international intervention and the state, *International Journal of Public* **29**, 1311–36

Burgess, R., M. Hansen, B. Olken, P. Potapov, and S. Sieber, 2011: The political economy of deforestation in the tropics, *MIT Working Paper*, Cambridge MA

Burke, J., 2000: Where state fails, others give poor a chance, *London Guardian*, February 28

Burns, J. P. and X. Wang, 2010: Civil service reform in China: impacts on civil servants' behaviour, *China Quarterly* **201**, 58–78

Bussell, J. L., 2012: *Corruption and Reforms in India: Public Services in the Digital Age*, Cambridge University Press

Cadot, O., 1987: Corruption as a gamble, *Journal of Public Economics* **33**, 223–44

Carrington, P. D., 2007: Law and transnational corruption: the need for Lincoln's law abroad, *Law and Contemporary Problems* **70**, 109–38

2010: Enforcing international corrupt practices law, *Michigan Journal of International Law* **32**, 129–64

Chang, E. C. and Y. Chu, 2006: Corruption and trust: exceptionalism in Asian democracies?, *Journal of Politics* **68**, 259–71

Chong, A. and F. López-de-Silanes, 2003: The truth about privatization in Latin America. *Research Network Working Paper*, Inter-American Development Bank, Washington, DC

Cole, S. and T. Ahn, 2011: Evidence from the firm: a new approach to understanding corruption, in S. Rose-Ackerman and T. Søreide (eds.), *The International Handbook on the Economics of Corruption*, Vol. 2, Edward Elgar, Cheltenham, 408–27

Colitt, R., 2004: Brazil probe reveals decade of corruption in health contracts, *Financial Times*, June 2

Dahlstrom, C., V. Lapuente, and J. Teorell, 2009: Bureaucracy, politics, and corruption, Paper presented at the Annual Meeting of the American Political Science Association, Toronto

de Figueirido, M. F. P., F. D. Hidalgo, and Y. Kasahara, 2013: When do voters punish corrupt politicians? Experimental evidence from Brazil, Working Paper, University of California, Berkeley and University of Oslo, www.dropbox.com/s/rzvvgyntmosndjr/SPCorruptionv52.pdf

de Michele, R., 2013: How can international financial institutions support countries' efforts to prevent corruption under international treaties and agreements?, in S. Rose-Ackerman and P. Carrington (eds.), *Anti-Corruption Policy: Can International Actors Play a Constructive Role*?, Carolina Academic Press, Durham, NC, 179–97

Di Gioacchino, D. and M. Franzini, 2008: Bureaucrats' corruption and competition in public administration, *European Journal of Law and Economics* **26**, 291–306

Dollar, D., M. Hallward-Driemeier, and T. Mengiste, 2006: Investment climate and international integration, *World Development* **34**, 1498–1516

Dreher, A. and T. Herzfeld, 2005: *The Economic Costs of Corruption: A Survey and New Evidence*, CESifo, Munich

Dubois, P. H. and A. E. Nowlan, 2010: Global administrative law and the legitimacy of sanctions regimes in international law, *Yale Journal of International Law Online 36*, 15-www.yjil.org/docs/pub/o-36-dubois-nowlan-global-administrative-law-sanctions.pdf

Dufwenberg, M. and G. Spagnolo, 2011: Legalizing bribes, *SITE Working Paper Series* 13, Stockholm School of Economics, http://swopec.hhs.se/hasite/papers/hasite0013.pdf

Engel, C., S. J. Georg, and G. Yu, 2012: Symmetric vs. asymmetric punishment regimes for bribery, Max Planck Institute for Research on Collective Goods, Bonn, Preprint 2012/1, http://ssrn.com/abstract=1983969; http://dx.doi.org/10.2139.ssrn.1983969

Escobar, F., 2004: Bolivia, in L. De Wulf and J. B. Sokol, *Customs Modernization Initiatives: Case Studies*, World Bank, Washington, DC, 7–18

Esty, D. and M. Porter, 2002: National environmental performance measurement and determinants, in D. Esty and P. K. Cornelius (eds.), *Environmental Performance Measurement: The Global Report 2001–2002*, Oxford University Press, New York

Evans, P. B. and J. E. Rauch, 2000: Bureaucratic structures and economic performance in less developed countries, *Journal of Public Economics* **75**, 49–71

Faccio, M., 2006: Politically connected firms, *American Economic Review* **96**, 369–86

Falk, A. and M. Kosfeld, 2006: The hidden costs of control, *American Economic Review* **96**, 1611–30

Ferraz, C. and F. Finan, 2010: Motivating politicians: the impacts of monetary incentives on quality and performance, *Working Paper*, University of California, Berkeley CA

2011: Electoral accountability and corruption: evidence from the audits of local governments, *American Economic Review* **101**, 1274–311

Ferraz, C., F. Finan, and D. B. Moreira, 2010: Corrupting learning: evidence from missing federal education funds in Brazil, *Working Paper*, University of California, Berkeley CA

Filmer, D. and D. L. Lindauer, 2001: Does Indonesia have a "low-pay" civil service?, *World Bank Policy Research Working Paper* **2621**, World Bank, Washington, DC

Fisman, R., 2001: Estimating the value of political connections, *American Economic Review* **91**, 1095–102

Fjeldsted, O., 2003: *Decentralisation and Corruption: A Review of the Literature*, U4 Report, Christian Michelsen Institute, Bergen

2005: *Revenue Administration and Corruption*, U4 Issue 2, Christian Michelson Institute, Bergen

Flyvberg, B. and E. Molloy, 2011: Delusion, deception and corruption in major infrastructure projects: causes, consequences and cures, in S. Rose-Ackerman and T. Søreide (eds.), *The International Handbook on the Economics of Corruption*, Vol. 2, Edward Elgar, Cheltenham, 81–107

Flyvbjerg, B., N. Bruzelius, and W. Rothengatter, 2003: *Megaprojects and Risk: an Anatomy of Ambition*, Cambridge University Press

Fried, B., P. Lagunes, and A. Venkataramani, 2009: Corruption and inequality at the crossroad: a multi-method study of bribery and discrimination in Latin America, *Latin American Research Review*, **45**, 76–97

Friedman, E., S. Johnson, D. Kaufmann, and P. Zoido-Lobaton, 2000: Dodging the grabbing hand: the determinant of unofficial activity in 69 countries, *Journal of Public Economics* **76**, 459–93

Fries, S., T. Lysenko, and S. Polanec, 2003: The 2002 Business Environment and Enterprise Performance Survey: results from a survey of 6,100 firms, *Working Paper* 84, European Bank for Reconstructions and Development, London, November

Goel, R. K. and D. P. Rich, 1989: On the economic incentives for taking bribes, *Public Choice* **61**, 269–75

Gómez Sabaini, J., 2006: Evolución y situación tributaria actual en América Latina: una serie de temas para la discusión, in Comisión Económica para América Latina y el Caribe (ed.), *Tributación en América Latina: En Busca de Una Nueva Agenda de Reformas*, Santiago de Chile Naciones Unidas: Comisión Económica para América Latina y el Caribe

Goorman, A., 2004: Peru, in L. De Wulf and J. B. Sokol, *Customs Modernization Initiatives: Case Studies*, World Bank, Washington, DC, 65–84

Gorodnichenko, Y. and P. K. Sabirianova Peter, 2007: Public sector pay and corruption: measuring bribery from micro data, *Journal of Public Economics* **91**, 963–99

Gyimah-Brempong, K., 2002: Corruption, economic growth, and income inequality in Africa, *Economics of Governance* **3**, 183–209

Hellman, J. S., G. Jones, and D. Kaufmann, 2003: Seize the state, seize the day: state capture, corruption, and influence in transition, *Journal of Comparative Economics* **31**, 751–73

Hoffmann, B., 2007: Why reform fails: the "politics of policies" in Costa Rican telecommunications liberalization, GIGA Research Unit, Institute of Latin American Studies, *Working Paper* **47**, Hamburg

Hunt, J., 2006: Why are some public officials more corrupt than others?, in S. Rose-Ackerman (ed.), *International Handbook on the Economics of Corruption*, Edward Elgar, Northampton, MA

Iversen, V., O. H. Fjeldstad, G. Bahiigwa, F. Ellis, and R. James, 2006: Private tax collection: remnant of the past or way forward? Evidence from rural Uganda, *Public Administration and Development* **26**, 317–28

Johnson, S., D. Kaufmann, J. McMillan, and C. Woodruff, 2000: Why do firms hide? Bribes and unofficial activity after Communism, *Journal of Public Economics* **76**, 495–520

Johnston, M., 2005: *Syndromes of Corruption*, Cambridge University Press

Kaufmann, D., 2003: Rethinking governance: empirical lessons challenge orthodoxy, Chapter 21, in *Global Competitiveness Report 2002–2003*, World Economic Forum, Geneva

Kenny, P., 2006: Measuring and reducing the impact of corruption in infrastructure, *Policy Research Working Paper*, World Bank, Washington, DC

Khwaja, A. I. and A. Mian, 2005: Do lenders favor politically connected firms? Rent provision in an emerging financial market, *Quarterly Journal of Economics* **120**, 1371–411

Kolstad, I. and A. Wiig, 2009: Is transparency the key to reducing corruption in resource-rich countries?, *World Development* **37**, 521–32

Kossick, R., 2004: *Best Practice Profile: CompraNet*, May 10, www.undp.org/surf-panama/egov/docs/programme_activities/bpractices/e-procurement_in_mexico-compranet.pdf

Kugler, M., T. Verdier, and Y. Zenou, 2005: Organized crime, corruption and punishment, *Journal of Public Economics*. **89**, 1639–63

Kunicová, J. and S. Rose-Ackerman, 2005: Electoral rules and constitutional structures as constraints on corruption, *British Journal of Political Science* **35**, 573–606

Laguna, M. I. D., 2011: The challenges of implementing merit-based personnel policies in Latin America: Mexico's civil service reform experience, *Journal of Comparative Policy Analysis* **13**, 51–73

Lambert-Mogiliansky, A., 2011: Corruption and collusion: strategic complements in procurement, in S. Rose-Ackerman and T. Søreide (eds.), *The International Handbook on the Economics of Corruption*, Vol. 2, Edward Elgar, Cheltenham, 108–40

Lambsdorff, J. G., 2003a: How corruption affects persistent capital flows, *Economics of Governance* **4**, 229–43

2003b: How corruption affects productivity, *Kyklos* **56**, 457–74

2006: Consequences and causes of corruption – what do we know from a cross-section of countries?, in S. Rose-Ackerman (ed.), *International Handbook on the Economics of Corruption*, Edward Elgar, Northampton, MA, 3–51

Lambsdorff, J. G. and M. Nell, 2007: Fighting corruption with asymmetric penalties and leniency, *CeGE-Discussion Paper* **59**, University of Göttingen

La Porta, R., F. López-de-Silanes, A. Shleifer, and R. Vishny, 1999: The quality of government, *Journal of Law, Economics, and Organization* **15**, 222–79

Lawson, L., 2009: The politics of anti-corruption reform in Africa, *Journal of Modern African Studies* **47**, 73–100

Loevinsohn, B. and A. Harding, 2005: Buying results? Contracting for health service delivery in developing countries, *Lancet* **366**, 676–81

Manzetti, L., 1999: *Privatization South American Style*, Oxford University Press, New York

Masclet, D., C. Noussair, S. Tucker, and M. C. Villeval, 2003: Monetary and non-monetary punishment in the voluntary contributions mechanism, *American Economic Review* **93**, 366–80

Mauro, P., 1998: Corruption and the composition of government expenditure, *Journal of Public Economics* **69**, 263–79

McMillan, J. and P. Zoido, 2004: How to subvert democracy: Montesinos in Peru, *Journal of Economic Perspectives* **18**, 69–92

McPake, B., D. Aslimwe, F. Mwesigye, M. Ofumbi, L. Ortenblad, P. Streefland, and A. Turinde, 1999: Informal economic activities of public health workers in Uganda: implications for quality and accessibility of care, *Social Science Medicine* **49**, 849–65

Meyer, O., 2011: The formation of a transnational ordre public against corruption, in S. Rose-Ackerman and P. Carrington (eds.), *Anti-Corruption Policy: Can International Actors Play a Constructive Role?*, Carolina Academic Press, Durham, NC, 229–46

Miller W., A. Grødeland, and T. Koshechkina, 2001: *A Culture of Corruption? Coping with Government in Post-Communist Europe?*, Central European University Press, Budapest

Mutebi, A. M., 2008: Explaining the failure of Thailand's anti-corruption regime, *Development and Change* **39**, 147–71

Olaya, J., 2010: *Good Governance and International Investment Law: The Challenge of Lack of Transparency and Corruption*, Paper presented at the Second Biennial SIEL Conference

Olken, B. A., 2006: Corruption and the costs of redistribution: micro evidence from Indonesia, *Journal of Public Economics* **90**, 853–70

2007: Monitoring corruption: evidence from a field experiment in Indonesia, *Journal of Political Economy* **115**, 200–49

2009: Corruption perceptions vs. corruption reality, *Journal of Public Economics* **93**, 950–64

Olken, B. A. and R. Pande, 2012: Corruption in developing countries, *Annual Review of Economics* **4**, 479–509

Organization for Economic Cooperation and Development (OECD), 2003: Trade facilitation reforms in the service of development, *Trade Committee Working Paper* TD/TC/WP(2003)11/FINAL, OECD, Paris

Panizza, U., 2000: The public sector premium and the gender gap in Latin America: evidence for the 1980s and 1990s, *IDB Research Department Working Paper* **431**, Inter-American Development Bank, Washington, DC, August

Pasuk, P. and P. Sungsidh, 1994: *Corruption and Democracy in Thailand* The Political Economy Centre, Faculty of Economics, Chulalongkorn University, Bangkok

Patrinos, H. and R. Kagia, 2006: Maximizing the performance of education systems: the case of teacher absenteeism, in J. E. Campos and S. Pradhan (eds.), *The Many Faces of Corruption: Tracking Vulnerabilities at the Sector Level*, World Bank, Washington, DC

Pauwelyn, J., 2013: Enforcing anti-corruption rules: limits and lessons of dispute settlement in trade and investment agreements, in S. Rose-Ackerman and P. Carrington (eds.), *Anti-Corruption Policy: Can International Actors Play a Constructive Role*?, Carolina Academic Press, Durham, NC, 247–66

Peisakhin, L. and P. Pinto, 2010: Is transparency an effective anti-corruption strategy? Evidence from a field experiment in India, *Regulation and Governance* **4**, 261–80

Peren Arin, K., V. Chmelarova, E. Feess, and A. Wohlschlegel, 2011: Why are corrupt countries less successful in consolidating their budgets?, *Journal of Public Economics* **95**, 521–30

Pieth, M., 2011: Contractual freedom v. public policy considerations in arbitration, in A. Büchler and M. Müller-Chen (eds.), *National–Global–Comparative, Festschrift für Ingeborg Schwenzer zum 60 Geburtstag*, Bern, 1375–85

Piga, G., 2011: A fighting chance against corruption in procurement, in S. Rose-Ackerman and T. Søreide (eds.), *The International Handbook on the Economics of Corruption*, Vol. 2, Edward Elgar, Cheltenham, 141–81

Pyman, M., R. Wilson, and D. Scott, 2009: The extent of single sourcing in defense procurement and its relevance as a corruption risk: a first look, *Defence and Peace Economics* **20**, 215–32, http://dx.doi.org/10.1080/10242690802016506

Rauch, J. E. and P. B. Evans, 2000: Bureaucratic structure and bureaucratic performance in less developed countries, *Journal of Public Economics* **75**, 49–71

Recanatini, F., 2011: Anti-corruption authorities: an effective tool to curb corruption?, in S. Rose-Ackerman and T. Søreide (eds.), *The International Handbook on the Economics of Corruption*, Vol. 2, Edward Elgar, Cheltenham, 528–66

Reinikka, R. and J. Svensson, 2004: Local capture: evidence from a central government transfer program in Uganda, *Quarterly Journal of Economics* **119**, 679–705

2006: Using micro-surveys to measure and explain corruption, *World Development* **34**, 359–70

2011: The power of information in public services: evidence from education in Uganda, *Journal of Public Economics* **95**, 956–66

Rock, M. T. and H. Bonnett, 2004: The comparative politics of corruption: accounting for the East Asian paradox in empirical studies of corruption, growth and investment, *World Development* **32**, 999–1017

Rodrik, D., 2006: Goodbye Washington Consensus, hello Washington Confusion? A review of the World Bank's *Economic Growth in the 1990s: Learning from a Decade of Reform, Journal of Economic Literature* **44**, 973–87

Rose-Ackerman, S., 1978: *Corruption: A Study in Political Economy*, Academic Press, New York

1999: *Corruption and Government: Causes, Consequences, and Reform*, Cambridge University Press

2010: The law and economics of bribery and extortion, in T. R. Hagan (ed.), *Annual Review of Law and Social Science* **6**, 217–38

Rusbridger, A., 2010: The splintering of the Fourth Estate, Andrew Olle Lecture, Sydney, published in *The Guardian*, November 19, www.guardian.co.uk/commentisfree/2010/nov/19/open-collaborative-future-journalism

Sandholtz, W. and W. Keotzle, 2000: Accounting for corruption: economic structure, democracy, and trade, *International Studies Quarterly* **44**, 31–50

Schulze, G. and B. Frank, 2003: Deterrence versus intrinsic motivation: experimental evidence on the determinants of corruptibility, *Economics of Governance* **4**, 143–60

Seligson, M., 2002: The impact of corruption on regime legitimacy: a comparative study of four Latin American countries, *Journal of Politics* **64**, 408–33

2006: The measurement and impact of corruption victimization: survey evidence from Latin America, *World Development* **34**, 381–404

Sequeira, S. and S. Djankov, 2010: An empirical study of corruption in ports, *MPRA Working Paper* **21791**, Munich University Library, http://ssrn.com/abstract=1592733

Serra, D., 2012: Combining top-down and bottom-up accountability: evidence from a bribery experiment, *Journal of Law, Economics and Organization* **28**, 569–87

Shah, A. and J. Huther, 2000: Anti-corruption policies and programs: a framework for evaluation, *World Bank Policy Research Working Paper* **2501**,World Bank, Washington, DC

Shaxson, N., 2010: *Treasure Islands: Tax Havens and the Men who Stole the World*, Bodley Head, London

Shleifer, A. and R. W. Vishny, 1993: Corruption, *Quarterly Journal of Economics* **108**, 599–617

Silva, P., 2010: *Learning to Fear the Inspector-General: Measuring Spillovers from Anti-Corrupt Policies*, Paper presented at the 2010 meeting of the American Political Science Association, Washington, DC

Søreide, T., A. Tostensen, and I. A. Skage, 2012: *Hunting for Per Diems: The Uses and Abuses of Travel Compensation in Three Developing Countries, NORAD Evaluation Report* **2/2012**, Norwegian Agency for Development Cooperation, Oslo, www.norad.no/en/tools-and-publications/publications/evaluations/publication?key=390706

Stein, E., M. Tommasi, K. Echebarría, E. Lora, and M. Payne, 2005: *The Politics of Policies: Economic and Social Progress in Latin America*, Inter-American Development Bank & the David Rockefeller Center for Latin American Studies at Harvard University, Washington, DC

Swamy, A., S. Knack, Y. Lee, and O. Azfar, 2001: Gender and corruption, *Journal of Development Economics* **64**, 25–55

Taliercio, R. Jr., 2001: *Unsustainably Autonomous?: Challenges to the Revenue Authority Model in Latin America Tax Agencies in Developing Countries*, World Bank, Washington, DC, Mimeo

2004: Designing performance: the semi-autonomous revenue authority model in Africa and Latin America, *World Bank Policy Research Working Paper* **3423**, World Bank, Washington, DC

Tanzi, V. and H. Davoodi, 2001: Corruption, growth, and public finances, in A. K. Jain (ed.), *Political Economy of Corruption*, Routledge, London, 89–110

Torgler, B., 2003: To evade taxes or not: that is the question, *Journal of Socio-Economics* **32**, 283–302

Transparency International (TI), 2010: *Global Corruption Barometer Report*, www.transparency.org/policy_research/surveys_indices/gcb/2010/press

Transparency International, Defense and Security Program, 2010: *Defence Offsets: Addressing the Risk of Corruption and Raising Transparency*, April, www.ti-defence.org/

2011a: *Building Integrity and Controlling Corruption in Defense and Security: 20 Practical Reforms*, September, www.ti-defence.org/

2011b: *The Transparency of Defence Budgets*, October, www.ti-defence.org/

Treisman, D., 2000: The causes of corruption: a cross-national study, *Journal of Public Economics* **76**, 399–457

2007: What have we learned about the causes of corruption from ten years of cross-national empirical research?, *Annual Review of Political Science* **10**, 211–44

Truex, R., 2011: Corruption, attitudes, and education: survey evidence from Nepal, *World Development* **39**, 1133–42

Truex, R. and T. Søreide, 2011: Why multi-stakeholder groups succeed and fail, in S. Rose-Ackerman and T. Søreide (eds.), *The International Handbook on the Economics of Corruption*, Vol. 2, Edward Elgar, Cheltenham, 478–98

Uslaner, E., 2007: Tax evasion, trust, and the strong arm of the law, in N. Hayoz and S. Hug (eds.), *Trust, Institutions, and State Capacities: A Comparative Study*, Peter Lang, Bern, 17–50

Vagliasindi, M., 2011: Public versus private governance and performance: evidence from public utility regulation, in S. Rose-Ackerman and T. Søreide (eds.), *The International Handbook on the Economics of Corruption*, Vol. 2 Edward Elgar, Cheltenham, 185–206 van Rijckeghem, C. and B. Weder, 2001: Bureaucratic corruption and the rate of temptation: do wages in the civil service affect corruption, and by how much?, *Journal of Development Economics* **65**, 307–31

Wade, R., 1982: The system of administrative and political corruption: canal irrigation in South India, *Journal of Development Studies* **18**, 287–328

Ware, G. T., S. Moss, J. E. Campos, and G. P. Noone, 2011: Corruption in procurement, in A. Graycar and R. G. Smith (eds.), *Handbook of Global Research and Practice in Corruption*, Edward Elgar, Cheltenham, 65–107

Wei, S. J., 2000: How taxing is corruption on international investors?, *Review of Economics and Statistics* **82**, 1–11

Weitz-Shapiro, R. and M. S. Winters, 2010: *Lacking Information or Condoning Corruption? Voter Attitudes Toward Corruption in Brazil*, APSA 2010 Annual Meeting Paper, Washington, DC

Wirth, C. J., 1997: Transportation policy in Mexico City: the politics and impacts of privatization, *Urban Affairs Review* **33**, 155–81

World Bank, 2012: *Fighting Corruption in Public Services: Chronicling Georgia's Reforms*, World Bank, Washington, DC

Wrong, M., 2013: How the media in developing countries can play a stronger role in combating corruption associated with international aid, in S. Rose-Ackerman and P. Carrington (eds.), *Anti-Corruption Policy: Can International Actors Play a Constructive Role?*, Carolina Academic Press, Durham, NC, 103–12

Yang, D., 2008: Integrity for hire: an analysis of a widespread customs reform, *Journal of Law and Economics* **51**, 25–57

You, J.-S. and S. Khagram, 2005: A comparative study of inequality and corruption, *American Sociological Review* **70**, 136–57

Zuleta, J. C., A. Leyton, and E. F. Ivanovic, 2006: Corruption in the revenue service: the case of VAT refunds in Bolivia, in J. E. Campos and S. Pradhan (eds.), *The Many Faces of Corruption: Tracking Vulnerabilities at the Sector Level*, World Bank, Washington, DC

CHAPTER 12

Trade Barriers and Subsidies

KYM ANDERSON*

Opening economies to international trade and investment, and reducing price-distorting subsidies, can generate enormous economic and social benefits relative to the costs of adjustment to such policy reform. Numerous barriers to trade in goods, in some services, and in capital flows have been reduced considerably over the past three decades, but many remain, as do many farm subsidies. Such price-distorting policies harm most the economies imposing them, but the worst of them (in agriculture and textiles) are particularly harmful to the world's poorest people. Addressing this challenge would therefore also reduce poverty and thereby assist in meeting several of the other challenges identified in the Copenhagen Consensus project, including malnutrition, disease, poor education, and air pollution.

This chapter focuses on how costly those anti-poor trade policies are, and examines possible strategies to reduce remaining price-distorting measures. Four opportunities in particular are addressed. The most beneficial involves multilaterally completing the stalled Doha Development Agenda (DDA) of the WTO. If that continues to prove to be too difficult politically to bring to a conclusion in the near future, the other three opportunities considered here involve prospective subglobal regional integration agreements. One involves the proposed Trans-Pacific Partnership (TPP) among a subset of member countries of the Asia Pacific Economic Cooperation (APEC) grouping; another involves extending the free-trade area (FTA) among the ten-member Association of South East Asian Nations to include China, Japan, and Korea (ASEAN+3); and the third opportunity is an FTA among all APEC countries.[1]

The chapter begins by defining the challenge. It then summarizes the arguments for removing price-distorting policies, along with critiques by skeptics, before discussing the various opportunities for reducing trade barriers and farm subsidies and explaining why we choose to focus on the four mentioned above. The core of the chapter is in the next two sections, which review the economic benefits and adjustment costs associated with these opportunities. That provides the foundation to undertake the CBA required to allow this set of opportunities to be ranked against those aimed at addressing the world's other key challenges. The chapter concludes with key caveats that suggest that taking up these opportunities could generate social BCRs that are even higher than the direct economic ones quantified in this study, not least because they would also go some way towards addressing several of the other challenges identified by the Copenhagen Consensus project.

The challenge

Despite the net economic and social benefits of reducing most government subsidies[2] and barriers

* This chapter draws on Anderson's papers for the 2004 and 2008 Copenhagen Consensus. Thanks are due to Nanda Aryal for research assistance with the benefit/cost calculus and to the Copenhagen Consensus Centre and the Australian Research Council for financial support. The views expressed are the author's alone.

[1] The nine current countries in TPP negotiations are Australia, Brunei, Chile, Malaysia, New Zealand, Peru, Singapore, the United States, and Vietnam. The twenty-one members of APEC include the TPP participants plus the other main ASEAN+3 economies plus Canada, Hong Kong, Mexico, Papua New Guinea, Russia, and Taiwan.

[2] Not all subsidies are welfare-reducing, and in some cases a subsidy-cum-tax will be the optimal government intervention to overcome a gap between private and social costs that cannot be bridged *à la* Coase (1960). Throughout this chapter

to international trade and investment, almost every national government intervenes in markets for goods, services, and capital in ways that distort international commerce.[3] To keep the task manageable, the policy instruments considered will be limited to those trade-related ones over which a government's international trade negotiators have some influence at both home and abroad. That thereby excludes measures such as generic taxes on income, consumption and value-added, government spending on mainstream public services, infrastructure and generic social safety nets in strong demand by the community, and subsidies (taxes) and related measures set optimally from the national viewpoint to overcome positive (negative) environmental or other externalities. Also excluded from consideration here are policies affecting markets for foreign exchange.

This challenge in its modern form has been with us for eight decades (Anderson, 2012). The latter part of the nineteenth century saw a strong movement toward laissez faire in goods and financial capital and widespread international migration, but that development was reversed following the First World War in ways that contributed to the Great Depression of the early 1930s and the conflict that followed (Kindleberger, 1989). It was during the Second World War, in 1944, that a conference at Bretton Woods in New Hampshire proposed an International Trade Organization (ITO). An ITO charter was drawn up by 1947 along with a General Agreement on Tariffs and Trade (GATT), but the ITO idea died when the United States failed to progress it through Congress (Diebold, 1952). Despite that, the GATT came into being from 1948 and during its forty-seven-year history (before it was absorbed into the WTO on 1 January 1995) oversaw the gradual lowering of many tariffs on imports of most manufactured goods by the governments of high-income countries. Manufacturing tariffs remained high in developing countries, however, and distortionary subsidies and trade policies affecting agricultural, textile, and services markets of both rich and poor countries, plus immigrations restrictions, continued to hamper efficient resource allocation, consumption choices, economic growth and poverty alleviation.

The GATT's Uruguay Round of multilateral trade negotiations led to agreements signed in 1994 that contributed to trade liberalization over the subsequent ten years. But even when those agreements had been fully implemented by early 2005, and despite additional unilateral trade liberalizations since the 1980s by a number of countries (particularly developing and transition economies), many subsidies and trade restrictions remained. They include not just trade taxes-cum-subsidies but also contingent protection measures such as antidumping, regulatory standards that can be technical barriers to trade, and domestic producer subsidies (allegedly decoupled from production in the case of some farm support programs in high-income countries, but in fact only partially so). Insufficient or excessive taxation or quantitative regulations in the presence of externalities such as environmental or food safety risks also lead to inefficiencies and can be trade-distorting. Furthermore, the on-going proliferation of preferential trading and bilateral or regional integration arrangements – for which there would be far less need in the absence of high barriers to trade – is adding complexity to international economic relations. In some cases those arrangements are leading to trade and investment diversion rather than creation, and may be welfare-reducing for some (especially excluded) economies.

The reluctance to reduce trade distortions is almost never because such policy reform involves government Treasury outlays. On the contrary, except in the case of a handful of low-income countries still heavily dependent on trade taxes for government revenue, such reform may well benefit the Treasury (by raising income or consumption/value-added tax revenues more than trade tax revenues fall, not to mention any payments forgone because of cuts to subsidy programs). Rather, trade distortions (and barriers to immigration) remain largely because further liberalization and subsidy cuts would redistribute jobs, income, and wealth in

all references to "cutting subsidies" refer to bringing them back to their optimal level (which will be zero in all but those relatively few exceptional cases).

[3] Labor market interventions also are rife, including barriers to international migration. For estimates of the potential global economic benefits from reducing the latter, see Anderson and Winters (2009).

ways that those in government fear would reduce their chances of remaining in power (and, in countries where corruption is rife, possibly their own wealth, see Chapter 11 in this volume). The challenge involves finding politically attractive ways to phase out remaining distortions to world markets for goods and services.

This challenge is even greater now than it was in the 2004 Copenhagen Consensus project (see Lomborg, 2004). One reason is that the WTO membership is struggling to address the DDA that was launched in the immediate aftermath of September 11, 2001 – a time when there was much more goodwill to cooperate multilaterally than seems to be the case now. More generally, in some regions there is a broader disenchantment with globalization that could result not just in a failure to reach agreement under the Doha Round to multilaterally liberalize trade, but also in the *raising* of current trade barriers. Such a reversal of past reforms could do huge damage to the global trading system and raise global inequality and poverty. That suggests the counterfactual to opening markets is not the status quo but something potentially much worse than the present, especially in the case of food (Anderson and Nelgen, 2011). It also underscores the need to re-emphasize the virtues of a more open global trading system – a system to which around seventy-five additional developing and transition economies have subscribed since the WTO came into being in 1995, with a further twenty-five+ currently striving to join. The case needs to be made within the context of the on-going ICT revolution that is ever-more rapidly globalizing the world's economies.[4]

Arguments for reducing trade barriers and subsidies

Even before examining the empirical estimates of the benefits and costs of grasping various trade-liberalizing opportunities, the case can be made that such reform in principle is beneficial economically.[5] It then remains to examine whether particular reforms are also positive or negative in terms of net social and environmental outcomes. The latter cannot be dealt with here in the same depth as the narrower economic analysis, but it is important because there are many who believe or assume that the net social and environmental consequences are sufficiently negative as to outweigh the net economic benefits of market opening. We begin with the static economic gains from trade arguments and then consider additional dynamic gains.

Static economic gains from own-country reform of trade and subsidy policies

The standard comparative static analysis of national gains from international trade emphasizes the economic benefits from production specialization and exchange so as to exploit comparative advantage in situations where a nation's costs of production and/or preferences differ from those in the rest of the world. This is part of the more general theory of the welfare effects of distortions in a trading economy, as summarized by Bhagwati (1971). Domestic industries become more productive on average, as those with a comparative advantage expand by drawing resources from those previously protected or subsidized industries that grow slower or contract following reform. The gains from opening an economy are larger, the greater the variance of rates of protection among industries – especially within a sector, insofar as resources are more mobile within than between sectors (Lloyd, 1974). Likewise, the more productive domestic firms *within* industries expand by drawing resources from less-productive firms that contract or go out of business. Indeed theory and empirical studies suggest that the

[4] So rapid is this phenomenon that one author felt the need to revise his popular book on the subject three times in three years (Friedman, 2007). Its influence on fragmenting the process of production has been sufficiently profound for economists to begin developing a theory of trade in "tasks," to capture the fact that firms are offshoring an increasing array of their activities (e.g. Grossman and Rossi-Hansberg, 2012). It is also increasing the demands by retailers for lower trade barriers which tend to be avoided by consumers buying foreign products online.

[5] This survey does not pretend to provide a comprehensive coverage of the gains-from-trade theory. For more, readers are referred to the handbooks by Grossman and Rogoff (1995) and Harrigan and Choi (2003) and the textbook by Feenstra (2003).

shifting of resources within an industry may be more welfare-improving than shifts between industries.[6]

The static gains from trade tend to be greater as a share of national output the smaller the economy, particularly where economies of scale in production have not been fully exploited and where consumers (including firms importing intermediate inputs) value variety so that intraindustry as well as interindustry trade can flourish. Less-than-full exploitation of scale economies is often the result of imperfect competition being allowed to prevail in the domestic market-place, which again is more common in smaller and poorer economies where industries have commensurately smaller numbers of firms. This is especially the case in the service sector. One example is subsectors such as utilities, where governments have been inclined to sanction monopoly provision.[7] The gain comes from firms having to reduce their mark-ups in the face of greater competition.

Those gains from opening up will be even greater if accompanied by a freeing-up of domestic markets and the market for currency exchange. The more stable is domestic macroeconomic policy, the more attractive will an economy be to capital inflows. And the more domestic microeconomic policies are friendly to markets and competition for goods, services and productive factors, the greater the likelihood that adjustments by firms and consumers to trade liberalization will lead to a more efficient utilization of national resources and greater economic welfare (Corden, 1997). If domestic policy reforms included improving the government's capacity to redistribute income and wealth more efficiently, and in ways that better matched society's wishes, concerns about the distributional consequences of trade liberalization would also be lessened.

With the vastly increased scope during the past decade to separate in time and space the various productive tasks along each value chain, thanks to the ICT revolution, firms are increasingly able to take advantage of factor-cost differences across countries for specific tasks without having to sacrifice gains from product specialization or move the whole of their production operation offshore (Hanson *et al.*, 2005). Trade in many tasks (e.g. emailing data files) is not even recorded in official trade statistics and so is not directly subject to trade policies. That suggests the variance of import protection across all traded items is even greater than across just recorded trade in goods, so the welfare gains from reducing the latter could well be greater than that captured by conventional trade models.

Dynamic economic gains from own-country reform of trade and subsidy policies

The standard comparative static analysis needs to be supplemented with links between trade and economic growth. The mechanisms by which openness contributes to growth are gradually getting to be better understood by economists, thanks to the pioneering work of such theorists as Grossman and Helpman (1991), Rivera-Batiz and Romer (1991), and the literature those studies spawned, including econometric papers based on firm-level databases. Channels through which openness to trade can affect an economy's growth rate include the scale of the market when knowledge is embodied in the products traded, the degree of redundant knowledge-creation that is avoided through openness, and the effect of knowledge spillovers (Romer, 1994; Taylor, 1999; Acharya and Keller, 2007). The latest surge of globalization has also been spurred by the technology "lending" that is involved in off-shoring an ever-rising proportion of production processes. As Baldwin (2011) points out, this joining of a supply chain has made industrialization potentially far less complex and far faster, especially for countries with reliable workers, a hospitable business environment, and located near large industrial countries.

The dynamic gains from openness can be greater when accompanied by reductions in domestic distortions. As one example, Helpman and Itskhoki (2010) develop a two-country two-sector model of

[6] Melitz (2003) provides the theory behind this point, and many econometricians have since provided strong empirical support for that theory.

[7] The argument for allowing such monopolies is that they could provide greater technical efficiency via their larger scale. The contrary argument is that, being sheltered from competition, they fall so short of that potential as to be less productive than two or more smaller-scale competing suppliers.

international trade in which one sector produces homogenous products while the other, which produces differentiated products, has firm heterogeneity, monopolistic competition, search, and matching in its labor market, and wage bargaining (so that some of the workers searching for jobs end up being unemployed). The two countries are similar except for frictions in their labor markets. They show that both countries gain from trade but that the country with lower labor market frictions gains proportionately more, and that its flexible labor market confers comparative advantage: the flexible country is a net exporter of differentiated products. Either country benefits by lowering frictions in its labor market, although that harms the other country; but a simultaneous proportional lowering of labor market frictions in both countries benefits both of them. With trade integration both countries benefit (even though it may raise their rates of unemployment), but the flexible country has higher TFP in this model.

When that trade reform includes financial markets, more is gained than just a lower cost of credit. The resulting financial deepening can stimulate growth, too (Townsend and Ueda, 2010). Kose *et al.* (2009) add two other indirect growth-enhancing benefits of financial reform: they discipline firms to look after the interests of shareholders better, and they discipline governments to provide greater macroeconomic stability.

Importantly from a policy-maker's viewpoint, the available empirical evidence strongly supports the view that open economies grow faster (see the surveys by USITC, 1997; Winters, 2004; Billmeier and Nannicini, 2009; and Francois and Martin, 2010). Notable early macroeconometric studies of the linkage between trade reform and the rate of economic growth include those by Sachs and Warner (1995) and Frankel and Romer (1999). More recent studies also provide some indirect supportive econometric evidence. For example, freeing-up the importation of intermediate and capital goods promotes investments that increase growth (Wacziarg, 2001). Indeed, the higher the ratio of imported to domestically produced capital goods for a developing country, the faster it grows (Lee, 1995; Mazumdar, 2001). Greater openness to international financial markets also boosts growth via the stimulation to investment that more risk-sharing generates.

Rodrigeuz and Rodrik (2001) examine a number of such studies and claim that the results they surveyed are not robust. However, in a more recent study that revisits the Sachs – Warner data and then provides new time-series evidence, Wacziarg and Welch (2008) show that dates of trade liberalization do characterize breaks in investment and GDP growth rates. Specifically, for the 1950–1998 period, countries that have liberalized their trade (raising their trade-to-GDP ratio by an average of 5 percentage points) have enjoyed on average 1.5 percentage points higher GDP growth compared with their pre-reform rate.

There have also been myriad case studies of liberalization episodes. In a survey of thirty-six of them, Greenaway (1993) reminds us that many things in addition to trade policies were changing during the studied cases, so ascribing causality is not easy. That, together with some econometric studies that fail to find that positive link, led Freeman (2004) to suggest that the promise of raising the rate of economic growth through trade reform has been overstated. But the same could be (and has been) said about the contributions to growth of such things as investments in education, health, agricultural research, and so on (Easterly, 2001). A more general and more robust conclusion that Easterly draws from empirical evidence, though, is that people respond to incentives. Hence getting incentives right in product, input, and factor markets is crucial – and removing unwarranted subsidies and trade barriers is an important part of that process. Additional evidence from thirteen new case studies reported in Wacziarg and Welch (2008) adds further empirical support to that view, as does the fact that there are no examples of autarkic economies that have enjoyed sustained economic growth, in contrast to the many examples since the 1960s of reformed economies that boomed after opening up.

Specifically, economies that commit to less market intervention tend to attract more investment funds, *ceteris paribus*, which raise their stocks of capital (through greater aggregate global savings or at the expense of other economies' capital stocks). This is consistent with the findings by Faini (2004) that trade liberalization in the 1990s fostered inward foreign investment (and both had a positive impact on investment in education) while backtracking on trade reform had a negative impact on foreign investment. More open economies also tend to be more innovative, because of greater trade in intellectual capital (a greater quantity and variety of information, ideas, and technologies, sometimes but not only in the form of purchasable intellectual property associated with product and process innovations), and because greater competition spurs innovation (Aghion and Griffith, 2005; Aghion and Howitt, 2006), leading to higher *rates* of capital accumulation and productivity growth (Lumenga-Neso *et al.* 2005).[8]

A growing body of industry studies, including ones based on firm-level survey data that capture the reality of firm heterogeneity, provides additional support for the theory that trade reform boosts the rate of productivity growth.[9] It appears that more productive firms are innately better at exporting, so opening an economy leads to their growth and the demise of the least productive firms (Bernard *et al.*, 2007). That leads to better exploitation of comparative advantage in terms not only of industries but also of firms within each industry. If those more productive firms are also foreign-owned, as is clearly the case in China (Whalley, 2010), then being open to FDI multiplies the gains from product-trade openness. And if those foreign firms are involved in retailing, and they enter a country with suppliers whose productivity is below best practise, they can put pressure on those suppliers to raise their productivity (and perhaps alert them as to ways to do that). Walmart's influence in Mexico provides one example of this force at work (Javorcik *et al.*, 2008). Furthermore, if the foreign firms are supplying lower-cost services inputs into manufacturing, that can boost the productivity growth of local manufacturers using those service inputs, according to a study of the Czech Republic (Arnold *et al.*, 2011).[10]

It need not be just the most productive firms that engage in exporting. For lower-productivity firms, incurring the fixed costs of investing in newly opened foreign markets may be justifiable if accompanied by the larger sales volumes that come with exporting. Lower foreign tariffs will induce these firms to simultaneously export and invest in productivity (while inducing higher-productivity firms to export without more investing, as in Melitz, 2003 and Melitz and Ottaviano, 2008). Lileeva and Trefler (2010) model this econometrically using a heterogenous response model. Unique "plant-specific" tariff cuts serve as their instrument for the decision of Canadian plants to start exporting to the United States. They find that those lower-productivity Canadian plants that were induced by the tariff cuts to start exporting increased their labor productivity, engaged in more product innovation, and had high adoption rates of advanced manufacturing technologies. These new exporters also increased their domestic (Canadian) market share at the expense of non-exporters, which suggests that the labor-productivity gains reflect underlying gains in TFP.

Liberalizing international financial flows also has been shown to have boosted economic growth, especially in the first wave of globalization up to 1913 (Schularick and Steger, 2010; Bordo and Rousseau, 2012). Study by Hoxha *et al.* (2011) examines the potential gains from financial integration and find that a move from autarky to full integration of financial markets globally could boost real consumption by 9 percent permanently in the median developing country, and up to 14 percent in the most capital-scarce countries.[11]

In short, international trade and investment liberalization can lead not just to a larger capital stock and a one-off increase in productivity but also to higher *rates* of capital accumulation and productivity growth in the reforming economy because of the way reform energizes entrepreneurs. For those higher growth rates to be sustained, though, there is widespread agreement that governments also need to (a) have in place effective institutions to efficiently allocate and protect property rights,

[8] More open economies also tend to be less vulnerable to foreign shocks such as sudden stops in capital inflows, currency crashes, and severe recessions (Frankel and Cavallo, 2008).

[9] For an overview of this new theory, see Helpman *et al.* (2008).

[10] For a survey of the growth effects of opening to trade in services, see Francois and Hoekman (2010).

[11] In a case study of Thailand, Townsend and Ueda (2010) estimate welfare gains from financial liberalization as high as 28 percent.

(b) allow domestic factor and product markets to function freely, and (c) maintain macroeconomic and political stability (Baldwin, 2004; Chang *et al.*, 2005; Rodrik, 2007; Wacziarg and Welch, 2008).

Perhaps the best single paper that first brought these ideas together using a numerical open-economy growth model is that by Rutherford and Tarr (2002). Their model allows for product variety, imperfect competition, economies of scale, and international capital flows. It is dynamic, so it can trace out an adjustment path to trade reform; and it is stochastic in that it draws randomly from uniform probability distributions for eight key parameters of the model. They simulate a halving of the only policy intervention (a 20 percent tariff on imports) and, in doing so, fully replace the government's lost tariff revenue with a lump-sum tax. That modest trade reform produces a welfare increase (in terms of Hicksian equivalent variation) of 10.6 percent of the present value of consumption in their central model. Systematic sensitivity analysis with 34,000 simulations showed that there is virtually no chance of a welfare gain of less than 3 percent, and a 7 percent chance of a welfare gain larger than 18 percent of consumption. Several modeling variants and sensitivity analysis on all the key parameters found that the welfare estimates for the same 10 percentage point tariff cut ranged up to 37 percent when international capital flows are allowed, and down to 4.7 percent when using the most inefficient replacement tax (a tax on capital). The latter result shows that even the very inefficient tax on capital is superior to the tariff as a revenue-raiser. Increasing the size of the tariff cuts results in roughly proportional increases in the estimated welfare gains. Large welfare gains in the model arise because the economy benefits from increased varieties of foreign goods, which dominate the decrease in varieties of domestic goods. In order to assess the importance of variety gains, they then assume that one of the two sectors is subject to constant returns to scale and perfect competition (CRS/PC) – and find in that case that the additional varieties do not increase TFP. Instead, a small welfare gain of about 0.5 percent of the PV of consumption emerges, which is of the same order of magnitude as in the many comparative static CRS/PC CGE studies. Their results also illustrate the importance of complementary reforms to fully realize the potential gains from trade reform. In particular, with the ability to access international capital markets the gains are roughly tripled; and use of inefficient replacement taxes significantly reduces the gains. These combined results underscore the point that complementary macroeconomic, regulatory, and financial market reforms to allow capital flows and efficient alternate tax collection are crucial to realizing the potentially large gains from trade liberalization.

Opportunities for reducing trade barriers and subsidies

Among the most feasible opportunities available today for encouraging trade negotiations to stimulate significant market opening, the most obvious is a non-preferential legally binding partial liberalization of goods and services trade following the WTO's current round of multilateral trade negotiations, the DDA. That continues to prove to be difficult politically to bring to a conclusion, however. Three other opportunities considered here involve prospective sub-global regional integration agreements. One is the proposed TPP among a subset of member countries of the Asia Pacific Economic Cooperation (APEC) grouping; another involves extending the FTA among the ten-member ASEAN grouping to include China, Japan, and Korea (ASEAN+3); and the third opportunity is an FTA among all APEC countries.[12]

The TPP began in 2006 when just four small APEC members (Brunei, Chile, New Zealand, and Singapore) got together to begin negotiations for greater economic integration. Being already open liberal economies, their leaders saw this not as an end in itself but rather as a pathway for a more expansive club. In September 2008 the United States announced its interest in joining the TPP, and by 2010 Australia, Malaysia, Peru, and

[12] Whether such reciprocal preferential trade agreements are stepping stones or stumbling blocks to freer global trade is a much-debated point among economists. For a survey of the impact of regionalism on the multilateral trading system, see Baldwin (2009).

Vietnam also joined in to make a total of nine of APEC's twenty-one members as of May 2012.[13]

Meanwhile, discussions have been under way between the ten members of ASEAN, who already have their own FTA (AFTA), and their three big northern neighbours (China, Japan, and Korea) with a view to forming the broader East Asian FTA that is generally referred to as ASEAN+3.

APEC, leaders have endorsed both of those regional integration tracks and see them as potential pathways to an FTA involving all APEC members (APEC, 2010). In what follows we therefore consider this more encompassing prospect as the third regional opportunity.

Economic effects of reducing trade barriers and subsidies

Empirical comparative static model simulation studies of the potential economic welfare gains from prospective multilateral or large regional trade liberalization agreements typically generate positive gains for the world and for most participating countries (as do econometric studies of past trade reforms). In this section we review the latest economy-wide analyses of those prospects.

All the estimates considered below of the costs of current policies and the potential economic welfare gains from these reform opportunities are generated using CGE models of the global economy. The CGE welfare gains refer to the equivalent variation in income (EV) as a result of each of the shocks described.[14] While not without their shortcomings (see Anderson, 2003, Francois and Martin, 2010 and the caveats below), CGE models are far superior for current purposes to partial-equilibrium models, which fail to capture the economy-wide nature of the adjustments to reform whereby some sectors expand when others contract and release capital and labor. They are also superior to macroeconometric models which typically lack sufficient sectoral detail and are based on time-series analysis of the past which may no longer be relevant for the near future (Francois and Reinert, 1997). CGE models were first used in multilateral trade reform analysis in *ex post* assessments of the Tokyo Round of GATT negotiations in the late 1970s/early 1980s (Cline *et al.*, 1978; Deardorff and Stern, 1979, 1986; Whalley, 1985). Since then they have been used increasingly during and following the Uruguay Round, as well as for *ex ante* assessments of the Doha Round, of bilateral and other preferential economic-integration agreements, and of unilateral reforms such as when a country considers acceding to the WTO.

Empirical comparative static economy-wide CGE model simulations of the potential economic welfare gains from prospective multilateral trade liberalization typically generate positive gains for the world and for most participating countries. In the case of subglobal preferential trade reform studies, the estimated gains to the countries involved are almost always smaller, and some excluded countries – and even some participating ones – may lose. When increasing returns to scale and monopolistic competition (IRS/MC) are assumed instead of CRS/PC, and firms are assumed to be heterogenous rather than homogenous, and when trade is liberalized not just in goods but also in services and investment flows, the estimates of potential gains can increase several-fold. Virtually all such studies are in the comparative static mode however, and so are unable to capture the crucially important growth-enhancing dynamic effects of trade reform described on pp. 677–80. It is therefore not surprising that they generate results for gains from trade reform that are typically only a small fraction of GDP.

Such low estimated gains seem to fly in the face of casual empiricism. Irwin (2002), for example, notes that three different countries in three different regions chose to liberalize in three different decades (Korea from 1965, Chile from 1974, and India from 1991 – see Irwin, 2002: Figures 2.3–2.5),

[13] At the APEC Summit in Honolulu in November 2011, Japan also indicated a possible interest. That idea has yet to be taken forward by Tokyo, however. Meanwhile, it was announced on 13 May 2012 that China, Korea, and Japan are to open talks on establishing a trilateral FTA.

[14] EV is defined as the income that consumers would be willing to forgo and still have the same level of well-being after as before the reform. For a discussion of the merits of EV versus other measures of change in economic welfare, see for example Just *et al.* (2004).

and per capita GDP growth in each of those countries accelerated markedly thereafter by several percentage points per year. Admittedly those historical liberalization experiences involved also complementary reforms to other domestic policies and institutions that would have contributed significantly to the observed boosts in economic growth. Even so, they support the point that trade can generate not only static efficiency gains but also important dynamic gains.

Some CGE modelers have tried to proxy that dynamic effect by adding an additional one-off TFP shock to their trade-reform scenarios. But reform may also raise the *rate* of factor productivity growth and/or of capital accumulation. Such endogenous growth has yet to be satisfactorily introduced into CGE models, and in any case it is unclear how to interpret a model's estimated welfare effects if households are reducing current consumption in order to boost their or their descendants' future consumption by investing more.

It should be kept in mind that all the experiments in the comparative static CGE studies surveyed below reduce only trade barriers plus agricultural production and export subsidies. The reasons for including subsidies only in agriculture are that they are the key subsidies explicitly being negotiated at the WTO (where non-agricultural export subsidies are illegal), they represented an estimated two-fifths of all government expenditure on subsidies globally during 1994–1998 (van Beers and de Moor, 2001: Table 3.1), and they are fully represented in the Global Trade Analysis Project (GTAP) database used by almost all economy-wide global modelers, whereas subsidies for most other sectors are not included in that database so it is not possible to estimate their welfare cost within the same framework. And the reason also for not explicitly estimating the welfare impacts of other domestic policies and institutions (even though, because of their complementarity, they can affect the pay-off from opening up) is that typically they are beyond the sphere of influence of international trade negotiators.

With this as background, we consider first the estimated economic consequences of Doha multilateral reform under the WTO, before turning to each of the identified opportunities for preferential trade reforms in the Asia-Pacific region.

Economic consequences of Doha multilateral reform

In the 2008 Copenhagen Consensus Project, hopes were still high that the Doha Round would be soon concluded, and numerous studies of the Round's possible economic effects were available. The one chosen for inclusion in the contribution to that project by Anderson and Winters (2009) was the modeling work of Anderson *et al.* (2006). That simulation exercise made use of the World Bank's Linkage Model of the global economy. With the stalling of the Round since 2008, there have been few new studies of its prospective effects. An important exception is a new pair of papers by Laborde *et al.* (2011, 2012) that not only analyses what is currently on the Doha negotiation table but also incorporates new and better ways of including estimates of the price distortions caused by trade and farm-subsidy policies. It again uses the World Bank's Linkage model (the latest version 7.1, see van der Mensbrugghe 2011), and again provides estimates of gains from partial global liberalization of all merchandise trade and subsidies, assuming constant returns to scale CRS and perfect competition in all product and factor markets.[15]

Laborde *et al.* (2011) estimate that if the basic formula approach to reducing trade barriers and subsidies, as currently proposed, were to be adopted by all WTO member countries, then global GDP would be 0.36 percent higher. However, that study notes that there are many flexibilities in the current Doha proposals, especially for developing countries. It is not possible to be certain as to how various countries might make use of those flexibilities, but the authors draw on political-economy reasoning to suggest likely take-up and then re-do their simulation. With that degree of flexibility the gains as a share of GDP drop to 0.22 percent globally, made up of 0.25 percent for high-income (including Europe's transition) economies and 0.17 percent for developing countries. This is considered here as the lower-bound estimate of the gains from this opportunity.

15 Laborde *et al.* (2011) provide three sets of results, but for simplicity here we include just the middle set ("sigma = 2") which they consider to be the most likely.

When economies of scale and monopolistic competition are assumed instead of CRS and perfect competition, and firms are assumed to be heterogenous rather than homogenous, and when trade is liberalized not just in goods but also in services and investment flows, the estimates of potential gains tend to be raised several-fold. Anderson and Winters (2009) reviewed the past literature of modeling efforts that added such features and concluded that an upper-bound estimate of those gains could be five times the lower-bound estimate. That would bring the gains as a share of GDP to 1.1 percent globally, made up of 1.25 percent for high-income countries and 0.85 percent for developing countries.

As for timing, again following Anderson and Winters (2009), it is assumed those gains would accrue fully after 2020, following an eight-year phase-in period during which the gains would begin in 2013 at one-eighth the full amount as of 2025 and rise by a further one-eighth each year until 2020.

There are dynamic gains from trade to consider in addition to the above comparative static ones. The past experiences of successful reformers such as Chile, China, India, and Korea suggest that trade opening immediately boosts GDP growth rates by several percentage points per year for many years. An estimate might be that reform boosts GDP growth rates – projected from 2010 to 2025 by the ADB (2011: 57) and Fouré *et al.* (2010) to be around 2.0 percent for high-income countries and 5.0 percent for developing countries and so 3.0 percent globally[16] – by one-fifth or 0.4 of a percentage point for high-income countries and 1.0 percentage points for developing countries, that is, to 2.4 and 6.0 percent, respectively, and hence from 3.0 to 3.6 percent globally through to 2025.[17] As for the period after 2025, a review of the literature by Winters (2004) suggests that while the growth increments due to trade liberalization will not go on forever, they could last several decades. Thus assume the dollar value of the boost to GDP declines linearly from its 2025 value to zero by 2050, so that there is just the continuing comparative static gain of 0.22 percent globally, 0.25 percent for high-income countries and 0.17 percent for developing countries from 2050 to 2100.

Economic consequences of preferential reforms in the Asia-Pacific region

The proposals and negotiations currently under way within the Asia-Pacific region that are considered here are a TPP among a subset of member countries of the APEC grouping (namely Australia, Brunei, Chile, Malaysia, New Zealand, Peru, Singapore, and Vietnam); an extension of the FTA that is already in place among the ten-member, ASEAN grouping to include China, Japan, and Korea (ASEAN+3); and an FTA among all the APEC countries. Each of these trade liberalization initiatives is assumed to be preferential, in the sense that trade is freed within the group but not between group members and the rest of the world.

Estimates of prospective gains from these three opportunities are provided by Petri *et al.* (2011). They use the latest GTAP database (preliminary version 8, with a 2007 baseline) but their CGE model of the global economy is, in several respects, more sophisticated than the one used in the Doha analysis (see Zhai, 2008). In particular, it is distinguished from the standard Linkage Model in two important ways. First, it assumes economies of scale and monopolistic competition in the manufacturing and private services sectors instead of CRS and perfect competition. Second, following Melitz (2003), firms are assumed to be heterogenous rather than homogenous: each industry with monopolistic competition consists of a continuum of firms that is differentiated by the varieties of products they produce and their productivity. Furthermore, trade is liberalized by these authors not just by reducing

[16] The growth rate of developing countries typically converges on that of high-income countries over time. Hence it is assumed in the baseline that the GDP of developing countries grows at a rate of 4.0 percent during 2025–2050 and at 3.0 percent during 2050–2100.

[17] Econometric support for the claim that this assumed increase in GDP growth rates is conservative is provided by Romalis (2007), who estimates that the elimination of just import tariffs, and only by high-income countries, would boost annual GDP growth in developing countries by up to 1.6 percentage points. In the model by Rutherford and Tarr (2002), their 10 percentage-point cut in tariffs led to a rise in the steady-state growth rate of 2 percent p.a. to 2.6 percent over the first decade and 2.2 percent over the first five decades (and even after fifty years their annual growth rate is 2.1 percent).

Table 12.1 Comparative static effects on economic welfare of trade reform under three different prospective Asia-Pacific preferential FTAs, 2025

	Baseline share of world GDP (%) 2025	US$ billion			Percent of GDP		
		TPP	ASEAN±3	FTAAP	TPP	ASEAN ±3	FTAAP
TPP9 countries	23	71	26	172	0.30	0.11	0.73
ASEAN+3 countries	28	71	219	596	0.25	0.78	2.12
All 21 APEC countries	57	109	216	912	0.19	0.37	1.57
All non-APEC countries	43	−5	−1	−50	−0.01	−0.00	−0.11
World	**100**	**104**	**215**	**862**	**0**	**0**	**0**

Note: Annual difference from baseline, 2007 US$ and percent
Source: Petri *et al.* (2011: Table 7).

applied bilateral tariffs on goods but also by raising utilization rates of tariff preferences, lowering non-tariff barriers (NTBs) to both goods and services, and reducing costs associated with meeting rules of origin (for details, see the Appendixes of Petri *et al.*, 2011). Even so, the results summarized below can be considered conservative in the sense that they do not include liberalization of foreign investment barriers, even though such reforms are an important part of the current proposals for economic integration in the Asia-Pacific region.

With these model refinements, the gains from preferential liberalization of trade within this region are non-trivial. This is in part because the Asia-Pacific region is projected to become a much more important part of the global economy by 2025. Specifically, the TPP9 countries are projected by Petri, Plummer, and Zhai to account for just under one-quarter of the global economy, the ASEAN+3 economies for just over one-quarter, and the whole of APEC's twenty-one members for nearly half of global GDP in 2025 (column (1) of Table 12.1).

The TPP, even if it involves just the current nine members and excludes the three large north-east Asian economies of China, Japan, and Korea, would get a 0.3 percent boost to their GDP if they removed their bilateral barriers to trade in goods and services. However, it would boost global GDP by just 0.1 percent. If those three north-east Asian countries formed an FTA with the ASEAN members, by contrast, global GDP would rise by twice as much (0.21 percent). Furthermore, if all twenty-one APEC members were to form an FTA (FTAAP), the global gains would be four times greater again (0.85 percent). The corresponding gains for all developing countries would be 0.1 percent of GDP from TPP, 0.33 percent from ASEAN+3, and 1.17 percent from FTAAP, and for all high-income and transition countries the gains would be 0.1, 0.1 and 0.56 percent of GDP (Table 12.2). This progression in gains is due to several factors: greater trade complementarity as the mix of economies broadened, greater trade barriers (especially in agriculture) between the full set of APEC economies and the two smaller subsets prior to their removal, and greater scope for exploiting gains within the manufacturing sectors among the ASEAN+3 countries than among the TPP9 countries.

Two other points are worth noting. One is that non-APEC countries lose very little in aggregate, reflecting the fact that trade-creation dominates trade-diversion in these three cases. The other is that the gain from full liberalization of trade among all APEC countries yields a higher global gain than that from the partial Doha multilateral reform summarized on pp. 682–3.

To make the PV of estimated gains from these prospective preferential reforms comparable with the above estimates of gains from partial multilateral reform under the WTO's Doha Agenda, it is assumed the gains would accrue fully after 2020, following an eight-year phase-in period during which the gains begin in 2013 at one-eighth the full amount as of 2025 and rise by a further one-eighth each year until 2020.

While these regional results are from more complete model simulations of proposed changes than was possible in the Doha analysis, they still

Table 12.2 Assumptions used in the benefit-cost calculus

Baseline GDP levels and assumed growth rates to 2100					
	Real GDP (US$ billion)		Real GDP growth rate, % p.a.		
	2010	2025	2010–2025	2025–2050	2050–2100
Developing countries	19,400	40,331	5.0	4.0	3.0
High-income countries[a]	38,800	52,220	2.0	2.0	2.0
World	**58,200**	**90,674**	**3.0**	**3.1**	**2.6**
Higher growth rates in alternative policy reform scenarios, 2010–25					
	Doha "low"	Doha "high"	TPP	ASEAN±3	FTAAP
Developing countries	6.0	6.0	5.1	5.5	5.6
High-income countries[a]	2.4	2.4	2.2	2.2	2.2
World	**3.6**	**3.6**	**3.1**	**3.3**	**3.4**
Additional comparative static gross benefit from reform (expressed as % of GDP for each year after 2020, and phased in linearly from 1/8 of that rate in 2013 and 1/8 more each year to 2020)					
	Doha "low"	Doha "high"	TPP	ASEAN±3	FTAAP
Developing countries	0.17	0.85	0.10	0.33	1.17
High-income countries[a]	0.25	1.25	0.10	0.10	0.56
World	**0.22**	**1.10**	**0.10**	**0.21**	**0.85**
Cost of reforms (US$ billion p.a.), for each year from 2013 to 2020 inclusive					
	Doha "low"	Doha "high"	TPP	ASEAN±3	FTAAP
Developing countries	7	17	4	13	24
High-income countries[a]	13	335	10	10	15
World	**20**	**50**	**14**	**23**	**39**

Note: [a] High-income includes Eastern European and FSU transition economies.
Source: See text, p. 683.

exclude proposed foreign investment liberalization. Furthermore, they do not fully capture the dynamic gains from trade reform. Consistent with the Doha analysis, we assume that reform boosts the GDP growth rates of the participating APEC countries and their key trading partners by one-fifth between 2010 and 2025. For the period after 2025, we assume, again very conservatively, that the dollar value of the dynamic boost to GDP growth diminishes linearly after 2025 and disappears by 2050 so the benefits from reform return to just the comparative static gains for the latter half of the century.

Economic costs of trade reform

The benefits from reform are not costless. Expenditure on negotiating, and on supporting policy think-tanks and the like to develop and disseminate a convincing case for reform, would be needed. But more significant in many people's eyes are the private costs of adjustment for firms and workers, as reform forces some industries to downsize or close to allow others to expand (Francois, 2003; Matusz and Tarr, 2000). Those costs are ignored in the CGE models discussed above, where the aggregate level of employment is held constant. There are also social costs to consider. They include social safety-net provisions in so far as such schemes are developed/drawn on by losers from reform (e.g. unemployment payments plus training grants to build up new skills so displaced workers can earn the same wage as before).

Those one-off costs, which need to be weighed against the non-stop flow of economic benefits from reform, tend to be smaller, the longer the phase-in period or smaller the tariff or subsidy cut per year (Furusawa and Lai, 1999). The adjustment required also tends to be small when compared with the changes due to exchange-rate fluctuations, technological improvements, preference shifts, and other economic shocks and structural developments associated with normal economic growth (Anderson *et al.*, 1997; Porto and Hoekman, 2010). In recent debates about trade and labor, analysts have not found a significant link between import expansion and increased unemployment. One example is a study of the four largest EU economies' imports from East Asia (Bendivogli and Pagano, 1999). Another is a study of the UK footwear industry, which found that liberalizing that market would incur unemployment costs only in the first year, because of the high job turnover in that industry, and they were less than 1.5 percent of the estimated benefits from cutting that protection (Winters and Takacs, 1991). A similar-sized estimate is provided by de Melo and Tarr (1990) using a CGE model that focuses on US textile, steel and auto protection cuts and draws on estimates of the cost of earnings lost by displaced workers (later reported by Jacobson *et al.*, 1993). For developing countries the evidence also seems to suggest low costs of adjustment, not least because trade reform typically causes a growth spurt (Krueger, 1983). In a study of thirteen liberalization efforts for nine developing countries, Michaely *et al.* (1991) found only one example where employment was not higher within a year.[18]

If the adjustment costs are so small and may lead to more rather than less jobs even during the adjustment period, why are governments so reluctant to open their economies? The reason is because the anticipated losses in jobs and asset values are very obvious and concentrated whereas the gains in terms of new job and investment opportunities are thinly spread, are less easily attributed to the trade reform, and are taken up often by people other than those losing from the reform. Moreover, there is considerable uncertainty as to who in fact will end up bearing the costs or reaping net benefits, leading all groups to be less enthusiastic about reform (Fernadez and Rodrik, 1991). As discussed on pp. 675–6, the few losers are prepared to support politicians who resist protection cuts, while the gains are sufficiently small per consumer and unassisted firm as to make it not worthwhile for those many potential gainers to get together to lobby for reform, particularly given their greater free-rider problem in acting collectively (Olsen, 1965). Thus reform has political, and possibly employment, costs for politicians and one should not underestimate the difficulties of political action to reduce/eliminate trade-protection measures. We do not factor these into the economic CBA for society as a whole, however, because they are not of a comparable form and the purpose of the Copenhagen Consensus process is to contribute

[18] A further impact of trade-policy reform about which concern is often expressed is the loss of tariff revenue for the government. This is of trivial importance to developed and upper middle-income countries where trade taxes account for only 1 and 3 percent of government revenue, respectively. For LMICs that share is 9 percent, and it is more than 20 percent for more than a dozen low-income countries for which data are available, so how concerned should those poorer countries be? The answer depends on whether/how much that revenue would fall and, if it does fall, on whether/how much more costly would be the next-best alternative means of raising government revenue. On the first of those two points, government revenue from import taxes will rise rather than fall with reform if the reform involves replacing, with less prohibitive tariffs, any of the import quotas or bans, or tariffs that are prohibitive (or nearly so), or which encourage smuggling or underinvoicing or corruption by customs officials. It is possible even in a tariff-only regime that lower tariffs lead to a sufficiently higher volume and value of trade that the aggregate tariff collection rises. Examples of trade policy reforms that led to increased tariff revenue are Chile and Mexico (Bacchetta and Jansen, 2003: 15) and Kenya (Glenday, 2002). See also Greenaway and Milner (1993) and Nash and Takacs (1998). Since the economy is enlarged by opening up, income and consumption tax collections will automatically rise too. On the second point, about the cost of raising government revenue by other means if tax revenue does fall, Corden (1997: Chapter 4) makes it clear that in all but the poorest of countries it will be more rather than less efficient to collect tax revenue in other ways. Even countries as poor as Cambodia have managed to introduce a value-added tax. Hence from a global viewpoint there is no significant cost that needs to be included in response to this concern. To the extent subsidies are also cut as part of the reform, the chances of government revenue rising are even greater. Income and consumption-tax revenue also will rise as the economy expands following reform. In any case CGE modelers typically alter those other tax rates when trade-tax revenues change so as to keep the overall government budget unchanged.

Table 12.3 NPV of benefits and costs to 2100, and BCRs, from reducing trade barriers and subsidies globally under the WTO's DDA

	3% discount rate						5% discount rate					
	Low			High			Low			High		
BCR												
World	**136**			**179**			**90**			**99**		
Developing countries	215			249			146			136		
NPV in 2013 of benefits and costs (2007 US$ billion)												
	Gross benefit	Cost	Net benefit	Gross benefit	Cost	Net benefit	Gross benefit	Cost	Net benefit	Gross benefit	Cost	Net benefit
World	**19,633**	**145**	**19,488**	**64,624**	**362**	**64,263**	**12,161**	**136**	**12,026**	**33,666**	**339**	**33,326**
Developing countries	10870	51	10,819	30,549	123	30,426	6,943	48	6,895	15,704	115	15,589

to their erosion. Nor do we count the transfers among people within each country as part of the gross benefits and costs of reform, since they are clearly transfers rather than net costs or benefits to each national society. Rather, we implicitly assume society costlessly compensates the losers using the extra tax revenue from those whose incomes rise.

The existing estimates of the adjustment costs to trade reform are very small, but they are concentrated on particular individuals and so perhaps deserve a large weight socially. It is certainly possible that those estimates omit some elements, too, such as the disutility of one-off uncertainty and disruption experienced by everyone in adjusting to policy changes. Hence, so as not to exaggerate the estimated net gains from trade reform, it is assumed here that there would be an adjustment period of eight years following the beginning of liberalization (assumed to start in 2013), and that in each of those years the adjustment costs would be 10 percent of the estimated annual comparative static benefits as of 2025 (and zero thereafter) in the case of Doha "low" and also in the cases of subregional FTA formation in the TPP and ASEAN+3 cases. For the more-comprehensive Doha "high" and the FTAAP cases, where benefits are far higher because reform is far more widespread, the costs of adjustment are assumed to be 2.5 times greater than in the other cases (that is, 5 percent of the 2025 comparative static benefit).

Net benefits and CBA

The assumptions used to calculate the present (i.e. 2013) value of the net benefits in real (2007) $US, and the BCRs associated with the policy reform opportunities described in the two previous sections, are summarized in Table 12.2 (p. 685). Those indicators are calculated using two alternative discount rates: 3 and 5 percent per year. In the Doha trade-reform scenarios, the "low" case refers to global comparative static gains of just 0.22 percent of GDP while the "high" case refers global gains five times that lower benefit, to take into account the unmeasured gains due to such things as economies and scale, imperfect competition, and services and foreign-investment reforms.

In PV terms the net benefit of a Doha Agreement are shown in Table 12.3 to range from $12 to $64 trillion. The costs are less than $400 billion in PV terms, but they are mostly private rather than government costs and are dwarfed by the gross benefits. Today's developing countries would reap just over half of those net gains, as their share of the global economy is assumed to grow throughout this century (although at a progressively slower rate after 2025). The BCRs from the trade-reform opportunity offered by the Doha Round are between 140 and 250, which means it is an extremely high-pay-off activity, if only the political will to bring about a successful conclusion to the Doha Round

Table 12.4 NPV of benefits and costs to 2100, and BCRs, from reducing trade barriers and subsidies under three alternative Asia-Pacific RTAs

BCR

	3% discount rate			5% discount rate		
	TPP	ASEAN±3	FTAAP	TPP	ASEAN±3	FTAAP
World	**65**	**89**	**174**	**38**	**54**	**95**
Developing countries	121	133	216	65	75	110

NPV in 2013 of benefits and costs, 3% discount rate: (2007 US$ billion)

	TPP			ASEAN±3			FTAAP		
	Gross benefit	Cost	Net benefit	Gross benefit	Cost	Net benefit	Gross benefit	Cost	Net benefit
World	**6,369**	**98**	**6,271**	**14,828**	**166**	**14,662**	**48,991**	**282**	**48,709**
Developing countries	3,489	29	3,460	12,515	94	12,421	37,430	174	37,257

Net present value in 2013 of benefits and costs, 5% discount rate: (2007 US$ billion)

	TPP			ASEAN±3			FTAAP		
	Gross benefit	Cost	Net benefit	Gross benefit	Cost	Net benefit	Gross benefit	Cost	Net benefit
World	**3,476**	**92**	**3,384**	**8,450**	**156**	**8,294**	**25,255**	**265**	**24,991**
Developing countries	1,764	27	1,737	6,619	88	6,530	17,926	163	17,763

Source: Author's calculations based on assumptions in text below.

can be found. The global BCRs from Doha are not much lower, at between 90 and 180.

If for political reasons the Doha Round cannot be brought to a successful conclusion with all the flexibilities demanded by developing countries and assumed in the above calculus, governments still have the opportunity to form preferential trade agreements. Of the three possibilities being discussed among countries in the Asia-Pacific region, Table 12.4 shows that the greatest estimated gain would come if all APEC member countries agreed to form a region-wide FTAAP. That is assumed to involve completely freeing all trade, albeit preferentially within the Asia-Pacific region (including Russia), in contrast to a Doha Agreement which would only partially open up trade, albeit non-preferentially so that all trading partners are involved (as the WTO membership now includes nearly 160 members and thus almost all of world trade). Since the APEC members are projected to comprise nearly three-fifths of global GDP by 2025 (see Table 12.1, p. 684), it is not surprising that an FTA among them could yield a benefit to the world that is three-quarters of what Doha is projected to deliver. Furthermore, the FTAAP is projected to deliver a slightly greater benefit to developing countries as a group than is Doha. This is partly because under Doha developing countries are assumed to reform less than high-income countries, and partly because by 2025 the APEC grouping will account for around two-thirds of the GDP of all developing countries.

The two other opportunities analyzed involve subregional FTAs in the Asia-Pacific region, and so necessarily yield smaller benefits than an FTA for the entire APEC region: fewer countries are liberalizing, and only for their trade with a subset of APEC members. Of those two, the ASEAN+3 proposal would yield more than twice the global and developing country benefits as the TPP between the United States and a number of small APEC economies (Table 12.4).

Social and environmental benefits and costs of reducing trade and migration barriers

Because trade reform generates large and on-going economic gains while incurring comparatively minor one-off adjustment costs, it would allow individuals and governments the freedom to spend more on other pressing problems, thereby *indirectly* contributing to the alleviation of other challenges facing society.[19] But, in addition, trade reform would also *directly* alleviate some of those challenges. This section first focuses on the impact of trade reform on poverty alleviation, since that is the solution to many of the world's problems. It then turns to trade reform's impact on the environment, before briefly commenting on its impact on several of the other specific challenges being addressed in this Copenhagen Consensus project, namely, communicable diseases, conflicts, underinvestment in education, corruption, and malnutrition and hunger.[20]

Poverty alleviation

Evidence presented by Dollar and Kraay (2002), Sala-i-Martin (2006), and others, and carefully surveyed in Ravallion (2006), suggests that aggregate economic growth differences have been largely responsible for the differences in poverty alleviation across regions. Initiatives that boost economic growth are therefore likely to be helpful in the fight against poverty, and trade liberalization is such an initiative. But cuts to trade barriers and subsidies also alter relative product prices domestically and in international markets, which in turn affect factor prices. Hence the net effect on poverty depends also in the way those price changes affect poor households' expenditure and their earnings net of remittances. If the consumer and producer price changes (whether due to own-country reforms and/or those of other countries) are pro-poor, then they will tend to reinforce any positive growth effects of trade reform on the poor.

The effects of trade reform on global poverty can be thought of at two levels: on the income gap between developed and developing countries, and on poor households within developing countries. On the first, CGE estimates such as by Anderson *et al.* (2006) and *Valenzuela et al.* (2009) suggest that current developing countries, which produce just one-fifth of global GDP, would enjoy nearly half of the NPV of the global static plus dynamic gains from reducing trade barriers. Clearly that will lower substantially the income gap between developed and poorer countries on average.

How poor households *within* developing countries are affected is more difficult to say (Winters, 2002; Winters *et al.*, 2004). We know that the agricultural policies of developed countries could provide a major source of developing-country gains from reform, and lowering barriers to textiles and clothing trade is also important. Both would boost the demand for unskilled labor and for farm products produced in poor countries. Since two-thirds of the world's poor live in rural areas and, in LDCs, the proportion is as high as 90 percent (OECD, 2003a: 3), and since many poor rural households are net sellers of farm labor and/or food, one would expect such reforms to reduce the number in absolute poverty. A set of analyses reported in Anderson *et al.* (2010, 2011), in which global and national CGE model results are carefully combined with household income and expenditure-survey data for nearly a dozen developing countries,[21] tests this hypothesis and finds strong support for it in most of the country case studies considered.

[19] On the intrinsic benefits of freedom of opportunity and action that freer markets provide people, apart from their positive impact in boosting income and wealth, see Sen (1999).

[20] The economic and social impacts of freeing up international migration are not discussed here, but they were explicitly included in the 2008 Copenhagen Consensus project, where they are shown to be potentially enormous in aggregate (Anderson and Winters, 2009). Not every small developing country will have less poverty if migration is freed up, because it will depend on the skill mix of the migrants and the extent of remittances they send back, among other things; but in most cases the evidence on international migration's impact on poverty is overwhelmingly positive (World Bank, 2006: Chapter 3).

[21] For more on this methodology, see Hertel *et al.* (2011).

The environment

The effects of trade reform on the environment have been the focus of much theoretical and empirical analysis since the 1970s and especially in the past dozen or so years (Beghin *et al.*, 2002; Copland and Taylor, 2003). Until recently, environmentalists have tended to focus mainly on the *direct* environmental costs they perceive from trade reform, just as they have with other areas of economic change.[22] That approach does not acknowledge areas where the environment might have been *improved*, albeit indirectly, as a result of trade reform (e.g. from less production by pollutive industries that were previously protected). Nor does it weigh the costs of any net worsening of the environment against the economic benefits of policy reform of the sort described above.

The reality is that while the environmental effects of reform will differ across sectors and regions of the world, some positive and some negative, there are many examples where cuts to subsidies and trade barriers would reduce environmental damage (Anderson, 1992; Irwin, 2002: 48–54). For some time the OECD has been encouraging analysis of these opportunities (OECD, 1996, 1997, 1998, 2003b). Environmental NGOs are increasingly recognizing them, too. They and the better-informed development NGOs seem to be coming to the view that the net social and environmental benefits from reducing subsidies and at least some trade barriers may indeed be positive rather than negative, and that the best hope of reducing environmentally harmful subsidies and trade barriers is via the WTO's multi-issue, multilateral trade negotiations process (see, e.g., Cameron, 2007; de Melo and Mathys, 2012).

If there remains a concern that the net effect of trade reform on the environment may be negative nationally or globally, that should be a stimulus to check whether first-best environmental policy measures are in place and set at the optimal level of intervention, rather than a reason for not reducing trade distortions. This is because if they are so set, we would then know that the direct economic gains from opening to trade would exceed society's evaluation of any extra environmental damage, other things equal (Corden 1997: Chapter 13).

Much environmental damage in developing countries is a direct consequence of poverty (e.g. the slash-and-burn shifting agriculture of landless unemployed squatters). In so far as trade reform reduces poverty, so it will reduce such damage. More generally, the relationships between per capita income and a wide range of environmental indicators have been studied extensively. Because richer people have a greater demand for a clean environment, income rises tend to be associated with better environmental outcomes once incomes rise above certain levels.[23] Even though more pollutive products are being consumed as incomes rise, many abatement practices have been spreading fast enough to more than compensate. And openness to trade accelerates that spread of abatement ideas and technologies, making their implementation in developing countries affordable at ever-earlier stages of development.

Estimating the global cost to society of all environmental damage that might accompany a reduction in subsidies and trade barriers, net of all environmental gains, is extraordinarily difficult both conceptually and empirically.[24] In the absence of any sufficiently comprehensive estimates it is safest to assume that the net effect of reform on the environment would be zero.

When the environmental impact is global rather than local, as with GHGs and their apparent impact

[22] See the critique by Lomborg (2001).

[23] This is the theme of the book by Hollander (2003). For statistical evidence of the extent to which different environmental indicators first worsen and then improve as incomes rise (sometimes called the environmental Kuznets curve), see the special issue of the journal *Environment and Development Economics*, Vol. 2, (4) in 1997 and the more recent papers by and cited in Harbaugh *et al.* (2002); Cole (2003); Johansson and Kristrom (2007); Vollebergh *et al.* (2009).

[24] A beginning nonetheless has been made, with several governments funding ex ante evaluations of the WTO Doha round's potential impact on the environment. The EU's efforts include a workshop on methodological issues which are laid out in CEPII (2003), and further work has been contracted to the University of Manchester whose progress can be traced at http://idpm.man.ac.uk/sia-trade/Consultation.htm. Ex post analyses are also being undertaken by NGOs. See, for example, Bermudez (2004) for WWF's sustainability impact assessment of trade policies during 2001–03.

on climate change, international environmental agreements may be required (see Cline, 2004; Yohe *et al.*, 2009; de Melo and Mathys, 2012). When developing countries are not party to such agreements, however, it is difficult to prevent "leakage" through a relocation of carbon-intensive activities to those non-signatories. An alternative or supplementary approach that is likely to achieve at least some emission reductions, and at the same time generate national and global economic benefits rather than costs, involves lowering coal subsidies and trade barriers. Past policies encouraged excessive production of coal in a number of industrial countries and excessive coal and petroleum product consumption in numerous developing countries, including transition economies. Phasing out those distortionary policies has both improved the economy and lowered GHG emissions globally – a "no regrets" outcome or win–win Pareto improvement for the economy and the environment (Anderson and McKibbin, 2000). Additional opportunities for reducing GHGs through cutting energy subsidies are pointed to in the UNEP study by von Moltke *et al.* (2004).

Communicable diseases

Communicable diseases are more common among the poor, so again trade reform's contribution to poverty alleviation will in turn impact on human health in general and the reduced incidence of diseases in particular. Furthermore, the greater openness of economies ensures that medicines and prevention technologies are more widespread and cheaper, particularly following the Doha WTO conference of trade ministers and the subsequent Decision of 30 August 2003 on the TRIPS Agreement and Public Health. That Decision by the WTO General Council ensures that developing-country governments can issue compulsory licenses to allow other companies to make a patented product or use a patented process under license without the consent of the patent owner, while developing countries unable to produce pharmaceuticals domestically can now import generic copies of patented drugs made under compulsory licensing by other developing countries.

Conflicts

Openness tends to break down the common prejudices that accompany insularity, and to broaden mutual understanding between people with different cultures and customs. It also expands economic interdependence among countries, which raises the opportunity cost of entering into conflicts with trading partners. In so far as it reduces income inequality across countries, then that too may diffuse tension between nations – a point that has even greater significance following the terrorist attacks of September 11, 2001. Indeed there is now statistical support for Immanuel Kant's hypothesis that durable peace is supported by representative democracy, trade, and membership of international organizations: Oneal and Russett (2000) find that all three contribute independently to more peaceful relationships with other countries. And casual observation suggests that more autarchic economies tend to be less democratic (Burma, Cuba, North Korea).

Education underinvestment

Parents and governments are less likely to underinvest in education the higher their incomes, other things equal. So to the extent that trade reform raises incomes, it contributes to better educational outcomes. That is especially so for the very poorest who cannot afford even primary education: a slight increase in the cash income of poor farm families, for example following a reform-induced increase in international prices of farm products, can make it possible to pay the (often relatively high) school fees that are otherwise unaffordable.

Poor governance and corruption

A tolerance for subsidies and trade barriers breeds rent-seeking by special interests seeking protectionist policies for their industry. If those policies include import licensing, that breeds corruption through encouraging bureaucrats responsible for allocating licenses to accept bribes from would-be importers. Together, those activities ensure that the welfare costs of trade barriers are higher than is typically measured, since a share of the private rents they generate is wasted in these lobbying activities. Tax-avoiding corruption is also encouraged in the case of import tariffs, for example through bribing customs officers or through smuggling. For these reasons it is not surprising that statistical analysis has found less-open economies to be more corrupt (Ades and Di Tella, 1999).

Malnutrition and hunger

Food security is always a great concern in poor countries, especially those dependent on food imports where there are fears that reducing agricultural subsidies and protectionism globally will raise the price of those imports. But food security is defined as always having access to the minimum supply of basic food necessary for survival, so enhancing food security is mainly about alleviating poverty. That suggests that this issue needs to be considered from a household rather than a national perspective. And the discussion on p. 689 argues that poverty is more likely than not to be alleviated by cuts to trade barriers.

Hunger and undernutrition can be eased by trade not only in goods but also in agricultural technologies, in particular newly bred varieties of staple crops. The introduction of high-yielding dwarf wheat and rice varieties during the "Green Revolution" that began in Asia in the 1960s is a previous case in point, whereby producers and consumers shared the benefits in terms of higher farm profits and lower consumer prices for cereals. A prospective case in point is the possibility of breeding crop varieties that are not only less costly to grow but are "nutriceuticals" in the sense that they contain vitamin and mineral supplements. The most promising is the so-called "golden rice." Consumers in many poor countries suffer from chronic vitamin A deficiency that can lead to blindness, weakened immune systems, and increased morbidity and mortality for children and pregnant and lactating women. Golden rice has been genetically engineered to contain a higher level of beta-carotene in the endosperm of the grain and thereby provide a vitamin A supplement. By being cheaper and/or more nutritionally beneficial, it would improve the health of poor people and thereby also boost their labor productivity. Anderson *et al.* (2005) estimate that the latter economic benefit from this new technology could be as much as ten times greater than just the traditional benefits of lower production costs – not to mention the fact that poor people would live longer and healthier lives. This new technology has yet to be adopted, however, because the European Union and some other countries will not import food from countries that may contain genetically modified organisms (GMOs) – even though there is no evidence that GM foods are a danger to human health (see, e.g., King, 2003). The cost of that trade barrier to developing countries – which is not included in the above estimates– has been very considerable (Anderson and Jackson, 2005).

Caveats

Measuring both the benefits and the costs of liberalizing subsidies and barriers to trade and migration is still an inexact science, despite the huge amount of progress that has been made over the past two decades in global CGE modelling.[25] We have tried to accommodate any shortcomings by providing a range of estimates and by erring on the conservative side in the above analysis. Nonetheless it is worth reviewing the key areas where analytical improvements are still needed. On the cost side, more empirical research on the real costs of adjustments to trade-policy changes, and how they are spread over time for different groups, would be helpful. On the benefit side, economists have made more progress but plenty of scope remains for further improvements, particularly on the size and longevity of dynamic gains from trade reform. Key areas, discussed in turn on p. 693, are the assumed policy counterfactual, the tariff-aggregation issue, product-quality differences, new products, measurement of distortions in markets for service products, and the behaviour of labor markets.

The standard approach used in evaluating the consequences of international trade agreements (ITAs) is to compare the agreed tariff binding with the previously applied tariff rate, and to treat the post-agreement tariff rate as the lesser of the two

[25] Parts of this section draw on the survey by Francois and Martin (2010).

rates. This essentially involves treating the current applied rate as a deterministic forecast of future protection rates in the absence of the agreement.

There are two potentially serious problems with this specification of the counterfactual. One is that the trend rate of protection responds systematically to underlying determinants that evolve over time. The second is that annual protection rates fluctuate substantially around that trend. Taking account of either or both of these counterfactuals can have large impacts on the estimated benefits of international trade liberalization agreements.

Anderson and Hayami (1986) and Lindert (1991) provide insights into the likely evolution of agricultural trade policies in the absence of international agreements. Key findings include a strong tendency for agricultural protection to rise with economic development because of fundamental changes in the structure of the economy. In particular, there is a tendency for agricultural protection to be low or negative in very poor countries because the number of farmers is large and it is difficult for them to organize to apply pressure on governments. Because farmers are mainly subsisting at that stage, their real incomes are not greatly affected by increases in farm-output prices. By contrast, the urban population in a poor country is far smaller and easier to organize, and food is an important part of consumer budgets.

As economies develop, however, all of these economic factors change in ways that shift the political–economy balance more towards agricultural protection. Farmers become fewer in number and find it easier to organize themselves. They also become more commercial in orientation, so that their real incomes are more strongly influenced by agricultural output prices. At the same time, the urban population becomes larger and hence harder to organize, and the importance of food in consumer budgets and hence in real wage determinations declines. The end result can be a very rapid increase in agricultural protection rates in high-growth economies. Without the new discipline of the Uruguay Round's Agreement on Agriculture, agricultural protection rates in Europe and Northeast Asia may well have kept rising over the past fifteen years, and may continue to rise in fast-growing middle-income countries whose tariff and subsidy bindings in the WTO are still well above applied rates (Anderson and Nelgen, 2011).

Also striking is the large variation in national rates of agricultural protection over time. This is because trade and subsidy policies are frequently also used to stabilize domestic agricultural prices in the face of variations in world prices (Tyers and Anderson, 1992; Anderson and Nelgen, 2012). The value of legal bindings on those policies via trade agreements, even when the bindings are well above applied rates at the time of the agreement, is non-trivial and yet is not captured in most models because those models are not stochastic. As Francois and Martin (2004) show, even bindings that are set well above average rates of protection may greatly diminish the costs of protection when international prices peak. They estimate, for example, that the European tariff binding on wheat, at 82 percent, reduced the cost of protection to this commodity by almost a third, despite being substantially above the average rate of protection prevailing during the preceding fifteen years for which data were available. This is another reason why current CGE models are understating the gains from reducing tariff and subsidy bindings, particularly for farm products.

Conclusion

The theory and available evidence surveyed above show that trade barriers and subsidies are very wasteful. Pre-announced, gradual reductions in them, especially if done multilaterally, would yield huge economic benefits and relatively little economic cost, and hence extremely high BCRs. Moreover, such reforms would contribute enormously to reducing global inequality and poverty. Furthermore, while some social and environmental effects of such reform may be perceived as negative, many more will be positive. Even where some of those effects are harmful, there are almost always cheaper ways of obtaining better social and environmental outcomes than via trade and subsidy measures. The reason that these inefficient measures persist is partly lack of understanding of the benefits being forgone, but mostly it is because a small number of vested interests are able to successfully lobby for their retention.

The challenge is to find politically feasible opportunities for ridding the world of trade barriers and distortionary subsidies. This chapter suggests that the most obvious way is currently before us in the form of the DDA of multilateral trade negotiations under the WTO. Seizing that opportunity for reform could reduce government outlays by hundreds of millions of dollars, and make it less attractive to seek preferential trade agreements which are prone to making excluded countries worse off. A successful Doha outcome would also make it less pressing to lower immigration barriers, insofar as trade in products is a substitute for international labor movements – although the global gains and inequality-reducing consequences of more migration are likely to be so large as to make that type of opening-up worthwhile, too (see Anderson and Winters, 2009). Cuts in trade barriers and subsidies also would provide a means for citizens to spend more on other pressing problems (because under freer trade the world's resources would be allocated more efficiently), thereby *indirectly* contributing to opportunities to alleviate other challenges facing the world; and they could also *directly* alleviate poverty and thereby reduce environmental degradation and address other challenges such as communicable diseases, conflicts and arms proliferation, education underinvestment, and hunger and malnutrition. All that is needed is the political will to agree to and implement such reforms.

Bibliography

Acharya, R. C. and W. Keller, 2007: Technology transfers through imports, *NBER Working Paper* **13086**, Cambridge, MA

Ades, A. and R. di Tella, 1999: Rents, competition, and corruption, *American Economic Review* **89**, 982–93

Aghion, P. and R. Griffith, 2005: *Competition and Growth: Reconciling Theory and Evidence*, MIT Press, Cambridge, MA

Aghion, P. and P. Howitt, 2006: Appropriate growth policy: a unified framework, *Journal of the European Economic Association* **4**, 269–314

Anderson, K., 1992: Effects on the environment and welfare of liberalising world trade: the cases of coal and food, in K. Anderson and R. Blackhurst (eds.), *The Greening of World Trade Issues*, Harvester-Wheatsheaf and University of Michigan, Ann Arbor, MI, London

2003: Measuring effects of trade policy distortions: how far have we come?, *The World Economy* **26**, 413–40

2013: Costing global trade barriers, 1900 to 2050, in B. Lomborg (ed.), *The Way the World Is: Past, Present and Future Challenges*, Cambridge University Press, New York

Anderson, K. and Y. Hayami, 1986: *The Political Economy of Agricultural Protection East Asia in International Perspective*, Allen & Unwin, London

Anderson, K. and L. A. Jackson, 2005: Some implications of GM food technology policies for Sub-Saharan Africa, *Journal of African Economies* **14**, 385–410

Anderson, K. and W. McKibbin, 2000: Reducing coal subsidies and trade barriers: their contribution to greenhouse gas abatement, *Environment and Development Economics* **5**, 457–81

Anderson, K. and S. Nelgen, 2011: What's the appropriate agricultural protection counterfactual for trade analysis?, in W. Martin and A. Mattoo (eds.), *Unfinished Business? The WTO's Doha Agenda*, Centre for Economic Policy Research and the World Bank, London

Anderson, K. and S. Nelgen, 2012: Trade barrier volatility and agricultural price stabilization, *World Development* **40**, 36–48

Anderson, K. and L. A. Winters, 2009: The challenge of reducing international trade and migration barriers, in B. Lomborg (ed.), *Global Crises, Global Solutions*, 2nd edn., Cambridge University Press

Anderson, K., J. Cockburn, and W. Martin, 2011: Would freeing up world trade reduce poverty and inequality? The vexed role of agricultural distortions, *The World Economy* **34**, 487–515

Anderson, K., J. Cockburn, and W. Martin (eds.), 2010: *Agricultural Price Distortions, Inequality and Poverty*, World Bank, Washington, DC

Anderson, K., L. A. Jackson, and C. P. Nielsen, 2005: GM rice adoption: implications for welfare and poverty alleviation, *Journal of Economic Integration* **20**, 771–88

Anderson, K., W. Martin, and D. van der Mensbrugghe, 2006: Market and welfare implications of the Doha reform scenarios, in K. Anderson and W. Martin (eds.), *Agricultural Trade Reform and the Doha Development Agenda*, Palgrave Macmillan, London (co-published with the World Bank)

APEC, 2010: *Leaders' Declaration*, www.apec.org/Meeting-Papers/Leaders-Declarations/2010/2010_aelm.aspx

Arnold, J. M., B. S. Javorcik, and A. Mattoo, 2011: Does services liberalization benefit manufacturing firms? Evidence from the Czech Republic, *Journal of International Economics* **85**, 136–46

Asian Development Bank (ADB), 2011: *Asian Development Outlook 2011*, ADB, Manila

Bacchetta, M. and M. Jansen, 2003: Adjusting to trade liberalization: the role of policy, institutions and WTO disciplines, *Special Studies* **7**, World Trade Organization, Geneva

Baldwin, R. E., 2004: Openness and growth: what's the empirical relationship?, in R. E. Baldwin and L. A. Winters (eds.), *Challenges to Globalization: Analysing the Economics*, University of Chicago Press for NBER and CEPR

2009: Big-think regionalism: a critical survey, in A. Estevadeordal, K. Suominen, and R. Teh (eds.), *Regional Rules in the Global Trading System*, Cambridge University Press, New York

2011: Trade and industrialization after globalization's, 2nd unbundling: how building and joining a supply chain are different and why it matters, *NBER Working Paper* **17716**, Cambridge, MA

Beghin, J., D. van der Mensbrugghe, and D. Roland-Holst, 2002: *Trade and the Environment in General Equilibrium: Evidence from Developing Economies*, Kluwer Academic Norwell, MA

Bendivogli, C. and P. Pagano, 1999: Trade, job destruction and job creation in european manufacturing, *Open Economies Review* **10**, 156–84

Bermudez, E., 2004: *Sustainability Assessments of Trade Policies and Programmes*, WWF International, Gland

Bernard, A. B., J. B. Jensen, S. J. Redding, and P. K. Schott, 2007: Firms in international trade, *Journal of Economic Perspectives* **21**, 105–30

Bhagwati, J. N., 1971: The generalized theory of distortions and welfare, in J. N. Bhagwati *et al.* (eds.), *Trade, Balance of Payments and Growth*, North-Holland, Amsterdam

Billmeier, A. and T. Nannicini, 2009: Trade openness and growth: pursuing empirical glasnost, *IMF Staff Papers* **56**, 447–75

Bordo, M. and P. Rousseau, 2012: Historical evidence on the finance–trade–growth nexus, *Journal of Banking and Finance* **36**, 1236–43

Cameron, H., 2007: The evolution of the trade and environment debate at the WTO, in A. Najam, M. Halle, and R. Melendez-Ortiz (eds.), *Trade and Environment: A Resource Book*, International Centre for Trade and Sustainable Development (ICTSD), Geneva, see www.trade-environment.org

CEPII, 2003: *Methodological Tools for SIA: Report of the CEPII Workshop held on 7–8 November 2002 in Brussels*, CEPIIo, Paris, *Working Paper* **2003–19**, www.cepii.fr/anglaisgraph/workpap/pdf/2003/wp03–19.pdf

Chang, R., L. Kaltani, and N. Loayza, 2005: Openness can be good for growth: the role of policy complementarity, *Policy Research Working Paper* **3763**, World Bank, Washington, DC, and *NBER Working Paper* **11787**, Cambridge, MA

Cline, W. R., 2004: Climate change, in B. Lomborg, (ed.), *Global Crises, Global Solutions*, Cambridge University Press

Cline, W. R., T. O. Kawanabe, M. Kronsjo, and T. Williams, 1978: *Trade Negotiations in the Tokyo Round: A Quantitative Assessment*, Brookings Institution, Washington, DC

Coase, R., 1960: The problem of social cost, *Journal of Law and Economics* **3**, 1–44

Cole, M. A., 2003: Development, trade, and the environment: how robust is the environmental kuznets curve?, *Environment and Development Economics* **8**, 557–80

Copland, B. and M. S. Taylor, 2003: *Trade and the Environment: Theory and Evidence*, Princeton University Press

Corden, W. M., 1997: *Trade Policy and Economic Welfare*, 2nd edn., Clarendon Press, Oxford

Deardorff, A. V. and R. M. Stern, 1979: *An Economic Analysis of the Effects of the Tokyo Round of Multilateral Trade Negotiations on the United States and Other Major Industrial Countries, MTN Studies* **5**, US Government Printing Office, Washington, DC

1986: *The Michigan Model of World Production and Trade: Theory and Applications*, MIT Press, Cambridge, MA

de Melo, J. and N. A. Mathys, 2012: Reconciling trade and climate policies, *CEPR Discussion Paper* **8760**, London

de Melo, J. and D. Tarr, 1990: Welfare costs of US quotas on textiles, steel and autos, *Review of Economics and Statistics* **72**, 489–97

Diebold, W., Jr., 1952: *The End of the ITO,* International Finance Section, *Essays in International Finance* **16**, Princeton University Press

Dollar, D. and A. Kraay, 2002: Growth is good for the poor, *Journal of Economic Growth* **7**, 195–225

Easterly, W., 2001: *The Elusive Quest for Growth*, MIT Press, Cambridge, MA

Faini, R., 2004: Trade liberalization in a globalizing world, *CEPR Discussion Paper* **4665**, London

Feenstra, R. C., 2003: *Advanced International Trade: Theory and Evidence*, Princeton University Press

Fernandez, R. and D. Rodrik, 1991: Resistance to reform: status quo bias and the presence of individual specific uncertainty, *American Economic Review* **81**, 1146–55

Fouré, J., A. Bénassy-Quéré, and L. Fontagné, 2010: The world economy in 2050: a tentative picture, *CEPII Working Paper* **2010–27**, CEPII, Paris

Francois, J. F., 2003: Assessing the impact of trade policy on labour markets and production, in *Methodological Tools for SIA, CEPII Working Paper* **2003–19**, CEPII, Paris, 61–88

Francois, J. F. and B. Hoekman, 2010: Services trade and policy, *Journal of Economic Literature* **48**, 642–92

Francois, J. F. and W. Martin, 2004: Commercial policy, bindings and market access, *European Economic Review* **48**, 665–79

2010: Ex ante assessments of the welfare impacts of trade reforms with numerical models, in H. Beladi and E. K. Choi (eds.), *New Developments in Computable General Equilibrium Analysis for Trade Policy*, Emerald Group Publishing, London

Francois, J. F. and K. A. Reinert (eds.), 1997: *Applied Methods for Trade Policy Analysis: A Handbook*, Cambridge University Press, New York

Frankel, J. A. and E. A. Cavallo, 2008: Does openness to trade make countries more vulnerable to sudden stops, or less? Using gravity to establish causality, *Journal of International Money and Finance* **27**, 1430–52

Frankel, J. A. and D. Romer, 1999: Does trade cause growth?, *American Economic Review* **89**, 379–99

Freeman, R. B., 2004: Trade wars: the exaggerated impact of trade in economic debate, *The World Economy* **27**, 1–23

Friedman, T. L., 2007: *The World is Flat: The Globalized World in the Twenty-First Century*, Penguin, London

Furusawa, T. and E. L. C. Lai, 1999: Adjustment costs and gradual trade liberalization, *Journal of International Economics* **49**, 333–61

Glenday, G., 2002: Trade liberalization and customs revenue: does trade liberalization lead to lower customs revenue? The Case of Kenya, *Journal of African Finance and Economic Development* **5**, 89–125

Greenaway, D., 1993: Liberalizing foreign trade through rose-tinted glasses, *Economic Journal* **103**, 208–22

Greenaway, D. and C. Milner, 1993: The fiscal implication of trade policy reform: theory and evidence, *UNDP/World Bank Trade Expansion Program Occasional Paper* **9**, World Bank, Washington, DC

Grossman, G. M. and E. Helpman, 1991: *Innovation and Growth in the Global Economy*, MIT Press, Cambridge, MA

Grossman, G. M. and E. Rossi-Hansberg, 2012: Task trade between similar countries, *Econometrica* **80**, 593–629

Grossman, G. M. and K. Rogoff (eds.), 1995: *Handbook of International Economics*, Vol. III, North-Holland, Amsterdam

Hanson, G. H., R. J. Mataloni, and M. J. Slaughter, 2005: Vertical production networks in multinational firms, *Review of Economics and Statistics* **87**, 664–78

Harbaugh, W. T., A. Levinson, and D. M. Wilson, 2002: Re-examining the empirical evidence for an environmental Kuznets curve, *Review of Economics and Statistics* **84**, 541–51

Harrigan, J. and E. K. Choi (eds.), 2003: *Handbook of International Trade*, Blackwell, Oxford

Helpman, E. and O. Itskhoki, 2010: Labor market rigidities, trade and unemployment, *Review of Economic Studies* **77**, 1100–37

Helpman, E., D. Marin, and T. Verdier (eds.), 2008: *The Organization of Firms in a Global*

Economy, Harvard University Press, Cambridge, MA

Hertel, T. W., M. Verma, M. Ivanic, and A. R. Rios, 2011: GTAP–POV: a framework for assessing the national poverty impacts of global economic and environmental policies, *GTAP Technical Paper* **31**, Purdue University, West Lafayette

Hollander, J., 2003: *The Real Environmental Crisis: Why Poverty, Not Affluence, is the Environment's Number One Enemy*, University of California Press, Berkeley, CA

Hoxha, I., S. Kalemli-Ozcan, and D. Vollrath, 2011: How big are the gains from international financial integration?, *CEPR Discussion Paper* **8647**, London

Irwin, D. A., 2002: *Free Trade Under Fire*, Princeton University Press

Jacobson, L. S., R. J. LaLonde, and D. G. Sullivan, 1993: Earnings losses of displaced workers, *American Economic Review* **83**, 685–709

Javorcik, B., W. Keller, and J. Tybout, 2008: Openness and industrial responses in a Walmart world: a case study of Mexican soaps, detergents and surfactant producers, *The World Economy* **31**, 1558–80

Johansson, P. and B. Kristrom, 2007: On a clear day you might see an environmental Kuznets curve, *Environmental and Resource Economics* **37**, 77–90

Just, R. E., D. L. Hueth, and A. Schmitz, 2004: *The Welfare Economics of Public Policy*, Edward Elgar, London

Kindleberger, C. P., 1989: Commercial policy between the wars, in Peter Mathias and Sidney Pollard (eds.), *The Cambridge Economic History of Europe*, Vol. 8, Cambridge University Press

King, D. K., 2003: *GM Science Review: First Report*, Prepared by the GM Science Review Panel under the chairmanship of Sir David King for the UK Government, July

Kose, M. A., E. Prasad, K. Rogoff, and S. Wei, 2009: Financial globalization: a reappaisal, *IMF Staff Papers* **56**, 8–62

Krueger, A. O., 1983: *Trade and Employment in Developing Countries, Volume, 3 Synthesis and Conclusions*, University of Chicago Press for NBER

Laborde, D., W. Martin, and D. van der Mensbrugghe, 2011: Potential real income effects of Doha reforms, in W. Martin and A. Mattoo (eds.), *Unfinished Business? The WTO's Doha Agenda*, Centre for Economic Policy Research, London and World Bank, Washington, DC

2012: Implications of the Doha market access proposals for developing countries, *World Trade Review* **11**. 1–25

Lee, J.-W., 1995: Capital goods imports and long-run growth, *Journal of Development Economics* **48**, 91–110

Lileeva, A. and D. Trefler, 2010: Improved access to foreign markets raises plant-level productivity . . . for some plants, *Quarterly Journal of Economics* **125**, 1051–99

Lindert, P., 1991: Historical patterns of agricultural protection, in P. Timmer (ed.), *Agriculture and the State*, Cornell University Press, Ithaca NY

Lloyd, P. J., 1974: A more general theory of price distortions in an open economy, *Journal of International Economics* **4**, 365–86

Lomborg, B., 2001: *The Skeptical Environmentalist: Measuring the Real State of the World*, Cambridge University Press, New York

(ed.), 2004: *Global Crises, Global Solutions*, Cambridge University Press, New York

Lumenga-Neso, O., M. Olarreaga, and M. Schiff, 2005: On "Indirect" Trade-Related R&D Spillovers, *European Economic Review* **49**, 1785–98

Matusz, S. and D. Tarr, 2000: Adjusting to trade policy reform, in A. O. Krueger (ed.), *Economic Policy Reform: The Second Stage*, University of Chicago Press

Mazumdar, J., 2001: Imported machinery and growth in LDCs, *Journal of Development Economics* **65**, 209–24

Melitz, M. J., 2003: The impact of trade on intra-industry reallocations and aggregate industry productivity, *Econometrica* **71**, 1692–725

Melitz, M. J. and G. I. P. Ottaviano, 2008: Market size, trade and productivity, *Review of Economic Studies* **75**, 295–316

Michaely, M., D. Papageorgiou, and A. Choksi (eds.), 1991: *Liberalizing Foreign Trade, 7: Lessons of Experience in the Developing World*, Basil Blackwell, Cambridge, MA and Oxford

Nash, J. and W. Takacs, 1998: Lessons from the trade expansion program, in J. Nash and W. Takacs, (eds.), *Trade Policy Reform: Lessons and Implications*, World Bank, Washington, DC

OECD, 1996: *Subsidies and the Environment: Exploring the Linkages*, OECD, Paris
1997: *Reforming Energy and Transport Subsidies: Environmental and Economic Implications*, OECD, Paris
1998: *Improving the Environment Through Reducing Subsidies*, OECD, Paris
2003a: *Agricultural Trade and Poverty: Making Policy Analysis Count*, OECD, Paris
2003b: *Environmentally Harmful Subsidies: Policy Issues and Challenges*, OECD, Paris
Olsen, M., 1965: *The Logic of Collective Action*, Harvard University Press, Cambridge, MA
Oneal, J. and B. Russett, 2000: *Triangulating Peace: Democracy, Interdependence and International Organizations*, W. W. Norton, New York
Petri, P. A., M. G. Plummer, and F. Zhai, 2011: The Trans-Pacific partnership and Asia-Pacific integration: a quantitative assessment, *East–West Center Economics Working Paper* **119**, Honolulu
Porto, G. and B. Hoekman (eds.), 2010: *Trade Adjustment Costs in Developing Countries: Impacts, Determinants and Policy Responses*, CEPR, London and World Bank, Washington, DC
Ravallion, M., 2006: Looking beyond averages in the trade and policy debate, *World Development* **34**, 1374–92
Rivera-Batiz, L. and P. Romer, 1991: International integration and endogenous growth, *Quarterly Journal of Economics* **106**, 531–56
Rodrigeuz, F. and D. Rodrik, 2001: Trade policy and economic growth: a skeptic's guide to cross-national evidence, in B. S. Bernanke and K. Rogoff (eds.), *NBER Macroeconomics Annual 2000*, MIT Press, Cambridge, MA
Rodrik, D., 2007: *One Economics, Many Recipes: Globalization, Institutions and Economic Growth*, Princeton University Press
Romalis, J., 2007: Market access, openness and growth, *NBER Working Paper* **13048**, Cambridge, MA
Romer, P., 1994: New goods, old theory, and the welfare costs of trade restrictions, *Journal of Development Economics* **43**, 5–38
Rutherford, T. F. and D. G. Tarr, 2002: Trade liberalization, product variety and growth in a small open economy: a quantitative assessment, *Journal of International Economics* **56**, 247–72
Sachs, J. D. and A. Warner, 1995: Economic reform and the process of global integration, *Brookings Papers on Economic Activity* **1**, 1–95
Sala-i-Martin, X., 2006: The world distribution of income: falling poverty and . . . convergence, period, *Quarterly Journal of Economics* **121**, 351–97
Schularick, M. and T. M. Steger, 2010: Financial integration, investment, and economic growth: evidence from two eras of financial globalization, *Review of Economics and Statistics* **92**, 756–68
Sen, A., 1999: *Development as Freedom*, Anchor Books, New York
Taylor, M. S., 1999: Trade and trade policy in endogenous growth models, in J. Piggott and A. Woodland (eds.), *International Trade Policy and the Pacific Rim*, Macmillan for the IAE, London
Townsend, R. M. and K. Ueda, 2010: Welfare gains from financial globalization, *International Economic Review* **51**, 553–97
Tyers, R. and K. Anderson, 1992: *Disarray in World Food Markets: A Quantitative Assessment*, Cambridge University Press, New York
USITC, 1997: *The Dynamic Effects of Trade Liberalization: An Empirical Analysis*, Publication **3069**, US International Trade Commission, Washington, DC
Valenzuela, E., D. van der Mensbrugghe, and K. Anderson, 2009: General equilibrium effects of price distortions on global markets, farm incomes and welfare, in K. Anderson (ed.), *Distortions to Agricultural Incentives: A Global Perspective, 1955–2007*, Palgrave Macmillan, London and World Bank, Washington, DC
van Beers, C. and A. de Moor, 2001: *Public Subsidies and Policy Failures: How Subsidies Distort the Natural Environment, Equity and Trade and How to Reform Them*, Edward Elgar, Cheltenham
van der Mensbrugghe, D., 2011: Linkage Technical Reference Document: Version 7.1, World Bank, Washington, DC, March, mimeo, http://go.worldbank.org/12JVZ7A910 or http://siteresources.worldbank.org/INTPROSPECTS/Resources/334934–1314986341738/TechRef7.1_01Mar2011.pdf
Vollebergh, H., B. Melenberg, and E. Dijkgraaf, 2009: Identifying reduced-form relations with panel data: the case of pollution and income,

Journal of Environmental Economics and Management **58**, 27–42

von Moltke, A., C. McKee, and T. Morgan, 2004: *Energy Subsidies: Lessons Learned in Assessing Their Impact and Designing Policy Reforms*, Greenleaf Books for UNEP, London

Wacziarg, R., 2001: Measuring the dynamic gains from trade, *World Bank Economic Review* **15**, 393–429

Wacziarg, R. and K. H. Welch, 2008: Trade liberalization and growth: new evidence, *World Bank Economic Review* **15**, 393–429

Whalley, J., 1985: *Trade Liberalization Among Major World Trading Areas*, MIT Press, Cambridge, MA

2010: China's FDI and non-FDI economies and the sustainability of future high chinese growth, *China Economic Review* **21**, 123–35

Winters, L. A., 2002: Trade liberalisation and poverty: what are the links?, *The World Economy* **25**, 1339–68

2004: Trade liberalization and economic performance: an overview, *Economic Journal* **114**, F4–F21

Winters, L. A., N. McCulloch, and A. McKay, 2004: Trade liberalization and poverty: the empirical evidence, *Journal of Economic Literature* **62**, 72–115

Winters, L. A. and W. E. Takacs, 1991: Labour adjustment costs and British footwear protection, *Oxford Economic Papers* **43**, 479–501

World Bank, 2006: *Global Economic Prospects 2006: Economic Implications of Remittances and Migration*, World Bank, Washington, DC

Yohe, G. W., R. S. J. Tol, R. G. Richels, and G. J. Blanford, 2009: Climate change, in B. Lomborg (ed.), *Global Crises, Global Solutions*, 2nd edn., Cambridge University Press, New York

Zhai, F., 2008: Armington meets melitz: introducing firm heterogeneity in a global CGE model of trade, *Journal of Economic Integration* **23**, 575–604

PART II

Ranking the Opportunities

Expert Panel Ranking

FINN E. KYDLAND, ROBERT MUNDELL, THOMAS SCHELLING, VERNON SMITH, AND NANCY STOKEY

The goal of the 2012 Copenhagen Consensus was to set priorities among a series of proposals for confronting ten of the world's most important challenges. These challenges were: Armed conflict; Biodiversity; Chronic disease; Climate change; Education; Hunger and malnutrition; Infectious disease; Natural disasters; Population growth; and Water and sanitation.

A Panel of economic experts, comprising five of the world's most distinguished economists, was invited to consider these issues. The members were:

- Finn E. Kydland, University of California, Santa Barbara (Nobel Laureate)
- Robert Mundell, Columbia University in New York (Nobel Laureate)
- Thomas Schelling, University of Maryland (Nobel Laureate)
- Vernon Smith, Chapman University (Nobel Laureate)
- Nancy Stokey, University of Chicago

The Panel was asked to address the ten challenge areas and to answer the question: "What are the best ways of advancing global welfare, and particularly the welfare of developing countries, illustrated by supposing that an additional $75 billion of resources were at their disposal over a 4-year initial period?"

Ten Challenge Papers (Chapters 1–10), commissioned from acknowledged authorities in each area of policy, set out thirty-nine proposals for the Panel's consideration. The Panel examined these proposals in detail. Each chapter was discussed at length with its principal author. The Panel was also informed by fourteen Alternative Perspective papers, providing critical appraisals of each chapter's assumptions and methodology. Based on the costs and benefits of the solutions, the Panel ranked the proposals, in descending order of desirability.

Final prioritized ranking

Table Pan.1 Prioritization of solutions: Expert Panel

	Challenge	Solution
1	Hunger and Education	Bundled Interventions to Reduce Undernutrition in Pre-Schoolers
2	Infectious Disease	Subsidy for Malaria Combination Treatment
3	Infectious Disease	Expanded Childhood Immunization Coverage
4	Infectious Disease	Deworming of Schoolchildren
5	Infectious Disease	Expanding Tuberculosis Treatment
6	Hunger and Biodiversity and Climate Change	R&D to Increase Yield Enhancements
7	Natural Disasters	Investing in Effective EWS
8	Infectious Disease	Strengthening Surgical Capacity
9	Chronic Disease	Hepatitis B Immunization
10	Chronic Disease	Acute Heart Attack Low-Cost Drugs
11	Chronic Disease	Salt-Reduction Campaign
12	Climate Change	Geo-Engineering R&D
13	Education	CCTs for School Attendance
14	Infectious Disease	Accelerated HIV Vaccine R&D
15	Education	Information Campaign on Benefits From Schooling
16	Water and Sanitation	Borehole and Public HandPump Intervention
17	Climate Change	Increased Funding for Green Energy R&D

(cont.)

Table Pan.1 (*cont.*)

	Challenge	Solution
18	Population Growth	Increase Availability of Family Planning
19	Chronic Disease	Heart Attack Risk Reduction Generic Pill
20	Water and Sanitation	CLTS
21	Water and Sanitation	Sanitation as a Business
22	Chronic Disease	Increasing Tobacco Taxation
23	Natural Disasters	Community Walls Against Floods
24	Water and Sanitation	The "Reinvented Toilet"
25	Biodiversity	Protecting All Forests
26	Natural Disasters	Retrofitting Schools to Withstand Earthquake Damage
27	Hunger	Crop Advisory Text Messages
28	Biodiversity	Extension of Protected Areas
29	Natural Disasters	Strengthening Structures Against Hurricanes and Storms
30	Natural Disasters	Elevating Residential Structures to Avoid Flooding

Budget

The Panel based its budget allocations on the proposals from authors, and on their own views of appropriate expenditure.

Methodology

The Panel considered the findings and arguments made in the Challenge Paper and Alternative Perspective Papers.

In ordering the proposals, the Panel was guided predominantly by consideration of economic costs and benefits. The Panel acknowledged the difficulties that CBA must overcome, both in principle and as a practical matter, but agreed that the cost-benefit approach was an indispensable organizing method. In setting priorities, the Panel took account of the strengths and weaknesses of the specific cost-benefit appraisals under review, and gave weight both to the institutional preconditions for success and to the demands of ethical or humanitarian urgency. As a general matter, the Panel noted that higher standards of governance and improvements in the institutions required to support development in the world's poor countries are of paramount importance.

For some of the proposals, the Panel found that information was too sparse to allow a judgment to be made. These proposals, some of which may prove after further study to be valuable, were therefore excluded from the ranking.

Each expert assigned his or her own ranking to the proposals. The individual rankings, together with commentaries prepared by each expert are on pp. 701–18. (The Challenge Papers, Alternative Perspective Papers, and Working Papers

Table Pan.2 Expert Panel's allocation of $75 billion

Solution	Amount allocated p.a., in $US billion
Bundled Interventions to Reduce Undernutrition in Pre-Schoolers	3.0
Subsidy for Malaria Combination Treatment	0.3
Expanded Childhood Immunization Coverage	1.0
Deworming of Schoolchildren	0.3
Expanding Tuberculosis Treatment	1.5
R&D to Increase Yield Enhancements	2.0
Investing in Effective EWS	1.0
Strengthening Surgical Capacity	3.0
Hepatitis B Immunization	0.12
Acute Heart Attack Low-Cost Drugs	0.2
Salt-Reduction Campaign	1.0
Geo-Engineering R&D	1.0
CCTs for School Attendance*	1.0
Accelerated HIV Vaccine R&D	0.1
Information Campaign on Benefits From Schooling*	1.34
Borehole and Public Handpump Intervention	1.89
Total	$18.75

Note:
* Estimate.

have already been placed in the public domain www.copenhagen consensus.com.) The Panel's ranking was calculated by taking the median of individual rankings. The Panel jointly endorses the median ordering shown above as representing their agreed view.

Notes about the challenges

Hunger and malnutrition (Chapter 6)

The Panel examined the following solutions to this challenge: Interventions to reduce chronic undernutrition in pre-schoolers, R&D to increase yield enhancements, Crop advisory text messages, Increased competition in the fertilizer market.

Based on very high BCRs, the Panel chose to give its highest ranking to Interventions to reduce chronic undernutrition in pre-schoolers. The Panel merged this with a similar proposed investment contained in the Education paper (Chapter 5). For about $100 per child, this bundle of interventions (including micronutrient provision, and also complementary foods, treatments for worms and diarrheal diseases, and behavior-change programs), could reduce chronic undernutrition by 36 percent in developing countries. The Panel noted that the educational benefits as well as the health benefits should be taken into consideration. Even in very poor countries and using very conservative assumptions, each dollar spent reducing chronic undernutrition has at least a $30 pay-off.

The Panel merged the intervention of R&D to increase yield enhancements with the similar investment from the Biodiversity topic (Chapter 2). The Panel noted accordingly that this investment would not lead only to a reduction in hunger, but also created benefits stemming from its effects on biodiversity and climate change. The BCRs are therefore very respectable for this intervention.

The Panel gave a comparatively low ranking to Crop advisory text messages, reflecting that this service is probably best left handled locally and by the private market.

In line with the unavailability of BCRs for the solution of Increasing Competition in the fertilizer market, and the author's views that this was not as promising as it had first appeared, the Panel chose not to rank it, while still emphasizing it as a relevant research consideration.

Education (Chapter 5)

The Panel examined the following solutions to this challenge: School-based health and nutrition programs, Conditional cash transfers (CCTs) for school attendance, Information campaign on benefits from schooling (extended field trial).

The first investment considered, School-based health and nutrition programs, shared many features with the interventions to Reduce chronic undernutrition in pre-schoolers under the heading of Hunger and malnutrition. As a result, the Panel combined these interventions into one investment proposal; further discussion of that investment is included under the previous heading of Hunger and malnutrition.

The Panel gave mid-rankings to the other two proposals considered. They found that there were considerable benefits to using CCTs to increase school attendance in some settings, and that there was a strong case to prioritize funding for an extended field trial of an information campaign on the benefits from schooling.

Infectious disease (Chapter 7)

The Panel examined the following solutions to this challenge: Subsidy for malaria combination treatment, Expanded childhood Immunization coverage, Deworming of schoolchildren, Expanding tuberculosis treatment, Strengthening surgical capacity, Accelerated HIV vaccine R&D.

The Panel was impressed by the high BCRs for the Infectious disease solutions, even with the conservative assumptions used.

A high priority for additional spending is to reduce the relative prices that poor countries face for new artemisinin combination therapies (through the so-called "Affordable Medicines Facility-malaria" or AMFM). Every $1 million spent on this financing mechanism of the Global Fund means about 300,000 more children treated, including 20,000 with severe malaria. This would prevent 1,000 deaths. Thus, spending $300 million a year on the subsidy for malaria combination treatment would prevent 300,000 child deaths, with benefits, put in economic terms, that are thirty-five times higher than the costs. This analysis suggests it is one of the best returns on health that could be made globally.

Another high priority is Expanded childhood immunization treatment, where spending about $1 billion annually would save 1 million child deaths and have benefits twenty times higher than the costs.

The Panel noted that the benefits from Deworming of schoolchildren would not just come from the health effects, but also from making education more productive.

While the benefits for Expanding tuberculosis treatment are lower than in the 2008 Copenhagen Consensus, this remains a very worthwhile investment.

The Panel noted a compelling need to Strengthen surgical capacity in the developing world, where very low-cost investments could be highly effective.

The Panel noted while there might be a considerable delay before an HIV vaccine is ready, this was a relatively cheap investment worthy of funds.

Biodiversity (Chapter 2)

The Panel examined the following solutions to this challenge: Agricultural productivity R&D, Extension of protected areas, Protecting all dense forests.

The Panel chose to merge Agricultural productivity R&D with the similar intervention proposed under the topic of Hunger and malnutrition, noting the combined benefits of this investment; discussion of this intervention is included under that heading, on p. 705.

The Panel questions the political viability of Protecting all dense forests over a thirty-year period. It is not clear that many countries are able to prevent forests from being converted to agriculture today; it is unclear that the investment would achieve this.

The Panel found that Extension of protected areas would have obvious benefits but also significant costs, principally the loss of output from the land that is taken out of use. The low BCR is reflected by its low ranking by the Panel. The Panel also notes that many of the benefits would be more relevant to the developed world, rather than the developing nations.

Natural disasters (Chapter 8)

The Panel examined the following solutions to this challenge: Investing in effective early warning systems (EWS), Community walls against floods, Retrofitting schools to withstand earthquake damage, Strengthening structures against hurricanes and storms, Elevating residential structures to avoid flooding.

Investing in Effective EWS was given a high ranking; it was substantially less costly, and more implementable than other interventions looked at in this topic, while it reaped significant benefits, not only from infrastructure damage reduction, but also from potentially large, reduced economic knock-on effects.

Of the two proposals to elevate structures and community walls (Community walls against floods, and Elevating residential structures to avoid flooding), the Panel noted that the Community wall was substantially more effective. However, both were very uncertain investments and hence were ranked low. The Panel also pointed out that a case-by-case approach was probably more useful than an overarching, global strategy. The Panel further noted the substantial challenges inherent in building sea walls, including the long time frames required for planning, agreement, and construction.

Based on the research presented, the Panel found that a global plan to Retrofit schools to withstand earthquake damage had a quite low BCR and while well-intentioned was therefore given a low ranking.

Strengthening structures against hurricanes and storms was given a low ranking by the Panel in keeping with the relatively modest BCRs calculated by the authors.

Chronic disease (Chapter 3)

The Panel examined the following solutions to this challenge: Hepatitis B immunization, Acute heart attack low-cost drugs, salt-reduction campaign, Heart attack risk reduction generic pill, Increasing tobacco taxation.

Hepatitis B immunization appears to be a straightforward and solid proposal, which the Panel found worthy of investment.

Acute heart attack low-cost drugs was a worthy investment, but seemed to be most relevant in countries in which infrastructure was already in place, suggesting there could be some challenges in low-income countries with less health care infrastructure.

Higher awareness of the risk factors of salt consumption is important, and the Panel found that there was a need for developed world experience in Salt-reduction campaigns to be shared with lower-income nations. This is a relatively low-cost intervention. Compared to Tobacco taxation, salt-reduction campaigns should face fewer barriers.

The Heart attack risk reduction generic pill was a rather expensive proposal at $32 billion per year, with a respectable but not high BCR.

The Panel found that Tobacco taxation was largely a question of political will rather than funds. They noted that a tax is a highly effective response to the health problems caused by smoking but a gradual tax would not be ideal. They noted that the proposed solution was more than simply taxation, but also included an information campaign which they found was important. Developed-world experience with tobacco control must be shared with developing nations.

Climate change (Chapter 4)

The Panel examined the following solutions to this challenge: Geo-engineering R&D, Increased funding for green energy R&D, Low global carbon tax, High global carbon tax, Adaptation planning.

The Panel found that Geo-engineering R&D, at low cost, was worthy of some funds, to explore the costs, benefits, and risks of this technology.

The panel found the Green energy R&D should be started at a lower level than that proposed, of $1 billion annually, which would likely imply a higher BCR. According to the Challenge Paper authors, the money should be distributed to the top green-technology countries, e.g. the United States, Canada, the United Kingdom, Germany, France, Brazil, China, India, Japan, Korea, and Russia, through cross-national research consortia, focusing on financing R&D across a portfolio of technologies.

While the Panel chose not to rank the carbon tax, it found that a low carbon tax (around $5/ton CO_2, $19/ton C, which is the damage estimate) increasing over time, would be a sensible policy that could help address the climate change challenge. The Panel also recognized that without significant technological breakthrough, significant CO_2 reduction remains unlikely.

The panel also chose not to rank the adaptation investment solution, but underscored the importance of adaptation in the future to decrease the vulnerability of the developing world to climate change.

Water and sanitation (Chapter 10)

The Panel examined the following solutions to this challenge: Borehole and public handpump intervention, Community-led total sanitation (CCTS), Sanitation as a business, The "reinvented toilet."

The solid but relatively modest BCRs of Borehole and public handpump intervention led to its mid-ranking.

The expert panel noted that CLTS was a "road-tested" solution, meaning that it carries a high degree of certainty in its ability to be expanded, as there is a good deal of previous experience and knowledge of its risks, costs, and benefits in different environments. However, like the Borehole and public handpump intervention, it had relatively low BCRs.

They noted that Sanitation as a business appeared to have a relatively short time frame to becoming available. In contrast, the "reinvented toilet" was a considerably longer time away from availability, involving R&D lasting fifteen–thirteen years followed by marketing, with an unclear pathway to success. The panel concluded that the "reinvented toilet" was a noble goal, but analysis of its costs and benefits remained highly speculative, while the necessary seed money had already been allocated by the Gates Foundation.

Population growth (Chapter 9)

The Panel examined the following solution to this challenge: Increase availability of family planning.

The Panel recognizes the importance of meeting the unmet need for family planning. They note that some households would be easier to reach with family planning services, and recommend that attention is focused on these households first.

Armed conflicts (Chapter 1)

The Panel examined the following solutions to this challenge: Conflict prevention, Conflict intervention, Post-conflict reconstruction.

The Panel chose not to include these interventions in its prioritized list. Conflict prevention is clearly important: peace is not an end to be achieved at the end of a conflict, but should be preserved. However, as with the solutions to Trade barriers and corruption (Chapters 12 and 11), this topic is largely political, rather than an economic question of resource allocation. The Panel notes that the chapter makes a valuable contribution to identifying the costs and benefits of responding to conflicts.

Corruption and trade barriers (Chapters 12 and 11)

Two Working Papers were commissioned by Copenhagen Consensus 2012 on corruption and reducing trade barriers. The Panel notes the importance of responding to both of these challenges, but notes that the barriers to response are political rather than financial in nature.

Corruption can have crippling effects on development and human welfare. There is a lack of good data on the relative effectiveness of most reform programs. Yet, even without definitive studies, some options look promising because the benefits seem clear and the costs are minimal. Even if the benefits cannot be precisely measured, the rates of return appear large. Collectively, improving top-down monitoring and punishment, fostering transparency and citizen involvement, adjusting bureaucratic incentives through civil-service reforms, improving the competitiveness of government asset sales and large purchases, and privatizing certain government services may provide the shock needed to push a country or sector towards a self-fulfilling cycle of good governance.

Because under freer trade the world's resources would be allocated more efficiently, the Panel finds that cuts in trade barriers and subsidies would provide a means for citizens to spend more on other pressing problems, thereby indirectly contributing to opportunities to alleviate other challenges facing the world. The NPV of the future benefits of a Doha Agreement ranges from $12 trillion to $64 trillion. The costs are less than $400 billion in PV terms, but they are mostly private rather than government costs and are dwarfed by the gross benefits.

Individual rankings

Finn E. Kydland

Ten of the first eleven solutions on the Panel's ranking are related to hunger and diseases. Implementing these solutions would be hugely important not only in saving lives and preventing various forms of agony among millions of people, but also in making educational attainment much more efficient and beneficial in the longer run. Personally I felt that this time, in comparison with the 2008 Copenhagen Consensus exercise, the estimates of BCRs had become more accurate and credible, removing some of the uncertainty that otherwise might make one reluctant to rank a particular solution highly.

Rather than talk in detail about these solutions, let me focus on the two for which the discrepancy between my ranking and that of the overall panel was the greatest. One is "Increase availability of family planning," ranked #5 by me and #18 by the Panel. While population growth doesn't seem to be a global problem any more (the Malthusian outlook is outdated), the micro-problem is that so many women don't have access to any kind of birth control. This is a huge problem for female education, productivity, and income, and is a financial burden when kids are not affordable. My reading from the experts is that estimates from smaller programs suggest the reduction in child and maternal mortality yields BCRs of 30:1 to 50:1. Estimates for larger programs that could change population dynamics predict significant impacts on GDP *per capita*. Reductions of population growth rates of 1 percent could increase the growth rate of GDP *per*

Table Pan.3 Prioritization of solutions: Finn Kydland

	Solution
1	Geo-Engineering R&D
2	Bundled Micronutrient Interventions
3	Sanitation as a Business
4	R&D to Increase Yield Enhancements
5	Increase Availability of Family Planning
6	Strengthening Surgical Capacity
7	Subsidy for Malaria Combination Treatment
8	Deworming of Schoolchildren
9	Expanded Childhood Immunization Coverage
10	Investing in Effective EWS
11	Acute Heart Attack Low-Cost Drugs
12	CCTs for School Attendance
13	Expanding Tuberculosis Treatment
14	The "Reinvented Toilet"
15	Information Campaign on Benefits From Schooling
16	Borehole and Public Handpump Intervention
17	Increased Funding for Green Energy R&D
18	Salt-Reduction Campaign
19	CLTS
20	Accelerated HIV Vaccine R&D
21	Heart Attack Risk Reduction Generic Pill
22	Hepatitis B Immunization
23	Community Walls Against Floods
24	Retrofitting Schools to Withstand Earthquake Damage
25	Protecting All Forests
26	Crop Advisory Text Messages
27	Increasing Tobacco Taxation
28	Elevating Residential Structures to Avoid Flooding
29	Strengthening Structures Against Hurricanes and Storms
30	Extension of Protected Areas

capita by about 1 percent in high-fertility countries. This suggests BCRs of 50:1 to 100:1. Combining the above analyses yields overall BCRs ranging from a little under to well over 100:1.

Admittedly, there is a great deal of uncertainty associated with such estimates. It's natural that different Panel members take that into account to various degrees. In my case, it was hard not to be influenced by something the others had not seen, namely a research paper by two of my most respected colleagues at the University of California at Santa Barbara, Henning Bohn and Charles Stuart, entitled "Global warming and the population externality." According to their abstract:

> We calculate the harm a birth imposes on others when greenhouse gas emissions are a problem and a cap limits emissions damage. This negative population externality, which equals the corrective Pigovian tax on having a child, is substantial in calibrations. In our base case, the Pigovian tax is 21 percent of a parent's lifetime income in steady state and 5 percent of lifetime income immediately after imposition of a cap, per child. The optimal population in steady state, which maximizes utility taking account of the externality, is about one quarter of the population households would choose voluntarily.

As always, such estimates are only as reliable as the model and the data on which they are based. But even much lower estimates would be worthy of note.

The largest ranking discrepancy, however, was for the solution "Sanitation as a business," ranked #3 by me and #21 overall by the Panel. (The reader may recall that, as the basis for the Panel ranking was medians of Panel members' rankings, once it was established that I was above the median, it didn't matter for the overall ranking whether my ranking was 3 or 20. If instead the mean had been the criterion, then that would have moved this solution up somewhat in the overall ranking.) By way of background, one-third of the world's population, 2.5 billion, does not have access to basic sanitation, and 1 billion defecate in the open. Improved sanitation could prevent 1.5 million deaths a year from diarrheal illness, enhance dignity, privacy, and safety, especially for women and girls. Modern indoor sanitation systems cost \$50–100 per month, putting this technology out of reach for those living on, say, \$1–2 per day. Conventional water waste-treatment plants are expensive to construct and operate. One must look to latrines and septic tanks, investments for which the home owner shoulders the responsibility of cost and maintenance. Developed nations use vacuum trucks for full septic tanks, but these trucks are expensive and not well suited for latrines. It is estimated that 200 million latrines and septic tanks are emptied manually, with a worker descending into the pit with a bucket and spade.

The "Sanitation as a business" solution proposes a service provided by entrepreneurs at a cost of no more than $10 per household per year. It consists of emptying sludge to a treatment plant and treating it to acceptable levels before dispersal into the environment. Assume it is feasible to invest in innovation to achieve the following: bring annual cost of a vacuum truck down from $35–90 to $20 as a result of more efficient markets, bring it down further to $10 with improved technology that is currently in the design state. As subsidies necessary for introduction of the services, one is looking at a $320 million investment for improving service for 200 million people in low-income urban areas, giving a BCR of 46:1. Assuming technological advancement does not pan out, so that it costs $20 per year instead of $10, then the BCR falls to 23:1. Even under that more conservative estimate, this strikes me as an eminently worthwhile solution.

The area of sanitation has received a welcome burst of visibility lately with the news of the engagement of the Gates Foundation. In particular, as reported by *The Economist*, Bill Gates will provide seed money for the reinvention of the toilet in an attempt to make it cost-effective in low-income countries. Of course, one of the solutions considered by our panel was the "reinvented toilet," ranked #14 by me and #24 overall by the Panel. But we were informed of Bill Gates' involvement, which suggests that, in spite of a high potential BCR (40:1, but with high risk), the involvement of the Copenhagen Consensus would not be crucial. Moreover, a factor, at least for me, is that it could take decades before this solution would be sufficiently cost-effective to make inroads, for example as an alternative to "Sanitation as a business."

Table Pan.4 Prioritization of solutions: Robert Mundell

	Solution
1	Bundled Micronutrient Interventions
2	Deworming of Schoolchildren
3	CCTs for School Attendance
4	CLTS
5	Subsidy for Malaria Combination Treatment
6	Expanded Childhood Immunization Coverage
7	Investing in Effective EWS
8	Increased Funding for Green Energy R&D
9	Expanding Tuberculosis Treatment
10	R&D to Increase Yield Enhancements
11	Salt-Reduction Campaign
12	Community Walls Against Floods
13	Geo-Engineering R&D
14	Increase Availability of Family Planning
15	Accelerated HIV Vaccine R&D
16	Information Campaign on Benefits From Schooling
17	Hepatitis B Immunization
18	Heart Attack Risk Reduction Generic Pill
19	Extension of Protected Areas
20	Retrofitting Schools to Withstand Earthquake Damage
21	Acute Heart Attack Low-Cost Drugs
22	Strengthening Structures Against Hurricanes and Storms
23	Strengthening Surgical Capacity
24	Increasing Tobacco Taxation
25	Borehole and Public Handpump Intervention
26	Crop Advisory Text Messages
27	Sanitation as a Business
28	Protecting All Forests
29	Elevating Residential Structures to Avoid Flooding
30	The "Reinvented Toilet"

Robert Mundell

The modern world is subdivided into nation-states with governments that at best try to maximize the well-being of their constituents. The nation-states typically have highly integrated economies while the WTO, IMF, World Bank and multilateral groupings of customs unions and FTAs. There are also supranational entities like the United Nations and its subgroups that contribute importantly to such challenges as war, disease, and poverty. But there is no world government or any other institution that specifically bridges the gap between global needs for public goods and global policies to close the gap.

The idea behind the Copenhagen Consensus – Bjorn Lomborg's idea – was to help bridge the gap by seeking out the "challenges" for global public spending and trying to determine the proportions of a given public sector budget that should be devoted to each challenge. A core panel of high-profile economists, including many Nobel Laureates, would make the final evaluations. The challenges settled on for study were in ten major fields: Armed Conflicts, Chronic diseases, Education, Infectious diseases, Population growth, Biodiversity, Climate change, Hunger and malnutrition, Natural disasters, and Water and sanitation. The idea was to prepare studies in these fields by experts and then have them discussed with a core group of five high-profile economists.

The next step was to divide these broad categories into subgroups associated with specific proposals. For example, the category of "Infectious diseases" was subdivided into four specific policies: A subsidy for malaria combination treatment; Expanded childhood immunization coverage; Deworming of schoolchildren; and Expanding Tuberculosis Treatment. Challenge Papers – it turned out there were thirty-nine such papers – were commissioned from acknowledged authorities in each field of policy and discussed at length with the core panel. There were also fourteen "Alternative Perspective Papers" providing critical appraisals of each Challenge Paper's assumptions and methodology. Based on the costs and benefits of the solutions the Panel ranked the proposals in descending order of desirability.

Another issue was the size of the budget. We were asked specifically how we would allocate $75 billion over four years to each production. That raised the question of how our choices would be affected by scale. The size of the budget is important for the results. $75 billion over four years would be just a drop in the bucket for some high-profile public projects (e.g. lowering global temperatures by control of hydrocarbon emissions).

In general, the rate of return on any investment or project depends on scale. The rate of return might for a time increase with scale as economies of coordination come into play (e.g. two men can lift a rock but not one). Eventually, increased investment will lead to a decline in the rate of return because of diminishing returns and limited absorptive capacity. We therefore allocated our budget of $18.75 billion per year (for four years) in a precise way such that the levels of spending chosen resulted in equal rates of return. Thus one of the largest programs we chose was $3 billion to reduce undernutrition for pre-schoolers but this does not mean that we valued this project more than the much smaller subsidies for malaria or accelerated HIV vaccine R&D; it means instead that those levels of spending make the rates of return on the two projects the same.

I believe our Panel did a good job in coping with the vast amount of information we had to absorb in the time available and I am happy to have been part of the project. Perhaps in the long run our contribution will point the way to a more sophisticated methodology for adjudicating global public policy projects that are crying out for attention.

Thomas Schelling

I am generally satisfied with the priority listing that I share with my colleagues. I have a few comments about the items above our "threshold" and one below.

The "conditional cash transfers (CCTs) for school attendance" program is especially oriented toward girls. The 2004 and 2008 Copenhagen Consensus identified numerous valuable outcomes for girls. Examples are reduced teenage pregnancy, reduced risk of HIV infection, enhanced social valuation of women, improved health of newborn offspring, and of course greater participation in the labor force. There is experimental evidence, furthermore, that CCTs actually work: where they are available for either boys or girls, the main impact is increased schooling for girls. CTs, thus, produce an important variety of benefits.

Geo-engineering R&D reflects a recent coming out of the closet for a potential extremely effective and almost ridiculously economical climatic intervention, the basis for which has been known for more than a hundred years, namely that certain particles introduced into the stratosphere that

Table Pan.5 Prioritization of solutions: Thomas Schelling

	Solution
1	Subsidy for Malaria Combination Treatment
2	Expanding Tuberculosis Treatment
3	Strengthening Surgical Capacity
4	Accelerated HIV Vaccine R&D
5	Expanded Childhood Immunization Coverage
6	Deworming of Schoolchildren
7	Bundled Micronutrient Interventions
8	Salt-Reduction Campaign
9	Increasing Tobacco Taxation
10	Acute Heart Attack Low-Cost Drugs
11	Hepatitis B Immunization
12	CCTs for School Attendance
13	Borehole and Public Handpump Intervention
14	R&D to Increase Yield Enhancements
15	Geo-Engineering R&D
16	Investing in Effective EWS
17	Increase Availability of Family Planning
18	Sanitation as a Business
19	Information Campaign on Benefits From Schooling
20	Increased Funding for Green Energy R&D
21	Heart Attack Risk Reduction Generic Pill
22	Crop Advisory Text Messages
23	CLTS
24	Extension of Protected Areas
25	Protecting All Forests
26	Retrofitting Schools to Withstand Earthquake Damage
27	Elevating Residential Structures to Avoid Flooding
28	Community Walls Against Floods
29	Strengthening Structures Against Hurricanes and Storms
30	The "Reinvented Toilet"

offset, by reflecting back into space about 1 or 2 percent of incoming sunlight, may offset the cooling effect of a doubling of the concentration of GHGs in the earth's atmosphere. Mount Pinatubo in the Philippines erupted in 1991 and spewed thousands of tons of sulfur into the stratosphere, reducing the temperature of the surface oceans for a couple of years. What cannot be known without experiment – on a small scale at first, too small to affect climate – is what the possible dangers are, what the different regional impacts will be, and whether the results may be exceedingly disadvantageous for some parts of the world. Our intention is not to promote the deployment of such measures, but to find out more about them. If geo-engineering of that kind is a bad idea, the sooner we find out the better. If there are alternative substances that may work in the stratosphere, knowing which ones are most favorable would be important if ever there were an agreed need to proceed. This kind of intervention does not wholly solve the "greenhouse problem" – continued growth of GHGs in the atmosphere leads, among other problems, to increasing acidity of the ocean, which is deleterious to all marine animals that require calcium absorption for the production of their shells.

I believe that both the improving incomes in the developing world (so that men can afford tobacco), and the gradual emancipation of women from social norms against female smoking, are leading to an "epidemic" of an addictive habit that is gradually being brought under control in much of the developed world. One of the proposals under chronic diseases was for increasing tobacco taxation. We have not included that proposal, I believe, not because we oppose it but because there are no identifiable costs in increasing tobacco taxes for which it makes sense to offer aid.

The 2004 and 2008 Copenhagen Consensus programs had separate proposals for delivering vitamin A, iodine, iron, and a variety of other "micronutrients" that are cheap to purchase but sometimes expensive to deliver, there not being a suitable established infrastructure for that purpose in many developing nations. Because the "delivery" of these cheap but vital nutrients is the same for most of them, we have in the 2012 Copenhagen Consensus exercise "bundled" them, thereby reducing the cost of delivery. Somewhat the same may prove feasible for the delivery of deworming pills and perhaps of some vaccines. This anticipated lowering of costs of delivery helps to account for the high ranking enjoyed by the "bundling" of those interventions.

Strengthening of surgical capacity may sound ambitious, but what is proposed is actually providing assistance, such as for simple injuries like fractures or childbirth problems, that require not highly specialized surgeons but general practitioners and trained assisting staff that can deal with a multitude of ailments that can be seriously debilitating or fatal but that can be dealt with fairly inexpensively. This is essentially a form of "infrastructure" to support a wide range of surgical benefits that are frequently unavailable or inaccessible.

Accelerated HIV vaccine R&D yields by far the most delayed benefits of any of our selected projects. Its success is uncertain; success, if it happens, will be years away, perhaps decades; and the benefits will be distributed over its own future through the reduced transmission of HIV over the succeeding decades. We were persuaded that our modest budget for HIV vaccine development, on top of the larger ongoing investment, made sense.

Vernon Smith

The key contribution of the Copenhagen Consensus meetings is to draw attention to a particular way of thinking about world problems that is not part of the mainstream political and media debate. The question is not whether a particular policy is likely to be beneficial, and command popular agreement; rather how it stacks up in comparison with the truly large and mind-boggling number of critical issues that might be on the table. These problems range from poverty to climate change, but each general topic contains a host of specific issues. The core idea in the Copenhagen Consensus is that we cannot do everything. This implies the need for a mechanism that allows specific proposals to be prioritized. A useful mechanism for focusing the mind on this task is to suppose that one has a limited budget, and the objective is to get the most out of the available resources – in this case, $75 billion over the next four years. In my view this is not intended as a central planner's exercise, but rather is directed to issues designed to sharpen the precision and centrality of that debate.

Toward that end, my prioritization reflects an attempt to answer the question: how to prioritize particular proposals to advance betterment in the quality of human life? For me, in this regard, our most pressing and continuing task is to deal with the ancient and continuing problem of poverty. Moreover, surely there must be substantial agreement that the most effective means of reducing poverty is through mechanisms that better enable people

Table Pan.6 Prioritization of solutions: Vernon Smith

	Solution
1	Bundled Micronutrient Interventions
2	Subsidy for Malaria Combination Treatment
3	Expanded Childhood Immunization Coverage
4	CCTs for School Attendance
5	R&D to Increase Yield Enhancements
6	Deworming of Schoolchildren
7	Hepatitis B Immunization
8	Expanding Tuberculosis Treatment
9	Salt-Reduction Campaign
10	Information Campaign on Benefits From Schooling
11	Protecting All Forests
12	Geo-Engineering R&D
13	The "Reinvented Toilet"
14	Increasing Tobacco Taxation
15	Borehole and Public Handpump Intervention
16	Strengthening Surgical Capacity
17	Heart Attack Risk Reduction Generic Pill
18	Investing in Effective EWS
19	Community Walls Against Floods
20	Acute Heart Attack Low-Cost Drugs
21	Strengthening Structures Against Hurricanes and Storms
22	Accelerated HIV Vaccine R&D
23	Sanitation as a Business
24	Increased Funding for Green Energy R&D
25	CLTS
26	Extension of Protected Areas
27	Retrofitting Schools to Withstand Earthquake Damage
28	Increase Availability of Family Planning
29	Elevating Residential Structures to Avoid Flooding
30	Crop Advisory Text Messages

to help themselves. Such programs are not only essential to individual self-fulfillment and actualization, but are also ultimately self-financing, perpetuating desirable outcomes without continued maintenance from external resources, enabling such resources to continue to be made available for other challenges.

Consequently, my top-ten list includes all the most promising, generally least uncertain, programs to alleviate lifelong suffering and improve lifelong performance in children: interventions that focus on the nearly 180 million children whose biological and mental development and maturation is stunted by undernutrition; childhood immunization; deworming of school children; and two programs designed to foster additional childhood years spent in school, investments that have a huge return that is especially large for girls. Once children are stunted, they become less reachable via investment programs.

The other five programs in my top ten include: Malaria treatment; R&D to enhance crop yields; Hepatitis B immunization; Tuberculosis treatment; and Salt reduction. Enhancing crop yields has well-proven claims of direct human benefit in avoiding mass starvation. Increasing crop yields also creates a direct bonus in climate benefits – an excellent example of doing good while doing well. Moreover, because of well-developed markets in agricultural commodity outputs and their inputs, basic new research findings in yield enhancement are likely to be properly calculated, evaluated, and efficiently implemented via a private sector response to any new discoveries.

My next-ten list largely overlaps that of the consensus rankings of other Panel members. I will use my limited space to discuss only one exception: I rated "Increase availability of family planning" near the bottom. This challenge might seem on first blush to be particularly deserving of high priority as a means to increasing human betterment and personal choice freedom; however, I found the Lam (2012) Alternative Perspective paper (Chapter 9.2) very persuasive in raising issues new to me, and effectively showcasing important weaknesses in the objective of isolating and estimating the benefits of extending family planning in regions with high fertility rates.

Kohler's (2012) Challenge Paper (Chapter 9) provides a well-documented summary of the impressive fifty-year history across a multiplicity of cultural groups – with the exception of SSA – attesting to decreases in the fertility rate as a historically common response to rising income and family economic betterment. Parents want fewer children, and to invest more in each child's preparation for life as they emerge from poverty. One's intuition is that this must surely mean that there is an important independent influence of birth control information provided by family planning programs.

As it turns out, evidence in support of this intuition is not that easy to demonstrate. The direct and most convincing evidence is in the Matlab program in Bangladesh (Joshi and Schultz, 2007) and the family planning program in Colombia (Miller, 2010) that have provided direct experimental measures of the direct effects of these programs on fertility, and indirectly on outcomes in health and education. As noted in Chapter 9, the critical link is the extent to which "it is lack of access to family planning services that explains why some women who want no more children are not using contraception" (Lam, 2012: Figure 9.2.1). If this link is weak, the benefit relative to cost of family planning is correspondingly diminished, and may pale in comparison with other Challenges. The many reasons women list for not using contraception imply that the availability of information is trumped by other considerations that are neither easily nor non-invasively changed by well-intentioned planning programs – i.e. additional contraceptive information is ineffective, whatever its potential benefits.

Turning to the Colombia experiments, Lam (2012: 590) notes that "the impact of Colombia's large family planning program was relatively modest, leading to a decline in fertility of about 1/3 of a child . . . in fertility over the 1964–93 period . . . The point is that estimates of unmet need and the cost of meeting that unmet need would almost surely lead to substantial overestimates of the actual impact of expanding family planning on fertility."

For future reference, a valuation issue that I have not been able to resolve deserves to be mentioned in this reflection. Kohler (2012: 554) identifies an important benefit from family planning: reduced expenditures on health and schooling. Yet health and schooling in both the 2008 and 2012 Copenhagen Consensus have been ranked very high in terms of their yield on investment. Hence, some fraction of the children not born fail to benefit from these high-yield investments, and to this extent are not a benefit but a cost of not being born; i.e. children are an intermediate input in these calculations. My point is that these interactions need to be taken into account, and spotlight the huge challenge in evaluating family planning as a desirable social expenditure.

Returning to the main theme, since the critical area of fertility concern is SSA, I could support a more limited program that would finance field experiments designed to measure the specific effects of birth control information on fertility in this region. The connection between information and realized fertility reduction would be the target of this exercise to be undertaken before embarking on a costly expansion of family planning programs into high-fertility regions. It seems likely that this causal relationship will interact with cultural norms, and indeed these considerations may help to account for the stubborn resistance of fertility to meaningful declines in the region. In the meantime, I believe that the resources are more efficaciously devoted to health and education investments, and other Copenhagen Consensus Challenges in the top-ten rankings.

Nancy Stokey

The 2012 Copenhagen Consensus ranking reaffirms many of the conclusions from the 2004 and 2008 Consensus, but it also offers a couple of new and noteworthy ideas: R&D in geo-engineering and an EWS for storms, floods, and tsunamis. My remarks will first discuss these new ideas in detail, and then look more briefly at the rest.

Table Pan.7 Prioritizing of solutions: Nancy Stokey

	Solution
1	Bundled Micronutrient Interventions
2	Subsidy for Malaria Combination Treatment
3	Geo-Engineering R&D
4	Expanded Childhood Immunization Coverage
5	Investing in Effective EWS
6	Expanding Tuberculosis Treatment
7	Acute Heart Attack Low-Cost Drugs
8	Deworming of Schoolchildren
9	Hepatitis B Immunization
10	Strengthening Surgical Capacity
11	R&D to Increase Yield Enhancements
12	Increased Funding for Green Energy R&D
13	Accelerated HIV Vaccine R&D
14	Heart Attack Risk Reduction Generic Pill
15	CLTS
16	Information Campaign on Benefits From Schooling
17	Increase Availability of Family Planning
18	Borehole and Public Handpump Intervention
19	Sanitation as a Business
20	Crop Advisory Text Messages
21	CCTS for School Attendance
22	Increasing Tobacco Taxation
23	Salt-Reduction Campaign
24	The "Reinvented Toilet"
25	Retrofitting Schools to Withstand Earthquake Damage
26	Community Walls Against Floods
27	Strengthening Structures Against Hurricanes and Storms
28	Extension of Protected Areas
29	Protecting All Forests
30	Elevating Residential Structures to Avoid Flooding

Geo-engineering R&D

I regret not ranking the proposal for R&D in geo-engineering as #1. This project deserves to have a flag waved to draw attention to it.

The proposal is to conduct additional laboratory investigations, followed by field trials, of a system for SRM. This proposal appeared in the 2009 Copenhagen Consensus on Climate change, where it was #1 in the overall group rankings.

Although geo-engineering sounds very high-tech and rather frightening, the main idea is in fact quite simple. It involves enhancing by a small amount an effect that occurs naturally, the reflection of sunlight before it reaches the surface of the earth. Both ordinary clouds in the lower atmosphere and aerosols in the upper atmosphere naturally reflect about 30 percent of the sunlight directed at the earth. Sunlight that is reflected does not warm, and slightly enhancing reflectivity, by 1–2 percent, can offset the additional warming produced by GHGs.

Funding is requested here for R&D on a system that uses rockets to inject small amounts of sulfites into the upper atmosphere, mimicking the effect produce by a large volcanic eruption. (The 2009 proposal also included R&D on a system that uses a flotilla of small, unmanned marine vessels, churning up seawater to "whiten" marine clouds.)

The total cost of the R&D proposed here is estimated to be about $500 million over ten years. The cost in the early years, which involve mostly laboratory experiments, is tiny: $5 million. The annual costs rise to $30 million and then $100 million for the field trials later in the ten-year window. To be conservative, the authors multiply all of these costs by 10.

We face enormous uncertainty about climate sensitivity – about the stability of ice shelves in the Antarctic, about methane gas in the Arctic tundra, about the rate at which glaciers will melt, about snowpack in the Himalayas. As Bickel and Lane point out in their subchapter of Chapter 4, "SRM is the only technology that could quickly cool the Earth should the need arise to do so" (Bickeland Lane, 2012: 204).

It is impossible to assess the expected benefits of a program like this one with any accuracy. The chance that it will need to be deployed in the next century may be small, how small? Is the chance 0.1 percent, or 0.01 percent ? Or is it 1.0 percent? The benefit in case the need arises are similarly difficult to quantify. Is it $0.1 trillion, or $1 trillion, or $10 trillion? The system to be investigated offers at least some insurance against a catastrophe, at very low cost. And as Tom Schelling pointed out in the discussion, if there are any as-yet-unknown reasons not to deploy SRM, we should find out now.

Investing in effective EWS

The second noteworthy addition is the proposal to provide upgraded hydro-meteorological services in developing countries. An EWS for storms, floods, and tsunamis would save both lives and property. The proposed system would use information from existing earth observation satellites and global weather forecasts, so the required investment consists of local infrastructure to assess risks and communicate warnings. For high-risk areas, investments of this type look very attractive.

Health, nutrition, sanitation

Infectious disease and Chronic disease are separate categories in the 2012 Copenhagen Consensus, and these two categories, together with Hunger, took many of the top positions. The Panel in 2012 unanimously agreed, as did the Panels in 2004 and 2008, that health and nutrition programs offer extremely attractive opportunities for improving the lives of people in low-income parts of the world. As in the developed world, early-childhood interventions are particularly effective, and many of these interventions are directed at young children.

Micronutrients (vitamin A, iodine, iron, zinc) got the top spot, this time in the form of a bundled package for infants under two years that also includes deworming and a highly nutritious peanut paste. Deworming appears again as a treatment for schoolchildren, who would probably benefit from the micronutrients as well. These interventions are directed at reducing infant mortality, preventing physical and cognitive stunting, and – for the older group – raising school attendance. There seems to be little or no question that these programs are feasible and that they are extremely cheap for the benefits they produce. Since early childhood begins *in utero*, pregnant women should also be a target group for these programs.

The Subsidy for malaria combination treatment is a program designed by a blue-ribbon commission of economists and health experts to deal with the problem of drug resistance in the malaria parasite. The typical treatment for malaria in many low-income countries consists of a single inexpensive drug. While the treatment is cheap and often effective, it has the unfortunate side-effect of promoting drug-resistant strains of the malaria parasite. The proposed intervention offers a subsidy to pharmaceutical companies, so they can sell a more expensive treatment that combines several drugs, at a similar low price. ACTs are more effective in treating malaria, and are in addition expected to reduce drug resistence. Thus, encouraging individuals to shift to ACTs is expected to produce global benefits by reducing child deaths, reducing transmission rates from infected individuals, and preventing the emergence of drug-resistant strains. The program would also undermine the growing supply of "fake" ACTs.

Expanded childhood immunization and hepatitis B immunization also got very high rankings. The former can reduce child mortality rates at very low cost, while the latter has lifelong benefits in terms of reduced morbidity from illness.

Several other health proposals were also very promising: Expanding tuberculosis treatment, Acute heart attack low-cost drugs, and Strengthening surgical capacity. The last involves training doctors or other medical personnel in existing health clinics to perform simple surgical procedures like Caesarian sections. Subsidizing the provision of generic pills to reduce the risk of heart attack is not a bad idea, but does seem more costly relative to its benefits.

Two of the Water and sanitation proposals are also health-related. Standpipes and latrines are old ideas, here offered with some new twists. CLTS proposes updated latrines, with an eye to insuring that they are actually used. The proposal for Boreholes and public handpumps involves chlorinating water at the public source. This seems like a good idea, but other parts of the Challenge Paper (Chapter 10) sent a somewhat mixed message, noting that handpumps often deteriorate and become inoperable after a few years.

Education, population growth

There is an on-going debate in the aid/development literature about the reluctance of individuals in low-income countries to make use of schools and family planning services. The debate revolves around whether the problem is supply (schools charge fees, family planning clinics are too far away) or demand (skepticism about the value of an education, religious or other objections to contraception).

The Education proposals for Information on returns and conditional cash transfers (CCTs) are attempts to work on the demand side. The former has been tried in only a couple of field experiments. The results are promising enough to make further trials worthwhile, although not to support a broad expansion on this front. The latter has been tried in a number of countries, and it seems to work, at least by the metric of better school attendance. The evidence for improved cognitive development or higher earnings after school completion is less solid, however. In addition programs of this type are expensive unless they are re-packaging existing transfers, so that only the "conditionality" is an incremental cost.

The proposal to Increase availability of family planning is an attempt to work on the supply side. Kohler in Chapter 9 defines "unmet need" as the number of women who are sexually active, who say that they do not want to become pregnant, and who nevertheless use no form of contraception (Kohler, 2012: 518). As one of the Alternative Perspective Paper authors (Chapter 9) points out, however, in the few areas where information is available, the "unmet need" seems to be less a supply issue than a demand issue. If this is so, simply increasing the availability of family planning clinics is probably not enough. Here, too, carefully planned field trials could be quite useful in determining what works. Until there is better evidence, a large investment is unwarranted.

R&D

Proposals were offered for funding R&D in a number of other areas, in addition to geo-engineering. Specifically, there were projects for R&D in yield enhancements, in a vaccine for HIV/AIDS, in green technologies, in non-piped technologies for waste removal in urban areas (Sanitation as a business), and in a "reinvented toilet."

Investment in yield enhancement has a long track record and, consequently, a fairly predictable payoff. The right question about further investment here is probably the extent to which public funds are needed, and how much can be left to the private sector.

For the other R&D projects, the Panel was offered little evidence to evaluate the expected return from additional funding. What particular green technologies would be investigated? Which aspects of waste removal require basic research? Is there a large portfolio of ideas for an HIV/AIDS vaccine that currently lack funding?

Not worth funding/inappropriate

Crop advisory text messages have been useful in some areas, providing farmers with information about the weather or about market prices for particular commodities. Cheap cell phones are widely available in the developing world, so large investments are not required to provide this kind of service. What is required is specialized local knowledge about what information is relevant. Private markets seem better suited to providing this kind of service.

Higher taxes on tobacco would surely reduce its consumption, and low-income individuals would be especially responsive to a large price increase. But taxing tobacco does not require any outside resources. On the contrary, such a tax would raise revenue. Nor does it require any particular expertise to levy an excise tax on tobacco. A government anywhere can do this on its own, if it feels that the health costs of tobacco are a high priority issue.

In the United States, about 70 million adults suffer from high blood pressure. About 50 percent control it with medication – most of which are inexpensive generics – and a much smaller fraction control it with diet. With this evidence as background, it is not at all clear that Salt reduction campaigns in the developing world are a worthwhile investment.

The "reinvented toilet," a machine that will – almost magically – deal with human waste without using water or sewer systems, is a dream for the future. Maybe it will happen, someday, but it is not a high priority for investment today.

Retrofitting schools to withstand earthquake damage, building Community walls against floods, Strengthening structures against hurricanes and Elevating residential structures are extremely expensive interventions, especially on the broad scale proposed here. At best, they would need to be targeted to regions with the highest risk. And the Community walls have another drawback, as well. With sea levels rising, how high should these walls be? Encouraging people to move to at-risk areas, by creating a false sense of security, could easily backfire.

Extension of protected areas and Protecting all forests are ideas that sound nice, but on closer inspection look impractical.

The Challenge Paper on Armed conflicts (Chapter 1), while admirable in many respects, did not offer a concrete proposal for an intervention. Syria? Sudan? Somalia? And what should be done? The Panel could not rank these proposals.

Carbon taxes

Several proposals for carbon taxes were offered, but the Panel chose – wisely – not to rank any of them. Our task was to allocate a (notional) budget of $75 billion over a four-year horizon. Two features make a carbon tax an unsuitable candidate for this exercise. First, as noted above, taxes require no funding. Indeed, a tax generates revenue. In addition, a carbon tax is a long-run policy and needs to be planned for decades or centuries, not four years.

Nevertheless, taxes on carbon dioxide and other GHGs are, in the end, the only serious way to deal with the problem of climate change. The geo-engineering ideas described above are short-run tools, useful for dealing with possible crises or for buying time while green technologies come on line. At some point, however, we will have to stop relying on fossil fuels, and the only way that this will happen is with a carbon tax.

A public commitment to such a tax, on a wide scale and with a rate that increases over time, is needed to provide the private sector with strong signals about the expected future returns from investment in such technologies. To be sure, there is a role for public investment in basic science in the relevant areas, but private funds will necessarily provide the bulk of the investment.

Reducing barriers to international trade was taken off the table for the 2012 Copenhagen Consensus, not because it is a bad idea. On the contrary, it is an outstanding idea. But, like taxing GHGs, reducing trade barriers requires no funding. It is a matter of political will, not lack of funds to invest. Negotiating trade reforms has been a painfully slow process, and negotiating a carbon tax will be, if anything, more difficult. The time to start is now.

Conclusion: Making Your Own Prioritization

BJØRN LOMBORG

This book represents the conclusion of several years of work since the Copenhagen Consensus Center started to approach the experts and authors whose work forms this book, and asked them to identify the best ways to solve the world's biggest problems.

Part I of this book brought together analyses of twelve global challenges, and proposals for their solution or mitigation. The authors used economic CBA to provide a coherent framework for evaluation.

Over the past decade, the developed world has increased its annual assistance corrected for inflation by $49 billion. Each year, $130 billion is spent globally. Countless more billions are spent trying to make the world better – investments in vaccine research, peacekeeping forces, and carbon taxes.

Much is spent, yet these funds are limited. We have to make choices. Not explicitly prioritizing means we still make choices but we just don't talk as clearly about them. My belief is that putting prices on the world's solutions makes our decisions better informed. They are still difficult, but it gives us a sounder basis to get them right. In particular, it provides a common framework of reference for comparing investment programs which might otherwise seem so far apart that comparison was not possible.

Part II provided one very smart perspective on prioritizing the research. The Copenhagen Consensus Center asked a panel of the world's top economists: "if you had $75 billion to spend over the next four years and your goal was to advance human welfare, especially in the developing world, how could you get the most value for money?" The amount of money represents a 15 percent increase in current spending.

One point that comes through clearly in both Part I and Part II of this book is that no problem is truly a stand-alone one. Many are directly related, and solutions proposed for one may have beneficial effects in other areas. Poor water supplies and air pollution inevitably increase rates of disease, while corruption and trade barriers reduce the funds available to address a whole range of problems. Other connections are less obvious. Lack of access to water can reduce the participation of women and children in education and the workforce because they spend many hours a day fetching and carrying. We still have to prioritize, because we can't do it all, but the academics have tried as best as the models allow to count all of the benefits and all of the costs, so that we can make the best decisions possible.

Sometimes smart investments are straightforward, such as expanding immunization programs or making malaria drugs available – two of the investments highlighted by the Panel. But sometimes, too, the best way to tackle challenges is not head-on. Two more of the investments highlighted by the Panel stand out for not only delivering high returns but providing smart solutions to difficult issues.

As Peter Orazem underscored (Chapter 5), massive advances have been made in the effort to educate all the world's children. The cost to parents of schooling has become cheaper and – unlike just a few years ago – most children now attend classes. The challenge now is to keep them in school and increase the quality of education they receive.

Research across several chapters demonstrated one way to improve the quality and quantity of learning. Malnourished children learn poorly. Ensuring proper nutrition when the brain is developing makes a significant difference. If we bundled nutrition interventions targeting pre-schoolers, we could get vital micronutrients to children who lack them – including combating vitamin A deficiencies, iodine deficiency, and reducing anemia caused by children and pregnant mothers not getting enough iron – but also pay for campaigns to improve long-term diet quality and behavior.

Chapter 6 by John Hoddinott, Mark Rosegrant, and Maximo Torero of the International Food Policy Research Institute (IFPRI) showed that spending $100 per child would decrease chronic undernutrition by 36 percent in developing countries. As shown in both this chapter and that by Peter Orazem (Chapter 5), this would also have a great impact on learning.

Long-term studies show that children would stay in school longer and learn more, and be more productive when they grow up, earning on average 24 percent more. In total, the benefits are likely to be much higher than $30 back on the dollar.

Similarly, we saw the interconnectivity of challenges highlighted when it came to the topics of biodiversity, malnutrition, and climate change.

Authors led by Salman Hussain and Anil Markandya (Chapter 2) showed that responding to the challenge of biodiversity has been difficult: so far, they told us, only 10 percent of land globally has been protected, and, often, protected areas are just "paper parks." Therefore, one of their proposed responses, which was endorsed by the Panel, was to increase the productivity of agriculture.

As the global population has increased to 7 billion, we have cut down more forest to grow our food. Without an increase in productivity growth, between now and 2050 we are likely to expand agricultural area by another 10 percent, and that land will mostly come from forests and grasslands. If we could increase agricultural productivity, we would need to take less and be able to leave more to nature, and generate more food at the same time.

Moreover, this would also help limit global warming because forests store carbon. And increasing agricultural productivity would make food cheaper, helping to solve the challenge of undernutrition. The research shows that for every $1 spent, we would probably produce more than $16 worth of benefits.

These investments show both new and overlooked ways to respond to global challenges. Together, they reveal a smarter middle path between those who argue that we should just dramatically increase aid and those who claim that, in the current economic climate, we have to cut ineffective aid – by focusing on smarter, more effective ways to help.

CBA also enables you, the reader, to make your own comparisons and judgments. We have seen how the Panel interprets the research. But, in a crucial sense, there is no "right answer." We all have to evaluate the evidence, make our choices of discount rates, values of DALYs, etc. The aim of this book is to encourage this debate and to help you, the reader, to think in a more structured way about the world's biggest problems. The challenges covered in this volume have been with us for a long time.

In an increasingly prosperous world, we can surely make a difference. Even against seemingly intractable problems, there is value in knowing what we cannot do, what we can do, and what the costs and benefits are. The next step is to decide what we should do first.

Index